DE SMITH's Judicial Review

AUSTRALIA
Law Book Co.
Sydney

CANADA and USA
Carswell
Toronto

HONG KONG
Sweet & Maxwell Asia

NEW ZEALAND
Brookers
Wellington

SINGAPORE and MALAYSIA
Sweet & Maxwell Asia
Singapore and Kuala Lumpur

De Smith's Judicial Review

Sixth Edition

The Rt Hon The Lord Woolf
Former Lord Chief Justice of England and Wales
Judge of the Court of Final Appeal. Hong Kong

Jeffrey Jowell, Q.C.
Professor of Law. Faculty of Laws, UCL
Barrister, Blackstone Chambers

Andrew Le Sueur
Professor of Public Law, Queen Mary,
University of London
Barrister

Assistant Editor:
Catherine M. Donnelly
Lecturer in Law,
University College. Dublin
Barrister

London
Sweet & Maxwell 2007

First edition	1959
Second impression	1960
Third impression	1961
Second edition	1968
Third edition	1973
Fourth edition	1980
Second impression	1986
Third impresion	1987
Fifth edition	1995
Supplement to the fifth edition	1998
Sixth edition	2007

Published in 2007 by Sweet & Maxwell Limited of
100 Avenue Road,
London NW3 3PF
http://www.sweetandmaxwell.co.uk
Typeset by LBJ Typesetting Ltd of Kingsclere
Printed and bound in Great Britain by
William Clowes Ltd, Beccles, Suffolk

"No natural forests were destroyed to make this product; only farmed
timber was used and re-planted"

ISBN: 9780421690301

A CIP catalogue record for this book is available from the British Library

PREFACE

This book was begun by Stanley de Smith in the 1950s as a doctoral thesis and then published in 1959. de Smith set out its aims in his original Preface as follows:

"It is to be hoped that [this book] will be helpful to practitioners, to public administrators and their legal advisers, and to students and their teachers in England and elsewhere. And those students of government who are not lawyers may also find in it material that has a bearing on the larger issues inherent in the relationship between the Administration and the individual."

de Smith's book was the first in the United Kingdom to describe and analyse this field of law with coherence. It quickly established a groundbreaking reputation here and in the Commonwealth. Professor de Smith produced two further editions in 1968 and 1973. After his untimely death, Professor John M. Evans (now Mr Justice Evans of the Federal Court of Canada) edited the 4th edition in 1980.

When two of the present authors (Woolf and Jowell) were asked to prepare a 5th edition of the work in the early 1990s, it soon became clear that the initial intention, which was merely to update the existing edition, was insufficient. Prompted by reforms to the procedures and remedies, and also by a changing intellectual climate, the 1980s and early 1990s saw dramatic changes in judicial review: the number of applications increased from a few hundred a year to several thousand; the judicial reasoning which creates the grounds for challenging the validity of governmental action grew in its sophistication; and there was by then a burgeoning academic literature about this area of law. The 5th edition of the work (ISBN 0 420 46620 7) was published in 1995 (with the assistance of Andrew Le Sueur) and consisted of a substantial restructuring and supple-mentation of the 1980 edition. A supplement, updating the 1995 text, was published in 1998 (ISBN 0 421 607904)). An abridged version of the work, intended more as a student text, was published in 1999 under the title *Principles of Judicial Review* (ISBN 0421 62020 X).

When work began on the present edition (with Le Sueur now a joint author), we recognised that new work would be required on the impact upon judicial review of the Human Rights Act 1998. We also agreed that the separate short surveys of the operation of judicial review in different contexts at the end of the 5th edition, excellent though they were, would be better integrated into the main body of the work. In other respects, however, we again initially assumed that a mere updating of the previous edition would suffice.

It soon became clear, however, that judicial review had altered in the past 12 years to an extent even more significant than between the previous editions and that a substantial re-arrangement, and major additions and reformulations were again required. These changes were driven, in particular, by the explicit recognition that individuals in a democracy possess rights against the state—as enunciated both by the common law as well as the Human Rights Act 1998 and in European Community law. In addition, the relationships between the courts and other branches of government have been clarified in important ways. The principle of the sovereignty of Parliament has been, if not been fatally undermined, at least substantially weakened as a shield against either unlawful administrative action or legislation which offends the rule of law. Constitutional principles such as the rule of law and separation of powers have been explicitly articulated as such, and their status has been enhanced. Above all, it has become clear that judicial review is not merely about the way decisions are reached but also about the substance of those decisions themselves. The fine line between appeal on the merits of a case and review still exists but we have moved, as we emphasise in various sections of this book, towards a "culture of justification".

In this edition, as in the last, we have, inevitably, deviated from some of de Smith's standpoints and approaches but not, we believe, in ways of which he would have disapproved, in the changed circumstances of these times. In three respects at least, we have attempted wherever possible to be faithful to de Smith's distinctive approach. First, by setting out the principles underlying each area of judicial review: de Smith's hallmark was, above all, the elucidation of principle. Never content merely to describe a line of cases, he would invariably sum up their underlying rationale through a series of "propositions". We have sought to do the same. Secondly, we have retained much of de Smith's unmatched historical researches (updating them were necessary), which are so important to a proper understanding of the context of judicial review today. As he wrote in his first Preface, "many of the peculiarities of judicial review in English administrative law are unintelligible unless viewed in the light of their historical origins". Thirdly, we have attempted to refer to the experience of other jurisdictions yet, again as in the previous editions, without any pretence at creating a work of comparative law. We have been struck by the increased readiness of our courts to consider (if not slavishly to follow) the decisions of courts in other countries. The requirement in some of the provisions of the European Convention on Human Rights that our decision-makers adhere to the necessary qualities of a "democratic society" is just one of the factors that have encouraged reference to the experience of democracies elsewhere. We have in this edition summarised at the end of a number of chapters the corresponding law and practice in some relevant Commonwealth countries.

Another of de Smith's hallmarks was his meticulous coverage of the case-law. He took pride in the fact that he had cited 1800 cases in the first edition. In the age before electronic databases this was a considerable achievement. Professor Evans was equally meticulous in his comprehensive coverage of developments in judicial review between 1973 and 1979. In those times it may have been possible to refer to virtually every case relevant to the subject (although some critics of the 4th edition queried the need for the routine citation of all relevant cases). To cite the mass of case law that exists today is, we believe, even if possible, unnecessary in a work of this nature. We hope not to have neglected the need to be comprehensive where desirable. We have, however, consciously been prepared to sacrifice coverage where it might impede de Smith's prime goal of clarity of exposition of principle.

Previous editions of the work were entitled *Judicial Review of Administrative Action*. We have in this edition dropped the reference to administrative action, which would today be partial and misleading, as some of judicial review (that under European Community law and in the interpretation of the rights under the European Convention on Human Rights as incorporated by the Human Rights Act 1998) involves review not only of administrative action (or the exercise of public functions, as we now prefer to say), but also of primary legislation.

SCHEME OF THE WORK

In Chapter 1 we set out the context of judicial review and its scope, considering at the outset a number of issues that guide our approach in so many of the later chapters. We therefore engage, more specifically than in the last edition, the constitutional foundations of judicial review. A raging debate on that subject erupted shortly after the 5th edition went to press. Our position is that courts in judicial review enunciate not merely the will of the legislature but the fundamental principles of a democratic (albeit unwritten) constitution. We also sketch at the outset another fundamental issue, namely, the respective roles of courts and other branches of government—the question of whether there are some matters that are simply beyond judicial review because they are not "justiciable". In addition, we consider the context in which judicial review is but one of a number of possible avenues of redress for aggrieved citizens, which include internal complaints procedures, mediation and other forms of ADR, ombudsmen and (reinvigorated by the Tribunals, Courts and Enforcement Act 2007) tribunals. In an era of "proportionate dispute resolution" there is a renewed appreciation that administrative justice may be achieved beyond the Administrative Court. As we argue, however, while other redress mechanisms may often provide cheaper, speedier and more convenient remedies, judicial review is usually best placed to ensure the rule of law.

Chapter 2 considers those who may initiate a claim for judicial review (claimants); those who have a right to be a party to the proceedings (interested parties), and those, often pressure groups, who may seek permission from the court to make submissions as interveners. Whatever may have been the case in the past, the operation of the rule on the standing of a person to bring a claim —which since 1976 has been based upon the need for "a sufficient interest in the matter" to which the claim relates—now excludes few people with well-presented grounds of challenge from commencing a review. Where a claimant seeks to rely on a Convention right as a ground of review, s.7 of the Human Rights Act 1998 modifies the standing test to include a requirement that the claimant be "a victim" (a development that has been subject to academic criticism and some judicial vacillation in its practical application).

In Chapter 3, we consider the often complex and controversial questions of which defendants and decisions are subject to judicial review. The court's choice as to whether to embark on review depends on its jurisdiction to do so; whether the decision is justiciable (on which, see Chapter 1) and whether there are any factors that indicate that the court should exercise its discretion to decline to review the matter. We see that the source of the public authorities' power in statute or a prerogative power continues to provide a clear basis for the court's jurisdiction in most cases, but the complementary "public function" test has not led to a widespread expansion of the ambit of judicial review. The court's approach to reviewing contracts—generally requiring there to be an "additional public element"—is less than satisfactory. The Human Rights Act has brought with it a new range of amenability problems as the courts and Parliament have struggled with the concept of "functions of a public nature" under s.6. Towards of end of Chapter 3 we note that a controversy of former years—whether a litigant must use the judicial review procedure rather than some other form of legal proceedings to raise a public law issue—has now subsided in the wake of the flexibility introduced by the Civil Procedure Rules.

Chapter 4 deals with concepts of jurisdiction and unlawful administration, including statutory provisions which seek to oust the courts' jurisdiction. The approach to ouster clauses is significantly affected by the Human Rights Act and the recently-endorsed common law right of access to justice. These developments have also affected the possibility of "collateral" challenge to official decisions (that is, in procedures other than judicial review).

Part II of the book (Chapters 5-14) deals with the grounds of review. As in the previous edition, we largely retain the categories which Lord Diplock set out, namely illegality (Chapter 5), lack of procedural fairness (Chapters 6-10) and irrationality or unreasonableness (Chapter 11—albeit, as discussed below, now renamed). Again, we recognise that these grounds are by no means self-contained, and that other grounds may well emerge in the future (the term "abuse of power" is often employed these days, either as a distinct ground of review or as a general term for unlawful action).

In the 5th edition the notion of "illegality" as a ground of review was regarded as relatively free of conceptual difficulties. In this edition we devote attention to the process of interpretation of statutory purpose, or relevancy, in respect of a number of issues, including problems raised by

Pepper v Hart, and the interaction between matters which engage Convention rights, European Community law and international law. New distinctions have been drawn recently between powers and duties (some of which are regarded as mere "target duties") and changing judicial approaches to what in the past may have been regarded as unenforceable "policies". Similarly, there have been significant developments in the notion of "relevancy", particularly the extent to which cost, or financial considerations may be lawfully relevant. Delegation of a power is also dealt with in this chapter.

Chapters 6-10 deal with the ground of procedural fairness. We retain the basic format of the 5th edition, dealing first with the history of the requirement that both sides be heard (Chapter 6), then proceeding to the situations giving rise to the fair decision-making process and the content of that entitlement (Chapter 7), then exceptions (Chapter 8). One of the situations which nowadays gives rise to a requirement of fair procedure is where there is a "legitimate expectation" of a hearing or benefit. In the 5th edition we dealt with the legitimate expectation in two parts of the book: in the section on procedural fairness and then again in respect of its relationship to the "unreasonable" decision, where it was then just emerging as a ground of substantive review. We felt in this edition that the legitimate expectation is best treated by considering both of its aspects together, and this is now done in Chapter 12.

Although there have perhaps been relatively few conceptual developments in the notion of fettering of discretion (Chapter 9), we were surprised at the extent of intense judicial examination given to the notion of bias and conflict of interest (as we now entitle Chapter 10). This issue has also been significantly affected by Convention law, especially Article 6 (I), which requires many tribunals to fulfil the qualities of "independence" and "impartiality".

In the 5th edition the chapter which contained for us the most surprises was the one we entitled "The Unreasonable Exercise of Power". De Smith had previously devoted little attention to the notion of "unreasonableness" but when we assembled the cases we discovered far more than we had expected in which decisions were held invalid on the ground of their substance, rather than procedure and we sought to make some sense of the categories in which such review took place. Substantive review is now fully recognised, prompted in particular by the more intense scrutiny that has been accorded to cases where human rights (or "constitutional rights" as they are now explicitly called) are engaged, and where the concept of proportionality is applied. As a result, we have retitled Chapter 11 "Substantive Review and Justification", and seek to show the relationship between the irrational, unreasonable and disproportionate decisions, the different senses of each of those terms, and how the courts have, in different circumstances, adopted different degrees of intensity of review and imposed different standards of justification.

Chapter 12, as we have said above, considers the legitimate expectation in both its procedural and substantive contexts and also considers the extent to which an unlawful representation may give rise to a legally enforceable expectation (as has increasingly been suggested).

This work cannot possibly cover the approach of the courts to each of the specific Convention rights, or the administrative law of the European Union. Other specialist texts admirably cover that extensive ground. However, we must at least outline the essence of those important areas of judicial review and this is done in Chapter 13 (drafted by Ivan Hare), which sets out the salient features of judicial review as it applies to Convention Rights under the Human Rights Act 1998, and in Chapter 14 (updated by Catherine Donnelly), which has the same purpose in respect of the law of the European Union.

Part III of the book is concerned with procedures and remedies. Since the 5th edition, the Civil Procedure Rules have been extended to claims for judicial review—RSC Ord.53 has been replaced by CPR Pt 54. In judicial review as in other types of litigation regard must now be had to "the overriding objectives" of the CPR. There have also been several changes in terminology: claims (rather than applications) for judicial review; the Administrative Court supersedes the Crown Office List; the ancient remedies of prohibition, mandamus and certiorari become prohibiting, mandatory and quashing orders. In Chapter 16, we have included some discussion of alternative dispute resolution, an outline of the Freedom of Information Act 2000 and the Data Protection Act 1998, funding and costs. Chapter 19 turns to monetary remedies against the background of a continuing Law Commission project on financial remedies against public authorities.

We have sought to state the law as it stood on June 1, 2007, though some later developments (to the end of October 2007) were incorporated at proof stage.

ACKNOWLEDGEMENTS

We are particularly grateful to Catherine M. Donnelly, who joined the team and has been responsible for the thorough updates of Chapters 6-8 and 14, and to Ivan Hare (of Blackstone Chambers, London) who contributed the text for Chapter 13 on Convention rights.

The comparative material we incorporate into this edition has been brought to our attention by our distinguished "foreign correspondents", to whom we express our gratitude for their prompt, detailed and expert guidance.

- Australia: Professor Cheryl Saunders and Garbrielle Appleby, University of Melbourne.

- Canada: Professor David Mullen, Queen's University, Ontario.

- India: Soli Sorabjee, former Attorney General of India.

- New Zealand: Professor Mike Taggart, University of Auckland.

- South Africa: Professor Hugh Corder, University of Cape Town and Professor Cora Hoexter, University of the Witwatersrand, Johannesburg.

We also thank Iqbal Jaffree (Pakistan), Justice Sri Ram (Malaysia), Roger Errera (France), Isaac Zamir (Israel) and J.A.S. Felix (Sri Lanka) for providing material relating to their jurisdictions.

We are grateful to the team of researchers who assisted us at various points during the project. They are (in alphabetical order): Caroline Bates; Anna Burne; Joanna Flower; Laura Johnson; Duncan Richards; Anne Street; Jason Varuhas; and Hermione Williams.

Our publishers at Sweet & Maxwell have been indulgent during the time that this edition grew from an update to a rewrite. We thank in particular (in chronological order of their direct involvement with the project): Kate Whetter; Sue Lewis; Caroline Shaw; Kate Auer; Vicky Wilson; and the editorial team who saw this book through its final stages of production.

Finally, as last time, we warmly thank Sylvia Lough for facilitating communication between the three authors and for her continued support and good humour throughout.

Harry Woolf
Jeffrey Jowell
Andrew Le Sueur
October 2007

CONTENTS

TABLE OF CASES

TABLE OF STATUTES

TABLE OF STATUTORY INSTRUMENTS

TABLE OF EUROPEAN LEGISLATION AND INTERNATIONAL CONVENTIONS

TABLE OF CIVIL PROCEDURE RULES

Part 1
THE CONTEXT OF JUDICIAL REVIEW

CHAPTER 1

THE NATURE OF JUDICIAL REVIEW

INTRODUCTION

Our approach

This book is concerned with judicial review of the lawfulness of the powers and duties of those exercising public functions in England and Wales.[1] Since the publication of the first edition of this book in 1959,[2] the circumstances in which the courts have been prepared to provide relief for unlawful administrative action have expanded in spectacular fashion. In the chapters that follow we shall see how, over a relatively short period, English courts reduced the zone of immunity from legal challenge formerly surrounding a great deal of action by public authorities. That task involved the jettisoning of many of the conceptual barriers and disfiguring archaisms which had inhibited the development of effective judicial review. It also required the articulation of acceptable principles governing the exercise of public functions and the vindication of the rights of the individual against the state. These principles and rights are now seen as fundamental features of a constitutional democracy.

European influences

A number of factors have influenced the development of coherent common law principles of judicial review. The effects of European integration have had and continue to have a profound impact. Since the United Kingdom's accession to the European Communities (now the European Union) in 1973, principles of Community law developed by the European Court of Justice, and directly effective rights contained in Community legislation, have provided grounds for judicial review in the national courts.[3] More recently, the enactment of the Human Rights Act 1998 has required our domestic courts to protect the rights set out in the European Convention of Human Rights (ECHR or Convention rights), taking into account the

1-002

---

[1] On the meaning of public function, see Ch.3.
[2] We refer to previous editions of this work, entitled *Judicial Review of Administrative Action*, in the Chapters which follow: the 5th edition (by Lord Woolf and J. Jowell, with the assistant editor A. Le Sueur) was published in 1995; an abridged and updated paperback version of that edition appeared in 1999 under the title *Principles of Judicial Review*; the 4th edition (by J.M. Evans) was published in 1980. Stanley de Smith's own editions were published in 1959 (1st edn), 1968 (2nd edn) and 1973 (3rd edn).
[3] See Ch.14.

case law of the European Court of Human Rights.[4] Both European influences have helped develop new approaches to statutory interpretation and the standards of judicial review.[5]

Common law comparative perspectives

1–003   The development of judicial review in these new contexts requires the courts to define and enunciate the necessary requirements of a democratic society. In so doing it is right to look to other democratic jurisdictions as aids to the development of domestic standards, as judicial review in England and Wales continues to share many features with others in the common law family of legal systems. While this book is not a fully-fledged work of comparative law, approaches adopted in other jurisdictions can provide useful reference points as we plot the development of our own law and practice. We therefore draw on the experience of other common law jurisdictions, especially those of Australia, Canada, India, New Zealand and South Africa, in our accounts of modern judicial review.[6] In relation to some aspects of judicial review, particularly those topics dealt with in Part III of the book, we have taken the view that comparisons are either of limited value or would require an expansive treatment that cannot be accommodated in a book with a primarily national focus. In relation to other aspects of judicial review, we present comparative material with two necessarily limited purposes in mind. First, there are situations where the law in another jurisdiction is so similar to that of England and Wales that a case could be of practical value as persuasive authority. Secondly and more broadly, an approach adopted in another jurisdiction may simply cast an interesting light on how the law in England and Wales operates or how it might develop in the future. We also make reference to judicial review as it is practised in Scotland[7] and Northern Ireland.[8]

Judicial review in the context of the administrative justice system

1–004   Like its predecessors, this edition is not a general treatise on the whole of administrative law in England and Wales. Nor is it a book on human rights and civil liberties. Nor even does it purport to give a complete account of that part of administrative law which is concerned with redress of citizens' grievances—though later in this Chapter we survey the range of avenues of

---

[4] See Ch.13.

[5] See Table 5 below and 5–020—5–048.

[6] Thanks to our "foreign correspondents" in those countries, details of whom are recorded in the Preface. For an explanation of the law reports from those jurisdictions and the rules governing the use of foreign material in the Courts of England and Wales, see Appendix A.

[7] See, e.g. in relation to standing (see 2–068) and amenability to review (see 3–106), in relation to which there are some stark differences with England and Wales. The grounds of review, given their constitutional character, can be assumed to be similar on both sides of the boarder.

[8] As with Scotland, the grounds of review in Northern Ireland and England and Wales are similar.

THE CONSTITUTIONAL CONTEXT OF JUDICIAL REVIEW

The purpose of judicial review

1–006 More than ever before, given the changes in constitutional practices and the notions of constitutionalism,[17] judicial review needs to be set in the context of mechanisms which seek to achieve broader political accountability. In some cases the courts have regarded Parliament's ability to call ministers to account for their decisions as a reason to be wary of intervening to scrutinise the lawfulness of an impugned action or omission, or at least as a fact shaping the development of the common law.[18] Nonetheless, there is a growing appreciation that the courts and Parliament have distinct and complementary constitutional roles so that the courts will no longer avoid adjudicating on the legality of a decision merely because it has been debated and approved in Parliament[19] or relates to nationally important policy pursued by a Minister accountable to Parliament.[20] The distinctive roles of judicial review and parliamentary (and other) oversight of executive action create opportunities for synergy, with aspects of a particular decision being scrutinised in different ways by different bodies. Thus, a government decision may be examined in judicial review proceedings, in an ombudsman complaint and by a parliamentary committee.[21] Judicial review proceedings may prompt parliamentary action, and vice versa.[22] Judicial review also goes some way to answering the age old question of "who guards the guards?" by ensuring that public authorities

[17] Lord Steyn, "The Weakest and Least Dangerous Department of Government" [1997] P.L. 84 (constitutionalism "is neither a rule or a principle of law. It is a political theory as to the type of institutional arrangements that are necessary in order to support the democratic ideal. It holds that the exercise of government power must be controlled in order that it should not be destructive of the very values which it was intended to promote").

[18] See, e.g. *Carltona Ltd v Commissioners of Works* [1943] 2 All E.R. 560 (Lord Greene M.R. emphasised that Ministers are accountable to Parliament for the work of officials).

[19] See, e.g. *R. (on the application of Javed) v Secretary of State for the Home Department* [2001] EWCA Civ 789; [2002] Q.B. 129 (delegated legislation approved by affirmative resolution of both Houses of Parliament could be subject to judicial review on the grounds of illegality, procedural impropriety or irrationality).

[20] See, e.g. *R. (on the application of Medway Council) v Secretary of State for Transport, Local Government and the Regions* [2002] EWHC 2516; [2003] J.P.L. 583 (challenge to decision to exclude Gatwick from proposals to expand airport capacity in southern England); see 7–025.

[21] See, e.g. the scheme for ex gratia payments to Second World War Far East internees was judicially reviewed (*R. (on the application of Association of British Civilian Internees (Far East Region)) v Secretary of State for Defence* [2003] EWCA Civ 473; [2003] Q.B. 1397), investigated by the Parliamentary Commissioner for Administration and was the subject of a special report by a select committee (House of Commons, Public Administration Committee, "*A Debt of Honour": the ex gratia scheme for British Groups interned by the Japanese in the Second World War* HC Paper No.735 (Session 2005/06)).

[22] See, e.g. *R. v Secretary of State for Foreign and Commonwealth Affairs Ex p. World Development Movement Ltd* [1995] 1 W.L.R. 386 was followed by an inquiry of the Foreign Affairs Select Committee, *Pergau Dam* HC paper No.271 (Session 1993/94).

responsible for ensuring accountability of government do so within the boundaries of their own lawful powers.[23]

A distinction which is now less clear than it was is between administrative law and constitutional law. We discuss below the constitutional foundations of judicial review and contend that both the exercise of judicial review and the principles enunciated through judicial review are constitutionally based. The constitution shapes administrative law and in turn is shaped by it. In earlier years, however, the purposes of constitutional and administrative law were considered distinct. Constitutional law was intended to define the powers of the State. Administrative law then had a subsidiary purpose, which was to regulate the exercise of those constitutionally established powers by ensuring that public officials acted within their scope. Most of the attention of administrative law was therefore absorbed in the interpretation of the power—express or implied—conferred upon administrators. Two questions predominated: should the grant of wide discretion be construed literally or purposively? And to what extent should a general duty of fairness or reasonableness be subsumed within the grant of official power? **1–007**

Initially, these questions were resolved within the overriding aim of enabling administrators to further the public interest. Public power should, it was said, self-evidently be exercised in the interest of the public as a whole, and not in the interest of any individual or group of individuals alone. Private concerns were not to obstruct that overall mission. A former Chief Justice considered judicial review to be founded on the principle that courts are the mere "handmaidens of public officials";[24] there to facilitate the work of bodies charged with acting in the public interest. **1–008**

As judicial review gained in confidence, another aim asserted itself, most often described as the promotion of "good public administration". This notion shifted the perspective of administrative law in the direction of the consumer—those persons affected by official decisions. However, the qualities of "the good" in public administration were not grounded in any clear theoretical or constitutional foundation. Later the courts articulated the "grounds" of administrative law as a failure to observe the principles of lawfulness, fairness and reasonableness. These more specific criteria were useful as guides to the content of the "good" in administrative action, but they were still considered duties of the administrator to provide, rather than rights of the individual to receive. **1–009**

[23] Thus the Audit Commission and the Independent Police Complaints Commission (to name but two) are amenable to judicial review. Decisions relating to public inquiries have also been subject to judicial review, as have regulators of the privatised industries (see Ch.3).
[24] A phrase used in 1962 by Lord Parker C.J., quoted in G. Williams, "The Donoughmore Report in Retrospect" (1982) 60 Pub.Admin. 273, 291.

1–010   In recent years, it is increasingly being realised that in a constitutional democracy the role of judicial review is to guard the rights of the individual against the abuse of official power.[25] This does not mean that the courts should necessarily be impeded in their ability to determine the public interest, or to achieve efficiency. Whether or not these rights are as clearly articulated as in countries with written constitutions, we have arrived at a situation described in an address by Lord Diplock delivered at a meeting to pay tribute to the work of the Professor de Smith. He said that our system of administrative law is "in substance nearly as comprehensive in its scope as *droit administratif* in France and gives effect to principles which, though not derived from Gallic concepts of *légalité* and *détournement de pouvoir*, are capable of achieving the same practical results".[26] Shortcomings and lacunae no doubt remain, but English administrative law is now one of the most celebrated products of our common law, and doubtless the fastest developing over the past half-century.

CONSTITUTIONAL JUSTIFICATIONS OF JUDICIAL REVIEW

Justification by the ultra vires principle

1–011   It is surprising that, during this period of development of judicial review, although its general purposes were articulated in the way we have seen, its constitutional justification was rarely articulated. It was perhaps generally assumed that judicial supervision over the exercise of official discretion was justified by the "central principle" of ultra vires.[27] Under this principle the role of the courts is to ensure that Parliament's will is enforced. Judicial review therefore simply involves the implementation of the express or implied intent of the legislature. It was only in 1987 that the ultra vires justification for judicial review was challenged in England and Wales,[28]

---

[25] See, e.g. T. Allan, *Law, Liberty and Justice* (1993). For a further account of the history of administrative law in the nineteenth and twentieth century see C. Harlow and R. Rawlings, Law and Administration, 2nd edn (1997), Chs 1–2. For a further history see J. Jowell, "Administrative Law" in V. Bognador (ed.), *The British Constitution in the Twentieth Century* (2004).

[26] [1974] C.L.J. 233, 244; and *R. v Inland Revenue Commissioners Ex p. National Federation of Self Employed* [1982] A.C. 617 at 641 (Lord Diplock: "the progress towards a comprehensive system of administrative law. . . I regard as having been the greatest achievement of the English courts in my judicial lifetime"); *Breen v Amalgamated Engineering Union* [1971] 2 Q.B. 175 at 189 (Lord Denning, himself an imaginative architect, "It may truly now be said that we have a developed system of administrative law"); *cf. Ridge v Baldwin* [1964] A.C. 40 at 72 (Lord Reid: "We do not have a developed system of administrative law-perhaps because until fairly recently we did not need it"). For the first appearance in an English statute of the term "administrative law", see State Immunity Act 1978 s.3(2).

[27] The late Professor Sir William Wade considered that the ultra vires doctrine was "the central principle of administrative law": H.W.R. Wade and C. Forsyth, *Administrative Law*, 9th edn (2004), p.35.

[28] D. Oliver, "Is the Ultra Vires Rule the Basis of Judicial Review?" [1987] P.L. 543.

initially mainly on the ground that judicial review supervises not only bodies created by statute, but also other regulatory bodies performing public functions, and indeed even bodies created under prerogative powers. These powers were not expressly created by the legislature, so it is not possible to discover the legislative intent behind their creation which might otherwise enable the vires of their actions to be determined.

It is only possible in this introduction briefly to sketch the heated debate that then ensued on this issue.[29] The principal attack on the ultra vires theory was that judges were not in practice merely interpreting the intent of a particular statute, but themselves fashioning independent principles of good administration under traditional methods of common law reasoning.[30] Adherents of this "common law" justification of judicial review argued that it should be openly acknowledged that principles such as "natural justice" or the requirement of a "fair hearing" were imposed by the courts in the face of legislative silence. It was artificial—a "fig leaf" or a "fairy tale"[31]—to suppose that the legislature had implicitly directed those procedures. The "common law" school concede the need to resolve many cases by reference to express or implied parliamentary intent. However, they pointed out that in some cases the courts would deliberately obstruct or evade legislative intent. For example, a clear legislative intention to exclude access to the courts had been subverted by employing the technical distinction between jurisdictional and non-jurisdictional errors. The common law school also accused the ultra vires school of lack of clarity: If the notion of legislative intent is so broad and indeterminate as to permit the implication of principles yet unarticulated (such as that legitimate expectations should not be disappointed), then it is of little use as a practical guide.

In response, the adherents of the ultra vires approach contended that the common law school wrongly justifies unconstrained judicial law-making, contrary to the principle of the separation of powers. Taken to its logical conclusion it was said that the common law approach could lead to judicial challenge to the supremacy of Parliament.

An attempt to reconcile the ultra vires and "common law" justifications of judicial review is provided by the "modified ultra vires" theory[32] (which just as easily could be called the "modified common law" theory). This justification accepts that part of the "common law" theory which acknowledges that judges create principles of good administration independent of specific parliamentary intent. However, it maintains that those principles should be applied consistently with a *general* intention attributed to

1–012

1–013

1–014

---

[29] A number of articles on this debate are collected together in C. Forsyth (ed.), *Judicial Review and the Constitution* (2000).

[30] P. Craig, "Competing Models of Judicial Review" [1999] P.L. 428; Sir John Laws, "Law and Democracy" [1995] P.L. 72.

[31] See the defence: C. Forsyth, "Of Fig Leaves and Fairy Tales: The Ultra Vires Doctrine, Sovereignty of Parliament and Judicial Review" [1987] P.L. 543; C. Forsyth and M. Elliott, "The Legitimacy of Judicial Review" [2003] P.L. 286.

[32] M. Elliott, "The Ultra Vires Doctrine in a Constitutional Setting: Still the Central Principle of Administrative Law" [1999] C.L.J. 129.

Parliament that power which it confers should be exercised in accordance with the rule of law. In other words, legislative silence or ambiguity is read in the context of a continuing consent by Parliament to be bound by the rule of law as interpreted by the courts.

Justification by constitutional principles

1–015 To the extent that the modified ultra vires justification seeks to weave judicial law-making into a constitutional context (under the principle of the rule of law) it is surely right. However, to the extent that it seeks to assign a general intent to Parliament, it is scarcely less artificial than the pure ultra vires justification. We prefer to place the justification of judicial review on a normative and constitutional basis: In our view Parliament *ought* to abide by the necessary requirements of a modern European constitutional democracy (one of which is the rule of law). From that proposition follows a second: that courts *ought* to make the assumption that the rule of law (and other necessary requirements of constitutional democracy) are followed by the legislature. These two propositions are qualified only to the extent that the courts may submit to the authority of Parliament when it seeks clearly and unambiguously to exclude the rule of law or other constitutional fundamentals.[33] Under what circumstances the courts are required so to submit depends upon the continuing validity of the sovereignty of Parliament as our governing constitutional principle.

1–016 In the chapters that follow we shall maintain that the standards applied by the courts in judicial review must ultimately be justified by constitutional principle, which governs the proper exercise of public power in any democracy.[34] This is so irrespective of whether the principles are set out in a formal, written document. The rule of law is one such principle of the greatest importance. It acts as a constraint upon the exercise of all power. The scope of the rule of law is broad and it incorporates different values. It has managed to justify—albeit not always explicitly—a great deal of the specific content of judicial review, such as the requirements that laws as

---

[33] This approach is supported by D. Dyzenhaus, *The Constitution of Law* (2006); J. Jowell, "Of Vires and Vacuums: The Constitutional Context of Judicial Review" [1999] P.L. 448; and "Beyond the Rule of Law: Towards Constitutional Judicial Review" [2000] P.L. 119; P. Joseph, "The Demise of Ultra Vires: Judicial Review in the New Zealand Courts" [2001] P.L. 354, 359 (who says "the concept of the rule of law has replaced ultra vires as the organising principle of administrative law", and cites in support the new Zealand Court of Appeal case *Peters v Davison* [1999] 2 N.Z.L.R. 164 at 188 where it was said that the court's judicial review powers "are based on the central constitutional role of the Court to rule on questions of law, rather than the ultra vires doctrine". For a view that partially shares this approach see T. Allan, "Constitutional Dialogue and the Justification of Judicial Review" (2003) 23 O.J.L.S. 563.

[34] The passages asserting this position in the 5th edition of this work were cited with approval by the South African Constitutional Court in *Pharmaceutical Manufacturer's Association of SA Ex p. President of the RSA* 2000 (3) B.C.L.R. 241 at 252, CC ("the finding that he [the decision-maker] acted ultra vires is a finding that he acted in a manner that was inconsistent with the Constitution").

enacted by Parliament be faithfully executed by officials; that orders of courts should be obeyed; that individuals wishing to enforce the law should have reasonable access to the courts; that no person should be condemned unheard; that decisions should be communicated before they are enforced, and that power should not be arbitrarily exercised. In addition, the rule of law embraces some internal qualities of all public law: that it should be certain, that is, ascertainable in advance so as to be predictable and not retrospective in its operation; and that it be applied equally, without unjustifiable differentiation.[35]

Other constitutional principles are perhaps less clearly identified but nevertheless involve features inherent in a democratic state. These include the requirements of political participation,[36] equality of treatment and freedom of expression.[37] A constitutional principle achieves practical effect as a constraint upon the exercise of all public power. Where the principle is violated it is enforced by the courts which define and articulate its precise content. As we shall see, English law now recognises three main "grounds" of judicial review, known as "procedural propriety", "rationality" and "legality".[38] These grounds are not isolated requirements of a discrete area of law; they refer to and attempt to impose upon all decision-makers standards that are inherent in a democracy. Procedural propriety imposes fair decision-making procedures necessary to the degree of participation which democracy requires. Rationality seeks the accuracy of decisions and prohibits arbitrariness and excessive burdens being imposed on individuals. The ground of legality involves the application both of the sovereignty of Parliament and the rule of law, by requiring Parliament's will to be respected and official action to be congruent with legislative purpose. In applying the ground of legality the courts are effectively acting as guardians of Parliament's intent.[39] Parliamentary sovereignty and the rule of law are

1–017

---

[35] On the rule of law, see 5–037; 11–059; 14–060 (in the context of European Community law); and J. Jowell, "The Rule of Law", Ch.1 in J. Jowell and D. Oliver (eds), The Changing Constitution, 6th edn (2007); P. Craig, "Formal and Substantive Conceptions of the Rule of Law: An Analytical Framework" [1997] P.L. 467; T. Allan, Constitutional Justice: A Liberal Theory of the Rule of Law (2001); Lord Bingham, "The Rule of Law" [2007] C.L.J. 67. The first Statutory reference to the rule of law as a constitutional principle is in the Constitutional Reform Act 2005 s.1, on which see House of Lords Select Committee on the Constitution, Relations between the Executive, the Judiciary and Parliament. HL Paper No.151 (Session 2006/07), para.23.

[36] An important debate about the USA Constitution, but which has relevance in the UK, is the extent to which the constitution seeks to further "process values" (permitting effective participation in the democratic process) or also deals in substantive or moral rights against the state. The argument for the former is put by J. Ely, Democracy and Distrust (1980); for criticism see P. Brest, "The Substance of Protest" (1982) 42 Ohio S.L.J. 131; L. Tribe, "The Puzzling Persistence of Process-based Constitutional Theories" (1980) 89 Yale L.J. 1037; R. Dworkin, "The Forum of Principle" (1982) 56 N.Y.U.L.R. 469; M. Tushnet, "Darkness on the Edge of Town" (1980) 89 Yale L.J. 1037. See also G. Richardson, "The Legal Regulation of Process", in Richardson and Genn (eds), Administrative Law and Government Action (1994), p.105.

[37] See 5–036; 11–057.

[38] Terms employed by Lord Diplock in Council of Civil Service Union v Minister for the Civil Service [1985] A.C. 374 and since employed widely by the courts.

[39] See 5–036.

therefore not inevitably mutually opposed, since a great deal of judicial review (and indeed the rule of law) is concerned with implementing Parliament's will.[40]

Reconciliation between parliamentary sovereignty and the rule of law

1–018 In some cases, however, courts have been faced with the challenge of having to adjudicate when the principle of the rule of law and the principle of the sovereignty of Parliament are in competition. This can occur when Parliament attempts to oust or limit the jurisdiction of the courts to determine the scope of a public authority's powers.[41]

1–019 From time to time it has also been suggested that the English courts ought to be prepared to modify the principle of parliamentary sovereignty by refusing to recognise as a valid law a statutory provision that violates a fundamental right recognised by the common law. Those who advocate this view stress that this judicial redefinition of the limits of parliamentary power would be justified only in an extreme case where the very foundations of democracy were at risk, or the rule of law was being undermined, by a legislative provision. Sir Robin Cooke, while President of the New Zealand Court of Appeal, expressed the view that some "common law rights presumably lie so deep that even Parliament could not override them".[42] Sir John Laws, writing extra-judicially, has alluded to "higher order" law, which "confers . . . and must of necessity limit" parliamentary sovereignty.[43] Lord Woolf has also recognised that, in extremis, the judiciary would have a constitutional responsibility to uphold the rule of law, even in the face of plain statutory words.[44] Lord Donaldson, a former Master of the Rolls, speaking in relation to an ouster clause proposed by the Government, speculated that had it been passed by Parliament "the judges would have said, 'We're not having this'".[45]

---

[40] A. Le Sueur, "The Influence of the House of Lords on the Administrative Court (and Vice Versa)", Ch.4 in R. Gordon (ed.), *Judicial Review in the New Millennium* (2003).

[41] See 4–014.

[42] *Taylor v New Zealand Poultry Board* [1984] 1 N.Z.L.R. 394, 398—an observation of the New Zealand Parliament but no doubt apt to apply also the UK Parliament. Robin Cooke, as Lord Cooke of Thorndon, sat occasionally as a Lord of Appeal in the HL and PC 1996–2001. See further: J. Goldsworth, *The Sovereignty of Parliament* (1999), Ch.1; R. Mullender, "Parliamentary Sovereignty, the Constitution, and the Judiciary" (1998) 49 N.I.L.Q. 138; M. Fordham, "Common Law Illegality of Ousting Judicial Review" [2004] J.R. 86.

[43] "Law and Democracy" [1995] P.L. 72, 87 (and see also 92).

[44] "Droit Public—English Style" [1995] P.L. 57, 68–69 ("However, if Parliament did the unthinkable, then I would say that the courts would also be required to act in a manner which would be without precedent. Some judges might choose to do so by saying that it was an unrebuttable presumption that Parliament could never intend such a result. I myself would consider there were advantages in making it clear that ultimately there are even limits on the supremacy of Parliament which it is the courts' inalienable responsibility to identify and uphold. They are limits of the most modest dimensions which I believe any democrat would accept. They are no more than are necessary to enable the rule of law to be preserved").

[45] *Hansard*, HL, col.746 (December 7, 2004). He continued: "How the judges could have done that is a different matter. One possibility would be that they might have grounded their opposition, and based their insistence on taking jurisdiction, on the rule of law. We have a

The matter was considered in a number of *obiter* dicta in *Jackson*.[46] **1–020** While Lord Bingham felt that Parliamentary sovereignty was still "the bedrock of the British constitution",[47] Lord Steyn said that while parliamentary sovereignty is the *general* principle of our constitution:

> "It is a construct of the common law. The judges created this principle. If that is so, it is not unthinkable that circumstances could arise where the courts may have to qualify a principle established on a different hypothesis of constitutionalism. In exceptional circumstances involving an attempt to abolish judicial review or the ordinary role of the courts, the Appellate Committee of the House of Lords or a new Supreme Court may have to consider whether this is a constitutional fundamental which even a sovereign Parliament acting at the behest of a complaisant House of Commons cannot abolish".[48]

Lord Hope, was even more unequivocal. He said that "The rule of law enforced by the courts is the ultimate controlling factor on which our constitution is based".[49]

Without however directly challenging the primacy of Parliamentary **1–021** sovereignty, the courts have, as we have discussed, finessed the apparent inconsistency between the rule of law and parliamentary supremacy by making the presumption that Parliament intended its legislation to conform to the rule of law as a constitutional principle. This presumption is powerful and is not easily rebutted; only express words or possibly necessary implication will suffice.[50] If officials refuse an individual reasonable access to the courts, or discriminate against a class of individuals, the courts will usually intervene to correct such breaches of the rule of law or other constitutional principle unless the language of the statute clearly and unambiguously prohibits this.[51]

Certainty and flexibility

The concrete application and elucidation of broad constitutional principles **1–022** are not self-evident or static. It is for the courts to articulate them. The general principles are specifically implemented in the context of

tripartite constitution, unwritten though it may be, under which it is not open to any two of the three components simply to close down the third. I make that point because I would not like the statement to go uncontradicted that in all circumstances Parliament is superior to the rule of law. It is in 99 out of 100 cases, yes, but not in all circumstances". The proposed ouster clause, which was not enacted, it is set out at Appendix C below.

[46] *Jackson v Attorney General* [2005] UKHL 56; [2006] 1 A.C. 262 at [102]; also Lord Hope at [120] and Baroness Hale at [36]. For analysis of the constitutional significance of *Jackson*, see J. Jowell, "Parliamentary Sovereignty under the New Constitutional Hypothesis" [2006] P.L. 562.
[47] *Jackson* [2005] UKHL 56; [2006] 1 A.C. 262 at [9].
[48] *Jackson* [2005] UKHL 56; [2006] 1 A.C. 262 at [102]; also Baroness Hale at [36].
[49] *Jackson* [2005] UKHL 56; [2006] 1 A.C. 262 at [107].
[50] See 5–00.
[51] See, e.g. *R. v Secretary of State for the Home Department Ex p. Leech (No.2)* [1994] Q.B. 198; 5–036.

contemporary standards of fairness as well as other values.[52] For example, that aspect of the rule of law that requires legal certainty and predictability is practically applied through the emerging requirement that "legitimate expectations" should be fulfilled in appropriate circumstances.[53] Values such as these are part of our general legal system, developed in accordance with accepted norms as to the proper role of the democratic state and the rights of individuals within it.[54]

1–023   However, many of the standards applied through judicial review are necessarily open-textured. It has been claimed that some of them, such as natural justice, fairness, or reasonableness, are so vague as to be practically meaningless. Lord Reid rightly regarded these claims as "tainted by the perennial fallacy that because something cannot be cut and dried or nicely weighed or measured therefore it does not exist".[55] Judicial review will naturally search for precision, as an aid to the prediction and prescription of administratively fair and correct practices. Yet it cannot afford entirely to abandon flexibility (a principle by no means inferior to that of certainty, aimed at individuated justice).[56] The search for precise standards will always need to be accompanied by a recognition of the particular circumstances of a special case, depending upon the breadth of the power conferred upon the decision-maker; the conditions of its exercise; the availability of alternative procedural protections, and the fairness to the parties involved (and to others affected by the decision). It is for these reasons that the courts themselves retain discretion in the grant of remedies in judicial review.[57]

1–024   The constitutional foundations of "administrative justice" are underlined by the fact that a number of national constitutions have embodied a right to "just" or "good" administrative action—starting with Namibia[58] and

---

[52] See, e.g. Lord Diplock's definition of the ground of review of irrationality as reflecting "accepted moral standards" in Council of Civil Service Union v Minister for the Civil Service [1985] A.C. 374.

[53] See Ch.12.

[54] During the 1990s a series of English judges, writing extra judicially, sought to place judicial review within the context of democratic rights: Lord Scarman, "The Development of Administrative Law: Obstacles and Opportunities" [1990] P.L. 490; Lord Browne-Wilkinson, "The Infiltration of a Bill of Rights" [1992] P.L. 397; Sir John Laws, "Judicial Remedies and the Constitution" (1994) 57 M.L.R. 213, and "Law and Democracy" [1995] P.L. 72; Lord Woolf, "Droit Public—English Style" [1995] P.L. 57; Sir Stephen Sedley, "The Sound of Silence: Constitutional Law Without a Constitution" (1994) 110 L.Q.R. 270.

[55] Ridge v Baldwin [1964] A. C. 40 at 64–65.

[56] D. Galligan, Discretionary Powers (1986). For further discussion on discretion, see 5–017; and for the tension between rules and discretion, see Chs 9 and 12.

[57] See 18–048.

[58] Constitution of the Republic of Namibia 1990 (as amended), Art.18: "Administrative bodies and administrative officials shall act fairly and reasonably and comply with the requirements imposed upon such bodies and officials by common law and any relevant legislation, and persons aggrieved by the exercise of such acts and decisions shall have the right to seek redress before a competent Court or Tribunal".

South Africa.[59] The Charter of Fundamental Rights of the European Union now incorporates the right to "good administrative practice".[60] In some jurisdictions, the grounds of judicial review have come to be codified in statute,[61] but as yet that has not been considered necessary here as there is thus far no quarrel that the incremental development of the common law has satisfactorily fashioned a balance between the need for efficiency and the need to prevent abuses of power.[62]

CONSTITUTIONAL AND INSTITUTIONAL LIMITS OF JUDICIAL REVIEW (JUSTICIABILITY)

Judicial review has developed to the point where it is possible to say that no power—whether statutory or under the prerogative—is any longer inherently unreviewable. Courts are charged with the responsibility of adjudicating upon the manner of the exercise of a public power, its scope and its substance.[63] As we shall see, even when discretionary powers are engaged, they are not immune from judicial review. Discretion has been described as the "hole in the [legal] doughnut",[64] but that hole is not automatically a lawless void. Nevertheless, there are certain decisions which courts cannot or should not easily engage. Courts are limited (a) by their constitutional role and (b) by their institutional capacity.   1–025

Limitations inherent in the courts' constitutional role

The principle of the separation of powers confers matters of social and economic policy upon the legislature and not the judiciary. Courts should, therefore, avoid interfering with the exercise of discretion by elected   1–026

---

[59] Constitution of the Republic of South Africa 1996 s.33: "(1) Everyone has the right to administrative action that is lawful, reasonable and procedurally fair. (2) Everyone whose rights have been adversely affected by administrative action has the right to be given written reasons. (3) National legislation must be enacted to give effect to these rights, and must—(a) provide for the review of administrative action by a court or, where appropriate, an independent and impartial tribunal; (b) impose a duty on the state to give effect to the rights in subsections (1) and (2); and (c) promote an efficient administration".

[60] Charter of Fundamental Rights of the European Union (see 14–028). The right here includes the right to have one's affairs handled impartially, fairly and within a reasonable time and the right to reasons and the right of access to your case file. There is no directly comparable right in ECHR, though Arts 6 and 13 go some way to ensuring effective judicial remedies (see 6–048, 7–032 and 13–010).

[61] e.g. in Australia: Administrative Decisions (Judicial Review) Act 1977 ss.5–7; in South Africa: Promotion of Administrative Justice Act, 2000; in Trinidad and Tobago: Judicial Review Act No.60 of 2000 s.5(3); in Barbados: Administrative Justice Act 1980. See further R. Ramlogen, *Judicial Review in the Commonwealth Caribbean* (2007).

[62] But see the Ministry of Justice's important Green Paper *The Governance of Britain* (Cm. 7170, July 2007), para.209: "A Bill of Rights and Duties could give people a clear idea of what we can expect from public authorities, and from each other, and a framework for giving practical effect to our common values".

[63] See Ch.11.

[64] R. Dworkin, *Taking Rights Seriously* (1977), p.82.

officials or their appointees when its aim is the pursuit of policy.[65] It is not for judges to weigh utilitarian calculations of social, economic or political preference.[66] Courts will not, therefore, make decisions on whether site A or B is suitable for the location of a new airport;[67] whether the United Kingdom should engage in a programme of nuclear disarmament;[68] whether there should be investment in a significant nuclear power programme[69]; or whether the programme to produce Trident nuclear warheads should be abandoned.[70]

[65] See e.g. *R. v Secretary of State for Trade and Industry Ex p. Lonrho Plc* [1989] 1 W.L.R. 525 at 536 (Lord Keith: "These provisions [that the Secretary of State may act against a proposed merger after a report by the Monopolies and Mergers Commission has so advised to Parliament and the Secretary of State acts by a draft order laid before Parliament] ensure that a decision which is essentially political in character will be brought to the attention of Parliament and subject to scrutiny and challenge therein, and the courts must be careful not to invade the political field and substitute their own judgment for that of the Minister. The courts judge the lawfulness not the wisdom of the decision"); *Wilson v First County Trust Ltd (No.2)* [2003] UKHL 40; [2004] 1 A.C. 816 at [70] (Lord Nicholls: "The more the legislation concerns matters of broad social policy the less ready will be a court to intervene"); *R. (on the application of Hooper) v Secretary of State for Work and Pensions* [2003] EWCA Civ 813; [2003] 1 W.L.R. 2623 at [63]–[64] (Laws L.J.: "A very considerable margin of discretion must be accorded to the Secretary of State. Difficult questions of economic and social policy were involved, the resolution of which fell within the province of the executive and the legislature rather than the courts"), reversed on appeal: [2005] UKHL 29; [2005] 1 W.L.R. 1681; *R. v Secretary of State for Education and Employment Ex p. Begbie* [2000] 1 W.L.R. 1115 at 1131 (Laws L.J., stating that less intrusive judicial review should apply to decisions in the "macro-political field"); see further 11–086.
[66] Dworkin's definition of policy: "Political Judges and the Rule of Law" (1978) 64 *Proceedings of the British Academy* 259. On his distinction between "principle" and "policy", see *Taking Rights Seriously* (1977), pp.82–87. Sometimes the term used is "political question", especially in the USA.
[67] *Essex CC v Ministry of Housing and Local Government* (1967) 66 L.G.R. 23 (it would be quite futile to impugn the government's decision that Foulness should be developed as the third London airport, merely by contending that the decision was unreasonable or that Cublington was more suitable); cf. *R. (on the application of Medway Council) v Secretary of State for Transport, Local Government and the Regions* [2002] EWHC 2516; [2003] J.P.L. 583 (decision to exclude Gatwick airport from consultation about expansion of air transport capacity in SE England was unreasonable).
[68] *Chandler v DPP* [1964] A.C. 763 at 798 (Lord Radcliffe said, that this was an issue of "policy" and that "the more one looks at it, the plainer it becomes, I think, that the question whether it is in the true interests of the country to acquire, retain or house nuclear armaments depends upon an infinity of considerations, military and diplomatic, technical, psychological and moral, and of decisions, tentative or final, which are themselves part assessments of fact and part expectations and hopes. I do not think that there is anything amiss with a legal ruling that does not make this issue a matter for judge or jury").
[69] *R. (on the application of Greenpeace Ltd) v Secretary of State for Trade and Industry* [2007] EWHC 311 Admin (a government review which, on the basis of a short period of consultation, recommended reversing the government's policy against nuclear power, was flawed for illegality; the consultation was not sufficient by the standards of Art.7 of the Aarhus Convention (UNECE Convention on Access to Information, Public Participation in Decision-making and Access to Justice in Environmental Matters); despite being a matter of "high policy", the review was so deficient in content and form that its process was "manifestly unfair").
[70] *R. (on the application of Marchiori) v Environment Agency* [2002] EWCA Civ 3; [2002] Eu. L.R. 225.

The constitutional status of the judiciary should not, however, excuse 1–027
the courts from any scrutiny of policy decisions. Courts are able, and
indeed obliged, to require that decisions, even in the realm of "high
policy"[71] are within the scope of the relevant power or duty,[72] and arrived
at by the standards of procedural fairness.[73] The courts display reserve in
impinging upon the substance of policy decisions, but even here they may
legitimately intervene if the decision is devoid of reason and not properly
justified.[74] Judges always possess the capacity to probe the evidence and
assess whether the reasons and motives for decisions are rationally related
to their aims. As will be shown in the Chapters that follow, public law has
rapidly advanced recently from a "culture of authority" to a "culture of
justification".[75]

Thus even where the courts recognise their lack of relative constitutional 1–028
capacity to make the primary decision of policy, they should nevertheless
not easily relinquish their secondary function of probing the quality of the
reasoning and ensuring that assertions are properly justified. As Lord
Nicholls said in *Ghaidan v Godin-Mendoza*[76] in respect of national housing
policy:

"Parliament has to hold a fair balance between the competing interests
of tenants and landlords, taking into account broad issues of social and
economic policy. But, even in such a field, where the alleged violation
comprises differential treatment based upon grounds such as race or sex
or sexual orientation the court will scrutinise with intensity any reasons
said to constitute justification".

In addition, it should be borne in mind that under the Human Rights Act 1–029
1998 no public authority may interfere with Convention rights and even
Parliament is expected to abide by their terms.[77] When adjudicating on the
scope of interference with Convention rights, therefore, the courts need

---

[71] *R. v Secretary of State for the Home Department Ex p. Everett* [1989] Q.B. 811 (Taylor
L.J.), such as making treaties, dissolving Parliament, mobilising the armed forces. See 3–034.
[72] On notion of "target duties", see 5–064; *R. (on the application of Bancoult) v Secretary of
State for Foreign and Commonwealth Affairs* [2007] EWCA Civ 498; (2007) 104 (23) L.S.G.
31 at [46] (Sedley L.J. considered that very broad latitude is given to the executive in deciding
what makes for the "peace, order and good government" of a colony but that the executive
must be open to challenge on grounds of jurisdictional error or malpractice or if the subject
matter "is manifestly not the peace, order or good government of the colony").
[73] See, e.g. Medway [2002] EWHC 2516; [2003] J.P.L. 583; Greenpeace [2007] EWHC 311
Admin. In other jurisdictions, see: *Peters v Davidson* [1999] 2 N.Z.L.R. 164 (New Zealand)
and *Operation Dismantle v The Queen* [1985] 1 S.C.R. 441 (Canada).
[74] A. Barak, "Foreword: A Judge on Judging: The Role of a Supreme Court in a Democracy"
(2002) Harv L.R. 16, 97–106 (the former President of the Israeli Supreme Court does not
admit that any decisions are inherently non-justiciable for this reason).
[75] The words of the late Professor Etienne Mureinik describing the transformation in post-
apartheid public law in South Africa: "A Bridge Too Far: Introducing the Interim Bill of
Rights" (1994) 10 S. African J. of Human Rights 31. See further 11–100.
[76] [2004] 2 A.C. 557 at [19].
[77] See Ch.13.

not defer to the executive on the ground of their responsibility to Parliament. Nor need they defer to Parliament on the ground that it is elected;[78] though deference to elected members may be legitimate on the ground that they, rather than the court, are better equipped at deciding particular questions requiring an assessment of the public interest.[79] The courts possess the legitimacy to guard the invasion of those rights that now form the basis of our constitutional democracy.

Limitations inherent in the courts' institutional capacity

1–030 In respect of the institutional capacity of the courts, there are some decisions which they are ill-equipped to review—those which are not ideally justiciable or, in other words, "not amenable to the judicial process",[80] or indeed those which are better able to be determined by other bodies, including Parliament.

Matters which are in essence matters of preference

1–031 These include decisions which cannot be impugned on the basis of any objective standard because their resolution is essentially a matter of individual (including political) preference. Where the Secretary of State

---

[78] *R. v Inland Revenue Commissioners Ex p. National Federation of Self-Employed and Small Businesses Ltd* [1982] A.C. 617 at 644 (Lord Diplock: "It is not, in my view, a sufficient answer to say that judicial review of the actions of officers or departments of central governments is unnecessary because they are accountable to Parliament for the way in which they carry out their functions. They are accountable to Parliament for what they do so far as regards efficiency and policy, and of that Parliament is the only judge; they are responsible to a court of justice for the lawfulness of what they do, and of that the court is the only judge"). This view towards judicial deference on constitutional grounds is shared by Lord Steyn, "Deference: A Tangled Story" [2005] P.L. 346; J. Jowell, "Judicial Deference and Human Rights: A Question of Competence", in P. Craig and R. Rawlings (eds), *Law and Administration in Europe, Essays in Honour of Carol Harlow* (2005), p.67; Jowell, "Judicial Deference: Servility, Civility to Institutional Capacity" [2003] P.L. 592. In respect of "common law" rights the courts may presume that Parliament did not intend to abrogate the right unless clearly enunciated—"the principle of "legality" (on which see 5–036). *cf. Rehman v Secretary of State for the Home Department* [2001] UKHL 47; [2003] 1 A.C. 153 at [62] (Lord Hoffmann contended that matters of national security "must be made by persons whom the people have elected and whom they can remove").

[79] See, e.g. in relation to local authorities: *R. v Brighton Corp Ex p. Tilling (Thomas) Ltd* (1916) 85 L.J.K.B. 1552 at 1555 (public transport licensing); *Sagnata Investments Ltd v Norwich Corp* [1971] 2 Q.B. 614 (amusement arcade permit); *Cumings v Birkenhead Corp* [1972] Ch. 12 (local educational policy); *Cannock Chase DC v Kelly* [1978] 1 W.L.R. 1 (allocation of tenancies of council houses); *Pickwell v Camden LBC* [1983] Q.B. 962 (allocation of salaries and wages even though strike still in progress). But note the caution expressed in *Huang v Secretary of State for the Home Department* [2007] UKHL 11; [2007] 2 W.L.R. 581 at [17] (HL found unpersuasive the submission of the Secretary of State that the decision-maker and the court should assume that the immigration rules adopted by the responsible minister and laid before Parliament "had the imprimatur of democratic approval and should be taken to strike the right balance between the interests of the individual and those of the community").

[80] *Council for the Civil Service Unions v Minister for the Civil Service* [1985] 1 A.C. 374 at 418 (Lord Roskill).

had the power to decide whether the expenditure of local authorities had been "excessive" and to penalise them if it had been, the House of Lords held that decision not suited to judicial determination because of the lack of "objective criteria" by which to determine the content of excessive expenditure.[81] Following the events of September 2001, the Government sought to derogate from ECHR Art.5 on the ground specified in Art.15 that there was a "public emergency threatening the life of the nation". The majority of the House of Lords held this to be a "pre-eminently political question", on the ground that it involved a prediction of what people around the world would do. The basis of this view was less that it was a question which lay, constitutionally, with the executive, than it required a judgment which admitted of no objective challenge.[82]

Matters in relation to which the court lacks expertise

A second institutional limitation of the courts is lack of relative expertise.[83]   1–032
Particularly as the review of fact, or the merits of a decision, is not routinely permitted in judicial review,[84] there are some matters which are best resolved by those with specialist knowledge (such as decisions about the rankings of university departments.)[85] Connected with the issue of expertise is that of risk-assessment.[86] National security is often said to be an

---

[81] *R. v Secretary of State for the Environment Ex p. Hammersmith and Fulham LBC* [1991] 1 A.C. 521 at 593, 597 (Lord Bridge); *Buttes Gas v Hammer* [1982] A.C. 888 (Lord Diplock, in a case involving relations with a foreign state, said that the court has "no justiciable or manageable standards by which to judge" the issue. To attempt such review, he said, the court would be in a "judicial no-man's land"); *Gillick v West Norfolk & Wisbech Area Health Authority* [1986] 1 A.C. 112 at 193 (the court should exercise its jurisdiction with the "utmost restraint" in cases involving "questions of social and ethical controversy"); *Airedale NHS Trust v Bland* [1993] A.C. 789 at 891 (Lord Mustill); *Roberts v Hopwood* [1925] A.C. 578 at 606–607 (Sumner L.J.); S. Sorabjee, "Decisions of the Supreme Court in *S.R. Rommai v Union of India* " (1994) 3 S.C.C. (Jour) 2.
[82] *X v Secretary of State for the Home Department* (Belmarsh detainees case) [2004] UKHL 56; [2005] 2 A.C. 68. Lord Hoffman, dissenting, held firmly that the events did not amount to a threat to the nation's life (which he considered included not only in the physical sense but in the sense of its entire cultural fabric, including its attachment to values of civil liberty).
[83] See, e.g. *R. v Secretary of State for the Home Department Ex p. Swati* [1986] 1 W.L.R. 477; *R. v Chief Constable of the Merseyside Police Ex p. Calveley* [1986] 1 Q.B. 424; *Pulhofer v Hillingdon LBC* [1986] A.C. 484; *R. v Secretary of State for Social Services Ex p. Stitt* [1990] C.O.D. 288; *R. (on the application of W) v Thetford Youth Justices* [2002] EWHC 1252; (2002) 166 J.P. 453 at [40] (Sedley L.J.: "A youth court has expertise which a higher court lacks"); *R. (on the application of Legal Remedy UK Ltd) v Secretary of State for Health* [2007] EWHC 1252 (Admin) (court wary of "donning the garb of policy maker" in challenge to restructuring of postgraduate medical training).
[84] On precedent fact, see 4–047; on mistake of fact, see 11–041.
[85] *R. v Higher Education Funding Council Ex p. Institute of Dental Surgery* [1994] 1 W.L.R. 242 (Sedley J. considered the question of rating the research of a university department not amenable to review on the ground of lack of the court's expertise); *cf. R. (on the application of Wooder) v Feggetter* [2002] EWCA Civ 554; [2003] Q.B. 219 at [40] (Sedley L.J. doubted whether he would necessarily reach that decision again). Lack of expertise on the part of the Administrative Court is one reason for the insistence that claimants use alternative means of legal challenge where they exist: 16–014.
[86] See, e.g. *R. (on the application of Farrakhan) v Secretary of State for the Home Department*

area in which the courts should not readily intervene,[87] not merely because the executive possess prime constitutional responsibility in this area, but because they may be best placed to assess, through their network of informers, the risk of the dangers involved.

However, here too the court will no longer unquestioningly accept the say-so of the executive or other experts, and will properly intervene if the decision is based on a material mistake of fact,[88] or is otherwise illegal or irrational.

Matters which are polycentric

1–033   A third limitation on the court's institutional capacity occurs when the matter to be determined is "polycentric". Most "allocative decisions"— decisions involving the distribution of limited resources—fall into this category. If the court alters such a decision, the judicial intervention will set up a chain reaction, requiring a rearrangement of other decisions with which the original has interacting points of influence.[89] Thus where it was alleged that the proposals of the Boundary Commission resulted in an "excessive disparity" between the number of electors in each constituency and the "electoral quota" (as required by the Rules), it was held that this was a question on which the courts should be reluctant to decide, there being "more than one answer", particularly since any adjustment to the boundaries would necessitate other compensating adjustments to the proposals (a typical polycentric problem, although not directly referred to as such).[90]

[2002] EWCA Civ 606; [2002] Q.B. 1391; *R. v Secretary of State for the Home Department Ex p. Turgut* [2001] 1 All E.R. 719 at 729 (Simon Brown L.J.: "The court is hardly less well placed than the Secretary of State himself to evaluate the risk once the relevant material is placed before it").
[87] In the Belmarsh detainees case *X v Secretary of State for the Home Department* [2004] UKHL 56; [2005] 2 A.C. 68, the HL held that preventive detention for non-nationals, designed for purposes of national security, was not sufficiently justified under the terms of ECHR Art.15. In relation to procedural fairness, see 8–007.
[88] See 11–041.
[89] *Council of Civil Service Unions v Minister for the Civil Service* [1985] A.C. 374 at 411 (Lord Diplock: decisions involving "competing policy considerations", involving "a balancing exercise which judges by their upbringing and their experience are ill-qualified to perform"). See L. Fuller, "The Forms and Limits of Adjudication" (1978–79) 92 Harv. L.R. 395, who likens a polycentric problem to that of a spider's web: "A pull on one strand will distribute tensions after a complicated pattern throughout the web as a whole. Doubling the original pull will, in all likelihood, not simply double each of the resulting tensions but rather create a different complicated pattern of tensions. This would certainly occur, for example, if the double pull caused one or more of the weaker strands to snap." These words were quoted in *R. v Secretary of State for the Home Department Ex p. P* [1995] 1 All E.R. 870 (Neill L.J.: non-statutory power establishing a scheme to provide compensation for criminal injuries was held not justiciable because it involved "a balance of competing claims on the public purse and the allocation of economic resources which the court is ill equipped to deal with"); J. Allison "Fuller's Analysis of Polycentric Disputes and The Limits of Adjudication" (1994) C.L.J. 367; *cf.* A. Le Sueur, "Justifying Judicial Caution: Jurisdiction, Justiciability and Policy", Ch.8 in B. Hadfield (ed.), *Judicial Review: A Thematic Approach* (1995). See generally: A. Chayes, "The Role of the Judge in Public Law Litigation" (1976) 89 Harv. L.R. 1281, 1288.
[90] *R. v Boundary Commission for England Ex p. Foot* [1983] Q.B. 600.

Another typical polycentric decision is one involving the allocation of **1–034** scarce resources among competing claims.[91] As will be discussed in Chapter 5, courts are asked to determine (a) whether the cost of a project is material to a decision; (b) whether the cost of a project is too high, or (c) too low.[92] The first issue to decide when these claims are made is whether the alleged duty is a mere "target duty" (such as to provide for the needs of children or the disabled in general) or an enforceable duty (to provide a particular service to the claimant). Once it has been decided that there is a duty to be engaged, or that a power is being neglected or ignored, should it then be for the courts to dictate how the resources ought to be allocated between the fulfillment of that duty and other competing responsibilities? In *R. v Cambridge DHA Ex p. B (No.1)*, the decision of a hospital not to provide expensive treatment to a child with cancer was upheld by the Court of Appeal.[93] Similarly, the House of Lords refused to interfere in a decision of a chief constable to deploy his resources in a manner that gave only partial and sporadic protection to exporters at risk of disruption of their trade from animal rights protesters.[94]

One of the reasons why a polycentric decision is not ideally amenable to **1–035** judicial review is that the re-allocation of resources in consequence of the court's judgment will normally involve the interests of those who were not represented in the initial litigation. Yet it should not always be assumed that the legislature always possesses an institutional capacity superior to that of the courts to take into account a wide variety of interests. In *Huang*,[95] the House of Lords acknowledged that in some areas the determination of policy by the legislative or executive branch is institutionally no better than that of the courts. Their Lordships distinguished between a case which concerns established housing policy[96]—where the result represented "a considered democratic compromise", and where all

---

[91] J. King, "The Justiciability of Resource Allocation" (2007) 70 M.L.R. 197; E. Palmer, "Resource Allocation, Welfare Rights—Mapping the Boundaries of Judicial Control in Public Administrative Law" (2000) 20 O.J.L.S. 63; S. Fredman, "Positive Rights Transformed: Positive Duties and Positive Rights" [2006] P.L. 498.

[92] See 5–124.

[93] [1995] 1 W.L.R. 898 at 906 (Sir Thomas Bingham M.R.: "Difficult and agonizing judgments have to be made as to how a limited budget is best allocated to the maximum advantage of the maximum number of patients. That is not a judgment which a court can make"); R. James and D. Longley, "Judicial Review and Tragic Choices: *Ex p. B* " [1995] P.L. 367.

[94] *R. v Chief Constable of Sussex Ex p. International Traders Ferry Ltd* [1999] 2 A.C. 418; also *R. (on the application of Pfizer Ltd) v Secretary of State for Health* [2002] EWCA Civ 1566; [2003] 1 C.M.L.R. 19 (CA upheld decision to provide the drug Viagra to a limited category of patients); K. Syrett, "Impotence or Importance? Judicial Review in an Era of Explicit NHS Rationing" (2004) 67 M.L.R. 289. *cf. R. (on the application of Rogers) v Swindon NHS Primary Care Trust* [2006] EWCA Civ 392; [2006] 1 W.L.R. 2649 (policy on funding breast cancer treatment with an unlicensed drug called Herceptin was irrational); K. Syrett, "Opening Eyes to the Reality of Scarce Health Care Resources? R (on the application of Rogers) v Swindon PCT and Secretary of State for Health" [2006] P.L. 664.

[95] *Huang v Secretary of State for the Home Department* [2007] UKHL 11; [2007] 2 W.L.R. 581.

[96] As in *Kay v Lambeth LBC* [2006] UKHL 10; [2006] 2 A.C. 465.

parties were represented in the debate and where the issue involved the allocation of finite resources—and the situation in immigration policy where those elements were not present. In the latter case, the courts have far less institutional reason to be diffident about intervening in order to protect the rights or interests of those who were not represented in the decision-making process.

1–036   Furthermore, budgetary decisions are not, invariably regarded by the courts as matters for the authority alone. The matter depends upon the relevant statute and context. While in *R. v Gloucestershire CC Ex p. Barry*,[97] the House of Lords held that the authority was entitled to take into account its limited resources when it considered whether it could fulfil "needs", in *R. v Sussex CC Ex p. Tandy*[98] the House of Lords took the opposite view in holding that the authority could not take its limited resources into account in considering whether it could provide "suitable education". As we shall see further when we consider these issues in greater detail in Chapters 5 and 11, so much in public law depends upon the context.[99]

Comparative approaches to justiciability

Australia

1–037 In Australia there are still a number of areas where a matter is considered *generally* non-justiciable. These include decisions with a "political" content or where there is a lack of explicit or manageable standards. Such areas have traditionally included treaty making, recognition of the government or boundaries of a foreign state, declaring war, dissolving Parliament, budgetary and financial decisions and decisions relating to national security, and the conduct of foreign policy.[100] Under the Administrative Decisions (Judicial Review) Act 1977, specific exercises of the prerogative and decisions and conduct of the Governor General are excluded from review.[101] However, Australia has generally followed the English position in respect that no power, even a prerogative power, is inherently non-justiciable at common law.[102] Thus the Federal Court has followed English authority[103] to the effect that the Act of State doctrine and the justiciability of "political" questions affecting foreign relations is not absolute and

[97] [1997] A.C. 206.
[98] [1998] A.C. 714.
[99] See 5–124; 11–001–012.
[100] *Horta v Commonwealth* (194) 181 C.L.R. 183 at 195–196.
[101] Administrative Decisions (Judicial Review) Act 1977 s.3(1) and Sch.1.
[102] Obiter comments in accord with *Council of Civil Service Unions v Minister for the Civil Service* [1985] A.C. 374 made in *R. v Toohey Ex p. Northern Land Council* (1981) 151 C.L.R. 170 (Mason J. at 219–221; Aicken J. at 261; Toohey at 282–3). The Full Federal Court endorsed the application of the *CCSU* case in *Minister for Arts Heritage and the Environment v Peko-Wallsend* (1987) 75 A.L.R. 224.
[103] *Kuwait Airways Corp v Iraqi Airways Company* [2002] 2 A.C. 883.

ought to be read down when there is a clear breach of an established standard of international law and where there are questions involving human rights.[104] Polycentric decisions tend to render a decision non-reviewable, but this has been challenged, especially in relation to the issue of whether a decision has been arrived at in accordance with procedural fairness.[105]

Canada

It is seldom that justiciability intrudes directly as a limiting principle in Canadian judicial review proceedings.[106] However, the courts have accepted, and s.2(1) of the Federal Courts Act 1985 provides, that exercises of prerogative power are not insulated from judicial review proceedings. However, in *Black v Canada (Prime Minister)*,[107] the Court of Appeal for Ontario did recognise that, on a subject matter basis, certain exercises of prerogative power could be immune from judicial review (in that instance, the Prime Minister's communication of the Canadian policy on honours to the Queen and his advice that Her Majesty not confer an honour on Conrad Black while he was still a Canadian citizen). In *Operation Dismantle*, the Supreme Court held that there was no such creature as a "political questions" doctrine in Canadian constitutional law and that the principle of justiciability should not prevent the Court from reviewing, on Charter grounds,[108] an executive decision to allow the United States to test planes possibly carrying nuclear warheads over Canada. However, the principle of justiciability does have an indirect impact on aspects of Canadian judicial review law. For example, it informs the factors that are taken into account in decisions about public interest standing. In *Operation Dismantle*[109] the Supreme Court rejected the challenge on the basis that the public interest plaintiff had not met the high evidential burden for obtaining standing in such cases. Justiciability also arises in respect of the constitutional relationship between the courts and the other branches of government,[110] and invites extreme deference ("patent reasonableness") when broad discretionary powers are conferred on the executive. Thus the Supreme Court has been reluctant to attribute improper motives to policy decision-making by collective bodies such as Cabinet (the Governor in Council) or even municipalities.[111] Traditional

1–038

---

[104] *Hicks v Ruddock* [2007] F.C.A. 299 at [14], [31]; also *Petrotimor v The Commonwealth of Australia* (2003) 126 F.C.R. 354 at 369. See C. Finn, "The Justiciability of Administrative Decisions: A Redundant Concept" (2002) 30 Federal Law Rev. 239.

[105] M. Aronson, B. Dyer and M. Groves, *Judicial Review of Administrative Action*, 3rd edn (2004), pp.423, 429. See Sir Anthony Mason, "Procedural Fairness: Its Development and Continuing Role of Legitimate Expectation" (2005) Australian J. of Admin. Law 103, 105.

[106] L. Sossin, *The Boundaries of Judicial Review; Justiciability in Canada* (1999).

[107] (2001), 54 OR. (3d) 215.

[108] The Canadian Charter of Rights and Freedoms, which forms the first part of the Constitution Act 1982.

[109] *Operation Dismantle v The Queen* [1985] 1 S.C.R. 441.

[110] *Finlay v Canada (Minister of Finance)* [1986] 2 S.C.R. 607.

[111] See, e.g. *Thorne's Hardware Ltd v Canada* [1983] 1 S.C.R. 106; *Consortium Developments (Clearwater) Ltd v Sarnia (City)* [1998] 3 S.C.R. 3.

limitations also continue to prevail where problems have a polycentric dimension, involving attempts to compel governments to spend money or to carry through with promises (election-based) or otherwise, and even when Charter rights are engaged.[112] A less deferential approach may, however, be foreshadowed by more recent cases,[113] where the Supreme Court stuck down provisions of provincial statutes that banned private medical insurance on the ground that the ban would breach the right to security of the person.[114] The majority were willing to make their own assessment of the factual impact of the ban and McLachlin C.J. and Major J. were adamant that the fact that the decision had "policy ramifications does not permit us to avoid answering it".[115]

India

1–039 In India, courts will not interfere with policy decisions of the government merely because it feels that another policy decision could have been fairer or wiser or more scientific or logical.[116] It is not the function of the courts to sit in judgment in matters of economic policy and that must necessarily be left to the expert bodies.[117] However, it has been firmly held that there is no unfettered discretion in public law, and that no decision which operates prejudicially to the rights and interests of a person is beyond judicial review.[118] Even in relation to policy decisions or those of experts, therefore, the courts will interfere if the decision is "patently arbitrary", discriminatory or *mala fide*.[119]

New Zealand

1–040 In *Curtis v Minister of Defence*, an attempt to judicially review the government's decision to disband the only air combat wing of the Royal New Zealand Air Force was upheld.[120] The further issue as to whether the

[112] D. Mullan, "Deference from Baker to Suresh and Beyond—Interpreting the Conflicting Signals", in D. Dyzenhaus (ed.), *The Unity of Public Law* (2004).

[113] See, e.g. *Mount Sinai Hospital v Quebec (Minister of Health and Social Services)* [2001] 2 S.C.R. 281 (judicial intervention in ministerial policy-making based on funding considerations).

[114] *Chaoulli v Quebec (Attorney General)* [2005] 1 S.C.R. 791. See J. King, "Constitutional Rights and Social Welfare: A Comment on the Canadian *Chaoulli* Health Care Decision" (2006) 69 M.L.R. 631.

[115] at 107.

[116] *BALCO Employees Union v Union of India* 2002 (2) S.C.C. 333 at 362.

[117] *Peerless General Finance and Investment Co Ltd v Reserve Bank of India* 1992 (2) S.C.C. 343 at 375.

[118] *Reliance Airport Developers v Airport Authority of India* 2006 (10) S.C.C. 1, 34, quoting Lord Denning in *Breen v Amalgamated Engineering Union* [1971] 2 Q.B. 175; *Tata Cellular v Union of India* 1994 (6) S.C.C. 651 at 686.

[119] *BALCO* 2002(2) S.C.C. 333 at 357.

[120] [2002] 2 N.Z.L.R. 744, CA. The principal argument that the Air Force would not satisfy the statutory requirement of an "armed force" without any fighter strike capacity was considered but rejected on the ground that it could not be said that the air force was no longer in existence. Tipping J. for the court said "[i]t has no doubt become a different sort of air force from which has hitherto existed but it nevertheless remains an air force" (at [18]).

minister's decision left the air force insufficiently armed was a "political" and therefore not a justiciable issue. In *Akatere v Attorney General*[121] the Court considered guidelines approved by the cabinet for the ex gratia payments for those wrongly convicted of crimes. In the event no reviewable error was found, but after considering cases pointing either way, Keane J. was inclined to hold the matter non-justiciable.[122]

South Africa

All power in South Africa must be exercised in accordance with constitu- 1–041 tional requirements, which include the rule of law. In *President of the Republic of South Africa v South African Rugby Football Union*[123] a decision of the President to appoint a commission of inquiry was challenged. The Constitutional Court held that:

> "the exercise of the powers is also clearly constrained by the principle of legality and, as is implicit in the Constitution, the President must act in good faith and must not misconstrue the powers. These are significant constraints upon the exercise of the President's power. They arise from provisions of the Constitution".

And in *Pharmaceutical Manufacturers Association of SA: Re Ex parte* 1–042 *President of the Republic of South Africa*,[124] the Constitutional Court held that the exercise of public power, and therefore its regulation by the courts, is always a constitutional matter.[125] A number of cases have also explicitly referred to the doubtful justiciability of polycentric decisions. In *Logbro Properties CC v Bedderson NO*[126] a challenge was made to the decision of a tender committee of which the cited respondent was chairperson. The Supreme Court held that both the complexity of the decision and the expertise of the committee meant that it was appropriate for the court to defer to the expertise and position of the committee. Cameron J.A. said:

---

[121] [2006] 3 N.Z.L.R. 705, HC.
[122] *cff. Peters v Davidson* [1999] 2 N.Z.L.R. 164 (NZCA held that a Commission of Inquiry (including the Chief Justice of New Zealand) was amenable to judicial review for material errors of law disclosed in the report's reasoning and conclusions). It should also be noted that the New Zealand approach is sometimes to require a deeper scrutiny of decisions than the traditional approach to unreasonableness, requiring "adequate consideration" and thus checking "poor public administration and inadequate, cursory and ill-considered decisions": *Thompson v Treaty of Waitingi Fisheries Commission* [2005] 2 N.Z.L.R. 9, CA, [219]; M. Taggart, "Administrative Law" [2006] N.Z.L.Rev. 75 at p.87; P. Joseph, *Constitutional and Administrative Law in New Zealand*, 2nd edn (2001), pp.833, 839.
[123] 2000 (1) S.A. 1, CC.
[124] 2000 (2) S.A. 674, CC.
[125] The rule of law, Chaskalson P. concluded, requires exercises of public power to be rational: "It is a requirement of the rule of law that the exercise of public power by the Executive and other functionaries should not be arbitrary. Decisions must be rationally related to the purpose for which the power was given, otherwise they are in effect arbitrary and inconsistent with this requirement".
[126] 2003 (2) S.A. 460, SCA.

"The fact is that the committee's performance of its duty in 1997 was a prime instance of what commentators have dubbed 'polycentric decision-making'. It was not a unilinear question involving the assertion of one subject's rights against the administration. . . . When, therefore, the committee set out to 'reconsider' the compliant tenders, it undertook the typically complex task of balancing all the public interests its mandate required it to fulfil. This included fair reconsideration of the appellant's tender—but not to the exclusion of considerations involving its broader responsibilities. These included the public benefit to be derived from obtaining a higher price by re-advertising the property".[127]

1-043　Two cases concerning the allocation of fishing quotas in accordance with complex mathematical formulae illustrate this further. In the *Foodcorp* case, Davis J. did not accept that the court should assume a role it has no competence to perform.[128] However, in the second case about fishing quotas, *Bato Star*,[129] O'Regan J. said in the Constitutional Court that that although "the distinction between appeals and reviews continues to be significant", and that courts of review must take care 'not to usurp the functions of administrative agencies",[130] review courts will not "rubber-stamp an unreasonable decision simply because of the complexity of the decision".[131] In the light of that authoritative judgment, Hoexter's leading text suggests therefore that it can no longer be said that polycentric decisions are unreviewable. Rather, the review of polycentric decisions should be undertaken with some caution and "the danger lies not in careful scrutiny but in "judicial overzealousness in setting aside administrative decisions that do not coincide with the judge's own opinions".[132]

THE INCIDENCE AND IMPACT OF JUDICIAL REVIEW

1-044　However crude a measure, the quantity of judicial review to some degree determines its potency as a constitutional constraint on the powers of public authorities and its practical utility as a means of dealing with

[127] At [20].
[128] The judgment in this second application is reported as *Foodcorp (Pty) Ltd v Deputy Director-General: Department of Environmental Affairs and Tourism: Branch Marine and Coastal Management* 2006 (2) S.A. 199 (C) at 211: "I have arrived at this conclusion reluctantly because this is the second time in which the allocation by first and second respondents has been found to have been unreasonable. However, given the polycentric nature of this task, prudence and the limits of institutional competence dictate that this Court should not assume the role of a fish allocator".
[129] *Bato Star Fishing (Pty) Ltd v Minister of Environmental Affairs* 2004 (4) S.A. 490, CC.
[130] At [45]. See also *Trinity Broadcasting (Ciskei) v Independent Communications Authority of South Africa* 2004 (3) S.A. 346 at [20], SCA.
[131] In the court below, it was held that "It is not our task to better his (the minister's) allocations, unless we should conclude that his decisions cannot be sustained on rational grounds": *Minister of Environmental Affairs and Tourism v Phambili Fisheries (Pty) Ltd; Minister of Environmental Affairs and Tourism v Bato Star Fishing (Pty) Ltd* 2003 (6) S.A. 407 at [53], SCA.
[132] C. Hoexter, *Administrative Law in South Africa* (2007), quoting Hoexter, "The Future of Judicial Review in South African Administrative Law" (2000) 117 *South African Law Journal* 484, 512.

individuals' grievances. Commentators have often pointed to the growth of judicial review—a fourteenfold increase in a 20 year period from the early 1980s.[133] This appears to be dramatic, but this stark statistic masks important features of the case load which mean that care is needed before ascribing too much weight to this trend. Judicial review is a two-stage procedure: claimants are required first to obtain the permission (formerly "leave") of the court; only cases regarded as arguable are set down for a full hearing.[134] Selected data are set out in Table 1.[135]

Table 1: The judicial review caseload

Year	Leave/ permission applications received	Success rate at filter stage	Full hearings disposed of during the year	Allowed	Dismissed	Withdrawn
1998	4,539	58%	1,346	47%	20%	33%
1999	4,959	49%	1,077	47%	19%	34%
2000	4,247	55%	1,429	55%	44%	1%
2001	4,732	28%	1,325	38%	39%	22%
2002	5,377	21%	458	36%	60%	5%
2003	5,949	27%	412	45%	50%	4%
2004	4,207	27%	345	45%	51%	3%
2005	5,381	31%	281	42%	55%	3%

[133] National Audit Office, *Citizen Redress: What citizens can do if thing go wrong with public services* (Report by the Comptroller and Auditor General, HC Paper No.21, Session 2004/05); and see M. Sunkin, "What is Happening to Applications for Judicial Review?" (1987) 50 M.L.R. 432; Sunkin, "The Judicial Review Case-Load 1987–1989" [1991] P.L. 491; Sunkin, "Trends in Judicial Review" [1993] P.L. 443; L. Bridges, G. Meszaros and M. Sunkin, *Judicial Review in Perspective* (1996).

[134] See Ch.16.

[135] Extrapolated from Department for Constitutional Affairs/Lord Chancellor's Department, *Judicial Statistics Annual Reports* for the years indicated. Methods for calculating the number of cases withdrawn after the grant of permission changed in 2000. Many claims are settled by consent *before* the court considers the permission application.

The case load

1–045 Why is caution needed in drawing inferences from these data? First, the quantity of litigation needs to put in context. In relation to the number of governmental decisions made each year, the overall number of review challenges commenced is infinitesimal (and the number receiving a fully reasoned judgment is even smaller). The scale of judicial review activity in redressing grievances is also modest compared to other avenues of complaint—the major tribunals heard more than 439,000 appeals in 2003–04,[136] and the various ombudsmen had a case load of over 35,000 a similar period.[137] The data in Table 1 also reveal that while in more recent years the annual number of judicial review cases initiated has fallen into the range of 4,000–5,000 a year, there has been a significant decrease in the number of these permitted to proceed to a full hearing (though success rates at the full hearing have remained fairly constant). Moreover, a large proportion of the annual judicial review caseload arises from a limited number of contexts—for many years it has been dominated by claims brought in relation to immigration and asylum decision-making (e.g. 53 per cent in 2004, 61 per cent in 2002); it remains to be seen whether the creation of a new immigration appeal system in 2005 will have the Government's desired effect of reducing the incidence of judicial review challenge.[138] Despite the creation of an alternative remedy against some aspects of local authority decisions relating to housing (in the form of an appeal on point of law to the county courts),[139] a significant proportion of judicial claims continue to be brought in relation to homelessness and housing matters.

1–046 Many people expected the coming into force of the Human Rights Act 1998 in October 2000 to lead to a significant increase in the number of judicial review claims. Reforms to the claim procedure and operation of the Administrative Court were in large made in order to "clear the decks" before October 2000 and have efficient systems in place to cope with this.[140] In fact, the impact of the HRA on case load numbers has been at most marginal. Research based on a sample of cases suggests that the HRA is cited in about half of claims, usually to supplement ordinary domestic law grounds of review rather than as the main ground; and that, typically, the inclusion of human rights arguments does not add significantly to the case or to the claimant's prospects of success.[141]

---

[136] DCA, *Transforming Public Services: Complaints, Redress and Tribunals*, Cm. 6243 (2004), para.3.28.
[137] See 1–066.
[138] Asylum and Immigration (Treatment of Claimants etc) Act 2004; see 17–004.
[139] See 17–045.
[140] See 15–095.
[141] Public Law Project (V. Bondy), *The Impact of the Human Rights Act 1998 on Judicial Review* (2003) (also published in summary at [2003] J.R. 14). See further on the impact of the HRA, 13–100.

Judicial review is not, of course, confined to claims at first instance in the **1–047** Administrative Court. Claimants and defendants appeal to the Court of Appeal (Civil Division) and the House of Lords.[142] As Table 2 shows, a considerable proportion of the appeals heard each year by the Law Lords are from judicial review claims.[143] Although the precise criteria on which leave to appeal to the House of Lords are granted and refused are far from clear, the relatively high incidence of judicial review cases shows that administrative law matters are often regarded as constituting points of law of general public importance.[144]

Table 2: Judicial review in the House of Lords

Year	Total number of judgments handed down by the House of Lords	Appeals from claims for judicial review	Percentage of total HL caseload
1998	52	13	25%
1999	51	14	27%
2000	70	13	19%
2001	71	10	14%
2002	47	14	30%
2003	74	13	16%
2004	56	10	18%
2005	75	23	31%
2006	59	8	14%
Total	555	118	21%

Central government responses to judicial review

The growth of judicial review during the 1980s and 1990s—in terms of **1–048** doctrinal sophistication, its theoretical base, the range of government functions amenable to review and the practical impact on governmental decisions—has not been universally welcomed. Although an approach of "partnership" between the courts and government has been advocated by the courts[145] (and often achieved), the potency of judicial review to

---

[142] See 17–077.
[143] The table does not include other public law cases, such as appeals from county court proceedings in homelessness cases and civil litigation invoking the Human Rights Act 1998.
[144] A. Le Sueur, "Panning for Gold: Choosing Cases for Top-level Courts", Ch.12 in Le Sueur (ed.), *Building the UK's New Supreme Court: National and Comparative Perspectives* (2004).
[145] *R. v Lancashire CC Ex p. Huddleston* [1986] 2 All E.R. 941 at 945; *R. v Monopolies and Mergers Commission Ex p. Argyll Group* [1986] 1 W.L.R. 763 at 774; H. Woolf, "Public Law-Private Law: Why the Divide?" [1986] P.L. 220, 30.

constrain government policy has led to a range of responses. Some can be welcomed as constructive engagements between the courts and the executive; others are regrettable and have at times risked undermining the important constitutional principles that ought to govern the relationship between the judges and ministers.[146]

1–049   During the 1980s, central government became increasingly concerned at the number of successful judicial review challenges and that departments seemed ill-equipped to respond effectively to actual or potential judicial reviews. Writing in 1983, the Treasury Solicitor drew attention to the fact that "senior administrators show a surprising ignorance of elementary legal principles" and "a lack of appreciation of the impact of legal considerations on administrative problems involving either considerable financial loss or embarrassment to Ministers".[147] A Cabinet committee endorsed this view and a strategy was formulated to deal with these problems. One aspect of the response was for the Treasury Solicitor's department and the Cabinet Office to distribute over 35,000 copies of a pamphlet called *The Judge Over Your Shoulder* to civil servants in 1987.[148] This set out some basic information about the judicial review process and some of the precautions which administrators could take to avoid the risk of challenge. A programme of legal awareness training was also organised for civil servants. Another aspect of the strategy was that departments and parliamentary counsel were urged to ensure that legislation was "expressed in the clearest possible language, even at the cost of drafting terms that are presentationally or politically unattractive".[149] In the years which followed, a marked change in the ethos of departments seemed to have occurred. Law and lawyers were no longer seen as peripheral to the process of administration. Administrators became more aware of the legal implications of their decisions and departmental lawyers tended to become involved at earlier stages of the policy-making process.[150] This does not however mean that government will always choose to avoid the risk of

[146] House of Lords Select Committee on the Constitution, *Relations between the Executive, the Judiciary and Parliament*. HL Paper No.151 (Session 2006/07), para.37.

[147] Sir Michael Kerry, "Administrative Law and the Administrator" (1983) 3 *Management in Government* 168, pp.170–171.

[148] A. Bradley, "The Judge Over Your Shoulder" [1987] P.L. 485. A second edition of the pamphlet was prepared in 1994, on which see D. Oliver [1994] P.L. 514. The 4th edn (January 2006) reflects changes following the coming into force of the Human Rights Act. There appear to two different versions of "JOYS", one for administrators and one for lawyers (Solicitor General, *Hansard* HC, col.101WA, July 4, 2000). For the Government's account of the training related to the HRA, see Joint Committee on Human Rights, *Government Responses to Reports from the Committee in the last Parliament*. HL Paper No.104/HC Paper No.850 (Session 2005/06), Appendix 2.

[149] Bradley [1987] P.L. 485.

[150] M. Sunkin and A. Le Sueur, "Can Government Control Judicial Review?" (1991) 44 C.L.P. 161 at p.171; A. Hammond, "Judicial Review: Continuing Interplay Between Law and Policy" [1998] P.L. 34 (where the former Treasury Solicitor writes of correction by the courts as being accepted in a "constructive spirit"). For an account of the provision of legal advice to Government, see T. Daintith and A. Page, *The Executive in the Constitution: Structure, Autonomy and Internal Control* (1999), Chs 7 and 9.

challenge: there is some evidence of public authorities pursuing policies despite receiving advice that there were good grounds for thinking that they are unlawful.[151]

Another approach to judicial review has been questionable. From time to **1–050** time senior Ministers have thought it fit to encourage and engage in hostile public comment about particular judges, judgments or the role of judicial review in general. Three particular episodes—all radiating from the Home Office—are of particular note. During the mid-1990s, the Conservative Home Secretary Mr Michael Howard Q.C. did little to hide his displeasure at judicial review judgments overturning government decisions and the tabloid newspapers poured venom over several named judges, portraying them as anti-democratic and contemptuous of public and parliamentary opinion.[152] Similar "ill-tempered outbursts" emanated from Labour Home Secretary Mr David Blunkett during 2003,[153] and again the tabloid press dispensed scorn on to some named judges and deplored "unaccountable and unelected judges" who were "usurping the role of Parliament, setting the wishes of the people at nought and pursuing a liberal, politically correct agenda of their own, in the zeal to interpret European legislation".[154] During 2006, while Mr John Reid was Home Secretary, further outbursts occurred. Following a decision of Sullivan J. that Afghan hijackers, released from prison on appeal, should not be deported to almost certain death in their home country,[155] the Prime Minister (Mr Tony Blair MP) told the news media "We can't have a situation in which people who hijack a plane, we're not able to deport back to their country. It's not an abuse of justice for us to order their deportation, it's an abuse of common sense, frankly, to be in a position where we can't do this".[156] Mr Reid added fuel to the fire: "When decisions are taken which appear inexplicable or bizarre to the general public, it only reinforces the perception that the system is not working to protect, or in favour of, the vast majority of ordinary, decent hard-working citizens in this country".[157] While such tactics of confrontation and denunciation of judicial review may enable politicians to vent frustration and a handful of journalists to fill column inches, they cannot provide a stable basis for a relationship between

---

[151] A. Le Sueur, "The Judicial Review Debate: From Partnership to Friction" (1996) 31 Govt & Opp. 8, 23–24.

[152] Le Sueur (1996) 31 Govt & Opp., 24–26. *The Times* wrote that "it is tempting to observe a pattern emerging, a potentially alarming hostility between an overmighty executive and an ambitious judiciary" (November 3, 1995).

[153] A. Bradley, "Judicial Independence Under Attack" [2003] P.L. 397. During a radio interview, Mr Blunkett said "Frankly, I'm personally fed up with having to deal with a situation where Parliament debates issues and the judges then overturn them" (quoted in *The Independent*, February 20, 2003).

[154] *Daily Mail*, February 21, 2003.

[155] *R. (on the application of S) v Secretary of State for the Home Department* [2006] EWHC 1111; [2006] A.C.D. 96.

[156] Press Conference with the French Prime Minister, May 10, 2006.

[157] BBC News on line, May 11, 2006.

executive and judiciary. That must be built upon mutual respect for the constitutional principles of the rule of law and separation of powers.[158]

1–051   In a constitutional system based on parliamentary supremacy, the government may be tempted to seek to oust the jurisdiction of the courts over some areas of decision-making. There is nothing new in this and for several decades the courts have taken a robust approach to minimising the practical effect of preclusive clauses in legislation.[159] In recent years it is the field of immigration and asylum policy that has given government most incentive and opportunity to introduce legislation restricting the scope of judicial review.[160] The Government's case (contested by many) has been that failed asylum-seekers "play the system" by making claims for judicial review tactically to delay their deportation from the United Kingdom. The Nationality, Immigration and Asylum Act 2002 created a greatly modified version of the claim for judicial review procedure for legal challenges to refusals of permission to appeal from one tier of the immigration appellate system to another.[161] Although this procedure appeared to be working well, in early 2003 the Government's Asylum and Immigration (Treatment of Claimants etc) Bill contained an ouster clause the like of which had never been seen. Amidst a great deal of criticism,[162] that the clause would undermine the rule of law, the Government withdrew it.

Local government responses

1–052 In local government, the 1980s also marked a greatly increased awareness on the part of local authority officers and councillors of the potency of judicial review as both a challenge to their decisions and as a weapon to be employed by them against central government.[163] As a result, relationships between central and local government altered, with increased emphasis

---

[158] House of Lords Select Committee on the Constitution, *Relations between the Executive, the Judiciary and Parliament*. HL Paper No.151 (Session 2006/07), para.51. Jack Straw MP said in one of his first speeches after his appointment as Lord Chancellor in 2007 that what ministers "must not do is gratuitously to criticise individual judgements, nor show a lack of respect for the institution of the judiciary or its members. After all, it is we in Parliament who ultimately make the law, and therefore have to accept its consequences" (Lord Mayor of London's annual judges dinner, July 17, 2007).

[159] See 4–014.

[160] A. Le Sueur, "Three Strikes and it's Out? The UK Government's Strategy to Oust Judicial Review from Immigration and Asylum Decision-making" [2004] P.L. 225; R. Rawlings, "Review, Revenge and Retreat" (2005) 68 M.L.R. 378

[161] See 17–004. Time limits were significantly shortened.

[162] Including that of the authors of this book: Lord Woolf, "The Rule of Law and a Change in the Constitution" (2004) 63 C.L.J. 317 (the clause "would be so inconsistent with the spirit of mutual respect between the different arms of government that it could be a catalyst for a campaign for a written constitution"); J. Jowell, "Immigration Wars", *The Guardian*, March 2, 2004 (it was "no longer self-evident . . . that our courts would inevitably concede Parliament's right to ride roughshod over fundamental rights and newly discovered constitutional principles"); Le Sueur [2004] P.L. 225.

[163] D. Cooper, "Institutional Illegality and Disobedience: Local Government Narratives" (1996) 16 O.J.L.S. 255.

being given to the definition of legal powers and duties, and adjudication given greater prominence alongside administrative bargaining and negotiation as a method of dispute resolution.[164] In short, "the courts and the legal process have become, seemingly, a necessary part of the political debate and decision-making".[165] In some authorities, this involved a trend towards greater formality in decision-making, particularly in committees, where councillors and officers are anxious to be able to demonstrate, should a decision be challenged, that all and only relevant factors were considered.[166] The opinions of independent counsel were frequently sought and some concern was expressed that "these can supplant the decision-making powers of an elected body unless there are members with the confidence and political will to resist".[167]

Recent research into judicial review claims against local authorities in **1–053** England and Wales has revealed some striking patterns.[168] The findings show that during 2000–05, 80 per cent of judicial review claims against local authorities were made against a group of councils that are less than 20 per cent of the total number. The top 20 authorities are all in London and the highest incidence of judicial review challenge is in areas of high multiple deprivations where there are relatively high numbers of solicitors with expertise in public law. The authors conclude that "For the inner city authority judicial review litigation typically involves a daily response to challenges by claimants seeking to protect their basic housing needs often in emergency situations. In this sense it is one part of the daily toil of resource management. This is a far cry from the more leisured engagement between citizen and authority in the High Court that is generally associated with the process".

The impact of judicial review on the quality of decision-making

Judicial review has a constitutional importance.[169] It may also have an **1–054** instrumental role in changing the behaviour of public authorities. The extent and character of that change is open to debate, but we can speculate (or hope) that judicial review improves the quality of decisions and decision-making processes by promoting compliance with law. Law, in this context, encompasses both adherence to criteria and procedures stipulated in legislation and the broad principles that are articulated through the common law. Judges who carry out the practical task of developing and

[164] M. Loughlin, *Local Government in the Modern State* (1986), pp.193–201.
[165] L. Bridges, C. Game, O. Lomas, J. McBride, *Legality and Local Politics* (1987), p.3.
[166] Bridges (1987), p.92. They comment that members are "deluged with paper on all aspects of the subject" under consideration and matters previously implicitly understood are now recorded.
[167] Bridges et al (1987), p.99.
[168] M. Sunkin, K. Calvo, L. Platt and T. Landman, "Mapping the Use of Judicial Review to Challenge Local Authorities in England and Wales" [2007] P.L. 545.
[169] See 1–006.

refining the judicial review case law certainly appear to work on the assumption that judicial review is capable of having a beneficial impact, both in relation to particular decisions and administrative processes more broadly.[170] The past decade has seen a burgeoning of studies of the relationships between judicial review and the political and administrative behaviour of public authorities and officials.[171] The impact of review is now understood for the complex phenomenon that it is; we appreciate that the size of the judicial review caseload, or the frequency with which government bodies are challenged, are not sure guides to assessing the various kinds of influence that may be exerted by judicial review. Nevertheless, there can be little doubt that the principles of judicial review, together with the requirements of Convention rights, have caused most bodies performing public functions to review their procedures and practices to comply with the principles of administrative justice, if for no other reason than to avoid the possibility of judicial review.

1-055   Drawing on a study of decision-making by local authorities about homeless people, Halliday has developed a useful model which seeks to identify the conditions which determine the degree to which public officials are likely to comply with administrative law norms.[172] He postulates three main variables. The first is the degree to which the decision-maker has knowledge about the law, cares about complying with the law and has competence in applying the law with appropriate sophistication. The second factor is the decision-making environment—which means the extent to which legal norms are in competition with other demands (such as requirements to reduce expenditure). The third element is the law itself, especially the extent to which it provides clear and consistent guidance. We draw from this the view that if judicial review is to achieve improvements in the quality of administrative decision-making, to give effect to the ideals of the rule of law as institutional morality, there does indeed need to be a partnership between public authorities and the courts. If the spirit of their judgments is to be embraced and translated into administrative practice, they need to show sensitivity to the tasks of officials in particular

---

[170] D. Feldman, "Judicial Review: A Way of Controlling Government?" (1988) 66 Pub. Admin. 21. cf. Justice/All Souls, Review of Administrative Law in the UK, Administrative Justice: Some Necessary Reforms (1988), Ch.2 on the need for codes setting out in positive form principles of good administration.

[171] See the valuable collection of essays in M. Hertogh and S. Halliday (eds), Judicial Review and Bureaucratic Impact: International and Interdisciplinary Perspectives (2004); S. Halliday, Judicial Review and Compliance with Administrative Law (2004); T. Daintith and A. Page, The Executive in the Constitution: Structure, Autonomy and Internal Control (1999), pp.335–340; G. Richardson and M. Sunkin, "Judicial Review: Questions of Impact" [1996] P.L. 79; M. Sunkin and K. Pick, "The Changing Impact of Judicial Review: The Independent Review Service of the Social Fund" [2001] P.L. 736; R. Thomas, "The Impact of Judicial Review on Asylum" [2003] P.L. 479.

[172] S. Halliday, Judicial Review and Compliance with Administrative Law (2004), esp. Ch.9.

contexts.[173] It is also important for the courts to articulate principles in such a way as to provide meaningful guidance to public officials.

The empirical evidence gathered so far tends to suggest that prudence is 1–056 needed before we can safely generalise that judicial review has a beneficial influence on administrative behaviour. In some organisations knowledge of the law, and empathy with values relating to the rule of law, appears to be thin on the ground.[174] Where judicial review has had some general influence, this seems more likely to be in relation to modifications of administrative procedure rather than changes to substantive entitlements.

ADMINISTRATIVE JUSTICE AND PROPORTIONATE DISPUTE RESOLUTION

In its 2004 White Paper *Transforming Pubic Services: Complaints Redress* 1–057 *and Tribunals*,[175] the Department for Constitutional Affairs (since May 2007 called the Ministry of Justice) coined the phrase "proportionate dispute resolution".[176] The strategy behind this slogan seeks "to transform civil and administrative justice and the way that people deal with legal problems and disputes".[177] The goal is to reduce the risk of administrative error in the first place by clarifying rights and responsibilities. Where disputes do arise, public authorities should offer internal methods to handle complaints. There should be a range of alternative dispute resolution services "so that different types of dispute can be resolved fairly, quickly, efficiently and effectively without recourse to the expense and

---

[173] Lord Donaldson M.R. spoke in several judgments of the need to establish a partnership between the courts and the administration "based on a common aim, namely the maintenance of the highest standards of public administration": see *R. v Lancashire CC Ex p. Huddleston* [1986] 2 All E.R. 941 at 945; *R. v Monopolies and Mergers Commission Ex p. Argyll plc* [1986] 1 W.L.R. 763 at 774.

[174] I. Loveland, "Housing Benefit: Administrative Law and Administrative Practice" (1988) 66 Pub. Admin. 57 and "Administrative Law, Administrative Processes, and the Housing of Homeless Persons: A View from the Sharp End" (1991) 13 J.S.W.F.L. 4—he notes in the former that in one of the authorities studied "decision-making processes are entirely uninformed by explicit reference to administrative law as such. Mention of the Wednesbury principles draws a blank stare from most officers" (at p.73). A similar, rather dismal picture of officials' view of law and lawyers emerges from other empirical studies: see S. Halliday, "Internal Review and Administrative Justice: Some Evidence and Research Questions from Homelessness Decision-making" (2001) 23 J.S.W.F.L 473; D. Cowan and J. Fionda, "Homelessness Internal Appeals Mechanisms: Serving the Administrative Process" (1998) 27 Anglo-American L.R. 66 (Pt 1) and 169 (Pt 2). G. Richardson and D. Machin, "Judicial Review and Tribunal Decision-Making: a Study of the Mental Health Review Tribunal" [2000] P.L. 494 conclude that "that the influence of judicial review on the decision making of MHRTs is patchy at best, even with regard to procedural fairness".

[175] Cm. 6243; see also National Audit Office, *Citizen Redress: What citizens can do if things go wrong with public services* (Report by the Comptroller and Auditor General, HC Paper No.21, Session 2004/05).

[176] For commentary, see M. Alder, "Tribunal Reform: Proportionate Dispute Resolution and the Pursuit of Administrative Justice" (2006) 69 M.L.R. 958; and A. Le Sueur, "Courts, Tribunals, Ombudsmen, ADR: Administrative Justice, Constitutionalism and Informality", Ch.13 in J. Jowell and D. Oliver (eds), *The Changing Constitution* (2007).

[177] Para.2.1.

complaint and redress which now exist, including: internal complaints procedures; mediation; recourse to the Ombudsmen; and appeals to the newly reinvigorated tribunals system.[9] Judicial review provides just one way to control the abuse of public power. In the 5th edition of this book we retained the reference to Professor de Smith's celebrated phrase that judicial review is "sporadic and peripheral", for the reason that the administrative process is not, and cannot be, a succession of justiciable controversies. Public authorities are set up to govern and administer, and if their every act or decision were to be reviewable by the courts, the business of administration could be brought to a standstill. Today, however, the principles developed through judicial review have become central to all of public administration in-so-far as those principles seek to enhance both the way decisions are reached and the quality of the decisions made.[10]

From "administrative action" to all public functions

The title of previous editions of this book was *Judicial Review of* 1–005 *Administrative Action*. Although this book still concentrates judicial review of what may broadly be described as "administrative action",[11] we have omitted from the title the words "of Administrative Action". This is because of the mounting importance of review of high-level policy decisions and of legislation.[12] Local authority byelaws have for many years been amenable to judicial review, but in more recent years the courts have with increasing vigour exercised jurisdiction over the lawfulness of other kinds of secondary legislation, including statutory instruments passed by affirmative resolution of Parliament.[13] Moreover, national courts are required by European Community law to disapply legislative provisions, including those in Acts of Parliament, where they are incompatible with Community law norms.[14] Section 4 of the Human Rights Act 1998 also provides the courts with power to make declarations of incompatibility in relation to primary legislation, which has given the higher courts a role in evaluating whether Parliament's enactments are consistent with Convention rights.[15] The courts have also been called upon to adjudicate on the application of the Parliament Acts.[16]

[9] See 1–087.
[10] See 1–054.
[11] On the once important classifications of fuctions as "legislative", "administrative", "judicial", "quasi judicial" and "ministerial" (now of mainly historical interest), see Appendix B, below.
[12] See 3–011.
[13] See 3–011.
[14] See 14–009.
[15] See 13–00; 3–00.
[16] *Jackson v Attorney General* [2005] UKHL 56; [2006] 1 A.C. 262.

formality of courts and tribunals where this is not necessary".[178] There is a growing realisation that "redress systems should be purposefully targeted to deliver valued benefits to citizens in a timely way, rather than just following through on established procedures whose added value for citizens remains unclear".[179]

1–058   This approach chimes well with the approach followed by the courts. The Civil Procedure Rules (CPR), governing all civil litigation including judicial review, have at their heart as an overriding principle the idea that dealing justly with a dispute, when litigation does occur, requires the court to deal with the case in ways which are proportionate to the importance and complexity of the case and the financial position of the parties.[180] In *R. (on the application of Anufrijeva) v Southwark LBC*,[181] the Court of Appeal considered what procedures should be followed to ensure that the costs of obtaining relief are proportionate to that relief. Although that case concerned a claim for damages under the Human Rights Act 1998, the approach advocated by the court has a general relevance.[182] Without intending to be prescriptive, the Court suggested that in appropriate cases a claimant should expect to have to explain to the Administrative Court why (if this be the case) any internal complaints procedure has not been pursued and why a complaint to the Ombudsman is not thought to be appropriate.[183]

1–059   The rationale for directing complaints to appropriate agencies (which on occasion may entail turning an aggrieved citizen away from pursing a judicial review claim) is two fold. First, it enables a match to be made between, on the one hand, the nature of the complaint and on the other the techniques and remedies needed to resolve it. Secondly, there is a growing recognition of the public interest in using collective resources wisely in the context of administrative justice. Attempts at quantifying the typical costs of the various redress mechanisms are inevitably rather impressionistic, but it has been suggested that the cost of an internal review by a public authority is £115; an appeal to a tribunal costs £455; and that ombudsman interventions typically cost in the region of £1,200–£1,500.[184] These are all relatively modest costs compared to that of a claim for judicial review (in which a non-publicly funded claimant also bears the risk of being ordered to pay the defendant public authority's legal costs in the event of losing).[185]

---

[178] Cm. 6243, Para.2.3.
[179] National Audit Office, *Citizen Redress: What citizens can do if thing go wrong with public services* (Report by the Comptroller and Auditor General, HC Paper No.21, Session 2004/05), para.8.
[180] CPR r.1.1; see 16–014.
[181] [2003] EWCA Civ 1406; [2004] Q.B. 1124; see further 19–085.
[182] *R. (on the application of Scholarstica UMO) v Commissioner for Local Administration* [2003] EWHC 3202 (Admin); [2004] E.L.R. 265 at [17].
[183] See 19–085.
[184] National Audit Office. HC Paper No.21 (Session 2004/05), para.14.
[185] See 16–080.

The notion of proportionate dispute resolution is still in its relative 1–060
infancy, but we nonetheless identify three practical propositions to guide
aggrieved citizens and their advisers. First, complainants should always
seek a local resolution of disputes. Many public authorities have in place
processes for internal reconsideration of specific decisions or dealing with
broader complaints about the conduct of public officials.[186] Complainants
who fail to use such mechanisms and instead take matters to an external
agency without first giving the public authority an opportunity to put
things right are likely to be turned away. Secondly, where a local resolution
of a dispute cannot be attained, there is a strong presumption that the
complainant must use any statutory appeals procedure that exists.[187]
Thirdly, investigation by the ombudsmen and a claim for judicial review
are avenues of last resort. There may however be some difficult questions
as to which—ombudsmen or judicial review—are most suitable in a
particular case, a point we consider below.[188]

INTERNAL COMPLAINT SYSTEMS

Most public authorities provide some form of internal complaints pro- 1–061
cedures for people dissatisfied with the outcome of a decision or the way in
which the decision was made.[189] Indeed, it is safe to assume that relatively
few grievances proceed beyond this kind of procedure. In some contexts
such complaint systems are relatively formalised and required by legislation. Thus, the Housing Act 1996 s.202 confers a right to request a review
by an officer of decisions relating to homelessness and regulations set out
the procedure to be followed, including the circumstances in which an oral
hearing must be provided.[190] The National Health Service (Complaints)
Regulations 2004 provides a detailed framework which must be followed
by NHS bodies for the handling complaints.[191] In other contexts public
authorities choose to provide internal complaints systems of their own
volition: these may be relatively informal (for example simply adopting a
practice at looking again at decisions when requested to do so) or more
systematised and elaborate.

There are some obvious benefits to encouraging internal resolution of 1–062
grievances within public authorities—including the relative speed and the
modest costs incurred in looking again at a decision or investigating a

---

[186] The LCA have published a useful guide to good practice "Running a Complaints System",
available on *http://www.lgo.org.uk.*
[187] See 16–014.
[188] See 1–081.
[189] D. Cowan and S. Halliday, *The Appeal of Internal Review* (2003).
[190] Allocation of Housing and Homelessness (Review Procedures) Regulations 1999 (SI
1999/71); Department for Communities and Local Government, *Homelessness Code of
Guidance for Local Authorities* (2006).
[191] SI 2004/1768.

complaint. Internal complaints are particularly well suited to cases where the aggrieved person is seeking an explanation for what has been decided or done, or an apology for poor service. Sometimes re-consideration of an application may result in a different outcome to the original determination. This said, in some contexts it may be open to doubt whether internal complaint systems are imbued with the values necessary to promote justice.[192] It has also been suggested that exposure to judicial review may have the effect of reducing willingness to carry out informal self-scrutiny of decisions.[193]

1–063   The Administrative Court looks favourably on the provision of internal complaint systems. A would-be judicial review claimant is likely to be refused permission to proceed with a claim for judicial review if he has failed to use a reasonably satisfactory internal complaints procedure.[194] The pre-action protocol for judicial review, published to accompany CPR Pt 54, requires that the claimant must in most situations write a letter before claim to the public authority "to identify the issues in dispute and establish whether litigation can be avoided".[195] Such a letter, in the absence of an established internal review system, ought normally to elicit a reconsideration of the initial decision. Would-be claimants need to bear in mind that claims for judicial review must be filed with the Administrative Court "promptly and in any event not later than 3 months after the grounds to make the claim first arose".[196] Arguably, grounds might "first arise" at the time of the initial decision by the public authority rather than at the conclusion of an internal review. It would however be antithetical to the idea of proportionate dispute resolution for a public authority which had failed to deal with an internal complaint promptly, or even within three months, to press the point that a subsequent claim for judicial review is out of time. What is more, the court has the power to extend time and is likely to do so if the complainant has acted reasonably.

1–064   On occasion, claimants have sought to challenge the lawfulness of an internal complaint or appeal system (rather than the initial decision by the public authority). The courts have shown little enthusiasm for intervening in such cases. Thus, in the homelessness context, it has been held that an internal review by a local authority officer of a homelessness application under the process required by s.202 of the Housing Act 1996 is not flawed by apparent bias on the ground that that officer had been involved in a

---

[192] Cowan and Fionda, "Homelessness Internal Appeals Mechanisms: Serving the Administrative Process" (1998) 27 Anglo-American L.R. 169, in their study of internal procedures relating to homelessness came to "the depressing conclusion that such systems have become cheap ways of denying justice. Nearly all the systems had design faults that make the walls of Jericho seem well constructed. Thus, the appeals processes become, in some instances, self-serving or an opportunity to adopt a view of the personal characteristics of the applicant" (pp.185–6).

[193] S. Halliday, "The Influence of Judicial Review on Bureaucratic Decision-Making" [2000] P.L. 110; D. Cowan and J. Fionda, (1998) 27 Anglo-American L.R. 169.

[194] See 16–021.

[195] See Appendix I.

[196] CPR r.54.5, discussed at 16–050.

previous review of the claimant's case.[197] Nor is there apparent bias where an officer refuses an application and the goes on to determine an application under s.184 for temporary accommodation pending a review.[198] In cases where "civil rights and obligations" within the meaning of ECHR Art.6(1) are at stake,[199] an internal review or appeal process cannot amount to a decision by an independent and impartial tribunal (which is the protection afforded by Art.6(1)). The English courts have however emphasised that what needs to be judged is not merely the initial decision and internal review, but also the possibility of any subsequent appeal or review by a court—and such composite processes has been held in several different contexts to comply with Art.6(1).[200]

MEDIATION

The courts have expressed a wish that before commencing a claim for judicial review the parties consider carefully whether mediation may resolve the dispute (and if so, to engage in mediation).[201] Despite judicial exhortation, the use of mediation in connection with judicial review claims is negligible. In 2007 the Public Law Project commenced a study of the value and limits of mediation in this context. The possibilities for mediation exist beyond judicial review. The ombudsmen now have express powers to appoint and pay for mediators.[202] And it is envisaged that mediation will play a role in the new tribunal system created by the Tribunals, Courts and Enforcement Act 2007.[203] **1–065**

[197] *Feld v Barnett* [2004] EWCA Civ 1307; [2005] H.L.R. 9.
[198] *R. (on the application of Abdi) v Lambeth LBC* [2007] EWHC 1565 (Admin); *The Times*, July 11, 2007.
[199] See 7–119.
[200] See, e.g. *Tower Hamlets LBC v Begum (Runa)* [2003] UKHL 5; [2003] 2 A.C. 430 (review officer clearly not independent and impartial for purposes of ECHR Art.6(1), but compliance was to be judged by looking at the composite process of internal review plus the possibility of appeal on point of law to the county court); *R. (on the application of Beeson) v Dorset CC* [2002] EWCA Civ 1812; [2003] H.R.L.R. 11 at [29] (emphasising that "even though the first decision-maker does not independently satisfy Art.6 the quality of his decision is by no means therefore rendered nugatory or valueless"). But see now the ECtHR ruling in*Tsfayo v UK* (Application No.60860/00), *The Times*, November 23, 2006, discussed at 8–031 and 10–083.
[201] *Cowl v Plymouth City Council* [2001] EWCA Civ 1935; [2002] 1 W.L.R. 803, discussed at 16–00; see M. Supperstone, D. Stilitz and C. Sheldon, "ADR in Public Law" [2006] P.L. 299; S. Boyron, "The Rise of Mediation in Administrative Law Disputes: Experiences from England, France and Germany" [2006] P.L. 320.
[202] See, e.g. in relation to the Parliamentary Ombudsmen, see Parliamentary Commissioner Act 1967 s.3(1A) (inserted by Regulatory Reform (Collaboration etc between Ombudsmen) Order 2007 (SI 2007/1889)).
[203] Tribunals, Courts and Enforcement Act 2007, s.24.

OMBUDSMEN AND SIMILAR GRIEVANCE-HANDLING SCHEMES

1–066 Over recent decades there has been a burgeoning of grievance-handling schemes independent of the public authority (or private enterprise) against which a complaint is made.[204] In recent years the main public sector ombudsmen have dealt with over 38,000 complaints per annum. The picture, as exemplified by Table 3 below, is complex. Some schemes are established by statute, others are non-statutory schemes set up by public authorities, and others are self-regulatory schemes run by particular private sector industries. All the grievance-handling schemes discussed here have the resolution of complaints from members of the public as one of their primary functions.[205] They are independent of bodies against which the complaint is made, and in this important respect different from internal grievance-handling mechanisms. Some have powers to make binding decisions, but many have formal powers only to make recommendations. They provide a free service to the aggrieved person and typically operate using techniques of investigation, though ever greater reliance is being placed on informal alternative dispute resolution techniques. The scope of their jurisdictions varies, but commonly includes injustice caused by "maladministration", as defined below, or failure to comply with a code of practice. Policies to encourage proportionate dispute resolution are likely to lead to a further proliferation of such agencies.[206] As well as providing individual redress, the ombudsmen often have a role in promoting principles and standards of good administration.

1–067 The popular term "ombudsman" has been informally adopted by the three main public sector agencies—the Parliamentary Commissioner for Administration (PCA or Parliamentary Ombudsman),[207] the Health Services Commissioner for England (HSC or Health Service Ombudsman)[208]; and

---

[204] M. Purdue, "Investigations by the Public Sector Ombudsmen", Ch.21 in D. Feldman (ed.), *English Public Law* (2004). On recent reform proposals, see M. Elliott, "Asymmetric Devolution and Ombudsman Reform in England" [2006] P.L. 84; and Regulatory Reform (Collaboration etc between Ombudsmen) Order 2007 (SI 2007/1889) amending primary legislation.

[205] Mainly regulatory bodies—such as the Competition Commission, General Medical Council, Electoral Commission, and the Audit Commission for Local Authorities and the National Health Service in England and Wales—are not dealt with here.

[206] And note also the recommendations of Lord Woolf's *Review of the Working Methods of the European Court of Human Rights* (2005), which calls on the Council of Europe to encourage greater use of national ombudsmen and other methods of alternative dispute resolution in relation to complaints of breaches of Convention rights.

[207] Not to be confused with the Parliamentary Commissioner for Standards, the non-statutory office established by the House of Commons in 1995 to oversee the Register of Members' Interests and offer guidance and training for MPs on matters of conduct, propriety and ethics; the activities of the PCS are not subject to judicial review as he is concerned with activities within Parliament: *R. v Parliamentary Commissioner for Standards Ex p. Al-Fayed* [1998] 1 W.L.R. 669.

[208] The offices of PCA and HSC are held by the same person and there is considerable integration of the two legally separate bodies. On the Healthcare Commission, a separate body, see 1–076.

the Commission for Local Administration in England (CLA or Local Government Ombudsman (LGO)). All these ombudsmen have powers to provide mediation to complainants and may work jointly.[209]

As a consequence of devolution, Wales now has its own statutory 1–068 ombudsman—the Public Services Ombudsman for Wales—dealing with complaints arising from matters relating the Assembly Government, health care in Wales, the work of local authorities and housing associations in Wales.[210] Similarly, an Act of the Scottish Parliament has established the Scottish Public Services Ombudsman with jurisdiction over complaints relating to the Scottish Parliament and Executive, local government in Scotland, health care, housing, further and higher education institutions and a range of other public authorities.[211] The Northern Ireland Ombudsman (the working-title of the Assembly Ombudsman for Northern Ireland and the Northern Ireland Commissioner for Complaints) provides a service in that part of the United Kingdom.[212] The European Ombudsman investigates complaints about maladministration by the institutions and bodies of the European Community.[213]

Table 3: Ombudsmen and similar grievance-redressing agencies in England and Wales

Statutory ombudsmen dealing with public sector		
Parliamentary Commissioner for Administration (also known as PCA or the Parliamentary Ombudsman)	Parliamentary Commissioner Act 1967—see 1–069 below	All-UK jurisdiction. Public authorities listed in Sch.2 (principally central government departments and non-departmental public bodies). Caseload: 1,853 in 2005–06. Only Members of Parliament may refer cases.
Health Services Commissioner for England (also known as HSC and the Health Service Ombudsman)	Health Service Commissioners Act 1993—see 1–076 below	England-only jurisdiction. Maladministration in failures to satisfactory service and also matters relating to clinical judgements. Caseload: 862 in 2006–07.
Commission for Local Administration in England (also known as LGO and the Local Government Ombudsman")	Local Government Act 1974—see 1–077 below.	England-only jurisdiction over local authorities. Caseload: 18,320 in 2006–07.

[209] Regulatory Reform (Collaboration etc between Ombudsmen) Order 2007 (SI 2007/1889).
[210] Public Services Ombudsman (Wales) Act 2005. M. Seneviratne, "A new ombudsman for Wales" [2006] P.L. 6.
[211] Scottish Public Services Ombudsman Act 2002.
[212] Ombudsman (Northern Ireland) Order 1996 (SI 1006/1298); Commissioner for Complaints (Northern Ireland) Order 1996 (SI 1996/1297).
[213] Decision of the European Parliament on the regulations and general conditions governing the performance of the Ombudsman's duties, adopted by Parliament on March 9, 1994 ([1994] O.J. L113/15) and amended by its decision of March 14, 2002 deleting Arts 12 and 16 ([2002] O.J. L92/p.13).

Housing Ombudsman Service	Housing Act 1996	England-only jurisdiction. Complaints relating to registered social landlords. Caseload: 503 in 2005–06.
Independent Police Complaints Commission	Police Reform Act 2002	Investigating allegations of misconduct by police officers
Public Services Ombudsman for Wales	Public Services Ombudsman (Wales) Act 2005	Wales-only jurisdiction. Matters relating the Assembly Government, health care in Wales, the work of local authorities and housing associations in Wales
Independent Review Service for the Social Fund	Social Security Act 1998	Discretionary Social Fund (community care grant, crisis loan, budgeting loan or overpayment decision); complaints must have exhausted JobCentre Plus decision-making and review procedures first
Information Commissioner		Regulates and enforces Data Protection Act 1998, Freedom of Information Act 2000, Privacy and Electronic Communications Regulations 2003, Environmental Information Regulations 2004, Re-use of Public Sector Information Regulations 2005.
Office of the Independent Adjudicator for Higher Education	Higher Education Act 2004	Students' complaints (see 4–035)
Office of Communications (Ofcom)	Communications Act 2003	In 2004 Ofcom replaced the Broadcasting Standards Commission (BSC), the Independent Television Commission (ITC), Oftel, the Radio Authority and the Radiocommunications Agency. It offers a complaints service in relation to standards and fairness.
Equality and Human Rights Commission	Equality Act 2006	Replacing the Commission for Racial Equality, Equal Opportunities Commission and Disability Rights Commission, the EHRC has power to investigate complaints relating to discrimination and to support litigation.
Standards Board for England	Local Government Act 2000	Ethical misconduct of individual elected members of local authorities (not corporate maladministration which is for the Local Government Ombudsman).
Judicial Appointments and Conduct Ombudsman	Constitutional Reform Act 2005, Sch.11	Judicial appointment complaints and the handling of judicial conduct complaints

Examples of non-statutory ombudsmen and similar agencies dealing with public sector	
The Adjudicator's Office	Formed in 1993, it investigates complaints relating to HM Revenue & Customs, The Valuation Office Agency, The Public Guardianship Office, and The Insolvency Service. *http://www.adjudicatorsoffice.gov.uk/*
Independent Case Examiners' Office	Formed in 1997, it provides a review and resolution service in relation to the Child Support Agency and the Northern Ireland Social Security Agency.
Independent Complaints Adjudicator for Ofsted and the Adult Learning Inspectorate	Investigates complaints about Ofsted and the Adult Learning Inspectorate. *http://www.ofsted-aliadjudicator.co.uk*
Independent Complaints Reviewer	Originally set up in 1998, the ICR investigates complaints about the Land Registry, The National Archives, the Charity Commission, the Audit Commission and the Housing Corporation. *http://www.icrev.org.co.uk*
Prisons and Probation Ombudsman for England and Wales	Established in 1994, it now investigates grievances relating to the Prison Service and National Probation Service. Its non-statutory basis has been much criticised. In the Management of Offenders and Sentencing Bill 2005 the Government sought to rectify this, but the Bill did not make progress because of the May 2005 General Election.
Waterways Ombudsman	Investigation of maladministration by British Waterways, the pubic corporation responsible for managing rivers and canals.

Examples of statutory ombudsmen dealing with private sector		
Legal Services Ombudsman	Courts and Legal Services Act 1990	Grievances about complaint-handling by the legal professional bodies' self-regulatory complaints systems.
Financial Services Ombudsman	Financial Services and Markets Act 2000	Dealing with complaints about a range of banking, mortgage and insurance activity.
Office of the Immigration Services Commission	Immigration and Asylum Act 1999	To ensure that all immigration advisers fulfil the requirements of good practice.
Pensions Ombudsman	Pension Schemes Act 1993	Deals with complaints and disputes about the way that pension schemes are run, and funded by registration levies on all occupational pension schemes.
Examples of non-statutory ombudsmen-type services dealing with private sector complaints		
Advertising Standards Authority		Established by the advertising industry to police the rules laid down in the advertising codes to ensure that advertising in all media are honest and decent. *http://www.asa.org.uk*
Press Complaints Commission		Established in 1991 (replacing the Press Council) to deal with complaints from members of the public about the editorial content of newspapers and magazines.
Telecommunications Ombudsman (Otelo)		Deals with disputes between customers and public communication providers who subscribe to the scheme.

The Parliamentary Ombudsman

1–069   The PCA was established in 1967 following a campaign for a new means of investigating complaints against administrative decisions where there was no tribunal or other procedure for dealing with complaints. In 2005–6, the PCA accepted 1,853 new cases for investigation,[214] with the largest case loads stemming from the Department for Work and Pensions, Inland Revenue and Home Office. The PCA lays annual and special reports before Parliament and has a relationship with the House of Commons Public Administration Select Committee (PASC), before whom the PCA appears at least once a year. This link with Parliament serves a dual function: it provides scrutiny of the PCA's work and PASC may support the PCA in pressing for government action.[215]

1–070   The function of the PCA is to investigate complaints from persons who claim to have "sustained injustice in consequence of maladministration" by specified central government bodies—including departments, executive agencies and non-departmental public bodies, or persons or bodies acting on their behalf, performing or failing to perform administrative (as distinct from judicial or legislative) functions.[216] Where authorities which are subject to the PCA's jurisdiction contract out services which are provided by other bodies, the ombudsman has the same power to investigate maladministration by the private contractor. This is important because of the widespread practice of "contracting out" public service provision to businesses and the voluntary sector.

1–071   "Injustice" has been widely interpreted so as to cover not merely injury redressible in a court of law, but also "the sense of out rage aroused by unfair or incompetent administration, even where the complainant has suffered no actual loss.[217] "Maladministration" was deliberately left undefined in the Parliamentary Commissioner Act 1967; the PCA was to work out its meaning in developing a body of case law. The term includes: corruption; bias and unfair discrimination; misleading a member of the public; failure to notify him of his rights; losing or mislaying documents; sitting on a decision or an answer to a request for information for an inordinate length of time; failing to explain why a decision was made or why a situation had arisen when it was unreasonable to refuse; making a decision on the basis of faulty information which should have been properly ascertained and assembled; the dilatory and superficial handling of complaints by public authorities; refusal to answer reasonable questions; offering no redress or manifestly disproportionate redress; omitting to

[214] Annual Report 2005–06, HC Paper 1363.
[215] For reform proposals, see O. Gay and B. Winetrobe, *Officers of Parliament—transforming the role* (UCL Constitution Unit, 2003).
[216] Parliamentary Commissioner Act 1967 s.5. The list of public authorities subject to investigation by the PCA is found in Sch.2 to the Act, and currently range from the Accounts Commission for Scotland to the Youth Justice Board for England and Wales, via Sir John Soane's Museum.
[217] *Hansard* HC, Vol.734 col.51 (October 18, 1966) (R. Crossman).

notify those who thereby lose rights of appeal and failing to advise on rights of appeal; failure by management to monitor compliance with adequate procedures; cavalier disregard of guidance which is intended to be followed in the interest of equitable treatment of those who use the service; failure to mitigate the rigid adherence to the letter of the law where that produces manifestly inequitable treatment.[218]

Complaints must be made within 12 months of the occurrence of the **1–072** events complained about, although this period may be extended. The PCA cannot conduct an investigation of its own initiative. Although the "filter" has been much criticised, it remains the case that a complaint may only be accepted for formal investigation if it is referred to the PCA by a Member of Parliament.

In recent years the PCA, like the other ombudsmen, has adopted a range **1–073** of informal methods of working which are not expressly referred to by the 1967 Act. Formal statutory investigations are therefore now the exception rather than the rule. Investigations are conducted in private. No set procedure is prescribed, but the officials concerned must be given an opportunity to comment on the relevant allegations. The PCA has power to administer oaths and to compel the attendance of witnesses and the production of documents. Wilful obstruction of their investigations is punishable in the same way as a contempt of court. The PCA has access to all relevant documents except those relating to the Cabinet and its committees. Public interest can be asserted to prevent further dissemination of information by the PCA, but not to prevent him from acquiring it in the first place.[219]

Gaps still remain in the PCA's terms of reference.[220] There can be no **1–074** investigation of: personnel matters in the public service; commercial or contractual transactions (subject to some exceptions relating to the acquisition and disposal of land); action taken for the investigation and prevention of crime and the institution and conduct of civil and criminal proceedings; external relations, the rendition of fugitive offenders or action taken for the protection of State security (including the withholding of passports).

The PCA has no power to make mandatory orders, merely recommenda- **1–075** tions.[221] Central government bodies under the jurisdiction of the PCA in almost all cases accept the findings of investigations and provide the recommended redress. In the rare cases where this does not happen, the PCA may publish a special report and the matter will be raised in

---

[218] Annual Report 1993 H.C. Paper No.290 (Session 1993/94), para.7.
[219] 1967 Act ss.7–9, 11(3).
[220] 1967 Act ss.4, 5 Schs 2, 3; 1993 Act ss.3(4), 4, 5, 6 and 7; 1974 Act ss.25, 26, Sch. 5.
[221] R. (on the application of Bradley) v Secretary of State for Work and Pensions [2007] EWHC 242; [2007] Pens. L.R. 87 at [50].

Parliament.[222] Since 2007, the PCA has formal powers to work collaboratively with the Health Service Ombudsman and the Local Government Ombudsman.[223]

Health Service Ombudsman for England

1-076 The PCA does not have jurisdiction to deal with complaints arising from the National Health Service. Instead, such complaints are dealt with by the HSC (a post that has been held by the same person as that of PCA).[224] In contrast to access to the PCA, aggrieved persons can apply directly to the HSC. They must first exhaust other avenues of complaint, which include "local resolution" and an "independent review" by the Healthcare Commission.[225] The HSC's jurisdiction extends beyond issues of maladministration to failures in providing a service and also includes matters relating to clinical judgements (for example receiving the wrong or poor treatment and errors in diagnosis or treatment). As with the PCA, the HSC has no jurisdiction over staff matters or complaints about which civil legal proceedings are pending or contemplated.

Local Government Ombudsman

1-077 The LGO investigates complaints of injustice resulting from maladministration from local authorities in England.[226] There are three Commissioners, each dealing with a different region of England. Complaints may be made directly to the LGO by aggrieved persons or by a councillor on their behalf. As well as handing individual complaints, the LGO issues guidance on good administrative practice.[227]

1-078 The formal legal powers of the LGO are to conduct investigations and issue reports recommending redress, including financial reparation if appropriate; and mediation services may be provided. As with the other

---

[222] For example, the Ministry of Defence did not accept all the findings, or agree to implement all the recommendations, of the PCA's investigation of failings in the *ex gratia* compensation scheme for British subjects interned by the Japanese during the Second World War. *"A Debt of Honour": the ex gratia scheme for British groups interned by the Japanese during the Second World War*, HC Paper No.324 (Session 2005). In 2006 the Department for Work and Pensions rejected all but one of the recommendations made by the PCA in relation to 75,000 people who lost all or part of their final salary occupational pensions on the winding up of their pension schemes (*Trusting in the Pensions Promise* (Cm. 6961) and for subsequent litigation see *Bradley* [2007] EWHC 242; [2007] Pens. L.R. 87.

[223] Primary legislation amended by Regulatory Reform (Collaboration etc between Ombudsmen) Order 2007 (SI 2007/1889).

[224] Health Service Commissioners Act 1993 (as amended). In Wales, health service complaints are dealt with the by Public Services Ombudsman for Wales (see Public Services Ombudsman (Wales) Act 2005).

[225] National Health Service (Complaints) Regulations 2004 (SI 2004/1768).

[226] Local government complaints in Wales are dealt with the by Public Services Ombudsman for Wales.

[227] ODPM: Housing, Planning, Local Government and the Regions Committee, *Ombudsmen for England*. HC Paper No.458 (Session 2004/05).

ombudsmen, a complainant is expected to use the local authority's internal complaints processes before calling up on the LGO to investigate. Decisions of local authorities from which an appeal lies to a Minister of the Crown may normally not be investigated by the LGO.[228]

If a local authority refuses to accept the recommendation, the LGO has power to issue a further report. As well as publicising the report and allowing it to be publicly available, the report has to be laid before and considered by the authority which must notify the LGO what it intends to do within specified time limits. If no notice is given or the LGO remains dissatisfied, it may issue a further report. Similar provisions apply to that further report and an unsatisfactory outcome may lead to the LGO requiring the authority to publish a statement in agreed form in the local press. Where this is refused, the Commissioner may publish such a statement at the authority's expense. Further reports must be considered by the Council where the action recommended in the report is not taken.[229] Monitoring Officers in each local authority have a duty to publicise cases of wilful refusal to accept a report or where an authority proposes to act unlawfully or with maladministration.[230]

1–079

Reform of the ombudsmen

There have been calls for significant reform of the PCA, HSC and LGO from inside and outside government, usually supported by the ombudsmen themselves.[231] In 2000, a review by the Cabinet Office found that the current legislative frameworks within which the three main ombudsmen operated were too restrictive and needed a thorough overhaul.[232] The review called for closer working between the ombudsmen and strongly recommended that the MP-filter be abolished. This is the requirement that complaints to the PCA may formally only be referred by MPs and not made by aggrieved citizens directly. In August 2005, the Cabinet Office announced that it would seek to carry out some reforms by means of a regulatory reform order (RRO) under the Regulatory Reform Act 2001, which it did in June 2007 in the Regulatory Reform (Collaboration etc. between Ombudsmen) Order. This did not, however, remove of the MP-filter. While the Government accepts that removal of this restriction is desirable, it takes the view that that reform must be carried out by an Act

1–080

---

[228] Local Government Act 1974 s.26(2)(b); however, it has been held that the Local Government Ombudsman was entitled to investigate the decisions of bodies hearing school admission appeals even though it was claimed the decision was made on the merits; he was investigating the process of decision: *R. v Commissioner for Local Administration Ex p. Croydon BC* [1989] 1 All E.R. 1033.

[229] Local Government Act 1974 s.31 (as amended).

[230] Local Government and Housing Act 1989 s.5.

[231] Parliamentary Ombudsman, *Redress in the round; remedying maladministration in central and local government*. HC Paper No.475 (Session 2005/06).

[232] P. Collcutt and M. Hourihan, *Review of the Public Sector Ombudsmen in England*, available at *http://www.cabinet-office.gov.uk*.

of Parliament; alas this seems unlikely to be a legislative priority for the Government.

Judicial review and the ombudsmen

1–081   There are two aspects to the relationship between judicial review and the ombudsmen—challenges to the ombudsmen and overlapping jurisdictions. We look at these in turn.

The PCA, HSC and LGO are public authorities carrying out a public function and thus in principle amenable to judicial review.[233] The absence of any statutory right of appeal against the findings of the ombudsmen makes judicial review the only process for questioning the lawfulness of their activity. This said, the court has indicated that it will not readily be persuaded to interfere with the broad discretionary powers of the ombudsmen, given their width and the high degree of subjective judgment involved.[234] Statistically, very few of the judicial review challenges brought against the LGO have been successful—not one of the 27 claims brought between 2001 and 2004.[235] Successful judicial review claims against the ombudsmen have involved: an investigation which failed to regard a public authority's refusal to exercise a power as maladministration;[236] the provision of inadequate reasons to explain a refusal to conduct and inquiry and refusal to disclose interview notes;[237] and issuing a report that went beyond the formal powers of the ombudsman.[238]

1–082   Decisions taken by ministers and local authorities to reject findings of fact made by an ombudsman are also amenable to judicial review;[239] subject to some *caveats*, they are generally to be regarded as binding.[240] The recommendations made by ombudsmen are not binding on the public

---

[233] See Ch.3.
[234] *R. v Parliamentary Commissioner for Administration Ex p. Dyer* [1994] 1 W.L.R. 621. *R. v Commissioner for Local Administration Ex p. Eastleigh BC* [1988] Q.B. 855; *R. v Commissioner for Local Administration Ex p. Croydon LBC* [1989] 1 All E.R. 1033.
[235] *Hansard* HC, col.761W (January 17, 2005).
[236] *R. v Parliamentary Commissioner for Administration Ex p. Balchin (No.1)* [1998] 1 P.L.R. 1; *R. v Parliamentary Commissioner for Administration Ex p. Balchin (No.2)* (2000) 2 L.G.L.R. 87.
[237] *R. (on the application of Turpin) v Commissioner for Local Administration* [2001] EWHC Admin 503; [2003] B.L.G.R. 133,
[238] *R. (on the application of Cavanagh) v Health Services Commissioner* [2005] EWCA Civ 1578; [2006] 1 F.C.R. 7.
[239] See, e.g. *R. (on the application of Bradley) v Secretary of State for Work and Pensions* [2007] EWHC 242; [2007] Pens. L.R. 87 (no reasonable minister could rationally disagree with the PCA's finding that a pamphlet about pensions was "sometimes inaccurate, often incomplete, largely inconsistent and therefore potentially misleading").
[240] *Bradley* [2007] EWHC 242; [2007] Pens. L.R. 87 at [58]. Subject to caveats laid down in *R. v Secretary of State for the Home Department Ex p. Danaei* [1997] EWCA Civ 2704; [1998] Imm. A.R. 84, (a) that the ombudsman's (in *Danaei*, the immigration adjudicator's) "factual conclusion was itself demonstrably flawed, as irrational or for failing to have regard to material considerations or for having regard to immaterial ones"; (b) fresh material has subsequently become available which could realistically have affected the findings of fact; and (c) the findings of fact are based only on documents rather than witnesses.

authority, but these too may be subject to judicial review if the discretion to reject has been exercised unlawfully.[241]

Maladministration (the province of the ombudsmen) and unlawfulness 1–083 (the jurisdiction of the Administrative Court) are overlapping categories of complaint:[242] for example, bias, fettering a discretion, taking into account irrelevant considerations, disproportionate decision, and failure to follow a code of practice may well constitute both maladministration and provide a basis for judicial review. This creates two interlinked problems. First, the main public sector ombudsmen have no jurisdiction to investigate a complaint if the complainant has or had a remedy by way of proceeding in any court of law unless the ombudsman is satisfied that, in the particular circumstances, it is not reasonable to expect the person aggrieved to have resorted or to resort to court proceedings.[243] In such cases, if a claim for judicial review is actually commenced, the ombudsman will be deprived of jurisdiction to investigate the matter.[244] In cases where legal proceedings have not yet started, both the ombudsmen and the Administrative Court have considerable latitude to form judgments as to which avenue the complainant should reasonably pursue. The ombudsmen have for their parts adopted a flexible approach.[245] A practical approach is required. In cases where extensive fact-finding is needed to deal with the complaint, an ombudsman will generally be a better route.[246] So too where the redress sought is relatively modest compensation.[247] The ombudsmen may also have regard to the emotional and financial cost of a claim for judicial review.[248] In contrast, judicial review is likely to be the more suitable

---

[241] *Bradley* [2007] EWHC 242; [2007] Pens. L.R. 87.

[242] *R. v Local Commissioner for Local Government for North and North East England Ex p. Liverpool City Council* [2001] 1 All E.R. 462 (Henry L.J.: "What may not have been recognised back in 1974 was the emergence of judicial review to the point where most if not almost all matters which could form the basis for a complaint of maladministration are matters for which the elastic qualities of judicial review might provide a remedy").

[243] Parliamentary Commissioner Act 1967 s.5(2); Local Government Act 1974 s.26(6).

[244] *R. (on the application of Scholarstica UMO) v Commissioner for Local Administration* [2003] EWHC 3202 (Admin); [2004] E.L.R. 265 (Beatson J.: "Accordingly, those advising individuals regarding matters potentially giving rise to both local commissioner investigations and to judicial review should first seek an investigation by the local commission"); this perhaps overlooks the practical difficulty that claims for judicial review must be made promptly and in any event within three months (see 16–050) while there is a 12 month time limit for complaints to the ombudsmen.

[245] E. Osmotherly, "The Local Government Ombudsman as an alternative to judicial review", published at *http://www.lgo.org.uk/judicial—review.htm*

[246] *R. v Local Commissioner for Local Government for North and North East England Ex p. Liverpool City Council* [2001] 1 All E.R. 462.

[247] *R. (on the application of Anufrijeva) v Southwark LBC* [2003] EWCA Civ 1406; [2004] Q.B. 1124; discussed at 19–085.

[248] Parliamentary Ombudsman, *"A Debt of Honour": the ex gratia scheme for British groups interned by the Japanese during the Second World War.* HC Paper No.324 (Session 2005/06), para.26. The Government in its response to the draft report took a different view, arguing that the complainant could reasonably have pursued judicial review proceedings (as others had done in *R. (on the application of Association of British Civilian Internees (Far East Region)) v Secretary of State for Defence* [2003] EWCA Civ 473; [2003] Q.B. 1397). The PASC supported the PCA's view: PASC, *"A Debt of Honour"*, HC Paper No.735 (Session 2005/06), para.20.

avenue where a case turns on a dispute about the correct interpretation of statutory provisions or where an interim remedy is needed. On occasion, the court has refused permission to proceed with a claim for judicial review on the ground that a complaint to an ombudsman is a satisfactory alternative remedy,[249] and the development of proportionate dispute resolution principles may well result in this becoming more common.[250]

TRIBUNALS

1–084   Judicial review and the tribunal system intersect in two main ways. First, the tribunal system provides a more specialised method of supervising the legality (and in many cases the merits) of decision-making by public authorities. Where an aggrieved person has the possibility of an appeal to a tribunal, the Administrative Court will be reluctant to grant permission to proceed with a claim for judicial review.[251] Secondly, judicial review is in some situations the appropriate means of challenging the lawfulness of decisions taken by the tribunals themselves—though following the Tribunals, Courts and Enforcement Act 2007 the role of the Administrative Court will be greatly diminished.[252]

Tribunals generally

1–085   In the design of an administrative justice system, a tribunal may be preferred to an ordinary court because its members have specialised knowledge of the subject-matter, because it will be more informal in its trappings and procedure, because it may be better at finding facts, applying flexible standards and exercising discretionary powers, and because it may be cheaper, more accessible and more expeditious than the High Court. Many of the decisions given to tribunals concern the merits of cases with relatively little legal content, and in such cases a tribunal, usually consisting of a legally qualified tribunal judge and two lay members, may be preferred to a court. Indeed dissatisfaction with the over-technical and allegedly unsympathetic approach of the courts towards social welfare legislation led to a transfer of functions to special tribunals; the Workmen's Compensation Acts were administered by the ordinary courts, but the National Insurance (Industrial Injuries) scheme was applied by tribunals. It is, however, unrealistic to imagine that technicalities and difficult legal issues can somehow be avoided by entrusting the administration of complex legislation to tribunals rather than the courts.[253] Until the coming into force

---

[249] See 16–021; R. v Lambeth LBC Ex p. Crookes (1997) 29 H.L.R. 28.
[250] R. (on the application of Anufrijeva) v Southwark LBC [2003] EWCA Civ 1406; [2004] Q.B. 1124.
[251] See 16–014.
[252] See 1–17–040.
[253] Research published by the Council on Tribunals suggests that tribunal users were often confused about procedures: M. Adler and J. Gulland, Tribunal Users' Esperience: Perceptions and Expectations: A Literature Review (2003).

of the Tribunals, Courts and Enforcement Act 2007, a wide range of grievances against public authorities were dealt with by a system of about 70 statutory tribunals, deciding over 1 million cases each year.[254] The case load is dominated by adjudication on welfare benefits and immigration and asylum. In addition to statutory tribunals, many self-regulatory and other non-statutory bodies performing public functions make appeal decisions though disciplinary and similar panels.

Table 4: Main areas of public sector tribunal activity prior to the TCEA 2007[255]

Tribunal	Case load in 2003–04
Appeals Service, then on further appeal to the *Social Security and Child Support Commissioners.*[256] Jurisdiction over decisions relating to Income Support; Jobseeker's Allowance; Incapacity Benefit; Disability Living Allowance; Attendance Allowance; and Retirement Pension. It also deals with disputes about Child Support Maintenance; Tax Credits; Housing Benefit; Council Tax Benefit	235,657 (Appeals Service) + 6,364 (Commissioners) = 242,021
Immigration Adjudicators, then on further appeal to the Immigration Appeal Tribunal. (Note: these have been replaced by the Asylum and Immigration Tribunal).	91,945 (Adjudicators) + 41,889 (Immigration Appeal Tribunal) = 133,834
Financial and Tax Tribunals (the collective name for four distinct tribunals: VAT and Duties Tribunals; Special Commissioners of Income Tax); Financial Services & Markets Tribunal; Pensions Regulator Tribunal	29,498 (General and Special Commissioners of Income Tax) + 2,496 (VAT & Duties Tribunal) = 31,994
Mental Health Review Tribunals[257]	20,408
Criminal Injuries Compensation Appeals Panel[258]	4,434
Special Educational Needs and Disability Tribunal (SENDIST)[259]	3,638
Pensions Appeals Tribunal[260]	3,372

In 1957, the Franks Committee considered that "tribunals should properly **1–086** be regarded as machinery provided by Parliament for adjudication rather than as part of the machinery of administration",[261] and it made a number

[254] Some tribunals are concerned for the most part with disputes between individuals and private bodies, e.g. Employment Tribunals and Leasehold Valuation Tribunals. Some tribunals are administered by government departments; others by local authorities (e.g. Parking Adjudicators and School Admission Appeals Panels).

[255] Adapted from DCA, *Transforming Public Services: Complaints, Redress and Tribunals* (Cm. 6243), p.15.

[256] T. Buck, D. Bonner and R. Sainsbury, *Making Social Security Law: The Role and Work of the Social Security and Child Support Commissioners* (2005). An appeal, with leave, on point of law lies from substantive decisions of the SSCSC to the Court of Appeal.

[257] Mental Health Act 1983. In September 2004 the Government published a revised Draft Mental Health Bill; if and when this reaches the statute book it will bring about significant reforms.

[258] This is a non-statutory tribunal with around 100 part-time panel members. It hears appeals from the Criminal Injuries Compensation Authority.

[259] Education Act 1993.

[260] Hears appeals from ex-servicemen or women who have had their claims for a War Pension rejected by the Secretary of State for Defence.

[261] Report of the Committee on Administrative Tribunals and Enquiries, Cmnd. 218 (1957), p.9.

of detailed recommendations (most of which were implemented) to achieve that object and to improve the procedure at statutory inquiries that preceded a ministerial decision.[262] The Franks Committee sought the qualities of "openness, fairness and impartiality" in tribunals. Nonetheless, until the 2007 Act there remained a great deal of dissatisfaction with the design and operation of tribunals. The structure of the system was widely regarded as haphazard and unnecessarily complex.[263] Doubts were also been expressed as to the degree of independence and impartiality of some tribunals, especially those that were administered by the government department against whose decisions they heard appeals.

Tribunals after the Tribunals, Courts and Enforcement Act 2007

1–087 The 2007 Act (TCEA) amalgamates almost all the jurisdictions of these tribunals (but not those dealing with immigration and asylum or the Employment Appeal Tribunal) into a new structure comprising a First-tier Tribunal and an Upper Tribunal (concerned mostly with appeals from the First-tier Tribunal), supported administratively by the Tribunals Service (an executive agency of the Department of Justice). The Upper Tribunal is a superior court of record[264] and many of its judges will be drawn from the High Court and Court of Appeal. Under secondary legislation, the First-tier Tribunal and Upper Tribunal are to be divided into chambers (each one headed by a judicial figured called the Chamber President), with jurisdiction over a specified subject or geographical area or a combination of the two. In future statutes creating administrative schemes will no longer need to create new tribunals if an appeal mechanism is required; the legislation will refer simply to the First-tier Tribunal and Upper Tribunal. The independence of tribunal judges is protected by a new statutory guarantee.[265] A judge is Senior President of Tribunals, with overarching responsibility for the new system.[266]

1–088   The 2007 Act has its origins in a report of a major review chaired by Sir Andrew Leggatt in 2001. A series of far-reaching recommendations were made.[267] The review was established because of concern by the then Lord Chancellor, Lord Irvine, that tribunals should provide "fair, timely and proportionate and effective arrangements for handling disputes" and a "coherent structure" for the delivery of administrative justice. Lord Justice Leggatt saw need for radical change. He observed that the present tribunal

[262] For the implementation of the Committee's recommendations, see esp. Tribunals and Inquiries Act 1958 (now Tribunals and Inquiries Act 1992) and the statutory rules of procedure promulgated for planning, compulsory purchase and highways inquiries.
[263] H. Woolf, "A Hotchpotch of Appeals—The Need for a Blender" [1988] C.J.Q. 44.
[264] TCEA s.3(5).
[265] TCEA s.1.
[266] TCEA s.2. (Lord Justice Carnwath was the first appointed).
[267] Sir Andrew Leggatt, Report of the Review of Tribunals: Tribunals for Users—One System, One Service http://www.tribunals-review.org.uk.

system had grown up in a "haphazard" way, providing no coherence and was "developed more to meet the needs and convenience of the departments and other bodies which run tribunals, rather than the needs of the user". He recommended that the tribunals should be rationalised and, in order to ensure their independence from government departments, administered by a new executive agency, reporting to the Department of Constitutional Affairs, in parallel with the new Court Service which has been established to administer the courts. He made a number of detailed arrangements for improvements to such matters as procedures, administration and routes of appeal.

Those recommendations were broadly accepted by the Government **1–089** which issued a White Paper in July 2004.[268] The White Paper was not, however, content with simply preserving the existing procedures and proposed an approach which would "re-engineer processes radically so that just solutions can be found without hearings at all" and be able not only to provide authoritative rulings where those were needed but also to "resolve disputes fairly and informally". The 2007 Act contains express provision for mediation, but subject to the safeguards that "(a) mediation of matters in dispute between parties to proceedings is to take place only by agreement between those parties; and (b) where parties to proceedings fail to mediate, or where mediation between parties to proceedings fails to resolve disputed matters, the failure is not to affect the outcome of the proceedings".[269]

Review and appeal in the new tribunal system

The First-tier Tribunal and the Upper Tribunal are public authorities **1–090** operating under the rule of law and it is important that parties aggrieved by their determinations are able to challenge them. In the new tribunal system, there are three main ways of challenging decisions. First, "reviews" may be carried out to identify and correct errors without the need for a full appeal. A First-tier Tribunal had discretion to carry out a review one of its decisions, either of its own motion or at the request of a party;[270] if a decision is set-aside, the First-tier Tribunal may make the decision again or refer the matter to the Upper Tribunal. The Upper Tribunal also has powers to review its own decisions on a similar basis.[271]

Secondly, there are rights of appeal. In most cases, parties have a right of **1–091** appeal, subject to permission, from the First-tier Tribunal to the Upper Tribunal.[272] If the Upper Tribunal holds that the decision was subject to an error of law, it may set aside the First-tier Tribunal decision and either take

---

[268] DCA, *Transforming Public Services: Complaints, Redress and Tribunals*, Cm. 6243 (2004).
[269] TCEA s.24.
[270] TCEA s.9 (subject to secondary legislation, yet to be made at the time of writing).
[271] TCEA s.10.
[272] TCEA s.11.

the decision itself or remit the case to the First-tier Tribunal for redetermination.[273] There is a further appeal on point of law, subject to permission, from the Upper Tribunal to the Court of Appeal, which may if it allows the appeal remit the matter back to the Upper Tribunal for re-decision or re-make a decision itself.[274]

1-092   Thirdly, the Upper Tribunal in most situations has powers to carry out "judicial review"[275] of decisions taken by the First-tier Tribunal.[276] Under this arrangement, the Upper Tribunal has a supervisory jurisdiction over First-tier Tribunals similar to that of the Administrative Court in terms of the grounds of review, the remedial orders that it may make and subject to similar limits on its jurisdiction. Four conditions have to be met before an applicant may seek "judicial review" from the Upper Tribunal in respect of a determination of the First-tier Tribunal. They are in effect as follows:[277] (a) the applicant seeks relief of the type normally available on judicial review claims under CPR Pt 54[278]—and nothing else; (b) the application does not call into question anything done in the Crown Court;[279] (c) the application falls within a class of cases specified by a direction made by the Lord Chief Justice of England and Wales or his nominee and approved by the Lord Chancellor;[280] and (d) the judge sitting in the Upper Tribunal is a High Court or Court of Appeal judge, or a judge agreed by the Lord Chief Justice of England and Wales and the Senior President of Tribunals.

1-093   The 2007 Act will have a significant impact on the role of the Administrative Court in hearing claims for judicial review against tribunal decisions. The Administrative Court will have no role at all in relation to decisions of the Upper Tribunal, which as superior court of record falls entirely outside the supervisory jurisdiction.[281] The conferral of powers of "judicial review" on the Upper Tribunal has the knock-on effect of limiting the role of the Administrative Court in relation to challenges to the lawfulness of decisions of the First-tier Tribunal. If a person makes a claim for judicial review to the Administrative Court under CPR Pt 54, in some circumstances the Administrative Court *must* transfer the claim to be dealt

---

[273] TCEA s.12.

[274] TCEA s.13. The grounds of appeal are the same as those applying in the court system: (a) that the proposed appeal would raise some important point of principle or practice, or (b) that there is some other compelling reason to hear the appeal.

[275] TCEA ss.15–18 are set out below. The quotation marks are used in the Act, presumably to signify that this "judicial review" is something distinct from that of the Administrative Court.

[276] TCEA s.15.

[277] TCEA s.18.

[278] A mandatory, prohibiting, or quashing order, a declaration or injunction; permission to apply for "judicial review"; costs; interest; and monetary remedies.

[279] 3–009; note that this is wider than the prohibition on the Adminsitrative Court hearing judicial reviews on matters "relating to trials on indictment".

[280] This direction-making power is contained in the Constitutional Reform Act 2005 Sch.2 Pt 1.

[281] See 3–019.

with by the Upper Tribunal;[282] in others it may order a transfer where it is thought just and convenient to do so.[283] The Administrative Court *may not* transfer claims relating to immigration and asylum.[284]

Immigration and asylum

As we have noted, immigration and asylum matters have been kept apart **1–094** from the new structures introduced by the 2007 Act. In April 2005, the Asylum and Immigration Tribunal (AIT) came into being, established by the Asylum and Immigration (Treatment of Claimants etc) Act 2004. It replaced the previous system of adjudicators (who made initial appeal decisions) and the Immigration and Asylum Tribunal. The judicial review case load in the Administrative Court has for several years been dominated by claims relating to immigration and asylum.[285] We consider the role of the Administrative Court in this context in Chapter 17.[286]

PUBLIC INQUIRIES AND INQUESTS

Town and Country Planning

One type of public inquiry provides a means of appealing to the Secretary **1–095** of State (in England) or National Assembly of Wales (in Wales) against decisions of local authorities in relation to planning and highways and transport proposals, rights of way and compulsory purchase.[287] Most appeals are in fact dealt with without a public inquiry—by exchange of written representations or a hearing; only some 4 per cent of appeals result in an inquiry. They are conducted by planning inspectors employed by the Planning Inspectorate, which is an executive agency under the auspices of the Department for Communities and Local Government in England (and the Welsh Assembly Government in Wales). At an inquiry, the developer

---

[282] Supreme Court Act (Senior Courts Act) 1981 s.31A(2) (inserted by TCEA s.19); set out in Appendix D below. There are four conditions that must be satisfied for a transfer to be mandatory, which may be paraphrased as follows: (1) the claimant is seeking only the normal judicial review remedies, damages, costs and interest; (2) the claim does not call into question anything done in the Crown Court; (3) the claim falls within the class of claims set out in a direction made by the Lord Chief Justice or his nominee; and (4) the claim does not call into question any decision made under the Immigration Acts or the British Nationality Act 1981, or any instrument having effect under those Acts, or law which determines British citizenship, British overseas territories citizenship, the status of a British National (Overseas) or British Overseas citizenship.
[283] Supreme Court Act (Senior Courts Act) 1981 s.31A(3). Transfer may take place where conditions 1, 2, and 4 described in n.282 are met. On the general approach to alternative remedies, see 16–041.
[284] Condition 4, described in n.282.
[285] See 1–045.
[286] See 17–004.
[287] See e.g. Town & Country Planning (Inquiries Procedure) Rules 1992 (SI 1992/2038).

and opposers are able to put their case by submitting written evidence and calling and cross-examining witnesses. The inspector's report makes findings of fact and recommendations to the relevant minister advising how statutory discretion should be exercised on the basis of law and government policy. In the vast majority of cases ministers accept the inspectors' recommendations. Neither inspectors nor ministers in the planning inquiry process constitute an "independent and impartial" tribunal for the purposes of determining civil rights and obligations under ECHR Art.6(1).[288] There is however a right of appeal to the Administrative Court, on point of law, and this has been held to provide sufficient judicial oversight of the lawfulness of decision-making to comply with Art.6(1).[289] In relation to aspects of the inquiry process from which there is no statutory appeal, a claim for judicial review under CPR Pt 54 may be made.

Other Public Inquiries

1–096 A different type of public inquiry is those established by ministers to investigate and make recommendations about events that have caused public concern.[290] The main legal basis for such inquiries is the Inquiries Act 2005, though ministers (and indeed other public authorities) may continue to establish ad hoc non-statutory investigative inquiries without formal legal powers. The 2005 Act provides ministers with a broad discretion to decide whether or not to call an inquiry, to determine terms of reference, appoint panel members[291] and restrict public access to information. Several bodies, including Amnesty International and the Law Society of England and Wales, have expressed disquiet about the degree of ministerial control over inquiries under the 2005 Act. Inquiries established under the 2005 Act must avoid ruling on any person's civil or criminal liability, though an inquiry panel is not to be "inhibited in the discharge of its functions by any likelihood of liability being inferred from facts that it determines or recommendations that it makes".[292]

1–097 Given the controversial contexts in which public inquiries arise it is perhaps unsurprising that decisions relating to public inquiries have been subject to judicial review challenges. The 2005 Act expressly anticipates such challenges and requires claims for judicial review of decisions made by a minister in relation to an inquiry or a by a member of an inquiry panel, must be brought within 14 days after the day on which the claimant became aware of the decision, unless that time limit is extended by the

---

[288] See 10–078.
[289] *R. v Secretary of State for the Environment, Transport and the Regions Ex p. Holdings & Barnes Plc (the Alconbury case)* [2001] UKHL 23; [2003] 2 A.C. 295; see 10–078.
[290] I. Steele, "Judging judicial inquiries" [2004] P.L. 738.
[291] Ministers have often chosen judges to chair inquiries: J. Beatson, "Should Judges Conduct Public Inquiries?" (2005) 121 L.Q.R. 221; R. Masterman, "A Supreme Court for the United Kingdom: Two Steps Forward, But One Step Back on Judicial Independence" [2004] P.L. 48.
[292] Inquiries Act 2005 s.1.

court.[293] The normal time limit for claims for judicial review (promptly and in any event within three months) applies to challenges to the contents of reports and decisions of which the claimant could not have become aware until the publication of the report.[294]

Judicial review may be directed at three main types of decisions relating to public inquiries. First, a claimant may seek to challenge a decision to hold or not hold an inquiry, or the basis on which the inquiry is to operate. Relatives of victims of Dr Harold Shipman successfully claimed that the Secretary of State for Health's decision to hold an internal departmental inquiry in the circumstances surrounding the multiple murders was irrational and a statutory public inquiry under the Tribunals of Inquiry (Evidence) Act 1921 (now repealed by the 2005 Act) was subsequently held.[295] This ruling has however been distinguished in later cases and it would seem doubtful whether there is any general proposition of law favouring public inquiries over internal government inquiries.[296] **1–098**

Secondly, judicial review challenges may be brought to question decisions relating to the procedures adopted by an inquiry (and it is in relation to this category that most challenges have been made).[297] **1–099**

Thirdly, it may be possible to challenge the findings of a report made by a public inquiry.[298] In *Mahon v Air New Zealand*, the Privy Council set aside a costs order of a Royal Commission (Justice Peter Mahon) into the crash of aircraft in the Antarctic in 1977 in which 257 people died. The report stated that there had been "an orchestrated litany of lies" by executives of Air New Zealand, and on that basis the costs order had been made. The Privy Council held that there was no probative evidence of such lies and no opportunity had been given to those implicated by the findings to make representations before the report was published. *Mahon*, arguably, does not provide clear authority for the amenability to judicial review of **1–100**

---

[293] Inquiries Act 2005 s.38(1).
[294] Inquiries Act 2005 s.38(2). On normal provisions for time limits, see 16–050.
[295] *R. (on the application of Wagstaff) v Secretary of State for Health* [2001] 1 W.L.R. 292. The internal inquiry under the chairmanship of Lord Laming of Tewin was stopped and a public inquiry under the terms of the 1921 Act was subsequently held under the chairmanship of Dame Janet Smith.
[296] See, e.g. *R. (on the application of Howard) v Secretary of State for Health* [2002] EWHC 396; [2003] Q.B. 830 (no presumption inquiries ordered under National Health Service Act 1977 s.84(1) would be public); *R. (on the application of Persey) v Secretary of State for the Environment, Food and Rural Affairs* [2002] EWHC 371; [2003] Q.B. 794 (Government to set up three separate independent inquiries, receiving evidence mainly in private, into a serious outbreak of foot and mouth disease in the UK).
[297] See, e.g. in relation to Lord Saville's Bloody Sunday inquiry: *R. v Lord Saville of Newdigate Ex p. B (No.1) The Times*, April 15, 1999, CA; *R. v Lord Saville of Newdigate Ex p. B (No.2)* [2000] 1 W.L.R. 1855; *R. (on the application of Widgery Soldiers) v Lord Saville of Newdigate* [2001] EWCA Civ 2048; [2002] 1 W.L.R. 1249; see further L. Blom-Cooper, "Procedures in Public Inquiries" [2002] P.L. 391.
[298] H. Quane, "Challenging the Report of an Independent Inquiry under the Human Rights Act" [2007] P.L. 529.

findings by a public authority.[299] Even if findings of fact are amenable, the court will be reluctant to intervene for the same reasons—and subject to the same caveats—as it is cautious about quashing findings of fact made by tribunals and ombudsmen.[300]

Coroners and Inquests

1–101 Inquests, by a coroner and jury, may be held to determine the cause of a death under the Coroners Act 1988. The conduct of inquests must, following the Human Rights Act 1998, take into account the requirements of ECHR Art.2 (right to life).[301] ECHR Art.2 creates a procedural obligation on the State to investigate deaths, but this may be satisfied by criminal proceedings or a coroner's inquest just as well as a public inquiry.[302] Where a coroner refuses to hold an inquest, or where justice requires that a further inquest be held and the coroner refuses, s.13 of the 1988 Act provides that an application may be made to the Administrative Court.[303] An ordinary claim for judicial review under CPR Pt 54 lies in respect of other matters to do with inquests.

CATEGORIES OF JUDICIAL REVIEW

1–102 So far in this Chapter, we have referred to judicial review in general terms. It is however useful to differentiate five different categories of review reflecting the sources of the rights and powers in issue. These categories are:

- where a ground of review in domestic law is advanced (other than a fundamental right)

- a fundamental right recognised by the common law is in issue

- Convention rights are advanced

- a directly effective right protected by European Community law exists

[299] Quane [2007] P.L. 529, argues that findings of a report may not be a "decision" amenable to judicial review). But the court's broad supervisory jurisdiction is broad and extends, e.g. to guidance and policy documents which do not directly affect any person's legal rights (see 3–025)

[300] See n.239.

[301] See 7–037; 7–128 and 13–060.

[302] *R. (on the application of Scholes) v Secretary of State for the Home Department* [2006] EWHC 1; (2006) 170 J.P. 243 (following an inquest, a coroner wrote to the minister recommending a public inquiry into sentencing policy and provision of local authority secure children's homes; held that while it was debatable whether or not it might be desirable to have a public inquiry, it was not unlawful for the minister to decline to do so).

[303] The procedure is considered at 17–043.

- there is a "devolution issue".

As we shall see in more detail in the Chapters which follow, although there   **1–103** may be increasing convergence between the standards applied under these different sources of review, the courts take a different approach to each of them, in relation to the fields summarised in Table 5. For example damages may be available for breach of a Community law right or a Convention right but not in relation to unlawful administrative action that is taken under domestic law. Other stark contrasts may arise in relation to statutory interpretation: the different obligations placed upon the court according to the rights in issue may in some cases result in the same legislation being given different meanings according to whether the matter is entirely one of domestic law or involves Convention rights or Community law.[304]

---

[304] *R. (on the application of Hurst) v HM Coroner for Northern District London* [2007] UKHL 13; [2007] 2 W.L.R. 726 at [12] (Lord Rodger: "legislation is interpreted differently, depending on whether or not Community rights are involved" and the same applies in relation to Convention rights).

Table 5

JUDICIAL REVIEW FEATURE →

	Standing (see Ch.2)	Amenability (Ch.3)	Statutory interpretation (Chs 5, 13, 14)	Procedural fairness (Chs 6-10, 13, 14)	Review of questions of fact (Chs 4, 11)	Substantive review (Ch.11; also Chs 13-14)	Legitimate expectations (Ch.12)	Remedial orders (Ch.18)	Monetary remedies (Ch.19)
Domestic law	Sufficient interest in the matter, liberally interpreted[i]	Source of power test (statute or prerogative),[ii] complemented by Datafin test of "public function"[iii] and justiciability requirement[iv]	Generally purposive, focusing on ordinary meaning of words to give effect to intent of Parliament[v]	General duty to act fairly according to the context[vi] – but as yet no general common law duty to give reasons[vii]	Where (a) fact is a condition precedent to decision;[viii] (b) misdirection on material fact;[ix] (c) decision unsupported by substantial evidence;[x] (d) inferences were unreasonably drawn or conclusions did not rationally relate to evidence available to a decision-maker[xi]	Variable intensity irrationality review,[xii] proportionality not yet accepted as a free-standing ground of review[xiii]	Common law now recognises substantive[xiv] as well as procedural[xv] legitimate expectations.	Quashing, prohibiting, mandatory orders; declarations; injunctions[xvi]	No right to damages for unlawful administration as such; must establish tortious wrong[xvii]
Fundamental rights recognised by the common law	As above	As above	"Principle of legality": rights cannot be limited or overridden except by express and unambiguous legislation[xviii]			"Anxious scrutiny" approach to irrationality review[xix]		As above. (Some speculation about power to set aside primary legislation)[xx]	As above; exemplary damages available for unconstitutional conduct[xxi]
Convention	Sufficient interest test	Decisions of "core" public	"So far as possible",	Art.6 rights in relation to	Greater scrutiny (a) to consider	Qualified Convention rights		Domestic remedies plus "declaration of	Damages under

← SOURCE OF RIGHTS OR POWERS

rights	modified to exclude those who are not "victims"[xxxii]	authorities[xxxiii] and "functions of a public nature"[xxxiv]	legislation must be read and given effect in way which is compatible with Convention rights;[xxv] court must "take into account" case law of the ECtHR[xxvi]	"civil rights and obligations" and "criminal charges",[xxviii] Art.2 (right to life) creates right to investigation of deaths[xxviii]	whether the public authority acted proportionately,[xxix] (b) factual basis necessary to justify action (such as detention or compulsory treatment) exists;[xxx] (c) court is required to have "full jurisdiction" for Art.6[xxxi]	(e.g. Arts.8-11) subject to proportionality review	incompatibility"[xxxii]	HRA s.8[xxxiii]
European Community law	As for domestic law.	As for domestic law; plus "emanations of the State" are subject to directly effective EC legislation.[xxiv]	Obligation of "conforming interpretation"[xxxv]	See generally 14-00 and 14-00. In relation to individual decisions affecting fundamental rights, duty to give reasons.[xxxvi]	See generally 14-00 and 14-00. Breach of general principles of EC law, including proportionality, non-discrimination, respect for fundamental rights, legal certainty and protection of legitimate expectations	Legitimate expectations protected as a general principle of Community law[xxxvii]	Domestic remedies plus power to "disapply" statutory provisions incompatible with Community law.[xxxviii]	Liability for breach of EC law under Francovich principles[xxxix]

Discussed in the following sections of the book:

Ordinary domestic situations

1–104 The first category may be regarded as the default position. The rights and duties at stake stem from English law: either statute or prerogative powers (or, if such thing exists, a residual freedom to act under common law powers).[305] No "constitutional rights" (as defined in the next section) are in issue and no questions of European Community or ECHR law arise. The grounds of judicial review here are the product of English common law. The court's general approach to statutory interpretation is to seek the intention of Parliament as expressed in words of enactment.[306] Substantive review is carried out under the head of review called "irrationality", according to the classic *Wednesbury* formula and its modern-day variants, focusing on the "reasonableness" (or otherwise) of the decision.[307] The court's role in fact-finding and correcting errors of law are limited.[308]

1–105 The scope of judicial review is governed by ss.29 and 31 of the Supreme Court Act (Senior Courts Act) 1981.[309] Standing to bring a claim for judicial review is expressed in terms of having a "sufficient interest in the matter to which the application relates" (SCA 1981 s.31), a provision that has been interpreted so liberally by the courts in recent years that it has ceased to be a bar.[310] Amenability to review is determined using a source of power test (is the power in question derived from statute or a prerogative power) supplemented by the *Datafin* approach of inquiring whether a

---

[305] On the Ram doctrine, see 5–022.
[306] See 5–020.
[307] See 11–018.
[308] See 4–047 (precedent fact) and 11–041 (mistake of fact).
[309] When Pt 3 of the Constitutional Reform Act 2005, establishing the Supreme Court of the United Kingdom, comes into force (the anticipated date for this is in October 2009) the Supreme Court Act will be renamed the Senior Courts Act to avoid confusion.
[310] See Ch.2.

"public function" is being carried out.[311] The remedial orders available are those specified in s.29 of the SCA 1981 (as amended): quashing orders; prohibiting orders; mandatory orders; declarations; and injunctions.[312] There is no right to damages for unlawful administrative action in and of itself; a claimant seeking financial recompense must establish that a tortious or other civil wrong has been committed.[313]

Constitutional rights under the common law

A second category of judicial review is where the claimant relies on a fundamental right recognised by the common law. Where in a claim for judicial review a common law fundamental right such as these is at stake, the court will adapt its approach to the task of statutory interpretation. Rights such as these recognised by the common law are fundamental in a more limited sense than comparable rights in many other constitutional systems. As we have discussed,[314] while "[t]here are not, under English domestic law, any fundamental constitutional rights that are immune from legislative change",[315] the court applies the "principle of legality", by which it is assumed that Parliament intended to legislate against a background of existing common law rights; only a specific provision in an Act of Parliament, or in regulations given specific power under an Act, can remove or limit a constitutional right.[316] This is an important safeguard for individual liberty so long as the principle of parliamentary sovereignty remains the basic rule of the British constitution.

1–106

Secondly, the recognition of a right as having a constitutional character calls for the court to modify its approach to substantive review. Where irrationality is used as a ground of review, the court adopts a stance of "anxious scrutiny".[317] Whereas in an ordinary domestic case, the burden of argument lies upon the claimant to demonstrate unreasonableness, here the public authority is called upon to justify its action. We contend that in this kind of case, the courts ought also to recognise that proportionality is an appropriate basis on which to judge official conduct.[318]

1–107

---

[311] See 3–041.
[312] See Ch.18.
[313] See 19.025.
[314] See 1–006.
[315] *Hooper v Secretary of State for Work and Pensions* [2005] UKHL 29; [2005] 1 W.L.R. 1681 at [92] (Lord Scott).
[316] See 5–036.
[317] See 11–007.
[318] See 12–00; see *Persimmon Homes (Thames Valley) Ltd v Taylor Woodrow Homes Ltd* [2005] EWCA Civ 1365; [2006] 1 W.L.R. 334 at [30] (Laws L.J.: "There are, of course, now familiar areas of our law in which the court's role in judicial review cases is much more intrusive than would be contemplated by the *Wednesbury* doctrine. In particular, we are accustomed to consider whether an executive decision is proportionate to a legitimate public interest aim; and it is elementary that the test of proportionality is closer to an adjudication of merits than is *Wednesbury*. But cases of that kind engage the court's duty to see to the protection of the citizen's constitutional rights (whether or not arising through the medium of the Human Rights Act 1998), where such a right is threatened by government action").

1–108   Thirdly, in a tort claim against a public authority, unconstitutional behaviour may permit the award of exemplary damages.[319]

Convention Rights Protected by the HRA

1–109   A third category of judicial review is where Convention rights are in issue. Since October 2000, when the Human Rights Act 1998 came into force, claimants have been able to use a breach of rights guaranteed by the European Convention on Human Rights as a ground of judicial review.[320] The ECHR does not itself expressly include the right to administrative justice but it has influenced administrative law in two important respects. First, it requires all public officials to respect Convention rights. Some of these rights are procedural (such as the right to a fair trial under Art.6), yet others are substantive (such as the right to free expression under Art.10, or equality under Art.14). The principles by which public officials act have therefore been expanded and specified to the extent that the ECHR provides. Although the courts do not have the authority under the HRA to strike down Acts of Parliament which do not conform to Convention rights, they may review such legislation and issue a declaration of incompatibility with Convention rights. This effect of the HRA has been said to provide a "new legal order"[321] and this is to a large extent true. Since even Parliament is expected, by virtue of its own concessions, to respect Convention rights, the notion of democracy as synonymous with majority rule is greatly weakened. The new model of democracy requires in accord with the rule of law that certain fundamental rights are respected, even in the face of popular opinion to the contrary.

1–110   The HRA has brought about a range of important practical changes to the scope and operation of judicial review. The rules of standing (who can be a claimant) are modified by the requirement of s.7 that only claimants who are "victims" of a breach of a Convention right may rely upon them. The question of what decisions "of a public nature" are subject to Convention right review under s.6 have proved to be complex and controversial (and is distinct from the issue of whether an activity is a "public function" amenable to judicial review).[322] Of great importance is the approach to statutory interpretation demanded by s.3, that the courts "so far as possible" interpret legislation so that it conforms with Convention rights.[323] Review of fact tends to be more intensive than in purely domestic law situations.[324]

1–111   A pervasive effect of the HRA has been to shift the focus of our courts away from purely domestic standards. Where Convention rights are relied upon directly, the courts must "take into account" the case law of the

[319] See 19–063.
[320] See Ch.13. More precisely, those Convention rights contained at the relevant time in Sch.1 to the HRA.
[321] *Jackson v Attorney General* [2005] UKHL 56; [2006] 1 A.C. 262 at [102] (Lord Steyn).
[322] See 3–075.
[323] HRA 1998 s.3(1); See 13–040.
[324] For example, in relation to proportionality see 11–079.

European Court of Human Rights (s.2).[325] There are also broader influences on domestic law. As we shall see in Chapter 11, what we call the "structured proportionality test" used in relation to qualified Convention rights may also be applicable to purely domestic contexts.[326] Convention rights have had an important role in creating a "culture of justification" in which the task of the courts is to ensure in an increasingly broad and deep way that there is a proper legal and factual basis for public authorities' actions.[327]

European Community law

A fourth category is where Community law rights and duties arise. Since **1–112** the United Kingdom's accession to the European Communities in 1973, judicial review has been one of the ways in which the domestic courts have been called upon to uphold Community law rights that are "directly effective" in our national legal system.[328] In a small number of cases this has required English courts to "disapply" provisions in primary legislation that are incompatible with such rights—a major modification to the principle of parliamentary sovereignty and the normal rule that courts do not question the validity of statute law.[329] New remedies have also been fashioned to ensure full protection of Community law rights, including damages where there has been a serious breach of Community law by a public authority[330]—this too is a significant innovation for a legal system that has generally set its face against compensation for public law wrongs.[331] Even where a claimant does not have a *directly* effective right under Community law, the domestic courts are obliged to adapt normal methods of statutory interpretation by ensuring that national legislation that deals with the same subject as Community law is construed in a manner that is consistent with it.[332]

Devolution issues and devolution-related questions

A final category of judicial review claim is those which raise a "devolution **1–113** issue".[333] Such issues are defined with some precision and differently (reflecting the asymmetric devolution arrangements) in each of the devolution Acts.[334] Devolution issues may relate to legislation (including primary

---

[325] See 13–034.
[326] See 11–079.
[327] See 11–098.
[328] See 14–010.
[329] See 3–011.
[330] See 14–066.
[331] See 19–025.
[332] See 14–044.
[333] G. Gee, "Devolution in the Courts", Ch.8 in R. Hazell and R. Rawlings (eds), *Devolution, Law Making and the Constitution* (2005).
[334] Scotland Act 1998 s.103(2) and Sch.6; Government of Wales Act 2006 s.149 and Sch.9; Northern Ireland Act 1998 ss.79–83 and Sch.10.

legislation) made by the Scottish Parliament, National Assembly of Wales and the Northern Ireland Assembly. Devolution issues may also relate to the exercise of functions by the Scottish Executive, the Welsh Assembly Government and the Northern Ireland Executive. There are three main ways in which a devolved institution may act outside its powers by legislating or exercising functions, namely (a) beyond the boundaries of the subject-matter competences conferred by the relevant devolution Act; (b) in way which is incompatible with Convention rights (which has the same meaning as under the Human Rights Act 1998); and (c) contrary to European Community law.[335] The definitions of "devolution issues" exclude some challenges to the lawfulness of decisions by or relating to the devolved institutions; these are dealt with as ordinary proceedings in the legal system in which they arise.[336]

1–114 To date, no "devolution issue" judicial review claims have arisen in the legal system of England and Wales; they have been confined to litigation in Scotland and in Northern Ireland. If and when a devolution issue arises in England and Wales, special procedures apply, including a requirement that a devolution issue notice be given to the Attorney General (the UK Government's Law Officer) and the relevant devolved institution, unless they are already a party to the proceedings. There is a provision for the court in which proceedings were initiated to make a reference of a devolution issue the Judicial Committee of the Privy Council; Law Officers may also directly refer to the Judicial Committee of the Privy Council/ Supreme Court of the United Kingdom questions relating to the legislative competence of a devolved legislature.[337]

1–115 In many legal systems, special techniques have been adopted in interpreting legislation that allocates powers to different levels of government. It remains to be seen to what extent a distinctive approach emerges in

---

[335] "Community law" is defined in Northern Ireland Act 1998 s.98 as "(a) all rights, powers, liabilities, obligations and restrictions created or arising by or under the Community Treaties; and (b) all remedies and procedures provided for by or under those Treaties".

[336] See, e.g. *Re Robinson's Application for Judicial Review* [2002] UKHL 32; [2002] N.I. 390 (time limits for election of First Minister and Deputy First Minister by the Northern Ireland Assembly); *Whalley v Lord Watson of Invergowrie* 2000 S.C. 340 (challenge to lawfulness of a member of the Scottish Parliament promoting, and introducing a bill to outlaw fox hunting on the grounds that the MSP had received legal, administrative and other assistance from a pressure group contrary to the Scotland Act 1998 (Members' Interests) Order 1999); *In the Matter of an application by Bairbre de Brun and Martin McGuinness for Judicial Review High Court of Northern Ireland*, January 30, 2001 (unrep.). (Two Sinn Fein Ministers of the Executive Committee of the Northern Ireland Assembly successfully challenged the legality of a decision by First Minister David Trimble not to nominate them for meetings of the North-South Ministerial Council; the case turned mainly on the proper interpretation of the Northern Ireland Act 1998 s.52(1)) under which the First Minister and Deputy First Minister are required to make nominations).

[337] e.g. Government of Wales Act 2006 s.96. Until such time as the United Kingdom Supreme Court, established under the Constitutional Reform Act 2005, begins operating, the final court of appeal for devolution issue cases is the Judicial Committee of the Privy Council (not the Appellate Committee of the House of Lords, which is the final court of appeal for all other judicial review proceedings). In this context, the Judicial Committee of the Privy Council sits as a court of the whole of the United Kingdom and its judgments are binding on all other courts (including the Appellate Committee of the House of Lords): Scotland Act 1998 s.103(1).

relation to the devolution Acts. There is much to commend in the approach of Lord Bingham of Cornhill, who held that the Northern Ireland Act 1998:

"does not set out all the constitutional provisions applicable to Northern Ireland, but it is in effect a constitution. So to categorise the Act is not to relieve the courts of their duty to interpret the constitutional provisions in issue. But the provisions should, consistently with the language used, be interpreted generously and purposively, bearing in mind the values which the constitutional provisions are intended to embody".[338]

He concluded that "Where constitutional arrangements retain scope for the exercise of political judgment they permit a flexible response to differing and unpredictable events in a way which the application of strict rules would preclude".[339]

Overlapping categories

A claimant's challenge to the lawfulness of a public authority's decision **1–116** may be based on more than one of the categories set out above: a Convention right, a European Community law right and a right under ordinary domestic law may all form grounds within a single claim for judicial review. A court may therefore have to adapt its approach during the course of its consideration of a claim. The English courts have often emphasised that application of ordinary domestic law may produce the same result as the application of Convention rights. In most cases, the categorisation of a ground of challenge will be relatively straightforward. Difficulties, however, occasionally arise.[340]

---

[338] *Re Robinson's Application for Judicial Review* [2002] UKHL 32; [2002] N.I. 390 [at 11]. See also Lord Hoffmann at [25]: "In choosing between these two approaches to construction, it is necessary to have regard to the background to the 1998 Act. . . . The 1998 Act is a constitution for Northern Ireland, framed to create a continuing form of government against the background of the history of the territory and the principles agreed in Belfast"; [at 33]: "According to established principles of interpretation, the Act must be construed against the background of the political situation in Northern Ireland and the principles laid down by the Belfast Agreement for a new start. These facts and documents form part of the admissible background for the construction of the Act just as much as the Revolution, the Convention and the Federalist Papers are the background to construing the Constitution of the United States". Lord Hutton and Lord Hobhouse dissented, stressing the need for an "ordinary construction of such a statutory provision".
[339] See n.338, [at 12].
[340] For example, it may not be clear whether a claimant is entitled to rely upon a Community law right if a measure is wholly internal to the United Kingdom (*R. v Secretary of State for the Home Department Ex p. Phull* [1996] Imm. A.R. 72); and Convention rights may overlap with fundamental rights recognised by English common law (*R. v Secretary of State for the Home Department Ex p. Daly* [2001] UKHL 26; [2001] 2 A.C. 532).

CHAPTER 2

CLAIMANTS, INTERESTED PARTIES AND INTERVENERS

SCOPE

This Chapter deals with the following issues.   2–001

- The requirement for a claimant to have standing in order to bring a claim for judicial review. Under CPR Pt 54, this is expressed as the need for the claimant to have "sufficient interest".[1] In relation to the ground of review that there is a breach of a Convention right, a further requirement that the claimant be a "victim" is imposed.[2] In some other forms of public law proceedings, the term "person aggrieved" is used.[3]

- The extent to which others, in addition to the claimant and defendant, may be involved in a claim for judicial review. They include "interested parties" who are directly affected by the claim and must be served with the claim form and may, as of right, participate in the proceedings.[4] Others (typically pressure groups and public authorities) may apply to the court for permission to intervene in proceedings to make written or oral submissions.[5] As with the requirement of standing, the approach adopted towards these interventions has an important impact on the constitutional purpose served by judicial review.

- Questions relating to the legal capacity of some claimants (for example, unincorporated associations) to institute proceedings.[6]

- Techniques used in some other jurisdictions to define standing.[7]

CONSTITUTIONAL SIGNIFICANCE OF STANDING RULES

All developed legal systems have had to face the problem of resolving the 2–002
conflict between two aspects of the public interest—the desirability of
encouraging people to participate actively in the enforcement of the law,

[1] See 2–006.
[2] See 2–042; and Ch.13 on Convention rights generally.
[3] See 2–055.
[4] See 2–063.
[5] See 2–064.
[6] See 2–012.
[7] See 2–067.

and the undesirability of encouraging meddlesome interlopers invoking the jurisdiction of the courts in matters in which they are not concerned.[8] The conflict may be resolved by developing principles which determine who is entitled to bring proceedings; that is who has *locus standi* or standing to make a claim. If those principles are satisfactory they should only prevent a would-be litigant who has no legitimate reason for bringing proceedings from doing so.

2–003   To deprive a person of access to the courts because of lack of standing can raise issues of constitutional significance. At its heart is the question whether it can ever be right, as a matter of principle, for a person with an otherwise meritorious challenge to the validity of a public authority's action to be turned away by the court on the ground that his rights or interests are not sufficiently affected by the impugned decision. To put this another way, if a decision which is otherwise justiciable is legally flawed, should the court prevent its jurisdiction being invoked because the litigant is not qualified to raise the issue? To answer "yes" to these questions presupposes that the primary function of the court's supervisory jurisdiction is to redress individual grievances, rather than that judicial review is concerned, more broadly, with the maintenance of the rule of law.[9] In recent years the courts have approached standing issues in a more flexible and liberal way than once was the case.

In favour of restricted access

2–004   A number of arguments are traditionally advanced for restricting access to the court by any member of the public for the purpose of challenging executive action of which he does not approve. First, it would be unwise to assume that the other safeguards that exist, the effect of the doctrine of precedent, the limited availability of public funding to assist would-be litigants,[10] and the power of the courts to award costs,[11] are sufficient to deter unmeritorious challenges. Secondly, the courts' resources should not be dissipated by the need to provide a forum for frivolous or academic proceedings. Thirdly, central and local government and other public authorities should not be disrupted unnecessarily, to the disadvantage of other members of the public, by having to contest unmeritorious proceedings. Fourthly, as a matter of prudence, the courts should reserve their

---

[8] How serious this conflict actually is, is open to question. As K. Scott has written, "The idle and whimsical plaintiff, a litigant who litigates for a lark, is a spectre which haunts the legal literature, not the courtroom": "Standing in the Supreme Court—A Functional Analysis" (1973) 86 Harv.L.R. 645.

[9] J. Miles, "Standing under the Human Rights Act 1998: Theories of Rights Enforcement and the Nature of Public Law Adjudication" (2000) 59 C.L.J. 133, 148–155 on underlying theoretical models; I. Hare, "The Law of Standing in Public Interest Adjudication", Ch.22 in M. Andenas (ed.), *Liber Amicorum in Honour of Lord Slynn of Hadley: Vol.II Judicial Review in International Perspective* (2000).

[10] On funding, see 16–080.

[11] On costs, see 16–087.

power to interfere with the workings of public authorities to those occasions when there is a claim before them by someone who has been adversely affected by the unlawful conduct of which complaint is made. Fifthly, particularly in relation to administrative action which can affect sections of the public, it is important that the claim should be brought by a person who, because he is sufficiently interested in the outcome of the proceedings or otherwise, is in a position to ensure that full argument in favour of the remedy which is sought is deployed before the court. Sixthly, it is important that the courts confine themselves to their correct constitutional role, and do not become involved in determining issues which are not justiciable by giving unlimited access to the courts.[12] Campaign groups will not necessarily properly reflect the interests or wishes of their members, or those they purport to protect, by undertaking legal action.[13]

In favour of a more open approach

On the other side of the argument there are substantial reasons for adopting a generous approach to standing in judicial review proceedings. It is usually important, in the interests of the public generally, that the law should be enforced. The policy should therefore be to encourage and not discourage public-spirited individuals and groups, even though they are not directly affected by the action which is being taken, to challenge unlawful administrative action. Other safeguards, besides restrictive rules as to standing, exist to protect the courts and administrators from unmeritorious challenges (including the requirement that claimants obtain permission from the court,[14] the relatively short time limits for commencing claims,[15] and in extreme circumstances provisions to bar vexatious litigants[16]). Where there are strict rules as to standing there is always the risk that no one will be in a position to bring proceedings to test the lawfulness of administrative action. It is hardly desirable that a situation should exist where because all members of the public are equally affected no one is in a position to bring proceedings. The fears that are sometimes voiced of the courts being overwhelmed by a flood of frivolous claims are unsupported by any evidence of this happening in practice. The costs of litigation are now so heavy that it is only the most determined litigant who will indulge

2–005

[12] See further K. Schiemann, "Locus Standi" [1990] P.L. 342 and his judgment in *R. v Secretary of State for the Environment Ex p. Rose Theatre Trust Ltd* [1990] 1 Q.B. 504; L. Bridges, M. Sunkin and G. Meszaros, *Judicial Review in Perspective* (1995), contains an analysis of claimants for judicial review. Applications were made in 84–88% of cases by individuals; of the remainder 50–60% are by companies, 6% by central government, 14–35% by local authorities and only 1–2% by non-governmental organisations (pp.34–5).
[13] C. Harlow, "Public Law and Popular Justice" (2002) 65 M.L.R. 1; P. Cane, "Standing, Representation and the Environment" in I. Loveland (ed.), *A Special Relationship? American Influences on Public Law in the UK* (1995).
[14] See 16–041.
[15] See 16–050.
[16] Supreme Court Act (Senior Court Act) 1981 s.42.

in legal proceedings which are without merit. The arguments in favour of a restrictive approach to standing nearly always confuse the question of the merits of the litigation with the question of who should be entitled to bring the proceedings. If there is a satisfactory mechanism for dealing with unmeritorious or frivolous claims most of the arguments for a restrictive approach to standing fall away.

THE "SUFFICIENT INTEREST" REQUIREMENT

2–006   Prior to the judicial review reforms of 1978, the standing rules (along with other matters such as time limits and procedural requirements) varied according to the particular remedy sought.[17] One of the objects of the new test was to save the courts from having to try to reconcile the multiplicity of conflicting authorities which governed the principles of *locus standi* under the previous procedure for obtaining the prerogative orders. For example, the old authorities indicate that the test varied depending on which prerogative order or area of the law was involved (the standard appeared to be higher if the application for the prerogative order related to a criminal cause or matter than if the application related to a planning matter).[18] In contrast, other old cases are of interest insofar as they indicate that prior to 1978 a very generous approach to standing was already being adopted in some contexts. Thus proceedings could be brought even by "strangers" for an order of prohibition.[19] In general on a modern day claim for judicial review, the old authorities provide only limited assistance and can be misleading. This said, the pre-1978 authorities should not always be ignored as being merely of historic interest. It can be stated with confidence that as the reforms introduced in 1978 were intended to liberalise the procedure for obtaining the prerogative orders, the approach to standing on a claim for judicial review is now at least as generous to the claimant as that which previously existed. So, if the pre-1978 authorities indicate that a claimant would have standing, this is almost certainly still the position.

2–007   The standing requirement for claims for judicial review made under CPR Pt 54 is now set out in s.31 of the Supreme Court Act (Senior Courts Act) 1981:[20]

"No application for judicial review shall be made unless the leave of the court has been obtained in accordance with the Rules of Court; and the

---

[17] See Ch.15.
[18] Such a distinction could be justified perfectly logically because in criminal proceedings there are normally only two parties, the prosecutor and the defendant, whereas planning procedures under the planning legislation allow for generous representation before the inquiry which the legislation normally contemplated would precede a decision on an appeal. For a modern application of a restricted approach to standing in criminal matters, see *R. (on the application of Bulger) v Lord Chief Justice* [2001] EWHC Admin 119; [2001] 3 All E.R. 449 at [18]–[24].
[19] See 15–029.
[20] See 16–002.

court shall not grant leave to make such an application unless it considers that the applicant has a sufficient interest in the matter to which the application relates."

The requirement is repeated by CPR r.54.4. The test is expressed in terms 2–008 of interests rather than rights because "What modern public law focuses upon are wrongs—that is to say, unlawful acts of public administration. These often, of course, infringe correlative rights, but they do not necessarily do so: hence the test of standing for public law claimants, which is interest-based rather than rights-based".[21] In Northern Ireland, a similar test based on sufficient interest applies under s.18(4) of the Judicature (Northern Ireland) Act 1978.[22]

The issue of whether a claimant has sufficient interest in the matter to 2–009 which the claim relates goes to the court's jurisdiction to entertain the application for judicial review, and is not merely a matter of discretion.[23] It follows that the defendant may not merely agree to the claimant having standing, as the parties are not entitled to confer jurisdiction, which the court may not have, by consent.[24] The court may also take the standing point of its own motion, even if not raised by the parties.[25] The interest must be "in relation to the matter to which the application relates". Assessment of the claimant's standing must therefore relate to the circumstances as they exist at the time at which permission is sought. A would-be claimant may have standing at an earlier point but have lost it by the time proceedings begin.[26] It has sometimes been suggested that a claimant may have standing to argue some grounds of review but be debarred by insufficient interest from advancing other related grounds. The better view is that a claimant who has standing for some grounds has it for all.[27]

---

[21] R. (on the application of Bancoult) v Secretary of State for Foreign and Commonwealth Affairs [2007] EWCA Civ 498 at [61] (Sedley L.J.).

[22] On the different approach in Scotland, see 2–068.

[23] R. v Secretary of State for Social Services Ex p. Child Poverty Action Group [1990] 2 Q.B. 540 at 556; R. v Secretary of State for Foreign and Commonwealth Affairs Ex p. World Development Movement Ltd [1995] 1 W.L.R. 386 at 395; R. v Secretary of State for the Environment Ex p. Rose Theatre Trust Co. Ltd [1990] 1 Q.B. 504 at 520.

[24] R. v Secretary of State for Social Services Ex p. Child Poverty Action Group [1990] 2 Q.B. 540 at 556E.

[25] See, e.g. R. (on the application of Bulger) v Lord Chief Justice [2001] EWHC Admin 119; [2001] 3 All E.R. 449 at [18].

[26] R. v North West Leicestershire DC Ex p. Moses (No.1) [2000] J.P.L. 733 (claimant objecting to extension of airport runway had moved six miles away); on appeal, permission was refused on grounds of delay rather than standing: [2000] EWCA Civ 125. cf. R. v Secretary of State for the Home Department Ex p. Salem [1999] 1 A.C. 450, where the HL held that it had a discretion to hear an appeal which concerned an issue involving a public authority as to a question of public law, even where there was no longer any live issue which would affect the rights and duties of the parties as between themselves. Note also provisions in Pt 19 of the CPR on the addition and substitution of parties.

[27] R. (on the application of Kides) v South Cambridgeshire DC [2002] EWCA Civ 1370, [2003] 1 P. & C.R. 19 at [132]–[136]. The court may, however, grant permission on certain grounds only but this is on the basis that the others lack merit: CPR r.54.12(1)(b)(ii).

Charity proceedings

2–010 Charities may perform public functions which are amenable to judicial review.[28] Where the would-be defendant is a charity, claimants in this context face a double hurdle. First, the claimant must obtain permission from the Charity Commissioners or a judge of the Chancery Division of the High Court before commencing legal action ("charity proceedings") against a charitable organisation. The purpose of this "protective filter" is to prevent charitable organisations from being "harassed and put to expense by a multiplicity of claims, which may or may not be well-founded".[29] A claim for judicial review may constitute "charity proceedings".[30] Standing rules are imposed by the Charities Act 1993 s.31(1) which regulates who may commence charity proceedings.[31] This general requirement has been interpreted more narrowly than the sufficient interest requirement of s.31(3) of the Supreme Court Act (Senior Courts Act) 1981[32] though in the particular context of an anticipated judicial review claim it is difficult to see why the test should be different from that applied in judicial review given that the overall purpose of the permission requirement is similar. Secondly, the claimant must obtain the permission of the Administrative Court to commence a judicial review claim.[33]

2–011 Bearing in mind the overriding aim of the CPR, there are clear advantages in combining both requirements into a single application dealt by a judge of the Chancery Division who is a nominated judge of the Administrative Court. If the permissions to proceed are granted, that judge can then decide whether the claim is most appropriately continued in the Chancery Division under CPR Pt 7 or Pt 8 or in the Administrative Court under CPR Pt 54.[34] Because of the availability of a procedure in the Chancery Division, and the greater experience of charity law in that part of the High Court, there is likely be a preference against proceeding by way

---

[28] See 3–042. Charities may also perform "functions of a public nature" under s.6(3)(b) HRA, on which see, e.g. *R. (on the application of Heather) v Leonard Cheshire Foundation* [2001] EWHC Admin 429; (2001) 4 C.C.L. Rep. 211 (Stanley Burnton J.); on appeal the CA heard no argument and expressed no view on the charity proceedings point: [2002] EWCA Civ 366; [2002] 2 All E.R. 936 at [38].

[29] *Scott v National Trust for Places of Historic Interest or Natural Beauty* [1998] 2 All ER 705, 714J (Robert Walker J.).

[30] *R. (on the application of Heather) v Leonard Cheshire Foundation* [2001] EWHC Admin 429; (2001) 4 C.C.L. Rep. 211 at [100].

[31] "Charity proceedings may be taken with reference to a charity either by the charity, or by any of the charity trustees, or by any person interested in the charity, or by any two or more inhabitants of the area if it is a local charity, but not by any other person".

[32] *Scott v National Trust for Places of Historic Interest or Natural Beauty* [1998] 2 All ER 705 at 714 (a person was "interested" in a charity within the meaning of s.33(1) of the 1993 Act if he had a materially greater interest in ensuring the due administration of the charity than that possessed by ordinary members of the public).

[33] *R. (on the application of Heather) v Leonard Cheshire Foundation* [2001] EWHC Admin 429; (2001) 4 C.C.L. Rep. 211 at [102]; *Scott* [1998] 1 W.L.R. 226 at 229. On the permission stage, see 16–041.

[34] *R. (on the application of Heather) v Leonard Cheshire Foundation* [2001] EWHC Admin 429; (2001) 4 C.C.L. Rep. 211 at [103].

of judicial review,[35] unless on the particular facts CPR Pt 54 provides a particularly suitable process for addressing the factual and legal issues in question.

CAPACITY AND STANDING

Unincorporated associations and companies

In English law, unincorporated associations generally lack legal capacity to **2–012** sue or be sued in their own name.[36] In some claims for judicial review brought by unincorporated associations it has been held that this is a bar to permission being granted.[37] A different approach has been adopted in other cases, where either no issue as to the legal capacity of the claimant has been being taken,[38] or the chairman, secretary or other member of the association was recognised as representing the association.[39] Indeed, it is possible formally to seek an order under CPR Pt 19.6 that a claim be begun or continued with one party representing the interests of others who have the same interest in the claim.[40] Given that the unincorporated status of a defendant has not been regarded as a bar to being subject to and defending judicial review proceedings,[41] a flexible approach is appropriate.[42]

---

[35] *Royal Society for the Prevention of Cruelty to Animals v Attorney General* [2002] 1 W.L.R. 448 at [22].
[36] *Halsbury's Laws*, 4th edn , Vol.9(2), para.1001.
[37] *R. v Darlington BC Ex p. Association of Darlington Taxi Owners* [1994] C.O.D. 424; *Alwoodly Golf Club v Leeds CC* [1995] N.P.C. 149.
[38] See, e.g. *R. v Director of Rail Franchising Ex p. Save Our Railways* [1996] C.L.C. 589 (strictly speaking the unincorporated association lacked capacity to sue but "no time should be taken up in this case resolving this somewhat arid issue"); *R. (on the application of Association of British Civilian Internees (Far East Region)) v Secretary of State for Defence* [2003] EWCA Civ 473; [2003] Q.B. 1397.
[39] See, e.g. *R. v Tower Hamlets LBC Ex p. Tower Hamlets Combined Traders Association* [1994] C.O.D. 325; *R. v Traffic Commissioner for the North Western Traffic Area Ex p. BRAKE* [1996] C.O.D. 248.
[40] In its 1994 report, *Administrative Law: Judicial Review and Statutory Appeals*, the Law Commission described recommended that unincorporated associations should be permitted to make claims for judicial review in their own name through one or more of their members applying in a representative capacity where the court is satisfied that members of the claimant association have been, or would be, adversely affected or are raising an issue of public interest warranting judicial review, and that the members of the association are appropriate persons to bring that challenge: Law Com. No.226, para.5.41.
[41] See, e.g. *R. v Panel on Takeovers and Mergers Ex p. Datafin Plc* [1987] Q.B. 815.
[42] Unincorporated associations have been allowed to be claimants in many cases, see e.g. *R. v Ministry of Agriculture, Fisheries and Food Ex p. British Pig Industry Support Group* [2000] Eu. L.R. 724; *R. (on the application of West End Street Traders Association) v Westminster City Council* [2004] EWHC 1167; [2005] B.L.G.R. 143; *R. (on the application of Western International Campaign Group) v Hounslow LBC* [2003] EWHC 3112; [2004] B.L.G.R. 536; *R. (on the application of Association of British Civilian Internees (Far East Region)) v Secretary of State for Defence* [2003] EWCA Civ 473; [2003] Q.B. 1397; *R. (on the application of British Aggregates Associates) v Customs and Excise Commissioners* [2002] EWHC 926; [2002] 2 C.M.L.R. 51; *R. v Coventry City Council Ex p. Coventry Heads of Independent Care Establishments (CHOICE)* (1997–98) 1 C.C.L. Rep. 379.

2–013   Pitfalls may also lie ahead for an unincorporated association that rushes to form itself into a company for the purpose of commencing a claim for judicial review.[43] First, it needs to be understood that incorporation will not of itself create a sufficient interest. One of the reasons why the Rose Theatre Trust Company Ltd was held to lack sufficient interest, in a challenge to a minister's refusal to designate a site as a protected ancient monument, was that it "would be absurd if two people, neither of whom had standing could, by an appropriately worded memorandum, incorporate themselves into a company which thereby obtained standing".[44] The judgment in *Rose Theatre* has been doubted, distinguished and not followed,[45] but on this point the case affirms the approach adopted by the majority of the House of Lords in *National*.[46] Secondly, the courts have in some cases been wary of unincorporated associations giving themselves limited liability specifically for the purpose of conducting litigation with the intention of avoiding the full force of any adverse costs order that might be made.[47]

Capacity and standing of public authorities

2–014   Many public authorities have capacity to institute legal proceedings. The Attorney General has an ancient power to make legal claims in the name of the Crown as an aspect of his role as guardian of the public interest. Proceedings may be commenced by the Attorney General in the name of the Attorney General; alternatively, the Attorney General may "consent to the use of his name, so as to enable proceedings to be brought by another party clothed with his authority in what are known as relator proceedings for the protection of the public interest in the civil courts".[48] A refusal by the Attorney General to "lend his *fiat*" to consent to a relator action has been thought to be not amenable to judicial review.[49] The liberalisation of

[43] See also 2–037.
[44] *R. v Secretary of State for the Environment Ex p. Rose Theatre Trust Co Ltd* [1990] 1 Q.B. 504 at 521D.
[45] *Rose Theatre* has been "not followed" in *R. v HM Inspectorate of Pollution Ex p. Greenpeace (No.2)* [1994] 4 All E.R. 329 and "distinguished" in *R. v Poole BC Ex p. Beebee* [1991] J.P.L. 643 and *R. v Somerset CC Ex p. Dixon* [1998] Env.L.R. 111. Although not overruled by the CA, there can be little doubt that a court faced with similar facts today would adopt a different approach. There were individuals who were involved in the Rose Theatre Co Ltd of acknowledged distinction in the field of archaeology who should, because of the nature of the issue before the court, have been regarded as being a significant factor in favour of there being standing.
[46] *Inland Revenue Commissioners v National Federation of Self-Employed and Small Businesses* [1982] A.C. 617 at 633D (Lord Wilberforce).
[47] *R. v Leicestershire CC Ex p. Blackfordby and Boothorpe Action Group Ltd* [2001] Env.L.R. 2 at [34]–[38] ("The costs position can be dealt with adequately by requiring the provision of security for costs in a realistically large sum"). In *R. (on the application of Legal Remedy UK Ltd) v Secretary of State for Health* [2007] EWHC Admin 1252 a pressure group of junior doctors was incorporated as a company limited by guarantee for the specific purpose of making a claim for judicial review and no point was taken on this).
[48] *Attorney General v Blake* [1998] Ch. 439 (Lord Woolf M.R.).
[49] *Attorney General v Gouriet* [1978] A.C. 435; *cf.* B. Hough, "Judicial review where the Attorney General refuses to act: time for a change" (1988) 8 L.S. 190.

the court's approach to the sufficient interest test has more or less brought an end to the use of relator actions in the public law context as there is now no impediment on a citizen commencing a claim in his own name to enforce a public duty. For local authorities, the statutory authorisation to institute legal proceedings rests on s.222 of the Local Government Act 1972 which authorises councils to initiate and defend civil proceedings where it is "expedient for the promotion or protection of the interests of the inhabitants of their area". The Commission for Equality and Human Rights is expressly stated to have capacity to institute and intervene in legal proceedings, whether for judicial review or otherwise.[50]

Child claimants and abuse of process

Where a decision affects a child (for example, in relation to schooling 2–015 arrangements) questions have arisen as to whether the child (acting through his "litigation friend")[51] should be the claimant, or the parents of the child. Where the child is the claimant, legal aid may be available in circumstances in which the parent would not be eligible for public funding and, if a claim is lost, an adverse costs order against a child claimant will have no practical affect. The Court of Appeal held, *obiter*, that in disputes about parental preference on school admissions the relevant claimant is the parent rather than the child; and any claims made in the name of the child in order to avoid potential adverse costs orders would be viewed as an abuse of process in the absence of special circumstances.[52] This approach has been doubted in subsequent cases in which the courts have taken the view that issues as to entitlement to legal aid are for the legal aid authorities, not the courts.[53] Even if it has some continuing relevance in the education field, a distinction ought to be drawn between situations where (a) rights of a parent are in issue (for example, the statutory right to express a preference about which school a child will attend) and (b) rights of a child.[54] Clear evidence would also be needed to demonstrate that a parent's claim is an abuse of process.[55]

---

[50] Equality Act 2006 s.30(1). *cf. Re Northern Ireland Human Rights Commission's Application for Judicial Review* [2002] UKHL 25; [2002] N.I. 236 (the NIHRC had been granted general powers to promote an understanding of human rights law and practice and to review its adequacy and effectiveness together with an incidental power to make, but not insist on making, submissions to courts and tribunals).

[51] CPR Pt 21.

[52] *R. v Richmond LBC Ex p. C (A Child)* [2001] B.L.G.R. 146.

[53] *R. (on the application of Edwards) v The Environment Agency* [2004] EWHC 736, discussed at 3–032.

[54] *In the matter of an application by JS for judicial review* [2006] NIQB 40 at [14].

[55] *R. (on the application of WB) v Leeds School Organisation Committee* [2002] EWHC 1927; [2003] E.L.R. 67 at [37].

HOW AND WHEN IS STANDING RELEVANT?

2–016 Questions relating to standing may be relevant (a) at the permission stage of the claim for judicial review;[56] (b) at the full hearing of the claim; and (c) in relation to the nature of the remedial orders that should be granted to the claimant.[57]

Standing at the permission stage

2–017 The language of s.31(3) SCA 1981 makes it clear that the statutory requirement for a claimant to have a sufficient interest is a threshold test of standing which applies when the claimant is seeking permission to apply.[58] If the claimant has an insufficient interest at that stage, the court is prohibited from granting permission. In the *National Federation* case, however, the House of Lords held that except in an obvious case, questions as to sufficient interest ought not to be dealt with as a preliminary issue at the permission stage but should be postponed until the full hearing of the claim. This is because except in the "simple" case "the question of sufficient interest cannot . . . be considered in the abstract, or as an isolated point: it must be taken together with legal and factual context".[59] The threshold for standing at the permission stage should be "set only at the height necessary to prevent abuse"—in other words, to exclude "cranks", "meddlesome busybodies" and "troublemakers".[60] Generally speaking, a person or body with a bona fide concern about the subject matter of the proceedings will not be regarded as a mere busybody.[61]

2–018 When assessing whether there is abuse, the claimant's motives for making the claim may be relevant.[62] Regard may also be had to obvious weaknesses in the grounds of challenge: if they are totally without

---

[56] See 16–041.

[57] See 17–054.

[58] An empirical study of the permission stage has shown that it is extremely rare for permission to be refused on the sole ground that a claimant lacks standing: see A. Le Sueur and M. Sunkin, "Applications for Judicial Review: The Requirement of Leave" [1992] P.L. 102.

[59] *Inland Revenue Commissioners v National Federation of Self-Employed and Small Businesses* [1982] A.C. 617 at 630 (Lord Wilberforce). The majority (Lord Diplock dissenting on this point) held that one taxpayer does not have standing to challenge the lawfulness of the Inland Revenue's treatment of another taxpayer. Exceptions to this proposition have been recognised in later cases: *R. v HM Treasury Ex p. Smedley* [1985] Q.B. 657 at 670, 667 and *R. v Attorney General Ex p. ICI Plc* [1985] 1 C.M.L.R. 588. More broadly, it may be said that Lord Diplock's general approach to standing now better represents the law and practice today.

[60] *R. v Monopolies and Mergers Commission Ex p Argyll Group plc* [1986] 1 W.L.R. 763 at 773; *R. (on the application of Dixon) v Somerset CC* [1997] EWHC Admin 393, [1998] Env. L.R. 111, [12].

[61] *Ex p. Argyll Group plc* [1986] 1 W.L.R. 763 at 773.

[62] *R. (on the application of Feakins) v Secretary of State for Environment, Food and Rural Affairs* [2003] EWCA Civ 1546 at [23]: "If the real reason why a claimant wishes to challenge a decision in which , objectively, there is a public interest is not that he has a genuine concern about the decision, but some other reason, then that is material to the question whether he should be accorded standing" (Dyson L.J.).

foundation or unarguable, any standing that a claimant might hypothetically have disappears.[63] Where the grounds of challenge are hopeless it is preferable for the court to refuse permission on that basis alone without making any ruling on standing.

A state not recognised by the United Kingdom government has no standing in the English courts.[64] 2–019

Standing at the full hearing

If a claimant has been granted permission, of what relevance is standing at the subsequent full hearing of the claim? One answer is that examination of the standing issue may be necessary to ensure that the Administrative Court has jurisdiction: as noted above, s.31 of the Supreme Court Act (Senior Courts Act) 1981 is regarded as making the claimant's "sufficient interest" a condition precedent to court having jurisdiction.[65] In practice, however, the courts rarely deal with the question of standing as a preliminary issue at hearings and many of the leading cases typically deal with the grounds of review first and relegate discussion of standing to the end of the judgment. Moreover, there are few if any reported cases in which the court has found for the claimant on the grounds of review while also holding that the claimant lacks sufficient interest. It is therefore perhaps open to question whether any practical purpose is served by discussion of standing at a full hearing, other than to prolong submissions and extend judgments. 2–020

The task of the court in assessing whether a particular claimant has standing has been described as "a balancing act between the various factors",[66] and these are discussed below. 2–021

Standing in relation to the grant of remedial orders

Suggestions have also been made in the past that the degree of interest required by a claimant will depend on the remedy which is claimed, for example a greater degree of interest is needed for a mandatory order than for a declaration. It is contended that this approach is misconceived and the test of standing is the same irrespective of the remedy which is claimed. This is, however, contrary to the views expressed by Lord Wilberforce and possibly Lord Scarman in *National Federation*.[67] It would be difficult in 2–022

---

[63] *R. v Secretary of State for the Home Department Ex p. Amnesty International (No.2)* 2000 W.L. 461 (challenge by human rights groups to gain access to Senator Pinochet's medical records was without foundation: "In legal, if somewhat peremptory terms, it is none of their business", Maurice Kay J.).

[64] *City of Berne v Bank of England* (1804) 9 Ves. 347; *cf. Gur Corporation v Trust Bank of Africa* [1987] 1 Q.B. 599 at 605; *R. (on the application of North Cyprus Tourism Centre Ltd) v Transport for London* [2005] EWHC 1698; [2005] U.K.H.R.R. 1231.

[65] See 3–016.

[66] *R. v North Somerset DC Ex p. Garnett* [1998] Env. L.R. 91 (Popplewell J.).

[67] *National Federation* [1982] A.C. 617 at 648E (Lord Scarman). It is not clear to what stage of the proceedings these statements referred.

practice to apply different principles of standing to different remedies at the permission stage. This is because claimants tend to include all relevant remedies in an application for permission and it is often only after the full hearing, often after judgment, that a claimant decides which remedial order to request. It would also be inconsistent with the intended comprehensive nature of the procedure of judicial review to have to apply different tests of standing for the different remedies. If Lords Wilberforce and Scarman were referring to the end of the hearing, then their views are perfectly acceptable since—when it comes to deciding in its discretion whether to grant relief—a court is going to be more hesitant in some situations in granting, for example, a mandatory order or an injunction (the disobedience of which can amount to contempt) than a declaration.[68] At this stage of the hearing the extent of the interest of the claimant is a factor to be considered when deciding what, if any, relief to grant.[69]

2–023   The court always has discretion to refuse a particular form of relief, or any relief, on a claim for judicial review. In deciding whether or not to grant relief, the court is required to have regard to all the circumstances. It is therefore sensible for the court not to isolate the question of the claimant's interest for separate treatment, but to take it into account when it comes to decide what, if any, relief it should grant, as a matter of discretion. The weight or importance which will be attached to the claimant's interest will differ depending on the circumstances.

Assessing the Claimant's Interest

2–024 As Lord Roskill pointed out in *National Federation*, the phrase "sufficient interest" was selected by the Rules Committee of the Supreme Court in 1977 "as one which could sufficiently embrace all classes of those who might apply and yet permit sufficient flexibility in any particular case to determine whether or not 'sufficient interest' was in fact shown".[70] This is precisely the approach which has been adopted in the vast majority of the cases which have come before the courts since that time, even if it creates considerable scope for differing judgments on the same facts as to whether a claimant has standing.[71]

---

[68] See Ch.18.
[69] See, e.g. *R. v Felixstowe Justices Ex p. Leigh* [1987] Q.B. 582 (after the full hearing, a journalist, who had not been present at the hearing, had sufficient standing to claim a declaration that a policy of not disclosing names of justices who had heard certain types of case was contrary to public interest and unlawful. On the other hand he was refused a mandatory order, ordering the court to reveal the names of the justices who had heard a particular case: the claimant was sufficiently interested in the point of principle but not in what had happened in the particular case which had given rise to the application).
[70] [1982] A.C. 617 at 658.
[71] For example in *National Federation* [1982] A.C. 617 Lord Diplock dissented on the issue of standing and held that the pressure group had standing; and in *Equal Opportunities Commission v Secretary of State for Employment* [1995] 1 A.C. 1 Lord Jauncey dissented on the issue whether the EOC had standing.

Section 31(3) SCA 1981 does not contain any express guidance as to the 2–025
factors to be taken into account in determining whether a claimant has
sufficient interest. The court will assess the claimant's interest against all
the factual and legal circumstances of the case. It is a "mixed question of
fact and degree".[72]

The legislative framework

The starting point for analysis of whether a claimant has sufficient interest 2–026
will normally be the legislative framework within which the public
authority's decision was taken. This may expressly or impliedly indicate
that the claimant has an interest in the subject matter of the claim. Thus, if
the statute gives the claimant the right to make representations before the
decision is reached this will be a strong indication that he has standing to
challenge the decision when it is made.[73] In *National Federation*, Lord
Frazer considered that one should look at the statute under which the duty
arises and see whether it gives any express or implied right to persons in
the position of the claimant to complain of the alleged unlawful act or
omission.[74] It is suggested that this is an unhelpful approach except in a
limited class of cases where the claimant's interest would in any event be
obvious. An example of this class of case is where the statute gives the
public authority seeking to make the claim special responsibility in the field
of activity to which the claim relates. Thus in a claim involving alleged sex
discrimination the Equal Opportunities Commission would have standing.[75] However claims for judicial review are usually made in situations
where the statute does not provide a remedy for the unlawful exercise of
the statutory discretion or power which is being challenged. In those
situations it is difficult, if not impossible, to apply satisfactorily the implied
right to complain test which Lord Frazer suggested.

The legislative framework may, however, be relevant in another sense. It 2–027
will sometimes be the case that legislation is intended to protect the section
of the public whose interests the claimant is seeking to defend.

---

[72] *R. v Sheffield City Council Ex p. Power* [1994] E.G.C.S. 101 (Turner J.).
[73] If the language of the statute is being considered in determining standing then again the
approach should not be too restrictive. Thus under the Immigration Act 1971 the Home
Secretary gives directions to the airline in respect of the removal of immigrants who are to be
deported, but the deportee is entitled to challenge the directions since the directions were
clearly of concern to the deportee.
[74] *National Federation* [1982] A.C. 617 at 646B.
[75] In the CA in *R. v Secretary of State for Employment Ex p Equal Opportunities Commission*
[1993] 1 W.L.R. 872, the majority of the Court took a different view from that expressed in
the text, but in the HL [1995] 1 A.C. 1 the judgment of Dillon L.J. was preferred and it was
decided that the EOC had standing in view of its statutory responsibilities.

Strength and importance of the grounds of challenge

2–028   The strength of the grounds of review is likely to be considered by the court in assessing whether or not the claimant has sufficient interest,[76] though this is not the dominant factor.[77] Indeed it is difficult to find any case where a claimant has been refused permission to proceed with a claim solely on the basis that he lacks sufficient interest where strongly arguable grounds of review are advanced. It is similarly hard to find cases where the court has at the full hearing refused to hear the substantive claim, on the grounds that he has no standing where relief would have been granted but for his lack of standing. Weight may also be attached to the importance of the point of law at issue and the public interest in the case.[78]

Impact and proximity interests

2–029   If the decision which the claimant wishes to challenge interferes directly with the claimant's personal or public rights or has adverse financial consequences for him then this will be an obvious case in which he will have standing. A public authority's treatment of a claimant's competitors or business rivals may also provide a sufficient interest.[79] A non-pecuniary concern may provide a claimant with sufficient interest. Thus, a claimant who uses public land in respect of which a challenge is made may have standing.[80] A parish council has standing to challenge planning permission for development three miles outside its area.[81] A claimant affected by the wrong-doing or negligence of a public official may have standing to

[76] *R. v Secretary of State for Foreign and Commonwealth Affairs Ex p. World Development Movement Ltd* [1995] 1 W.L.R. 386 at 395G.
[77] *R. v North Somerset DC Ex p. Garnett* [1998] Env. L.R. 91 at [11].
[78] *World Development Movement Ltd* [1995] 1 W.L.R. 386 at 395F; *R. (on the application of Bulger) v Lord Chief Justice* [2001] EWHC Admin 119; [2001] 3 All E.R. 449 at [24].
[79] See, e.g. *R. v Canterbury City Council Ex p. Springimage Ltd* (1994) 68 P. & C.R. 171 (claimant, who intended to apply for permission to develop its own land, had standing to challenge legality of grant of planning permission to another person in respect of other land); *R. v Attorney General Ex p. ICI Plc* [1985] 1 C.M.L.R. 588 (ICI had standing to seek judicial review of the way the Inland Revenue proposed to value business goods used by Shell, Esso and BP which ICI alleged would have provided its competitors with an artificially favourable fiscal regime); *R. v Department of Transport Ex p. Presvac Engineering Ltd* (1992) 4 Admin. L.R. 121 (a trade competitor would normally have sufficient interest in the subject matter of an order which was intended to benefit a rival). cf. *R. v Hereford Corporation Ex p. Harrower* [1970] 1 W.L.R. 1424 (would-be contractors excluded from tendering process had standing if they were ratepayers, but not if they were mere contractors; this pre-1978 judgment needs to be treated with caution: see 2–006); *R. v Pembrokeshire CC Ex p. Coker* [1999] 4 All E.R. 1007, [15] (potential purchasers of council land had no standing to challenge the council's decision to sell to another party); *R. (on the application of Rockware Glass Ltd) v Chester City Council* [2005] EWHC 2250; [2006] Env. L.R. 30.
[80] *R. v Dyfed CC Ex p. Manson* [1994] C.O.D. 366 (claimant lived in a house which directly adjoined a beach to which the impugned byelaws applied and he used the beach for a number of purposes, some of which he was concerned might be affected by the byelaws). cf. *R. v North Somerset DC Ex p. Garnett* [1998] Env.L.R. 91 (two local residents lacked standing to challenge grant of permission for quarrying in a large public park).
[81] *R. v Cotswold DC Ex p. Barrington Parish Council* (1998) 75 P. & C.R. 515.

challenge the conduct of subsequent disciplinary proceedings.[82] An architect with a rural practice has an interest in the proper administration of planning law and the proper administration of the planning law which directly impacts on his clients and on his business.[83] "Not without hesitation", the Northern Ireland Court of Appeal held that the mother of a youth murdered by members of the British Army had sufficient interest to challenge a decision of the Army Board to retain them after their release from prison.[84]

The following have been held not to have a sufficient interest. An agent   2–030
for six musicians (which sought to hire their services to perform at a concert) who had been refused work permits or entry clearance in circumstances where the musicians had a statutory right of appeal or could themselves make a claim for judicial review.[85] In a challenge to the grant of a licence, a person who was not a contender for the grant of the licence may lack standing.[86]

Public interest

It may not be necessary for the claimant to show any personal proximity to   2–031
the decision or special impact or interest over an above that "shared with the generality of the public".[87] The Court of Appeal has drawn a distinction between "a person who brings proceedings having no real or genuine interest in obtaining the relief sought" (who accordingly will not have sufficient interest) and one "who, whilst legitimately and perhaps passionately interested in obtaining the relief sought, relies as grounds for seeking that relief on matters in which he has no personal interest".[88] Thus, for example, a former editor of The Times was held to have standing to challenge the Foreign Secretary's decision to ratify the Treaty on European Union "because of his sincere concern for constitutional issues".[89] The World Development Movement, none of whose supporters were directly affected by a particular grant of overseas aid to the government of Malaysia, was held to have standing.[90] The Howard League for Penal

---

[82] R. v North Thames RHA Ex p. L (An Infant) [1996] 7 Med. L.R. 385.
[83] Re Ward, Application for Judicial Review [2006] NIQB 67 (application for leave).
[84] In the Matter of an Application for Judicial Review by Jean McBridge (No.2) [2003] NICA 23 at [27].
[85] R. (on the application of R70 World Ltd) v Visa Section, British Deputy High Commission, Lagos [2006] EWHC 330.
[86] R. (on the application of Wildman) v Office of Communications [2005] EWHC 1573; The Times, September 28, 2005.
[87] R. (on the application of Dixon) v Somerset CC [1997] EWHC Admin 393, [1998] Env. L.R. 111 at [13] (Sedley J.).
[88] R. (on the application of Kides) v South Cambridgeshire DC [2002] EWCA Civ 1370, [2003] 1 P. & C.R. 19 at [132].
[89] R. v Secretary of State for Foreign and Commonwealth Affairs Ex p Rees-Mogg [1994] Q.B. 552 at 562.
[90] Ex p. World Development Movement Ltd [1995] 1 W.L.R. 386. On campaign groups see 2–035.

Reform had standing to challenge the Home Secretary's policy guidance on the treatment of children less than 18 years of age held in young offender institutions.[91]

2–032   Importance may be attached to a track record of concern and activity by the claimant in relation to the area of government decision-making under challenge.[92] But in assessing whether a claimant has sufficient interest, a failure to make representations before a decision was made, or be actively involved in a campaign, is unlikely to be fatal.[93] Equally, the fact that a claimant has made representations to the public authority and has received responses may not in and of itself signify that the claimant has standing subsequently to commence a claim for judicial review.[94] The fact that a claimant appears to have been "put up" by others to bring a claim in order to secure public funding from the Legal Services Commission, or to avoid exposure to an adverse order for costs, is not generally relevant to the question of standing.[95]

Presence or absence of other challengers

2–033   The courts have also regarded the presence or absence of challengers— apart from the claimant in question—as relevant. The existence of other potential claimants who have consciously or unwittingly decided not to bring proceedings need not however be a bar to another claimant being recognised as having sufficient interest.[96] The fact that nobody else apart from the claimant is likely to be sufficiently concerned by the impugned decision to bring legal proceedings may weigh in the claimant's favour, the rationale being that otherwise there would be a gap in the vindication of the law.[97]

[91] R. (on the application of on the application of the Howard League for Penal Reform) v Secretary of State for the Home Department (No.2) [2002] EWHC 2497; [2003] 1 F.L.R. 484.
[92] R. v Secretary of State for Social Services Ex p. Child Poverty Action Group [1990] 2 Q.B. 540 at 546; World Development Movement Ltd [1995] 1 W.L.R. 386.
[93] R. (on the application of Edwards) v The Environment Agency [2004] EWHC Admin 736 at [16] (Keith J.: "You do not have to be active in a campaign yourself to have an interest in its outcome. If the consultation exercise ends with a decision which affects your interests, you are no less affected by that decision simply because you took no part in the exercise but left it to others to do so. You should not be debarred from subsequently challenging the decision on the ground of inadequate consultation simply because you chose not to participate in the consultation exercise, provided that you are affected by its outcome").
[94] R. v Secretary of State for the Environment Ex p. Rose Theatre Trust Co Ltd [1990] 1 Q.B. 504 (Schiemann J.: "The very fact that the Secretary of State has answered with care the representations made by those whose will the applicant embodies gives them a sufficient interest for the purpose of this application").
[95] Edwards [2004] EWHC Admin 736.
[96] See, e.g. R. v Lambeth LBC Ex p. Crookes (1999) 31 H.L.R. 59 (landlord had standing to challenge failure to pay housing benefits to tenants, who would have paid the money over to him); R. v HM Pollution Inspectorate Ex p. Greenpeace Ltd (No.2) [1994] 4 All E.R. 329 at 350E (residents of Cumbria would also have had standing); cf. R. (on the application of Grierson) v Office of Communications (OFCOM) [2005] EWHC 1899; [2005] E.M.L.R. 37 at [20]–[23] (where a company had decided not to make a judicial review claim in respect of a licensing decision, the managing director and a minority shareholder of that company lacked sufficient interest to bring a claim).
[97] World Development Movement Ltd [1995] 1 W.L.R. 386 at 395; cf. Rose Theatre Trust Co Ltd [1990] 1 Q.B. 504 at 522.

Standing of local taxpayers

For many years, taxation levied by local authorities in England and Wales, based on a notional rental value of domestic and business premises, was known as rates. Business rates continue to be levied, but taxation of domestic dwellings is now called Council Tax. Naturally, ratepayers and Council Tax payers have standing to challenge decisions about rates and Council Tax.[98] A ratepayer in one London borough was held to be aggrieved by the rateable value ascribed to premises situated in a neighbouring borough on the ground that part of the rates collected from both boroughs was used to maintain services supplied by the Greater London Council.[99] Beyond this, the courts have generally adopted a generous approach to the standing of ratepayers to challenge the legality of local authority action in judicial review proceedings.[100] It is said that "Local authorities are not, of course, trustees for their ratepayers, but they do . . . owe an analogous fiduciary duty to their ratepayers in relation to the application of funds contributed by the latter".[101] Thus, even before 1978, standing was accorded to local ratepayers seeking to challenge a breach of standing orders relating to the placing of contracts even though they had suffered no more detriment *qua* ratepayers than other members of their class.[102] Reliance on the claimant's status as a ratepayer to obtain standing appears to have fallen somewhat out of fashion, no doubt because of the general relaxation of the "sufficient interest" test.

2–034

The role of campaign and interest groups as claimants

Campaign and interest groups are the claimants in only a relatively small proportion of judicial review claims each year.[103] The basis on which they are accorded standing varies:

2–035

---

[98] See, e.g. *R. v Waltham Forest LBC Ex p. Baxter* [1988] Q.B. 419; Local Government Finance Act 1982 s.4.

[99] *Arsenal Football Club Ltd v Ende* [1979] A.C. 1. A ratepayer's standing was stated to depend as much upon his interest in the uniformity and fairness of rating assessments as upon any increased financial burden resulting from an under-assessment; thus, it was not necessary that the ratepayer establish any demonstrable material loss beyond that suffered by other ratepayers. A taxpayer, however, is not aggrieved by an erroneous valuation, even though he contributes through his taxation to the rate support grant administered by central government on the basis of total rateable value.

[100] The position is different in other types of legal proceedings: *Barrs v Bethell* [1982] Ch. 294.

[101] *Prescott v Birmingham Corporation* [1955] Ch. 210 at 234–6 (unlawful for local authority to charge differential bus fares without specific statutory powers to do so).

[102] *R. v Hereford Corp Ex p Harrower* [1970] 1 W.L.R. 1424 (contractors excluded from tendering process had standing as ratepayers, but not as competitors of the firm awarded the contract).

[103] Claims bought in the name of an individual may be brought behalf of a campaign group, see e.g. *R. (on the application of Smeaton) v Secretary of State for Health* [2002] EWHC 610; [2002] 2 F.L.R. 146 (claim by the Society for the Protection of Unborn Children).

(a) in some claims, they may themselves have been directly affected, as an organisation, by the challenged decision and so be afforded standing on the basis of impact and proximity[104];

(b) they may be bringing the claim in a representative capacity, where some or all of the organisation's members are personally affected by the decision being challenged[105]; and

(c) in some other cases, the group brings a "pure" public interest challenge in circumstances where neither the organization itself, nor any of its members, are personally or directly affected.[106] As we have noted, individuals may be afforded standing on the basis of public interest but public interest challenges by groups requires further comment.[107]

2–036 In *National Federation*, Lord Wilberforce considered that a body which represents a group of claimants who are seeking to establish standing are in no better position than an individual, "since an aggregate of individuals, each of whom has no interest, cannot of itself have an interest".[108] In *Ex p. Rose Theatre*,[109] Schiemann J. applied the same principle to a body of individuals who, because they were interested in preserving a site of historical theatrical remains from development, formed a company to

---

[104] See, e.g. *R. v Radio Authority Ex p. Amnesty International* [1998] Q.B. 294 (Radio Authority refused AI permission to advertise on the radio about the distress of victims of human rights violations overseas, on the basis that the objects of the organisation were "mainly of a political nature" within the meaning of the Broadcasting Act 1990); *R. (on the application of National Union of Journalists) v Central Arbitration Committee* [2004] EWHC 2612; [2005] I.C.R. 493; [2005] I.R.L.R. 28 (judicial review of a decision of the Central Arbitration Committee denying NUJ's recognition under the Trade Union and Labour Relations (Consolidation) Act 1992 by an employer).

[105] See, e.g. *R. (on the application of West End Street Traders Association) v Westminster City Council* [2004] EWHC 1167; [2005] B.L.G.R. 143 (judicial review of a decision of local authority to implement changes in relation to charges for street trading); *R. (on the application of National Association of Colliery Overmen Deputies and Shotfirers) v Secretary of State for Work and Pensions* [2003] EWHC 607; [2004] A.C.D. 14 (judicial review of the Secretary of State's decision not to immediately modify and revise the guidance given in the Notes on the Diagnosis of Prescribed Diseases on the use of the Cold Water Provocation Test as a diagnostic tool for vibration induced white finger in claims for industrial injuries benefits under the Social Security Contributions and Benefits Act 1992); *R. (on the application of United Kingdom Renderers Association Ltd) v Secretary of State for the Environment, Transport and the Regions* [2002] EWCA Civ 749; [2003] Env. L.R. 7 (judicial review of a Process Guidance Note issued by the Secretary of State which recommended, in the case of authorisations to carry out the rendering of animals, the imposition of an "odour boundary condition"); *R. (on the application of Association of British Civilian Internees (Far East Region)) v Secretary of State for Defence* [2003] EWCA Civ 473; [2003] Q.B. 1397 (judicial review of Secretary of State's refusal to make *ex gratia* compensation payment to individuals had been interned by foreign powers as British civilians during World War II); *Greenpeace Ltd (No.2)* [1994] 4 All E.R. 329 (in a challenge to the grant of a licence for a nuclear reprocessing plant at Sellafield, importance attached to the fact that 2,500 members of Greenpeace lived in Cumbria). On representation orders under CPR r.19.6, see 2–012.

[106] See, e.g. *World Development Movement Ltd* [1995] 1 W.L.R. 386.

[107] See 2–031.

[108] *National Federation* [1982] A.C. 617 at 633.

[109] [1990] 1 Q.B. 504. *cf. R. v Stroud DC Ex p Goodenough* (1980) 43 P. & C.R. 59.

challenge the failure of the minister to prevent the development. The company failed in its claim on the merits but the judge carefully considered the question of standing before coming to the conclusion the company did not have standing. In his judgment Schiemann J. identified eight principles which were "not inconsistent" with the speeches in *National Federation*. Two of those principles were:

"7. The fact that some thousands of people join together and assert that they have an interest does not create an interest if the individuals did not have an interest.

8. The fact that those without an interest incorporate themselves and give the company in its memorandum power to pursue a particular object does not give the company an interest".

No doubt there can be circumstances where both of these principles can be applied without producing undesirable results. However it would be wrong to regard them as being of general application. The simple act of incorporation may not improve the status of a claimant. There is no magic in the act of incorporation for public law purposes.[110] However the fact that a group of persons combine to make a claim may give them enhanced authority to speak on a subject on behalf of a section of the public. As a group or a company they may acquire a special status of acknowledged expertise.[111] It is possible for there to be situations where there are persons who are directly affected by administrative action who are for reasons of poverty, ignorance or lack of an incentive incapable of bringing proceedings. In such situations an appropriate body or, if necessary, an appropriate individual should be regarded by the court as having the necessary standing.   2–037

In *Rose Theatre*, counsel for the claimant did not submit that an "agglomeration of individuals might have a standing which any one individual lacked".[112] It is suggested he was wrong not to do so. Indeed that there were individuals who were involved in the Rose Theatre company of acknowledged distinction in the field of archaeology who should, because of the nature of the issue before the court, have been regarded as being a significant factor in favour of there being standing. A specialist body which has the authority to speak collectively on behalf of its membership can carry greater weight than any one individual, no matter how distinguished. Similarly a trade union or a professional body is the obvious litigant to make a claim as to an administrative decision which affects its members generally.   2–038

---

[110] See 2–013.
[111] *Greenpeace Ltd (No.2)* [1994] 4 All E.R. 329; *R. v Secretary of State for Social Security Ex p. Joint Council for the Welfare of Immigrants* [1997] 1 W.L.R. 275.
[112] *Rose Theatre Trust Co Ltd* [1990] 1 Q.B. 504 at 521.

2–039   The preferable approach was adopted by Otton J. in *R. v HM Inspectorate of Pollution Ex p. Greenpeace Ltd (No.2)*.[113] He decided that Greenpeace was entitled to challenge the Secretary of State's decision as to the discharge and disposal of radioactive waste at Sellafield. He pointed out if Greenpeace did not have standing an application would have to be made by an employee or neighbour of the establishment who would not be as well qualified as Greenpeace to make the application. The judge declined to follow the decision in *Rose Theatre*.

2–040   A subsequent case took the trend of liberalising the requirement of standing a step further. In *R. v Secretary of State for Foreign Affairs Ex p. World Development Movement Ltd*[114] the Divisional Court held that the claimant had sufficient interest to apply for judicial review. The WDM was a non-partisan pressure group, over 20 years old, which campaigned to improve the quality and quantity of overseas aid given by the British government. In the past it had given evidence to Parliamentary select committees, had regular contact with the Overseas Development Administration (the government department responsible for overseas aid) and internationally it had consultative status with United Nations organisations. In one respect, however, the WDM differed from Greenpeace; whereas in the *Greenpeace* application challenging the legality of testing THORP, individual members of Greenpeace who lived in Cumbria would have been directly affected by the testing, and so have sufficient interest to make an application themselves, no individual member of the WDM was any more or less affected by the grant to build a power station on the Pergau dam in Malaysia than other members of the public. Nevertheless, the court held that the WDM had sufficient interest, referring to a range of factors: the merits of the application (here the impugned decision was held to be unlawful); the importance of vindicating the rule of law; the importance of the issue raised; the likely absence of any other challenger; the nature of the breach of duty against which relief was sought; and the prominent role of these claimants in giving advice, guidance and assistance with regard to all.

2–041   The process of liberalising the standing requirements for pressure groups has reached the stage where in *R. v Secretary of State for Trade and Industry Ex p. Greenpeace*[115] Laws J. commented that litigation of this kind was now an "accepted and greatly valued dimension of the judicial review jurisdiction". The corollary of this, however, is that a pressure group bringing a public interest challenge had to "act as a friend to the court," meaning that its conduct in making an application has to be controlled with particular strictness—especially as regards the requirement that applications for permission be made promptly and in any event within three months of the impugned decision. In summary, it can be said that today the

[113] *Ex p. Greenpeace Ltd (No.2)* [1994] 4 All E.R. 329: Greenpeace's primary objectives include the protection of wildlife and the elimination of threats to the environment.
[114] [1995] 1 W.L.R. 386.
[115] [1998] Env L.R. 415.

court ought not to decline jurisdiction to hear a claim for judicial review on the ground of lack of standing to any responsible person or group seeking, on reasonable grounds, to challenge the validity of governmental action. The good sense of this approach is emphasised by the ability of the courts to give permission to a third party to intervene in the proceedings to assist the court, which is happening with increasing frequency.[116]

HUMAN RIGHTS ACT 1998 AND THE VICTIM REQUIREMENT

Where a claim for judicial review seeks to rely on breach of a Convention right as a ground of review, in relation to that ground the meaning of "sufficient interest" is modified by s.7 of the HRA, which provides: 2–042

"(1) A person who claims that a public authority has acted (or proposes to act) in a way which is made unlawful by section 6(1) may—

(a) bring proceedings against the authority under this Act in the appropriate court or tribunal, or
(b) rely on the Convention right or rights concerned in any legal proceedings,

but only if he is (or would be) a victim of the unlawful act".

Subsection 7(3) states: "If the proceedings are brought on an application for judicial review, the applicant is to be taken to have a sufficient interest in relation to the unlawful act only if he is, or would be, a victim of that act".   2–043

The effect is to incorporate into English law the approach adopted by the European Court of Human Rights under Art.34 ECHR (formerly Art.25), which sets out the standing requirement for access that court in the following terms: "The Court may receive applications from any person, non-governmental organisation or group of individuals claiming to be a victim of a violation . . .". The requirement to follow Strasbourg case law appears to be stronger here, by virtue of s.7, than the general obligation under s.2 HRA that courts "must take into account" this case law.   2–044

The rationale for including the victim requirement in the HRA appeared to be two-fold. In part, it reflected the government's general aim for the HRA that it should "bring rights home" by closely mirroring the ECHR and not creating new kinds of rights. The victim requirement was also clearly intended to restrict the capacity of campaign groups to use Convention rights as a ground for judicial review.[117]   2–045

---

[116] See 2–064.
[117] See, e.g. *Re Application by the Family Planning Association of Northern Ireland for Judicial Review* [2003] NIQB 48 at [58]–[67] (Kerr J. held that FBANI was prevented from making submissions in relation to whether Minister had contravened Convention rights).

When is the victim requirement relevant?

2–046 There is uncertainty as to when the victim requirement is brought into play. On one analysis it is necessary, by reason of the words of the HRA, to differentiate between claims (a) in which the claimant argues that there has been a breach by a public authority of s.6 of the HRA (to which the victim requirement applies) and (b) where a claimant is seeking a declaration of incompatibility under s.4 of the HRA in respect of a statutory provision (in which the victim requirement does not apply).[118] In other cases, however, the courts have held or assumed that the victim requirement applies to claims for a declaration of incompatibility.[119] In our view the former approach is the better one.

Strasbourg case law on meaning of "victim"

2–047 In transplanting the case law of the European Court of Human Rights into the domestic setting, it needs to be borne in mind that the Strasbourg rule and its interpretation have been crafted for the purposes of controlling access to an international tribunal. That is a rather different purpose from the role of the "sufficient interest" test used in judicial review. When determining individual applications, the ECtHR is concerned with concrete review and eschews abstract review of legislation, policy or administrative action. Moreover, applications that amount to an *actio popularis* are excluded.[120]

2–048 Generally, the term "victim" in ECHR Art.34 denotes a person directly affected by the specific act or omission in issue. It is not however necessary that the victim have suffered damage, which is an issue in relation to "just

---

[118] *R. (on the application of Countryside Alliance) v Attorney General* [2006] EWCA Civ 817; [2006] 3 W.L.R. 1017 at [64]–[66] (Lord Phillips C.J.—claim for declaration of incompatibility of the Hunting Act 2004: the HRA "does not purport to prescribe rules for standing if a declaration like this is sought, in contrast to the rule in s.7(1)(a), which entitles a person who claims that a public authority has acted (or proposed to act) in a way which is made unlawful by s.6(1) to bring proceedings against that authority in the appropriate court, but only if he is (or would be) a victim of the unlawful act". The claimant in a claim for judicial review must still satisfy the requirement of having "sufficient interest" (albeit not modified to include a victim test); *cf. R. (on the application of Morris) v Westminster City Council (No.3)* [2005] EWCA Civ 1184; [2006] 1 W.L.R. 505 at [54] (Sedley L.J., "Although the claim for a declaration of incompatibility requires a sufficient interest on the part of the claimant, the decision to make a declaration if the conditions are met depends not on the claimant's interest alone but on the general compatibility of the measure with the Convention right in question").

[119] *R. (on the application of Rusbridger) v Attorney General* [2003] UKHL 38; [2004] 1 A.C. 357, discussed below. See also *Taylor v Lancashire CC* [2005] EWCA Civ 284; [2005] 1 W.L.R. 2668 (appellant sought to raise as a defence to an order for possession of an agricultural holding that certain provisions of the Agricultural Holdings Act 1986, which did not apply to his case, were incompatible with Convention rights; held not to be a victim because he "has not been and could not be personally adversely affected by the repealed legislation on which he seeks to rely").

[120] An *actio popularis* is an action "in which any member of the public may be entitled as such to vindicate certain forms of public right" (*MacCormick v Lord Advocate* 1953 S.C. 396 at 413, Lord Cooper L.P.).

satisfaction" under Art.41.[121] If a national authority makes a decision or measure favourable to the applicant, that is not sufficient to deprive him of his status as a victim unless (a) the national authorities acknowledges, either expressly or in substance, and then (b) affords redress for, the breach of the Convention.[122] It is no answer for a national authority to say that the person has, in the end, suffered no detriment under national law.[123] Where, however, an administrative order is retrospectively quashed by a national court a person can no longer claim to be a victim of interference.[124] The ECtHR has regarded a person falling within the ambit of legislation affecting a Convention right to be a victim, even in the absence of enforcement of that legislation against the person.[125] The repeal of national legislation violating a Convention right does not preclude a person being a victim in subsequent proceedings before the ECtHR if he suffered disadvantage during the time the legislation was in force.[126]

Close family relationships may form the basis of a claim to be a victim; **2–049** this is not a general principle, rather all the circumstances of a case must be considered. Thus, the father of a son who had disappeared may himself be the victim of inhuman and degrading treatment under Art.3, having regard to the way in which national authorities responded when the disappearance was brought to their attention.[127]

The ECtHR has not been particularly generous in its interpretation of **2–050** "victim" in relation to the deportation of foreign nationals. An applicant cannot claim to be the victim of a deportation measure if the measure is

---

[121] *Ilhan v Turkey* (2002) 34 E.H.R.R. 36 (brother of person injured by police could make application; but ECtHR noted that it would generally be appropriate for an application to name the injured person as the applicant and for a letter of authority to be provided allowing another member of the family to act on his or her behalf). On just satisfaction and damages, see 19–088.

[122] *Eckle v Germany* (1983) 5 E.H.R.R. 1.

[123] *Posokhov v Russia* (2004) 39 E.H.R.R. 21 (P complained about appointment of judge, his conviction was quashed on the basis of an unrelated procedural irregularity); *Ryabykh v Russia* (2005) 40 E.H.R.R. 25 (R successfully claimed that the State had failed to fulfil a legal requirement to revalue her savings to counter the effects of inflation; she suffered detriment because of a period of uncertainty during the litigation caused by a review of the case contrary to Art.6(1)).

[124] *Akkoc v Turkey* (2002) 34 E.H.R.R. 51; *Amuur v France* (1996) 22 E.H.R.R. 533.

[125] See, e.g. *Klass v Federal Republic of Germany* (1978) 2 E.H.R.R. 214, para.33 (secret surveillance legislation), *Dudgeon v United Kingdom* (1982) 4 E.H.R.R. 149 (law prohibiting sex between men) *Burden v United Kingdom* (2007) 44 E.H.R.R. 51, para.25 (liability to pay inheritance tax had not yet accrued, but there was "every high probability" that applicants would become liable). *cff. Leigh v United Kingdom* (1982) 38 D.R. 74 (journalist claiming to be affected by "chilling effect" of House of Lords' judgment on contempt of court was not a victim). In relation to Art.8 and secret surveillance, the ECtHR has accepted that an applicant does not need to contend that measures of surveillance were actually applied to him and that it is therefore inappropriate to apply a reasonable likelihood test to determine whether he may claim to be a victim: *Case of the Association for European Integration and Human Rights v Bulgaria* (62540/00), para.58.

[126] *SL v Austria* (2003) 37 E.H.R.R. 3 (S was a victim of legislation prohibiting sex between males, since repealed, as he had suffered disadvantage during the time it was in force).

[127] *Timurtas v Turkey* (2001) 33 E.H.R.R. 6. See also *Kurt v Turkey* (1999) 27 E.H.R.R. 373. *cf. Akdeniz v Turkey* (23954/94).

not enforceable.[128] Similarly, where execution of the deportation order has been stayed indefinitely or otherwise deprived of legal effect and where an appeal lies to a court, the person will not be regarded as a victim.[129] Removal from a register of residents did not make applicants victims when this did not result in the applicants facing any real and imminent risk of deportation.[130]

2–051 The ECtHR has attached considerable importance to the legal personality of applicants. Piercing of the corporate veil or disregarding the company's personality is justified only in exceptional circumstances: where it is the interests of a company that have been affected, and that company (or its liquidators) are able to bring proceedings, shareholders of the company are unlikely to be regarded as victims.[131] A distinction was made between a national political party (which had applied to the court) and a regional organisation of that party (which had not, yet had been the legal entity directly affected).[132]

2–052 In several respects, the standing rule in Art.34 ECHR is more limited than the Administrative Court's approach to the test for sufficient interest. Government bodies fall outside the ambit of Art.34, cannot be victims and therefore cannot use violation of Convention rights as a ground of review.[133] Moreover, the European Court does not permit pure public interest claims: to bring proceedings a non-governmental organisation (NGO) must itself be directly affected by the alleged violation of a Convention right.[134]

Application of "victim" requirement in the HRA

2–053 The meaning of "victim" in s.7 of the HRA has been considered in only a handful of cases. The House of Lords held (*obiter*) that a person who, in proceedings before the European Court of Human Rights, obtained the award of a payment by way of just satisfaction, remained a "victim" for the

---

[128] *Vijayanathan v France* (1993) 15 E.H.R.R. 62 (applicants remained in France beyond the time set for their deportation order; if they had been arrested, the order would be subject to annulment for obvious error of assessment on appeal within 24 hours to the French courts. Lodging an appeal had a suspensive effect on deportation orders).

[129] See cases cited in *Sisojeva v Latvia* (60654/00), para.93.

[130] *Sisojeva* (60654/00), para.100.

[131] *Agrotexim v Greece* (1996) 21 E.H.R.R. 250.

[132] *Vatan v Russia* (2006) 42 E.H.R.R. 7.

[133] *Ayuntamiento de M v Spain* (1991) 68 D. & R. 209; and 3–071.

[134] See, e.g. *Norris and National Gay Federation v Ireland* (1984) 44 D.R. 132 (NGF was not itself directly affected by legislation prohibiting sex between males); *Purcell v Ireland* (1991) 70 D.R. 262 (broadcasting unions could not bring proceedings to challenge probation on transmissions of interviews with paramilitary groups); cf. *Open Door Counselling Ltd and Dublin Well Woman Centre v Ireland* (1993) 15 E.H.R.R. 244 (two Irish counselling organisations assisting clients to have abortions in England were restrained by an injunction claimed by the Attorney General; as directly affected NGOs, there were recognised as victims). An NGO may however be permitted to make an application on behalf of a group of named individuals who are themselves victims if it is acting on specific instructions from those named individuals.

purposes of claim made under the HRA in respect of a continuing breach of a Convention right.[135] In another case, in which the editor of the *Guardian* sought declarations in respect of s.3 of the Treason Felony Act 1848, which appeared to criminalise advocacy of republicanism in Britain, the House of Lords was divided as to whether the editor should be held to be a victim (an issue that had, in fact, been conceded by the defendant).[136] As noted above, there is some doubt as to whether the victim requirement should apply where the only remedy sought is a declaration of incompatibility under s.4 of the HRA.[137] In *Hooper v Secretary of State for Work and Pensions* the claimant widowers challenging the lawfulness of refusal to pay them social security and pension payments, to which they would have been entitled had they been widows, were held to be victims because each claimant had done something which identified him as having wished to make a claim[138] In *Austin Hall Building Ltd v Buckland Securities Ltd*,[139] the client of a building contractor was held not to be a victim in a challenge to a decision of an adjudicator appointed under the Housing Grants, Construction and Regeneration Act 1996 as it had not objected to the manner of the decision-making process at the time.

Criticism of the victim requirement in the HRA

The policy of s.7(3) HRA was opposed during the passage of the Human Rights Bill and has been subject to academic criticism.[140] It may be thought undesirable to have different standing rules for purely domestic and Convention right grounds of review—particularly as these two categories of ground will often be combined in a single claim. An environmental pressure group may therefore have standing to advance (say) a claim of illegality but not to argue that Art.8 ECHR has been violated by a

2–054

---

[135] *Re McKerr's Application for Judicial Review* [2004] UKHL 12; [2004] 1 W.L.R. 807 (*obiter*, because the HL held that the HRA did not operate retrospectively to create a continuing obligation under ECHR Art.2 to investigate unlawful killings that occurred before the HRA came into force).

[136] *Rusbridger* [2003] UKHL 38; [2004] 1 A.C. 357: Lord Steyn, at [21], emphasised this was a threshold question and applied *Norris v Ireland* (1989) 13 E.H.R.R. 186 in which a "homosexual man complained that the criminalisation of homosexual conduct in Ireland violated his Art.8 right to respect for his private life, although he accepted that the risk of being prosecuted was remote"; Lord Rodger of Earlsferry, at [55], described the present proceedings as "in substance an actio popularis" and stressed that *Norris* required "that an individual applicant should be able to claim to be actually affected by the measure of which he complains" (which was not so in the case of the editor).

[137] See 2–046.

[138] [2005] UKHL 29; [2005] 1 W.L.R. 1681 at [53]–[59] (Lord Hoffmann, *obiter*, citing *Cornwell v United Kingdom* (1999) 27 E.H.R.R. CD 62 in which the Court treated an inquiry about the availability of benefits as sufficient).

[139] [2001] B.L.R. 272, QBD.

[140] J. Marriott and D. Nicol, "The Human Rights Act, Representative Standing and the Victim Culture" (1998) 6 E.H.R.L.R. 730; J. Miles, "Standing under the Human Rights Act 1998: Theories of Rights Enforcement and the Nature of Public Law Adjudication" [2000] C.L.J. 133.

development. Similarly a group campaigning for the rights of immigrants and asylum seeks may have standing in relation to a procedural impropriety point but not (say) an allegation that there has been a breach of Art.6(1). A policy that permits only individuals to advance Convention right points in judicial review claims undermines the pragmatic good sense of Otton J.'s recognition in *Ex p. Greenpeace (No.2)* of the advantages to the court of having a well-qualified claimant, rather than "an employee or neighbour", or other individual, bring the challenge.[141] The Commission for Equality and Human Rights may rely on Convention rights in judicial review claims it makes or intervenes in without itself being a victim or potential victim of the unlawful act, provided that there are one or more other people who are victims.[142] Moreover, a campaign group that is not a victim may nevertheless be able to seek permission to intervene to raise Convention right points in a claim begun by someone else.[143]

STANDING OF "PERSONS AGGRIEVED"

2–055   In some contexts, legislation provides a procedure distinct from a claim for judicial review under CPR Pt 54, enabling those affected by the activities of public authorities to appeal or make an application to quash an order or other administrative decision.[144] The legislation may specify who is entitled to bring the proceedings, and when this happens as long as the legislation is not ambiguous and sufficiently specific there should be no difficulty in determining who has standing.[145] It frequently happens, however, that the legislation uses some general description to describe who may bring proceedings and in this situation the courts have to determine who falls within that description. A longstanding favourite description in legislation of those who are entitled to challenge the validity of or appeal against administrative acts is a "person aggrieved".[146] Judicial protests against the continued use of this vague expression have gone unheeded;[147] and in its

---

[141] See 2–039.

[142] Equality Act 2006 s.30(3).

[143] A possibility anticipated by the Government during the passage of the Human Rights Bill: *Hansard* HC, col.1058 (November 24, 1997). On interventions, see 2–064.

[144] See 17–025.

[145] See, e.g. Town and Country Planning Act 1990 s.289(1), which provides that in respect of a decision by the Secretary of State in respect of an enforcement notice, the person who appealed to the Secretary of State, the local authority or any other person having an interest in the land to which the notice relates may appeal to the High Court.

[146] See, e.g. Town and Country Planning Act 1990 ss.287 and 288; Planning and Compulsory Purchase Act 2004 s.100; Human Tissue Act 2004 s.22; Petroleum Act 1998, s.42. No doubt the reason for this is that at common law, before the introduction of the universal test of "sufficient interest" in the 1978 procedural reforms, it was generally the test for determining whether a person had standing to apply for certiorari and prohibition to ask whether he was a person aggrieved. The use of the term "person aggrieved" in relation to appeals to tribunals or courts other than the Administrative Court falls outside the scope of this chapter.

[147] *Ealing Corp v Jones* [1959] 1 Q.B. 384 at 390; *Buxton v Minister of Housing and Local Government* [1961] 1 Q.B. 278 at 282–3.

1994 report, the Law Commission concluded that "we do not wish to widen the test of standing under these statutes and, in the circumstances, make no recommendations for reform".[148] A "person aggrieved" may authorise an agent to commence and conduct proceedings on his behalf.[149]

The task of interpretation has been left to the judge.[150] The results in the **2–056** past have not been entirely coherent. It is, of course, to be expected that the meaning attributed to such an expression will vary according to the context in which it is found,[151] and this partly explains why in the past there was an undesirable lack of consistency in decisions as to the meaning of this term. The sheer number of different statutes which use the term is also a contributing factor.[152] The purpose for which a right of appeal or to make an application was conferred in a particular situation will often be a decisive factor in answering the question who is entitled to exercise the right.[153]

The courts did for a time give an unduly restrictive interpretation to the **2–057** expression "person aggrieved". They took the view that to be legally aggrieved a person must not be merely dissatisfied with or even prejudiced by an act or decision, but must have been deprived of or refused something to which he was legally entitled[154] or subjected to a legal burden (for example, a duty to pay costs or execute works).[155] In accord with the developments which were taking place on applications for judicial review, there was a clearly discernible trend away from the restrictive and highly technical approach to who is a person aggrieved.

---

[148] *Administrative Law: Judicial Review and Statutory Appeals* (Law Com. 226), para.12.18.
[149] *General Legal Council (on the application of Whitter) v Frankson* [2006] UKPC 42; [2006] 1 W.L.R. 2803.
[150] See, e.g. *Swansea City and County Council v Davies* (2001) 165 J.P. 156.
[151] *Arsenal Football Club Ltd v Ende* [1979] A.C. 1 at 27 (Viscount Dilhorne).
[152] Examples appear in Annex 2 to the Law Commission's Consultation Paper No.126 *Administrative Law: Judicial Review and Statutory Appeals* (1993).
[153] Cf. *R. v Ministry of Health Ex p. Ellis* [1968] 1 Q.B. 84; *R. v Dorset Quarter Sessions Appeals Committee Ex p. Weymouth Corp* [1960] 2 Q.B. 230. See also *R. v Ipswich Justices Ex p. Robson* [1971] 2 Q.B. 340 (driver refused licence could not be person who "feels aggrieved" by decision if licensing authority had no power to grant licence on particular facts); *General and Municipal Workers' Union v Certification Officer* [1977] I.C.R. 183 (right of appeal to Employment Appeal Tribunal against a decision of Certification Officer limited to a "trade union aggrieved" by the refusal of its application for or revocation of its certificate of independence).
[154] *Ex p. Sidebotham* (1880) 14 Ch.D. 458 at 465 (James L.J.), *cf.* at 466 (Bramwell L.J.); *Ex p. Official Receiver; Re Reed, Bowen & Co* (1887) 19 Q.B.D. 174; *R. v London Quarter Sessions Ex p. Westminster Corp* [1951] 2 K.B. 508 (overruled in *Cook v Southend BC* [1990] 2 Q.B. 1); *Burke v Minister of Housing and Local Government* (1957) 8 P. & C.R. 25 at 27–8.
[155] *R. v Nottingham Quarter Sessions Ex p. Harlow* [1952] 2 Q.B. 601; *R. v Lancaster Quarter Sessions Ex p. Huyton-with-Roby UDC* [1955] 1 Q.B. 52; *Re Hurle-Hobbs' Decision* [1944] 2 All E.R. 261; *Ealing Corp v Jones* [1959] 1 Q.B. 384; *R. v Dorset Quarter Sessions Appeals Committee Ex p. Weymouth Corp* [1960] 2 Q.B. 230; *R. v Boldero Ex p. Bognor Regis UDC* (1962) 60 L.G.R. 292; *Phillips v Berkshire CC* [1967] 2 Q.B. 991. However this approach was rejected in *Cook v Southend BC* [1990] 2 Q.B. 1 in respect of appeals from magistrates' courts.

2–058   Normally, "a public authority which has an adverse decision made against it in an area where it is required to perform public duties, is entitled to be treated as a person aggrieved".[156] A local authority may be a "person aggrieved";[157] so also may the Crown or the Attorney General acting on its behalf.[158] However, it may still be the case that if the decision is in favour of the local authority and that body only objects to the reasons given for the decision the local authority is not a "person aggrieved".[159] It is suggested that this view underestimates the importance which can attach to the reasons for a decision being given. The absence of reasons or the provision of unsatisfactory reasons can result in a local authority having to adopt in another case an approach of which it disapproves, for example to maintain consistency. At least in some cases a local authority should be able to challenge the reasons given for a decision in its favour, if those reasons create an undesirable precedent.

2–059   In some contexts the term "person aggrieved" necessarily has a wider meaning. Thus, if a local authority refuses in its discretion to grant or to renew a licence, or revokes such a licence, the applicant or licensee is entitled to appeal as a "person aggrieved" to a magistrates' court;[160] though in some circumstances where there has not been an actual refusal of a licence or the actual grant of a licence subject to a condition, a person fearing an adverse decision may not be a person aggrieved.[161]

2–060   The narrow view previously adopted[162] as to who may be regarded as a "person aggrieved" by a decision on a planning appeal has been rejected. A statutory remedy was held to be available not only to those with a statutory right to appear at the inquiry but also those who have, in the discretion of the inspector, been permitted to make representations.[163] Furthermore a successor in title of the person who was involved at the outset in a planning application can be entitled to appeal to the High Court even if he

---

[156] *Cook v Southend BC* [1990] 2 Q.B. 1.
[157] *R. v Surrey Quarter Sessions Ex p. Lilley* [1951] 2 K.B. 749.
[158] *Attorney General of the Gambia v N'Jie* [1961] A.C. 617; *Buxton v Minister of Housing and Local Government* [1961] 1 Q.B. 278.
[159] *GLC v Secretary of State for the Environment* [1985] J.P.L. 868 (Woolf J.); a claim for judicial review (rather than a statutory application to quash under the Town and Country Planning Acts) may be possible.
[160] *Ferrant v Stepney BC* (1964) 62 L.G.R. 182.
[161] *Peddubriwny v Cambridge City Council* [2001] EWHC Admin 200; [2001] R.T.R. 31.
[162] *Ealing* [1959] 1 Q.B. 384 and *Dorset* [1960] 2 Q.B. 230; *London Quarter Sessions* [1951] 2 K.B. 508; *Buxton* [1961] 1 Q.B. 278 (neighbour who appeared at planning appeal denied standing); *Gregory v Camden LBC* [1966] 1 W.L.R. 899.
[163] *Turner v Secretary of State for the Environment* (1974) 28 P. & C.R. 123 (local amenity group); *Bison v Secretary of State for the Environment* (1976) 239 E.G. 281 (preliminary objection to locus standi of neighbour rejected; the court was prepared to assume without deciding that the applicant was a person aggrieved); *Jones v Secretary of State for Wales* (1974) 28 P. & C.R. 280 at 287. In *Murphy (J) & Sons Ltd v Secretary of State for the Environment* [1973] 1 W.L.R. 560, the locus standi of a neighbour to challenge planning appeal and confirmation of a compulsory purchase order was not raised. In *Times Investment Ltd v Secretary of State for the Environment and Tower Hamlets LBC* (1990) 3 P.L.R. 111, the phrase was applied to a successor in title of an appellant.

did not appear at the planning inquiry.[164] These developments are, no doubt, influenced by the opportunities available to objectors at local public inquiries.[165] When statutory recognition has been given to the desirability of public participation in the administrative process, it would seem appropriate that those qualified to question the validity of the decision or order should include those who participated in the inquiry which preceded the order.[166] The availability of judicial review to impugn planning decisions may have helped to widen the categories of persons with standing, since it would be a nonsense to prevent a person from exercising a statutory right of appeal in circumstances where the same remedy would be available on a claim for judicial review.[167] Hence a householder anticipating a serious loss of amenity as a result of an administrative decision to permit the building of a high block of flats nearby was entitled to appeal against the decision as "a person aggrieved".[168]

REFORM OF STANDING

In its 1994 report on remedies in administrative law, the Law Commission 2–061 noted that "the fluid nature of the requirement of sufficiency means that it is uncertain what precisely is required".[169] It recommended that rules of court and s.31 of the Supreme Court Act 1981 (Senior Courts Act 1981) be amended to make special provision for the standing requirements in cases where the claimant is a representative or pressure group or where there is a public interest in a matter being litigated but no individual has standing. It proposed that a "two track" system be established.[170] The first track would cover situations where a person has a direct interest in the impugned

---

[164] *Times Investment Ltd* (1990) 3 P.L.R. 111. *cf. Eco-Energy (GB) Ltd v First Secretary of State* [2004] EWCA Civ 1566; [2005] 2 P. & C.R. 5 (a person may be denied the status of a "person aggrieved" if he did not take a sufficiently active role in the planning process and did not hold an interest in the land at the relevant time).

[165] *Turner* [1974] 28 P. & C.R. 123 at 134–5 (*Buxton* is not followed for this reason). It may be noted that Major Buxton was permitted to appear at the inquiry and that the applicants in *Turner* only did so at the discretion of the inspector. But the statutory basis of modern inquiry procedure and the broad range of factors relevant to the exercise of planning powers can be seen as conferring legal recognition to interests other than those of the applicant and the planning authority. Whether a person has a legally protected "right" may involve a more sophisticated appreciation of the purposes underlying the legislative scheme than was assumed in the earlier decisions.

[166] *Wilson v Secretary of State for the Environment* [1973] 1 W.L.R. 1083, where an appropriation certificate was quashed for lack of proper public notice at the instance of members of the public who would have objected had the statutory requirements for notice been observed.

[167] *Cook v Southend BC* [1990] 2 Q.B. 1 at 18.

[168] *Maurice v London CC* [1964] 2 Q.B. 362; *cf. Buxton* [1961] 1 Q.B. 278. In *Maurice* there was no question of interference with an easement or any other proprietary interest; and *R. v Surrey (Mid-Eastern Area) Assessment Committee* [1948] 1 All E.R. 856.

[169] Law Com. 226, para.5.16 (see 15–092).

[170] Law Com. 226, para.5.20. A proposal supported by Lord Woolf in *Access to Justice: final report* (1995), p.255.

decision, in the sense that he has had his legal rights or legitimate expectations affected or there has been a refusal to confer some discretionary benefit. Here standing should be accorded as a matter of course. The second track would cover public interest challenges, i.e. applications in which no person is affected more than the public generally and also challenges by a group rather than an individual where the decision nevertheless affects an individual.[171] In such cases, the court would have regard to a wider range of factors than under the first track in deciding whether there is standing, including: the importance of the legal point: the chances of the issue being raised in any other proceedings; the allocation of scarce judicial resources; and the concern that in the determination of issues the courts should have the benefit of the conflicting points of view of those most directly affected by them. Implementation of the Law Commission proposals now seems unnecessary in the light of developments in the *WMD* and other cases mentioned above,[172] which have moved the court's approach to a position which is not dissimilar.

2–062   Finally, we need to remember that issues as to standing are issues of procedure of the court. Issues of procedure have a primary purpose and that is to facilitate the achievement of justice. Because of this, the rules always have to be applied with the degree of flexibility necessary to assist the achievement of this purpose.

INTERESTED PARTIES AND INTERVENERS

Interested parties

2–063   Persons other than the claimant and defendant may participate in a claim for judicial review. One important category is "interested parties", upon whom the claimant is obliged to serve the claim form,[173] and who should receive a letter before the claim is started.[174] An interested party "means any person (other than the claimant and defendant) who is directly affected by the claim".[175] Being inevitably or necessarily affected by the outcome of the claim for judicial review is insufficient to make a person *directly* affected; he must (also) be "affected without the intervention of any

---

[171] The report gives as an illustration of this type of challenge *R. v Chief Adjudication Office Ex p. Bland and the TUC, The Times*, February 6, 1985 where the Trades Union Congress was held not to have standing to challenge the legality of reductions of state welfare benefits to striking miners.

[172] See 2–040.

[173] CPR rr.54.6 and 54.7. PD 54 provides "Where the claim for judicial review relates to proceedings in a court or tribunal, any other parties to those proceedings must be named in the claim form as interested parties".

[174] CPR r.54 Pre-Action Protocol.

[175] CPR r.54.1(2)(f).

intermediate agency".[176] Interested parties are parties to the claim and may therefore appeal against the judgment of the court.

Interveners

Secondly, a person may apply for permission to make written and/or oral submissions—"interventions"—at the hearing of the judicial review.[177] Prior to the adoption of the CPR, the rules relating to first instance claims for judicial review provided only for intervention by persons seeking to oppose the application for judicial review, not to support it. Since 2000 there has been a noticeable increase in the number of interventions, in judicial review and other proceedings in the Administrative Court, Court of Appeal and before the House of Lords.[178] Interveners may include campaign groups, government departments,[179] the Commission for Equality and Human Rights,[180] and business enterprises indirectly affected by the outcome of the claim. This trend—especially the role of campaign groups[181]—has attracted both supporters[182] and critics.[183] On the one hand, the court's decision-making may benefit from the perspectives of interveners, who typically will make different or broader legal points, or provide additional facts, to those raised by the claimant and defendant. On the other hand, the courts have only begun to articulate the principles that should govern when interventions should be permitted and when refused. The main criterion ought to be whether would-be interveners, though their expertise, are likely to be able to assist the court in understanding either the legal issues in question or the factual basis of the claim and the consequences that may flow from the court's judgment.

2–064

---

[176] *R. v Rent Officer Service Ex p. Muldoon* [1996] 1 W.L.R. 1103, interpreting a similar provision (RSC, Ord.53 r.5(3)) in the precursor to the current rules; the Secretary of State for Social Security reimbursed local authorities for up to 95% of their expenditure on housing benefit but was not "directly affected" by a judicial review of the refusal or failure of a local authority to determine claims for benefits where rent officers had been denied entry to the dwelling in circumstances where there had been no deliberate denial of entry by the applicant.
[177] CPR r.54.17(1). Such applications must be made promptly. PD 54, para.13.3: "An application for permission should be made by letter to the Administrative Court office, identifying the claim, explaining who the applicant is and indicating why and in what form the applicant wants to participate in the hearing".
[178] See Sir Henry Brooke, "Interventions in the Court of Appeal" [2007] P.L. 401.
[179] See, e.g. the Secretary of State for Health in *R. v North and East Devon HA Ex p. Coughlan* [2001] Q.B. 213; M. Havers and C. Mellor, "Third Party Interventions for Government" [2004] J.R. 130.
[180] Equality Act 2006 s.30(1).
[181] Among the organisations intervening in judicial review claims in recent years are: Liberty; Joint Council for the Welfare of Immigrants; Stonewall; League Against Cruel Sports.
[182] M. Arshi and C. O'Cinneide, "Third Party Interventions: the Public Interest Reaffirmed" [2004] P.L. 69; Sir Konrad Schiemann, "Interventions in Public Interest Cases" [1996] PL. 240.
[183] S. Hannett, "Third Party Intervention: in the Public Interest?" [2003] P.L. 128; C. Harlow, "Public Law and Popular Justice" (2002) 65 M.L.R. 1.

2-065   Instead of merely intervening, in some circumstances a person may seek to be joined as a second claimant or defendant.[184] The same criteria should apply. The advantages of becoming a party are that you may obtain relief if you succeed or appeal if you do not. The principle disadvantage is your possible liability for costs.

Joining the Crown as a party to proceedings

2-066   Where the court is considering whether to make a declaration of incompatibility under s.4 of the Human Rights Act 1998, the Crown is entitled to be given notice and thereafter a minister of the Crown is entitled to be joined as a party to the proceedings.[185] No award of damages may be made against the Crown under s.9(3) HRA unless the appropriate person is joined in the proceedings.[186]

COMPARATIVE PERSPECTIVES

2-067   In this section, we bring together summaries of the approaches to standing adopted in several other jurisdictions—Scotland, Australia, Canada, India, New Zealand and South Africa. The purpose of doing so is to illustrate the variety of legislative and judicial techniques that are employed in common law jurisdictions.[187] The fact that a person or organisation has been held to having standing in one jurisdiction does not, of course, necessarily imply that the same outcome ought to follow in other legal systems. A range of constitutional, political and procedural factors may justify different outcomes.

Scotland

2-068   There are no distinct rules governing standing in relation to judicial review in Scotland. Ordinary principles apply; the respondent may enter pleas of "no title to sue" (the petitioner must be a party, in the widest sense, to some legal relation which has been infringed) and "no interest to sue" (there must be a real rather than merely an academic question of law), though in some cases it has been recognised that these elements "very much run into each other".[188] The Scots law approach, based on private

---

[184] *R. v Secretary of State for the Home Department Ex p. O'Byrne* [2000] C.P. Rep. 9 (local authority joined as second respondent, but attaching a restriction as to costs).
[185] HRA s.5; CPR r.19. The notice given under r.19.4A must be served on the person named in the list published under s.17 of the Crown Proceedings Act 1947 (typically but not invariably the Treasury Solicitor).
[186] HRA s.9(4).
[187] See 1–003.
[188] Lord Clyde and D. Edwards, *Judicial Review* (2000), Ch.10; Lord Hope of Craighead, "Mike Tyson comes to Glasgow—A Question of Standing" [2001] P.L. 294.

law principles, has in the past led to the Court of Session refusing to hear petitions in situations where, on similar facts, the Administrative Court in England applying the broadly interpreted rules of "sufficient interest" would have accepted jurisdiction.

Australia

The Australian test for standing both at common law and under the **2–069** Administrative Decisions (Judicial Review) Act 1977 has developed more narrowly than in the England and Wales. Strictly speaking, there is no single test for standing in the various types of review available in Australia.[189] It is generally accepted that, at the discretion of the court, a "stranger" may bring an action for the writs of prohibition, certiorari and habeas corpus;[190] although it appears from *Re McBain; Ex parte Catholic Bishops Conference* the court may be less inclined to exercise its discretion in favour of a stranger.[191] The standing requirements for mandamus require a "special interest".[192] Similarly an ordinary member of the public will have to show that they have a "special interest in the subject matter of the action" to have standing to bring an action for an injunction or declaration.[193] The test for standing under ADJR Act is the applicant is a person whose interests are adversely affected by a decision or determination to which the Act applies.[194] This test has been described as no "narrower" than the "special interest" test.[195]

The "special interest" test is considered to be stricter than the position **2–070** in England and Wales in relation to public interest litigation. Gaudron J. has noted its limiting effect on the availability of the equitable remedies.[196] Kirby J. has advocated the adoption of a more flexible approach to standing,[197] which critics have argued amounts to nothing short of abolishing standing requirements altogether.[198]

---

[189] *Bateman's Bay Local Aboriginal Land Council v Aboriginal Community Benefit Fund Pty Ltd* (1998) 194 C.L.R. 247; *Truth About Motorways Pty Ltd v Macquarie Infrastructure Investment Management Ltd* (2000) 200 C.L.R. 591.
[190] Administrative Review Council, *The Scope of Judicial Review* (2006) Report No.47, paras 2.2.3 and 2.2.6; *Truth About Motorways Pty Ltd v Macquarie Infrastructure Investment Management Ltd* (2000) 200 C.L.R. 591; *Re McBain; Ex parte Catholic Bishops Conference* (2002) 209 C.L.R. 372.
[191] (2002) 209 C.L.R. 372 at [422] (McHugh J.).
[192] Administrative Review Council *The Scope of Judicial Review* (April 2006) Report No.47, para.2.2.4.
[193] *Australian Conservation Foundation (ACF) v Commonwealth* (1980) 146 C.L.R. 493; *Bateman's Bay* (1998) 194 C.L.R. 247 at 256 (Gaudron, Gummow and Kirby JJ.).
[194] ADJR Act s.3(4) defines a "person aggrieved" for the purposes of ss.5(1), 6(1) and 7(1).
[195] *Australian Institute of Marine and Power Engineers v Secretary, Department of Transport* (1986) 71 A.L.R. 73 at 81 (Gummow J.).
[196] *Enfield City v Development Assessment Commission* (2000) 199 C.L.R. 135 at [57] (Gaudron J.).
[197] *Re McBain* (2002) 209 C.L.R. 372 at 449–50.
[198] M. Aronson, B. Dyer and M. Groves, *Judicial Review of Administrative Action*, 3rd edn (2004), p.656.

2–071   The Attorney General always has standing to seek equitable relief to enforce *public rights* either on his or her own account or upon the relation of a third party.[199] Perhaps because of the stricter standing rules that have developed, the grant of the Attorney's fiat to commence a relator action to individuals or entities without the requisite standing is still used in Australia relatively frequently.[200] The effectiveness of the role of the Attorney General as the enforcer of public rights in the current political environment where he or she acts as both a Minister of the executive and the first law officer of the State was criticised sharply by Gaudron, Gummow and Kirby JJ. in *Bateman's Bay Local Aboriginal Land Council v Aboriginal Community Benefit Fund Pty Ltd*.[201] Their broad suggestion was that standing may not be required to be demonstrated to obtain equitable relief in public interest litigation if increased reliance is placed on questions of justiciability and other doctrines.[202] The appropriateness of the Attorney General to act as the enforcer of public rights was defended by McHugh J.[203]

2–072   The dual faceted role of the Attorney General in *Re McBain* was extraordinary. The proceedings were brought to quash a decision of a single judge of the Federal Court regarding the validity of the Infertility Treatment Act 1995 (Vic). The parties to the proceedings did not challenge the decision on appeal. The Australian Catholic Bishops Conference and the Australian Episcopal Conference of the Roman Catholic Church (the Bishops) appeared as amicus curiae. The Bishops subsequently sought relief in the High Court's original jurisdiction for a grant of certiorari to quash the decision. The standing of the Bishops was challenged by the Women's Electoral Lobby (Vic), who was granted leave to intervene in the proceedings for this purpose. Due to the challenge, the Bishops sought and were granted the fiat of the Attorney General to challenge the finding of invalidity of the Infertility Treatment Act on the basis of inconsistency with Sex Discrimination Act 1984 (Cth) only under s.109 of the Constitution. The Bishops also sought to argue, in the alternative, that the relevant provisions of the Sex Discrimination Act were beyond the power of the Commonwealth Parliament but the fiat was not granted with respect to this argument. The Attorney General intervened[204] to argue in favour of the validity of the Sex Discrimination Act. The dual role of the Attorney General was criticised by Gaudron and Gummow JJ.[205] but supported by Kirby J.[206] Gaudron and Gummow JJ. also commented on the use of the

---

[199] *Bateman's Bay* (1998) 194 C.L.R. 247 at 259 (Gaudron, Gummow and Kirby JJ.).
[200] See, e.g. *Re McBain* (2002) 209 C.L.R. 372 in which the Attorney General was both the plaintiff in the relator action and an intervener. Recent statistics have been compiled in C. Saunders and P. Rabbat, "Relator Actions: Practice in Australia and New Zealand" (2002) 13 *Public Law Review* 292, 296.
[201] *Bateman's Bay* (1998) 184 C.L.R. 247 at 262–3 (Gaudron, Gummow and Kirby JJ.).
[202] *Bateman's Bay* (1998) 184 C.L.R. 247 at 263–4.
[203] *Bateman's Bay* (1998) 184 C.L.R. 247 at 276–80.
[204] Pursuant to s.78A of the Judiciary Act 1903 (Cth).
[205] *Re McBain* (2002) 209 C.L.R. 372 at [53] (Gaudron and Gummow JJ.).
[206] *Re McBain* (2002) 209 C.L.R. 372 at [214] (Kirby J.).

Attorney General of the fiat and the right to intervene in the Judiciary Act to attack the integrity of Federal Court decisions through judicial review.[207]

The ADJR Act provides for parties to be joined if the person is a "person 2–073 interested",[208] which is easier to satisfy than the general standing test.[209] Pursuant to the requirements of natural justice, the Australian courts have an inherent power to give leave for non-parties to intervene.[210] Where an applicant's rights are *substantially* affected leave will be granted as of right.[211] Otherwise, leave will be a matter of discretion.[212] The court also has an *absolute* discretion to grant leave to appear as amicus curiae.[213] Kirby J. in *Attorney General (Cth) v Breckler* compared the approach of other jurisdictions and commented on the less embracing and sometimes inconsistent approach of the Australian High Court with respect to amicus curiae.[214]

There also exist statutory rights to intervene. For example, the Attorney 2–074 General has a right to intervene under the ADJR Act[215] and the Human Rights and Equal Opportunity Commission has a statutory function to intervene, if leave is granted, in proceedings that involve human rights and discrimination issues.[216]

Canada

Standing is not a major impediment in Canada to public interest litigation. 2–075 The Supreme Court of Canada extended public interest standing from the constitutional to the administrative law domain in *Finlay v Canada (Minister of Finance)*.[217] While it remains a matter of judicial discretion contingent on a range of factors identified in that decision, for the most part, those factors do not operate to prevent worthy public interest cases being litigated: Is there a justiciable issue (see above)? Is the applicant raising a serious issue? Does the applicant have a genuine interest in the matter? Is there any more effective or appropriate manner or forum for the litigation of these issues? Of these factors, the most significant has been the

---

[207] *Re McBain* (2002) 209 C.L.R. 372 at [76](Gaudron and Gummow J.J). See also C. Maxwell, "In the Line of Fire: Re McBain and the Role of the Attorney General as a Party" (2002) 13 *Public Law Review* 283, 291.
[208] Section 12 of the Administrative Decisions (Judicial Review) Act 1977.
[209] *Lord v Commissioner of Australian Federal Police* (1997) 74 F.C.R. 61 (Lindgren J.), 78.
[210] *Levy v State of Victoria* (1997) 189 C.L.R. 579 at 601 (Brennan C.J.).
[211] *Levy* (1997) 189 C.L.R. 579 (Brennan C.J.) at 603.
[212] *Levy* (1997) 189 C.L.R. 579 (Brennan C.J.) at 603.
[213] *Levy* (1997) 189 C.L.R. 579 (Brennan C.J.) at 604. See also S. Kenny, "Interveners and Amici Curiae in the High Court" (1998) 20 *Adelaide Law Review* 159 and A.F. Mason, "Interveners and Amici Curiae in the High Court: A Comment" (1998) 20 *Adelaide Law Review* 173.
[214] (1999) 197 C.L.R. 83 at 134–7 (Kirby J.).
[215] s.18.
[216] Human Rights and Equal Opportunity Commission Act 1986 (Cth) ss.11(1)(o) and 31(j). See, e.g. *Al-Kateb v Godwin* (2004) 219 C.L.R. 562.
[217] [1986] 2 S.C.R. 607.

last; in *Canadian Council of Churches v Canada (Minister of Employment and Immigration)*,[218] it was used controversially in a constitutional case to deny the Council the ability to mount a broadly-based challenge to provisions in amendments to Canada's immigration legislation. Individual refugee claimants were already before the courts challenging discrete provisions in that legislation. However, it has not proved all that much of an obstacle in subsequent litigation.[219] In fact, the real deterrents to public interest litigation in administrative law settings in Canada are the cost of mounting judicial review applications, the unavailability of legal aid, and exposure to costs awards in the event of the dismissal of the application.

2–076   Third party intervention in judicial review proceedings is permissible in all Canadian jurisdictions, subject to what are a variegated set of rules of courts. In general, the test is the familiar one that those seeking intervener status must have something to contribute to the proceedings beyond what could be expected of the parties. In addition the intervention must not, in effect, amount to a taking over of the applicant's case. Under some rules of court (such as the Supreme Court Rules) the intervention may be confined to submitting a written brief.

India

2–077 Standing does not constitute an important impediment in applications for judicial review. The concept of locus standi has been substantially relaxed.[220] However if the application for judicial review has been filed for personal gain or private profit or political motivation or other oblique considerations the court will not allow its process to be abused.[221] Under Ord.1 r.8A of the Code of Civil Procedure 1908 the Court may, if satisfied that a person or body of persons is interested in any question of law which is directly and substantially in issue in the suit and that it is necessary in the public interest to allow the person or body of persons to present his or its opinion on that question of law, permit that person or body of persons to present such opinion and to take such part in the proceedings of the suit as the Court may specify. This provision will also apply to an application for judicial review. Apart from the aforesaid statutory provision a court may permit an intervention if the court is satisfied that the intervener has a genuine interest in the pending litigation and may be affected one way or the other by its outcome.

---

[218] [1992] 1 S.C.R. 236.
[219] *Vriend v Alberta* [1998] 1 S.C.R. 493 (another constitutional case); *Harris v Canada* [2000] 4 F.C. 37 (administrative law) (and notwithstanding the Federal Courts Act's provision seemingly requiring that applicants for relief be "directly affected"); and *Canadian Egg Marketing Agency v Richardson* [1998] 3 S.C.R. 157 (seemingly accepting that the courts possess an overriding discretion to allow an application to proceed even where the challenger does not meet the normal *Finlay* requirements).
[220] *Guruvayoor Dewaswom Managing Committee v CK Rajan* 2003 (7) S.C.C. 546 at 569(iv)
[221] *Kushum Lata v Union of India* 2006 (6) S.C.C. 180 at 187 para.18.

New Zealand

In New Zealand, standing as a threshold issue is almost a dead letter. In a **2–078** small country with a judicial review caseload of less than a hundred cases a year the floodgates have not opened without any noticeable standing requirement operating since the mid-1980s.[222] (Moreover, there are no time limits—short of the six years statute of limitations—and no requirement to obtain leave to bring review proceedings). The liberalising trend (in line with the *National Federation* case)[223] has meant that questions of standing will normally require examination of the substantive issues and does not preclude ventilation of the merits of the challenge. Concerns about standing are rolled into the exercise of judicial discretion at the end of the proceedings as to what if any remedy to grant.[224] Standing as a preliminary requirement remains theoretically available as a filter at the outset for crazy cases and people, but is very rarely invoked.[225]

Standing in New Zealand has never recovered from the ill-fated attempt **2–079** in 1985 of the New Zealand Rugby Union to defeat a challenge to the constitutionality of the Union's decision to accept an invitation to tour the (then) apartheid South Africa. In a somewhat controversial decision the Court of Appeal held two rugby players to have standing to challenge the decision.[226] The upshot was delay and ultimately the substantive litigation was settled and the 1985 tour abandoned by the Rugby Union.[227] One of the last significant cases where the courts refused judicial review for lack of standing was *Wall v Livingston*,[228] where a third party (a paediatrician who had seen the expectant mother in hospital on an matter unrelated to her pregnancy) sought unsuccessfully to challenge on review the certification of two consultants that an abortion was necessary on health grounds. The judicial review proceeding foundered at first instance on the ground that the applicant had no standing, a view upheld by way of *obiter* in the Court of Appeal. It was said there that only those involved in the statutory decision-making could be regarded as having sufficient interest and therefore standing to challenge the certification. Nearly 25 years later, a High Court judge refused to strike out a wide-ranging challenge to the discharge of the Abortion Supervisory Committee's statutory obligations.[229] The earlier case of *Wall v Livingston* was distinguished as that was a challenge to a particular abortion decision by consultants whereas the pro-life

---

[222] See Sir Ivor Richardson, "Public Interest Litigation" (1995) 3 *Waikato Law Review* 1 at 12.
[223] See 2–017.
[224] See, e.g. *Murray v Whakatane District Council* [1997] N.Z.R.M.A. 433 at 465–6 (HC, Elias J.) and *Society for the Protection of Auckland City and Waterfront Inc v Auckland City Council* [2001] N.Z.R.M.A. 209 (HC, Morris J.).
[225] cf. *Holloway v Auckland City Council* (1988) 7 N.Z.A.R. 271 (HC, Barker J.).
[226] *Finnigan v New Zealand Rugby Football Union Inc* [1985] 2 N.Z.L.R. 159, CA.
[227] See generally M. Taggart, "Rugby, the Anti-Apartheid Movement and Administrative Law" in R. Bigwood (ed.), *Law, Social Policy and the Role of the Courts* (2006), p.69.
[228] [1982] 1 N.Z.L.R. 734, CA.
[229] *Right to Life New Zealand Inc v Rothwell* [2006] 1 N.Z.L.R. 531.

charitable society in *Rothwell* was seeking review of the performance of the Committee' statutory functions to oversee the process and indirectly protect the interests of the unborn child.[230]

2–080   At the High Court level in the case reported on appeal as *Curtis v Minister of Defence*,[231] the Crown challenged the standing of the applicant-organiser of a "Save our Squadrons" campaign created to persuade the government to change its decision to disband the air combat wing of the air force. The trial judge, Heron J., said there was "some force" in his counsel's submission that the applicant represented "a responsible public interest group and that unless people like him had standing "there may be no effective way of establishing whether or not the executive is acting within its lawful powers".[232] The trial judge preferred to deal with the substantive challenge, which he struck out as non-justiciable (a finding upheld on appeal).

South Africa

2–081 In the pre-democratic era (i.e. before the coming into force of the interim Constitution in 1994), the common-law rules of standing imposed a strict requirement of "sufficient interest", which was a very significant impediment in the area of public law. The interest held had to be personal and direct.[233] But after 1994, the South African courts recognised that the rules of standing operated differently in the private and public arenas. In *Ferreira v Levin NO*, O'Regan J. said that while the interest which parties have in private litigation is often direct and intimate, the harm alleged in litigation of a public nature "may often be quite diffuse or amorphous".[234]

2–082   The Constitution adopted in 1996 now offers far more liberal grounds on which to approach courts for relief. Section 38 of the Constitution lists five classes of persons who may approach a competent court alleging that a right in the Bill of Rights has been infringed or is threatened. These classes include classes familiar to the common law, such as anyone acting in his or her own interest (s.38(a)), anyone acting on behalf of another who cannot act in his or her own name (s.38(b)), and an association acting on behalf of its members (s.38(e)). But s.38 also introduces new standing provisions into South African law: s.38(c) and (d) respectively allow that "anyone acting as a member of, or in the interest of, a group or class of persons" and "anyone acting in the public interest" may approach a court alleging that a breach of rights in the Bill of Rights has occurred or is imminent. Academic

---

[230] At [39].
[231] [2002] 2 N.Z.L.R. 744, CA.
[232] *Curtis v Minister of Defence*, High Court Wellington, CP 253/01, November 20, 2001, [16].
[233] *Jacobs v Waks* 1992 (1) S.A. 521 (A) at 534–6, *Independent Food Processors (Pty) Ltd v Minister of Agriculture* 1993 (4) S.A. 294 (C) *Verstappen v Port Edward Town Board* 1994 (3) S.A. 569 (D).
[234] 1996 (1) S.A. 984, CC, para.229.

commentators have suggested that the generous standing provisions of s.38 of the Constitution must be "read into" the Promotion of Administrative Justice Act 2000 (the statute passed to give effect to the right to just administrative action in the Bill of Right).[235] Indeed, the Act itself seems to contemplate a wider approach to standing than previously available at common law. Section 33 of the Constitution confers on everyone the right to administrative action that is lawful, reasonable and procedurally fair. The PAJA gives effect to this right, and defines "administrative action" in doing so. One of the requirements of administrative action is that it "adversely affects the rights of any person". Wherever action affects the rights of any person—and meets all the other criteria of "administrative action"—it must comply with the requirements of the right to administrative justice. In addition, s.6(1) of the PAJA provides that "any person may institute proceedings in a court or a tribunal for the judicial review of an administrative action". Anyone can approach a court for review of an administrative action, even where it is not his or her own right that is adversely affected.[236] This is clearly what is contemplated in s.38 of the Constitution where the right affected is a right in the Bill of Rights, since the section establishes class actions and a right of action in the public interest. But the PAJA seems to create a class action or cause of action in the public interest even where ordinary, non-Bill of Rights rights are concerned.

---

[235] C. Hoexter, *Administrative Law in South Africa* (2007), p.441; J. De Ville, *Judicial Review of Administrative Action in South Africa* (2005), p.401.

[236] Courts have softened the "adverse" requirement, however, indicating that an effect on rights will be sufficient to meet the requirements of the definition. See *Greys Marine Hout Bay (Pty) Ltd v Minister of Public Works and others* [2005] All S.A. 33 (SCA), where it was stated that the definition "was probably intended rather to convey that administrative action is action that has the capacity to affect legal rights".

CHAPTER 3

DEFENDANTS AND DECISIONS SUBJECT TO JUDICIAL REVIEW

SCOPE

This chapter examines the law, principles and policy relating to the 3–001 following questions.

- Which functions[1] of public authorities are amenable to judicial review? A wide range of governmental decision-making is potentially challengeable by judicial review claims. The Administrative Court may, however, decline to review the exercise of a function on the basis that it lacks jurisdiction; challenges to some functions of public authorities may be regarded as non-justiciable; and the court may refuse to hear a case in the exercise of its discretion having regard to a range of factors including the existence of alternative remedies.

- In what circumstances may public functions of office-holders and bodies which are not formal institutions of the State be subject to judicial review?[2] In recent years challenges have been brought against the exercise of functions of (for example) non-statutory self-regulatory bodies, members' clubs, religious organisations, universities, and front-line service providers with which public authorities have contracted.

- Which public functions may be subject to judicial review claims on the ground that they unlawfully interfere with a Convention right, contrary to s.6 of the HRA?[3]

- What is the territorial reach of the Administrative Court's supervisory jurisdiction and the HRA?

- Where a matter falls within the Administrative Court's judicial review jurisdiction, is it mandatory for a claimant to use CPR Pt 54 (the claim for judicial review procedure) or is it permissible to use one of the

[1] We use "functions" as a collective term for the whole array of decisions, actions, omissions, legislation, etc that may be the subject of challenge in judicial review proceedings. As has been noted, "The question in any particular case is not whether the decision-maker is, in general terms, amenable to judicial review, but whether a particular decision is": M. Supperstone and E. Laing, "The Ambit of Judicial Review", Ch.5 in M. Supperstone, J. Goudie and P. Walker (eds), *Judicial Review*, 3rd edn (2005).
[2] See 3–041.
[3] See 3–069.

other ways of commencing a civil claim?[4] If this is not permissible this would be an example of what is known as the principle of procedural exclusivity.[5]

- How, in outline, do other jurisdictions deal with issues of amenability to review?[6]

In the past these questions have often been addressed in terms suggesting that there is a divide separating public law and private law. For several years this distinction caused more controversy between distinguished commentators than any other aspect of English administrative law. While most, if not all, developed legal systems recognise some degree of distinction between public and private law,[7] in England and Wales the law and procedural rules relating to judicial review have now developed in ways which make broad references to "public law" and "private law" less helpful than they may have been in the past because these terms beg important questions. In contrast, the terms "public authority", "public function" and "functions of a public nature" are terms now recognised in the common law developments and legislation.[8] In many contexts with which we are concerned, the term "public" is a synonym for "governmental" rather than referring to a decision affecting the general public, though in many situation these two senses coincide.[9]

RANGE OF PUBLIC AUTHORITIES SUBJECT TO JUDICIAL REVIEW

3–002 British constitutional law does not have any single "juristic conception of the State".[10] Nor is there any precise concept of "the executive" or "executive power"; central government is "more plural than unitary".[11] In recent times, governance is said to be "multi-level" and "fragmented", with interventions

---

[4] The alternatives to CPR Pt 54 are Pt 7 ("How to start proceedings") and Pt 8 ("Alternative procedure for claims", used primarily where a claimant seeks "the court's decision on a question which is unlikely to involve a substantial dispute of fact"). Pt 54 takes Part 8 as its starting point but greatly modifies it: see 16–008.

[5] See 3–097. See also collateral challenges (where public law issues are raised by way of a defence to a civil claim or criminal prosecution), dealt with at 4–064.

[6] See 3–105.

[7] See C. Szladits, *International Encyclopaedia of Comparative Law*, Vol.2, paras 25, 31, 57. As was pointed out by Lord Goff in *Re Norway's Application*, "the identification of public law matters differs from country to country, sometimes in minor respects and sometimes in major respects" [1990] 1 A.C. 723, at 802–3. See further 1–003.

[8] CPR Pt 54.1 and HRA ss.6–7, discussed at 3–041 and 3–69.

[9] *Aston Cantlow v Aston Cantlow and Wilmcote with Billesley Parochial Church Council* [2003] UKHL 37; [2004] 1 A.C. 546, at [6]–[7] (Lord Nicholls of Birkenhead, in the context of HRA s.6); *Mullins v The Board of Appeal of the Jockey Club* [2005] EWHC 2197 (Burnton J., in the context of amenability to judicial review generally).

[10] J. McLean, "The Crown in Contract and Administrative Law" (2004) 24 O.J.L.S. 129, 131.

[11] T. Daintith and A. Page, *The Executive in the Constitution: Structure, Autonomy and Internal Control* (1999).

from central and local government, actions by the voluntary sector (charities) and much practical delivery of public services contracted out to business enterprises. Across many fields, laws and decisions taken at European Union level—and sometimes also at international level—also have influence. It is therefore unsurprising that a wide range of public authorities and other organisations carrying out public functions find themselves subject to judicial review claims. Almost all judicial review claims are brought against functions exercised by office-holders and institutions that are clearly part of the formal machinery of government,[12] though as we examine below in a relatively small number of cases issues arise as to the amenability of non-State actors.

Central government

The Secretary of State is the mostly commonly challenged office-holder in **3–003** central government.[13] There is in constitutional law a single office of Secretary of State; unless stated otherwise in an Act, any of the various Secretaries of State in existence at a given time (. . . for the Home Department, . . . for Health) may lawfully exercise powers conferred on "the Secretary of State".[14] Convention and practice may dictate otherwise, however. The office of Lord High Chancellor of Great Britain is distinct from that of Secretary of State,[15] though since 2003 the minister holding the post of Lord Chancellor has held office as Secretary of State as well (first, as Secretary of State for Constitutional Affairs then, since May 2007, as Secretary of State for Justice). The naming of the relevant Secretary of State as the defendant is different from the practice in relation to "civil proceedings" (typically claims for damages) where the defendant is normally the Department.[16] Since the 1980s, there has been a split throughout central

[12] In accordance with Crown Proceedings Act 1947 s.17, the Cabinet Office from time to time prepares a list (published on the Treasury Solicitor's Department website) of authorised government departments for the purpose of identifying the department by and against which "civil proceedings" may be brought. Claims for judicial review are not "civil proceedings" (see 18–007); the defendants specified on that list are in the main *Departments* whereas in judicial review the *Secretary of State*, as the person empowered to carry out the impugned function, should be the defendant; but that list contains useful information about addresses for service.

[13] For an overview of central government, see D. Feldman (ed.), *English Public Law* (2004), Ch.3. Overall, challenges to decisions taken by central government departments amount on average to 20% of the total case load (leaving aside immigration and asylum applications): see M. Sunkin, K. Calvo, L. Platt and T. Landman, "Mapping the Use of Judicial Review to Challenge Local Authorities in England and Wales" [2007] P.L. 545.

[14] A. Simcock, "One and Many: the Office of Secretary of State" (1992) 70 Pub. Admin. 535.

[15] Constitutional Reform Act 2005 ss.2, 17. Certain functions of the Lord Chancellor are, by the 2005 Act, entrenched and cannot be transferred to other ministers by order under the Ministers of the Crown Act 1975. A claimant proposing to seek judicial review of a decision taken within the Ministry of Justice, or one of its executive agencies, will need to identify whether the function in question is one that is exercised by the Lord Chancellor or the Secretary of State for Justice; on this division of responsibilities, see House of Lords Select Committee on the Constitution, *Relations Between the Executive, Judiciary and Parliament*, HL Paper No.151 (Session 2006/07), Appendix 7.

[16] Civil Proceedings Act 1947 s.17. Judicial review claims are not "civil proceedings": see 18–007.

government between policy-formation (dealt with by Departments directly) and the delivery of services and practical administration dealt with by "executive agencies", staffed by civil servants but working under a chief executive at arm's length from the Department. In some situations it may be appropriate for an executive agency rather than a Secretary of State to be the defendant.[17] Many different non-departmental public bodies (NDPBs) also find the exercise of their functions challenged by judicial review.[18] In cases of doubt as to which public authority is the appropriate defendant, claims may be made against the Attorney General.[19] In British constitutional law, the civil service have no legal or constitutional personality separate from the Government or ministers.[20]

Local and devolved government

3–004 There are, at the time of writing, some 410 local authorities in England and Wales, with plans to encourage more parish councils as a tier of decision-making in each local authority area.[21] Challenges to decisions taken by local authorities typically constitute some 46 per cent of the annual judicial review case load (leaving aside immigration and asylum applications). Local author-

---

[17] See, e.g. *R. (Ann Summers Ltd) v Jobcentre Plus* [2003] EWHC 1416—the defendant being an executive agency of the Department for Work and Pensions—and *R. v Vehicle Inspectorate Ex p. Healy* [2001] R.T.R. 17. Practice seems to vary; in many other cases a Secretary of State under whose Department the executive agency operates is the defendant. Some executive agencies have legal personality (and in these cases may be made the defendant) whereas others lack a distinct legal personality (and here the relevant Secretary of State should be the defendant). See *R. (on the application of National Association of Health Stores) v Secretary of State for Health* [2005] EWCA Civ 154, at [40]–[41], where the potential difficulties are noted.

[18] The following have all been subject to judicial review challenge in recent years: Agriculture Wages Board of England and Wales; Audit Commission; British Broadcasting Corporation; Boundary Commission for England; Central Arbitration Committee (responsible for adjudicating on the recognition of trade unions); Commissioners of Customs and Excise, Special Commissioners of Income Tax and the Inland Revenue Commissioners; Civil Aviation Authority; Competition Commission; Construction Industry Training Board; Criminal Cases Review Commission; Criminal Injuries Compensation Appeals Board; Housing Corporation; English Nature; Environment Agency; Food Standards Agency; Forestry Commissioners; Gaming Board for Great Britain; Home Office Policy Advisory Board for Forensic Pathology; Horseracing Betting Levy Board; Human Fertilisation and Embryology Authority; Independent Police Complaints Authority; Legal Services Commission; Licensing Authority established under the Medicines Act 1968; Postal Services Commission; Rent Assessment Committees and panels; Medical Referees; National Asylum Support Service; National Care Standards Commission (superseded by two other inspectorates in 2004); several of the National Park Authorities; NHS Trusts and Primary Care Trusts; Office of the Schools Adjudicator; Rail Regulator; Standards Board for England (promoting ethical conduct in local government). A database of all NDPBs is published by the Cabinet Office.

[19] See e.g. *R. (on the application of Countryside Alliance) v Attorney General* [2005] EWHC 1677; [2006] Eu. L.R. 178 (whether Hunting Act 2005 breached Convention rights). This follows the practice specified by Crown Proceedings Act 1947 s.17(3) (though claims for judicial review are not "civil proceedings").

[20] On the *Carltona* principle, see 5–162.

[21] For an overview, see S. Bailey, "The Structure, Powers and Accountability fo Local Government", Ch.4 in D. Feldman (ed.), *English Public Law* (2004).

ities exercise statutory functions across a broad spectrum, the most challenged being: housing; homelessness;[22] community care; environmental planning; education; housing benefit; and family-related.[23]

The National Assembly for Wales and the Welsh Assembly Government are amenable to judicial review.[24]

Criminal justice system

Where the dispute as to the lawfulness of the exercise of a public function 3–005 relates to the criminal justice system, in addition to the Secretary of State for the Home Department and the Secretary of State for Justice (the ministers with responsibilities for this field), defendants may include: Chief Constables of Police;[25] the Crown Prosecution Service; the Director of Public Prosecutions (DPP); the Director of the Serious Fraud Office; prison governors; the National Parole Service; the Parole Board; the Criminal Cases Review Commission; and the Serious Organised Crime Agency.

Some of decisions made by HM Attorney General in relation to instituting 3–006 and stopping prosecutions may fall outside the court's supervisory jurisdiction altogether.[26] Even where matters are within the court's jurisdiction, there is a marked reluctance exercise that supervisory jurisdiction over police decisions to investigate,[27] charge, and administer cautions;[28] and decisions of the DPP to prosecute, continue or discontinue criminal prosecutions.[29] The court will generally do so only if there is a grave abuse of power or a clear breach of the police or prosecuting authority's settled policy. Claimants will also be expected to use other alternative remedies (such as an application to the relevant criminal court to dismiss or stay the criminal proceedings on the ground that they are an abuse of the process, or to utilise any route of appeal that may exist).[30]

[22] Despite the existence of a remedy in the form of an appeal on point of law to the county courts: see 17–045.

[23] Sunkin et al ([2007] P.L. 545); there is a concentration on challenges in the London Boroughs.

[24] So far, the challenges to the National Assembly for Wales (established by the Government of Wales Act 1998; now the Government of Wales Act 2006) have mainly concerned environmental planning matters.

[25] See, e.g. R. (on the application of R) v Durham Constabulary [2005] UKHL 21; [2005] 1 W.L.R. 1184 (whether warning given to young offender compatible with ECHR Art.6).

[26] See, 3–019.

[27] cf. R. v Commissioner of Police of the Metropolis, Ex p Blackburn [1968] 2 Q.B. 118 (unlawful for Commissioner to issue instructions to officers not to enforce provisions of the Betting, Gaming and Lotteries Act 1963, except with his approval, because of manpower constraints and legal complexities).

[28] See, e.g. R. (on the application of Mondelly) v Commissioner of Police of the Metropolis [2006] EWHC 2370 (Admin); (2007) 171 J.P. 121; R. v Chief Constable of Kent Ex p. L [1993] 1 All E.R. 756; R. v Commissioner of Police of the Metropolis Ex p. Thompson [1997] 1 W.L.R. 1519.

[29] R. v DPP Ex p. Kebilene [2000] 2 A.C. 326 (absent "dishonesty or mala fide or an exceptional circumstance" decisions by the DPP to consent to a prosecution are not amenable to judicial review); cf. R. v DPP Ex p. Manning [2001] Q.B. 330 (challenge to decision not to bring prosecution); R. v DPP Ex p. Duckenfield [2000] 1 W.L.R. 55.

[30] See 16–018.

Administrative justice system

3–007 Public authorities that handle peoples' grievances also fall within the supervisory jurisdiction of the Administrative Court. Thus, judicial review claims may be brought against tribunals,[31] ombudsmen[32] and public inquiries.[33]

Courts

3–008 The Administrative Court's jurisdiction over other courts generally extends only to courts and tribunals of inferior jurisdiction; decisions of the superior courts of record—the House of Lords, Court of Appeal and the High Court—are outside the scope of judicial review (though judges of the higher courts may be subject to judicial review when exercising specific statutory power separate from the courts in which they sit).[34]

Criminal cases

3–009 A significant proportion of the Administrative Court's load is judicial review claims and appeals by way of case stated against the decisions of the criminal courts.[35] The prosecution and defence may challenge magistrates' courts' decision, or decision of the Crown Court on appeal from the magistrates, by claim for judicial review. In 2001 Sir Robin Auld's review of the criminal courts of England and Wales recommended that the Adminsitrative Court's supervisory jurisdiction over criminal courts be replaced with with new routes of appeal to the Court of Appeal (Criminal Appeal).[36] The Government accepted this and the Law Commission is currently (in 2007) considering how this may best be achieved.[37] There are, however, several different existing appeal routes and judicial review will only be permitted in the absense of such an appropriate alternative remedy.[38] The position of the Crown Court (the highest level criminal trial court in England and Wales) requires special analysis. Although it is a superior court of record, some of its decisions are amenable to judicial review.[39] The situation is regulated by

[31] See 1–093.
[32] See 1–081.
[33] See 1–097.
[34] For example, the Master of the Rolls, when exercising his powers in relation to appeals under the Solicitors Act 1974, is subject to judicial review: *R. v Master of the Rolls Ex P. McKinnell* [1993] 1 W.L.R. 88. *cf. R. (on the application of Bulger) v Secretary of State for the Home Department* [2001] EWHC Admin 119; [2001] 3 All E.R. 449 (decision of Lord Chief Justice of England and Wales on tariff).
[35] See 1–045.
[36] *Review of the Criminal Courts of England and Wales*, Ch.12.
[37] Law Commission, *Judicial Review of Decisions of the Crown Court* (July 2005).
[38] See 16–016 and 17–036. *cf. R. v Hereford Magistrates' Court Ex p. Rowlands* [1998] Q.B. 110 in which the Divisional Court held that the existence of a right of appeal by way of retrial in the Crown Court did not preclude a person convicted in a magistrates' court from applying for judicial review on the grounds of procedural impropriety, unfairness or bias.
[39] The historical explanation for this is that the Crown Court was created by the amalgamation of one court that was and another that was not subject to the High Court's supervisory jurisdiction: see *In re Smalley* [1985] A.C. 622, at 640 (Lord Bridge).

s.29(3) of the Supreme Court Act (Senior Courts Act) 1981, derived from s.10 of the Courts Act 1971: "In relation to the jurisdiction of the Crown Court, other than its jurisdiction in matters relating to trial on indictment, the High Court shall have all such jurisdiction to make mandatory, prohibiting or quashing orders as the High Court possesses in relation to the jurisdiction of an inferior court".[40] The phrase "matters relating to trials on indictment" has proved to be problematic.[41] The restriction applies even when a claimant seeks only a declaration.[42]

Civil cases

The Administrative Court has jurisdiction to determine judicial review claims   3–010
against decisions of the county courts; s.54(4) of the Access to Justice Act 1999, which provides for appeals from county courts and restricts *appeals* against the refusal of permission to pursue such an appeal, does not oust that jurisdiction.[43] But the statutory appeal routes will in almost all cases be a more appropriate remedy than judicial review, and the Administrative Court will refuse permission for a judicial review claim save in the most exceptional circumstances.[44]

Legislation

As noted in Chapter 1, whereas in the past judicial review challenges focused   3–011
on administrative action, the court's supervisory jurisdiction now clearly covers legislation.[45] Byelaws made by local authorities and other public authorities have for many years been amenable to judicial review.[46] So too

---

[40] R. Ward, "Judicial Review and Trials on Indictment" [1990] P.L. 50; *R. v Crown Court at Leeds Ex p. Hussain* [1995] 1 W.L.R. 1329; *R. v Crown Court at Manchester Ex p. H* [2000] 1 W.L.R. 760.

[41] It has been considered by the House of Lords five times over the past 20 years; for detailed analysis see Law Commission, *Judicial Review of Decisions of the Crown Court* (July 2005). For a survey see *R. (on the application of H) v Wood Green Crown Court* [2006] EWHC 2683; [2007] 2 All E.R. 259.

[42] *R. v Chelmsford Crown Court Ex p. Chief Constable of Essex* [1994] 1 W.L.R. 359.

[43] *R. (on the application of Sivasubramaniam) v Wandsworth County Court* [2002] EWCA Civ 1738; [2003] 1 W.L.R. 475.

[44] *Sivasubramaniam* [2002] EWCA Civ 1738; [2003] 1 W.L.R. 475; the "possibility remains that there may be very rare cases where a litigant challenges the jurisdiction of a circuit judge giving or refusing permission to appeal on the ground of jurisdictional error in the narrow, pre-*Anisminic* sense, or procedural irregularity of such a kind as to constitute a denial of the applicant's right to a fair hearing. If such grounds are made out we consider that a proper case for judicial review will have been established" (Lord Phillips of Matravers M.R. at [54]); see also *Gregory v Turner* [2003] EWCA Civ 183; [2003] 1 W.L.R. 1149, at [29]–[31], [37]–[46], where even though the CA expressed "serious concern that something may have gone wrong in connection with the district judge's handling of the case", and acknowledged that the judge refusing permission to appeal had not had the "crucial errors" drawn to his attention, the case was not one in which judicial review was appropriate.

[45] See 1–005.

[46] See e.g. *R. (on the application of Mott) v Ministry of Agriculture, Fisheries and Food* [2000] C.O.D. 183 (National Salmon Byelaws 1999 made by the Environment Agency); *Boddington v British Transport Police* [1999] 2 A.C. 143 (British Railways Board Byelaws 1965, on smoking); *R. v Ministry of Agriculture, Fisheries and Food Ex p. Bray* [1999] C.O.D. 187 (byelaw made by the Sussex Sea Fisheries Committee regulating fishing vessels).

are Statutory Instruments made by ministers,[47] including those passed by affirmative resolution of Parliament.[48] All grounds of review, substantive as well as procedural, may be invoked against secondary legislation.[49] The court is not confined to giving declaratory relief; a quashing order may be made,[50] either of the whole instrument or, if an offending provision is severable, of that provision.[51]

3–012   Although parliamentary supremacy remains a general principle of the British constitution, the court's supervisory jurisdiction now—in important albeit limited ways—extends to primary legislation. European Community law requires national courts to disapply legislative provisions, including those in Acts of Parliament, where they are incompatible with Community law norms.[52] Section 4 of the Human Rights Act 1998 also provides the courts with power to make declarations of incompatibility in relation to primary legislation: though this stops well short of creating judicial review of Acts of Parliament, it nonetheless has given the higher courts a role in evaluating whether Parliament's enactments are consistent with Convention rights.[53]

"Judicial review" outside CPR Pt 54

3–013   The primary focus of this Chapter is on amenability to claims for judicial review under CPR Pt 54,[54] but some public authorities are subject to judicial review independently of CPR Pt 54. Several Acts of Parliament provide that various tribunals and courts other than the Administrative Court have specific powers to adjudicate by "applying the principles applied by the court on an application for judicial review". These include: the Information Tribunal; [55] the High Court exercising supervisory jurisdiction over the making of non-derogating control orders;[56] the Competition Appeal Tribunal;[57] the tribunal established by the Regulation of Investigatory Powers Act 2000;[58] the Proscribed Organisations Appeal Commission;[59] and the Pathongens Access Appeal Commission.[60]

[47] See, e.g. *R. (Middlebrook Mushrooms Ltd) v Agricultural Wages Board of England and Wales* [2004] EWHC 1447 (Admin) (Agricultural Wages Order 2003 (No.1)); *R. v Secretary of State for Education and Employment Ex p. National Union of Teachers* [2000] Ed. C.R. 603; *R. v Secretary of State for Employment Ex p. Seymour-Smith* [1996] All E.R. (EC) 1.
[48] See, e.g. *R. (on the application of Javed) v Secretary of State for the Home Department* [2001] EWCA Civ 789; [2002] Q.B. 129 (Asylum (Designated Countries of Destination and Designated Safe Third Countries) Order 1996).
[49] *Javed* [2001] EWCH Civ 789; [2002] Q.B. 129.
[50] *R. v Secretary of State for Social Services Ex p. Association of Metropolitan Authorities* [1986] 1 W.L.R. 1 (quashing order refused in court's discretion); *R. v Secretary of State for Health Ex p. US Tobacco International* [1992] 1 Q.B. 353 (quashing order made).
[51] *Middlebrook Mushrooms*, [2004] EWHC 1447 at [90]. On severability, see 5–135.
[52] See 14–009.
[53] See 13–045.
[54] See Ch.16.
[55] Adjudicating on rights under the Data Protection Act 1998 and the Freedom of Information Act 2000 (on which, see 16–026).
[56] Prevention of Terrorism Act 2005 s.3(11).
[57] Enterprise Act 2002 ss.120, 179.
[58] s.67.
[59] Terrorism Act 2000 ss.5(3), 9(3).
[60] Anti-Terrorism, Crime and Security Act 2001 s.70.

There are also appeals on a point of law to the county courts in   3–014
homelessness cases.[61] In addition, various applications and appeals can be
made to the High Court.[62] They can be brought on grounds of appeal that
are basically the same as the grounds for judicial review. The Tribunals,
Courts and Enforcement Act 2007 empowers the Upper Tribunal to carry
out "judicial review" (quotation marks are used in the Act) in respect of
decisions of the First-tier Tribunal if certain conditions are met; not only is
adjudication on the basis of the substantive principles of judicial review, but
the Upper Tribunal follows a procedure similar to that of the Administrative
Court and may grant judicial review remedies.[63]

JURISDICTION, JUSTICIABILITY AND DISCRETION

There is an obvious need to set a boundary— for practical and constitutional   3–015
reasons—on the reach of the Administrative Court's role. In the past, the
development of English administrative law was impeded by rigid distinctions
made by the court between functions which were classified as "legislative",
"administrative", "judicial", and "quasi-judicial".[64] These categories no
longer determine whether a function is amenable to judicial review. The
boundary is now set using three main techniques by: defining the jurisdiction
of the court; holding some functions to be "non-justiciable" (even though
not falling outside the court's jurisdiction); and exercising the court's
discretion to refuse permission to proceed with a claim.[65] The courts have
regrettably not always maintained a clear distinction between these techniques, for example describing a function as "non-justiciable" when it is
more properly to be thought of as falling outside the courts' jurisdiction.

Jurisdiction of the Administrative Court

A starting point for analysing which functions are, and are not, amenable to   3–016
judicial review is to ascertain the extent of the Administrative Court's
supervisory jurisdiction.[66] In this context the term jurisdiction means the
"courts have power to enquire into such a claim and consider whether any
relief is called for".[67] The court's jurisdiction stems from the common law, is

---

[61] See 17–045. But note that the Lord Chancellor is prohibited from making Orders allocating
claims for judicial review to the county court: see Courts and Legal Services Act 1990 s.1(10).
[62] See Ch.17.
[63] ss.15–21.
[64] See Appendix B, below.
[65] On these terms, see A. Le Sueur, "Justifying Judicial Caution: Jurisdiction, Justiciability and
Policy", Ch.8 in B. Hadfield (ed.), *Judicial Review: A Thematic Approach* (1995), where it was
argued that the justification for not intervening in cases has shifted from reliance on the
concept of jurisdiction to discretionary factors and non-justiciability. See also M. Beloff,
"Judicial Review—2001: A Prophetic Odyssey" (1995) 58 M.L.R. 143.
[66] For a historical account of the development of the supervisory jurisdiction see Ch.15.
[67] *Bahamas District of the Methodist Church in the Caribbean and the Americas v Symonette*
[2000] UKPC 31; (2002–03) 5 I.T.E.L.R. 311 at [32]. The recognition of jurisdiction is
distinct from the question whether a claimant has a cause of action or grounds of judicial
review (see [36]). On questions relating to so-called jurisdictional and non-jurisdictional
errors *by public authorities*—where the focus is on the powers (or jurisdiction) of the
decision-maker rather than of the court—see 4–007.

subject to precedent, and may be restricted by statute. This constitutional arrangement is reflected in s.29 of the Supreme Court Act (Senior Courts Act) 1981, as amended, which provides:

"(1A) The High Court shall have jurisdiction to make mandatory, prohibiting and quashing orders in those classes of case in which, immediately before 1st May 2004, it had jurisdiction to make orders of mandamus, prohibition and certiorari respectively."[68]

3–017 The forerunners of this statutory provision provided that judicial review remedial orders could be granted by the High Court "in those classes of case which it had power to do so immediately before the commencement of this Act".[69] This statutory statement is declaratory of the existing jurisdiction and should not be regarded as exhaustive. It is capable of development by the courts in response to changing circumstances because ultimately its source lies in the prerogative or inherent power of the judiciary of the High Court, which has never been comprehensively defined.

3–018 As we shall discuss below, the main touchstones for determining that a function falls within the court's supervisory jurisdiction are now (a) that the source of the decision-maker's authority is a statutory provision or prerogative power[70] and (b) that the function has a public character.[71] The question is not so much whether there is power to award one of the public law remedial orders, but whether in a more general sense the matter in dispute falls within the court's public law supervisory jurisdiction.

Public functions outside the court's jurisdiction

3–019 Despite the expansion of judicial review,[72] there are situations in which the court has no jurisdiction. Matters falling into these "forbidden areas"[73] or "Alsatia",[74] include the following categories in which, as a matter of law, the

---

[68] The significance of the date May 1, 2004 is that it was on this day that the Supreme Court Act 1981 was amended to alter the names of some of the remedies available on claims for judicial review: orders of certiorari became quashing orders; prohibition, prohibiting orders; and mandamus, mandatory orders. See The Civil Procedure (Modification of Supreme Court Act 1981) Order 2004.

[69] Supreme Court Act 1981 s.29 (before amendment); Administration of Justice (Miscellaneous Provisions) Act 1938.

[70] See 3–029.

[71] See 3–041.

[72] See 1–005.

[73] A term used in *R. (on the application of Abassi) v Secretary of State for Foreign and Commonwealth Affairs* [2002] EWCA Civ 1598; [2003] U.K.H.R.R. 76, at [106] (Lord Phillips M.R.).

[74] A reference to an area adjacent to the Temple in London where during the 15th–17th centuries the courts' writs did not run and which accordingly provided sanctuary for criminals. See, e.g. *R. (on the application of UMBS Online Ltd v Serious Organised Crime Agency* [2007] EWCA Civ 406, at [58] (Sedley L.J.: "In setting up the Serious Organised Crime Agency, the state has set out to create an Alsatia—a region of executive action free of judicial oversight. Although the statutory powers can intrude heavily, and sometimes

court may not embark on an inquiry into a claim beyond satisfying itself that the case does truly fall within the relevant no-go area.

(a) Challenges to decisions relating to the internal procedures of the United Kingdom Parliament, reflecting the constitutional principle of parliamentary privilege.[75]

(b) Challenges to decisions relating to the validity of provisions contained in Acts of Parliament, reflecting the constitutional principle of the supremacy of Parliament. This is now subject to several exceptions: the court's duty to disapply provisions which are not in compliance with European Community law;[76] the court's discretion to make a declaration of incompatibility with Convention rights under s.4 of the Human Rights Act 1998;[77] questions of implied repeal of an earlier provision by a later one;[78] and questions relating to the application of the Parliament Acts 1911 and 1949.[79]

(c) Challenges to decisions made by the superior courts of England and Wales (the Upper Tribunal,[80] High Court, Court of Appeal and House of Lords). Historically, the prerogative writs[81] extended only to inferior courts (today, principally in the form of magistrates' courts and the county courts) and tribunals.[82] The Crown Court is a superior court of record but is made amenable to judicial review to some extent by s.29(3) of the Supreme Court Act (Senior Courts Act) 1981.[83]

---

ruinously, into civil rights and obligations, the supervisory role which the court would otherwise have is limited by its primary obligation to give effect to Parliament's clearly expressed intentions. But, except where the statute prevents it, the scheme must also accommodate what Byles J. in *Cooper v Wandsworth Board of Works* (1863) 14 C.B.N.S. 180 called the justice of the common law. That is the duality we have sought to recognise in deciding this case").

[75] *Prebble v Television New Zealand Ltd* [1995] 1 A.C. 321 at 332, PC (Lord Browne-Wilkinson) (parliamentary privilege prevents the use of statements made in Parliament being used as evidence of justification in libel proceedings); *R. v Parliamentary Commissioner for Standards Ex p. Fayed* [1998] 1 W.L.R. 669 (it fell to Parliament, not the courts, to supervise the work of the PCS). Bill of Rights 1689 Art.9 provides "That the freedom of speech and debates or proceedings in Parliament ought not to be impeached or questioned in any court or place out of Parliament"; *R. (on the application of Bradley) v Secretary of State for Work and Pensions* [2007] EWHC 242; [2007] Pens. L.R. 87 at [26]–[35] (Parliamantary Commission for Administration).

[76] See 14–009.

[77] See 13–045 (a declaration under s.4 does not, in formal terms, affect the validity of the provision in question).

[78] See *Thorburn v Sunderland City Council* [2002] EWHC 195 (Admin; [2003] Q.B. 151.

[79] *Jackson v Attorney General* [2005] UKHL 56; [2006] 1 A.C. 262. The Parliament Acts set out legal requirements as to the manner and form of an Act passed under their provisions and only the courts—not Parliament—can resolve any dispute as the validity of such an Act. The court's jurisdiction is necessary to guarantee the rule of law and involves no breach of constitutional propriety (see Lord Bingham at [51]).

[80] See 1–087.

[81] See 18–023.

[82] *In re A Company* [1981] A.C. 374 at 392.

[83] See 3–009.

(d) Matters falling outside the territorial reach of the High Court of England and Wales (of which the Administrative Court is part) and the ambit of the HRA.[84]

(e) Questions over which the court's jurisdiction has been expressly removed or limited by statute. Statutory restrictions on judicial review in "ouster" or "preclusive" clauses are construed narrowly.[85]

(f) Challenges to certain decisions made by the HM Attorney General may also fall outside the court's supervisory jurisdiction. These are the functions, some derived from prerogative powers, others from statute, in respect of which the Attorney General makes decisions independently of ministerial colleagues and for which he is responsible to Parliament including: entering a nolle prosequi to stop a prosecution on indictment (very rarely exercised, usually on the ground of the defendant's ill health); he may institute a prosecution; direct the Director of Public Prosecutions to take over a prosecution; and give or withhold his consent ("fiat") to a relator action brought by a person to enforce the law. The House of Lords in *Gouriet* held that "in the exercise of these powers he is not subject to direction by his ministerial colleagues or to control and supervision by the courts",[86] though the Privy Council has subsequently highlighted that since the *GCHQ* case put the matter beyond doubt, prerogative powers do generally fall within the court's jurisdiction,[87] and there is no inherent objection to the court's jurisdiction being invoked where the Attorney General is exercising a statutory power.[88]

3–020 A claimant's lack of standing goes to the jurisdiction of the court, but the liberalisation of the "sufficient interest" test means that this will rarely now be a practical bar for a claimant who in other respects has a meritorious case.[89] Until comparatively recently, the courts worked upon the assumption that they had no jurisdiction to review decisions taken under prerogative powers, but it is now understood that this is not so:[90] whether a function under a prerogative power is or is not reviewable is determined by inquiring whether the issue at stake is justiciable or not. Some aspects of the Crown's power—when exercised directly by the Sovereign—remain outside the reach of the courts' jurisdiction but this is of little practical importance in the field of public law.[91]

---

[84] See 3–088.
[85] See 4–051.
[86] *Attorney General v Gouriet* [1978] A.C. 435 at 487 (Viscount Dilhorne).
[87] See 3–32. *R. v Criminal Injuries Compensation Board Ex p. Lain* [1967] 2 Q.B. 864, Div. Ct.; *Council of Civil Service Unions v Minister for the Civil Service* [1985] A.C. 374 HL. See 3–032 (on prerogative powers) and 1–025 (on justiciability).
[88] *Mohit v The Director of Public Prosecutions of Mauritius* [2006] UKPC 20 at [14] (Lord Bingham). In July 2007, the Attorney General announced that she would no longer make key prosecution decisions in individual cases except where the law or national security requires it: *The Governance of Britain: a Consultation on the Role of Attorney General* (Cm 7192)
[89] See 2–007.
[90] See 3–033.
[91] See 3–038.

The Administrative Court operates subject to the general limits governing 3–021 the capacity of the courts of England and Wales to deal with matters of international law. Questions of interpretation of international legal instruments,[92] unless they relate to the court's determination of some domestic law right or interest,[93] are not matters of English law and fall outside the courts' jurisdiction. This reflects the dualist character of the United Kingdom's constitution in which domestic law is seen as wholly distinct from international treaties, until such time as a treaty provision is expressly incorporated into domestic law. The English courts also avoid determining questions relating to actions by a foreign sovereign state,[94] reflecting the international law principle of comity.

Procedural point

Where a claim and a defendant's acknowledgement of service reveal a 3–022 dispute about court's jurisdiction, it will often be convenient for court to grant permission and order the case to proceed by way of the preliminary issue as to jurisdiction.

Non-justiciable decisions

It is a "wholesome development"[95] that the Administrative Court deals with 3–023 many matters that even in the recent past would have been regarded as inappropriate for judicial determination. The fact remains, however, that there are some issues which are inherently unsuited to adjudication. In this category of case, the court acknowledges that the litigation process and the expertise of the court are unsuited to resolving the question in hand. This constraint is most evident where the court is called on to review the exercise of a function on grounds of rationality and proportionality. We discuss non-justiciability in Chapter 1.[96] However, even if a particular issue is not ideally suited to the judicial determination of its substance, it may be amenable to the court's jurisdiction on the ground that it was insufficiently justified.

---

[92] See, e.g. *R. (on the application of Gentle) v Prime Minister* [2006] EWCA Civ 1690; [2007] 2 W.L.R. 195 (relatives of soldiers killed during the UK's occupation of Iraq sought judicial review of the refusal of the Government to hold an independent inquiry into the circumstances that led to the invasion; court could not consider questions of international law); *R. (on the application of Campaign for Nuclear Disarmament) v Prime Minister* [2002] EWHC 2777; [2003] A.C.D. 36 (court could not rule on true meaning of true meaning of United Nations Security Council Resolution 1441 on Iraq); *Buttes Gas & Oil Co v Hammer (No.3)* [1982] A.C. 888, HL.
[93] See 5–043.
[94] *Abassi* [2002] EWCH Civ 1598; [2003] U.K.H.R.R. 76 (no remedy in the English courts for a British citizen detained in Guantanamo Bay the by US government).
[95] *R. (on the application of the Howard League for Penal Reform) v Secretary of State for the Home Department (No.2)* [2002] EWHC 2497; [2003] 1 F.L.R. 484 at [140] (Munby J.: challenge to the legality of the Secretary of State's policy guidance on the treatment of children under 18 years of age held in young offender institutions).
[96] See 1–025.

Judicial discretion

3–024 Even if a matter falls within the supervisory jurisdiction of the Administrative Court and is justiciable, there are a number of good reasons why the court may quite properly exercise its discretion to refuse to consider a claim for judicial review.[97] Ideally this is a decision that ought to be made at the permission stage of the claim procedure.[98] Perhaps the most common reason for declining to hear a claim—usually at the point of the application for permission[99]—is that there is another more appropriate court procedure[100] or the claimant has a satisfactory alternative remedy outside the court system (for example an appeal to a tribunal[101] or a complaint to an ombudsman[102]). Discretion may also be exercised to refuse to determine a case whether the claim is filed outside the time requirement of "promptly and in any event within 3 months".[103] Discretion is also important at the point when the court considers what if any remedial order to make.[104]

No Decision or Decisions Without Legal Effect

3–025 In some cases it has been suggested that the court should not consider a claim for judicial review because the public authority has not actually taken any decision amenable to review.[105]

Informal action

3–026 First, there are situations where a public authority seeks to deal with a problem by informal action outside the expected statutory procedures[106] or in the absence of any statutory regime.[107] It is submitted that where a public

---

[97] On the difference between discretion *and judgment*, see F. Bennion, "Distinguishing judgment and discretion" [2000] P.L. 368 ("What then is the difference, in summary? With judgment the requirement is to assess and pronounce upon a factual or legal question; with discretion it is to determine how to exercise a power of choice. Broadly, discretion is subjective while judgment is objective. Discretion is free, except for limitations placed upon it by the defining formula. Judgment is necessarily restricted, because its purpose is to arrive at a conclusion which registers reality. Discretion necessarily offers choice; judgment registers the functionary's assessment of a situation offering no choice. Discretion analytically presents a variety of possibilities; judgment but one. Discretion offers looseness of outcome and scope for variation; judgment does not").

[98] See 16–041.

[99] See 16–041.

[100] See 16–014.

[101] See 1–087 and 16–019.

[102] See 1–066 and 16–021.

[103] See 16–050.

[104] See 18–048.

[105] On binding effects of policy, see Ch.12.

[106] See, e.g. *R v Devon CC Ex p. L* [1991] 2 F.L.R. 541; *R v Harrow LBC Ex p. D* [1990] Fam. 133; *R. v Norfolk CC Ex p. M* [1989] Q.B. 619 (all dealing with child protection).

[107] *R. v Secretary of State for Health Ex p. C* [2000] 1 F.L.R. 627 CA: lawful for Department to maintain a list ("Consultancy Service Index") of people about whom there were doubts as to their suitability to work with children; inclusion on the list had significant impact upon the appellant's chances of obtaining employment but it did not interfere with his right to apply for or to accept such employment

authority takes such action to further its public functions this should, in principle, be reviewable.[108] Moreover, since the HRA, it should be clear that where action interferes with a qualified Convention right (such as ECHR Art.8 on respect for family life), such action needs to be taken "in accordance with law".[109]

Decisions without direct legal effect

In other cases the court has been invited to decline exercise its powers of review because the public authority's action is characterised as being without legal effect. The courts now take a broad view and it is no longer necessary for a claimant to demonstrate that a decision or action has direct legal consequences upon the claimant. Thus, a press release may constitute a reviewable decision.[110] Similarly, the court may review policy guidance issued by public authorities.[111]   **3–027**

Chains of decisions

A series of decisions may be made in relation to a claimant; the question may arise as to which of them is amenable to review. Thus, a preparatory step on the way to making a formal, legally binding decision may not be reviewable.[112] A decision may be part of a two-tier process, so that an initial determination is superseded by a later one, with the effect that the first decision may no longer be challenged;[113] or what purports to be a second decision may in reality be only a confirmation of an initial decision and so not itself reviewable.[114] There is also the question whether a decision not to alter an earlier administrative decision is itself a reviewable decision. There is "no formulaic or straightforward answer", and each case must to an extent   **3–028**

---

[108] See, e.g. *R. v Liverpool CC Ex p. Baby Products Association* (2000) 2 L.G.L.R. 689 (issue of press release following investigation into safety of a product held to be reviewable).
[109] See 13–023.
[110] *Baby Products* (2000) 2 L.G.L.R.; *R. v Secretary of State for Trade and Industry Ex p. Greenpeace Ltd (No.1)* [1998] Eu. L.R. 48.
[111] See, e.g. *R. (on the application of Burke) v General Medical Council* [2005] EWCA Civ 1003; [2006] Q.B. 273 (review of guidance on withdrawal of artificial feeding, though noting that the "court should not be used as a general advice centre" [21]); *R. (on the application of Axon) v Secretary of State for Health* [2006] EWHC 37; [2006] Q.B. 539 (review of guidance entitled "Guidance for Doctors and other Health Professionals on the Provision of Advice and Treatment to Young People under 16 on Contraception, Sexual and Reproductive Health"). cf. *R. (on the application of United Cooperatives Ltd) v Manchester City Council* [2005] EWHC 364 at [21] (Elias J. noting that. "the courts are in principle reluctant to permit mere advice to be the subject of review"), discussed at 8–032.
[112] cf. *R. (on the application of The Garden and Leisure Group Ltd) v North Somerset Council* [2003] EWHC 1605; [2004] 1 P. & C.R. 39 (review permitted of resolution by local authority committee that planning permission should in principle be formally granted if certain conditions were met).
[113] *R. v Secretary of State for Education Ex p. B (A Child)* [2001] E.L.R. 333.
[114] See, e.g. *R. v Secretary of State for the Home Department Ex p. Kaygusuz (Ibrahim)* [1991] Imm. A.R. 300.

turn on its own particular facts.[115] If there has been no significant change of circumstances since the original decision, especially if the court views the request to the public authority to reconsider its earlier decision as a ploy to circumvent the time limit for commencing a judicial review claim,[116] the court is likely to decline to hear the matter.

AMENABILITY TESTS BASED ON THE SOURCE OF POWER

3–029 The courts have adopted two complementary approaches to determining whether a function falls within the ambit of the supervisory jurisdiction. First, the court considers the legal source of power exercised by the impugned decision-maker. In identifying the "classes of case in which judicial review is available",[117] the courts place considerable importance on the source of legal authority exercised by the defendant public authority. Secondly and additionally, where the "source of power" approach does not yield a clear or satisfactory outcome, the court may consider the characteristics of the function being performed. This has enabled the courts to extend the reach of the supervisory jurisdiction to some activities of non-statutory bodies (such as self-regulatory organisations). We begin by looking at the first approach, based on the source of power.

Statutory powers

3–030 The court now operates on the assumption that "If the source of power is a statute, or subordinate legislation under a statute, then clearly the body in question will be subject to judicial review".[118] There must be some "compelling reason to infer that such a presumption is excluded".[119] In the large proportion of claims commenced, there is no doubt that the decision in question is susceptible to review because the source of power exercised is statutory.

3–031   Decisions of bodies deriving their power from Private Acts of Parliament (that is, legislation promoted through special procedure by organisations to obtain powers in excess or in conflict with the general law) are not however, for this reason alone, subject to judicial review. Thus, Lloyd's of London and

---

[115] *R. (on the application of Lambeth LBC) v Secretary of State for Work and Pensions* [2005] EWHC 637; [2005] B.L.G.R. 764 at [38] (fresh facts may justify the court intervening; but "A subsequent change of English law or a change of the policy of our government that is not retrospective to the earlier decision will not, in general, justify treating a refusal to alter a previously undisputed decision as a new decision").

[116] See 16–050.

[117] See 3–016.

[118] *R. v Panel on Take-overs and Mergers Ex p. Datafin Plc* [1987] Q.B. 815 at 847 (Lloyd L.J.).

[119] *Mohit v The Director of Public Prosecutions of Mauritius* [2006] UKPC 20 at [20] (Lord Bingham).

Cambridge University, both institutions established by Private Act of Parliament, are not for that reason alone susceptible to judicial review;[120] a particular public function must also be identified. If, however, they perform public functions those functions will be reviewable. This approach accords with one of the roles of judicial review which is to ensure decisions are taken lawfully. When applied here this means in accordance with the statutory power and purpose.

Prerogative powers

Nature of prerogative powers

The courts recognise that the Crown (a term we consider shortly) possesses **3–032** common law powers and immunities. There is no definitive list of these prerogative powers and central government departments appear not to keep records about their exercise.[121] Nor is there consensus about the definition of prerogative powers. Some commentators take the view that only those governmental powers which are unique to the Crown should be called prerogative,[122] whereas others adopt a more all-encompassing definition and include all the non-statutory powers of the Crown.[123] A practical example of the difference is that the action of making ex gratia payments falls within the latter but not the former definition of prerogative powers, because it is open

---

[120] See, e.g. *R. v University of Cambridge Ex p. Evans (No.2)* [1999] Ed. C.R. 556; *R. (on the application of West) v Lloyd's of London* [2004] EWCA Civ 506; [2004] 3 All E.R. 251.

[121] D. Feldman (ed.), *English Public Law* (2004), paras 3.109–3.117. Prerogative powers include: making treaties; issuing and withdrawing passports; recognising foreign governments; conducting diplomatic relations; declaring war and committing UK armed forces; requisitioning ships in times of war; destroying property to prevent it falling into enemy hands; the appointment of judges; establishing Royal Commissions and some other committees of inquiry; granting the prerogative of mercy; appointment of Bishops of the Church of England; the regulation of the civil service; the dissolution of Parliament; the Prime Minister and other ministers; and to grant Royal Assent to Bills passed by Parliament. There also exist prerogative powers relating to colonial governance of the UK's remaining British Overseas Territories (formerly called dependent territories): see *R. (on the application of Bancoult) v Secretary of State for Foreign and Commonwealth Affairs (No.1)* [2001] Q.B. 1067 and *R. (on the application of Bancoult) v Secretary of State for Foreign and Commonwealth Affairs (No.2)* [2007] EWCA Civ 498.

[122] See, e.g. H.W.R. Wade and C. Forsyth, *Administrative Law*, 9th edn (2004), p.216 ("'Prerogative' power is, properly speaking, legal power that appertains to the Crown but not to its subjects"), drawing on Blackstone (Bl.Comm. 1.239). Wade stressed the requirement for there to be *legal* power to to alter people's rights, duties and status and, thus, he did not regard the issue of passports as based on prerogative power (*Constitutional Fundamentals* (1980), p.46). See *R. (on the application of Heath) v Home Office Policy and Advisory Board for Forensic Pathology* [2005] EWHC 1793 at [25] (Newman J. drawing a distinction between prerogative power and "executive power" as the basis for setting up the Board).

[123] A. Dicey, *Introduction to the Study of the Law of the Constitution*, 8th edn (1915), p.421 ("The prerogative is the name for the remaining portion of the Crown's original authority, and is therefore, as already pointed out, the name for the residue of discretionary power left at any moment in the hands of the Crown, whether such power be in fact exercised by the King himself or by his ministers.") This definition was quoted with approval in *Attorney General v de Keyser's Royal Hotel Ltd* [1920] A.C. 508 at 526, and by Lord Fraser in *Council of Civil Service Unions v Minister for the Civil Service* [1985] A.C. 374.

to any citizen to make donations of money. Prerogative powers are residual powers—new ones cannot be created,[124] and they "remain in existence to the extent that Parliament has not expressly or by implication extinguished them".[125] Despite uncertainty about the definition of prerogative powers it has long been clear that "the King hath no prerogative, but that which the law of the land allows him";[126] the existence of a prerogative power is ultimately a question for the determination of the courts, not mere assertion by government. Prerogative and statutory powers may both govern a field,[127] though where there is conflict statute prevails. There have been suggestions that the scope of a prerogative power cannot be extended by the representations of a public authority in ways which might, in other contexts, have created a legitimate expectation.[128] In July 2007, the Government announced proposals for reform of prerogative powers.[129]

3–033   Until the mid-1970s, the courts took the view that the exercise of prerogative powers fell outside the court's supervisory jurisdiction, except in the narrowest senses of determining whether a prerogative power existed, and if so, its extent, whether it was being exercised in the appropriate form and as to how far it has been superseded by statute.[130] The courts were not normally prepared to examine the appropriateness or adequacy of the grounds for exercising the power,[131] or the fairness of the procedure

[124] *British Broadcasting Corp v Johns* [1965] Ch. 32 (Diplock L.J.: it was "three hundred and fifty years and a civil war too late for the Queen's courts to broaden the prerogative" in respect of the Crown's right to a monopoly).

[125] *R. v Secretary of State for the Home Department Ex p. Fire Brigades Union* [1995] 2 A.C. 513 at 552 (Lord Browne-Wilkinson).

[126] *Case of Proclamations* (1611) 12 Co. Rep. 74 at 76 (Sir Edward Coke).

[127] For example, the Immigration Act 1971 s.33(5) expressly preserves prerogative powers relating to immigration control of aliens.

[128] *R. v Criminal Injuries Compensation Board Ex p. M (A Minor)* [1998] P.I.Q.R. P107; [1998] C.O.D. 128.

[129] See *The Governance of Britain* Green Paper (Cm 7170) and *The Governance of Britain— War Powers and Treaties: Limiting Executive Powers* (CP 26/07). The Government's prposals follow on from several years of calls for reform, e.g. by the House of Commons Public Administration Committee, *Taming the Prerogative: Strengthening Ministerial Accountability to Parliament.* HC Paper No.422; (Session 2003/04) *A Matter of Honour: Reforming the Honours System*, HC Paper No.212–I (Session 2003/04); *A Draft Civil Service Bill: Completing the Reform.* HC Paper No.128–I (Session 2003/04); *Hansard* HL, (March 3, 2006): 2nd reading debate of Lord Lester's Constitutional Reform (Prerogative Powers and Civil Service etc.) Bill.

[130] See, e.g. *Willion v Berkley* (1561) Plow. 223; *Case of Monopolies* (1602) 11 Co.Rep. 84b; *Prohibitions del Roy* (1607) 12 Co.Rep. 63; *Case of Proclamations* (1611) 12 Co.Rep. 74; *Burmah Oil Co v Lord Advocate* [1965] A.C. 75; *Attorney General v De Keyser's Royal Hotel Ltd* [1920] A.C. 508; *Walwin (LE) and Partners Ltd v West Sussex CC* [1975] 3 All E.R. 604; *Laker Airways Ltd v Department of Trade* [1977] Q.B. 643.

[131] See, e.g. *R. v Allen* (1862) 1 B. & S. 850 (*nolle prosequi*); *Musgrove v Chun Teeong Toy* [1918] A.C. 272 (exclusion of alien); *Bugsier Reederei-und-Bergungs A/G v SS Brighton* [1951] 2 T.L.R. 409 (licence granted to enemy company to sue in British court); *Chandler v DPP* [1964] A.C. 763 at 790–2, 796, 800–1, 814 (disposition of forces); *Hanratty v Lord Butler of Saffron Walden* (1971) 115 S .J. 386 and *de Freitas v Benn* y [1976] A.C. 239 (prerogative of mercy); *Jenkins v Attorney General* (1971) 115 S.J. 674 (dissemination of official information); *Blackburn v Attorney General* [1971] 1 W.L.R. 1037 (treaty-making power); *Secretary of State for the Home Department v Lakdawalla* [1972] Imm. A.R. 26 (issue of passport). Lord

followed before the power was exercised,[132] and they would not allow bad faith to be attributed to the Crown.[133] The unwillingness of the courts to review prerogative powers could be explained partly on the basis of the close relationship those powers were regarded as having with the monarch personally, the Crown being the source of the powers, and partly because the courts regarded prerogative powers as being those common law powers of the Crown which had no statutory source. In addition, there are some prerogative powers which were considered within the appropriate constitutional realm of the executive, or which required unrestricted discretion for their effective exercise (such as the power to declare war).

Shift from jurisdiction to justiciability to set limits on court's powers to supervise legality prerogative powers

In the *GCHQ* case,[134] a decision of great constitutional importance, the   3–034
majority of the House of Lords were of the opinion that it was no longer constitutionally appropriate to deny the court supervisory jurisdiction over a governmental decision merely because the legal authority for that decision rested on prerogative rather than statutory powers.[135] The courts' intervention should be governed by whether or not, in the particular case, the subject-matter of the prerogative power was justiciable.[136] Lord Roskill listed examples of non-justiciable decisions those "such as those relating to the making of treaties, the defence of the realm, the prerogative of mercy, the grant of honours, the dissolution of Parliament and the appointment of Ministers".[137]

Denning M.R. in *Laker Airways* [1997] Q.B. 643 at 705–7 anticipated a change in the law by assimilating a review in which the review of the prerogative with that of statutory power, so that its exercise may be impugned for "misdirection in fact or in law". The majority, however, proceeded on a narrower basis, concluding that the Civil Aviation Act 1971 had impliedly superseded the Crown's prerogative in foreign affairs, and that the holder of a licence under the statute could not be deprived of its commercial value by a decision on the part of the Secretary of State to revoke the licensee's status as a designated carrier under the Bermuda Agreement. In other respects the majority accepted the orthodox position on the unreviewability of the exercise of the prerogative: at 718 (Roskill L.J.) and, it appears, at 727–8 (Lawton L.J.).
[132] *de Freitas v Benny* [1976] A.C. 239 at 247–8.
[133] *Duncan v Theodore* (1917) 23 C.L.R. 510 at 544; *Australian Communist Party v Commonwealth* (1951) 83 C.L.R. 1 at 257–8.
[134] *Council of Civil Service Unions v Minister for the Civil Service* [1985] A.C. 374. The case concerned the decision of the Minister for the Civil Service (a post held by the Prime Minister, at the time Mrs Thatcher) to give instructions to affect the terms and conditions of Civil Servants at GCHQ, the government agency responsible for signals intelligence, so as to exclude them from membership of any trade union other than a department staff association approved by the Director of GCHQ; it was held that the unions had a legitimate expectation of being consulted but that whether national security considerations outweighed the need for fair procedures was a matter for the executive rather than the courts.
[135] Lords Scarman, Diplock and Roskill. The minority (Lords Fraser and Brightman) preferred to leave open the question as to whether prerogative powers were reviewable until it had to be determined.
[136] Lord Scarman, at 407 ("The controlling factor in determining whether the exercise of prerogative power is subjected to judicial review is not its source but its subject matter.").
[137] At 418.

3–035   In the ensuing years, some of these fields have upon further analysis come to be regarded as potentially justiciable. The question "is simply whether the nature and subject matter of the decision is amenable to the judicial process. Are the courts qualified to deal with the matter or does the decision involve such questions of policy that they should not intrude because they are ill-equipped to do so?"[138] The general concept of justiciability is examined elsewhere;[139] here we can simply set out those prerogative powers which have been regarded as susceptible to judicial review: civil servants' conditions of service;[140] *ex gratia* payments to victims of crime;[141] *ex gratia* payments to a person convicted and imprisoned and then subsequently acquitted on appeal;[142] the power to issue and withdraw passports;[143] the issue of a warrant to intercept telephone communications signed by the Secretary of State for the Home Department;[144] the prerogative of mercy;[145] the duty of the Foreign and Commonwealth Office to render diplomatic assistance to a British citizen abroad in respect of miscarriage or denial of justice;[146] the form of declaration to be made upon appointment as Queen's Counsel;[147] and an Order of Council in relation to a British Overseas Territory.[148]

[138] *R. v Secretary of State for the Home Department Ex p. Bentley* [1994] Q.B. 349 at 453 (Watkins L.J.) An example was given: "If. . . it was clear that the Home Secretary had refused to pardon someone solely on the grounds of their sex, race or religion, the courts would be expected to interfere and, in our judgment, would be entitled to do so". See also *R. (on the application of Bancoult) v Secretary of State for Foreign and Commonwealth Affairs* [2007] EWCA Civ 498 at [46] (Sedley L.J.) "It can be observed without disrespect, particularly since Lord Roskill was careful to express himself tentatively, that a number of his examples could today be regarded as questionable: the grant of honours for reward, the waging of a war of manifest aggression or a refusal to dissolve Parliament at all might well call in question an immunity based purely on subject-matter".

[139] See 1–025.

[140] *Council of Civil Service Unions v Minister for the Civil Service* [1985] A.C. 374; see 3–00 below for discussion of review relating to employment.

[141] *R. v Criminal Injuries Compensation Board Ex p. Lain* [1967] 2 Q.B. 864 (pre-dating the landmark ruling in the CCSU case); *R. v Secretary of State for the Home Department Ex p. Fire Brigades Union* [1995] 2 A.C. 513. In Great Britain the scheme now operates on a statutory basis under the Criminal Injuries Compensation Act 1995.

[142] See, e.g. *R. v Secretary of State for the Home Department Ex p. Harrison* [1988] 3 All E.R. 86; *Re McFarland* [2004] UKHL 17; [2004] 1 W.L.R. 1289;

[143] *R. v Secretary of State for Foreign and Commonwealth Affairs Ex p. Everett* [1989] Q.B. 811 (Taylor L.J. distinguished those acts at "the top of the scale of executive functions under the prerogative" involving "high policy", which were not justiciable, from "administrative decisions, affecting the rights of individuals and their freedom of travel", which are justiciable).

[144] *R. v Secretary of State for the Home Department Ex p. Ruddock* [1987] 1 W.L.R. 1482. The power is now governed by the Interception of Communications Act 1985.

[145] *R. v Secretary of State for the Home Department Ex p Bentley* [1994] Q.B. 349 (Home Secretary's failure to consider the grant of a posthumous pardon when the previous Home Secretary's decision had been wrong was held to be a clear error of law).

[146] *R. (on the application of Abassi) v Secretary of State for Foreign and Commonwealth Affairs* [2002] EWCA Civ 1470; [2003] 1 W.L.R. 741 at [106].

[147] *Re Treacy's Application for Judicial Review* [2000] N.I. 330.

[148] *Bancoult* [2007] EWCH Civ 498. The Order in Council conferred a broad power to act for the "peace, order and good government" of the territory. The term "Order in Council" is used in relation to two quite distinct types of legislation—some forms of delegated legislation (typically where a statute confers law-making powers upon Her Majesty in Council) and, or relevance to present context, a form of *primary* legislation made under prerogative powers (examples of which include the Civil Service Order in Council).

Prerogative powers in respect of which the court may have supervisory jurisdiction

Despite the general shift away from jurisdiction to justiciability marked by the *GCHQ* case, there may still be some areas where the supervisory jurisdiction of the court will still not run.[149] First, some prerogative powers are exercised in the sphere of international relations and the courts of England and Wales do not consider questions of pure international law as these are not, for the purposes of the national legal system, "law" at all.[150] Secondly, the prerogative power of Royal Assent to legislation may fall outside the court's jurisdiction as being concerned with the processes of Parliament.[151] 3–036

Thirdly, in some circumstances the court may lack jurisdiction because the prerogative power in question has been exercised directly by the Sovereign (rather than by Her ministers) and as a matter of general constitutional principle, the Sovereign cannot be subject to legal process.[152] These powers, called "personal" or "direct" prerogatives, "can be exercised legally by the person of the monarch him or herself".[153] The main examples are the appointment of the Prime Minister, the dissolution of Parliament, and the Royal Assent to legislation. The traditional constitutional justification for immunity of the Crown (as Sovereign) from public law remedies was "both because there would be an incongruity in the Queen commanding herself to do an act, and also because the disobedience to a writ of mandamus is to be enforced by attachment".[154] The Crown is, however, only the nominal claimant in claims for judicial review.[155] The provisions of the Crown Proceedings Act 1947, which permitted claims to be brought against the Crown in the more general sense of the Crown as executive government, do not apply to the Monarch personally;[156] nor do they apply to claims for 3–037

---

[149] Or if the courts do have jurisdiction, they defer to the authority of those exercising the powers of the Crown. If the exercise of a prerogative power were to offend human rights or was clearly irrational, the courts would find it difficult not to intervene.

[150] See, e.g in relation to treaty-making *R. v Secretary of State for Foreign and Commonwealth Affairs Ex p. Rees-Mogg* [1994] Q.B. 552 (no jurisdiction to consider ratification of Title V of the Treaty on European Union which established a common foreign and security policy and involved no question of domestic law); *Ex p. Molyneaux* [1986] 1 W.L.R. 331 (Anglo-Irish Agreement was akin to a treaty); *cf. R. v HM Treasury Ex p. Smedley* [1985] Q.B. 657 (review of draft Order in Council that sought to bring treaty provisions into national law).

[151] See 3–019. See generally A. Twomey, "The Refusal or Deferral of Royal Assent" [2006] P.L. 580; R. Blackburn, "The Royal Assent to Legislation and a Monarch's Fundamental Human Rights" [2003] P.L. 205.

[152] On the changing nature of the legal status of the Crown, see J. Jacob, *The Republican Crown: Lawyers and the Making of the State in Twentieth Century Britain* (1996); M. Sunkin and S. Payne (eds), *The Nature of the Crown* (1999); also P. Sales, "Crown Proceedings", Ch.13 in M. Supperstone, J. Goudie and P. Walker (eds), *Judicial Review*, 3rd edn (2005).

[153] R. Blackburn, "Monarchy and the Personal Prerogatives" [2004] P.L. 546 at 548; R. Brazier, "'Monarchy and the Personal Prerogatives': a personal response to Professor Blackburn" [2005] P.L. 45.

[154] *R v Powell* (1841) 1 Q.B. 352 at 361 (Lord Denman C.J.) quoted with approval by Lord Woolf in *M v Home Office* at 415.

[155] *R. (on the application of Ben-Abdelaziz) v Haringey LBC* [2001] EWCA Civ 803; [2001] 1 W.L.R. 1485.

[156] s.40, in relation to tort claims.

judicial review or other public law proceedings on the Crown side of the Queen's Bench Division of the High Court.[157] Moreover, the principal norms regulating the exercise of these "sovereign acts" (in distinction to merely executive acts) are also more in the nature of constitutional conventions than legal principles; and conventions are, broadly speaking, not enforceable by the courts.[158]

3–038   To the extent that an area of sovereign immunity continues to exist, it causes few practical problems.[159] Whereas until 1714 (when George I acceded to the throne) it could be thought that "the King or Queen governed through Ministers, now Ministers govern through the instrumentality of the Crown".[160] Most prerogative powers are now exercised by ministers of the Crown. Here, "any amenability to judicial review in relation to the use of the royal prerogative is that of ministers, not of the Monarch in whose name they govern" and the theoretical source of executive action in the Crown does not protect it from judicial review.[161] For this reason, it is of little practical importance that neither the prerogative remedies (quashing orders, prohibiting orders and mandatory orders) nor injunctions can be obtained against the Crown directly because they will clearly issue against Ministers of the Crown. Ministers of the Crown do not share the immunity of the Crown as Sovereign.[162]

3–039   The mere fact that an institution has been incorporated by Royal Charter does not necessarily make its decisions susceptible to judicial review;[163] it will be necessary to show that its decision engages with a public function.

Other sources of power

3–040   Statute and the prerogative do not exhaust the possible sources of power for office-holders in the public sphere. Powers may also be exercised pursuant to contracts, a subject examined below.[164] Ministers also lay claim under the so-

---

[157] s.38(2). The confusion which arose as to whether the court had jurisdiction to order an interim injunction against a Minister on an application for judicial review was rectified by the HL in *M v Home Office* [1994] 1 A.C. 377.

[158] K. Keith, "The Courts and the Conventions of the Constitution" (1967) 16 I.C.L.Q. 542; J. Jaconelli, "Do Constitutional Conventions Bind?" [2004] C.L.J. 149.

[159] Note also, in relation to that statutory power, that Acts of Parliament only rarely impose public law duties or confer functions on "the Crown" (and where they do, it will normally relate to an executive act); instead it is normal for "the Secretary of State" to be given such responsibilities: *M v Home Office* [1994] 1 A.C. 377 at 417.

[160] Anson, *Law and Custom of the Constitution*, 3rd edn (1907), II.i, p.41 (cited by Sedley J. in *R. (on the application of Bancoult) v Secretary of State for Foreign and Commonwealth Affairs* [2007] EWCA Civ 498 at [32]).

[161] *R. (on the application of Bancoult) v Secretary of State for Foreign and Commonwealth Affairs* [2007] EWCA Civ 498 at [31]–[36] (Sedley L.J.) (in relation to an Order in Council made under prerogative powers, which was held to be an act of the executive and as such is amenable to any appropriate form of judicial review, whether anticipatory or retrospective).

[162] *M v Home Office* (n.157).

[163] *R. v Royal Life Saving Society Ex p. Howe* [1990] C.O.D. 440; *cf. R. v Royal Pharmaceutical Society of Great Britain Ex p. Mahmood* [2001] EWCA Civ 1245; [2002] 1 W.L.R. 879.

[164] See 3–056.

called "Ram doctrine" to have at their disposal all the legal powers enjoyed by a corporation sole.[165]

JUDICIAL REVIEW OF PUBLIC FUNCTIONS

The previous section considered susceptibility to judicial review based on the *source of the power*—statute or prerogative. The courts came to recognise that an approach based solely on the source of the public authority's power was too restrictive. Since 1987 they have developed an additional approach to determining susceptibility based on by the type of *function performed* by the decision-maker.[166] The "public function" approach is, since 2000, reflected in the Civil Procedure Rules: CPR.54.1(2)(a)(ii), defines a claim for judicial review as a claim to the lawfulness of "a decision, action or failure to act in relation to the exercise of a public function". (Similar terminology is used in s.6(3)(b) of the Human Rights Act 1998 to define a public authority as "any person certain of whose functions are functions of a public nature", but detailed consideration of that provision is postponed until later).[167] As we noted at the outset,[168] the term "public" is usually a synonym for "governmental". 3–041

The public functions approach brings within the court's judicial review supervisory jurisdiction some actions of some bodies—including self-regulatory organisations, charities and business enterprises—which would otherwise fall outside public law scrutiny if only the traditional "source of power" approach were deployed. Applying a public functions test in this context, the courts have held decisions taken by the following, among others, to be susceptible to review: the Takeover Panel;[169] Advertising Standards Authority;[170] Press Complaints Commission;[171] the Code of Practice Committee of the Association of the British Pharmaceutical Indus- 3–042

---

[165] See 5–022.
[166] Notably in *R. v Panel on Takeovers and Mergers Ex p. Datafin Plc* [1987] 1 Q.B. 815, CA. See further: C. Forsyth, "The Scope of Judicial Review: 'public duty' not 'source of power'" [1987] PL. 356; D. Pannick, "Who is Subject to Judicial Review and in Respect of What?" [1992] P.L. 1; N. Bamforth, "The Scope of Judicial Review: Still Uncertain" [1993] P.L. 239.
[167] See 3–069.
[168] See 3–001.
[169] *Datafin* [1987] 1 Q.B.815. The Panel is a non-statutory body, set up in 1968, which administers the City Code on Takeovers and Mergers; its central objective is to ensure equality of treatment and opportunity for all shareholders in takeover bids. Since *Datafin*, the Panel has been designated as a supervisory authority under the EC Directive on Takeover Bids (2004/25/EC) and has Statutory functions under Pt 28 of the Companies Act 2006.
[170] *R. v Advertising Standards Authority Ltd Ex p. Insurance Services Plc* [1990] C.O.D. 42. The ASA is the self-regulatory body of the advertising industry, hearing complaints from members of the public about adverts in the print media. Since 2004 Ofcom, the statutory regulator for radio and television, has contracted out some of its regulatory functions to the ASA.
[171] *R. v Press Complaints Commission Ex p. Stewart-Brady* (1997) 9 Admin. L.R. 247. The PCC is a self-regulatory body dealing with complaints from members of the public about the editorial content of newspapers and magazines.

try;[172] Life Assurance Unit Trust Regulatory Organisation;[173] London Metal Exchange Ltd;[174] the managers of a privately-owned psychiatric hospital;[175] and Hampshire Farmers Markets Ltd.[176] Sir John Donaldson M.R. urged that it is important for the courts to "recognise the realities of executive power" and not allow "their vision to be clouded by the subtlety and sometimes complexity of the way in which it can be exerted".[177] Non-statutory bodies are as capable of abusing their powers as is government.[178]

3-043   The adoption of the public functions approach has not led to a widespread expansion of the ambit of judicial review. More often than not, submissions that a body's decision falls within the sphere of public functions have been unsuccessful, leading to dismissal of claims against (for example) organisations regulating sports,[179] decisions by religious bodies,[180] and in the commercial sphere.[181] In some of these cases what was

---

[172] *R. v Code of Practice Committee of the Association of the British Pharmaceutical Industry Ex p. Professional Counselling Aids* [1991] C.O.D. 228. The ABPI is a is the trade association for about a hundred companies in the UK producing prescription medicines.

[173] *R. v Life Assurance Unit Trust Regulatory Organisation Ex p. Ross* [1993] Q.B. 17. LAUTRO was a recognised self-regulating organisation for the purposes of s.8 of the Financial Services Act 1986. It functions are now part of the Personal Investment Authority (PIA), a directorate of the Financial Services Authority (FSA) established by the Financial Services and Markets Act 2000.

[174] *R. v London Metal Exchange Ltd Ex p. Albatros Warehousing Ltd*, unreported March 30, 2000, Richards J. (unrep.). The LME is now a "recognised investment exchange" (RIE); regulated by the FSA.

[175] *R. (on the application of A) v Partnerships in Care Ltd* [2002] EWHC 529; [2002] 1 W.L.R. 2610. The impugned decision was to change the focus of the ward on which the claimant was accommodated from treatment of patients with personality disorders to the treatment of mental illness.

[176] *R. (on the application of Beer (t/a Hammer Trout Farm)) v Hampshire Farmers Markets Ltd* [2003] EWCA Civ 1056; [2004] 1 W.L.R. 233. The company was set up on the initiative of Hampshire County Council to help producers in its area run farmers markets.

[177] *Datafin* [1987] 1 Q.B. 815 at 838–9.

[178] See J. Black, "Constitutionalising Self Regulation" (1996) 59 M.L.R. 24; A. Ogus, "Rethinking Self-Regulation" (1995) 15 O.J.L.S. 95.

[179] In relation to horse racing: see *Mullins v The Board of Appeal of the Jockey Club* [2005] EWHC 2197 (Admin), Burnton J.; *R. v Disciplinary Committee of the Jockey Club Ex p. Massingberd-Mundy* [1993] 2 All E.R. 207, DC; *R. v Jockey Club Ex p. RAM Racecourses Ltd* (1990) [1993] 2 All E.R. 225, DC; *R. v Disciplinary Committee of the Jockey Club Ex p. Aga Khan* [1993] 1 W.L.R. 909, CA. Note that in 2001 the Disciplinary Committee was superseded by an Appeal Board and since 2006 regulatory functions have been carried out by the independent Horseracing Regulatory Authority. But *cf. Nagle v Feilden* [1966] 2 Q.B. 633 (review of practice of Jockey Club to refuse trainer's licences to women). In relation to other sports, see: *R. v Football Association Ltd Ex p. Football League Ltd* [1993] 12 All E.R. 833 (Rose J.); *Law v National Greyhound Racing Club* [1983] 1 W.L.R. 1302; and see J. Anderson, "An Accident of History: Why the Decisions of Sports Governing Bodies are not Amenable to Judicial Review" (2006) 35 *Common Law World Review* 173; the position is different in Scotland: C. Munro, "Sports in the Courts" [2005] P.L. 681 and 3–106 below.

[180] *R. v Chief Rabbi of the United Hebrew Congregations Ex p. Wachmann* [1992] 1 W.L.R. 1036; *R. v London Beth Din (Court of Chief Rabbi) Ex p. Bloom* [1998] C.O.D. 131; *R. v Imam of Bury Park Mosque, Luton Ex p. Ali (Sulaiman)* [1994] C.O.D. 142; *R. v St Edmundsbury and Ipswich Diocese (Chancellor) Ex p. White* [1948] 1 K.B. 195. *cf. R. v Bishop of Stafford Ex p. Owen* [2001] A.C.D. 14.

[181] *R. v Insurance Ombudsman Ex p. Aegon Life Assurance Ltd* [1994] C.O.D. 426; *R. v Panel of the Federation of Communication Services Ltd Ex p. Kubis* [1998] C.O.D. 56; *R. v*

---

fatal to the claim was the presence of a contractual nexus between the claimant and the defendant.[182] In others, the activity in question was assessed not to have the characteristics of a public function.

There is much to commend a function-based approach to determining the **3–044** scope of judicial review. Not only does it enable the courts to articulate more explicitly the modern constitutional role of judicial review—the common law control of public functions[183]—but it may provide redress for grievance where no other remedy exists. As it is through the principles of judicial review that the rule of law and other constitutional principles are given practical effect, the supervisory jurisdiction of the Administrative Court should ensure that bodies, whether nominally public or private, when performing public functions comply with the law and achieve acceptable standards of administration. While some public functions fall outside the scope of judicial review,[184] nevertheless there exists a wide and growing—if sometimes uncertain—range of public functions which are potentially subject to the supervisory scrutiny of the courts.

Various characteristics of a public function

Where the courts do employ the broad test based on the existence of public **3–045** functions, it is not always clear what criteria are relevant. Some judgments focus on the nature of the specific task carried out (which ought to be the dominant consideration) whereas others examine the general characteristics of the decision-making body. In *Ex p. Datafin Plc*, Sir John Donaldson M.R. suggested that possibly "the only essential elements are what can be described as a public element, which can take many different forms, and the exclusion from jurisdiction of bodies where the sole source of power is the consensual submission to its jurisdiction".[185] He warned that even as the law then stood, in the law reports it was possible to find enumerations of factors giving rise to the jurisdiction, but it was a fatal error to regard the presence of all those factors as essential or as being exclusive of other factors. In subsequent cases, the courts have gone on to elaborate a variety of overlapping criteria designed to particularise the broad-based functional approach of the Master of the Rolls in *Datafin*. The following points are relevant.

"But for"

The "but for" test—whether, but for the existence of a non-statutory body, **3–046** the government would itself almost inevitably have intervened to do or regulate the activity in question. Here the court poses a hypothetical

---

Association of British Travel Agents Ex p. Sunspell Ltd (t/a Superlative Travel) [2001] A.C.D. 16; *R. v Lloyd's of London Ex p. Briggs* [1993] 1 Lloyd's Rep. 176; *R. (on the application of West) v Lloyd's of London* [2004] EWCA Civ 506; [2004] 3 All E.R. 251.
[182] See 3–050.
[183] See 1–015.
[184] On non-justiciability, see 1–025.
[185] [1987]1 Q.B. 815 at 838.

question.[186] Evidence as to the position of comparable bodies in other countries has sometimes been regarded as relevant, and sometimes not.[187] Given the huge changes in the scope of government activity, and disputes about its proper scope, it is open to doubt whether this criterion is a satisfactory one.

Statutory underpinning

3–047 Where the government has acquiesced or encouraged the activities of the body under challenge by providing "underpinning" for its work, has woven the body into the fabric of public regulation[188] or the body was established under the authority of government",[189] this can constitute statutory underpinning. Here the court is concerned not with what might happen, but with what has actually occurred.[190] The mere fact that existence of the body is explicitly or implicitly recognised in legislation is insufficient.[191]

---

[186] A factor present in, e.g. *R. v Advertising Standards Authority Ex p. Insurance Services Plc* [1990] C.O.D. 42 where it was held that in the absence of a self-regulatory body such as the ASA, its functions "would no doubt be exercised by the Director General of Fair Trading" (Glidewell L.J. at 86). *cf.*, e.g. *R. v Football Association Ltd Ex p. Football League Ltd* [1993] 2 All E.R. 833 (television or other commercial company more likely than government to step in to regulate football if the FA did not exist). The but-for test is not conclusive. In *Ex p. Aga Khan* [1993] 1 W.L.R. 909, the Master of the Rolls was "willing to accept that if the Jockey Club did not regulate horse racing the government would probably be driven to create a public body to do so," but went on to hold that the Club "is not in its origin, its history, its constitution or (least of all) its membership a public body" (at 923); the other members of the CA differed, holding that the government would not have intervened.

[187] The fact that outside England some governments regulated the sport of horse racing was not regarded as significant in *Ex p. Aga Khan* [1993] 1 W.L.R. 909 at 932. *cf. Datafin* [1987] 1 Q.B. 815 where the Panel's lack of a direct statutory base was regarded as "a complete anomaly, judged by the experience of other comparable markets world wide" (at 835).

[188] An expression used by Sir Thomas Bingham M.R. in *Ex p. Aga Khan* [1993] 1 W.L.R. 909 at 921.

[189] *Ex p. Lain* [1967] 2 Q.B. 864 at 884 (Diplock L.J.), cited with approval in *Ex p. Datafin plc* [1987] 1 Q.B. 815 at 849 (Lloyd L.J.).

[190] See, e.g. *R. (on the application of A) v Partnerships in Care Ltd* [2002] EWCH 529. The claimant was compulsorily detained under Mental Health Act 1983 s.3(1), the defendant private hospital was registered as a mental nursing home under Registered Homes Act 1984 Pt 2, and a statutory instrument imposed a duty directly on the hospital to provide adequate professional staff and treatment facilities.

[191] See, e.g. *Ex p. Wachmann* [1992] 1 W.L.R. 1036 (existence and some functions of Chief Rabbi recognised by United Synagogues Act 1870 and Slaughter Houses Act 1974); *Ex p. Aegon Life Insurance Ltd* [1994] C.O.D. 426 (under Financial Services Act 1986 LAUTRO recognised by Secretary of State as self-regulatory organisation; rather than itself carrying out a complaints investigation function, as required by the Act, LAUTRO recognised the Insurance Ombudsman as performing that task); *Ex p. Football Association Ltd* [1993] 2 All E.R. 833 where the EA had been recognised by Football Spectators Act 1989 s.4. In none of these cases was the presence of the legislation sufficient to make the body reviewable.

Extensive or monopolistic powers

The fact that the body was exercising extensive or monopolistic powers, for **3–048** instance by effectively regulating entry to a trade or profession can be significant.[192] The Takeover Panel was said to have "a giant's strength".[193] Decisions of Lough Neagh Fishermen's Co-operative Society Ltd, a friendly society that by historical accident owns the rights to eel fishing on Lough Neagh and the River Bann, was carrying out a public function when it refused a boat-owners licence to someone who had fished there as a boat-helper for 47 years.[194]

Monopolistic power is not, however, necessarily to be equated with the **3–049** performance of public functions; nor will increases in scale lead to a change in the nature of the function in question. Extensive power over others is often exercised in the private sphere and here judicial review is not available.[195] The seriousness of the impact of the decision on those affected,[196] or the number of people affected by the action,[197] have not been regarded as necessarily significant; nor is the importance of the body in national life.[198]

---

[192] As with the other criteria, the existence of monopolistic power is not in itself sufficient to make a decision-maker subject to judicial review. Rose J. accepted that the FA had "virtually monopolistic powers" (see *Ex p. Football League Ltd* [1993] 2 All E.R. 833 at 848), and so did the Court of Appeal in *Ex p. Aga Khan* [1993] 1 W.L.R. 909. Sporting-relating businesses may be subject to oversight by the Office of Fair Trading, which enforces competition law.

[193] *Datafin* [1987] 1 Q.B. 815 at 845, Lloyd L.J.

[194] *In the Matter of an Application for Judicial Review by Patrick Wylie* [2005] NIQB 2 at [19] (Weatherup J.: "the regulation of the fishing involves an implied duty to act in the public interest; the issues that arise are matters of public concern and interest and the regulatory control arises in a public sphere where direct governmental regulatory control is absent and the regulatory activities are providing a public service").

[195] See, e.g. Ex.p. *Aga Khan* [1993] 1 W.L.R. 909 at 932–3 where Hoffmann L.J. stated: "the mere fact of power, even over a substantial area of economic activity, is not enough. In a mixed economy, power may be private as well as public. Private power may affect the public interest and livelihoods of many individuals. But that does not subject it to the rules of public law. If control is needed, it must be found in the law of contract, the doctrine of restraint of trade, the Restrictive Trade Practices Act 1976, Arts 85 and 86 of the EEC treaty and all the other instruments available in law for curbing excesses of private power." See also *Mullins* [2005] EWCH 2197 (Admin) at [31].

[196] See, e.g. *Ex p. Wachmann* [1992] 1 W.L.R. 1036 (whether or not a decision had "public law consequences" must be determined otherwise than by reference to the seriousness of its impact upon those affected).

[197] For example, *Ex p. Football League Ltd* [1993] 2 All E.R. 833 Rose J. noted at 841 that "FA's powers extend beyond contract to affect the lives of many hundreds of thousands who are not in any contractual relationship . . . though the same could be said about large public companies".

[198] See *Ex p. Football League Ltd* [1993] 2 All E.R. 833 where Rose J. at 840 notes that the important role of the EA. had been recognised by official government reports. *cf. Ex p. Massingberd-Mundy* [1993] 2 All E.R. 207, DC where Neill L.J. stated that, had the matter been free of authority, he would have held that the Jockey Club was judicially reviewable because it held a position of major public importance and "near monopolistic powers in an area in which the public generally have an interest and many persons earn their livelihoods".

Absence of consensual submission

3–050 Whether the aggrieved person has consensually submitted to be bound by the decision-maker. This is closely linked to the previous criterion. In considering the position of the Panel on Takeovers and Mergers in *Datafin*, Lloyd L.J. stated that "the City is not a club which one can join or not at will . . . The panel regulates not only itself, but all others who have no alternative but to come to the market in a case to which the code applies".[199] The question of whether there has been consensual submission ought not to be merged with that of whether a contract *entirely* regulates the relationship between the parties. It has always been the case that private or domestic tribunals are performing no public function when their "authority is derived solely from contract, that is the agreement of the parties concerned".[200] Their functions are therefore outside the scope of judicial review. Whether or not a contract exists between the aggrieved person and the body, in some situations the body may be performing regulatory or other functions which create a situation where the person is left with the stark choice of either submitting himself to the control of the body or not participating in the activity concerned.[201] Here, it is submitted, judicial review ought in principle to be available to an aggrieved person, though if a contract exists a contractual claim will normally be an appropriate alternative remedy which may bar judicial review.

Public funding

3–051 The fact that a body receives substantial funding from government to carry out its activities is of only marginal relevance in determining whether it is carrying out a public—that is, governmental—function. Many cultural

---

[199] *Datafin* [1987] 1 Q.B. 815 at 846.
[200] See, e.g. *R. v Criminal Injuries Compensation Board Ex p. Lain* [1967] 2 Q.B. 864 at 882 (Lord Parker C.J.) and 884–5 (Diplock L.J.). Many self-regulatory organisations include arbitration provisions in their contracts with members, which may involve a waiver of any rights under ECHR Art.6 to a determination by an independent and impartial tribunal established by law: see, e.g. *Stretford v Football Association Ltd* [2007] EWCA Civ 238; *The Times*, April 13, 2007. When dealing with claims for breach of contract of terms relating to discipline, it would be "surprising and unsatisfactory if a private law claim in relation to the decision of a domestic body required the court to adopt a materially different approach from a judicial review claim in relation to the decision of a public body. In each case the essential concern should be with the lawfulness of the decision taken: whether the procedure was fair, whether there was any error of law, whether any exercise of judgment or discretion fell within the limits open to the decision maker, and so forth": *Bradley v Jockey Club* [2004] EWHC 2164 at [37] (Richards J.), considered by the CA [2005] EWCA Civ 1056; *The Times*, July 14, 2005; *Flaherty v National Greyhound Racing Club Ltd* [2005] EWCA Civ 1117; (2005) 102(37) L.S.G. 31.
[201] See, e.g. *Ex p. Wachmann* [1992] 1 W.L.R. 1036 (judicial review not excluded because the applicant had consensually submitted to the Chief Rabbi's jurisdiction; the exclusion from judicial review of those who consensually submit to some subordinate jurisdiction properly applied only to arbitrators or private and domestic tribunals. Other reasons were, however, given for not subjecting the Chief Rabbi's decision to judicial review). There is much to be said for this view. *cf.* the statement of Farquharson L.J. in *Ex p. Aga Khan* [1993] 1 W.L.R. 909 at 928: "The fact is that if the applicant wishes to race his horses in this country he had no choice but to submit to the Jockey Club"s jurisdiction. This may be true but nobody is obliged to race his horses in this country and it does not destroy the element of consensuality". See also *Ex p. Professional Counselling Aids Ltd* [1991] C.O.D. 228.

organisations are heavily subsidised from taxation, but quite clearly that does not, in and of itself, make them susceptible to judicial review.[202]

Impact on the court's caseload

Suggestions have also been made from time to time that the court ought to have regard to the limited number of judges and the growing judicial review case load in deciding whether a class of body is susceptible to judicial review.[203] To take account of this factor appears to be wrong in principle and creates potential problems as to the independence of the judiciary. The number of the judiciary is of no relevance to the scope of judicial review. By failing to fill vacancies the executive could reduce the number of judges and thus, if the factor is relevant, theoretically reduce the scope of judicial review. 3–052

Broad and flexible approach

Undue reliance upon any one of the above criteria, while perhaps helpful in promoting certainty in this area of law, should be avoided. The test of public function should be overriding and the qualities enumerated in the criteria should be weighed and balanced in the context of each specific case. This will avoid the formalism that might otherwise develop and that has, in the past, inhibited the proper development of so much of administrative law.[204] It may however be going too far in the other direction to suggest that "The boundary between public law and private law is not capable of precise definition, and whether a decision has a sufficient public law element to justify the intervention of the Administrative Court by judicial review is often as much a matter of feel, as deciding whether any particular criteria are met".[205] 3–053

The application of the principles of judicial review can have the effect of extending the rights of the individual. For example, it can give an individual a right to be consulted which he would not have in private law.[206] On the other hand, the extent of redress that is available in judicial review may be less extensive than that available in private law. 3–054

English law recognises that a public body can act in more than one capacity. This is unlike the situation in most civil legal systems, such as the French system, where all the activities of public bodies are governed by 3–055

[202] *Mullins v The Board of Appeal of the Jockey Club* [2005] EWHC 2197 (Admin) at [35].
[203] *Ex p. Football League Ltd* [1993] 2 All E.R. 833 at 849 (Rose J.) it would be "a misapplication of scarce judicial resources" to hold the FA. amenable to the court's public law supervisory jurisdiction" and dicta in *R. v Panel on Take-overs and Mergers Ex p. Guinness plc* [1990] 1 Q.B. 146 at 177–8 (Lord Donaldson M.R.). *cf.* D. Pannick, "Who is Subject to Judicial Review and in Respect of What?" [1992] P.L. 1 at pp.6–7.
[204] Consider, e.g., the judicial/administrative/quasi-judicial categories (on which see Appendix B).
[205] *R. (on the application of Tucker) v Director General of the National Crime Squad* [2003] EWCA Civ 2; [2003] I.C.R. 599 at [13] (Scott L.J.).
[206] *Council for Civil Service Unions v Minister for the Civil Service* [1985] A.C. 374.

public law; or in relation to Convention rights, which apply to all functions of a "core" public authority.[207] Conversely, not all the activities of private bodies (such as business enterprises) are subject only to private law. For example, the activities of a private body such as a privatised former state-owned enterprise, may be governed by the standards of public law when its decisions are subject to duties conferred by statute[208] or when, by virtue of the function it is performing or possibly its dominant position in the market, it is under an implied duty to act in the public interest.[209]

AMENABILITY OF FUNCTIONS RELATING TO PRE-CONTACTUAL AND CONTRACTUAL POWERS

Contractual capacity of public authorities

3–056 Most public authorities in England and Wales have powers to make contracts. For statutory bodies, including local authorities, the legal capacity to enter into contractual relations can only stem from express or implied powers in legislation.[210] The powers of central government to enter into contracts may in some instances derive from specific statutory powers but may alternatively arise from the Crown's inherent common law powers as a corporation sole.[211] Some bodies (such as self-regulatory organisations and members' clubs) carrying out public functions are limited liability companies, the contractual powers of which are governed by the articles and memoranda of association; others are unincorporated associations which have no separate legal personality from that of their individual members and so cannot enter into contracts in their own name. It is important to note that some of the judicial review challenges brought have related not directly to a contract but to pre-contractual matters (such as tender processes) in relation to which the claimant may not have any other private law redress. Where a public authority lacks power to make a contract, the contract may as a matter of *private* law be unenforceable.[212]

---

[207] See 3–070.

[208] See, e.g. Gas Act 1986, s.9 (to supply gas).

[209] *Mercury Energy Ltd v Electricity Corp of NZ Ltd* [1994] 1 W.L.R. 521.

[210] See, For example, the Local Government (Contracts) Act 1997, which sought to put the contracting powers of local authorities on a firmer legal footing; the Local Authorities (Goods and Services) Act 1970 enables local authorities to supply goods and services, subject to certain restrictions, to other local authorities and to public bodies; and where no more specific provision exists, Local Government Act 1972 s.111 provides local authorities with a subsidiary power "to do any thing (whether involving the expenditure, borrowing, or lending of money, or the acquisition or disposal of any property or rights) which is calculated to facilitate, or is conducive or incidental to, the discharge of any of their functions". Legislation may also make provision for imposing charges for the provision of services pursuant to statutory powers, though not duties (e.g. Local Government Act 2003 s.92), though this will not always lead to the creation of a contractual relationship. A police force may charge for services and goods under Police Act 1996 ss.18, 25, 26 (e.g. where policing is provided for football and other sports events or to agencies such as Immigration Service).

[211] Under the so-called "Ram doctrine": see 5–022.

[212] See 19–077.

Variety of contracts entered into by public authorities

Public authorities enter into a wide range of contracts to equip themselves   3–057
to carry out their basic functions, including employment contracts and
commercial contracts for the supply of goods and services to the authority.
In more recent years, contracts have also assumed a more important
general role in governance in many Western democracies, including the
United Kingdom. Planning agreements have a role in relation to environment and planning development control.[213] Between 1980 and 1998 local
authorities were required by legislation to put out a range of activities and
services (including refuse collection, grounds maintenance, personnel management and legal services) to competitive tender. As a result of this
"contracting out", the practical delivery of statutory duties came to be
done by businesses and not-for-profit organisations.[214] The Local Government Act 1999 replaced compulsory competitive tendering with a duty of
to secure "best value" on a wider range of public authorities. The aim was
no longer to achieve simply the lowest cost but "to make arrangements to
secure continuous improvement in the way in which its functions are
exercised, having regard to a combination of economy, efficiency and
effectiveness".[215] The outcome of these developments is that local authorities now fulfil many of their core public functions by entering into
contracts for services with businesses and charities (for example, in respect
of making arrangements for providing residential accommodation to
persons who by reason of age, illness, disability or any other circumstances
are in need of care and attention which is not otherwise available under
s.21 of the National Assistance Act 1948).

   At national level, a strategic policy of "Public Private Partnerships" (PPP)   3–058
has been promoted as one means of providing capital investment for public
services. This entails various kinds of private sector ownership of formerly
wholly state-owned functions; the Private Finance Initiative (PFI) under
which private sector businesses takes responsibility for providing public
services, including providing and maintaining the necessary infrastructure;
and the marketing of government services to the private sector.[216] European Community law imposes obligations and rights in relation to public
procurement, but consideration of that regime falls outside the scope of
this book.[217]

[213] See, e.g. "planning obligations" entered into under Town and Country Planning Act 1990
s.106. Such agreements must be made by deed and constitute a local land charge.
[214] This has resulted in judicial review claims in two main kinds of situation: first, in relation
to complaints of unlawful tendering processes (See, e.g. *R. v Secretary of State for the
Environment, Transport and the Regions Ex p. Bury MBC* [1998] 2 C.M.L.R. 787 and *R. v
Avon CC Ex p. Terry Adams Ltd* [1994] Env L.R. 442); secondly, by citizens who deal directly
with the business or not-for-profit organisation delivering services which a local authority or
other public body is under a statutory obligation to provide (e.g. *R. (on the application of
Heather) v Leonard Cheshire Foundation* [2002] EWCA Civ 366; [2002] 2 All E.R. 936)
[215] s.3(1).
[216] HM Treasury, *Public Private Partnerships—the Government's Approach* (2000).
[217] See S. Arrowsmith, *The Law of Public and Utilities Procurement* (2005); Public Contracts
Regulations 2006 (SI 2006/5).

Amenability tests for contractual situations

3–059 The range and growth of contractual relationships in the public sector has presented a challenge for judicial review law. The current position on amenability to judicial review of situations involving contracts is the product of two policies. One is that judicial review, as a remedy of last resort, is inappropriate where there is another field of law governing the situation. Thus, contract disputes are normally to be left to the general law of contract and CPR Pt 7 proceedings (or, in relation to employment contracts, recourse to an Employment Tribunal) rather than judicial review.[218] The Unfair Terms in Consumer Contracts Regulations 1999 may apply to the contracting activities of public authorities, including those relating to housing.[219] The existence of a private cause of action does not by itself, however, make judicial review inappropriate.[220] The other policy is to recognise that some public functions may be carried out through the medium of contractual relationships, which justifies the use of the Administrative Court's judicial review supervisory jurisdiction. It should be noted that the contracting process may give rise to tort claims, including for misfeasance in public office.[221]

3–060 The tests applied by the courts to determine whether a function involving a contract is susceptible to judicial review have been criticised as overly complex and liable to divert the attention of the court away from the substance of the complaint.[222] In the orthodox approach, the court assumes that the fact that the source of a public authority's power is statutory is in and of itself insufficient to make a dispute about a contract amenable to judicial review; the court therefore goes on to consider whether there is some additional "sufficient public element, flavour or character" to the situation.[223] A more straightforward approach (though not one widely applied by the courts) would be to say that if the contractual decision in issue involves that exercise of a statutory power, then in principle it should be subject to judicial review and the court should consider whether any of the grounds of review have been made out.[224]

---

[218] It is inappropriate to start two sets of proceedings seeking the similar remedies on similar grounds: *Cookson & Clegg Ltd v Ministry of Defence* [2005] EWCA Civ 811; [2006] Eu. L.R. 1092 (claimant commenced Pt 7 and Pt 54 claims).

[219] *R. (on the application of Khatun) v Newham LBC* [2004] EWCA Civ 55; [2005] Q.B. 37.

[220] *R. (on the application of London Corp) v Secretary of State for the Environment, Food and Rural Affairs* [2004] EWCA Civ 1765; [2005] 1 W.L.R. 1286 (a decision of the minister to give consent to the to grant leases for the purpose of selling meat or fish at New Covent Garden Market in London, a market set up as a horticultural market, was a public law matter).

[221] See, e.g. *Harmon CFEM Facades (UK) Ltd v Corporate Officer of the House of Commons* [1999] EWHC Technology 199; (2000) 2 L.G.L.R. 372 (unlawful tender award).

[222] S. Bailey, "Judicial Review of Contracting Decisions" [2007] P.L. 444.

[223] *R. (on the application of Beer (t/a Hammer Trout Farm)) v Hampshire Farmers Markets Ltd* [2003] EWCA Civ 1056; [2004] 1 W.L.R. 233 at [16] (Dyson J.); and see, e.g. *R v Lord Chancellor Ex p. Hibbit & Saunders* [1993] C.O.D. 326; *R. v Camden LBC Ex p. Hughes* [1994] C.O.D. 253; *R. v Bolsover DC Ex p. Pepper* (2001) 3 L.G.L.R. 20.

[224] Bailey [2007] P.L. 444, p.451.

As in other contexts, in working out whether a decision is susceptible to **3–061** judicial review the court considers two main factors. It will have regard to the source of the power under which the impugned decision is made.[225] If this is "purely" contractual, judicial review is unlikely to be appropriate; some close statutory (or prerogative) underpinning of the contract will normally be needed. Alternatively, the court may consider whether the function being carried out by the defendant is a public function. Having decided that a decision is susceptible to judicial review, the court will go on to examine the grounds advanced by the claimant for the decision's unlawfulness.[226]

Identifying the "additional public element"

So long as the courts approach the issue of amenability by requiring a **3–062** sufficient "public element" in the contractual dispute, there is much to be said for adopting a pragmatic method and reasoning by analogy from previously decided cases rather than attempting to identify broad overarching principles (an exercise that soon risks imploding in a sea of generalisations). The cases set out in the following paragraphs demonstrate that different *types* of consideration are capable of providing the necessary "public element"—in some it is the intrinsic public importance of the contract-related decision; in others it is the ground of review ("bad faith" scoring more highly than irrationality, for example).

Situations where there was an insufficient "additional public element"

The courts have held the following contractual situations *not* to be **3–063** susceptible to judicial review: where a pupil at an independent, fee-paying school was excluded following an alleged theft;[227] where a sports regulatory body disciplined a member with whom it is in a contractual relationship;[228] where a disappointed tenderer for court reporting services alleged that they had a legitimate expectation that other tenderers would not be invited to submit lower bids;[229] alleged irrationalities in a marking scheme used to assess pre-qualification questionnaires from prospective

---

[225] See, e.g. *R. v Pembrokeshire CC Ex p. Coker* [1999] 4 All E.R. 1007 (whether the council had contravened the Local Government Act 1972 s.123 in failing to obtain the best consideration reasonably obtainable for the letting of land).

[226] The PC in *Mercury Energy v Electricity Corp of New Zealand* [1994] 1 W.L.R. 521 held that decisions of a "state enterprise" (as defined by NZ legislation) were in principle susceptible to review, though the court would not interfere with a decision to enter into or determine a commercial contract to supply goods or services "in the absence of fraud, corruption or bad faith" (at 530).

[227] *R. v Incorporated Froebel Educational Institute Ex p. L* [1999] E.L.R. 488 (although the school operated within a statutory framework, the relationship between the school and its students was founded on the contract between the school and the parents).

[228] *Law v National Greyhound Racing Club* [1983] 1 W.L.R. 1302; *R. v Disciplinary Committee of the Jockey Club Ex p. Aga Khan* [1993] 1 W.L.R. 909.

[229] *R. v Lord Chancellor Ex p. Hibbit & Saunders* [1993] C.O.D. 326.

141

tenderers for options to lease land for a wind farm;[230] decisions of the Business Conduct Committee of Lloyd's of London to approve four minority buyouts of his memberships in four syndicates at Lloyd's;[231] other decisions by Lloyd's of London to make cash calls on members of certain syndicates;[232] a decision of the British Standards Institution to circulate a letter to the chief fire officers' association stating that the claimant manufacturer had made false claims that its door release mechanisms met BSI standards;[233] a decision of the British Council to withdraw a language school's accreditation under a scheme designed to identify schools of good quality;[234] where a mobile phone dealer was contractually bound by terms of an anti-theft scheme, supported by the police and promoted by a trade association (of which the dealer was not a member);[235] a refusal of the local authority to sell certain land to the claimant on the basis that he had a legitimate expectation, either to be sold the land or at least to be allowed to make representations before any decision not to sell it was taken.[236]

Situations where there was a sufficient "additional public element"

3–064   In contrast, the courts have held (or assumed) there to be a sufficient public law element: in a challenge by a disappointed tenderer to the Legal Aid Board's decision to award a contract to represent claimants seeking compensation for Gulf War Syndrome to two other firms;[237] where a building contractor was removed from a local authority's approved list of contractors following disputes about the quality of work;[238] where a local

---

[230] *R. (on the application of Gamesa Energy UK Ltd) v National Assembly for Wales* [2006] EWHC 2167; at [76] (Gibbs J.): ("the stated aims of the pre-qualification procedure are not and could not be criticised. It follows that the complaints on the basis of irrationality and unfairness are confined to the nuts and bolts of parts of the exercise and their effect on the individual application of the claimant"). See also *Mass Energy Ltd v Birmingham CC* [1994] Env. L.R. 298, CA; *R. (on the application of Menai Collect Ltd) v Department for Constitutional Affairs* [2006] EWHC 724 at [47] (McCombe J.: "It is not every wandering from the precise paths of best practice that lends fuel to a claim for judicial review. It is, I think, for this reason that the examples given of cases where commercial processes such as these are likely to be subject to review are such as they are in the reported cases, namely bribery, corruption, implementation of unlawful policy and the like. In such cases, there is a true public law element").

[231] *R. (on the application of West) v Lloyd's of London* [2004] EWCA Civ 506; [2004] 3 All E.R. 251.

[232] *R. v Lloyd's of London Ex p. Briggs* [1993] 1 Lloyd's Rep. 176; and see also *Doll-Steinberg v Society of Lloyd's* [2002] EWHC 419 (Admin) (renewed application for permission—determinations of its Settlement Panel not subject to judicial review).

[233] *R. v British Standards Institution Ex p. Dorgard Ltd* [2001] A.C.D. 15 (the dispute arose from a commercial contract under which the BSI had agreed to test the claimant's product).

[234] *R. (on the application of Oxford Study Centre Ltd) v British Council* [2001] EWHC Admin 207; [2001] E.L.R. 803 (the scheme was voluntary; the British Council had acted in breach of an implied term in its contract to act fairly).

[235] *R. v Panel of the Federation of Communication Services Ltd Ex p. Kubis* (1999) 11 Admin. L.R. 43.

[236] *R. v Bolsover DC Ex p. Pepper* (2001) 3 L.G.L.R. 20.

[237] *R. v Legal Aid Board Ex p. Donn & Co* [1996] 3 All E.R. 1 at 10–11 (the board were allocating a very large sum of public money; there was an obvious public important in making the right decision; and the board is the sole and final arbiter of selection).

[238] *R. v Bristol City Council Ex p. DL Barrett & Sons* (2001) 3 L.G.L.R. 11, following *R. v Enfield LBC Ex p. TF Unwin (Roydon) Ltd* [1989] C.O.D. 466.

authority terminated an informal arrangement permitting a hot-food take-away caravan to be located at a market;[239] where a local authority refused to vary a lease to permit the use of premises as a café after the council had lost an appeal against the change of use under planning legislation;[240] where a group of former tenants of market units sought to challenge a council's decision not to select them as tenants for a new smaller market which was to replace the existing market.[241]

Where the contract-related decision is the promulgation of a broad 3–065 policy, taken under the exercise of statutory powers, the courts have often assumed without argument that the decision is susceptible to judicial review. For instance: where a local authority resolved not to contract in future with a company, on the ground of its links with South Africa during the apartheid era;[242] and where a local authority boycotted the publications of a particular newspaper company on the ground of the company's employment practices.[243]

Employment situations

Where a public authority takes action in relation to an employee, such as 3–066 disciplinary action or termination of an employment relationship, this will normally be matter for contract or employment law rather than judicial review.[244] Complications have arisen in relation to civil servants who hold office under the Crown, terminable at will, as it has not been clear whether a contract of employment exists in this context, but that is a rather different question to the one in hand, namely whether the Administrative Court should intervene.[245] Police officers, similarly are office-holders rather

[239] R. v Wear Valley DC Ex p. Binks [1985] 2 All E.R. 699.
[240] R. (on the application of Molinaro) v Kensington and Chelsea RLBC [2001] EWHC Admin 896; [2002] B.L.G.R. 336 at [63] (Elias J.) ("Manifestly, the council was not simply acting as a private body when it sought to give effect to its planning policy through the contract. Again, the decision not to permit a change of use, albeit one involving the exercise of discretion under a contract, was taken for the purpose of giving effect to its planning objectives").
[241] R. (on the application of Western International Campaign Group) v Hounslow LBC [2003] EWHC 3112; [2004] B.L.G.R. 536 (the council had specific statutory powers in relation to the market, the market was on publicly-owned land, and the council's powers emanated not solely from the lease but also its byelaws).
[242] R. v Lewisham LBC Ex p. Shell UK [1988] 1 All E.R. 938. See also Bromley v GLC [1983] 1 A.C. 768 at 813 and Wheeler v Leicester CC [1985] A.C. 1054. See further 5–083.
[243] R. v Ealing LBC Ex p. Times Newspapers Ltd (1987) 85 L.G.R. 316.
[244] R. v BBC Ex p. Lavelle [1983] 1 W.L.R. 23 (claimant sought stay of BBC disciplinary proceedings pending conclusion of a criminal trial); R. v East Berkshire HA Ex p. Walsh [1985] Q.B. 152; R. v Derbyshire CC Ex p. Noble [1990] I.C.R. 808 (local authority terminated appointment of deputy police surgeon without given reasons or allowing representations); McLaren v Secretary of State for the Home Department [1990] I.C.R. 824; R. v Lord Chancellor's Department Ex p. Nangle [1991] I.R.L.R. 343; R. (on the application of Arthurworry) v Haringey LBC [2001] EWHC Admin 698; [2002] I.C.R. 279; Evans v University of Cambridge [2002] EWHC 1382; [2003] E.L.R. 8; R. (on the application of Tucker) v Director General of the National Crime Squad [2003] EWCA Civ 2; [2003] I.C.R. 599 (termination of secondment of police office to the NCS).
[245] See S. Fredman and G. Morris, "Judicial Review and Civil Servants: Contracts of Employment Declared to Exist" [1991] P.L. 485.

than employees under contract. Following precedent, the court also probably has jurisdiction over claims made by Church of England clergymen complaining about lack of fairness in the procedures adopted by their superiors,[246] though not in respect of employment-type issues arising in other religious organisations.[247]

3-067   It will perhaps be easiest to establish that an employment decision amounts to a public function where what is at stake is a general policy, taken under statutory or prerogative powers. The following situations have been held to be susceptible to judicial review: a local authority's decision restricting how educational psychologists could consult other professionals before producing their advisory reports;[248] delegated legislation by which a minister sought to change teachers' contracts of employment to implement a system of performance-related pay;[249] an exercise of prerogative powers to change terms of employment to ban trade union membership at CGHQ;[250] a redeployment and redundancy policy adopted by a local authority;[251] a ministerial decision to close collieries without following an agreed consultation procedure;[252] a wage settlement when it is claimed that the authority exceeded or abused its conferred powers;[253] and a decision of the Army Board, pursuant to Queen's Regulations, to retain two guardsmen in the Army after they had been released from prison after conviction for murdering a youth while on duty.[254]

3-068   Judicial review may also be possible in relation to disciplinary proceedings which are specifically provided for in legislation, as opposed to being wholly informal or domestic matters.[255] The role of the Administrative Court here is analogous to its supervisory jurisdiction over other inferior tribunals. As in other contexts, the claimant is however expected to have exhausted other available remedies before resorting to judicial review.[256]

---

[246] R. v Bishop of Stafford Ex p. Owen [2001] A.C.D. 14 (CA, Schiemann L.J. stating that he so assumed "without finally ruling on the point").

[247] R. v Chief Rabbi of the United Hebrew Congregations of Great Britain and the Commonwealth Ex p. Wachmann [1992] 1 W.L.R. 1036.

[248] R. v Sunderland City Council Ex p. Baumber [1996] C.O.D. 211.

[249] R. v Secretary of State for Education and Employment Ex p. National Union of Teachers [2000] Ed. C.R. 603.

[250] Council of Civil Service Unions v Minister for the Civil Service [1985] A.C. 374; McLaren v Secretary of State for the Home Department [1990] I.C.R. 824 (obiter).

[251] R. v Hammersmith and Fulham LBC Ex p. NALGO [1991] I.R.L.R. 249.

[252] R. v Secretary of State for Trade and Industry Ex p. Vardy [1993] I.C.R. 720.

[253] Pickwell v Camden LBC [1983] Q.B. 962.

[254] In the Matter of an Application for Judicial Review by Jean McBride (No.2) [2003] NICA 23 at [25].

[255] McClaren v Home Office [1990] I.C.R. 824; and, e.g. R. (on the application of Bennion) v Chief Constable of Merseyside [2001] EWCA Civ 638; [2001] I.R.L.R. 442; R. v Ministry of Defence Police Ex p. Byrne [1994] C.O.D. 429; R. v Deputy Chief Constable of North Wales Ex p. Hughes [1991] 3 All E.R. 414; R. v Chief Constable of Merseyside Ex p. Merrill [1989] 1 W.L.R. 1077.

[256] R. v Chief Constable of the Merseyside Police Ex p. Calveley [1986] Q.B. 424.

Judicial review may also be used to challenge the compatibility of UK employment legislation with European Community law.[257]

AMENABILITY AND THE HUMAN RIGHTS ACT

Having examined issues relating to amenability to judicial review generally, **3–069** we now turn to consider which functions may be subject to judicial review claims on the specific ground that they unlawfully interfere with a Convention right, contrary to s.6 of the Human Rights Act 1998 (HRA).[258] Three basic categories can be distinguished: (a) functions of "core public authorities";[259] (b) "functions of a public nature" carried out by other organisations and persons;[260] and (c) decisions of courts and tribunals.[261] Section 6 of the HRA provides:

"6.—(1) It is unlawful for a public authority to act in a way which is incompatible with a Convention right.

(2) Subsection (1) does not apply to an act if —

(a) as the result of one or more provisions of primary legislation, the authority could not have acted differently; or

(b) in the case of one or more provisions of, or made under, primary legislation which cannot be read or given effect in a way which is compatible with the Convention rights, the authority was acting so as to give effect to or enforce those provisions.

(3) In this section 'public authority' includes —

(a) a court or tribunal, and

(b) any person certain of whose functions are functions of a public nature, but does not include either House of Parliament or a person exercising functions in connection with proceedings in Parliament.

(4) In subsection (3) 'Parliament' does not include the House of Lords in its judicial capacity.

(5) In relation to a particular act, a person is not a public authority by virtue only of subsection (3)(b) if the nature of the act is private.

(6) 'An act' includes a failure to act but does not include a failure to—

---

[257] See, e.g. R. v Secretary of State for Employment Ex p. Seymour-Smith (No.2) [2000] 1 W.L.R. 435; R. v Secretary of State for Employment Ex p. Seymour-Smith (No.1) [1997] 1 W.L.R. 473; R. v Secretary of State for Employment Ex p. Equal Opportunities Commission [1995] 1 A.C. 1.
[258] See Ch. 13.
[259] See 3–070.
[260] See 3–075.
[261] HRA s.6(3)(a).

(a) introduce in, or lay before, Parliament a proposal for legislation; or

(b) make any primary legislation or remedial order."

Core public authorities

3–070 It has been said that the HRA fails to provide an exhaustive definition of what is meant by the term "public authority" because "there are certain bodies that so obviously have the character of a public authority that it is not necessary to mention them".[262] These bodies have come to be called "core", "true", "pure", "standard" or "through-and-through" public authorities. Put in terms of the structure of the HRA, we can say that core public authorities are those public authorities falling within s.6 without reference to s.6(3)(b).[263]

3–071 Categorising an organisation or person as a core public authority has several consequences. Under ECHR law, such institutions of the State are bound to respect Convention rights *in all aspects* of their activities. This being so, for the purposes of the HRA it is unnecessary to consider whether a particular act or function of a core public authority is or is not "of a public nature".[264] Thus, if a local authority provides accommodation and nursing care for elderly people in a council-run home, that function—and all acts connected with that function—fall within the scope of s.6 of the HRA simply because the local authority is a "core public authority" and regardless of whether the function is regarded as being public or private. Another consequence of classifying a body as a core public authority is that it will fall outside the protective scope of the ECHR as the State cannot benefit from or exert the protections offered by Convention rights.[265]

3–072 As in the interpretation of other aspects of the HRA, the courts must in determining whether a body is a core public authority take into account the text of the ECHR and the case law of the European Court of Human Rights (ECtHR).[266] The purpose of the HRA was to "bring rights home",[267] and the national courts will accordingly attempt to define a core public authority as one that "carries out a function of government that

---

[262] *R. (on the application of Quark Fishing Ltd) v Secretary of State for Foreign and Commonwealth Affairs (No.2)* [2005] UKHL 57; [2006] 1 A.C. 529 at [85] (Lord Hope of Craighead).

[263] *Aston Cantlow v Aston Cantlow and Wilmcote with Billesley Parochial Church Council* [2003] UKHL 37; [2004] 1 A.C. 546 at [8] (Lord Nicholls).

[264] *YL (by her litigation friend the Official Solicitor) v Birmingham CC* [2007] UKHL 27; [2007] 3 W.L.R. 112 at [110] (Lord Mance: "All such functions and activities are subject to the Convention, because the authority is a core public authority. It only becomes necessary to analyse their nature, if and when they are contracted out to a person who is not a core public authority"); [at 131] (Lord Neuberger of Abbotsbury: ". . . there is therefore no need to distinguish between private and public acts or functions of a core public authority"). See further J. Landau, "Functional public authorities after *YL* " [2007] P.L. 630.

[265] *Aston Cantlow* [2003] UKHL 37; [2004] 1 A.C. 546 at [8].

[266] HRA s.2; and see, e.g. *YL* [2003] UKHL 27; [2007] 3 W.L.R. 112 at [119] (Lord Mance).

[267] See 13–030.

would engage the responsibility of the United Kingdom before the Strasbourg organs"[268]—subject to the important qualification that Parliament and a person exercising functions in connection with proceedings in Parliament, are expressly excluded from the definition of public authority in s.6(3) and 6(6), in order to preserve the constitutional principle of parliamentary supremacy. The limitation of this approach, however, is that the ECtHR takes little general interest in the internal governance arrangements within Member States: "It is only the responsibility of the [Member] State itself—not that of a domestic authority or organ—that is in issue before the Court. It is not the Court's role to deal with a multiplicity of national authorities or courts or to examine disputes between institutions or over internal politics".[269] The ECtHR has held that Convention rights bind "governmental organisations established for public administration purposes".[270] Responsibility is not confined to central government but extends to lower tiers as well.[271] Of particular importance is the question whether the organisation in question might be a "non-governmental organisation" for the purposes of Art.34.[272] Non-governmental organisations have the right to invoke Convention rights before the ECtHR and cannot therefore be part of the State (which cannot benefit from the protection of Convention rights).[273] The concept of "emanation of the State" in European Community law,[274] is not relevant in this context.[275]

There is relatively little national case law on the ambit of the concept of core public authority for the simple reason that in most cases the answer is fairly obvious. "The most obvious examples are government departments, local authorities, the police and the armed forces".[276] In addition: "Health authorities and NHS trusts and their staff";[277] a local education authority, **3–073**

---

[268] *Aston Cantlow* [2003] UKHL 37; [2004] 1 A.C. 546 at [160] (Lord Rodger).

[269] *Assanide v Georgia* [2004] E.C.H.R. 140, para.149.

[270] *Holy Monasteries v Greece* (1995) 20 E.H.R.R. 1, para.49 (holding that monasteries of the Greek Orthodox Church did not exercise governmental power: "Their objectives—essentially ecclesiastical and spiritual ones, but also cultural and social ones in some cases—are not such as to enable them to be classed with governmental organisations established for public administration purposes").

[271] *Ayuntamiento de Mula v Spain*, Application No.55346/00, February 1, 2001 (ECtHR) ("the Court reiterates that in international law the expression 'governmental organisations' cannot be held to refer only to the Government or the central organs of the State. When powers are distributed along decentralised lines, it refers to any national authority which exercises public functions").

[272] Discussed at 2–052.

[273] *Aston Cantlow* [2003] UKHL 37; [2004] 1 A.C. 546 in holding a parochial church council of the Church of England was not a core public authority, the HL attached significance to the fact that if were such a public authority, it would be incapable of seeking protection for Convention rights, notably freedom of religion (which by HRA s.12 is afforded especial recognition in domestic law).

[274] See 14–024.

[275] *Aston Cantlow* [2003] UKHL 37; [2004] 1 A.C. 546 at [55]

[276] *Aston Cantlow* [2003] UKHL 37; [2004] 1 A.C. 546 at [7].

[277] *R. (on the application of Wilkinson) v Broadmoor Special Hospital Authority* [2001] EWCA Civ 1545; [2002] 1 W.L.R. 419 at [61]; *Grampian University Hospitals NHS Trust v Her Majesty's Advocate* [2004] ScotHC 10.

the governing body of a maintained school and a head teacher.[278] The following has been held *not* to be a core public authority: parochial church councils (PCCs) of the Church of England, responsible for the financial affairs of the Church and the care and maintenance of the church fabric.[279]

3–074   Although (as noted above) for the purposes of liability under the HRA it is unnecessary to consider whether a core public authority is carrying out a public function (because all its functions are subject to the HRA), it may, however, still be necessary to consider whether *for the purposes of making a claim for judicial review* the act or function in question is a public function.[280] So, for example, an employment dispute with a local authority which raises an issue of Convention rights may lack a sufficient public element to make it amenable to judicial review; and in any event proceedings before the Employment Tribunal may be a more appropriate alternative remedy.[281] In short, we can say that while all acts and functions of core public authorities fall within s.6 of the HRA, some disputes about whether they are compatible with Convention rights may fall outside the scope of judicial review and should be pursued in other forms of legal claim.

"Functions of a public nature" under the HRA

3–075   The second type of act falling within the ambit of s.6 of the HRA is where a person or organisation that is not a core public authority carries out a "function of a public nature". This phrase is used in other legislation with increasing frequency.[282] Convention rights regulate only that public function, not all functions of the body in question; "if the nature of the act is private" (HRA s.6(5), then it falls outside the scope of s.6. The HRA does not create a system of direct "horizontal effect" for Convention rights

---

[278] *A v Headteacher and Governors of Lord Grey School* [2004] EWCA Civ 382; [2004] Q.B. 1231 at [36]–[38] (but Sedley J. expressing "a visceral unease at the conclusion that the headteacher of a maintained school is a public authority"); decision on Convention rights issues reversed by HL: [2006] UKHL 14; [2006] 2 A.C. 363. In relation to "trust schools" established under the Education and Inspections Act 2006, the Government takes the view that they are within the ambit of the HRA, though it is not entirely clear whether this is because they are "core" or "functional": see *Hansard* HL, col.WA46 (January 31, 2006) "The governing bodies of all maintained schools are public authorities for the purposes of the Human Rights Act 1998, and the governing bodies of trust schools will be no different in this respect. Although the matter has not been judicially determined, in the department's view academies exercise functions of a public nature by providing education at public expense and are therefore public authorities for the purposes of the Human Rights Act 1998".
[279] *Aston Cantlow* [2003] UKHL 37; [2004] 1 A.C. 546: despite its close links to the State, "the Church of England remains essentially a religious organisation" [at 13], and its concerns were for the "congregation of believers in the parish" rather than the general public [at 86].
[280] See 3–041.
[281] See 16–018.
[282] See, e.g. Equality Act 2006 s.52; Sex Discrimination Act 1975 new s.21A; London Olympic Games and Paralympic Games Act 2006 s.35; Government of Wales Act 2006 s.63 and Sch.7; Education and Inspections Act 2006 Sch.13; Companies Act 2006 s.54; and Police and Justice Act 2006 s.28. And see *YL* [2007] UKHL 27; [2007] 3 W.L.R. 112 [106].

(*unmittlebare Drittwirkung*) in which they can be invoked in purely private relationships. In respect of its private functions and acts, such a body is capable of being a victim of breaches of Convention rights.[283] "Functions of a public nature" are defined by HRA s.6(3)(b) and 6(5), which requires "a two-fold assessment, first of the body's functions, and secondly of the particular act in question".[284]

The YL decision in the House of Lords

The leading decision on the meaning of "functions of a public of a public   3–076
nature" is YL,[285] a test case. The claimant was an elderly woman suffering from Alzheimer's disease living in a residential home operated by Southern Cross Healthcare Ltd (a business providing accommodation and nursing services, subject to regulation under the Care Standards Act 2000). The claimant lived at the home under the terms of a contract. There were three parties to this "placement agreement": the claimant (through her daughter); Southern Cross; and Birmingham City Council (the local authority with statutory responsibilities in relation to the claimant for care in the community). There was a further contract (a "third party funding agreement") between Southern Cross and the council, under which the council undertook to pay a certain sum towards the fee charged to the claimant by Southern Cross (£478 a week), the balance (£35 a week) being paid by the claimant's daughter. The local NHS Trust contributed a further sum towards the claimant's nursing care.

Following a dispute with the claimant's family, Southern Cross exercised   3–077
its contractual right to terminate for "good reason" the placement agreement by giving four weeks notice. The claimant's lawyers argued that the termination notice violated her rights under Art.8 (right to respect for home). Clearly, Southern Cross could not be a "core" public authority. The council was, but it was not the organisation which had served notice on the claimant and nor was it suggested that the council had failed to carry out any of its statutory duties. The claimant's only recourse under the HRA was therefore to demonstrate that Southern Cross were carrying out functions and acts of a public nature. The rival contentions took place against the contractual background, described above, and the statutory duties and powers that government the arrangements. The council was required to (and did) carry out an assessment of the claimant's needs under Pt 3 of the National Health Service and Community Care Act 1990 in relation to "community care". The local NHS Primary Care Trust was also

---

[283] *Aston Cantlow* [2003] UKHL 37; [2004] 1 A.C. 546 at [11]. On the victim requirement, see 2–053.
[284] *Aston Cantlow* [2003] UKHL 37; [2004] 1 A.C. 546 [85] (Lord Hobhouse). His Lordship added "The nature of the person's functions are not to be confused with the nature of the act complained of, as s.6 makes clear" [at 88]. See also YL [2007] UKHL 27; [2007] 3 W.L.R. 112 at [25], [34] (Lord Scott).
[285] *YL (by her litigation friend the Official Solicitor) v Birmingham CC* [2007] UKHL 27; [2007] 3 W.L.R. 112.

required to assess the claimant's health care needs under the National Health Service Act 1977 (and did so). The National Assistance Act 1948 placed a duty on the council to "make arrangements for providing" residential accommodation and nursing care for people assessed to be in need, to be paid in whole or in part by the council and the NHS according to means testing—payments being made directly to the operator of the care home (which it had done). Under the Health and Social Care Act 2001, the council agreed to fund most of the claimant's costs.

3–078   For the reasons examined below, Lords Scott of Foscote, Mance and Neuberger of Abbotsbury held that Southern Cross were not performing a pubic function; Lord Bingham of Cornhill and Baroness Hale of Richmond dissented. The division within the Appellate Committee in YL provides amble evidence that "There is room for doubt and for argument"[286] about the meaning of the phrase "function of a public nature" and thus the ambit of the HRA. There have been sharp differences of opinion within the judiciary and between the courts and parliamentarians.[287]

3–079   These differences of view, which are unlikely to be settled by the House of Lords' ruling in YL, is a particular instance of a broader debate the overall aims of the HRA. The narrower view is that purpose of the HRA is limited to making available though the UK courts the rights and remedies that previously had to be obtained by individual petition to the ECtHR. There should therefore, on this view, be as great an equivalence as possible between what can and cannot be obtained in Strasbourg and in the national courts. The broader view sees the ECHR as providing simply a minimum starting point from which national courts, applying the HRA, may extend in order to achieve a higher degree of respect for Convention rights in a domestic setting—which necessarily entails outcomes where Convention rights in the United Kingdom are not completely aligned with how those rights are applied and defined in Strasbourg.

3–080   In the particular context of interpreting "functions of a public nature", those supporting a narrower interpretation eschew reliance on what was said about the scope of s.6 in parliamentary debates reported in *Hansard*.[288] Another methodological concern is to avoid making simplistic assumptions about what is the preferable policy to pursued: while there may be policy arguments in favour of extending the protection of Convention rights (for example, as in YL, to people being cared for by charitable organisations or

---

[286] *Aston Cantlow* [2003] UKHL 37; [2004] 1 A.C. 546 [36] (Lord Hope).
[287] Two reports of the Joint Committee on Human Rights have been critical of the courts' approach: *The Meaning of Public Authority under the Human Rights Act*, HL Paper No.39/HC Paper No.382; (Session 2003/04) and *The Meaning of Public Authority under the Human Rights Act*, HL Paper No.77/HC (Session 2006/07) 410; and a Private Members Bill has sought to address the perceived problem: see *Hansard* HC, col.1036 (June 15, 2007).
[288] *Aston Cantlow* [2003] UKHL 37; [2004] 1 A.C. 547 at [37] (Lord Hope), [161]–[162] (Lord Rodger); *YL* [2007] UKHL 27; [2004] 3 W.L.R. 112 at [89]–[90] (Lord Mance). The point is that there is no ambiguity in the expression "functions of a public nature" that brings into play the limited rule in *Pepper v Hart* [1993] A.C. 593 allowing *reference* to ministerial statements.

in privately-owned care homes under arrangements made and funded by local government), there are also countervailing considerations (for example, that extension of liability under the HRA may risk driving voluntary sector organisations and businesses away from contracting with the state to carry out functions, or may inhibit effective deployment of resources within organisations).[289] Another consideration is that all residents of a home—whether their places are arranged by government and publicly funded or arranged by themselves or their families and privately funded (or, as is often the case, a mix of the two)—should have similar rights and protections. This would not be so if those residents (and only those residents) whose places are arranged and funded by government were to have Convention rights directly enforceable the care home provider.[290] An important article by Professor Dawn Oliver has influenced the courts, especially her argument that the characteristics which give some functions (of non-core authorities) a public nature should be confined to "specifically legally authorised coercion or authority over others which would normally be unlawful for a private body to exercise".[291] Furthermore, the structure of some of the Convention rights is ill-suited to deal with claims against non-State bodies: where a qualified right exists (as in Arts 8–11), most of the limitations on that right can only be relied upon by high-level institutions of the State.[292]

Critics—including the Government[293]—say that the decisions of the House of Lords in the test case of YL[294] and the Court of Appeal in Leonard Cheshire[295] are based on too narrow a conception of function of a public nature.[296] The Joint Committee on Human Rights in reports made in 2003–04 and 2006–07 argued for a broad interpretation, to give better effect to what was intended by the provision, as evidenced by the parliamentary debates at the time.[297] A failure to adopt such an approach has, it is said, led to a gap in human rights protection, especially for people vulnerable to ill-treatment.[298] The Joint Committee's view in 2003–04 was that "a function is a public one when government has taken responsibility 3–081

---

[289] YL [2007] UKHL 27; [2004] 3 W.L.R. 112 [152] (Lord Neuberger).
[290] YL [2007] UKHL 27; [2004] 3 W.L.R. 112 [151] (Lord Neuberger).
[291] D. Oliver, "Functions of a Public Nature under the Human Rights Act" [2004] P.L. 328 at 330, and "Frontiers of the State: Public Authorities and Public Functions under the Human Rights Act" [2000] P.L. 476.
[292] See 13–023. See YL [2007] UKHL 27; [2004] 3 W.L.R. 112 at [74] for a reply.
[293] The Secretary of State for Constitutional Affairs was an intervener in YL, supporting a broad interpretation.
[294] [2007] UKHL 27; [2007] 3 W.L.R. 112.
[295] [2002] EWCA Civ 366; [2002] 2 All E.R. 936.
[296] See Hansard HC, col.1311 (November 21, 2005) (Vera Baird); col.1302 (Mr Burstow); col.1266 (Sandra Gidley); Hansard HL, col.WA70 (February 2, 2006).
[297] See, e.g. Hansard HL, col.1232 (November 3, 1997): "We also decided that we should apply the Bill to a wide rather than a narrow range of public authorities, so as to provide as much protection as possible to those who claim that their rights have been infringed" (Lord Irvine L.C.).
[298] See n.287 and M. Sunkin, "Pushing Forward the Frontiers of Human Rights Protection: The Meaning of Public Authority under the Human Rights Act" [2005] P.L. 643.

for it" in the public interest.[299] In this context, it was argued that "institutional links with a public body are not necessary to identifying a public function";[300] the question ought instead to be whether the activity has "its origins in governmental responsibilities, in such a way as to compel individuals to rely on that body for realisation of their Convention human rights".[301]

Overview of the case law up to and including YL

3–082   The following table summarises the principal decisions on "functions of a public nature" up to an including the House of Lords' decision in *YL*.

Case	Date	Court	"function"	"act"	Outcome
Poplar Housing (a housing association)[302]	4/01	CA	Registered Social Landlord to which the local authority had transferred all its housing stock	Decision to issue proceedings for possession	Was a public authority (but no breach of Convention rights)
Austin Hall Building Ltd (case concerned an adjudicator)[303]	4/01	QBD	Adjudication about payment for building works under the Housing Grants, Construction and Regeneration Act 1996 s.108	Had been given insufficient opportunity to present case etc	Not a public authority

[299] Joint Committee on Human Rights, HL Paper No.39/HC Paper No.302 (Session 2003/04) Ch.8.
[300] Joint Committee on Human Rights HL Paper No.39/HC Paper No.302 (Session 2003/04) para.143. By way of illustration: "Under s.6 . . . , there should be no distinction between a body providing housing because it itself is required to do so by statute, and a body providing housing because it has contracted with a local authority which is required by statute to provide the service" (para.142).
[301] HL Paper No.39/HC Paper No.382 (Session 2003/04) para.157. In the 2006–07 report the Joint Committee on Human Rights suggested that an interpretive statute could provide "For the purposes of s.6(3)(b) of the Human Rights Act 1998, a function of a public nature includes a function performed pursuant to a contract or other arrangement with a public authority which is under a duty to perform the function" (para.150). Would this cover the situation in *YL*? The local authority's duty under the National Assistance Act 1949 s.21 is to make arrangements, not to provide directly, accommodation and care.
[302] *Poplar Housing & Regeneration Community Association Ltd v Donoghue* [2001] EWCA Civ 595; [2002] Q.B. 48; *cf.*, e.g. *Smart v Sheffield City Council* [2002] EWCA Civ 4; [2002] H.L.R. 34 (possession proceedings by a local authority subject to the HRA because it was a "core" public authority).
[303] *Austin Hall Building Ltd v Buckland Securities Ltd* [2001] B.L.R. 272.

Case	Date	Court	"function"	"act"	Outcome
Partnerships in Care (a private hospital provider)[304]	4/02	Admin Court	Provision of treatment in private psychiatric hospital to person compulsorily detained under Mental Health Act 1983	Decision of managers to "change the focus of one of its wards"	Was an act of a public nature
Leonard Cheshire Foundation[305] (a charity providing accommodation and care to the elderly)	4/02	CA	Provision of accommodation plus care to elderly under contract with local authority (which is fulfilling duties to make such arrangements under National Assistance Act 1948)	Decision to close home where claimants had lived for more than 17 years and move them to alternative accommodation	Not a function of a public nature
Parochial Church Council of the Parish of Aston Cantlow etc[306]	6/03	HL	Ensuring the maintenance and repair of Church of England churches	Decision to enforce a lay rector's obligation to meet the cost of chancel repairs	Not a function of a public nature
Hampshire Farmers Markets Ltd[307] (private company limited by guarantee set up by local authority to regulate markets)	7/03	CA	Controlling the right of access to a public market	Decision to reject application by claimant trout farmer to participate in programme of farmers markets	Was a public function
Malcolm[308] (trustee in bankruptcy)	4/05	CA	Role of insolvency practitioner appointed trustee of bankrupt's estate under Insolvency Act 1986	Decision to obtain a lump sum benefit of a retirement annuity contract	Was a public function

[304] R. (on the application of A) v Partnerships in Care Ltd [2002] EWHC 529; [2002] 1 W.L.R. 2610; see also R. (on the application of Wilkinson) v Broadmoor Special Hospital Authority [2001] EWCA Civ 1545; [2002] 1 W.L.R. 419 at [61] (HRA s.6(3) "is apt to cover the actions of private doctors and others carrying out statutory functions under the Mental Health Act").
[305] R. (on the application of Heather) v Leonard Cheshire Foundation [2002] EWCA Civ 366; [2002] 2 All E.R. 936.
[306] Wallbank v Aston Cantlow and Wilmcote with Billesley Parochial Church Council [2003] UKHL 37; [2004] 1 A.C. 546 (4:1 decision on this point, Lord Scott of Foscote dissenting).
[307] R. (on the application of Beer (t/a Hammer Trout Farm)) v Hampshire Farmers Markets Ltd [2003] EWCA Civ 1056; [2004] 1 W.L.R. 233. The judgment does not identify which Convention right was at stake. See further B. Hough, "Public Law Regulation of Markets and Fairs" [2005] P.L. 586.
[308] Malcolm, Re; Malcolm v Benedict Mackenzie (A Firm) [2004] EWCA Civ 1748; [2005] 1 W.L.R. 1238 at [30].

Case	Date	Court	"function"	"act"	Outcome
Network Rail Infrastructure Ltd (formerly Railtrack Plc)[309]	5/06	QBD	Role as an "infrastructure controller" under the Railways (Safety Case) Regulations 2000 and owner and controller of track, signalling and bridge works on the stretch of line on which Potters Bar accident occurred	A failure to maintain points on the track	Was not a public function
YL[310] (challenge to Southern Cross Health-care, a business running care homes for the elderly)	6/07	HL	Provision of accommodation plus care to elderly people (arranged by and subsidised by local authorities under duties imposed by National Assistance Act 1948)	Decision to terminate elderly resident's contractual right to remain in care home	Was not a public function

Step 1—assessing the body's functions

3–083   As we have noted, assessment of the reach of the HRA is a two step process: assessing the body's functions and then considering the nature of the "act". Here we consider the first step, which involves examination of the overall work of the body in question. "Function" has a more conceptual and less specific meaning than "act" (which falls for consideration at step 2).[311] Only if the body is carrying out a mix of public and private functions does it fall within the scope of s.6 of the HRA.[312] If *none* of its functions are of a public nature then it is incapable of perpetrating breaches of Convention rights. The use of the terms "hybrid public authority" and "functional public authority"[313] has been

[309] *Cameron v Network Rail Infrastructure Ltd (formerly Railtrack Plc)* [2006] EWHC 1133; [2007] 1 W.L.R. 163 at [29]: the company was set up in 1994, when the British Rail Board was privatised, and the railway infrastructure was vested in it by the Railway Act 1993. At first the company had statutory powers to regulate safety (and may during that time have been a public authority) but those were removed in December 2000 and transferred to the Health and Safety Executive and subsequently to the Office of Rail Regulation. *cf. In the Matter of an Application for Judicial Review by Ronald Wadsworth* [2004] NIQB 8 (a dispute about the exclusion of a licensed public hire taxi driver from a designated taxi rank) where Weatherup J. held that the Northern Ireland Railways Company Ltd, a railway company authorised under the Transport Act (Northern Ireland) 1967, and the Northern Ireland Transport Holding Company (owner of the lands at Central Station Belfast), established under the 1967, were carrying out "functions of a public nature" for the purposes of the HRA.
[310] *YL (by her Litigation friend the Official Solicitor) v Birmingham CC* [2007] UKHL 27; [2007] 3 W.L.R. 112.
[311] *YL* [2007] UKHL 27; [2007] 3 W.L.R. 112 at [130] (Lord Neuberger).
[312] "The body must be one of which at least some, but not all, of its functions are of a public nature", *Aston Cantlow* [2003] UKHL 37; [2004] 1 A.C. 547 at [85].
[313] The terms "functional public authority" and "hybrid public authority" have been coined in the context of the institutional approach (see *Aston Cantlow* [2003] UKHL 37; [2004] 1 A.C. 547 at [34]), which has now been disapproved: see n.322.

deprecated,[314] but in relation to this stage of the inquiry it is useful shorthand for the kind of body that falls within ambit of the HRA. Certainly, it would be wrong to focus only on what is "done" without considering the institutional and relational context in which it is done.[315] How then do and should the courts approach the task of identifying functions of a public nature? There are two possible sources of assistance.

Relevance of the judicial review case law on public functions

The first is the case law following from *Datafin* on "public functions" for **3–084** the purposes of amenability to judicial review.[316] The language is similar, as are the purposes of the tests—respectively, to extend the ambit of the HRA beyond core public authorities[317] and to extend judicial review generally beyond those public authorities exercising statutory and prerogative powers. Some early judgments assumed that the tests were the same.[318] On more mature reflection it can however be seen that the tests are in fact distinct.[319] In many cases a decision will be susceptible to judicial review and the HRA. There are, however, situations in which a decision will be subject to the HRA but judicial review will not be an appropriate way of making a challenge (e.g. an issue to do with whether a decision in relation to an official's employment is compatible with Convention rights ought to be taken on appeal to the Employment Tribunal).[320] Nonetheless, provided a cautious approach is adopted, the case law relating to judicial review may be helpful in identifying, though not determinative of, the factors that need to be taken into account.[321] Too great an emphasis on the institutional and relational characteristics of the decision-maker must, however, be avoided.

---

[314] The Joint Select Committee on Human Rights has pointed out use of such terms is unhelpful as they deflect attention away from the nature of the functions performed to the intrinsic character of the body (HL Paper No.39/HC Paper No.382 (Session 2003/04) para.7).
[315] *YL* [2007] UKHL 27; [2007] 3 W.L.R. 112 at [102] (Lord Mance: "There is, for example, a clear conceptual difference between the functions of a private firm engaged by a local authority to enforce the Road Traffic Regulation Act 1984, as amended, on a public road and the activities of the same firm engaged by a private land-owner or a local authority to enforce a private scheme or parking restrictions of which notice have been given on a private property or estate"). cf. *Akumah v Hackney LBC* [2005] UKHL 17; [2005] 1 W.L.R. 985.
[316] See 3–041.
[317] Joint Committee on Human Rights HL Paper No.39/HC Paper No.382 (Session 2003/04) para.4 ("to apply human rights guarantees beyond the obvious government bodies").
[318] *Poplar Housing & Regeneration Community Association Ltd v Donaghue* [2001] EWCA Civ 595; [2002] Q.B. 48 at [65(i)]; *R. (on the application of Heather) v Leonard Cheshire Foundation* [2001] EWHC Admin 429 at [65] (Stanley Burnton J.).
[319] *R. (on the application of Heather) v Leonard Cheshire Foundation* [2002] EWCA Civ 366; [2002] 2 All E.R. 936 at [36] (Lord Woolf C.J.); *R. (on the application of A) v Partnerships in Care Ltd* [2002] EWHC 529; [2002] 1 W.L.R. 2610 at [27]; *Aston Cantlow* [2007] UKHL 27; [2007] 3 W.L.R. 112 at [52] (Lord Hope of Craighead); *YL* (n.315) at [87] (Lord Mance).
[320] See 16–017.
[321] In *YL* [2003] UKHL 37; [2004] 1 A.C. 547 at [12] (Lord Bingham: "it will not ordinarily matter whether the body in question is amenable to judicial review").

In some of the early cases courts fell into this trap[322] and as a result perhaps focused insufficiently on the inherent characteristics of the function, which ought to be the main object of the inquiry under the HRA.[323]

Relevance of the ECtHR case law

3–085 A second source of assistance is the case law of the European Court of Human Rights.[324] As with the identification of "core" public authorities,[325] so too with the ambit of "functions of a public nature": there is a link to the responsibility of Member States under the ECHR.[326] That said, the concept of "functions of a public nature" is one of national law that has no exact counterpart in ECHR case law. In *YL*, two "relevant principles" in the ECHR case law were identified, though it was conceded that the ECtHR has not always distinguished clearly between them.[327] First, there are circumstances in which Member States are responsible for a failure to take positive steps to prevent a person or non-state body from directly and immediately affecting a person's Convention rights. An example of this is a local authority's failure to protect children known to be being ill-treated by relatives (contrary to ECHR Art.2).[328] Another illustration might be where the management of a commercially-owned shopping centre refuses to allow a campaign group permission to distribute leaflets to shoppers.[329] Secondly,

---

[322] For example, in *Poplar Housing* [2001] EWCA Civ 595; [2002] Q.B. 48. In *YL*, the HL criticised *Poplar Housing*: [105] (Lord Mance: "The deployment in *Poplar Housing*, apparently as a decisive factor in favour of the application of s.6(3)(b), of the close historical and organisational assimilation of Poplar Housing with the local authority is in my view open to the objection that this did not bear on the function or role that Poplar Housing was performing"); at [61] (Baroness Hale: "It is common ground that it is the nature of the function being performed, rather than the nature of the body performing it, which matters under s.6(3)(b).The case of *Poplar Housing* relied too heavily upon the historical links between the local authority and the registered social landlord, rather than upon the nature of the function itself which was the provision of social housing").

[323] An approach adopted by Lord Hope in *Aston Cantlow* [2003] UKHL 37; [2004] 1 A.C. 547 at [34]–[64]. See also *YL* [2007] UKHL 27; [2007] 3 W.L.R. 112 at [148] (Lord Neuberger of Abbotsbury: "s.6(3)(b) appears to me to be concerned primarily with 'functions', or services, as such, rather than with the identity of the person who is paying for the provision of the services, or the reason for payment (although such factors are not, in my view, irrelevant)").

[324] H. Quane, "The Strasbourg Jurisprudence and the Meaning of 'Public Authority' under the Human Rights Act" [2006] P.L. 106; *R. (on the application of Beer (t/a Hammer Trout Farm)) v Hampshire Farmers Markets Ltd* [2003] EWCA Civ 1056; [2004] 1 W.L.R. 233 at [28].

[325] See 3–070.

[326] See, e.g. *YL* [2007] UKHL 27; [2007] 3 W.L.R. 112 at [87] (Lord Mance).

[327] *YL* [2007] UKHL 27; [2007] 3 W.L.R. 112 at [92] (Lord Mance).

[328] *Z v United Kingdom* (29392/95) [2001] 2 F.L.R. 612 (failure of State in its positive obligation to prevent breaches of Art.3 (prohibition of cruel and degrading treatment) by private third party).

[329] *Appleby v United Kingdom* (44306/98) (2003) 37 E.H.R.R. 38. The applicants argued that there was a breach of Art.10 (freedom of expression). The ECtHR held: "The Court does not find that the authorities bear any direct responsibility for this restriction on the applicants' freedom of expression. It is not persuaded that any element of State responsibility can be derived from the fact that a public development corporation transferred the property to Postel or that this was done with ministerial permission. The issue to be determined is whether the respondent State has failed in any positive obligation to protect the exercise of the applicants' Art.10 rights from interference by others—in this case, the owner of the Galleries" (para.41). The State had not so failed.

a Member State may remain responsible for the activities of non-State body to which it has delegated state powers. An example here would be a privately-managed "contracted out" prison or probation services (which may engage a number of Convention rights).[330]

Possible factors indicating a "function of a public nature"

The approach of the national courts has been to enumerate various factors, **3–086** in the light of the ECtHR case law, and drawing lightly upon some of the factors relevant to determining amenability to judicial review,[331] which may indicate that a function is a "function of a public nature". In doing so, the courts have been careful to stress that "there is no single litmus test".[332] In the following table we set out some of the main factors that may need to be considered. No list can be comprehensive as each case necessarily turns on its own facts. In any case where there is disagreement over whether a function is or is not public in nature, it will be important to identify whether the source of that disagreement is about the relevance of a factor, the application of a factor to the facts in the case in hand, or the overall (and somewhat impressionistic) assessment as to the outcome that is suggested by the overall mix of factors. These factors are summarised in the following table.

Factor	Comment
Public funding—often necessary but never sufficient. "The extent to which in carrying out the relevant function the body is publicly funded" (*Aston Cantlow* at [12]). "The greater the State's involvement in making payment for the function in question, the greater (other things being equal) is its assumption of responsibility" (*Aston Cantlow* at [10]). "It may well be that an activity of an entity which is not a core public authority is often unlikely to be a 'function of a public nature' if it is not ultimately funded by a core public authority, but, again as a matter of logic and language, it cannot be a sufficient condition, in my view" (*YL*, [142]).	In *YL*, the majority drew a distinction between public subsidy (which may imply a public function) and payment by a core public authority for a service provided by a third party (at [27]); "The injection of capital or subsidy into an organisation in return for undertaking a non-commercial role or activity of general public interest may be one thing; payment for services under a contractual arrangement with a company aiming to profit commercially thereby is potentially quite another" (*YL*, [105]). *cf.* Baroness Hale in *YL* at [67]).

---

[330] See, e.g. Offender Management Act 2007. Examples given in *YL* are *Wós v Poland* (2005) (Polish-German Reconciliation Foundation, a private body, had powers to provide compensation provided from Germany to compensate Nazi victims engaged the responsibility of the State); *Sychev v Ukraine* (2005) (powers to execute court judgments delegated to private law commission; held that it exercised State powers).

[331] See 3–084.

[332] *YL* [2007] UKHL 27; [2007] 3 W.L.R. 112 at [66]; *Aston Cantlow* [2003] UKHL 37; [2004] 1 A.C. 547 at [11].

Factor	Comment
Statutory powers. Whether the body is "exercising statutory powers" (*Aston Cantlow* at [12]); whether the body possesses "special powers and enjoys immunities which might have been indications of "publicness" (*Railtrack* at [29]); "Conversely, the absence of any statutory intervention will tend to indicate parliamentary recognition that the function in question is private and so an inappropriate subject for public regulation" (*Aston Cantlow* at [8]). "The existence and source of any special powers or duties must on any view be a very relevant factor when considering whether State responsibility is engaged in Strasbourg or whether s.6(3)(b) applies domestically" (*YL* at [102]).	But "the mere possession of special powers conferred by Parliament does not by itself mean that a person has functions of a public nature. Such powers may have been conferred for private, religious or purely commercial purposes" (*YL* at [101]).
Coercive and regulatory powers. "The use or potential use of statutory coercive powers is a powerful consideration in favour of this being a public function" (*YL* at [70]). "The regulatory or coercive powers of the state" (*YL* at [63])	In *YL*, the majority distinguished this factor from situations in which a person may have powers under the common law doctrine of necessity and where statutory powers of coercion applied to people working in both the public and private sector (at [84]).
Delegation—standing in the shoes of a core public authority. Whether the body is "taking the place of central government or local authorities" (*Aston Cantlow* at [12]).	In *YL*, the majority held that "no delegation of that sort exists in relation to the council's functions under s.21 of the 1948 Act" (at [104]).
Public service. Whether the body "is providing a public service" (*Aston Cantlow* at [12]).	The majority on *YL* held "It is necessary to look *also* at *the reason why* the person in question, whether an individual or corporate, is carrying out those activities. A local authority is doing so pursuant to public law obligations. A private person, including local authority employees, is doing so pursuant to private law contractual obligations" (at [31]).

Factor	Comment
Public rights of access. The function relates to a building or land over which the public have rights of access (*Aston Cantlow* at [130]).[333] Markets held on publicly owned land to which the public have access (*Hampshire Farmers Markets* at [33]).	
Core State responsibilities. Whether the function is "intrinsically an activity of government" (*Railtrack* at [29]); "the role and responsibility of the state in relation to the subject matter in question" (*Aston Cantlow* at [7]); "the fact that a function is or has been performed by a core public authority for the benefit of the public" (*YL* at [72]).	In *YL*, the majority held that it was wrong to regard "the actual provision, as opposed to the arrangement, of care and accommodation for those unable to arrange it themselves as an inherently governmental function" (at [115]). "While it would be wrong to be didactic in this difficult area, I suspect that it would be a relatively rare case where a company could be performing a 'function of a public nature' if it was carrying on an activity which could not be carried out by any core public authority. On the other hand, I would not accept that the mere fact that a core public authority, even where it is the body funding the activity, could carry out the activity concerned must mean that the activity is such a function. Apart from anything else, there must scarcely be an activity which cannot be carried out by some core public authority" (*YL* at [144]).
Beyond core State responsibilities: the assumption of responsibility by the State. "Whether the State has assumed responsibility for seeing that this task is performed" (*YL* at [66]).	

[333] Lord Scott of Foscote, dissenting.

Factor	Comment
The public interest. Whether there is an obligation "to conduct its operations in a manner subservient to the public interest" (*Railtrack* at [29]), "The contrast is between what is 'public' in the sense of being done for or by or on behalf of the people as a whole and what is 'private' in the sense of being done for one's own purposes" (*YL* at [62], and [67]); "Democratic accountability, an obligation to act only in the public interest and (in most cases today) a statutory constitution exclude the sectional or personally motivated interests of privately owned, profit-earning enterprises" (*YL* at [105]).	It goes against a function being public where there is a "a clear commercial objective" of making profits for shareholders (*Railtrack* at [29]). "The fact that a service can fairly be said to be to the public benefit cannot mean, as a matter of language, that it follows that providing the service itself is a function of a public nature. Nor does it follow as a matter of logic or policy. Otherwise, the services of all charities, indeed, it seems to me, of all private organisations which provide services which could be offered by charities, would be caught by s.6(1)" (*YL* at [135]).
Democratic accountability. Whether the body is "democratically accountable to central or local government" (*Railtrack* at [29]); "democratic accountability" (*YL* at [103]).	
Government control. Whether those appointed to run the body are subject to government influence or control (*Railtrack* at [29]).	
Regulation. The "extent to which the state, directly or indirectly, regulates, supervises and inspects the performance of the function in question, and imposes criminal penalties on those who fall below publicly promulgated standards in performing it" (*Aston Cantlow* at [9]).	In *YL*, the majority doubted this factor: "Regulation by the State is no real pointer towards the person regulated being a state or governmental body or a person with a function of a public nature, if anything perhaps even the contrary" (at [161]). "There is no identity between the public interest in a particular service being provided properly and the service itself being a public service. As a matter of ordinary language and concepts, the mere fact that the public interest requires a service to be closely regulated and supervised pursuant to statutory rules cannot mean that the provision of the service, as opposed to its regulation and supervision, is a function of a public nature" (at [134]).

Factor	Comment
Risk of breaching rights. "The extent of the risk, if any, that improper performance of the function might violate an individual's Convention right" (*YL* at [11]). "The close connection between [the] service and the core values underlying the Convention rights and the . . . risk that rights will be violated unless adequate steps are taken to protect them" (*YL* at [71]).	

Step 2—assessing the nature of the particular act complained of

If the court's analysis leads to the conclusion that there is a "function of a 3–087 public nature", a second step is then to consider the precise act in question. If "the nature of the act is private" (s.6(5)), then it falls outside the protective scope of the HRA. The following have been held to be private acts: the enforcement of a civil debt;[334] the exercise of a contractual notice to terminate a licence.[335]

TERRITORIAL REACH OF JUDICIAL REVIEW AND THE HRA

Almost all functions challenged in judicial review claims in the Administra- 3–088 tive Court are exercised in England and Wales in respect of claimants based in England and Wales. In a small number of cases, however, the court has had to consider whether decisions relating to other geographical areas are amenable to review.

Public functions exercised in Scotland or Northern Ireland

Within the United Kingdom there are three separate legal jurisdictions:[336] 3–089 England and Wales (with which this book is primarily concerned);[337] Scotland; and Northern Ireland. As we note, judicial review law in Scotland differs in some significant respects, for example in relation to the time limit for commencing proceedings (no general limit is set by legislation), standing[338] and as to amenability.[339] Despite this, attempts at tactical "forum shopping" are rare.[340]

---

[334] *Aston Cantlow* UKHL 37; [2004] 1 A.C. 547 at [64] (Lord Hope).
[335] *YL* [2007] UKHL 27; [2007] 3 W.L.R. 112 at [34] (Lord Scott).
[336] And on devolution, see 1–113.
[337] On the emerging differentiation between England and Wales, see T. Jones and J. Williams, "Wales as a Jurisdiction" [2004] P.L. 78.
[338] See 2–068.
[339] See 3–016.
[340] Cf. *Sokha v Secretary of State for the Home Office, The Times*, August 15, 1991 (Outer House).

3–090   The questions that arise are (a) whether the Administrative Court has jurisdiction and (b) if so, whether discretion should be exercised to allow or require the claim to be dealt with in another legal system. Where a conflicts of law situation does arise, the Administrative Court will not necessarily adopt the same approach to determining the most convenient forum as English courts do in private law disputes as there are constitutional considerations at stake, not merely issues of private expediency.[341] One such constitutional factor is Art.19 of the Treaty and Act of Union with Scotland 1706, which should make the English and Scottish courts wary of exercising jurisdiction over cases which properly belong to the other legal system.

3–091   Where the impugned decision is taken by a public authority with decision-making powers stretching across Great Britain[342] or the whole United Kingdom, the approach of the English courts faced, for example, with a claimant with strong links to Scotland has, however, varied. In some cases, the English courts have accepted jurisdiction. Thus the Court of Appeal heard, without detailed discussion of the jurisdictional issue, an appeal in a judicial review claim brought by Scottish Power Plc (an electricity power supply company operating exclusively in Scotland) against a decision of the Director General of Electricity Supply, a regulator with a remit covering Great Britain (whose head office was in Birmingham, England).[343] If jurisdiction does exist, discretion may be exercised to refuse or stay English proceedings brought by a person whose circumstances have an insufficiently strong connection to England.[344] There are, however, also cases in which jurisdiction has been declined by the English court.[345]

3–092   In immigration and asylum matters the substantive law is uniform throughout the United Kingdom. In this context, where a judicial review challenge is made to a decision of a tribunal which has jurisdiction in all parts of the United Kingdom, the superior courts in each part of the United Kingdom should correspondingly have jurisdiction; generally, the court in the part of the United Kingdom where the tribunal made its decision should hear any challenge.[346] In relation to criminal justice, there are some significant differences between different parts of the United Kingdom and

[341] R. (on the application of Majead) v Immigration Appeal Tribunal [2003] EWCA Civ 615; [2003] A.C.D. 70 at [13].
[342] Great Britain consists of England and Wales and Scotland.
[343] R. v Director General of Electricity Supply Ex p. Scottish Power Plc, unreported, February 3, 1997. Neither party took a point on jurisdiction.
[344] R. v Special Commissioners Ex p. RW Forsyth Ltd [1987] 1 All E.R. 1035.
[345] R. v Secretary of State for Scotland Ex p. Greenpeace, May 24, 1995 unreported, in which, citing Art.19, Popplewell J. held that he had no jurisdiction to hear a challenge to a decision by the minister to grant a licence to Shell UK to dispose of the Brent Spa oil platform in deep water off Scotland.
[346] Tehrani v Secretary of State for the Home Department [2006] UKHL 47; [2007] 1 A.C. 521; C. Himsworth, "Inter-jurisdictional questions in judicial review" (2007) 11 Edin. L.R. 277 (who argues that "it may yet be found preferable to seek solutions not in terms of choice of jurisdiction, but by ensuring that, whichever jurisdiction is adopted, the result to be obtained from both the substance and procedural rules is the same").

where the court's jurisdiction is called into question it will be necessary to consider the particular decision that raises the jurisdiction issue.[347]

Devolution issues

There has been remarkably little cross-boarder litigation over "devolution 3–093 issues" since the coming into force of the Scotland Act 1998, the Northern Ireland Act 1998 and the Government of Wales Act 1998.

Public functions exercised outside the United Kingdom

The Administrative Court's jurisdiction to issue judicial review remedial 3–094 orders in respect of the exercise of functions in the name of the Crown extends beyond the United Kingdom "to overseas territories subject to the Queen's dominion", at least where in substance (if not in form) the decision is taken on the orders or direction of United Kingdom Ministers.[348] Thus, it may be possible to commence judicial review proceedings in respect of functions exercised by Ministers based in the United Kingdom in respect of the Isle of Man, the Bailiwicks of Jersey and Guernsey, and British Overseas Territories. The Administrative Court may, however, exercise its discretion to decline to hear the claim on the ground the local courts provide a more convenient forum.[349] The Administrative Court will not, as a matter of international comity, hear a claim for judicial review which amounts to an unwarranted interference in the affairs of an independent member of the British Commonwealth.[350]

Territorial jurisdiction and the HRA

Where a judicial review claim includes the ground of breach of s.6 of the 3–095 HRA, further considerations must be taken into account. By ECHR Art.1, Convention rights extend to everyone within the "jurisdiction" of the signatory State. The concept of jurisdiction is essentially territorial. For present purposes, the signatory State and territorial area is that of the

---

[347] *In the matter of an application by Samuel Surgenor for judicial review* [2003] NIQB 62.
[348] *R. (on the application of Bancoult) v Secretary of State for the Foreign and Commonwealth Office* [2001] Q.B. 1067 at [21]–[29] (granting judicial review of a decision of the Commissioner for the British Indian Ocean Territory to banish inhabitants from the Chagos Islands). *cf. R. (on the application of Quark Fishing Ltd) v Secretary of State for Foreign and Commonwealth Affairs (No.1)* [2002] EWCA Civ 1409 where no jurisdictional issue arose in relation to the refusal of a fishing licence in relation to the South Georgia and South Sandwich Islands and the Court of Appeal quashed a direction given by the Foreign Secretary. On the jurisdictional position in relation to the HRA, see 3–095.
[349] *Bancoult* [2001] Q.B. 1067 at [27].
[350] *Fitzgibbon v Attorney General* [2005] EWHC 114; *The Times*, March 15, 2005 (the claimant sought declarations in relation to the power of the Queen to issue letters patent in respect of her functions under the Commonwealth of Australia Constitution Act 1900 (Australia)).

United Kingdom of Great Britain and Northern Ireland. The United Kingdom has acted under ECHR Art.56, or the various Protocols to the ECHR, to extend the application of the ECHR to many of the territories which are not part of the United Kingdom but for whose international relations the United Kingdom is responsible (essentially the British Overseas Territories[351] and the Crown dependencies of the Isle of Man and Bailiwicks of Jersey and Guernsey).[352] If the ECHR or a Protocol has not been formally extended to a British Overseas Territory (whether by oversight or deliberately), there is no possibility of a claim under HRA s.6 and consequently for damages under s.7.[353] The reach of the HRA is the same as the ECHR.

3–096   The ECtHR has recognises two general extensions to the principle of territoriality.[354] The House of Lords has followed this case law on the application of Convention rights, rejecting the narrower view that the HRA, as a domestic statute, has territorial application only within the United Kingdom.[355] First, where a State exercises control though its agents (for example its armed forces or consular and diplomatic officers abroad) over persons or property outside its national borders.[356] Second, where a State has "effective control" of an area outside its territory which is part of the territory of another contracting state.[357]

PROCEDURAL EXCLUSIVITY

3–097   Between 1983 and 2000 (when the CPR Pt 54 claim for judicial review procedure came into force), issues relating to "procedural exclusivity" often arose. This term referred to the issue of whether a litigant wishing to challenge the legality of a decision made by an authority amenable to judicial review was *required* to use the RSC, Ord.53 application for judicial review procedure to challenge the lawfulness of a public authority's

[351] British Overseas Territories Act 2002.
[352] Jersey, Guernsey and the Isle of Man have each adopted human rights laws broadly similar in structure to that of the HRA.
[353] *R. (on the application of Quark Fishing Ltd) v Secretary of State for Foreign and Commonwealth Affairs (No.2)* [2005] UKHL 57; [2006] 1 A.C. 529 (UK had not extended the application of ECHR Protocol 1 Art.1 (right to enjoyment of property) to the South Georgia and South Sandwich Islands; accordingly, the claimant had no basis for a claim for damages under HRA s.7).
[354] *R. v Special Adjudicator Ex p. Ullah* [2004] UKHL 26; [2004] 2 A.C. 323, [29] (Lord Steyn).
[355] *R. (on the application of Al-Skeini) v Secretary of State for Defence* [2007] UKHL 26; [2007] 3 W.L.R. (Lord Bingham dissenting).
[356] *R. (on the application of B) v Secretary of State for Foreign and Commonwealth Affairs* [2004] EWCA Civ 1344; [2005] Q.B. 643 (two young Afghan brothers sought refuge in British Consulate in Melbourne; HRA applied but there had been no violation of any Convention right); *Al-Skeini* [2007] UKHL 26 (claims by families of Iraqi civilians who had been killed in Basrah whilst the UK was an occupying power).
[357] *Al-Skeini* [2007] UKHL 26; P. Leach, "The British military in Iraq—the applicability of the *espace juridique* doctrine under the ECHR" [2005] P.L. 448.

action,[358] or whether it was permissible to commence litigation using some other procedure (a writ action or originating summons). Procedural exclusivity also concerned itself with the circumstances where a person wished to raise issues of public law by way of a defence in general civil proceedings or in a criminal trial (sometimes called "collateral challenges"), a question that we consider in Chapter 4.[359] The extent to which public law submissions may be advanced outside RSC, Ord.53 proceedings was highly contentious.

Under CPR.54.2 there remains a requirement that "the judicial review 3–098 procedure must be used" if the claimant is seeking one or more of the distinctly "public law" remedies of a mandatory, prohibiting or quashing order or an injunction restraining a person from acting in an office in which he is not entitled to act. Although the language of CPR.54.2 is similar to that used in the former RSC, Ord.54, a rather different approach now needs to be taken in the light of the overarching changes brought about the CPR. The CPR seek to end the old wholly unproductive demarcation disputes.[360]

The justification for procedural exclusivity under RSC, Ord.53

When recommending in 1976 the creation of a new procedure for judicial 3–099 review the Law Commission contemplated the co-existence of judicial review proceedings and actions brought by issuing a writ or originating summons for a declaration (private law proceedings) in relation to public law issues.[361] This was not, however, a realistic approach. The application for judicial review procedures had the safeguard of the requirement for leave (now called "permission") and a limited period in which to make applications, which would serve no purpose if they could be bypassed by issuing an ordinary claim for a declaration which was not subject to the same safeguards.

The much-criticised decision in the House of Lords in *O'Reilly v* 3–100 *Mackman*[362] was therefore the logical consequence[363] of the procedure included in RSC, Ord.53. In that case Lord Diplock set out the general rule.

[358] The main features of the RSC, Ord.53 procedure are examined at 15–087; on the CPR Pt 54 procedure which superseded it, see Ch.16.

[359] See 4–064.

[360] *R. (on the application of Heather) v Leonard Cheshire Foundation* [2002] EWCA Civ 366; [2002] 2 All E.R. 936 at [36]–[39] (Lord Woolf C.J.).

[361] Remedies in Administrative Law (Law Commission No.73 (1976)), paras 34, 58(a). (The issue of "writs" and "summons" has been replaced by "claim forms" in the Civil Procedure Rules enacted in 1999).

[362] [1983] 2 A.C. 237. See also the companion case *Cocks v Thanet District Council* [1983] 2 A.C. 287 (where private law rights depended on prior public law decisions they too must ordinarily be litigated by judicial review).

[363] *cf.* e.g. Justice/All Souls, *Administrative Justice-Some Necessary Reforms* (1988), para. 6.18, which describes it as "an unfortunate decision". Wade and Forsyth say it "must be accounted a serious setback for administrative law.. .a step back towards the time of the old forms of action which were so deservedly buried in 1852." (*Administrative Law* 7th edn (1994), p.682.)

"Now . . . all remedies for infringement of rights protected by public law can be obtained upon an application for judicial review, as can also remedies for infringement of rights under private law if such infringement should also be involved, it would in my view as a general rule be contrary to public policy, and as such an abuse of the process of the court, to permit a person seeking to establish that a decision of a public authority infringed rights to which he was entitled to protection under public law to proceed by way of ordinary action and by this means to evade the provisions of Ord.53 for the protection of such authorities. . . I have described this as a general rule; for, though it may normally be appropriate to apply it by the summary process of striking out the action, there may be exceptions, particularly where the invalidity of the decision arises as a collateral issue in a claim for infringement of a right of the plaintiff arising under private law, or where none of the parties object to the adoption of the procedure by writ or originating summons. Whether there should be other exceptions should, in my view, at this stage in the development of procedural public law, be left to be decided on a case to case basis."

3–101 It is important to note that in the passage of his speech just cited Lord Diplock was setting out a general rule and a rule which was to be the subject of exceptions which were to be worked out on a case-by-case basis.[364] In addition *O'Reilly v Mackman* typified the sort of case which it could be expected would result in the misgivings which had been expressed in earlier cases about the undesirability of bypassing judicial review being reiterated. It involved four prisoners who, after the Hull Prison Riots, brought an action claiming declarations that the disciplinary awards which had been made against them by the Prison Visitors were invalid as being in breach of the Prison Rules and as contravening the principles of natural justice. If the proceedings had been by way of judicial review, it is most unlikely that permission would have been granted for them to be commenced since the applicants were short on merits.

3–102 O'Reilly v Mackman represented something of a high-water mark in the courts' insistence on procedural exclusivity. In a series of subsequent cases, encouraged by Lord Scarman's dicta, the courts identified exceptions to the rule, allowing judicial review issues to be advanced outside the RSC, Ord.53 procedure. The exceptions included: where public and private law decisions were not separate and distinct;[365] where the public law aspect of the claim was collateral to an issue which was the proper subject matter of private law proceedings;[366] where private law aspects of the claim

---

[364] [1983] 2 A.C. 237 at 284–285.

[365] *An Bord Bainne Co-op Ltd v Milk Marketing Board* [1984] 2 C.M.L.R. 584 at 587–8.

[366] In *Davy v Spelthorne BC* (1983) 81 L.G.R. 580 the CA did not permit the plaintiff to proceed with a claim for an injunction in ordinary civil proceedings to prevent the implementation of an enforcement notice and the setting aside of the notice, but did allow a claim for damages for negligent advice by the Council to proceed arising out of the same matter. The HL dismissed the authority's appeal in relation to the claim for damages since liability for damages did not directly raise any question of public law [1984] A.C. 262. See also *Steed v Home Office* [2000] 1 W.L.R. 1169.

dominated the proceedings;[367] where a person sought to challenge the validity of a public authority's decision as a defence in a civil claim;[368] and where the parties did not contest the appropriateness of the chosen procedure.[369] The courts stressed the general need for flexibility[370] and pragmatism.[371] Nevertheless, parties frequently engaged in ferocious litigation as to whether the right procedure has been adopted purely for tactical purposes. Their indulging in this activity was made worthwhile by the fact that, depending on the nature of the issue involved, there could be substantial advantages in an applicant choosing one form of procedure rather than another. Unfortunately, although the House of Lords had a number of opportunities to improve the situation, a case by case approach prevented the development of a formula which might have injected some commonsense into the position.

Procedural exclusivity in the era of the Civil Procedure Rules

The replacement of RSC, Ord.53 by the new CPR 54 claim for judicial review procedure in October 2000 called for a fresh approach to procedural exclusivity. In all types of civil proceedings, the CPR gave judges new powers to manage litigation and in several respects the differences between judicial review (Pt 54) and the other ways of starting civil proceedings (Pt 7 and Pt 8) have been significantly reduced. The main difference nowadays is in the time period within which a claim must be made. For judicial review the requirement is that claims be made promptly and in any event within three months, whereas in relation to other types of civil claim the limitation period will typically be three, six or even 12 years.[372] What matters under the CPR regime is not the mode of commencement of proceedings but whether the choice of procedure may have a material effect on the outcome. To prove an abuse of process, it is now necessary to do more than merely show that a civil claim started under Pt 7 or Pt 8 could have been brought by way of judicial review.[373]

3–103

---

[367] *Roy v Kensington and Chelsea and Westminster Family Practitioner Committee* [1992] 1 A.C. 624 (GP brought action against his family practitioner committee for withholding part of his practice allowance).

[368] *Wandsworth LBC v Winder* [1985] A.C. 461. This principle applies even where the litigation is between two private parties: *Dwr Cymru Cyfyngedig v Corus UK Ltd* [2006] EWHC 1183, Ch D—this point was not challenged on a subsequent appeal ([2007] EWCA Civ 285).

[369] This could be considered as being the explanation for the ability of the plaintiffs in*Gillick v West Norfolk and Wisbech AHA* [1986] A.C. 112 and *Royal College of Nursing v Department of Health and Social Security* [1982] A.C. 800 to make claims and not apply for permission to seek judicial review when challenging ministerial guidance.

[370] *Mercury Communications Ltd v Director General of Telecommunications* [1996] 1 W.L.R. 48.

[371] *Trustees of the Dennis Rye Pension Fund v Sheffield City Council* [1998] 1 W.L.R. 840.

[372] See 16–050.

[373] *Clark v University of Lincolnshire and Humberside* [2000] 1 W.L.R. 1988 (and see also *Phonographic Performance Ltd v Department of Trade and Industry* [2004] EWHC 1795; [2004] 1 W.L.R. 2893).

The Court of Appeal, doubting the continuing relevance of *O'Reilly v Mackman*, held:[374]

> "The court's approach to what is an abuse of process has to be considered today in the light of the changes brought about by the CPR. Those changes include a requirement that a party to proceedings should behave reasonably both before and after they have commenced proceedings. Parties are now under an obligation to help the court further the over-riding objectives which include ensuring that cases are dealt with expeditiously and fairly. (CPR 1.1(2)(d) and 1.3) They should not allow the choice of procedure to achieve procedural advantages".

Adopting this approach, sterile and expensive procedural disputes which may be of no practical significance to the outcome of a case may be avoided. There are many illustrations of the new flexible approach.[375]

3–104 The practical question remains as to what a claimant ought to do in a case where he asserts that the defendant is carrying out a public function amenable to judicial review and the defendant does not accept that this is so.[376] One option is to commence claims both a claim for judicial review and an ordinary civil claim, which the court could order be consolidated and heard together; alternatively, a claimant may commence a judicial review claim and—if unsuccessful on the jurisdiction point—seek an order transferring the matter to continue as if it had not been commenced under CPR Pt 54.[377] Where delay is an issue, it may be addressed by the court either in ordinary civil proceedings,[378] or under CPR Pt 54.

COMPARATIVE PERSPECTIVES

3–105 In this section, we bring together summaries of the approaches to amenability to review adopted in several other jurisdictions—Scotland, Australia, Canada, India, New Zealand and South Africa. The purpose of

---

[374] *Clark* [2000] 1 W.L.R. 1988 [34] (Lord Woolf MR).

[375] See, e.g. *R. (on the application of Wilkinson) v Broadmoor Special Hospital Authority* [2001] EWCA Civ 1545; [2002] 1 W.L.R. 419 at [62] ("it cannot and should not matter whether proceedings in respect of forcible treatment of detained patients are brought by way of an ordinary action in tort, an action under s.7(1) of the [HRA], or judicial review"); *R. (on the application of P) v Secretary of State for the Home Department* [2001] EWCA Civ 1151; [2001] 1 W.L.R. 2002 at [120] (challenge to lawfulness of Prison Service policy on mother and baby units should be made in the Family Division unless relief which only the Administrative Court may grant is sought); *D v Home Office* [2005] EWCA Civ 38; [2006] 1 W.L.R. 1003 at [104] (civil claim for damages for false imprisonment); *Rhondda Cynon Taff CBC v Watkins* [2003] EWCA Civ 129; [2003] 1 W.L.R. 1864 (possession action); *Bunney v Burns Anderson Plc* [2007] EWHC 1240, Ch D at [25] (direction of Financial Services Ombudsman).

[376] *Mullins* at [47]–[49] (noting that this was an issue that deserves the attention of the Rules Committee); and see also *Cookson & Clegg Ltd v Ministry of Defence* [2005] EWCA Civ 811; [2006] Eu. L.R. 1092.

[377] On transfers, see CPR.54.20.

[378] In civil proceedings the court of its own motion or on the application of a party may, under CPR Pt 24, give summary judgment in the claim or on an issue if it considers that it has no real prospect of succeeding. See, e.g. *Dwr Cymru Cyfyngedig (Welsh Water) v Corus UK Ltd* [2006] EWHC 1183, Ch D.

doing so is to illustrate the variety of legislative and judicial techniques that are employed in common law jurisdictions to draw the dividing line between what falls within and outside the courts' supervisory jurisdiction. The fact that a particular function has been held to be within the scope of the court's jurisdiction in one jurisdiction does not, of course, imply that it ought to be within the jurisdiction of courts of other legal systems. A range of constitutional, political and procedural factors may justify difference.[379]

Scotland

In 1992, the Inner House restated the scope of judicial review in Scotland **3–106** in *West v Secretary of State for Scotland*.[380] Lord President Hope (as he then was) made it clear that the scope of the judicial review in Scotland depended not on a "public" element that determines the reach of English judicial review, but rather on the presence of what became known as a "tripartite" or "triangular" relationship. The three elements are (i) a body that delegates or entrusts power, whether by statute, agreement or other instrument to (ii) a person who exercises that power (iii) in relation to a person or persons. The approach adopted in *West*—which eschews reference to the public/private divide—has allowed judicial review in some situations in Scotland that would not be amenable to judicial review in England and Wales under CPR Pt 54. Thus, decisions of sports clubs[381] and religious associations[382] have been held to be reviewable. Commentators now argue that the formula laid down in *West* "should not be treated as definitive"[383] and "scope of review in Scotland is thus every bit as vague and contradictory as it is in England".[384] Review of decisions of the Scottish inferior criminal courts falls outside the jurisdiction of the Court of Session; there are dealt with instead by the High Court of Justiciary.[385]

---

[379] See, e.g. *Aga Khan* [1993] 1 W.L.R. 909 (Hoffmann L.J. notes that "different countries draw the line between public and private regulation in different places. The fact that certain functions of the Jockey Club could be exercised by a statutory body and that they are so exercised in some other countries does not make them governmental functions in England").
[380] 1992 S.C. 385. The case concerned a prison officer who was refused discretionary reimbursement of removal expenses following the transfer from one prison to another. West lost: there was no tripartite relationship.
[381] See C. Munro, "Sports in the Courts" [2005] P.L. 681. See, e.g. *Irvine v Royal Burgess Golfing Society of Edinburgh* 2004 S.C.L.R. 386 (no recognised principle that the courts should refrain from exercising judicial review with regard to a sporting body); *Wiles v Bothwell Castle Golf Club* 2005 S.L.T. 785; *Crocket v Tantallon Golf Club* 2005 S.L.T. 663.
[382] This does not extend to the Church of Scotland, which has its own system of courts. But other religious bodies may fall within the supervisory jurisdiction of the Court of Session: see, e.g. *M'Milan v The Free Church* (1859) 22D. 290; *M'Donald v Burns* 1940 S.C. 376.
[383] Lord Clyde and D. Edwards, *Judicial Review* (2000), para.8.33.
[384] A. McHarg, "Border Disputes: the Scope and Purposes of Judicial Review" Ch.11 in A. McHarg and T. Mullen (eds), *Public Law in Scotland* (2006), p.236. McHarg argues that "It is not that one jurisdiction rejects while the other accepts the relevance of the distinction; rather each emphasises different aspects of publicness and privateness. Thus, while *West* stressed the importance of non-consensual relationships and decision-making constraints, the English courts are interested primarily in identifying decisions made on behalf of the public collectively, and which affect the public interest" (p.238).
[385] *Law Hospital NHS Trust v Lord Advocate* 1996 S.C. 301 at 311.

Australia

3–107   As a general summary of the factors that will affect the justiciability of actions for the purpose of judicial review, Professor Allars proposes the following eight criteria: "(i) source or nature of power to make decision; (ii) status of decision-maker; (iii) nature of decision, by reference to its character as administrative rather than legislative or judicial; (iv) nature of decision, by reference to its place in the decision-making process; (v) subject-matter of decision; (vi) interests of applicant affected; (vii) source of power by which decision-maker established; and (viii) whether the decision has a public element or is a matter for private law".[386] Professor Allars notes that the Administrative Decisions (Judicial Review) Act 1977 adopts a combination of elements (i) to (iv).

3–108   Debate in the courts as to whether non-statutory bodies are subject to judicial review in Australia has largely played out under the Administrative Decisions (Judicial Review) Act 1977 and whether these bodies are making decisions "under an enactment". This has attracted criticism of the criterion.[387] Two recent cases demonstrate the limitations. In *NEAT Domestic Trading Pty Ltd v AWB Ltd*[388] the High Court considered whether a "veto" power given to AWB (International) Ltd (AWBI) over the Wheat Export Authority's power to consent to bulk export of wheat outside the statutory scheme established by the Wheat Marketing Act 1989 (Cth). The court held that the decision of AWBI was not justiciable as it was not made under the Wheat Marketing Act, but pursuant to a common law power as an incorporated body under the corporations legislation, it was of a "private character" and could be exercised for purely commercial interests that did not take into account "public law considerations".[389] Kirby J., dissenting, adopted the English approach in *Datafin* and the "public function" test.[390] In *Griffith University v Tang* the High Court substantially narrowed the circumstances in which a decision will be "under an enactment".[391] It was argued that the decision of the university to exclude a PhD candidate on the grounds of academic misconduct was made under the Griffith University Act 1998 (Qld). The court developed two criteria to be met for a decision to be made "under an enactment". The decision must: (a) expressly or impliedly required or authorised by the enactment; and (b) confer, alter or otherwise affect legal rights or

---

[386] M. Allars, "Public Administration in Private Hands" (2005) 12 *Australian Journal of Administrative Law* 126 at 127.
[387] M. Aronson, "Is the ADJR Act hampering the development of Australian administrative law?" (2004) 15 *Public Law Review* 202 at 207–9.
[388] (2003) 216 C.L.R. 277.
[389] (2003) 216 C.L.R. 277 (McHugh, Hayne and Callinan JJ.) at [51].
[390] (2003) 216 C.L.R. 277 (Kirby J) at [96], [99] and [133].
[391] A. Cassimatis, "Statutory judicial review and the requirement of a statutory effect on rights or obligations: 'Decisions under an enactment'" (2006) 13 *Australian Journal of Administrative Law* 169; C. Mantziaris and L. McDonald, "Federal judicial review jurisdiction after *Griffith University v Tang*" (2006) 17 *Public Law Review* 22.

obligations, and in that sense the decision must derive from the enactment.[392] Under general law, federal jurisdiction over judicial review is limited by the requirements that the decision be of an "officer of the Commonwealth".[393]

Canada

Surprisingly, there is very little case law on the subject of amenability to 3–109 judicial review in Canada. Aside from the general proposition that public law judicial review is confined to bodies exercising powers derived from statute or the prerogative, there is not much else. Assuming, however, that the Court of Appeal for Ontario was correct in *Black v Canada (Prime Minister)*,[394] it is likely that the Canadian courts will be primarily interested in the nature of the power rather than its specific source. The one context in which it has arisen is that of the Canadian Charter of Rights and Freedoms 1982 and the question of what constitutes a governmental function for the purposes of triggering the application of the Charter. In *McKinney v University of Guelph*,[395] the Supreme Court held that "government" as used in the Charter was not co-extensive with the reach of judicial review in holding that the mandatory retirement rules of a public university were not subject to direct attack; they did not constitute government action even though universities were in general subject to the remedies of judicial review. Subsequently, however, in *Eldridge v British Columbia*[396] the Supreme Court accepted that the Charter could reach a non-governmental body performing a truly governmental function under a legislative delegation of power.

India

The position in India has been explained in the following way: "Although, 3–110 it is not easy to define what a public function or public duty is, it can reasonably be said that such functions are similar to or closely related to those performable by the State in its sovereign capacity".[397] The concept of public law function is yet to be crystallised. However "it may be safely inferred that when essential government functions are placed or allowed to be performed by a private body they must be held to have undertaken a public duty or public function".[398]

---

[392] *Griffith University v Tang* (2005) 221 C.L.R. 99 at [89], [149] (Gummow, Callinan and Heydon JJ.).
[393] s.39B(1) of the Judiciary Act 1903 (Cth) and s.75(v) of the Constitution.
[394] (2001) 54 O.R. (3d) 215.
[395] [1990] 3 S.C.R. 229.
[396] [1997] 3 S.C.R. 624.
[397] *G. Bassi Reddy v International Crops Research Institute* 2003 (4) S.C.C. 225 at 237.
[398] *Zee Telefilms Ltd v Union of India* 2005 (4) S.C.C. 649 at 712–13 (Sinha J. dissenting, Majority not taking a contrary view).

New Zealand

3–111 The New Zealand cases have followed *Datafin*[399] and in determining whether a body or particular decision is susceptible to judicial review the courts can look not only at the source of the power but also at the "public" function exercised and its public consequences. In *Royal Australasian College of Surgeons v Phipps*, the Court of Appeal said that over recent decades "courts have increasingly been willing to review exercises of power which in substance are public or have important public consequences, however their origins and the persons or bodies exercising them might be characterised. . . The Courts have made it clear that in appropriate cases, even although there may be no statutory power of decision or the power may in significant measure be contractual, they are willing to review the exercise of the power".[400] In *Electoral Commission v Cameron,* the Advertising Standards Complaints Board, an unincorporated body set up under the rules of a self-regulatory incorporated society representing the major advertising industry groups, was held to be carrying out public regulatory functions and was subjected to judicial review.[401] As Cooke P. said in *Finnigan v New Zealand Rugby Football Union Inc*"in the New Zealand context, a sharp boundary between public and private law cannot be realistically be drawn".[402]

3–112　　Three recent examples illustrate this. *Dunne v CanWest TVWorks Ltd* goes further than any case so far, subjecting a publicly-licensed but privately-owned free-to-air broadcaster to judicial review.[403] In *Sky City Auckland Ltd v Wu*, but for explicit statutory override, Blanchard and Anderson JJ. (McGrath J. to the contrary) were inclined to accept that a monopolistic, state-licensed casino was a "business affected with a public interest" and therefore could not exclude patrons arbitrarily and without good reason.[404] In *Velich v Body Corporate No.164980* the issue was whether the owner of a top-level apartment could complete a partially constructed deck that had not been completed by a previous owner within the time stipulated by the body corporate.[405] The body corporate asserted an unfettered discretion under the rules to refuse to allow the deck to be completed. After construing the rules of the body corporate so as to avoid that result, William Young P. said for the Court that "a public law dimension" to the case had been overlooked. A decision by a body corporate to withhold consent under either rule would involve the exercise of a statutory power of decision under s.3 of the Judicature Amendment

---

[399] See 3–041.
[400] [1999] 3 N.Z.L.R. 1 at 11–12. This aspect of the case is untouched by the PC's overturning on another point: *Phipps v Royal Australasian College of Surgeons* [2000] 2 N.Z.L.R. 513.
[401] [1997] 2 N.Z.L.R. 241, CA.
[402] [1985] 1 N.Z.L.R. 159 at 179.
[403] [2005] N.Z.A.R. 577, HC.
[404] [2002] 3 N.Z.L.R. 621, CA, [33].
[405] (2005) 5 N.Z .Conv.C. 194 at 138 CA.

Act 1972 (NZ). This would bring into play administrative law principles that would require the body corporate to give proper effect to the rules and the statutory scheme. It could not exercise its consent power essentially to prevent a unit owner from exercising his property right. It might be that it would also satisfy the *Wednesbury* test that no reasonable body corporate could object to the minor works necessary to complete the deck. Although William Young P. added the caveat that the application of the 1972 Act "does not mean that the body corporate must act as if the rules provided that consent not be declined unreasonably", that is logic of the application of administrative law principles and there is excellent authority for the proposition.[406]

Section 3 of the New Zealand Bill of Rights Act 1990 "applies only to acts done . . . (a)[b]y the legislative, executive, or judicial branches of the government of New Zealand; or (b) [b]y any person or body in the performance of any public function, power, or duty conferred or imposed on that person or body by or pursuant to law". For example, in *Television New Zealand Ltd v Viewers For Television Excellence Inc* the Broadcasting Standards Authority was held to be within s.3(b) when determining complaints made under a statutorily recognised and industry-created Code of TV Programme Standards.[407]   **3–113**

South Africa

In *Sarfu* the Constitutional Court held that the source of a power, for example its source in legislation, is not determinative of whether the exercise of the power should be subject to judicial review.[408] Similarly, the identity of the functionary or the person exercising the power is not determinative. Rather, the nature of the power itself must be closely examined in an effort to discover if the power, by its very nature, attracts the controls of administrative justice.[409] Two situations exist where the controls of administrative law have been extended. The first is in the exercise of powers of a public nature by private bodies, or the privatisation of public functions, and the second is the private relationships of public bodies and institutions.   **3–114**

Private bodies

South African common law has even since the pre-constitutional era recognised that private bodies may exercise administrative powers and must comply with principles of administrative justice when they do so.[410]   **3–115**

---

[406] See, e.g. *Webster v Auckland Harbour Board* [1983] N.Z.L.R. 646 at 650 (Cooke and Jeffries JJ.), CA; *Webster v Auckland Harbour Board* [1987] 2 N.Z.L.R. 129, 131 (Cooke P.), CA; *R. v Tower Hamlets LBC Ex p Chetnik Developments Ltd* [1988] 1 A.C. 858, 872 (Lord Bridge).

[407] [2005] N.Z.A.R. 1, HC.

[408] *President of the RSA v SARFU* 2000 (1) S.A. 1, CC.

[409] paras.141, 143.

[410] *Johannesburg Stock Exchange v Witwatersrand Nigel Ltd and Another* 1988 (3) S.A. 132 (A), *Dawnlaan Beleggings (Edms) Bpk v Johannesburg Stock Exchange* 1983 (3) S.A. 344 (W), *Theron en Andere v Ring van Wellington van die NG Sendingskerk in Suid-Afrika en Andere* 1976 (2) S.A. 1 (A), and *Turner v Jockey Club of South Africa* 1974 (3) S.A. 633 (A).

In the constitutional era there are a number of cases that refine the approach to the private exercise of public power. *AAA Investments (Pty) Ltd v Micro Finance Regulatory Council* raised the question of whether a private and voluntary body with the power to make rules regulating the micro-loan industry nevertheless exercised public power when making rules.[411] The applicant submitted that in making rules regulating the micro-finance industry the Council exercised public power and had to comply with the principles of the doctrine of legality when doing so. In the court below, the Supreme Court of Appeal, it was held that the Council was not a "public regulator", but a "private regulator" of moneylenders who consent to its authority.[412] It was important to decide whether the Council exercised public power, Yacoob J. said in the Constitutional Court: "The exercise of public power is always subject to constitutional control and to the rule of law or, to put it more specifically, the legality requirement of our Constitution. The Council would therefore be bound by this requirement if it exercised public power". An important aspect of the Constitutional Court judgment is that it puts to rest any notion that the exercise of a power or function can escape the controls of administrative justice and scrutiny against the requirements of the Constitution simply because it is a private body that is involved. The approach in the SCA was that the rules made by the Council applied only to those participants in the micro-lending industry who chose to participate in the industry, that the rules operated in the private sphere by reason of the contractual relationship, and had no effect or impact on the public at large. The Constitutional Court rejected this formalistic and categorical approach, recognising that traditionally governmental functions are to an increasing degree being outsourced to private entities. The inquiry must then be focused on the nature of the power, rather than the nature of the functionary:

"The fundamental difference between a private company registered in terms of the Companies Act and the Council is that the private company, while it has to comply with the law, is autonomous in the sense that the company itself decides what its objectives and functions are and how it fulfils them. The Council's composition and mandate show that although its legal form is that of a private company, its functions are essentially regulatory of an industry. . . . I strain to find any characteristic of autonomy in the functions of the Council equivalent to that of an enterprise of a private nature. The Council regulates in the public interest and in the performance of a public duty. Its decisions and Rules are subject to constitutional control. The Council is subject to the principle of legality".[413]

---

[411] 2006 (11) B.C.L.R. 1255, CC.
[412] The Supreme Court of Appeal judgment is reported as *Micro Finance Regulatory Council v AAA Investment (Pty) Ltd and Another* 2006 (1) S.A. 27, SCA, see para.24.
[413] para.45.

Private powers of public bodies

The second situation concerns the extent to which contractual relation- **3–116** ships to which the state or other public entities are party are subject to the constraints and controls of administrative law. Historically the approach to this question was dominated by reliance on the source of the power: if the exercise of the power was authorised in the terms of a contract, or the contract explicitly conferred the power concerned, then the exercise of the power was to be considered private—even where a statutory or public power authorised the conclusion of the contract in the first place.[414] The dominance of this categorical and formalistic approach has been eroded in the constitutional era. In *Cape Metropolitan Council v Metro Inspection Services (Western Cape) CC* the Supreme Court of Appeal found that although the appellant Council's power to enter into a contract with the respondent came from statute, the power to terminate the contract arose only from the terms of the contract and common law.[415] The cancellation of the contract was thus not a public duty or function, did not amount to a public power, and was not subject to the controls on public power. The court did hold, however, that an important element of the reason for this conclusion was that the terms of the contract were not prescribed by statute and "could not be dictated by the [the Council] by virtue of its position as a public authority". In *Logbro Properties CC v Bedderson NO* Cameron J.A. emphasised this nuanced approach relying on the nature of the relationship between the contracting parties over the formalism of a contract per se.[416] He stated that the *Cape Metro case* established the principle that "a public authority's invocation of a power of cancellation in a contract concluded on equal terms with a major commercial undertaking, without any element of superiority or authority deriving from its public position, does not amount to an exercise of public power".[417]

However, the formalism this statement seeks to banish retains a hold **3–117** over South African legal reasoning, particularly in the area of public sector employment law. A number of cases have held that the regulation of employment relationships by contract is a purely private matter, even when the employer is a department or organ of state whose power to employ is founded on statutory or public power.[418] Most recently a judgment forming

---

[414] *Mustapha v Receiver of Revenue, Lichtenburg*, 1958 (3) S.A. 343 (A). See also C. Hoexter, "Contracts in Administrative Law: Life after Formalism?" (2004) 121 *South African Law Journal* 595, D. Pretorius, "The defence of the Realm: Contract and Natural Justice'" (2002) 119 *South African Law Journal* 374.

[415] 2001 (3) S.A. 1013, SCA.

[416] 2003 (2) S.A. 460, SCA.

[417] para.10.

[418] See, e.g. *Public Servants' Association obo Haschke v MEC for Agriculture* [2004] 8 B.L.L.R. 822, LC and *Hlope v Minister of Safety and Security* [2006] 3 B.L.L.R. 297, LC. In *SA Police Union v National Commissioner of the SA Police Service* (2005) 26 I.L.J. 2403, LC Murphy A.J. concluded that the National Police Commissioner's decision to unilaterally change employees' shift hours was not public power on more or less the same terms that a similar conclusion was reached in *Cape Metropolitan Services* above. He held that the decision was the exercise of apower in terms of collective agreement between the two parties and that the agreement was eneterd into on equal terms without any element of superiority or authority deriving from the SAPS's public position (para.53).

part of a plurality decision in the Supreme Court of Appeal displays this formalism. In *Transnet Limited v PNN Chirwa*[419] Mthiyane J.A. held that although Transnet is an organ of state and derives its authority to enter into contracts from statute,[420] its power to terminate contracts does not derive from the same source. The judge went on to conclude that "the nature of the conduct involved here is the termination of a contract of employment. It is based on contract and does not involve the exercise of any public power or performance of a public function in terms of legislation".[421]

---

[419] (2006) 27 I.L.J. 2294, SCA.
[420] See in this regard *Transnet Ltd v Goodman Brothers (Pty) Ltd* 2001 (1) S.A. 853, SCA, paras 37–38.
[421] At the time of writing the matter is before the Constitutional Court.

CHAPTER 4

CONCEPTS OF JURISDICTION AND LAWFUL ADMINISTRATION

SCOPE

The following issues are discussed in this Chapter, which concludes with **4–001** some comparative perspectives.[1]

- The historical development of the concepts of jurisdiction and vires of public authorities;[2]

- Ouster clauses and similar statutory provisions which seek to exclude or restrict the powers of the court to carry out judicial review of some decisions;[3]

- The *Anisminic* case and its aftermath;[4]

- The concepts of jurisdiction and vires today—we argue that the foundation of judicial review is no longer ultra vires but rather the principles of lawful or legitimate administration;[5]

- The distinction between "void and voidable" decisions, which has now largely been superseded by a more straightforward distinction between "lawful and unlawful";[6]

- Collateral challenge—situations in which a defendant in civil or criminal proceedings seeks to argue that delegated legislation or a decision of a public authority is unlawful.[7]

INTRODUCTION

Judicial review of administrative action was founded upon the premise that **4–002** an inferior tribunal or administrative public authority is entitled to decide wrongly, but is not entitled to exceed the jurisdiction it was given by

---

[1] The 5th edition of this work considered here the power of the courts to review findings of fact. This section, as amended, is now at Ch.11, except for brief discussion of "precedent fact" at 4–047.
[2] See 4–007.
[3] See 4–014.
[4] See 4–028.
[5] See 4–039.
[6] See 4–056; and on the effect of void decision, see 4–077.
[7] See 4–064; and see also 3–097 on the principle of procedural exclusivity.

statute. The statutory jurisdiction (later referred to also as "vires") permitted the public authority to make errors of fact, or errors of law *within* its jurisdiction, provided that such an error of law was not manifest "on the face of the record". In this respect judicial review is to be distinguished from an appeal. It was largely restricted to review for *excess* of jurisdiction, while an appeal would usually enable errors either of fact or of law to be rectified. Ultra vires, or excess of jurisdiction, in the narrow or strict sense, was thus the organising principle which both justified judicial review (by declaring all power to be derived power) and constrained it (by permitting a degree of autonomy to the reviewed public authority).

4–003   The concept of jurisdictional error has become one of the most elusive in administrative law, largely because it calls for analytical distinctions which have, as judicial review has developed, become difficult if not impossible to sustain. There is the vexed distinction between jurisdictional error and error of law within jurisdiction. There is also a related distinction between "preliminary" or "collateral" requirements[8] which have to be fulfilled before a public authority's jurisdiction exists (which therefore go to a public authority's jurisdiction, being preliminary or collateral to the "merits" of the decision), and requirements (of law or fact or merits) which do not. Finally, there is the equally contested distinction between a "void" and "voidable" decision: that is, a decision which is invalid or void in the sense that it is a nullity, or voidable in that it can be set aside but until it is set aside gives rise to legal consequences.

4–004   At the heart of these seemingly technical distinctions there lie fundamental constitutional issues concerning the rule of law (to what extent should administrative bodies be able to determine the scope of their own powers? To what extent may Parliament prevent access to justice? To what extent ought invalid decisions be able to survive once successfully challenged?); the relationship between the courts and the administration (to what extent should courts exercising powers of review refrain from correcting the administration's factual or legal errors?), and the sovereignty of Parliament (to what extent do the courts possess an inherent power to review the legality of official action despite parliamentary legislation purporting to exclude or limit such review?).

4–005   Although these traditional distinctions and labels cannot yet be declared obsolete, they are today largely of historic interest for four reasons. First, after a stage during which the courts only tentatively asserted their right to insist on the legality of administrative action, they have now become more confident in their constitutional responsibility of enforcing the rule of law, thus generally requiring all administrative action to be simply lawful, whether or not it is technically outwith a public authority's so-called jurisdiction in the narrow sense. Secondly, the claim for judicial review

---

[8] Collateral in this sense should not be confused with collateral used in another sense involving jurisdiction, namely, a challenge of the lawfulness of a decision in collateral or indirect proceedings, that is, other than by judicial review, e.g. by way of a defence in criminal or civil proceedings (see also 4–064).

procedure[9] enables the courts to conduct more thorough investigation of the way in which administrative decisions are reached than was previously possible by means of an application for the prerogative writs before 1978.[10] The existence of such procedures means that there is little sense in retaining the former distinction between errors of law that are and those that are not patent-on the face of the record since latent errors are accessible to investigation. Thirdly, the courts have now developed a series of principles, under the rubric of a number of "grounds" of review, that are accepted as governing the exercise of official power and which the courts legitimately enforce upon all bodies exercising public functions. Fourthly, the passing of the Human Rights Act 1998 requires our courts to apply the principles of the ECHR, which in many respects expand both the substance ad approach to judicial review.[11] Judicial review is thus engaged with new principles and new challenges and is no longer very concerned with the notion of jurisdictional rectitude or vires, in the narrow sense of those terms. Yet because the old distinctions do occasionally arise it is still necessary to consider their history and background, which supply the intellectual foundations of so much of modern judicial review.

Before doing so, however, it should be borne in mind that the terms "jurisdiction" and "vires" are both at times confused by the fact that they can refer to the power either of the public authority reviewed or of the reviewing court. The assertion that the courts have no "jurisdiction" to review "non-jurisdictional" error committed by an administrative tribunal raises questions both about the power to review of the court and the power to err of the tribunal. When Parliament seeks to oust the jurisdiction of the courts to review decisions of a public authority, the question arises as to whether the intention was to preclude the court reviewing even for a jurisdictional error committed by the public authority. Here again two questions are raised: (a) the power of the court to review, and (b) the kind of determination (or non-determination) that the public authority is entitled to make with impunity. These different senses of jurisdiction interlock and overlap. Although they may be kept conceptually distinct, we believe that they require common treatment and cannot be fully understood in isolation one from the other. **4–006**

HISTORICAL DEVELOPMENT OF THE CONCEPT OF JURISDICTION

From the earliest times the influence of the common law permeated the local courts and the local communities, and proceedings instituted before borough courts were removable into the King's courts at Westminster.[12] **4–007**

[9] See Ch.16.
[10] See 15–087.
[11] See Ch.13; 11–079.
[12] Holdsworth, *History of English Law*, ii, pp.395–405; Ch.15 below.

Usurpations of authority by municipal corporations gave rise to actions to impugn the validity of byelaws,[13] *quo warranto* proceedings,[14] and later, applications for writs of scire facias to repeal borough charters. When the justices of the peace emerged as the principal organ of local administration, the Court of King's Bench (which of all the common law courts was the one most closely associated with the business of government) assumed superintendence over their proceedings—a superintendence that was facilitated by the fact that the administrative functions of the justices were discharged in a judicial form. During the course of the 17th century a distinction gradually came to be drawn, as we shall see, between acts done without jurisdiction, which might be collaterally impeached in civil proceedings brought against the justices for trespass and which could be quashed by a writ of certiorari, and erroneous acts done within jurisdiction, which could not ordinarily be impugned in collateral proceedings and which were immune from the reach of certiorari unless an error was apparent on the face of the "record". The essential features of this distinction survived to condition the scope of judicial control over the successors of the justices of the peace in the work of public administration.[15]

4–008   The courts of common law had at the outset asserted a right to determine the proper jurisdiction of courts administering other systems of law and to contain them within that jurisdiction by writs of prohibition.[16] But it was not until the 17th century that what was to become the modern conception of judicial review took shape.[17] In actions for trespass and other civil wrongs against the Commissioners of Sewers and the judges and officers of other inferior courts, a distinction began to be drawn between a court which proceeded erroneously or *inverso ordine* within its jurisdiction, and a court which proceeded without jurisdiction of the cause. Only in the latter class of case could the order of the court be collaterally impeached and its judges or officers subjected to civil liability.[18] The jurisdiction of a court might be limited with respect to place, persons or subject-matter; and the conferment of a limited or stinted jurisdiction, so Hale held, implied a negative, namely, that the court should not proceed at all in other cases. "But if they should commit a mistake in a matter that were within their power, that would not be examinable here".[19]

[13] Holdsworth, pp.398, 400, giving illustrations from the 14th and 15th centuries.
[14] See 15–057.
[15] See 15–020.
[16] See 15–017.
[17] A. Rubinstein, *Jurisdiction and Illegality* (1965), Ch.4; E. Henderson, *Foundations of English Administrative Law* (1963); L. Jaffe, *Judicial Control of Administrative Action* (1933), pp.205–208, 329–334, 624–629; L. Jaffe and E. Henderson , "Judicial Review and the Rule of Law" (1956) 72 L.Q.R. 345; L. Jaffe, "Judicial Review: Constitutional and Jurisdictional Fact" (1957) 70 Harv. L.R., 953.
[18] See esp. Coke's dicta in the case of the *Marshalsea* (1613) 10 Co.Rep. 68b, 76. But Coke himself did not always follow this distinction; see *Dr Bonham's case* (1610) 8 Co.Rep. 113b.
[19] *Terry v Huntington* (1668) Hardres 480 at 483; see also *Commins v Massam* (1643) March 196 at 197–198 (Heath J.); *Groenvelt v Burwell* (1700) 1 Ld.Raym. 454 at 467–468 (Holt C.J.).

After 1700 certiorari to quash became the regular mode of impugning **4–009** the decisions of inferior courts. At first it was not easy to distinguish between certiorari to quash for want of jurisdiction and certiorari to quash for a defect on the face of the record.[20] The inferior court was required to incorporate in its record all the facts which invested it with jurisdiction, and often a wide range of other facts besides,[21] and if any material fact was omitted the record was bad on its face. In so far as the exercise of the power to quash was clearly referable to jurisdictional defects, errors committed by inferior courts were almost invariably assumed to go to jurisdiction.[22] That a distinction between errors within jurisdiction and errors going to jurisdiction was still recognised was demonstrated by the establishment in the latter part of the 18th century of the practice that findings on jurisdictional matters, though not on other matters, could be impugned by affidavit evidence.[23] But it was not until the first half of the 19th century that a reaction set in against the prevalent tendency to treat nearly all of an inferior court's findings as touching its jurisdiction.[24] This reaction made it possible to construct a coherent theory of the concept of jurisdiction which, had it but prevailed, would have seriously limited the scope of judicial review both in magisterial law and in administrative law.

The pure theory of jurisdiction

This "pure" theory of jurisdiction may be stated as follows.[25] Jurisdiction **4–010** means authority to decide. Whenever a judicial tribunal is empowered or required to inquire into a question of law or fact for the purpose of giving a decision, its findings cannot be impeached collaterally or on an application for judicial review but are binding until reversed on appeal. Moreover, "Where a court has jurisdiction to entertain an application, it

---

[20] See 15–014.

[21] Both in summary convictions and in orders the adjudication had to be stated, and in summary convictions the court was also required to set out the evidence and its conclusions drawn therefrom.

[22] Not till about 1720 was it clearly settled that not every statutory requirement was to be treated as jurisdictional (Henderson, (1963) p.157). For the development of the distinction between jurisdictional and non-jurisdictional matters in prohibition and in mandamus cases, see Henderson (1963), Ch.4.

[23] As late as 1735 extrinsic evidence to disprove the existence of jurisdictional facts was held inadmissible (*R. v Oulton Inhabitants* (1735) Cas.t.Hard.169). The distinction between the two classes of errors came to be drawn more sharply in the second half of the 19th century, when the recital of evidential facts was omitted from the records of summary convictions.

[24] *Brittain v Kinnaird* (1819) 1 B. & B. 432; *Cave v Mountain* (1840) 1 Mon. & G. 257; *R. v Bolton* (1841) 1 Q.B. 66; *R. v Rotherham (Inhabitants)* (1842) 3 Q.B. 776; *R. v Buckinghamshire Justices* (1843) 3 Q.B. 800. The relevant authorities are examined in *R. v Mahony* [1910] 2 J.R. 695 and *R. v Nat Bell Liquors Ltd* [1922] 2 A.C. 128; see L. Jaffe, *Judicial Control of Administrative Action* (1965), pp.624–30.

[25] D. Gordon, "The Relation of Facts to Jurisdiction" (1929) 45 L.Q.R. 459; D. Gordon, "Tithe Redemption Commission v Gwynne" (1944) 60 L.Q.R. 250; D. Gordon, "Conditional or Contingent Jurisdiction of Tribunals" (1960) 1 U. of B.C.L. Rev. 185. For a reply to criticisms of his views see: H.W.R. Wade, "Anglo-American Administrative Law: More Reflections" (1966) 82 L.Q.R. 263 at 515.

does not lose its jurisdiction by coming to a wrong conclusion, whether it was wrong in law or in fact".[26] It does not lose its jurisdiction even if its conclusion on any aspect of its proper field of inquiry is entirely without evidential support.[27] The question whether a tribunal has jurisdiction depends not on the truth or falsehood of the facts into which it has to inquire, or upon the correctness of its findings on these facts, but upon their nature, and it is determinable "at the commencement, not at the conclusion, of the inquiry".[28] A preliminary or collateral question is said to be one that is collateral to "the merits"[29] or to "the very essence of the inquiry";[30] it is "not the main question which the tribunal have to decide".[31] Thus, a tribunal empowered to determine claims for compensation for loss of office has jurisdiction to determine all questions of law and fact relating to the measure of compensation and the tenure of the office, and it does not exceed its jurisdiction by determining any of those questions incorrectly; but it has no implied jurisdiction to entertain a claim for reinstatement or damages for wrongful dismissal, and it will exceed its jurisdiction if it makes an order in such terms, for it has no legal power to give any decision whatsoever on those matters. A tribunal may also lack jurisdiction if it is improperly constituted, or (possibly) if it fails to observe certain essential preliminaries to the inquiry.[32] But it does not exceed its jurisdiction by basing its decision upon an incorrect determination of any question that it is empowered or required (i.e. has jurisdiction) to determine.

The ultra vires doctrine

4–011 In essence, the doctrine of ultra vires permits the courts to strike down decisions made by bodies exercising public functions which they have no power to make. Acting ultra vires and acting without jurisdiction have

[26] *R. v Central Criminal Court Justices* (1886) 17 Q.B.D. 598 at 602; *R. v Grant* (1850) 19 L.J.M.C. 59; *Kemp v Neville* (1862) 10 C.B.(n.s.) 523 at 549–52; *R. v St Olave's Southwark, District Board of Works* (1857) 8 E. & B. 659; *R. v Bradley* (1894) 70 L.T. 349; *Shridramappa Pasare v Narhari Bin Shivappa* (1900) L.R. 27 I.A. 216 at 225; *R. v Cheshire Justices Ex p. Heaver* (1913) 108 L.T. 374; *R. (Limerick Corp) v LGB* [1922] 2 I.R. 76, 93; *R. v Weston-Super Mare Justices. Ex p. Barkers (Contractors) Ltd* [1944] 1 All E.R. 747; *R. v Minister of Health* [1939] 1 K.B. 232; *R. v Minister of Transport Ex p. Beech-Allen (WH) Ltd* (1964) 62 L.G.R. 76; *Punton v Ministry of Pensions and National Insurance (No.2)* [1964] 1 W.L.R. 226;
[27] *R. v Shropshire Justices Ex p. Blewitt* (1866) 14 L.T. 598; *Ex p. Hopwood* (1850) 15 Q.B. 121; *R. v Mahony* [1910] 2 I.R. 695; *R. v Nat Bell Liquors Ltd* [1922] 12 A.C. 128; *R. v Ludlow Ex p. Barnsley Corp* [1947] K.B. 634 at 639.
[28] *R. v Bolton* (1841) 1 Q.B. 66 at 74.
[29] *Bunbury v Fuller* (1853) 9 Ex. 111 at 140; *R. v Lincolnshire Justices Ex p. Brett* [19261 2 K.B. 192 at 202; *R. (Limerick Corp) v LGB* [1922] 12 I.R. 76 at 93.
[30] *Ex p. Vaughan* (1866) L.R. 2 Q.B. 114 at 116.
[31] *R. v Fulham, etc. Rent Tribunal Ex p. Zerek* [1951] 2 K.B. 1 at 6. A tribunal that proceeds in a matter that is *res judicata* has also been said to exceed its jurisdiction: *Jowett v Bradford (Earl)* [1977] 2 All E.R. 33.
[32] *Colonial Bank of Australasia Ltd v Willan* (1874) L.R. 5 at 417, 422, PC. D. Gordon has even challenged the validity of the last-mentioned proposition in "Observance of Law as a Condition of Jurisdiction" (1931) 47 L.Q.R. 386, 557.

essentially the same meaning, although in general the term "vires" has been employed when considering administrative decisions and subordinate legislative orders, and "jurisdiction" when considering judicial decisions, or those having a judicial flavour.[33]

The evolution of a specific concept of ultra vires did not take place in the context of the power of public authorities. The term was first generally used to denote excess of legal authority by independent statutory bodies and railway companies in the middle years of the 19th century;[34] though the main features of the doctrine to which this name was given had already been taking shape over a long period in relation to the powers of common-law corporations.[35] The term came to be used in relation to municipal corporations, then to the other new types of local government authorities,[36] and finally to the Crown and its servants and even to inferior judicial bodies.   **4–012**

The ultra vires doctrine has had a restricted application to corporations created otherwise than by or under statute. Although such corporations are subject to the doctrine in areas regulated by legislation, they seem to be as capable of performing other transactions (e.g. entering into contracts, acquiring land or providing new services) as any natural person.[37] But they may be restrained from committing acts infringing their charter of incorporation;[38] they cannot perpetrate any direct interference with the rights of individuals without specific legal authority; and in the case of such municipal corporations as owed their origin to the royal prerogative, it was doubtful whether they could expend money save in circumstances defined by statute.[39] Subordinate legislative instruments, as well as administrative acts and decisions, may be ultra vires on substantive as well as procedural grounds.[40]   **4–013**

[33] cf. R. v Secretary of State for the Environment Ex p. Ostler [1977] 1 Q.B. 122 at 135, 138 (distinction drawn between the effect of a breach of the rules of natural justice and fraud upon the jurisdiction of a judicial tribunal and upon the vires of an administrative decision, albeit one to which the rules of natural justice applied).

[34] H. Street, A Treatise on the Doctrine of Ultra Vires (1930), pp.1–3. Ultra Vires has been largely eroded in modern company law. H. Rajak, "Judicial Control: Corporations and the decline of Ultra Vires" [1995] Cambrian L.R. 9.

[35] Holdsworth viii, pp.59–61.

[36] I. Jennings in H. Laski, I. Jennings and W. Robson (eds), A Century of Municipal Progress (1935), p.418.

[37] Sutton Hospital case (1612) 10 Co.Rep. 23a at 30b; Wenlock (Baroness) v River Dee Co (1887) 36 Ch.D. 675 at 685; Attorney General v Manchester Corp [1906] 1 Ch. 643 at 651; Attorney General v Leeds Corp [1929] 2 Ch. 291 at 295; Attorney General v Leicester Corp [1943] 1 Ch. 86 at 93. The authority of the rule was strongly criticised by Street (1930), pp.18–22.

[38] A member of the incorporated body may sue: Jenkin v Pharmaceutical Society of Great Britain [1921] 1 Ch. 392; Dickson v Pharmaceutical Society of Great Britain [1970] A.C. 403.

[39] Subject to the "Ram doctrine" discussed at 5–022. In Hazell v Hammersmith & Fulham LBC [1992] A.C. 1, although the local authority had been incorporated by royal charter, the charter did not confer on the borough any greater power than the statutory power exercisable by any other local authority, since the grant of incorporation had been made by virtue of the royal prerogative and in pursuance of the 1963 Act, the combined effect of which was to create a statutory corporation. It followed that the council had no power to carry out the swap transaction whether in its own name or in the name of the borough.

[40] See 3–005.

STATUTORY RESTRICTION OF JUDICIAL REVIEW

4–014 Before considering the extent to which the "pure" theory of jurisdiction has any relevance today, and, if so, the type of legal error that constitutes an error of jurisdiction in the strict sense, we consider the way the courts have approached statutory restrictions upon judicial review. This will allow us to view in tandem the two interlocking aspects of jurisdiction that we have identified: the jurisdiction of the public authority reviewed to commit errors of law or fact (the issue we have just been considering) and the jurisdiction of the court to review the decision of public authorities in the face of legislation which attempts to restrict such review.

4–015 In matters of public law, the role of the courts is of high constitutional importance. It is a function of the judiciary to determine the lawfulness of the acts and decisions and orders of public authorities exercising public functions, and to afford protection to the rights of the citizen. Legislation which deprives them of these powers is inimical to the principle of the rule of law, which requires the citizen to have access to justice.[41]

4–016 The courts have, therefore, long been zealous to resist encroachments upon their jurisdiction. An attitude which may have originally been conditioned by the solicitude of the judges for their emoluments (which were dependent largely on fees paid by suitors) has been reinforced by traditions stemming from the battles successfully waged against the pre-rogative courts in the seventeenth century and by the authority that the superior judges have since acquired. The view is widely held that "the proper tribunals for the determination of legal disputes in this country are the courts, and they are the only tribunals which, by training and experience, and assisted by properly qualified advocates, are fitted for the task".[42] It is a common law presumption of legislative intent[43] that access to the courts in respect of justiciable issues is not to be denied save by clear words in a statute. Subordinate legislation purporting to restrict or exclude access to the courts has been held to be ultra vires in the absence of express authorisation of such provisions in the enabling Act.[44]

---

[41] See 1–016; 5–036 et seq; 11–059.

[42] Lee v Showmen's Guild of Great Britain [1952] 2 Q.B. 329 at 354 (Romer L.J.). cf. R. v Medical Appeal Tribunal Ex p. Gilmore [1957] 1 Q.B. 574 at 587.

[43] See 1–016 and 5–036 et seq; and see, e.g. Goldsack v Shore [1950] 1 K.B. 708 at 712; Bennett & White (Calgary) Ltd v Municipal District of Sugar City (No.5) [1951] A.C. 786 at 808–9, 812; London Hospital Governors v Jacobs [1956] 1 W.L.R. 662 at 669, 676; R. v Medical Appeal Tribunal Ex p. Gilmore (n.34); Francis v Yiewsley & West Drayton UDC [1957] 2 Q.B. 136, 148; Pyx Granite Co v Ministry of Housing and Local Government [1958] 1 Q.B. 554 at 571; [1960] A.C. 260 at 286; Re Parliamentary Privilege Act 1770 [1958] A.C. 331 at 353; Customs and Excise Commissioners v Cure & Deeley Ltd [1962] 1 Q.B. 340 at 357–9, 369 (cf. Marsh (B) (Wholesale) Ltd v Customs and Excise Commissioners [1970] 2 Q.B. 206); Baron v Sunderland Corp [1966] Q.B. 56 at 66; Ealing LBC v Race Relations Board [1972] A.C. 342; Re Boaler [1915] 1 K.B. 21 at 36; R. v Secretary of State for the Home Department Ex p. Leech [1994] Q.B. 198.

[44] Chester v Bateson [1920] 1 K.B. 829; Newcastle Breweries Ltd v R., ibid., 854; Paul (R & W) Ltd v Wheat Commission [1937] A.C. 139; Cure & Deeley [1962] 1 Q.B. 340; though cf. Postmaster-General v Wadsworth [1939] 4 All E.R. 1, an unsatisfactory decision of the CA; Re Kellner's Will Trusts [1949] 2 All E.R. 43; Leech [1994] Q.B. 198; Raymond v Honey [1983] 1 A.C. 1; and R v Lord Chancellor Ex p. Witham [1998] Q.B. 575.

Section 11 of the Tribunals and Inquiries Act 1958 reinforced judicial **4–017** attitudes towards "finality clauses" by enacting that, subject to four exceptions,[45] any provision in an Act passed before August 1958, to the effect that an order or determination was not to be "called into question in any court" (and any such provision which "by similar words" excluded any of the powers of the High Court), was not to prevent the issue of certiorari or mandamus.[46] This section was re-enacted as s.14 of the Tribunals and Inquiries Act 1971 and s.12(1) of the 1992 Act. The section applies to all forms of finality clauses, howsoever worded (subject to the exceptions listed), and covers other remedies (such as the declaratory judgment[47]) as well as certiorari and mandamus (now known as declaratory order, quashing order and mandatory order). It does not extend to exclusionary clauses contained in statutes passed after July 1958.

Various means have been devised by Parliament to seek to restrict **4–018** judicial review. Indirect means include the establishment of a prescribed appeals procedure,[48] conferring of wide "subjective" discretion upon the decision-maker,[49] and designating an appellate body as a superior court of record.[50] These indirect means are considered elsewhere.[51] Direct means have included legislation employing a variety of formulae: "finality clauses", "no certiorari" clauses, "conclusive evidence" clauses, time-limited clauses and general formulae purporting to exclude review. Each can constitute a threat to the rule of law, which the Lord Chancellor is under a duty to uphold. These will now be considered in turn.

Finality clauses

By the end of the 17th century it had been settled that a conviction or **4–019** order made by any inferior tribunal could be removed by certiorari into the Court of King's Bench to be quashed for excess or want of jurisdiction or error on the face of the record. The court, viewing with disfavour the process of conviction without indictment[52] and applying the principle that

[45] Now there are only two exceptions under s.12(3) of the Tribunals and Inquiries Act 1992: (a) an order or determination of a court of law, and (b) where an Act makes special provision for application to the High Court within a specified time.

[46] The Franks Committee on Administrative Tribunals and Enquiries had recommended in 1957 that no statute should contain words purporting to oust certiorari, prohibition or mandamus in respect of statutory tribunals (Cmnd. 218 (1957), pp.27, 93). The House of Commons Select Committee on Statutory Instruments was already required to consider whether to draw the attention of the House to instruments made under statutes purporting to exclude them from challenge in the courts.

[47] *Anisminic Ltd v Foreign Compensation Commission* [1969] 2 A.C. 147, where the plaintiffs successfully claimed a declaration.

[48] See 16–018 and Ch.17.

[49] See 5–017 *et seq.*

[50] A. Le Sueur, "Three strikes and it's out? The UK government's strategy to oust judicial review from immigration and asylum decision-making" [2004] P.L. 225.

[51] On alternative remedies, see 16–015 and Ch.17; subjective discretion is considered at 5–017.

[52] *R. v Corden* (1769) 4 Burr. 2279.

statutes creating new jurisdictions ought to be strictly construed[53] tended to combine lack of discrimination with excess of zeal and quashed convictions and orders for minor technical defects. Parliament therefore incorporated into a number of statutes conferring summary jurisdiction provisions that were designed to take away the right to apply for certiorari to quash decisions, either by using express words to that effect,[54] or by providing that the matter was to be finally determined by the justices.

4-020   The King's Bench, however, held that a general finality clause was insufficient to deprive the courts of their power to award the beneficial remedy of certiorari for patent errors of law[55] or for jurisdictional defects,[56] unless the right to a certiorari had itself been conferred by statute.[57] These precedents were followed in later cases, and it became settled law that a finality clause did not restrict in any way whatsoever the power of the courts to issue certiorari to quash either for jurisdictional defects[58] or for error of law on the face of the record.[59] It was clear, furthermore, that a finality clause did not affect their power to award a declaration that a decision or order made by a statutory body is invalid.[60] Even such words as "final and conclusive" were ineffective to abridge or attenuate judicial review.[61] The only practical effects of a finality clause were to take away a right of appeal where one already exists—e.g. rights of appeal to the High Court by way of case stated from inferior courts[62]—and

[53] *Warwick v White* (1722) Bunb. 106.
[54] This practice began towards the end of the 17th century, shortly after it had become usual to give a right of appeal from justices sitting out of sessions to Quarter Sessions: *W. Paley on Summary Convictions*, 9th edn (1926), p.800. See generally *R. v Mahony* [1910] 2 I.R. 695 at 730 *et seq.* (Gibson J.).
[55] As distinct from errors on questions of fact: *R. v Plowright* (1686) 3 Mod. 95.
[56] See, e.g. *R. v Plowright* (1686) 3 Mod. 95; *R. v Moreley* (1760) 2 Burr. 1041; *R. v Jukes* (1800) 8 T.R. 542.
[57] *R. v Hunt* (1856) 6 E. & B. 408; D. Yardley, "Statutory Limitations on the Power of Prerogative Orders in England" (1957) 3 U. of Queensld L.J. 103.
[58] *R. v Nat Bell Liquors Ltd* [1922] A.C. 128 at 159–60; *R. v Minister of Transport Ex p. HC Motor Works Ltd* [1927] 2 K.B. 401; *R. v Minister of Health* [1939] 1 K.B. 232 at 246, 249; *R. v Medical Appeal Tribunal Ex p. Gilmore* [1957] 1 Q.B. 574 at 583–585–588.
[59] *Gilmore* [1957] 1 Q.B. 574; Notes [1957] P.L. 89; S.A. de Smith, "Administrative Finality and Judicial Review" (1957) 20 M.L.R. 394. As a result of this decision a right of appeal on questions of law was statutorily provided to the Industrial Injuries Commissioner by the Family Allowance and National Insurance Act 1959 s.2.
[60] *Taylor v National Assistance Board* [1956] P 470; [1957] P 101 at 111 (dictum); *Pyx Granite Co v Ministry of Housing and Local Government* [1958] 1 Q.B. 554; [1960] A.C. 260; *Ridge v Baldwin* [1964] A.C. 40; *Watt v Lord Advocate* 1977 S.L.T. 130; *Smith v East Sussex CC* (1977) 76 L.G.R. 332.
[61] *Fenwick v Croydon Union Rural Sanitary Authority* [1891] 2 Q.B. 216; *Attorney General v Hanwell UDC* [1900] 1 Ch. 51; [1900] 2 Ch. 377 ("binding and conclusive"). In so far as any effect at all was attributable to a finality clause, it could often be circumvented by limiting its operation to matters other than those in issue before court: see *St Lucia Usines Co v Colonial Treasurer* [1924] A.C. 508 at 513; *Gateshead Union Guardians v Durham CC* [1918] 1 Ch. 146; *Seabrooke v Grays Thurrock Local Board* (1891) 8 T.L.R. 19; *Gillow v Durham CC* [1913] A.C. 54 at 57.
[62] *Westminster Corp v Gordon Hotels Ltd* [190711 K.B. 910; [1908] A.C. 142; *Hall v Arnold* [1950] 2 K.B. 543; *Kydd v Liverpool Watch Committee* [1908] A.C. 327; *Piper v St Marylebone Licensing Justices* [1928] 2 K.B. 221. See also *Re McCosh's Application* [1958] N.Z.L.R. 731; *Dean v District Auditor for Ashton-in-Makerfield* [1960] 1 Q.B. 149; cf. *Tehrani v Rostron* [1972] 1 Q.B. 182.

to preclude a public authority from rescinding or rectifying one of its own valid decisions.[63]

"No certiorari" clauses

Even where the right to certiorari had been expressly taken away by 4–021 statute, the courts relying on one or other of the restrictive rules of interpretation already mentioned, or upon the proposition that Parliament could not have intended a tribunal of limited jurisdiction to be permitted to exceed its authority without the possibility of direct correction by a superior court, persistently declined to construe the words of the statute literally. It was held that certiorari would issue, notwithstanding the presence of words taking away the right to apply for it, if the inferior tribunal was improperly constituted (as where some of its members had a disqualifying interest),[64] or if it lacked or exceeded jurisdiction because of the nature of the subject-matter or failure to observe essential preliminaries,[65] or if a conviction or order had been procured by fraud or collusion.[66] Such language would also be ineffective to exclude certiorari or a declaration of invalidity for breach of either rule of natural justice.[67] Legislation purporting to exclude review by other named remedies (e.g. prohibition, injunction) was equally ineffective to prevent the courts from containing inferior tribunals within the limits of their jurisdiction.[68]

Conclusive evidence clauses

A clause making the confirmation of a compulsory purchase order final and 4–022 of effect as if enacted in the Act and "conclusive evidence that the requirements of this Act have been complied with, and that the order is duly made and is within the powers of this Act," has been held to exclude

[63] R. v Agricultural Land Tribunal (South Eastern Area) Ex p. Hooker [1952] 1 Q.B. 182.
[64] R. v Cheltenham Commissioners (1841) 1 Q.B. 467; R. v L & NW Ry (1863) 9 L.T. (N.S.) 423.
[65] R. v Somersetshire Justices (1826) 5 B. & C. 816; R. v St Albans Justices (1853) 22 L.J.M.C. 142; R. v Wood (1855) 3 E. & B. 49; Ex p. Bradlaugh (1878) 3 Q.B.D. 509 at 512; R. v Hurst Ex p. Smith [1960] 2 Q.B. 133; R. v Worthington-Evans Ex p. Madan [1959] 2 Q.B. 145 at 152; R. v Bloomsbury and Marylebone County Court Ex p. Villerwest Ltd [1975] 1 W.L.R. 1175.
[66] R. v Gillyard (1848) 12 Q.B. 527; Colonial Bank of Australasia Ltd v Willan (1874) L.R. 5 PC 417. Nor does an express privative clause affect the right of the Crown, or of a private prosecutor in criminal proceedings, to apply for the order.
[67] Ridge v Baldwin [1964] A.C. 40 at 120–121.
[68] On prohibition, see Jacobs v Brett (1875) L.R. 20 Eq. 1. On injunctions, see Andrews v Mitchell [1905] A.C. 78; cf. Catt v Wood [1910] A.C. 404 (where the error of law did not go to jurisdiction); see also Wayman v Perseverance Lodge [1917] 1 K.B. 677. There appears to be no statute expressly excluding review by an action for a declaration, but the same principles would surely have applied; see Ridge v Baldwin [1964] A.C. 40; Anisminic Ltd v Foreign Compensation Commission [1969] 2 A.C. 147, although it was assumed throughout Anisminic that a no certiorari clause would remove the power to quash for patent error of law not going to jurisdiction.

the six week period the validity of the action "shall not be questioned in any legal proceedings whatsoever".

Once the period in which a statutory remedy is available has expired, the circumstances in which a decision or order protected by a preclusive clause has been successfully challenged in proceedings other than specific statutory one are extremely limited, if they exist at all. In *Smith v East Elloe RDC*,[76] the House of Lords held a compulsory purchase order immune from judicial review on the ground of alleged bad faith after a time limit had expired. **4–024**

The principal justification for regarding a clause containing a time limit as an effective bar to review after the time limit has expired is that the legislator, having created a statutory remedy, is entitled to limit the availability of that remedy. This can be the case even where the time limit is too short to enable the order or decision to be challenged in some situations. The use of limitation periods to prevent the assertion of legal rights is, after all, a perfectly familiar feature of the legal system. Furthermore, there can be an obvious public interest in enabling public or private works to be commenced and resources to be committed in reliance upon the legal invulnerability of an apparently valid order. In *East Elloe* it was suggested that an order that is patently ultra vires may be impugned outside the six-week period.[77] **4–025**

Formulae purporting to exclude judicial review by general but comprehensive language

Formulae of this character were the principal statutory device adopted for giving the impress of finality to administrative action by the direct prohibition of judicial review. The legal effects attributable to such formulae varied according to the contexts in which they appeared. **4–026**

Where exclusionary formulae were contained in statutes dealing with foreign relations or the working of the parliamentary system, there was a much stronger probability that the courts would give the prohibitive words a literal interpretation.[78] In other contexts, however, the courts have declined to give literal effect to generally worded clauses apparently intended totally to exclude from judicial review the determinations of administrative tribunals. This question was raised in the case of *Anisminic*,[79] which also dealt a blow to the distinction between jurisdictional and non-jurisdictional error from which it has scarcely recovered. **4–027**

---

[76] [1956] A.C. 736 (action for declaration).
[77] *Smith v East Elloe RDC* [1956] A.C. 736 (Viscount Simonds), 769–70 (Lord Radcliffe); *cf.* *Graddage v Haringey LBC* [1975] 1 W.L.R. 241 at 250; *R. v Secretary of State for the Environment Ex p. Ostler* [1977] Q.B. 122.
[78] See, e.g. Extradition Act 1870 s.5 (relating to Orders in Council that apply the provisions of the Act to any foreign State); Parliament Act 1911 s.3 (making a certificate given by the Speaker under the Act conclusive for all purposes and immune from challenge in any court of law); *cf. Harper v Home Secretary* [1955] Ch. 238.
[79] *Anisminic v Foreign Compensation Commission* [1969] 2 A.C. 147.

THE ANISMINIC CASE

4–028 The *Anisminic* case concerned decisions of the Foreign Compensation Commission (which heard and determined claims for compensation out of payments received by the Crown from foreign governments for measures taken by them against the property of British subjects). The statute stated that the Commission's decisions were not to be "called in question in any court of law".[80] The reasons for excluding judicial review were that payments awarded to claimants were discretionary and that it would be undesirable for the calculations made by the Commission for distribution of the limited sums at its disposal to be upset by successful applications to the courts. More important, perhaps, instituting judicial proceedings might seriously retard distribution to successful claimants. Nevertheless, the House of Lords held that the exclusionary formula did not apply to a purported "determination" that was a nullity because it was not one that the Commission had jurisdiction to make. The effect of the clause was merely to protect valid decisions that might otherwise have been impugned for a non-jurisdictional error of law on the face of the record.[81]

4–029 The most important breakthrough in *Anisminic* was the emphatic rejection by the House of Lords[82] of the idea[83] that the jurisdiction of an inferior tribunal was determinable only at the outset of its inquiry. It was observed[84] that a tribunal having jurisdiction over a matter in the first instance might exceed its jurisdiction by breaking the rules of natural justice,[85] applying a wrong legal test and answering the wrong question,[86] failing to take relevant considerations into account or basing the decisions

---

[80] Foreign Compensation Act 1950 s.4(4). The Tribunals and Inquiries Act 1958 s.11(3) exempted the Commission from the scope of the section.

[81] The 1950 Act was subsequently amended to provide a right of appeal from the Commission to the CA on jurisdictional and other questions of law. Foreign Compensation Act 1969; the former provision exempting decisions of the Commission from the scope of the 1958 Act was omitted from the Tribunals and Inquiries Act 1971 s.14(3); see now Tribunals, Courts and Enforcement Act 2007 Sch.23.

[82] *Anisminic* [1969] 2 A.C. 147, Lords Reid, Pearce and Wlberforce; Lords Morris and Pearson dissenting); see H.W.R. Wade (1969) 85 L.Q.R. 198, Lord Diplock (1971) 24 C.L.P 1; D.M. Gordon (1971) 34 M.L.R. 1; B. Gould [1970] P.L. 358; de Smith [1969] C.L.J. 161.

[83] Already rejected in a number of earlier cases, e.g. *R. v Nat Bell Liquors Ltd* [1922] 2 A.C. 128 at 156.

[84] Most of the observations about to be noted were strictly *obiter*, since their Lordships held that the appellants, who had claimed to be entitled to a share in a compensation fund for British-owned property nationalised in Egypt had established their claim on the true construction of the relevant legislation, and that the Commission had erred in applying to the claimants a test of eligibility that they were not required to comply with and had dismissed the claim on this preliminary point. However, Lord Morris and all the members of the CA ([1968] 2 Q.B. 862) agreed that if the Commission had erred, its error went to the merits and not to jurisdiction. See also Gordon, (1971) 34 M.L.R. 1.

[85] [1969] 2 A.C. 147 at 171, 195, 207, 215.

[86] [1969] 2 A.C. 147 at 171, 195, 215; *cf.* the more guarded formulation by Lord Wilberforce at 210.

on legally irrelevant considerations.[87] Although they accepted the survival of the rule that a judicial tribunal has power to err within the limits of its jurisdiction, it was not easy to identify errors of law which, in the light of their analyses, would not be held to go to jurisdiction.

Subsequent cases

In *Pearlman v Keepers and Governors of Harrow School*[88] the relevant 4–030 statute provided that the determination of a county court judge on the question of the rateable value of a house was to be "final and conclusive". The Court of Appeal nevertheless, by a majority, overruled the county court's holding that a new central heating system was not a "structural alteration or addition to the house'. The county court judge's misconstruction of those words was held to be an error of law which went to his jurisdiction. Lord Denning, however, made it clear that the difference between jurisdictional and non-jurisdictional error could not be sustained logically, and considered that no inferior court or administrative tribunal has jurisdiction to make an error of law "on which the decision of the case depends".[89]

Pearlman was considered in two cases decided within a short time of 4–031 each other the following year. In the first, the Privy Council held[90] that a clause that provided that an award of the Industrial Court in Malaysia shall be "final and conclusive"[91] was effective to preclude judicial review if the inferior tribunal "made an error of law which does not affect its jurisdiction". Lord Denning's view in *Pearlman* of the coincidence of error of law and error of jurisdiction was therefore not accepted and Lord Lane's dissent in that case preferred. In the second case, *Re Racal Communications Ltd*,[92] the House of Lords considered a challenge to an order of the High

---

[87] [1969] 2 A.C. 147 at 171, 195, 198, 215. See also *R. v Southampton Justices. Ex p. Green* [1976] Q.B. 11 (decision that recognisance should be forfeit held to be in excess of jurisdiction because magistrates ignored a relevant factor and took into account an irrelevant consideration: but Browne L.J. (at 22) doubted whether an exercise of discretion on wrong legal principles could be brought within *Anisminic*). cf. *R. v Secretary of State for the Environment Ex p. Ostler* [1977] Q.B. 122, where a distinction appears to have been drawn between the jurisdictional control exercised over judicial tribunals and the application of the ultra vires doctrine to administrative decisions made in the exercise of a wide discretion, although Lord Denning has extra-judicially expressed regret at "some unguarded" statements made by him in this case: *The Discipline of Law* (1979), p.108.
[88] [1979] Q.B. 56.
[89] Lord Denning at 69–70. Eveleigh L.J., agreeing, held, at 77 that "before the tribunal could embark on its inquiry, it was necessary for it to decide the meaning of the question it was required to answer. This was a collateral matter. It had nothing to do with the merits of the case". But see the dissent of Geoffrey Lane L.J. who said, at 75–6: "The question is not whether he had made a wrong decision, but whether he inquired into and decided a matter which he had no right to consider".
[90] *South East Asia Fire Bricks Sdn Bhd v Non-Metallic Mineral Prouducts Manufacturing Employees Union* [1981] A.C. 363.
[91] Malaysian Industrial Relations Act 1967 s.29(3)(a) continuing that "no award shall be challenged, appealed against, reviewed, quashed or called in question in any court of law".
[92] [1981] A.C. 374.

Court under the Companies Act 1948 to authorise the inspection of the company's books. The majority held that the ouster clause[93] was effective to exclude the power of the Court of Appeal to review the High Court judge's decision. Lord Diplock made a distinction, however, between cases where a legal error is made by an administrative tribunal or authority and the case of an error made by a court of law. In the former case, there is a presumption that Parliament did not intend the administrative body to be the final arbiter of questions of law. There is, however, no such presumption in relation to courts of law. In respect of administrative bodies the distinction between errors of law that went to jurisdiction and errors of law that did not "was for practical purposes abolished". In respect of inferior courts, however, the "subtle distinctions . . . that did so much to confuse English administrative law before *Anisminic*" might survive and the superior court conducting the review "should not be astute to hold that Parliament did not intend the inferior court to have jurisdiction to decide for itself the meaning of ordinary words used in the statute involving, as many do, inter-related questions of law, fact and degree".[94]

4–032   It should be noted that *Racal Communications* by no means exempted all courts or judicial decisions from review for non-jurisdictional error of law. The case was limited to a consideration of the scope of a statutory provision attempting to oust the jurisdiction of the courts to review mistakes of law made by a judge of the High Court, which it was held could only be corrected by means of appeal to an appellate court.[95]

4–033   Two years later, Lord Diplock, in his celebrated *obiter* in *O'Reilly v Mackman*,[96] emphasised this point. He referred to *Anisminic* as:

"A landmark decision . . . which has liberated English public law from the fetters that the courts had therefore imposed on themselves so far as determinations of *inferior courts and statutory tribunals* were concerned, by drawing esoteric distinctions between errors of law committed by such tribunals that went to their jurisdiction, and errors of law committed by them within their jurisdiction. The breakthrough that *Anisminic* made was the recognition by the majority of this House that if a tribunal . . . mistook the law applicable to the facts as it had found them, it must have asked itself the wrong question, *i.e.* one into which it was not empowered to inquire and so had no jurisdiction to determine.

[93] Companies Act 1948 s.441(3): "The decision of a judge of the High Court. . . on an application under this section shall not be appealable".
[94] *Re Racal Communications* [1981] A.C. 374 at 383. In evaluating what was said in Re Racal, it is important to remember that decisions of High Court judges are not subject to judicial review and the CA's jurisdiction is statutory and so can be limited by statute.
[95] Lord Salmon said that the Anisminic principle was confined "to decisions made by commissioners, tribunals or inferior courts which can now be reviewed by the High Court of Justice, just as the decisions of inferior courts used to be reviewed by the old Court of King's Bench under the prerogative writs". *Re Racal Communications* [1981] A.C. 374 at 386.
[96] [1982] 2 A.C. 237 at 278, and agreed to by the remainder of their Lordships.

Its purported "determination", not being a 'determination' within the meaning of the empowering legislation, was accordingly a nullity."[97]

In *R. v Manchester Coroner Ex p. Tal*[98] the question was raised as to **4–034** whether a decision of a coroner's inquest was subject to judicial review for jurisdictional error alone. Despite the statement by Lord Diplock in *Re Racal Communications* to the effect that courts would be so treated, his clearer statement in *O'Reilly v Mackman* was preferred, Goff L.J. stating that "Lord Diplock did not intend to say [in *Racal Communications*] that the *Anisminic* principle did not extend to inferior courts as well as tribunals".[99] It was therefore held that all errors of law committed during the course of the coroner's inquest were reviewable by the court,[100] and that "as a matter of principle, the *Anisminic* principle applies to inferior courts as well as inferior tribunals, nevertheless we do not wish to be understood as expressing any opinion that the principle will apply with full force in the case of every inferior court".[101]

Visitors

In *R. v Hull University Visitor Ex p. Page*[102] the majority of the House of **4–035** Lords accepted "the general rule that any misdirection or error of law made by an administrative tribunal or inferior court in reaching its decision can be quashed for error of law.[103] In the case of an ouster clause, however, the majority in *Page* accepted the distinction made by Lord Diplock in *Racal Communications* that the presumption that a "final and conclusive" clause was not intended to oust the power to review the decision (including errors of law) applied to administrative bodies but not to courts. These comments were, however, strictly obiter, since the question to be decided in *Page* was not that of an ouster clause but whether a University Visitor had exclusive jurisdiction to determine disputes arising under the domestic law of the university. It was held that the visitor of an eleemosynary charity, applying the internal laws of the charity, and not applying the general law of the land" occupied an "exceptional" and "anomalous" position and was therefore not subject to the general rule that judicial review would lie to impeach decisions taken within a public authority's

---

[97] *O'Reilly v Mackman* [1982] 2 A.C. 237 at 278 (emphasis added). In *Racal Communications* [1981] A.C. 374 at 386.
[98] [1985] Q.B. 67.
[99] [1985] Q.B. 67 at 81.
[100] Contrary to an earlier decision of the Divisional Court, *R. v Surrey Coroner Ex p. Campbell* [1982] Q.B. 661. In *Renfrew DC v McGourlick* [1987] S.L.T. 538 a total ouster clause did not present challenge to a decision of the Sheriff.
[101] The case of *R. v Ipswich Justices Ex p. Edwards* (1979) 143 J.P 699 was cited, where the principle was not applied in the case of committing justices.
[102] [1993] A.C. 682.
[103] Lord Browne-Wilkinson at 702. See also *R. v Chancellor of Chichester Consistory Court Ex p. News Group Newspapers* [1992] C.O.D. 48.

jurisdiction in the narrow sense.[104] Judicial review would only lie to the visitor "in cases where he has acted outside his jurisdiction (in the narrow sense) or abused his powers or acted in breach of the rules of natural justice".[105] This body of case law, at least in its application to universities, is now of little more than historical interest. In almost all universities in the United Kingdom complaints that in the past would have fallen to be determined by a visitor are now handled by the Independent Adjudicator for Higher Education.[106]

Criminal proceedings

4–036   There are other situations where some important principle will permit review for jurisdictional error alone. One such principle is the avoidance of double jeopardy in relation to criminal proceedings. Normally—subject now to Pt 10 of the Criminal Justice Act 2004—when a person has been acquitted, the prosecution is not entitled to go behind that acquittal, and if they do the defendant will be entitled to rely on a plea of *autrefois acquit*. This does not, however, apply where the previous proceedings were a nullity. For the proceedings to be a nullity they will have to be shown to be "no trial at all".[107] For this to happen the decision has to be made without jurisdiction in the narrow sense. Thus in *R. v Hendon Justices. Ex p. DPP*[108] the decision of the magistrate was held to be a nullity when the defendant

---

[104] A similar view has been taken in respect of decisions of judges of the High Court acting as visitors to the Inns of Court. *R. v Visitors to the Inns of Court Ex p. Calder* [1994] Q.B. 1 and *R. v Honourable Society of the Middle Temple Ex p. Bullock* [1996] C.O.D. 376 (in an educational matter the judges qualified to sit as Visitors did not have an unfettered power to overrule decisions made by an expert review body under statutorily approved regulations and the Visitor was therefore right to conclude that he should only interfere if satisfied that the review board has acted irrationally or unlawfully). On the powers of Visitors, see *R. v Visitor of the University of London Ex p. Vijayatunga* [1990] 2 Q.B. 444; *R. v University of Nottingham Ex p. Ktorides* [1998] C.O.D. 26; *R. v University College London Ex p. Christofi*, September 12, 1997, CA unreported; *R. (on the application of Deman) v Lord Chancellor's Department* [2004] EWHC 930; [2004] E.L.R. 484.

[105] *R. v Hull University Visitor Page* [1993] A.C. 682 at 704, Lord Griffiths (692–694) agreeing, would permit judicial review of the visitor decision which amounted to an "abuse of his powers" (a term he had used in *Thomas v University of Bradford* [1987] A.C. 795 at 825.) Abuse of power was contrasted by Lord Griffiths with a "mistake of law", which, in the case of the university visitor, was not reviewable. "In such a case the judge is not abusing his powers: he is exercising them to the best of his ability albeit some other court thinks he was mistaken. I used the phrase "abuse of his powers" to connote some form of misbehaviour that was wholly incompatible with the judicial role that the judge was expected to perform. I did not intend it to include a mere error of law"(at 693). *cf.* the dissent of Lord Slynn, with whom Lord Mustill agreed, who could see no reason in principle for limiting the availability of certiorari to a patent excess of power and "excluding review on other grounds recognised by law", and no reason for excluding review on grounds generally available in the case of the decision of a visitor (at 710). He also said that "If the individual's rights are affected he should be entitled to the same protection by the courts as he would be in respect of the decisions of a wide range of other tribunals and bodies to whom decisions involving questions of law are assigned" (at 710).

[106] Higher Education Act 2004; *http://www.oiahe.org.uk/*.

[107] *Harrington v Roots* [1984] A.C. 743 at 753 (Lord Roskill).

[108] [1994] Q.B. 167.

was quite irrationally acquitted because of the late arrival in the court of the prosecuting lawyer through no fault of his own.

Habeas corpus

During the 1990s, there were suggestions that the scope of review in an application for habeas corpus (which continues to be a separate remedy outside the normal CPR Pt 54 claim for judicial review procedure) is confined to want of jurisdiction in the narrow sense.[109] In *R. v Secretary of State for the Home Department Ex p. Cheblak*[110] Lord Donaldson M.R. drew a distinction, obiter, between habeas corpus and judicial review. In his view "A writ of habeas corpus will issue where someone is detained without any authority or the purported authority is beyond the powers of the person authorising the detention and so is unlawful".[111] In *R. v Secretary of State for the Home Department Ex p. Muboyayi* it was held[112] that, where the applicant for habeas corpus was not alleging the absence of precedent fact[113] but was challenging the reasons for the underlying decision, then habeas corpus could not lie. This view was, however, contradicted by Law Commission[114] and other strong authority to the effect that both habeas corpus and judicial review are dealt with "under a common principle".[115] Moreover, it is difficult to see how limiting the scope of review in habeas corpus applications is compatible with the requirements of ECHR Art.5. Since the coming into force of the HRA, the Administrative Court is now itself (as a public authority) under a duty to ensure compliance with Convention rights and this is likely to entail review of both law and fact.[116]

4–037

Time-limited ouster clauses

In respect of time-limited ouster clauses, although the logic of *Anisminic* cast doubt upon their efficacy to preclude review for excess of jurisdiction (as defined in that case) the courts have been inclined to prevent all

4–038

---

[109] See 17–017.

[110] [1991] 1 W.L.R. 890.

[111] [1991] 1 W.L.R. 890 at 894. Judicial review on the other hand was available where the decision "is within the power of the person taking it but, due to procedural error, a misappreciation of the law, failure to take account of relevant matters, a taking account of irrelevant matters or the unreasonableness of the decision or action, it should never have been taken" (at 894).

[112] [1992] 1 Q.B. 244 at 254–255 (Lord Donaldson M.R., with whom Glidewell and Taylor L.JJ. agreed).

[113] See 4–047–048.

[114] Law Com. No.226 *Administrative Law: Judicial Review and Statutory Appeals* (1994) Part XI.

[115] *R. v Secretary of State for the Home Department Ex p. Khawaja* [1984] A.C. 74 at 99 (Lord Scarman).

[116] *R. (on the application of MH) v Secretary of State for Health* [2005] UKHL 60; [2006] 1 A.C. 441 at [31] (Baroness Hale, reviewing the relevant case law). In *Guisto v Governor of Brixton Prison* [2003] UKHL 19; [2004] 1 A.C. 101 at [62] Lord Hutton referred to the distinction between habeas corpus on judicial review without expressing a view on its correctness (on the facts, there was a jurisdictional error by the district judge in an extradition case).

challenges after the expiration of a reasonable limitation period,[117] even in cases where the claimant does not or is not able to discover the grounds for challenging the decision until after the statutory period has elapsed,[118] or because he does not learn of the decision until it is too late to challenge it.[119] In *Enterprise Inns Plc v Secretary of State for the Environment, Transport and the Regions*[120] the court rejected a challenge to the six-week statutory period for challenges under the Acquisition of Land Act 1981. Kay J. held that Art.6(1) of the ECHR was not an absolute right and that the interests of certainty and good public administration justified the time limit for challenges.

JURISDICTION AND VIRES TODAY

4–039 It has been suggested that *Anisminic* freed the courts to adopt a "functional"[121] or "pragmatic"[122] approach to the question of jurisdiction. This approach, it will be suggested below, may be helpful in those few instances where those "subtle distinctions"[123] between jurisdictional or non-jurisdictional error survive today.[124]

4–040 There is, however, a preliminary question that must be asked: namely, under what circumstance does the distinction between jurisdictional and non-jurisdictional error survive? That preliminary question, it is submitted, should not be approached on the basis of pragmatism. It should rather be based upon principle.[125] The apposite principles are deeply embedded in our constitutional law, but have rarely been explicitly applied to admin-

---

[117] See, e.g. *R v Secretary of State for the Environment Ex p. Ostler* [1977] Q.B. 122; *R v Secretary of State for the Environment Ex p. Kent* [1988] J.P.L. 706; *R v Cornwall CC Ex p. Huntington* [1994] All E.R. 694; *Martin v Bearsden and Milngavie DC* 1987 S.L.T. 300. cf. *Greater London Council v Secretary of State for the Environment* [1985] J.P.L. 868 (reasoning underpinning the decision which was otherwise in the applicant's favour could be challenged when it damaged some further interest of the applicant); *Lenlyn Ltd v Secretary of State for the Environment* (1985) 50 P & C.R. 129 (failure of the decision-maker to exercise his discretion by refusing to make a decision); *R v Carmarthen DC Ex p. Blewin Trust Ltd* [1990] C.O.D. 5; cf. *Pollway Nominees Ltd v Croydon LBC* [1987] A.C. 79 (21–day limitations clause ineffective). But see *Renfrew DC v McCorlick* [1987] S.L.T. 538. See *Century National Merchant Bank Ltd v Davies* [1998] A.C. 628 (10–day appeal from minister's action to CA carried "a necessary implication" of finality; *Barraclough v Brown* [1897] A.C. 615 applied).
[118] *Smith v East Elloe* [1986] A.C. 736 and *Ostler* [1977] 1 Q.B. 122
[119] *Kent* [1988] J.P.L. 706. Similarly, if the claimant wrongly begins judicial review proceedings and loses time, there is nothing to be done: see 17–00 and 18–00.
[120] (2001) 81 P. & C.R. 18.
[121] L. Jaffe, "Judicial Review : Constitutional and Jurisdictional Fact" (1957) 70 Harv. L. Rev 953; *Judicial Control of Administrative Action* (1965), pp.631–663; J. Beatson, "The scope of judicial review for error of law" (1984) 4 O.J.L.S. 22.
[122] G. Peiris, "Judicial review and judicial policy: the evolving mosaic" (1987) 103 L.Q.R. 66; C. Emery and B. Smythe, "Error of Law in Administrative Law" (1984) 100 L.Q.R. 612.
[123] *Re Racal Communications* [1981] A.C. 374 at 390–1 (Lord Diplock).
[124] See 4–044.
[125] Goff L.J. in *Tal* considered that "as a matter of principle" the *Anisminic* principle applied to both inferior courts and tribunals. See also Sir John Laws, "Illegality: The Problem of Jurisdiction" in M. Supperstone and J. Goudie (eds), *Judicial Review*, 2nd edn (2005), p.51.

istrative law. The principle of the rule of law is one such, which addresses two relevant issues.[126] The first of these is the legality of decisions of public authorities; the rule of law does not permit bodies performing public functions by determining their own powers to alter their scope. Any excess of their powers should be subject to restraint. The second issue addressed by the rule of law relates to legal certainty; where possible, individuals ought to be able to rely upon the validity of official decisions.[127] Another constitutional principle is the sovereignty of Parliament.[128] Under this principle Parliament may (in the interest perhaps of certainty and finality) permit a public authority to determine its own powers. The courts should attempt to reconcile these various principles when they appear superficially to compete. The courts thus presume, in the absence of clear words to the contrary, that Parliament does not intend to offend the rule of law.[129]

Identifying the relevant principles does not of course automatically solve the difficult problems in this area, particularly those relating to interpretation of parliamentary intent and to the scope and context of particular powers. Nevertheless, reference back to these principles will allow the issues to be resolved in a more coherent manner than can be achieved through a purely functional or pragmatic approach that leads to confusion and a wilderness of single instances.[130] Attempting to refer to and utilise these principles in the light of the recent developments, the following propositions can now be advanced. **4–041**

Foundation of judicial review no longer ultra vires

The doctrine of ultra vires, to the extent that it implies that all administrative power is derived from a specific statutory source, can no longer be considered the sole justification for review of the powers of bodies exercising public functions. Certain of these functions are today carried out under common law powers or under powers, like that of self regulatory bodies, with "no visible means of legal support".[131] These days an increasing amount of regulatory activity is carried out by the use of powers created by contract, or by means of the manipulation of rights to property. These powers "do not lend themselves to the language of ultra vires".[132] Insistence upon ultra vires as the basis for judicial review inhibits review when the powers of the public authority are not derived from a defined statutory source. Even prerogative powers, formerly immune from judicial **4–042**

[126] On rule of law generally, see 1–016, 5–036 and 11–059.
[127] See Ch.12 on legitimate expectations.
[128] See 1–015.
[129] See 1–015.
[130] H.W.R. Wade, "Crossroads in Administrative Law" (1968) 21 C.L.P 75, 85; D. Galligan, "Judicial Review and the Textbook Writers" (1982) 2 O.J.L.S. 257; J. Beatson, "The Scope of Judicial Review for Error of Law" (1984) 4 O.J.L.S. 22.
[131] *R. v Panel on Takeovers and Mergers Ex p. Datafin* [1987] 1 Q.B. 815 at 824 (Sir John Donaldson M.R.); See 3–041.
[132] D. Oliver, "Is the ultra vires rule the basis of judicial review?" [1987] P.L. 543 at 545.

review, have been brought within its ambit.[133] The review of such powers cannot easily be justified by the ultra vires principle. Yet, the courts have recognised that it is important to the rule of law that the abuse of those powers be controlled irrespective of their source and that the nature of the control should be the same as the control of more conventional administrative powers conferred by statute. Accordingly, the foundation for judicial review should no longer be regarded as ultra vires.[134] In general therefore, in a claim for judicial review it is no longer of any significance whether the source of alleged invalidity of administrative action is based upon an excess of jurisdiction or error of law within jurisdiction. Nor does it matter whether the error is or is not an error disclosed on the face of the record.[135]

Review in accordance with principles of lawful administration

4-043 All power can be appropriately reviewed today under what might be described as the principles of lawful or legitimate administration. These principles were enunciated as "grounds" of judicial review, by Lord Diplock in the GCHQ case[136] (a case itself involving review of prerogative power). The grounds he conveniently set out—"legality", "procedural propriety" and "rationality"—may not be watertight categories, and may include others such as proportionality and abuse of power. However, these requirements of lawful administration, together with the Convention rights and rights under European Community law, form a firm foundation upon which to review the public functions of modern administration and do not depend upon the limited notion of jurisdiction or vires in its narrow sense.[137]

---

[133] See 3–034.

[134] See 1–011 et seq. on the constitutional foundations of judicial review. It is noteworthy that Lord Steyn appeared to favour the ultra vires approach in Boddington v British Transport Police [1999] 2 A.C. 143 at 173. However, in his article "Democracy Through Law" (2002) 6 E.H.R.L.R. 723 at 725 he says that "By overwhelming weight of reasoned argument the ultra vires theory of judicial review has been shown to be a dispensable fiction" and "In a democracy, the rule of law itself legitimises judicial review". See also J. Jowell, "Beyond the Rule of Law: Towards Constitutional Review" [2000] P.L. 110; P. Joseph, "The Demise of Ultra Vires—Judicial Review in the New Zealand Courts" [2001] P.L. 354.

[135] R. v Hull University Visitor Ex p. Page [1993] A.C. 682 at 701 (Lord Browne-Wilkinson): "In my judgment the decision in Anisminic Ltd v Foreign Compensation Commission . . . rendered obsolete the distinction between errors of law on the face of the record and other errors of law by extending the doctrine of ultra vires. Thenceforward it was to be taken that Parliament had only conferred the decision making power on the basis that it was to be exercised on the correct legal basis: a misdirection in law in making the decision rendered the decision ultra vires".

[136] Council for Civil Service Unions v Minister for the Civil Service [1985] A.C. 374.

[137] This view has much support, e.g. Lloyd L.J. in Datafin [1987] 1 Q.B. 815 "The express powers conferred on inferior tribunals were of critical importance in the early days when the sole or main ground for intervention by the courts was that the inferior tribunal had exceeded its powers. But those days are long since past". See also Oliver [1987] P.L. 547; Sir John Laws and Ben Hooper, "Illegality: The Problem of Jurisdiction", in M. Supperstone, J. Goudie and

Residual categories of exceptional and anomalous situations

There are, however, very exceptional situations where the court's powers **4–044** of review may be limited to jurisdictional errors in the narrow sense. These include decisions involving the acquittal of a criminal offence (where the principle of double jeopardy is in play)[138] and cases governed by a special historical tradition in relation to a particular institution (such as visitors).[139] These are, however, strictly exceptional and anomalous situations. Habeas corpus is not one of them.[140] In general the rule of law requires that "there must be no Alsatia in England where the King's writ does not run".[141] In these few remaining situations where the distinction between jurisdictional and non-jurisdictional error survives, the question as to what is a non-jurisdictional error cannot be based upon any clear predetermined criteria that will serve as a test for all bodies. The test is must depend upon the context of the particular power and the function being performed.

After *Anisminic* virtually every error of law is a jurisdictional error, and **4–045** the only place left for non-jurisdictional error is where the components of the decision made by the public authority include matters of fact and policy as well as law, or where the error was evidential (concerning for example the burden of proof or admission of evidence).[142] Perhaps the most precise indication of jurisdictional error is that advanced by Lord Diplock in *Racal Communications*, when he suggested that a tribunal is entitled to make an error when the matter "involves, as many do, interrelated questions of law, fact and degree".[143] Thus it was for the county court judge in *Pearlman*[144] to decide whether the installation of central heating in a dwelling amounted to a "structural alteration extension or addition". This was a

> "typical question of mixed law, fact and degree which only a scholiast
> would think it appropriate to dissect into two separate questions, one for

P.Walker (eds) *Judicial Review*, 2nd edn (2005), p.91. See Ivan Hare's consideration of error of law based on the separtation of powers; I. Hare, "The Separation of Powers and Judicial Review for Error of Law", in C. Forsyth and I. Hare (eds) *The Golden Metwand and the Crooked Cord: Essays in Honour of Sir William Wade* (1998), p.112; Sir William Wade, "Habeas Corpus and Judicial Review" (1997) 113 L.Q.R. 55. *cf.* P Craig, "Ultra Vires and the Foundations of Judicial Review" [1998] C.L.J. 63. And see the helpful discussion by Lord Cooke of the concept of jurisdiction in *R. v Bedwellty Justices Ex p. Williams* [1997] A.C. 225 (although remedy for error of law at court's discretion, where a committal procedure was so influenced by inadmissible evidence as to amount to an irregularity, a remedy would normally follow (although express use of "jurisdiction" was avoided). See M. Taggart, "The Contribution of Lord Cooke to Scope of Review Doctrine in Administrative Law: A Comparative Common Law Perspective", in P. Rishworth (ed.), *The Struggle for Simplicity in the Law: Essays for Lord Cooke of Thorndon* (1997), p.189; D. Dyzenhaus, "The Politics of Deference: Judicial Review and Democracy" in M. Taggart (ed.), *The Province of Administrative Law* (1997), p.279.
[138] See 4–036.
[139] See 4–035; *R. v Visitors to the Inns of Court Ex p. Calder* [1994] Q.B. 1.
[140] See 4–037 and 17–010.
[141] *Czamikow v Roth Schmidt and Co* [1922] 2 K.B. 478 at 488 (Scrutton L.J.); and see 3–022.
[142] See 4–022.
[143] *Re Racal Communications* [1981] A.C. 374 at 390–1.
[144] [1979] Q.B. 56.

decision by the superior court, viz. the meaning of these words, a question which must entail considerations of degree, and the other for decision by a county court, viz. the application of words to the particular installation, a question which also entails considerations of degree."

4–046 It is, however, doubtful whether any test of jurisdictional error will prove satisfactory. The distinction between jurisdictional and non-jurisdictional error is ultimately based upon foundations of sand. Much of the superstructure has already crumbled. What remains is likely quickly to fall away as the courts rightly insist that all administrative action should be simply, lawful, whether or not jurisdictionally lawful.

Precedent fact

4–047 In Chapter 11 we consider what is a question of fact, as opposed to a question of law, a question of mixed law and fact, a question of judgment or a question of degree.[145] These all depend greatly upon the particular statutory scheme and its context. For example, whether a councillor was "disqualified" has been held to be a precedent fact.[146] However, whether a person is a "refugee" was considered to be just one of a number of facts which the decision-maker could take into account.[147] And whether a project had "likely significant effects on the environment", so as to necessitate an environmental impact assessment, was held to be a matter of "judgment" only.[148]

4–048 One of the exceptions to the general prohibition on courts reviewing the facts upon which decisions of public authorities are based is where it is alleged that there is an absence of required "jurisdictional fact" (sometimes called "precedent fact"). Where a set of facts must exist for the exercise of the jurisdiction of the decision-maker (in the strict sense of permitting the decision-maker to enter into its inquiry) the courts are entitled to inquire into the existence of those facts.[149] The language of jurisdiction is not necessary to justify such intervention.[150] The statute in such a case imposes a condition as precedent to the exercise of the public authority's power and it is the duty of the court to ensure that the condition has been met. The exercise of the decision-maker's power is dependent upon the existence of a fact or set of facts; the court is entitled to ensure that those facts exist.

---

[145] See 11–041.

[146] *Islington LBC v Camp* [2004] L.G.R. 58, 67; *R. (on the application of Brittannic Asset Management Ltd) v Pensions Ombudsman* [2002] EWCA Civ 1405; [2002] 4 All E.R. 860 ("administrators of the pension scheme").

[147] *R v. Secretary of State for the Home Department ex p. Bugdaycay* [1987] A.C. 514 at 522–3 (Lord Bridge). In *R v. Hillingdon BC Ex p. Pulhofer* [1986] A.C. 484 "accommodation" was not considered a precedent fact (at 513).

[148] *R. (on the application of Jones) v Mansfield DC* [2003] EWCA Civ 1408; [2004] Env. L.R. 21.

[149] See, e.g. cases such as *White and Collins v Minister of Health* [1934] 2 K.B. 838.

[150] For support of this view see Laws and Hooper, n.137 above.

This point was not fully appreciated in *Zamir v Secretary of State for Home Affairs*,[151] where the question for the House of Lords was whether an appellant was an "illegal entrant".[152] It was held that the matter was one for the immigration officer although the court could "see whether there was evidence on which the immigration officer, acting reasonably, could decide as he did".[153] This approach was, however, overruled in *R. v Secretary of State for the Home Department Ex p. Khawaja*[154] where it was held that it was the court's duty to inquire whether the immigration officer's belief that the entry had been illegal was correct.[155]

Presumption that all errors of law are reviewable

Where a statute seeks to oust the jurisdiction of the courts to review the 4–049 decisions of a public authority, there is a compelling inference that Parliament did not intend that public authority to be the final arbiter of its own powers. There is therefore a presumption that any error of law committed by that public authority is reviewable, whether or not the error is one of jurisdiction in the narrow sense.[156] As has been noted, the rule of law and parliamentary sovereignty are both engaged as principles in these situations. The courts are loath to relinquish their inherent power to review for jurisdictional error. While it may be possible for Parliament to bar judicial review for "any determination or purported determination", the fact that this has never been done indicates the persuasive force of the rule of law as a principle endorsing the power of the courts to require administrative legality.[157]

---

[151] [1980] A.C. 930.
[152] Immigration Act 1971 s.33(1).
[153] At 949 (Lord Wilberforce).
[154] [1984] A.C. 74. But see *Re S (Minors)* [1995] E.L.R. 98, where Butler-Sloss L.J said that the decision in *Khawaja* is only applicable to cases involving the liberty of the person.
[155] Where precedent fact is a condition to the exercise of power, the courts are not confined to intervening only when the fact-finding body has acted "unreasonably". They should themselves assess whether, the decision was sufficiently justified. Where precedent fact was held not to be present see *R. v Secretary of State for the Home Department Ex p. Naheed Ejaz* [1994] Q.B. 496, CA; *Silver Mountain Investments Ltd v Attorney General of Hong Kong* [1994] 1 W.L.R. 925, PC; *R. v Secretary of State for the Home Department Ex p. Onibiyo* [1996] Q.B. 768 (*Bugdaycay* and *Khawaja* considered; court had no power to review as an objective precedent fact whether fresh "claim for asylum" had been made). But see *Tan Te Lam v Superintendent of Tai A Chau Detention Centre* [1997] A.C. 97, PC (question whether applicant could be repatriated to Vietnam from Hong Kong is a matter of jurisdiction for the court) and see also *Re Rahman (Saidur)* [1998] Q.B. 136.
[156] *Jacmain v Attorney General of Canada* [1978] 2 S.C.R. 15 at 29 (Can.), [1978 2 S.C.R. 15 at 29 (Dickson J., dissenting): "It is hard to conceive that a legislature would create a tribunal with a limited jurisdiction and yet bestow on such tribunal an unlimited power to determine the extent of its jurisdiction". See I. Hare n.137 above, who raises the principle of separation of powers in this context.
[157] *cf.* the outser clause in the Asylum and Immigration (Treatment of Claimants etc) Bill, discussed at 1–019 and set out at Appendix C below.

4–050   Parliamentary draftsmen have, however, repeatedly devised a variety of formulae to restrict judicial review. Some simply provide that a document issued shall be "final and conclusive".[158] Others provide that a statutory duty imposed by the Act shall not "be read as imposing either directly or indirectly, any form of duty or liability enforceable by proceedings before any court".[159] The Local Government Finance Act 1987 even sought to confer validity on action taken by the Secretary of State that might otherwise be held unlawful.[160] Section 7(8) of the Interception of Communications Act 1985 provides that "The decisions of the Tribunal (including any decisions as to their jurisdiction) shall not be subject to appeal or liable to be questioned in any court". We saw in Chapter 1 that proposals to evade judicial review in immigration and asylum cases was threatened but eventually withdrawn.[161] Convention rights also provide safeguards against disproportionate exclusion of recourse to the courts. ECHR Art.6 requires access to a court where civil rights and obligations or criminal charges are in issue.[162] And in relation to Convention rights themselves, Art.13 requires national authorities to provide effective remedies.[163]

4–051   In situations where the jurisdiction of the courts is ousted or limited, the courts now take account not the concept of jurisdictional error, but a number of practical matters. These include the need in the circumstances

---

[158] See, e.g. *R. v Registrar of Companies Ex p. Central Bank of India* [1986] Q.B. 1114, CA held a certificate of the registration of a charge provided by the Registrar of Companies was "conclusive evidence" under the Companies Act 1948 s.98(2) and was therefore not reviewable by the court even if the Registrar had made an error of fact or law or mixed fact and law in the course of determining the question. The words of the statute were held thus to override Tribunals and Inquiries Act 1971 s.14(1) which in effect itself overrides provisions in a pre-1958 statute seeking to oust the court's jurisdiction. The court was informed in that case that there were about 300 such clauses ("conclusive evidence" clauses) in existence. *R. v Secretary of State for Foreign and Commonwealth Affairs Ex p. Trawnik* (1985) 82 L.S.G. 2739.

[159] London Regional Transport Act 1984 s.2(6). The Act provides various duties, e.g. to provide for efficient, economic and safe transportation (s.2(1)–(2)) and to provide for the needs of the disabled (s.2(7)). Mental Health Act 1983 s.139(1) provides that "No person shall be liable, whether on the ground of want of jurisdiction or on any other ground, to any civil or criminal proceedings to which he would have been liable apart from this section in respect of any act purporting to be done in pursuance of this Act or any regulations or rules made under this Act. . . unless the act was done in bad faith or without reasonable care". In *Re Waldron* [1986] Q.B. 824 it was held that "civil proceedings" did not refer to judicial review.

[160] s.13(1) of the Act provides that "the validity of anything done, whether before or after the passing of this Act, by the Secretary of State under or for the purposes of paragraph 1 or 3 of Schedule 1 to the Local Government (Scotland) Act 1966 in relation to the financial years 1983–84 or any subsequent financial year shall not be called into question in any legal proceedings on the ground that in ascertaining the actual expenditure or the estimated expenditure of a local authority the Secretary of State took into account the transfer of any sum between the authority's general fund and any special account or account maintained by them under any enactment". The same Act provides in s.4(1) that "Anything done by the Secretary of State before the passing of this Act for the purposes of the relevant provisions in relation to any of the initial years or intermediate years shall be deemed to have been done in compliance with those provisions".

[161] See 1–019 and Appendix C.

[162] See 6–048, 7–032 and 10–077.

[163] See 13–010.

for legal certainty and the need for finality on which the affected person may rely;[164] the degree of expertise of the decision-making body; the esoteric nature of the traditions or legal provisions decided by the decision-making body; and the extent to which interrelated questions of law, fact and degree are often best decided by the body which hears the evidence at first hand, rather than the courts on judicial review. In particular, account will be taken as to whether there has been previous appropriate opportunity for the claimant to challenge the relevant decision. The House of Lords considered whether the validity of a decision by the Secretary of State for Social Security on the question of a maintenance assessment under the Child Support Act 1995 could be challenged in a magistrates' court.[165] Section 33(4) of the Act provides that "the court . . . shall not question the maintenance assessment". It was held that since the Secretary of State's decision could be challenged by way of appeal to an appeal tribunal, the scheme "provided an effective means" to challenge the Secretary of State's decision: "Given the existence of this statutory right of review and appeal, it would be surprising and undesirable if the magistrate's court were to have parallel jurisdiction to adjudicate upon the same question".[166] In other cases where challenge to courts is precluded but challenge to an appropriate tribunal is provided, the courts have upheld the preclusive clause on the ground that the statutory scheme provides "proportionate and adequate protection to the rights of the litigant".[167]

As we have seen,[168] there are two situations where the presumption that 4–052 a statute does not seek to oust the court's jurisdiction has substantially reduced force: first, where the statute seeks to preclude judicial review of the decision of a court; and secondly, where a statute permits a reasonable time to challenge a decision of a public authority but then purports, in the interest of finality, thereafter to preclude challenge to its validity.

Limitation of review of decisions of courts

As to the first of these exceptions, the question of what is a court is not 4–053 always clear cut, and the distinction between courts and other bodies invites a resuscitation of the discredited dichotomy between "judicial" and "administrative" decisions.[169] Nevertheless, where a public authority has

[164] The need for certainty in commercial dealings was very much a factor influencing the court in *Central Bank of India* [1986] Q.B. 1114. See also the importance attached to certainty in respect of the assumption of management of a bank in *Century National Merchant Bank Ltd* [1998] A.C. 628.
[165] *Farley v Secretary of State for Work and Pensions (No.2)* [2006] UKHL 31; [2006] 1 W.L.R. 1817.
[166] Lord Nicholls at [25].
[167] *Sinclair Gardens Investments Ltd v Lands Tribunal* [2005] EWCA Civ 1305; [2006] 3 All E.R. 650; see R. Kellar, "Judicial review of Refusals to Grant Permission to Appeal" [2005] J.R. 244; and the requirement for claimants for judicial review to use alternative remedies, see 16–014.
[168] See 4–030 *et seq.*
[169] See Appendix B and the discussion in respect of natural justice and the fair hearing in Ch.7 and Ch.8.

undoubted legal expertise, and where a right of appeal against its decisions has not been provided, it is perhaps not unacceptable for that public authority to be accorded a broader degree of deference and autonomy than that accorded to a public authority lacking those attributes.[170]

4–054   The limitation of review in s.54(4) of the Access to Justice Act 1999 provides that "No appeal may be made against a decision of a court under this section to give or refuse permission" for an appeal from a District Court to the County Court". Did this statutory bar oust the jurisdiction of the Administrative Court on a challenge in judicial review to a refusal of such permission? The Court of Appeal held that judicial review should not be taken away except by clear and explicit words, which s.54(4) did not provide, and therefore held that Administrative Court's jurisdiction should not be taken away in the circumstances of this case.[171] It was made clear however that a challenge by way of judicial review could not normally be made on the merits of a refusal of permission for an appeal to the county court. This was because the Act had established a system of fair and proportionate protection against the risk of error. However there may be exceptional circumstances of "jurisdictional error" in the narrow, pre-*Anisminic* sense or procedural irregularity such as to constitute a denial of the applicant's right to a fair hearing".[172] The Court of Appeal revisited this question in *Gregory v Turner*[173] where Brooke L.J. said that judicial review would only be available where the judge below had acted in complete disregard of his duties or in fundamental departure from the rules of natural justice.[174]

Time-limited ouster clauses

4–055   When the opportunity for judicial challenge is closed off after a period of time, the requirement of the rule of law is met to the extent that an affected person has some reasonable time to challenge the decision.[175] The time limit is imposed in order to accommodate the needs of legal certainty.[176] Nevertheless, and despite authority to the contrary,[177] not all

---

[170] See 4–051.
[171] *R. (on the application of Sivasubramaniam) v Wandsworth County Court* [2002] EWCA Civ 1738; [2003] 1 W.L.R. 475.
[172] *Sivasubramaniam* [2002] EWCA Civ 1738; [2003] 1 W.L.R. 475 at [54].
[173] [2003] EWCA Civ 183; [2003] 1 W.L.R. 1149.
[174] Citing *Re McC* [1985] A.C. 528, where the HL held that an action for false imprisonment could only lie against justices if they acted without jurisdiction or in excess of jurisdiction, which Lord Bridge described as "some gross and obvious irregularity of procedure". See R. Kellar [2005] J.R. 244 and *R. (on the application of G) v Immigration Appeal Tribunal* [2004] EWCA Civ 1731; [2005] 1 W.L.R. 1445 where the refusal of the High Court to review a decision of the IAT to refuse permission to appeal was upheld by the CA. Again here, it was held that statutory review provided adequate and proportionate protection of asylum seekers' rights.
[175] See 17–025 on procedures for statutory review under "six week clauses" and similar.
[176] As in *Enterprise Inns Plc v. Secretary of State for the Environment, Transport and the Regions*: six week statutory period for challenge held by Kay J. not to offend ECHR Art.6(1) and in the interest of certainty and good public administration.
[177] See 4–023.

decisions of lower courts, nor all decisions taken by other bodies after the expiry of a time-limited ouster clause, should be exempt from judicial review. It would seem right in principle that decisions that lack jurisdiction in "the narrow and original sense of not being entitled to enter on the inquiry in question"[178] (for example, if a public authority is wrongly constituted) should be amenable to judicial review. It is also suggested, despite the authorities to the contrary,[179] that if it is not possible for a claimant to ascertain the existence of a ground for challenging a decision during the period in which a challenge is permitted, the claimant should be permitted, at least for excess of jurisdiction, to make a claim for judicial review. The court could then decide whether, in all circumstances, permission should be granted.

FROM "VOID AND VOIDABLE" TO "LAWFUL AND UNLAWFUL"

The position in the past

Behind the simple dichotomy of void and voidable acts (invalid and valid **4–056** until declared to be invalid) lurk terminological and conceptual problems of excruciating complexity.[180] The problems arose from the premise that if an act, order or decision is ultra vires in the sense of outside jurisdiction, it was said to be invalid, or null and void. If it is intra vires it was, of course, valid. If it is flawed by an error perpetrated within the area of authority or jurisdiction, it was usually said to be voidable;[181] that is, valid till set aside on appeal or in the past quashed by certiorari for error of law on the face of the record.[182]

Is it correct to say that "there are no degrees of nullity"?[183] If so, does it **4–057** follow that "out of nothing comes nothing"? The notion that void acts are destitute of legal effect is and always has been subject to major qualifications. Thus, although the courts refused to entertain appeals against void

---

[178] Lord Reid in *Anisminic* [1969] 2 A.C. 147.
[179] See, e.g. *Ostler* [1977] 1 Q.B. 122.
[180] A. Rubinstein, *Jurisdiction and Illegality* (1963); D. Gordon, "Observance of Law as a Condition of Jurisdiction" (1931) 47 L.Q.R. 386 and (1931) 47 L.Q.R 557; H.W.R. Wade, "Unlawful Administrative Action: Void or Voidable" (1967) 83 L.Q.R. 499; Wade, "Unlawful Administrative Action" (1968) 84 L.Q.R. 95; M. Akehurst, "Void or Voidable? Natural Justice and Unnatural Meanings" (1968) 31 M.L.R. 2 and (1968) 31 M.L.R.138.
[181] See 5–053.
[182] Unless an error on the face of the record goes to jurisdiction, the decision in question was undoubtledly voidable, not void (e.g. *Punton v Ministry of Pensions and National Insurance (No.2)* [1964] 1 W.L.R. 226; *DPP v Head* [1959] A.C. 83 at 109, 112); but in *R. v Paddington Valuation Officer Ex p. Peachey Property Corp Ltd* [1966] 1 Q.B. 380 at 402, Lord Denning M.R. appeared to assume that patent error would have rendered the impugned decision void.
[183] *Anisminic Ltd v Foreign Compensation Commission* [196912 A.C. 147 at 170 (Lord Reid).

decisions because they were nugatory,[184] and have even refused to award certiorari to quash such acts and decisions,[185] it was inappropriate for a court to decline to hear an appeal or an application to set aside an ostensibly valid act which was in reality void.[186]

4–058   Again, although an ultra *vires* decision was ineffective against the party aggrieved, he might need, for his own protection, a formal pronouncement of a court setting the decision aside or declaring it to be void. Meanwhile, he could be enjoined from disregarding the decision until its validity had been finally determined.[187] If he took no judicial proceedings at all within a prescribed statutory timelimit, the void decision could become as impregnable as if it had been valid in the first place.[188] And until he obtained such a judicial pronouncement in an appropriate form of proceedings, third parties (unable to impugn the invalid decision) would be obliged to treat it as if it were valid.[189]

4–059   In addition, the courts have in practice had sufficient room for manoeuvre to be able to avoid being driven to reach unsatisfactory conclusions by the pressure exerted by conceptual reasoning. They often employed the elasticity provided by the discretionary nature of most of the judicial remedies, particularly where the claimant had not been prejudiced.[190]

The situation today

4–060   The erosion of the distinction between jurisdictional errors and non jurisdictional errors has, as we have seen, correspondingly eroded the distinction between void and voidable decisions. The courts have become increasingly impatient with the distinction,[191] to the extent that the situation today can be summarised as follows.

---

[184] *R. v Jones (Gwyn)* [1969] 2 Q.B. 33; and *Chapman v Earl* [1968] 1 W.L.R. 1315; *Metropolitan Properties Co (FGC) Ltd v Lannon* [1969] 1 Q.B. 577 (application for certiorari regarded as the appropriate means of challenge rather than an appeal); *Campbell v Rochdale General Commissioners* [1975] 2 All E.R. 385 (breach of rules of natural justice: court could only affirm or reverse on appeal, thus rendering the matter *res judicata* on the merits: certiorari regarded as the appropriate remedy); *cf.* B. Schwartz and H.W.R. Wade, *Legal Control of Government* (1972), pp.159–60. See also *Hanson v Church Commissioners for England* [1978] Q.B. 823 (relief both by way of appeal and certiorari was sought for breach of the rules of natural justice. Certiorari was granted, and the matter remitted to a differently constituted tribunal: semble the appeal was dismissed. An appeal was allowed for breach of the rules of natural justice by an industrial tribunal in *Wilcox v HGS* [1976] I.C.R. 306).

[185] See, e.g. *R. v Barnstaple Justices. Ex p. Carder* [1938]1 K.B. 385.

[186] For example, where X has been invalidly removed from an office and Y has been appointed in his place; or where P's licence has been invalidly revoked and allocated to Q, it may be futile for X and P to carry on as if nothing has happened.

[187] *Hoffmann-La Roche (F) & Co AG v Secretary of State for Trade and Industry* [1975] A.C. 295 (defendants failed to rebut presumption of validity of ministerial order).

[188] *Re Gale* [1966] Ch. 236 at 242, 247. See also *Ridge v Baldwin* [1964] A.C. 40 at 125 (Lord Morris).

[189] *Re F (Infants)* [1977] Fam. 165.

[190] See 18–048.

[191] See, e.g. *Hoffmann-La Roche* [1975] A.C. 295 at 366 (Lord Diplock considered the terms "concepts developed in the private law of contract which are ill adapted to the field of public

Presumption of validity

All official decisions are presumed to be valid until set aside or otherwise **4–061** held to be invalid by a court of competent jurisdiction.[192] Under the terminology of void and voidable decisions, this proposition raises a paradox, namely, that a decision, although technically void, is in practice voidable. Such a paradox is, however, circumvented if we abandon those terms which "lead to confusion"[193] and instead use the terms lawful and unlawful decisions.[194] Decisions are thus presumed lawful unless and until a court of competent jurisdiction declares them unlawful. There is good reason for this: the public must be entitled to rely upon the validity of official decisions and individuals should not take the law into their own hands.[195] These reasons are built into the procedures of judicial review, which requires for example an application to quash a decision to be

---

law". In *London and Clydeside Estates Ltd v Aberdeen DC* [1980] 1 W.L.R. 182 at 189–90 (Lord Hailsham considered the existence of "stark categories such as 'mandatory' and 'directory', 'void' and 'voidable', a 'nullity' and 'purely regulatory' . . . useful but . . . misleading in so far as it may be supposed to present a court with the necessity of fitting a particular case into one or other of mutually exclusive and starkly contrasted compartments, . . . which in some cases (e.g. 'void' and 'voidable') are borrowed from the language of contract or status and are not easily fitted to the requirements of administrative law"). Lord Denning, as we have seen, initially supported the void-voidable distinction and terminology but in *Lovelock v Minister of Transport* (1980) 40 P. & C.R. 336 at 345 said "I have got tired of all the discussion about 'void' and 'voidable'. It seems to be a matter of words-of semantics-and that is all." See also Lord Denning, *The Discipline of Law* (1979) p.77 where he said: "I confess that at one time I used to say that such a decision was not void but only voidable. But I have seen the error of my ways"; see also his retraction of remarks in *Ostler* [1977] 1 Q.B. 122 p.108.

[192] Lord Radcliffe in *Smith v East Elloe RDC* [1986] A.C. 736; Lord Denning in *Lovelock* (1980) 40 P. & C.R. 336 went on to say that "The plain fact is that, even if such a decision as this is 'void' or a 'nullity', it remains in being unless and until some steps are taken before the courts to have it declared void". Lord Diplock in *Hoffmann-La Roche* [1975] A.C. 295 said that "the presumption that subordinate legislation is intra vires prevails in the absence of rebuttal, and . . . it cannot be rebutted except by a party to legal proceedings in a court of competent jurisdiction who has locus standi to challenge the validity of the subordinate legislation in question" (at 366). See also the decision of the PC in *Calvin v Carr* [1980] A.C. 574 where Lord Wilberforce stated (at 589–590) that a decision made contrary to natural justice is void, "but that, until it is so declared by a competent body or court, it may have some effect, or existence, in law" He preferred the term "invalid or vitiated" to void, and felt that it would be "wholly unreal" to hold that the decision made was totally void in the sense of being legally non-existent. The Master of the Rolls in *R. v Panel on Takeovers and Mergers Ex p. Datafin Plc* [1987] Q.B. 815 at 840 referred to "a very special feature of public law decisions" to be the fact that "however wrong they may be, however lacking in jurisdiction they may be, they subsist and remain fully effective unless and until they are set aside by a court of competent jurisdiction".

[193] Lord Diplock in *Hoffmann-La Roche* [1975] A.C. 295 at 366.

[194] *Palacegate Properties Ltd v Camden LBC* (2000) 4 P.L.R. 59 at 80 (Laws L.J.).

[195] For a consideration of the presumption of regularity (*ommia praesumantur rite et solemniter esse acta donec probetur in contrarium*), see *R. v Inland Revenue Commissioners Ex p. TC Coombs & Co* [1991] 2 A.C. 283. Although an individual in the case in which "a fundamental obligation may have been so outrageously and flagrantly ignored or defied", may "safely ignore what has been done and treat it as having no legal consequences upon himself. In such a case it may be that the subject is entitled to use the defect in procedure simply as a shield or defence without having taken any positive action of his own": *London and Clydeside Estates Ltd v Aberdeen DC* [1980] 1 W.L.R. 182 at 190 (Lord Hailsham).

brought within a limited time.[196] A decision not challenged within that time, whether or not it would have been declared unlawful if challenged, and whether or not unlawful for jurisdictional error, retains legal effect.[197] So does a decision found to be unlawful but where a remedy is, in the court's discretion, withheld.[198] The language of void and voidable cannot, however, accommodate such an effect, as it would insist that a void decision, being void ab initio, is devoid of legal consequences and that a voidable decision is capable of being set aside.

Nature of unlawfulness irrelevant

4–062 Outside of the rare exceptions we have identified,[199] decisions may be unlawful whether or not they exceed a public authority's jurisdiction in the narrow sense, or are flawed by an error of law within the public authority's jurisdiction or an error of law on the face of the record.

Residual categories

4–063 There are a limited number of situations where the use of the word "nullity", coupled with the distinction between jurisdictional and non-jurisdictional error, survives. Here, some important principle justifies the retention of these concepts. We have seen that one such principle is the need to avoid double jeopardy in relation to criminal proceedings.[200] Thus a previous acquittal may only be challenged where it is a nullity in the sense of being made without jurisdiction in the narrow sense.[201]

COLLATERAL CHALLENGE

4–064 To what extent may a person seeking to challenge the validity of an official decision do so in proceedings not specially "designated by law for the purpose of having . . . a[n] official decision set aside, reversed or

---

[196] See 17–025.

[197] *Mclauglin v His Excellency the Governor of the Cayman Islands* [2007] UKPC 50 at [14] (Lord Bingham: "it is a settled principle of law that if a public authority purports to dismiss the holder of a public office in excess of its powers,. . . the dismissal is . . null, void and without legal effect, at any rate once a court of competent jurisdiction so declares or orders").

[198] *Mclaughin* [2007] UKPL 50 at [16] ("since public law remedies are, for the most part, discretionary, it necessarily follows that a claimant may be disabled from obtaining the full relief he seeks whether on grounds of lack of standing, delay or his own conduct, or grounds pertaining to the facts of a particular case"). For examples of two such cases: *Chief Constable of the North Wales Police v Evans* [1982] 1 W.L.R. 1155; *Jhagroo v Teaching Service Commission* (2002) 61 W.I.R. 510.

[199] See 4–044 *et seq.*

[200] See 4–036.

[201] *Harrington v Roots* [1984] A.C. 743 at 753; *R. v Hendon Justices. Ex p. DPP* [1994] Q.B. 167. In planning law the distinction between "invalidity" and "nullity" survives. See, e.g. *McKay v Secretary of State for the Environment* [1994] J.P.L. 806. And see the new distinction between "procedural" and "substantive" invalidity discussed at 4–070.

modified"?[202] In Chapter 3 we consider the principle of "procedural exclusivity"—now much diminished in its importance following the introduction of the Civil Procedure Rules—which concerns the question of whether a claimant may raise public law issues in proceedings other than the CPR Pt 54 claim for judicial review procedure.[203] Here we consider the different question of whether a defendant in (for example) a civil claim for damages or criminal proceedings may assert by way of a "collateral" challenge that a public authority's decision, or subordinate legislation, is unlawful.

In principle it would seem wrong for a person to be prosecuted for **4–065** breach of a decision or a byelaw or a regulation that was invalid, whatever the source of its invalidity. Two difficulties, however, arise: first, the ordinary civil proceedings or criminal trial may be inappropriate to handle public law questions (for example, because they do not, as in judicial review, possess discretion to refuse relief; or have short time limits, or because of lack of expertise on the part of the judge called upon to determine the issue).[204] Secondly, in the past, because of the distinction between void and voidable, the only decisions open to collateral attack were void decisions. Errors of law within a public authority's jurisdiction—even including those on the face of the record—were regarded as valid and effective for all purposes unless successfully impugned through direct attack. Thus, here again the issue of jurisdictional and non-jurisdictional error of law raises its head.

Although over the years the courts have not been entirely consistent on **4–066** the point, in general, collateral challenges have been allowed.[205] And even after *O'Reilly v Muckman*[206] which, as we have seen,[207] held that challenges to the validity of action by public authorities must be brought by way of judicial review, and that it is an abuse of process not to do so, it was recognised both in *O'Reilly v Mackman* and in *Cocks v Thanet BC*[208] that a public law challenge could be permitted if it arose collaterally in the course of an ordinary civil action. Today a far more flexible approach is taken in any situation as the courts now have powers under the Civil Procedure Rules to decide how claims ought to be decided.[209]

---

[202] A. Rubinstein, *Jurisdiction and Illegality* (1963), pp.37–8.
[203] See 3–097.
[204] See H. Woolf, *Protection of the Public: a New Challenge* (1990), p.80.
[205] See, e.g. *DPP v Head* [1959] A.C. 83; *Customs and Excise Commissioners v Cure & Deeley Ltd* [1962] 1 Q.B. 340; *R. v Commissioners of Customs and Excise Ex p. Hedges and Butler Ltd* [1986] 2 All E.R. 164; *Musson v Emile* [1964] 1 W.L.R. 337; *Heptulla Bros Ltd v Thakore* [1956] 1 W.L.R. 289; *R. v Pugh (Judge) Ex p. Graham* [1951] 2 K.B. 623; *R. v Sheffield Area Rent Tribunal Ex p. Purshouse* (1957) 121 J.P 553. *West Glamorgan CC v Rafferty* [1987] 1 W.L.R. 457.
[206] [1983] 2 A.C. 237.
[207] See 3–100.
[208] [1983] 2 A.C. 286.
[209] See 3–103.

4-067   In *Chief Adjudication Officer v Foster*,[210] the House of Lords considered whether social security commissioners (an appellate body) had jurisdiction to determine any challenge to the validity of regulations made by the Secretary of State when they were given statutory jurisdiction under an Act[211] to hear an appeal on the ground that the decision of a social security appeal tribunal was erroneous on a "point of law". Leaving open the question of whether procedural and substantive validity should receive different treatment, it was held that the commissioners did have such jurisdiction whenever it is necessary to do so in determining whether a decision under appeal was erroneous in point of law".[212] Lord Bridge, for a unanimous House, held that such a conclusion avoids "a cumbrous duplicity of proceedings" and welcomed the prior view of one of the commissioners "who have great expertise in this esoteric area of the law" which would benefit the superior court upon appeal or review. He also explained why the commissioners and indeed the tribunal were not an inappropriate body to determine such an issue where the Secretary of State's views could be put before the tribunal by the adjudicating officer. Under the provisions of the Tribunals, Courts and Enforcement Act 2007 it is possible for cases to be transferred from the Upper Tribunal to the Administrative Court, and vice versa, which will ensure that important questions relating to the lawfulness of delegated legislation can be decided by a tribunal or court with the relevant expertise.

4-068   Whatever the limits today upon collateral challenge (and we shall see these shortly), the distinction between void and voidable decisions is no longer one of them. In *London & Clydeside Estates v Aberdeen DC*,[213] Lord Hailsham, attacking that "misleading" language, made it clear that except in "flagrant" and "outrageous" cases, a statutory order such as a byelaw remains effective until it is quashed.[214] The question today therefore is whether the court or tribunal in question is competent to be seised of a collateral challenge to the validity of an official decision, rather than whether the decision challenged is or is not a jurisdictional error.

---

[210] [1993] A.C. 754.

[211] Social Security Act 1975 s.101.

[212] Lord Bridge at 712; Lord Bridge also referred to the distinction between substantive and procedural invalidity in *Bugg* (discussed at 4–070), but considered it unnecessary to decide that point since the issue in Foster was "one of pure statutory construction unaffected by evidence".

[213] [1980] 1 W.L.R. 182.

[214] [1980] 1 W.L.R. 182 at 189–90. See also Lord Radcliffe in Smith v East Elloe RDC [1956] A.C. 736 at 769–70 who said that "An order, even if not made in good faith, is still an act capable of legal consequences. It bears no brand of invalidity upon its forehead. Unless the necessary proceedings are taken at law to establish the cause of invalidity and to get it quashed or otherwise upset, it will remain as effective for its ostensible purpose as the most impeccable of orders". See also *Hoffmann-La Roche and Co AG v Secretary of State for Trade and Industry* [1975] A.C. 295 at 366 (Lord Diplock: "the presumption that subordinate legislation is intra vires prevails in the absence of rebuttal, and . . . cannot be rebutted except by a party to legal proceedings in a court of competent jurisdiction who has locus standi to challenge [its] validity)".

The matter received attention in the context of criminal enforcement of **4–069** official decisions, regulations and byelaws. In *Quietlynn Ltd v Plymouth City Council*[215] it was held that a licence for a sex establishment, challenged collaterally before justices for procedural irregularity, was presumed to be valid unless it was invalid on its face, and that in the case of such a challenge the correct proceedings was for the matter to be adjourned to enable an application for judicial review to be made and determined. However, in R. *v Reading Crown Court Ex p. Hutchinson*,[216] the Court of Appeal held that "justices have always had jurisdiction to inquire into the validity of a byelaw. They are not only entitled, but bound to do so when the defendant relies on the invalidity of the byelaw by way of defence".[217]

In *Bugg v DPP*[218] the defendants, charged with entering a military area **4–070** contrary to hyelaws,[219] pleaded not guilty on the ground, inter alia, that the byelaws were not valid because of non-compliance with certain procedural requirements. The Divisional Court held that all subordinate legislation, whether "void" or "voidable", was in principle open to collateral challenge on the grounds of "substantive invalidity" (where the byelaws were on their face outside the scope of their powers or patently unreasonable). A challenge, however, on the ground of "procedural invalidity" was not normally an appropriate matter to be investigated in a magistrates' court since such an investigation required evidence in proceedings to which the byelaw-making authority was not to be a party. In such a case, the byelaws were, until set aside, to be treated as valid.[220] However, strong doubts were expressed about *Bugg* in R. *v Wicks*[221] and in *Boddington v British Transport Police*[222] the House of Lords held that a defendant in criminal proceedings was entitled to challenge the invalidity of a byelaw whether on procedural or substantive grounds. Lord Steyn found the consequences of *Bugg* "too austere and indeed too authoritarian to be compatible with the traditions of the common law".[223] He thought that a person had a right to defend himself against an unlawful provision.

[215] [1988] Q.B. 114.
[216] [1988] Q.B. 384.
[217] Lloyd L.J. at 391. This case went to the HL ([1990]) 12 A.C. 783, but the issue of invalidity was not there considered, but see Lord Bridge at 804. See also R. *v Oxford Crown Court Ex p. Smith* (1989) 154 J.P 422 (following the approach of Lloyd L.J. in *Ex p. Hutchinson*, [1988] Q. B. 384; R. *v Parking Adjudicator for London Ex p. Bexley LBC* [1998] C.O.D. 116 (parking adjudicator exercising appellate functions under Road Traffic Act 1984 s. 32 was entitled and bound to consider validity of byelaw; he had correctly held that a provision was *Wednesbury* unreasonable).
[218] [1993] Q.B. 473.
[219] Byelaw 2(b) of the Byelaws 1985 under s.17(2) of the Military Lands Act 1892 (the "Greenham Common byelaws").
[220] This distinction was adopted by Lord Taylor C.J. in respect of regulations in R. *v Blackledge* [1996] 1 Cr. App. R. 326.
[221] [1998] A.C. 92; A.W. Bradley, "Collateral Challenge to Enforcement Decisions—a Duty to Apply for Judicial Review?" [1997] P.L. 365.
[222] [1999] 2 A.C. 143.
[223] At 64.

4–071   In *Boddington*,[224] Lord Irvine said that the rule of law raised a "strong presumption" that individuals should have a "fair opportunity" to vindicate their rights in court proceedings. However, in respect of collateral challenge both the rule of law (in respect of its value of certainty and stability of decisions which on their face seem valid and which may have been acted upon by others) as well as other values, such as that of public confidence, may invite principled exceptions to the possibility of collateral review.

4–072   In *Bunney v Burns Anderson Plc*,[225] Lewison J., in a case about a determination of the Financial Services Ombudsman, provided a succinct summary of the current position.

"i) The original procedural reasons which led to the formulation of the principle in *O'Reilly v Mackman* have lost much of their force since the introduction of the CPR;

ii) They never applied to defendants who wished to challenge public law decisions upon which a private cause of action against them was asserted in proceedings which they wished to defend;

iii) There is no longer any difference in principle between a challenge based on substantive validity and one based on procedural invalidity;

iv) Where a defendant to a claim wishes to challenge a public law decision as part of his defence, the court does not have any discretion to refuse to allow him to do so, unless either the raising of the defence is an abuse of process or it has no reasonable prospect of success;

v) It will have no reasonable prospect of success if, as a matter of construction of the statute under which the impugned act was done, the legislation forbids any challenge (or the particular type of challenge that the defendant wishes to make) to be made otherwise than by judicial review;

vi) In construing statutory schemes which enable decisions to be made under them there is a strong presumption, based on the importance of the rule of law, against concluding that the only permissible means of challenge is by judicial review."

Summary

4–073   The position in relation to collateral attack appears today to be as follows.

- Except possibly for a decision which is clearly invalid on its face, all official decisions are presumed to be valid until impugned by a court of competent jurisdiction.

- An individual should in principle be able to rely on any invalidity as a defence in collateral proceedings before an appellate body,

---

[224] See n.222.
[225] [2007] EWHC 1240 at [47], Ch D.

whether or not the source of invalidity is alleged to arise out of a jurisdictional or non-jurisdictional error (or whether the decision or instrument is "void" or "voidable").

- To avoid "cumbrous duplicity of proceedings", that challenge should where possible take place in the forum in which it is made, without having to adjourn the proceedings in order to enable a claim to be made for judicial review.[226]

There may be some exceptions to the above. First, there will be some cases **4–074** where the proceedings are simply inappropriate to decide the matter in question, for example: where evidence is needed to substantiate the claim;[227] where the decision-maker is not a party to the proceedings;[228] or where the claimant has not suffered any direct prejudice as a result of the alleged invalidity.[229]

Secondly, Parliament may have established a scheme which precludes **4–075** collateral attack, explicitly or implicitly. The latter arose in the case of *Wicks*[230] where the House of Lords held that the defendant, who was prosecuted for breach of planning restrictions, could not challenge a planning enforcement notice as the statute provided an exclusive and comprehensive scheme of appeal.

Thirdly, a well-established exception to the possibility of collateral **4–076** challenge relates to judges and other official decision-makers acting under "colour of authority". Where there is a flaw in the appointment or authority of some officer or judge, such that he has no legal power at all, his acts may nevertheless be unchallengeable. The term employed to describe such a judge or officer is "judge *de facto*".[231] The doctrine of the

---

[226] See now the provisions for transfer contained in the Tribunal, Courts and Enforcement Act 2007.

[227] *Hunter v Chief Constable of the West Midlands Police* [1982] A.C. 529.

[228] Although in *Dwr Cymru Cyfyngedig (Welsh Water) v Corus UK Ltd* [2006] EWHC 1183, Ch, Hart J. seems to imply that collateral challenge of this type is permissible.

[229] See the suggestion of Keene L.J. that a powerful factor influencing the court's decision whether to permit a collateral attack will be whether the attack is aimed at an instrument directed specifically at him (such as an enforcement notice under planning legislation) or a generally applicable instrument (such as a byelaw or statutory instrument): "Collateral Challenge: Some Observations" [1999] J.R. 170. In the former case he will generally have had the opportunity to challenge the validity of the instrument at the time of its service (by way of appeal or judicial review—as in *Quietlynn* [1988] Q.B. 114 and *R. v Wicks* [1988] A.C. 92. However, in a respect of an instrument of general application, he may have been unaware of its existence, and the time limit in which to challenge it under judicial review may well have passed.

[230] *R. v Wicks* [1988] A.C. 92; *cf. Dilieto v Ealing* LBC [2000] Q.B. 381. See also *R. v Davey* [1899] 2 Q.B. 301.

[231] See e.g. *Scadding v Lorant* (1851) 3 H.L.C. 418; *cf. R. v Bedford Level Corp* (1805) 6 East 356; *Adams v Adams* [1971] P 188; Rubinstein (n.202), pp.205–8; Sir Owen Dixon, *Jesting Pilate* (1965), p.229.

de facto judge or officer has been confirmed in three recent cases[232]. As the Court of Appeal noted in *Coppard*, the *de facto* holder of the office must have some basis for the office (variously expressed as "colourable title" or "colourable authority"),[233] but must not be a "usurper".[234] As Hale L.J. put it in *Fawdry*,[235] the doctrine "protects the individual citizen, who had good reason to think that he was appearing before a properly constituted court, acted accordingly and should not without more be deprived of the rights he has established as a result". Or as put by Laws L.J. in *Baldock*:[236]

> ". . . the general reputation of the law and the public's confidence in it must be protected as surely as the interests of individual parties who have proceeded on the assumption that a judgment in their case is perfectly valid, where that is exactly how it seems to all the world. Public confidence as well as individual parties are, in my judgment, protected by the requirement. . .".

The effect of a judgment that a decision is void

4–077 When an act or decision is held to be unlawful, and if the effect of that holding is that the matter is void ab initio then, as we have seen, there may be what has been called a "domino effect" on a number of other decisions or acts which were made on the assumption that the first act or decision was lawful. For example, where byelaws have been successfully challenged as unlawful, are all persons who were previously convicted on the basis of those byelaws entitled to damages against the police for false arrest?[237] In *Percy*, the answer to that question was held to be no, due to the fact, as we have discussed, that at the time of the arrest the presumption of validity applied. In similar situations, however, damages for false imprisonment have been awarded despite the fact that the prison had been following the law as it reasonably seemed at the time.[238] Retrospective application could lead to administrative chaos and also deprive individuals of their benefits (albeit that those benefits, obtained under the colour of a void act, may not strictly be regarded as rights). In practice this conundrum does not cause much problem, because the courts have discovered other principles to deal

---

[232] *Fawdry and Co v Murfitt* [2002] EWCA Civ 643; [2003] Q.B. 104, where the de facto doctrine was described as a "long standing doctrine of the common law" (Hale L.J. at [18]); *Coppard v Customs and Excise Commissioners* [2003] EWCA Civ 511; [2003] Q.B. 1428; where Sedley L.J. at [15] described the doctrine as "an ancient one" not confined to judges but to offices, including the monarchy itself by persons later held not have lawfully occupied them; *Baldock v Webster* [2004] EWCA Civ 1869; [2006] Q.B. 315.
[233] *Fawdry* at [21] (Hale L.J.).
[234] Described by the Court in *Coppard* [2003] EWCA Civ 511; [2003] Q.B. 1428 at [18] as a person who knew he had no title or legal authority.
[235] At [36].
[236] At [15], with whom Arden and Kennedy L.JJ agreed.
[237] *Percy v Hall* [1997] Q.B. 924.
[238] *R. v Governor of Broakhill Prison Ex p. Evans (No.2)* [2001] 2 A.C. 19; see 19–00.

with this situation, but it has engaged intense debate, particularly in the light of the possibility, after *Boddington*[239] of collateral attack on a decision via a court not subject to the time limits and other constraints of a the procedures of judicial review.

Forsyth suggests that where an initial act (in the above example, the 4–078 byelaw) appears to be valid and people have acted on that assumption, then the validity of the later act (the arrest) depends on the legal powers of the "second actor" (the police who made the arrest).[240] By looking at the relationship between the two acts the question of the validity of the second actor's legal powers will be determined. In some cases (as in *Percy*[241]) the second act will be valid because it had not been challenged before the first act was struck down as void. Thus is the theoretical integrity of the void-voidable distinction preserved, and the domino effect avoided.

Forsyth's approach has been called "a tissue of pseudo-conceptualism 4–079 behind which lurks what is in reality a pragmatic conclusion".[242] In *Percy*, it was clear that considerations of what was called "policy" were invoked to preserve the arrests from nullity.[243] Yet in some cases Forsyth's analysis may be helpful provided that (and it is a major proviso) the interpretation of the second actor's power is capable of a clear solution. Craig, while believing that retrospective nullity should be the rule, disapproves of the "mask" of the void-voidable distinction in favour of a frank admission on the part of the courts that the decision is void, but would then employ discretion to refuse or limit a remedy to ensure that it only operates prospectively in an appropriate case.[244] As Lord Browne-Wilkinson said in *Boddington*, an ultra vires act may be capable of having some legal effect and the "subsequent recognition of its invalidity cannot rewrite history as to all other matters done in the meantime in reliance on its validity".[245] There are four ways in which the courts are able to prevent history being rewritten, all of them perfectly within the realm of public law principle.

First, there is clear authority for a recognition of the saving of *de facto* 4–080 authority, as we have seen in respect of judges and officials acting under the colour of authority. Surely the same justification applies outside the area of official appointments (such as the arrest carried out in *Percy*)? To seek to avert the hardship that a rigorous imposition of the *de iure* situation would impose on countless people is not, as Lord Wilberforce said in *Butte*[246] a mere matter of discretion, but a matter of applying principles of

[239] [1999] 2 A.C. 143.
[240] "The Metaphysics of Nullity: Invalidity, Conceptual Reasoning and the Rule of Law" in C. Forsyth and I. Hare (eds), *The Golden Metwand and the Crooked Cord* (1998), p.141.
[241] [1997] Q.B. 924.
[242] M. Elliott, *Beatson, Matthew and Elliott's Administrative Law, Text and Materials* (2005), p.100.
[243] See e.g. Simon Brown L.J. and Schiemann L.J. at 951–952.
[244] *Administrative Law*, 5th edn (2003), pp.710–13; "Collateral Attack, Procedural Exclusivity and Judicial Review" (1998) 114 L.Q.R. 535.
[245] [1999] 2 A.C. 143 at 164; Lord Slynn at 165.
[246] [1999] 2 A.C. 143.

public law that seek to avoid needless unfairness. He regarded the application of these principles as "inherent in the judicial process". Of course that does not mean that there will not be occasions where an individual or authority who had acted apparently lawfully will have to pay for the legal mistakes of others.[247]

4–081   Secondly, the courts should take into account the context of an invalidity. This was done in a case where certain procedural requirements were not complied with to the letter in an immigration appeal (a declaration of truth was omitted). Lord Woolf M.R. considered whether there had been substantial compliance with the requirements, whether non-compliance was capable of being waived, and the practical consequences of non-compliance.[248]

4–082   Thirdly, where the court has discretion to refuse to provide a remedy, or to provide a remedy that is prospective in effect (in the form of a declaration), it may in appropriate situations refuse to quash an unlawful decision. This can happen where there is a lack of prejudice to the claimant, or where to quash the decision would prejudice third parties who have relied on the validity of the decision.[249] The maintenance of "public confidence"[250] is, as we shall see in different parts of this book, an important value of public law.

4–083   Finally, in some cases a person who has been adversely affected by an unlawful official decision may be entitled to restitution for consequential loss.[251] The House of Lords have held that money paid to the Revenue pursuant to a demand based upon an invalid regulation was prima facie recoverable.[252] The majority of the Lords held that the claimant was entitled in "common justice" to restitution and that the court should seek to "do justice between the parties".[253] Lord Goff's *obiter* in that case, to the effect that the principle of recovery may not apply in cases where the authority had "misconstrued a relevant statute or regulation" or had "simply . . . paid the money under a mistake of law"[254] fails to recognise the full effect of the collapse of the distinction between jurisdictional and non-jurisdictional error. As Lord Slynn said in that case, it is where the demand is based upon a mistake of law that the principle of recovery is "most likely to be needed".[255]

---

[247] See, e.g. *R v Governor of Her Majesty's Prison Brockhill Ex p. Evans (No.2)* [2001] A.C. 19.
[248] *R. v Immigration Appeal Tribunal Ex p. Jeyeanthan* [2000] 1 W.L.R. 354, CA.
[249] See 18–048.
[250] *Baldock* (Laws L.J.).
[251] See 19–075.
[252] *Woolwich Equitable Building Society v Inland Revenue Commission (No.2)* [1993] A.C. 70.
[253] Lord Goff at 761.
[254] Lord Goff at 763–4.
[255] Lord Goff at 787.

COMPARATIVE PERSPECTIVES

Australia

In Australia, the categories of "jurisdictional" and "non-jurisdictional   4–084
error" still apply. The distinction was reaffirmed in *Craig v South
Australia;*[256] *Coal and Allied Operations Pty Ltd v Australian Industrial
Relations Commission*[257] and *Minister for Immigration and Multicultural
Affairs v Yusuf.*[258] The High Court has held that its entrenched jurisdiction
to grant the writs under s.75(v) of the Constitution is limited only to
review of jurisdictional errors.[259] The increase in the number of ouster
clauses (referred to below), particularly in migration matters, has meant
that there has been an increased reliance on the constitutional writs.[260] The
distinction sometimes appears arbitrary due to the increased scope of what
will amount to a "jurisdictional error". Kirby J. has expressed the strong
view that the retention of the distinction in Australia is a historical
anomaly and ought to be disregarded, consistently with the position in the
United Kingdom.[261] The consequence of finding jurisdictional error in a
decision was considered in *Minister for Immigration and Multicultural
Affairs v Bhardwaj.*[262] Gaudron and Gummow JJ. held that a decision
involving a jurisdictional error has "no legal foundation" and should be
regarded as "no decision at all". Consequently, the decision may be
remade without the existing decision being first set aside by the court.[263]

In relation to ouster clauses, the main developments recently have been   4–085
in relation to the Migration Act 1958 (Cth). The government introduced a
new legislative scheme in 2001 which limited the judicial review of
decisions made under the Migration Act by purporting to remove "privative clause decisions" from the scope of the Administrative Decisions
(Judicial Review) Act 1977, the High Court's jurisdiction under s.75(v) of
the Constitution and the Federal Court's jurisdiction under s.39B(1) of the
Judiciary Act 1903 (Cth). In *Plaintiff S157/2002 v Commonwealth*, the
High Court upheld the constitutional validity of the ouster clause.
However, the effect of the clause was significantly curtailed: "privative
clause decisions" in respect of which there was to be no judicial review did

---

[256] (1995) 184 C.L.R. 163.
[257] (2000) 203 C.L.R. 194.
[258] (2001) 206 C.L.R. 323.
[259] *Darling Casino Ltd v NSW Casino Control Authority* (1997) 191 C.L.R. 602, 633; *Re
McBain; Ex parte Australian Catholic Bishops Conference* (2002) 209 C.L.R. 372.
[260] D. Jackson Q.C., "'Development of judicial review in Australia over the last 10 years: The
growth of the constitutional writs" (2004) 12 *Australian Journal of Administrative Law* 22, at
26–7; e.g. *Abebe v Commonwealth* (1999) 197 C.L.R. 510; *Re Refugee Review Tribunal; Ex
parte Aala* (2000) 204 C.L.R. 82.
[261] *Minister for Immigration and Multicultural Affairs Ex p. Miah* (2001) 206 C.L.R. 57 at
[211]–[212].
[262] (2002) 209 C.L.R. 597.
[263] (2002) 209 C.L.R. 597 at 616.

not include decisions involving jurisdictional error; they were not decisions made "under" the Act, but "purported decisions". The court based its decision upon the separation of powers entrenched in the Constitution and the violation of that doctrine by the conferral on a "non-judicial body the power to conclusively determine the limits of its own jurisdiction".[264] The court went so far to say that s.75(v) introduced "into the Constitution of the Commonwealth an entrenched minimum provision of judicial review".[265]

4–086 Following this decision, further amendments were introduced by the government in 2005. Among other things, the changes excluded "purported privative clause decisions" from judicial review under the Administrative Decisions (Judicial Review) Act 1977. Further, strict time limits for bringing an application to the High Court for a writ of mandamus, prohibition or certiorari or an injunction or declaration were introduced for a "purported privative clause decision". A "purported privative clause decision" was defined to mean a decision purportedly made under the Act that would be a privative clause decision if there were not a failure to exercise jurisdiction or an excess of jurisdiction in the making of the decision. The High Court was prohibited by s.486A(2) from making an order allowing, or having the effect of allowing, an applicant to make an application outside the statutory time period. The validity of s.486A was tested in *Bodrudazza v Minister for Immigration and Multicultural Affairs*. The court struck the clause down, holding that the imposition of the inflexible time limits "subverts the constitutional purpose of the remedy provided by s 75(v)".[266] In *Shergold v Tanner* the High Court considered whether a "conclusive" certificate clause under the Freedom of Information Act 1982 (Cth) operated to remove the federal court's jurisdiction under the Administrative Decisions (Judicial Review) Act 1977. The court held that in the absence of clear legislative intent, the court's jurisdiction was not impliedly withdrawn or limited.[267] In several subsequent cases, the High Court considered the operation of a state privative clause that provided, subject to an appeal by leave to the Full Bench of the New South Wales Industrial Relations Commission, a decision or purported decision of the Commission was final and could not be appealed against or otherwise reviewed by any court or tribunal.[268] The majority held that because the application to the Court of Appeal was instituted before any hearing in or decision by the Commission the privative clause had no operation.[269]

[264] *Plaintiff S157/2002 v Commonwealth* (2003) 211 C.L.R. 476 at 512.
[265] *Plaintiff S157/2002*, (2003) 211 C.L.R. 476 at 513.
[266] *Bodrudazza v Minister for Immigration and Multicultural Affairs* [2007] HCA 14 at [58].
[267] (2002) 209 C.L.R. 126 at [34].
[268] *Fish v Solution 6 Holdings Ltd* (2006) 225 C.L.R. 180, *Batterham v QSR Ltd* (2006) 225 C.L.R. 237, *Old UGC Inc v Industrial Relations Commission of New South Wales in Court Session* (2006) 225 C.L.R. 274.
[269] *Fish v Solution 6 Holdings Ltd* (2006) 225 C.L.R. 180 at [44] (Gleeson C.J., Gummow,

Canada

The place of jurisdictional error in Canadian judicial review law is in a **4–087** state of considerable uncertainty. It does, however, still exist as a category. In *Pushpanathan v Canada (Minister of Citizenship and Immigration)*, Bastarache J. stated: "[J]urisdictional error" is simply an error on an issue with respect to which, according to the outcome of the pragmatic and functional analysis, the tribunal must make a correct interpretation to which no deference will be shown".[270] In other words, it seemed as though the Supreme Court was accepting that the term "jurisdiction" was simply an ex post facto way of describing an issue that a statutory authority had to get correct on pain of being set aside, that status being determined by the series of factors that the Court had identified as relevant in the reaching of that conclusion. However, in its subsequent cases, the Court has clearly not adhered to that perspective. Rather the Court has seemingly accepted that there are certain questions that a priori are jurisdictional in character. In some of those instances, this has led the Court to automatically engage in correctness review.[271] However, in other instances, the Court has characterised an issue as jurisdictional on an a priori basis and then treated this as no more than a factor in conducting the pragmatic and functional analysis to establish a standard of review. In other words, just because a question is jurisdictional in nature does automatically lead to correctness review.[272]

Ouster clauses remain one factor that the Courts take into account in **4–088** conducting the pragmatic and functional approach. The stronger the ouster clause, the more likely it is that the Court will use the most deferential standard of review: patent unreasonableness. Since *Crevier v Quebec (Attorney General)*[273] and *MacMillan Bloedel Ltd v Simpson*,[274] accepting that judicial review of administrative action at least for jurisdictional error is a constitutionally guaranteed right (arising out of ss.96–101 of the Constitution Act 1981), a right that cannot removed by either the provincial legislature or Federal Parliament, there is no incentive to enact

---

Hayne, Callinan and Crennan JJ.); *Batterham v QSR Ltd* (2006) 225 C.L.R. 237 at [28] (Gleeson C.J., Gummow, Hayne, Callinan and Crennan JJ.); *Old UGC Inc v Industrial Relations Commission of New South Wales in Court Session* (2006) 225 C.L.R. 274 at [28] (Gummow, Hayne, Callinan and Crennan JJ.).
[270] [1998] 1 S.C.R. 982.
[271] *Nova Scotia (Workers' Compensation Board) v Martin* [2003] 2 S.C.R. 504 (whether a tribunal had authority to consider a challenge on Charter grounds to its constitutive legislation); *United Taxi Drivers' Fellowship of Southern Alberta v Calgary (City)* [2004] 1 S.C.R. 427 (use of correctness review on a traditional ultra vires basis in dealing with challenge to municipal increase in number of taxi licences); and various duelling jurisdiction cases such as *Regina Police Association v Regina (City) Board of Police Commissioners* [2000] 1 S.C.R. 360.
[272] See, e.g. *Chieu v Canada (Minister of Citizenship and Immigration)* [2002] 1 S.C.R 84; *Zenner v Prince Edward Island College of Optometrists* [2005] 3 S.C.R. 645; and also *ATCO Gas & Pipelines Ltd v Alberta (Energy & Utilities Board)* [2006] 1 S.C.R. 140, where ironically, Bastarache J. wrote the majority judgment.
[273] [1981] 2 S.C.R. 220.
[274] [1995] 4 S.C.R. 725.

privative clauses that have as their objective the total removal of access to judicial review.[275] It should, however, be noted that this constitutional guarantee has not led to the striking down of "impediments" to judicial review such as limitation periods, leave requirements, or procedural and evidential restrictions favouring the "government" in judicial review and statutory appeals.

New Zealand

4–089   The categories of "jurisdictional" and "non-jurisdictional error" no longer apply in New Zealand.[276] The concept of jurisdiction was effectively jettisoned in favour of an error of law standard of review in *Bulk Gas Users Group v Attorney General*,[277] a direction confirmed by the Court of Appeal.[278] Following Lord Diplock's lead, there is a suggestion in *Bulk Gas* that the concept of jurisdiction might still have some operation in relation to inferior courts of law of general jurisdiction, primarily to prevent appeal rights from being circumvented by judicial review,[279] but this has had no significant impact in subsequent case law.

4–090   In relation to ouster clauses, the New Zealand courts have consistently followed *Anisminic* and not given effect to privative clauses that purport to exclude judicial review altogether unless there is a good policy reason for the exclusion.[280] But they have upheld privative clauses delaying judicial review until appeal rights and the like are exhausted where this is sensible policy.[281] In contrast to the position in Canada, New Zealand courts have disregarded the presence of privative clauses in "determining, as a matter of statutory interpretation, what questions of law, if any, have been remitted to the conclusive decision of the tribunal".[282] Extra-judicially, Sir Robin Cooke frequently expressed the view that privative clauses are ineffectual, useless and best repealed.[283]

---

[275] *Quaere* whether *Crevier* guarantees in some form the perpetuation of "jurisdictional error" as a ground of review in Canadian law.

[276] See generally M. Taggart, "The Contribution of Lord Cooke to Scope of Review Doctrine in Administrative Law: A Comparative Common Law Perspective" in P. Rishworth (ed.), *The Struggle for Simplicity in the Law: essays for Lord Cooke of Thorn* (1998), p.189.

[277] [1982] N.Z.L.R. 129 (CA).

[278] *Hawkins v Minister of Justice* [1991] 2 N.Z.L.R. 530, CA; *Peters v Davison* [1999] 2 N.Z.L.R. 164, CA.

[279] *Martin v Ryan* [1990] 2 N.Z.L.R. 209, 225 (HC, Fisher J.).

[280] *New Zealand Rail Ltd v Employment Court* [1995] 3 N.Z.L.R. 179 (CA); Ramsay v Wellington District Court [2006] NZAR 136, CA.

[281] *Love v Porirua City Council* [1984] 2 N.Z.L.R. 308, CA; *McGuire v Hastings District Council* [2002] 2 N.Z.L.R. 577 at [25] PC (Lord Cooke of Thorndon).

[282] *Bulk Gas Users Group v Attorney General* [1982] N.Z.L.R. 129 at 134 CA; and *Mobil Oil New Zealand Ltd v Motor Spirits Licensing Appeal Authority* (1985) 5 N.Z.A.R. 412, CA.

[283] See e.g. R. Cooke, "Administrative Law: The Vanishing Sphinx" [1975] N.Z.L.J. 529, 530; R. Cooke, "The Struggle for Simplicity" in Michael Taggart (ed.), *Judicial Review of Administrative Action: Problems and Prospects* (1986) 1, p.8 ("[t]heir disuse by legislative draftsmen would be a further advance in the struggle for simplicity").

South Africa

The South African courts have largely followed the English example in collapsing the distinction between jurisdictional and non-jurisdictional errors. The case taking the decisive step in this regard is *Hira v Booysen*,[284] decided in the pre-constitutional era.[285] The approach taken in *Hira* was essentially that courts of review need to pay attention to the intention of the legislature in determining whether the tribunal or administrator had exclusive authority to decide the question of law concerned. The focus of the inquiry as described in *Hira* has to an extent been superseded by the provisions of the Promotion of Administrative Justice Act. Section 6(2)(d) allows a court to review an administrative action if it is "materially influenced by an error of law". The focus of the inquiry is thus, in the constitutional era, whether the error materially influenced the decision, rather than whether the administrator was "empowered" to err.   4-091

There was at first some division in the views of the academy and the judiciary. In the first edition of her book Hoexter suggested that the Constitution contemplated that every error of law would be reviewable.[286] Currie and Klaaren,[287] Burns,[288] Beukes[289] and De Ville[290] are of the view that only material errors of law are reviewable. In the latest edition of her book, Hoexter states that an error will lead to reviewability if it affects the outcome.[291] In *Liberty Life Association of Africa Ltd v Kachelhoffer NO and Others* Van Reenen J "inclined to the view" that only errors of law that "materially influence the outcome of administrative action, should be reviewable".[292] The judge went on to explain the concept of materiality by saying that an error is not material "if the decision is justifiable on the facts despite such an error". *Governing Body, Mikro Primary School, v Minister of Education, Western Cape* is a case where the error of law was found to be material and constituted a reason for the setting aside of the decision: "The error of law was that the first respondent thought that the second respondent was entitled to issue the directive".[293] The decision was confirmed on appeal by the Supreme Court of Appeal of South Africa. An excellent account of the history of the distinction between jurisdictional and non-jurisdictional errors appears in the judgment of Malan J. in *South African Jewish Board of Deputies v Sutherland NO*.[294]   4-092

[284] 1992 (4) S.A. 69 (A).
[285] For an account of this case and the English decisions relied on it its reasoning, see C. Hoexter, *Administrative Law in South Africa* (2007), pp.256–258.
[286] *The New Constitutional and Administrative Law*: Vol.2—*Administrative Law* (2002), p.154.
[287] *The Promotion of Administrative Justice Act Benchbook* (2001), p.163.
[288] *Administrative Law under the Constitution* 2nd edn (1996), p.175.
[289] "Review as a Tool for the Development of a Culture of Accountability in the Public Administration" (2002) *South African Public Law* 244 at 256–257.
[290] *Judicial Review of Administrative Action in South Africa* (2003), p.152.
[291] *Administrative Law in South Africa* (2007), p.258.
[292] 2005 (3) S.A. 69 (C), para.48.
[293] 2005 (3) S.A. 504 (C); and *Jicama 17 (Pty) Ltd v West Coast District Municipality* 2006 (1) S.A. 116 (C).
[294] 2004 (4) S.A. 368 (W) at paras 26–27.

4-093   In relation to ouster clauses, the right of access to court in s.34 of the Constitution provides that "everyone has the right to have any dispute that can be resolved by the application of law decided in a fair public hearing before a court or. . . another independent and impartial tribunal". This right probably makes direct and unambiguous ouster clauses unconstitutional. The Constitutional Court has not yet ruled on legislative provisions which may indirectly narrow considerably the review jurisdiction of the courts.

Part II
GROUNDS OF JUDICIAL REVIEW

CHAPTER 5

ILLEGALITY

SCOPE

This Chapter considers the question of legality in relation to the following **5–001** issues.

- A discussion of the history of discretionary power.[1]
- Statutory interpretation in the context of pubic authorities' powers and duties.[2]
- Mandatory and "directory" powers and duties.[3]
- The interpretation of policies.[4]
- Exercise of power for extraneous purposes.[5]
- The failure of a public authority to have regard to a relevant consideration and the taking into account of a legally irrelevant consideration.[6]
- Partial illegality and severance.[7]
- The lawfulness of delegation by a public authority.[8]

INTRODUCTION

An administrative decision is flawed if it is illegal. A decision is illegal if it: **5–002**

(a) contravenes or exceeds the terms of the power which authorises the making of the decision;

(b) pursues an objective other than that for which the power to make the decision was conferred;

[1] See 5–007.
[2] See 5–020.
[3] See 5–049,
[4] See 5–073.
[5] See 5–075.
[6] See 5–010.
[7] See 5–135.
[8] 5–138.

(c) is not authorised by any power;

(d) contravenes or fails to implement a public duty.[9]

5–003 The task for the courts in evaluating whether a decision is illegal is essentially one of construing the content and scope of the instrument conferring the duty or power upon the decision-maker. The instrument will normally be a statute or statutory instrument, but it may also be an enunciated policy, and sometimes a prerogative or other "common law" power.[10] The courts when exercising this power of construction are enforcing the rule of law, by requiring administrative bodies to act within the "four corners" of their powers or duties. They are also acting as guardians of Parliament's will, seeking to ensure that the exercise of power is in accordance with the scope and purpose of Parliament's enactments.

5–004 At first sight this ground of review seems a fairly straightforward exercise of statutory interpretation, for which courts are well suited. It is for them to determine whether an authority has made an error of law. Yet there are a number of issues that arise in public law that make the courts' task more complex. First, is the fact that power is often conferred, and necessarily so in a complex modern society, in terms which grant the decision-maker a broad degree of discretion. Statutes abound with expressions such as: "the Secretary of State may" (do some act); conditions may be imposed as the authority "thinks fit"; action may be taken "if the Secretary of State believes" circumstances to exist or "considers it appropriate" to take action. These formulae, and others like them, appear on their face to grant the decision-maker infinite power, or at least the power to choose from a wide range of alternatives, free of judicial interference. The courts, however, insist that such seemingly unconstrained power is confined by the purpose for which the statute conferred the power. This task is made easier where the purpose is clearly defined, or where the considerations which the body must take into account in arriving at its decisions are clearly spelled out. In such cases the courts require the decision-maker to take into account the specified considerations and ignore the irrelevant. But many

---

[9] Compare this definition, albeit slightly extended from the 5th edition of this work, with the variety of instances of illegality specified under the South African Promotion of Administrative Justice Act 2000, s.6 of which permits judicial review of an administrative action if the administrator who took it was "not authorised to so by the empowering provision" (s.6(2)(a)(i)); or "acted under a delegation of power which was not authorised by the empowering provision" (s.6(2)(a)(ii)); or if " a mandatory and material procedure or condition prescribed by an empowering provision was not complied with" (s.6(2)(b)); or "the action was materially influenced by an error of law" (s.6(2)(d)); or the action was taken: "for a reason not authorised by the empowering provision; for an ulterior purpose or motive; because irrelevant considerations were taken into account or relevant considerations were not considered; because of the unauthorised or unwarranted dictates of another person or body; in bad faith; or arbitrary or capriciously (s.6(2)(e)(i)-(vi)). In addition, review is available if the action itself "contravenes the law or is not authorised by the empowering provision" (s.6(2)(f) i)), and finally "if the action concerned consists of a failure to take a decision" (s.6(2)(g)). Other provisions deal with irrationality and procedural fairness.

[10] See 3–032(on prerogative powers) and 5–022(on the "Ram doctrine").

statutes provide only the framework for subsequent decisions,[11] or delegate power to the executive further to specify those considerations. In any event the distinction between considerations which are "relevant" from those which are not is not always immediately obvious.

Secondly, statutes do not exist in a vacuum.[12] They are located in the 5–005 context of our contemporary European democracy. As has been discussed above, the rule of law and other fundamental principles of democratic constitutionalism should be presumed to inform the exercise of all official powers unless Parliament expressly excludes them.[13] There may even be some aspects of the rule of law and other democratic fundamentals which Parliament has no power to exclude.[14] The courts should therefore strive to interpret powers in accordance with these principles. International law, both customary and treaty obligations are also part of the context which cannot be ignored. European Community Law is part of our law, as now is the European Convention on Human Rights. Breach of European Community law and Convention rights thus amounts to illegality.

It is because of these considerations that for a substantial part of this 5–006 chapter it is necessary to focus closely on issues as to the appropriate manner in which legislation should be construed. This is necessary in order to identify the all important dividing line between decisions that can be reached lawfully and those that are unlawful.

DISCRETIONARY POWER: A BRIEF HISTORY OF JUDICIAL ATTITUDES

The concept of discretion in its legal context implies power to make a 5–007 choice between alternative courses of action or inaction.[15] If only one course can lawfully be adopted, the decision taken is not the exercise of a discretion but the performance of a duty. To say that somebody has a discretion presupposes that there is no unique legal answer to a problem. There may, however, be a number of answers that are wrong in law. And even in cases where the power is discretionary, circumstances can exist which mean the discretion can only be exercised in one way. There are

[11] See, e.g. 5–033–34 on planning powers where, under the Town and Country Planning Acts over the years, the term "planning" has never been given statutory definition.
[12] *R. v Secretary of State for the Home Department Ex p. Pierson* [1998] A.C. 539 at 587 (Lord Steyn: "Parliament does not legislate in a vacuum. Parliament legislates for a European liberal democracy based upon the traditions of the common law . . . and . . ., unless there is the clearest provision to the contrary, Parliament must be presumed not to legislate contrary to the rule of law").
[13] See 1–015–021 See also 11–059–061.
[14] *Jackson v Attorney General* [2005] UKHL 56; [2006] 1 A.C. 262 at [120] (Lord Hope), [102] (Lord Steyn), [159] (Baroness Hale suggest that the rule of law may have become "the ultimate controlling factor in our unwritten constitution"; and see J. Jowell, "Parliamentarys Sovereignty under the New Constitutional Hypothesis" [2006] P.L. 262.
[15] *cf.* K.C. Davis, *Discretionary Justice*(1969), p.4: "A public officer has discretion whenever the effective limits of his power leave him free to make a choice among possible courses of action or inaction".

degrees of discretion, varying the scope for manoeuvre afforded to the decision-maker.[16]

5–008   At the outset it should be emphasised that the scope of judicial review of the exercise of discretion will be determined mainly by the wording of the power and the context in which it is exercised.[17] Parliament employs a great variety of different formulae to confer discretion and to guide the exercise of that discretion. Sometimes, a statute exhaustively specifies the ways in which a discretion may be deployed, such as by enumerating the types of conditions which an authority may attach to the grant of a licence. In such cases, the attachment of any other type of condition may be illegal. Or it may lay down general standards to which the exercise of a power must conform.[18] Sometimes, however, the exercise of a statutory discretion is not limited by the express provisions of the Act and in those cases the courts embark upon an interpretation of the objects and purposes of the statute in order to identify the limitations to which the discretion is subject.

5–009   As was said by Lord Upjohn in *Padfield*,[19] even if a statute were to confer upon a decision-maker an "unfettered discretion";

"[T]he use of that adjective [unfettered], even in an Act of Parliament, can do nothing to unfetter the control which the judiciary have over the executive, namely, that in exercising their powers the latter must act lawfully and that is a matter to be determined by looking at the Act and

[16] Ronald Dworkin makes the distinction between "strong discretion" (the sergeant's discretion to pick "any five men" for a patrol) and "weak discretion" (the sergeant's discretion to pick "the most five experienced men"): *Taking Rights Seriously* (1977), p.32. See also D. Galligan, *Discretionary Powers* (1986); G. Richardson, A. Ogus and P. Burrows, *Policing Pollution: A Study of Regulation and Enforcement* (1982); K. Hawkins, *Environment and Enforcement: Regulation and the Social Definition of Pollution* (1984); B. Hutter, *The Reasonable Arm of the Law: The Law Enforcement Procedures of Environmental Health Officers* (1988); K. Hawkins (ed.), *The Uses of Discretion* (1992) and its review by D. Feldman, "Discretion, Choices and Values" [1994] P.L. 279; T. Buck, D. Bonner and R. Sainsbury, *Making Social Security Law: The Role and Work of the Social Security and Child Support Commissioners* (2005); F. Bennion, "Judgment and Discretion Revisited: Pedantry or Substance?" [2005] P.L. 368; T. Endicott, *Vagueness in Law* (2000); J. King, "The Justiciability of Resource Allocation" (2007) M.L.R. 197, 201–207.
[17] *Secretary of State for Education and Science v Tameside MBC* [1977] A.C. 1014 at 1047 (Lord Wilberforce: "there is no universal rule as to the principles on which the exercise of a discretion may be reviewed: each statute or type of statute must be individually looked at").
[18] The extent to which discretionary power should be confined by rule in any particular context will not be considered here. For concern with the "optimal precision" of rules, see R. Posner, *An Economic Analysis of Law*, 6th edn (2003); T. Endicott, *Vagueness in Law*(2000); J King (2007) M.L.R. 197 For earlier accounts of the need to confine discretion see: D. Oliver, "Regulating Precision" in A. Hawkins and J. Thomas (eds), *Making Regulatory Policy* (1985); C. McRudden, "Codes in a Cold Climate: Administrative Rule-Making by the Commissions for Racial Equality" (1988) 51 M.L.R. 409; R. Baldwin "Why Rules Don't Work" (1990) 53 M.L.R. 321; D. McBarnet and C. Whelan, "The Elusive Spirit of the Law: Formalisation and the Struggle for Legal Control" (1991) 54 M.L.R. 848; C. Reich, "The New Property" 73 Yale L.J. 733; J. Jowell, *Law and Bureaucracy* (1975) and "The Legal Control of Administrative Discretion" [1973] P.L. 178; R. Baldwin and K. Hawkins, "Discretionary Justice: Davis Reconsidered" [1984] P.L. 570. *cf.* G. Mashaw, *Bureaucratic Justice* (1983).
[19] *Padfield v Minister of Agriculture Fisheries and Food* [1968] A.C. 997.

its scope and object in conferring a discretion upon the minister rather than by the use of adjectives."[20]

Those words are true today and to some extent have always been true, subject to some notable decisions to the contrary in the past, particularly during times of war or public emergency. The criteria by which the exercise of a discretion could be judged were indicated early in the 17th century. Lambard's advice to justices—"no way better shall the Discretion of a Justice of the Peace appear than if he (remembering that he is *lex loquens*) do contain himself within the listes of the law, and (being soberly wise) do not use his own discretion, but only where both the law permitteth, and the present case requireth it"[21]—was fortified by dicta and decisions of the courts. Discretion, said Coke, was *scire per legem quod sit justum;*[22] it was "a science or understanding to discern between falsity and truth, between right and wrong, between shadows and substance, between equity and colourable glosses and pretences, and not to do according to their wills and private affections".[23] In 1647 it was laid down by the King's Bench that "wheresoever a commissioner or other person hath power given to do a thing at his discretion, it is to be understood of sound discretion, and according to law, and that this Court hath power to redress things otherwise done by them".[24] The concept of a judicial discretion, which was not confined to courts in the strict sense, was later stated by Lord Mansfield to import a duty to be "fair, candid, and unprejudiced; not arbitrary, capricious, or biased; much less, warped by resentment, or personal dislike".[25] In 1591 the discretion of licensing justices was expressed to mean that they were to act "according to the rules of reason and justice, not according to private opinion . . . according to law, and not humour". Their discretion was to be "not arbitrary, vague, and fanciful, but legal and regular".[26]

5–010

[20] [1968] A.C. 997 at 1060. For interpretation of a statute which came close to conferring unfettered discretion, but which nevertheless permitted judicial review, see *R. v Secretary of State for the Environment Ex p. Norwich CC* [1982] Q.B. 808 ("Where it appears to the Secretary of State that tenants . . . have or may have difficulty in exercising the right to buy [council houses]"; held that evidence of such difficulty existed); *R. (on the application of Mehanne) v Westminster Housing Benefit Review Board* [2001] UKHL 11; [2001] 1 W.L.R. 539 at [13] (the power to decide as the Board "considers appropriate" is the "language of discretion"); *R. (on the application of G) v Barnet LBC* [2003] UKHL 57; [2004] 2 A.C. 208 (local authority's duties in relation to children under Children Act 1989).
[21] W. Lambard, *Eirenarcha or of the Office of the Justices of Peace* (1581), p.58.
[22] *Keighley's case* (1609) 10 Co.Rep. 139a at 140a.
[23] *Rooke's case* (1598) 5 Co.Rep. 99b at 100a (assessment by Commissioners of Sewers); and R. Callis, *Readings upon the Statute of Sewers*, 2nd edn, pp.112–113; *Hetley v Boyer* (1614) Cro. Jac. 336: *case of Commendams* (1617) Hob. 140 at 158–159.
[24] *Estwick v City of London* (1647) Style 42 at 43 (suspension of a councillor).
[25] *R. v Askew* (1768) 4 Burr. 2186 at 2189 (determination by College of Physicians as to competence to practise medicine).
[26] *Sharp v Wakefield* [1891] A.C. 173 at 179 (Lord Halsbury L.C., substantially recapitulating a dictum of Lord Mansfield C.J., in *R. v Wilkes* (1770) 4 Burr. 2528 at 2539, concerning discretions exercised by courts of justice). *Roncarelli v Duplessis* [1959] S.C.R. 122 at 140; *Ward v James* [1966] 1 Q.B. 273 at 293–295; and *Birkett v James* [1978] A.C. 297, 317 (discretion on interlocutory order reviewable on appeal to promote consistency).

5–011   It follows that a discretionary power which is prima facie unfettered has always been held to be subject to implied limitations set by the common law.[27] Indeed, at an early date the courts drew a distinction between judicial discretions and executive discretions, recognising that it would be inappropriate to apply the same criteria to all classes of discretions;[28] and the courts would sometimes characterise a discretion as judicial when they wish to assert powers of review,[29] but as executive or administrative when they wished to explain their inability or unwillingness to measure it by reference to any objective standard.[30]

5–012   Various formulae have been drafted over the years to stretch administrative discretion to its outer limits, and even with the intention of making public officials "judge-proof". Some authorise an authority to take a prescribed course of action if *satisfied* that the action is "necessary" or "appropriate". Initially in this situation the courts held that they could not go behind a statement by the competent authority (in the absence of proof of bad faith) that it was satisfied that the statutory condition for the exercise of the power existed.[31] But it was later conceded that if prima facie grounds could be established for the proposition that the authority could not have been so satisfied, a court will be entitled to hold the act or decision to be invalid unless the authority itself persuades the court that it did in fact genuinely form the opinion which it claims to have held.[32] However, in any event, the burden cast upon a person seeking to impugn such an act or decision was likely to be a heavy one to discharge.[33]

[27] A. Barak, *Judicial Discretion* (1989); and *The Judge in a Democracy* (2006).
[28] D. Gordon, "Administrative" Tribunals and the Courts' (1933) 49 L.Q.R. 419 (where, however, the degree of immunity of discretionary powers from judicial review is overstated).
[29] *R. v Manchester Legal Aid Committee Ex p. Brand (RA) & Co* [1952] 2 Q.B. 413.
[30] *Johnson (B) & Co (Builders) Ltd v Minister of Health* [1947] 2 All E.R. 395 at 399–400 (Minister's decision whether or not to confirm a compulsory purchase order) and *Attorney General v Bastow* [1957] 1 Q.B. 514 (Attorney General's decision to sue for injunction to restrain continuance of criminal offence); *Robinson v Minister of Town and Country Planning* [1947] K.B. 702; *Holmes (Peter) & Son v Secretary of State for Scotland* 1965 S.C. 1 (designation of large areas as subject to comprehensive redevelopment and compulsory purchase); *Webb v Minister of Housing and Local Government* [1964] 1 W.L.R. 1295 at 1301. Cf. *R. v Secretary of State for the Environment Ex p. Ostler* [1977] Q.B. 122 (administrative nature of minister's discretion to confirm a compulsory purchase order offered as one reason for the court's inability to review its legality outside the statutory time limitation for impugning it).
[31] *Re Beck & Pollitzer's Application* [1948] 2 K.B. 339 (order stopping up a highway); *Land Realisation Co v Postmaster-General* [1950] Ch. 435 (compulsory purchase order); *Shand v Minister of Railways* [1970] N.Z.L.R. 615 (closure of railway line); *Secretary of State for Education and Science v Tameside MBC* [1977] A.C. 1014, 1025 (Lord Denning M.R. commenting to the effect that the statements in the wartime and post-war cases "do not apply to-day").
[32] cf. *R. v Brixton Prison Governor Ex p. Soblen* [1963] 2 Q.B. 243 at 302, 307–308 (Home Secretary alleged to have used his power to order the deportation of an alien, a power exercisable whenever he deemed it to be "conductive to the public good", for the ulterior purpose of effecting an unlawful extradition).
[33] In *Soblen* [1963] 2 Q.B. 243, evidence relating to intergovernmental communications was withheld from production when the Secretary of State certified that its production would be injurious to good diplomatic relations.

In *Liversidge v Anderson*[34] the House of Lords held that the Secretary of 5–013
State's power to order the detention of any person whom he had
"reasonable cause to believe" to be of hostile origins or associations, and
over whom it was therefore necessary to exercise control, was validly
exercised unless it was shown that he had not honestly considered that he
had had reasonable cause for his belief.[35]

In 1970 powers were given to the tax authorities to issue a warrant to 5–014
enter premises where they have "reasonable ground" for suspecting an
offence. Having entered the premises they had the power to seize and
remove items found there which they had "reasonable cause to believe"
may be required as evidence of the offence.[36] Suspecting tax fraud, the
Inland Revenue officials obtained search warrants, entered premises and
seized documents without informing the applicants of the offences suspected or the persons suspected of having committed them. The House of
Lords upheld the Inland Revenue's actions and held that the applicants had
no right to be informed of the alleged offences, or of the "reasonable
ground" for suspecting an offence.[37] Nevertheless, it was held that the
existence of "reasonable cause to believe" was a question of objective fact,
to be tried on evidence, and Lord Diplock said that "the time has come to
acknowledge openly that the majority of this House in *Liversidge v
Anderson* were expediently and, at that time perhaps, excusably wrong and
the dissenting speech of Lord Atkin was right.[38]

In the immediate aftermath of the Second World War judicial deference 5–015
to the executive and other public authorities was still the norm, even where
the statutory purposes were defined with close precision. In cases involving
public control over land use and housing accommodation, one could point
to dicta to the effect that an order shown to be perverse or otherwise
lacking in any evidentiary support might be held ultra vires because the
competent authority could not be deemed to have been genuinely satisfied
that it was appropriate for a purpose sanctioned by legislation.[39] Yet if
persons claimed to be aggrieved they invariably failed in the courts; and the
judgments persistently laid a heavier emphasis on the amplitude of the
discretionary power than on the need to relate it to the purposes of the
Act.[40] The incantation of statements denying the absoluteness of

---

[34] [1942] A.C. 206; see Lord Atkin (at 225–247) who delivered a powerful dissenting
judgment. The nature of the "objective" test that Lord Atkin thought appropriate has
sometimes been misrepresented; see 246–247 of his judgment, in which he gave his reasons
for agreeing with the other members of the HL in the analogous case of *Green v Home
Secretary* [1942] A.C. 284.
[35] The only other admissible ground for challenge was that the detention order was
improperly made out; see *R. v Home Secretary Ex p. Budd* [1942] 2 K.B. 1 at 22.
[36] Taxes Management Act 1970 s.20C (now Finance Act 2006 s.174).
[37] *R. v I.R.C. Ex p. Rossminster* [1980] A.C. 952.
[38] At 1011.
[39] *Robinson v Minister of Town and Country Planning* [1947] K.B. 702 at 724; *Demetriades v
Glasgow Corp* [1951] 1 All E.R. 457 at 463.
[40] *Minister of Agriculture and Fisheries v Price* [1941] 2 K.B. 116; *Robinson* [1947] K.B. 702;
Taylor v Brighton Corp [1947] K.B. 736; *Swindon Corp v Pearce* [1948] 2 All E.R. 119;
Holmes (Peter) & Son v Secretary of State for Scotland 1965 S.C. 1.

administrative discretion in such cases was little more than a perfunctory ritual to satisfy the consciences of the judges.

5–016   Sometimes the question before a court is whether words which apparently confer a discretion (words such as "may", or "it shall be lawful if") are instead to be interpreted as imposing a duty. The word "may" has, over the years, primarily been construed as permissive, not imperative.[41] However, exceptionally, it was construed as imposing a duty to act, and even a duty to act in one particular manner.[42]

5–017   Conversely, an apparently absolute duty cast by statute upon a public authority may be interpreted as granting a discretion as to the manner and extent of its performance. Thus, a local authority required by statute to provide suitable alternative accommodation for those displaced by a closing order was held not to be obliged to place them at the top of its housing waiting list.[43] The local authority was in effect given discretion in relation to which it had to use its best endeavours to deal with the result of a housing shortage in the most satisfactory way. Similarly, the manner and timing of the performance by a highway authority of its statutory duty to remove obstructions from the highway are to a large extent within the discretion of the authority.[44] Discretion, in other words, may be conferred implicitly as well as expressly.

---

[41] *Julius v Bishop of Oxford* (1880) 5 App.Cas. 214. Students may wish to consider the following problem: "I learned afterwards that in the scholarship examination another man had obtained more marks than I had, but Whitehead had the impression that I was the abler of the two. He therefore burned the marks before the examiners' meeting, and recommended me in preference to the other man" (*The Autobiography of Bertrand Russell, 1872–1914* (1967), p.57). Discuss. (Notes for Guidance: (1) Assuming that there were no formal rules prescribing criteria for the award of scholarships, do you think the examiners had an implied duty to award them to the highest placed candidates, or did they have a discretion? (2) If the former, what legal remedy, if any, would the candidate with higher marks have had, and against whom? (3) If the latter, did the exercise of Whitehead's discretion taint the subsequent proceedings with invalidity? (4) If not, why not? (5) If yes, what legal remedies would the other candidate have had, and against whom? (The answers to these questions are not provided in this book.))

[42] *Iderman Blackwell's case* (1683) 1 Vent. 152; and authorities cited in *Stroud's Judicial Dictionary* (4th edn), Vol.3 ("May") and examined in *Julius v Bishop of Oxford* (1880) 5 App. Cas. 214. See also *Shelley v LCC* [1949] A.C. 56; *Peterborough Corp v Holdich* [1956] 1 Q.B. 124; *Re Shuter* [1960] 1 Q.B. 142; *Annison v District Auditor for St Pancras BC* [1962] 1 Q.B. 489; *R. v Derby Justices Ex p. Kooner* [1971] 1 Q.B. 147; *Lord Advocate v Glasgow Corp* 1973 S.L.T. 3, HL; *Re Pentonville Prison Governor Ex p. Narang* [1978] A.C. 247; *R. v Secretary of State for the Home Department Ex p. Phansopkar* [1976] Q.B. 606. For an analysis of the uses of "may" and "shall", "duty" and "power" see *R. v Berkshire CC Ex p. Parker* [1997] C.O.D. 64.

[43] *R. v Bristol Corp Ex p. Hendy* [1974] 1 W.L.R. 498; *Thornton v Kirklees MBC* [1979] Q.B. 626; *cf. Salford CC v McNally* [1976] A.C. 379; *R. v Kerrier DC Ex p. Guppys (Bridport) Ltd* (1976) 32 P. & C.R. 411, where it was held that local authorities have no discretion to serve abatement notices under the Public Health Act 1936 or to discharge their obligations under the Housing Act 1957 in respect of houses unfit for human habitation: the duties imposed by both statutes are cumulative. See also *R. v Hillingdon AHA Ex p. Wyatt* (1978) 76 L.G.R. 727 (duty to provide home nurses).

[44] *Haydon v Kent CC* [19781 Q.B. 343.

Change of approach

More than a decade was to elapse after the Second World War before the 5–018
pendulum swung and the emphasis shifted. In New Zealand in 1959 a
power vested in the Governor-General to make such regulations as he
"thinks necessary in order to secure the due administration" of an
Education Act was held to be invalidly exercised in so far as his opinion as
to the necessity for such a regulation was not reasonably tenable.[45] In
England in 1962 the power of the Commissioners of Customs and Excise
to make regulations for "any matter for which provision appears to them
necessary for the purpose of giving effect" to the Act was not construed as
constituting them as the sole judges of what was in fact necessary for the
purposes of the Act; and a regulation in which they gave themselves power
to determine conclusively the amounts of tax payable was held to be ultra
vires.[46] Again, in 1964, the courts were not deterred by a subjectively
worded formula from holding that a compulsory purchase order made
ostensibly for the purpose of coast protection work was invalid because the
land in question was not in fact required for such a purpose.[47] As was
observed in a leading Canadian case, "there is always a perspective within
which a statute is intended to operate".[48]

The decision in 1968 of the House of Lords *Padfield*[49] was an important 5–019
landmark.[50] The minister had refused to appoint a committee, as he was
statutorily empowered to do at his discretion, to investigate complaints
made by members of the Milk Marketing Board that the majority of the
Board had fixed milk prices in a way that was unduly unfavourable to the
complainants. The House of Lords held that the minister's discretion was
not unfettered and that the reasons that he had given for his refusal
showed that he had acted ultra vires by taking into account factors that
were legally irrelevant and by using his power in a way calculated to
frustrate the policy of the Act.[51] The view was also expressed by four of

[45] *Reade v Smith* [1959] N.Z.L.R. 996; *Low v Earthquake and War Damages Commission*
[1959] N.Z.L.R. 1198 at 1207 (dicta).
[46] *Customs and Excise Commissioners v Cure and Deeley Ltd* [1962] 1 Q.B. 340. A number of
the authorities referred to in the preceding pages were considered in the judgment at 366–
368. But on different facts, a similarly worded provision of a subsequent Act was interpreted
literally in *Marsh (B) (Wholesale) Ltd v Customs and Excise Commissioners* [1970] 2 Q.B. 206.
[47] *Webb v Minister of Housing and Local Government* [1964] 1 W.L.R. 1295; [1965] 1
W.L.R. 755 (a complicated case, in which the enabling legislation was couched partly in
subjective and partly in objective terms); J. Bennett Miller, "Administrative Necessity and the
Abuse of Power" [1966] P.L. 330; A.W. Bradley, "Judicial Review and Compulsory
Purchase" [1965] C.L.J. 161.
[48] *Roncarelli v Duplessis* [1959] S.C.R. 122 at 140 (Rand J.); *Rogers v Jordan* (1965) 112
C.L.R. 580 (dicta).
[49] *Padfield v Minister of Agriculture, Fisheries and Food* [1968] A.C. 997.
[50] For some critical comments upon this decision and, more generally, upon judicial
willingness to imply limitations upon the scope of subjectively worded discretion, see R.
Austin, "Judicial Review of Subjective Discretion" (1975) 28 C.L.P 150, 167–173.
[51] The minister's reasons for refusing to accede to the complainants' request had been that it
was the purpose of the statutory scheme that issues of the kind raised by the complainants

their Lordships that even had the minister given no reasons for his decision, the court would not have been powerless to intervene: for once a prima facie case of misuse of power had been established, it would have been open to the court to infer that the minister had acted unlawfully if he had declined to supply any justification at all for his decision.[52] In the years that followed the Court of Appeal[53] and the House of Lords[54] set aside as ultra vires the exercise of discretion that included a substantial subjective element. It is interesting to note that important as the decision in *Padfield* has been in the evolution of judicial attitudes, the minister was ultimately able to uphold the Board's decision without resorting to legislation. Another feature of those decisions was the willingness of the courts to assert their power to scrutinise the factual basis upon which discretionary powers have been exercised.[55]

STATUTORY INTERPRETATION

5–020 The law reports abound with cases involving challenges to the interpretation by public officials of statutory power. Sometimes the exercise of interpretation by the courts of the statutory provision in question involves

should be settled by the representatives of the producers from the different regions who sat on the Board, and that were the committee to uphold the complainants, it would be politically embarrassing for him if he decided not to implement the committee's recommendations. After the decision of the HL the minister complied with the order by referring the complaint to a committee of investigation. The committee reported in favour of the complainants; the minister declined to follow the recommendation.

[52] [1968] A.C. 997 at 1032–1933 (Lord Reid), 1049 (Lord Hodson), 1053–1054 (Lord Pearce), 1061–1062 (Lord Upjohn).

[53] See, e.g. *Congreve v Home Office* [1976] Q.B. 629 (subjective power to revoke television licences not validly exercisable to prevent avoidance of prospectively announced fee increase); *Laker Airways Ltd v Department of Trade* [1977] Q.B. 643 (neither statutory power to give directions to Civil Aviation Authority nor non-statutory power conferred by treaty validly exercisable to defeat legislative scheme); *R. (on the application of Quark Fishing Ltd) v Secretary of State for Foreign and Commonwealth Affairs (No.1)* [2002] EWCA 1409.

[54] See, e.g. *Daymond v Plymouth CC* [1976] A.C. 609 (statutory power to make charges for sewerage services as the authority thought fit did not authorise charging those not in receipt of the services): *Secretary of State for Education and Science v Tameside MBC* [1977] A.C. 1014 (minister improperly exercised power to give directions to a local education authority when satisfied that the authority was proposing to act unreasonably).

[55] For review on the basis of fact is see 4–047 et seq. and see the discussion of review for mistake of fact at 11–041. See *Tameside* [1977] A.C. 1014, especially at 1047 at 1065–1066, 1072; but the statutory standard on which the minister had to be satisfied was by no means wholly subjective. Their Lordships did not indorse the wider scope of inquiry into the underlying facts advanced in the CA by Scarman L.J. at 1030–1031. *cf.* Sir Leslie Scarman, *English Law—The New Dimension* (1974), pp.48–50. See also *Laker Airways* [1977] Q.B. 643 at 706. But see the "Draconian" powers given to the Secretary of State under s.23 of the Housing Act 1980 to intervene to exercise the powers of a local housing authority to do "all such things as appear to him necessary or expedient" to enable tenants to exercise the right to buy. Under that statute he may exercise those powers "Where it appears [to him] that [the tenants] have or may have difficulty in exercising their right to buy effectively or expeditiously". In *R. v Secretary of State for the Environment Ex p. Norwich CC* [1982] Q.B. 808 (Kerr L.J., it was held that this formula did not require the Secretary of State to intervene only when the authority had acted "unreasonably" but, it seems, there had to be some objective evidence that the tenants were experiencing "difficulty").

no more than a search for the "natural and ordinary meaning" of a word or term. For example, a number of cases under various statutes requiring local authorities to house the homeless have considered the meaning of terms such as "homelessness",[56] or "intentionally homeless".[57] Others have considered the duty to provide "adequate accommodation" to gypsies "residing in or resorting to the area".[58] The term "ordinarily resident in the United Kingdom" has also been construed in various contexts.[59] Planning authorities, when deciding whether to grant permission in conservation areas, are required to pay special attention to the desirability of "preserving or enhancing the character or appearance" of the designated conservation area.[60] Do those words require that permission be granted only for development which positively improves the area, or do they merely require that the standards of amenity in the area are maintained at their existing level and not harmed? The House of Lords, after various interpretations in the courts below,[61] held the latter interpretation to be correct.[62]

Where discretion is conferred on the decision-maker the courts also have 5–021 to determine the scope of that discretion and therefore need to construe the statute purposefully.[63] We have seen that the expression "may" can mean "must" in the context of the purpose of the statute as a whole, and we shall see below that the opposite may also apply.[64] Where the statute gives power to the decision-maker to act as he "thinks appropriate", or as he "believes", or "thinks fit", the courts nowadays tend to require those thoughts or beliefs to be "reasonably and objectively justified by relevant facts".[65] Although in judicial review the courts should not put themselves into the position of the primary decision-maker and reassess the facts or decide the merits of the original decision, we shall see in Chapter 11 that there is growing "culture of justification",[66] where even the broadest

---

[56] See, e.g. *R. v Hillingdon LBC Ex p. Islam* [1981] 1 A.C. 688.
[57] See, e.g. *R. v Secretary of State for the Environment Ex p. Tower Hamlets LBC* [1993] Q.B. 632.
[58] Caravan Sites Act, 1968 s.6 (repealed by the Criminal Justice and Public Order Act 1994, s.80); *W Glamorgan v Rafferty* [1987] 1 W.L.R. 457; *R. v Gloucester CC Ex p. Dutton* [1992] C.O.D. 1.
[59] See, e.g. *Shah v Barnet LBC* [1983] 2 A.C. 309 (in the context of a student seeking non-overseas status).
[60] Planning (Listed Buildings and Conservation Areas) Act 1990 s.72.
[61] See, e.g. *Steinberg v Secretary of State for the Environment* (1988) 58 P. & C.R. 453.
[62] *South Lakeland DC v Secretary of State for the Environment* [1992] A.C. 141.
[63] Sir Rupert Cross, *Statutory Interpretation*, 13th edn. (1995), pp.172–75; J. Burrows, *Statute Law in New Zealand*, 3rd edn. (2003), pp.177–99. For a recent example in Canada see *ATCO Gas and Pipelines Ltd v Alberta (Energy and Utilities Board)* [2006] S.C.R. 140.
[64] See 5–049–072.
[65] *Office of Fair Trading v IBA Health Ltd* [2004] EWCA Civ 142; [2004] 4 All E.R. 1103 at [45].
[66] See 11–04 and 098–102.

discretionary formula will not justify an arbitrary decision, or one that is not demonstrably justified (or at least demonstrably unjustified).[67]

Non-statutory sources of power and the Ram Doctrine

5-022 Virtually all of interpretation of legality engages statutory sources, but to what extent is government permitted to achieve its aims by "extra-statutory" means? The power of the Executive is derived from statute, but also, as we have seen, from the royal prerogative.[68] We also consider below that local authorities may enjoy implied powers to achieve objectives which are "incidental" to their other activities.[69] They must surely be able to employ staff, convey property and buy stamps and cleaning equipment and may not need specified power for that kind of activity (although it is sometimes granted). However, there is another source of power, known variously as a "*de facto*",[70] or "common law discretionary"[71] power, which is employed for the kind of "incidental" activities which are required at the level of central government. This authority is derived from what is known as the "Ram doctrine",[72] which states that a minister of the Crown may exercise any powers that the Crown may exercise, except in so far as the minister is precluded from doing so, either expressly or by necessary implication.

5-023 In a written reply to Lord Lester's question in the House of Lords about the scope of the doctrine, Baroness Scotland of Asthal explained that under the Ram doctrine ministers and their departments, "like many other persons" have common law powers which derive from the Crown's status as a corporation sole. She said that to require parliamentary authority for every exercise of the common law powers exercisable by the Crown "either would impose upon Parliament an impossible burden or produce legislation in terms that simply reproduced the common law".[73] The Ram doctrine has also been commented on by the Cabinet Office's Performance and Innovation Unit which claimed that doctrine permitted "a department [to] do anything a natural person can, provided it is not forbidden from doing so".[74]

---

[67] Although sometimes the court will not consider decisions (e.g. of elected local authorities in respect of the issuance of taxi licenses) "with over-refinement": R. v Great Yarmouth BC Ex p. Sawyer [1989] R.T.R. 297, [55]; R. (on the application of Johnson) v Reading BC [2004] EWHC 765; [2004] A.C.D. 72.

[68] See Ch.3.

[69] See 5-091.

[70] M. Elliott, The Constitutional Foundations of Judicial Review (2001), p.166; P. Cane, Administrative Law, 4th edn. (2004), p.50.

[71] P. Craig, Administrative Law, 5th edn. (2003), p.555.

[72] After Sir Granville Ram, First Parliamentary Counsel 1937–47, who set out the doctrine in a memorandum of November 2, 1945; it was first made public in a written parliamentary answer on January 22, 2003, HL Hansard, Vol.643, col.WA98. See B. Harris, "The 'Third Source' of Authority for Government Action Revisited" (2007) 123 L.Q.R. 225; M. Cohn, "Medieval Chains, Invisible Inks: On Non-Statutory Powers of the Executive" (2005) 25 O.J.L.S.97.

[73] HL Hansard, Vol.645, col.WA12 (February 25, 2003).

[74] Cabinet Office, Report on Privacy and Data Sharing (2002).

As Lester and Weait and point out,[75] these interpretations of the Ram 5–024
doctrine appear to be based upon the approach taken in *Malone v
Metropolitan Police Commissioner*, where Sir Robert Megarry V.C. permitted telephone tapping by the police on the ground that England "is not a
country where everything is expressly permitted; it is a country where
everything is permitted except what is expressly forbidden".[76] The European Court of Human Rights subsequently held that the actions of the
police violated Art.8.[77]

While government must be able to carry out incidental functions that are 5–025
not in conflict with its statutory powers, it is wrong to equate the principle
pertaining to private individuals—that they may do everything which is not
specifically forbidden—with the powers of public officials, where the
opposite is true. Any action they take must be justified by a law which
"defines its purpose and justifies its existence".[78] The extension of the Ram
doctrine beyond its modest initial purpose of achieving incidental powers[79]
should be resisted in the interest of the rule of law.[80] However, in any
event it seems that the courts are, also in accordance with the rule of law,
increasingly insisting that all powers, whatever their source, are
reviewable.[81]

[75] Lord Lester and M. Weait, "The Use of Ministerial Powers Without Parliamentary
Authority: The Ram Doctrine" [2003] P.L. 415, p.421.
[76] [1979] Ch. 344 at 357.
[77] *Malone v UK* (1984) 7 E.H.R.R. 14 at paras 67–68 (action was not "in accordance with
law" for the purposes of ECHR Art.8). The Interception of Communications Act 1985 was
enacted to provide a statutory framework for telephone tapping.
[78] *R. v Somerset CC Ex p. Fewings* [1995] 1 All ER 513 at 524 (Laws L.J.), where he made the
distinction between the powers of the private citizen "which are not conditional upon some
affirmative justification for which he must burrow in the law books" and the powers of a
public body, which has no rights of its own . . . beyond its public responsibility which defines
its purpose and justifies its existence"; also Sir Thomas Bingham M.R. in the CA [1995] 1
W.L.R. 1037 at 1042.
[79] Lester and Weait [2003] P.L. 415, pp.417, 421.
[80] Cases where the doctrine has been liberally construed are *R. v Secretary of State for Health
Ex p. C* [2000] 1 F.L.R. 627 and *R. v Worcester CC Ex p. SW* [2000] 3 F.C.R. 174, both cases
which considered the legality of the Consultancy Services Index (CSI), a database maintained
by the Secretary of State for Health without statutory authority. In both cases the CA and
High Court respectively held that the Secretary of State could maintain the database just as a
natural person could (see 3–026). The matter was considered in *R. v Secretary of State for
Work and Pensions Ex p. Hooper* [2005] UKHL 29; [2005] 1 W.L.R. 1681, in the context of
the "common law" power of the Secretary of State to make extra-statutory payments to
widowers in order to achieve equality with the pensions provided solely to widows. The CA
had rejected the submissions [2003] EWCA Civ 875; [2003] 1 W.L.R. 2623 at [135] and the
Ram doctrine was not specifically considered in the HL but Lord Hoffmann at [47] felt that
they contained "a good deal of force".
[81] See, e.g. *R. (on the application of Abassi) v Secretary of State for Foreign and Commonwealth Affairs* [2002] EWCA Civ 1598; [2003] U.K.H.R.R. 76 at [106] ("It is not an answer
to a claim for judicial review to say that the source of the power of the Foreign Office is the
prerogative. It is the subject-matter that is determinative"); *Secretary of State for Foreign and
Commonwealth Affairs v Bancoult* [2007] EWCA Civ 498.

The discovery of Parliament's intent and use of Hansard

5–026   Because a body like Parliament can have no mind, it is not possible to "consolidate individual intentions into a collective, fictitious group intention".[82] Therefore the provisions of a statute need to be understood in the context of the purpose of the statute as a whole. This first requires an understanding of the context in which it was enacted and the "mischief" at which it was aimed. In *Pepper v Hart*,[83] the term in dispute was that of "cost" in s.63 of the Finance Act 1976. The question was whether teachers at independent schools whose children were educated at the school at much reduced fees should be taxed on the "marginal cost" to the school of educating those children (which would be a small sum), or on the "average cost" (which would be significantly higher). The issue had implications for the in-house benefits of many other employees as well. It was decided that the statutory purpose favoured the interpretation most favourable to the teachers. Departing from previous authority,[84] the House of Lords referred to parliamentary material to assist the construction of the ambiguous provision. Reference may now therefore be made to the parliamentary record to aid the construction of legislation. However, as Lord Browne Wilkinson made plain the exclusionary rule should be relaxed to permit reference to parliamentary materials only where: "(a) legislation is ambiguous or obscure, or leads to an absurdity; (b) the material relied on consists of one or more statements by a minister or other promoter of the Bill together if necessary with such other parliamentary material as is necessary to understand such statements and their effect; (c) the statements relied on are clear".[85]

5–027   This important step may aid the "purposive" or "teleological" approach to statutory interpretation. There are however, dangers: it encourages the artificial manufacture of parliamentary intent. Lobby groups seeking a particular interpretation of a statutory provision seek "Pepper v Hart" statements from the minister. The rule may even lead to the confounding of the presumption of parliamentary respect for certain fundamental constitutional principles where the intention clearly reveals that Parliament

---

[82] R. Dworkin, *Law's Empire* (1986), pp.335–336.

[83] [1993] A.C. 593.

[84] *Practice Statement (Judicial Precedent)* [1966] 1 W.L.R. 1234; *Davis v Johnson* [1979] A.C. 264; *Hadmor Productions Ltd v Hamilton* [1983] A.C. 191. *Hansard* reports have been directly referred to in some cases, e.g. *Pickstone v Freemans Plc* [1989] A.C. 66, and *Owen Bank v Bracco* [1992] A.C. 443 and in others (mainly involving national security issues) the Crown has referred to *Hansard* see, e.g. *R. v Secretary of State for the Home Department Ex p. Brind* [1991] A.C. 696.

[85] [1993] A.C. 640. It was not foreseen that any statement other than that of the minister or other promoter of the bill was likely to meet those criteria. The Australian Acts Interpretation Act 1901 (Cth) s.15AB(1) provides that extrinsic material may be referred to ascertain the meaning of a statutory provision where there is ambiguity or obscurity or where the ordinary meaning of the text leads to a result that is manifestly absurd or unreasonable. A non-exhaustive list of material may be considered which includes the second-reading speech of the minister (s.15AB(2)). Australian States have similar legislation.

wished, say, to oust the court's jurisdiction or to breach the rule of law.[86] It no doubt increases the cost of litigation in certain cases. Perhaps its most troubling aspect has been pointed out extra-judicially by Lord Steyn: "To give the executive, which promotes a Bill, the right to put its own gloss on a Bill is a substantial inroad on a constitutional principle, shifting legislative power from Parliament to the Executive".[87]

The House of Lords in *Spath Holme* sought to mitigate some of these 5–028 negative effects of *Pepper v Hart* by permitting reference to ministerial statements only to clarify the meaning of a statutory expression (such as the term "cost of a benefit" in *Pepper v Hart*), and not to clarify the scope of the ministerial power (such as, in *Spath Holme*, whether a statutory power to make delegated legislation to restrict rent levels could be employed for a purpose other than the control of inflation).[88] In the latter case, only if a minister were to give a "categorical assurance" to Parliament that a power would be used in a particular way, could the statement be admissible.[89]

While *Spath Holme* restricted recourse to statements in Parliament, the 5–029 House of Lords in *Wilson v First County Trust Ltd*[90] somewhat extended it in cases where the courts are, under the Human Rights Act 1998, considering whether a statute may be incompatible with the ECHR. Since the courts have to consider, in the context of some Convention rights, whether the legislation pursued a legitimate objective and did so proportionately, it was necessary to assess the "practical effect" of the legislation and thus it might occasionally be necessary to consider the words spoken by a minister in the course of a debate on a Bill. The House of Lords was clear that such a resort to the parliamentary record was only for the purpose of "background information". Lord Nicholls said that "the court is called upon to evaluate the proportionality of the legislation, not the adequacy of the minister's exploration of the policy options or of his explanations to Parliament. The Latter would contravene Art. 9 of the Bill of Rights 1689" (which provides that "the freedom of speech and debates

---

[86] D. Oliver, "*Pepper v Hart*: A Suitable Case for Reference to Hansard?" [1993] P.L. 5; T. Bates, "Parliamentary Material and Statutory Construction: Aspects of the Practical Application of *Pepper v Hart*" (1993) 14 Stat.L.R. 46, p.54; F. Bennion, "Executive Estoppel: *Pepper v Hart* Revisited" [2007] P.L.1.
[87] Lord Steyn, "*Pepper v Hart*; A Re-Examination" (2001) 21 O.J.L.S. 59. Lord Nicholls sought in *Jackson v Attorney General* [2005] UKHL 56; [2006] 1 A.C. 262 to rescue *Pepper v Hart* from the "cloud" under which Lord Steyn had placed it; his Lordship sought to invoke the post-enactment history of the Parliament Acts as an aid in their construction, a course which Lord Steyn "emphatically rejected" (at [99]), as did Lord Cooke in "A Constitutional Retreat" (2006) 122 L.Q.R. 224. See also Lord Nicholls' dicta in *R. (on the application of Spath Holme Ltd) v Secretary of State for the Environment, Transport and the Regions* [2001] 2 A.C. 349 at 396 and in *Wilson v First County Trust Ltd (No.2)* [2003] UKHL 40; [2004] 1 A.C. 816 at 827.
[88] *Spath Holme* [2001] 2 A.C. 349, Lords Nicholls and Cooke dissenting. Which also held that in interpreting a consolidated statute, reference could be had to earlier versions of the various consolidated acts.
[89] *Spath Holme* [2001] 2 A.C. 349 at 212 (Lord Bingham of Cornhill).
[90] *First County Trust Ltd* [2003] UKHL 40; [2004] 1 A.C. 816.

or proceedings in Parliament ought not to be impeached or questioned in any court or place out of Parliament").[91]

5–030   The European Court of Human Rights has, however, been more willing to have recourse to the reasoning (or lack of reasoning) of parliamentary debates. In *Hirst v United Kingdom (No.2)*[92] the Court considered whether the United Kingdom's blanket ban on convicted prisoners voting in general and local elections breached ECHR Art.3 of Protocol 1. It held that the *failure* by Parliament to give adequate reasons for the relevant statutes displayed lack of evidence that Parliament had assessed the proportionality of the ban.[93] The absence of the required justification led the Court to hold that the ban violated the prisoners' Convention rights. This approach is diametrically opposed to that of the House of Lords in *Wilson*, and may well violate Art.9 of the Bill of Rights 1689 if employed by a domestic court in the future.

5–031   The practice, since 1999, of publishing Explanatory Notes, prepared by departmental lawyers to accompany all bills and updated during the course of the bills' passage through Parliament, provide contextual information on the Bill that may be helpful in interpreting its provisions and purpose.

Always-speaking statutes

5–032   Reference to the parliamentary record and the "original intent" of a statute may be of limited value, especially in cases where its purpose is not defined, or in the case of a "framework Act", which deliberately leaves the definition of purpose to be developed in the course of the statute's implementation. However, even in cases where a term seems at the time of enactment relatively specific, its meaning over time may alter. For example, in *McCartan Turkington Breen v Times Newspapers Ltd*, the question was whether "public meeting" could include a press conference; Lord Bingham said, in relation to the Defamation Act (Northern Ireland) 1955: "Although the 1955 reference to "public meeting" derives from 1888, it must be interpreted in a manner which gives effect to the intention of the legislature *in the social and other conditions which obtain today*".[94] And Lord Steyn said that, unless they reveal a contrary intention, statutes are to be interpreted as always speaking.[95] The notion of the "always speaking" statute or constitution has been applied in a number of recent cases considering the interpretation of Commonwealth constitutions,[96] but it has

[91] *First County Trust Ltd* [2003] UKHL 40; [2004] 1 A.C. 816.
[92] (2006) 42 E.H.R.R. 41.
[93] At [78]–[85].
[94] [2001] 2 A.C. 277 at 292 (emphasis added).
[95] [2001] 2 A.C. 277 at 296.
[96] See, e.g. *Balkissoon Roodal v The State* [2003] UKPC 78; *Matthew v State of Trinidad and Tobago* [2004] UKPC 33; *R. v Ireland* [1998] A.C. 147; *Robinson v Secretary of State for Northern Ireland* [2002] UKHL 32; [2002] N.I. 390.

relevance to statutory interpretation in different contexts.[97] As we shall soon consider, courts should of course be careful in accepting ministerial or other statements of policy as the best evidence of a change in a statute's meaning.[98] However, especially in cases where the purpose of a statute has never been defined, either generally, or by reference to any particular relevant considerations, its purposes may well change over time. The area of land-use planning provides a vivid example.

Since 1947, when the systematic control of land use and development 5–033 was introduced by the Town and Country Planning Act of that year, local authorities and the Secretary of State for the Environment[99] on appeal, have possessed seemingly unlimited power to grant and refuse planning permission. The governing statute[100] requires "regard to be had" to the development plan as drafted by the local authority, but it has always allowed "other material considerations" also to be considered.[101] Conditions may be imposed upon permissions as the authority "think fit".[102]

The judicial construction of the Town and Country Planning Act over 5–034 time shows that the purposes pursued by a statutory scheme may not be static. When first enacted, the Act was concerned largely with what have been called physical criteria: questions such as access to the site, siting of the buildings, their height, bulk, set-back, mass, design and external appearance. It was held unequivocally that the "character of the use of the land, not the particular purposes of a particular occupier"[103] was the concern of planning, and therefore the authority could not seek to pursue social policies through its planning policies, for example, requiring developers to provide housing for the less well-off.[104] Over time, however, policies changed, and the courts accepted that the pursuit of "affordable housing" may be a material planning consideration.[105]

---

[97] In re McFarland [2004] UKHL 17; [2004] 1 W.L.R. 1289 at [25] (Lord Steyn: "legislation, whether primary or secondary, must be accorded an always-speaking construction unless the language and structure of the statute reveals an intention to impress on the statute a historic meaning. Exceptions to the general principle are a rarity"). For cases displaying a similar approach in New Zealand, see J. Burrows, Statute Law in New Zealand, 3rd edn. (2003), pp.177–199.
[98] On interpretation of policies, see 5–073–074.
[99] Formerly the Minister of Housing and Local Government; currently Secretary of State for Communities and Local Government, via the First Secretary of State (the official office of the Deputy Prime Minister).
[100] Now the Town and Country Planning Act 1990.
[101] Formerly the development plan and other material considerations had equal influence. Since 1991, however, the development plan shall be followed unless other material considerations "indicate otherwise"; Town and Country Planning Act 1990 s.54A.
[102] Town and Country Planning Act 1990 s.70(1).
[103] East Barnet UDC v British Transport Commission [1962] 2 Q.B. 484 (Lord Parker C.J.).
[104] R. v Hillingdon LBC Ex p. Royco Homes Ltd [1974] Q.B. 720.
[105] Mitchell v Secretary of State for the Environment [1994] J.P.L. 916, CA (upheld the refusal of permission to change the use of a house in multiple occupation to self-contained flats in order to meet the need for cheap rental accommodation); ECC Construction Ltd v Secretary of State for the Environment (1994) 69 P. & C.R. 51. Since these cases the law has changed to the extent that if a policy (such as to pursue affordable housing) is articulated in the development plan, then if the policy is lawful there is a presumption (under s.54A of the Act)

5-035   The experience of the interpretation of planning powers over time provides a salient reminder of the fluid nature of statutory purposes and the danger of freezing their purpose for all time through undue reliance upon the so-called "original intent" of the legislature (even if such intent is capable of discovery).[106] The goals of a scheme of public regulation can be gauged by a number of sources of public law. In the planning area these include statutory instruments as well as various policy documents known as Planning Policy Guidance (PPGs) issued by the relevant department from time to time on different subjects. Although not having the force of law, they nevertheless are considerations to which the decision-maker must have regard and therefore themselves fall within the scope of the statutory power. Interpretation of the contemporary scope of planning therefore requires some understanding of what planners on the ground actually do. The court will therefore need to be guided by those who keep abreast of changing social and professional expectations and approaches.

Interpretation in relation to constitutional principles and constitutional rights

5-036   The Human Rights Act 1998 now incorporates provisions of the European Convention on Human Rights into domestic law.[107] Breach of Convention rights by anyone exercising public functions therefore offends legality. However, what we now explicitly call constitutional rights, based on constitutional principle such as the rule of law, have always been acknowledged in the common law. In *Simms* the common law "principle of legality" was enunciated.[108] It means that, in the absence of express language or implication to the contrary, the courts will assume that even the most general statutory words were intended to be subject to the basic rights of the individual (in that case freedom of expression).

5-037   The rule of law as a fundamental constitutional principle will be considered in more detail in Chapter 11.[109] Of the common-law presumptions, the most influential in modern administrative law is one based on the rule of law, namely, that the courts should have the ultimate jurisdiction to pronounce on matters of law. Accordingly, only in the most exceptional

that the development plan should be followed: *Persimmon Homes (North West) Ltd v First Secretary of State and West Lancashire DC* [2006] EWHC 2643 (Admin). In addition, Local Government Act 2000 s.4 requires every local authority to prepare a "community strategy" for "promoting or improving the economic, social and environmental well-being of their area". Under the Planning and Compulsory Purchase Act 2004, s.62(5) local planning authorities must have regard to the "community strategy".

[106] If parliamentary records are resorted to in cases such as these they may well inhibit, if not used sensibly, the kind of incremental development of purpose seen in planning law.

[107] See Ch.13.

[108] *R. v Secretary of State for the Home Department Ex p. Simms* [2000] 2 A.C. 115 at 131 (Lord Hoffmann).

[109] See 11-059; and W. Sadurski, "Judicial Review of the protection of constitutional Rights (2002) 22 O.J.L.S. 275.

circumstances will the courts construe statutory language so as to endow a public body with exclusive authority to determine the ambit of its own powers.[110] Access of the individual to the courts, another fundamental requirement of the rule of law, is similarly recognized.[111] In *Raymond v Honey* it was held that the Home Secretary had no power to make prison rules to "authorise hindrance or interference with so basic a right" as the citizen's right of access to the court.[112] In *Leech (No.2)*,[113] the Court of Appeal held unlawful a regulation which permitted a prison governor to read and stop correspondence between a prisoner and his legal advisor. Despite a generally worded governing statute,[114] it was held, following *Raymond v Honey* that a prisoner retains all his rights which are not taken away expressly or by necessary implication. It was also held that a prisoner's right of unimpeded access to his solicitor was an inseparable part of the right of access to the courts themselves.[115]

Well before the principle of legality had been expressly articulated, the 5–038 courts made the presumption that Parliament does not intend to deprive the subject of his or her common-law rights and therefore, in the absence of express words or necessary intendment, statutes are not to be interpreted so as to authorise their interference. Among other rules of construction, express words are necessary to empower a public authority to

---

[110] See Ch.4.

[111] *See, e.g. In re Boaler* [1915] 1 K.B. 21 at 36 (Scrutton J.: "One of the valuable rights of every subject of the King is to appeal to the King in his Courts if he alleges that a civil wrong has been done to him, or if he alleges that a wrong punishable criminally has been done to him, or has been committed by another subject of the King"); *R. v Secretary of State for the Home Department Ex p. Leech* [1994] Q.B. 198, 210; *R. v Lord Chancellor Ex p. Witham* [1998] Q.B. 575 at [13] (Laws L.J.: "the common law has clearly given special weight to the citizens' right of access to the courts"). *Witham* distinguished in *R. v Lord Chancellor Ex p. Lightfoot* [2000] Q.B. 597 and *R. (on the application of Ewing) v Department for Constitutional Affairs* [2006] EWHC 504; [2006] 2 All E.R. 993. See also ECHR Art.6 on fair trails (See 7–119) and Art.13 on effective remedies (See 13–010).

[112] [1983] A.C. 1 at 11 (Lord Wilberforce).

[113] *R. v Secretary of State for Home Affairs Ex p. Leech (No.2)* [1994] Q.B. 198.

[114] Prison Act 1952 s.47(1), conferring power on the Home Secretary to make rules for the "regulation and management" of prisons and for the "classification, treatment, employment, discipline and control of persons required to be detained therein". The material part of the disputed rr.33(3) and 37A of the Prisons Rules 1964 provided that the prison governor could read every letter to or from a prisoner and stop any letter that was "objectionable or of inordinate length", except for correspondence between a prisoner who was party to proceedings in which a writ had been issued and his legal advisor.

[115] See also *Golder v UK* (1975) 1 E.H.R.R. 524 In *Drew v Attorney General* [2002] 1 N.Z.L.R. 58, the New Zealand CA struck down a prison regulation as ultra vires the Penal Institutions Act 1954. The regulation purported to deny prisoners legal representation in every disciplinary hearing. The empowering provision was in general terms, authorising the making of regulations to ensure "the discipline of inmates" including "prescribing the procedures for the hearing of such complaints". The Court reached this result by "applying common law principles of construction guided by the principles of natural justice", and did not need to refer to the guarantee of the observance of natural justice in the New Zealand Bill of Rights Act, s.27.

raise money from the subject,[116] or to warrant the exercise of a statutory power with retroactive effect.[117]

5-039   In Chapter 1 we outlined the constitutional justification for recognising and protecting rights in this way which, in the absence of a codified constitution or a domestic bill of rights, might otherwise seem perplexing.[118] For many years the courts have recognised rights such as the privilege against self-incrimination,[119] limitations on searches of premises and seizure of documents,[120] and even the ancient right to fish in tidal waters.[121] We now see "the common law's emphatic reassertion in recent years of the importance of constitutional rights",[122] among which are the following.[123]

- The right to life.[124]

[116] *Attorney General v Wilts United Dairies Ltd* (1921) 37 T.L.R. 884; *Brocklebank (T & J) Ltd v R.* [1924] 1 K.B. 647 (reversed on other grounds, [1925] 1 K.B. 252); *Liverpool Corp v Maiden (Arthur) Ltd* [1938] 4 All E.R. 200; *Davey Paxman & Co v Post Office, The Times,* November 16, 1954, which made it necessary to pass the Wireless Telegraphy (Validation of Charges) Act 1954; *City Brick & Terra Cotta Co v Belfast Corp* [1958] N.I. 44; *Daymond v Plymouth CC* [1976] A.C. 609 (see Water Charges Act 1976 ss.1, 2); *Congreve v Home Office* [1976] Q.B. 629; *Clark v University of Melbourne* [1978] V.R. 457 at 463–465. Unparliamentary taxation for the use of the Crown contravenes the Bill of Rights 1689; *cf. Cobb & Co v Kropp* [1967] 1 A.C. 141; *Customs and Excise Commissioners v Thorn Electrical Industries Ltd* [1975] 1 W.L.R. 1661 at 1673 (Kilbrandon L.J.: the presumption may have outlived its usefulness, "A modern Hampden would in many quarters be pilloried as a tax-evader"); *McCarthy and Stone (Developments) Ltd v Richmond-upon-Thames LBC* [1992] A.C. 48.
[117] See 5–00.
[118] *Watkins v Home Office* [2006] UKHL 17; [2006] 2 A.C. 395 at [47]–[64] (Lord Rogers).
[119] *Master Ladies Tailors Organisation v Minister of Labour and National Service* [1950] 2 All E.R. 525 at 528; *Howell v Falmouth Boat Construction Co* [1951] A.C. 837; *cf. Sabally and Njie v Attorney-General* [1965] 1 Q.B. 273. See also *R. v Pentonville Prison Governor Ex p. Azam* [1974] A.C. 18; *Scott v Aberdeen Corp* 1976 S.L.T. 141; *Re O (Disclosure Order)* [1991] 2 Q.B. 520.
[120] *Marcel v Commissioner of Police* [1992] Ch. 225 (approving the words of Lord Browne-Wilkinson in *Re O*); Lord Browne-Wilkinson, "The Infiltration of a Bill of Rights" [1992] P.L 397, 407.
[121] *Anderson v Alnwick DC* [1993] 1 W.L.R. 1156 (byelaws invalid for restricting digging for lugworms—if not ragworms—from the foreshore as bait). Another ancient right, the right to hunt, was referred to by Laws J. in *R. v Somerset CC Ex p. Fewings* [1995] 1 All E.R. 513. In the late 19th century the validity of a number of byelaws prohibiting the playing of musical instruments in the street was challenged by the Salvation Army. Sometimes the challenges were successful, e.g. *Powell* (1884) 51 L.T. 92 (Stephen J.: "the liberty of the subject always consists in doing something that a man is not forbidden to do"); *cf. Johnson v Croydon Corp* (1886) 16 Q.B.D. 708; *Slee v Meadows* (1911) 75 J.P 246; *Kruse v Johnson* [1898] 2 Q.B. 91.
[122] *D v Secretary of State for the Home Department* [2005] EWCA Civ 38; [2006] 1 W.L.R. 1003 at [130] (Brooke L.J.).
[123] For a somewhat different attempt to catalogue the rights, see Lord Lester of Herne Hill and D. Oliver (eds), *Constitutional Law and Human Rights* (1997). For an account of judicial review that reject rights, and promotes legitimacy, as the basis for judicial review, see T. Poole, "Legitimacy, Rights and Judicial Review" (2005) 25 O.J.L.S. 697.
[124] See, e.g. *R. v Secretary of State for the Home Department Ex p. Bugdaycay* [1987] A.C. 514 at 531 (Lord Bridge, in a deportation case "The most fundamental of human rights is the individual's right to life and when an administrative decision under challenge is said to be one which may put the applicant's life at risk, the basis of the decision must surely call for the most anxious scrutiny"); *R. v Secretary of State for the Home Department Ex p. Khawaja* [1984] A.C. 74 at 110–111 (Lord Scarman). See also ECHR Art.2, discussed at 7–128. For 'anxious scrutiny' see 11–086.

- The liberty of the person.[125]

- The doing of justice in public[126]

- The right to a fair hearing.[127]

- The prohibition on the retrospective imposition of criminal penalty.[128]

- Freedom of expression[129]

- The rights of access to legal advice and to communicate confidentially with a legal adviser under the seal of legal professional privilege.[130]

[125] See, e.g. *Bowditch v Balchin*(1850) 5 Exch. 378 (Pollock C.B.: "In a case in which the liberty of the subject is concerned, we cannot go beyond the natural construction of the statute"); *R. v Thames Magistrate Ex p. Brindle* [1975] 1 W.L.R. 1400, CA (Roskill L.J.: "When [a court] has to consider a matter involving the liberty of the individual, it must look at the matter carefully and strictly, and it must ensure that the curtailment of liberty sought is entirely justified by the Act relied on by those who seek that curtailment"); *Liversidge v Anderson* [1942] A.C. 206 (Lord Atkin, in his courageous dissent: "It has always been one of the pillars of freedom, one of the principles of liberty for which on recent authority we are now fighting, that the judges are no respecters of persons and stand between the subject and any attempted encroachments on his liberty by the executive, alert to see that any coercive action is justified in law; *Raymond v Honey* [1983] 1 A.C. 1 at 13 (Lord Wilberforce: "a basic right" of prisoners to enjoy liberty not necessary for their custody); "). See also ECHR Art.5, discussed at 13–070.
[126] See, e.g. *Scott v Scott* [1913] A.C. 417 at 477 (Lord Shaw of Dunfermline: "To remit the maintenance of constitutional right to the region of judicial discretion is to shift the foundations of freedom from the rock to the sand"); *R. (on the application of Malik) v Central Criminal Court* [2006] EWHC 1539; [2006] 4 All E.R. 1141 at [30]. See also ECHR Art.6 (see 7–119).
[127] See, e.g. *R. (on the application of McCann) v Manchester Crown Court* [2002] UKHL 39; [2003] 1 A.C. 787 at [29] (Lord Steyn: "Moreover, under domestic English law they undoubtedly have a constitutional right to a fair hearing in respect of such proceedings"—for a breach of an anti-social behaviour order).
[128] See, e.g. *Pierson v Secretary of State for the Home Department* [1998] A.C. 539 (Lord Steyn: "It is a general principle of the common law that a lawful sentence pronounced by a judge may not retrospectively be increased").
[129] See, e.g. *Attorney-General v Guardian Newspapers Ltd (No.2)* (the "Spycatcher case")[1990] 1 A.C. 109 at 283–284 (Lord Goff, remarking that in the field of freedom of speech there is no difference in principle between English law on the subject and ECHR Art.10); *Derbyshire CC v Times Newspapers Ltd* [1993] A.C. 534 at 547 (Lord Keith, in a case in which a local authority sought to sue for defamation: "it is of the highest public importance that a democratically elected body should be open to uninhibited criticism. The threat of a civil action for defamation must inevitably have an inhibiting effect on free Speech"); *R. v Secretary of State for the Home Department Ex p. Simms* [2000] 2 A.C. 115 (Lord Steyn, in a case concerning restrictions on prisoners communicating with journalists: "The starting point is the right of freedom of expression. In a democracy it is the primary right: without it an effective rule of law is not possible. Nevertheless, freedom of expression is not an absolute right. Sometimes it must yield to other cogent social interests"). See also ECHR Art.10, discussed at 13–089.
[130] See, e.g. *R. v Secretary of State for the Home Department Ex p. Daly* [2001] UKHL 26; [2001] 2 A.C. 532, [5] (Lord Bingham of Cornhill); *Colley v Council for Licensed Conveyancers (Right of Appeal)* [2001] EWCA Civ 1137; [2002] 1 W.L.R. 160 at [26] ("The right of access to a court is of fundamental constitutional importance. It is scarcely necessary to refer to authority for that obvious proposition"). See also ECHR Art.8 (discussed at 13–084).

245

- Limitations on searches of premises and seizure of documents.[131]

- Prohibition on the use of evidence obtained by torture.[132]

- That a British citizen has a fundamental right to live in, or return to, that part of the Queen's territory of which he is a citizen.[133]

- The deprivation of property rights without compensation.[134]

- The privilege against self-incrimination.[135]

- A duty on the State to provide subsistence to asylum-seekers.[136]

- Freedom of movement within the United Kingdom.[137]

5–040 The foundation in precedent for the presumption against the infringement of human rights in English domestic law is therefore solid. The foundation in theory is less apparent in the absence of a written constitution or

---

[131] See, e.g. *Marcel v Commissioner of Police* [1992] Ch. 225, CA, approving the words of Sir Nicholas Browne-Wilkinson V.-C. reported at [1991] 2 W.L.R. 1118 ("Search and seizure under statutory powers constitute fundamental infringements of the individual's immunity from interference by the state with his property and privacy—fundamental human rights"). See also ECHR Art.8 (discussed at 13–084).

[132] *A v Secretary of State for the Home Department* [2005] UKHL 71; [2006] 2 A.C. 221 at [11]–[12](Lord Bingham of Cornhill, holding the prohibition of evidence received through torture "more aptly categorized as a constitutional principle than as a rule of evidence" and "In rejecting the use of torture, whether applied to potential defendants or potential witnesses, the common law was moved by the cruelty of the practice as applied to those not convicted of crime, by the inherent unreliability of confessions or evidence so procured and by the belief that it degraded all those who lent themselves to the practice").

[133] See, e.g. *R v Secretary of State for the Foreign and Commonwealth Office Ex p. Bancoult* [2001] Q.B. 1067.

[134] See, e.g. *Central Control Board v Cannon Brewery Co* [1919] A.C. 744 at 752; *Bournemouth-Swanage Motor Road & Ferry Co v Harvey & Sons* [1929] 1 Ch. 686, 697; *Colonial Sugar Refining Co v Melbourne Harbour Trust Commrs* [1927] A.C. 343; *Consett Iron Co v Clavering Trustees* [1935] K.B. 42, 65; *Foster Wheeler Ltd v Green (E) & Son Ltd* [1946] Ch. 101, 108; *Hall v Shoreham-by-Sea UDC* [1964] 1 W.L.R. 240; *Hartnell v Minister of Housing and Local Government* [1965] A.C. 1134; *Langham v City of London Corp* [1949] 1 K.B. 208 at 212, 213; *Burmah Oil Co v Lord-Advocate* [1965] A.C. 75 (prerogative powers; *cf.* War Damage Act 1965). The presumption is still stronger where powers conferred by delegated legislation are in question: *Newcastle Breweries Ltd v R.* [1920] 1 K.B. 854. But the force of the presumption is weak in the context of modern planning legislation: *Westminster Bank Ltd v Beverley BC* [1971] A.C. 508; *Hoveringham Gravels Ltd v Secretary of State for the Environment* [1975] Q.B. 754; *R. v Hillingdon LBC Ex p. Royco Homes Ltd* [1974] Q.B. 720. See also ECHR Protocol 1, Art.1.

[135] See, e.g. *W v P* [2006] EWHC 1226, Ch; [2006] Ch. 549 (principle extends not only to the right to refuse to answer questions but also to incriminating material); *Master Ladies Tailors Organisation v Minister of Labour and National Service* [1950] 2 All E.R. 525 at 528; *Howell v Falmouth Boat Construction Co* [1951] A.C. 837. *cf. Sabally and Njie v Attorney General* [1965] 1 Q.B. 273; *R. v Pentonville Prison Governor Ex p. Azam* [1974] A.C. 18; *Scott v Aberdeen Corp* 1976 S.L.T. 141; *Re O* [1991] 2 W.L.R. 475 at 480.

[136] *R. v Secretary of State for Social Security Ex p. Joint Council for the Welfare of Immigrants* [1997] 1 W.L.R. 275, CA (Simon Brown L.J., citing Lord Ellenborough, C.J. in *R v Inhabitants of Eastbourne* (1803) 4 East 103: "As to there being no obligation for maintaining poor foreigners before the statutes ascertaining the different methods of acquiring settlements, the law of humanity, which is anterior to all positive laws, obliges us to afford them relief, to save them from starving").

[137] *R. v Secretary of State for the Home Department Ex p. McQuillan* [1995] 4 All E.R. 400 (Sedley J.).

enumerated bill of rights. However, fundamental rights can be properly viewed as integral features of a democratic state.[138] Freedom of speech is an obvious component of any democratic society, as are other rights, both those which address democratic procedures and those which address the treatment of individuals in a democracy.[139] Courts in other countries have recognised this explicitly.[140]

Interpretation of Convention rights

The Human Rights Act 1998 at s.3(1) places the following interpretive 5–041 obligation on courts: "So far as it is possible to do so, primary legislation and subordinate legislation must be read and given effect in a way which is compatible with the Convention rights".[141] The courts are also under an obligation, under s.2, to "take into account" the case law of the European Court of Human Rights and the former Commission.[142] These issues are considered in Chapter 13. What is important to note at this point is that the interpretive obligation created by s.3 of the HRA applies only where a Convention right, as defined by the HRA, exists; legislation may therefore be interpreted differently depending on whether or not a Convention right is involved.[143]

[138] See, e.g. R. Dworkin, "Equality, Democracy and the Constitution" (1990) Alberta L.R. 324 This view was enunciated in the UK By Lord Browne-Wilkinson, "The Infiltration of a Bill of Rights" [1992] P.L. 406, 406 ("Can it really be suggested that Parliament intended to authorise, for example a directive prohibiting broadcasts which are critical of the government for the time being in power, or of the Home Secretary himself?"); R. Cooke, "Fundamentals" [1988] N.Z.L.J. 158; Sir John Laws, "Is the Constitution the Guardian of Fundamental Rights?" [1993] P.L. 59; "Law and Democracy" [1995] P.L. 72; Sir Stephen Sedley, "The Sound of Silence: Constitutional Law without a Constitution" (1994) 110 L.Q.R. 270; M. Kirby, "Lord Cooke and Fundamental Rights", in P. Rishworth (ed.), *The Struggle for Simplicity in Law: Essays in Honour of Lord Cooke of Thorndon* (1998), p.331; M. Elliott, *The Constitutional Foundations of Judicial Review* (2001); M. Hunt, *Using Human Rights Law in English Courts* (1997), Ch.6; T. Allan, *Constitutional Justice: A Liberal Theory of the Rule of Law* (2001);); M. Kirby, "Deep-Lying Rights—A Constitutional Conversion Continues" (2004) 3 N.Z.J. of International and Public Law 195; D. Dyzenhaus, *The Constitution of Law* (2006). cf. T. Poole, "Legitimacy, Rights and Judicial Review" (2005) O.J.L.S. 697.
[139] T. Allan, *Law, Liberty and Justice* (1993).
[140] See, e.g. Israel—D. Kretzmer, "The New Basic Laws and Human Rights: A Mini-Revolution in Israeli Constitutional Law?" (1992) *Israel Law Review* 238; S. Goldstein, "Protection of Human Rights by Judges: The Israeli Experience" (1994) St Louis U.L.J. 605; A. Barak, The *Judge in a Democracy* (2006). Australia—H.P. Lee, "The Australian High Court and Implied Fundamental Guarantees" [1993] P.L. 606. South Africa—C. Hoexter, "The Principle of Legality in South African Administrative Law" (2004) Macquarie L.J. 165. See the endorsement of this approach in New Zealand in *R. v Pora* [2001] 2 N.Z.L.R. 37 at [53], [157], CA (Elias C.J., Tipping and Thomas JJ.); *Ngati Apa Ki Te Waipounama Trust v R* [2000] 2 N.Z.L.R. 659 at [82].
[141] See 13–040.
[142] See 13–034.
[143] *R. (on the application of Hurst) v HM Coroner for Northern District London* [2007] UKHL 13; [2007] 2 W.L.R. 726 at [10]–[12] (Lord Rodger).

Interpretation of European Community law

5–042　European Community law requires national courts interpreting national legislation to apply the principle of "conforming interpretation" in those situations in which there is a potential infringement of Community law, a matter we consider in Chapter 14.[144]

Interpretation and international law

5–043　In considering the approach of the domestic courts to international law,[145] a distinction must be drawn between (a) interpretive questions relating to treaties and similar instruments of international law which have been incorporated into national law—in the United Kingdom's dualist legal system, international treaties are not part of domestic law unless and until they are expressly incorporated by legislation; (b) the use that the domestic courts may make of treaties that have been ratified but not expressly incorporated into national law; and (c) customary international law.[146]

Incorporated treaties

5–044　The constitutional importance and complexity of two bodies of treaties require special consideration—the reception of Convention rights from the ECHR into domestic law by the Human Rights Act 1998[147] and the treaties establishing the European Union and European Community.[148] Here we focus on other treaties. It is wrong to think of incorporation as a single phenomenon; a treaty may be received into and given effect in the law of England and Wales in more than one way. The most straightforward situation is where an Act of Parliament is enacted to bring a treaty into English law, but even here there are various drafting techniques. In some Acts, the text or part of the text, of a treaty has been "copied out"; in others parliamentary counsel have used English statutory language to give general effect to the treaty (but which may, upon proper interpretation, confer rights that are narrower or broader than those contained in the treaty). There are other ways of bringing about incorporation—including

[144] See 14–046.
[145] We deal with the following aspects of the relationship between judicial review and international law: see 3–043(the extent to which questions international law falls outside the jurisdiction of the Administrative Court or is non-justiciable); interpretation of international law (see 5–043); whether international law may be a relevant consideration to which a public authority ought to have regard in exercising a public function (see 5–123); and the court's adaptation of the unreasonableness test to "anxious scrutiny" to decisions which affect fundamental rights, some of which may be reflected in unincorporated treaty provisions (See 11–086).
[146] See generally S. Fatima, *Using International Law in Domestic Courts* (2005); D. Feldman, "The internationalization of public law and its impact on the United Kingdom", Ch.5 in J. Jowell and D. Oliver (eds), *The Changing Constitution*, 6th edn (2007).
[147] See Ch.13.
[148] See Ch.14.

what may variously be called "indirect" or "for practical purposes" or an "informal mode" of incorporation. Thus, s.2 of the Asylum and Immigration Act 1993 provides, under the heading "Primacy of the Convention" that "Nothing in the immigration rules [made under the Immigration Act 1971] shall lay down any practice which would be contrary to the Convention"—a reference to the Convention and Protocol relating to the Status of Refugees.[149]

If a treaty has been incorporated (by whatever technique) into domestic law, the question then is how should the courts approach the task of interpreting the treaty. The language of treaties is often broader and more open-textured than the precise wording that is the earmark of English statutory drafting. The Vienna Convention on the Law of Treaties 1969, especially Arts 31–33, provides the basic guidelines.[150] Generally, it can be said that:[151] the starting point is the language and structure of the text in question; words should be given the natural and ordinary meaning, avoiding over-sophisticated analysis and "prolonged debate about the niceties of language";[152] treaties may contain implied as well as express provisions;[153] where a provision is ambiguous, "the interpretation which is less onerous to the State owing the Treaty obligation is to be preferred"[154] and regard may be had to the traveaux préparatoires; good faith is required in the interpretation and performance of a treaty;[155] the provisions "must be read together as part an parcel of the scheme" of the treaty;[156] relevant reservations and derogations must be considered;[157] and, above all, a broad, purposive interpretation is required.[158] The court must not lose sight of the fact that it is an international legal instrument that is being interpreted, and that its concepts have a meaning that is autonomous of the particularities of a domestic legal system.[159] Interpretations reached by courts in other national systems is of persuasive authority;[160] inevitably, however, courts in different legal systems may reach interpretations that are difficult to reconcile.

5–045

---

[149] Cmnd 9171 and Cmnd 3906. See *R. (on the application of European Roma Rights Centre) v Immigration Officer, Prague Airport* [2004] UKHL 55; [2005] 2 A.C. 1.

[150] In force since January 27, 1980 and strictly speaking applying only to treaties in force after that date—but the main provisions concerning interpretation (Arts 31 and 32) reflect customary international law: see European Roma Centre [2004] UKHL 55; [2005] 2 A.C. 1 at [18].

[151] Fatima (2005) Ch.4 and the cases surveyed there.

[152] *Horvath v Secretary of State for the Home Department* [2001] 1 A.C. 489 at 508.

[153] As the ECHR and its interpretation by the European Court of Human Rights amply illustrate: see Ch.13.

[154] *R. (on the application of Marchiori) v Environment Agency* [2002] EWCA Civ 3; [2002] Eu. L.R. 225 at [58].

[155] *European Roma Centre* [2004] UKHL 55; [2005] 2 A.C. 1 at [19].

[156] *R. (on the application of Mullen) v Secretary of State for the Home Department* [2004] UKHL 18; [2005] 1 A.C. 1 at [38].

[157] *R. v Secretary of State for the Home Department Ex p. Ahmed (Mohammed Hussain)* [1999] Imm. A.R. 22, 33 (Lord Woolf M.R.).

[158] *Horvath* [2001] 1 A.C. 489 at 494–495.

[159] *R. (on the application of Adan (Lul Omar)) v Secretary of State for the Home Department* [2001] 2 A.C. 477 at 515–516; *Mullen* [2004] UKHL 18; [2005] 1 A.C. 1 at [36].

[160] *Forthergill v Monarch Airlines* [1981] A.C. 251 at 284.

Unincorporated treaties

5-046 The dualist principles that underpin the British constitution—which require a divide between ratifying treaties (an action of the executive branch of government) and law-making (the province of Parliament and the courts)—has the consequence of limiting the scope for utilising unincorporated treaties as part of a judicial review claim.[161] Unincorporated treaties have no direct effect in the courts of England and Wales and the courts accordingly generally lack jurisdiction to interpret them (on which point see Chapter 3).[162] That is not to say, however, that they have no effect. First, circumstances may arise in which a minister, by ratifying a treaty, creates a legitimate expectation that government decision-making and policy will follow the terms of that treaty; we consider this possibility in Chapter 12.[163] Secondly, unincorporated treaties may be used as an aid to interpretation of domestic legislation (and in interpreting the treaty, the approach described above in relation to incorporated treaties applies). Where an ambiguity in domestic legislation arises, the English courts will—in the absence of clear statutory words to the contrary—presume that Parliament intended to legislate in conformity with the international law obligations of the United Kingdom on the same subject matter.[164] The courts adopt a similar approach in relation to developing the common law.[165]

Customary international law

5-047 Customary international law is a source of English common law;[166] none of the issues relating to incorporation are therefore relevant. Customary international law consists of those norms about which there is clear consensus among States, which are based on general and consistent practice and a sense of legal obligation.[167]*Jus cogens* (peremptory norms) is that body of customary international law comprising fundamental principles which cannot be derogated from by States.[168]

[161] Whether this constitutional principle ought to continue to apply to human rights treaties has been questioned: Dame Rosalind Higgins, "The Relationship between International and Regional Human Rights Norms and Domestic Law" (1992) 18 *Commonwealth Law Bulletin* 1268; *Re McKerr's Application for Judicial Review* [2004] UKHL 12; [2004] 1 W.L.R. 807 at [49]–[50] (Lord Steyn).

[162] *R. v Lyons (Isidore Jack) (No.3)* [2002] UKHL 44; [2003] 1 A.C. 976 at [27]; see further 3–021.

[163] See 12–025.

[164] A.V. Dicey, *An Introduction to the Study of the Law of the Constitution*, 10th edn. (1959), pp.62–63; *R. v Secretary of State for the Home Department Ex p. Brind* [1991] 1 A.C. 696 at 747, 760.

[165] Sir John Laws, "Is the High Court the Guardian of Fundamental Human Rights? [1993] P.L. 59, 66–67; *Lyons* [2002] UKHL 44; [2003] 1 A.C. 976 at [27]; *Reynolds v Times Newspapers Ltd* [2001] 2 A.C. 127 at 223.

[166] R. Jennings and A. Watts (eds), *Oppenheim's International Law*, 9th edn (1992), p.57; *R. v Jones (Margaret)* [2006] UKHL 16; [2007] 1 A.C. 136 at [11] (Lord Bingham, citing "old and high authority").

[167] *European Roma Rights Centre* [2004] UKHL 55; [2005] 2 A.C. 1 at [23].

[168] See, e.g. prohibition of torture *(A v Secretary of State for the Home Department* [2005] UKHL 71; [2006] 2 A.C. 221).

It falls outside the scope of this book to give a comprehensive account of 5–048
this field, but the following are illustrations of how customary international
law may be used. Principles of customary international law were recognised
in relation to: the immunity from criminal process of a head of state;[169] the
right to admit, exclude and expel aliens;[170] and prohibition of torture.[171]
But the courts have held that: there is no right of conscientious objection
to military service;[172] no duty on governments to provide diplomatic
assistance to protect citizens from actions of foreign states;[173] and maintenance of nuclear weapons is not contrary to international law.[174]

Mandatory and directory duties and powers

When Parliament prescribes the manner or form in which a duty is to be 5–049
performed or a power exercised, it seldom lays down what will be the legal
consequences of failure to observe its prescriptions. The courts have
therefore formulated their own criteria for determining whether the
prescriptions are to be regarded as mandatory, in which case disobedience
will normally render invalid what has been done, or as directory, in which
case disobedience may be treated as an irregularity not affecting the
validity of what has been done.[175]

These terms, like others we have been considering in this chapter, often 5–050
cause more problems than they solve. The law relating to the effect of
failure to comply with statutory requirements thus resembles an inextrica-
ble tangle of loose ends and judges have often stressed the impracticability
of specifying exact rules for the assignment of a provision to the appropri-

[169] R. v Bow Street Metropolitan Stipendiary Magistrate Ex p. Pinochet Ugarte (No.3) [2000] 1
A.C. 147 at 201, 265, 268.
[170] European Roma Rights Centre [2004] UKHL 55; [2005] 2 A.C. 1 at [11].
[171] A [2005] UKHL 71; [2006] 2 A.C. 221 at [34].
[172] R. (on the application of Septet) v Secretary of State for the Home Department [2003]
UKHL 15; [2003] 1 W.L.R. 856.
[173] R. (on the application of Abassi) v Secretary of State for Foreign and Commonwealth Affairs
[2002] EWCA Civ 1598; [2003] U.K.H.R.R. 76.
[174] R. (on the application of Marchiori) v Environment Agency [2002] EWCA Civ 3; [2002] Eu.
L.R. 225.
[175] In some cases it has been said that there must be "substantial compliance" with the
statutory provisions if the deviation is to be excused as a mere irregularity, e.g. Coney v
Choyce [1975] 1 W.L.R. 222 (where the attempt bona fide to comply and the absence of
prejudice from the non-compliance are also emphasised). Grunwick Processing Laboratories
Ltd v ACAS [1978] A.C. 655 at 691–692 (where mandatory duties in absolute form were
contrasted with duties to be performed "as far as reasonably practicable"); Donnelly v
Marrickville Municipal Council [1973] 2 N.S.W.L.R. 390 at 398. Authorities are reviewed in
Cullimore v Lyme Regis Corp [1962] 1 Q.B. 718; Graham v Attorney General [1966]
N.Z.L.R. 937 at 953–961; Parisienne Basket Shoes Pty Ltd v Whyte (1938) 59 C.L.R. 369;
Scurr v Brisbane City Council (1973) 133 C.L.R. 242 (an approach that still applies where the
Act specifies that substantial compliance suffices); Queensland v Queensland Land Council
Aboriginal Corp (2002) 195 A.L.R. 106 at 169. For further comment on the Australian
approach see See 12–080 et seq. and M. Aronson, B. Dyer and M. Groves, Judicial Review of
Administrative Action, 3rd edn. (2004), pp.323–325.

ate category. Nevertheless, it is possible to state the main principles that the courts have generally followed and to illustrate their application in a few settings. In brief, the principles are as follows:

(a) A decision or action is in general to be treated as valid until struck down by a court of competent jurisdiction. This issue has been discussed above[176] and need not be repeated now.

(b) Statutory words requiring things to be done as a condition of making a decision, especially when the form of words requires that something "shall" be done, raise an inference that the requirement is "mandatory" or "imperative" and therefore that failure to do the required act renders the decision unlawful.

(c) The above inference does not arise when the statutory context indicates that the failure to do the required act is of insufficient importance, in the circumstances of the particular decision, to render the decision unlawful.

(d) The courts, in appropriate cases and on accepted grounds may, in their discretion refuse to strike down a decision or action or to award any other remedy.

5–051　One of the causes of the loose ends entangling this area of the law is the failure to distinguish factors that rebut the presumption that a requirement is legally required (proposition (c) above) from factors that justify the court's exercise of discretion to excuse the breach of a legal requirement (proposition (d) above). The first set of factors raises questions about the lawful consequence of the requirement, which is not dependent upon the exercise of judicial discretion. The second set of factors raises questions about the appropriate use of judicial discretion in relation to the grant of a remedy.

5–052　A second reason for the tangle in this area is the use of the terms "mandatory" and "directory"; the latter term is especially misleading. All statutory requirements are prima facie mandatory. However, in some situations the violation of a provision will, in the context of the statute as a whole and the circumstances of the particular decision, not violate the objects and purpose of the statute. Condoning such a breach does not, however, render the statutory provision directory or discretionary. The breach of the particular provision is treated in the circumstances as not involving a breach of the statute taken as a whole. Furthermore, logically, a provision cannot be mandatory if a court has discretion not to enforce it.

5–053　Lord Hailsham expressed this point well in *London and Clydeside Estates v Aberdeen District Council* where he distinguished two ends of a spectrum. At the one end are cases "where a fundamental obligation may have been so outrageously and flagrantly ignored or defied that the subject

[176] See 4–061 et seq.

may safely ignore what has been done and treat it as having no legal consequence". At the other end of the spectrum the defect may be "so nugatory or trivial" that the authority can proceed on the assumption that "if the subject is so misguided as to rely on the fault, the courts will decline to listen to his complaint". Lord Hailsham considered that language like "mandatory", "directory", "void", "voidable" and "nullity" only served to confuse the situation and stretch or cramp the facts of a case into rigid legal categories or "on a bed of Procrustes invented by lawyers for convenient exposition".[177]

In order to decide whether a presumption that a provision is "manda- 5–054 tory" is in fact rebutted, the whole scope and purpose of the enactment must be considered, and one must assess "the importance of the provision that has been disregarded, and the relation of that provision to the general object intended to be secured by the Act".[178] In Assessing the importance of the provision, particular regard should be given to its significance as a protection of individual rights; the relative value that is normally attached to the rights that may be adversely affected by the decision, and the importance of the procedural requirement in the overall administrative scheme established by the statute. Breach of procedural or formal rules is likely to be treated as a mere irregularity if the departure from the terms of the Act is of a trivial nature,[179] or if no substantial prejudice has been suffered by those for whose benefit the requirements were introduced.[180] But the requirement will be treated as "fundamental" and "of central

[177] [1980] 1 W.L.R. 182 at 189–90 (the issue was whether under the Town and Country Planning legislation it was a mandatory requirement that a certificate issued by a local authority include a statement setting out the applicant's right of appeal to the Secretary of State—it was). See also *R. v Tower Hamlets LBC Ex p. Tower Hamlets Combined Traders Association* [1994] C.O.D. 325 (Sedley J. analyses the *obiter* remark of Lord Hailsham in *Clydeside* and concludes that two points were being made: first, that the consequences of non-compliance are variable, and secondly, that the grant of relief is discretionary). On discretion to withhold remedies, see 18–048.
[178] *Howard v Bodington* (1877) 2 P.D. 203 at 211; *Spicer v Holt* [1977] A.C. 987 (compliance with procedure for administering breath-tests, a condition precedent for valid conviction); *Grunwick Processing* [1978] A.C. 655; *Sheffield City Council v Graingers Wines Ltd* [1978] 2 All E.R. 70; *Tower Combined Traders Association [1994] C.O.D. 325; Wang v Commissioner of Inland Revenue* [1994] 1 W.L.R. 1286, PC.
[179] *R. v Dacorum Gaming Licensing Committee Ex p. EMI Cinemas and Leisure Ltd* [1971] 3 All E.R. 666 (minor typographical error in notice of application for licence could be disregarded, despite general strictness of statutory requirements); *R. v Inner London Betting Licensing Committee Ex p. Pearcy* [1972] 1 W.L.R. 421 (unimportant additional words added to advertisement and notice of application).
[180] See, e.g. *R. v Liverpool City Council* [1975] 1 W.L.R. 701; *Coney v Choyce* [1975] 1 W.L.R. 222; *George v Secretary of State for the Environment* (1979) 250 E.G. 339; *Main v* (1985) 49 P. & C.R. 26, CA; cf. *London and Clydeside Estates* [1980] 1 W.L.R. 182 at 195 (Lord Fraser: "The validity of a certificate is not in my opinion dependent on whether the appellants were actually prejudiced by it or not").

importance" if members of the public might suffer from its breach.[181] Another factor influencing the categorisation is whether there may be another opportunity to rectify the situation; of putting right the failure to observe the requirement.[182]

5–055   The principle that the whole scope and purpose of the Act must be looked at is illustrated by a decision of the Court of Appeal in which the validity of a reference to a rent tribunal was challenged on the ground that the tenant had given the name of the wrong landlord. The minister, who had power to make regulations with regard to proceedings before these tribunals, had made regulations requiring (among other things) that the name of the landlord be specified in an application. The court held that the regulations were directory only and that the reference was therefore valid; the minister had no power to impose conditions of validity when Parliament itself had not done so, and it could be assumed to have omitted to do so because it had contemplated that applications would often be made by tenants who had "no lawyers to advise them and no regulations by their side".[183] If, on the other hand, the primary purpose is to promote the public interest rather than the interests of individuals,[184] the courts are likely to take a strict view of minor deviations from a statutory code of procedure on the part of persons seeking to obtain exemption from the prescribed system of regulation.[185]

5–056   Some classes of procedural requirements are so important that they will nearly always be held to be "mandatory". For example, an authority which fails to comply with a statutory duty to give prior notice or hold a hearing or make due inquiry or consider objections in the course of exercising discretionary powers affecting individual rights will seldom find the courts casting an indulgent eye upon its omissions.[186] Non-compliance or

---

[181] *R. v Lambeth LBC Ex p. Sharp* (1988) 55 P. & C.R. 232 (notice published by local authority failed to specify the period within which representation should be made to a planning application. The CA held that these requirements were "fundamental" and "strict").
[182] *Brayhead (Ascot) Ltd v Berkshire CC* [1964] 2 Q.B. 303; *London & Clydeside Estates* [1980] 1 W.L.R. 182.
[183] *Francis Jackson Development Ltd v Hall* [1951] 2 K.B. 488 at 493; distinguished in *Chapman v Earl* [1968] 1 W.L.R. 1315 where, on somewhat similar facts, a different intent was attributed to the provisions of a subsequent Rent Act; *cf. R. v Devon and Cornwall Rent Tribunal Ex p. West* (1975) 29 P. & C.R. 316.
[184] *cf. Kammins Ballrooms Co Ltd v Zenith Investments (Torquay) Ltd* [1971] A.C. 850; *Mercantile and General Reinsurance Co Ltd v Groves* [1974] Q.B. 43 (time limit imposed for the benefit of one party waivable by him); *cf. Meah v Sector Properties Ltd* [1974] 1 W.L.R. 547, *Gyle-Thompson v Wall Street (Properties) Ltd* [1974] 1 W.L.R. 123; *Dedman v British Building etc. Ltd* [1974] 1 W.L.R. 171.
[185] See, e.g. *R. v Pontypool Gaming Licensing Committee Ex p. Risca Cinemas Ltd* [1970] 1 W.L.R. 1299 (time limit for submitting advertisement of bingo licence application exceeded). *cf. Howard v Secretary of State for the Environment* [1975] Q.B. 235 (only the filing of the notice but not the statement of the grounds of appeal to the minister against an enforcement notice was held to be mandatory); *Button v Jenkins* [1975] 3 All E.R. 585; *R. v Urbanowski* [1976] 1 W.L.R. 455 (time limitations within which magistrates must state a case and accused person be tried only directory: judge of Crown Court may extend time).
[186] *Grunwick* [1978] A.C. 655 (statutory duty was to ascertain the opinions of affected workers; the means by which this was to be done, however, were entrusted to the discretion

inadequate compliance with an express duty to give particulars of rights of appeal may render an administrative determination invalid.[187] A provision requiring consultation with named bodies before a statutory power is exercised is also likely to be construed as mandatory.[188]

The practical effects of the exercise of a power upon the rights of 5–057 individuals will often determine whether the relevant formal and procedural rules are to be classified as mandatory. Thus, where powers are conferred to issue orders or certificates that affect civil liberties or rights to compensation, the courts have insisted that the decision-maker must closely observe all material requirements as to form.[189] For many years the formalities surrounding the issue, service and content of enforcement notices (preliminary to taking measures to secure compliance with planning controls) were construed rigorously and literally by the courts; later they tended to consider whether disregard of a formal or procedural requirement by the local planning authority might have substantially prejudiced the developer.[190] The principle that failure to observe formal or procedural rules in the administrative process may be venial if no substantial prejudice

of the authority); *Donnelly v Marrickville Municipal Council* [1973] 2 N.S.W.L.R. 390. However, substantial compliance with statutory provisions prescribing the method of giving notice may suffice: *Smith v East Sussex CC* (1977) 76 L.G.R. 332. For an illustration of the vitiating effect of failure to give sufficient notice where this entailed a breach of a statutory duty to afford interested parties a genuine opportunity of making representations against a proposed scheme for comprehensive schools, see *Lee v Department of Education and Science* (1967) 66 L.G.R. 211; *Lee v Enfield LBC* (1967) 66 L.G.R. 195; *Legg v ILEA* [1972] 1 W.L.R. 1245; cf. *Coney v Choyce* [1975] 1 W.L.R. 422; *R. v Southwark Juvenile Court Ex p. J* [1973] 1 W.L.R. 1300 (provision for attendance at hearing by a non-party directory, but decision quashed for lacking appearance of fairness).
[187] See, e.g. *London and Clydeside Estates* [1980] 1 W.L.R. 182; *Agricultural, Horticultural and Forestry Industry Training Board v Kent* [1970] 2 Q.B. 19; *Rayner v Stepney Corp* [1911] 2 Ch. 312; cf. *Jones v Lewis* (1973) 25 P. & C.R. 375; *George v Secretary of State for the Environment* (1979) 250 E.G. 339; *Skinner and King v Secretary of State for the Environment* [1978] J.P.L. 842 (statutory duty to serve notice on both joint tenants not discharged by service on one, although relief may not be granted in the absence of substantial prejudice); *R. v Chief Immigration Officer, Manchester Airport Ex p. Insah Begum* [1973] 1 W.L.R. 141 (statutory duty to give notice of refusal of entry to immigrant discharged by delivery to agent); *Re Bowman* [1932] 2 K.B. 621.
[188] *May v Beattie* [1927] 2 K.B. 353; *R. v Minister of Transport Ex p. Skylark Motor Coach Co* (1931) 47 T.L.R. 325; *Agricultural etc. Industry Training Board v Aylesbury Mushrooms Ltd* [1972] 1 W.L.R. 190; *Hamilton City v Electricity Distribution Commission* [1972] N.Z.L.R. 605.
[189] *Hill v Ladyshore Coal Co* (1930) Ltd [1936] 3 All E.R. 299; Enraght v Lord Penzance (1881) 6 Q.B.D. 376 at 461, 463, 471–472; *R. v Secretary of State for the Home Department Ex p. Budd* [1942] 2 K.B. 14.
[190] Town and Country Planning Act 1990 s.174(2) empowering the Secretary of State on an appeal against an enforcement notice to correct immaterial informalities, defects and errors. For the scope of this amending power, see *Miller-Mead v Minister of Housing and Local Government* [1963] 2 Q.B. 196; *R. v Endersby Properties Ltd* (1976) 32 P. & C.R. 399 (distinguishing *East Riding CC v Park Estate (Bridlington) Ltd* [1957] A.C. 223); *Graddage v Haringey LBC* [1975] 1 W.L.R. 241 (omission of official's signature invalidated notice demanding payment for work done to make houses fit for human habitation—an example of an application of the strict approach to formal irregularities).

has been caused to those immediately affected now appears in a number of statutory contexts.[191]

5-058   In *Wang v The Commissioner of Inland Revenue*,[192] the Privy Council held that the breach of a time provision by the Inland Revenue of Hong Kong would not "deprive the decision-maker of jurisdiction and render any decision which he purported to make null and void". It is noteworthy that although the terms "mandatory" and "directory" were used in argument, they were nowhere employed in the judgment. Two principal reasons were given for the Board's decision. The first was that the Inland Revenue's decision resulted in "no real prejudice for the taxpayer in question by reason of the delay". The second reason was that to invalidate the decision "would not only deprive the Government of revenue, it would also be unfair to other taxpayers who need to shoulder the burden of Government expenditure"[193] (a more dubious reason, as we shall presently suggest).

5-059   In a number of more recent cases our highest courts have displayed flexibility in the face of breaches of imperative language. In *R. v Immigration Appeal Tribunal Ex p. Jeyeanthan*[194] the Court of Appeal considered the consequence of the Secretary of State failing to use a prescribed form for applying for leave from the Special Adjudicator to the Immigration Appeals Tribunal. The only difference between the form used and the prescribed form was the absence of a declaration of truth. Lord Woolf, for the Court, adopted the dictum of Lord Hailsham in *London & Clydesdale Estates*.[195] Eschewing a rigid adherence to the language of "mandatory" and "directory" (although it was to be regarded as a "first step"),[196] it was held that the matter should be judged upon the overall intent of the legislation, and the interests of justice In particular, if there had been "substantial compliance" with the requirement, and if the irregularity was capable of being waived, then whether the non-compliance could be justified depended upon the consequences of non-compliance which, in the circumstances of that case, did not materially prejudice the appellants.

---

[191] See, e.g. Town and Country Planning Act 1990 s.288(1). For an illustration of non-compliance with minor formal statutory requirements being held not to have caused substantial prejudice, see *Gordondale Investments Ltd v Secretary of State for the Environment* (1971) 70 L.G.R. 15; *cf. McCowan v Secretary of State for Scotland*, 1972 S.L.T. 163 (property-owner deprived of opportunity to object to compulsory purchase order through failure to serve notice on him).

[192] [1994] 1 W.L.R. 1286.

[193] *cf. London & Clydesdale Estates* [1980] 1 W.L.R. 182 at 195 (Lord Fraser): "the validity of the certificate is not in my opinion dependent on whether the appellants were actually prejudiced by it or not". See also: *Devan Nair v Yong Kuan Teik* [1967] 2 A.C. 31; *James v Minister of Housing and Local Government* [1966] 1 W.L.R. 171, C.A; *R. v Inspector of Taxes Ex p. Clarke* [1974] Q.B. 220; *cf. R. v Liverpool City Council Ex p. Liverpool Taxi Fleet Operators' Association* [1975] 1 W.L.R. 701 at 706 (requirement to state reasons directory only, but decision could be set aside if applicant showed that he had been thereby prejudiced); *R. v Fairford Justices Ex p. Brewster* [1976] Q.B. 600 (magistrates may lose jurisdiction by a delay in issuing a summons that prejudices the accused, despite the absence of a statutory time limitation).

[194] [2000] 1 W.L.R. 354; also *Credit Suisse v Allerdale BC* [1997] Q.B. 306.

[195] [1980] 1 W.L.R. 182.

[196] At [16].

A similar approach was taken by the Privy Council in *Charles*,[197] where 5–060
the Board upheld a failure to observe time limits laid down by regulations
dealing with discipline in the public service in Trinidad and Tobago. In
Attorney General's Reference (No.3 of 1999),[198] the House of Lords
considered a breach of a duty to destroy the fingerprints and DNA samples
of a defendant cleared of an offence. The DNA samples then led to his
subsequent conviction for rape. Again the mandatory/directory distinction
was ignored in favour of a test based upon the intent of Parliament and the
consequence of non-compliance. A unanimous House held that the prosecution was valid[199] and this approach was repeated in *R v Soneji* where the
House of Lords, again unanimously, refused to quash two confiscation
orders despite a clear defect in the procedure,[200] Lord Steyn considering
that the mandatory/directory distinction had "outlived its usefulness".[201]

A similar approach has been adopted in the courts of Australia, New 5–061
Zealand and Canada. The Australian High Court has criticised the "elusive
distinction between directory and mandatory" as well as the division of
directory acts into those which have substantially been complied with and
those which have not. The Court considers the test for determining the
issue of validity is "to ask whether it was a purpose of the legislation that
an act done in breach of the provision should be invalid".[202] In New
Zealand Cooke J. said that whether non-compliance with a procedural
requirement is fatal depends upon "its place in the scheme of the Act or
regulations and the degree and seriousness of the non-compliance".[203] In
Canada too the mandatory/directory distinction has been departed from
and the question asked: "would it be seriously inconvenient to regard the
performance of some statutory direction as an imperative?"[204]

The breakdown of inappropriate technical distinctions is obviously to be 5–062
applauded, as is the need to concentrate upon legislative purpose and the
requirements of justice, but there is danger in the courts readily arrogating
to themselves the power to dispense with procedural or other duties. In the
mind of the public, law-breaking should not be condoned, especially by
courts of law. On the other hand, excessive legalism serves no useful
purpose. In the result, the circumstances in which a flawed decision should
be held valid should be narrowly drawn. The criteria suggested by Tipping
J. in *Charles* would seem acceptable: endorsing the validity of a breach of a
time limit, he noted that "in the present case the delays were in good faith,

---

[197] *Charles v Judicial and Legal Services Commission* [2002] UKPC 34; [2003] 1 L.R.C. 422.
[198] [2001] 2 A.C. 91.
[199] Lord Steyn (at 117–118); Lord Cooke (at 120–121); Lord Clyde (at 121).
[200] [2005] UKHL 49; [2006] 1 A.C. 340 (the statute provided that the orders could be
postponed only where there were established exceptional circumstances. Since these had not
been established, the CA had held that the postponement rendered the orders invalid).
[201] At [23].
[202] *Project Blue Sky Inc v Australian Broadcasting Authority* (1998) 194 C.L.R. 355 at para.93.
[203] *New Zealand Institute of Agricultural Science Inc v Ellesmere County* [1976] 1 N.Z.L.R.
630 at 636.
[204] *British Columbia (Attorney General) v Canada (Attorney-General): An Act respecting the
Vancouver Island Railway (Re)* [1994] 2 S.C.R. 41 (Iacobucci J.).

they were not lengthy and they were entirely understandable. The appellant suffered no material prejudice; no fair trial considerations were or could have been raised, and no fundamental human rights are in issue".[205]

5–063   Evans J.A. approached the criteria from a different perspective in the Canadian Federal Court of Appeal: "the more serious the public inconvenience and injustice likely to be caused by invalidating the resulting administrative action, including frustrating the purposes of the legislation, public expense and hardship to third parties, the less likely it is that a court will conclude that legislative intent is best implemented by a declaration of invalidity".[206] This statement is helpful except perhaps in the value it places upon "inconvenience" and "expense" as a factor to be taken into account on the question of validity. As we noted,[207] these utilitarian considerations were also raised by Lord Slynn in the Privy Council to justify the validity of a breach of a time limit in *Wang*.[208] Is administrative inconvenience a proper reason for rebutting the presumption that a decision which violates a statutory provision is unlawful? Administrative inconvenience is an accepted criterion in relation to remedies provided by the courts in judicial review. For example, where a series of commercial transactions have been undertaken in reliance upon the impugned decision the court may, in its discretion, fail to quash that decision in view of the administrative chaos that would result from such a remedy.[209] Judicial discretion is employed here to balance fairness to the individual against the general public interest. The task, however, of deciding the force of a statutory provision does not involve judicial discretion. It involves the faithful construction of the objects and purposes of an Act of Parliament in the context of the particular decision. Although aspects of public policy may play a part in this exercise,[210] it would be wrong of the courts to impute any general implication that Parliament may intend administrative inconvenience, or indeed expense,[211] to excuse in advance the violation of its statutes. Such an implication invites careless administration and assumes that the legislature would too easily excuse a breach of its statutes.

---

[205] [2002] UKPC 34; [2003] 1 L.R.C. 422 at [12].
[206] *Society Promoting Environmental Conservation v Candada (Attorney General)* (2003) 228 D.L.R. (4th) 693 at 710.
[207] See 5–054.
[208] [1994] 1.W.L.R. 1286. See also the celebrated New Zealand case where the Governor-General had issued his warrant for the holding of a general election later than the date specified by statute. A challenge directed against the validity of the election failed on the ground that a contrary decision would have had the catastrophic effect of nullifying a number of Acts of Parliament, together with all actions already taken under them. *Simpson v Attorney General* [1955] N.Z.L.R. 271. cf. *Transport Ministry v Hamill* [1973] 2 N.Z.L.R. 663.
[209] See 18–053.
[210] See 5–068.
[211] On financial considerations, see 5–124.

Target duties: "directory" rather than "mandatory"?

In some cases where what appears to be a clear (mandatory) duty is **5–064** imposed upon an authority, the courts have held that is not directly enforceable by any individual.[212] Such a duty was called a "target duty" by Woolf L.J. in *R. v Inner London Education Authority Ex p. Ali*.[213] Such a duty seeks to achieve more an aspiration than an obligation. The authority is simply required to "do its best"[214] and failure to achieve the duty does not result in illegality. Examples include:

- Education Act 1996, s.14 ("A local education authority shall secure that sufficient schools for providing—(a) primary education, and (b) education that is secondary education . . . , are available for their area . . . ").

- National Assistance Act 1948, s.21 ("a local authority may with the approval of the Secretary of State, and to such extent as he may direct shall, make arrangements for providing—(a) residential accommodation for persons aged eighteen or over who by reason of age, illness, disability or any other circumstances are in need of care and attention which is not otherwise available to them").

- Children Act 1989, s.17 ("It shall be the general duty of every local authority (in addition to the other duties imposed on them by this Part)—(a) to safeguard and promote the welfare of children within their area who are in need; and (b) so far as is consistent with that duty, to promote the upbringing of such children by their families, by providing a range and level of services appropriate to those children's needs".

Courts allow great flexibility to authorities to achieve this kind of duty, as **5–065** long as they are not "outside the tolerance" of the statutory provision.[215] And since these duties normally require the decision to allocate scarce resources among competing needs, the courts will not interfere readily,[216] although a target duty may "crystallise" into an enforceable duty in certain

[212] C. Callaghan, "What is a Target Duty?" [2000] J.R. 184; L. Clements, *Community Care and the Law* (2004), pp.11–13; J. King, "The Justiciability of Resource Allocation" (2007) 70 M.L.R. 197, 214–216.
[213] (1990) 2 Admin. L.R. 822.
[214] *R. v Islington LBC Ex p. Rixon* [1997] E.L.R. 66 at 69; *R. v Radio Authority Ex p. Bull* [1998] Q.B. 294 at 309.
[215] *Ali* (n.213 above).
[216] On resource allocation see 1–025 and 5–124.

circumstances.[217] At the other extreme is what has been called a "proactive duty".[218]

5–066   While it is clear that not all duties phrased in general terms are intended to be readily enforceable, there is a danger that target duties will devalue the notion of a duty and permit Parliament to reassure the public with empty gestures and the executive to sit back and take no further notice. Duties incorporated in a statute ought not to be treated the way some constitutions (such as the Indian and Irish) treat certain rights (normally the "socio-economic rights" such as the right to "an adequate means of livelihood").[219] Unlike the fundamental rights enumerated in the Constitution, these are regarded simply as "Directive Principles of State Policy"— aspirations, rather than directly enforceable duties, although they may, like a preamble to a statute, inform the interpretation of the constitution.[220]

5–067   Is the duty imposed upon all ministers of the Crown under the Constitutional Reform Act 2005 to "uphold the continued independence of the judiciary"[221] a mere target duty? The same Act imposes "particular duties" for the purpose of upholding that independence. One of those duties requires the Lord Chancellor to "have regard to the need for the judiciary to have the support necessary for them to exercise their functions".[222] Are these target or enforceable duties? As with all powers framed in terms that are mandatory, the courts should presume that they mean what they say and are intended to be implemented. There will of course be cases where limited resources might (depending on the scheme) excuse some degree of implementation. However, the courts ought to examine each case in its context and rigorously apply the standards of public law.[223] They ought not therefore permit the decision-maker simply to sleep on the

---

[217] See, e.g. *R. (on the application of G) v Barnet LBC* [2003] UKHL 57; [2004] 2 A.C. 208, where Lord Hope (for the majority) at [80] held that a target duty to promote the welfare of children in need under Children Act 1989 s.17(1) was concerned with general principles and not designed to confer rights upon individuals. Nor could it easily crystallise in into an enforceable duty, [88].

[218] M. Fordham, *Judicial Review Handbook*, 4th edn (2004), pp.753–754. Such duty requires an authority under a duty, e.g. to reassess periodically the chronically sick and disabled, even in the absence of a request to do so. *R. v Bexley LBC Ex p. B* (2000) 3 C.C.L.R. 15 at 22; *R v Gloucester CC Ex p. RADAR* (1998) 1 C.C.L.R. 476 (duty to reassess needs for community care requires more than a letter inviting a request for an assessment).

[219] Art.39(a) of the Constitution of India.

[220] A. Datar, *Commentary on the Constitution of India* (2001), Pt IV, p.339. Under the South African Constitution most of the socio-economic rights are qualified to the extent that there is a right only to "access" to the right (such as health care) and its "progressive realisation", "within available resources".

[221] Constitutional Reform Act 2005 s.3(1).

[222] ss.3(4) and 3(6)(b).

[223] See, e.g. the South African case *Minister of Works v Kyalami Ridge Environmental Assoc* 2001 (3) S.A. 1151, CC where it was held that it was a constitutional duty to provide relief to victims of natural disasters even in the absence of authorising legislation. However, the majority decision in the recent case of *Constitutional Court Doctors for Life International v Speaker of the National Assembly* 2006 (6) S.A. 416, CC suggests that the court will defer to the legislature's decision on how to meet a duty.

target duty and fail to put his mind to its implementation;[224] or fail to take relevant considerations into account, or to take irrelevant considerations into account.[225] Nor should the courts excuse the pursuit of the purpose of the relevant scheme, or the cogent justification of its non-implementation.[226] However, this approach does not mean that non observance of a requirement will mean that the failure results inevitably in a non conforming action being necessarily void. This is more likely to be true in circumstances where the consequences of the failure to comply with the requirement does not cause injustice, or where any injustice can be remedied by other means.

Public policy

A related question to that of administrative inconvenience is the extent to which public policy might be employed to rebut the presumption that a statutory provision is mandatory. Public policy is employed here as the public law equivalent of private law equitable principles, such as that which states that no person may benefit from his own wrong. Thus the courts will presume that Parliament did not intend to imperil the welfare of the state or its inhabitants.   **5–068**

This question arose in the case of *R. v Registrar General Ex p. Smith.*[227] **5–069** Charlie Smith, the appellant, was detained in a secure mental hospital following his conviction for murder and the manslaughter of a cellmate during a psychotic bout under a belief that he was killing his adoptive mother. He had no knowledge of his natural mother's identity and applied under s.51 of the Adoption Act 1976 to the Registrar General for a copy of his birth certificate. The application was refused on the ground that the Registrar General, after receiving medical advice, believed that Smith's natural mother might be in danger if he were ever released and her identity known to him. Under the statute the duty of the Registrar General to supply the information was in terms absolute.[228] Nevertheless, the Court of Appeal held that this duty may be vitiated by public policy. In this case the public policy involved the prevention of crime. Parliament is thus presumed not to have intended that a statutory duty should be enforced either

---

[224] *R. v Secretary of State for the Home Department Ex p. Fire Brigades Union* [1995] 2 A.C. 513 (requiring the minister to implement an *ex gratia* scheme for compensating victims of crime).

[225] On the notion of relevancy, see See 5–110.

[226] For example, the enforcement of the right to housing (South African Constitution s.26) on the basis of familiar public law principles in *Government of South Africa v Grootboom* 2001 (1) S.A .46, CC. On justification, see 11–098 et seq.

[227] [1991] 2 Q.B. 393; A. Le Sueur, "Public Policies and the Adoption Act" [1991] P.L. 326.

[228] ". . . the Registrar-General shall on an application made in the prescribed manner by an adopted person a record of whose birth is kept by the Registrar-General and who has attained the age of 18 years supply to that person on payment of the prescribed fee (if any) such information as is necessary to enable that person to obtain a certified copy of the record of his birth".

to reward serious crime in the past, or to promote serious crime in the future.[229] Nor should the duty be enforced if there is "a significant risk"[230] or "current and justified apprehension" that to do so would facilitate "crime resulting in danger to life".[231]

5-070   In *Smith* it was made clear that the decision of the Court of Appeal was "in no way connected with the discretion of the court to refuse relief in judicial review cases".[232] Nor was the language of a directory (as opposed to a mandatory) statutory provision employed. In effect, the court held that a mandatory provision may simply be vitiated by the dictates of public policy[233] and rightly emphasised that such a result is founded upon the interpretation of statutory purpose, rather than upon any strained distinction between mandatory and directory statutory provisions. Today, under the terms of the Human Rights Act 1998, Convention rights might have been specifically invoked in a such a case, as public policy is an "unruly horse"[234] which must be ridden with care, as policy is within the proper realm of the legislature and not the courts. Such care was taken in a subsequent case where the Court of Appeal would not employ public policy to enable the Registrar General to refuse to provide a marriage certificate to a prisoner to enable him to marry his long-term girlfriend on the ground that that girlfriend would no longer be a compellable witness at the prisoner's forthcoming murder trial.[235]

Discretionary power in the context of law enforcement

5-071   When a public officer has discretion to prosecute an unlawful act, should that power be interpreted to be mandatory rather than directory? The rule of law suggests the law ought to be enforced and the power therefore

---

[229] *R. v National Insurance Commissioner Ex p. Connor* [1981] Q.B. 758 (applicant unable to recover the widow's allowance under the Social Security Act 1975 because she had unlawfully killed her husband); *R. v Secretary of State for the Home Department Ex p. Puttick* [1981] Q.B. 767 (applicant denied the benefit of registration of the United Kingdom and Colonies under the British Nationality Act 1948 although she was lawfully married to a citizen, because she had committed perjury and forgery in the course of procuring the marriage). For a summary of the private law principle that the courts will not enforce a contract if to do so would enable the plaintiff to benefit from his own crime see *Euro-Diam Ltd v Bathhurst* [1990] 1 Q.B. 1 at 35 (Kerr L.J.).

[230] Staughton and McCowan L.JJ.

[231] McCowan L.J.

[232] Staughton L J.

[233] For earlier cases where public policy has been engaged, see *Nagle v Feilden* [1966] 2 Q.B. 633 (Jockey Club's refusal of horse trainer's licence to woman held against public policy); *Edwards v SOGAT* [1971] Ch. 354 (unfair discrimination in withdrawal of collective bargaining rights).

[234] *Enderby Town Football Club v Football Association* [1971] Ch. 591 (Lord Denning M.R.: "I know that over 300 years ago Hobart C.J. said that "Public policy is an unruly horse". It has often been repeated since. So unruly is the horse, it is said [Burrough J. in *Richardson v Mellish* (1824) 2 Bing 229 at 252], that no judge should ever try to mount it lest it run away with him. I disagree. With a good man in the saddle, the unruly horse can be kept in control. It can jump over obstacles. It can leap the fences put up by fictions and come down on the side of justice, as indeed was done in *Nagle v Feilden* [1966] 2 Q.B. 633. It can hold a rule to be invalid even though it is contained in a contract").

[235] *R. (on the application of the Crown Prosecution Service) v Registrar General of Births, Deaths and Marriages* [2002] EWCA Civ 1661; [2003] Q.B. 1222.

interpreted as mandatory rather than directory. On the other hand, there are many reasons why prosecutors should be able to engage in "selective enforcement", in the public interest. The reasons include the fact that the authority may only possess limited resources and therefore need to concentrate on prosecutions of strategic importance.[236] There are also questions of public interest which the prosecutor is uniquely qualified to judge; such as the need to avoid defendants espousing unpopular causes having a hearing in the court, with the resultant elevation of the defendant to the status of a martyr.[237] Furthermore, full enforcement of a law may not fulfil its ultimate purpose (for example, the purpose of road safety will not be served by requiring the prosecution of a doctor who narrowly exceeded the speed limit while driving to the scene of an accident in the early hours of the morning). Political, rather than legal accountability is therefore generally thought to be the better method of controlling discretion in these cases, and the courts have generally refrained from intervening to require the discretion of a prosecutor[238] or other law enforcement officer to be exercised, outside of cases of bad faith or manifest unreasonableness.[239]

Enforcement decisions are not, however, entirely immune from attack 5–072 on the ground of illegality. If enforcement of a particular law were simply abandoned, the rule of law could be offended.[240] And where guidelines as to prosecution have been made, it has been held that judicial review may lie where the guidelines themselves are based upon an unlawful policy, or where the prosecutor fails to follow his own guidelines.[241]

---

[236] *R. v Chief Constable of Sussex Ex p. International Traders' Ferry Ltd* [1999] 2 A.C. 418 (decision partially to withdraw police protection from protestors against the export of animals upheld as lawful and not disproportionate or irrational). On limited resources, see 5–124; on justiciability, see 1–025.

[237] *Gouriet v Union of Post Office Workers* [1978] A.C. 435 (refusal of the Attorney-General to support a private action to restrain breach of the law by the Union held not justiciable on that ground).

[238] *R. v Director of Public Prosecutions Ex p. Kebilene* [2000] 2 A.C. 326 (in the absence of "dishonesty or mala fide or an exceptional circumstance" decisions by the DPP to consent to a prosecution are not amenable to judicial review").

[239] Y. Dotan, "Should Prosecutorial Discretion Enjoy Special Treatment in Judicial Review? A Comparative Analysis of the Law in England and Israel" [1997] P.L. 513; *Raymond v Attorney-General* [1982] Q.B. 839; and *R. (on the application of UMBS Online Ltd) v Serious Organised Crime Agency* [2007] EWCA Civ 406 at [58] (see 3–00).

[240] *F Hoffmann La Roche & Co AG v Secretary of State for Trade and Industry* [1975] A.C. 295 at 364 (Lord Diplock: "The Crown does owe a duty to the public at large to initiate proceedings to secure that the law is not flouted"); *R. v Coventry Airport Ex p. Phoenix Aviation* [1995] 3 All E.R. 37 (failure to provide any police protection to secure safety of exporters affected by animal rights protests a breach of the rule of law).

[241] *R. v Chief Constable of Kent Ex p. L* [1993] All E.R. 756; *R. v DPP Ex p. C* [1995] Cr. App. R. 136 at 141 (Kennedy L.J.). It appears too that a decision to prosecute an accused for an offence in circumstances in which an alternative and more serious offence could have been charged is also susceptible to judicial review: G. Dingwall, "Judicial Review of Public Prosecutions" [1995] C.L.J. 265.

THE INTERPRETATION OF POLICIES

5-073   We shall below consider to what extent policies or guidance, promulgated by ministers, departments and other public authorities must or may be taken into account as "relevant considerations".[242] What should the approach of the courts be to the interpretation of policy? Clearly the policy must not fall outside the terms and purpose of the relevant power. Nor will policies be subjected to the fine analysis of a statute.[243] But to whom does it fall to interpret the meaning of the policy? Is it for the courts to pronounce upon the natural meaning of the language used, or for the decision-maker, subject only to the constraints of rationality?[244] In other words, should the courts defer to the decision-maker's own interpretation of his policy or should the court apply its plain meaning?

5-074   In *R. (on the application of Springhall) v Richmond on Thames LBC*, it was said that the decision-maker's "approach to policy will only be interfered with by the court if it goes beyond the range of reasonable meanings that can be given to the language used".[245] The opposite view was expressed in *R. v Derbyshire CC Ex p. Woods* where it was said that it is for the court, as a matter of law, to determine a policy's meaning and that if the decision-maker failed properly to understand that meaning then it will have made an error of law.[246] The approach of *Woods* was accepted in *First Secretary of State v Sainsbury's Supermarkets Ltd* where Sedley L.J. made clear that "the interpretation of policy is not a matter for the Secretary of State. What a policy says, it is".[247] This approach is surely correct. Although, as Sedley L.J. said, a policy is "a rule not a guide" and thus may be balanced against countervailing principles, policies do have legal consequences. Decision-makers take them into account as "relevant considerations".[248] And, as we shall later see, they may not lightly abandon policies that have created legitimate expectations or that breach the principle of consistency.[249] For that reason, when they fall to be interpreted in the courts, their ordinary meaning should prevail.[250]

[242] See 5–110–134
[243] *R. v Secretary of State for the Home Department Ex p. Urmaza* [1996] C.O.D. 479.
[244] On policy see 12–023, 031, 037 *et seq*; and 9–008–013. N. Blake, "Judicial Interpretation of Policies Promulgated by the Executive" [2006] J.R. 298.
[245] [2006] EWCA Civ 19; [2006] B.L.G.R. 419 at [7] (Auld L.J.).
[246] [1997] J.P.L. 958 at 967–968 (Brooke L.J.).
[247] [2005] EWCA Civ 520; [2005] N.P.C. 60. *cf. R. v Director of Passenger Rail Franchising Ex p. Save Our Railways* (1996) C.L.C. 589 at 610 (Sir Thomas Bingham M.R. said of the Secretary of State's directions: "the Court cannot . . . abdicate its responsibility to give the document its proper meaning. It means what it means, not what anyone would like it to mean").
[248] See 5–120–122.
[249] See Ch.12 and 11–059–061.
[250] On policies as "relevant considerations", see 5–120–122.

EXERCISE OF A DISCRETIONARY POWER FOR EXTRANEOUS PURPOSE

If a power granted for one purpose is exercised for a different purpose, **5–075** that power has not been validly exercised. In administrative law[251] this elementary proposition was first laid down in cases concerning the exercise of powers of compulsory acquisition. These cases held that when persons were authorised by Parliament to take compulsorily the lands of others, paying to the latter proper compensation, they cannot be allowed to exercise the powers conferred on them for any collateral object; that is, for any purposes except those for which the legislature has invested them with extraordinary powers.[252]

An expression of judicial solicitude for private property rights[253] was **5–076** thus enlarged into a fundamental principle of English administrative law, possibly even based upon an implied constitutional principle. Most of the reported cases deal with the misapplication of powers by local authorities, though the same general principle governed the exercise of subordinate legislative power by the executive.[254]

When a decision-maker pursues a purpose outside of the four corners of **5–077** his powers, he may do so by taking an "irrelevant consideration" into account (the term "relevant" referring to the purpose of the statute). The interpretation of purpose, and the relevance of considerations taken into account in pursuing that purpose, are therefore often inextricably linked. However, in some cases neither the motive for the decision, nor the considerations taken into account in reaching that decision, are apparent. In such a case the purpose pursued is judged alone, without reference to the considerations by which it was influenced. The definition of purpose and the relevance of considerations must therefore be considered as separate aspects of the illegal decision.[255]

The abandonment of purpose has been expressed in different ways. **5–078** Sometimes it is said that decision-makers should not pursue "collateral objects", or that they should not pursue ends which are outside the "objects and purposes of the statute". On other occasions it is said that power should not be "exceeded" or that the purposes pursued by the

---

[251] The doctrine of a fraud upon a power is well known in equity.

[252] *Galloway v London Corp* (1866) L.R. 1 HL 34 at 43.

[253] For other early dicta, see *Webb v Manchester & Leeds Ry* (1839) 4 Myl. & Cr. 116 at 118; *Dodd v Salisbury & Yeovil Ry* (1859) 1 Giff. 158; *Stockton & Darlington Ry v Brown* (1860) 9 H.L.C. 246 at 254, 256; *Biddulph v St George's, Hanover Square, Vestry* (1863) 33 L.J.Ch. 411 at 417; *Hawley v Steele* (1877) 6 Ch.D. 521 at 527–529. See also *Marshall Shipping Co v R.* (1925) 41 T.L.R. 285: 'You can never beat into the heads of people exercising bureaucratic authority that they must exercise their powers singly, and not for collateral objects".

[254] For byelaws, see e.g. *Scott v Glasgow Corp* [1899] A.C. 470 at 492; *Baird (Robert) Ltd v Glasgow Corp* [1936] A.C. 32, 42; *Boyd Builders Ltd v City of Ottawa* (1964) 45 D.L.R. (2nd) 211; *Re Burns and Township of Haldimand* (1965) 52 D.L.R. (2nd) 101; *Prince George (City of) v Payne* [1978] S.C.R. 458; *R. v Toohey Ex p. Northern Land Council* (1981) I.S.I. C.L.R. 170, where the majority of the court regarded legislative and administrative powers as equally susceptible to judicial review.

[255] On irrelevant considerations, see 5–110–134.

decision-maker should not be "improper", "ulterior", or "extraneous" to those required by the statute in question. It is also said that "irrelevant considerations" should not be taken into account in reaching a decision. All these terms of course "run into each other" and "overlap".[256]

5-079   However, the designation of a purpose as "improper" is distinct because of its connotation of *moral* impropriety. In most cases where the term "improper" has been employed the decision-maker either knowingly pursues a purpose that is different from the one that is ostensibly being pursued, or the motive behind the decision is illicit (based for example on personal factors such as financial gain, revenge or prejudice). Because, therefore, of its adverse moral imputation, the notion of improper purposes is more akin to that of bad faith, which will now be considered separately.

Bad faith and improper motive

5-080   Fundamental to the legitimacy of public decision-making is the principle that official decisions should not be infected with improper motives such as fraud or dishonesty, malice or personal self-interest. These motives, which have the effect of distorting or unfairly biasing the decision-maker's approach to the subject of the decision, automatically cause the decision to be taken for an improper purpose and thus take it outside the permissible parameters of the power.

5-081   A power is exercised *fraudulently* if its repository intends for an improper purpose, for example dishonestly, to achieve an object other than that which he claims to be seeking. The intention may be to promote another public interest or private interests. A power is exercised *maliciously* if its repository is motivated by personal animosity towards those who are directly affected by its exercise.

5-082   Bad faith[257] is a serious allegation which attracts a heavy burden of proof.[258] Examples of cases involving fraudulent or dishonest motives include those where a local authority acquired property for the ostensible purpose of widening a street or redeveloping an urban area but in reality for the purpose of reselling it at a profit;[259] or preventing the owner from

---

[256] *Associated Provincial Picture Houses v Wednesbury Corp* [1948] 1 K.B. 223 at 228 (Lord Greene M.R.).

[257] Bad faith has been defined rarely, but an Australian case defined it as "a lack of honest or genuine attempt to undertake the task and involves a personal attack on the honesty of the decision-maker": *SCA v Minister of Immigration* [2002] F.C.A.F.C. 397 at [19]. Recklessness was held not to involve bad faith (*NAFK v Minister of Immigration* (2003) 130 F.C. 210, [24]).

[258] *Daihatsu Australia Pty Ltd v Federal Commission of Australia* (2001) 184 A.L.R. 576 (Finn J. at 587).

[259] *Gard v Commissioners of Sewers for the City of London* (1885) 28 Ch.D. 486; *Donaldson v South Shields Corp* [1899] W.N. 6; *Fernley v Limehouse Board of Works* (1899) 68 L.J. Ch. 344; *Denman & Co v Westminster Corp* [1906] 1 Ch. 464 at 475; *R. v Minister of Health Ex p. Davis* [1929] 1 K.B. 619 at 624. Contrast *CC Auto Port Pty Ltd v Minister for Works* (1966)

reaping the benefit of the expected increment in land values;[260] or giving an advantage to a third party.[261] Licensing powers cannot be used to augment public funds.[262] An authority, purporting to exercise powers of compulsory acquisition for the purpose of widening streets, proposed to widen a street only to a minute extent, its true purpose being to alter the street level.[263] A local authority empowered to acquire unfit houses purported to do so in order to provide temporary accommodation pending their demolition, but in reality intended to render them fit for habitation and add them to its permanent housing stock.[264] An authority purporting to dismiss school teachers on educational grounds, in reality dismissed them for reasons of economy.[265] An authority claiming to raise the salaries of its employees to reflect an increase in their duties, in reality did so in order to grant an employee a salary increase unrelated to the changes in his duties.[266] A police authority which called its former chief constable, who was living abroad, ostensibly for medical examination (and cancelled his pension when he failed to appear) in reality called him so as to facilitate the execution of a warrant of arrest issued against him by the Bankruptcy Court.[267] A local authority sought to acquire land for its benefit, when its true motive was to remove gypsies from the land.[268]

113 C.L.R. 365. But see the puzzling decision, *Robins (E) & Son Ltd v Minister of Health* [1939] 1 K.B. 520 (CA held the local authority had an unfettered discretion in its choice of method (clearance or demolition) of dealing with compulsorily acquired land. Mackinnon L.J. (at 537–538) also observed that, even had the property owners succeeded in establishing that the local authority had adopted the method of compulsory purchase in order to be able to resell the land to the owners (who wished to develop it) at a high price, that would not have affected the validity of the decision). *cf. Merrick v Liverpool Corp* [1910] 2 Ch. 449 at 463.
[260] *Sydney Municipal Council v Campbell* [1925] A.C. 338; *Grice v Dudley Corp* [1958] Ch. 329 and other authorities there cited at 341–342.
[261] *Bartrum v Manurewa Borough* [1962] N.Z.L.R. 21.
[262] *R. v Bowman* [1898] 1 Q.B. 663; *R. v Birmingham Licensing Planning Committee Ex p. Kennedy* [1972] 2 Q.B. 140: *R. v Shann* [1910] 2 K.B. 418 at 434.
[263] *Lynch v Commissioners of Sewers for the City of London* (1886) 32 Ch.D. 72. Attempts to impugn compulsory purchase orders in the English courts for improper purpose were successful in *Grice v Dudley Corp* [1958] Ch.329, *London & Westcliff Properties Ltd v Minister of Housing and Local Government* [1961] 1 W.L.R. 519, *Webb v Minister of Housing and Local Government* [1965] 1 W.L.R. 755, *Meravale Builders Ltd v Secretary of the Environment* (1978) 36 P. & C.R. 87; *Victoria Square Property Co Ltd v Southwark LBC* [1978] 1 W.L.R. 463; and unsuccessful in *Hanks v Minister of Housing and Local Government* [1963] 1 Q.B. 999; *Simpsons Motor Sales (London) Ltd v Hendon Corp* [1964] A.C. 1088; *Moore v Minister of Housing and Local Government* [1966] 2 Q.B. 602. See also *Birmingham & Midland Motor Omnibus Co v Worcestershire CC* [1967] 1 W.L.R. 409 (diversion of traffic for unauthorised purpose).
[264] *Victoria Square Property Co Ltd v Southwark LBC* [1972] 1 W.L.R. 463; *R. v Birmingham City Council Ex p. Sale* (1983) 9 H.L.R. 33.
[265] *Hanson v Radcliffe UDC* [1922] 2 Ch. 490; *Sadler v Sheffield Corp* [1924] 1 Ch. 483. See also *Smith v McNally* [1912] 1 Ch. 816 at 825–826; *Martin v Eccles Corp* [1919] 1 Ch. 387 at 400 ("grounds connected with the giving of religious instruction"). Contrast *Price v Rhondda UDC* [1923] 2 Ch. 377; *Short v Poole Corp* [1926] Ch. 66.
[266] *R. (Wexford CC) v Local Government Board* [1902] 2 I.R. 349. See also the leading Australian case *Brownells Ltd v Ironmongers' Wages Board* (1950) 81 C.L.R. 108 at 120, 130 (wages board fixed high overtime rates in reality to bring about closure of shops at hours different from those required by statute).
[267] *R. v Leigh (Lord)* [1987] 1 Q.B. 582; *R. v Brixton Prison Governor Ex p. Soblen* [1963] 2 Q.B. 243 (where it was unsuccessfully alleged that the true purpose of deportation was to

5–083   A decision based on *malice* is usually one that is directed to the person, e.g. where a byelaw or order has been made especially to thwart an individual application for a permit.[269] The malice may arise out of personal or political animosity built up over a series of past dealings.[270] For instance, in a Canadian case the cancellation of a liquor licence was held to be an abuse of power where the decision was prompted by the proprietor's support of a religious sect which was considered a nuisance by the police.[271] In another Canadian case the court inferred mala fides from the fact that a byelaw was made for the compulsory purchase of land which was the subject of pending litigation between the owner and the local authority.[272] And in a third it was held that a local authority cannot use its licensing power to prohibit lawful businesses of which it disapproves.[273] In an English case the decision of Derbyshire County Council to cease advertising in journals controlled by Times Newspapers which had written articles critical of its councillors was explicitly held to have been motivated by bad faith and therefore declared invalid for that reason alone.[274] In a

comply with a request for extradition); *R. v Secretary of State for the Environment Ex p. Ostler* [1977] Q.B. 122 (applicant was issued with false information which misled him not to appear at a public inquiry. But judicial review was excluded by an ouster clause. In other cases it has been said that where bad faith is established, the courts will be prepared to set aside a decision procured or made fraudulently, despite the existence of a formula purporting to exclude judicial review); *Lazarus Estates Ltd v Beasley* [1956] 1 Q.B. 702 at 712, 713 (Denning L.J.), 722 (Parker L.J.: fraud "vitiates all transactions known to the law of however high a degree of solemnity"); cases cited by counsel in *Smith v East Elloe RDC* [1956] A.C. 736 at 740 where it was held that the statutory language was sufficiently clear to exclude challenge for bad faith to a compulsory purchase order outside the short statutory limitation period. See further 4–00.

[268] *Costello v Dacorum DC* (1980) 79 L.G.R. 133.

[269] *Lubrizol Corp Pty Ltd v Leichhardt Municipal Council* [1961] N.S.W.R. 111; *Boyd Builders Ltd v City of Ottawa* (1964) 45 D.L.R. (2nd) 211.

[270] The allegation by Mrs Smith in *Smith v East Elloe RDC* [1986] A.C. 736. Personal animosity towards a party may also disqualify an adjudicator: *R. (Donoghue) v Cork County Justices* [1910] 2 I.R. 271; *R. (Kingston) v Cork County Justicesm* [1910] 2 I.R. 658; *R. (Harrington) v Clare County Justices* [1918] 2 I.R. 116; *Law v Chartered Institute of Patent Agents* [1919] 2 Ch. 276; *R. v Handley* (1921) 61 D.L.R. 656; *Re "Catalina" and "Norma"* (1938) 61 Ll. Rep. 360.

[271] *Roncarelli v Duplessis* (1959) 16 D.L.R. (2nd) 689 at 705. For further proceedings see [1959] S.C.R. 121.

[272] *Re Burns and Township of Haldimand* (1966) 52 D.L.R. (2nd) 101.

[273] *Prince George (City of) v Payne* [1978] 1 S.C.R. 458. In any event a power to regulate will not normally be constructed to allow total prohibition: *Tarr v Tarr* [1973] A.C. 254 at 265–268. For another interesting Canadian case, see *Re Doctors Hospital and Minister of Health* (1976) 68 D.L.R. (3rd) 220 (power to revoke approval as public hospital wrongfully exercised in the interests of economy). More recently, see *Canadian Union of Public Employees v Ontario (Minister of Labour)* [2003] 1 S.C.R. 539 (the use of a ministerial appointment power for an improper purpose).

[274] *R. v Derbyshire CC Ex p. The Times Supplement Ltd* [1991] C.O.D. 129. In *R. v Ealing LBC Ex p. Times Newspaper Ltd* (1986) 85 L.G.R. 316, councils imposed a ban on purchasing the publications of the Times Newspapers in their libraries. Watkins L.J., without going so far as to label the "shadowy" reasons for imposing the ban (to punish a "tyrannical employer") as bad faith—he called them "a transparent piece of camouflage"—did hold the decision both irrational and an abuse of power (as well as illegal, as discussed at 5–086). *Cf. R. v Lewisham LBC Ex p. Shell UK Ltd* [1988] 1 All E.R. 938 (ban on purchasing Shell's products to pressure

case concerning hijackers from Afghanistan, the Home Secretary refused any form of leave to enter to the claimants (to which they were entitled) but had instead granted them "temporary admission". Since his motive was, according to Sullivan J., to thwart a decision of the Immigration Appellate Authority by giving himself time "in the hope that something would turn up", his decision was void and an abuse of power.[275]

Specified purposes

Even when purposes are specified in a statute, it is often difficult to determine their scope, as the following examples show. The case of *Spath Holme* typifies the search for purpose and also demonstrates how difficult it is to draw general rules from individual statutory powers.[276] In 1999 the Secretary of State made Orders to cap the rents of regulated tenants who, as a result of judicial decisions, faced increases in their rents. The Order was made under a consolidated statute which had originally conferred temporary powers on the Secretary of State directed to preventing inflation in the economy. The landlord challenged the Order on the ground that it was outwith the power of the statute which had at its purpose the countering of general inflation in the economy and not the alleviation of hardship. Having first decided (by majority) that it was not appropriate to seek the general purpose of the statute by reference to the parliamentary record,[277] the House of Lords held that the earlier legislation was not confined to the specific anti-inflationary purpose. 5–084

Where a statute conferred power upon local authorities to incur expenditure for the "publication within their area of information on matters relating to local government", an expensive media and poster campaign mounted by the Inner London Education Authority was invalidated on the ground that it was made with the dual purpose both of informing the public of the detail of the education service and also of persuading the public to support the authority's opposition to the government's "rate-capping" policy. The first objective of the campaign (information) was lawful, but the second objective (persuasion) was held to be an unlawful purpose, which materially influenced the decision.[278] 5–085

The legality of sanctions imposed by local authorities for various motives has arisen in a number of cases. Where a statute imposed a duty upon every Library authority to provide a comprehensive and efficient library service",[279] the action of three London local authorities in banning from 5–086

parent company to sever links with South African subsidiary illegal but not unreasonable, although "very near the line").
[275] *R. (on the application of S) v Secretary of State for the Home Department* [2006] EWCA Civ 1157; [2006] I.N.L.R. 575 at [102].
[276] *R. (on the application of Spath Holme Ltd) v Secretary of State for the Environment, Transport and the Regions* [2001] 2 A.C. 349.
[277] See 5–026–031.
[278] *R. v ILEA Ex p. Westminster CC* [1986] 1 W.L.R. 28. On plurality purposes, see 5–099.
[279] Public Libraries and Museums Act 1964 s.7(1).

their libraries all publications of the Times Newspaper Group was held unlawful.[280] The ban was imposed to demonstrate support for the trade unions involved in a long and bitter dispute with the newspaper's proprietors. It was held that the ban pursued an "ulterior purpose" which was "set by a political attitude to a so-called workers' struggle against a tyrannical employer with the object of punishing the employer".[281] In an earlier case Lord Denning indicated that the closure of schools during a prolonged labour dispute could, if influenced by trade union pressure, amount to an unlawful extraneous purpose.[282]

5–087   Where local authorities have sought to impose conditions upon the use of their land, the courts have required them to further the purposes authorised by the statutes under which the land was acquired. A London authority attached a condition to permission for the holding of a community festival in a park.[283] The condition required the banning at the festival of "any political party or organisation seeking to promote or oppose any political party or cause". It was held that those restrictions were extraneous to the purpose of the statute under which the authority had purchased the park, namely "for the purpose of being used as public walks or a pleasure ground".[284]

5–088   Prior to the Hunting Act 2004, which banned the hunting of various mammals with dogs, the Somerset County Council had passed a resolution to ban hunting on their (council-owned) land on the Quantock Hills. The ban was motivated by the "moral repugnance" of the majority of the council towards hunting. The land had been acquired under a statute generally authorising acquisition of land for "the benefit, improvement or development of their area".[285] That purpose was interpreted as permitting the council to pursue objects which would "conduce to the better management of the estate". Had the ban been introduced to protect rare flora damaged by the hunt, or to eliminate physical interference with the enjoyment of others of the amenities offered on the land, it might have been lawful. However, since the ban was fuelled by the "ethical perceptions of the councillors about the rights and wrongs of hunting", the purposes it sought were outwith that of the governing statute.[286]

5–089   The power of the Foreign Secretary to grant assistance to overseas countries was subjected to judicial scrutiny in relation to the funding of the Pergau dam hydro-electric project in Malaysia. The Overseas Development and Co-operation Act 1980 confers such power on the Secretary of State

[280] *R. v Ealing LBC Ex p. Times Newspapers Ltd* (1986) 85 L.G.R. 316.
[281] The ban was also held to be unreasonable: see 11–072, n.250.
[282] *Meade v Haringey LBC* [1979] 1 W.L.R. 637.
[283] *R. v Barnet LBC Ex p. Johnson* [1989] C.O.D. 538.
[284] Public Health Act 1865 s.164. The ban was also held to be an unreasonable infringement of the right of association.
[285] Local Government Act 1972 s.120(1).
[286] *R. v Somerset CC Ex p. Fewings* [1995] 1 All E.R. 513 (Laws J.). The CA upheld this decision, although on different grounds [1995] 1 W.L.R. 1037. See D. Cooper, "For the Sake of the Deer: Land, Local Government and the Hunt (1997) 45 *Sociological Review* 668.

"for the purpose of promoting the economy of a country or territory outside the United Kingdom, or the welfare of its people".[287] It was clear that the Pergau project was not economically "sound" and was a "very bad buy". However, it was contended for the Secretary of State that wider political and economic interest were and could have been taken into account, including an alleged undertaking by the Prime Minister to provide the assistance (perhaps, as alleged in the press—although not directly alluded to in the judgments—as part of a wider arrangement involving an agreement to purchase defence items in the United Kingdom). The court, however, held that these wider purposes were not sufficient in themselves to qualify as a project for assistance under the statute. Although the statute did not specifically require an assisted project to be economically "sound", so much had to be implied. Had there been a "developmental promotion purpose" within s.1 of the Act, only then would it have been proper to take into account the wider political and economic considerations, including the impact which withdrawing from the offer would have had on commercial relations with Malaysia. In the circumstances, however, there was, at the time when assistance was provided, "no such purpose within the section".[288]

In a number of recent South African cases the courts have impugned decisions because they pursued extraneous purposes. In *Minister of Home Affairs v Watchenuka*[289] it was held that the power to regulate the granting of asylum did not include a power to prevent asylum seekers from taking up employment or studying.[290] 5–090

Incidental powers

Even when purposes are clearly specified in a statute, the law permits authorities to undertake tasks that are "reasonably incidental" to the achievement of those purposes,[291] provided that they do not contradict any statutory power. We have seen[292] how the common law under the Ram doctrine may apply in respect of the powers of the executive and the problems associated with this for the rule of law. In respect of the activities of local authorities, statutory recognition is given to the rule of common 5–091

---

[287] Overseas Development and Co-operation Act 1980 s.1(1).
[288] *R. v Secretary of State for Foreign Affairs Ex p. World Development Movement Ltd* [1995] 1 W.L.R. 386.
[289] 2004 (4) S.A. 326, SCA.
[290] See also *Minister of Correctional Services v Kwakwa* 2002 (4) S.A. 455, SCA; *Vorster v Dep. of Economic Development, Environment and Tourism* 2006 (5) S.A. 291 (T) (conditions attached to hunting permit beyond the scope of the power); *Chairperson: Standing Tender Committee v JFE Sapela Electronics (Pty) Ltd* [2005] 4 All SA 487 (unacceptable tender invalid act).
[291] *Ashbury Railway Carriage and Iron Co Ltd v Riche* (1875) L.R. 7 HL 653; *Attorney General v Great Eastern Railway Company* (1880) 5 App. Cas. 473; *Attorney General v Fulham Corp* [1912] 1 Ch. 440.
[292] See 5–022.

law, authorising them to do any thing which is "calculated to facilitate, or is conducive or incidental to, the discharge of any of their functions".[293] This phrase has itself been the subject of statutory construction in cases where, for example, local authorities have attempted to raise revenue by charging fees or speculating on the financial markets. When a local education authority decided to charge fees for individual and group music tuition, that decision was held unlawful as the duty under the statute to provide "education" without charge[294] included the duty to provide music tuition.[295] Similarly, a local authority was held not entitled to charge for consultations with developers prior to applications for planning permission being lodged. The House of Lords held that, although pre-application advice was not a duty or a discretionary power, but an incidental power authorised by the statute, the power to charge for that incidental power was not authorised.[296] The courts also struck down the power of a local authority to enter into interest rate swap transaction, which involved speculation as to future interest trends, with the object of making a profit to increase the available resources of the authority. That activity was held inconsistent with the borrowing powers of local authorities and not "conducive or incidental' to the discharge of those limited powers.[297]

5-092   In *Stennett*[298] the question before the House of Lords was whether a duty to provide after-care services for those discharged from compulsory detention under the Mental Health Act 1983 also authorised the authority to charge for those services. Despite the huge cost to local authorities of providing this service free of charge (estimated at between £30 million and £80 million), the House of Lords agreed with the Court of Appeal[299] that that a public authority could not charge for services unless it was explicitly authorised to do so and it was held that s.117 of the 1983 Act did not so authorise any charge as it was a "free-standing" section, and did not act as

---

[293] Local Government Act 1972 s.111; Local Government Act 2003 s.93(7); see also Local Government Act 2003 s.92 (charges for provision of services for local authorities' powers, though not duties); Police Act 1996 ss.18, 25, 26 (powers to police to charge for services and goods).
[294] Education Act 1949 s.61.
[295] *R. v Hereford and Worcester Local Education Authority Ex p. Jones* [1981] 1 W.L.R. 768. In general authorities require specific authorisation to raise revenue. *Attorney General v Wilts United Dairies Ltd* (1921) 37 T.L.R. 884.
[296] *McCarthy and Stone (Developments) Ltd v Richmond-upon-Thames LBC* [1992] 2 A.C. 48.
[297] *Hazell v Hammersmith & Fulham LBC* [1992] 2 A.C. 1. See also: *Credit Suisse v Allerdale BC* [1997] Q.B. 306; *Credit Suisse v Waltham Forest LBC* [1997] Q.B. 362; *Sutton London LBC v Morgan Grenfell and Co Ltd* (1997) 9 Admin. L.R. 145. cf. *R. v Greater Manchester Police Authority Ex p. Century Motors (Farnworth) Ltd, The Times* May 31, 1996 (necessary implication that power to levy charges for vehicle recovery operation); *R. v Powys CC Ex p. Hambidge, The Times*, November 5, 1997 (Local authority may charge for services under Chronically Sick and Disabled Persons Act 1970, s.2).
[298] *R. (on the application of Stennett) v Manchester City Council* [2002] UKHL 34; [2002] 2 A.C. 1127.
[299] [2001] Q.B. 370.

a "gateway" to the incorporation of provisions of other legislation which did authorise charging.[300]

Unspecified purposes

If a discretionary power is conferred without express reference to purpose, it must still be exercised in accordance with such implied purposes as the courts attribute to the legislation.[301] We have seen that the minister who, in reliance upon an ostensibly unfettered discretionary power, refused to refer a complaint by milk producers to a committee of investigation because this might lead him into economic and political difficulties, was held to have violated the unexpressed purpose, or the "policy and objects" of the Act, for which the power of reference had been conferred[302] and (according to a somewhat hyperbolical interpretation of their Lordships' comments) was "roundly rebuked by the House of Lords for his impudence".[303] In order to avoid paying an announced (but not yet enacted) increase in the fee for a television licence, some licence-holders obtained another licence at the old rate before their existing licence expired. The Court of Appeal held that the minister could not use his power to revoke the licences, despite the lack of apparent limits on that power, in order to deprive licensees of the advantage that they had secured from the gap between the Government's announcement and parliamentary authorisation of the change in fees.[304]

5-093

In the case of *Magill v Porter*,[305] the Conservative leaders of Westminster City Council had used their powers to increase the number of owner-occupiers in marginal wards for the purpose of encouraging them to vote for the Conservative Party in future elections. The District Auditor held that this was an unlawful purpose and, through wilful conduct, had lost the Council money which the leaders of the Council should pay by way of

5-094

---

[300] National Assistance Act 1948 s.21; see A. Scully, "Scarce Resources Again" [2003] C.L.J. 1, 2 who makes the point that the result of charging could mean delay in releasing a person from detention, as if no after-care has been arranged detention may be continued under the authority of *R. (on the application of J) v Ashworth Hospital Authority* [2002] EWCA Civ 923.
[301] See, e.g. *Liversidge v Anderson* [1942] A.C. 206 at 220, 248, 261, 278; *Barber v Manchester Regional Hospital Board* [1958] 1 W.L.R. 181 at 193; *Potato Marketing Board v Merricks* [1958] 2 Q.B. 316 at 331; *Smith v East Elloe RDC* [1956] A.C. 736 at 740. The proposition stated in the text has nevertheless been doubted or contradicted (see *Yates (Arthur) & Co Pty Ltd v Vegetable Seeds Committee* (1945) 72 C.L.R. 37 at 68 (Latham C.J.) by some authorities. The decision in *R. v Paddington & St Marylebone Rent Tribunal Ex p. Bell London & Provincial Properties Ltd* [1949] 1 K.B. 666 (block reference of 555 tenancies by local authority to rent tribunal without considering wishes of tenants or circumstances of particular cases; reference held invalid in that council was using tribunal as a general rent-fixing agency) has generally been regarded as a good illustration of the proposition in the text, but the case has now been explained as an example of a merely capricious reference: *R. v Barnet & Camden Rent Tribunal Ex p. Frey Investments Ltd* [1972] 2 Q.B. 342, CA. See also *Rowling v Takaro Properties Ltd* [1975] 2 N.Z.L.R. 62, NZCA; and [1988] A.C. 473, PC where the NZCA and PC took different views as to the implied purposes of the regulations.
[302] *Padfield v Minister of Agriculture, Fisheries and Food* [1968] A.C. 997; see 5-009.
[303] *Breen v Amalgamated Engineering Union* [1971] 2 Q.B. 175 at 191 (Lord Denning M.R.).
[304] *Congreve v Home Office* [1976] Q.B. 629.
[305] [2001] UKHL 67; [2002] 2 A.C. 357.

surcharge. The House of Lords upheld the District Auditor's decision. It was held that although the powers under which the Council could dispose of the land was very broad,[306] and although elected politicians were entitled to act in a manner which would earn the gratitude and support of their electorate,[307] they could only act to pursue a "public purpose for which the power was conferred". The purpose of securing electoral advantage for the Conservative Party was, it was held, no such "public purpose".[308]

5-095   When an authority which is clothed with powers to regulate an activity and accompanies its regulations with a sanction or penalty, the courts look carefully at the restrictions and penalties to ensure that they are within the policy and objects of the empowering statute. This is true even where the power permits conditions to be attached to the regulations or licences. Thus where conditions in an ice-cream vendors' licence restricted their right to open shops at times of their choosing, the conditions were held to be unlawful.[309] A local authority was not entitled to lay down conditions relating to the customers of a licensee of a caravan site as it interfered with the licensee's freedom to contract with his customers and to matters that did not relate to the manner of the use of the site.[310] A similar approach was taken in a recent case where the House of Lords held that a Scottish local authority which had power to regulate second-hand car dealing acted unlawfully when it failed to renew a licence to a dealer who had failed to provide pre-sales information and inspection reports to his customers. Lord Hope held that the principal mischief to which the power was directed was the handling of stolen property and that the conditions imposed pursued a policy of consumer protection, which was not one of the objects and purposes of the statute.[311]

5-096   Another case concerned Afghans fleeing from the Taliban regime by means of a hijacked plane which landed in England and where they requested asylum. Criminal convictions against them for hijacking were quashed because of misdirection by the judge. The Home Secretary had rejected their claim for asylum and this was upheld by a panel of adjudicators. The Home Secretary was unable to deport them as their lives

[306] Housing Act 1985 s.32.
[307] [2001] UKHL 67; [2002] 2 A.C. 357 at [20](Lord Bingham).
[308] *R. v Tower Hamlets LBC Ex p. Chetnick Developments Ltd* [1988] A.C. 858 at 872 (Lord Bridge: "Statutory power conferred for public purposes is conferred . . . upon trust, not absolutely—that is to say, it can validly be used only in the right and proper way which Parliament when conferring it is presumed to have intended"); *Credit Suisse v Allerdale BC* [1997] Q.B. 306 at 333 (Neill L.J. described that principle as "a general principle of public law").
[309] *Rossi v Magistrates of Edinburgh* (1904) 7 F 85, HL *Spook Erection Ltd v City of Edinburgh DC*, 1995 S.L.T. 107, Sh Ct.
[310] *Mixnam's Properties Ltd v Chertsey UDC* [1965] A.C. 735 at 763 (Lord Upjohn), 755 (Lord Reid).
[311] *Stewart v Perth and Kinross Council* [2004] UKHL 16; 2004 S.C. 71, HL. It was held too that the conditions were not intended to interfere with the relationship between the dealer and his contractors, and that consumer legislation of this could kind should preferably be introduced through national legislation, in order to be consistently applied.

would be at risk on their return to Afghanistan. The Home Secretary then decided not to allow the claimants discretionary leave, which he was entitled to do under his policy on "humanitarian grounds" and granted them instead "temporary admission". The Court of Appeal held that the purpose of temporary admission had not been sanctioned by Parliament. There had been ample time for the Home Secretary to obtain parliamentary authority for this new measure, but he had not done so and therefore his policy was unlawful.[312]

Other cases made it clear that the imposition of a penalty in the absence 5–097 of a legal wrong pursues an extraneous purpose. Purporting to be acting under the general duty under s.61 of the Race Relations Act 1976 to "promote good race relations", and also purporting to act under its broad powers to manage its own land, Leicester City Council withdrew the licence of a local rugby club to use the council-owned recreation ground. The council did this as a mark of their disapproval that the club had been unable to persuade some of its members to withdraw from the English rugby footballers' tour of South Africa, at the time of apartheid and as a demonstration of their effort to promote good relations between persons of different racial or ethnic groups. The House of Lords held the council's action unlawful, Lord Templeman considering it to be a "misuse of power . . . punishing the club where it had done no wrong".[313] Similar reasons (the opposition to apartheid and the promotion of good race relations) motivated the London Borough of Lewisham which decided to boycott the products of Shell UK Ltd so as to put pressure on the parent companies of the group to withdraw their interests from South Africa. It was held that the dominant purpose of the boycott was to penalise the applicant for the fact that the group to which it belonged had trading links with South Africa. These links were not unlawful and the council's decision had therefore been influenced by an "extraneous and impermissible purpose".[314] Another boycott was considered by the courts when Liverpool City Council threatened to withdraw grant aid from organisations which might consider joining a (voluntary) employment training scheme

---

[312] R. (on the application of S) v Secretary of State for the Home Department [2006] EWCA Civ 1157; [2006] I.N.L.R. 575.
[313] Wheeler v Leicester City Council [1985] A.C. 1954. Cf. the approach of Lord Browne-Wilkinson in his dissenting judgment in the CA (at 1064–1065), where he raised the conflict between "two basic principles of a democratic society", one that allowed a "democratically elected body to conduct its affairs in accordance with its own views" and the other "the right to freedom of speech and conscience enjoyed by each individual". Basing his decision on illegality rather than on unreasonableness (the council having taken a "legally irrelevant factor" into account), he came close to deciding the matter on the ground of the council's acting inconsistently with "fundamental freedoms of speech and conscience". cf. the New Zealand decision of Ashby v Minister of Immigration [1981] 1 N.Z.L.R. 222 (refusal of Minister to bar the entry of the South African rugby football team into New Zealand upheld on the ground that the public interest, a relevant consideration in the context of the Minister's power, allowed the decision—although it was not the role of the court to second-guess the minister on that question in the context of foreign relation).
[314] R. v Lewisham LBC Ex p. Shell UK Ltd [1988] 1 All E.R. 938.

introduced by the Government. The Court of Appeal held the purpose (punishment or coercion) to be unlawful.[315]

5-098   When two school governors were removed by the Inner London Education Authority because they had opposed the Authority's educational policy, the House of Lords considered whether the broad discretion conferred on the authority permitted this action. The statute simply provided that a governor "shall be removable by the authority by whom he was appointed".[316] It was held that the power could not be exercised in a way that usurped the governor's independent function and that such a usurpation was in effect extraneous to the power conferred.[317]

Plurality of purposes

5-099   We now take hold of a legal porcupine which bristles with difficulties as soon as it is touched. In a case where the actor has sought to achieve unauthorised as well as authorised purposes, what test should be applied to determine the validity of his act? At least six separate tests have been applied where plural purposes or motives are present. The choice of one test in preference to another can materially affect the decision. Despite this, it is not uncommon to find two or more of the tests applied in the course of a single judgment.[318] The following tests, none of which is entirely satisfactory, have been formulated.

Test 1: What was the true purpose for which the power was exercised

5-100   If the actor has in truth used his power for the purpose for which it was conferred, it is immaterial that he achieved as well a subsidiary object. Thus, if a power to construct an underground public convenience is exercised in such a way as to provide a subway leading to the convenience that can also be used by pedestrians who do not wish to take advantage of its facilities, the power has been validly exercised. The position would have been different if the construction of the conveniences was a colourable device adopted in order to enable a subway to be built.[319] A local authority

---

[315] R. v Liverpool CC Ex p. Secretary of State for Employment [1988] C.O.D. 404.

[316] Education Act 1944 s.21(1) (now Education Act 1986 ss.56,67).

[317] Brunyate v Inner London Education Authority [1989] 1 W.L.R. 542. But when eight recalcitrant councillors were removed from a local authority housing committee ostensibly to reduce the size of that committee (and not to punish their behaviour), the decision was not held unlawful. R. v Greenwich LBC Ex p. Lovelace [1990] 1 W.L.R. 18; affirmed [1991] 1 W.L.R. 506. See also Champion v Chief Constable of the Gwent Constabulary [1990] 1 W.L.R. 1 (refusal of membership of school appointments committee to police constable governor held unlawful as it was not "likely" to give the appearance of partiality); R. v Warwickshire CC Ex p. Dill-Russell (1991) 3 Admin. L.R. 415; affirmed (1991) 3 Admin. L.R. 415 (lawful for all governors of school to resign simultaneously so as to achieve proportionality with political representation on reappointment).

[318] See, e.g. Webb v Minister of Housing and Local Government [1965] 1 W.L.R. 755 at 773-774, 777H (test (5)), 778G (test (2)); Grieve v Douglas-Home 1965 S.C. 313 (tests (1) and (2)); R. v Inner London Education Authority Ex p. Westminster CC [1986] 1 W.L.R. 28 (tests (1) and (5)).

[319] Westminster Corp v L & NW Ry [1905] A.C. 426.

empowered to spend money upon altering and repairing streets "as and when required" acts lawfully in resurfacing a road that is in fact in need of repair, although the immediate occasion for carrying out the work is the hope of attracting an automobile club to use it for racing trials.[320] If the Home Secretary is honestly satisfied that the deportation of an alien is conducive to the public good and there is some basis for his belief, his deportation order is valid although the practical effect (and perhaps a secondary desired effect) of the order is to secure the extradition of the alien to another country seeking his rendition for a non-extraditable offence.[321]

Test 2: What was the dominant purpose for which the power was exercised

If the actor pursues two or more purposes where only one is expressly or impliedly permitted, the legality of the act is determined by reference to the dominant purpose. This test, based on an analogy with the law of tortious conspiracy,[322] has been applied in several cases.[323] In substance it may often prove to be nothing more than a different verbal formulation of the "true purpose" test. Where several purposes coexist, attempts to single out the "true" purpose have an air of unreality. If, of course, the avowed purpose is shown to be a mere sham, the "true purpose" test can readily be applied. It is of some interest that in *Soblen* the courts concentrated their analysis on the question of whether the deportation order was a sham, or a pretext for procuring an unlawful extradition; they abstained from asking themselves what was the Home Secretary's dominant purpose in making the order, though this would not appear to have been an irrelevant question.[324] 5-101

In the Pergau dam case[325] it was held that the minister's dominant purpose in funding the uneconomic project was not the authorised one of furthering the "economy" or "welfare" of the people of Malaysia. In the stag hunting ban case[326] it was held that the dominant purpose of fulfilling the "ethical perceptions" of the councillors did not fulfil the statute's 5-102

---

[320] *R. v Brighton Corp Ex p. Shoosmith* (1907) 96 L.T. 762.
[321] *R. v Brixton Prison Governor Ex p. Soblen* [1963] 2 Q.B. 243. It is to be noted that the Home Secretary's discretion was couched in subjective terms and was exercisable on "policy" grounds.
[322] *Crofter Hand Woven Harris Tweed Co v Veitch* [1942] A.C. 435.
[323] *Earl Fitzwilliam's Wentworth Estates Co v Minister of Town and Country Planning* [1951] 2 K.B. 284 at 307 (Denning L.J., dissenting). The HL did not give any ruling on this point on appeal ([1952] A.C. 362). For subsequent formulations of a similar test, *Webb* [1965] 1 W.L.R.755 at 778; *Grieve v Douglas-Home* 1965 S.C. 313 *R. v Immigration Appeals Adjudicator Ex p. Khan* [1972] 1 W.L.R. 1058 (whether primary purpose of entering UK as full-time student was to take up permanent residence); *R. v Ealing LBC Ex p. Times Newspapers Ltd* (1986) 85 L.G.R. 316 (dominant purpose in imposing ban on purchase of publications for library was to interfere in industrial dispute).
[324] See n.321.
[325] *R. v Secretary of State for Foreign Affairs Ex p. World Development Movement* [1995] 1 W.L.R. 386.
[326] *R. v Somerset CC Ex p. Fewings* [1995] 1 W.L.R. 1037.

authorised purpose that of improvement of the amenity of the area. Perhaps in both these cases the sole purpose was unauthorised.

5–103   The House of Lords adopted a combination of the "true" and "dominant" purpose tests in a case where an accountant challenged an application by the police to produce documents relating to her dealings with a client. The statute under which the police made the application provided that it could be made for purposes of investigation into whether a person has "benefited from any criminal conduct".[327] However, the accountant submitted that the predominant reason for seeking the documents was to investigate, under a power provided in different legislation,[328] whether "the conduct from which the person had benefited was criminal". It was held that since "true and dominant purpose" of the application was to investigate the proceeds of criminal conduct in order to obtain evidence for the prosecution, the application should therefore be granted. Furthermore, the application should be granted even if an incidental consequence might be that the police would obtain evidence relating to the commission of an offence.[329]

5–104   In the New Zealand case *Attorney General v Ireland*[330] it was held that when a power was exercised for two purposes, one of which was authorised and the other not, the exercise of the one purpose is valid if the statute does not limit the power to "only" the explicitly authorised purpose and the additional purpose does not thwart or frustrate the purpose of the Act. However, in South Africa it was held that a minister's exercise of a power to regulate the granting of asylum did not extend to preventing asylum seekers from taking up employment or studying.[331]

Test 3: Would the power still have been exercised if the actor had not desired concurrently to achieve an unauthorised purpose?

5–105   This test was applied by the High Court of Australia.[332]

Test 4: Was any of the purposes pursued an authorised purpose?

5–106   If so, the presence of concurrent illicit purposes does not affect the validity of the act. This test appears to have been applied in only one English case, and even then somewhat equivocally.[333] It is submitted that in English law

---

[327] Criminal Justice Act 1988 s.93H.
[328] Police and Criminal Evidence Act 1984 s.9(1).
[329] *R. v Southwark Crown Court Ex p. Bowles* [1998] A.C. 641.
[330] [2002] 2 N.Z.L.R. 220, CA—citing this para. in the 5th edition of this work, at [38].
[331] *Minister of Home Affairs v Watchenukam* 2004 (4) SA 326.
[332] *Thompson v Randwick Municipal Council* (1950) 81 C.L.R. 87 at 106. It may have the disadvantage of requiring the courts to speculate about motives for which it is ill-equipped, but it is not very different from test (6) below. The leading Australian text suggests that Australian cases now suggest a "substantial purpose' test, "in the sense that the decision would not have been made without the illegitimate purpose": M. Aronson, B. Dyer and M. Groves, *Judicial Review of Administrative Action*, 3rd edn. (2004), pp.298–299.
[333] *Earl Fitzwilliam* [1951] 1 K.B. 203 at 217–219 (Birkett J.); see also Lord MacDermott's observations in the HL [1952] A.C. 362 at 385.

the existence of one legitimate purpose among illegitimate purposes will only save the validity of an act if the purpose for which the power was granted has been substantially fulfilled.

Test 5: Were any of the purposes pursued an unauthorised purpose?

If so, and if the unauthorised purpose has materially influenced the actor's **5-107** conduct, the power has been invalidly exercised because irrelevant considerations have been taken into account. The effect of applying such a test may be directly opposed to that produced by the preceding test.[334] This is a curious state of affairs, for the concepts of improper purpose and irrelevancy are intimately related and are often analytically indistinguishable.[335] That the possibility of a sharp conflict between them exists has seldom been recognised. The question was considered in a case where the validity of a compulsory purchase order was impugned and the court preferred the test of irrelevancy: had the making of the order been significantly or substantially influenced by irrelevant considerations.[336]

Cases have affirmed this approach. When irrelevant considerations have **5-108** been taken into account, the courts have invalidated the decision if those considerations have had a "substantial" or "material" influence upon the decision.[337]

Test 6: Would the decision-maker have reached the same decision if regard had only been had to the relevant considerations or to the authorised purposes?

This is a subtle variation of the previous (material influence) test. It was **5-109** applied when the Broadcasting Complaints Commission refused to investigate a complaint for a number of reasons, only one of which was bad (that the investigation would impose too great a burden on the Commission's limited staff). It was held that where the bad reason was not mixed and

---

[334] Thus, in *Sadler v Sheffield Corp* [1924] Ch. 483, where notices of dismissal served on teachers were held to be invalid because they have been served not on "educational grounds" (as was required by the Act) but in reality on financial grounds, Lawrence J. said obiter (at 504–505) that even if bona fide educational grounds for dismissal had coexisted with the financial grounds, it would have been wrong to try to separate them, and that mixed educational and financial grounds were not educational grounds within the meaning of the Act, which were the only grounds that could lawfully be taken into account (applying dictum in *R. v St Pancras Vestry* (1890) 24 Q.B.D. 375.

[335] As In *Padfield* [1968] A.C. 997.

[336] *Hanks v Minister of Housing and Local Government* [1963] 1 Q.B. 999 at 1018–1020 (Megaw J.); cf. *Meravale Builders Ltd v Secretary of State for the Environment* (1978) 36 P. & C.R. 87. In practice the result of analysing a situation by reference to the effect of irrelevant considerations will often be the same as that produced by applying the "dominant purpose" test; cf. *Fawcett Properties Ltd v Buckingham CC* [1958] 1 W.L.R. 1161 at 1167–1168.

[337] See e.g. *R. v Inner London Education Authority Ex p. Westminster CC* [1986] 1 W.L.R. 28 (advertising campaign for the purposes of: (a) information about rate-capping and (b) persuasion against it. Persuasion held an extraneous purpose which materially influenced the decision); *R. v Lewisham LBC Ex p. Shell UK Ltd* [1983] 1 All E.R. 938 (boycott in order to induce Shell to sever its trading links with South Africa held "substantial influence" on decision); and *R. v Ealing LBC Ex p. Times Newspapers Ltd* (1986) 85 L.G.R. 316.

could be disentangled from the good, then the decision could stand if the Commission would have reached precisely the same decision on the other valid reasons".[338]

DECISIONS BASED UPON IRRELEVANT CONSIDERATIONS OR FAILURE TO TAKE ACCOUNT OF RELEVANT CONSIDERATIONS

5–110 When exercising a discretionary power a decision-maker may take into account a range of lawful considerations. Some of these are specified in the statute as matters to which regard may be had. Others are specified as matters to which regard may not be had. There are other considerations which are not specified but which the decision-maker may or may not lawfully take into account.[339] If the exercise of a discretionary power has been influenced by considerations that cannot lawfully be taken into account, or by the disregard of relevant considerations required to be taken into account (expressly or impliedly), a court will normally hold that the power has not been validly exercised.

5–111 It may be immaterial that an authority has considered irrelevant matters in arriving at its decision if it has not allowed itself to be influenced by those matters [340] and it may be right to overlook a minor error of this kind even if it has affected an aspect of the decision.[341] However, if the influence of irrelevant factors is established, it does not appear to be necessary to prove that they were the sole or even the dominant influence. As a general rule it is enough to prove that their influence was material or substantial. For this reason there may be a practical advantage in founding a challenge to the validity of a discretionary act on the basis of irrelevant considerations rather than extraneous purpose, though the line of demarcation between the two grounds of invalidity is often imperceptible.[342]

5–112 In cases where the reasons for the decision are not available, and there is no material either way to show by what considerations the authority was influenced, the court may determine whether their influence is to be

---

[338] *R. v Broadcasting Complaints Commission Ex p. Owen* [1985] Q.B. 1153; *R. v Rochdale MBC. Ex p. Cromer Ring Mill Ltd* [1982] 3 All E.R. 761 (misconceived guidelines "substantially influenced" decision not to refund rates, despite good reasons which could not be disentangled).

[339] These three considerations were set out by Simon Brown L.J. in *R. v Somerset CC Ex p. Fewings* [1995] 1 W.L.R. 1037, at 1049.

[340] *R. v London (Bishop)* (1890) 24 Q.B.D. 213 at 226–227 (affd. on grounds not identical, *sub nom. Allcroft v Bishop of London* [1891] A.C. 666); *Ex p. Rice; Re Hawkins* (1957) 74 W.N. (N.S.W) 7, 14; *Hanks v Minister of Housing and Local Government* [1963] 1 Q.B. 999 at 1018–1020; *Re Hurle-Hobbs' Decision* [1944] 1 All E.R. 249.

[341] *Hounslow LBC v Twickenham Garden Developments* Ltd [1971] Ch. 233, 271; *R. v Barnet & Camden Rent Tribunal Ex p. Frey Investments Ltd* [1972] 2 Q.B. 342; *Bristol DC v Clark* [1975] 1 W.L.R. 1443 at 1449–1450 (Lawton L.J.); *Asher v Secretary of State for the Environment* [1974] Ch. 208 at 221, 227.

[342] *Marshall v Blackpool Corp* [1935] A.C. 16; *Padfield v Minister of Agriculture, Fisheries and Food* [1968] A.C. 997; *R. v Rochdale MBC Ex p. Cromer Ring Mill Ltd* [1992] 2 All E.R. 761.

inferred from the surrounding circumstances. In such cases the courts may infer that an extraneous purpose was being pursued.[343]

If the ground of challenge is that relevant considerations have not been taken into account, the court will normally try to assess the actual or potential importance of the factor that was overlooked,[344] even though this may entail a degree of speculation. The question is whether the validity of the decision is contingent on strict observance of antecedent requirements. In determining what factors may or must be taken into account by the authority, the courts are again faced with problems of statutory interpretation. If relevant factors are specified in the enabling Act it is for the courts to determine whether they are factors to which the authority is compelled to have regard.[345] If so, may other, non-specified considerations be taken into account or are the specified, considerations to be construed as being exhaustive?

5–113

This question arose in a case where members of the Labour Party challenged the recommendations of the Boundary Commission.[346] The Commission was under a duty to make recommendations to the Home Secretary about the boundaries of parliamentary constituencies (though the final decision rested with Parliament). The statute set out a series of rules to which the Commission were required to give effect. These included the requirements (a) that "so far as practicable" the constituencies are not to cross London borough boundaries and (b) that the electorate shall be as near to the electoral quota" as possible.[347] If it appeared, however, that it was desirable to avoid an "excessive disparity" between the electoral quota and the actual electorate of any constituency, the Commission had a discretion to take (c) "geographical considerations" into account. The Commission were also permitted to take account, in so far as they reasonably could, of (d) "inconvenience attendant on alterations of constituencies and of any local ties broken by such alterations". The applicants considered that the Commission had laid undue emphasis on the

5–114

---

[343] Or that the exercise of discretion was unreasonable: *Lonrho Plc v Secretary of State for Trade and Industry* [1989] 1 W.L.R. 525 at 539 (Lord Keith said that where reasons for a decision were absent "and if all other known facts and circumstances appear to point overwhelmingly in favour of a different decision, the decision-maker . . . cannot complain if the court draws the inference that he had no rational reason for his decision"); *R. v Civil Service Appeal Board Ex p. Cunningham* [1991] 4 All E.R. 310 (absence of reasons for low compensation award and no reasons given inference made that decision irrational); *Padfield* [1968] A.C. 997 at 1032–1033, 1049, 1053–1054, 1061–1062 (Lords Reid, Hodson, Pearce and Upjohn).

[344] *R. v London (Bishop)* (1890) 24 Q.B.D. at 266–227, 237, 244; *Baldwin & Francis Ltd v Patents Appeal Tribunal* [1959] A.C. 663 at 693 (Lord Denning); *R. v Paddington Valuation Officer Ex p. Peachey Property Corp Ltd* [1966] 1 Q.B. 380.

[345] On mandatory and directory considerations, see 5–049; e.g. *Yorkshire Copper Works Ltd v Registrar of Trade Marks* [1954] 1 W.L.R. 554 (HL held that the Registrar was bound to have regard to specific factors to which he was prima facie empowered to have regard); *R. v Shadow Education Committee of Greenwich BC Ex p. Governors of John Ball Primary School* (1989) 88 L.G.R. 589 (failure to have regard to parental preferences).

[346] *R. v Boundary Commission for England Ex p. Foot* [1983] 1 Q.B. 600, CA.

[347] House of Commons (Redistribution of Seats) Act 1949 s.2(1)(a) Sch.2 rr.4, 5.

requirement of not crossing local boundaries and insufficient emphasis on the requirement of achieving equality of numbers in the electorates of their constituents. It was held that although the Acts set out requirements to which the Commission had to have regard, the burden on the applicants of showing that the commission had exercised their powers wrongly was heavy as the rules themselves were no more than guidelines. Despite the wide disparity in some constituency boundaries, there was no evidence that the Commission had misunderstood or ignored Parliament's instructions.

5–115   If the relevant factors are not specified (e.g. if the power is merely to grant or refuse a licence, or to attach such conditions as the competent authority thinks fit), it is for the courts to determine whether the permissible considerations are impliedly restricted, and, if so, to what extent,[348] although when the courts conclude that a wide range of factors may properly be considered, they will be reluctant to lay down a list with which the authority will be required to comply in every case.[349] In *R. v Secretary of State for Transport Ex p. Richmond LBC*,[350] Laws J. said that where relevant considerations are not specified in a statute the decision-maker's consideration of what is a relevant consideration can only be subject to review on the ground of unreasonableness. With respect, this ignores the fact that the (non-specified) considerations adopted by the decision-maker may be matters that are extraneous to the purpose of the statute, and therefore reviewable for illegality.

5–116   The question of relevancy may relate not to specified factors that need to be taken into account by the decision-maker, but to the decision-maker's approach to the evidence before him. In *R. (on the application of National Association of Health Stores) v Department of Health*[351] the minister decided to accept the view of the Medicines Commission that a herbal remedy ought to be banned. The Commission, unusually, informed the minister that one of its members was opposed to the ban, but failed to inform him that that member was especially qualified in psychomarmacology and had recently completed a meta-analysis of the scientific evidence of the remedy. Nor was the minister informed of the conclusions of the review. Were these factors "relevant considerations" which the minister had ignored? In the circumstances of this case it was held that the minister must know, or be told "enough" to ensure that no relevant considerations are ignored, but need not know "everything that is relevant". The court followed Lord Cooke's distinction in *CREEDNZ Inc v Governor General*[352] between "matters which are so relevant that they must be taken into

---

[348] 5–084.
[349] See e.g. *Elliott v Southwark LBC* [1976] 1 W.L.R. 499 at 507; *Bristol DC v Clark* [1975] 1 W.L.R. 1443 (the court looked for guidance on the factors relevant to the exercise of a statutory discretion to a departmental circular issued after the enactment of the legislation).
[350] [1994] 1 W.L.R. 74 at 95.
[351] [2005] EWCA Civ 154; *The Times*, March 9, 2005; I. Steele, "Note on *R. (National Association of Health Stores) v Department of Health*" [2005] J.R. 232.
[352] [1981] 1 N.Z.L.R. 172. CREEDNZ was endorsed by Lord Scarman in *Re Findlay* [1985] A.C. 318. See also *Minister of Aboriginal Affairs v Peko-Wallsend* (1986) 162 C.L.R. 24.

account" (which included the Commission's report and the matters about which he was informed) and "matters which are not irrelevant and therefore may legitimately be taken into account" (which included the matters about which he was not informed). Sedley L.J. held that "only a failure to take into account something in the former class would vitiate a public law decision",[353] and the minister had sufficient information to make a decision. The second category surely begs the question of whether the "not irrelevant" matter ought to have been taken into account so as to give the minister a complete picture of the weight he ought to have accorded to the dissenting expert's view.[354]

Examples of discretionary powers having been unlawfully exercised on legally irrelevant grounds are multitudinous. Many of the earlier cases are concerned with magistrates refusing to issue summonses for extraneous reasons,[355] or failing to consider relevant factors before ordering a surety to forfeit a recognisance,[356] or with tribunals improperly refusing or agreeing to adjourn proceedings before them,[357] and with licensing justices refusing applications,[358] granting them subject to irrelevant conditions,[359] or even granting them unconditionally on irrelevant grounds.[360] There are decisions on the unlawful expenditure of public funds by local authorities,[361] and a

5–117

---

[353] *National Association of Health Stores* [2005] EWCA Civ 154; *The Times*, March 9, 2005 at [63] and [75] (Keene L.J.); and see the approach of Gibbs C.J. in *Peko-Wallsend Ltd* [2005] EWCA Civ 154; *The Times*, March 9, 2005 at 31 (distinction made between "insignificant or insubstantial matters" which are not brought to the attention of the minister, and "material facts which he is bound to consider"), and Brennan J. at 61 (makes the distinction between "minutiae", which the minister need not consider, and "salient facts which give shape and substance to the matter"). For a discussion of the *weight* to be attached to relevant considerations, see 11–033–036.

[354] On mandatory and discretionary requirements, see 5–059–072.

[355] *R. v Adamson* (1875) 1 Q.B.D. 201; *R. v Boteler* (1864) 33 L.J.M.C. 101; *R. v Mead Ex p. National Health Insurance Commrs* (1916) 85 W.K.B. 1065 (refusals based on disapproval of conduct of complainants or of the policy or application of the legislation concerned); *R. v Bennett and Bond* (1908) 72 J.P 362; *R. v Nuneaton Borough Justices* [1954] 1 W.L.R. 1318 (refusal on ground that other proceedings more appropriate).

[356] See e.g. *R. v Southampton Justices Ex p. Green* [1976] Q.B. 11; *R. v Horseferry Road Stipendiary Magistrate Ex p. Pearson* [1976] 1 W.L.R. 511.

[357] On the question whether a tribunal is entitled to adjourn a matter because a change in the law is pending, see *R. v Whiteway Ex p. Stephenson* [1961] V.R. 168, 171; *Boyd Builders Ltd v Ottawa* (1964–45 D.L.R. (2nd) 211 (adjournment improper); but the position may be different if the change in the law is imminent and reasonably certain; *cf. Clifford Sabey (Contractors) Ltd v Long* [1959] 2 Q.B. 290 at 298–300. For non-judicial exercise of discretion to postpone operation of demolition order, see *Pocklington v Melksham UDC* [1964] 2 Q.B. 673. See also *Royal v Prescott-Clarke* [196611 W.L.R. 788; *Walker v Walker* [1967] 11 W.L.R. 327.

[358] See e.g. *R. v de Rutzen* (1875) 1 Q.B.D. 55.

[359] e.g. *R. v Bowman* [1898] 1 Q.B. 663; *R. v Birmingham Licensing Planning Committee Ex p. Kennedy* [1972] 2 Q.B. 140 (refusal to allow application to proceed unless irrelevant condition complied with); see too *Fletcher v London (Metropolis) Licensing Committee* [1976] A.C. 150.

[360] See e.g. *R. v Cotham* [1898] 1 Q.B. 802.

[361] *Attorney General v Tynemouth Poor Law Union Guardians* [1930] 1 Ch. 616; *Roberts v Hopwood* [1925] A.C. 578; *Prescott v Birmingham Corp* [1955] Ch. 210; *Taylor v Munrow* [1960] 1 W.L.R. 151.

miscellany of decisions which illustrate the general rule in a wide range of contexts.[362]

5–118   As we have seen, the interpretation of statutory purpose and that of the relevancy of considerations are closely related, since the question in regard to the considerations taken into account in reaching a decision is normally whether that consideration is relevant to the statutory purpose. This is seen in respect of the considerations taken into account by planning authorities as a basis of a refusal of planning permission. Is it relevant to refuse an application for permission to change the use on the site from use A to use B on the ground that the authority wishes to preserve the use of site as A (and have no inherent objection to use B)? It has been held that the preservation of an existing use may be a material planning consideration, but only if, on the balance of probabilities, there is a fair chance of use A being continued.[363] Where, however, the authority wished to retain the existing use so that it could be kept in their own occupation, it was held that that consideration was not a legitimate planning consideration.[364] Other disputed considerations in the area of planning law involve the regard that has been had to factors such as precedent (it has been held that permission may be refused because it would be difficult to resist similar applications in the future);[365] to the fact that alternative sites would be more appropriate for the development, or to the personal circumstances of the applicant.

5–119   Where a university, after consultation with the police, refused to permit a meeting on its premises addressed by members of the South African Embassy during the apartheid regime, it did so in the belief that the meeting would provoke public violence in the neighbouring area. The statute required universities to ensure that freedom of speech was secured and that the use of university premises was not denied to any individual body on the ground of their beliefs, policy or objectives. It was held that in taking into account the likelihood of violence outside of their premises the decision had been influenced by an irrelevant consideration and was therefore ultra vires.[366] The action of a local trading standards officer was held to have been unlawful when, three days after a children's toy was found to have been dangerous, he suspended the manufacturer from supplying the toy for six months. He claimed to have had regard to a regulation which would have permitted the suspension, but which was not

---

[362] See e.g. *Padfield* [1968] A.C. 997; and many of the cases on improper purpose.

[363] *Westminster CC v British Waterways Board* [1985] A.C. 676: *London Residuary Body v Lambeth LBC* [1990] 1 W.L.R. 744; *Clyde & Co v Secretary of State for the Environment* [1977] 1 W.L.R. 926 (desirability of maintaining the possibility that land would be used to relieve housing shortage a material consideration); cf. *Granada Theatres Ltd v Secretary of State for the Environment* [1976] J.P.L. 96.

[364] *Westminster CC v British Waterways Board* [1985] A.C. 676 (Lord Bridge).

[365] *Collis Radio Ltd v Secretary of State for the Environment* (1975) 29 P. & C.R. 390.

[366] *R. v Liverpool University Ex p. Caesar Gordon* [1991] 1 Q.B. 124; *R. v Coventry Airport Ex p. Phoenix Aviation* [1995] 3 All E.R. 37, DC (unlawful surrender to the dictates of pressure groups opposed to the export of live animals). cf. *R. v Chief Constable of Sussex Ex p. International Traders Ferry* [1999] 2 A.C. 418.

yet in force. The court held that consideration to be irrelevant.[367] Where a statute gave the power to the minister to licence medicines for importation into the United Kingdom when it was "expedient" to do so, it was held that his taking into account of trade mark (private) rights was a consideration irrelevant to the public law powers in the circumstances of that case.[368]

Government policy as a relevant consideration

In a number of cases the question has arisen of whether regard may or **5–120** must be had to various forms of government advice or indication of government policy. Normally such policy will be expressed through a government circular or a code of practice which lacks binding effect.[369] A number of questions may arise in respect of non-statutory guidance which are addressed elsewhere in this work, such as the method of their interpretation,[370] possible effect in creating legitimate expectations,[371] or whether their effect is to fetter the decision-maker's discretion.[372] The question has also arisen as to whether or not a circular may amount to an authoritative account of the law at all, and thus be subject to judicial review.[373]

The House of Lords considered the status of a code of practice which **5–121** the Secretary of State for Health was required to prepare under the terms of the Mental Health Act 1983 in order to guide the treatment of patients in hospitals dealing with mental disorders.[374] The code then required hospitals to produce their own codes, and the question was whether a local hospital trust's code was unlawful because it was not in conformity with the Secretary of State's code.[375] The House of Lords held that although the Secretary of State's code did not have the binding effect of a statutory provision, and purported to be "guidance", not "instruction", it was

---

[367] *R. v Birmingham CC Ex p. Ferrero Ltd* (1991) 3 Admin. L.R. 613.

[368] *R. v Secretary of State for Social Services Ex p. Wellcome Foundation* [1987] 2 All E.R. 1025.

[369] R. Baldwin and J. Houghton, "Circular Arguments: The Status and Legitimacy of Administrative Rules" [1986] P.L. 239; G. Ganz, *Quasi-legislation* (1986). For the distinction between direction and guidance see *Laker Airways v Department of Trade* [1977] Q.B. 643, 714. See also *R. v Secretary of State for Social Services and the Social Fund Inspector Ex p. Stilt* (1992) 4 Admin. L.R. 713. On what constitutes "policy", see 5–073–074.

[370] See 5–075 et seq.

[371] See 12–023; 031; 037 et seq.

[372] See 9–013.

[373] *Gillick v West Norfolk & Wisbech AHA* [1986] A.C. 112. Lord Bridge, doubting the correctness of the decision: in appropriate circumstances a misleading or manifestly inaccurate circular may be reviewed. But see *R. v Secretary of State for the Environment Ex p. Greenwich LBC* [1989] C.O.D. 530, where the applicants sought judicial review to prohibit the distribution by the Secretary of State for the Environment of a leaflet on the community charge. The application was refused on the ground that the document, although perhaps misleading by omission, was not literally inaccurate.

[374] *R. (on the application of Munjaz) v Mersey Care NHS Trust* [2005] UKHL 58; [2006] 2 A.C. 148.

[375] See 9–120–122.

guidance which should be given "great weight" from which the hospital could only depart with "great care".[376] Similarly, circulars or "Planning Policy Guidance" issued by the Department, although only advisory in nature, have been held to be material planning considerations to which regard must be had by both local authorities and the Secretary of State in making decisions about development control.[377]

5-122 To what extent can a failure to have regard to a government non-statutory policy invalidate a decision for disregard of a material consideration? An authority is entitled to ignore or act contrary to a policy circular which misstates the law.[378] A policy cannot make a matter that is an irrelevant consideration, or outside the purpose of the statute, relevant or lawful. If the decision-maker attaches a meaning to the words of the policy which they are not capable of bearing, he will have made an error of law.[379] If there has been a change in the policy, it has been held that the decision must relate to the new policy, even if it has not been published and is not known to the parties.[380] However, this proposition may be subject to any legitimate expectation on their part.[381] If the decision-maker departs from the policy, clear reasons for doing so must be provided, in order that the recipient of the decision will know why the decision is made as an exception to the policy and the grounds upon which the decision is taken.[382] In *Munjaz*, the House of Lords held that the hospital could only depart from the Secretary of State's code if it had provided "cogent

---

[376] Lord Bingham at [21]; and see *R. (on the application of Khatun) v Newham LBC* [2004] EWCA Civ 55; [2005] Q.B. 37 at [47] (Laws L.J.).

[377] A policy need not normally have been promulgated in any particular way, but after-dinner speeches do not qualify: *Dinsdale Developments Ltd v Secretary of State for the Environment* [1986] J.P.L. 276. Draft policy statements may qualify: *Richmond-upon-Thames LBC v Secretary of State for the Environment* [1984] J.P.L. 24; but may not: *Pye JA (Oxford) Estates Ltd v Secretary of State for the Environment* [1982] J.P.L. 577.

[378] *R. v Secretary of State for the Environment Ex p. Tower Hamlets LBC* [1993] Q.B. 632 (Code of Guidance to Local Authorities on Homelessness by Department of the Environment held to misstate the law); *R. v Secretary of State for the Environment Ex p. Lancashire CC* [1994] 4 All E.R. 165 (policy guidance issued to local government Commissioners to replace their authorities with unitary authorities held more in the nature of directions than guidance and therefore unlawful).

[379] *Horsham DC v Secretary of State for the Environment* [1992] 1 P.L.R. 81; *Virgin Cinema Properties Ltd v Secretary of State for the Environment* [1998] 2 P.L.R. 24; and *R. (on the application of Howard League for Penal Reform) v Secretary of State for the Home Department (No.2)* [2002] EWHC 2497; [2003] 1 F.L.R. 484; *R. (on the application of Burke) v General Medical Council* [2005] EWCA Civ 1003; [2006] Q.B. 273 at [21] (review of guidance on the withdrawal of artificial feeding. Noting that "the court should not be used as a general advice centre"); Cf. *R. (on the application of Lambeth LBC) v Secretary of State for Work and Pensions* [2005] EWHC 637; [2005] B.L.G.R. 764 (change in government policy will not in general justify treating a refusal to alter a previous decision).

[380] *Newham LBC v Secretary of State for the Environment* (1986) 53 P. & C.R. 98.

[381] On legitimate expectations, see Ch.12.

[382] *EC Gransden & Co Ltd v Secretary of State for the Environment* (1987) 54 P. & C.R. 86; *Carpets of Worth Ltd v Wye Forest DC* (1991) 62 P. & C.R. 334. For application of these principles outside of planning law, in relation to police negotiating machinery, see *R. v Secretary of State for the Home Department Ex p. Lancashire Police Authority* [1992] C.O.D. 161.

reasoned justification" for so doing, which the court "should scrutinize with the intensity which the importance and sensitivity of the subject matter requires".[383]

International law and relevancy

We have already drawn a distinction between (a) incorporated treaty provisions, (b) unincorporated treaty provisions and (c) customary international law.[384] The question whether a public authority has acted unlawfully in the exercise of its discretion by failing to take into account international law relates to (b). The concern of the courts has often been that if such an argument is accepted, it is tantamount to incorporation of the treaty "through the back door"—in other words, it would in practice be giving effect to a treaty provision (the making of which is an executive action) which Parliament has not expressly provided should be part of domestic law. The high water mark for such an approach is the House of Lords' decision in *Brind*,[385] in which—before the Human Rights Act 1998— their Lordships rejected an argument that a minister should exercise his discretion within the limitations imposed by the ECHR. Lord Bridge said that the contrary conclusion "would be a judicial usurpation of the legislative function".[386] This approach has been softened in recent years. While it still remains the case that a decision will not be held unlawful just because a public authority has failed to take into account an unincorporated treaty provision, in such situations the courts will now subject the decision to "anxious scrutiny" in testing its reasoning and calling for a justification from the public authority.[387]

5–123

Financial considerations and relevancy

There are three ways in which the relevance of financial considerations may be engaged: (a) whether the cost of a project may be taken into account as a factor relevant to the decision; (b) whether the expenditure of public funds is simply too extravagant, and (c) whether the authority's lack

5–124

---

[383] *R. (on the application of Munjaz) v Mersey Care NHS Trust* [2005] UKHL 58; [2006] 2 A.C. 148 at [21] (Lord Bingham); see also *Argos Ltd v Office of Fair Trading* [2006] EWCA Civ 1318; [2006] U.K.C.L.R. 1135 (Competition Act 1998 s.38(1) required the OFT to prepare and publish guidance and s.38(8) required it to "have regard" to the guidance in setting penalties. It was held that the OFT must give reasons for departing from the guidance); *Royal Mail Group Plc v The Postal Services Commission* [2007] EWHC 1205 (Admin) (PSC unlawfully departed from its policy on penalties).
[384] See 5–043–048.
[385] *R. v Secretary of State for the Home Department Ex p. Brind* [1991] A.C. 696; and *R. (on the application of Hurst) v HM Coroner for Northern District London* [2007] UKHL 13; [2007] 2 W.L.R. 726 at [53]–[59] (Lord Browne.
[386] *Brind* [1991] A.C. 696 at 748; also *R. v Ministry of Defence Ex p. Smith* [1996] Q.B. 517 at 558 (Sir Thomas Bingham M.R.).
[387] See 11–086–102.

of resources may justify the non-implementation of a power or duty. Under (b) and (c) particularly, the question of the amenability of the courts to pronounce on the matter of resource allocation comes into sharp focus.[388]

Cost as a relevant consideration

5–125   In the area of planning, the question of cost has been raised in different contexts. It has been held that the likelihood that a development would, because of its excessive cost, never be implemented, may be a material consideration in refusing planning permission.[389] Yet the question of whether a development was a good investment proposition for the developer was held not to be material.[390] The refusal of planning permission because of the absence in the proposal of any "planning gain" (a benefit by means of a voluntary material contribution to the authority) has also been held to be a non-material consideration.[391] Westminster City Council granted planning permission to the Directors of the Covent Garden Opera House for an office development near (but not on) its site, on the ground that the profits from the development would be devoted to improving the facilities of the opera house. Although the office development would not have been given planning permission on its own, the fact that it enabled an otherwise unaffordable development was held by the Court of Appeal to be a material consideration which justified the permission.[392]

Excessive expenditure

5–126   At the other extreme are cases where an authority's expenditure has been challenged for being excessive.[393] The attempt of the Poplar Borough Council in 1925 to raise the wages and salaries of its employees, and to pay

---

[388] On justiciability, see 1–025–043.

[389] *Sovmots Investments Ltd v Secretary of State for the Environment* [1979] A.C. 144.

[390] *Murphy (J) & Sons Ltd v Secretary of State for the Environment* [1973] 1 W.L.R. 560; *Walters v Secretary of State for Wales* [1979] J.P.L. 171 (cost of development not a material planning consideration); *cf. Sovmots Investments Ltd v Secretary of State for the Environment* [1977] Q.B. 411 at 422–425; *Hambledon and Chiddingfold PC v Secretary of State for the Environment* [1976] J.P.L. 502; *Niarches (London) Ltd v Secretary of State for the Environment* (1978) 35 P. & C.R. 259).

[391] *Westminster Renslade Ltd v Secretary of State for the Environment* [1983] J.P.L. 454.

[392] *R. v Westminster City Council Ex p. Monahan* [1990] 1 Q.B. 87, although it was doubted whether such a consideration would be material or relevant if the benefit was not in physical proximity to the development (e.g. if the benefit was in the form of a swimming pool at the other end of the town). On the use of planning obligations (formerly planning agreements) to achieve this kind of benefit, see 5–00. *cf. R. v Camden LBC Ex p. Cram, The Times*, January 25, 1995 (relevant for Council to seek to make a profit from a car parking scheme).

[393] See e.g. *R v. Secretary of State for the Environment Ex p. Hammersmith and Fulham LBC* [1991] A.C. 521 at 593, 597 (Lord Bridge: local authorities' claim that the Secretary of State's determination of their expenditure as "excessive" was not capable of resolution by the courts as it admitted of no objective justification); *R. v Secretary of State for Health Ex p. Keen* (1991) 3 Admin. L.R. 180 (lawful for resources to be allocated in anticipation of a new scheme proposed in a parliamentary Bill, provided the authority's discretion was not fettered).

women employees rates equal to that of men, was held contrary to law. The House of Lords in that case came close to holding that expenditure unreasonable,[394] but the ratio of the case was based upon the view that the amounts paid were at a time of falling cost of living, more in the nature of a gratuity than the wages and salaries which the authority was authorised to pay.[395] In 1983 the question of local authority expenditure arose again in respect of the decision of the Greater London Council to reduce transport fares by 25 per cent.[396] The fare cuts would have lost the council approximately £50 million of the rate support grant which they would otherwise have been entitled to receive from the central government sources. Although the governing statute gave wide discretion to promote the provision of "integrated, efficient and economic transport facilities",[397] it also required the authorities to make up any deficit incurred in one accounting period in the next such period.[398] This provision was held to limit the authorities' discretion and subject them to a duty to run the system on ordinary business principles, which the drastic reductions in the fares contravened.[399]

The courts have, from time to time, invoked the principle that local 5–127 authorities owe an implied "fiduciary duty" to their ratepayers. The breach of such a duty has rarely formed the ratio of a decision to strike down the expenditure concerned.[400] The fiduciary duty could be interpreted in two ways: first, it could imply a duty to act on ordinary business principles and not to be "thriftless"[401] with ratepayers" money. Such a meaning of the fiduciary duty comes close to permitting the courts themselves to decide the levels of expenditure which meet those standards. As the House of Lords has reminded us in a different context, courts are not, in judicial review, equipped to make such decisions.[402] A second interpretation views the fiduciary duty as a duty to take into account, in reaching a decision on expenditure, the interests of the ratepayers.[403] Since the ratepayers' inter-

---

[394] *Roberts v Hopwood* [1925] A.C. 578.
[395] A point made by Ormrod L.J. in *Pickwell v Camden LBC* [1983] Q.B. 962. See also Sir David Williams, "Law and Administrative Discretion" (1994) Indiana J. of Global Legal Studies 191. For a consideration of the "fiduciary principle" raised in *Roberts v Hopwood* and other cases, see 11–00; *Prescott v Birmingham Corp* [1955] Ch. 210; *Taylor v Monrow* [1960] 1 W.L.R. 151.
[396] *Bromley LBC v Greater London Council* [1983] 1 A.C. 768.
[397] Transport (London) Act 1969 s.1.
[398] Transport (London) Act 1969 s.7(3)(b).
[399] A subsequent scheme, known as the "balanced fare scheme", was held to be lawful: *R. v London Transport Executive Ex p. Greater London Council* [1983] Q.B. 484.
[400] For example, in *Roberts v Hopwood* [1925] A.C. 578, or *Bromley LBC v GLC* [1983] 1 A.C. 768. Both these cases were decided on the basis of "illegality". See also *Re Westminster CC* [1986] A.C. 668 (grants by GLC unlawful but not unreasonable). *cf. Prescott v Birmingham* [1995] Ch. 210.
[401] *Bromley LBC v GLC* [1983] 1 A.C. 768 at 899 (Lord Diplock); cf. *Hazell v Hammersmith and Fulham LBC* [1992] 2 A.C. 1 at 37 (Lord Templeman referred to the duty of the local authority to be "prudent" with ratepayers' money.
[402] *R. v Secretary of State for the Environment Ex p. Hammersmith and Fulham LBC* [1991] 1 A.C. 521 at 593, 597 (Lord Bridge), at least in relation to unreasonableness. On justiciability, see 1–025–043.
[403] Today, commercial ratepayers and domestic council taxpayers.

ests are likely to be adversely affected by a decision to increase expenditure, it is surely right that those interests should be considered by the local authority (although not necessarily slavishly followed). This second meaning of the fiduciary duty does not involve the courts in a function to which, in judicial review, they are unsuited. It merely involves them in requiring that considerations which are relevant to the local authority's powers, namely, the interests of the local taxpayers, be taken into account. This function is perfectly suited to judicial review. It is noteworthy that in *Magill v Porter*,[404] a case in which members of Westminster Council were held to have incurred unlawful expenditure on behalf of the Council, the fiduciary concept was not employed and the House of Lords were content to find simply that the councillors' actions failed to pursue a "public purpose" in seeking to obtain party-political gain at the expense of the ratepayers.[405]

Limited resources

5–128 Public authorities have frequently pleaded lack of resources as an excuse for not fulfilling their duties or powers. Whether this excuse is lawful, as we have seen, depends in the first instance on whether the duty is a mere "target duty", or whether it is, or has crystallised into, an enforceable duty.[406] In *Barnett*,[407] considering whether a local authority owed a duty to provide resources to children "in need", the majority of the House of Lords held that the duty was a mere "target duty" and therefore the Lords could not require the expenditure of additional resources. A similar view was taken in *R v Gloucestershire CC Ex p. Barry*[408], where the House of Lords held that the authority was entitled to take into account its limited resources when it considered whether it could fulfill the "needs" of disabled persons. Later, the House of Lords refused to interfere in a decision of a chief constable to deploy his resources by withdrawing full-time protection from animal exporters threatened by demonstrations by

[404] *Magill v Porter* [2001] UKHL 67; [2002] 2 A.C. 357.
[405] In *Bromley* [1983] 1 A.C. 768 a further question concerned the relevance to the decision of the council's so-called "mandate". It was argued that the promise to reduce transport fares was the major part of the manifesto on which the new ruling party had fought the recent election. The House of Lords clearly held, however, that a so-called mandate from the electorate can have no influence on the *legality* of a decision, which must fulfil the purposes authorised by the statute which governs the power in question. Compare the influence of the mandate upon the reasonableness of a decision, discussed at 11–00; *cf. R. v Merseyside CC Ex p. Great Universal Stores Ltd* (1982) 80 L.G.R. 639. In New Zealand there is a line of cases in which the fiduciary concept has been applied: *Lovelock v Waitakere CC* [1996] 3 N.Z.L.R. 310; *Waitakere CC v Lovelock* [1997] 2 N.Z.L.R. 385, CA.
[406] See 5–064–67.
[407] *R. (on the application of G) v Barnet LBC* [2003] UKHL 57; [2004] 2 A.C. 208.
[408] [1997] A.C. 206; see E. Palmer, "Resource Allocation, Welfare Rights—Mapping the Boundaries of Resource Allocation in Public Administrative Law" (2000) O.J.L.S. 63; *R. v Southwark LBC Ex p. Udu* (1996) 8 Admin. L.R. 25 (policy of refusing grants to courses at private colleges, including the College of Law; held, local authority was a political body with limited funds, and it was entitled to have policies and to decide how to allocate those funds).

animal welfare groups.[409] However, in *R. v Sussex CC Ex p. Tandy*[410] the House of Lords took the opposite view in holding that the authority could not take its limited resources into account in considering whether it could provide "suitable education" to children in need. In that case the council did have the resources to perform the duty but preferred to expend it in different ways. Lord Browne-Wilkinson said that permitting the authority to follow that preference would, wrongly, "downgrade a statutory duty to a discretionary power. . . . over which the court would have very little control".[411] More recent cases under the Human Rights Act, where "positive duties" are increasingly recognised, have also held irrelevant the excuse of lack of resources.[412]

The statement of Lord Nicholls in *Barnet*,[413] that the existence of an **5–129** "absolute duty" (as opposed to a "target duty") always "precludes the . . . authority from ordering its expenditure priorities for itself"[414] is, however, only a starting point, for three further factors need to be considered.

(a) Even if the duty is strictly enforceable, it is not always clear whether, or to what extent, the courts may disallow, amend or reorder the allocation of the authority's budgetary decisions and allocation of resources.

(b) Even if the authority possesses a discretionary power, there is a question as to what extent it possesses the discretion to ignore or

---

[409] *R. v Chief Constable of Sussex Ex p. International Traders Ferry Ltd* [1999] 2 A.C. 418; also *R. (on the application of Pfizer Ltd) v Secretary of State for Health* [2002] EWCA Civ 1566; [2003] 1 C.M.L.R. 19 (CA upheld decision to provide the drug Viagra to a limited category of patients); K. Syrett, "Impotence or Importance?" Judicial Review in an Era of Explicit NHS Rationing" (2004) 67 M.L.R. 289. *cf. R. (on the application of Rogers) v Swindon NHS Primary Care Trust* [2006] EWCA Civ 392; [2006] 1 W.L.R. 2649 (policy on funding breast cancer treatment with an unlicensed drug called Herceptin was irrational); K. Syrett, "Opening Eyes to the Reality of Scarce Health Care Resources? *R. (on the application of Rogers) v Swindon PCT and Secretary of State for Health*" [2006] P.L. 664.
[410] [1998] A.C. 714; and *R. v Sefton MBC Ex p. Help the Aged* [1997] 4 All E.R. 532, CA (lack of financial resources does not entitle a local authority to defer compliance with their duty under Chronically Sick and Disabled Persons Act 1970 s.2); *R. v Cheshire CC Ex p. C* [1998] E.L.R. 66 (decision about special educational needs should be made on purely educational grounds without reference to financial considerations); Case C–44/95 *R. v Secretary of State for the Environment Ex p. RSPB* [1997] Q.B. 206 (ECJ held that economic considerations are not relevant to determining wild bird protection areas under Directive 79/409); *R. v Secretary of State for the Environment Ex p. Kingston-Upon-Hull City Council* [1996] Env. L.R. 248 (cost of the treatment of waste water was not a relevant consideration); *Cf. R. v National Rivers Authority Ex p. Moreton* [1996] Env. L.R. D17 (investment budget relevant to decision of NRA to allow discharge); *R. v Hillingdon LBC Ex p. Governing Body of Queensmead School* [1997] E.L.R. 331 (budgetary constraints and lack of funds could play no part in the assessment of a child's special educational needs);
[411] *Tandy* [1998] A.C. 714 at 749.
[412] J. King, "The Justiciability of Resource Allocation" (2007) 70 M.L.R. 197; S. Fredman, "Positive Rights and Transformed: Positive Duties and Positive Rights" [2006] P.L. 498; see e.g. *R. v Secretary of State for the Home Department Ex p. Limbuela* [2005] UKHL 66; [2006] 1 A.C. 396.
[413] *Barnet LBC* [2003] UKHL 57; [2004] 2 A.C. 208. Lord Nicholls and Lord Steyn dissented, regarding the duty as an "absolute" and not "target duty".
[414] *Barnet LBC* [2003] UKHL 57; [2004] 2 A.C. 208 at [13].

neglect the sufficient allocation of its scarce resources in pursuit of that power.

(c) A further (and somewhat separate question) is the extent to which the courts ought to avoid making judgments or imposing remedies which cause the expenditure of public funds.[415]

5–130 In Chapter 1, we saw that the allocation of resources is regarded as a matter which is not normally amenable to judicial review for one or more of four reasons.[416] First, the question of expenditure often goes hand in hand with a "policy" question (e.g. whether to devote additional resources to a space or nuclear programme rather than university education), which lies squarely within the constitutional competence of the legislature or executive and not the courts. Secondly, the decision of the court to increase or reduce expenditure may not be able to be made by reference to any objective standards. Thirdly, the courts may not have the expertise to decide the question. Fourthly, the decision may be "polycentric" in character, namely, it will require a series of adjustments in the decision-maker's other budgetary allocations (in the context of finite resources) which the courts are not competent either to set in motion or to decide.[417] Examples of polycentric situations are discussed in Chapter 1, and reflected in the approach in *R. v Cambridge DHA Ex p. B (No.1)*, where the decision of a hospital not to provide expensive treatment to a child with cancer was upheld by the Court of Appeal. Acknowledging that in the "real world . . . difficult and agonising judgments have to be made as to how a limited budget is best allocated to the maximum advantage of the maximum number of patients" (for example making decisions as to whether kidney dialysis over a period of months should be sacrificed to the urgent cancer operation in that case), Sir Thomas Bingham M.R. held "that is not a judgment which a court can make".[418]

5–131 Nevertheless, there are a number of different situations where the courts have required the allocation of resources, even where no particular duty was engaged. Parliament had enacted a statute to implement a new criminal injuries compensation scheme. The statute conferred upon the Home Secretary discretion as to when to bring the new scheme into effect. Before implementing the new scheme, the Home Secretary sought to introduce, under his prerogative powers (by means of which the previous scheme had been administered), a scheme different from that envisaged by the legislation. The House of Lords held that the courts should "hesitate long" before holding the Home Secretary under a duty to implement the scheme contemplated by the statute. However, he did not have absolute and

---

[415] The first two questions (which he considers as one) are referred to by King as questions of "discretionary allocative decision-making" and the third as a question of "allocative impact": King (2007) M.L.R. 197.

[416] See 1–025 *et seq*.

[417] See 1–033–036.

[418] [1995] 1 W.L.R. 898; and see the South African case *T. Soobramoney v Minister of Health Kwazula Natal* 1997 (12) BCL.R. 1696 CCSA.

unfettered discretion not to do so. The cost of implementing the statutory scheme was a factor relevant to his decision as to when the new scheme might be implemented. But the cost was not decisive, and would not justify the frustration of the statutory purpose by a scheme inconsistent with that approved by Parliament.[419] Another case where a power rather than duty was in issue involved the Broadcasting Complaints Commission, which decided not to investigate a complaint on the ground that to do so would be burdensome and perhaps require the employment of additional staff. These reasons were held not to excuse the failure to investigate the complaint.[420]

In addition, the issue of allocation of resources presents itself in different 5–132 guises. It by no means always rests on the distinction between target duties and enforceable duties. General principles of public law may be engaged, as was the case where a company had overpaid rates to a local authority. The local authority claimed unfettered discretion whether or not to refund the rates, which it was reluctant to do because of its own poor financial situation and the adverse effect of the expenditure on the situation of the ratepayers. It was held that, in the circumstances, the authority should, as a prime consideration, have had regard to the unfairness to the company.[421] In some cases the issue may rest upon the interpretation of a particular statutory provision rather than the category of duty (target or enforceable). For example the Court of Appeal considered whether a local authority had given the applicant a "reasonable opportunity" to secure accommodation. It was held that the expression "reasonable opportunity" referred to what was reasonable from the standpoint of the applicant, and did not permit the authority to take into account its own lack of resources.[422] And even when a duty is clearly engaged, such as the duty to award social security benefit, the courts have held that delay in processing claims for the benefit could be excused by the lack of sufficient funds or resources.[423]

The lack of resources has sometimes been pleaded to excuse a delay 5–133 particularly (but not confined to) situations concerning the right under Art.5(4) of the ECHR to a "speedy" decision and under Art 6(1) ECHR to a hearing "within a reasonable time". The court will not "shut their eyes to the practicalities of litigious life",[424] nor to the fact that in general the court

[419] R. v Secretary of State for the Home Department Ex p. Fire Brigades Union [1995] 2 A.C. 583. cf. R. v Blackledge (1995) 92 L.S.G. 32 (prosecutions made under orders made pursuant to a statute contemplating their existence only for the period of the "emergency" (following the declaration of war in 1939) not ultra vires). See also Willcock v Muckle [1951] 2 K.B. 844.
[420] R. v Broadcasting Complaints Commission Ex p. Owen [1985] Q.B. 1153.
[421] Tower Hamlets LBC v Chetnik Developments Ltd [1988] A.C. 858; R. v Rochdale MBC Ex p. Cromer Ring Mill Ltd [1982] 3 All E.R. 761.
[422] R. (on the application of Conville) v Richmond upon Thames LBC [2006] EWCA Civ 718; [2006] 1 W.L.R. 2808.
[423] R. v Secretary of State for Social Services Ex p. Child Poverty Action Group [1990] 2 Q.B. 570, CA.
[424] Procurator Fiscal v Watson and Burrows [2002] UKPC D1; [2004] 1 A.C. 379 at [52] (Lord Bingham). Lord Bingham was there summarising the jurisprudence of the ECtHR on the matter, but also endorsed, at [29], the approach of the PC in Darmalingum v The State [2002] 1 W.L.R. 2303; see also Dyer v Watson [2002] UKPC DI [2004] 1 A.C. 379 at [55] (Lord Bingham).

is not well equipped to consider the adequacy of resources. However, adequacy of resources or "administrative necessity" will not automatically excuse delay. Therefore, if it has been established that the delays were inconsistent with the standard of "speed" or "reasonable time", then the onus of justifying the delay will be on the authority,[425] and the court will carry out a careful analysis of the reasons underlying the justification,[426] if necessary requiring that "further resources must be found".[427]

5–134   In general, therefore, public authorities are limited in the circumstances in which they can plead lack of resources as an excuse to judicial intervention. However, the courts too are limited in the circumstances in which they can order the re-allocation of an authority's finite resources. The issue is fundamental to the separation of powers and the rule of law and requires delicate handling for the following reasons:

- In the real world, limited resources must play a part in the exercise of powers and duties.

- However, in the interest of the rule of law the courts should not hesitate to require public duties to be implemented, even where that requires additional expenditure.[428]

- Courts should, however, be sensitive to their constitutional limitations to make policy decisions involving allocation of resources and to their institutional limitations in themselves deciding how (rather than whether) additional expenditure is required. The courts can order additional expenditure but should be wary of reordering the detail of an authority's budget.

- Even when the authority possesses a mere power, or target duty (rather than an enforceable or crystallised duty), the authority should not be able simply to sit on its hands and ignore the implementation of that power or target duty, whether or not that implementation requires expenditure.

[425] *Procurator Fisal* [2002] UKPC D1; [2004] 1 A.C. 379 at [52] (Lord Bingham: "a marked lack of expedition, if unjustified, will point towards a breach of the reasonable time requirement, and the authorities make clear that while, for purposes of the reasonable time requirement, time runs from the date when the defendant is charged, the passage of any considerable period of time before charge may call for greater than normal expedition thereafter"); see further S. Lambert and A. Strugo, "Delay as a Ground of Review" [2005] J.R. 253; 11–072.

[426] *R. (on the application of KB) v Mental Health Review Tribunal* [2002] EWHC 639; (2002) 5 C.C.L. Rep. 458 at [47] (Stanley Burnton J.); and *R. (on the application of Murray) v Parole Board* [2003] EWCA Civ 1561; (2004) 101(1) L.S.G. 21.

[427] *R. (on the application of Noorkoiv) v Secretary of State for the Home Department* [2002] EWCA Civ 770; [2002] 1 W.L.R. 3284 at [58] (Simon Brown L.J.).

[428] Or, as King rightly points out (2007) M.L.R. 197 courts ought not to refuse to award remedies such as damages or compensation on the ground of expense to the authority. In *R. (on the application of Stennett) v Manchester City Council* [2002] UKHL 34; [2002] 2 A.C. 1127, it was held that, despite a burden of between £30 million and £80 million on local authorities of providing after-care services to those released from detention under the Mental Health Act 1983, charging for those services was not authorised under that Act. The case also underlined the point that the existence of a duty does not inevitably mean that the authority has the (incidental) power to implement that duty by charging for it (see 5–019).

PARTIAL ILLEGALITY AND SEVERANCE

What if an act or decision is partly legal and partly illegal? Suppose that an 5–135
authority has power to revoke a person's licence? It revokes X's licence, and
proceeds to order that he shall be disqualified from applying for a new
licence for five years. It has no power to impose such a disqualification. In
this case, X will be able to obtain a quashing order in respect of the five-year
disqualification, or a declaration that the disqualification is void; but the
court can still hold that the revocation of his licence is valid, for the two
limbs of the tribunal's order are severable from one another.

Cases of partial invalidity are often more complicated than this because 5–136
the good and the bad elements are not clearly distinct. The typical problem
in this area of the law arises where a permit or licence has been granted
subject to void conditions. Three approaches may be followed by the court,
assuming that the jurisdiction of the court (e.g. to enter in an appeal against
the conditions alone) has not been demarcated by statute. First, it may set
aside the entire decision because the competent authority might well have
been unwilling to grant unconditional permission; the applicant must
therefore start again.[429] Secondly, it may simply sever the bad from the good.
In such a case the effect will be to give unconditional permission if all the
conditions are struck down, and this may frustrate the intentions of the
competent authority.[430] Thirdly, the court may adopt an intermediate
position, and sever the invalid condition only if it is trivial, or if it is quite
extraneous to the subject matter of the grant, or perhaps if there are other
reasons for supposing that the authority would still have granted permission
had it believed that the conditions might be invalid. This approach has
recommended itself to the House of Lords in a case involving the validity of
planning conditions.[431] But it involves the courts in a speculative attribution
of intent to an administrative body.

Until recently, it was difficult to elicit any clear principle from the cases on
partly invalid byelaws, though the courts had less compunction about
striking out only the invalid words if the character of what remained was

---

[429] *Hall & Co v Shoreham-by-Sea UDC* [1964] 1 W.L.R. 240; *Pyx Granite Co v Ministry of
Housing and Local Government* [1958] 1 Q.B. 554 at 578–579 (Hodson L.J); *R. v Hillingdon
LBC Ex p. Royco Homes Ltd* [1974] Q.B. 720.
[430] Nevertheless, this course has been adopted in a number of cases, e.g. *Ellis v Dubowski*
[1921] 3 K.B. 621 (though this was a prosecution for breach of a invalid condition and the
question of severability did not directly arise); *Mixnam's Properties Ltd v Chertsey UDC*
[1965] A.C. 735; *Hartnell v Minister of Housing and Local Government* [1965] A.C. 1134;
Lowe (David) & Sons Ltd v Provost, etc. of Burgh of Musselburgh 1974 S.L.T. 5.
[431] *Kingsway Investments (Kent) Ltd v Kent CC* [1971] A.C. 72 at 90–91, 102–103, 112–114;
though cf. [1971] A.C. 106–107 (Guest L.J.); *Allnatt London Properties Ltd v Middlesex CC*
(1964) 62 L.G.R. 304. See also *Transport Ministry v Alexander* [1978] 1 N.Z.L.R. 306 at
311–312 (invalid part severable because it was "not fundamental or part of the structure of
the regulation").

unaltered by a decision to sever the bad from the good.[432] In *DPP v Hutchinson*,[433] the House of Lords considered the validity of byelaws prohibiting entry onto the Greenham Common where there were military installations. The enabling legislation permitted such byelaws to be made, provided that rights of common were not interfered with. The appellants claimed that the byelaws did interfere with the rights of common and this contention was upheld. Could the bad parts of the byelaw be severed from the good? The House of Lords considered whether, in order to be severable, the test was that of "textual severability" or "substantial severability" If textual severability was the correct test, then the bad part of the instrument could be disregarded as exceeding the lawmaker's power, provided what remained was still "grammatical and coherent".[434] If, however, the proper test was that of substantial severability, then what remained after severance could survive as lawful provided that is was "essentially unchanged in its legislative purpose, operation and effect".[435] The majority of their Lordships accepted the test of "substantial severability" and it was held that this could be achieved in the following two situations:

(a) Where the text could be severed so that the valid part could operate independently of the invalid part, then the test of substantial severability would be satisfied when the valid part is unaffected by, and independent of, the invalid part.

(b) Where severance could only be effected by modifying the text, this can only be done "when the court is satisfied that it is effecting no change in the substantial purpose and effect of the impugned provision".[436]

---

[432] *Potato Marketing Board v Merricks* [1958] 2 Q.B. 316 at 333 (Devlin J.) (a case of a partly unauthorised demand for information under the threat of a penalty). The cases on byelaws are generally unhelpful, e.g. *R. v Lundie* (1862) 31 L.J.M.C. 157; *Reay v Gateshead Corp* (1886) 55 L.T. 92 at 103; *Strickland v Hayes* [1896] 1 Q.B. 290 at 292; *Rossi v Edinburgh Corp* [1905] A.C., 21.

[433] [1990] 2 A.C. 783; A. Bradley, "Judicial Enforcement of Ultra Vires Byelaws: The Proper Scope of Severance" [1990] P.L. 293.

[434] Sometimes called the "blue pencil test": *R. v Company of Fisherman of Faversham* (1799) 8 Dwrn & E. 352 at 356.

[435] *Dunkley v Evans* [1981] 1 W.L.R. 1522; *Daymond v Plymouth CC* [1976] A.C. 609. See also the Australian approach followed in *R. v Commonwealth Court of Conciliation and Arbitration Ex p. Whybrow and Co* (1910) 11 C.L.R. 1; *Owners of SS Kalibav Wilson* (1910) 11 C.L.R. 689. In Australia severability is governed by legislation; Interpretation Act 1901 s.46(1)(b) and s.15(a) which expressly recognise severability in the context of judicial review of administration and constitutional review respectively.

[436] Lord Bridge at 811; cf. Lord Lowry, dissenting, at 819: "To liberalise the [severance] test would be anarchic, not progressive". For an example of the severance of an invalid part of a statutory instrument (void for unreasonableness) under situation (a) above, *R. v Immigration Appeal. Tribunal Ex p. Begum Manshoora* [1986] Imm. A.R. 385. *cf. R. v Inland Revenue Commissioners Ex p. Woolwich Equitable Building Society* [1990] 1 W.L.R. 1400, HL (alteration of substance by textual severance too great); *R. v North Hertfordshire DC Ex p. Cobbold* [1985] 3 All E.R. 486 (unreasonable conditions attached to license for pop concert. Severance would alter whole character of licence). See also *Mouchell Superannuation Fund Trustees v Oxfordshire CC* [1992] 1 P.L.R. 97, CA.

Omissions

The corollary of severance by "blue pencilling" arises when some required 5–137 provision is omitted from a regulation. Is it open to the court to supply that omission? Can the court write in an exemption? The Court of Appeal held that an omission was curable in a case where it "appears to have affected nobody" and therefore, "however cogent the case in legal theory" for striking down the regulation, to do so "would represent a triumph of logic over reason".[437] The omission related to the failure in the regulation (which banned a herbal medicine) to exempt goods in transit. Sedley L.J. recognised that there may be occasions where it is simply too late, or simply insufficient, to allow the rule-maker to supply the omission. In such a case, the test would be the same as that in *Hutchinson*, namely, would the new provision be "totally different in character" from the impugned one? However, if the omission can be made good without doing harm, or disrupting the existing, lawful text, then the court could permit the rule-maker to "insert the missing brick", rather than pull down the entire structure.[438] This new doctrine of "innocuous amendment"[439] is a pragmatic response to a difficult situation. However, care must be exercised lest it encourage lax drafting and encourages litigation in order to fill in the gap.

DELEGATION OF POWERS

The rule against delegation

A discretionary power must, in general, be exercised only by the public 5–138 authority to which it has been committed. It is a well-known principle of law that when a power has been conferred to a person in circumstances indicating that trust is being placed in his individual judgment and discretion, he must exercise that power personally unless he has been expressly empowered to delegate it to another.[440] This principle has been applied in the law of agency, trusts and arbitration as well as in public law. The former

[437] R. *(on the application of National Association of Health Stores) v Department of Health* [2005] EWCA Civ 154.
[438] At [18]–[20].
[439] I. Steele, "Note on R.(National Association of Health Stores) v Department of Health" [2005] J.R. 232.
[440] Sometimes expressed in the form of the maxim *delegatus non potest delegare* (or *delegan*), a maxim which, it has been suggested, "owes its origin to medieval commentators on the Digest and the Decretals, and its vogue in the common law to the carelessness of a sixteenth-century printer": P. Duff and H. Whiteside, "The Maxim in American Constitutional Law: A Study in Delegation of Legislative Power" (1929) 14 Cornell L.Q. 168, 173. The authors suggest that the maxim, recited by Coke in his Institutes (ii, 597), was probably taken from an incorrect rendering in a passage in an early printed edition of Bracton. But see H. Ehmke, "'Delegatus Potestas Non Potest Delegare: A Maxim of American Constitutional Law" (1961) 47 Cornell L.Q. 50, 54–55, pointing out that Bracton was indeed addressing himself to the impropriety of sub-delegating judicial power delegated by the King.

assumption that the principle applies only to the sub-delegation of delegated *legislative* powers and to the sub-delegation of other powers delegated by a superior *administrative* authority, is unfounded. It applies to the delegation of *all* classes of powers, and it was indeed originally invoked in the context of delegation of judicial powers. It is therefore convenient to travel beyond the delegation of discretionary powers in the strict sense and to view the problem as a whole.

5–139 The cases on delegation have arisen in diverse contexts, and many of them turn upon unique points of statutory interpretation. The judgments are not always consistent. The principle does not amount to a rule that knows no exception; it is a rule of construction which makes the presumption that "a discretion conferred by statute is prima facie intended to be exercised by the authority on which the statute has conferred it and by no other authority, but this presumption may be rebutted by any contrary indications found in the language, scope or object of the statute".[441] Courts have sometimes wrongly assumed that the principle lays down a rule of rigid application, so that devolution of power cannot (in the absence of express statutory authority) be valid unless it falls short of delegation. This has resulted in an unreasonably restricted meaning often being given to the concept of delegation.[442]

Delegation of "Judicial" Powers

5–140 The principle has been applied most rigorously to proceedings of courts,[443] requiring a judge to act personally throughout a case except in so far as he is expressly absolved from this duty by statute.[444] Special tribunals and public bodies exercising functions broadly analogous to the judicial are also precluded from delegating their powers of decision unless there is express authority to that effect.[445] This may be the case where judicial functions are

[441] J. Willis, "Delegatus non potest delegare" (1943) 21 Can. B.R. 257, 259.
[442] See cases cited by Willis (1943) 21 Can. B.R. 257, 257–258.
[443] *Caudle v Seymour* (1841) 1 Q.B. 889 (depositions taken by justices' clerk). cf. *Hunt v Allied Bakeries Ltd (No.2)* [1959] 1 W.L.R. 50 at 56; *R. v Brentford Justices Ex p. Catlin* [1975] Q.B. 455; *R. v Majewski* [1977] A.C. 443 at 449–451 (registrar's power to refer criminal appeals for summary dismissal); *R. v Gateshead Justices Ex p. Tesco* [1981] Q.B. 470 (power of single justice or justices' clerk to issue summonses could not be delegated to court official); approved in *Hill v Alderton* (1982) 75 Cr. App. R. 346, HL; *Olympia Press Ltd v Hollis* [1973] 1 W.L.R. 1520 where it was held that each magistrate did not have to read all the books that were the subject of forfeiture proceedings provided that they collectively discussed them before making a decision (*Burke v Copper* [1962] 1 W.L.R. 700 distinguished).
[444] On implied power to sub-delegate ministerial functions: *Allam & Co v Europa Poster Services Ltd* [1968] 1 W.L.R. 638 (where the sub-delegated function, though not the decisions culminating in it, was merely "ministerial").
[445] *GMC v UK Dental Board* [1936] Ch. 41; *Barnard v National Dock Labour Board* [1953] 2 Q.B. 18; *Vine v National Dock Labour Board* [1957] A.C. 488; *Labour Relation Board of Saskatchewan v Speers* [1948] 1 D.L.R. 340; *Turner v Allison* [1971] N.Z.L.R. 833. cf. *Re S. (a Barrister)* [1970] 1 Q.B. 160 (jurisdiction to disbar, though ostensibly delegated, was in truth original); *Re Schabas and Caput of University of Toronto* (1975) 52 D.L.R. (3rd) 495; *Re Bortolotti and Ministry of Housing* (1977) 76 D.L.R. (3rd) 408 (chairman of tribunals has no inherent power to make rulings on points of law that bind the other members). Legislation may be construed to define the tribunal as those members who sit in a particular case. See *Howard v Borneman (No.2)* [1976] A.C. 301.

expressly "privatised" or "contracted out". In countries with written constitutions the question has arisen as to whether certain disciplinary or quasi-judicial functions can ever be devolved. For example, is prison discipline involving the imposition of penalties a core state function, or can it be devolved to private companies running prisons?[446] Generally, in spite of the retreat from a rigid conceptual distinction between administrative, judicial, and quasi-judicial functions, it is still the case that the courts will be more ready to find a necessary implication of delegation in respect of a body that does not exercise strictly "judicial" functions.[447]

But, as we shall see in the discussion on procedural propriety,[448] the courts will sometimes concede that a public body has an implied power to entrust a group of its own members with authority to investigate, to hear evidence and submissions and to make recommendations in a report, provided that (a) it retains the power of decision in its own hands and receives a report full enough to enable it to comply with its duty to "hear" before deciding,[449] and (b) the context does not indicate that it must perform the entire "adjudica-

5–141

---

[446] This issue was discussed in the South African Constitutional Court in *AAA Investments Ltd v The Micro Finance Regulatory Council and the Minister of Trade and Industry* [2006] C.C.T. 51/05 (July 26, 2006), where it was held that such delegation of governmental functions was not "overbroad" provided that responsibility for the functions lay ultimately with the government.

[447] *Young v Fife Regional Council*, 1986 S.L.T. 331 (Scottish Teachers Salaries Committee and no power to delegate decision regarding teachers' pay to sub-committee, because since functions was "at least" quasi judicial, there was no implied power of delegation); *R. v Gateshead Justices Ex p. Tesco* [1981] Q.B. 470 (court officials could lawfully carry out non-judicial duties of justices' clerk, but no judicial duties). South African courts allowed implied delegation of "purely administrative" or "ministerial" functions but not of "legislative" or "judicial" functions: *United Democratic Front v Staatspresident*, 1987 (4) S.A. 649 (W).

[448] *cf. Osgood v Nelson* (1872) L.R. 5 H.L. 636 (council could validly empower one of its committees to investigate charges against an official, the council itself retaining the power of decision); *Devlin v Barnett* [1958] N.Z.L.R. 828 (promotions board entitled to entrust another body with conduct of tests); *Attorney General (ex rel. McWhirter) v Independent Broadcasting Authority* [1973] Q.B. 629 at 651, 657–658 (Authority normally able to rely on staff reports except when credible evidence contradicting a report is received): *R. v Commission for Racial Equality Ex p. Cottrell and Rothon* [1980] 1 W.L.R. 1580 (CRE allowed to delegate formal investigation into alleged discrimination and hence could rely and act on evidence received in reports); *Vine* [1957] A.C. 488, 512; *cf. Re Sarran* (1969) 14 W.L.R. 361.

[449] It seems that if a public authority is required to be satisfied of the existence of certain facts before exercising a power but is not obliged to afford any hearing beforehand, its satisfaction may be sufficiently expressed by formally adopting findings made by its committees even though these findings do not fully record the materials on which they were based: *Goddard v Minister of Housing and Local Government* [1958] 1 W.L.R. 1151; *Savoury v Secretary of State for Wales* (1976) 31 P. & C.R. 344 (also illustrates the difficulty of reviewing the validity of the resolution for lack of evidence when the applicant is unable to discover upon what evidence the council acted); *cf. Electronic Industries Ltd v Oakleigh Corp* [1973] V.R. 177 (court prepared to infer that the council had not considered a particular matter). But in some contexts (e.g. where bodies making decisions significantly affecting individual rights perfunctorily adopt findings by officials) the courts may hold that failure to exercise independent judgment or discretion constitutes an unlawful abdication of authority; *R. v Chester CC Ex p. Quietlynn Ltd* (1984) 83 L.G.R. 308; *R. v Birmingham CC Ex p. Quietlynn Ltd* (1985) 83 L.G.R. 461.

tory" process itself.[450] Determinations by ministers, however, stand in a special class;[451] not only may the hearing be conducted by a person authorised on their behalf, but the decision may be made by an authorised official in the minister's name.[452]

Delegation of "Legislative" Powers

5-142 There is a strong presumption against construing a grant of delegated legislative power as empowering the delegate to sub-delegate the whole or any substantial part of the law-making power entrusted to it.[453] In New Zealand cases this presumption was invoked as a ground for holding regulations and orders made by the sub-delegate to be invalid.[454] But the presumption is not irrebuttable, and in a Canadian wartime case the power of the Governor General in Council to make such regulations as he might by reason of the existence of war deem necessary or advisable for the defence of Canada was held to be wide enough to enable him to sub-delegate to the Controller of Chemicals power to make regulations.[455] There seems to be no English authority directly in point in constitutional or administrative law. In the First World War the sweeping legislative powers vested by the Defence of the Realm Acts in the King in Council were extensively sub-delegated to ministers and others; the validity of such sub-delegation was not, apparently, challenged in the courts. In the Second World War the King in Council was

[450] Delegation of purely investigatory or fact-finding functions may therefore be lawfully delegated, e.g *R. v North Thames RHA Ex p. L (An Infant)* [1996] Med. L.R. 385; *R. v Hertsmere BC Ex p. Woolgar* (1995) 27 H.L.R. 703.
[451] On the *Carltona* principle.
[452] *Doody v Secretary of State for the Home Department* [1994] 1 A.C. 531, HL (a decision required to be taken by the Home Secretary on the period which a life sentence prisoner should serve for the purposes of retribution and deterrence may be taken by a Minister of state at the Home Office on his behalf. However, any advice on that question given by the Lord Chief justice must be given by the holder of that office, as his function cannot be delegated. The Home Secretary no longer has this function but has power not to release prisoners after the minimum term has been served: Criminal Justice Act 2003 ss.224–236).
[453] *King-Emperor v Benoari Lal Sarma* [1945] A.C. 14 at 24; *R. v Lampe Ex p. Maddolozzo* [1966] A.L.R. 144 (dicta); B. Fox and O. Davies, "Sub-Delegated Legislation" (1955) 28 A.L.J. 486.
[454] *Geraghty v Porter* [1917] N.Z.L.R. 554 (distinguished in *Hookings v Director of Civil Aviation* [1957] N.Z.L.R. 929); *Godkin v Newman* [1928] N.Z.L.R. 593; *Jackson (FE) & Co v Collector of Customs* [1939] N.Z.L.R. 682 at 732–734; *Hawke's Bay Raw Milk Producers' Co-operative Co v New Zealand Milk Board* [1961] N.Z.L.R. 218 (distinguished in *Van Gorkom v Attorney-General* [1977] 1 N.Z.L.R. 535). See C. Aikman, "Subdelegation of the Legislative Power" (1960) 3 Victoria Uni. of Wellington L. Rev 69 for an authoritative analysis of these still relevant cases. More recently, see *Videbeck v Auckland City Council* [2002] 3 N.Z.L.R. 842 (court would not permit 'rubber stamping' by decision-maker of recommendations by officials, nor de facto delegation contrary to statutory requirements).
[455] *Reference Re Chemicals Regulations* [1943] S.C.R. 1; but see *Attorney General of Canada v Brent* [1956] S.C.R. 318 (powers of Governor-General in Council to make regulations with respect to immigration restrictions not validly exercised by making of regulations which in substance transferred to public officers the effective power to make the necessary rules); with which contrast *Hookings v Director of Civil Aviation* [1957] N.Z.L.R. 929 (delegation of dispensing power); and *Arnold v Hunt* (1943) 67 C.L.R. 429; *cf. Croft v Rose* [1957] A.L.R. 148; J. Merralls, "Note" (1957) 1 Melbourne Univ. L.R. 105.

expressly empowered by s.1(3) of the Emergency Powers (Defence) Act 1939 to sub-delegate his legislative powers under the Act. It is doubtful whether implied authority to subdelegate legislative powers would ever be conceded by the English courts save in time of grave emergency.[456] For when Parliament has specifically appointed an authority to discharge a legislative function, a function normally exercised by Parliament itself, it cannot readily be presumed to have intended that its delegate should be free to empower another person or body to act in its place. Nevertheless, one can envisage circumstances in which a carefully delimited sub-delegation of rule-making power could more reasonably be upheld than a sub-delegation of uncontrolled administrative discretion to be exercised in relation to individual cases.[457]

Delegation of "Administrative" Powers

Most of the practical problems concerned with sub-delegation have been related to the exercise of powers of a discretionary character—to regulate, to grant licences and permits, to requisition, to require the abatement of nuisances and to institute legal proceedings. **5–143**

Delegation and Agency

In this context, sharp differences of opinion have been expressed on the relationship between the concepts of delegation and agency. They have sometimes been treated as being virtually indistinguishable[458] but in many cases a distinction has been drawn between them, particularly where the court is acting on the assumption that an authority can validly employ an agent but cannot delegate its powers **5–144**

The correct view seems to be that the distinctions drawn between delegation and agency are frequently misconceived in so far as they are based on the erroneous assumption that there is never an implied power to delegate. However, some relationships that are properly included within the concept of delegation are substantially different from those which typify the relationship of principal and agent. There are three main characteristics of agency. First, the agent acts on behalf of his principal, he does so in his name, and the acts done by the agent within the scope of his authority are attributable to the principal. These principles are broadly applicable to delegation in administrative law, and it would generally be held to be unlawful for an authority to invest a delegate with powers exercisable in his **5–145**

---

[456] Reference to extrinsic documents in delegated legislation is common, and is not considered to involve sub-delegation unless the document is not in existence when the instrument is approved, and its content is beyond the control of the minister; see criticisms of the Joint Committee on Statutory Instruments. HC Paper No. 21–XI (Session 1974/75); *cf.* R. v Secretary of State for Social Services Ex p. Camden LBC [1987] 1 W.L.R. 819.

[457] *Aikman* (1960) 3 Victoria Uni. of Wellington L. Rev. 69 82–83.

[458] See, e.g. *Huth v Clarke* (1890) 25 Q.B.D. 391; *Lewisham Borough v Roberts* [1949] 2 K.B. 608, 622; *Gordon, Dadds & Co v Morris* [1945] 2 All E.R. 616.

own name. But where legislative powers are delegated by Parliament, or validly sub-delegated by Parliament's delegate, the delegate or subdelegate exercises his powers in his own name. And in the schemes of administrative delegation drawn up in local government law, the relationships between the local authorities concerned have often been far removed from those connoted by the relationship of principal and agent.[459]

Secondly, the agent can be—given detailed directions by his principal and does not usually have a wide area of discretion. On the other hand one to whom statutory discretionary powers are delegated often has a substantial measure of freedom from control in exercising them. But the degree of freedom from control with which he is vested may be a decisive factor in determining the validity of the delegation made to him.

5–146   The more significant are the effective powers of control retained by the delegating authority, the more readily will the courts uphold the validity of the delegation; and they may choose to uphold its validity by denying that there has been any delegation at all, on the ground that in substance the authority in which the discretion has been vested by statute continues to address its own mind to the exercise of the powers.[460]

Thirdly, in agency the principal retains concurrent powers. This principle was generally applicable to delegation by a local authority to its committees. Thus, the local authority retained power to make decisions in relation to matters comprised within the delegation[461]—a rule now expressly restated by statute[462]—and it could (and presumably still can) revoke the authority of a delegate.[463] Nevertheless, it has sometimes been stated that delegation implies a denudation of authority.[464] Such a statement was made by the Employment Appeal Tribunal in *Robertson v Department for the Environment, Food and Rural Affairs*.[465] This cannot be accepted as an accurate general proposition.[466] On the contrary, the general rule is that an authority which delegates its powers does not divest itself of them indeed, if it purports to abdicate it may be imposing a legally ineffective fetter on its own discretion[467]—and can resume them. But if it has validly delegated an

---

[459] Inter-delegation between local authorities was considerably diminished by the Local Government Act 1972.
[460] As in *Devlin v Barnett* [1958] N.Z.L.R. 828; cf. *Winder v Cambridgeshire CC* (1978) 76 L.G.R. 549.
[461] *Huth v Clarke* (1890) 25 Q.B.D. 391; *Gordon, Dadds & Co v Morris* [1945] 2 All E.R. 616 at 621; *Winder v Cambridgeshire CC* (1978) 76 L.G.R. 549 (local authority retained residual discretion to exercise a power that it had delegated under a statutorily required instrument of college government, when the refusal of the delegate to act would otherwise frustrate the discharge of the authority's overall educational responsibilities).
[462] Local Government Act 1972 s.101(4) as amended by Local Government Act 2003 s.99.
[463] *Manton v Brighton Corp* [1951] 2 K.B. 393 (power of council to revoke authority of member of sub-committee).
[464] *Blackpool Corp v Locker* [1948] 1 K.B. 349 at 377–378 (Scott and Asquith L.JJ.).
[465] [2005] EWCA Civ 138; [2005] I.C.R. 750.
[466] Strong support for the position here, and criticism of *Robertson and Blackpool Corp* is provided by S. Bailey, "Delegation and Concurrent Exercises of Power" [2005] J.R. 84.
[467] On the general rule that a public authority cannot fetter itself in the exercise of discretionary powers, see Ch.9.

executive power to make decisions, it will normally be bound by a particular decision, conferring rights on individuals (and possibly one derogating from those rights), made in pursuance of the delegated power and will be incapable of rescinding or varying it;[468] nor will it be competent to "ratify" with retroactive effect a decision made by the delegate in excess of the powers so delegated, even though the delegating authority could validly have made the decision itself in the first place.[469]

It must be explained that in local government law there may be delegation **5–147** either of executive power[470] (in which case the delegating-authority may be bound by the delegate's decisions and the degree of supervision exercisable over the delegate may sometimes be minimal) or of power to make recommendations or decisions subject to the approval of the delegating authority. In the latter class of case (which is not always categorised as true delegation) difficult marginal problems of interpretation have arisen where a delegate or subdelegate has taken action e.g. to require the execution of works on private property or to institute legal proceedings), without antecedent approval and the authority whose approval is required has purported to ratify the action already taken.[471] Other difficult problems, peripheral to the general question of delegation, have arisen in cases where it has been contended that a local government officer, acting without a formal grant of authority, has imposed legally binding obligations on his employers by virtue of undertakings, assurances or other conduct.[472]

---

[468] *Battelley v Finsbury BC* (1958) 56 L.G.R. 165; *Morris v Shire of Morwell* [1948] V.L.R. 83. *cf.* the unsettled question of whether the Home Secretary may disregard a decision by an immigration officer to grant leave to enter that is not consistent with the immigration rules: *R. v Secretary of State for the Home Department Ex p. Choudhary* [1978] 1 W.L.R. 1177; *R. v Secretary of State for the Home Department Ex p. Ram* [1979] 1 W.L.R. 148.

[469] This appears to be the best explanation of the decision in *Blackpool Corp v Locker* [1948] 1 K.B. 349. A minister delegated requisitioning powers, subject to restrictive conditions, to local authorities or their clerks by a departmental circular. A town clerk requisitioned L's house without complying with certain conditions. It was unsuccessfully contended that a subsequent letter from the minister had cured the invalidity by ratification. It was doubtful, moreover, whether the purported ratification was to be construed as anything more than an act of affirmance, or whether the local authority or its clerk was to be regarded as an agent of the minister, who was himself acting "on behalf of His Majesty". But the assertion (at 379) that the minister was incompetent to requisition the house anew because he had not reserved powers to himself in the instrument of delegation cannot be supported. See also *Attorney General Ex rel. Co-operative Retail Services Ltd v Taff-Ely BC* (1979) 39 P. & C.R. 223, CA, affirmed 42 P. & C.R. 1, HL (council could not ratify purported grant of planning permission by district clerk, since ultra vires act could not be ratified; *quaere* whether in any case council had power to grant planning permission). And see the discussion on estoppel, 12–063 et seq.

[470] The power of local authorities to delegate to committees, sub-committees and officers, and of committees to sub-delegate was greatly extended by the Local Government Act 1972 Pt VI, esp. s.101.

[471] On the one hand, *Firth v Staines* [1897] 2 Q.B. 70; *R. v Chapman Ex p. Arlidge* [1918] 2 K.B. 298; and *Warwick RDC v Miller-Mead* [1962] Ch. 441 applied by the CA in *Stoke on Trent CC v B & Q Retail Ltd* [1984] Ch. 1; on the other hand, St Leonard's Vestry v Holmes (1885) 50 J.P 132 and Bowyer, *Philpott & Payne Ltd v Mather* [1919] 1 K.B. 419. *cf. Attorney General Ex rel. Co-operative Retail Services Ltd v Taff-Ely BC* (1979) 39 P. & C.R. 223.

[472] M. Freedland, "The Rule Against Delegation and the Carltona doctrine in an Agency Context" [1996] P.L. 19.

General Principles of Delegation

5-148 The following are some of the principles elicited from the cases in which devolution of statutory discretions has been considered.

Vesting Authority Without Supervisory Control

5-149 Where an authority vested with discretionary powers empowers one of its committees or subcommittees, members or officers to exercise those powers independently without any supervisory control by the authority itself, the exercise of the powers is likely to be held invalid. Thus, where the Minister of Agriculture had validly delegated to a war agricultural executive committee power to give directions with respect to the cultivation, management or use of land, and the committee sub-delegated to its officer power to determine in which fields a specified crop should be grown and to issue a direction to the farmer without reference to the committee, a direction issued by the officer was held to be invalid.[473] A byelaw by which a local authority hands over its own regulatory powers to an official by vesting him with virtually unrestricted discretion may be held to be void.[474] A delegation of power to review prosecutions to decide whether there was sufficient evidence to proceed, from the Director of Public Prosecutions to non-lawyers, was held unlawful since the statute by giving the power to the DPP clearly contemplated that it would only be delegated to a member of the Crown Prosecution Service, who would be a lawyer.[475] The powers to determine the state of health of a child, in relation to the question of whether free transport to school should be provided, could not be delegated to the school medical officer but had to be exercised by the education committee as a whole.[476]

Degree of control maintained may be material

5-150 The degree of control (before or afterwards) maintained by the delegating authority over the acts of the delegate or subdelegate may be a material factor in determining the validity of the delegation. In general the control preserved (e.g. by a power to refuse to ratify an act or to reject a recommendation) must be close enough for the decision to be identifiable as that of the delegating authority.[477] That the decision of the delegate is not

[473] *Allingham v Minister of Agriculture and Fisheries* [19481] All E.R. 780; *High v Billings* (1903) 67 J.P 388.
[474] *Madoc Township v Quinlan* (1972) 21 D.L.R. (3rd) 136; *R. v Sandler*, 286.
[475] *R. v DPP Ex p. Association of First Division Civil Servants, The Times,* May 24, 1988. However, the HL did not hold invalid power exercised by a subordinate officer of a rating authority when the power was conferred on the authority itself: *Provident Mutual Life Assurance Association v Derby CC* [1981] 1 W.L.R. 173, HL.
[476] *R. v Devon CC Ex p. G* [1989] A.C. 573. On the *Carltona* principle and whether delegation or devolution may not be permitted if the function requires particular competence or qualifications, see 5–00.
[477] *Hall v Manchester Corp.* (1915) 84 L.J. Ch. 734 at 741 and *Cohen v West Ham Corp* [1933] Ch. 814 at 826–827 on the duty of local authorities to exercise independent discretion before acting on reports by their officers; *R. v Board of Assessment, etc.* (1965) 49 D.L.R. (2nd) 156 (tax assessment board, by simply adopting valuations made by official, failed to perform statutory duties).

final or conclusive because of control exerted by a third party, in the form of an appeal or review from the decision of the delegating authority and/or delegate, may also be an important factor in determining the validity of the delegation.[478]

Amplitude, impact and importance

How far, if at all, delegation of discretionary power is impliedly authorised 5–151 may also depend on the amplitude of the power, the impact of its exercise upon individual interests and the importance to be attached to the efficient transaction of public business by informal delegation of responsibility.[479] If authorisation is permitted, the choice of one officer over another for the exercise of the delegated power is a matter for the holder of the power, within the limits of rationality, and the choice of the level of the delegated office-holder will depend not primarily on rank, but on matters such as "resources, availability, skills, contacts, experience, knowledge and so forth".[480]

Generally improper to delegate wide powers

It is improper for an authority to delegate wide discretionary powers to 5–152 another authority over which it is incapable of exercising direct control, unless it is expressly empowered so to delegate.[481] Thus, the Minister of Works could not allocate to the Minister of Health part of his functions in the system of building licensing.[482] A Canadian provincial marketing board, exercising delegated authority, could not sub-delegate part of it regulatory

---

[478] *Provident Mutual Life Assurance Assn v Derby* CC [1981] 1 W.L.R. 173, 181, HL (principal rating assistant could serve completion notice without consulting borough treasurer; right of appeal to county court existed).

[479] *Ex p. Forster, re University of Sydney* (1963) 63 S.R. (N.S.W) 723 at 733–734; Willis; *R. v Monopolies and Mergers Commission Ex p. Argyll Group Plc* [1986] 1 W.L.R. 763, CA held that the Chairman of the MMC did not have authority to act on his own to request the Secretary of State to lay the reference about the company aside. However, a properly constituted group of MMC members would have reached the same conclusion and therefore the act was valid. But where a chairman of a local education committee designated the date for the closure of a school, that was held an unlawful delegation: *R. v Secretary of State for Education and Science Ex p. Birmingham CC* (1984) 83 L.G.R. 79.

[480] *R. (on the application of Chief Constable of the West Midlands Police) v Gonzales* [2002] EWHC 1087 (Admin) at [18] (Sedley L.J.).

[481] cf. *Kyle v Barbor* (1888) 58 L.T. 229.

[482] *Jackson, Stansfield & Sons v Butterworth* [1948] 2 All E.R. 558 at 564–566 (dicta); but is it true that the Minister of Works in that case had done anything more than use the Minister of Health as a convenient channel of communication with local authorities? And see *Lavender (H) & Son Ltd v Minister of Housing and Local Government* [1970] 1 W.L.R. 1231 (Minister X determining planning appeal by mechanically applying policy of Minister Y; decision in effect that of Minister Y, and therefore ultra vires). cf. *Kent CC v Secretary of State for the Environment* (1977) 75 L.G.R. 452, where the minister was held to have decided a planning appeal himself although he had had regard to the opinion of another minister on an important issue in the appeal. If a minister delays the making or implementation of a discretionary decision till the matter has been debated in Parliament he is not, of course, delegating his power of decision at all: *R. v Brixton Prison Governor Ex p. Enaharo* [1963] 2 Q.B. 455.

powers to an inter-provincial authority.[483] Nor could a local authority, empowered to issue cinematograph licences subject to conditions, attach a condition that no film shall be shown which had not been certified for public exhibition by the British Board of Film Censors,[484] unless the authority has expressly reserved to itself power to dispense with that requirement in any individual case.[485] It is doubtful how far a minister would be held to have an implied power to devolve discretionary functions upon local authorities and their officers, over whom he is constitutionally enabled to exercise indirect control. One may surmise that the courts would not readily uphold the validity of a devolution of very wide discretionary powers, but that if the devolution of discretion covered a relatively narrow field they might characterise the relationship as agency rather than delegation and hold that it had been validly created.[486]

Named officers

5–153 Where the exercise of a discretionary power is entrusted to a named officer—e.g. a chief officer of police, a medical officer of health or an inspector—another officer cannot exercise his powers in his stead unless express statutory provision has been made for the appointment of a deputy or unless in the circumstances the administrative convenience of allowing a deputy or other subordinate to act as an authorised agent very clearly outweighs the desirability of maintaining the principle that the officer designated by statute should act personally.[487] But where statute permitted discharge of disciplinary functions of the Law Society Council to "an individual (whether or not a member of the Society's staff)", there was nothing which required the Council to familiarise itself with the name of the delegatee; the Council could delegate to the holder from time to time of an office.[488] The presumption of deliberate selection is not an independent normative principle, but is merely a principle of statutory construction which will readily give way to legislative indications to the contrary.[489]

---

[483] *Prince Edward Island Potato Marketing Board v Willis* (HB) Inc [1952] 2 S.C.R. 391.

[484] *Ellis v Dubowski* [1921] 3 K.B. 621. See also *R. v Burnley Justices* (1916) 85 L.J.K.B. 1565.

[485] *Mills v LCC* [1925] 1 K.B. 213; *R. v Greater London Council Ex p. Blackburn* [1976] 1 W.L.R. 550.

[486] *Jackson, Stansfield & Sons v Butterworth* [1948] 2 All E.R. 558 564–565.

[487] *Nelms v Roe* [1970] 1 W.L.R. 4, 8; *Mason v Pearce, The Times*, October 7, 1981; *R. v Majewski* [1977] A.C. 443 at 449–451. This passage was cited with approval in *R. (on the application of WH Smith Ltd) v Croydon Justices* [2001] E.H.L.R. 12 at [15] (Elias J.); and in *R. v Chief Constable of Greater Manchester Police Ex p. Lainton, The Times*, April 4, 2000. Sedley L.J. in *Chief Constable of West Midlands Police* [2002] EWHC 1087 (Admin) overruled *Nelms v Roe* insofar as Parker C.J. said in that case that the power in question was not subject to the *Carltona* principle, but had to be expressly or impliedly delegated.

[488] *R. v The Law Society Ex p. Curtin* (1994) 6 Admin. L.R. 657.

[489] *R v Law Society Exp. Curtin* (1994) 6 Admin L.R. 657 (Steyn L.J.).

Further sub delegation

The restrictions on the power to delegate have on the whole been applied 5–154
more strictly to the further sub-delegation of sub-delegated powers than to
the sub-delegation of primary delegated powers.[490] This is in accordance
with the maxim that the expression of one excludes the other:[491] where
Parliament has expressly authorised sub-delegation of a specific character, it
can generally be presumed to have intended that no further sub-delegation
shall be permissible.

Exercise of deliberate judgment

Again, it may generally be presumed that express authority to sub-delegate 5–155
powers is to be construed as impliedly excluding authority to sub-delegate
the performance of duties involving the exercise of deliberate judgment,
unless the performance of the duty is inextricably interwoven with the
exercise of the power.[492]

Delegation in accordance with statute

Where power to sub-delegate prescribed functions has been conferred by 5–156
statute, strict requirements to the form of delegation must normally be
observed.[493] Delegation must therefore be conveyed in an authorised form[494]
to the designated authority,[495] and must identify sufficiently what are the
functions thus delegated instead of leaving the sub-delegate to decide the
ambit of his own authority.[496]

Comparative perspectives on delegation

In Australia it has been held that delegation to an office-holder does not 5–157
require renewal each time there is a change in the holder of that office; it has
also held that revocation of a delegation does not affect the validity of

---

[490] See e.g. *Cook v Ward* (1877) 2 C.P.D. 255. Powers of sub-delegation are greatly extended
by the Local Government Act 1972 at s.101.
[491] *Expressio unius est exclusio alterius.*
[492] *Mungoni v Attorney General of Northern Rhodesia* [1960] A.C. 336; *R. v DPP Ex p.
Association of First Division Civil Servants, The Times*, May 24, 1988.
[493] *B (A Solicitor) v Victorian Lawyers RPA Ltd* (2000) 6 V.R. 642.
[494] For the manner of conveying such authorisation within a police force: *Nelms v Roe* [1970]
1 W.L.R. 4; *Pamplin v Gorman* [1980] R.T.R. 54; *cf. Record Tower Cranes Ltd v Gisbey*
[1969] 1 W.L.R. 148.
[495] *cf. Esmonds Motors Pty Ltd v Commonwealth* (1970) 120 C.L.R. 463 (minister acted ultra
vires by designating himself); *R. v Secretary of State for the Environment Ex p. Hillingdon LBC*
[1986] 1 W.L.R. 192, aff'd [1986] 1 W.L.R. 807 (power under s.101(1) of the Local
Government Act 1972 to delegate to a committee does not give the power to delegate to a
committee of one); *cf. R. v Secretary of State for Education and Science Ex p. Birmingham CC*
(1984) 83 L.G.R. 79 (no power to delegate to a member of an authority).
[496] *Ratnagopal v Attorney General* [1970] A.C. 972 (Governor-General, empowered to
appoint a commissioner of inquiry, left terms of reference excessively vague). *cf. R. v Law
Society Ex p. Curtin* (1994) 6 Admin. L.R. 657; delegation to a named official may not be
required. See also the situations in which the authority may be estopped from denying the
authority of an officer to whom power has not been officially delegated: See 12–063 et seq.

the delegate's acts until the moment of revocation.[497] In addition, the delegation by an office holder does not require renewal each time there is a change in the holder of that office.[498]

5-158 Canadian courts have in the past taken a restrictive view of the competence of local authorities to confer a free discretion on their members or officials to dispense with prohibitions embodied in byelaws. Thus, Montreal could not make a byelaw providing that nobody was to run a business in the city without an official permit; this was analysed as an invalid sub-delegation.[499] And in another case,[500] a marketing board (itself a sub-delegate) was empowered to make regulations on certain matters; the regulations that it made were held invalid on the ground that they contained no standards, but reserved to the board the power to exercise its discretion case by case. The board was said not to have exercised the legislative function delegated to it but to have sub-delegated to itself an administrative function.[501]

5-159 The New Zealand decisions are conflicting; sometimes such provisions have been construed as valid conditional prohibitions, and sometimes as sub-delegations the validity of which may be dependent on the prescription of standards governing the exercise of the dispensing power.[502] Issues such

[497] *Fyfe v Bordoni* [1998] SACS 6860.

[498] *Johnson v Veteran's Review Board* (2002) 71 A.L.D. 16.

[499] *Vic Restaurant Inc v Montreal* [1959] S.C.R. 58 (distinguished in *Lamoureux v City of Beaconsfield* [1978] 1 S.C.R. 134).

[500] *Brant Dairy Co Ltd v Milk Commission of Ontario* [1973] S.C.R. 131; *Re Canadian Institute of Public Real Estate Companies and City of Toronto* (1979) 25 N.R. 108, SCC. Cf., however, *Re Bedesky and Farm Products Marketing Board of Ontario* (1976) 58 D.L.R. (3rd) 484 at 502–504.

[501] This reasoning reflects to a limited degree the argument advanced in K.C. Davis, *Discretionary Justice: a Preliminary Inquiry* (1969), pp.57–59, that bodies and officials in whom discretion is vested should be under an obligation to confine and structure it by the promulgation of decisional criteria so as to strike the best balance in the context between rules and discretion. This is a variation on the non-delegation doctrine at one time used by the Supreme Court of the United States to render invalid statutes that delegated legislative power without setting sufficiently precise limits upon its exercise, e.g. *Field v Clark* 143 U.S. 649 (1892). See Jaffe, "An Essay on Delegation of Legislative Power" (1947) 47 Colum. L. Rev. 359, 561. It later reappeared in other contexts, e.g. *Shuttlesworth v Birmingham* 394 U.S. 147 (1969) (byelaw requiring that permit be obtained before holding public demonstration, invalid because of the broad discretion entrusted to an official); *Furman v Georgia* 408 U.S. 238 (1972); *Profitt v Florida* 428 U.S. 242(1976), where the constitutionality of capital punishment was attacked in part because of the broad discretion "delegated" to the judge and jury in imposing it. Cf. *Francis v Chief of Police* [1973] A.C. 761 at 773, where the PC held that a statutory requirement that the permission of the Chief of Police be obtained before "noisy instruments" could lawfully be used at public meetings did not delegate so much discretion as to infringe the freedom of speech and assembly provisions of a constitution of St Christopher, Nevis and Anguilla.

[502] *Mackay v Adams* [1926] N.Z.L.R. 518; *Jackson (FE) & Co v Collector of Customs* [1939] N.Z.L.R. 682; *Hazeldon v McAra* [1948] N.Z.L.R. 1087; *Ideal Laundry Ltd v Petone Borough* [1957] N.Z.L.R. 1038; *Hookings v Director of Civil Aviation*, ibid., 929. See also *Hanna v Auckland City Corp* [1945] N.Z.L.R. 622 (unfettered dispensing power). For a review of these and other Commonwealth decisions, see C. Aikman, (1960) 3 Victoria Univ of Wellington L. Rev. 85–95. See also *Attorney General v Mount Roskill Borough* [1971] N.Z.L.R. 1030. For a penetrating analysis of the New Zealand approach which does not permit delegation of unfettered or overbroad discretion see P. Joseph, *Constitutional and Administrative Law in New Zealand*, 2nd edn (2001), paras 24.6.3, 24.6.4 and 21.3.6(2).

as these have seldom arisen in the English courts.[503] If an absolute prohibition would be valid, then prima facie a conditional prohibition should be upheld;[504] but it may be relevant in some cases to consider the context, the persons to whom the dispensing or regulatory power are delegated and the scope of the authority "delegated" to them.

In India the principle of non-delegation has also been upheld,[505] however 5-160 "due to the enormous rise in the nature of activities to be handled by statutory authorities, the maxim *delegates non potest delegare* is not being applied especially when there is a question of exercise of administrative discretionary power".[506]

In South Africa, the principle of non-delegation is more strictly applied, 5-161 although "it is not every delegation of power that is [prohibited] but only such delegations as are not, either expressly or by necessary implication, authorised by delegated powers".[507]

The Carltona principle

Special considerations arise where a statutory power vested in a minister or 5-162 a department of state is exercised by a departmental official. The official is not usually spoken of as a delegate, but rather as the *alter ego* of the minister or the department;[508] power is devolved rather than delegated.[509] (A different analysis must, of course, be adopted where powers are explicitly conferred upon or delegated to an official by a law-making instrument.[510]) Under the "*Carltona* principle the courts have recognised that "the duties imposed on ministers and the powers given to ministers are normally exercised under the authority of the ministers by responsible officials of the department. Public business could not be carried on if that

---

[503] See, the decision of the PC in *Francis v Chief of Police* [1993] A.C. 761 In England licensing powers are nearly always conferred directly by statute or under explicit statutory authority.

[504] *Williams v Weston-super-Mare UDC* (1907) 98 L.T. 537 at 540.

[505] *Sahni Silk Mills (P) Ltd v ESI Corp* [1994] 5 S.C.C. 346 at 352.

[506] Ibid at 350.

[507] *Attorney General OFS v Cyril Anderson Investments (Pty) Ltd* 1965 (4) SA 628 (A), 639–D); *AAA Investments* [2006] C.C.T. 51/05 (july 26, 2006).

[508] See e.g. *Lewisham Borough v Roberts* [1949] 2 K.B. 608, 629 at *R. v Skinner* [1968] 2 Q.B. 700; *Re Golden Chemical Products Ltd* [1976] Ch. 300 at 307; cf. *Woollett v Minister of Agriculture and Fisheries* [1955] 1 Q.B. 103. The harmless fiction of the "alter ego principle" (D. Lanham, "Delegation and the Alter Ego Principle" (1984) 100 L.Q.R. 587) does, however, have its limits. Admissions by a civil servant will not necessarily be treated as admissions by his minister, *Williams v Home Office* [1981] 1 All E.R. 1121. Similarly, evidence of receipt of a letter by a minister's department will not satisfy a requirement that advice be received by a minister of the Crown, although evidence of receipt by an official with responsibility for the matter in question will suffice: *Air 2000 Ltd v Secretary of State for Transport* (No.2) 1990 S.L.T. 335.

[509] *R. v Secretary of State Ex p. Oladehinde* [1991] 1 A.C. 254 at 283–284, CA.

[510] As where power to decide certain classes of planning appeals have been vested in inspectors by legislation.

were not the case".[511] In general, therefore, a minister is not obliged to bring his own mind to bear upon a matter entrusted to him by statute but may act through a duly authorised officer[512] of his department.[513] The officer's authority need not be conferred upon him by the minister personally;[514] it may be conveyed generally and informally by the officer's hierarchical superiors in accordance with departmental practice.[515] Whether it is necessary for the authorised officer explicitly to profess to act on behalf of the minister is not certain, but it is suggested that this will not usually be required.[516]

5–163   In *R. (on the application of National Association of Health Stores) v Department of Health*, the Court of Appeal considered whether the knowledge within the department should in law be imputed to the minister (who made the decision to prohibit the use of a herbal remedy in foodstuffs in ignorance of the special expertise of a particular adviser). Sedley L.J. held that to impute the knowledge would be "antithetical to good government".[517] and result in a situation where "the person with knowledge decides nothing and the person without knowledge decides everything". Modern departmental government, he felt, required ministers to be properly briefed about the decisions they must take. He was not willing to accept that the collective knowledge of the civil servants in his department or their collective expertise would necessarily be treated as the minister's own knowledge and expertise.[518]

---

[511] *Carltona Ltd v Commissioners of Works* [1943] 2 All E.R. 560 at 563 (Lord Greene M.R.); *West Riding CC v Wilson* [1941] 2 All E.R. 827 at 831 (Viscount Caldecote C.J.); *Re Golden Chemical Products Ltd* [1976] Ch. 300. Cf. *R. v Secretary of State for the Home Department Ex p. Phansopkar* [1976] Q.B. 606 where the minister was held to have no power to require applicants for certificates of partiality to obtain them from British Government officials in the applicant's country of origin rather than from the Home Office in London.

[512] Cf *Customs and Excise Commissioners v Cure & Deeley Ltd* [1962] 1 Q.B. 340 (manner of authorization prescribed by statute held, not complied with).

[513] *West Riding* [1941] 2 All E.R. 827 , *Point of Ayr Collieries Ltd v Lloyd-George* [1943] 2 All E.R. 546; *Carltona* [1943]2 All E.R. 560 ; *Lewisham* [1949] 2 K.B. 608 ; *Woollett* [1955]1 Q.B. 103.

[514] *Lewisham* [1949] 2 K.B. 608 ; *Woollett* [1995] 1 Q.B. 103; *R. v Skinner* [1968] 2 Q.B. 700 *Cf. Horton v St Thomas Elgin General Hospital* (1982) 140 D.L.R. (3rd) 274.

[515] ibid.; see esp. *Woollett* [1955] 1 Q.B. 103 at 124–126 (Jenkins L.J.); *Golden Chemical* [1996] Ch. 300, 305.

[516] Cf. *Woollett* [1955] 1 Q.B. 103 at 120–121, 132, 134 (Denning and Morris L.JJ.); *Re Reference Under Section 11 of the Ombudsman Act* (1979) 2 A.L.D. 86, 94. In *Golden Chemical* [1976] Ch. 300 at 311, it was said to be preferable for the departmental officer who had in fact taken the decision to state that he had been satisfied that the statutory criterion for exercising the power had been met. It has been suggested for Australia that the officer may possess ostensible authority. M. Aronson, B. Dyer and M. Groves, *Judicial Review of Administrative Action*, 3rd edn (2004), p.311; E. Campbell, "Ostensible Authority in Public Law" (1999) 27 F.L.Rev 1.

[517] [2005] EWCA Civ 154 at [26].

[518] Thus distinguishing Lord Diplock's assertion to the contrary in *Bushell v Secretary of State for the Environment* [1981] A.C. 75 at 95. It was held that the considerations of which the minister had no knowledge were not "relevant". See also M.Freedland, "The Rule Against Delegation and the *Carltona* Doctrine in an Agency Context" [1996] P.L. 19 (who argues that in conferring a discretionary power on a minister, the parliamentary draftsmen are in effect

It may be that there are, however, some matters of such importance that **5–164** the minister is legally required to address himself to them personally,[519] despite the fact that many dicta that appear to support the existence of such an obligation are at best equivocal.[520] It is, however, possible that orders drastically affecting the liberty of the person—e.g. deportation orders,[521] detention orders made under wartime security regulations[522] and perhaps discretionary orders for the rendition of fugitive offenders[523] require the personal attention of the minister.[524]

On the other hand, the minister was not required personally to approve **5–165** breath-testing equipment, despite its importance to the liberty of motorists suspected of driving after consuming alcohol,[525] and a decision on the question of a life sentence prisoner's tariff period may be taken on behalf of the Home Secretary by a Minister of State at the Home Office.[526] Objection to the production of documentary evidence in legal proceedings on the ground that its production would be injurious to the public interest must be taken by the minister or the permanent head of the department, certifying that personal consideration has been given to the documents in

employing a formula that the discretion is conferred upon the government department). Sedley L.J. considered that such a proposition would have the effect that "ministers need to know nothing before reaching a decision so long as those advising them know the facts" at [37]—which he called "the law according to Sir Humphrey Appleby" (an illusion to the permanent secretary in the television comedy "Yes Minister"); I. Steele, "Note on R. (National Association of Health Stores) v Department of Health" [2005] J.R. 232.

[519] *In Golden Chemical* [1976] Ch. 300 the judge denied that such a category existed. But see *Ramawad v Minister of Manpower and Immigration* [1978] 2 S.C.R. 375 and *R. (on the application of Tamil Information Centre) v Secretary of State for the Home Department* [2002] EWHC 2155; (2002) 99 L.S.G. 32 where it was held that ministerial authorisation was an impermissible delegation as the statute required the minister personally to exercise his judgment.

[520] *In Golden Chemical* [1946] Ch. 300 at 309–310, Brightman J. concluded that the dicta in *Liversidge Anderson* [1942] A.C. 206 should be understood as referring to political expediency and to the minister's personal responsibility to Parliament, rather than to his legal obligation.

[521] *R. v Chiswick Police Station Superintendent Ex p. Sacksteder* [1918] 1 K.B. 578 at 585–586, 591–592 (dicta). The decision has in fact been taken by the Home Secretary personally (Cmnd 3387 (1967), 16). In *Oladehinde v Secretary of State for the Home Department* [1991] 1 A.C. 254, which concerned the provisional decision to deport, the HL appeared to accept that the final decision to deport had to be taken by the Secretary of State personally or by a junior Home Office minister if he was unavailable. *R. v Secretary of State for the Home Department Ex p. Mensah* [1996] Imm. A.R. 223.

[522] *Liversidge v Anderson* [1942] A.C. 206 at 223–224, 265, 281; *Point of Ayr* [1943] 2 All E.R. 546 at 548 (dicta).

[523] *R. v Brixton Prison Governor Ex p. Enahoro* [1963] 2 Q.B. 455 at 466.

[524] Had he believed that such a category existed, the judge in Re Golden Chemicals might well have included in it the power to present a petition for the compulsory winding up of a company (Companies Act 1967 s.10). See D. Lanham, "Delegation and the Alter Ego Principle" (1984) 100 L.Q.R. 587, 592–594 (who argues that where life or personal liberty are at stake, the *alter ego* principle may not apply).

[525] *R. v Skinner* [1968] 2 Q.B. 700: it might, of course, be argued that the reliability of the equipment raises technical questions to which the minister will normally bring no special expertise.

[526] *Doody v Secretary of State for the Home Department* [1994] 1 A.C. 531.

question.[527] Statutory instruments are signed by senior officials acting under a general grant of authority from the minister.[528]

5-166   Similarly, it is uncertain whether the courts will examine the suitability of the official who performs the work. The *Carltona* case emphasised that Parliament, not the courts, was the forum for scrutiny of the minister's decision,[529] but more recently it has been accepted that the courts may also examine the devolvement of authority, by way of judicial review.[530] At the very least, it would seem that the official must satisfy the test of *Wednesbury* unreasonableness: he must not be so junior that no reasonable minister would allow him to exercise the power.[531] There may be some tasks which by their nature ought not to allow of delegation or devolution, such as some disciplinary powers.[532] And different tasks conferred on a decision-maker may be delegable to different levels within the organisation.[533]

5-167   The *Carltona* principle may be expressly excluded by legislation,[534] but whether it may in addition be excluded by statutory implication remains uncertain. Two situations should be distinguished. Where a power of delegation is expressly conferred by Parliament on a minister, it may compel the inference that Parliament intended to restrict devolution of power to the statutory method, thus impliedly excluding the *Carltona* principle.[535] Commonwealth authority, however, suggests that such an

---

[527] *Duncan v Cammell, Laird & Co* [1942] A.C. 624, 638.

[528] E.C. Page, *Governing by Numbers: Delegated Legislation and Everyday Policy-Making* (2001). Departmental practice varies; in some departments all or nearly all statutory instruments are signed by the minister personally (Report of the Joint Committee on Delegated Legislation. HC Paper No. 475 (Session 1971/72), Minutes of Evidence, 196–203). In *Lewisham Borough v Roberts* [1949] 2 K.B. 608 at 621–622 Denning L.J. indicated that legislative functions had to be performed by the minister personally; but Bucknill and Jenkins L.JJ. at 619, 629–630) were of the contrary opinion.

[529] *Oladehinde*, 281–282, CA.

[530] *Oladehinde* QBD at 260; CA at 282.

[531] In the HL, Lord Griffiths perhaps went further in stating that development of authority to officials under the *Carltona* principle was permissible "providing . . . that the decisions are suitable to their grading and experience" at 303); *R. (on the application of Chief Constable of the West Midlands Police) v Birmingham Magistrate's Court* [2002] EWHC 1087; [2003] Crim. L.R. at 37 [10] (Sedley L.J. considered that delegation had to be to "somebody suitable" but that question was for the official subject to the test of irrationality).

[532] *R. v North Thames Regional Health Authority and Chelsea and Westminster NHS Trust Ex p. L* [1996] Med L.R. 385 (Sedley J., although the Trust had no express power to delegate disciplinary powers to the Regional Health Authority, certain stages of the disciplinary process might be delegated, although the Trust alone had the duty to evaluate the findings of the inquiry).

[533] For example, the application task and the consultation task in *Chief Constable of the West Midlands Police* [2002] EWHC 1087,[2003] Crim. L.R. 37 and the different tasks involved in the disciplinary functions in *North Thames RHA* [1996] Med. L.R. 385 ; *E v Hertsmere BC Ex p. Woolgar* [1996] 2 F.C.R. 69 (powers of investigation, but not ultimate decision, may be delegated).

[534] See e.g. Immigration Act 1971, ss.13(5), 14(3) and 15(4), which referred to action by the minister "and not by a person acting under his authority".

[535] *Customs and Excise Cmrs v Cure and Deeley Ltd* [1962] 1 Q.B. 340 (conferment by Parliament of express power of delegation on Commissioners deprived them of previously existing benefit of Carltona principle): but compare *Carltona* itself.

implication will not readily be drawn.[536] It has also been suggested that the principle may be impliedly excluded where it appears inconsistent with the intention of Parliament as evinced by a statutory framework of powers and responsibilities.[537] However, where the Immigration Act 1971 apparently clearly divided responsibilities between immigration officers and the Secretary of State, the Court of Appeal and House of Lords held that the *Carltona* principle enabled powers of the Secretary of State to be exercised by immigration officers. In the Court of Appeal it was said that the *Carltona* principle was not merely an implication which would be read into a statute in the absence of any clear contrary indication, but was a common law constitutional principle, which could not be excluded by implication unless "a challenge could be mounted on the possibly broader basis that the decision to devolve authority was *Wednesbury* unreasonable".[538] The House of Lords allowed the devolution of power on the narrower ground that the implication to exclude could not be drawn; the devolution did "not conflict with or embarrass [the officers] in the discharge of their specific statutory duties under the Act".[539] Although their statutory analysis may be questioned,[540] the approach of the House of Lords accorded greater weight than the Court of Appeal to Parliament's intent.

Does the *Carltona* principle apply to public authorities or officers besides ministers?[541] Powers of the Queen or Governor in Council may be exercised by a minister or official in his department, although any formal decision necessarily will be made by the Queen in Council.[542] Powers conferred on senior departmental officers may be devolved to more junior officials in the department.[543] In *Nelms v Roe*[544] the Divisional Court **5–168**

---

[536] *O'Reilly v Commissioner of State Bank of Victoria* (1982) 44 A.L.R. 27; (1983) 153 C.L.R. 1. Cf. *Re Reference Under s.11 of the Ombudsman Act* (1979) 2 A.L.D. 86; cf. *Lanham* 600–603.

[537] *Ramawad v Minister of Manpower and Immigration* (1978) 81 D.L.R. (3rd) 687; *Sean Investments v MacKellar* (1981) 38 A.L.R. 363.

[538] *Oladehinde* CA, 282 (Lord Donaldson M.R.).For unreasonableness, see Ch.11.

[539] *Oladehinde* HL, 303 (Lord Griffiths). This conclusion was influenced by the fact that the minister retained a personal role in reviewing and signing each deportation order.

[540] Weight was placed on several explicit limitations of the minister's powers to him personally, as excluding further implicit limitations; yet it was surely consistent of Parliament to intend some powers to be exercised by the minister personally, some to be exercised by the minister or his civil servants in the department, and others to be exercised by immigration officers as the statutory scheme appeared to require.

[541] See e.g. *Lanham* 604 *et seq.*

[542] *FAI Insurances Ltd v Winneke* (1982) 41 A.L.R. 1; (1982) 151 C.L.R. 342; *South Australia v O'Shea* (1987) 163 C.L.R. 378; Cf. *Attorney-General v Brent* [1956] 2 D.L.R. (2nd) 503.

[543] *Commissioners of Customs and Excise v Cure and Deeley* [1962] 1 Q.B. 340; *O'Reilly v Commissioners of State Bank of Victoria* (1982) 44 A.L.R. 27; (1983) 153 C.L.R. 1; *R. v Secretary of State for the Home Department Ex p. Sherwin* (1996) 32 B.M.L.R. 1. (*Carltona* applied to the Benefits Agency which was held to be part of the Department of Social Security and the agency staff belonged to the Civil Service). See also *R. v Greater Manchester Police Authority Ex p. Century Motors (Farnworth) Ltd, The Times,* May 31, 1996; Cf. *R. v Oxfordshire CC Ex p. Pittick* [1995] C.O.D. 397 (Education Act 1981 s.7(2)—council had not improperly delegated its duty to provide special needs education to the school); *R. v Harrow LBC Ex p. M* [1997] 3 F.C.R.. 761 (obligations on a local education authority under

upheld a decision of a police inspector acting on behalf of the Metropolitan Police Commissioner, on whom the power had been conferred. However, Lord Parker did not think that the inspector could be considered the alter ego of the Commissioner and preferred to base the case on implied delegated authority.

5-169   However, the Court of Appeal has held that the *Carltona* principle is transferable to non-ministerial bodies and that applications for antisocial behaviour orders (ASBOs) could be made by junior police officers despite the fact that the power was conferred upon a local council or chief officer of police. Sedley L.J. stressed that *Carltona* was based not only on convenience (the alter ego aspect) but also upon the fact that the minister continued to be responsible for the decision taken by the official in his department. Provided that (a) the power is delegable, and (b) is not required to be performed by a particularly qualified individual (such as a medical officer of health or a statutory inspector), it may be exercised at different levels. The delegation or devolution of powers was, in those circumstances, for the Chief Constable to decide, and the court could not second-guess him unless his choice was irrational or beyond his powers.[545]

Acting under dictation

5-170   An authority entrusted with a discretion must not, in the purported exercise of its discretion, act under the dictation of another body or person. In at least two Commonwealth cases, licensing bodies were found to have taken decisions on the instructions of the heads of government who were prompted by extraneous motives.[546] But, as less colourful cases illustrate, it is enough to show that a decision which ought to have been based on the exercise of independent judgment was dictated by those not entrusted with the power to decide,[547] although it remains a question of fact whether the repository of discretion abdicated it in the face of external pressure.[548] And it is immaterial that the external authority has not sought to impose its policy. For instance, where a local authority, in assessing compensation for loss of office, erroneously made certain deductions because it thought it was obliged to do so, having regard to the practice

Education Act 1993 s.168 to arrange that special educational provision be made for a child was not delegable); *MFI Furniture Centre Ltd v Hibbert* (1996) 160 J.P. 178 (validity of council's Minutes of Delegation).
[544] [1970] 1 W.L.R. 4 at 8 (Lord Parker C.J.).
[545] *R. (on the application of Chief Constable of the west Midlands) v Birminghan Magistrates Court* [2002] EWHC 1087(Admin); [2003] Gin L.R. 37, [16].
[546] *Roncarelli v Duplessis* [1959] S.C.R. 121: *Rowjee v State of Andhra Pradesh*, AIr 1964 S.C. 962. And see *Ellis-Don Ltd v Ontario (Labour Relations Board)* [2001] 1 S.C.R. 221; *Canada (Minister of Citizenship and Immigration) v Thamotharem*, 2007 F.C.A. 198 (cases involving the interference with the decision-making independence of adjudicators).
[547] *McLoughlin v Minister for Social Welfare* [1958] I.R. 1 at 27.
[548] *Hlookoff v City of Vancouver* (1968) 65 D.L.R. (2nd) 71; 63 W.W.R. 129; *Malloch v Aberdeen Corp (No.2)* 1974 S.L.T. 253 at 264.

followed in such cases by the Treasury (to which an appeal lay from its decisions), mandamus issued to compel it to determine the claim according to law.[549] Where a minister entertaining a planning appeal dismissed the appeal purely on the strength of policy objections entered by another minister, it was held that his decision had to be quashed because he had, in effect, surrendered his discretion to the other minister.[550] Authorities directly entrusted with statutory discretions, be they executive officers or members of distinct tribunals, are usually entitled and are often obliged to take into account considerations of public policy, and in some contexts the policy of a minister or of the Government as a whole may be a relevant factor in weighing those considerations;[551] but this will not absolve them from their duty to exercise their personal judgment in individual cases,[552] unless explicit statutory provision has been made for them to be given binding instructions by a superior,[553] or (possibly) unless the cumulative effect of the subject-matter and their hierarchical subordination[554] (in the case of civil servants and local government officers)[555] make it clear that it is constitutionally proper for them to receive and obey instructions conveyed in the proper manner and form.[556]

---

[549] R. v Stepney Corp [1902] 1 K.B. 317; Buttle v Buttle [1953] 1 W.L.R. 1217.

[550] Lavender (H) & Son Ltd v Minister of Housing and Local Government [1970] 1 W.L.R. 1231 (where the other minister might be said to have imposed his policy); Cf. Kent CC v Secretary of State for the Environment (1977) 75 L.G.R. 452. See also R. v Secretary of State for Trade and Industry Ex p. Lonrho Plc [1989] 1 W.I.R. 525 at 583 (Lord Keith said that "the discretion . . . must be exercised by him and not at the dictation of another minister or body"); Ainooson v Secretary of State for the Home Department [1973] Imm.A.R. 43.

[551] Cf. R. v Mahony Ex p. Johnson (1931) 46 C.L.R. 131 at 145; R. v Anderson Ex p. Ipec-Air Pty Ltd (1965) 113 C.L.R. 177; Ansett Transport Industries (Operations) Pty Ltd v Commonwealth (1977) 17 A.L.R. 513; Re Innisfi (Township of) and Barrie (City of) (1977) 80 D.L.R. (3rd) 85. See also Roberts v Dorset CC (1977) 75 L.G.R. 462 (adoption by local authority of central government circular). Cf. Re Multi-Malls Inc and Minister of Transportation and Communications (1977) 73 D.L.R. (3rd) 18 (minister's refusal of permit for proposed development invalid because he had regard to general government planning policy, rather than limiting his decision to road traffic matters).

[552] See Ipec-Air (1965) 113 C.L.R. 177 for divergent expressions of opinion on the question of how far a decision of the Director-General of Civil Aviation (a public officer) to refuse permission to import aircraft and to refuse a charter licence to operate an inter-state air service could properly be predetermined by current government policy. On government policy as a "relevant consideration", R. v Parole Board Ex p. Watson [1996] 1 W.L.R. 906 (Parole Board must make up its own mind and not simply review Secretary of State's reasons for revocation of parole); Cf. R. (on the application of S (A Child)) v Brent LBC [2002] EWCA Civ 693; [2002] E.L.R. 556 (a view that statutory guidance re pupil exclusion should "normally" be upheld was not an unlawful exercise of discretion).

[553] Laker Airways Ltd v Department of Trade [1977] Q.B. 643 at 698–700, 713, 714, 724–725, considering the Civil Aviation Act 1971 at s.4(3) (power of Secretary of State to give specific directions to licensing authority for certain purposes); and s.3(2) authorising the Secretary of State to issue guidance to the authority on the performance of its statutory functions which it must perform "as it considers is in accordance with the guidance".

[554] I. Zamir, "Administrative Control of Administrative Action" (1969) 57 California L.R. 866.

[555] But in local government, treasurers have been obliged to obey the law and to disobey the council's instructions if contrary to law.

[556] Cf. Simms Motor Units Ltd v Minister of Labour and National Service [1946] 2 All E.R. 201 (where instructions were communicated to the officers in an unauthorised form).

5–171   The rule against acting under dictation—as a "puppet" of another authority does not however mean that authority X cannot, if it possesses the power, authorise a decision by authority Y , so long as authority X maintains control of the ultimate decision. In *Audit Commission for England and Wales v Ealing LBC*[557] the Audit Commission, in carrying out its performance assessment of local authorities, relied on the Commission for Social Care Inspection to conduct an assessment of performance in the social services. The Court of Appeal held that the Audit Commission had maintained control over the assessment principles and the ultimate decision, to which it had applied its mind, and therefore had not acted under the dictation of the Social Care Commission.[558]

5–172   Needless to say, a duty not to comply with executive instructions[559] to decide individual cases in a particular way is always strictly cast upon courts.[560]

---

[557] [2005] EWCA Civ 556; (2005) 8 C.C.L. Rep. 317.
[558] J. Brair, "When is a Fetter not a Fetter?" [2005] J.R. 217.
[559] Or advice: *Sankey v Whitlam* [1977] 1 N.S.W.L.R. 333.
[560] *Evans v Donaldson* (1909) 9 C.L.R. 140; *Ex p. Duncan* (1904) 4 S.R. (N.S.W) 217; *R. (Courtney) v Emerson*.[1913] 2 I.R. 377. See also *Buttle v Buttle* [1953] 1 W.L.R. 1217.

CHAPTER 6

PROCEDURAL FAIRNESS:
INTRODUCTION, HISTORY AND COMPARATIVE
PERSPECTIVES

SCOPE

Chapters 6 to 10 are concerned primarily with the manner in which 6–001
functions are performed by public authorities, rather than the validity of
the decisions themselves. The chapters deal with issues of procedural
justice. An important concern of procedural justice is to provide the
opportunity for individuals to participate in decisions by public authorities
that affect them. Another is to promote the quality, accuracy and
rationality of the decision-making process. Both concerns aim at enhancing
the legitimacy of that process while at the same time improving the quality
of decisions made by public authorities.

Procedural justice, or procedural fairness, has to be contrasted with 6–002
substantive justice. The general objective of substantive justice is to ensure
that the decisions of public authorities are within the scope of the powers
conferred on those authorities. Substantive justice ensures that those
powers are not exceeded. Procedural justice aims to provide individuals
with a fair opportunity to influence the outcome of a decision and so
ensure the decision's integrity. It deals with issues such as the requirement
to consult, to hear representations, to hold hearings and to give reasons for
decisions. It addresses the nature of those consultations, representations
and hearings, so as to ensure that they are appropriate in the circumstances, meaningful, and that they assist and do not hinder the administrative process.

Chapter 7 examines the circumstances that give rise to *an entitlement* to 6–003
procedural fairness and *the content* of that entitlement. The entitlement
can arise from a statutory duty to follow a particular procedure or from the
relationship between the person or body taking the decision and the person
or body who could be affected adversely by the decision. It may arise out
of a "legitimate expectation" encouraged by the decision-maker, but our
main examination of this aspect of procedural fairness is postponed until
Chapter 12. Depending upon the situation, the content of the procedural
protection may range from the mere right to be consulted, to a full public
hearing containing most of the features of a judicial trial.

6–004   Chapter 8 considers the situations in which there would normally be an entitlement to fair procedure, but where the circumstances (such as those involved in a decision concerning questions of national security) may negate or curtail the right.

6–005   Chapters 9 and 10 consider the principal techniques that ensure that the procedures provided are meaningful. These include the rule against the fettering of discretion (Chapter 9) and the entitlement to an unbiased decision-maker (Chapter 10).

6–006   The remainder of this chapter will: first, examine the concept of natural justice or fairness from a theoretical perspective; secondly, describe the different stages in the historical evolution of this concept in this jurisdiction; and thirdly, present a brief comparative overview of procedural fairness.

Introduction

6–007   A minority of administrative decisions do not permit any participation; those for example that require speed and despatch and cannot be delayed. A hearing may not be able to be held about whether a fire brigade, in the course of a fire, should destroy a building.[1] In cases where participation is appropriate, the content of the procedure will vary in accordance with the nature of the decision to be made: in some circumstances a full public inquiry may be required,[2] whereas in others there will only be a bare entitlement to consultation.[3] Courts, in deciding the scope and limits of procedural fairness, must be alert to the interests of good administration, and therefore sensitive to the subject-matter of the decision. Participation should not however be seen as opposed to the interests of effective administration. On the contrary it can greatly improve the quality of official decisions by providing the decision-makers with information they might not otherwise receive; information about the quality of the decision, as well as its perceived impact upon individuals or groups.

6–008   The interest of individuals in participation in decisions by which they could be affected is obvious: they will wish to influence the outcome of the decision. Fairness requires that, in appropriate circumstances, they should have the opportunity of doing so. Among the reasons for this are; procedural fairness may improve the quality of the decision, serve the purpose of protecting human dignity[4] and assist in achieving a sense that

---

[1] See 8–015; *R. (on the application of Louis Brehony) v Chief Constable of Greater Manchester Police* [2005] EWHC 640; (2005) 149 S.J.L.B. 393 at [17] (Bean J. distinguishing between an "on-the-spot" decision of a police officer not to permit an assembly, and a decision regarding an intention to hold a future assembly).

[2] On public inquiries, see 1–095.

[3] See 7–039.

[4] R. Dworkin, *Taking Rights Seriously* (1977), Ch.4; G. Maher, "Natural Justice as Fairness",

justice has both been done and seen to be done; it may promote objectivity and impartiality,[5] or, as just noted, increase the likelihood of an accurate substantive outcome.[6] But of course, the exercise of the opportunity to make representations will not automatically result in the representations made being accepted. Nor does the existence of fair procedures guarantee the open mind of the decision maker. There is always room for "symbolic reassurance",[7] and for the cynical manipulation of procedural forms on the part of a decision-maker who has no intention of being persuaded and whose mind is closed. The procedure that is required to be followed can provide protection against this. The decision must usually be taken by an individual who is free from bias.[8] The fettering of discretion is normally not allowed thus ensuring that the decision-maker keeps an open mind.[9] Most importantly, the duty to give reasons for decisions, where it exists, assists in ensuring the rationality of the decision[10] and that the arguments presented to the decision-maker are seen to be taken into account.

Ch.6 in N. MacCormick and P. Birks (eds), *The Legal Mind: Essays for Tony Honoré* (1986); J. Mashaw, *Due Process in the Administrative State* (1985), Chs 4–7. The difference between instrumental and non-instrumental accounts of procedural fairness are discussed in P. Craig, *Administrative Law*, 5th edn. (2003), pp.408–409; M. Aronson, B. Dyer and M. Groves, *Judicial Review of Administrative Action*, 3rd edn (2004), pp.375–379; Lord Millett "The Right to Good Administration in European Law" [2002] P.L. 309 (distinguishing between common law and civil law systems); D. Galligan, *Due Process and Fair Procedures: A Study of Administrative Procedures* (1996) (prioritising instrumental rationales); T. Allan, "Procedural Fairness and the Duty of Respect" (1998) 18 O.J.L.S. 497 and *Constitutional Justice: A Liberal Theory of the Rule of Law* (2001) (defending a more dignitarian, non-instrumental rationale). See also P. Cane, *Administrative Law*, 4th edn (2004), pp.133–143. For a full account of fair procedures in discretionary decisions, see D. Galligan, *Discretionary Powers* (1986), Ch.7. See also L. Sossin, "An Intimate Approach to Fairness, Impartiality and Reasonableness in Administrative Law" (2002) 27 Queen's L.J. 809; L. Solum, "Procedural Justice" (2004) 78 S. Cal. L. Rev. 181, for a general theoretical defence of the importance of participation in decision-making procedures. For an example of the influence of instrumental and non-instrumental justifications on judicial reasoning, see *R. v Secretary of State for the Home Department Ex p. Doody* [1994] A.C. 531 at 551 (Lord Mustill noting that a prisoner, given a life sentence for murder, would wish to know the reasons for his imprisonment term, "partly from an obvious human desire to be told the reason for a decision so gravely affecting his future, and partly because he hopes that once the information is obtained he may be able to point out errors of fact or reasoning and thereby persuade the Secretary of State to change his mind, or if he fails in this to challenge the decision in the courts"). See also *Sengupta v Holmes* [2002] EWCA Civ 1104 at [38] (Laws L.J. referring to "the central place accorded to oral argument in our common law adversarial system. This I think is important, because oral argument is perhaps the most powerful force there is, in our legal process, to promote a change of mind by the judge. That judges in fact change their minds under the influence of oral argument is not an arcane feature of the system; it is at the centre of it").
[5] J. Rawls, *A Theory of Justice* (1972), p.239 ("the rule of law requires some form of due process . . . designed to ascertain the truth . . . The precepts of natural justice are to insure that the legal order will be impartially and regularly maintained"). See also H.L.A. Hart, *The Concept of Law* (1961), pp.156, 202.
[6] Rawls (1972); J. Resnick "Due Process and Procedural Justice" in J. Pennock and J. Chapman (eds), *Due Process* (1977), p.217.
[7] M. Edelman, *The Symbolic Uses of Politics* (1964).
[8] See Ch.10.
[9] See Ch.9.
[10] See 7–087. For a theoretical consideration of the duty to give reasons, see D. Dyzenhaus and M. Taggart, "Reasoned Decisions and Legal Theory", Ch.5 in D. Edlin (ed.), *Common Law Theory* (2007).

6–009   Historically, the principle of natural justice appropriated most of procedural fairness, but, as we shall see, eventually unnecessarily confined itself to situations where a body was acting "judicially", and where "rights" rather than "privileges" were in issue.[11] Although often retained as a general concept, the term natural justice has since been largely replaced and extended by the more general duty to act "fairly".[12] In 1984, Lord Diplock adopted the term "procedural propriety" to describe one of the three "grounds" of judicial review.[13] Such a term extends the exclusively common law ambit of natural justice and fair hearings to situations where there are procedures that are provided by statute. His term did not include other aspects of fair procedures, such as the duty not to fetter discretion, a duty which requires a decision-maker, even where a policy has been announced, to consider representations arguing for an exception to be made to the policy (thus ensuring the continuous possibility of effective participation in the decision-making process).

THE CONCEPT OF NATURAL JUSTICE

6–010   The expression "natural justice", which is the source from which procedural fairness now flows, has been described as one "sadly lacking in precision".[14] It has been consigned more than once to the lumber room. Thus, it has been said that in so far as it "means that a result or process should be just, it is harmless though it may be a high-sounding expression; in so far as it attempts to reflect the old *jus naturale*, it is a confused and unwarranted transfer into the ethical sphere of a term employed for other distinctions; and, in so far as it is resorted to for other purposes, it is vacuous".[15] No one who has the slightest acquaintance with the medieval English legal system[16] or with legal systems in other parts of the world[17]

---

[11] See 6–020.
[12] For an early discussion of the transition from natural justice to procedural fairness, see M. Loughlin, "Procedural Fairness: A Study of the Crisis in Administrative Law Theory" (1978) 28 U. of Toronto L.J. 215; D. Mullan, "Fairness: the New Natural Justice?" (1975) 25 U. of Toronto L.J. 281; R. MacDonald, "Judicial Review and Procedural Fairness in Administrative Law" (1979–1980) 25 McGill L.J. 520 and (1980–1981) 26 McGill L.J. 1. More recently, see Craig (2003), pp.415–418; and H. Delany, *Judicial Review of Administrative Action: A Comparative Analysis* (2001), pp.150–153.
[13] *Council of Civil Service Unions v Minister for the Civil Service* [1985] A.C. 374 at 410; and *R. v Oxford Regional Mental Health Review Tribunal Ex p. Secretary of State for the Home Department* [1988] A.C. 120 at 126 (Lord Bridge referring to a "decision . . . made in breach of the rules of natural justice, which in a word means unfairly").
[14] *R. v Local Government Board* [1914] 1 K.B. 160; *Norwest Holst Ltd v Secretary of State for Trade* [1978] Ch. 201 at 226 (Ormrod L.J.: "natural" adds nothing to justice "except perhaps a hint of nostalgia").
[15] *Local Government Board v Arlidge* [1915] A.C. 120 at 138 (Lord Shaw); and *Maclean v Workers' Union* [1929] 1 Ch. 602 at 624; *McInnes v Onslow-Fane* [1978] 1 W.L.R. 1520 at 1530; and *Norwest Holst* [1978] Ch. 201 at 226 (a "mesmerising" effect is attributed to the phrase "the requirements of natural justice").
[16] D. Gordon, "Observance of Law as a Condition of Jurisdiction" (1931) 47 L.Q.R. 386, 403–404.
[17] J. Wigmore, *A Kaleidoscope of Justice* (1941).

will suggest that those elements of judicial procedure which are now regarded as the hallmark of a civilised society have been generally enforced or even generally regarded as proper. But courts and commentators who decline to accept any form of justice as natural may take their choice from among "substantial justice",[18] "the essence of justice",[19] "fundamental Justice",[20] "universal justice",[21] "rational Justice",[22] the "principles of British justice",[23] or simply "justice without any epithet",[24] "fair play in action"[25] or "fairness writ large and juridically"[26] as phrases which express the same idea. And in any event "natural justice" was written into the statute book in 1969.[27] Moreover, "natural justice" is said to express the close relationship between the common law and moral principles.[28] Certainly it has an impressive ancestry. That no man is to be judged unheard was a precept known to the Greeks",[29] inscribed in ancient times upon images in places where justice was administered,[30] proclaimed in Seneca's Medea,[31] enshrined in the scriptures,[32] mentioned by St. Augustine,[33] embodied in Germanic[34] as well as African[35] proverbs, ascribed in the Year

[18] *Smith v R.* (1878) 3 App.Cas. 614 at 623.
[19] *Spackman v Plumstead District Board of Works* (1883) 10 App.Cas. 229 at 240.
[20] *Hopkins v Smethwick Local Board of Health* (1890) 24 Q.B.D. 712 at 716.
[21] *Drew v Drew* (1855) 2 Macq. 1 at 8.
[22] *R. v Russell* (1869) 10 B. & S. 91 at 117.
[23] *Errington v Minister of Health* [1935] 1 K.B. 249 at 280.
[24] *Green v Blake* [1948] I.R. 242 at 248; *Norwest Holst* [1978] Ch. 201 at 226 (Ormrod L.J.: "the ordinary principles of justice").
[25] *Ridge v Baldwin* [1963] 1 Q.B. 539 at 578 (Hannan L.J., a much-quoted phrase); and *Fairmount Investments Ltd v Secretary of State for the Environment* [1976] 1 W.L.R. 1255 at 1266 (for another vaguely sporting metaphor, "a fair crack of the whip").
[26] *Furnell v Whangarei High Schools Board* [1973] A.C. 660 at 679 (Lord Morris of Borthy-Gest, adding that it was not "a leaven to be associated only with judicial or quasi judicial occasions").
[27] Foreign Compensation Act 1969 s.3(10) (ground for impugning purported determination by Foreign Compensation Commission); and Mental Capacity Act 2005 Sch.4 Pt IV para.19; Anatomy Act 1984 s.7A(3)(c); Licensing (Scotland) Act 2005 s.131. In Canada, see Federal Court Act, R.S.C. 1970 s.28(1)(a); and in New Zealand s.27(1) of the New Zealand Bill of Rights Act 1990. See also 6–052.
[28] A. Goodhart, *English Law and the Moral Law* (1953), p.65.
[29] J. Kelly, "Audi Alteram Partem" (1964) 9 *Natural Law Forum* 103; he points out, however, that the Greeks tended to regard the principle as a practical aid to making good decisions rather than an abstract principle of justice. But since equal application of the law to similar situations is an important aspect of justice, there is a significant overlap between good decision-making and justice. See also A. Harrison, *The Law of Athens* (1971) Vol.2.
[30] G. Del Vecchio, *Justice: An Historical and Philosophical Essay* (1878), pp.172–173.
[31] "Qui statuit aliquid, parte inaudita altera, Aequum, licet stuerit, Haud aequus fuerit", lines 199–200, cited in *Boswell's Case* (1606) 6 Co.Rep. 48b at 52a, *Bagg's Case* (1615) 11 Co.Rep. 93b at 99a, and in several 19th century cases.
[32] "Doth our law judge any man, before it hear him, and know what he doeth?" (John, vii, 51). But *Cf.* n.37, below.
[33] *De Duabus Animabus*, xiv, ii.
[34] "Fines Mannes Rede ist Keines Marines Rede, Man soll sie billig horen beede"; "Richter sollen zwei gleiche Ohren haben" (Lotmar, Die Gereclitigkeit, 77, 92).
[35] Thus, it is commended in proverbs and songs of the Lozi tribe in Barotseland (M. Gluckman, *The Judicial Process Among the Barotse of Northern Rhodesia* (1967), p.102). See also the Kiganda proverb referred to by E. Haydon, *Law and Justice in Buganda* (1960),

Books to the law of nature,[36] asserted by Coke to be a principle of divine justice,[37] and traced by an 18th-century judge to the events in the Garden of Eden.[38] Of course, if the concept of "natural justice" is vulnerable to rational criticism, so too are the "unalienable rights" of the Founding Fathers of the American Constitution or the notion of "due process". The view that "natural justice is so vague as to be practically meaningless" is tainted by "the perennial fallacy that because something cannot be cut and dried or nicely weighed or measured therefore it does not exist".[39]

6–011   Certainly, "natural justice" did exist in English law, and it became identified with the two constituents of a fair hearing; (a) that the parties should be given a proper opportunity to be heard and to this end should be given due notice of the hearing[40] and (b) that a person adjudicating should be disinterested and unbiased.[41]

HISTORICAL DEVELOPMENT BEFORE THE FIRST WORLD WAR

Early development of the right to a fair hearing[42]

6–012 In 1850 it was said that "No proposition can be more clearly established than that a man cannot incur the loss of liberty or property for an offence by a judicial proceeding until he has had a fair opportunity of answering the case against him,[43] unless indeed the Legislature has expressly or impliedly given an authority *to act* without that necessary preliminary".[44]

p.333. The Kiganda proverb corresponding to the maxim *nemo judex in causa sua* means literally "a monkey does not decide an affair of the forest" (p.333). Practice did not always conform to precept.

[36] "In lege naturae requiritur ques les parties soient presentes ou que ils soient absentes *per contumacie*" ((1469) Y.B. 9 Edw. 4, Tin. pl. 9). *Cf. R. v Clegg* (1721) 8 Mod. 3 at 4. See also H. Marshall, *Natural Justice* (1959), Ch.2.

[37] Institutes, iii, 35. Rhadamanthus, the cruel judge of Hell, punished before he heard. "But far otherwise doth Almighty God proceed . . . 1. Vocat 2. Interrogat, 3 Judicat".

[38] *R. v Chancellor of the University of Cambridge* (1723) 1 Str. 557 at 567 (Fortescue J.: "even God himself did not pass sentence upon Adam, before he was called upon to make his defence. 'Adam' (says God) 'where art thou? Hast thou not eaten of the tree, whereof I commanded thee that thou shouldst not eat?'"). But the biblical precedents are conflicting: see R. Heuston, *Essays in Constitutional Law*, 2nd edn (1964), p.185, and Kelly (1964), p.110.

[39] *Ridge v Baldwin* [1964] A.C. 40 at 64–65 (Lord Reid).

[40] *Audi alteram partem*. Fair hearings are considered in Ch.7.

[41] *Nemo judex in causa sua*. Bias is dealt with in Ch.10.

[42] For an overview of the evolution of procedural fairness, see: H.W.R. Wade and C.F. Forsyth, *Administrative Law*, 9th edn. (2004), pp.480–494; M. Beloff, "Natural Justice and Fairness: the Audi Alteram Partem Rule" in M. Supperstone, J. Goudie and P. Walker (eds), *Judicial Review*, 3rd edn (2005), paras 10.4–10.11. For a general historical overview of administrative law, including procedural fairness, see: G. Drewry, "Judicial Review: the Historical Background" also in Supperstone, Goudie and Walker, Ch.2.

[43] The rule was said by Hawkins to be implied in the construction of all penal statutes (Pleas of the Crown, i, 420); and *Painter v Liverpool Oil Gas Light Co* (1836) 3 A. & E. 433 at 448–449 ("a party is not to suffer in person or in purse without an opportunity of being heard").

[44] *Bonaker v Evans* (1850) 16 Q.B. 162 at 171 (Parke B.). See also Ch.8.

Most of the earliest reported decisions in which natural justice was **6–013** applied[45] concerned summary proceedings before justices. Service of a summons upon the party affected was regarded as a condition of the validity of such proceedings[46] not only in criminal matters but also in applications for the issue of distress warrants and orders for the levying of taxes and the charges imposed by public authorities upon the subject.[47] Justices who adjudicated summarily without having issued a summons were at one time punishable in the Court of King's Bench for a misdemeanour.[48] Decisions on the effect of non-service of process were numerous and not always reconcilable,[49] but instances were not wanting of the strict application of the general principle that service is mandatory in civil as well as criminal proceedings before judicial tribunals.[50]

A second line of cases relates to the deprivation of offices and other **6–014** dignities. Here the effective starting-point is 1615, when James Bagg, a chief burgess of Plymouth, who had been disfranchised for singularly unbecoming conduct,[51] was reinstated by mandamus because he had been removed without notice or hearing.[52] In 1723 mandamus was issued to restore Dr Bentley to his academic degrees in the University of Cambridge, of which he had been deprived without a summons.[53] It became established with respect to offices that removal had to be preceded by notice and hearing if the office was a freehold or was to be forfeited only for cause,[54]

---

[45] See cases collected in note (a) to 8 Mod. 154.
[46] *R. v Dyer* (1703) 1 Salk. 181; *R. v Benn and Church* (1795) 6 T.R. 198. A more modern example is *R. v Dudley JJ Ex p. Payne* [1979] 1 W.L.R. 891 (no notice of hearing given to a defendant before sentence).
[47] *R. v Benn and Church* (1795) 6 T.R. 198; *Harper v Carr* (1797) 7 T.R. 270; *Gibbs v Stead* (1828) 8 B. & C. 528; *Painter v Liverpool Oil Gas Light Co* (1836) 3 A. & E. 433; *R. v Totnes Union* (1854) 14 Q.B. 349; *R. v Cheshire Lines Committee* (1873) L.R. 8 Q.B. 344; see also Hankins, "The Necessity for Administrative Notice and Hearing" (1940) 25 Iowa L. Rev. 457,pp 460–462.
[48] *R. v Venables* (1725) 2 Ld.Raym. 1405; *R. v Alington* (1726) 2 Str. 678.
[49] Early authorities are reviewed in *Marsh v Marsh* [1945] A.C. 271 and more fully in *Posner v Collector for Inter-State Destitute Persons (Victoria)* (1946) 74 C.L.R. 461. See also D. Gordon, "Observance of Law as a Condition of Jurisdiction" (1931) 47 L.Q.R. 386,pp 557– 563, 579–582.
[50] See, e.g. *R. v North Ex p. Oakey* [1927] 1 K.B. 491; *Craig v Kanssen* [1943] K.B. 256; *Chettiar v Chettiar* [1962] 1 W.L.R. 279; *R. v London County Q.S. Appeals Committee Ex p. Rossi* [1956] 1 Q.B. 682 (appealed in *R. v Industrial Court Ex p. George Green & Thomson Ltd* (1967) 2 K.I.R. 259); *R. v Havering JJ. Ex p. Smith* [1974] 3 All E.R. 484. But statutorily prescribed detail on the manner of service may not be mandatory: *R. v Devon and Cornwall Rent Tribunal Ex p. West* (1975) 29 P. & C.R. 316. In criminal law: Magistrates' Courts Act 1980 s.1 (issue of summons); s.14 (invalidity of proceedings where accused was unaware of them); Criminal Procedures and Investigations Act 1996 ss.3, 7A (disclosure obligations of the prosecutor).
[51] As by saying to the mayor "You are a cozening knave" and "I will make thy neck crack"; and by "turning the hinder part of his body in an inhuman and uncivil manner" towards the mayor. saying "Come and kiss".
[52] *Bagg's Case* (1615) 11 Co.Rep. 93b.
[53] *R. v Chancellor of the University of Cambridge* (1723) 1 Str. 557.
[54] *Bagg's Case* (1615) 11 Co.Rep. 13b; *Protector v Colchester* (1655) Style 446 at 452; *R. v Wilton (Mayor)* (1697) 2 Salk. 428; *R. v Ipswich (Bailiffs)* (1705) 2 Ld.Raym. 1233; *R. v Smith* (1844) 5 Q.B. 614; *Re Fremington School* (1846) 10 Jur. (o.s.) 512; *Ex p. Ramshay* (1852) 21 L J.Q.B. 238 at 239; *Osgood v Nelson* (1872) L. R. 5 H.L. 636; *Fisher v Jackson* [1891] 2 Ch. 84.

but not if there was a discretionary power to remove the holder at pleasure.[55] These principles, which extended even to dismissals of school-masters and parish clerks, came to be largely forgotten, partly, perhaps, because of the decline of the concept of a freehold *office*, and partly because the tenure of public office was usually determinable either at pleasure or in accordance with specific statutory, contractual or customary procedures. In 1963 they were rescued from oblivion, dressed in modern garb, by the House of Lords.[56]

6–015   Linked with this group of cases are the decisions on the regulation of the clergy. Where a bishop issued an order for the sequestration of the profits of a benefice without having given the vicar notice of the charges of neglect that had been made against him or an opportunity to refute them, and where the Archbishop of Canterbury dismissed an appeal by a curate against the revocation of his licence without having afforded him an adequate hearing, the courts gave redress for violation of natural justice.[57] One of the most remarkable illustrations of the right to be heard (*audi alteram partem*) principle in a reported case was *Capel v Child*,[58] where a bishop, empowered by statute to order a vicar to appoint a curate (to be paid by the vicar) when satisfied, either of his own knowledge or by affidavit, that the vicar had neglected his duties, was held to be under an absolute duty to give the vicar notice and opportunity to be heard before making the order. This was a high-water mark of, at that time, judicial intervention; in later cases the courts generally showed themselves disinclined to require investigations conducted by ecclesiastical authorities to conform to judicial standards.[59]

6–016   Nineteenth and early twentieth century decisions established that the right to be heard (*audi alteram partem*) rule was to govern the conduct of arbitrators,[60] of professional bodies and voluntary associations in the exercise of their disciplinary functions,[61] and indeed of "every tribunal or body of persons invested with authority to adjudicate upon matters involving civil consequences to individuals".[62] An individual who was

---

[55] *R. v Stratford-on-Avon (Mayor)* (1671) 1 Lev. 291; *R. v Andover* (1701) 1 Ld.Raym. 710; *R. v Darlington Free Grammar School Governors* (1844) 6 Q.B. 682; *Re Poor Law Commissioners* (1850) 19 L.J.M.C. 70; *Dickson v Viscount Combermere* (1863) 3 F. & F. 527 at 548, note (a).

[56] *Ridge v Baldwin* [1964] A.C. 40 (chief constable, removable only for statutory cause, dismissed without notice of charges against him or adequate opportunity to be heard; dismissal declared invalid).

[57] *Bonaker v Evans* (1850) 16 Q.B. 163; *R. v Canterbury (Archbishop)* (1859) 1 E.&E. 545.

[58] (1832) 2 Cr. & J. 558; but *Cf. Re Hammersmith Rent Charge* (1849) 4 Ex. 87 at 94, 100.

[59] *Abervavenny (Marquis) v Llandaff (Bishop)* (1888) 20 Q.B.D. 460; *R. v Canterbury (Archbishop) Ex p. Morant* [1944] K.B. 282; cf. *R. v North Ex p. Oakey* [1927] 1 K.B. 491.

[60] *Re Brook* (1864) 16 C.B. (n.s.) 403; see now D. Sutton and J. Gill *Russell on Arbitration*, 22nd edn. (2003), pp.172–177, paras 5–050–5.064.

[61] D. Lloyd, "The Discretionary Powers of Professional Bodies" (1950) 13 M.L.R. 281; Z. Chafee, "The Internal Affairs of Associations not for Profit" (1930) 43 Harv. L.R. 993; D. Lloyd, *Law Relating to Unincorporated Associations* (1938), pp.127–129.

[62] *Wood v Woad* (1874) L.R. 9 Ex. 190 at 196.

expelled from membership of a club[63] or similar association,[64] or from a trade union,[65] was prima facie entitled to have the decision set aside by the courts unless he had been given adequate notice of the allegations made against him and a fair opportunity to reply to them. This principle was subsequently applied with particular vigour where the sanction imposed would deprive a person of his livelihood[66] or where there was a charge of discreditable conduct.[67]

With the extension of the franchise and the decline of the doctrine of laissez faire in the latter half of the 19th century came a vast increase in the regulatory functions of public authorities, especially in the fields of housing and public health. Where a statute authorising interference with property or civil rights was silent on the question of notice and hearing, the courts, drawing upon the authority of the older cases, invoked "the justice of the common law" to "supply the omission of the legislature".[68] In a long line of cases on demolition orders, beginning with *Cooper v Wandsworth Board of Works*,[69] the rule, said to be "of universal application and founded on the plainest principles of justice",[70] was laid down that public authorities must either give the person concerned "notice that they intend to take this matter into their consideration with a view to coming to a decision, or, if they have come to a decision, that they propose to act upon it, and give him an opportunity of showing cause why such steps should not be

6–017

[63] *Innes v Wylie* (1844) 1 Car. & Kir. 257; *Dawkins v Antrobus* (1881) 17 Ch.D. 615; *Fisher v Keane* (1878) 11 Ch.D. 353; *Gray v Allison* (1909) 25 T.L.R. 531; *Lamberton v Thorpe* (1929) 141 L.T. 638.

[64] *Wood v Woad* (1874) L.R. 9 Ex. 190 (mutual insurance society); see also *Lapointe v L'Association de Bienfai-sance et de Retraite de la Police de Montreal* [1906] A.C. 535 (denial of pension to member of police friendly society); *John v Rees* [1970] Ch. 345 (suspension or expulsion from political party). This decision was distinguished in *Lewis v Heffer* [1978] 1 W.L.R. 1061 on the ground that the suspension was imposed pending an inquiry and not as a punishment. Nor was the rule applied in *Gaiman v National Association for Mental Health* [1971] Ch. 317 (exclusion from membership of a company).

[65] *Parr v Lancashire & Cheshire Miners' Federation* [1913] 1 Ch. 366; *Burn v National Amalgamated Labourers' Union* [1920] 2 Ch. 364. See also *Abbott v Sullivan* [1952] 1 K.B. 189 at 199; *Amalgamated v Oilfield Workers' Trade Union* [1961] A.C. 945; *Lawlor v Union of Post Office Workers* [1965] Ch. 712; *Taylor v National Union of Seamen* [1967] 1 W.L.R. 532; *Hiles v Amalgamated Society of Woodworkers* [1968] Ch. 440; *Leary v National Union of Vehicle Builders* [1971] Ch. 34; *Edwards v SOGAT* [1971] Ch. 354; see also *Roebuck v National Union of Mineworkers* [1977] I.C.R. 573 (bias).

[66] *Russell v Duke of Norfolk* [1949] 1 All E.R. 109 at 119; *Abbott v Sullivan* [1952] 1 Q.B. 189, 199 (Denning L.J.); *Edwards v SOGAT* [1971] Ch. 354. After a number of years of dormancy, this jurisprudence has been revived by the courts: *Bradley v Jockey Club* [2005] EWCA Civ 1056, *The Times*, July 14, 2005 at [13] and [2004] EWHC 2164 and *Mullins v McFarlane* [2006] EWHC 986 at [38].

[67] *G.M.C. v Spackman* [1943] A. C. 627 at 637–638 (Lord Atkin); *Breen v AEU* [1971] 2 Q.B. 175 (dicta).

[68] *Cooper v Wandsworth Board of Works* (1863) 14 C.B. (N.S.) 180 at 194.

[69] *Cooper v Wandsworth Board of Works* (1863) 14 C.B. (N.S.) 180 at 194; *Brutton v St George's, Hanover Square, Vestry* (1871) L.R. 13 Eq. 339; *Masters v Pontypool Local Government Board* (1878) 9 Ch.D. 677; *Hopkins v Smethwick Board of Health* (1890) 24 Q.B.D. 712; *Sydney Municipal Council v Harris* (1912) 14 C.L.R. 1. See also *Urban Housing Co v Oxford City Council* [1940] Ch. 70; *Delta Properties Pty Ltd v Brisbane City Council* (1955) 95 C.L.R. 11 at 18; *Police Commissioner v Tanos* (1958) 98 C.L.R. 383 at 395–396.

[70] *Cooper v Wandsworth Board of Works* (1863) 14 C.B. (N.S.) 180 at 190.

taken".[71] An authority empowered to postpone the operation of a demolition order on the owner's application had to permit him adequately to present his case for postponement.[72] The general rule, which was applied in a variety of legislative contexts,[73] might be satisfied if an opportunity was available of obtaining a full review of the initial decision[74] or of making other representations[75] before the order became finally operative or was enforced; and it was, of course, displaced by express statutory provisions dispensing with the need to serve notice.[76]

6-018   Maitland had pointed out in 1888 that England and Wales was becoming "a much governed nation, governed by all manner of councils and boards and officers, central and local, high and low Exercising the powers which have been committed to them by modern statutes", and that half the reported cases in the Queen's Bench Division had to do with aspects of administrative law such as rating, licensing, public health and education.[77] At this time it was usual to confer new adjudicatory functions upon the existing departments of State and local authorities; special tribunals had been established for the regulation of railway traffic and the determination of income tax appeals, but the proliferation of ad hoc tribunals was to be a 20th-century phenomenon. The courts, while recognising that it would be hopeless to require government departments, making institutional decisions, to follow the procedure of courts of justice, nevertheless superimposed upon their statutory responsibilities the duty to act judicially, in certain situations, in the manner prescribed by the rules of natural justice. The best-known statement of the right to be heard rule in English administrative law was formulated by the House of Lords in relation to the appellate functions of a government department; but it is of broad application:

"Comparatively recent statutes have extended, if they have not originated, the practice of imposing upon departments or officers of State the

[71] *Urban Housing Co v Oxford City Council* [1940] Ch. 70 at 85 (Sir Wilfrid Greene M.R.). For local colour and the aftermath of this case, see R. Heuston, *Essays in Constitutional Law*, 2nd edn. (1964), pp.186–188.
[72] *Broadbent v Rotherham Corp* [1917] 2 Ch. 31.
[73] For example, closing orders in respect of houses unfit for human habitation (*Hall v Manchester Corp* (1915) 84 L.J.Ch. 732 at 741–742); forfeiture of a lease of Crown land in Australia (*Smith v R.* (1878) 3 App.Cas. 614); transfer of indentures of immigrants from one employer to another in Trinidad (*De Verteuil v Knaggs* [1918] A.C. 557); applications to present a case before a wages board (*R. v Amphlett (Judge)* [1915] 2 K.B. 223); confirmation of grant of liquor licence (*R. v Huntingdon Confirming Authority* [1929] 1 K.B. 698).
[74] *St James and St. John, Clerkenwell, Vestry v Feary* (1890) 24 Q.B.D. 703 (order to supply sanitary installations); but this exception is untypical.
[75] *Attorney-General v Hooper* [1893] 3 Ch. 483 (removal of projection over highway); *Robinson v Sunderland Corp* [1899] 1 Q.B. 751 at 757–758 (supply of sanitary installation); *De Verteuil v Knaggs* [1918] A.C. 557. See also *Knuckey v Peirce* [1964] W.A.R. 200 (notice requiring removal of rubbish from site). In principle however, a duty to give prior notice and opportunity to be heard arises when an individual will suffer direct detriment from the act or decision (*Delta Properies* (1955) 95 C.L.R. 11).
[76] *Cheetham v Mayor of Manchester* (1875) L.R. 10 C.P. 249.
[77] F.W. Maitland, *Constitutional History of England* (1888), pp.501, 505; and H. Arthurs, *"Without the Law": Administrative Justice and Legal Pluralism in Nineteenth Century England* (1985).

duty of deciding or determining questions of various kinds . . . In such cases . . . they must act in good faith and fairly listen to both sides, for that is a duty lying upon everyone who decides anything. But I do not think they are bound to treat such a question as though it were a trial . . . They can obtain information in any way they think best, always giving a fair opportunity to those who are parties in the controversy for correcting or contradicting any relevant statement prejudicial to their view."[78]

Operation of the rule reviewed

These dicta by Lord Loreburn in *Board of Education v Rice* must 6–019 nevertheless be viewed with caution. The Board in that case had been required to determine a dispute between a local education authority and the managers of a school, that is a *lis inter partes*.[79] Had the education authority complied with its statutory duty to maintain the school efficiently when it was discriminating against the teachers in the school by paying them lower salaries than those paid to teachers in other schools doing similar work? The determination of this question involved the ascertainment of questions of law and fact as well as the exercise of judicial discretion. It is doubtless true to say that in such situations the deciding authority is under an implied duty to listen fairly to both sides. It does not follow that "everyone who decides anything" is subject to a similar duty, or that persons involved in a controversy must always be given an opportunity of rebutting statements prejudicial to them. A decision to increase the rate of income tax, to arrest a participant in an armed robbery, to pull down a building to prevent the spread of a fire, may have serious adverse effects on those directly concerned, but there is no duty to give prior notice or opportunity to be heard. Moreover, only four years after the decision in *Board of Education v Rice*,[80] the House of Lords held in *Arlidge*[81] that a government department determining a housing appeal was not obliged to divulge one of its inspector's reports to the appellant, even though the report might well have contained relevant statements prejudicial to his case which he might have wished to controvert. This decision marked the beginning of a partial retreat by the English courts from their earlier position—a retreat which was not halted till the 1960s. For nearly half a century they were to show a marked reluctance to hold that an implied duty to give prior notice and opportunity to be heard was imposed on persons and authorities empowered to make decisions in the general field of administrative law.

[78] *Board of Education v Rice* [1911] A.C. 179 at 182 (Lord Loreburn L.C.) See also *Local Government Board v Arlidge* [1915] A.C. 120 at 132–134; *Spackman v Plumstead District Board of Works* (1885) 10 App.Cas. 229 at 240; *Parsons v Lakenheath School Board* (1889) 58 L J.Q.B. 371 at 372.
[79] See 6–037.
[80] [1911] A.C. 179.
[81] [1915] A.C. 120.

HISTORICAL DEVELOPMENT AFTER THE FIRST WORLD WAR

The path of deviation

6–020 The state of the law at the outbreak of the First World War can be briefly restated. Judicial tribunals empowered to deprive persons of their liberty, impose financial burdens on them and ascertain their legal rights had to observe the requirements of a fair hearing, or the *audi alteram partem* rule. So did arbitrators and government departments when called upon to decide questions of law and fact in situations resembling a legal action between two parties. The rule would also normally be held to apply where the trappings of adjudication were present although the decision involved the exercise of wide discretion. It was prima facie applicable in various other situations where there was nothing resembling a dispute determinable by a third party: removal from an office not tenable merely at pleasure, the disciplining of the clergy, the exercise of disciplinary powers by professional authorities and voluntary organisations, and administrative intrusions (e.g. by demolition, destruction and compulsory execution of works) upon private property rights. In the aftermath of the First World War, however, the principles of natural justice experienced a notable demise.[82]

Venicoff's Case

6–021 The first leading case in which the courts refused to apply the rule at all in a situation where it clearly ought to have been applied was *Venicoff's* case.[83] The Home Secretary had been empowered by recent legislation to deport an alien whenever he deemed this to be "conducive to the public good".[84] When a deportation order was impugned, it was held that he was exercising purely executive functions, importing no duty to act judicially.[85] The court laid emphasis on the amplitude of the Secretary of State's discretion, the context of an emergency[86] and the impracticability of giving prior notice in such a case; the impact of a deportation order on personal liberty was treated as an irrelevant consideration,[87] and the feasibility of

---

[82] Of the impact of the First World War on civil liberties more generally, Gearty and Ewing note the following: "The First World War offers a fascinating study of a state in crisis and of the ease with which liberal values may be surrendered in times of emergency. It also offers a valuable insight into the role of the different institutions of government, tending to reveal a largely unaccountable executive restrained only be a sometimes quiescent legislature and a compliant judiciary" (C. Gearty and K. Ewing, *The Struggle for Civil Liberties. Political Freedom and the Rule of Law in Britain 1914–1945* (2001)).

[83] *R. v Leman Street Police Station Inspector Ex p. Venicoff* [1920] 3 K.B. 72.

[84] Art.12(1) of the Aliens Order 1919, made under the Aliens Restriction Act 1914 (passed immediately after the outbreak of war).

[85] On the distinctions between "administrative", "judicial" and "ministerial" and "legislative", see 6–031.

[86] *Venicoff* [1920] 3 K.B. 72 at 80 (Earl of Reading C.J.),

[87] It was observed that the validity of a still more drastic curtailment of personal freedom, the summary preventive detention of British subjects by administrative order, had been upheld only three years earlier: *R. v Halliday* [1917] A.C. 260. For discussion of *Halliday*, see D. Foxton, "*R. v Halliday Ex parte Zadig* in Retrospect" (2003) 119 L.Q.R. 455.

requiring a hearing after the order had been made but before it had been executed was not canvassed in the judgments.[88] In 1962 the Court of Appeal reaffirmed the rule established in *Venicoff's* case that an alien deportee has no implied legal right to any hearing,[89] but this rule has now been modified by statute.[90]

The tenor of the judgments in *Venicoff's* Case foreshadowed the **6–022** debilitation of the *audi alteram partem* rule as a common-law standard applied by the court to administrative decision-making. In the first place, there were the references to emergency situations. During wartime, enormous powers over persons and property were vested in the Government, and the courts showed an understandable reluctance to scrutinise the exercise of essential powers in such a way as to make it more difficult for the Government to govern. Not surprisingly, it was hard to persuade the courts that war emergency powers were subject to an implied qualification that persons adversely affected by their exercise were entitled to prior notification and an opportunity to be heard.[91] But the climate of judicial opinion engendered by the exigencies of war tended to persist long after hostilities had ended.[92]

Secondly, the existence of a wide policy discretion vested in a minister **6–023** responsible to Parliament was thought to dictate not only abstention from judicial review of the merits of particular decisions but also (and with less justification) the impropriety of setting minimum procedural standards to be observed in the course of reaching or before executing such decisions.

Thirdly, there was the implicit assumption that the role of the courts in **6–024** relation to the administrative process should be one of rigorous self-restraint; the administration ought not to be embarrassed by well-meaning judicial intruders. Such an assumption had already been clearly articulated in *Arlidge*.[93] It was to be revealed in other contexts.

[88] Though the Home Secretary had offered to entertain representations informally: [1920] 3 K.B. 72 at 78.
[89] *R. v Brixton Prison Governor Ex p. Soblen* [1963] 2 Q.B. 243 (interpreting art.20(2)(b) of the Aliens Order 1953 (SI 1953/1671), which reproduced the words construed in *Venicoff's* case). Lord Denning M.R. (at 298–299) reserved his opinion on the question whether the deportee might have a legal right to be heard after the order had been made but before it had been executed. See also, for dicta to the same effect, *Schmidt v Home Secretary* [1969] 2 Ch. 149, 171, where it was held that an alien had no right to a hearing before a refusal of either initial entry or renewal of leave to remain.
[90] Pursuant to s.82 of the Nationality, Immigration and Asylum Act 2002, where an "immigration decision" is made in respect of a person, he may appeal to the Asylum and Immigration Tribunal. An "immigration decision" includes refusal of leave to enter the UK (s.82(2)(a)), refusal of entry clearance (s.82(2)(b)), refusal to vary a person's leave to enter or remain if the result of the refusal is that the person has no leave to enter or remain in the UK (s.82(2)(d)) and a decision to remove a person who is unlawfully in the UK (s.82(2)(g)). Limitations and exceptions to the right of appeal, for example, where an immigration decision is made on grounds of national security, are found in ss.88, 89–92, and 94–99.
[91] In the following cases persons aggrieved by the exercise of executive powers were held to be unprotected by the *audi alteram partem* rule: *Irving v Paterson* [1943] Ch. 180; *Howell v Addison* [1943] 1 All E.R. 29, 32 (consent by Minister to determination of agricultural tenancy (though cf. *West Riding CC v Wilson* [1941] 2 All E.R. 827 at 832); *Carltona Ltd v Commissioners of Works* [1943] 2 All E.R. 560 at 562 (requisitioning of factory).
[92] On the legality of discretionary powers, see Ch.5.
[93] [1915] A.C. 120.

6–025   Fourthly, the characterisation of the Secretary of State's functions as executive and non-judicial was understood to exclude any implied obligation on his part to act in accordance with natural justice, despite the impact of his decisions on individual rights. The importance of analytical labels in restricting the scope of the obligation to act judicially was to be underlined in the years that followed, perhaps most notably by Atkin L.J.'s much-quoted judgment in the *Electricity Commissioners* case, defining the circumstances in which the writ of certiorari would issue to quash the decisions of public authorities. Certiorari (and prohibition) would issue to "any body of persons having legal authority to determine questions affecting the rights of subjects, and having the duty to act judicially".[94] In natural justice cases this dictum was generally understood to mean that a duty to act judicially was not to be inferred merely from the impact of a decision on the "rights of subjects"; such a duty would arise only if there were "superadded" an express obligation to follow a judicial-type procedure in arriving at the decision.[95] In pursuit of a circuitous (and sometimes circular) line of reasoning the courts lost sight of the older cases;[96] in which a duty to act judicially in accordance with natural justice had been held to arise by implication from the nature and effect of the powers exercised.[97]

The rise of statutory procedures and the demise of the audi alteram partem principle

6–026   Paradoxically, the decline of the *audi alteram partem* principle as an implied common-law requirement of administrative procedure was hastened by its embodiment in statutory forms. Twentieth-century statute law reflected the disfavour with which the common law viewed administrative claims to be entitled to take direct action against private property without giving prior notice or opportunity to be heard. Public health, housing, highways and town planning legislation in particular spell out the procedural conditions under which enforcement powers are exercisable.[98] Where no statutory provision is made for prior notice to be given, it may sometimes be assumed that the omission is deliberate; so, too, where statutory provision is made for a hearing that falls short of the requirements of natural justice, the statutory procedure can often be assumed to be exhaustive. In Victorian times detailed codes were exceptional, and the

---

[94] *R. v Electricity Commissioners* [1924] 1 K.B. 171 at 204–205 (where the contention was not that natural justice had been contravened, but that the impugned order was ultra vires).
[95] *Nakkuda Ali v Jayaratne* [1951] A.C. 66, another decision which gave extremely influential support for this approach.
[96] See 6–012; through the ratio of *Cooper v Wandsworth Board of Works* was momentarily glimpsed in 1939: *Urban Housing Co v Oxford City Council* [1940] Ch. 70.
[97] A point emphasised by H.W.R. Wade, "The Twilight of Natural justice?" (1951) 67 L.Q.R. 103 and later elaborated by Lord Reid in *Ridge v Baldwin* [1964] A.C. 40 at 74–76.
[98] See Ch.7.

courts supplied the omissions, in the interests of justice to individuals, by importing common-law principles.

Of more general significance in the reshaping of judicial attitudes was the fact that in the 1930s and 1940s the typical administrative law controversy in the superior courts was a challenge directed against the validity of a slum clearance or compulsory purchase order. The procedure for the compulsory acquisition of land by public authorities almost invariably provides for prior notice and opportunity to be heard. It was largely standardised by the Acquisition of Land (Authorisation Procedure) Act 1946 (which substantially reproduced earlier legislation on the matter), supplemented by statutory rules.[99] The acquiring authority (normally a local authority) must give public notice of its intentions, and must also notify owners, lessees and occupiers individually. Objections to the order may be lodged within a prescribed period by the persons individually served. If an objection so made is not withdrawn, the Minister who will have to decide whether or not to confirm the order must (unless the objection relates only to compensation) either cause a public local inquiry to be held or afford the objector an opportunity of being heard before a person appointed for the purpose, and must consider the objections and the report on the inquiry or hearing. Broadly similar rules govern clearance orders to secure the demolition of slum property in an area.[100]   6–027

Persons who had not expressly been given the right to prior notice or opportunity to be heard found difficulty in persuading the courts that implications affording them such a right ought to be read into the enabling Acts.[101] As far as the courts were concerned, the obligations of the acquiring authority had been codified by statute. To be sure, the inspector conducting the public local inquiry or private hearing had to act in conformity with natural justice even though he had no power to make an initial decision[102] but for the rest, judicial review was to be interstitial; and   6–028

[99] Now see the Acquisition of Land Act 1981. See also Compulsory Purchase by Non-Ministerial Acquiring Authorities (Inquiries Procedure) Rules 1990 (SI 1990/512); Compulsory Purchase by Ministers (Inquiries Procedure) Rules 1994 (SI 1994/3264); Compulsory Purchase of Land (Written Representations Procedure) (Ministers) Regulations 2004/(SI 2004/2594); Compulsory Purchase of Land (Vesting Declarations) Regulations 1990/(SI 1990/497); and Compulsory Purchase of Land (Prescribed Forms) (Ministers) Regulations 2004/(SI 2004/2595).
[100] Housing Act 1985 ss.269, 269A, 272, 317, 318; and Housing Act 2004 Pt I.
[101] *Fredman v Minister of Health* (1935) 154 L.T. 240 (owner not entitled to be heard by the local authority before it declared a building to be included in a clearance area); *Cohen v West Hain Corp* [1933] Ch. 814 at 827 (a somewhat anomalous decision; no right to be heard before issue of notice to execute works). For the position today in which natural justice may supplement a statutory code, see 7–013 and 7–041.
[102] *Marriott v Minister of Health* (1935) 154 L.T. 47 at 50; *Denby (William) & Sons Ltd v Minister of Health* [1936] 1 K.B. 337 at 342–343. Where the holding of a hearing or a local inquiry was provided for by statute, it was always open to the courts to hold that the proceedings were too defective to constitute a hearing (see *Ealing Borough Council v Minister of Housing and Local Government* [1952] Ch. 856) or an inquiry within the meaning of the Act, even though the functions of the Minister under the Act in question were characterised as purely administrative (*Franklin v Minister of Town and Country Planning* [1948] A.C. 87 at 102, 105–106; *Wednesbury Corp v Ministry of Housing and Local Government (No.2)* [1966] 2 Q.B. 275 at 302–303 (dicta)).

to the courts the interstices seemed very narrow. Decisions in the 1940s and 1950s showed a persistent tendency to substitute for the presumption that the *audi alteram partem* principle conditioned the exercise of powers in relation to persons and property a still stronger presumption that unless a procedural duty was expressed (e.g. to consider objections,[103] or to decide "after due inquiry"[104]), none was to be implied.[105] Power to obtain information from any source was assumed to be inconsistent with the existence of any duty to notify the person affected by the information obtained.[106]

The rise of analytical distinctions and the demise of the audi alteram partem principle

The distinctions adopted

6–029 More significant to the demise of natural justice than the increase in statutory procedures, however, was the distinction drawn in *Venicoff's* case, as noted above, between "executive" and "non-judicial";[107] and this case heralded an era of increased focus on analytical distinctions in determining the applicability of natural justice. A sharp distinction was drawn between the deprivation of a right and the deprivation of a mere privilege, the latter function importing no duty to act fairly.[108] Distinctions were also drawn between "judicial" and "quasi-judicial" functions, which attracted the duty to act in accordance with the requirements of natural justice, and "administrative" and "legislative" decisions, which did not attract such a duty. The impact of the distinctions is well-illustrated by the decision in the 1951 case of *Nakkuda Ali v Jayaratne*.[109] The Controller of

---

[103] Cf. *R. v British Columbia Pollution Control Board* (1967) 61 D.L.R. (2nd) 221.
[104] This is generally understood to mean an inquiry conducted in accordance with natural justice: *Leeson v General Medical Council* (1890) 43 Ch.D. 366 at 383; *General Medical Council v Spackman* [1943] A.C. 627; *Memudu Lagunju v Olubadan-in-Council* [1952] A.C. 387 at 399; *Cf. Patterson v District Commissioner of Accra* [1948] A.C. 341 ("after inquiry, if necessary"); *Beetham v Trinidad Cement Co* [1960] A.C. 132 (government's power to "inquire" into facts of trade dispute and then appoint a board of inquiry, held purely administrative); *Abergavenny (Marquis) v Llandaff (Bishop)* (1880) 20 Q.B.D. 460 at 472; *R. v Staines Union* (1893) 69 L. 714. And *Cf Ross-Clunis v Papadopoullos* [1958] 1 W.L.R. 546 at 560–562 (power of Commissioner to conduct inquiry as he thinks fit, subject to his being satisfied as to its fairness; limited scope of judicial review).
[105] See wartime cases cited at n.91; *Patterson v District Commissioner of Accra* [1948] A.C. 341 (levying of differential charges on inhabitants for extra police protection); *Nakkuda Ali v Jayaratne* [1951] A.C. 66 (revocation of trader's licence); *Musson v Rodriguez* [1953] A.C. 530 (deportation of prohibited immigrant); *R. v Metropolitan Police Commissioner Ex p. Parker* [1953] 1 W.L.R. 1150 (revocation of taxi-cab driver's licence); *R. v St Lawrence's Hospital, Caterham, Statutory Visitors Ex p. Pritchard* [1953] 1 W.L.R. 1158 at 1162.
[106] *R. v Central Professional Committee for Opticians Ex p. Brown* [1949] 2 All E.R. 519 at 521; (*Musson v Rodriguez* [1993] A.C. 530; *R. v Metropolitan Police Commissioner* [1953] 1 W.L.R. 1150. Contrast *Capel v Child* (1832) 2 Cr. & J. 558.
[107] See 6–021.
[108] *Nakkuda Ali v Jayaratne* [1951] A.C. 66; and *R. v Metropolitan Police Commissioner* [1953] 1 W.L.R. 1150.
[109] [1951] A.C. 66.

Textiles in Ceylon had cancelled a textile dealer's licence in pursuance of a power to revoke a licence when he had "reasonable grounds" for believing its holder to be unfit to continue as a dealer. The dealer applied for certiorari to quash the order, contending that the Controller had not held an inquiry conducted in conformity with natural justice. The Judicial Committee of the Privy Council dismissed his appeal, holding that the Controller, although obliged to act on reasonable grounds,[110] was under no duty to act judicially, so that certiorari could not issue and compliance with natural justice was unnecessary. Two reasons were given for the decision: first, that certiorari would issue only to an authority that was required to follow a procedure analogous to the "judicial" procedure in arriving at its decision; and second, that the Controller was not determining a question affecting the rights of subjects but was merely "taking executive action to withdraw a privilege".[111] Yet the first assertion was contradicted in many cases on the scope of certiorari;[112] and the second served only to demonstrate the limitations of a conceptualistic approach to administrative law. Demolition of a property owner's uninhabitable house might be for him a supportable misfortune; deprivation of a licence to trade might mean a calamitous loss of livelihood; but the judicial flavour detected in the former function was held to be absent from the latter. The decision, whilst not unique,[113] was inconsistent with the previously-adopted attitude of the English courts towards the licensing and regulation of trades and occupations[114] and in general towards the right to earn one's living.[115]

Servitude to the classifications between "right" and "privilege" and "judicial" and "administrative" has now been abandoned, and the notion that a fair hearing is reserved to a "judicial" or "quasi-judicial" situation has been firmly "scotched" as a "heresy".[116] Nonetheless, these distinctions are worth examining briefly,[117] since they had a significant impact on the   6–030

[110] Distinguishing *Liversidge v Anderson* [1942] A.C. 206 on this point.
[111] [1951] A.C. 66 at 78. The Judicial Committee also held that the dealer had in fact been given an adequate opportunity to put his case against revocation; but this finding clearly did not reduce the other grounds for the decision to the status of obiter dicta. The reasons for holding that there was no duty to observe natural justice have been almost universally criticised by academic writers. They were trenchantly criticised by Lord Reid in *Ridge v Baldwin* [1964] A.C. 40 at 77–79; his Lordship was prepared, however, to explain the decision as one resting on the wording of defence regulations (at 73, 78). The decision was restrictively distinguished by Lord Parker C.J. in *Re HK (An Infant)* [1967] 2 Q.B. 617 at 630, 631, and disapproved by Lord Denning M.R. in *R. v Gaming Board for Great Britain Ex p. Benaim and Khaida* [1970] 2 Q.B. 417 at 430; though in *Durayappah v Fernando* [1967] 2 A.C. 337 at 349, the PC observed, rather opaquely, that it did not "necessarily agree" with Lord Reid's comments.
[112] See, e.g. *R. v Manchester Area Legal Aid Committee Ex p. Brand (RA) & Co* [1952] 2 Q.B. 413 and cases there cited at 427–428.
[113] *R. v Metropolitan Police Commissioner Ex p. Parker* [1953] 1 W.L.R. 1150; and *Cf. Ex p. Fry* [1954] 1 W.L.R. 730.
[114] See 6–016.
[115] See, e.g. *Abbott v Sullivan* [1952] 1 K.B. 189.
[116] Words used by Lord Denning in *R. v Gaming Board Ex p. Benaim and Khaida* [1970] 2 Q.B. 417 at 430 in respect of the decision of the HL in *Ridge v Baldwin* [1964] A.C. 40. See also Lord Diplock in *O'Reilly v Mackman* [1983] A.C. 23, 279. And see Ch.7.
[117] For a detailed discussion of the distinctions, see the Appendix to the 5th edition of this work.

evolution of natural justice, and are relevant to aspects of the discussion in the subsequent chapters.

Understanding the distinctions

6–031 It is fair to say that the meanings attributed by the courts to the terms "judicial", "quasi-judicial", "administrative", "legislative" and "ministerial" for administrative law purposes were often inconsistent. Terms were used loosely and without deliberation; sometimes the method of characterisation could be seen as a contrivance to support a conclusion reached on non-conceptual grounds; and it was sometimes impossible to discern why a court characterised a given function as "judicial" or "administrative". Broadly speaking, though, the characterisations described in the following paragraphs applied.

6–032   The term "ministerial" was used to describe any duty, the discharge of which involved no element of discretion or independent judgment; to describe the issue of a formal instruction, in consequence of a prior determination which may or may not be of a judicial character, that direct action be taken in relation to another's person or property;[118] or to describe the execution of such an instruction by an inferior officer (sometimes called a ministerial officer). Alternatively, the term was sometimes used loosely to describe any act that was neither "judicial" nor "legislative", and in this sense the term was used interchangeably with "executive" or "administrative".[119]

6–033   A wide range of meanings was capable of being attached to the term "administrative". A distinction often made between "legislative" and "administrative" acts was that between the general and the particular: while a legislative act entails the creation and promulgation of a general rule of conduct without reference to particular cases; an administrative act cannot be exactly defined, but it includes the adoption of a policy, the making and issue of a specific direction, and the application of a general rule to a particular case in accordance with the requirements of policy or expediency or administrative practice. For example, every measure duly enacted by Parliament is regarded as legislation, so if land was compulsorily acquired by means of a Private Act of Parliament or a Provisional Order Confirmation Act, the acquisition was deemed to be a legislative act; though if the acquisition was effected by means of a compulsory purchase order made under enabling legislation, it would usually be classified as an administrative act. Similarly, departmental instruments or announcements

---

[118] D. Gordon, "Administrative' Tribunals and the Courts" (1933) 49 L.Q.R. 94, P 98 *et seq.* Thus the duty of an official to notify an applicant for planning permission of the decision made by the local planning authority might aptly be described as ministerial: see *R. v Yeovil Corp. Ex p. Elim Pentecostal Church Trustees* (1971) 70 L.G.R. 142. On whether an estoppel may arise if the official errs in the performance of his duty, see *Norfolk CC v Secretary of State for the Environment* [1973] 1 W.L.R. 1400.

[119] *Haridas v Khan* [1971] 1 W.L.R. 507 at 512; *Dean v District Auditor for Ashton-in-Makerfield* [1960] 1 Q.B. 149 at 156.

which, although general in application, normally neither create legally enforceable rights nor impose legally enforceable obligations were usually referred to as examples of "administrative action".[120]

The term "quasi-judicial" could have any one of three meanings. It could describe a function that was partly judicial and partly administrative—e.g. the making of a compulsory purchase order (a discretionary or administrative act) preceded by the holding of a judicial-type local inquiry and the consideration of objections. It could, alternatively, describe the "judicial" element in a composite function; holding an inquiry and considering objections in respect of a compulsory purchase order are thus "quasi judicial" acts. Or it could describe the nature of a discretionary act itself where the actor's discretion is not unfettered.   6–034

In determining whether a function was 'judicial', a number of factors were considered, albeit that none of these factors was determinative in itself. The first test that was applied turned upon whether the performance of the function terminated in an order that had conclusive effect;[121] and a body exercising powers which were of a merely advisory,[122] deliberative,[123] investigatory[124] or conciliatory[125] character, or which did not have legal effect until confirmed by another body,[126] or involved only the making of a preliminary decision,[127] as not normally held to have judicial capacity.   6–035

A second test turned primarily on the presence or absence of certain formal and procedural attributes. The manner in which courts proceed is distinguished by a number of special characteristics. They determine   6–036

---

[120] See, e.g. Bizony v Secretary of State for the Environment [1976] 239 E.G. 281 at 283; Birdi v Home Secretary, The Times, February 12, 1975; Purewal v Entry Clearance Officer [1977] Imm. A.R. 93 (Immigration Appeal Tribunal: amnesty provisions not within jurisdiction of immigration appellate authorities). Cf. Salemi v MacKellar (No.2) (1977) 137 C.L.R. 396.

[121] See, e.g. Stow v Mineral Holdings (Australia) Pty Ltd (1977) 51 A.L.J.R. 672.

[122] Re Clifford and O'Sullivan [1921] 2 A.C. 570; R. v MacFarlane Ex p. O'Flanagan and O'Kelly (1923) 32 C.L.R. 518; R. v St Lawrence's Hospital, Caterham, Statutory Visitors Ex p. Pritchard [1953] 1 W.L.R. 1158.

[123] R. v Legislative Committee of the Church Assembly Ex p. Haynes-Smith [1928] 1 K.B. 411.

[124] See, e.g. Re Grosvenor & West-End Railway Terminus Hotel Co (1897) 76 L.T. 337; Hearts of Oak Assurance Co v Attorney General [1932] A.C. 392; O'Conner v Waldron [1935] A.C. 76; St John v Fraser [1935] S.C.R. 441; Lockwood v Commonwealth (1954) 90 C.L.R. 177; Ex p. Mineral Deposits Pty Ltd; re Claye and Lynch (1959) S.R. (N.S.W.) 167; R. v Fowler Ex p. McArthur [1958] Qd.R 41; R. v Coppel Ex p. Viney Industries Pty Ltd [1962] V.R. 630; Testro Bros Pty Ltd v Tait (1963) 109 C.L.R. 353; Guay v Lafleur [1965] S.C.R. 12; R. v Collins Ex p. ACTU-Solo Enterprises Pty Ltd (1976) 8 A.L.R. 691. Contrast Re Pergamon Press Ltd [1971] Ch. 388; Cf. however, the subsequent decision in Maxwell v Department of Trade and Industry [1974] Q.B. 523.

[125] Ayriss (FF) & Co v Alberta Labour Relations Board (1960) 23 D.L.R. (2nd) 584 at [9]; R. v Clipsham Ex p. Basken (1965) 49 D.L.R. (2nd) 747; R. v Race Relations Board Ex p. Selvarajan [1975] 1 W.L.R. 1686.

[126] R. v Hastings Local Board of Health (1865) 6 B. & S. 401; Re Local Government Board Ex p. Kingstown Commissioners (1885) 16 L.R.Ir. 150; (1886) 18 L.R.Ir. 509; Re Zadrevec and Town of Brampton (1973) 37 D.L.R. (3rd) 326.

[127] Jayawardane v Silva [1970] 1 W.L.R. 1365; Pearlberg v Varty [1972] 1 W.L.R. 534 (cf. however, Wiseman v Borneman [1971] A.C. 297).

matters in cases initiated by parties; they must normally sit in public;[128] they are empowered to compel the attendance of witnesses, who may be examined on oath; they are required to follow the rules of evidence; they are entitled to impose sanctions by way of imprisonment, fine, damages or mandatory or prohibitory orders, and to enforce obedience to their own commands. The fact that a body has been endowed with many of the "trappings of a court" may not always be sufficient to establish conclusively that it has been invested with judicial power;[129] but the presence of such trappings tended to support that conclusion. Thus, in seeking to establish that the proceedings (or the functions) of a body are to be classified as judicial for any given purpose, it may be material to show that the body is called a "tribunal" which holds "sittings" and makes "decisions" in relation to "cases" before it,[130] that it is empowered to summon witnesses and administer oaths,[131] that it is normally required to sit in public,[132] that its members are debarred from sitting if personally interested in a matter before them,[133] or that it has power to award costs[134] or to impose sanctions to enforce compliance with its orders.[135]

6–037   Perhaps the most obvious characteristic of ordinary courts though is that they determine, on the basis of evidence and arguments submitted to them, disputes between two or more parties about their respective legal rights and duties, powers and liabilities, privileges and immunities.[136] If, then, the functions of a body include the determination of issues that closely resemble *lis inter partes*, it could be expected that those functions would be classified as judicial. Of course, in administrative law many of the issues that arise between contending parties are different in character from those typically determined by courts. An applicant may appear before a licensing tribunal to seek a legal privilege; a member of the public may appear to oppose the application. Superficially the tribunal seems to be deciding a *lis*

---

[128] *Scott v Scott* [1913] A.C. 417; *McPherson v McPherson* [1936] A.C. 177; *Stone v Stone* [1949] P. 165; *Re Agricultural Industries* [1952] 1 All E.R. 1188; *B (otherwise P) v Attorney-General* [1967] P. 119. Cf. *Hearts of Oak* [1932] A.C. 392.

[129] Cf. *Shell Co of Australia Ltd v Federal Commission of Taxation* [1931] A.C. 275 at 296–297 (dealing with judicial power under the Australian Constitution).

[130] *Jackson (FE) & Co v Price Tribunal (No.2)* [1950] N.Z.L.R 433 at 448–449; *New Zealand United Licensed Victuallers' Association of Employers v Price Tribunal* [1957] N.Z.L.R. 167, 204, 207.

[131] *ibid.* And see *Attorney General v BBC* [1978] 1 W.L.R. 477 at 481.

[132] *ibid. Copartnership Farms v Harvey-Smith* [1918] 2 K.B. 405 at 411.

[133] *Copartnership Farms* [1918] 2 K.B. 405.

[134] *R. v Manchester JJ* [1899] 1 Q.B. 571; *R. v Sunderland JJ* [1901] 2 K.B. 357 at 369.

[135] The power of the Commonwealth Court of Conciliation and Arbitration to impose penalties for breaches or non-observance of its orders and awards was held by the PC in the *Boilermakers'* case to be "plainly judicial": *Attorney General of Australia v R.* [1957] A.C. 288 at 322.

[136] *Labour Relations Board of Saskatchewan v John East Iron Works Ltd* [1949] A. C. 134, 149. See also *Boulter v Kent JJ.* [1897] A.C. 556 at 569; *Huddart Parker & Co Pty Ltd v Commonwealth* (1908) 8 C.L.R. 330 at 357 (Griffith C.J.). Cf. *Re Rubber Plastic and Cable Making Industry Award* 8 F.L.R. 396 (Commonwealth Industrial Court exercising judicial power of the Commonwealth in interpreting award although no dispute between parties bound by the award).

inter partes; but if it decides to refuse the application it is not deciding only in favour of the objector; it is deciding that it is not in the public interest to grant the licence, and the decision may in effect be in favour of the public at large, who are not directly represented at the hearing.[137] Nevertheless, functions may become reviewable as "judicial" because of statutory interpolation of a procedure bearing a superficial resemblance to a *lis inter partes*. Thus, the proceedings of licensing authorities that were required to conduct hearings were sufficiently judicial to be amenable to review by certiorari and prohibition and must be conducted in conformity with natural justice. A tribunal or other deciding body was therefore likely to be held to be acting in a judicial capacity when, after investigation and deliberation, it determined an issue conclusively by the application of a pre-existing legal rule or another objective legal standard to the facts found by it. Likewise, where the decision-maker was interpreting, declaring and applying the law.[138]

Applying the distinctions

The application of these distinctions often created significant complica- 6–038
tions. To illustrate in the context of the statutory schemes regarding housing and planning, described above. Between 1935 and 1947, a number of property owners endeavoured, with scant success, to impugn compulsory purchase orders and clearance orders on the ground that the Minister as confirming authority had failed to observe the rules of natural justice. The courts held that the Minister's functions were essentially administrative, but that once objections were lodged he assumed a quasi judicial role which imposed upon him the duty to follow the rules of natural justice when considering the objections and the report on the inquiry.[139] Before objections were lodged he could offer advice to the local authority on housing matters[140] and even express tentative approval of the proposed order.[141] He could obtain information from other departments[142] or from the local authority,[143] which he was not obliged to disclose to the objector although it might be prejudicial to the latter's case.[144] To this

---

[137] *Boulter v Kent JJ* [1897] A.C. 556 at 569 (Lord Herschell); *R. v Howard* [1902] 2 K.B. 363; *Tynemouth Corp v Attorney General* [1899] A.C. 293 at 307; *R. v Ashton Ex p. Walker* (1915) 85 L.J.K.B. 27 at 30.
[138] *Moses v Parker* [1896] A.C. 245; *United Engineering Workers; Union v Devanayagam* [1968] A.C. 356 for acknowledgements of this principle.
[139] *Stafford v Minister of Health* [1946] K.B. 621 (where under a temporary Act the Minister was empowered to dispense with a local inquiry, he was still obliged in considering objections to act in conformity with natural justice).
[140] *Frost v Minister of Health* [1935] 1 K.B. 286; *Offer v Minister of Health* [1936] 1 K.B. 40.
[141] *Re Manchester (Ringway Airport) Compulsory Purchase Order* (1935) 153 L.T. 219.
[142] *Miller v Minister of Health* [1946] K.B. 626; *Summers v Minister of Health* [1947] 1 All E.R. 184.
[143] *Price v Minister of Health* [1947] 1 All E.R. 47; *Summers* [1947] 1 All E.R. 184; *Johnson (B) & Co (Builders) Ltd v Minister of Health* [1947] 2 All E.R. 395.
[144] *Johnson* [1947] 2 All E.R. 395; *Bushell v Secretary of State for the Environment* [1981] A.C. 75 (Minister both proposing and affirming authority for compulsory purchase order under the Highways Act 1959).

extent the objector was denied part of the protection afforded by the *audi alteram partem* rule.[145] After objections had been lodged the Minister had to hold himself aloof from the parties, in so far as he was not to receive *ex parte* statements from the local authority relating to the subject matter of objections examined at the inquiry.[146] But he was not precluded from discussing with the local authority matters not related to the order,[147] or (possibly) matters related to the order but not made the subject of objections at the inquiry. He was apparently entitled after the inquiry to consult with other departments on matters relevant to his decision whether or not to confirm the order, but—the point was never cleared up by the courts—the character of the information thus obtained might be such as to impose on him an obligation to disclose it to the objector to enable him to challenge its accuracy.[148] He was under no implied legal duty to disclose the contents of the inspector's report to the parties;[149] here again the courts diluted the *audi alteram partem* rule. His decision whether or not to confirm the order was "administrative," inasmuch as it could not be impeached for lack of evidence to support it.[150] If no objections were lodged his function was said to be administrative throughout.[151]

6–039   Where the Minister was both confirming authority and initiator of the order the courts showed an even stronger disinclination to review the discharge of his statutory duties in terms of judicial standards. Under the New Towns Act 1946 the Minister was empowered to make orders designating areas as the sites of satellite towns. If objections were lodged against a draft order, he had to cause a public local inquiry to be held with respect thereto and to consider the inspector's report before finally making the order.[152] Before the New Towns Bill had been introduced into

[145] *Cf. Board of Education v Rice* [1911] A.C. 179 at 182; *R. v City of Westminster Assessment Committee* [1941] 1 K.B. 53.
[146] *Errington v Minister of Health* [1935] 1 K.B. 249.
[147] *Horn v Minister of Health* [1937] 1 K.B. 164.
[148] *Darlassis v Minister of Education* (1954) 118 J.P. 452 at 466 (dictum). This issue was directly raised in *Buxton v Minister of Housing and Local Government* [1961] 1 Q.B. 278 (arising out of a planning appeal, but the application was dismissed on a preliminary point of law because the applicant lacked *locus standi*). The circumstances in which information obtained by the Minister after the inquiry must be disclosed, and the consequences of disclosure, are now specified by regulations, e.g. Town and Country Planning (Major Infrastructure Project Inquiries Procedure) (England) Rules 2005 (SI 2005/2115). The Secretary of State is required to go back to the parties where he (a) differs from the inspector or on any matter of fact mentioned in, or appearing to him to be material to, a conclusion reached by the inspector, or (b) takes into consideration any new evidence or new matter of fact (not being a matter of government policy): (SI 2005/2115, r.21). See also Town and Country Planning Appeals (Determination by Inspectors) (Inquiry Procedures) (England) Rules 2000 (SI 2000/1625) r.18.
[149] *Denby (William) & Sons Ltd v Minister of Health* [1936] 1 K.B. 337; *Steele v Minister of Housing and Local Government* (1956) 6 P. & C.R. 386, following *Local Government Board v Arlidge* [1915] A.C. 120. Disclosure or inspection of the report is now required: Town and Country Planning (Major Infrastructure Project Inquiries Procedure) (England) Rules 2005 (SI 2005/2115) r.22.
[150] *Johnson* [1947] 2 All E.R. 395; *Re Falmouth Clearance Order 1936* [1937] 3 All E.R. 308; *Re LCC Order 1938* [1945] 2 All E.R. 484.
[151] *Errington v Minister of Health* [1935] 1 K.B. 249 at 259; *Johnson* [1947] 2 All E.R. 395.
[152] Sch.1; now New Towns Act 1981 Sch.1.

Parliament, the Government had expressed its intention of designating Stevenage as the first of the new towns. In *Franklin v Minister of Town and Country Planning*[153] an attempt was made to impugn an order relating to Stevenage in that the Minister had not called evidence at the inquiry in support of the draft order and had been biased in favour of the order when he had finally made it. The House of Lords rejected these contentions; the inquiry, it held, was directed to the objections, not to the order itself, and was prescribed for the further information of the Minister[154] and the criterion of bias, appropriate to measure the conduct of a quasi-judicial officer, had no relevance to the functions of the Minister which were "purely administrative". Provided that a properly conducted inquiry had been held, the only grounds of challenge could be that the Minister had not in fact considered the report or the objections or "that his mind was so foreclosed that he gave no genuine consideration to them".[155] Whilst it was undoubtedly proper to conclude from the nature of the legislative scheme that the Minister was entitled to approach his statutory duty to consider objections with a strong inclination to implement his own policy, the House of Lords used terminology which could be regarded as lending countenance to the view that a public authority did not act in a judicial capacity, in the sense of being required to observe the rules of natural justice, unless it occupied the role of an adjudicator determining something approximating to a *lis inter partes*, in which case a duty to observe natural justice might be superimposed upon the procedural requirements already prescribed by statute.[156]

The impact of the distinctions

These lines of cases profoundly influenced the attitude of English courts 6–040 towards the procedural duties of public authorities invested with statutory powers in relation to individual rights. As was considered above, the courts tended to assume that a duty to observe the rules of natural justice arose only where the authority was already under a statutory duty to consider objections or conduct an inquiry in a "triangular" situation with two other contending parties before it; and that where no such statutory duty was imposed the functions of the authority could not be characterised as

---

[153] [1948] A.C. 87.
[154] Following *Re Trunk Roads Act 1936* [1939] 2 K.B. 515; distinguished in *Magistrates of Ayr v Lord Advocate* 1950 S.C. 102. See also *Wednesbury Corp v Ministry of Housing and Local Government (No.2)* [1966] 2 Q.B. 275 (inquiries in connection with objections to proposals for review of local government).
[155] [1948] A.C. 87 at 102, 103. See, to like effect, *Robinson v Minister of Town and Country Planning* [1947] K.B. 702; *Cf. Magistrates of Ayr v Lord Advocate* 1950 S.C. 102.
[156] *Cf.* H.W.R. Wade, *Towards Administrative Justice* (1963), p.67: "the right result was reached by the wrong road." Cf. K.C. Davis, "English Administrative Law—An American View" [1962] P.L. 139, 154–155, approving the terminology used.

judicial for this purpose.[157] They overlooked the reasons that lay behind the somewhat artificial system of characterisation adopted in the Housing Act cases. There the courts had a threefold purpose in stressing the "essentially administrative" nature of the Minister's functions: to emphasise that the Minister had an overriding political responsibility for matters of housing policy, for which he was answerable to Parliament, so that in reviewing his functions in confirming individual orders it would be inappropriate to impose upon him standards appropriate to a judge determining *lites inter partes*; to protect from disclosure departmental files and communications made to and by him in his political capacity; and to resist the contention that his final decision upon an order involved the exercise of a "quasi judicial" discretion that might be reviewed on its merits. The housing and town planning cases achieved so much prominence that older cases establishing a right to notice and hearing despite the absence of a *lis inter partes* or express procedural requirements lurked, neglected and half-forgotten, in the shadows of the past.

HISTORICAL DEVELOPMENT SINCE THE 1960S

Revisionism revised

6–041 By this stage, valedictory addresses to the *audi alteram partem* rule in English administrative law were becoming almost commonplace. It was nevertheless suggested in the first edition of this work that the time had "not yet arrived to think of pronouncing obsequies or writing obituary notices", and that "the comatose must not be assumed to be moribund";[158] and in the 1960s, the rule recovered much of its former vitality as an implied common-law requirement of fair administrative procedure. Perhaps the state of its debility had been slightly exaggerated. Its revival was indirectly stimulated by a growing awareness among practitioners and judges of old forsaken paths, of more imaginative judicial achievements in other English-speaking countries, and of academic legal literature. Undoubtedly the enactment of the Tribunals and Inquiries Act 1958, which extended the scope of judicial review in other directions, modified the general climate of judicial opinion. Above all, there had been a growth of informed interest in problems of administrative adjudication and judicialised administration generated by the publication of the Franks Report

---

[157] Statutory rules impose upon Ministers who initiate compulsory purchase orders almost exactly the same procedural duties as are prescribed in connection with orders initiated by local authorities: Compulsory Purchase by Ministers (Inquiry Procedure) Rules 1994 (SI 1994/3264); cf. Compulsory Purchase by Non-Ministerial Acquiring Authorities (Inquiries Procedure) Rules 1990 (SI 1990/512). Analogous rules now also apply to the confirmation of highway schemes inititated by the Minister: Highways (Inquiries Procedure) Rules 1994 (SI 1994/3263).

[158] (1959), p.136.

(1957), the establishment of the Council on Tribunals, the proliferation of statutory procedural rules in administrative law and the controversies aroused by the decision-making process in town and country planning. Judges do not inhabit an intellectual vacuum, and they were impelled to do some hard thinking about their own role in administrative law.

There were some indications in the first years of the 1960s, both from English courts[159] and the Privy Council, that considerations of the need for fairness in the administrative process had not been entirely eliminated from judicial thinking. Particular mention should be made of Lord Denning who, in a series of cases involving the powers of voluntary associations was concerned to ensure that these powers were tempered by corresponding responsibilities, of which the duty to hold fair inquiries was one.[160] Characteristically, Lord Denning was not concerned with the formal nature of the decision but with the fact that voluntary associations have monopoly powers and that their decisions in effect deprived individuals of their livelihoods.   6–042

Then in 1963 the House of Lords restored the law to the path from which it had deviated. For in *Ridge v Baldwin*,[161] it was held by a majority that a chief constable, dismissible only for cause prescribed by statute,[162] was impliedly entitled to prior notice of the charge against him and a proper opportunity of meeting it before being removed by the local police authority for misconduct.[163] In an illuminating review of the   6–043

[159] *R. v Registrar of Building Societies* [1960] 1 W.L.R. 669; *Hoggard v Worsbrough UDC* [1962] 2 Q.B. 93. In a number of other cases, proceedings before courts and regularly constituted tribunals were set aside for non-compliance with the *audi alteram partem* rule: *Chettiar v Chettiar* [1962] 1 W.L.R. 279; *R. v Birkenhead JJ. Ex p. Fisher* [1962] 1 W.L.R. 1410; *Brinkley v Brinkley* [1965] P. 75; *Fowler v Fowler* [1963] P. 311; *Abraham v Jutsun* [1963] 1 W.L.R. 658; *Disher v Disher* [1965] P. 31; *Appuhamy v R.* [1963] A.C. 474; *Sheldon v Bromfield JJ.* [1964] 2 Q.B. 573; *S v S* (1964) [1965] 1 W.L.R. 21; *Hodgkins v Hodgkins* [1965] 1 W.L.R. 1448; *R. v Aylesbury JJ. Ex p. Wisbey* [1965] 1 W.L.R. 339 (courts); *The Seistan* [1960] 1 W.L.R. 186; *R. v Deputy Industrial Injuries Commissioner Ex p. Jones* [1962] 2 Q.B. 677; *R. v Industrial Tribunal Ex p. George Green & Thomson Ltd* (1967) 2 K.I.R. 259 (other statutory tribunals). Decisions on non-statutory arbitrations and domestic tribunals have been omitted.

[160] See, e.g. *Russell v Duke of Norfolk* (1949) 65 T.L.R. 225 (withdrawal of horse trainer's licence by jockey Club); *Abbott v Sullivan* [1952] 1 K.B. 189 (dockworker struck off Union's register and therefore could no longer be employed); *Lee v Showman's Guild* [1952] 2 Q.B. 329 (expulsion from a trade association). See generally, J. Jowell, "Administrative Law" in J. Jowell and P. McAuslan (eds), *Lord Denning: The Judge and The Law* (1983).

[161] [1964] A.C. 40.

[162] Negligence or other unfitness (Municipal Corporations Act 1882 s.191(4)), repealed by Police Act 1964 s.64(3) and Sch.10. See now Police Act 1996 s.11 (chief constable may be called upon to retire or resign in the interests of efficiency and effectiveness; before seeking approval of Secretary of State for retirement or resignation, the chief constable is entitled to reasons and an opportunity to make representations).

[163] The implications of the decision were much discussed, e.g. A. Bradley, "Failure of Justice and Defect of Police" [1964] Cam. L.J. 83; A. Goodhart, "*Ridge v Baldwin*: Administrative and Natural Justice" (1964) 80 L.Q.R. 105. The decision was criticised by some New Zealand writers because of the omission of a "superadded" requirement to act judicially: J. Northey, "The Electricity Commissioners and the Chief Constable" [1963] N.Z.L.J. 448; D. Patterson, "Natural justice and licensing applications: Hohfeld and the Writ of Certiorari" [1966] N.Z.L J. 107; but see J. Farmer, "Natural justice and licensing applications: Hohfeld and the Writ of Certiorari" (1967) 2 N.Z.U.L.Rev. 282.

authorities,[164] Lord Reid repudiated the notions that the rules of natural justice applied only to the exercise of those functions which were analytically judicial, and that a "superadded" duty to act judicially had to be visible before an obligation to observe natural justice could arise in the exercise of a statutory function affecting the rights of an individual. He emphasised that the duty to act in conformity with natural justice could, in some situations, simply be inferred from a duty to decide "what the rights of an individual should be".[165]

6–044   This decision gave a powerful impetus to the emergent trend,[166] an impetus which is not yet spent in administrative law. It opened an era of activism in which the courts have subjected the working of government to a degree of judicial scrutiny, on substantive as well as procedural grounds, which shows little sign yet of diminishing; and which has received renewed impetus with the advent of the Human Rights Act 1998.[167]

The duty to act fairly

6–045 In the case law since the late 1960s, the courts have demonstrated considerable flexibility in their manipulation of the principal criteria used for determining the circumstances in which a duty to observe the rules of natural justice would be implied. As long as it was remembered that the degree of procedural formality required by the rules was capable of considerable variation according to the context,[168] an extension of the range of situations to which they were applied did not attract the criticism that the courts were "over judicialising" administrative procedures. Since 1967 the courts began to employ the term "duty to act fairly" to denote an implied procedural obligation—the content of which may fall considerably short of the essential elements of a trial or a formal inquiry—accompanying the performance of a function that could not readily be characterised as judicial in nature.[169]

6–046   Thus, before refusing leave to enter, immigration officers were not required to hold a judicial hearing at which the individual could produce witnesses and evidence to support his claim: this would unduly burden the administration of the system of immigration control in which officers at the

[164] [1964] A.C. 40 at 71–79.
[165] [1964] A.C. 40 at 75–76.
[166] PC decisions in the 1960s applying the *audi alteram partem* rule to set aside administrative action included: *Kanda v Government of Malaya* [1962] A.C. 322; *Shareef v Commissioner for Registration of Indian and Pakistani Residents* [1966] A.C. 47; *Alaradana Mosque Trustees v Mahmud* [1967] 1 A.C. 13; *Jeffs v New Zealand Dairy Production and Marketing Board* [1967] 1 A.C. 551. See also *Durayappah v Fernando* [1967] 2 A.C. 337 (implied duty to observe natural justice, but appeal dismissed on a technical point. Cf. *Vidyodaya University Council v Silva* [1965] 1 W.L.R. 77; *Pillai v Singapore City Council* [1968] 1 W.L.R. 1278.
[167] See Ch.13 and 7–032 and 7–119.
[168] Dicta to this effect in *Russell v Duke of Norfolk* [1949] 1 All E.R. 109 at 118 were cited with predictable regularity.
[169] On similar developments in other jurisdictions, see 6–051.

ports are required, within a relatively short period of time, to make a large number of decisions.[170] However, they were under a legal obligation to exercise their powers fairly, and this meant that they must inform a person who claims a legal right to enter why they are disposed to refuse and allow him an opportunity to allay their suspicions.[171] Similar obligations were imposed upon inspectors conducting inquiries into allegations of improprieties committed against companies by their officers.[172] While the damage to reputations that might be suffered as a result of the publication of a report containing adverse criticisms required that affected individuals have a prior opportunity to be informed of and to comment upon any serious allegations made against them, to insist on an adjudicative hearing would be inconsistent with the public interest in protecting the confidentiality of evidence given to the inspector, and in ensuring that the inquiry is conducted with reasonable expedition. Moreover, an adverse report does not directly deprive a person of any legal rights in the strict sense. The duty to act fairly also extended the scope of the hearing to situations where a "privilege" rather than a "right" was in issue. For example, an applicant for a renewal of gaming licence cannot be refused on grounds of personal unacceptability unless the board has first intimated to him its concerns in such a way that allows the applicant to respond, but without prejudicing the confidentiality of the board's sources of information.[173]

The principal benefit of the introduction of the duty to act fairly into the court's vocabulary was to extend the benefit of basic procedural protections to situations which it would be inappropriate to describe the decision makers functions as judicial, or even quasi-judicial, and inappropriate to insist on a procedure analogous to a trial.[174]   6–047

---

[170] Immigration Act 1971 Sch. 2.

[171] *Re HK (An Infant)* [1967] 2 Q.B. 617: applicant had a legal right to enter if he could establish his claim to be the son, under the age of 16, of a Commonwealth citizen settled in the UK. The reason for Lord Parker C.J.'s doubt over the proper characterisation of the immigration officer's function arose from the exigencies of the administration of immigration control at the ports of entry, rather than from the nature of the decision to be made. Those without a legal entitlement (or, it should now be added, a legitimate expectation) to enter or remain in the UK may be refused without the benefit of any implied procedural rights: *Schmidt v Home Office* [1969] 2 Ch. 149. Since 1969, there has been a right to a hearing on an appeal against many immigration decisions to independent tribunals. This is one context in which statutory justice has, to an extent at least, supplied the omission of the common law. However, the statutory duty to give reasons for refusal, before a notice of appeal is given, has been construed narrowly: *R. v Secretary of State for for the Home Department Ex p. Swati* [1986] 1 W.L.R. 477; *R. (on the application of Hicks) v Secretary of State for the Home Department* [2005] EWHC 2818; [2006] A.C.D. 47.

[172] Companies Act 1985 Pt.14 and Companies Act 2006 Pt.10; *Re Pergamon Press Ltd* [1971] Ch. 388; *Maxwell v Department of Trade and Industry* [1974] Q.B. 523. Cf. *Norwest Holst Ltd v Secretary of State for Trade* [1978] Ch. 201 (appointment of inspectors), and *R. v Secretary of State for Trade Ex p. Perestrello* [1981] Q.B. 19 (exercise of power under Companies Act 1967 s.109 (now Companies Act 1985 s.447), to require the production of corporate documents), where the duty to act fairly was given hardly any independent content.

[173] *R. v Gaming Board of Great Britain Ex p. Benaim and Khaida* [1970] 2 Q.B. 417.

[174] See 6–029. As will be seen in Ch.7, courts now tend to reason in terms of a general duty to

European influences

The ECHR

6-048 More recently , the incorporation of Art.6 of the ECHR into English law in 2000 as a result of the Human Rights Act 1998 has proved to be an important stimulus to the evolution of procedural fairness.[175] In summary, Art.6 requires a "fair and public hearing within a reasonable time" by an "independent and impartial tribunal established by law" for the determination of an individual's "civil rights and obligations".[176] As is evident from the wording of the provision and, as is discussed in Chapter 7, the entitlement to Art.6 protection only arises where "civil rights and obligations" are in issue.[177] The term "civil rights and obligations" is clearly "rooted in a paradigm of private law rights",[178] and the Strasbourg Court has experienced considerable difficulty in determining its scope.[179] Initially interpreted very restrictively,[180] over time Art.6 has been given a more

act fairly. However, for earlier cases on the relationship between classification of a function as administrative and importation of a duty to act "fairly" rather than "judicially," e.g. *Pearlberg v Varty* [1972] 1 W.L.R. 534 at 547 (Lord Pearson); *Bates v Lord Hailsham of St Marylebone* [1972] 1 W.L.R. 1373 at 1378 (Megarry J.); *R. v Liverpool Corp Ex p. Liverpool Taxi Fleet Operators' Association* [1972] 2 Q.B. 299 at 307–308, 310 (Lord Denning M.R. and Roskill L.J.); *Herring v Templeman* [1973] 3 All E.R. 369 at 584 (no duty to disclose academic assessments to student liable to expulsion), *R. v Race Relations Board Ex p. Selvarajan* [1973] 1 W.L.R. 1686 at 1693–1696, 1700 (delegation of decision-making by a body whose functions were largely investigative and conciliatory). While judges often adopted different characterisations of the same power, and used different terms to describe the applicable procedural duty, they could still agree on whether the authority was obliged to afford to the applicant the procedural right in question, e.g. *Re H.K.* [1967] 2 Q.B. 617 at 630–631 (Lord Parker C.J., "fairly") 632–633 (Salmon L.J., "natural justice"), (Blain J., neutral); *Re Pergamon Press Ltd* [1971] Ch. 388 at 399–400 (Lord Denning M.R., "fairly"), 402–403 (Sachs L.J., "natural justice"), 407 (Buckley L.J. "not a judicial function"); *Breen v AEU* [1971] 2 Q.B. 175 at 190 (Lord Denning M.R., "fairly"), 195 (Edmund Davies L.J., "natural justice"), 200 (Megaw L.J., neutral); and *Grunwick Processing Laboratories Ltd v ACAS* [1978] A.C. 633 at 660, 667 (Lord Denning M.R.: "judicial", "natural justice"), 677 (Geoffrey Lane L.J.: "unfair or contrary to the rules of natural justice"); but on appeal Lord Diplock, speaking for the majority in the HL, disposed of the questions of statutory interpretation in issue without reference to either term.

[175] For the impact of Art.6 on common law procedural fairness, see 7–032 and 7–119; S. Juss, "Constitutionalising Rights without a Constitution: The British Experience under Article 6 of the Human Rights Act 1998" (2006) 27 Statute L. Rev. 29. On Art.6 specifically, see Lord Lester and D. Pannick, *Human Rights Law and Practice*, 2nd edn. (2004), para.4.6; C. Ovey and R. White, *Jacobs and White The European Convention on Human Rights*, 4th edn. (2006).

[176] See 7–032, 7–119 and 10–077.

[177] See 7–032; P. Craig, "The Human Rights Act, Article 6 and Procedural Rights" [2003] P.L. 753; J. Herberg, A. Le Sueur and J. Mulcahy, "Determining Civil Rights and Obligations" in J. Jowell and J. Cooper (eds), *Understanding Human Rights Principles* (2001), p.91, at pp.112, and 114–121.

[178] Craig [2003] P.L. 753,P 754.

[179] Craig [2003] P.L. 753; Lester and Pannick (2004), paras 4.6.8–4.6.12; Ovey and White (2006), pp.163–169. The jurisprudence relating to the applicability of Art.6 to civil service disputes has been particularly protracted: *Massa v Italy* (1994) 18 E.H.R.R. 266; *De Santa v Italy* (App. No.25574/94); *Lapalorcia v Italy* (App. No. 25586/94); *Abenavoli v Italy* (App. No.25587/94), Judgments of September 2, 1997; *Neigel v France* (2000) 30 E.H.R.R. 310; *Pellegrin v France* (2001) 31 E.H.R.R. 26.

[180] See 7–032; *Ringeisen v Austria* (1979–80) 1 E.H.R.R. 455.

generous application. For example, it has been applied to the determination of welfare benefits[181] and the revocation of a licence to operate a taxi. Now it is certainly not as restricted in its scope as the *Nakudda Ali* formulation considered above. Nonetheless, the Article is clearly not of unrestricted scope,[182] and in this respect, it lacks the flexibility of application of the common law duty to act fairly.[183] The content of the protection provided by Art.6 will be considered in detail in Chapters 7, 8 and 10, but for present purposes, it is worth noting that the provision's most notable impact has been due to its requirement of an "independent" tribunal, to accompany the common law principle that no one should be a judge in his own cause or "*nemo judex in causa sua*".[184] The influence of Art.6 has resulted in an "independent" tribunal being declared to be a requirement of common law procedural fairness;[185] while an important jurisprudence has evolved regarding the extent to which judicial review can remedy the absence of institutional or structural independence on the part of the decision-maker.[186]

European Community law

European Community law has undoubtedly had a very important impact 6–049 on English administrative law, which is explored in detail in Chapter 14. However, its impact has been more notable in the context of substantive review and legitimate expectations, than it has been in the context of procedural fairness. Aside from the example of a duty to give reasons, which applies both in respect of acts of the Community and in respect of national measures which interfere with Community law rights,[187] there is a stronger case for asserting that European Community law on procedural fairness has been inspired more by, and borrowed more from, English common law, than vice versa.[188]

---

[181] See 7–035 and, e.g. *Salesi v Italy* (1998) 26 E.H.R.R. 187; *Tsfayo v UK* App. No.60860/00, [2007] H.L.R. 19.

[182] See 7–033 and, e.g. *Charalambos v France* App. No.49210/99, admissibility decision of February 8, 2000 (determination of tax liability); *Maaouia v France* (2001) 33 E.H.R.R. 1037 (proceedings to challenge an exclusion order); *R. v Richmond upon Thames LBC Ex p. JC* [2001] E.L.R. 21 (school admission decision).

[183] On occasion, English courts have deliberately avoided the issue altogether, and decided cases on alternative grounds: *Begum v Tower Hamlets LBC* [2003] UKHL 5: [2003] 2 A.C. 430.

[184] See 10–00.

[185] *R. (on the application of Bewry) v Norwich City Council* [2001] EWHC Admin 657; [2002] H.R.L.R. 2.

[186] See 10–00.

[187] See 14–107 and 14–117.

[188] Case 17/74 *Transocean Marine Paint Association v Commission* [1974] E.C.R. 1063 at 1088–90 (AG Warner noting that in English law, the right to be heard was a "rule of natural justice", regardless of whether there was a written obligation to provide a hearing). On process rights in the EU, see further P. Craig, *EU Administrative Law* (2006), Ch.11.

COMPARATIVE PERSPECTIVES

Historical comparisons

6–050 When reviewing the evolution of procedural fairness in comparative historical context, the debt owed in England and Wales, and the Commonwealth more generally, to the large body of American case-law and the sophisticated writings of American commentators[189] on the right to a hearing is worthy of note. While the impact of American experience and thought on English courts was neither immediate nor obvious, its influence on English academics was marked. That said, the *audi alteram partem* principle did find vibrancy in courts across the Commonwealth from the 1950s onwards. The High Court of Australia reaffirmed the presumption in favour of the maxim in two cases where summary action derogating from private property rights had been taken in reliance on legislation which afforded no procedural safeguard.[190] The Supreme Court of Ceylon, although bound by *Nakuuda Ali v Jayaratne*,[191] contrived to give effect to the maxim in a range of situations extending from the disqualification of a university student for misconduct to the removal of local councillors.[192] The vitality of the maxim had survived in Canada as well. The Supreme Court applied the *audi alteram partem* rule to a decision of a Labour Relations Board to decertify a trade union as the bargaining agent for employees.[193] And in a striking decision the Appellate Division of the South African Supreme Court demonstrated its independence by invalidating a restriction order served by a minister under the Suppression of Communism Act, the person affected not having been given the opportunity of making representations against it in accordance with the "sacred maxim," *audi alteram partem*.[194] Finally, the New Zealand courts, whilst regarding

[189] See, e.g. K.C. Davis, *Administrative Law Treatise* (1958), and now R. Pierce, 4th edn. (2002); W. Gellhorn and C. Byse, *Administrative Law: Cases and Comments*, 10th edn. (2003) Chs 3–7; R. Stewart, "The Reformation of American Law" (1974–5) 88 Harv. L.R. 1667; J. Mashaw, *Due Process in the Administrative State* (1985).

[190] *Delta Properties Pty Ltd v Brisbane City Council* (1956) 95 C.L.R. 11 at 18 (resolution prohibiting erection of dwellings on land); *Police Commissioner v Tanos* (1958) 98 C.L.R. 383 at 385–386 (judge declaring restaurant a disorderly house on an ex parte application).

[191] [1951] A.C. 66.

[192] *Fernando v Ceylan University* (1957) 59 NLR 265 (reversed on the merits [1960] 1 W.L.R. 223).

[193] *Alliance des Professeurs Catholiques de Montreal v Labour Relations Board of Quebec* [1953] 2 S.C.R. 140. See also *Saltfleet Board of Health v Knapman* [1956] S.C.R. 877; *Wisell v Metropolitan Corp of Greater Winnipeg* [1965] S.C.R. 512; *Re Nicholson and Haldimand-Norfolk Police Commissioners* (1979) 88 D.L.R. (3rd) 671. But the line has not always been firmly held, e.g. *Calgary Power Ltd Copitliorne* [1959] S.C.R. 24; *Howarth v National Parole Board* [1976] 1 S.C.R. 453; *Martineau and Butters v Matsqui Institution Inmate Disciplinary Board* [1978] 1 S.C.R. 118 (although the latter two cases turn specifically on the interpretation of the Federal Court Act 1970 s.28(1)).

[194] *R. v Ngwevela* 1954 (1) S.A. 123 (rule not excluded by Parliament expressly or by necessary implication, and no exceptional circumstances, such as paramount need for swift preventive action, present). See also *Saliwa v Minister of Native Affairs*, 1956 (2) S.A. 310; contrast, however, *South African Defence and Aid Fund v Minister of Justice*, 1967 (1) S.A. 263, indicating a retreat by the judges from their bold attitude towards executive encroachments on individual freedom.

themselves bound by *Nakkuda Ali*, were nonetheless prepared to apply the rule to situations far removed from that of a judge deciding a *lis inter partes*, by finding statutory indications of a duty to act judicially, albeit that the legislation did not expressly require notice or hearing.[195]

Contemporary comparisons

Generally, across common law jurisdictions, recognition of the importance 6–051 of observing the requirements of procedural fairness continues apace. Perhaps the most definitive statement that can be made though is that, while similar procedural fairness questions appear to have occupied courts across jurisdictions, the precise solutions reached by those courts have not always been uniform.

As in England and Wales, elsewhere, the common law duty to act in 6–052 accordance with natural justice has generally been overtaken by a duty to act fairly.[196] Just as in England and Wales, procedural fairness has been affected by the incorporation of Convention rights into domestic law, across the common law world principles of procedural fairness continue to be influenced by constitutional and statutory developments. Well-established examples include:

- s.7 of the Canadian Charter of Rights and Freedoms 1990, which states that the right to life, liberty and security of the person may only be deprived "in accordance with the principles of fundamental justice";[197]

- s.27(1) of the New Zealand Bill of Rights Act 1990;

- s.18.1(4)(b) of the Canadian Federal Court Act 1970, which, like the New Zealand Bill of Rights Act, refers expressly to "natural justice";

---

[195] *New Zealand Dairy Board v Okitu Co-operative Dairy Co Ltd* [1953] N.Z.L.R. 366 at 403–405, 417, 422; *New Zealand United Licensed Victuallers' Association of Employers v Price Tribunal* [1957] N.Z.L.R. 167 at 203–205, 207; *Low v Earthquake Commission* [1959] N.Z.L.R. 1198.

[196] See, e.g. in New Zealand: *Chandra v Minister of Immigration* [1978] 2 N.Z.L.R. 559 at 564 reviewing authorities on the relationship between fairness and natural justice. In Australia the term "procedural fairness" has normally been invoked in preference to "natural justice". *Kioa v West* (1985) 159 C.L.R. 550 at 583, although the Australian Administrative Decisions (Judicial Review) Act 1977 ss.5(1)(a); 6(1)(a) prescribes natural justice as a ground of review. The applicability and content of natural justice under the Act are however the same as at common law. *Kioa* (1985) 159 C.L.R. 550 at 576, 583–584.

[197] *Singh v Minister of Employment and Immigration* [1985] 1 S.C.R. 177. For a general discussion, see D. Mullan and D. Harrington, "The Charter and Administrative Decision-Making" (2002) 27 Queen's L.J. 879. Section 7 has had a particular influence on the question of a right to legal representation: *Howard v Presiding Officer of Inmate Disciplinary Court of Stony Mountain Institution* (1985) 19 D.L.R. 502. The constitutional duty to provide procedural fairness in Canada may be overridden by statute however: *Ocean Port Hotel Ltd. v British Columbia (General Manager, Liquor and Control Licensing Branch)* [2001] 2 S.C.R. 781. See also the jurisprudence regarding the concept of "constitutional justice", deriving from Art.40.3 of the Irish Constitution: Delany (2001), pp.236–238.

- in South Africa, the Promotion of Administrative Justice Act 2000 ("the PAJA") implements the call in s.33(3) of the South African Constitution for national legislation to give effect to the rights to administrative justice listed in s.33(1) and s.33(2). The Act provides the default pathway for judicial review, and, like all the s.33 rights in the Constitution, applies to "administrative action". However, a distinction is drawn between "administrative action" affecting an individual,[198] and "administrative action" which affects "the rights of the public".[199] Procedural fairness in the former context is broad in nature and involves notice, an opportunity to be heard and in the latter context, may entail recourse to public inquiries or notice and comment procedures.

6–053 In terms of entitlement to procedural fairness, different trends are to be noted. Generally, the former distinction between quasi-judicial and administrative acts has now been abandoned,[200] and in India, for example, the

---

[198] PAJA s.3.

[199] PAJA s.4; see *Earthlife Africa (Cape Town v Director-General: Department of Environmental Affairs and Tourism and Another* 2005 (3) S.A. 156 (C); *Chairpersons' Association v Minister of Arts and Culture and Others* 2006 (2) S.A. 32 (T); *Minister of Health v New Clicks South Africa (Pty) Ltd (Treatment Action Campaign and Another as Amici Curiae)* 2006 (2) S.A. 311, CC.

[200] See nn.190–195; *Canada Nicholson v Haldimand-Norfolk Regional Board of Commissioners of Police* [1979] 1 S.C.R. 311 (probationary constable entitled to procedural fairness before being let go, even though the statutory rules prescribing a hearing before dismissal did not apply to a power to dispense with services of a probationer); *Syndicat des Employés de production du Québec et de l'Acadie v Canadian Human Rights Commission* (1989) 62 D.L.R. (4th) 383 at 425; and *Elliott v Burin Peninsula School Board—District 7* (1998) 161 D.L.R. (4th) 112, 119. But on the continuing survival of a category of "legislative" decisions, see *Cardinal v Kent Institution* (1985) 24 D.L.R. (4th) 44 at [14] (Le Dain J): "There is as a general common law principle a duty of procedural fairness lying on every public authority making an administrative decision which is not of a legislative nature and affects the rights, privileges or interests of an individual". The distinction between "quasi-judicial" and "administrative" has been abandoned in Australia since *Bankes v Transport Regulation Board* (1968) 119 C.L.R. 222, but the seminal case was *Kioa v West* (1985) 159 C.L.R. 550. The Australian Administrative Appeals Tribunal has stated that it is a clear principle that all parties whose interests may be affected have a right to be heard by a decision-maker: *Hawker de Havilland v Australian Securities Commission* (1991) 10 A.C.L.C. 34 at 38. See also *Annetts v McCann* (1990) 170 C.L.R. 596, citing with approval Deane J. in *Haoucher v Minister for Immigration and Ethnic Affairs* (1990) 169 C.L.R. 648 at 680 that the law was "moving towards a . . . position where the common law requirements of procedural fairness will, in the absence of clear contrary legislative intent, be recognised as applying generally to governmental executive decision-making". *Annetts*, (1990) 170 C.L.R. 596 at 598. See also M. Aronson, B. Dyer and M. Groves, *Judicial Review of Administrative Action*, 3rd edn. (2004), pp.381–387 and 390–391, noting that procedural fairness applies even to application cases, "such that the Australian courts have now moved beyond the point where the interests protected by procedural fairness can be defined by reference to deprivation". In New Zealand, see *Fowler & Roderique Ltd v A-G* [1987] 2 N.Z.L.R. 56; *Lower Hutt City Council v Bank* [1974] 1 N.Z.L.R. 545; and *Daganayasi v Minister of Immigration* [1980] N.Z.L.R. 130 at 141 (Cooke J. noting that "the requirements of natural justice vary with the power that is exercised and the circumstances. In their broadest sense, they are not limited to occasions which might be labelled judicial or quasi-judicial"). Some jurisdictions appear to have afforded procedural protection to the right to drink alcohol: *R. v McArthur Ex p. Cornish* [1966] Tas. S.R. 157

distinction has "withered away".[201] Even an administrative order with what have been described as "civil consequences" must be consistent with the requirements of natural justice;[202] and the phrase "civil consequences" has been interpreted to include "infraction of not merely property or personal rights but of civil liberties, material deprivations and non-pecuniary damages. In its comprehensive connotation, everything that affects a citizen in his civil life inflicts civil consequences".[203]

Meanwhile, in New Zealand, s.27(1) of the New Zealand Bill of Rights   6–054 Act 1990, states that natural justice applies to determinations in respect of rights, obligations and interests. While this clearly rejects the "right"-"privilege" distinction discussed above,[204] the courts have generally followed the intent of the drafters that the requirements of natural justice should only be applied by courts in the individuated decision-making paradigm.[205] Moreover, courts have often regarded "legislative" decisions,[206] or to use the term used more frequently now, "decisions affecting many"[207] as not being subject to the requirements of procedural fairness.

As for the content of procedural fairness, as a general observation, the   6–055 importance of flexibility in this context has been widely recognised;[208] and this flexibility has even survived statutory codification—albeit that any

(police superintendent, empowered to order licensees to stop serving alcohol to habitual drunkard on basis of information supplied, issues orders in respect of C upon information supplied by C's wife; held orders void because C was denied opportunity to rebut accusation); *Re Liquor Control Board of Ontario and Keupfer* (1974) 47 D.L.R. (3rd) 326. See also *Wisconsin v Constantineau* 400 U.S. 433 (1971).

[201] *SL Kapoor v Jagmohan* A.I.R. 1981 A.C. 136 at 140.

[202] *Rajesh Kumar v Dy CIT* 2007 (2) S.C.C. 181 at 192, 193, [96].

[203] *Mohiner Singh Gill v Chief Election Commissioner* A.I.R. 1978 S.C. 851 at 870; See also *Canara Bank v VK Awasthy* 2005 (6) S.C.C. 32 331–332 at [14]; *Erusian Equipment and Chemicals v State of West Bengal* A.I.R. 1975 S.C. 266 (trader on government blacklist involves civil consequences because it tarnishes reputation and prevents trading with government). See S.J. Sorabjee, "Obliging Government to Control Itself: Recent Developments in Indian Administrative Law" [1994] PL. 39.

[204] See 6–029.

[205] *Chisholm v Auckland City Council* [2005] N.Z.A.R. 661 at [32] (Tipping J., CA); *Henderson v Director, Land Transport Safety Authority* [2006] N.Z.A.R. 629 at [70]–[71]; *Air Nelson Ltd v Minister of Transport* [2007] N.Z.A.R. 266, HC. At common law, the courts had rejected the judicial-administrative distinctions: see n.200.

[206] *Attorney-General of Canada v Inuit Tapirisat of Canada* [1980] 2 S.C.R. 735; G. Carter, "Procedural Fairness in Legislative Functions: The End of Judicial Abstinence?" (2003) 53 U.T.L.J. 217.

[207] PAJA s.4; and see Aronson, Dyer and Groves (2004), pp.411–418.

[208] In Australia, e.g. *Kioa v Minister for Immigration and Ethnic Affairs* (1985) 62 A.L.R. 321 at 368 (Brennan J commenting that "the principles of natural justice have a flexible quality which, chameleon-like, evokes a different response from the repository of a statutory power according to the circumstances in which the respository is to exercise that power"); *Mobil Oil Australia Pty Ltd v FCT* (1963) 113 C.L.R. 475 at 504. Likewise in Ireland, see *Mooney v An Post* [1994] E.L.R. 103 at 116 (Keane J. noting that "the concept is necessarily an imprecise one and what its application requires may differ significantly from case to case"). In Canada see *Knight v Indian Head School Division No.19* (1990) 69 D.L.R. (4th) 489 at 510 (L'Heureux-Dubé J noting that the concept of procedural fairness is "eminently variable"); *Baker v Canada* (1999) 174 D.L.R. (4th) 193 at 212 (L'Heureux-Dubé J. noting that "the more important the decision is to the lives of those affected and the greater its impact is on that person or persons the more stringent the procedural protections that will be mandated"); and *Martineau v Matsqui Institution Disciplinary Board* [1980] 1 S.C.R. 602 at [61]–[63].

given statutory scheme will provide the most important starting point in determining the procedure to be followed.[209] In South Africa, s.2 of the PAJA even stipulates that a "fair administrative procedure depends on the circumstances of each case". Section 3 of the PAJA divides the demands of fairness in individual cases into five minimum requirements and three discretionary cases, and the courts have drawn freely on the common law in developing their jurisprudence on the meaning and content of the various requirements.[210] In India, given the courts' presumption that Parliament did not intend to contravene fundamental rights,[211] the principle of *audi alteram partem* has regularly been implied into statutory schemes.[212] In the US, the extent of due process protection required is usually determined by a number of factors: first, the private interest that will be affected by the official action; second, the risk of an erroneous deprivation of such interest through the procedures used, and the probable value, if any, of additional or substitute procedural safeguards; and finally, the government's interest, including the function involved and the fiscal and administrative burdens that the additional or substantive procedural requirement would entail.[213] However, US federal courts also frequently apply a more general test of assessing what is "reasonable" in the circumstances.[214] In Canada, five non-exhaustive factors have been identified as relevant to determining the content of procedural fairness: the nature of the decision being made and the process followed in making that decision; the nature of the statutory scheme and the terms of the statute pursuant to which the body operates; the importance of the decision to the individual affected (the more important the decision is to the lives of those affected and the greater its impact on that person or persons, the more

---

[209] *Waitemata County v Local Government Commission* [1964] N.Z.L.R. 689; *Brettingham-Moore v St Leonards Municipality* (1969) 121 C.L.R. 509; *French v Law Society of Upper Canada* [1975] 2 S.C.R. 767 at 783–786; *Salemi v McKellar (No.2)* (1977) 137 C.L.R. 396; *Bourke v State Services Commission* [1978] 1 N.Z.L.R. 633 at 644–646; *CREEDNZ Inc v Governor General* [1981] 1 N.Z.L.R. 172 at 177–178. *Cf.*, however, *Re Cardinal and Board of Commissioners of Police of the City of Cornwall* (1974) 42 D.L.R. (3rd) 323; *Twist v Randwick Municipal Council* (1976) 136 C.L.R. 106. In the United States the Supreme Court, in a landmark case, *Vermont Yankee Nuclear Power Corp v Natural Resources Defense Council, Inc* 435 U.S. (1978) 519 at 543 it was held that absent constitutional contraints or extremely compelling circumstances, courts may not force agencies to utilise rulemaking procedures beyond those prescribed in the Administrative Procedure Act 1946 or other statutory or constitutional provisions.

[210] See, e.g. *Minister of Health v New Clicks South Africa (Pty) Ltd (Treatment Action Campaign as Amici Curiae)* 2006 (2) S.A. 311 at [147], CC; *Bato Star Fishing (Pty) Ltd v Minister of Environmental Affairs* 2004 (4) S.A. 490 at [45], CC; *Premier, Mpumalanga v Executive Committee, Association of State-Aided Schools, Eastern Transvaal* 1999 (2) S.A. 91 (CC) [39]; *President of the Republic of South Africa v South African Rugby Football Union* 2000 (1) S.A. 1 at [219], CC.

[211] *IR Coelho v State of TN* 2006 (8) S.C.C. 212 at 240, 241.

[212] See, e.g. *Rajesh Kimar v Dy CIT* 2007 (2) S.C.C. 1 at 79.

[213] *Mathews v Eldridge* 424 U.S. 319 (1976) at 335.

[214] *Mullane v Central Hanover Bank & Trust Co* 339 U.S. 306 (1950) at 339 (stating that notice must be "reasonably calculated, under all the circumstances, to apprise interested parties of the pendency of the action and afford them an opportunity to present their objections"). See also *Dusenbery v United States*, 534 U.S. 161 (2002) at 167–168.

stringent the procedural protections that will be mandated); the legitimate expectation of the person challenging the decision; and the choice of procedure made by the decision-maker itself when the statute leaves to the decision-maker the ability to choose its own procedures.[215]

More specifically, the importance of prior notice has been universally accepted.[216] It has been equally widely accepted that an oral hearing will not always be required to comply with a duty to act fairly,[217] and various factors have been identified regarding when an oral hearing will be necessary.[218] One notable divergence of view between the Canadian and Australian courts on this question has arisen in the context of asylum-seekers, who are entitled to oral hearings in Canada, but not in Australia.[219] The importance in certain circumstances of being able to call and cross-examine witnesses and to legal representation at oral hearings has been recognised; but these rights are certainly not absolute and whether they are necessary to ensure procedural fairness depends on the circumstances.[220]

6–056

[215] *Baker* (1999) 174 D.L.R. (4th) 193 (L'Heureux-Dubé J.); see also *The Board of Education of the Indian Head School Division No.19 of Saskatchewan v Knight* [1990] 1 S.C.R. 653 at [28].

[216] See 7–062 and e.g. *Murdoch v New Zealand Milk Board* [1982] N.Z.L.R. 108; *Birss v Secretary of State for Justice* [1984] 1 N.Z.L.R. 513 (notice required where suspension under consideration); *Gage v Attorney-General for Onatario* (1992) 90 D.L.R. (4th) 537 at 552 (stating that "notice is an essential component of natural justice" and that it will be a mixed question of fact and law in each case whether the notice given is adequate); *TV3 v Independent Radio and television Commission* [1994] 2 I.R. 439.

[217] See Ch.7. In Canada, even where the word "hearing" is used in statute, which "almost always" indicates an oral hearing, written representations may suffice on occasion: *Re Attorney-General of Manitoba and National Energy Board* (1974) 48 D.L.R. 73 at 89; see also *US v Florida East Coat Rly Co* 410 U.S. 224 (1973); *Zhang de Yong v Minister for Immigration* (1993) 118 A.L.R. 165, 187. See also *Johns v Release on Licence Board* (1987) 9 N.S.W.L.R. 103 at 113 (Kirby P. mentioning the need for a cost-benefit analysis).

[218] See Ch.7. It has been suggested in Canada that an oral hearing is required where there is threat to life or liberty (*Singh v Minister of Employment and Immigration* (1985) 17 D.L.R. (4th) 433); where there is a loss of an existing right or privilege (*Maple Ridge (District) v Thornhill Aggregates Ltd* (1998) 162 D.L.R. 203 at 217); or where there is a "serious issue of credibility" (*Singh v Canada* (1985) 17 D.L.R. (4th) 422; *Khan v University of Ottawa* (1997) 148 D.L.R. (4th) 577. In the Australian case of *Zhang de Yong v Minister for Immigration* (1993) 118 A.L.R. 165 at 188, it was suggested that an oral hearing may be required where inconsistencies between written submissions and information available to the decision cannot be resolved. In India, where issues are complex or technical, fairness may demand a hearing: *Travancore Rayons v India* A.I.R. 1971 S.C. 862. See Delany (2001) pp.194–199.

[219] Contrast: *Zhang v Minister for Immigration Local Government and Ethnic Affairs* (1993) 45 F.C.R. 384 and *Singh v Minister of Employment and Immigration* (1985) 17 D.L.R. (4th) 433. See also *Dagi v The Broken Hill Proprietary Company Ltd* [2000] V.S.C. 486, *Daguio v Minister for Immigraiton and Ethnic Affairs* (1986) 71 A.L.R. 173 and *Muhazi v Minister of Employment and Immigration* (2004) 42 Imm. L.R. (3rd) 292; S. Kneebone "Natural Justice and Non-Citizens: A Matter of Integrity?" (2002) 26 Melb. U. L. Rev. 355.

[220] See, e.g. *Innisfil v Township of Vespra* [1981] 2 S.C.R. 145 at 166; *Finch v Goldstein* (1981) 36 A.L.R. 287 at 304; *Badger v Whangarei Commission of Inquiry* [1985] 2 N.Z.L.R. 688 at 697; *Freedman v Petty* [1981] V.R. 1001. In Canada, the right to legal representation has been considered important where a penalty is at stake (*Re Husted and Ridley* (1981) 58 C.C.C. (2nd) 156; *Howard v Presiding Ofice of Inmate Disciplinary Court of Stony Mountain Institution* (1985) 19 D.L.R. 502) and in "factual situations which are closer or analogous to criminal proceeding" (*Dehghani v Canada* (1993) 101 D.L.R. (4th) 654).

6–057　　While the duty to consult has been established in the United States since the introduction of notice and comment rule-making procedures in the Administrative Procedure Act 1946,[221] recently, it has been increasing in importance across other jurisdictions.[222] For example, a duty to consult in the context of a power to modify corporations legislation, where only a small number of persons was affected, has been worded by the Australian High Court in sufficiently broad terms to import a duty to consult even where a larger number of persons are affected.[223] Meanwhile, in South Africa, as noted above, s.4 of the PAJA makes provision for public inquiries, notice and comment proceedings and other forms of public participation. Likewise, in India, it has been held that a delegated legislative function may require consideration of the viewpoint of those affected by the exercise of power,[224] while if a ban order is to be introduced, those affected should have the opportunity of meeting the facts.[225] More generally, in the absence of a statutory requirement, pre-existing practice or policy, or a representation creating a legitimate expectation that consultation will be conducted, the circumstances in which a common law duty to consult will arise are likely to remain limited.[226]

6–058　　The absence of an over-arching common law duty on administrative decision-makers to give reasons[227] continues to cause strain, and the absence of a duty is increasingly superseded by a growing number of statutory requirements of reason-giving, of greater or less generality.[228] For example, in South Africa, the omission of the common law has largely been overtaken by s.5 of the PAJA, which establishes the duty to give reasons in

---

[221] 5 U.S.C. §553. For discussion, see M. Shapiro "Trans-Atlantic: Harlow Revisited" in P. Craig and R. Rawlings (eds) *Law and Administration in Europe: Essays in Honour of Carol Harlow* (2003), Ch.12. See also T. Ziamou "Alternative Modes of Administrative Action: Negotiated Rule-Making in the United States, Germany and Britain" (2000) 6 *European Public Law* 45; P. Cane *Administrative Law*, 4th edn. (2004), pp.170–175.

[222] See 7–052.

[223] *Australian Securities and Investments Commission v DB Management Pty Ltd* (2000) 199 C.L.R. 321 at 341 (Gleeson C.J., Gaudron, Gummow, Hayne and Callinan JJ.); M. Aronson, B. Dyer and M. Groves, *Judicial Review of Administrative Action*, 3rd edn. (2004), p.431, and pp.429–432.

[224] *State of Tamil Nadu v K Sabanayagam* [1998] (1) S.C.C. 318.

[225] *Godawat Pan Masala Products IP Ltd v Union of India* [2004] (7) S.C.C. 68 at 105, [76].

[226] Aronson, Dyer and Groves (2004), 430.

[227] Although see *Baker v Canada (Minister of Citizenship & Immigration)* (1999) 174 D.L.R. (4th) 193; *Suresh v Canada (Minister of Citizenship and Immigration)* (2002) 208 D.L.R. (4th) 1; *R. v Sheppard* (2002) 210 D.L.R. (4th) 608; M. Liston, "'Alert, alive and sensitive': Baker, the Duty to Give Reasons, and the Ethos of Justification in Canadian Public Law" in D. Dyzenhaus, ed., *The Unity of Public Law* (2004), p.113; D. Dyzenhaus and E. Fox-Decent, "Rethinking the Process/Substance Distinction: *Baker v Canada*" (2001) 51 U.T.L.J. 193. See also *R. v Sheppard* [2002] 1 S.C.R. 869 (trial judges).

[228] See, e.g. s.23 of the Official Information Act 1982 (NZ) (although s.2(6) excludes from the coverage of the Act "[a] Court" and "[i]n relation to its judicial functions, a Tribunal"); and in Australia Administrative Decisions (Judicial Review) Act 1977 s.13, Administrative Appeals Tribunal Act 1975 s.28 and Administrative Law Act 1978 (Victoria). On the requirement to give reasons, see 7–087. See also D Dyzenhaus and M. Taggart, "Reasoned Decisions and Legal Theory" in Ch.5 in D.E. Edlin (ed.), *Common Law Theory* (2007).

respect of "administrative action"; while in Ireland, s.18(1) of the Freedom of Information Act 1997 places a far-reaching duty on public authorities to provide reasons when requested.[229] However, more limited statutory interventions can have the consequence of uneveness in coverage. As for the case law, individual judges from many jurisdictions have reviewed a requirement to give reasons favourably.[230] In New Zealand, although not imposing an enforceable general common law obligation to give reasons,[231] courts have indicated an openness to hearing argument on the issue,[232] and have imposed a duty to give reasons in particular contexts. In Australia, it is still the case that there is no common law duty on administrative decision-makers to give reasons, with the position taken in the 1986 case of *Osmond* holding firm,[233] although Kirby J. has indicated his dissatifaction with the law[234] and Aronson, Dyer and Groves have suggested that other members of the High Court may also be prepared to make a partial retreat from the position taken in *Osmond*.[235] In India, although there has been significant judicial support for imposing a requirement to provide reasons[236] and although the duty to give reasons has regularly been implied into statutory schemes,[237] the development of a more comprehensive obligation to give reasons has not been entirely uncontested.[238]

[229] See s.2 and Sch.1 for the definition of "public body".
[230] See, e.g. *Re Northwestern Utilities and the City of Edmonton* (1978) 89 D.L.R. (3rd) 161 at 175 (Estey J); *Potter v New Zealand Milk Board* [1983] N.Z.L.R. 620 at 624.
[231] See, e.g., *Lewis v Wilson & Horton Ltd* [2000] 3 N.Z.L.R. 546, CA (upholding the position taken in *R. v Awatere* [1982] 1 N.Z.L.R. 644, CA and *R. v MacPherson* [1982] N.Z.L.R. 650, CA (cases which had refused to establish a legally enforceable obligation on the part of inferior courts to give reasoned decisions).
[232] *Lewis* [2000] 3 N.Z.L.R. 546 at 567 (Elias C.J.: "Whether it is time to say that as a general rule Judges must give reasons, is a matter this court would wish to consider at an early opportunity").
[233] *Osmond v Public Service Board* [1984] 3 N.S.W.L.R. 447. It should be noted however though that Australia has a long tradition of imposing reason-giving obligations on courts: see Dyzenhaus and Taggart (2007) for discussion.
[234] Kirby J. (dissenting) in *Re Minister for Immigration and Multicultural and Indigenous Affairs Ex p. Palme* [2003] 216 C.L.R. 212 at [64] noting that: "[I]n other common law countries, the law has moved in recent times, with general consistency, to insist on the importance of the giving of reasons for valid and just decisions, not only by judges but also administrators".
[235] *Public Service Board of New South Wales v Osmond* (1986) 159 C.L.R. 656; M. Aronson, B. Dyer and M. Groves, *Judicial Review of Administrative Action*, 3rd edn. (2004), p.559. See also *Edwards v Giudice* (1999) 169 A.L.R. 89. Australian courts have required reasons to be given by judges when the appellant's right of appeal would otherwise be rendered nugatory: e.g. *Pettitt v Dunkley* [1971] 1 N.S.W.L.R. 376; *Pinkstone v Goldrick* [1979] 1 N.S.W.L.R. 279; *Australian Timber Workers Union v Monaro Sawmills Pty Ltd* (1980) 29 A.L.R. 322; *Perkins v County Court (Vic.)* (2000) 115 A Crim R 528 at [54]–[69] (Buchanan J.A.) In some cases this reasoning has been extended to cover quasi-judicial or administrative decisions which are subject to appeal, e.g. *Edwards v Giudice* (1999) 94 F.C.R 561; *Yung v Adams* (1997) 80 F.C.R. 453 at 481–482 (decision regarding duty to give reasons upheld on appeal: *Adams v Yung* (1998) 83 F.C.R. 248).
[236] *Siemens Engineering v Union of India* [1976] (2) S.C.C. 981 (holding that giving of reasons is part of the requirement of natural justice); *CB Gautam v Union of India* 1993 (1) S.C.C. 78 at 105; *Bhagat Raja v Union of India* A.I.R. 1967 S.C. 1607.
[237] See, e.g. *Rajesh Kimar v Dy CIT* 2007 (2) S.C.C. 179.
[238] *Rajesh Kumar v Dy CIT* 2007 (2) S.C.C. 181 at 191; *Ramachandra Murarilal v State of Maharashtra* 2007 (2) S.C.C. 588 at 608.

6–059   Finally, on the issue of exceptions to the availability of procedural fairness,[239] if the common law requirements of procedural fairness are to be excluded by statute, it is settled that legislatures must state that they are doing so explicitly.[240] Traditional dichotomies such as between categories of mandatory and directory requirements have also fallen out of favour,[241] and for example, the preferred approach in Australia now is to determine whether it was a "purpose of the legislature" that an act done in breach of the statutory provision should be deemed to be invalid.[242] It has also been increasingly accepted that a procedurally fair appeal can cure an initial procedurally unfair procedure; although again, everything depends on the circumstances.[243]

[239] See 8–003.
[240] In Australia the rules of procedural fairness are regarded as fundamental requirements of the common law and therefore their exclusion by statute will normally require a clear expression of legislative intent. See *Kioa v West* (1985) 159 C.L.R. 550 at 585; *South Australia v O'Shea* (1987) 163 C.L.R. 378 at 415; *Re Minister for Multicultural Affairs; Ex p. Miah* (2001) 206 C.L.R. 57 (McHugh J.), 102 (Kirby J.) 114 (it was held that the Codes of Procedure relating to fair and efficient administrative decision making under the Migration Act 1958 (Cth) did not exclude common law natural justice). In response to the decision, the government amended the Act to the effect that the Codes of Procedure contained in the Act did constitute an exhaustive statement of the requirements of the natural justice rules. And see *Fraser v State Services Commission* [1984] 1 N.Z.L.R. 116 at 121 where Cooke J. questioned whether the legislature could exclude the common law rules of natural justice even by express enactment.
[241] For the distinction between "mandatory" and "directory" requirements, See 5–049.
[242] *Project Blue Sky v Australian Broadcasting Authority* (1998) 194 C.L.R. 355 at 390–391 (McHugh, Gummow, Kirby and Hayne JJ.).
[243] *Slipper Island Resort Ltd v Number One Town and Country Planning Appeal Board* [1981] 1 N.Z.L.R. 143 at 145; *Twist v Randwick Municipal Council* (1976) 136 C.L.R. 106; *Ainsworth v Criminal Justice Commission* (1992) 175 C.L.R. 564; *McNamara v Ontario Racing Commission* (1998) 164 D.L.R. (4th) 99. See also Aronson, Dyer and Grove (2004).

CHAPTER 7

PROCEDURAL FAIRNESS: ENTITLEMENT AND CONTENT

SCOPE

This Chapter examines, first, entitlement to procedural fairness. There are 7–001
three broad bases on which a public authority may owe a duty to exercise
its functions in accordance with fair procedures: (a) where legislation
imposes a duty to follow fair procedures;[1] (b) where the common law
requires fair procedures to be followed in order to safeguard rights and
interests;[2] and (c) since the Human Rights Act 1998, to meet the
procedural requirements of Convention rights, notably Art.6 (in relation to
determination of "civil rights and obligations" and "criminal charges")[3]
and Art.2 (right to life, in respect of investigations of deaths).[4] Entitlement
may also arise from a legitimate expectation created by a public authority's
assurances or conduct, a possibility that we consider in Chapter 12.

Secondly, this Chapter considers the *content* of fair procedures. There is 7–002
a broad range of requirements, which vary according to the context in
which the public function is exercised, including: (a) to give notice of a
proposed decision before making it;[5] (b) to consult and receive written
representations;[6] (c) to disclose information before a final decision is
reached;[7] (d) to provide oral hearings,[8] at which (e) the person is offered
legal representations or other assistance,[9] and (f) has the right to cross
examine witnesses;[10] and (g) a right to be given reasons explaining why a
decision or action was taken.[11] Public inquiries raise additional considerations[11a]; while ECHR Art.6 and Art. 2, in the situations to a ECHR Art.6
and Art. 2, in the situations to which they apply, impose further
requirements.[12]

[1] See 7–011.
[2] See 7–017.
[3] See 7–032.
[4] See 7–037.
[5] See 7–043.
[6] See 7–052.
[7] See 7–057.
[8] See 7–062.
[9] See 7–074.
[10] See 7–083.
[11] See 7–087.
[11a] See 7–116.
[12] See 7–119 and 7–128.

ENTITLEMENT TO PROCEDURAL FAIRNESS: OVERVIEW

From "natural justice" to "the duty to act fairly"

7–003 Procedural fairness, as we have seen, is no longer restricted by distinctions between "judicial" and "administrative" functions or between "rights" and "privileges".[13] This "heresy was scotched"[14] in *Ridge v Baldwin*.[15] The term "natural justice" has largely been replaced by a general duty to act fairly, which is a key element of procedural propriety.[16] On occasion, the term "due process" has also been invoked.[17] Whichever term is used, the entitlement to fair procedures no longer depends upon the adjudicative analogy, nor whether the authority is required or empowered to decide matters analogous to a legal action between two parties.[18] The law has moved on; not to the state where the entitlement to procedural protection can be extracted with certainty from a computer, but to where the courts are able to insist upon some degree of participation in reaching most official decisions by those whom the decisions will affect in widely different situations, subject only to well-established exceptions.[19] Procedural fairness is therefore not these days rationed at its source—blocked at the outset on the ground of a decision being administrative rather than judicial, or governing a privilege rather than a right. It may, in exceptional situations, be diverted during the course of its flow where special circumstances, such as national security excuse a right to a fair hearing.[20] And the breadth of the flow will depend upon the circumstances surrounding the decision. As we will see, some decisions require full adjudicative-type hearings, others only narrowly permit the mere right to make representations.[21] Increasing resort to the open-textured standard of fairness is not, though, without its drawbacks. There is a point at which the benefits of its flexible application

---

[13] See 6–029.

[14] *R. v Gaming Board for Great Britain Ex p. Benaim and Khaida* [1970] 2 Q.B. 417 at 430 (Denning M.R.).

[15] [1964] A.C. 40.

[16] See 6–045. In *O'Reilly v Mackman* [1983] 2 A.C. 237 at 275 (Lord Diplock: the rules of natural justice "mean no more than the duty to act fairly . . . and I prefer so to put it"). For academic debate on whether a general duty to act fairly should be melded with the concept of natural justice, see: D. Mullan, "Fairness: The New Natural Justice" (1975) 25 U.T.L.J. 281; M. Loughlin, "Procedural Fairness: A Study of the Crisis in Administrative Law Theory" (1978) 28 U.T.L.J. 215; G. Taylor, "Fairness and Natural Justice" (1977) 3 Mon LR 191; R. Macdonald, "Judicial Review and Procedural Fairness in Administrative Law" (1980) 25 McGill L.J. 520 and (1980) 26 McGill L.J. 1; G. Cartier, "Procedural Fairness in Legislative Functions: The End of Judicial Abstinence?" (2003) 53 U.T.L.J. 217.

[17] *R. v Secretary of State for the Home Department Ex p. Hindley* [2000] 1 QB 152 at 163–164, CA (Lord Woolf M.R.); *R. v Camden LBC Ex p. Paddock* [1995] C.O.D. 130; *R. v Secretary of State for the Home Department Ex p. Moon* (1996) 8 Admin. L. R. 477, 485; *Flannery v Halifax Estate Agencies Ltd* [2000] 1 W.L.R. 377 at 381.

[18] See 6–029.

[19] *R. v Secretary of State for the Environment Ex p. Kirkstall Valley Campaign Ltd* [1996] 3 All E.R. 304 at 324 (Sedley J. noting that "Since *Ridge v Baldwin*, although not without occasional deviations, public law has returned to the broad highway of due process across the full range of justiciable decision-making").

[20] See 8–007.

[21] See 7–039.

may be outweighed by the costs of uncertainty. The courts are perhaps creating "a surrogate political process to ensure the fair representation of a wide range of affected interests in the administrative process".[22] Doubts have been expressed as to whether the courts are institutionally equipped for such tasks,[23] and whether the unconstrained expansion of participation might paralyse effective administration.[24]

Attempts to categorise boundaries of procedural fairness

In response to these doubts, various attempts have been made in recent time to devise categories or criteria of relative precision to determine the bounds of procedural fairness. In *Ridge v Baldwin*[25] it was stated that the duty to observe the rules of natural justice should be inferred from the nature of the power conferred upon the public authority. It has been suggested[26] that whether the nature of the power requires such an inference to be drawn may be determined by considering the following three factors: first, the nature of the complainant's interest; secondly, the conditions under which the public authority is entitled to encroach on those interests; and thirdly, the severity of the sanction that can be imposed. These factors offer some guidance as to which interests should be protected by fair procedures, but leave a great deal open to speculation.

A more precise classification was provided in *McInnes v Onslow Fane*,[27] where the following three situations were distinguished: (a) "forfeiture" or "deprivation" cases, where a vested interest (such as a licence to trade) has been withdrawn; (b) "application" cases, where no interest yet exists, but

7–004

7–005

---

[22] R. Stewart, "The Reformation of American Administrative Law" (1975) 88 Harv. L.R. 1669, 1670.

[23] Loughlin (1978) 28 U.T.L.J. 215; MacDonald (1980) 25 McGill L.J. 520 and (1980) 26 McGill L.J. 1 where the development of the duty to act fairly is regarded as a major theoretical departure in the law of procedural review. Contrast P. Craig, *Administrative Law*, 5th edn. (2003), pp.415–418. And for a judicial recognition of the limited nature of the courts' role, see *R. v Brent LBC Ex p. Gunning* (1985) 84 L.G.R. 168 at 180.

[24] See, e.g. the comments of Mr Michael Barnes Q.C. who conducted an inquiry into the proposal for a nuclear reactor at Hinkley Point in Somerset under the Electricity Act 1957 and the Electricity Generating Stations and Overhead Lines (Inquiries Procedures) Rules 1987 (SI 1987/2182) (now 2007 (SI 2007/841)). The inquiry lasted 182 days and there were nearly 10,000 objectors ("section 34 parties") with a right to appear. In Ch.4 of his Report on the inquiry Mr Barnes warned that in the effort to ensure a proper hearing in inquiries of this scale there is a danger that the inquiry will become an "engine of delay in reaching administrative decisions"; and P. Cane, *Administrative Law*, 4th edn. (2004), p.181, citing the Sizewell water reactor inquiry (1983–85), which cost £25 million and lasted 340 days, and the inquiry on Heathrow Terminal 5, which lasted for four years and cost in the region of £80 million; and the difficulties entailed in ensuring fairness in other important inquiries: Sir R. Scott "Procedures at Inquiries: The Duty to be Fair" (1995) 111 L.Q.R. 596; B. Hadfield, "*R. v Lord Saville of Newdigate Ex p. Anonymous Soldiers*: What is the Purpose of a Tribunal of Inquiry?" [2003] P.L. 663; L. Blom-Cooper, "Tribunals under Inquiry" [2000] P.L. 1; L. Blom-Cooper, "Public Interest in Public Inquiries" [2003] P.L. 578.

[25] [1964] A.C. 40 at 76.

[26] *Durayappah v Fernando* [1967] 2 A.C. 337 at 349; *Lloyd v McMahon* [1987] A.C. 625 at 702–703 (Lord Bridge). For comparative perspectives, see 6–050.

[27] [1978] 1 W.L.R. 1520.

is merely being sought (such as an application for a licence, passport or a council house); and (c) "expectation" cases, where there is a reasonable expectation of a continuation of an existing benefit which falls short of a right. A fair hearing, it was suggested, should be granted in cases involving "forfeiture" and (normally) "expectation", but not in those involving a mere "application". This analysis would, if strictly applied, result in anomalies and injustice for there are situations where the refusal of an application could adversely affect an interest deserving of protection by means of a fair hearing. For example, the refusal of an application for a passport not only prevents the exercise of a basic liberty to travel, but may also cast aspersions on a person's character.[28] It would seem unfair to deny an applicant for planning permission procedural protection (as is provided by statute)[29] so that he may argue in favour of his interest in developing his land. It would also seem unfair to deny an applicant for a licence to export goods the opportunity to make representations in support of his application (again, such an opportunity is presently provided by statute[30]).

7-006   In addition, some decisions deserving of a fair hearing do not fall into any of the three categories set out in *McInnes*. For example, it has been held that in some circumstances an interested person such as a neighbour is entitled to object to a proposed development of land despite the absence of a statutory right to make representations and the absence of any legitimate expectation of so doing.[31] That kind of situation fits none of the categories in *McInnes*, as the interested person is neither in the position of an applicant, nor someone deprived of an existing right, interest or legitimate expectation.

7-007   In general there are practical reasons why a hearing cannot be given to every applicant for a licence, for the same reason that the hearing cannot be given to all applicants for scarce resources (such as hospital beds, or university places). The task of allocation in these circumstances requires

[28] *R. v Secretary of State for Foreign and Commonwealth Affairs Ex p. Everett* [1989] Q.B. 811 at 820 (Taylor L.J.: a passport was a "normal expectation of every citizen"); cf. *R. v Huntingdon DC Ex p. Cowan* [1984] 1 W.L.R. 501. In *R. v Secretary of State for the Home Department Ex p. Fayed* [1998] 1 W.L.R. 763 at the CA held (Woolf M.R., Phillips L.J., Kennedy L.J. dissenting), that the applicants for British citizenship were wrongly deprived of an opportunity to make representations in advance of the refusal of their applications. The statute itself precludes a requirement for reasons. The ratio appears to be (Lord Woolf at 237–238; Phillips L.J. at 251) that, although the applicants had no vested rights to citizenship (as in *Attorney General v Ryan* [1980] A.C. 718, PC, constitutional entitlement to citizenship of the Bahamas), the refusal of the application would in the circumstances of this case lead to adverse inferences being drawn about the applicants' characters. For a similar case where an applicant was afforded the right to a fair hearing see *R. v Secretary of State for the Home Department Ex p. Moon* [1997] I.N.L.R. 165; *Murungaru v Secretary of State for the Home Department* [2006] EWHC 2416 (procedural fairness would normally require that reasons be given where a decision was made to exclude someone from the UK who had recently been granted a visa, although considerations of national security or the dictates of diplomacy may justify a departure from normal procedure).
[29] Town and Country Planning Act 1990 s.78.
[30] Export of Goods, Transfer of Technology and Provision of Technical Assistance (Control) Order 2003 (SI 2003/2764) Art. 15.
[31] *R. v Great Yarmouth BC Ex p. Botton Bros* (1988) 56 P. & C.R. 99.

despatch, and the class of applicant may be entirely open-ended.[32] However, on occasion, the unfairness of the summary refusal of a licence or the summary award of a licence to a competitor will be so manifest (e.g. because the worthiness of the applicant rather than the availability of resources is the dominant factor shaping a decision),[33] that it will be right for a court to hold that the deciding body is under a duty to give the applicant an opportunity to make representations (whether in writing or orally) and of being apprised of all information on which the decision may be founded.[34] In express reliance on these considerations, it was held in *R. (on the application of Quark Fishing Ltd) v Secretary of State for Foreign and Commonwealth Affairs* that the applicant for an extremely valuable licence to fish for Patagonian Toothfish was entitled not to be left in any doubt about the criteria upon which the licence would be granted.[35]

Other situations where applicants may be accorded the benefits of a fair   7–008 hearing include those where the licensing authority is constituted as a distinct tribunal, or is expressly required to entertain representations or objections or appeals, or to conduct hearings or inquiries, when deciding whether or not to grant a licence.[36] A duty to act fairly may also be imposed even upon "application" cases when policy guidelines have been established (especially if published) within which discretion will normally be exercised. They may raise an expectation of benefit in those who believe that they fall within the guidelines.[37] In addition, an opportunity to be heard, both on the application and the merits of the policy, may be required in order to prevent a fettering of discretion.[38]

The recognition of a general duty of fairness

There are, therefore, situations which are not covered by the *McInnes*   7–009 approach which, like other attempts at classification, has its shortcomings. It is therefore preferable to adopt a more comprehensive approach, recognising that the duty of fairness cannot and should not be restricted by artificial barriers or confined by inflexible categories. The duty is a general one, governed by the following propositions.

[32] On non-justiciability, see 1–00.
[33] See, e.g. *R. v Aston University Senate Ex p. Roffey* [1969] 2 Q.B. 538 at 554 (university places); and *Stininato v Auckland Boxing Assocation* [1978] 1 N.Z.L.R. 1; *Trivett v Nivison* [1976] 1 N.S.WL.R. 312; and H. Friendly, "Some Kind of Hearing" (1975) 123 U. Penn.L.Rev. 1267.
[34] In *R. v Huntingdon DC Ex p. Cowan* [1984] 1 W.L.R. 501 it was held that an applicant for an entertainments licence was entitled to know the substance of objections and to have an opportunity of responding to those objections in writing; cf. *R. v Independent Television Commission Ex p. TSW Broadcasting Ltd* [1996] E.M.L.R. 291.
[35] [2001] EWHC Admin 1174; [2002] A.C.D. 197 at [67]–[68] and [2002] EWCA Civ 1409.
[36] Though the obligation may be qualified by a right to refrain from disclosing the source and precise content of highly confidential information: *R. v Gaming Board for Great Britain Ex p. Benaim and Khaida* [1970] 2 Q.B. 417 at 431.
[37] See Ch.12.
[38] See 9–00; *British Oxygen Co Ltd v Board of Trade* [1971] A.C. 610 at 625; *R. v Criminal Injuries Compensation Board Ex p. Ince* [1973] 1 W.L.R. 1334 at 1345.

- Whenever a public function is being performed there is an inference, in the absence of an express requirement to the contrary, that the function is required to be performed fairly.[39]

- The inference will be more compelling in the case of any decision which may adversely affect a person's rights or interests or when a person has a legitimate expectation of being fairly treated.

- The requirement of a fair hearing will not apply to all situations of perceived or actual detriment. There are clearly some situations where the interest affected will be too insignificant, or too speculative, or too remote to qualify for a fair hearing.[40] Whether this is so will depend on all the circumstances but a fair hearing ought no longer to be rejected out of hand, for example, simply because the decision-maker is acting in a "legislative" capacity.[41]

- Special circumstances may create an exception which vitiates the inference of a duty to act fairly. The inference can be rebutted by the needs of national security, or because of other characteristics of the particular function. For example, a decision to allocate scarce resources amongst a large number of contenders which needs to be made with despatch may be inconsistent with an obligation to hold a

---

[39] English law must now take note of ECHR Art.6, which requires a fair hearing in the "determination" of "civil rights and obligations" or of "criminal charges" (on which see 7–032).

[40] In such cases where there has been a claim for judicial review the claimant may not qualify for standing on the ground of not possessing a "sufficient interest" in the matter to which the application relates. Alternatively, the applicant may have failed to suffer any "substantial prejudice" from any lack of procedural propriety where the statute requires it, see, e.g. *Save Britain's Heritage v Number One Poultry Ltd* [1991] 1 W.L.R. 153, HL. Cf. *R. v Swansea City Council Ex p. Elitestone Ltd* [1993] 2 P.L.R. 65 at 70; *R. v Westminster City Council Ex p. Ermakov* [1996] 2 All E.R. 302; and see below on the extent to which it is necessary to show prejudice.

[41] *Leech v Parkhurst Prison Deputy Governor* [1988] A.C. 533 at 538 (Lord Oliver); *R. v Secretary of State for Health Ex p. United States Tobacco International Inc* [1992] Q.B. 353. cf. *R. v Lord Chancellor Ex p. The Law Society* (1994) 6 Admin L.R. 833. For discussion of the rule against imposing natural justice requirements in "legislative" contexts see G. Craven, "Legislative Action by Subordinate Authorities and the Requirements of a Fair Hearing" (1988) 16 M.U.L.Rev. 596 and G. Cartier, "Procedural Fairness in Legislative Functions: The End of Judicial Abstinence?" (2003) 53 U.T.L.J. 217. For comparative perspectives, see 6–052. "Legislative" decisions, or "decisions affecting many" (see 6–031), continue however to be subject to different treatment and the full rigours of procedural fairness will often not apply: *Bates v Lord Hailsham of St Marylebone* [1972] 1 W.L.R. 1373 (affirmed in: *Bapio Action Ltd v The Secretary of State for the Home Department* [2007] EWHC 199 at [47] and *R. (on the application of the British Casino Association Ltd v Secretary of State for Culture Media & Sport* [2007] EWHC 1312 at [82]); and *R. (on the application of British Waterways Board) v The First Secretary of State* [2006] EWHC 1019, [23] (no duty to consult in respect of rating demand arising out of regulation, but defendants, having chosen to consult, had to conduct the consultation fairly). In Canada, see *Cardinal v Kent Institution* (1985) 24 D.L.R. (4th) 44 at para.14 (Le Dain J.).

fair hearing.[42] The inference may also not be drawn if the protection is to be achieved another way. For example, in the case of a "legislative" decision, at least where participation is built into the decision-making process elsewhere, the safeguard which would be provided by a fair hearing can be achieved by other means; as in cases where the decision is taken by democratically elected representatives accountable to Parliament or to the electorate for the exercise of the relevant power.[43]

- What fairness requires will vary according to the circumstances.[44] We shall see that some decisions, while attracting the duty to be fair, will permit no more to the affected person than a bare right to submit representations.[45] In other cases however there will be a right to an oral hearing with the essential elements of a trial.[46] In between these extremes come a large variety of decisions which, because of the nature of the issues to be determined or the seriousness of their impact upon important interests, require some kind of a hearing (which may not even involve oral representations), but not anything that has all the characteristics of a full trial.[47]

- Whether fairness is required and what is involved in order to achieve fairness is for the decision of the courts as a matter of law. The issue is not one for the discretion of the decision-maker. The test is not whether no reasonable body would have thought it proper to

[42] On the other hand, local authorities are now statutorily required to maintain for public inspection their rules for determining priority among applicants for council housing and their procedural rules for allocating it: Housing Act 1985 s.106. A local authority that has made and published its rules of procedure may well be held to have acted unlawfully if, in some material respect, it does not apply them fairly (e.g. by an officer's failing to disclose some unfavourable impression gained as a result of a home visit or from the third party and to allow the applicant an opportunity to respond).

[43] The exceptions to the requirement of fair hearing are considered fully in Ch.8.

[44] See 7–039.

[45] For a minimalist view of fairness, as involving no more than a duty to act without bias, see, e.g. *R. v Secretary of State for Trade Ex p. Perestrello* [1981] Q.B. 19; and 7–035.

[46] Decision-making that formerly would have been characterised as "judicial" fall into this category (see 6–035); e.g. *R. v Immigration Tribunal Ex p. Mehmet* [1977] 1 W.L.R. 795. In the US case of *Mathews v Eldridge* 424 U.S. 319 (1976), it was held that whether the constitutional guarantee of due process requires an evidentiary hearing depends on the individual interest at stake, the extent to which a trial procedure was more likely than the procedure actually used to avoid an erroneous decision, and the government's interest, including the extra cost of the procedure requested. It has been argued that this kind of utilitarian approach fails adequately to take account of the moral harm or sense of injustice suffered by a person who is wrongly deprived of a right without a hearing, as opposed, for example, to the reaction engendered by a contested policy decision such as the siting of a motorway: see R. Dworkin, "Principle, policy, procedure" in C. Tapper (ed.), *Crime Proof and Punishment: Essays in Memory of Sir Rupert Cross* (1981), pp.193 and 221 *et seq.*; and 6–008, n.4.

[47] *Lloyd v McMahon* [1987] A.C. 625 at 702 (Lord Bridge: "the so-called rules of national justice are not engraved on tablets of stone." A similar approach has been adopted in other jurisdictions: see 6–055 and in Canada: *Martineau v Matsqui Institution Disciplinary Board* [1980] 1 S.C.R. 602 at paras 61–63.

dispense with a fair hearing.[48] The *Wednesbury*[49] reserve has no place in relation to procedural propriety.

7–010 The significance of this approach is that at first sight it imposes on all administrators an obligation to act fairly. Without acknowledging this expressly, the majority of the recent decisions of the courts are in practice no more than conscious or unconscious illustrations of the approach. They can be conveniently examined under the following four headings.

• Where the terms of a statute confirm the inference of a fair hearing.

• Where the inference of a fair hearing is confirmed by the need to safeguard a right or interest.

• Where the inference of a fair hearing is confirmed by the need to safeguard an expectation induced by the decision-maker.

• Art.6 of the ECHR.

• Art.2 of the ECHR.

STATUTORY REQUIREMENTS OF FAIR PROCEDURES

Express statutory requirements

7–011 When a mandatory procedure is set out in a statute, it must be followed.[50] Many areas of public administration provide elaborate procedural codes. Town and country planning legislation, for example, permits public participation at the stage of drafting development plans,[51] requires notification of applications for planning permission,[52] requires consultation with

---

[48] *R. v Panel on Takeovers and Mergers Ex p. Guinness* [1990] Q.B. 146 (Woolf and Lloyd L.JJ. who said that "the court is the arbiter of what is fair"). However, in limited circumstances, the court may give great weight to the decision-maker's view of what is fair, see, e.g. *R. v Monopolies and Mergers Commission Ex p. Matthew Brown Plc* [1987] 1 W.L.R. 1235 at 1242 (test was whether the MMC "had adopted a procedure so unfair that no reasonable commission or group would have adopted it"); *R. v Monopolies and Mergers Commission Ex p. Stagecoach Holdings Ltd, The Times*, July 23, 1996 ("The court is the arbiter of what is fair", although the court would give great weight to the MMC's own view of fairness); *Interbrew SA and Interbrew UK Holdings Ltd v The Competition Commission and the Secretary of State for Trade and Industry* [2001] EWHC Admin 367; [2001] E.C.C. 40 at [70]–[72].

[49] See 11–014 for discussion of the *Wednesbury* case and the margin of discretion accorded the decision-maker in cases involving abuse of discretion.

[50] For the distinction between requirements which are "mandatory" and "directory" see 5–049.

[51] Planning and Compulsory Purchase Act 2004 ss.1, 6, 8, 15; Town and Country Planning Act 1990 Sch.4A.

[52] Town and Country Planning (General Development Procedure) Order 1995 (SI 1995/419) art.5; and arts 7, 8, 13, 16 and 18, and Town and Country Planning Act 1990 s.71; Town and Country Planning General Development Order 1988 art.2B; Planning (Listed Buildings and Conservation Areas) Act 1990 s.73.

given bodies[53] and provides the opportunity for applicants to appeal a refusal of a planning application or a condition attached to an application.[54] The appeal may be by way of written representations or a full structured inquiry.[55] In the context of health care provision, health authorities, Primary Care Trusts and NHS Trusts have duties to involve and consult, either directly or through representatives, those who use their services.[56]

Supplementing statutory procedures

Even where the procedural code is comprehensive in its scope, the courts are called upon to adjudicate on the extent to which the statutory procedure has been fulfilled. For example, are the reasons, required of the Secretary of State on a planning appeal, "proper adequate and intelligible"?[57] Has the consultation required been "genuine"?[58] In these cases there are no express statutory requirements in relation to the adequacy, intelligibility or genuineness of the reasons or consultations, but the courts employ these criteria so as to ensure the correct standards of fairness. In doing so, the courts are not imposing additional requirements but are instead ensuring the effectiveness of existing requirements.   **7–012**

Can the courts supplement the statutory procedures with requirements over and above those specified? For example, can the courts impose a requirement upon a local planning authority to consult on a planning application with neighbours where no such requirement is provided in the statute? There have been cases where the courts have supplemented a statutory scheme.[59] However, in others the maxim *expressio unius exclusio*   **7–013**

---

[53] Town and Country Planning (General Development Procedure) Order 1995 (SI 1995/419) arts 10, 10A, 11, 11B.
[54] Town and Country Planning Act 1990 ss.78, 78A, 79. On inquiries, see 7–116.
[55] Town and Country Planning (Appeals) (Written Representations Procedure) (England) Regulations 2000 (SI 2000/1628); Town and Country Planning (Hearings Procedure) (England) Rules 2000 (SI 2000/1626); Town and Country Planning Appeals (Determination by Inspectors) (Inquiries Procedure) (England) Rules 2000 (SI 2000/1625).
[56] R. (on the application of Morris) v Trafford Healthcare NHS Trust [2006] EWHC 2334; (2006) 9 C.C.L. Rep. 648; R. (on the application of Smith) v North Eastern Derbyshire Primary Care Trust [2006] EWCA Civ 1291; [2006] 1 W.L.R. 3315; see also Local Government and Public Involvement in Health Bill 2007 Pt 11 ("Local involvement networks").
[57] Save Britain's Heritage v Number One Poultry Ltd [1991] 1 W.L.R. 153 at 166; Westminster City Council v Great Portland Estates Plc [1985] A.C. 661 at 663; Vicarage Gate Ltd v First Secretary of State, Royal Borough of Kensington and Chelsea [2007] EWHC 768 at [8]; George Wimpey UK Ltd v Tewkesbury Borough Council [2007] EWHC 628 at [69]; Chris Jaram Developments Ltd v First Secretary of State [2004] EWHC 1220; Next Generation Clubs, Bernard George Stacy Bush v Secretary of State for the Environment Transport and the Regions, London Borough of Havering [2000] E.G.C.S. 109 at [10], CA.
[58] R. v Secretary of State for Social Services Ex p. Association of Metropolitan Authorities [1986] 1 W.L.R. 1 (Webster J.); R. v North and East Devon Health Authority Ex p. Coughlan [2001] Q.B. 213 at [108]; see 7–052.
[59] See 7–014 and 7–041; R. (on the application of S) v Brent LBC [2002] EWCA Civ 693;

alterius (the express mention of one thing excludes all others) has been invoked to avoid doing so.[60] Lord Reid unusually expressed an inclination in favour of judicial restraint when he warned against the use by the courts of "this unusual kind of power" (extending statutory procedures) which he felt should be exercised only when it is "clear that the statutory procedure is insufficient to achieve justice and that to require additional steps would not frustrate the apparent purpose of the legislation".[61] But the maxim *expressio unius*, like other aids to interpretation, may be "a valuable servant, but a dangerous master to follow . . . [and] ought not to be applied when it leads to inconsistency or injustice.[62] A bolder approach has been suggested by Lord Bridge, who said that "the courts will not only require the procedure prescribed by the statute to be followed, but will readily imply so much and no more to be introduced by way of additional procedural safeguards as will ensure the attainment of fairness".[63]

[2002] E.L.R. 556 at [14]; *Raji v General Medical Council* [2003] UKPC 24; [2003] 1 W.L.R. 1052 (even though Medical Act 1983 s.41(1) and (6) permitted consideration of suspension and restoration together, the two issues should have been considered separately); *Fairmount Investments Ltd v Secretary of State for the Environment* [1976] 1 W.L.R. 1255; *Lake District Special Planning Board v Secretary of State for the Environment* [1975] J.P.L. 220; *Hambledon and Chiddingfold Parish Council v Secretary of State for the Environment* [1976] J.P.L. 502; *Reading BC v Secretary of State for the Environment* [1986] J.P.L. 115; *Nicholson v Secretary of State for Energy* (1977) 76 L.G.R. 693. *Coleen Properties Ltd v Minister of Housing and Local Government* [1971] 1 W.L.R. 433; *Lithgow v Secretary of State for Scotland* 1973 S.L.T. 81; *R. v Huntingdon L.C. Ex p. Cowan* [1984] 1 W.L.R 501; and elsewhere: *Rich v Christchurch Girls' High School Board of Governors (No.1)* [1974] 1 N.Z.L.R. 1 at 9, 18–20; *Birss v Secretary of State for Justice* [1984] 1 N.Z.L.R. 513; *Heatley v Tasmanian Racing and Gaming Commission* (1977) 137 C.L.R. 487.

[60] See, e.g. *Pearlberg v Varty* [1972] 1 W.L.R. 534; *Furnell v Whangarei High Schools Board* [1973] A.C. 660 at 679; *Wiseman v Borneman* [1971] A.C. 297; *R. (on the application of Venture Projects Ltd) v Secretary of State for the Home Department* October 20, 2000, CA (although the maxim was not invoked, a duty to give reasons was held not to arise where an EC Directive required reasons for certain decisions, but not this type of decision); *R. v Aylesbury Vale District Council Ex p. Chaplin* [1997] 3 P.L.R. 55 at 60; *R. v Secretary of State for the Home Department Ex p. Abdi* [1996] 1 W.L.R. 298 at 314; *Re Findlay* [1985] A.C. 318; *Maynard v Osmond* [1977] Q.B. 240; *Lewis v Heffer* [1978] 1 W.L.R. 1061; *R. v Raymond* [1981] Q.B. 910; *Bird v St Mary Abbotts Vestry* (1895) 72 L.T. 599; *Hutton v Att.-Gen.* [1927] 1 Ch. 427 at 437–438. See, 6–026 and, see, e.g. *Waitemata County v Local Government Commission* [1964] N.Z.L.R. 689; *Brettingham-Moore v St. Leonards Municipality* (1969) 121 C.L.R. 509; *French v Law Society of Upper Canada* [1975] 2 S.C.R. 767 at 783–786; *Salemi v McKellar (No.2)* (1977) 137 C.L.R. 396; *Bourke v State Services Commission* [1978] 1 N.Z.L.R. 633 at 644–646; *CREEDNZ Inc v Governor General* [1981] 1 N.Z.L.R. 172 at 177–178. In the USA, the Supreme Court, in a landmark case, *Vermont Yankee Nuclear Power Corp v Natural Resources Defense Council, Inc* 435 U.S. 519 (1978) at 543 it was held that absent constitutional constraints or extremely compelling circumstances, courts may not force agencies to utilise rulemaking procedures beyond those prescribed in the Administrative Procedure Act 1946 or other statutory or constitutional provisions. Contrast however, *Re Cardinal and Board of Commissioners of Police of the City of Cornwall* (1974) 42 D.L.R. (3rd) 323; *R. v Crown Court at Bristol Ex p. Cooper* [1990] 1 W.L.R. 1031 (Bingham L.J.); *R. v Secretary of State for the Environment Ex p. Hammersmith and Fulham LBC* [1991] 1 A.C. 521.

[61] *Wiseman v Borneman* [1971] A.C. 297 at 308.

[62] *Colquhoun v Brooks* (1887) 19 Q.B.D. 400 at 406; on appeal (1888) 21 Q.B.D. 52.

[63] *Lloyd v McMahon* [1987] A.C. 625 at 702–703.

The test today of whether to supplement statutory procedures is no **7–014** longer whether the statutory procedure alone could result in manifest unfairness.[64] The preferable view is that fairness must, without qualification, be attained, and that the "justice of the common law" may supplement that of the statute unless by necessary implication the procedural code must be regarded as exclusive.[65] Under either test, similar factors are likely to be relevant: the comprehensiveness of the code, the degree of deviation from the statutory procedure required, and the overall fairness of the procedures to the individual concerned.[66]

Where legislation, instead of placing a duty on a body to hold a hearing, **7–015** merely gives a *discretion* to do so, the inference must normally be that no duty to hear exists in that context, particularly if the legislation explicitly requires that body to conduct hearings or inquiries in the performance of other functions.[67] However, where the merits of a planning proposal were the subject of intense controversy, it was held that the minister's refusal to hold a hearing was an improper exercise of discretion.[68]

Statutory requirements and legitimate expectations

The existence of a statutory scheme will also have an impact on whether a **7–016** particular legitimate expectation as to procedure can arise, and may have the effect of preventing the expectation from arising.[69]

FAIRNESS NEEDED TO SAFEGUARD RIGHTS AND INTERESTS

There is a presumption that procedural fairness is required whenever the **7–017** exercise of a power adversely affects an individual's rights protected by common law or created by statute. These include rights in property,

---

[64] *Furnell* [1973] A.C. 660 at 679.
[65] *Furnell* [1973] A.C. 660 at 686 (Viscount Dilhorne and Lord Reid, dissenting); *Wiseman v Borneman* [1971] A.C. 297 at 308, 317; *R. (on the application of Khatun) v Newham LBC* [2004] EWCA Civ 55; [2005] Q.B. 37, para.30 (Laws L.J.: "a right to be heard [can] be inserted or implied into the statutory scheme not by virtue of the statute's words, but by force of our public law standards of procedural fairness"); *R. v Parole Board Ex p. Wilson* [1992] 2 Q.B. 740; see 7–041; *Heatley* (1977) 137 C.L.R. 487; *Re Hamilton; Re Forrest* [1981] A.C. 1038; *Re Northern Ireland Housing Executive's Application for Judicial Review* [2006] N.I. 234, QBD (NI).
[66] Examples of cases where the courts considered that it would have frustrated the statutory purpose to supplement the statutory procedures include: *R. v Birmingham City Council Ex p. Ferrero Ltd* [1993] 1 All E.R. 530; *Abdi* [1996] 1 W.L.R. 298 at 315; *R. v Secretary of State for Education and Employment and the North East London Education Authority Ex p. M* [1996] E.L.R. 162 at 208.
[67] *cf. Ronaki v Number One Town and Country Planning Appeal Board* [1977] 2 N.Z.L.R. 174.
[68] *Binney v Secretary of State for the Environment* [1984] J.P.L. 871.
[69] See 12–00; *R. v DPP Ex p. Kebilene* [2000] 2 A.C. 326, HL; *R. v Secretary of State for Education Ex p. Begbie* [2000] 1 W.L.R. 1115, CA.

personal liberty, status and immunity from penalties or other fiscal impositions. The right or immunity may be enjoyed by either a private person (including a corporation) or a public authority.[70]

7–018   The duty to afford procedural fairness is not however limited to the protection of legal rights in the strict sense: it also applies to more general interests, of which the interest in pursuing a livelihood and in personal reputation have received particular recognition.[71] The interests also extend, however, to personal freedom (of a prisoner seeking parole)[72] and other benefits and advantages the conferral of which are in the discretion of the decision-maker (and were formerly regarded as "privileges",[73] and thus not meriting procedural protection).

Licences and similar benefits

7–019   Because the interest of the claimant, rather than the discretionary power of the decision-maker, now founds a right to a fair hearing, a hearing is required in most situations where licences or other similar benefits are revoked, varied, suspended or refused; even where the decision-making power affords wide discretion to the decision maker. Thus a strong presumption exists that a person whose licence is threatened with revocation should receive prior notice of that fact and an opportunity to be heard. The presumption should be especially strong where revocation causes deprivation of livelihood or serious pecuniary loss, or carries an implication of misconduct. Variation of the terms of an existing licence to the licensee's detriment will also prima facie attract the duty to act fairly.[74] A decision to increase the number of licences, with the effect of diminishing the value of existing licences, may in some situations also attract the duty.[75]

7–020   Whether a suspension of a licence should be preceded by notice and opportunity to be heard may depend on various factors, for example, the degree of urgency involved, the duration of the suspension, whether

---

[70] See, e.g. *Durayappah v Fernando* [1967] 2 A.C. 337; *R. v Secretary of State for the Environment Ex p. Norwich City Council* [1982] Q.B. 808 at 824 (dicta): *R. v Secretary of State for the Environment Ex p. Brent LBC* [1982] Q.B. 593 at 642–643; *R. v Secretary of State for Transport Ex p. Greater London Council* [1986] Q.B. 556.

[71] *Ridge v Baldwin* [1964] A.C. 40; *McInnes v Onslow-Fane* [1978] 1 W.L.R. 1520 at 1527–1528; *R. v Barnsley M.BC Ex p. Hook* [1976] 1 W.L.R. 1052; *Re Pergamon Press Ltd* [1971] Ch. 388 at 399; *Rees v Crane* [1994] 2 A.C. 173, PC. Cf. *Lloyd v McMahon* [1987] A.C. 625 at 702–703 (Lord Bridge, where fairness appears confined to decisions which "affect the rights of individuals"); cf. *Leech v Parkhurst Prison Deputy Governor* [1988] A.C. 533 at 578.

[72] See, e.g. *R. v Secretary for the Home Department Ex p. Doody* [1994] 1 A.C. 531; *R. v Secretary of State for the Home Department Ex p. Duggan* [1994] 3 All E.R. 277 (a classification of a prisoner directly affected his liberty and thus a fair hearing was required). *R. (on the application of West) v Parole Board* [2005] UKHL 1; [2005] 1 W.L.R. 350 (on revocation of release on licence).

[73] See 6–029; *Nakkudo Ali v Jayarante* [1951] A.C. 66; *R. v Metropolitan Police Commissioner Ex p. Parker* [1953] 1 W.L.R. 1150.

[74] *Re CTV Television Network Ltd* (1980) 116 D.L.R. (3rd) 741.

[75] *R. v Liverpool Corp. Ex p. Liverpool Taxi Fleet Operators' Association* [1972] 2 Q.B. 299 (Lord Denning, whose view was not expressed by the other members of the CA).

suspension implies a finding of guilt, whether it entails material financial loss and whether it is a purely temporary measure pending full review.[76]

Non-renewal of an existing licence is usually a more serious matter than refusal to grant a licence in the first place. Unless the licensee has already been given to understand when he was granted the licence that renewal is not to be expected, non-renewal may seriously upset his plans, cause him economic loss and perhaps cast a slur on his reputation. It may therefore be right to imply a duty to hear before a decision not to renew irrespective of whether there is a legitimate expectation of renewal,[77] even though no such duty is implied in the making of the original decision to grant or refuse the licence.[78]

7–021

Applicants for new licences are in a different position from those whose existing licences are revoked, suspended, varied or not renewed.[79] The reason why applicants for new licences or other permissions may be denied a hearing is because in many cases there is no vested interest involved to defend. The applicant will be adversely affected by a refusal of something which he does not yet have only to the extent that he is disappointed and may have suffered some "transaction costs" in the process of the application.[80]

7–022

[76] See, e.g. *Hlookoff v City of Vancouver* (1968) 67 D.L.R. (2nd) 119 (summary suspension of licence of premises for publishing newspaper on account of gross misconduct; suspension invalid). Cf. *Furnell v Whangarei High Schools Board* [1973] A.C. 660; on preliminary hearings, see 8–032.

[77] See 12–00.

[78] This paragraph was cited with approval in *Hook* [1976] 1 W.L.R. 1052, 1058 (Scarman L.J.). Supporting this distinction: *Schmidt v Secretary of State for Home Affairs* [1969] 2 Ch. 149 at 171, 173; *Breen v AEU* [1971] 2 Q.B. 175 at 191; *Liverpool Taxi* [1972] 2 Q.B. 299 (reduction in value of existing licences); *Hook* [1976] 1 W.L.R. 1052 at 1057; *McInnes v Onslow-Fane* [1978] 1 W.L.R. 1520. Cf. *Salemi v MacKellar (No.2)* (1977) 137 C.L.R. 396; and *Re Holden* [1957] Tas. S.R. 16; *Delmonico v Director of Wildlife* (1969) 67 W.W.R. 340; *Board of Regents v Roth* 408 U.S. 564 (1972). Generally, in the US, a benefit is not a protected entitlement if officials have discretion to grant or deny it: *Kentucky Department of Corrections v Thompson* 490 U.S. 454 (1989) at 462–463; *Town of Castle Rock Colorado v Gonzales* 545 U.S. 748 (2005).

[79] *McInnes v Onslow Fane* [1978] 1 W.L.R. 1520; *FAI Insurances Ltd v Winneke* (1982) 151 C.L.R. 342.

[80] That the considerations applicable to the revocation of licences may be different from those applicable to the refusal of licences has been recognised in a number of cases, e.g. *McInnes v Onslow Fane* [1978] 1 W.L.R. 1520, and particularly in Canadian provincial cases, holding that licensees have an implied right to be heard before revocation, see *Re Watt and Registrar of Motor Vehicles* (1958) 13 D.L.R. (2nd) 124 (driving licences); *Klymchuk v Cowan* (1964) 45 D.L.R. (2nd) 587 (used car dealer's permit); *R. v Calgary Ex p. Sanderson* (1966) 53 D.L.R. (2nd) 477 (store licence); *Re Halliwell and Welfare Institutions Board* (1966) 56 D.L.R. (2nd) 754 (rest home licence); though *cf. Re Foremost Construction Co. and Registrar of Companies* (1967) 61 D.L.R. (2nd) 528. And see *Re North Coast Air Services Ltd* [1972] EC. 390 at 404. For Australian decisions applying the rule, see *Bankes v Transport Regulation Board (Vic.)* (1968) 119 C.L.R. 222 (taxi driver's licence); *Stollery v Greyhound Racing Control Board* (1972) 128 C.L.R. 509 (revocation of greyhound owner's licence for misconduct); and *James v Pope* [1931] S.A.S.R. 441 (licence for dried fruit packing shed); *R. v Melbourne Corp Ex p. Whyte* [1949] VL.R. 257 (taxi driver's licence); contrast *Election Importing Co Pty Ltd v Courtice* (1949) 80 C.L.R. 657 at 663–664 (import licence); and *Hecht v Monaghan* 121 N.E.2d 421 (1954), where, on facts almost identical to those in *Parker* [1953] 1 W.L.R. 1150 the court reached the opposite conclusion.

7–023   Nevertheless, as has been discussed,[81] there may be a number of situations in which the decision to grant or refuse an application for a licence may attract a fair hearing. Even in the absence of a legitimate expectation, the refusal of an application may cast aspersions on a person's character. In such a case fairness dictates that the individual ought to be able to defend his interest in his reputation.[82]

The scope of interests protected by fair procedures

7–024   The right to a fair procedure is not confined to those who are direct parties to a decision.[83] However, the right does not extend to every vested right or interest. Some may be too remote or too speculative to justify their having an opportunity of being heard.[84] However, care should be exercised that decision-makers do not prejudge the impact of the decision which is in issue.[85] To what extent should a fair procedure be provided to individuals whose interests in library use are threatened by a local authority's proposal to close a local public library? Or to shopkeepers whose business interests may be threatened by a proposed car parking scheme?[86] Before a decision is taken to increase the number of taxi licences, should a local authority hear representations from the existing licensees, who have a private interest in preserving the commercial value of their licences?[87] Should the authority also be required to hear from those concerned that any increase in traffic

---

[81] See 7–007; *Fayed* [1998] 1 W.L.R. 763.

[82] *Doody v Secretary of State for the Home Department* [1994] 1 A.C. 531 at 566 (Lord Mustill: where the applicant is treated differently from other similarly placed applicants it has been suggested that the applicant has a right to a hearing in order to defend his interest in equal treatment).

[83] See, e.g. *R. v LAUTRO Ex p. Ross* [1993] Q.B. 17 (self-regulatory body was required to consult a non-member who was not a party to the decision but whose reputation could have been adversely affected by the decision); cf. *Cheall v Association of Professional Executive and Computer Staff* [1983] 2 A.C. 180. A. Lidbetter, "Financial Services: The Right to Make Representations" [1992] P.L. 533.

[84] See, e.g. *R. (on the application of Niazi) v Secretary of State for the Home Department* [2007] EWCA Civ 1495, DC (applicants for *ex gratia* payments, paid to victims of miscarriages of justice pursuant to a discretionary scheme, which was withdrawn before they made their claim, were not entitled to be consulted before the scheme was withdrawn).

[85] *R. v Ealing Justices Ex p. Fanneran* (1996) 8 Admin. L.R. 351 (applicant not informed of a hearing before justices at which they made a destruction order in relation to her pit bull terrier following her nephew's conviction of having the dog in a public place without a muzzle. Held that even though the applicant's presence at a hearing may not have made any difference to the outcome, it was important that justices acted in accordance with the rules of natural justice. The destruction order was quashed).

[86] *R. v Camden LBC Ex p. Cran* [1995] R.T.R. 346 (failure adequately to consult residents on proposed car parking zone).

[87] *R. v Liverpool Corp Ex p. Liverpool Taxi Fleet Operators' Association* [1972] 2 Q.B. 299 (corporation's assurance created what was in essence a legitimate expectation of a hearing. Lord Denning M.R., alone in the CA, further suggested that even in the absence of any legitimate expectation, the taxi drivers would have a sufficient interest by virtue of their existing licences to be entitled to consultation before a decision to increase the number of licences was taken). On the distinction between interests and legitimate expectations, see 7–005 and 12–00.

may add to congestion and levels of pollution, and adversely affect public transport?[88]

Resource allocation decisions

In the past exemption from the duty of fairness has been accorded to 7–025 decisions regarded as essentially allocative,[89] or inherently non-justiciable[90] because of their substantial policy content or "managerial" qualities.[91] However, the courts are increasingly insisting that even decisions of this kind ought to provide those whose interests are affected the opportunity to participate at least in some degree. For example, decisions of prison governors, formerly considered as falling outside the ambit of judicial review, are now within its ambit.[92] A consultation on the future development of air transport was quashed as unfair because the Secretary of State excluded any options relating to the possibility of expansion of Gatwick airport.[93] A minister's decision to support building nuclear power stations as part of the national future "electricity generating mix" was quashed on the ground that the consultation process leading to the decision was procedurally flawed.[94]

Legislative decisions

In the 4th edition of this work in 1979 it was contended that the decision 7–026 of a minister to close a coal pit would, because government economic policy was involved, not attract the duty to act fairly.[95] In a later case, however, it has been held that just such a decision was void for failure to consult the unions and others who had a legitimate expectation of being consulted prior to the pit closures.[96] Nevertheless, aside from situations where a legitimate expectation exists, decisions such as these, and others categorised as "legislative", have remained relatively immune from the assault that has been made upon the distinction between duties that are analytically "judicial" and those that are "purely administrative".[97] English

---

[88] Of course, those motivated by self-interest to make representations may bring to the attention of the decision-maker whatever considerations support their position, including matters relevant to the wider public interest that might otherwise have been overlooked: *R. v Bromley Licensing Justices Ex p. Bromley Licensed Victuallers' Association* [1984] 1 W.L.R. 585, 589.

[89] A term used by L. Fuller, *The Morality of Law* (1969), pp.46–47, 170–177.

[90] On justiciability, see 1–00.

[91] *R. v Secretary of State for the Environment Ex p. Hammersmith and Fulham LBC* [1991] A.C. 521 at 585 (Lord Bridge).

[92] *R. (on the application of West) v Parole Board* [2005] UKHL 1; [2005] 1 W.L.R. 350; *Leech v Deputy Governor of Parkhurst Prison* [1988] 1 A.C. 533.

[93] *R. (on the application of Medway Council) v Secretary of State for Transport, Local Government and the Regions* [2002] EWHC 2516; [2003] J.P.L. 583; see n.234 below.

[94] *R. (on the application of Greenpeace Ltd) v Secretary of State for Trade and Industry* [2007] EWHC 311; [2007] N.P.C. 21.

[95] G. Evans (ed.), *de Smith: Judicial Review of Administrative Action*, 4th edn. (1979), p.180.

[96] *R. v British Coal Corporation and Secretary of State for Trade and Industry Ex p. Vardy* [1993] I.C.R. 720, DC. See Ch.12.

[97] See 6–029.

courts have been reluctant to impose the duty to consult on ministers exercising powers delegated under legislation to issue orders or directions.[98] Nor is such a duty imposed upon the procedures for making policy of a less formal kind,[99] although where consultation is required by statute the courts will police its implementation and insist that it is adequate and genuine.[100] By contrast, in the United States full opportunity for notice and comment for most administrative rule-making is provided by statute.[101]

7–027   There are two reasons why "legislative" decisions[102] have been held exempt from the duty to provide a fair hearing: first, where the decision is taken by a minister or other elected official who is accountable to Parliament or a local authority, the courts will be chary of adding an additional forum of participation where one is already in place as part of the process of political accountability. The second reason is a practical one: bodies may be exempt from the duty to provide a hearing where the potential of adversely affected interests is too diverse or too numerous to permit each individual to participate.

7–028   The participation of both public interest groups and individuals asserting general interests, for example, in the environment, is accepted in areas such as planning and education.[103] The planning legislation allows interested parties the opportunity to participate in planning appeals.[104] Where, however, discretion exists to deny a hearing the courts have intervened, for example to require the Secretary of State for the Environment not to dispense with an inquiry as unnecessary, when the merits of the proposal were the subject of acute local controversy among the champions of conflicting facets of the public interest.[105] It has also been held that a

---

[98] See, e.g. *Bates v Lord Hailsham of Marylebone* [1972] 1 W.L.R. 1373.

[99] G. Ganz, *Quasi Legislation: Recent Developments in Secondary Legislation* (1987).

[100] For example, an express statutory obligation to consult has been held to require the public authority to give to those entitled to be consulted a fair opportunity to participate in a meaningful way in the exercise of the power to which the duty relates. See 7–052, for a detailed discussion of consultation rights.

[101] S. Breyer, R. Stewart, C. Sunstein and A. Vermeule, *Administrative Law and Regulatory Policy*, 6th edn (2006), Ch.6. A distinction has been drawn between trial-type hearings which are appropriate for the determination of "adjudicative facts" (facts about particular parties) and argument-type hearings to help a tribunal determine "legislative facts" (matters pertaining to questions of law, policy or discretion): R. Pierce, *Administrative Law Treatise* 4th ed (2002), Ch.7. This distinction is broadly acceptable in an English context, and although it has not fully been adopted by the law its effect can be seen, for example, in the inquiry procedure followed in the making of planning, compulsory purchase and highway decisions, e.g. *Bushell v Secretary of State for the Environment* [1981] A.C. 75. A duty to consult specified or other interested bodies before a regulation-making power is exercised is not an uncommon feature of British legislation, see e.g. Companies Act 2006 s.789; Anti-terrorism Crime and Security Act 2001 s.103. See generally, M. Asimov, "Delegated Legislation: United States and United Kingdom" (1983) 3 O.J.L.S. 253; B. Bracha, "The Right to be Heard in Rule Making Proceedings in England and Israel: Judicial Policy Reconsidered" (1987) Fordham International L.J. 613.

[102] See 6–031.

[103] See 7–011 and 7–054.

[104] See 7–011.

[105] *Binney v Secretary of State for the Environment* [1984] J.P.L. 871; cf. *R. v Secretary of State for the Environment Ex p. Greenpeace Ltd* [1994] 4 All E.R. 352.

prominent objector to a proposed development had a right to be positively consulted prior to the holding of an appeal.[106]

When it is appropriate for the courts, rather than the legislature or the administration, to extend rights of participation to these kinds of situations is an issue of some difficulty. Undoubtedly, increasing public participation in decision-making causes delay, hinders the conferral of the intended benefits of a particular programme and imposes burdens upon governmental resources.[107] The preparation and presentation of effective representations also takes time and money, commodities that are not evenly spread among all segments of society. Whether, and how, procedural arrangements should be made to enable broader ranges of interest to be represented raises fundamental issues about the adequacy of existing institutional arrangements for ensuring that government hears the concerns of the governed, and is sufficiently responsive and accountable to them.   7-029

While taking care not to hamper unduly effective administration, the common law duty of fairness surely has a useful role in opening new channels of public participation, while leaving their precise contours to be defined by legislative or administrative action. As the *British Coal* case shows,[108] a legislative-type decision,[109] and one involving issues of national economic policy, is not *ipso facto* exempt from the duty to act fairly. Even in the absence of a legitimate expectation of a hearing, it would seem fair to allow representations by at least some of those objecting to the decisions whose interests are substantially threatened by an adverse outcome.   7-030

Legitimate expectations

Finally, in broad terms, the existence of a legitimate expectation can affect procedural fairness in two ways: first, a representation or practice or policy indicating that a particular procedure will be followed can give rise to an entitlement that the procedure be followed;[110] and second, if there is a legitimate expectation of a substantive benefit, this may give rise to an entitlement to a fair procedure before the benefit can be withheld.[111] The impact of legitimate expectations on procedural fairness is discussed in detail in Chapter 12.[112]   7-031

[106] *Wilson v Secretary of State for the Environment* [1988] J.P.L. 540; *Mancetter Developments Ltd v Secretary of State for the Environment* [1993] J.P.L. 439. Interested parties have a right to be consulted when a decision to hold a new inquiry is made. *R. v Secretary of State for the Environment Ex p. Fielder Estates (Canvey) Ltd* (1989) 57 P. & C.R. 424.
[107] See n.24.
[108] [1993] I.C.R. 720.
[109] See 6-029.
[110] *R. v Liverpool Corporation Ex p. Liverpool Taxi Fleet Operators Association* [1972] 2 Q.B. 299 (representation); *Attorney-General of Hong Kong v Ng Yuen Shiu* [1983] 2 A.C. 629 (representation); *Nichol v Gateshead Metropolitan Borough Council* (1988) 87 L.G.R. 435 (past practice); *R. v Secretary of State for Trade and Industry Ex p. Vardy* [1993] I.C.R. 720 (past practice).
[111] *McInnes v Onslow-Fane* [1978] 1 W.L.R. 1520.
[112] See P. Craig, *Administrative Law*, 5th edn (2003), pp.419–421 for a discussion of the different ways in which legitimate expectations affect the entitlement to procedural fairness.

FAIR PROCEDURES UNDER ECHR ART.6: THRESHOLD ISSUES

7–032 Article 6(1) of the ECHR provides that:

"In the determination of his civil rights and obligations or of any criminal charge against him, everyone is entitled to a fair and public hearing within a reasonable time by an independent and impartial tribunal established by law. Judgement shall be pronounced publicly but the press and public may be excluded from all or part of the trial in the interest of morals, public order or national security in a democratic society, where the interests of juveniles or the protection of the private life of the parties so require, or the extent strictly necessary in the opinion of the court in special circumstances where publicity would prejudice the interests of justice."[113]

7–033 Thus, the procedural fairness protection conferred by Art.6 applies only to the determination of "civil rights or obligations" or of a criminal charge; and as was noted in Chapter 6, the boundaries of these terms have required much judicial consideration, at both the Strasbourg and the domestic level.[114] The terms have autonomous meanings, and domestic interpretations of the terms are not determinative.[115] Moreover, to engage Art.6, there should be a dispute,[116] although, generally, this requirement is not interpreted too restrictively.[117]

7–034　The result of the proceedings must be decisive of the "civil rights or obligations".[118] The mere fact that an official investigation makes findings detrimental to the applicant, where it is not dispositive of a civil right or obligation, will not bring the investigation within the scope of Art.6.[119]

---

[113] Lord Lester and D. Pannick, *Human Rights Law and Practice*, 2nd edn (2004), paras 4.6.8–4.6.12; C. Ovey and R.C.A. White, *Jacobs and White The European Convention on Human Rights*, 4th edn. (2006) pp.163–169; P. Craig, "The Human Rights Act, Article 6 and Procedural Rights" [2003] P.L. 753; J. Herberg, A. Le Sueur and J. Mulcahy, "Determining Civil Rights and Obligations" in J. Jowell and J. Cooper (eds), *Understanding Human Rights Principles* (2001), pp.91–138; P. Van Dijk, "The interpretation of 'civil rights and obligations' by the ECtHR—One more Step to Take" in F. Matscher and H. Petzold (eds), *Protecting Human Rights: The European Dimension: Studies in Honour of Gérard J. Wiarda* (1990) (considering the legislative history of the provision).

[114] See 6–00; Lester and Pannick (2004), paras 4.6.8–4.6.12; Ovey and White (2006), pp.163–169.

[115] *König v Federal Republic of Germany* (1979–80) 2 E.H.R.R. 469 at paras 88–89; *Baraona v Portugal* (1991) 13 E.H.R.R. 329, para.42; *Malige v France* (1999) 28 E.H.R.R. 578 at para.34; *Maaouia v France* (2001) 33 E.H.R.R. 1037 at para.34.

[116] This requirement appears to derive from the French version of Art.6.1, which reads "contestations sur ses droits et obligations de caracter civil"; Herberg, Le Sueur and Mulcahy (2001), p.93.

[117] *Moreira de Azevedo v Portugal* (1991) 13 E.H.R.R. 721 at para.66.

[118] *Le Compte, Van Leuven and De Meyere v Belgium* (1982) 4 E.H.R.R. 1; *Obermeier v Austria* (1990) 13 E.H.R.R. 290.

[119] *Fayed v UK* (1994) 18 E.H.R.R. 393; *Saunders v UK* (1996) 23 E.H.R.R. 313; *R. v Secretary of State for Health Ex p. C* [2000] 1 F.L.R. 627 (inclusion in a list of people about whom there were doubts as to their suitability to work with children was not determinative of civil rights and obligations).

Interim proceedings will not usually engage Art.6,[120] but may do so where they cause "irreversible prejudice" to the applicant's interests;[121] while determinations of preliminary points on liability, costs or quantum of damages[122] and proceedings to enforce a settlement agreement are considered to engage Art.6.[123]

The rights and obligations of private persons in their relations as **7–035** between themselves are civil rights and obligations, such as in tort,[124] family law,[125] employment law[126] and the law of real property.[127] With regard to relations between the individual and the state, it appears that Art.6 applies to the determination of all rights of a pecuniary nature, including for example, rights to real[128] and personal[129] property, the right to engage in a commercial activity,[130] the right to practise a profession,[131] and the right to compensation for illegal state acts.[132] Disciplinary proceedings resulting in professional suspension,[133] questions relating to children

---

[120] See, e.g. *R. (on the application of Kenny) v Leeds Magistrates Court* [2003] EWHC 2963 (Owen J. dismissed a challenge to an interim anti-social behaviour order made without notice).

[121] *Markass v Cyprus* [2002] E.H.R.L.R. 387; cf. *R. (on the application of M) v Secretary of State for Constitutional Affairs* [2004] EWCA Civ 312; [2004] 1 W.L.R. 2298 at [39(5)] (interim anti-social behaviour orders were not a determination of a civil right or obligation, since they were merely interim and short-term); *Elanay Constructs Ltd v The Vestry* [2001] B.L.R. 33 (adjudicator dealing with construction contract disputes was not subject to Art.6 because he was not making a "final determination); *R. (on the application of Aggregate Industries UK Ltd) v English Nature* [2002] EWHC 908; [2003] Env. L.R. 3 at [56] (decision-making proceess should be "directly decisive" of the civil rights or obligation in question).

[122] *Obermeier* (1990) 13 E.H.R.R. 290 at paras 66–67; *Robins v UK* (1997) 26 E.II.R.R. 527 at paras 28–29; *Silva Pontes v Portugal* (1994) 18 E.H.R.R. 156 at paras 30–36.

[123] *Pérez de Rada Cavanilles v Spain* (1998) 29 E.H.R.R. 109 at para.39; *R. (on the application of Mitchell) v Horsham District Council* [2003] EWHC 234 Admin at [32]–[33].

[124] *Axen v Germany* (1983) 6 E.H.R.R. 195.

[125] *Airey v Ireland* (1979) 2 E.H.R.R. 305.

[126] *Bucholz v Germany* (1980) E.H.R.R. 597.

[127] *Langborger v Sweden* (1989) 12 E.H.R.R. 416.

[128] *Holy Monasteries v Greece* (1994) 20 E.H.R.R. 1 at para.85; *Bryan v UK* (1995) 21 E.H.R.R. 342 at para.31; *Friends Provident Life and Pensions Ltd v Secretary of State for Transport, Local Government and Regions* [2001] EWHC Admin 820; [2002] 1 W.L.R. 1450 at [70] (planning decision a determination of civil rights and obligations of corporate objector, given the latter's property interests). cf. *Bovis Homes Ltd v New Forest DC* [2002] EWHC 483 at [300] (decision to make a local plan so that development of the claimant's land was less likely, was not a determination of a civil right or obligation.

[129] *Anca v Belgium* App. No.10259/83, 40 D.R. 170 (1984) (bankruptcy proceedings); *X v Austria*, App. No.7830/77, 14 D.R. 200 (1978) (patent rights).

[130] *The Tre Traktörer Aktiebolag v Sweden* (1989) 13 E.H.R.R. 309 (withdrawal of an alcohol licence from a restaurant); *Pudas v Sweden* (1988) 18 E.H.R.R. 188 (licence to operate a taxi); *R. (on the application of Chief Constable of Lancashire) v Preston Crown Court* [2001] EWHC Admin 928; [2002] 1 W.L.R. 1332 at [17] (liquor licensing decision a determination of a civil right or obligation because it goes to the right to make a living or economic activity); *R. (on the application of Thompson) v Law Society* [2004] EWCA Civ 167; [2004] 1 W.L.R. 2522 at [80] (Art.6 applies to disciplinary proceedings where the right to exercise a profession is at stake).

[131] *König* (1979–80) 2 E.H.R.R. 469.

[132] *Editions Périscope v France* (1992) 14 E.H.R.R. 597 at paras 35–40.

[133] *Fredin v Sweden* (1991) 13 E.H.R.R. 784 (medical profession); *Le Compte, van Leuven and de Meyere v Belgium* (1982) 4 E.H.R.R. 1. In this context, it has been held that the

taken into care;[134] decisions relating to planning and the environment;[135] conditions of detention;[136] and an application for release from detention in a prison psychiatric wing[137] also engage Art.6. Even a first-time applicant for a licence may be entitled to Art.6 protection.[138] In addition, Art.6 applies in the field of social insurance, not only to assistance linked to private employment contracts,[139] but also where the benefit is non-contributory, provided it is not entirely discretionary.[140] By contrast, however, it appears that the Strasbourg Court is reluctant to extend the protection of Art.6 to certain non-pecuniary benefits;[141] and school exclusions,[142] asylum or citizenship applications[143] and questions regarding tax liability,[144] generally do not engage Art.6. There has also been a complicated and unsatisfactory series of cases regarding civil service employment.

relevant consideration is whether the decision of the disciplinary body *could* result in a determination of civil rights and obligations, such as through suspension, rather than considering whether the outcome of the disciplinary hearing may be admonishment: *Tehrani v UK Central Council for Nursing, Midwifery & Health Visiting* [2001] I.R.L.R. 208 at [33]; *R. (on the application of Thompson) v Law Society* [2004] EWCA Civ 167; [2004] 1 W.L.R. 2522 at [83]; *Threlfall v General Optical Council* [2004] EWHC 2683; [2005] Lloyd's Rep. Med. 250 at [33]–[35].

[134] *McMichael v UK* (1995) 20 E.H.R.R. 205.

[135] *Mats Jacobsson v Sweden* (1991) 13 E.H.R.R. 79; *Taskin v Turkey* (2006) 42 E.H.R.R. 50.

[136] *Ganci v Italy* (2005) 41 E.H.R.R. 16; *Musumeci v Italy* App. No.33695/96, January 11, 2005.

[137] *Aerts v Belgium* (2000) 29 E.H.R.R. 50.

[138] *Benthem v Netherlands* (1985) 8 E.H.R.R. 1 (an application for a grant of a statutory licence to operate an installation for the supply of liquefied petroleum gas was rejected, and this was found to constitute a "civil right" given that it was a pre-condition for the exercise of business activity: para.36); *McInnes v Onslow-Fane* [1978] 1 W.L.R. 1520.

[139] See, e.g. *Lombardo v Italy* (1992) 21 E.H.R.R. 188 at paras 14–17 (pension linked to employment).

[140] *Salesi v Italy* (1993) 26 E.H.R.R. 187; *Tsfayo v UK* App. No.60860/00; [2007] B.L.G.R. 1 (discussed further at 10–00); *R. (on the application of Husain) v Asylum Support Adjudicator* [2001] EWHC Admin 852 [2002] A.C.D. 61 at [25] (termination of asylum support engaged Art.6).

[141] See, e.g. *Pierre-Bloch v France* (1997) 26 E.H.R.R. 202 at paras 50–55 (holding that the right to stand for election to the National Assembly in France was a "political" and not a "civil" right); *Adams and Benn v UK* (1997) 23 E.H.R.R. C.D. 160 (Commission) (holding that the right to move within the European Community pursuant to Art.18 of the EC Treaty did not engage Art.6.1; see 14–096 and 14–119).

[142] *R. (on the application of B) v Head Teacher of Alperton Community School* [2001] EWHC Admin 229; [2002] B.L.G.R. 132; (no private right to education, therefore Art.6 not engaged); *R. (on the application of M-P) v Barking LBC* [2002] EWHC 2483; [2003] E.L.R. 144 at [28] (the decision to remove a pupil from a school register was not a determination of a civil right or obligation) *R. v Richmond upon Thames LBC Ex p. JC* [2001] E.L.R. 21 at [59] (primary school admissions decision was not a determination of "civil rights"). cf. *R. (on the application of S) v Brent LBC* [2002] EWCA Civ 693, [2002] E.L.R. 556 at [30] (considering and assuming that a school exclusion does engage Art.6).

[143] *Maaouia v France* (2001) 33 E.H.R.R. 1037 (proceedings to challenge an exclusion order); *MNM v Secretary of State for the Home Department* [2000] I.N.L.R. 576 (Art.6 not applying to immigration appeals because these involve public law rights); *R. (on the application of Ullah) v Secretary of State for the Home Department* [2003] EWCA Civ 1366 at [20]; *R. (on the application of Harrison) v Secretary of State for the Home Department* [2003] EWCA Civ 432, [2003] I.N.L.R. 294 (where it was doubted whether citizenship decisions were capable of constituting determinations of civil rights or obligations)

[144] *Charalambos v France* App. No.49210/99, admissibility decision of 8 February 2000 (determination of tax liability).

Initially, the ECtHR held that "disputes relating to the recruitment, careers and termination of service of civil servants are as a general rule outside the scope of Article 6(1)".[145] However, after a number of cases,[146] the position that has now emerged is that the only civil service disputes excluded from Art.6(1) are "those which are raised by public servants whose duties typify the specific activities of the public service in so far as the latter is acting as the depository of public authority responsible for protecting the general interests of the State or other public authorities".[147]

In determining whether the proceedings are determinative of a criminal charge, it is necessary to consider: the classification of the proceedings in domestic law; the nature of the offence itself; and the severity of the penalty which may be imposed.[148] If the proceedings are categorised as "criminal" in domestic law, this will be decisive. If however, the proceedings are categorised as "civil", the ECt HR will conduct an independent examination of the nature of the proceedings. The severity of the penalty will often be decisive[149] and in particular, if there is a power to impose imprisonment, this will generally suffice to categorise the proceedings as "criminal", unless the "nature, duration or manner of execution of the imprisonment" is not "appreciably detrimental".[150] Certain prison disciplinary proceedings may engage Art.6, if they are sufficiently serious.[151] Even in cases where the penalty is in the nature of a fine rather than

7–036

---

[145] *Massa v Italy* (1994) 18 E.H.R.R. 266 at para.26.
[146] See, e.g. *De Santa v Italy* App. No.25574/94; *Lapalorcia v Italy* (App. No.25586/94); *Abenavoli v Italy* App. No.25587/94, Judgments of September 2, 1997; *Neigel v France* (2000) 30 E.H.R.R. 310.
[147] *Pellegrin v France* (2001) 31 E.H.R.R. 26 at para.66.
[148] *Engel v Netherlands* (1976) 1 E.H.R.R. 647 at para.82: *MB(FC) v Secretary of State for the Home Department: AF v Secretary of State for the Home Department* [2007] UKHL 46 [23]–[24] (holding that non-derogating control orders issued pursuant to the prevention of Terrorism Act 2005, do not involve "criminal change". Even though there may be devastating consequences for the individuals and their families, there is: no assertion of criminal conduct only a foundation of suspicion: no identification of any specific criminal offence is provided for: the order made is preventative, not punitive or retributive: and the obligations imposed must be no more restrictive than are judged necessary to achieve the preventative object of the order).
[149] *Brown v UK* (1998) 28 E.H.R.R. CD 233.
[150] *Engel* (1976) 1 E.H.R.R. 647 at para.82; *R. (on the application of Napier) v Secretary of State for the Home Department* [2004] EWHC 936; [2004] 1 W.L.R. 3056 (the decision to impose additional days on a prisoner was "criminal" for the purposes of Art.6); *R. v H* [2003] UKHL 1, [2003] 1 W.L.R. 41 (jury procedure for dealing with a defendant unfit to stand trial was not the determination of a criminal charge because it could not culminate in a penal sanction); *R. (on the application of West) v Parole Board* [2005] UKHL 1; [2005] 1 W.L.R. 350 (the decision to recall a determinative sentence prisoner, released on licence, not the determination of a criminal charge so as to render an oral hearing for that reason necessary); *R. (on the application of Manjit Singh Sunder) v Secretary of State for the Home Department* [2001] EWHC Admin 252 at [22] (reclassification of a prisoner did not engage Art.6, there being no determination of a criminal charge).
[151] *Campbell and Fell v UK* (1984) 7 E.H.R.R. 165; *Ezeh v UK* (2002) 35 E.H.R.R. 691; see 7–076.

imprisonment,[152] if a punitive and deterrent penalty is attached, it is likely that the proceedings will be regarded as criminal in character, rather than disciplinary. However, where the offence is limited to a restricted group, as is generally the case in relation to disciplinary offences, a court would be unlikely to characterise the charge under the applicable disciplinary or regulatory code as criminal, at least unless it involves or may lead to loss of liberty.[153]

FAIR PROCEDURES REQUIRED BY ECHR ART.2: THRESHOLD ISSUES

7–037 Art.2 requires a state to conduct an adequate and effective investigation, wherever there is a breach of the right to life through the use of lethal force.[154] A violation of Art.2 may arise from the absence of procedural safeguards even where the applicant has failed to provide sufficient evidence to conclude that the deceased was intentionally killed by the state.[155] Thus lack of state protection, rather than just direct state involvement, will trigger the Art.2 procedural duty,[156] and where authorities are informed of a death, this in itself can give rise to an obligation to carry out an effective investigation into the circumstances surrounding the death.[157] The fact that a security situation exists in the country will not relieve the state of its obligation.[158]

CONTENT OF PROCEDURAL FAIRNESS: OVERVIEW

7–038 The content of procedural fairness in any given context may be determined by statute, the common law, the ECHR and European Community law. As a general observation, the position of the English courts is that the requirements of Art.6 and the common law are equivalent;[159] albeit that, as

---

[152] *Han (t/a Murdishaw Supper Bar) v Customs and Excise Commissioners* [2001] EWCA Civ 1048; [2001] 1 W.L.R. 2253 at [66] (holding that proceedings before the Securities and Futures Authority, which could result debarment from earning one's livelihood, were not "criminal" for the purposes of Art.6).

[153] *Han* [2001] EWCA Civ 1048; [2001] 1 W.L.R. 2253.

[154] *McCann v UK* (1995) 21 E.H.R.R. 97; *R. (on the application of Middleton) v West Somerset Coroner* [2004] UKHL 10; [2004] 2 A.C. 182 at [3]; *R. (on the application of A) v Lord Saville of Newdigate* [2001] EWCA Civ 2048; [2002] 1 W.L.R. 1249 at [10]–[11]; *R. (on the application of Green) v Police Complaints Authority* [2004] UKHL 6; [2004] 1 W.L.R. 725 at [11].

[155] *Kaya v Turkey* (1998) 28 E.H.R.R. 1; *Tanrikulu v Turkey* (2000) 30 E.H.R.R. 950; *Kiliç v Turkey* [2001] 33 E.H.R.R. 1357; *Mahmut Kaya v Turkey*; unreported (March 28, 2000,).

[156] *R. (on the application of Challender) v Legal Services Commission* [2004] EWHC 925; [2004] A.C.D. 57 at [49].

[157] *Tanrikulu v Turkey* (2000) 30 E.H.R.R. 950; *Menson v UK* (2003) 37 E.H.R.R. C.D. 220; *Ergi v Turkey* (2001) 32 E.H.R.R. 388; *Yasa v Turkey* (1998) 28 E.H.R.R. 408 at para.[100].

[158] *Tanrikulu v Turkey* (2000) 30 E.H.R.R. 950.

[159] See, e.g. *R. (on the application of Bright) v Central Criminal Court* [2001] 1 W.L.R. 662 at 679 (Judge L.J. noting that "by now we surely fully appreciate that the principles to be found in ECHR Arts 6 and 10 are bred in the bone of the common law").

was noted in Chapter 6 and just discussed, common law procedural fairness is broader in its scope of application.[160] ECHR Art.2 has a very specific impact on the content of procedural fairness: it requires an effective official investigation where an individual is killed as a result of the use of force and identifies the elements which must be satisfied in order for an investigation to be deemed "effective".[161] Meanwhile, as was also noted in Chapter 6, the most notable contribution of European Community law to the content of procedural fairness is the requirement to give reasons where the decision of a national authority has the effect of denying a fundamental European Community right, and this requirement is discussed in Chapter 14.[162]

A flexible and evolving concept

The content of procedural fairness is infinitely flexible.[163] It is not possible to lay down rigid rules and everything depends on the subject-matter.[164] The requirements necessary to achieve fairness range from mere consultation at the lower end, upwards through an entitlement to make written representations, to make oral representations, to a fully fledged hearing with most of the characteristics of a judicial trial at the other extreme. What is required in any particular case is incapable of definition in abstract terms. As Lord Bridge has put it "the so-called rules of natural justice are not engraved on tablets of stone. To use the phrase which better expresses the underlying concept, what the requirements of fairness demand when any body, domestic, administrative or judicial, has to make a decision which will affect the rights of individuals depends on the character of the decision-making body, the kind of decision it has to make and the statutory or other framework in which it operates."[165] Procedural fairness is also a   7–039

---

[160] See Ch.6 and 7–017; *R. (on the application Wooder) v Feggetter* [2002] EWCA Civ 554; [2003] Q.B. 219 at [46] ("the common law sets high standards of due process in non-judicial settings to which the European Court of Human Rights at Strasbourg declines to apply Art.6").

[161] See 7–128.

[162] See 6–009, 14–107 and 14–117.

[163] *Re Pergamon Press Ltd* [1971] Ch. 388 at 403 (Sachs L.J. noting the need for "real flexibility"); *Russell v Duke of Norfolk* [1949] 1 All E.R. 109 at 1188 (Tucker L.J. noting "There are, in my view, no words which are of universal application to every kind of inquiry and every kind of domestic tribunal. The requirements of natural justice must depend on the circumstances of the case, the nature of the inquiry, the rules under which the tribunal is acting, the subject-matter under consideration and so on"). For comparative perspectives, see 6–055.

[164] *R. v Gaming Board for Great Britain Ex p. Benaim and Khaida* [1970] 2 Q.B. 417 at 439 (Lord Denning M.R.); *Sheridan v Stanley Cole (Wainfleet) Ltd* [2003] EWCA Civ 1046; [2003] 4 All E.R. 1181 at [33] (Ward L.J. noting that "[e]verything depends on the subject matter and the facts and circumstances of each case").

[165] *Lloyd v McMahon* [1987] A.C. 625 at 702; *R. v Secretary of State for the Home Department Ex p. Doody* [1994] 1 A.C. 531 at 560 (Lord Mustill noting that what fairness requires is "essentially an intuitive judgment"); *R. v Leicester Crown Court Ex p. Phipps* [1997] C.O.D. 299 (where there is no customary general practice, an individual judge will

"constantly evolving concept",[166] and in implementation of Government policy on "proportionate dispute resolution",[167] adjudicatory bodies have recently started working in new and more flexible ways to resolve grievances through alternative dispute resolution mechanisms. The content of procedural fairness in these contexts has yet to be settled.[168]

7–040   The content of a hearing is easier to determine in cases where it is based upon a legitimate expectation of a hearing[169]—but even in such a case the scope of the expected hearing may not be easy to define. Where the right to procedural fairness has a statutory source[170] then substantial guidance as to what should be provided can be obtained, usually by construction of the legislation in question.[171] Even in such a case, however, terms such as "consultation" need elaboration[172] and degrees of disclosure or candour will differ in different circumstances. Furthermore, as was discussed above, the courts may be prepared to supplement the statutory code.[173] In the case of *Doody*,[174] Lord Mustill in summarising the effect of the authorities said:

> "The principles of fairness are not to be applied by rote identically in every situation. What fairness demands is dependent on the context of the decision, and this is to be taken into account in all its aspects. An essential factor of the context is the statute which creates the discretion, as regards both its language and the shape of the legal and administrative system within which the decision is taken."

7–041   While the statute is an essential factor it is not the only feature and where the statutory procedure is "insufficient to achieve justice", the courts will supplement the statutory code to the extent necessary to ensure that it operates fairly,[175] or if the statute is silent, add or imply a code.[176] Rules

have to devise a procedure that is fair and just and meets the particular circumstances of the case); *R. (on the application of X) v Secretary of State for the Home Department, Governor of HMP Drake Hall, Governor of HMP East Sutton Park* [2005] EWHC 1616 at [31]. But for the dangers of excessive informality, see *Dyason v Secretary of State for the Environment, Transport and the Regions* (1998) 75 P. & C.R. 506.

[166] *R. v H* [2004] UKHL 3, [2004] 2 A.C. 134 at [11] (Lord Bingham).
[167] See 1–00.
[168] G. Richardson and H. Genn, "Tribunals in Transition: Resolution or Adjudication?" [2007] P.L. 116.
[169] See 12–00.
[170] See 7–011.
[171] See, e.g. *Kioa v Minister for Immigration and Ethnic Affairs* (1985) 62 A.L.R. 321 at 369 ("to ascertain what must be done to comply with the principles of natural justice in a particular case, the starting point is the statute creating the power").
[172] See, e.g. *R. v Secretary of State for Social Services Ex p. Association of Metropolitan Authorities* [1986] 1 W.L.R. 1.
[173] See 7–013.
[174] *R. v Secretary of State for the Home Department Ex p. Doody* [1994] 1 A.C. 531 at 560.
[175] *Wiseman v Borneman* [1971] A.C. 297 at 298; *R. (on the application of S) v London Borough of Brent* [2002] EWCA Civ 693; [2002] E.L.R. 556 at [14]; *Raji v General Medical Council* [2003] UKPC 24; [2003] 1 W.L.R. 1052, PC (even though Medical Act 1983 ss.41(1) and (6) permitted consideration of suspension and restoration together, the two issues should have been considered separately); *R. (on the application of Cheltenham Builders Ltd) v South*

and regulations may also be supplemented with fair procedures.[177] In all cases though, any implied or inserted procedures must not frustrate the statutory scheme.[178]

Consequences of following flawed procedures

The consequence of non-compliance with a statutory requirement for fair 7–042
procedure should be derived from the legislator's intention, which should be assessed on a consideration of the language of the legislation against the factual circumstances of the non-compliance.[179] Where the procedure followed by the decision-maker is found to be flawed it will usually, but not always, be appropriate to quash the decision. If a decision-maker can demonstrate to the court that the same decision would have been reached even if consultation had been carried out properly, the court may exercise its discretion to withhold a remedy.[180]

PRIOR NOTICE OF THE DECISION

The importance of prior notice

Procedural fairness generally requires that persons liable to be directly 7–043
affected by proposed administrative acts, decisions or proceedings be given adequate notice of what is proposed, so that they may be in a position:

Gloucestershire DC [2003] EWHC 2803; [2003] 4 P.L.R. 95 at [34]–[36].
[176] *Doody* [1994] 1 A.C. 531 at 562; *R. (on the application of Khatun) v Newham LBC* [2004] EWCA Civ 55; [2005] Q.B. 37 at [30] (Laws L.J. noting that "a right to be heard [can] be inserted or implied into the statutory scheme not by virtue of the statute's words, but by force of our public law standards of procedural fairness"). *R. v Parole Board Ex p. Wilson* [1992] 2 Q.B. 740; *Wiseman v Borneman* [1971] A.C. 297 at 308, 311, 312, 317G and 320; *Lloyd v McMahon* [1987] A.C. 625 at 702H–703A (Lord Bridge); *Pearlberg v Varty* [1972] 1 W.L.R. 534, 551A–B (Lord Salmon—but *cf.* Lord Hailsham 540C–D); *Wooder* [2003] Q.B. 219 at [44] (Sedley L.J. noting that "[t]he process is not one of discerning implied terms but of adding necessary ones").
[177] *R. (on the application of Bentley) v HM Coroner for Avon* [2001] EWHC Admin 170; (2002) 166 J.P. 297 (held that the refusal of the Coroner to give advance disclosure of documents to the family of the deceased was unlawful, even though the relevant rules made no provision for such disclosure); and n.176 above.
[178] *R. v Birmingham CC Ex p. Ferrero Ltd* [1993] 1 All E.R. 530, 542 (Taylor L.J.); *Wiseman v Borneman* [1971] A.C. 297 at 308; and n.60 above.
[179] See 5–00.
[180] See 18–00.

- to make representations on their own behalf;[181] or

- to appear at a hearing or inquiry (if one is to be held); and

- effectively to prepare their own case and to answer the case (if any) they have to meet.[182]

7–044 Individuals should not be taken unfairly by surprise.[183] In disciplinary and analogous situations, there will often be a further reason why adequate prior notice should be given to the party to be charged—to give him the opportunity of offering to resign[184] or (for example) surrender his licence, rather than face the prospect of formal condemnation. The duty to notify also includes the duty to take into consideration any representations made in response to notification.[185]

7–045 In a large majority of the reported cases where breach of the requirements of fairness has been alleged, no notice whatsoever of the action taken or proposed to be taken was given to the person claiming to be

---

[181] See, e.g. *Hoggard v Worsbrough UDC* [1962] 2 Q.B. 93 (insufficient warning given of what was proposed to be done to plaintiff's detriment; plaintiff's abstention from making immediate representations excusable because he was left under a misapprehension); *R. v Secretary of State for the Home Department Ex p. Doody* [1994] 1 A.C. 531 at 563 where Lord Mustill described it as a proposition of common sense; *R. v (Banks) v Secretary of State for the Environment, Food and Rural Affairs* [2004] EWHC 416, [2004] N.P.C. 43 at [95] (noting that "[i]n order to be able to make meaningful representations the claimants had to be told what concerns they had to answer" and as such it was procedurally unfair for Secretary of State for the Environment, Food and Rural Affairs not to disclose information on which she relied in deciding to maintain cattle movement restriction notice); *R. (on the application of C) v Sunderland Youth Court* [2003] EWHC 2385, [2004] 1 Cr.App.R.(S.) 76 at [31]; *R. v Secretary of State for the Home Department Ex p. Fayed* [1998] 1 W.L.R. 763 (applicant for British citizenship entitled to be told of Secretary of State's concerns, notwithstanding statutory provision excluding duty to give reasons); *Lewis v Attorney-General of Jamaica* [2001] 2 A.C. 50 (a prisoner sentenced to death had a right to information and documents regarding the prerogative of mercy); *R. v Governors of Dunraven School Ex p. B* [2000] E.L.R. 156 (it was unfair for school governors to have access to material to which an accused pupil did not have access); *R. (on the application of Dermott) v SENDIST, Liverpool City Council* [2005] EWHC 2722 at [15] (finding that it was unfair for a tribunal to rely on its own expertise, thereby depriving the parties "of the opportunity of producing material which might have been relevant"); *R. v Haringey LBC Ex p. Haringey Consortium of Disabled People and Carers Association* (2000) 58 B.M.L.R. 160.

[182] *In re D (Minors) (Adoption Reports: Confidentiality)* [1996] A.C. 593 at 603–604 (Lord Mustill, describing it as the "first principle of fairness").

[183] *R. (on the application of Anufrijeva) v Secretary of State for the Home Department* [2003] UKHL 36; [2004] 1 A.C. 604 at [30] (Lord Steyn noting that "[i]n our system of law surprise is regarded as the enemy of justice"); *MacDonald v Western Isles Licensing Board* 2001 S.C. 628 (Board acted unlawfully in founding it decision upon Sabbath observance without informing the applicant of this and allowing her to address the matter).

[184] See, e.g. Comment, "Judicial Control of Acts of Private Associations" (1963) 76 Harv. L.R. 983, p.1028. Of course, it does not necessarily follow that the competent authority is obliged to accept such a resignation or withdrawal.

[185] *R. (on the application of Wainwright) v Richmond upon Thames LBC* [2001] EWCA Civ 2062; (2002) 99(9) L.S.G. 29 at [6] (the purpose of notification of the public of the proposal means that the council must have a duty to consider representations made in response to notification); *R. v North Yorkshire County Council Ex p. M* [1989] Q.B. 411 (there was a "duty on the part of the local authority, not only to disclose proposals for change in relation to the child, but also to listen to the views of the guardian ad litem").

aggrieved,[186] and failure to give him prior notice was tantamount to a denial of an opportunity to be heard.[187] The requirement that prior notice be given, therefore, usually follows automatically from a right to be consulted or heard (whether in writing or orally).

The degree of notice required

If there is a duty to give prior notice, it does not invariably follow that notice must actually be served and received;[188] it is not uncommon for legislation to provide that it is sufficient if reasonable steps are taken to give notice.[189] If the number of persons affected is indeterminate,[190] to give public notice in a manner fairly and reasonably calculated to alert those likely to be interested in the subject matter may be enough to satisfy the rule.[191] But where a person is likely to suffer particular loss from the decision, the duty of "candour" is that much higher.[192] If a person upon whom notice ought to be served, or his representative, obstructs service[193]   7-046

---

[186] See, e.g. *Bagg's Case* (1615) 11 Co.Rep. 93b; *Cooper v Wandsworth Board of Works* (1863) 14 C.B.(N.S.) 180; *Ridge v Baldwin* [1964] A.C. 40; *Glynn v Keele University* [1971] 1 W.L.R. 487; *R. v Havering Justices Ex p. Smith* [1974] 3 All E.R. 484. It should be noted, however, that as the knowledge of the basic requirements of fairness has increased among both potential applicants and respondents, the proportion of cases involving a complete failure to give notice or to hear has fallen, as compared to those cases involving a challenge to the extent or nature of the hearing.

[187] *Annamunthodo v Oilfield Workers' Trade Union* [1961] A.C. 945; *Maradana Mosque Trustees v Mahmud* [1967] A.C. 13; *Lau Liat Meng v Disciplinary Committee* [1968] A.C. 391; *Fairmount Investments Ltd v Secretary of State for the Environment* [1976] 1 W.L.R. 1255; and *Hadmor Productions v Hamilton* [1983] 1 A.C. 191 at 233B–C. *Cf. R. v Secretary of State for Health Ex p. US Tobacco International Inc* [1992] Q.B. 353 at 370F–G; *Chief Constable of North Wales Police v Evans* [1982] 1 W.L.R. 1155; *R. v Hampshire CC Ex p. K* [1990] 2 Q.B. 71.

[188] But the general rule is that it must be: see, See, e.g. *Re Wykeham Terrace, Brighton* [1971] Ch. 204; *cf. R. v Kensington and Chelsea Rent Tribunal Ex p. MacFarlane* [1974] 1 W.L.R. 1486 (notice served but not received: proceedings valid, but tribunal has discretion to reconsider its decision in light of representations subsequently made by absent party).

[189] For example, under the Town and Country Planning Act 1990 s.65, and Art.6 of the Town and Country Planning (General Development Procedure) Order 1995 (SI 1995/419), a local planning authority shall not entertain an application for planning permission unless the applicant has certified that he is the sole owner of all the land to which the application relates, or has notified the owner of the land or any tenant of the land. Where, however, the applicant has been unable to identify the owner or tenant, he must show that he has taken reasonable steps to do so and has advertised the notice locally. It may still be wrong to proceed if it is known that notice has not in fact been received, at least where the statute makes the time at which notice is received important: *R. v London County QS Appeals Committee Ex p. Rossi* [1956] 1 Q.B. 682. *cf. R. v Devon and Cornwall Rent Tribunal Ex p. West* (1975) 29 P. & C.R. 316; *Willowgreen Ltd v Smithers* [1994] 1 W.L.R. 832.

[190] And not merely large; cf. *Young v Ladies Imperial Club Ltd* [1920] 2 K.B. 523 (irregularly constituted meeting; fact that a committee member was known to wish not to attend did not justify failure to summon her).

[191] See, e.g. *Wilson v Secretary of State for the Environment* [1973] 1 W.L.R. 1083; *Waitemata County v Local Government Commission* [1964] N.Z.L.R. 689 at 698–699.

[192] *R. v Secretary of State for Health Ex p. US Tobacco International Inc* [1992] Q.B. 353, DC. *R. v Ealing Magistrates' Court Ex p. Fanneran* (1996) 8 Admin. L.R. 351 (dog owner entitled to be heard before destruction order is made).

[193] *De Verteuil v Knaggs* [1918] A.C. 557 at 560–561.

or negligently fails to notify a change of address,[194] non-service of notice may be excused.[195] If the matter is one of special urgency, non-service of notice may also be excused.[196] Other possible exceptions to the general rule—where the person claiming to be aggrieved must be assumed to have known or did in fact know what was being alleged or what was likely to happen to him,[197] or that he suffered no real detriment by the omission[198] or impliedly waived the defect by appearing at a subsequent hearing[199]— must be viewed with some reserve.[200] Seldom will the absence of prior notice leave a person with an adequate opportunity of preparing his own case or his answers.

7–047   As the reason for imposing an obligation to give prior notice is usually to afford those who will be affected an opportunity to make representations, the notice must be served in sufficient time to enable representations to be made effectively.[201] Where a decision-maker's exercise of its power to adjourn is reviewed, there is no margin of appreciation for the decision-maker and the court itself will decide whether fairness required an adjournment.[202] If an oral hearing is to be held, the time and place must be properly notified.[203] If charges are to be brought, they should be specified

---

[194] *James v Institute of Chartered Accountants* (1907) 98 L.T. 225; *Glynn v Keele University* [1971] 1 W.L.R. 487; *Al-Mehdawi v Secretary of State for the Home Department* [1990] 1 A.C. 876 (where the negligence was that of the appellant's solicitor); *R. (on the application of Mathialagan) v Southwark LBC* [2004] EWCA Civ 1689; *R. (on the application of R) v Secretary of State for the Home Department* [2005] EWHC 520.

[195] See nn.193–194. *Cf. R. v The Criminal Injuries Compensation Board Ex p. A* [1999] 2 A.C. 330 at 345 ("[i]t does not seem to me to be necessary to find that anyone was at fault"); *Haile v Immigration Appeal Tribunal* [2001] EWCA Civ 663; [2002] Imm. A.R. 170 at [26] (Simon Brown L.J. noting that aspects of *Al-Mehdawi* [1990] 1 A.C. 876 "may in any event now need to be reconsidered"); *FP (Iran) v. Secretary of State for the Home Department* [2007] EWCA Civ 13 at [45] (suggesting that *Al-Mehdawi* does not apply to asylum cases and not applying it given potentially serious consequences for the applicants caused by legal representative's error); 7–051.

[196] *De Verteuil v Knaggs* [1918] A.C. 557.

[197] *cf. Robinson v Sunderland Corp* [1899] 1 Q.B. 751 at 757, 758; *Russell v Duke of Norfolk* [1949] 1 All E.R. 109 at 117–118; *Byrne v Kinematograph Renters Society Ltd* [1958] 1 W.L.R. 762 at 785.

[198] *cf. Davis v Carew-Pole* [1956] 1 W.L.R. 833 at 838–840. See generally on this point, *John v Rees* [1970] Ch. 345 at 402.

[199] *Noakes v Smith* (1942) 107 J.P 101.

[200] See, e.g. *Hibernian Property Co Ltd v Secretary of State for the Environment* (1973) 27 P. & C.R. 197 at 213; *Fairmount Investments Ltd v Secretary of State for the Environment* [1976] 1 W.L.R. 1255 at 1266; and *Rees v Crane* [1994] 2 A.C. 173, PC, and see the discussion at 8–023 and 8–043 below.

[201] *R. v Thames Magistrates Court Ex p. Polemis* [1974] 1 W.L.R. 1371 (refusal of an adjournment); *R. v Guildford Justices Ex p. Rich* [1997] 1 Cr. App. R. (S) 49 (sufficient notice of distress order must be given to allow affected individual opportunity to make representations); *R. v Devon County Council Ex p. Baker* [1995] 1 All E.R. 73 (insufficient notice given to residents of proposed closure of old people's home to enable proper representations or objections); *R. v Secretary of State for the Home Department Ex p. Moon* (1996) 8 Admin. L.R. 477; *R. v Northern & Yorks Regional Health Authority Ex p. Trivedi* [1995] 1 W.L.R. 961 at 975.

[202] *R. v Cheshire CC Ex p. C* [1998] E.L.R. 66 at 73 (Sedley J.); see 7–066.

[203] *Hopkins v Smethwick Board of Health* (1890) 24 Q.B.D. 712 at 715; *Wilson v Secretary of State for the Environment* [1988] 3 P.L. 520; *cf. Ostreicher v Secretary of State for the Environment* [1978] W.L.R. 810 (date of hearing inconvenient for religious reasons).

with particularity,[204] and in any event an interested party ought not to be taken by surprise by being expected to give an immediate answer to an important point raised for the first time at the hearing.[205]

A breach of fairness will also be found where an individual has been **7–048** informed of only one charge, although there are two;[206] or where the person is found guilty of a different offence from the one with which she was actually charged.[207] Nevertheless, sometimes decision-makers have been accorded a considerable degree of latitude in such matters.[208]

Statutory requirements for notice

Statutory rules may set out in varying detail the requirements for the giving **7–049** of notice and for consultation. There is no set form, and procedures will differ for different decisions. Under current regulations on proposals for development plans[209] the local planning authority is required to carry out consultations with a list of named consultees.[210] This duty carries with it a duty to "consider any representations made by the consultees before finally determining the contents of the proposal".[211] If additional persons are consulted voluntarily, the planning authority is required to prepare a statement of those consultees, and of any steps it took to publicise the proposals and to provide persons with an opportunity of making representations in respect of those proposals.[212] Planning applications must be publicised by the local planning authority, either by a site notice or notification of neighbours.[213] In addition, an advertisement in a newspaper is required in some specified cases,[214] and in all cases of "major develop-

---

[204] *Ex p. Daisy Hopkins* (1891) 61 L.J.Q.B. 240; *R. v LAUTRO Ex p. Tee* (1995) 7 Admin. L.R. 289; *McDonald v Lanarkshire Fire Brigade Joint Committee* 1959 S.C. 141. On duty of adequate disclosure, see 7–057.

[205] *R. v Chance Ex p. Coopers & Lybrand* (1995) 7 Admin. L.R. 821 at 835 (surprise as the enemy of justice); *R. v Rodney and Minister of Manpower and Immigration* (1972) 27 D.L.R. (3rd) 756;

[206] *Board of Trustees of the Marandana Mosque v Mahmud* [1967] 1 A.C. 13 at 24–25. See further *Singleton v The Law Society* [2005] EWHC 2915 at [12]–[13] (where it was unfair not to give a solicitor timely notice that the allegation of "conduct unbefitting a solicitor" was being made on the basis of dishonesty).

[207] *Lau Liat Meng v Disciplinary Committee* [1968] A.C. 391 (notice given of proposed action on ground X but action taken on ground Y of which no notice, or inadequate notice, had been given).

[208] See, e.g. *Sloane v GMC* [1970] 1 W.L.R. 1130; *Norman and Moran v National Dock Labour Board* [1957] 1 Lloyd's Rep. 455 (imprecise charges); *cf. Stevenson v United Road Transport Union* [1977] I.C.R. 893.

[209] Town and Country Planning (Development Plan) (England) Regulations 1999 (SI 1999/3280).

[210] SI 1999/3280 reg.10. The consultees include the Secretary of State, other local planning authorities for the area or adjacent areas, the Environment Agency, the Countryside Agency and English Nature and the Historic Buildings and Monuments Commission.

[211] SI 1999/3280 reg.10(2).

[212] SI 1999/3280 reg.10(3).

[213] Art.8 para.5 of the Town and Country Planning (General Development Procedure) Order 1995 (SI 1995/419); and s.16(2) of the Planning and Compensation Act 1991, amending s.71 of the Town and Country Planning Act 1990.

[214] Where the application is accompanied by an environment statement, departures from a development plan, or development affecting a public right of way. See art.8 para.2.

ment".[215] These requirements of publicity are backed up by a duty to "take into account" any representations that are made in response to them, and the authority is forbidden from determining the application before 21 days from the posting of a site notice or 14 days from the date of the publication of a newspaper notice.[216]

7–050   Statutory notice requirements are also imposed in the education context.[217] If a local education authority wishes to invite proposals for a new school, it must notify with a number of interested parties, including: any schools which are proposed to be discontinued[218]; and any local education authority which may be affected by the establishment of the new school.[219] It must also hold at least one public meeting to inform the public of the proposals.[220] The notice inviting proposals for the new school must be published in at least one newspaper circulating in the area,[221] and the proposals received sent to a number of parties including the Secretary of State.[222] Notice and consultation obligations also exist in the context of re-organisation of the NHS[223] and the formulation of health strategy.[224]

Consequences of inadequate notice

7–051   Although the non-issue or the inadequacy of the notice can invalidate the subsequent proceedings,[225] exceptions to the general rule have been introduced by statute. For example, under a number of statutes procedural defects will only be a ground for setting aside an order if a defect has resulted in the applicant being substantially prejudiced thereby.[226] Non-service or inadequacy of a notice depriving the applicant of a proper

---

[215] Defined under arts 2, 7(1) of the Town and Country Planning (General Development Procedure) (Amendment) (England) Order 2006 (SI 2006/1062).

[216] SI 1995/419 art.19.

[217] School Organisation (Establishment and Discontinuance of Schools) (England) Regulations 2007 (SI 2007/1288).

[218] 2007/1288 reg 5(1)(h).

[219] 2007/1288 reg 5(1)(a).

[220] 2007/1288 reg 10(2).

[221] 2007/1288 reg 5(2)(3).

[222] 2007/1288 reg 10(6)(h).

[223] See, e.g. Primary Care Trusts (Consultation on Establishment, Dissolution and Transfer of Staff) 1999 (SI 1999/2337).

[224] National Health Service Act 2006 s.24.

[225] See 7.00 the consequences of failing to comply with a statutory requirement to give prior notice should be determined from a consideration of the legislation.

[226] See, e.g. Town and Country Planning Act 1990 s.288. In *Wilson v Secretary of State for the Environment* [1988] J.P.L. 540, it was held that the failure by the authority to notify of an appeal those who were consulted or notified of the original proposal, or who had made representations, might not result in substantial prejudice. However in that case the applicant, being the leader of local opposition to the development, was substantially prejudiced by the authority's failure to notify him of the appeal; and s.176(5) Town and Country Planning Act 1990 which permits the Secretary of State of the Environment on an enforcement appeal to disregard a failure by the local authority to serve any person with an enforcement notice if neither the appellant nor that person has been "substantially prejudiced" by the failure. In the absence of such express provision, however, the courts will not normally imply a requirement that prejudice be shown.

opportunity to put his case will normally constitute substantial prejudice. In the context of a parole board hearing, however, the parole board is required to make a practical judgment which balances the interests of the prisoner, the public and the informant; and the use of a specially appointed advocate is deemed to mitigate any disadvantage faced by the prisoner due to the lack of notice.[227] Thus, a parole board has been permitted by s.32 of the Criminal Justice Act 1991 to rely on evidence provided by an informant, which had not been disclosed to the prisoner or to his legal representative and which had only been disclosed to a special advocate.[228]

CONSULTATION AND WRITTEN REPRESENTATIONS

In some situations it is sufficient if written representations are considered.[229] Where a duty of "consultation" is placed upon the decision-maker, this is almost always interpreted by the courts to require merely an opportunity to make written representations, or comments upon announced proposals. However, where the words "hearing" or "opportunity to be heard" are used in legislation, they usually[230] require a hearing[231] at which oral submissions and evidence can be tendered. In general, fairness is more likely to require an oral hearing in proceedings before the High Court, as opposed to an administrative tribunal, bearing in mind the kinds of issues that are determined by the court, as opposed to the issues determined by administrative tribunals.[232]   7–052

Standards of consultation

When a duty to entertain written representations is imposed by statute, by way of a duty to consult, what is required of the decision maker in each case to comply with the duty will depend upon the statutory context. But the fundamental requirements of the duty of consultation have been summarised by Lord Woolf: 7–053

---

[227] *R. (on the application of Roberts) v Parole Board* [2005] UKHL 45; [2005] 2 A.C. 738, HL; note Lord Steyn's strong dissent.

[228] *Roberts* [2005] UKHL 45; [2005] 2 A.C. 738, HL at [43], [52]–[56], [60]–[62].

[229] See, e.g. *Naraynsingh v Commissioner of Police* [2004] UKPC 20; (2004) 148 S.J.L.B. 510 (no obligation to hold an oral hearing in relation to revocation of a firearms certificate although on the facts, a more extensive written procedure should have taken place); *R. (on the application of Jemchi) v Visitor of Brunel University* [2003] E.L.R. 125 (not unfair for University Visitor to proceed without an oral hearing). For an example of an oral hearing being required, see *R. v Immigration Tribunal Ex p. Mehmet* [1977] 1 W.L.R. 795.

[230] cf. *R. v Housing Appeal Tribunal* [1920] 3 K.B. 334; and *Lloyd v McMahon* [1987] A.C. 625; *R. v Army Board of the Defence Council Ex p. Anderson* [1992] 1 Q.B. 169; cf. *R. v Hull Prison Board of Visitors Ex p. St Germain (No.2)* [1979] 1 W.L.R. 1401.

[231] Not merely an informal meeting: *Ealing BC v Minister of Housing and Local Government* [1952] Ch. 856.

[232] *R. (on the application of Ewing) v Department for Constitutional Affairs* [2006] EWHC 504; [2006] 2 All E.R. 99 [32].

"To be proper, consultation must be undertaken at a time when proposals are still at a formative stage; it must include sufficient reasons for particular proposals to allow those consulted to give intelligent consideration and an intelligent response; adequate time must be given for this purpose; and the product of consultation must be conscientiously taken into account when the ultimate decision is taken."[233]

7–054 Essentially, in developing standards of consultation, and applying those standards to particular statutory contexts, the courts are using the general principles of fairness to ensure that the consulted party is able properly to address the concerns of the decision-maker.[234] Although consultation must take place at the formative stage, it does not require consultation on every possible option, although there should be consultation on every viable option.[235] Consultation may be phased.[236] It is clearly necessary to consult sufficiently widely;[237] and to give adequate time to those consulted to

[233] *R. v North and East Devon Health Authority Ex p. Coughlan* [2001] Q.B. 213 at [108]; and *R. v Brent LBC Ex p. Gunning* (1985) 84 L.G.R. 168; *R. v Secretary of State for Social Services Ex p. Association of Metropolitan Authorities* [1986] 1 W.L.R. 1, 4 (Webster J. noting that consultation requires that "sufficient information must be supplied by the consulting to the consulted party to enable it to tender helpful advice. Sufficient time must be given by the consulting to the consulted party"); *R. v Gwent CC and Secretary of State for Wales Ex p. Bryant* [1988] C.O.D. 19 (consultation arising from legitimate expectation), where Hodgson J. considered the requirements of fair consultation, and stressed that the process must take place at a sufficiently early stage in the decision-making process for the exercise to be meaningful. cf. *R. v Camden LBC Ex p. Cran* [1995] R.T.R. 346; *R. v Devon CC Ex p. Baker* [1995] 1 All E.R. 73; *R. v Lambeth LBC Ex p. N* [1996] E.L.R. 299; *R. v Secretary of State for Trade and Industry Ex p. UNISON* [1996] I.C.R. 1003; *Desmond v Bromley LBC* (1996) 28 H.L.R. 518 (distinguishing *Ex p. AMA*); *R. v Secretary of State for Transport Ex p. Richmond-upon-Thames* LBC [1996] 1 W.L.R. 1460 (level of detail in consultation sufficient to enable representations).
[234] See, e.g. *R. (on the application of Medway Council) v Secretary of State for Transport, Local Government and the Regions* [2002] EWHC 2516; [2003] J.P.L. 583 at [28] (Maurice Kay J. rejecting the submission that fairness had ceased to be an aspect of consultation: "It is an aspect of what is 'proper'—the word used in Coughlan [108] . . . it is axiomatic that consultation, whether it is a matter of obligation or undertaken voluntarily, requires fairness."); *R. (on the application of Edwards) v Environment Agency* [2006] EWCA Civ 877; [2007] Env. L.R. 9 at [90]–[94], [102]–[106]; *R. (on the application of Greenpeace Ltd) v Secretary of State for Trade and Industry* [2007] EWHC 311; [2007] N.P.C. 21 at [61] (Sullivan J. noting that "the overriding requirement that any consultation must be fair is not in doubt").
[235] *R. (on the application of Montpeliers and Trevors Association v City of Westminster* [2005] EWHC 16; [2006] B.L.G.R. 304; *R. (on the application of Partingdale Lane Residents Association) v Barnet LBC* [2003] EWHC 947. Cf. *R. (on the application of Tinn) v Secretary of State for Transport* [2006] EWHC 193 (claimant had no legitimate expectation that the Secretary of State would have consultation on more than one alignment for a proposed new road); *Medway Council* [2002] EWHC 2516; [2003] J.P.L. 583 (irrational to exclude Gatwick from consultation exercise over future development of air transport in south-east England).
[236] *R. (on the application of Parents for Legal Action Ltd) v Northumberland CC* [2006] EWHC 1081; [2006] B.L.G.R. 646.
[237] See, e.g. *R. (on the application of Wainwright) v Richmond upon Thames LBC* [2001] EWCA Civ 2062 (criticising, although not invalidating due to other circumstances, a consultation in respect of a toucan crossing in which the council had not ensured that one letter per flat was mailed).

respond.[238] Proper consultation requires the "candid disclosure of the reasons for what is proposed"[239] and that consulted parties are aware of the criteria to be adopted and any factors considered to be decisive or of substantial importance.[240] Consultation documents "should be clear as to their purpose".[241] The consultation must also be in respect of proposals, rather than merely a bland generality. Where the decision-maker has access to important documents which are material to its determination whose contents the public would have a legitimate interest in knowing, these documents should be disclosed as part of the consultation process.[242] While consultation requires that sufficient reasons be given for the particular proposals to enable those consulted to give intelligent consideration and an intelligent response to the proposals, it does not usually require that sufficient information be given about any objections to the proposals to enable those consulted to give intelligent consideration and an intelligent response to the objections.[243] Moreover, in general, there is no duty to re-consult unless there is a "fundamental difference" between the proposals consulted on and those which the consulting party subsequently wishes to adopt,[244] or if, after consultation has concluded, the decision-maker becomes aware of some internal material or a factor of potential significance to the decision to be made.[245] A consultation may be vitiated

---

[238] *R. v Secretary of State for Education and Employment Ex p. National Union of Teachers* [2000] Ed. C.R. 603 (four days was an insufficient period for consultation in respect of imposing an obligation on teachers to engage in assessment of their peers); *R. (on the application of Anvac Chemical UK Ltd) v Secretary of State for Environment, Food and Rural Affairs* [2001] EWHC Admin 1011; [2002] A.C.D 219 at [63] (noting that a period of notification of two days was too short, even taking into account the urgent situation prior to suspension of use of a pesticide).

[239] *R. (on the application of L) v Barking and Dagenham LBC* [2001] EWCA Civ 533 at [13] (Schiemann L.J.); and *R. (on the application of Madden) v Bury MBC* [2002] EWHC 1882 at [58]; *R. v Secretary of State for Transport Ex p. Richmond Upon Thames LBC* [1995] Env L.R. 390 at 405 (misleading consultation paper rendering the consultation process flawed); *R. (on the application of Westminster City Council) v Mayor of London* [2002] EWHC 2440; [2003] L.G.R. 611 at [27] (noting that adequate information had been provided in a consultation as to the Congestion Charging Scheme for London as to enable consultees to make an "intelligent response").

[240] *R. (on the application of Capenhurst) v Leicester City Council* [2004] EWHC 2124 at [46].

[241] *Greenpeace* [2007] EWHC 311; [2007] N.P.C. at [74] (Sullivan J. distinguishing between putting an "issues paper" to the public and putting "policy proposals" to the public).

[242] *Edwards* [2006] EWCA Civ 877 [2007] Env L.R. 9 at [94].

[243] *R. (on the application of Beale) v Camden LBC* [2004] EWHC 6 at [19] (Munby J.). See further *R. (on the application of Ramda) v Secretary of State for the Home Department* [2002] EWHC 1278 at [25] ("the Home Secretary is not required to be drawn into a never-ending dialogue"); *R. v Secretary of State for Wales Ex p. Williams* [1997] E.L.R. 100 (no duty to prolong consultation to allow everybody to comment on everybody else's comments).

[244] *R. (on the application of Smith) v East Kent Hospital NHS Trust* [2002] EWHC 2640 at [45]. *cf. R. (on the application of Carton) v Coventry City Council* (2001) 4 C.C.L.R. 41 at 44 (further consultation was required where a fundamental change in day-care charging arrangements from those originally proposed).

[245] *Edwards* [2006] EWHC 877; [2007] Env L.R. 9 at [103]; *Interbrew SA and Interbrew UK Holdings Ltd v The Competition Commission and the Secretary of State for Trade and Industry* [2001] E.C.C. 40 at [33]–[35]; *R. v Secretary of State for Health Ex p. United States Tobacco International Inc* [1992] Q.B. 353 at 370–371, 376; *Greenpeace* [2007] EWHC 311; [2007] N.P.C. 21 at [116]. *cf. Withers v First Secretary of State* [2005] EWCA Civ 1119 (no additional factual findings made).

however where errors have been made by either the consulted party or the adviser.[246]

Considering the representations

7–055   It is necessary for proper consideration to be given to representations made in the consultation and the government authority must "have embarked on the consultation process prepared to change course, if persuaded by it to do so".[247] This is not however a duty not to make a decision without prior agreement of the consulted parties.[248] As is the case where written representations are required, the courts may be in a poor position to ensure that the decision-maker considers those representations. At the lowest, the courts will attempt to ensure that all written representations are before the decision-maker when the decision is made, and will quash a decision made in disregard of representations.[249] Nevertheless, where a large-scale consultation exercise has been carried out, the courts may be effectively powerless to ensure that representations have been read and digested unless the decision-maker is required to address representations received by way of reasons.[250] Furthermore, where consultations are invited upon detailed proposals which have already been arrived at, the duty of the court to ensure that genuine consideration has been given to critical representations is taxed to the utmost.[251]

[246] R. (on the application of Goldsmith) v Wandsworth LBC [2004] EWCA Civ 1170; (2004) 7 C.C.L. Rep. 472 at [66]–[77] (decision to terminate residential placement was vitiated by flaws by the Care Panel whose recommendations it adopted, since the Panel had failed to keep minutes, give reasons, take account of a relevant care assessment and allow the claimant's daughter to attend a meeting). But if the error had no effect on the final outcome, a court may declare the consultation unfair but refuse relief: Edwards [2006] EWHC 877; [2007] Env L.R. 9 (the Environment Agency had breached its common law duty of fairness by relying on internal reports which it failed to disclose, but the court was entitled to refuse relief since there was, on the evidence no environmental harm from the plant and the relevant regulatory systems enabled assessment made on what was known rather than predicted by old assessments, such that it would be pointless to quash the permit simply to enable the public to be consulted on data which was now out of date). On refusal of relief, see 18–00.
[247] R. v Barnet LBC Ex p. B [1994] E.L.R. 357 at 375.
[248] R. (on the application of Smith) v East Kent Hospital NHS Trust [2002] EWHC 2640; (2003) 6 C.C.L. Rep. 251 at [61].
[249] See e.g. R. v Manchester Metropolitan University Ex p. Nolan, The Independent, July 15, 1993 (examination board's disciplinary decision taken in ignorance of written testimonials and psychiatric evidence quashed, where applicant had no right to attend and was "entirely dependent" on what was placed before the board).
[250] See 7–087.
[251] See, e.g. R. v Hillingdon Health Authority Ex p. Goodwin [1984] I.C.R. 800 for the extent to which a proposed scheme may be developed in advance of a consultation process; compare Rollo v Minister of Town and Country Planning [1948] 1 All E.R. 13. But see R. v Camden LBC Ex p. Cran [1995] R.T.R. 346 (consultation should have taken place before the Council's "mind was made up").

The increasing importance of consultation

Finally, the importance of an appropriate consultation procedure has been **7–056** given greater emphasis by the government in recent times. The Cabinet Office Code of Practice on Written Consultation[252] applies to consultation documents issued after January 1, 2001. It sets out six "consultation criteria" which require government departments and agencies to: first, consult widely throughout the process, allowing a minimum of 12 weeks for written consultation at least once during the development of the policy; second, be clear about what the proposals are, who may be affected, what questions are being asked and the timescale for responses; third, ensure that the consultation is clear, concise and widely accessible; fourth, give feedback regarding the responses received and how the consultation process influenced the policy; fifth, monitor the department's effectiveness at consultation, perhaps including the use of a designated consultation co-ordinator; and sixth, ensure that the consultation follows better regulation best practice, including carrying out a Regulatory Impact Assessment if appropriate. Though the code does not have legal force, and cannot prevail over statutory or mandatory external requirements,[253] it should otherwise generally be regarded as binding on UK departments and their agencies, unless Ministers conclude that exceptional circumstances require a departure from it.[254]

DUTY OF ADEQUATE DISCLOSURE BEFORE A DECISION IS TAKEN

The level of disclosure required

If prejudicial allegations are to be made against a person, he must normally, **7–057** as we have seen, be given particulars of them before the hearing so that he can prepare his answers.[255] The level of detail required must be such as to

---

[252] Revised edition, January 2004, *http://www.cabinetoffice.gov.uk/regulation/consultation/code/index.asp* (last accessed July 6, 2007).
[253] See, e.g. European Community law (see 14–009); on the binding force of policy, see 8–032, 12–00 (legitimate expectation).
[254] For discussion of whether there is a need for greater consultation rights, see: P. Cane, *Administrative Law*, 4th edn. (2004); R. Baldwin and J. Houghton, "Circular Arguments: The Status and Legitimacy of Administrative Rules" [1986] P.L. 239; P. Craig *Public Law and Democracy in the United Kingdom and in the United States* (1990), pp.160–182.
[255] See 7–043. In *Council of Civil Service Unions v Minister for the Civil Service* [1985] A.C. 374 at 415 (Lord Roskill: legitimate expectations can take many forms including, "an expectation of being allowed time to make representations"); *Hadmor Productions v Hamilton* [1983] 1 A.C. 191 at 233 (Lord Diplock—one of the most fundamental rules of natural justice "[is] the right . . . to be informed of any point adverse . . . that is going to be relied upon . . . and to be given an opportunity of stating what his answer to it is"); *Bushell v Secretary of State for Environment* [1981] A.C. 75 at 96 (Lord Diplock); *McDonald v Lanarkshire Fire Brigade Joint Committee* 1959 S.C. 141 (particulars of disciplinary allegations

enable the making of "meaningful and focused representations".[256] In order to protect his interests, the person must also be enabled to controvert, correct or comment on other evidence or information that may be relevant to the decision and influential material on which the decision-maker intends to rely;[257] including, in certain cases, disclosure of representations or information provided by third parties.[258] At least in some circumstances there will also be a duty on the decision-maker to disclose information favourable to the applicant, as well as information prejudicial to his case.[259] If material is available before the hearing, the right course will usually be to give him advance notification; but it cannot be said that there is a hard and fast rule on this matter, and sometimes natural justice will be held to be satisfied if the material is divulged at the hearing, which may have to be adjourned if he cannot fairly be expected to make his reply

communicated only after undue delay); *R. v Department of Health Ex p. Gandhi* [1991] 1 W.L.R. 1053. Reference should also be made to the requirement to give reasons for a decision, 7–087. A reaffirmation of the courts' approach was provided in *R. v Secretary of State for the Home Department Ex p. Duggan* [1994] 3 All E.R. 277 (Div Ct held that prisoner serving a life sentence for murder is entitled, subject to necessary exceptions due to public interest immunity, to be informed of the gist of any matter of facts or opinion relevant to his security re-categorisation and to reasons for any decision to maintain him as a "category A" prisoner); *R. (on the application of Lord) v Secretary of State for the Home Department* [2003] EWHC 2073 at [60] (gist of the security report should state in terms whether the views expressed are unanimous or not; where views are divided, should indicate the numbers of views pro and con; and should set out the gist of each of the reported views); *R. v Hampshire CC Ex p. K* [1990] 2 Q.B. 71 (duty of local authorities in child abuse cases to be open and to disclose all relevant material); *R. (on the application of Ramda) v Secretary of State for the Home Department* [2002] EWHC 1278 at [25] (Sedley L.J. noting that in extradition proceedings the Home Secretary "must not rely on potentially influential material which is withheld from the individual affected").

[256] *R. v Secretary of State for the Home Department Ex p. Harry* [1998] 1 W.L.R. 1737 at 1748.

[257] *R. (on the application of Ramda) v Secretary of State for the Home Department* [2002] EWHC 1278 at [25]; *R. (on the application of Banks) v Secretary of State for the Environment, Food and Rural Affairs* [2004] EWHC 416; [2004] N.P.C. 43 at [104] (noting that DEFRA deliberately refused to disclose highly material information to the claimants); *Wiseman v Borneman* [1971] A.C. 297 at 309; *R. (on the application of O'Leary) v Chief Constable of the Merseyside Police* [2001] EWHC Admin 57 at [16] (noting that it was unfair not to disclose and allow comment on departmental report relied on in imposing employment restrictions); *R. (on the application of Bentley) v HM Coroner District of Avon* [2001] EWHC Admin 170; (2002) 166 J.P. 297; (unfair to coroner not to have made advance disclosure of witness statements); *Sheridan v Stanley Cole (Wainfleet) Ltd* [2003] EWCA Civ 1046; [2003] 4 All E.R. 1181 (unfair for EAT not to allow chance to make representations on new authorities relied on, if central to its decision); *cf. R. (on the application of Bedford) v Islington LBC* [2002] EWHC 2044; [2003] Env L.R. 463 at [102] (no unfairness in non-disclosure of confidential information relating to planning application).

[258] See, e.g. *R. (on the application of Anglian Water Services Ltd) v Environment Agency* [2003] EWHC 1506; [2004] Env. L.R. 15 at [26] (unfair for EA not to disclose residents' representations for sewerage company to comment, where there was a dispute as to whether to impose a requirement to provide a public sewer).

[259] *Re D (Minors) (Adoption Reports: Confidentiality)* [1996] A.C. 593 at 603 (Lord Mustill: "It is a first principle of fairness that each party to a judicial process shall have the opportunity to answer by evidence and argument any adverse material which the tribunal may take into account when forming its opinion"); *R. v Secretary of state for the Home Department Ex p. Fayed* [1998] 1 W.L.R. 763 (duty on Secretary of State to disclose his concerns in application for citizenship).

without time for consideration.[260] In deciding whether fairness does or does not require an adjournment in order to allow further time to consider such material and to prepare representations, a court or other decision-maker should take into account the importance of the proceedings and the likely adverse consequences on the party seeking the adjournment; the risk that the applicant would be prejudiced; the risk of prejudice to any opponent if the adjournment were granted; the convenience of the Court and the interests of justice in ensuring the efficient despatch of business; and the extent to which the applicant has been responsible for the circumstances leading to the request for an adjournment.[261]

Failure to made adequate disclosure

If relevant evidential material is not disclosed at all to a party who is 7–058 potentially prejudiced by this, there is *prima facie* unfairness, irrespective of whether the material in question arose before, during or after the hearing. This proposition can be illustrated by a large number of cases involving the use of undisclosed reports by decision-makers.[262] If the deciding body is or has the trappings of a judicial tribunal and receives or appears to receive evidence *ex parte* which is not fully disclosed, or holds *ex parte* (without notice to others involved) inspections during the course or after the conclusion of the hearing, the case for setting the decision aside is obviously very strong; the maxim that justice must be seen to be done can readily be invoked.[263] If an appellate tribunal has communications with a

---

[260] See 7–066.

[261] *R. v Kingston-upon-Thames Justices Ex p. Martin* [1994] Imm. A.R. 172; and 7–066; *R. (on the application of Turner) v Highbury Corner Magistrates' Court* [2005] EWHC 2568; [2006] 1 W.L.R. 220 at [35]–[38].

[262] See, e.g. *Kanda v Government of Malaya* [1962] A.C. 322; *R. (on the application of A) v Liverpool City Council* [2007] EWHC 1477; *R. v Milk Marketing Board Ex p. North* (1934) 50 T.L.R. 559; *R. v Westminster (City of) Assessment Committee* [1941] 1 K.B. 53; *R. v Architects' Registration Tribunal Ex p. Jaggar* [1945] 2 All E.R. 131; *R. v Kent Police Authority Ex p. Godden* [1971] 2 Q.B. 662; *Fairmount Investments Ltd v Secretary of State for the Environment* [1976] 1 W.L.R. 1255; *Chief Constable for North Wales Police v Evans* [1982] 1 W.L.R. 1155; *R. v Hampshire CC Ex p. K* [1990] 2 Q.B. 71; *R. v Enfield LBC Ex p. TF Unwin (Roydon) Ltd* (1989) 46 B.L.R. 1, DC. For the general rule, see *Board of Education v Rice* [1911] A.C. 179 at 182. And see *Shareef v Commissioner for Registration of Indian and Pakistani Residents* [1966] A.C. 47 (inadequate disclosure of relevant reports).

[263] See, e.g. *R. v Bodmin Justices Ex p. McEwen* [1947] K.B. 321; *Fowler v Fowler* [1963] 2 W.L.R. 155 (courts); *R. v Birmingham City Magistrate Ex p. Chris Foreign foods (Wholesalers) Ltd* [1970] 1 W.L.R. 1428 (magistrate condemning food); *Eastcheap Dried Fruit Co v NV Gebroeders Catz' Handelsvereeniging* [1962] 1 Lloyd's Rep. 283 (arbitrators); *R. v Newmarket Assessment Committee* [1945] 2 All E.R. 371; *R. v Deputy Industrial Injuries Commissioner Ex p. Jones* [1962] 2 Q.B. 677 (statutory tribunals); *Taylor v National Union of Seamen* [1967] 1 W.L.R. 532 (trade unions); *R. v Home Secretary Ex p. Georghiades* (1992) 5 Admin L.R. 457 (parole board); and *Re Gregson and Armstrong* (1894) 70 L.T. 106 and *Goold v Evans* [1951] 2 T.L.R. 1189; *Errington v Minister of Health* [1935] 1 K.B. 249; *Hibemian Property Co Ltd v Secretary of State for the Environment* (1974) 27 P. & C.R. 197; and; *Barrs v British Wool Marketing Board* 1957 S.C. 72; *Clark v Wellington Rent Appeal Board* [1975] 2 N.Z.L.R. 24 at 28–30 on the impropriety of ex parte views; *cf. Salsbury v Woodland* [1970] 1

tribunal of first instance with a view to altering the original decision, the parties to the proceedings before that tribunal ought to be notified so that they can make further submissions.[264] *A fortiori*, it can be a breach of fairness for an appellate authority, or a body receiving the report of the appellate authority, to hold private interviews with witnesses.[265] In relation to central government decision-making, especially on issues of policy, the duty of disclosure may be lessened in respect of information originating within the government department. When a minister considers whether to grant a planning application following a local inquiry and consequent report by the inspector, he is under no obligation to disclose to objectors or to give them an opportunity of commenting on advice, expert or otherwise, which he receives from the department in the course of making up his mind.[266] And where the Parliamentary Commissioner for Administration has produced a draft report pursuant to an individual's complaint passed to him by the complainant's Member of Parliament, the Ombudsman does not act unfairly or contrarily to natural justice in sending a copy of the draft report to the government department involved but not to the complainant, since it is the department rather than the complainant which is being investigated and which may have to justify its conduct before a parliamentary select committee and face public criticism.[267]

Q.B. 324 and *Gibbons (Tony) v DPP* December 12, 2000 on the circumstances in which an unaccompanied view is permissible; *R. v Lilydale Magistrates' Court Ex p. Ciccone* [1973] V.R. 122 on the suspicions of bias that may arise from the travelling arrangements; compare *R. v Ely Justices Ex p. Burgess* [1992] Crim.L.R. 888; *R. v Green* [1950] 1 All E.R. 38 and *R. v Furlong, ibid.* at 636 on the impropriety of private communications between judge and jury: see also the discussion on bias in relation to the limits of propriety in communications between justices and their clerks in 10–00; and *Fisher v Keane* (1879) 11 Ch.D. 353 on ex parte (without notice) hearings in club expulsion cases.

[264] *R. v Huntingdon Confirming Authority* [1929] 1 K.B. 698. Cf. *The Corchester* [1957] P. 84.
[265] *Palmer v Inverness Hospitals Committee* 1963 S.C. 311; *Wilcox v H.G.S* [1976] I.C.R. 306; *Fairmount Investments Ltd v Secretary of State for the Environment* [1976] 1 W.L.R. 1255 at 1266 (Lord Russell) (a person concerned has the right not to be "taken by surprise in a relevantly unfair way by the conclusions of the inspector"). But where a minister legitimately declines to hold a public inquiry in respect of a planning application, it would appear that he need not give to objectors the written representations of those supporting the scheme: *Binney v Secretary of State for the Environment* [1984] J.P.L. 871 (although Webster J. did not reach a final conclusion on the point).
[266] *Bushell v Secretary of State for the Environment* [1981] A.C. 75 at 102, HL (Lord Diplock); and *R. v Secretary of State for Education and Science Ex p. S* [1995] C.O.D. 48; *R. v Secretary of State for the Environment, Transport and the Regions Ex p. Holdings & Barnes Plc* ("*Alconbury*") [2001] UKHL 23; [2003] 2 A.C. 295. Further, the HL held in Bushell that even where the post-inquiry evidence contradicts or modifies evidence given at the inquiry, the Secretary of State is not obliged to reopen the inquiry. However, if the new evidence is on a matter of central importance rather than (as in *Bushell*) on a matter held to be tangential or irrelevant to the inquiry, there would be a duty to reopen the inquiry, or to afford individuals the right to make further written representations; *R. v Secretary of State for Health Ex p. US Tobacco International Inc* [1992] Q.B. 353, DC; *R. (on the application of Edwards) v Environment Agency* [2006] EWCA Civ 877; [2007] Env. L.R. 9 at [92]–[94] see n.245.
[267] *R. v Parliamentary Commissioner for Administration Ex p. Dyer* [1994] 1 W.L.R. 621 (applied in *R. (on the application of Cavanagh) v Health Service Commissioner* [2004] EWHC 1847, overturned on other grounds in [2005] EWCA Civ 1578; [2006] 1 W.L.R. 1229 (but consider whether in some circumstances the complainant's interest in receiving fair consideration of his or her complaint might not in fairness demand that the draft report be disclosed to him or her)).

Exceptions

To the general rule there are various exceptions, some of which have **7–059** already been indicated. There are cases where disclosure of evidential material might inflict serious harm on the person directly concerned (e.g. disclosure of a distressing medical report to a claimant for a social security benefit)[268] or other persons;[269] where disclosure would be a breach of confidence or might be injurious to the public interest (e.g. because it would involve the revelation of official secrets, inhibit frankness of comment and the detection of crime, and might make it impossible to obtain certain classes of essential information at all in the future);[270] or where disclosure is sought of sensitive intelligence information.[271] Where a committee is entitled to sit in private session, it is not obliged to disclose legal advice of its officers to persons with a right to be heard, or to invite representations on the advice.[272] In such situations the person claiming to be aggrieved should nevertheless be adequately apprised of the case he has to answer, subject to the need for withholding details in order to protect other overriding interests.[273] An argument relying upon mere administrative inconvenience—for example, in having to prepare and disclose summaries of evidence which cannot itself be disclosed—is unlikely to succeed.[274]

---

[268] *R. v Kent Police Authority Ex p. Godden* [1971] 2 Q.B. 662 (undisclosed official psychiatric report on police officer; court ordered disclosure to officer's own medical adviser but not to the officer himself). *cf. Re WLW* [1972] Ch. 456 (report on condition of mental patient).

[269] *R. v Harrow Borough Ex p. D* [1990] 2 All E.R. 12 (mother not told that she was suspected child abuser justified by need to protect interests of the child). This case has been criticised: Beloff n.378.

[270] *R. v Lewes Justices Ex p. Gaming Board of Great Britain* [1973] A.C. 388; *R. v Secretary of State for the Home Department Ex p. Hickey* [1995] Q.B. 43, CA; *cf. R. v Poole BC Ex p. Cooper* (1995) 27 H.L.R. 605 (information received by local authority during statutory inquiries about homelessness of housing applicant could not be protected from disclosure on ground of confidentiality). *R. v Joint Higher Committee on Surgical Training Ex p. Milner* (1995) 7 Admin L.R. 454 (Committee not obliged to disclose references to applicant for accreditation as surgeon; interests of confidentiality outweighed applicant's interest in disclosure).

[271] *R. (on the application of Tucker) v Director General of the National Crime Squad* [2003] EWCA Civ 2; [2003] I.C.R. 599 (although the decision to terminate the appellant's secondment to the National Crime Squad did not involve sufficient public law elements to justify susceptibility to judicial review (see 3–00), the CA added that fairness did not require that reasons should be given for the termination given the sensitivity of the work of the National Crime Squad).

[272] *Stoop v Kensington and Chelsea LBC* [1992] 1 P.L.R. 58 (local authority planning and conservation committee).

[273] *R. v Gaming Board for Great Britain Ex p. Benaim and Khaida* [1970] 2 Q.B. 417 (how much information ought to be disclosed to applicants for consents to run gaming clubs); *R. v Secretary of State for the Home Department Ex p. Hosenball* [1977] 1 W.L.R. 766 (intelligence information and deportation); *R. v Secretary of State for the Home Department Ex p. Duggan* [1994] 3 All E.R. 277.

[274] *Ex p. Duggan* [1994] 3 All E.R. 277.

JUDICIAL AND OFFICIAL NOTICE

7–060 Against this background one must consider the concept of judicial notice, which in administrative law shades off into what is known in the United States as "official notice".[275] Courts, which are required to decide cases on the basis of the rules of evidence, are also allowed to take judicial notice of matters of common knowledge, and these need not be put to the parties before them. How far judicial notice can properly extend is not altogether clear. The general principle is "that a person exercising judicial functions is not justified in noticing directly or indirectly by statement or otherwise facts within his private knowledge. He ought to be sworn and state them as a witness".[276] Exceptionally (if, for example, magistrates propose to take into account their impressions of a party before them, derived from earlier proceedings in which he was involved),[277] an adjudicator may be permitted to use his personal knowledge, provided that there is no real danger of bias and the matter to be taken into account is clearly disclosed to the party concerned.[278] In one case,[279] an appeal was lodged against an acquittal by lay magistrates, on the ground that one of them had used his medical expertise during their retirement to consider their verdict, to persuade them to reject the only evidence given on a particular issue. The appeal was dismissed; such expertise may properly be used to evaluate evidence given, but not to contradict evidence or introduce new evidence that should be made available to the parties.[280] Characteristic of the standards appropriate for administrative adjudication was the attitude adopted towards arbitrators deciding workmen's compensation cases, who were permitted to draw on their own accumulated knowledge of general and local labour conditions to supplement evidence, but were obliged to disclose their thoughts to the claimant if non-disclosure would unfairly deprive him of his right to lead evidence or tender submissions on specific facts in issue.[281]

[275] For a critical survey of the American doctrine, see R. Pierce, *Administrative Law Treatise*, 4th edn. (2002), pp.741–758; J. Smillie, "The Problem of 'Official Notice'" [1975] P.L. 64.

[276] *R. (on the application of Giant's Causeway, etc., Tramway Co) v Antrim Justices* [1895] 2 I.R. 603. 649; and *Re Frank Bros Ltd and Hamilton Board of Police Cmrs* (1967) 63 D.L.R. (2nd) 309.

[277] *Thomas v Thomas* [1961] 1 W.L.R. 1; *Brinkley v Brinkley* [1965] P. 75; cf. *Munday v Munday* [1954] 1 W.L.R. 1078; *Dugdale v Kraft Foods Ltd* [1977] I.C.R. 487 at 54–55.

[278] See Ch.10.

[279] *Wetherall v Harrison* [1976] Q.B. 773. The court did warn, however, against the expert's unduly pressing his opinion upon his non-expert colleagues.

[280] For a stricter approach to the problem see *R. v Prosser* (1836) 7 C. & P 648; and *R. v Field Ex p. White* (1895) 64 L.J.M.C. 158. Cf. Minister's duty to disclose evidence upon which he relies when disagreeing with a finding of fact by an inspector in a planning or compulsory purchase appeal.

[281] See, e.g. *Peart v Bolckow, Vaughan & Co* [1925] 1 K.B. 399; *Reynolds v Llanelly Associated Tinplate Co* [1948] 1 All E.R. 140; and generally, *Learmonth Property Investment Co v Aitken* 1971 S.L.T. 349 at 356; on industrial tribunals, see, e.g. *Dugdale v Kraft Foods Ltd* [1976] 1 W.L.R. 1288 at 1294–1295; *Adda International Ltd v Curcio* [1976] I.C.R. 407; *Spurling v Development Underwriting (Vic.) Pty Ltd* [1973] V.R. 1 at 10; *Bowman v DPP*

Public authorities may be set up because they already have or can be 7–061
expected to acquire specialised expertise. Clearly they are entitled to use
their expertise to draw inferences from evidence. If a decision-maker is
under an obligation to observe the rules of evidence it cannot use its own
expert opinion as a substitute for evidence,[282] though it may still be able to
rely on an extended concept of judicial notice to supplement evidence. But
a number of special tribunals are not bound by the strict rules of evidence.
They are charged with the task of actively finding the material facts by any
appropriate means; they may be permitted to adopt inquisitorial procedures,[283] undertake unaccompanied inspections,[284] consult experts[285] and
use their own technical and local knowledge[286] and their past experience
which may be based on evidence given in previous cases;[287] their final
decision may, in some cases, be based on broad considerations of public
policy. They are nevertheless obliged to act fairly. And this means that, in
the absence of contrary intendment, they must not place a party at a
disadvantage by depriving him of an adequate opportunity of commenting
on material relevant to their decision if it is gleaned from an outside
source[288] or in the course of their own investigations,[289] or from evidence

---

[282] *Moxon v Minister of Pensions* [1945] K.B. 490.
[283] cf. *R. v Medical Appeal Tribunal (North Midland Region) Ex p. Hubble* [1958] 2 Q.B. 228
at 240 241; affirmed [1959] 2 Q.B. 408.
[284] cf. *R. v Brighton & Area Rent Tribunal Ex p. Marine Parade Estates (936) Ltd* [1950] 2 K.B.
410. cf. *Halsey v Esso Petroleum Co* [1961] 1 W.L.R. 683 at 689; *Salsbury v Woodlund*
[1970] 1 Q.B. 324 (unaccompanied view by judge). For recognition of the greater flexibility
given in this respect to inspectors conducting public local inquiries, see *Fairmount Investments
Ltd v Secretary of State for the Environment* [1976] 1 W.L.R. 1255 at 1264; *Hickmott v
Dorset CC* (1977) 35 P. & C.R. 195.
[285] cf. *R. v Deputy Industrial Injuries Commissioner Ex p. Jones* [1962] 2 Q.B. 677; and
Wislang v Medical Practitioners Disciplinary Committee [1974] 1 N.Z.L.R. 29 (no duty to
disclose legal advice obtained from outside the tribunal on a point of law upon which the
individual had addressed the tribunal).
[286] *Croft on Investment Trust Ltd v Greater London Rent Assessment Committee* [1967] 2 Q.B.
955; also *R. v Brighton Rent Officers Ex p. Elliott* (1975) 29 P. & C.R. 456 (rent officer not
required to disclose before the statutory consultation with the parties, the properties with
which he proposed to compare the premises in question); *Kalil v Bray* [1977] 1 N.S.W.L.R.
256 (specialist tribunal may rely on its own expertise to reject otherwise uncontradicted lay
evidence).
[287] cf. *R. v Deputy Industrial Injuries Commissioner Ex p. Moore* [1965] 1 Q.B. 456.
[288] As in *Jones* [1962] 2 Q.B. 677; *Hibernian Property Co Ltd v Secretary of State for the
Environment* (1974) 27 P. & C.R. 197 (views of occupiers favouring demolition of unfit
houses).
[289] *R. v Paddington & St Marylebone Rent Tribunal Ex p. Bell, London & Provincial Properties
Ltd* [1949] 1 K.B. 666 at 682 (important evidential point commented on during inspection
but not properly put to landlords); *Croft on Investment Trust Ltd v Greater London Rent
Assessment Committee* [1967] 2 Q.B. 955 at 968 (dictum); *Fairmount* [1976] 1 W.L.R. 1255
1265 (inspection revealed evidence of an aspect of unfitness not relied upon at inquiry); and
Hickmott v Dorset CC (1977) 35 P. & C.R. 195; *Edward Ware New Homes Ltd v Secretary of
State for Transport, Local Government and the Regions* [2003] EWCA Civ 566; [2004] 1 P. &
C.R. 6 at [22]–[23]; *Wigan MBC v Secretary of State for the Environment* [2001] EWCA
Admin 587; [2002] J.P.L. 417, 425; *Castleford Homes v Secretary of State for the
Environment* [2001] P. L.C.R. 470 at [65].

given in earlier cases.[290]An important consideration is whether the person who is affected by the decision could or could not be expected to anticipate what happened. That person should be mindful of his own interests. Accordingly, the doctrine of "official notice" is more readily applicable where the information relied upon is drawn from the general, accumulated experience of the decision-maker, rather than from an identifiable source upon which he has relied, whether it be another person, particular documents or specific prior events. As yet the case law gives no clear indication of the extent to which decision-makers will be permitted to abstain from disclosing during the hearing their own expert opinions, or information relevant to the exercise of their discretion.[291] The courts will lean in favour of imposing judicial standards as far as practicable,[292] so that if a person is misled as to the basis on which the decision-maker is likely to decide and is thus placed at a material disadvantage in putting his case, he may be held to have been denied procedural fairness.[293]

HEARINGS

7–062 A fair "hearing" does not necessarily mean that there must be an opportunity to be heard orally: "one is entitled to an oral hearing where fairness requires that there should be such a hearing, but fairness does not require that there should be an oral hearing in every case".[294]

---

[290] *Moore* [1965] 1 Q.B. 456 at 466–468, 489–490 (dicta); *Re Martin (John) & Co Ltd* (1974) 8 S.A.S.R. 237, where on the facts an opportunity to rebut the evidence was found to have been given.

[291] *cf.* R. Pierce. Davis's general position (see n.275) that matters of policy and material affecting the exercise of discretion should, as far as is practicable, be disclosed but be controvertible by argument rather than the adduction of evidence.

[292] See, e.g. *Learmonth* 1971 S.L.T. 349 *Brighton Rent Officers* (n.286), (tribunal entitled to use local knowledge but not undisclosed knowledge of particular facts in issue). *cf.* however, *Wetherall* [1976] Q.B. 773.

[293] *Shareef v Commissioner for Registration of Indian and Pakistani Residents* [1966] A.C. 47 (applicant's advocate misled as to importance attached by tribunal to specific item of evidence; decision quashed); *Societe Franco-Tunisienne d'Ammement-Tunis v Government of Ceylon* [1959] 1 W.L.R. 787 (arbitration; giving the decision on basis of point of law not raised at the hearing is misconduct; quaere whether this would be regarded as a breach of natural justice in proceedings before an administrative tribunal); *Re Chien Sign-Shou* [1967] 1 W.L.R. 1155; *Re Simeon* [1935] 2 K.B. 183; and *R. v Criminal Injuries Compensation Board Ex p. Ince* [1973] 1 W.L.R. 1334 at 1344–1345; *cf.* *British Oxygen Co Ltd v Board of Trade* [1971] A.C. 610; *Withers v The First Secretary of State* [2005] EWCA Civ 1119; [2002] 4 P.L.R. 102 at [27] (noting that this was not a case where the inspector had made factual findings without permitting the parties to comment). *cf.* *Drewitt v Price Tribunal* [1959] N.Z.L.R. 21 (parties inadequately aware of basis of decision, but no fault attributable).

[294] *R. (on the application of Ewing) v Department for Constitutional Affairs* [2006] EWHC 504; [2006] 2 All E.R. 99 at [27]; *R. (on the application of West) v Parole Board* [2005] UKHL 1; [2005] 1 W.L.R. 350 (where a Parole Board is resolving challenges to licence revocations, whether an oral hearing is necessary depends on the circumstances of each case; and it is likely to be necessary where facts are in issue that could affect the outcome or where it might otherwise contribute to achieving a just decision). On the importance of an oral hearing

Requirements at an oral hearing

A person who is entitled to be heard orally, or who is given an oral hearing   7-063
as a matter of discretion under a power conferred by statutory or other
formal rules,[295] must be allowed an adequate opportunity of putting his
own case. As noted above, he will normally be entitled to that opportunity,
particularly where there is some dispute as to material facts or other matter
on which oral argument will be of assistance to the decision-maker.[296] If he
has a right to appear, it will, of course, be a breach of that right, in
addition to being unfair, for the decision-maker to refuse, deliberately or
through inadvertence, to hear him[297] or even to allow him to be present.[298]
His right to be heard must not be stultified by constant interruptions.
Nevertheless, the right to an oral hearing does not in all cases confer the
right to be personally present at the hearing, if the case is being conducted
by a representative. Thus the Secretary of State was entitled to require a

though, see: *Sengupta v Holmes* [2002] EWCA Civ 1104 at [38] (Laws L.J. referring to "the
central place accorded to oral argument in our common law adversarial system. This I think is
important, because oral argument is perhaps the most powerful force there is, in our legal
process, to promote a change of mind by the judge. That judges in fact change their minds
under the influence of oral argument is not an arcane feature of the system; it is at the centre
of it").

[295] On "voluntary" hearings, see 7–00, and for situations where there is no right to an oral
hearing, see *Lloyd v McMahon* [1987] A.C. 625 and 7–00.

[296] *R. (on the application of Thompson) v Law Society* [2004] EWCA Civ 167; [2004] 1
W.L.R. 2522 at [51] (asking whether any "disputed issue of fact which was central to the
Adjudication Panel's assessment in [the claimant's] case and which could not fairly be resolved
without hearing oral evidence and without an oral hearing"); *R. v Criminal Injuries
Compensation Board Ex p. Dickson* [1997] 1 W.L.R. 58 (applicant not entitled to oral hearing
because no dispute as to primary facts); *R. v Criminal Injuries Compensation Board Ex p.
Cook* [1996] 1 W.L.R. 1037, CA; *cf. R. v Criminal Injuries Compensation Board Ex p. Singh
(Amrik)* [1996] C.O.D. 149; *R. v Secretary of State for Wales Ex p. Emery* [1996] 4 All E.R. 1
(conflict of documentary evidence as to footpath should have been tested at public inquiry;
Secretary of State acted unfairly in deciding without convening inquiry); *R. v Secretary of
State for the Home Department Ex p. Khanafer* [1996] Imm. A.R. 212; *R. v Cardinal
Newman's School, Birmingham Ex p. S* [1998] E.L.R. 304.

[297] *R. v Birkenhead Justices Ex p. Fisher* [1962] 1 W.L.R. 1410; *R. v Gravesend Justices Ex p.
Sheldon* [1968] 1 W.L.R. 1699; *R. v Kingston-upon-Hull Rent Tribunal Ex p. Black* (1949) 65
T.L.R. 209; *Chettiar v Chettiar* [1962] 1 W.L.R. 279; *Malloch v Aberdeen Corp* [1971] 1
W.L.R. 1578; similarly where the tribunal will not hear a party on an essential issue: *Sheldon
v Bromfield Justices* [1964] 2 Q.B. 573; *Hodgkins v Hodgkins* [1965] 1 W.L.R. 1448; *R. v
Hendon Justices Ex p. Gorchein* [1973] 1 W.L.R. 1502 (*R. v Woking Justices Ex p. Gossage*
[1973] Q.B. 448 distinguished); and see *R. v Hopkins Ex p. Haywood* [1973] 1 W.L.R. 965;
R. v Worcester Justices Ex p. Daniels (1997) 161 J.P 121 (magistrate appearing not to pay
attention); *Jones v Welsh Rugby Football Union, The Times*, March 6, 1997 (noted [1997] P.L.
340) (arguable that failure by RFU to let applicant challenge by question or evidence the
factual basis of the evidence against him, or to vary procedure for viewing video evidence, was
unfair); *R. v Clerkenwell Metropolitan Stipendiary Magistrate Ex p. Hooper* [1998] 1 W.L.R.
800 (oral hearing before bindover and/or order for surety); see also *Hooper v UK* (2005) 41
E.H.R.R. 1.

[298] *R. v Dewsbury Magistrates Court Ex p. K, The Times*, March 16, 1994; *R. v Ely Justices Ex
p. Burgess* [1972] Crim. L.R. 888 (Div Ct held that a view was part of a criminal trial, and
that the absence of the accused, unless there were special circumstances, was a fatal matter.
The fact that the justices travelled to the view in the same car as the prosecutor, even though
there was no evidence that they discussed the issue, meant a fair trial was not possible,
applying Ackner L.J. in *R. v Liverpool City Justices Ex p. Topping* [1983] 1 W.L.R. 119).

prisoner to meet the costs of his production at court for an application for judicial review, since there was no fundamental right to be present.[299]

7–064   The fact that there is a right to an oral hearing usually indicates that the hearing is to be in public.[300] This enables the public to see that justice is done and plays a significant part in the maintenance of proper standards. In the case of judicial-type bodies the circumstances in which the public can be excluded from the substantive hearing are strictly circumscribed. This does not however apply to preliminary hearings, which are frequently held in private. When a hearing should normally be heard in public there is usually a discretion to exclude the public for good reason, such as national security, but the public should not be excluded to any greater extent than is necessary in the interests of justice.[301]

7–065   An oral hearing will not necessarily be conducted as though it was a hearing in court.[302] In some cases, it will merely involve the right to deliver oral representations, untrammelled by rules of evidence or rights to produce or cross-examine witnesses. In other cases, an oral hearing will be afforded in the context of a fully judicialised procedure. Unless the proceedings are criminal it is unlikely the decision-maker will be bound by strict rules of evidence. Today, in civil proceedings, as result of the Civil Procedure Rules (Pts 1, 32 and 33) a judge, as long as no injustice is caused, has considerable discretion to control evidence, determine what evidence is called and decide how matters are to be proved. In the past the rejection of relevant and admissible evidence was considered a mere "error of law", but nowadays it may constitute denial of a fair hearing according to the requirements of procedural fairness.[303] Again, procedural fairness may be violated by a refusal to allow a party (or his legal representative) to address the decision-maker on the law or the facts[304] or, after a finding of guilt, on the penalty to be imposed.[305]

---

[299] R. v Secretary of State for the Home Department Ex p. Wynne [1992] 1 Q.B. 406, CA; also R. v Morley [1988] Q.B. 601. For the right to be present at an oral hearing pursuant to ECHR Art.6(1), see 7–122 below.
[300] See, e.g. Storer v British Gas Plc [2000] 1 W.L.R. 1237 (decision of industrial tribunal quashed and remitted because not conducted in public). cf. Meerabux v Attorney-General of Belize [2005] UKPC 12; [2005] 2 A.C. 513 at [39]–[41].
[301] Scott v S [1913] A.C. 417; Attorney General v Leveller Magazine Ltd [1979] A.C. 440; R. v Malvern Justices Ex p. Evans [1988] Q.B. 540 (unruly persons may be excluded from an inquiry); Lovelock v Minister of Transport (1980) 39 P. & C.R. 468; R. v Morley [1988] Q.B. 601 (even a defendant who is disruptive and is appearing in person can be removed during his trial for a criminal offence). On the right to a public hearing under ECHR Art.6, see 7–122.
[302] See, e.g. Mahon v Air New Zealand Ltd [1984] A.C. 808 at 821 (Lord Diplock: "[t]he technical rules of evidence applicable to civil or criminal litigation form no part of the rules of natural justice"); R. (on the application of B) v Merton LBC [2003] EWHC 1689; [2003] 4 All E.R. 280 at [50] ("[j]udicialisation of relatively straightforward decisions is to be avoided").
[303] General Medical Council v Spackman [1943] A.C. 627; Bond v Bond [1967] P. 39.
[304] Disher v Disher [1965] P 31; Mayes v Mayes [1971] 1 W.L.R. 679.
[305] Ex p. Kelly, re Teece [1966]2 N.S.WR. 674; Ex p. Kent, re Callaghan [1969] 2 N.S.W.R. 84; see also Fullbrook v Berkshire Magistrates' Courts Committee (1970) 69 L.G.R. 75 (clerk dismissed for misconduct, entitled to opportunity to be heard on question whether pension should be forfeited).

Adjournments

Wrongful refusal of an adjournment to a party unable to attend the **7–066** hearing[306] or denying time to produce a witness or other important evidence may be tantamount to a denial of justice.[307] It may also be contrary to the rules of procedural fairness for a decision-maker to refuse to grant an adjournment where the continuation of the proceedings may prejudice the fairness of the trial of other proceedings, at least if there is a real risk of injustice.[308] In such a situation, the decision-maker, or reviewing court, must balance the potential prejudice to the claimant against the public and/or private interest in the speedy determination of the proceedings[309] and the "overiding objective" of the Civil Procedure Rules which can sensibly be applied by analogy to tribunal proceedings and decision-making generally as long as this is not inconsistent with doing justice in relation to the determination of which complaint is made. It has been emphasised that the power to adjourn is one "which has to be exercised with great care and only when there is a real risk of serious prejudice which may lead to injustice".[310] It would appear that, in practice, the test is difficult to satisfy.[311]

The language of "consultation" usually finds no place in the vocabulary **7–067** of procedural protection where the entitlement derives from the common law duty of natural justice or fairness (except where the source of the entitlement is a legitimate expectation[312]). Nevertheless, in this situation too, the opportunity to make written representations may on occasion be held to be all that fairness requires.[313] For example, when considering a

---

[306] *Re M (an Infant)* [1968] 1 W.L.R. 1897; *Rose v Humbles* [1972] 1 W.L.R. 33; and *R. v Llandrindod Wells Justices Ex p. Gibson* [1968] 1 W.L.R. 598; *Priddle v Fisher & Sons* 1478 (tribunal should have granted adjournment though not expressly requested); *R. v Kingston-upon-Thames Justices Ex p. Martin, The Times,* March 25, 1993.

[307] *R. v Medical Appeal Tribunal (Midland Region) Ex p. Carrarini* [1966] 1 W.L.R. 883; *R. v Thames Magistrates' Court Ex p. Polemis* [1974] 1 W.L.R. 1371; *R. v Panel on Takeovers and Mergers Ex p. Guinness Plc* [1990] 1 Q.B. 146.

[308] *R. v Panel on Takeovers and Mergers Ex p. Fayed* [1992] B.C.C. 524 at 531; *R. v Institute of Chartered Accountants Ex p. Brindle* [1994] B.C.C. 297, CA.

[309] *Brindle* [1994] B.C.C. 297, CA (Hirst L.J.).

[310] *Fayed* [1994] B.C.C. 524 at 531 (Neill L.J.).

[311] In addition to the above cases: *R. v Chairman of the Regulatory Board of Lloyds Ltd Ex p. Macmillan* [1995] L.R.L.R. 485; *R. v Chance Ex p. Smith, Coopers & Lybrand* (1995) 7 Admin. L.R. 821; *R. (on the application of Turner) v Highbury Corner Magistrates' Court* [2005] EWHC 2568; [2006] 1 W.L.R. 220 at [35]–[38] (exceptional circumstances justifying adjournment existed where the claimant, against whom a closure order under s.1 of the Anti-social Behaviour Act 2003 has been sought, had mental health problems and was not legally represented).

[312] For example, in *Council for Civil Service Unions v Minister for the Civil Service* [1985] 1 A.C. 374; see Ch.12.

[313] *R. v Amphlett (J)* [1915] 2 K.B. 223; *R. v Central Tribunal Ex p. Parton* (1916) 32 T.L.R. 476; *R. v Housing Appeal Tribunal* [1920] 3 K.B. 334; *Stuart v Haughley Parochial Church Council* [1935] Ch. 452 affirmed [1936] Ch. 32); *R. (on the application of Cairns) v Local Government Board* [1911] 2 I.R. 331; *Brighton Corp v Parry* (1972) 70 L.G.R. 576; *Kavanagh v Chief Constable of Devon and Cornwall* [1974] Q.B. 624 at 634; *Fairmount Investments Ltd*

first application for an entertainments licence a local authority was held to be under no duty to give the applicant an oral hearing, although it was necessary to inform him of objections made and to give him an opportunity to reply.[314] A school governor could not be dismissed by his local authority without being given an opportunity to reply in writing to the complaints made against him.[315] The Army Board of the Defence Council was entitled to deal with a complaint of racial discrimination by way of written representations.[316] The true question in every case is whether the decision-maker acted fairly in all the circumstances, and therefore written representations may be sufficient in a particular case although the nature of the right or interest affected would normally indicate that an oral hearing was necessary.[317] In many cases, it is the impracticality of requiring the decision-maker to hold oral hearings which leads the courts to hold that written representations are sufficient. Thus in the case of the first-time applicant for an entertainment licence, the court could not but take account of the danger of requiring that oral hearings be held for a completely open-ended category of applicants.[318] Similarly, a series of cases has decided that fairness requires that the opportunity to make representations be afforded to prisoners in a number of situations; for example, mandatory[319] and discretionary[320] life sentence prisoners now have an opportunity to make representations before the "tariff" period is fixed, and high security "category A" prisoners may make representations before any review of the security classification.[321] In all such cases, it has been held that written representations are appropriate. In so far as the statutory

v Secretary of State for the Environment [1976] 1 W.L.R. 1255 at 1266; Ayanlowo v IRC [1975] I.R.L.R. 253; R. v Whalley Ex p. Bordin & Co [1972] V.R. 748. See generally Local Government Board v Arlidge [1915] A.C. 120. If, however, the deciding body conveys the impression that it will accord an oral hearing but then determines the issue on the basis of preliminary written submissions, it may be held to have contravened natural justice: R. v Secretary of State for Wales Ex p. Green (1969) 67 L.G.R. 560; and R. v Liverpool Corp Ex p. Liverpool Taxi Fleet Operators' Association [1972] 2 Q.B. 299 (no proper opportunity to make any submissions); Lloyd v McMahon [1987] A.C. 625 (proceedings for surcharging councillors only given an opportunity to make written representations upheld).

[314] R. v Huntingdon DC Ex p. Cowan [1984] 1 W.L.R. 501 (decision quashed because of failure to give the applicant an opportunity to reply to the objections).

[315] R. v Brent LBC Ex p. Assegai (1987) 151 L.G. Rev 891 (obiter).

[316] R. v Army Board of the Defence Council Ex p. Anderson [1992] 1 Q.B. 169; see also R. v Department of Health Ex p. Gandhi [1991] 1 W.L.R. 1053 (Secretary of State hearing appeal from Medical Practices Committee under s.33(5) NHS Act 1977 on issue of racial discrimination could dispense with oral hearing).

[317] See, e.g. Lloyd v McMahon [1987] A.C. 625, HL (a district auditor had not acted unfairly in not offering oral hearings to councillors before certifying that financial losses of the council were the result of their wilful misconduct, since the councillors had made extensive written representations. However, for at least some of their Lordships, the determining factor was that the applicants had not requested an oral hearing. "If any had asked to be heard orally and the auditor had refused, there would have been clear ground for a complaint of unfairness" (Lord Bridge at 706); see also Lord Templeman at 714D).

[318] R. v Huntingdon DC Ex p. Cowan [1984] 1 W.L.R. 501.

[319] R. v Secretary of State for the Home Department Ex p. Doody [1994] 1 A.C. 531.

[320] R. v Secretary of State for the Home Department Ex p. McCartney [1994] C.O.D. 528; R. v Secretary of State for the Home Department Ex p. Chapman (1994) 138 S.J.L.B. 216.

[321] R. v Secretary of State for the Home Department Ex p. Duggan [1994] 3 All E.R. 277.

procedures for planning appeals by means of written representations codify the common law, these require the exchange of representations between the local authority and the appellant.[322] They also require the notification of all persons who were consulted or notified of the original application, or who made representations.[323]

Failure to appear at an oral hearing

It should not be assumed that entitlement to an oral hearing means that the applicant can choose to make written representations instead. A litigant has no basic right to conduct his case in writing without attending the hearing, and a decision-maker may therefore be justified in disregarding written submissions where an applicant has failed to appear.[324] Although this may be thought surprising, it should not be forgotten that an oral hearing may not be helpful. The decision-maker may form an adverse impression of the applicant. **7–068**

Statutory tribunals and inquiries may be required to conduct oral hearings.[325] Sometimes an appellant may be able to waive his right to an oral hearing in favour of a hearing by means of written representations.[326] If a tribunal has a general discretion to proceed by way of written representations, it should not have an inflexible policy of declining requests for oral hearings, but must consider whether there are circumstances—for example substantial disputes on questions of fact—which should lead it to depart from its usual course of action.[327] Administrative convenience must **7–069**

[322] Town and Country Planning (Appeals) (Written Representations Procedure) Regulations 2000 (SI 2000/1628). Under reg.6 the local authority shall submit a questionnaire to the Secretary of State and to the appellant, to which the appellant may reply (reg.7).

[323] SI 2000/1628 regs 5 and 8.

[324] *Banin v MacKinlay* [1985] 1 All E.R. 842, CA (taxpayer who did not attend hearing of Special Commissioners but merely sent materials marked "Pleadings and Affidavit" could not complain when the Commissioners dismissed his appeal solely on the evidence and arguments put forward by the Crown. There was no breach of natural justice, and a statutory privilege for barristers and solicitors (s.50(5) Taxes Management Act 1970) entitling them to plead in writing did not extend to litigants in person). *Per contra*, it may be unfair to require written evidence when the individual is not at liberty to provide it: *R. v South Western Magistrates Ex p. Doyle* [1996] C.O.D. 309.

[325] See, e.g. Town and Country Planning Act 1990 ss.78 and 79(2).

[326] See, e.g. Town and Country Planning (Appeals) (Written Representations Procedure) (England) Regulations 2000 (SI 2000/1628).

[327] *R. v Army Board of the Defence Council Ex p. Anderson* [1992] Q.B. 169. The Secretary of State for the Environment has a discretion not to hold a public inquiry under the Highways Act 1980, instead merely entertaining written representations. But he may not refuse to hold a hearing simply because he considers that all the necessary information is before him and that the issues raised are clear to him; he must also be satisfied that he can properly weigh any two or more conflicting issues, and that those with the right to make representations can have their representations properly taken into account: see *Binney v Secretary of State for the Environment* [1984] J.P.L. 871 where it was held that the minister in question had misdirected himself as to the factors to take into account; and, *Shorman v Secretary of State for the Environment* [1977] J.P.L. 98. It was suggested by Webster J. in *Binney* (without so deciding) that it might be more important to allow objectors to a scheme to make oral representations to a scheme where that scheme had been proposed by the minister himself rather than by a local authority (at 873).

not be allowed to override the exigencies of a particular case.[328] If there are contending parties before a tribunal and one is permitted to give oral evidence, the same facility must, of course, be afforded to the others.[329]

7–070   If a person who is entitled to request an oral hearing abstains from so doing, how far does he waive entitlement to other procedural protection—such as the opportunity to make written representations which fairness would have afforded him? In one case it was indicated that he impliedly abandons his right to be apprised of and comment on evidential material obtained by the decision-maker.[330] This may be a reasonable interpretation in special situations where the proceedings are essentially inquisitorial; but it should not be accepted as a general principle of law.[331]

Right to call witnesses

7–071   Where a party is entitled to an oral hearing before a decision is taken which materially affects his rights or interests, he may be entitled to call witnesses to support his case.[332] A decision-maker will normally have a discretion whether or not to grant such a request, but the discretion must be exercised reasonably and in good faith, so that, for example, the decision of a prison board of visitors at a disciplinary hearing not to allow a prisoner to call witnesses because of administrative inconvenience was held to be contrary to procedural fairness.[333] The failure of prosecution authorities to inform the defendant of potential witnesses may also invalidate a decision,[334] although such cases have been explained (at least in the criminal context) as resting not upon a breach of procedural fairness but upon a breach of duty owed by the prosecution to the court and defence.[335] Where magistrates declined to issue warrants for the arrest of

---

[328] *R. v Department of Health Ex p. Gandhi* [1991] 1 W.L.R. 1053 at 1063 (Taylor L.J.).

[329] *R. v Kingston-upon-Hull Rent Tribunal Ex p. Black* (1949) 65 T.L.R. 209.

[330] *R. v Deputy Industrial Injuries Commissioner Ex p. Moore* [1965] 1 Q.B. 456, CA, 476 at 490.

[331] And see *Lloyd v McMahon* [1987] A.C. 625 where there was no suggestion that the fact that the applicants had failed to request oral hearings meant that the district auditor was not under a duty to consider their written representations.

[332] *Vye v Vye* [1969] 1 W.L.R. 588. Natural justice does not require that witnesses be excluded while other witnesses are giving evidence; *Moore v Lambeth County Court Registrar* [1969] 1 W.L.R. 141.

[333] *R. v Board of Visitors of Hull Prison Ex p. St Germain (No.2)* [1979] 1 W.L.R. 1401. Similarly, it was held that the attendance of witnesses could not be refused because the tribunal thought there was ample evidence against the prisoner. *R. v Gartree Prison Visitors Ex p. Mealy, The Times*, November 14, 1981 (decision of prison board of visitors quashed where prisoner not allowed to question his own witness or to comment on the evidence presented); cf. *Cheung v Minister of Employment and Immigration* [1981] 2 F.C. 764 (1981) 122 D.L.R. (3rd) 41 (immigration adjudicator wrong to refuse to allow applicant to call for purposes of cross-examination an immigration officer who had made a damaging statutory statement about the applicant.)

[334] *R. v Leyland Magistrates Ex p. Hawthorn* [1979] Q.B. 283; *R. v Blundeston Prison Board of Visitors Ex p. Fox-Taylor* [1982] 1 All E.R. 646.

[335] *Al-Mehdawi v Secretary of State for the Home Office* [1990] A.C. 876, HL; see 9–00.

reluctant defence witnesses whose evidence was plainly material, a defendant succeeded in establishing a breach of procedural fairness.[336] In child care cases, a local authority has a duty to weigh fairly and objectively its discretion to authorise or refuse a medical examination of a child requested by parents in the hope of obtaining expert evidence in their favour,[337] and the authority must also allow evidence to be brought and witnesses to be called at a hearing for an interim care order where the order is opposed.[338]

However, the courts will allow tribunals a certain latitude in deciding 7–072 whether to permit witnesses to be called. In *R. v Panel on Takeovers and Mergers Ex p. Guinness Plc*, the Court of Appeal felt the "greatest anxiety" about the Panel's decision not to grant an adjournment to allow witnesses for Guinness to attend, but found it impossible to say that that decision was wrong, bearing in mind the "overwhelming" evidence in favour of the Panel's view, and the fact that the Panel did not see itself as exercising a disciplinary function, regarding its procedures as inquisitorial rather than adversarial.[339] Even in disciplinary cases, there can be limitations on the right to allow witnesses to attend. A taxi driver suspended for life from a radio-paging service failed to impugn the proceedings of the Board hearing his case (in private law proceedings alleging a breach of procedural fairness), since the Board's refusal to grant an adjournment at the close of the proceedings to allow the applicant to seek possible witnesses did not breach the implied contractual right to procedural fairness, but was a proper exercise of its discretion.[340]

Finally, it may be a breach of procedural fairness for a decision-maker to 7–073 refuse to allow a person to call his witnesses in the order that he thinks best, if there is a real possibility of prejudice to the effective presentation of the case.[341]

RIGHT TO LEGAL REPRESENTATION AND OTHER ASSISTANCE

Fairness may require that a person be permitted to be legally represented at 7–074 a hearing, have an interpreter or the assistance of a non-legally qualified person (a "litigation friend" formerly called a "McKenzie friend").

---

[336] *R. v Bradford Justices Ex p. Wilkinson* [1990] 1 W.L.R. 692.
[337] *R. v Hampshire CC Ex p. K* [1990] 2 Q.B. 71; *R. v Hereford Magistrates Court Ex p. Rowlands* [1998] Q.B. 110 (magistrates' refusal of an adjournment to enable "vital" defence witnesses to attend deprived the applicant of a reasonable opportunity to present his defence).
[338] *R. v Birmingham City Juvenile Court Ex p. Birmingham CC* [1988] 1 W.L.R. 337 (this result was reached both, it would seem, on construction, and on natural justice grounds).
[339] [1990] 1 Q.B. 146 (see Lord Donaldson M.R.'s comments on the "remarkable" nature of the panel in general).
[340] *Bradman v Radio Taxicabs Ltd* (1984) 134 New L.J. 1018 (the driver had been told before the hearing began that he could call witnesses).
[341] *Briscoe v Briscoe* [1968] P. 501; *Barnes v BPC (Business Forms) Ltd* [1975] 1 W.L.R. 1565.

Legal representation

7–075   There is some authority for the proposition that a person who is entitled to appear before an adjudicatory body is also usually entitled, in the absence of express or implied provision to the contrary,[342] to be represented by a lawyer or by any other appropriate spokesman of his choice.[343] However this puts the case too high, and it is more accurate to say that the decision-maker possesses a discretion whether to allow legal representation and everything depends on the circumstances of the particular case.[344] The courts may then scrutinise the exercise of that discretion according to the ordinary principles of review.[345]

7–076   Thus in a series of cases concerning the right of prisoners to be represented at disciplinary hearings before Boards of Visitors (the former adjudicatory body within prisons),[346] the courts quashed decisions where there was a refusal to allow representation where the charge and potential penalty were particularly grave, or where relevant factors such as the ability of the prisoner to present his case, the availability of witnesses, the complexity of the case in fact and law, and the necessity for even-handedness between prisoners and prison officers had not been properly considered.[347] Where the charge had a straightforward factual and legal basis,[348] and where the prisoner was intelligent, articulate and had a clear appreciation of the proceedings,[349] courts declined to interfere with

[342] *Maynard v Osmond* [1977] Q.B. 240 (disciplinary proceedings against police officer). On the right to legal representation where ECHR Art.6 applies, see 7–120.
[343] *R. v St Mary Abbotts Assessment Committee* [1891] 1 Q.B. 378; *R. v Board of Appeal Ex p. Kay* (1916) 22 C.L.R. 183; and *R. v Birmingham Justices Ex p. Wyatt* [1976] 1 W.L.R. 260. The scope of the rule is not, however, clear either in England or in some other jurisdictions. See *Fraser v Mudge* [1975] 1 W.L.R. 1132 (disciplinary proceedings against a prison inmate) and below, n.345; *Maynard v Osmond* [1977] Q.B. 240 at 253 (dicta); cf. *Robinson v R.* [1985] A.C. 956 and *R. v Board of Visitors Maze Prison Ex p. Hone* [1988] A.C. 379. And see *Golder v U.K.* (1975), where the ECtHR upheld prisoner's right of access to his solicitor; *Murray v UK* (1996) 22 E.H.R.R. 29 (lack of access to lawyer during first 48 hours in detention violated right to fair hearing under Art.6(1) and (3)). In some cases the matter is put more narrowly as being a matter of discretion for an adjudicator to allow the individual to appear in person or through an agent; see *R. v Visiting Justice at Her Majesty's Prison, Pentridge Ex p. Walker* [1975] V.R. 883, where the principal authorities are considered. Cf. *Maynard v Osmond* [1977] Q.B. 240 (appearance "in person" does not include representation by a lawyer).
[344] *R. v Board of Visitors of HM Prison, The Maze Ex p. Hone* [1988] A.C. 379 at 392 (Lord Goff).
[345] See, e.g. *R. v Secretary of State for the Home Department Ex p. Tarrant* [1985] Q.B. 251 (board of visitors' refusal to allow legal representation unreasonable on charge of mutiny); *R. v Rathbone Ex p. Dikko* [1985] Q.B. 630; *R. v Secretary of State for the Home Department Ex p. Vera Lawson* [1994] Imm. A.R. 58. On legal representation at public inquiries, see 7–117.
[346] Prison Boards of Visitors have had their name changed to Independent Monitoring Boards and since 1992, have not had responsibilities for adjudicating on prison discipline: Prison (Amendment) Rules 1992 (SI 1992/514) (since repealed) and Prison Rules 1999 (SI 1999/728) rr.75–78.
[347] *R. v Secretary of State for the Home Department Ex p. Tarrant* [1985] Q.B. 251; approved in *R. v Board of Visitors of H.M. Prisons, The Maze Ex p. Hone* [1988] A.C. 379, HL.
[348] *R. v Board of Visitors of HM Remand Centre Risley Ex p. Draper, The Times*, May 24, 1988.
[349] *R. v Board of Visitors of Parkhurst Prison Ex p. Norney* [1990] C.O.D. 133.

decisions not to allow representation. It is now clear however, that Art.6 is presumed to apply to any prison disciplinary proceedings which may result in the award of additional days of detention for a prisoner.[350] Such an award constitutes a fresh deprivation of liberty imposed for punitive reasons after a finding of culpability and should be categorised as "criminal" rather than disciplinary within the meaning of Art.6.[351] This presumption of the applicability of Art.6 can only be rebutted entirely exceptionally, and only if the deprivation of liberty cannot be considered appreciably detrimental given its nature, duration or manner of execution.[352] The Prison Rules were amended in 2002 to comply with Art.6, and where the governor of a prison determines that the charge against a prisoner is sufficiently serious to warrant the award of additional days of detention, he must refer it to an adjudicator, who is to inquire into the offence.[353] At the relevant inquiry, the prisoner who has been charged is given the opportunity to be legally represented.[354]

As regards informal proceedings before a decision-maker, it is similarly 7–077 the case that decision-makers possess a discretion as to whether to allow representation, although the courts will be less willing to intervene where representation is refused[355] even where the character of the hearing is disciplinary.[356] However, it may be that where the allegation is an "infamous" one, the decision-maker can only reasonably exercise its discretion in one way, and there is therefore a duty to allow legal representation.[357] Furthermore, where the case before the disciplinary committee is legally complex, again, legal representation may be required.[358] There may be no requirement to allow legal representation at

---

[350] See 7–036.
[351] *Ezeh v UK* (2004) 39 E.H.R.R. para.124; see 7–036.
[352] *Ezeh* (2004) 39 E.H.R.R. 1, para.125.
[353] Prison Rules 1999 (SI 1999/728) r.53A, as inserted by para.3 of the Sch. to Prison (Amendment) Rules 2002 (SI 2002/2116).
[354] Prison Rules 1991 (SI 1999/728) r.54(3), as inserted by para.4 of the Sch. to Prison (Amendment) Rules 2002 (SI 2002/2116).
[355] *Re Macqueen and Nottingham Caledonian Society* (1861) 9 C.B. (N.S.) 793; *Enderby Town Football Club Ltd v Football Association Ltd* [1971] Ch. 591, CA; *Pett v Greyhound Racing Association Ltd (No.2)* [1970] 1 Q.B. 46; *Ex p. Death* (1852) 18 Q.B. 647. There is some authority for the proposition that when a body has made no formal rule on the matter, it cannot refuse to exercise its discretion to consider allowing legal representation to a person whose ability to pursue his livelihood is in jeopardy: *Pett v Greyhound Racing Association Ltd (No.1)* [1969] 1 Q.B. 125 (as explained by Lord Denning M.R. in *Enderby Town* [1971] Ch. 591 at 605–606). However, it would appear possible for legal representation to be excluded altogether, whether as of right or in the discretion of the tribunal, by the exercise of an express rule-making power (e.g. *Enderby Town* [1971] Ch. 591 at 609 (Cairns L.J); *Maynard v Osmond* [1977] Q.B. 240 at 252, 256, where it was held that legal representation had effectively been excluded by a rule made under a statutory power).
[356] *Tait v Central Radio Taxis* 1989 S.L.T. 217 (member of taxi radio company not entitled to representation before disciplinary committee which debarred him from membership).
[357] *Manchanda v Medical Eye Centre Assn* (1987) 131 S.J. 47 (natural justice required that doctor be represented before Medical Eye Centre Association committee hearing allegation of unbecoming conduct).
[358] *R. (on the application of S) v Knowsley NHS Primary Care Trust* [2006] EWHC 26; [2006] Lloyd's Rep. Med. 123.

professional disciplinary hearings which lead to temporary suspension without financial penalty.[359]

7–078   No matter what the status or functions of the decision-maker, it would be contrary to the requirements of procedural fairness to allow one side to be legally represented but to refuse the same right to the other. And where legal representation is permitted or granted, a party may be entitled to confer with non-legally qualified advisors, although such persons would be barred from fully representing the party.[360] Further, the right to legal representation will where appropriate extend beyond the courtroom or hearing venue, and will be subsumed into the general principle that every citizen has a right of unimpeded access to a court and to legal advice. Thus, prison rules which authorised a prison governor or officer designated by him, to open and read any communication to a prisoner, and to intercept any communication of objectionable content or inordinate length, were held to be ultra vires the Prison Act 1952 to the extent that they authorised intrusion beyond the minimum necessary to ensure that correspondence was bona fide legal correspondence.[361]

7–079   In considering whether procedural fairness implies a right to legal representation (if a party is able to obtain it), it should be borne in mind that only reasonable standards of fair adjudication, and not ideal standards, are required. Whether, and if so when, legal representation ought to be permitted before a decision-maker, can raise difficult questions of policy. The reasons for excluding legal representatives (or permitting them to appear only with the decision-maker's consent) are various. It is said that they tend to introduce too much formality and an inappropriate adversarial element into the proceedings, which are apt to become unnecessarily prolonged;[362] they disturb witnesses and inexpert members of the decision-making body by asking awkward questions and making "technical" points; their presence increases the likelihood of subsequent proceedings in the courts to impugn the decision. Not-withstanding these points, in general, legal representation of the right quality before statutory tribunals is

[359] *R. (on the application of Malik) v Waltham Forest Primary Care Trust* [2006] EWHC 487, [2006] 3 All E.R. 71.
[360] *R. v Leicester City Justices Ex p. Barrow* [1991] 2 Q.B. 260, CA (poll tax protestors allowed to have non-legally qualified assistants in magistrates' court). See also *R. v Secretary of State for the Home Department Ex p. Tarrant* [1985] Q.B. 251 at 282–283, 298; *R. v London Borough of Newham Ex p. Ajayi* (1996) 28 H.L.R. 25 at 29 (absence of anyone present at interview underlined unfairness).
[361] *R. v Secretary of State for the Home Department Ex p. Leech (No.2)* [1994] Q.B. 198, CA; see now r.39, the Prison Rules 1999 (SI 1999/728) which permits a prisoner to correspond with his legal adviser and any court (including the European Commission and Court of Human Rights) without the correspondence being read, whether or not legal proceedings have commenced subject to restrictions where the governor has reason to believe the communication may contain an illicit enclosure, or may endanger prison security, the safety of others, etc. cf.*Murray v UK* (1996) 22 E.H.R.R. 29; *R. v Governor of Whitemoor Prison Ex p. Main* [1997] C.O.D. 400 (search of correspondence did not prevent free flow of information between applicant and solicitor).
[362] An argument used in connection with the imposition of punishment on members of disciplined organisations, see, e.g. *Fraser v Mudge* [1975] 1 W.L.R. 1132.

desirable, and a person threatened with social or financial ruin by disciplinary proceedings in a purely domestic forum may be gravely prejudiced if he is denied legal representation.

Since the Franks Report the right to legal representation before statutory 7–080 tribunals has been extended;[363] and it has found its way into disciplinary procedures in universities and national sporting organisations.[364] Development of the case law on implied rights to legal representation in non-statutory environments should be guided by a realistic appraisal of the interests of the person claiming it, as well as of the interests of the organisation to which he belongs.

Interpreter

In asylum proceedings, although an asylum claimant has no right to be 7–081 accompanied by an interpreter at interview, a refusal to permit an interpreter has been quashed for irrationality.[365] Generally, a party who is unable to understand the English language should be allowed to engage (and in serious cases ought to be provided with) an interpreter.[366] Where neither a legal representative nor an interpreter is present at the asylum interview, the interviewee must be permitted to tape record the interview in order to provide the applicant with an adequate means of ensuring that the record is adequate and reliable.[367]

Litigation friend

Although the relevant decision-maker has the discretion to permit the 7–082 individual to be assisted by an adviser, an individual does not have a right to have a friend or advisor attend a hearing.[368] However, a party to proceedings has the right to present his own case and should be afforded all reasonable facilities to do so, including the assistance of a friend to give advice and take notes unless, in the interests of justice and in order to maintain order and regulate proceedings.[369] It has also been held in the

---

[363] For a right to legal aid in the context of a criminal trial or appeal, see *Boner v UK* (1995) 19 E.H.R.R. 246 (ECtHR found that the refusal of legal aid was a violation of Art.6(3)(c), which provides for the right, for any person charged with a criminal offence, where "he has not sufficient means to pay for legal assistance, to be given it free when the interests of justice so require").

[364] In 1972 legal representation was permitted at certain disciplinary hearings before the stewards of the Jockey Club and the Greyhound Racing Association, and before the Football Association authorities; see n.355.

[365] *R. v Secretary of State for the Home Department Ex p. Bostanci* [1999] Imm. A.R. 411.

[366] Cf. *Re Fuld's Estate (No.2)* [1965] 1 W.L.R. 1336; *R. v Merthyr Tydfil Justices Ex p. Jenkins* [1967] 2 Q.B. 21 at 23 (dictum) (see now Welsh Language Act 1993 ss.22, 24).

[367] *R. (on the application of Dirshe) v Secretary of State for the Home Department* [2005] EWCA Civ 421; [2005] 1 W.L.R. 2685.

[368] *R. v Secretary of State for the Home Department Ex p. Tarrant* [1985] Q.B. 251 at 282–283, 298.

[369] *R. v Leicester City Justices Ex p. Barrow* [1991] 2 Q.B. 260 at 289.

context of family law proceedings that if a litigant in person apply to use the services of an unpaid adviser, the applciation should only be refused for compelling reasons.[370]

RIGHT TO CROSS-EXAMINATION

7–083 Refusal to permit cross-examination of witnesses may amount to procedural unfairness,[371] especially if a witness has testified orally and a party requests leave to confront and cross-examine him[372] or if the evidence is fundamental or highly contested.[373] The fact that the proceedings may be inquisitorial and informal is inconclusive.[374] As with the question of entitlement to legal representation, the matter is one for the discretion of the decision-maker. However, where a "judicialised" procedure has been adopted and witnesses are called to give evidence, the courts will be very ready in the absence of strong reasons to the contrary to find unfairness where a decision-maker declines to allow the evidence of those witnesses to be tested in cross-examination, and indeed it may be unfair for the decision-maker not to grant an adjournment to allow witnesses to attend for the purpose of being cross-examined.[375] As Lord Edmund-Davies has

---

[370] Re O (Children) [2005] EWCA Civ 759; [2006] Fam. 1.
[371] Re Fremington School (1846) 10 Jur. (O.S.) 512; Osgood v Nelson (1872) L.R. 5 HL 636 at 646, 660; Marriott v Minister of Health (1936) 154 L.T. 47 at 50; R. v Newmarket Assessment Committee [1945] 2 All E.R. 371 at 373; Magistrates of Ayr v Lord Advocate 1950 S.C. 102 at 109. Refusal to permit cross-examination of a witness in proceedings in a court will be a denial of justice; see R. v Edmonton Justices Ex p. Brooks [1960] 1 W.L.R. 697; Blaise v Blaise [1969] 2 W.L.R. 1047; cf. though R. v Wells Street Stipendiary Magistrate Ex p. Seillon [1978] 1 W.L.R. 1002 (refusal to permit cross-examination of witness in committal proceedings not reviewable by prerogative order prior to their termination). Procedural codes for statutory tribunals and inquiries normally give an express right of cross-examination.
[372] R. (on the application of S) v Knowsley NHS Primary Care Trust, The Secretary of State for Health [2006] EWHC 26; [2006] Lloyd's Rep. Med. 123 (where there was a serious dispute of fact between a witness and the doctor, questioning of the witness by the chair was unlikely to be an effective way of probing the witness's evidence, compared with cross examination).
[373] R. (on the application of Sim) v Parole Board [2003] EWCA Civ 1845; [2004] Q.B. 1288 at [59] (parole board recall decision). cf. R. (on the application of B) v Secretary of State for Education and Employment [2001] EWHC Admin 229; [2002] A.C.D. 15 (school expulsion hearing).
[374] R. v Brighton & Area Rent Tribunal [1950] 2 K.B. 410 at 419; Ceylon University v Fernando [1960] W.L.R. 223 at 235 (dicta). In the Fernando case (involving disciplinary charges) it was held that a fair hearing had been given although witnesses had been heard in Fernando's absence; he had been given a sufficient account of what they had said and he had not asked to confront or cross-examine them. But quaere whether it was reasonable in the circumstances to make Fernando's right to cross-examine contingent on his taking the initiative in making such a request; he was not legally represented. Nor, indeed, was he represented at the hearing of the appeal before the PC. In R. v Commission for Racial Equality Ex p. Cottrell & Rothon [1980] 1 W.L.R. 1580, it was held that a hearing held pursuant to s.58(5) of the Race Relations Act 1976 (where the CRE was minded to issue a non-discrimination notice) was more investigative than judicial in character, and consequently fairness did not require that the applicants should have the opportunity to cross-examine witnesses.
[375] R. v Criminal Injuries Compensation Board Ex p. Cobb [1995] C.O.D. 126.

pointed out, "there is a massive body of accepted decisions establishing that procedural fairness requires that a party be given an opportunity of challenging by cross-examination witnesses called by other parties on relevant issues".[376] The true question in every case is whether the absence of cross-examination renders the decision unfair in all the circumstances. If no useful purpose is likely to be served by allowing cross-examination then the courts will be slow to disturb that decision.[377] Thus in *Bushell v Secretary of State for the Environment*, the majority of the House of Lords held that an inspector at a motorway planning inquiry had not acted unfairly in refusing to allow cross-examination of witnesses from the Department of Transport in relation to traffic flow forecasts, because such evidence "was Government policy in the relevant sense of being a topic unsuitable for investigation by individual inspectors upon whatever material happens to be presented to them at local inquiries held throughout the country".[378] It is submitted that there is no conflict of principle between such reasoning and the dicta of Lord Edmund-Davies, who dissented in the case. The difference between their Lordships simply concerned whether such evidence was indeed a "relevant issue" for the inquiry.

Even if cross-examination of some witnesses is permitted, the decision-   7–084
maker is not necessarily obliged to allow cross-examination of every other witness by every party,[379] and there may exceptionally be valid grounds for disallowing questions to a witness on a particular matter.[380] It has been suggested that the proper approach of the courts to all these questions is to ask whether the decision-maker's exercise of its discretion can be faulted on normal judicial review grounds for example, has it, in considering whether to allow cross-examination, had regard to irrelevant considerations, or is its decision unreasonable?[381] However, such an approach is only

---

[376] *Bushell v Secretary of State for the Environment* [1981] A.C. 75 at 116, there citing *Marriott v Minister of Health* (1935) 52 T.L.R. 63 at 67 (Swift J., compulsory purchase orders inquiry); *Errington v Minister of Health* [1935] 1 K.B. 249 at 272 (Maugham L.J., clearance order); *R. v Deputy Industrial Injuries Commissioner Ex p. Moore* [1965] 1 Q.B. 465 at 488, 490 (Diplock L.J.); *Wednesbury Corp v Ministry of Housing and Local Government (No.2)* [1966] 2 Q.B. 275 at 302 (Diplock L.J., local government inquiry); *Errington v Wilson* 1995 S.C. 550 (Outer House of the Court of Session, justices' food destruction order where conflicting scientific evidence).

[377] *Bushell v Secretary of State for the Environment* [1981] A.C. 75 at 108 (Viscount Dilhome).

[378] Bushell [1981] A.C. 75 at 100H–101A; 123 (Lord Lane). It might be asked why, this being the case, it was that the inspector permitted evidence to be led at the inquiry in relation to the traffic forecasts. It is submitted that in an ordinary case, if a tribunal allows a witness to lead evidence which is not strictly relevant, it ought also to allow cross-examination on such evidence. *Bushell* is perhaps unusual in that the ultimate decision-maker was not the tribunal (the inspector) but the Secretary of State, who had indicated that such evidence was not a matter appropriate for the inquiry. There was therefore no prejudice in allowing the untested evidence to stand, since the decision-maker (the Secretary of State) appreciated that it was not relevant to the decision which he had to make.

[379] *R. v London Regional Passengers Committee Ex p. Brent LBC, The Times*, May 23, 1985.

[380] As where questions are put to a civil servant on the merits of government policy (*Bushell* [1981] A.C. 75. The immunity from cross-examination conceded to the civil servant witness in *Re Trunk Roads Act 1936* [1939] 2 K.B. 515 seems to have been more extensive than this.

[381] See *R. v London Regional Passengers Committee Ex p. Brent LBC, The Times*, May 23, 1985.

justifiable in those situations where the decision in all the circumstances complies with the minimum requirements of procedural fairness. In respect of decisions which are subject to the requirements of procedural fairness, the decision-maker has no discretion to adopt a procedure which will not comply with the minimum standards of fairness applicable.

7–085   If a party to proceedings claims that he has suffered an injustice because the non-appearance of a witness has made it impossible to cross-examine him, an attack on the validity of the proceedings may seem to be justified but may well prove to be abortive. A decision-maker may be entitled to base its decision on hearsay, written depositions or medical reports.[382] In these circumstances a person aggrieved will normally be unable to insist on oral testimony by the original source of the information, provided that he has had a genuine opportunity to controvert that information.[383] It is the responsibility of the decision-maker to make due allowance for the lack of an opportunity to cross-examine when assessing the evidence.

7–086   Three final points can be made. First, often a party cannot effectively exercise his right to cross-examine unless he is represented by a lawyer. Secondly, in proceedings culminating in the imposition of a penalty, procedural fairness requires that after the case has been proved, or even if there is no dispute as to the law and facts in the first place,[384] that there should be a right to address the decision-maker in mitigation[385] unless the penalty is automatic. Thirdly, there may well be questions of law or opinion on which a party cannot properly claim any right to lead evidence or to cross-examine witnesses but on which he can fairly claim an implied right to make submissions to the deciding body.

RIGHT TO REASONS

7–087   A failure by a public authority to give reasons, or adequate reasons, for a decision may be unlawful in two ways. First, it may be said that such a failure is *procedurally* unfair. Secondly, a failure to give adequate reasons may indicate that a decision is *irrational*.[386] We look at these in turn.

---

[382] *R. v Epping and Harlow Justices Ex p. Massaro* [1973] Q.B. 433 (prosecution not obliged to produce for cross-examination at committal proceedings witnesses who will be called at trial).

[383] *Wilson v Esquimait & Nanaimo Ry* [1922] 1 A.C. 202; *R. v War Pensions Entitlement Appeal Tribunal Ex p. Bott* (1933) 50 C.L.R. 228; *Miller (TA) Ltd v Minister of Housing and Local Government* [1968] 1 W.L.R. 992 (enforcement notice appeal). In these cases the relevant evidential material was disclosed in writing; and *Kavanagh v Chief Constable of Devon and Cornwall* [1974] Q.B. 624 (Crown Court, on an appeal from a refusal to register a person under the Firearms Act 1968, may, like the original decision-maker, rely upon hearsay evidence). Cf. *Re WLW* [1972] Ch. 456, where production of the author of a report for cross-examination was held to be a requisite of natural justice in a proceeding in a court of law.

[384] *Ridge v Baldwin* [1964] A.C. 40 at 68; *Burn v National Amalgamated Labourers Union* [1920] 2 Ch. 364 at 374; *Edgar v Meade* (1917) 23 C.L.R. 29 at 43; cf. *Weinberger v Inglis* [1919] A.C. 606 at 632.

[385] *Fullbrook v Berkshire Magistrates' Court Committee* (1970) 69 L.G.R. 75.

[386] On irrationality generally, see Ch.11.

Reasons as an aspect of procedural fairness

It has long been a commonly recited proposition of English law that there 7–088
is no general rule of law that reasons should be given for administrative
decisions.[387] On this view, a decision-maker is not normally required to
consider whether fairness or procedural fairness demands that reasons
should be provided to an individual affected by a decision because the
giving of reasons has not been considered to be a requirement of the rules
of procedural propriety. This situation has changed enormously.[388]

The absence of a duty to give reasons has sometimes been explained as 7–089
following from the fact that the courts themselves are not obliged at
common law to give reasons for their decisions.[389] However, today not
only the higher courts, but all courts, at least in relation to some of their
decisions, are under such an obligation, for

"It is the function of professional judges to give reasons for their
decisions and the decisions to which they are a party. This court would
look askance at the refusal by a judge to give reasons for a decision
particularly if requested to do so by one of the parties . . . it may well be
that if such a case should arise this court would find that it had power to
order the judge to give his reasons for his decision".[390]

---

[387] See, e.g. *Stefan v General Medical Council* [1999] 1 W.L.R. 1293 at 1300 (Lord Clyde:
"the established position of the common law [is] that there is no general duty, universally
imposed on all decision-makers"); *R. v Gaming Board of Great Britain Ex p. Benaim and
Khaida* [1970] 2 Q.B. 417 at 431 (where, however, the need to keep confidential the sources
of the board's information was a paramount consideration); *Cannock Chase DC v Kelly*
[1978] 1 W.L.R. 1 at 4; *McInnes v Onslow-Fane* [1978] 1 W.L.R. 1520 at 1532–1535 (a non-
statutory tribunal); *R. v Bristol Ex p. Pearce* (1984) 83 L.G.R. 711; *Antaios Compañia Naviera
SA v Salen Rederiema A.B. ("The Antaios")* [1985] A.C. 191 at 199 (Lord Diplock); *R. v
Secretary of State for Social Services Ex p. Connolly* [1986] 1 W.L.R. 421 at 431 (Slade L.J.).
[388] For the duty to give reasons under ECHR Art.6, see 7–121.
[389] See, e.g. the 4th edition of this book, at p.195 ("Minimum standards [of fairness] cannot
be higher than those prescribed by the courts for themselves. Courts are not obliged to give
reasons . . .").
[390] *R. v Knightsbridge Crown Court Ex p. International Sporting Club* [1982] Q.B. 304
(Griffiths L.J.); *Norton Tool Co Ltd v Tewson* [1973] 1 W.L.R. 45 at 49; *Capital and
Suburban Properties Ltd v Swycher* [1976] Ch. 319 at 326; *Tramountana Armadora SA v
Atlantic Shipping Co SA* [1978] 2 All E.R. 870 at 872; *Hoey v Hoey* [1984] 1 W.L.R. 464
(reasons for decisions should be stated in custody cases); *Eagil Trust Co v Pigott-Brown* [1985]
3 All E.R. 119 at 122, CA; *R. v Crown Court at Harrow Ex p. Dave* [1994] 1 W.L.R. 98; *R. v
Ministry of Defence Ex p. Murray* [1998] C.O.D. 134 (court-martial). However, cf. *Macdonald
v R.* [1977] 2 S.C.R. 665 (although judges are normally expected to give reasons for their
decisions, the absence of reasons is not in itself a ground of appeal). In relation to decisions of
magistrates: *R. v Southend Stipendiary Magistrate Ex p. Rochford DC* [1995] Env L.R. 1 (no
general duty on magistrates to give judgments or reasons for decisions); *R. v Haringey
Magistrates Ex p. Cragg* [1997] C.O.D. 160 (no general duty to give reasons, even where no
appeal from magistrates' decision); *Harrison v Department of Social Security* [1997] C.O.D.
220. See generally, M. Taggart, "Should Canadian Judges Be Legally Required to Give
Reasoned Decisions in Civil Cases" (1983) 33 U.T.L.J. 1.

7–090 Judges are under a general duty to provide reasons,[391] and the number of exceptions to the duty are progressively decreasing;[392] even the formerly well-established exception on a judge's refusal of leave to appeal to the Court of Appeal from his decision to refuse leave to appeal from the decision of an arbitrator[393] has been doubted.[394] ECHR Art.6 requires that "adequate and intelligible reasons must be given for judicial decisions".[395] Reasons have been required on costs decisions;[396] decisions refusing an extension of time in respect of leave to appeal;[397] on application for an interim remedy;[398] where the crown court is sitting in an appellate capacity;[399] and when issuing warrants.[400] If a judge does not give reasons, his decision may be quashed and remitted for a rehearing.[401]

7–091 As a general proposition, it is still accurate to say that "the law does not at present recognise a general duty to give reasons for an administrative decision".[402] But the increasing number of so-called "exceptional"

---

[391] *Flannery v Halifax Estate Agencies Ltd* [2000] 1 W.L.R. 377 at 381B (Henry L.J. noting that "today's professional judge owes a general duty to give reasons is clear"); *Eagil Trust Co v Pigott-Brown* [1985] 3 All E.R. 119 at 122, CA (Griffiths L.J., in application to strike out action for want of prosecution, judge should give sufficient reasons to show the CA the principles on which he has acted and the reasons that have led to his conclusion).

[392] See, e.g. *Moran v Director of Public Prosecutions* [2002] EWHC 89; (2002) 166 J.P. 467 (magistrates not required to give reasons for rejecting a submission of no case to answer); cf. *R. v Secretary of State for the Home Department Ex p. Berhe* [2000] Imm. A.R. 463 (no duty on the IAT to give reasons for deciding to extend time for giving its decision).

[393] *Antaios Compañia Naviera SA v Salen Rederiema AB (The Antaios)* [1985] A.C. 191, HL (judges ought not to give reasons for such a refusal of leave); *Mousaka Inc v Golden Seagull Maritime Inc* [2002] 1 W.L.R. 395, QBD (Comm).

[394] *North Range Shipping Ltd v Seatrans Shipping Corp* [2002] EWCA Civ 405; [2002] 1 W.L.R. 2397 at [27] (Tuckey L.J.).

[395] *Anya v University of Oxford* [2001] EWCA Civ 405; [2001] I.C.R. 847 at [12].

[396] *English v Emery Reimbold and Strick Ltd* [2002] EWCA Civ 605; [2002] 1 W.L.R. 2409; *R. (on the application of Cunningham) v Exeter Crown Court* [2003] EWHC 184; [2003] 2 Cr. App. R. (S.) 64 at [14] (Crown Court should give reasons for costs decisions in criminal cases).

[397] *R. (on the application of Tofik) v Immigration Appeal Tribunal* [2003] EWCA Civ 1138; [2003] I.N.L.R. 623, [17].

[398] *Douglas v Hello! Ltd (No.1)* [2001] Q.B. 967 at [9].

[399] *R. v Snaresbrook Crown Court Ex p. Lea, The Times,* April 5, 1994.

[400] *R. v Central Criminal Court Ex p. Propend Finance Property Ltd* [1996] 2 Cr.App.R. 26 (reasons particularly important where the court was "exercising a draconian jurisdiction").

[401] As is now the case in relation to Crown Court decisions (save perhaps for some interlocutory or procedural decisions): *R. v Crown Court at Harrow Ex p. Dave* [1994] 1 W.L.R. 98; *R. v Snaresbrook Crown Court Ex p. Lea, The Times,* April 5, 1994; *R. v Stafford Crown Court Ex p. Reid, Independent,* March 13, 1995 (no duty to give reasons for Crown Court refusal to extend time for appealing against conviction before magistrates); *R. v Southwark Crown Court Ex p. Samuel* [1995] C.O.D. 249; *R. v Winchester Crown Court Ex p. Morris* [1996] C.O.D. 104; *R. v Southwark Crown Court Ex p. Brooke* [1997] C.O.D. 7 (following *Dave*); *R. v Bozat* (1997) 9 Admin. L.R. 125 (Crown Court Judge should give reasons for recommending deportation).

[402] *R. v Secretary of State for the Home Department Ex p. Doody* [1994] 1 A.C. 531 at 564 (Lord Mustill); Sir Patrick Neill Q.C., "The Duty to Give Reasons: The Openness of Decision-Making" in C. Forsyth and I. Hare (eds), *The Golden Metwand and the Crooked Cord* (1998), p.161; *Stefan v General Medical Council* [1999] 1 W.L.R. 1293 at 1300 (Lord Clyde: "the established position of the common law [is] that there is no general duty, universally imposed on all decision-makers"); *Rey v Government of Switzerland* [1999] 1 A.C.

circumstances[403] in which fairness or procedural fairness does now require that reasons be afforded to an affected individual means that the general proposition is meaningless apart from demonstrating that the mere fact that a decision-making process is held to be subject to the requirements of fairness does not automatically lead to the further conclusion that reasons must be given. However, it is certainly now the case that a decision-maker subject to the requirements of fairness should consider carefully whether, in the particular circumstances of the case, reasons should be given. Indeed, so fast is the case law on the duty to give reasons developing, that it can now be added that fairness or procedural fairness usually will require a decision-maker to give reasons for its decision.[404] Overall, "the trend of the law has been towards an increased recognition of the duty to give reasons"[405] and there has been a strong momentum recently in favour of greater openness in decision-making.[406] What were once seen as exceptions to the rule which stated that reasons were not required, are now becoming examples of the norm; while the cases where reasons are not required may be taking on the appearance of exceptions.[407]

54 at 66 (Lord Steyn); *R. (on the application of Asha Foundation) v The Millennium Commission* [2003] EWCA Civ 88; [2002] A.C.D. 79, CA; *R. v Ministry of Defence Ex p. Murray* [1998] C.O.D. 134. *cf. R. v Lambeth LBC Ex p. Walters* [1994] 2 F.C.R. 336, where Sir Louis Blom-Cooper Q.C., sitting as a deputy judge, suggested that English law has now arrived at a point where there is at least a general duty to give reasons wherever the statutorily impregnated administrative process is infused with the concept of fair treatment to those potentially affected by administrative action. But see *R. v Kensington and Chelsea R.LBC Ex p. Grillo* (1996) 28 H.L.R. 94, CA, where Neill L.J. doubted the proposition of the judge at first instance (also Sir Louis Blom-Cooper Q.C.) that there was a general duty to give reasons "in every aspect of the homeless persons legislation". Neill L.J. did, however, foresee that "there may come a time when English law does impose a general obligation on administrative authorities to give reasons . . ." (at 105); Sir Louis Blom-Cooper Q.C. in *R. v Islington LBC Ex p. Hinds* (1995) 27 H.L.R. 65; (1996) 28 H.L.R. 302, CA; and *Public Service Board of New South Wales v Osmond* (1986) 159 C.L.R. 656 where the High Court of Australia held that for discretionary administrative decisions there was no general common law obligation to give reasons, even for those decisions made under statute and which could adversely affect individual interests or defeat legitimate expectations, and that the question of whether reasons should be given in such a context was best left to the legislature.

[403] *R. v Universities Funding Council Ex p. Institute of Dental Surgery* [1994] 1 W.L.R. 242 (Divisional Court rejected the contention that the duty to give reasons could any longer be described as an "exceptional one").

[404] *Ex p. Murray* [1998] C.O.D. 134; *R. v Secretary of State for Education Ex p. G* [1995] E.L.R. 58 at 67 (Latham J.).

[405] *North Range Shipping Ltd v Seatrans Shipping Corp* [2002] EWCA Civ 405; [2002] 1 W.L.R. 2397 at [15] CA, (Tuckey L.J.).

[406] See, e.g. *R. v Higher Education Funding Council Ex p. Institute of Dental Surgery* [1994] 1 W.L.R. 242 at 259 (Sedley J. in a case where reasons were not required—but Sedley L.J. has since suggested that, if decided today, reasons would be required even in that context: see *R. (on the application of Wooder) v Feggetter* [2002] EWCA Civ 554; [2003] Q.B. 219 at [40]); *R. v Ministry of Defence Ex p. Murray* [1998] C.O.D. 134 (Hooper J. referring to the "perceptible trend towards an insistence on greater openness in the making of administrative decisions").

[407] *Stefan v General Medical Council* [1999] 1 W.L.R. 1293 at 1301.

Advantages of a duty to give reasons

7–092   The absence of a general duty to give reasons has long been condemned as a major defect of our system of administrative law. As the Justice-All Souls Committee concluded, "no single factor has inhibited the development of English administrative law as seriously as the absence of any general obligation upon public authorities to give reasons for their decisions".[408] The beneficial effects of a duty to give reasons are many.[409] To have to provide an explanation of the basis for their decision is a salutary discipline for those who have to decide anything that adversely affects others.[410] The giving of reasons is widely regarded as one of the principles of good administration[411] in that it encourages a careful examination of the relevant issues, the elimination of extraneous considerations, and consistency in decision-making. If published, reasons can provide guidance to others on the body's likely future decisions, and so deter applications which would be unsuccessful. The giving of reasons may protect the body from unjustified challenges, because those adversely affected are more likely to accept a decision if they know why it has been taken.[412] Basic fairness and respect

[408] Justice-All Souls Committee Report, *Administrative Justice, Some Necessary Reforms* (1988), p.71, quoting the earlier Justice Committee Report, *Administration Under Law* (1971), p.23. See further, H.W.R. Wade and C. Forsyth, Administrative Law, 9th edn (2004), pp.523–525; H. Woolf, *Protection of the Public—A New Challenge* (1990), p.92; P. Craig *Administrative Law*, 5th edn. (2003), pp.436–437; the important survey in *Ex. p. Murray* [1998] C.O.D. 134; *Ex p. Hinds* (1995) 27 H.L.R. 65; P. Craig, "The Common Law, Reasons and Administrative Justice" (1994) 53 C.L.J. 282; F. Schauer, "Giving Reasons" (1995) 47 Standford L.R. 633.

[409] See, e.g. *Osmond v Public Service Board* [1984] 3 N.S.W.L.R. 447 at 463 where Kirby P. gives several reasons why giving reasons is desirable: (a) assists in seeing if a reviewable or appeal able error has occurred; (b) giving of reasons adds legitimacy; (c) provides a disincentive for arbitrariness; (d) the discipline of giving reasons will make administrators more careful and rational; and (e) reasons give guidance for future cases.

[410] *Tramountana Annadora SA v Atlantic Shipping Co SA* [1978] 2 All E.R. 870 at 872 (Donaldson J.: "Having to give reasons concentrates the mind wonderfully"); *R. v Islington LBC Ex p. Hinds* (1995) 27 H.L.R. 65 at 75 (noting that "[g]iving reasons is also a self-disciplining exercise"); *Cullen v Chief Constable of the Royal Ulster Constabulary* [2003] UKHL 39; [2003] 1 W.L.R. 1763 at [7] (Lord Steyn noting that the statutory duty to give reasons for deferring access to a solicitor "impose[s] a discipline . . . which may contribute to such refusals being considered with care"); *R. (on the application of O'Brien) v Independent Assessor* [2004] EWCA Civ 1035 at [77] (Auld L.J. noting that the purpose of the giving of reasons is to focus the Independent Assessor's mind on the relevant statutory criteria, guidance and principles of law on the make-up of his awards before and when considering their totality; appeal dismissed at [2007] UKHL 10; [2007] 2 W.L.R. 544); *Flannery v Halifax Estate Agencies Ltd* [2000] 1 W.L.R. 377 at 381 (Henry L.J. noting that "a requirement to give reasons concentrates the mind").

[411] See, e.g. G. Richardson, "The Duty to Give Reasons: Potential and Practice" [1986] P.L. 437; J. Garton, "The Judicial Review of the Decisions of Charity Trustees" (2006) 20 *Trust Law International* 160, 177; A. Le Sueur "Taking the Soft Option? The Duty to Give Reasons in the Draft Freedom of Information Bill" [1999] P.L. 419, 423. On good administration generally.

[412] See, e.g. *R. v Secretary of State for the Home Department Ex p. Singh, The Times*, June 8, 1987, QBD, where Woolf L.J. explained that it was highly undesirable for the Home Office not to give written notification of a decision on an application for asylum, not only because of the potential unfairness to the applicant, but because without notice, an applicant would be likely to receive leave to move for judicial review, whatever the real merits of his case, if he indicated that as far as he was aware no decision had been taken on his case.

for the individual often requires that those in authority over others should tell them why they are subject to some liability or have been refused some benefit: in short, "justice will not be done if it is not apparent to the parties why one has won and the other has lost".[413] The giving of reasons increases public confidence in the decision-making process.[414] The giving of reasons can also render it easier to determine if a decision is irrational or erroneous.[415]

In addition to helping to ensure the fairness of an initial hearing, a requirement of reasons is of particular importance where decisions are subject to a right of appeal on questions of law.[416] A reasoned decision is necessary to enable the person prejudicially affected by the decision to know whether he has a ground of appeal,[417] or alternatively, a ground of challenge by way of judicial review.[418] Reasons will also assist the appellate court to scrutinise effectively the decision for relevant error, without necessarily usurping the function of the decision-maker by itself re-determining the questions of fact and discretion which Parliament entrusted to the decision-maker.[419] Without reasons, it can be extremely difficult to detect errors.[420]   7–093

It is because of these very real benefits which result from the giving of reasons that a legal duty to give reasons has become an integral part of the model of administration that has dominated English administrative law since the publication of the Franks Report.[421] If those entitled to be heard   7–094

---

[413] *English v Emery Reimbold and Strick Ltd* [2002] EWCA Civ 605; [2002] 1 W.L.R. 2409 at [16]; *Flannery v Halifax Estate Agencies Ltd* [2000] 1 W.L.R. 377 at 381 (Henry L.J. noting that "fairness surely requires that the parties—especially the losing party—should be left in no doubt why they have won or lost").

[414] *Stefan v General Medical Council* [1999] 1 W.L.R. 1293 at 1300.

[415] See, e.g. *Edwards v Bairstow* [1956] A.C. 14 at 36 (reasoning setting out the facts found and the determination revealed irrationality constituting error of law); *R. v Director of Public Prosecutions Ex p. Manning* [2001] Q.B. 330 (a note indicated that relevant matters had not been considered); *R. (on the application of Kelsall) v Secretary of State for the Environment, Food and Rural Affairs (No.1)* [2003] EWHC 459 at [35] ("if [the] reasons do not bear scrutiny they add substance to the argument that the provisions of the Order are so flawed as to be irrational and unfair"); *R. (on the application of Quark Fishing Ltd) v Secretary of State for Foreign and Commonwealth Affairs (No.1)* [2002] EWCA Civ 1409 (unlawful approach became clear from documents disclosed following the court order).

[416] See, e.g. Tribunals and Inquiries Act 1992 s.10.

[417] See, e.g. *R. v London Borough of Islington Ex p. Hinds* (1995) 27 HLR 65 at 75 (noting that reasons enable the claimant to determine if the decision is "legally challengeable").

[418] *R. (on the application of O'Brien) v Independent Assessor* [2004] EWCA Civ 1035 at [77] (appeal dismissed at [2007] UKHL 10; [2007] 2 W.L.R. 544).

[419] *Cullen v Chief Constable of the Royal Ulster Constabulary* [2003] UKHL 39; [2003] 1 W.L.R. 1763 at [7] (Lord Steyn).

[420] *R. v Nat Bell Liquors Ltd* [1922] 2 A.C. 128 at 159 (Lord Sumner); *O'Reilly v Mackman* [1983] 2 A.C. 237 at 277 (Lord Diplock noting that judicial review for error of law on the face of the record "was liable to be defeated by the decision-making body if it gave no reasons for its determination"); *R. v Islington LBC Ex p. Hinds* (1995) 27 H.L.R. 65, 75 (noting that reasons facilitate review as "adequate reasons . . . expose any errors of law, unsubstantial findings and extraneous considerations").

[421] Cmnd. 218 (1957), para.98; similar recommendations had been made 25 years earlier by the Donoughmore Committee Cmd. 4060 (1932) p.100, but they were not implemented. The

have no right to know how a tribunal resolved the issues in dispute at the hearing, they may well regard as an empty ritual their legally conferred opportunity to be heard and to influence the tribunal by producing witnesses and other evidence to establish the relevant facts, advancing arguments on the proper exercise of any discretion and the resolution of any legal questions, and challenging their opponents' case. Unless the tribunal makes findings on disputes as to fact, explains the exercise of its discretion (by indicating the considerations that it has taken into account and relative weight assigned to them, for example) and gives its answers to any questions of law, there can be no assurance that the tribunal has discharged its obligation to correctly decide issues of law and base its decision upon the material presented at the hearing, rather than on extraneous considerations.[422]

Disadvantages of a duty to give reasons

7–095 There are, however, some significant objections which can be raised to the courts extending a general requirement to provide reasons and findings of fact to all administrative bodies that are in any case obliged by the duty of fairness to inform those whom they may prejudicially affect of the case that they have to meet and to offer them an opportunity to submit representations. These include the possibility that reasons, especially if published, will unduly increase "legalisation" and the formal nature of the decision making process,[423] place burdens upon decision makers that will occasion administrative delays, and encourage the disappointed to pore over the reasons in the hope of detecting some shortcoming for which to seek redress in the courts.[424] In addition, a reluctance to give reasons perhaps because they may occasion harm (by, for example, causing personal

---

US Administrative Procedure Act's requirement of reasons applies principally to formal adjudication, although the courts have imposed a duty to make findings of fact and to state reasons in some other situations: see R. Pierce, *Administrative Law Treatise*, 4th edn. (2002), pp.546–551. In contrast, all regulations, decisions and directives of the EU Council and Commission must be supported by reasons.

[422] cf. *R. v Mental Health Review Tribunal Ex p. Clatworthy* [1985] 3 All E.R. 699 at 703–704.

[423] cf. *Verndell v Kearney & Trecker Marwin Ltd* [1983] I.C.R. 683 at 694–695 (warning to tribunals not to reduce questions of facts, degree and discretion to legal propositions by excessively elaborate reasons); *Stefan v General Medical Council* [1999] 1 W.L.R. 1293 at 1300 (noting that "there are dangers and disadvantages in a universal requirement for reasons. It may impose an undesirable legalism into areas where a high degree of informality is inappropriate and add to delay and expense").

[424] *McInnes v Onslow-Fane* [1978] 1 W.L.R. 1520 at 1535; *R. v Chief Registrar of Friendly Societies Ex p. New Cross Building Society* [1984] Q.B. 227 at 245 (detailed reasons may tempt a reviewing court erroneously to assume an appellate of de novo jurisdiction); and the disadvantages listed by Hooper J. in *R. v Ministry of Defence Ex p. Murray* [1998] C.O.D. 134; *R. v Mayor, Commonality and Citizens of the City of London Ex p. Matson* (1996) 8 Admin. L.R. 49 at 70 (Swinton Thomas L.J. cast doubt upon the argument that it would be wrong to require a collegiate body to articulate a reason or set of reasons for its decision).

distress,[425] revealing confidences, or endangering national security[426]) could discourage the making of difficult or controversial decisions or result in the production of anodyne, uninformative and standard reasons. In addition, the determination of an issuer may not lend itself to reasoning, being a matter of impression, or taste, or a matter on which no objective justification is possible or useful.[427] Nonetheless, apart from the exceptional case, the advantages of providing reasons so clearly outweigh the disadvantages that fairness requires that the individual be informed of the basis of the decision.

Distinction between duty to give reasons and disclosure

The duty to give reasons for a decision must be distinguished from the fundamental principle of procedural fairness already considered[428] which imposes an obligation to provide information about the case which a party affected may want to answer. Some cases which appear to suggest that reasons are required by natural justice or fairness are in reality examples of this more basic requirement. For example, a local authority must not suspend a contractor from its list of approved contractors without giving detailed reasons immediately (or as soon as is practicable in a case where serious impropriety is suspected).[429] This is not an example of a case where reasons are required, but rather safeguards of the contractor's right to make further representations: the authority must disclose the case against the contractor so that it may be able to answer the allegation as quickly as possible. Thus the right to information protects the right to make representations, but does not by itself automatically entitle the contractor to a reasoned justification of the final decision.[430]

7-096

---

[425] *McInnes v Onslow-Fane* [1978] 1 W.L.R. 1520 at 1533; cf. *Grundy (Teddington) Ltd v Plummer* [1983] I.C.R. 367 at 373–374.

[426] cf. Regulation of Investigatory Powers Act 2000 s.69, which enables the Secretary of State to make rules enabling the Tribunal to hear proceedings without the person who has brought the proceedings being given reasons. See *R. v Secretary of State for the Home Department Ex p. Adams* [1995] All E.R. (E.C.) 177 (reasons not required where, to be meaningful, they would have to reveal sensitive intelligence information).

[427] *Institute of Dental Surgery* [1994] 1 W.L.R. 242.

[428] See 7–043.

[429] *R. v Enfield LBC Ex p. TF Unwin Ltd* [1989] C.O.D. 466; cf. *Cinnamond v British Airports Authority* [1980] 1 W.L.R. 582 at 591.

[430] See, e.g. *R. v Secretary of State for the Home Office Ex p. Thirukumar* [1989] Imm. A.R. 270, CA (applicant for asylum should be made aware of reasons why his application is being at least provisionally refused; in reality so that he can make further representations); cf. *R. v Secretary of State for Foreign and Commonwealth Affairs Ex p. Everett* [1989] Q.B. 811, CA (O'Connor L.J., Secretary of State did not have to afford applicant opportunity to be heard before refusing application for a passport, but "was entitled to refuse the passport but to give his reason for so doing" and "tell him that if there were any exceptional grounds which might call for the issue of a passport he would consider them"); *Breen v AEU* [1971] 2 Q.B. 175 at 190–191 (Lord Denning M.R. stated that fairness may require that a person who is being deprived of an important right should be given a hearing and reasons)—this again may be understood as referring to disclosure of the case against the individual. An important example of the distinction is *R. v Secretary of State for the Home Department Ex p. Fayed* [1997] 1 W.L.R. 228, CA (no duty to give reasons because of statutory exclusion, but duty to disclose to applicant the subject matter of the decision-maker's concern to allow meaningful representations).

Circumstances in which reasons will be required

7–097 The catagories of situations where reasons are required are not closed but a failure to provide reasons may give grounds for challenging an administrative decision on the ground that this amounts to procedural impropriety in the following circumstances.[431]

Required by statute

7–098 Reasons for a decision may be expressly or impliedly required by statute.[432] A duty to supply reasons when requested to do so is imposed by the Tribunals and Inquiries Act 1992 on a large number of statutory tribunals and on Ministers notifying decisions after the holding of a statutory inquiry or in cases where the person concerned could have required the holding of such an inquiry.[433] This duty, which is qualified by a narrow range of exceptions,[434] is enforceable by a mandatory order.[435] A similar duty has been imposed on various other tribunals and public authorities by statute or regulations.[436] There are indications, for example, that in deciding a planning appeal on the basis of written representations, an inspector is obliged to give reasons dealing with the parties' major contentions, even though the statutory duty to give reasons without a request from a party applies only to decisions made after an inquiry.[437]

7–099 Although not strictly speaking obligations to give reasons, public authorities are also subject to qualified statutory obligations to disclose information under the Freedom of Information Act 2000, the Data Protection Act 1998 and regulations on environmental information.[438]

---

[431] *R. v University of Cambridge Ex p. Evans (No.1)* [1998] E.515 at 521–523 (Sedley J.); *R. (on the application of Wooder) v Feggetter* [2002] EWCA Civ 554; [2003] Q.B. 219 at [40] (Sedley L.J.).

[432] A. Le Sueur, "Legal Duties to Give Reasons" (1999) 52 C.L.P. 150; *Stefan v Medical Council* [1999] 1 W.L.R. 1293 at 1297 (implied statutory duty).

[433] Tribunals and Inquiries Act 1992, s.10, Sch.1.

[434] The duty does not apply to ministerial decisions in connection with orders and schemes of a legislative character: Tribunals and Inquiries Act 1992 s.10(5). Where the duty applies, a statement of reasons may still be refused or restricted by the tribunal or Minister on grounds of national security; and it may also be withheld in the interests of a party to the decision if it is asked for by someone not primarily concerned with the decision. Orders may be made after consultation with the Administrative Justice and Tribunals Council excluding particular classes of decisions from the scope of s.10 (s.10(7)); there have been few such Orders.

[435] *Parrish v Minister of Housing and Local Government* (1961) 59 L.G.R. 411 at 418; *Brayhead (Ascot) Ltd v Berkshire CC* [1964] 2 Q.B. 303 at 313–314; *Mountview Court Properties Ltd v Devlin* (1970) 21 P. & C.R. 689 at 693.

[436] See, e.g. Enterprise Act 2002 ss.22, 38(2) (considered in *Somerfield Plc v Competition Commission* [2006] CAT 4; [2006] Comp. A.R. 390 and *IBA Health Ltd v Office of Fair Trading* [2004] EWCA Civ 142, [2004] 4 All E.R. 1103); Town and Country Planning (Inquiries Procedure) Rules 1992 (SI 1992/2038); Animal Welfare Act 2006 s.34(8)(a); Anti-Terrorism, Crime and Security Act 2001 Sch.3 para.11; Criminal Justice Act 2003 s.110.

[437] *Grenfell-Baines v Secretary of State for the Environment* [1985] J.P.L. 256.

[438] See 16–00.

To enable effective right of appeal

Where statute or regulation provides a right of appeal from a decision, **7–100** reasons may be required so as to enable the affected individual to exercise effectively that right. A right to reasons in these circumstances may be explained either by reference to the rules of procedural fairness, or, more usually, by a necessary implication from the rules which provide for the appeal.[439] Thus in one group of cases, tribunals when stating a case on an award of costs have been required to give reasons if their award departs from normal practice;[440] and more generally, reasons may also be required where the body is departing from a previous decision or from a policy guidance.[441] Licensing justices empowered to refuse liquor licences on specified grounds were held to have failed to hear and determine according to law when they failed to specify the ground for refusal.[442] The courts may even imply a right to reasons into a well-developed statutory framework which is silent on the question of an entitlement to reasons.[443] The courts have recently demonstrated a greater willingness to intervene in such circumstances (provided always that they do not discern a statutory intention *to exclude* reasons) simply on the basis that procedural fairness requires that reasons be given.[444]

[439] *Norton Tool Co Ltd v Tewson* [1973] 1 W.L.R. 45 at 49; *Alexander Machinery (Dudley) Ltd v Crabtree* [1974] I.C.R. 120 at 122 (in *R. v Civil Service Appeal Board Ex p. Cunningham* [1991] 4 All E.R. 310 at 317 (Lord Donaldson M.R. rejected the suggestion of Gibbs C.J. in *Public Service Board of New South Wales v Osmond* (1986) 159 C.L.R. 656 at 664 that the above two cases could be explained by the existence of a statutory duty to give reasons).

[440] *Smeaton Hanscomb & Co Ltd v Sassoon I Setty, Son & Co (No.2)* [1953] 1 W.L.R. 1481; *Lewis v Haverfordwest RDC* [1953] 1 W.L.R. 1486 (arbitrator); *Pepys v London Transport Executive* [1975] 1 W.L.R. 234 (Land Tribunal), disapproving dicta to the contrary in *Hood Investment Co Ltd v Marlow UDC* (1964) 15 P. & C.R. 229 at 232.

[441] *Westminster CC v Great Portland Estates Plc* [1985] A.C. 661 (planning authority must give reasons for deciding exceptionally to take into account personal circumstances); *R. v Islington LBCl Ex p. Rixon* [1997] E.L.R. 66 (a duty to comply with statutory guidance unless there is good reason for departure which has been properly articulated); *Ynyforgan and Glais Gypsy Site Action Group v Secretary of State for Wales* [1981] J.P.L. 874 (particularly clear reasons to be given for departure from development plan); *Panjehali v City and County of Swansea, Mr Anthony Osbourne Davies, The Times,* December 1, 2000.

[442] *R. v Sykes* (1875) 1 Q.B.D 52; *Ex p. Smith* (1878) 3 Q.B.D 374; *Tranter v Lancashire Justices* (1887) 51 J.P 454; *R. v Thomas* [1892] 1 Q.B. 426. In *Ex p. Gorman* [1904] A.C. 23 at 28 (Lord Herschell described the decision in *Ex p. Smith*, where the applicant had not demanded that the justices give their reasons, as "somewhat peculiar"); cf. *Minister of National Revenue v Wrights' Canadian Ropes Ltd* [1947] A.C. 109.

[443] *Doody* [1994] 1 A.C. 531; cf. *R. v Secretary of State for the Home Office Ex p. Stitt, The Times,* February 3, 1987, DC (Secretary of State did not have to give reasons for conclusion that a person was "concerned in the commission, preparation, or instigation of acts of terrorism" within the meaning of the Prevention of Terrorism (Temporary Provisions) Act 1976 and 1984 in making an exclusion order, in part because the 1976 Act accorded a comprehensive package of rights to candidates for exclusion, which did not include the right to reasons). In *R. v Civil Service Appeal Board Ex p. Cunningham* [1991] 4 All E.R. 310 Lord Donaldson M.R. rejected the argument that since Parliament had required some tribunals to give reasons by statute, therefore the common law was unable to impose a similar requirement upon other tribunals if justice so required.

[444] *R. v Ministry of Defence Ex p. Murray* [1998] C.O.D. 134. Interestingly, that case also suggested that the converse situation, i.e. where the statutory framework does not provide for any appeal—may also be a factor in favour of requiring the provision of reasons (relying on *Cunningham* and *Doody*).

Required by the common law

7–101 Whether the above decisions are explainable on the basis of a statutory implication or not, it is now clear that fairness may itself require, in a wide range of circumstances, that reasons be given. In a landmark decision, the Court of Appeal in *R. v Civil Service Appeal Board Ex p. Cunningham* held that the Civil Service Appeal Board, a "judicialised" tribunal established under the royal prerogative, was under a duty to give outline reasons for its decisions, sufficient to show to what it has directed its mind and to indicate whether its decisions are lawful, and a failure to do so is a breach of procedural fairness.[445] This decision demonstrates the falsity of the argument that procedural fairness concerns only procedure *at* the hearing, and accordingly cannot require the provision of reasons, which are part of the form of the determination made *after* the hearing. Natural justice should not be viewed so narrowly; the form of a determination is part of the procedure of a hearing, and is no less subject to the requirements of procedural fairness than any other part.[446] One ground upon which fairness may require that reasons be provided in such a case is that reasons enable a person aggrieved by a decision to know not only whether he may appeal, but also—as in *Cunningham*[447]—whether he may maintain in action for judicial review on an independent ground such as illegality or irrationality.[448] But the House of Lords has made it clear that this is only one ground for the imposition of a duty to give reasons. In addition, their Lordships held, it may be that the very importance of the decision to the individual—for example, a decision concerning personal liberty—is such that the individual cannot be left to receive an unreasoned decision, as if "the distant oracle has spoken".[449] It is submitted that it is preferable not

---

[445] *R. v Civil Service Appeal Board Ex p. Cunningham* [1991] 4 All E.R. 310; see J. Herberg, "The Right to Reasons: Palm Trees in Retreat" [1991] P.L. 340; *R. (on the application of Viggers) v Pensions Appeal Tribunal* [2006] EWHC 1066; [2006] A.C.D. 80.

[446] [1991] 4 All E.R. 310 at 322 (McCowan L.J.).

[447] *R. v Civil Service Appeal Board Ex p. Cunningham* [1991] 4 All E.R. 310; *R. v Secretary of State for the Home Department Ex p. Chetta* [1996] C.O.D. 463 (court criticised the practice of only giving reasons after a challenge had been brought for this reason).

[448] The Australian Administrative Decisions (Judicial Review) Act, 1977 s.13 entitles applicants for judicial review to a statement of reasons from the decision maker.

[449] *R. v Secretary of State for the Home Department Ex p. Doody* [1994] 1 A.C. 531 at 565 (Lord Mustill); applied to security categorisation of prisoners in *R. v Secretary of State for the Home Department Ex p. Duggan* [1994] 3 All E.R. 277; *R. v Secretary of State for the Home Department Ex p. Follen* [1996] C.O.D. 169 (decision to refuse release on licence quashed where no adequate reasons given for not following recommendations of Parole Board); *R. v Secretary of State for the Home Department Ex p. Lillycrop, The Times*, December 13, 1996 (Parole Board should summarise in decision letter reasons why parole not recommended); *cf.* the analysis of Sedley J. in *R. v Universities Funding Council Ex p. Institute of Dental Surgery* [1994] 1 W.L.R. 242 (reasons not required for decision of UFC where based upon "pure academic judgment", even though the decision had substantial financial implications for the applicant; Sedley L.J. has, however, subsequently doubted whether this case would be decided the same way today: *R. (Wooder) v Feggetter* [2002] EWCA Civ 554; [2003] Q.B. 219 at [41]). The "oracular" effect of an unreasoned decision will, naturally, be greater in a case where there is no right of appeal, and this has led to the suggestion that the fact that there is

to attempt to separate out the different grounds upon which a duty to give reasons may arise; rather, there is a "unitary test"[450] which rests on familiar considerations of fairness;[451] within such a test, regard may be had, where appropriate, to the multiple grounds which may exist, such as a need for reasons to know whether to challenge the decision (by appeal or judicial review), the importance of the decision on the individual's liberty or livelihood, the advantage of concentrating the decision-maker's mind and ensuring that the issues have been conscientiously addressed, the general nature of the adjudicating process,[452] and so on.[453] Where an authority decides to depart from a legitimate expectation, fairness requires that the authority articulate its reasons so that their propriety may be tested by the court.[454]

Since the duty to give reasons may now be seen simply as yet another 7–102 aspect of the requirements of procedural fairness, it would be wrong to imagine that the duty may be artificially confined to situations in which the decision-maker is acting in a "judicial" or "quasi-judicial" capacity. Although in *Cunningham*, some reliance was placed upon the fact that the Civil Service Appeal Board is a fully "judicialised" tribunal, and one that is almost unique among tribunals in not falling under a statutory duty to give reasons, subsequent decisions have made it clear that reasons may be required of a body exercising "quasi-judicial" functions, such as that of the Home Secretary in relation to the tariff period to be served by life sentence prisoners,[455] and "administrative" functions, such as a local authority making decisions regarding an individual's housing application.[456] Fairness

no right of appeal may be a factor in favour of requiring reasons: see *Murray* [1998] C.O.D. 134. The position would therefore appear to be that both the existence of a right of appeal (or judicial review), and the absence of any appeal, may be factors predisposing the courts to require reasons.

[450] *Institute of Dental Surgery* [1994] 1 W.L.R. 242 (Sedley J.).

[451] In *Cunningham* [1991] 4 All E.R. 310 Lord Donaldson M.R. relied in his judgment upon the general words of guidance offered by Lord Bridge in *Lloyd v McMahon* [1987] A.C. 625 and cited at the opening of this chapter, that the requirements of fairness in every case must be determined by a consideration of the character of the decision making body and the framework within which it operates (to which may be added, the effect which the decision is likely to have upon the affected individual).

[452] *R. v Kensington and Chelsea R.LBC Ex p. Grillo* (1996) 28 H.L.R, 94, CA (Neill L.J., where the court, in holding that fairness did not require the provision of reasons, relied on the fact that the appellate procedure in question was voluntary); *Murray* [1998] C.O.D. 134.

[453] See, e.g. the duty to give reasons in the context of disciplinary proceedings: *Brabazon-Drenning v UK Central Council for Nursing Midwifery and Health Visiting* [2001] H.R.L.R. 91 at [24]–[29] (UK Central Council for Nursing Midwifery and Health Visiting). However, it has been held that there is no general duty to give reasons for a disciplinary committee's findings of fact (although on occasion the principle of fairness may require reasons for decisions even on matters of fact). There is a duty to give reasons in respect of the penalty: *Gupta v General Medical Council* [2001] UKPC 61; [2002] 1 W.L.R. 1691.

[454] *R. (on the application of Bibi) v Newham LBC* [2001] EWCA Civ 607; [2002] 1 W.L.R. 23 at [59].

[455] *Doody* [1994] 1 A.C. 531; since the Criminal Justice Act 2003, the Home Secretary no longer exercises this function.

[456] *R. v Islington LBC Ex p. Trail* [1994] 2 F.C.R. 1261; *R. v Lambeth LBC Ex p. Walters* [1994] 2 F.C.R. 336 (both decisions of Sir Louis Blom-Cooper Q.C.); but see *R. v Bristol CC*

may also require that a body explain why it is rejecting or preferring particular evidence[457] or why it is failing to give effect to a legitimate expectation.[458] The distinction between judicial, quasi-judicial and administrative functions may be consigned to history in this context, as well as more generally. As Sedley J. has put it, in rejecting such a submission in the context of the duty to give reasons, "[i]n the modern state the decisions of administrative bodies can have a more immediate and profound impact on people's lives than the decisions of courts, and public law has since *Ridge v Baldwin* been alive to that fact".[459]

Brief survey of case law on reason giving

7–103 The following brief survey of the case law not mentioned above further demonstrates some of the situations in which reasons have, and have not, been required.

- In the criminal justice context, reasons were required where the DPP had decided not to prosecute despite the fact that an inquest jury had decided that there had been an unlawful killing and that a prima facie case had been established against an identifiable individual.[460] But no reasons were required for the Solicitor-General's decision not to institute contempt proceedings against newspaper editors.[461]

- The Criminal Injuries Compensation Authority should give reasons for its conclusion that an applicant's conduct had "caused or contributed to the incident".[462]

Ex p. Bailey (1995) 27 H.L.R. 307 (local authority subcommittee determining appeal against authority's refusal to award renovation grant not required to give reasons); and, in the housing context, *R. v Camden LBC Ex p. Adair* (1997) 29 H.L.R. 236 (nature of duty to give reasons under s.64 of the Housing Act 1985 for decision that applicant not in priority need); *R. v Kensington and Chelsea RLBC Ex p. Campbell* (1996) 28 H.L.R. 160; *R. v Lambeth LBC Housing Benefit Review Board Ex p. Harrington The Times*, December 20, 1996 (duty to supply material facts and reasoning); *R. v Housing Benefit Review Board of South Tyneside MBC Ex p. Tooley* [1996] C.O.D. 143.

[457] See, e.g. *R. (on the application of Beeson) v Dorset County Council* [2002] H.R.L.R. 368 at [39] (reversed or other grounds [2002] EWCA Civ 1812); *R. (on the application of H) v Ashworth Hospital Authority Council* [2002] EWCA Civ 923; [2003] 1 W.L.R. 127 at [81]; cf. *R. (on the application of Alliss) v Legal Services Commission* [2002] EWHC 2079; [2003] A.C.D. 16 at [65].

[458] *R. (on the application of Bibi) v Newham LBC* [2002] 1 W.L.R. 237 at [59].

[459] *Institute of Dental Surgery* [1994] 1 W.L.R. 242 at 258.

[460] *R. v DPP Ex p. Manning* [2001] Q.B. 330 at [33].

[461] *R. v Solicitor-General Ex p. Taylor and Taylor* [1996] 1 F.C.R. 206. On the jurisdiction of Law Officer's decisions.

[462] *R. v Criminal Injuries Compensation Authority Ex p. Leatherland* [2001] A.C.D 76 (criticising the CICA for the "the closed and defensive manner" that it had adopted); *R. (on the application of Mahmood) v Criminal Injuries Compensation Appeal Panel* [2005] EWHC 2919 (panel failed to give any reasons for its departure from the guidelines); *R. v Criminal Injuries Compensation Board Ex p. Cook* [1996] 1 W.L.R. 1037, CA.

- A doctor's decision forcibly to administer medication to a competent non-consenting adult should have been accompanied by written reasons.[463]

- A rent officer should give reasons for a determination whereby a local reference rent fell below the contractual rent and affected housing benefit.[464]

- The Court of Aldermen was required to give reasons, in relation to a decision not to confirm the election of an Alderman following victory in a ward vote.[465]

- The Home Secretary's decision not to extend exceptional leave to remain in the United Kingdom,[466] and to refuse exceptional leave to remain, required reasons.[467] But no reasons were required for refusal to exercise extra statutory discretion.[468]

- A local authority's decision as to community care and educational provision for a disabled person, where it was departing from guidelines, required reasons.[469]

- No reasons are generally required for the General Medical Council's refusal to re-register a doctor on register of General Practitioners.[470]

- An Admissions Appeal Panel allowing an appeal from a local education authority's decision on the ground that it was unreasonable had to supply reasons.[471]

The standard of reasons required

It remains difficult to state precisely the standard of reasoning the court **7–104** will demand. Much depends upon the particular circumstances[472] and the statutory context in which the duty to give reasons arises. It is clear that

---

[463] *R. (on the application of Wooder) v Feggetter* [2002] EWCA Civ 554; [2003] Q.B. 219.
[464] *R. (on the application of Cumpsty) v Rent Service* [2002] EWHC 2526 at [86]–[87]; cf. *Friends Provident Life and Pensions Ltd v Secretary of State for Transport, Local Government and the Regions* [2001] EWHC Admin 820; [2002] 1 W.L.R. 1450 at [103] (no general duty on the Secretary of State to give reasons for refusing to call-in a planning application).
[465] *R. v Mayor, Commonality and Citizens of the City of London Ex p. Matson* [1997] 1 W.L.R. 765.
[466] *R. v Secretary of State for the Home Department Ex p. Erdogan (Resul)* [1995] Imm. A.R. 430.
[467] *R. v Secretary of State for the Home Department Ex p. Quaquah (No.2)* September 1, 2000 (unrep).
[468] *R. v Secretary of State for the Home Department Ex p. Owalabi (Paul)* [1995] Imm. A.R. 400.
[469] *R. v Islington LBC Ex p. Rixon* [1997] E.L.R. 66.
[470] *R. v General Medical Council Ex p. Salvi* (1999) 46 B.M.L.R. 167 (though fairness may require reasons in relation to some individual circumstances).
[471] *R. (on the application of Reading BC) v Admissions Appeal Panel for Reading BC* [2005] EWHC 2378; [2006] E.L.R. 186.
[472] *R. (on the application of The Asha Foundation) v The Millennium Commission* [2003] EWCA Civ 88 at [27] (Lord Woolf C.J.); *Flannery and Flannery v Halifax Estate Agencies Ltd* [2000] 1 W.L.R. 377 at 382 (Henry L.J. noting that "[t]he extent of the duty, or rather the reach of what is required to fulfil it, depends on the subject matter").

the reasons given must be intelligible and must adequately meet the substance of the arguments advanced.[473] It will not suffice to merely recite a general formula or restate a statutorily-prescribed conclusion.[474] It is also preferable if the reasons demonstrate that a systematic analysis has been undertaken by the decision-maker.[475] However, the courts have not attempted to define a uniform standard or threshold which the reasons must satisfy, and on occasion, courts have expressed concern that decision-makers be granted "a certain latitude in how they express themselves".[476] The reasons must generally state the decision-maker's material findings of fact (and, if the facts were disputed at the hearing, their evidential support[477]), and meet the substance of the principal arguments that the decision-maker was required to consider. If a decision is made on the basis of the evidence of witnesses or experts, reasons for preferring one witness or expert over another should generally be explained.[478] In short, the reasons must show that the decision-maker successfully came to grips with the main contentions advanced by the parties,[479] and must tell the parties in

---

[473] *Re Poyser and Mills' Arbitration* [1964] 2 Q.B. 467 at 477–478 is the most frequently cited judicial articulation of the test of the adequacy of reasons; approved in *Westminster CC v Great Portland Estates Plc* [1985] A.C. 661 at 673; cf. *Save Britain's Heritage v Number One Poultry Ltd* [1991] 1 W.L.R. 153 at 165; and *Edwin H. Bradley & Sons Ltd v Secretary of State for the Environment* (1982) 47 P. & C.R. 374 (same standard was applied despite the subjective element in the minister's duty under the Town and Country Planning Act 1971 s.9(8) to give such statement as he considers appropriate of the reasons for his decision); *Bolton MBC v Secretary of State for the Environment (No.2)* [1995] 3 P.L.R. 37.

[474] *R. v Birmingham City Council Ex p. B* [1999] E.L.R. 305 at 311 (Scott Baker J. noting that the letter sent did "nothing more than make ritual incantation of the two-stage process that is applicable for deciding these appeals"). However, where the decision involves a clear application of policy, "[t]he reason is the policy": *R. (on the application of Thompson) v Secretary of State for the Home Department* [2003] EWHC 538 at [41].

[475] See, e.g. *R. (on the application of Lowe) v Family Health Services Appeal Authority* [2001] EWCA Civ 128 at [18] (reasons inadequate because they did not deal with the question in correct "logical sequence"); *R. v Crown Court at Cantebury Ex p. Howson-Ball* [2001] Env L.R. 36 at [32] (referring to a need for the Crown Court to provide "some analysis" of the relevant matters); *Curtis v Lodon Rent Assessment Committee* [1999] Q.B. 92 at 118–119 (the rent assessment committee's duty to give reasons required some "working through", i.e. an arithmetical explanation, of the assessment).

[476] *R. v Brent London LBC Ex p. Baruwa* (1997) 29 H.L.R. 915 at 929, approved in *William v Wandsworth LBC* [2006] EWCA Civ 535; [2006] H.L.R. 42 at [18].

[477] Cf. *R. v Secretary of State for the Home Department Ex p. Swati* [1986] 1 W.L.R. 477 (passenger refused entry entitled only to be told the ground for refusal; statement of facts required only after notice of appeal is given).

[478] *R. (on the application of H) v Ashworth Hospital Authority* [2002] EWCA Civ 923; [2003] 1 W.L.R. 127 at [81]; *R. (on the application of Bushell) v Newcastle Upon Tyne Licensing Justices* [2004] EWHC 446 at [41]; cf. *R. (on the application of Alliss) v Legal Services Commission* [2002] EWHC 2079 at [65].

[479] In addition to *Re Poyser* [1964] 2 Q.B. 467 authority for the proposition in the text can be found, e.g. in: *R. v Immigration Appeal Tribunal Ex p. Khan* [19831 Q.B. 790; *Knights Motors Ltd v Secretary of State for the Environment* [1984] J.P.L. 584; *R. v Mental Health Tribunal Ex p. Pickering* [1986] 1 All E.R. 99; *Bolton MBC* [1995] 3 P.L.R. 37; *MIT Securities Ltd v Secretary of State for the Environment* (1998) 75 P. & C.R. 188, CA; *S v Special Educational Needs Tribunal* [1995] 1 W.L.R. 1627 at 1636; *R. v Immigration Appeal Tribunal Ex p. Jebunisha Patel* [1996] Imm. A.R. 161 at 167; *Arulandandam v Secretary of State for the Home Department* [1996] Imm. A.R. 587 at 592; *R. v Secretary of State for Education Ex p. G*

broad terms why they lost or, as the case may be, won'.[480] Provided the reasons satisfy these core criteria, they need not be lengthy.[481] Judicial review may be inappropriate where the dispute relates to issues about the precise drafting of a decision.[482] Courts should also not scrutinise reasons with the analytical rigour employed on statutes or trust instruments,[483] and ought to forgive obvious mistakes that were unlikely to have misled anyone.[484]

Some general guidance on the standard of reasons required may also be   7–105
derived from a consideration of the purposes served by a duty to give reasons. Thus, reasons should be sufficiently detailed as to make quite clear to the parties—and especially the losing party—why the decision-maker decided as it did, and to avoid the impression that the decision was based upon extraneous considerations, rather than the matters raised at the hearing.[485] Reasons must be sufficient to reveal whether the tribunal made any error of law.[486] Reasons must also enable the court to which an appeal lies to discharge its appellate function, and when this is limited to questions of law, it will only be necessary to explain the exercise of discretion and to set out the evidence for the findings of fact in enough detail to disclose that the decision-maker has not acted unreasonably.[487] The reasons should refer

[1995] E.L.R. 58 at 67; *R. v Lancashire CC Ex p. Maycock* (1995) 159 L.G. Rev. 201 ("standard letter" with individual variations sufficient in circumstances); *R. v Islington LBC Ex p. Hinds* (1996) 28 H.L.R. 302; *R. v Criminal Injuries Compensation Board Ex p. Cook* [1996] 1 W.L.R. 1037 at 1043; *R. v Secretary of State for Transport Ex p. Richmond-upon-Thames LBC* [1996] 1 W.L.R. 1460, CA.

[480] *UCATT v Brain* [1981] I.R.L.R. 224 at 228 (Lord Donaldson M.R.: reasons required of industrial tribunal); *Piggott Brothers & Co Ltd v Jackson* [1991] I.R.L.R. 309 at 313; *Ex p. Ross, The Times,* June 9, 1994, CA (prison governor giving reasons for transfer of disruptive prisoner did not need to give "chapter and verse" of prisoner's conduct relied upon. See also *R. (on the application of Bahrami) v Immigration Appeal Tribunal* [2003] EWHC 1453 at [8] (Maurice Kay J.: "what is essential is not that an adjudicator should deal with every point at length, but that the determination should be sufficiently reasoned to enable a claimant, his advisers, and any appellate or reviewing body, to see why the claimant lost on a particular issue").

[481] *Stefan v General Medical Council* [1999] 1 W.L.R. 1293 at 1304 (reasons "need not be elaborate nor lengthy").

[482] *R. (on the application of W) v Acton Youth Court* [2005] EWHC 954; (2006) 170 J.P. 31.

[483] *Seddon Properties Ltd v Secretary of State for the Environment* (1978) 42 P. & C.R. 26; *UCATT v Brain* [1981] I.R.L.R. 224.

[484] *Elmbridge BC v Secretary of State for the Environment* (1980) 39 P. & C.R. 543 at 547–548.

[485] See, e.g. *R. v Mental Health Review Tribunal Ex p. Clatworthy* [1985] 3 All E.R. 699; *R. (on the application of Ashworth Hospital Authority) v Mental Health Review Tribunal for West Midlands and North West Region* [2001] EWHC Admin 901 at [77]; *South Bucks DC v Porter (No.2)* [2004] UKHL 33; [2004] 1 W.L.R. 1953 at [36].

[486] *Ashworth Hospital* [2001] EWHC Admin 901 at [77]; *South Bucks* [2004] UKHL 33; [2004] 1 W.L.R. 1953 at [36].

[487] *Varndell v Kearney & Trecker Marwin Ltd* [1983] I.C.R. 683 at 693–694, criticising the possibly more stringent test propounded in *Alexander Machinery (Dudley) Ltd v Crabtree* [1974] I.C.R. 120 at 122; cf. *Thameside MBC v Secretary of State for the Environment* [1984] J.P.L. 180, where the court may have set a high standard to ensure that a peripheral consideration in the determination of a planning appeal had not been given undue importance. And see *R. v Chief Registrar of Friendly Societies Ex p. New Cross Building Society* [1984] Q.B. 227.

to the main issues in the dispute, but need not necessarily deal with every material consideration.[488] Brevity is an administrative virtue, and elliptical reasons may be perfectly comprehensible when considered against the background of the arguments at the hearing.[489] Some decisions (such as the refusal of planning permission by an inspector) should be accompanied by reasons that are sufficiently precise to permit the individual to make the modifications necessary to secure a favourable decision in the future, or (where a Secretary of State disagrees with an inspector) to enable an objector to know what, if any, impact the planning considerations taken into account in a grant of planning permission may have in relation to the determination of future applications.[490]

7–106   The standard of reasons required in certain specific contexts has been considered. For example, a mental health review tribunal should explain why one witness is preferred to another; the reasons should sufficiently inform the patient and the hospital of the findings of the tribunal; and the court should take into account the fact that the tribunal has a legally qualified chairman and that reasons do not have to be given immediately.[491] As for immigration adjudicators, it has been held that there is no duty on the adjudicator to deal with every argument raised by the advocate in the case,[492] but the critical matters must be explained sufficiently clearly for the "thought processes" of the adjudicator on "material findings" to be understood.[493]

7–107   However, whilst concern for the quality of administrative justice does not require that all tribunals in all circumstances comply with some universally applicable standard, it is, nonetheless, essential that the courts do not allow the duty to give reasons to atrophy. In principle a remedy ought to lie for failure to give reasons,[494] unless the court is satisfied that

---

[488] South Bucks [2004] UKHL 33; [2004] 1 W.L.R. 1953 at [36]; R. v Criminal Injuries Compensation Board Ex p. Cook [1996] 1 W.L.R. 1037 at 1043.

[489] Elliot v Southwark LBC [1976] 1 W.L.R. 499; R. v Mental Health Tribunal Ex p. Pickering [1986] 1 All E.R. 99; Great Portland Estates Plc v Westminster City Council [1985] A.C. 661 at 673. The courts have recognised that the decision letters of inspectors are generally more succinct than the report and recommendations by inspectors together with letter of decision from the Secretary of State in non-devolved appeals. Nonetheless, in devolved decisions inspectors are held to much the same standard; see Hope v Secretary of State for the Environment (1975) 31 P. & C.R. 120; cf. Ellis v Secretary of State for the Environment (1974) 31 P. & C.R. 130; and Hatfield Construction Ltd v Secretary of State for the Environment [1983] J.P.L. 605. And see A. Barker and M. Couper, "The Art of Quasi-judicial Administration: The Planning Appeal and Inquiry System in England" (1983) 6 Urban Law and Policy 363, pp.454–455, where the increase in court challenges to inspectors' decisions in the early 1980s is attributed to deficiencies in inspectors' skills in writing decision letters.

[490] Save Britain's Heritage v Number 1 Poultry Ltd [1991] 1 W.L.R. 153 at 167. A mental health review tribunal should give sufficiently precise reasons to enable patients and medical advisors to cover the matters on a renewed application.

[491] Ashworth Hospital [2001] EWHC Admin 901 at [77].

[492] Eagil Trust Co Ltd v Piggott-Brown [1985] 3 All E.R. 119 at 122 (Griffiths L.J.).

[493] English v Emery Reimbold and Strick Ltd [2002] EWCA Civ 605; [2002] 1 W.L.R. 2409 at [19] (Lord Phillips M.R.).

[494] On an appeal from a decision on a question of law the courts may well have an inherent jurisdiction to direct the minister or tribunal to give adequate reasons although no formal application for mandamus has been made; see Iveagh (Earl) v Minister of Housing and Local Government [1964] 1 Q.B. 395 at 410.

no real prejudice has been caused to the applicant.[495] The reasons given by the reviewing court can often remedy the shortcomings of the original decision maker.

Whatever standards are applied by judges to the adequacy of reasons **7–108** given under a duty, it seems likely that reasons given voluntarily—where there is no duty—will be reviewed in accordance with the same standards as are applied to compulsory reasons.[496] It is no answer to an attack on the reasons for a decision on the grounds that they disclose a failure to take into account a relevant consideration or that an irrelevant consideration was taken into account or an error of law was made, that there is no requirement to give reasons. The unlawfulness in such a case lies not in the failure to give proper reasons, but in the unlawful nature of the decision, reasoning, or failure to reason, thereby disclosed.[497] On applications for judicial review it is the practice of government departments and public bodies to explain their reasons for their actions irrespective of any legal obligation to do so, where the outcome of the applications will depend on these reasons. As Lord Donaldson M.R. has said, judicial review "is a process which falls to be considered with all the cards face upwards on the table and the vast majority of the cards start in the authority's hands".[498] But in those cases where it is only because of the demands of procedural fairness or fairness that reasons are given, it may be that a lower standard applies; reasons may be as brief as a few sentences if that is enough to convey the substance of the decision.[499]

---

[495] *R. v Liverpool CC Ex p. Liverpool Taxi Fleet Operators' Association* [1975] 1 W.L.R. 701 at 706; *cf. Preston BC v Secretary of State for the Environment* [1978] J.P.L. 548 (omission of significant part of reasoning normally prejudicial); *Save Britain's Heritage* [1991] 1 W.L.R. 153. Outside the planning field, however (where the requirement to demonstrate substantial prejudice is required by statute), the courts will not readily conclude that an applicant is not prejudiced by an inadequately reasoned decision. The test may be whether any other conclusion than that reached was realistically possible: *R. v Ministry of Defence Ex p. Murray* [1998] C.O.D. 134, or whether it is "obvious" that there is no injustice (*R. v Winchester Crown Court Ex p. Morris* [1996] C.O.D. 104).

[496] *Elmbridge BC v Secretary of State for the Environment* (1980) 39 P. & C.R. 543; *Westminster City Council v Secretary of State for the Environment* [1984] J.P.L. 27 at 29–30; also *Grenfell-Baines v Secretary of State for the Environment* [1985] J.P.L. 256. *cf. Kentucky Fried Chicken Pty Ltd v Gantidis* (1979) 140 C.L.R. 675. In *R. v Secretary of State for Transport Ex p. Richmond-upon-Thames LBC*, the CA ([1996] 1 W.L.R. 1460) did not rely upon the suggestion of Jowitt J. at first instance ([1996] 1 W.L.R. 1005) that there was no duty to give reasons in respect of a voluntary consulation.

[497] See, e.g. *R. v Criminal Injuries Compensation Board v Gambles* [1994] P.I.Q.R. 314 (CICB's reasons contained a defect such that the decision could not stand, in failing to establish or disclose a rational and proportionate nexus between the conduct of the applicant and the decision not to offer him even a discounted award). But see now *R. v Criminal Injuries Compensation Board Ex p. Cook* [1996] 1 W.L.R. 1037, CA.

[498] *R. v Lancashire CC Ex p. Huddleston* [1986] 2 All E.R. 941; *OFT v IBA Healthcare* [2004] I.C.R. 1364.

[499] *R. v Civil Service Appeal Board Ex p. Cunningham* [1991] 4 All E.R. 310.

The rationality of the reasons given

7-109 When reasons are required, either by statute or by the growing common law requirements, or where they are provided, even though not strictly required, those reasons must be both "adequate and intelligible". They must therefore both rationally relate to the evidence in the case,[500] and be comprehensible in themselves.[501] The reasons for a decision must not be "self contradictory".[502] The reasons will not be construed in the same way as courts would construe a statute, but a decision may be struck down where an applicant can show substantial prejudice resulting from a failure on the part of the decision-maker to demonstrate how an issue of law had been resolved or a disputed issue of fact decided, or by "demonstrating some other lack of reasoning which raised substantial doubts over the decision-making process",[503] or by indicating "that the tribunal had never properly considered the matter . . . and that the proper thought processes have not been gone through".[504]

The implications which can be drawn from a failure to provide reasons

7-110 Where an applicant seeks to impugn a decision of an administrative authority other than by claiming non-compliance with a duty to give reasons—for example by challenging the legality or rationality of the decision—a failure by that authority to offer any answer to the allegations may justify an inference that its reasons were bad in law or that it had

---

[500] In *Re Poyser and Mills' Arbitration* [1964] 2 Q.B. 467 at 478 (Megaw J., speaking of the duty to give reasons imposed by s.12 of the Tribunals and Inquiries Act 1958, said that the required reasons "must be read as meaning that proper adequate reasons must be given . . . which deal with the substantial points that have been raised"); *Westminster City Council v Great Portland Estates Plc* [1985] A.C. 661 at 673 (Lord Scarman).

[501] *Hope v Secretary of State for the Environment* (1975) 31 P. & C.R. 120 at 123 (Phillips J., referring to a decision of a planning inspector which "must be such that it enables the appellant to understand on what grounds the appeal has been decided and be in sufficient detail to enable him to know what conclusions the inspector has reached on the principal important issues"); *Ward v Secretary of State for the Environment* (1989) 59 P. & C.R. 486 at 487 (Woolf L.J.: "With regard to the requirement to give reasons it suffices to say that the reasons must be ones which are understandable to those who will receive those reasons"), cited with approval in *Save Britain's Heritage v Number 1 Poultry Ltd* [1991] 1 W.L.R. 153 at 165 (Lord Bridge), *Bolton MDC v Secretary of State for the Environment* (1996) 71 P. & C.R. 309; *R. v Hammersmith & Fulham LBC Ex p. Earls Court Ltd*, *The Times*, September 7, 1993 (a condition imposed upon an entertainment licence which was so obscure that it necessitated the issue of a construction summons was "unreasonable in the *Wednesbury* sense" (Kennedy L.J.)).

[502] *Mahon v Air New Zealand Ltd* [1984] A.C. 808 at 835 (Lord Diplock required the finding to be based on some material that tends logically to show the existence of facts consistent with the finding).

[503] *Save Britain's Heritage v Number 1 Poultry Ltd* [1991] 1 W.L.R. 153 at 168 (Lord Bridge, emphasising, however, that the adequacy of reasons depended upon the legislative context and could not be answered in vacuo. It used to be said that it was a requirement of natural justice that the material logically relates to the finding); *Lord Diplock in Mahon v Air New Zealand Ltd* [1984] A.C. 808.

[504] *Crake v Supplementary Benefits Commission* [1982] 1 All E.R. 498 at 508.

exercised its powers unlawfully. "Absurd" or "perverse" decisions may be presumed to have been decided in that fashion, as may decisions where the given reasons are simply unintelligible.[505] However, the absence of reasons does not automatically give rise to the inference that none exist,[506] and there is a conflict of authorities at the highest level as to the strength of the evidence of collateral unlawfulness which the applicant must adduce in order to benefit from the inference of unlawfulness if no justification of the decision is given. In *Padfield v Minister of Agriculture, Fisheries and Food*, where the challenge was to the purpose to which the Minister had applied the regulations in question, the House of Lords suggested that if a prima facie case of unlawfulness was established by the applicant, then in the absence of reasons the court could infer that the power was exercised outside of the legislative purpose.[507]

A more restrictive approach was adopted in *R. v Secretary of State for*   7–111
Trade and Industry Ex p. Lonrho, where, upon a challenge for irrationality, it was held that the absence of reasons could provide no support for the suggested irrationality of the decision unless, "if all other known facts and the circumstances appear to point overwhelmingly in favour of a different decision, the decision-maker cannot complain if the court draws the inference that he has had no rational reason for his Decision".[508] Although there is some support for the restrictive *Lonrho* test, at least where an authority has a specific exemption from a statutory duty to give reasons, (in which case the courts ought not to force the authority to choose between waiving the exemption and risking an adverse inference[509]) in general, recent authority has favoured the *Padfield* approach, even in cases where the ground of review is irrationality (as in *Lonrho*) rather than illegality.

Thus where a local authority made a very meagre disclosure of reasons in   7–112
response to an application for judicial review of a decision not to award a student grant, the Court of Appeal suggested that if the applicant could

[505] *R. v Higher Education Funding Council Ex p. Institute of Dental Surgery* [1994] 1 W.L.R. 242 at 258 (referring to "an apparently inexplicable decision") and 261 (noting that a decision may be "so aberrant as in itself to call for an explanation").
[506] *R. (on the application of Farrakhan) v Secretary of State for the Home Department* [2002] EWCA Civ 606; [2002] Q.B. 1391 at [7].
[507] [1968] A.C. 997 at 1053, 1061, 1032–1033, 1049 (Lords Pearce, Upjohn, Reid and Hodson; *R. v Brixton Prison Governor Ex p. Soblen (No.2)* [1963] 2 Q.B. 243 at 302, 307–308 (Lord Denning M.R. and Donovan L.J.).
[508] [1989] 1 W.L.R. 525 at 539; *Eagil Trust Co Ltd v Piggott-Brown* [1985] 3 All E.R. 119 (tribunal presumed to have acted properly when court can see how a point could have been answered, despite failure of reasons to deal with it expressly).
[509] *R. v Secretary of State for Social Services Ex p. Connolly* [1986] 1 W.L.R. 421, CA (since social security commissioners have been specifically exempted by art.2 of the Tribunals and Inquiries (Social Security Commissioners) Order 1980 from the general requirement under s.10 of the Tribunals and Inquiries Act 1992 to give reasons when refusing leave to appeal from a determination of the attendance allowance board, no adverse inference should be drawn from a failure to give reasons, and the court ought not to confront the commissioners with the embarrassing choice of either complying with the court's wishes and thus waiving their statutory exemption or declining to comply and thus running the risk of apparent discourtesy to the court and of adverse inferences being drawn (Slade L.J.); *cf. R. v Inland Revenue Commissioners Ex p. TC Coombs & Co* [1991] 2 A.C. 283.

merely show that the facts were sufficient to obtain leave to apply for judicial review then, even though there was no obligation on the decision-maker to give reasons to the applicant, the authority would be under a duty to make full and fair disclosure to the court.[510] And where the Civil Service Appeal Board had awarded an inexplicably low sum in compensation for unfair dismissal, the failure of the Board to provide reasons to the court to dispel the "arguable" case of the applicant led the court to presume that the prima facie irrational decision was in fact irrational.[511] The *Padfield* approach can also be supported by reference to more general principles of the law of evidence. As Lord Lowry has pointed out, in another case concerning a challenge for irrationality in the absence of justification by the decision-maker:

> "In our legal system generally, the silence of one party in face of the other party's evidence may convert that evidence into proof in relation to matters which are, or are likely to be, within the knowledge of the silent party and about which that party could be expected to give evidence. Thus, depending on the circumstances, a prima facie case may become a strong or even an overwhelming case."[512]

7–113   It should be noted, however, that in the absence of reasons it will often be difficult to establish a prima facie case that a wide discretionary power has been improperly exercised,[513] so a claimant may not be able to obtain

[510] *R. v Lancashire CC Ex p. Huddleston* [1986] 2 All E.R. 941 (court did not on the facts infer that the authority had erred in exercising its discretion or that it had acted irrationally; Parker L.J. and Sir George Waller did not share Lord Donaldson's unease about the lack of disclosure in the case, but "I do not understand them to have disagreed with the principle" (Lord Donaldson M.R. in *Cunningham* [1991] 4 All E.R. 310). *cf. New Zealand Fishing Industry Assn v Minister of Agriculture and Fisheries* [1988] 1 N.Z.L.R. 544, CA (minister's failure to file affidavit giving reasons for decision could serve to strengthen misgivings as to lawfulness of action).

[511] *Cunningham* [1991] 4 All E.R. 310; *R. v Criminal Injuries Compensation Board Ex p. Cummins* [1992] C.O.D. 297 (although the CICB is not under statutory duty to give reasons, failure to show basis of fact on which it relied in making award to victim of crime rendered the award perverse); *R. v Secretary of State for the Home Department Ex p. Sinclair* [1992] Imm. A.R. 293 (decision of Home Secretary to sign extradition warrant *Wednesbury* unreasonable); *R. v Secretary of State for Education Ex p. Standish, The Times*, November 15, 1993 (ground upon which teacher debarred from his employment was not identified by the Secretary of State by reasons or by his affidavit, and hence the decision quashed for irrationality); *cf. R. v Criminal Injuries Compensation Board Ex p. Gambles* [1994] P.I.Q.R. 314 (reasoning which omitted one important step was defective and hence decision must be quashed).

[512] *Coombs* [1991] 2 A.C. 283 at 300 (sparseness of evidence provided by the Revenue to justify a notice compelling the disclosure of documents should not lead to the conclusion that the Revenue had acted irrationally); it is suggested that the decision turned on special circumstances which justified the failure to provide reasons: the fact that the notice had been scrutinised by a Commissioner and hence the presumption of regularity *omnia praesumuntur rite et solenniter esse acta donec probelur in contrarium* applied; the fact that there was a general duty of confidentiality on the Revenue; and that on the facts there had been an express promise of anonymity and confidentiality.

[513] See, e.g. *Cannock Chase DC v Kelly* [1978] 1 W.L.R. 1. Cf. *Secretary of State for Employment v ASLEF (No.2)* [1972] 2 Q.B. 455; also *British Airways Board v Laker Airways Ltd* [1985] A.C. 58, 92 (ultra vires difficult to establish in decision concerning international relations).

permission and thereby pressure the decision maker to justify the decision to the court. The readiness of the courts to infer unlawfulness is therefore no substitute for a duty on public bodies to give reasons for their decisions to affected individuals.

Remedy for lack or insufficiency of reasons

Usually, the remedy given in a case of breach of duty to give reasons or adequate reasons is an order quashing the unreasoned decision,[514] rather than an order to require provision of the reasons. The former remedy is usually deemed preferable as it reflects the purpose of reasons to encourage focused decision-making and avoids the risk of reconstruction of reasons after the decision.[515] Given that there is a lapse of time between the original decision and the judicial review proceedings, it may also be impractical to order a remedy requiring reasons to be provided.[516]   **7–114**

It is unsettled whether the absence or inadequacy of reasons can be remedied by provision of further fresh reasons in evidence when the decision is challenged.[517] However, "It is well-established that the court should exercise caution before accepting reasons for a decision which were not articulated at the time of the decision but were only expressed later, in particular after the commencement of proceedings".[518] Where there is a statutory duty to provide reasons, such that the adequacy of reasons is central to the legality of the decision itself, this caution also applies.[519] The types of considerations that should be taken into account in deciding whether to accept subsequent evidence of the reasons include:[520] whether   **7–115**

---

[514] See, e.g. *Flannery v Halifax Estate Agencies Ltd* [2000] 1 W.L.R. 377 at 383; *Cedeno v Logan* [2001] 1 W.L.R. 86; *R. (on the application of Nash) v Chelsea College of Art and Design* [2001] EWHC Admin 538 at [27]. *cf.English v Emery Reimbold and Strick Ltd* [2002] EWCA Civ 605; [2002] 1 W.L.R. 2409 at [25].

[515] M. Fordham, *Judicial Review Handbook*, 4th edn. (2004), para.62.5.

[516] See, e.g. *Flannery v Halifax Estate Agencies Ltd* [2000] 1 W.L.R. 377 at 383 (Henry L.J.: since "more than a year had passed since the hearing. It would not have been realistic for the judge to reconstitute his reasons").

[517] See, e.g. *R. (on the application of Young) v Oxford City Council* [2002] EWCA Civ 990; [2002] 3 P.L.R. 86 at [20] (Pill L.J. noting the dangers in permitting a planning authority to provide an explanatory statement); *cf. Hijazi v Kensington and Chelsea R. LBC* [2003] EWCA Civ 692; [2003] H.L.R. 1113 at [32] ("nothing objectionable in a decision-maker making a subsequent statement in which he identifies the material that he took into account in the course of the decision-making process"); also *Lewis v Havering LBC* [2006] EWCA Civ 1793; (2006) 150 S.J.L.B. 1569, CA.

[518] *R. (on the application of D) v Secretary of State for the Home Department* [2003] EWHC 155; [2003] 1 F.L.R. 979 at [18] (Maurice Kay J.), [19]; also *R. v Westminster City Council Ex p. Ermakov* [1996] 2 All E.R. 302; *R. (on the application of August) v Criminal Injuries Compensation Appeals Panel* [2001] Q.B. 774 at [86]; *R. (on the application of S) v Brent LBC* [2002] EWCA Civ 693; [2002] E.L.R. 556 at [26]; *R. (on the application of Wandsworth LBC) v Schools Adjudicator* [2003] EWHC 2969; [2004] E.L.R. 274 at [79]; *R. (on the application of Goldsmith) v Wandsworth LBC* [2004] EWCA Civ 1170; (2004) 7 C.C.L. Rep. 472 at [91]; *R. (on the application of Richards) v Pembrokeshire CC* [2004] EWCA Civ 1000; [2005] B.L.G.R. 105.

[519] *R. v Westminster City Council Ex p. Ermakov* [1996] 2 All E.R. 302 at 312; *R. (on the application of Nash) v Chelsea College of Art and Design* [2001] EWHC Admin 538 at [34]

[520] *Nash* [2001] EWHC Admin 538 at [34].

the new reasons are consistent with the original reasons; whether it is clear that the new reasons are indeed the original reasons or whether there is a real risk that the new reasons have been composed subsequently to support the decision; the delay before the later reasons were put forward; and the circumstances in which the later reasons were put forward. In particular, reasons put forward after the commencement of proceedings should be treated especially carefully. Where the later reasons merely elucidate reasons given contemporaneously with the decision, they will normally be considered by the court.[521] The courts have also considered whether the decision-maker would have been expected to state in the decision document the reason that he is seeking to adduce later and whether it would be just in all the circumstances to refuse to admit the subsequent reasons.[522]

PUBLIC INQUIRIES

7–116 As we noted in Chapter 1, public inquiries can take a number of forms and may be established in different contexts.[523] Public inquiries engage a duty to act fairly,[524] and the precise procedures to be followed usually depend on the particular circumstances of the inquiry.[525] The difficulty often lies in "securing an acceptable balance between the thorough investigation of a matter of 'urgent public importance' so as to ascertain the truth, on the one hand, and on the other the need fully to accord implicated individuals a fair procedure".[526]

7–117 What has happened more recently at certain public inquiries, does however illustrate a change of emphasis in the role of the person conducting an inquiry. The traditional approach in the past, much favoured by planning inquiry inspectors, was to let anyone who had an interest appear, call every witness he wished, and be separately represented if he was prepared to meet the expenses involved. Now a much more "hands on" approach is sometimes adopted by the inspector or other person in charge of the inquiry. Thus in the case of both the Taylor Inquiry into the Hillsborough football disaster and the Woolf Inquiry into the

---

[521] R. (on the application of B) v Merton LBC [2003] EWHC 1689; [2003] 4 All E.R. 280 at [42]; R. v South Bank University Ex p. Coggeran [2001] E.L.R. 42 at [36] (evidence rejected because it was used to alter or contract the contemporaneous minutes).

[522] R. (on the application of Leung) v Imperial College of Science, Technology and Medicine [2002] EWHC 1358; [2002] E.L.R. 653 at [29]–[30] (Silber J.).

[523] See 1–001.

[524] Bushell v Secretary of State for the Environment [1981] A.C. 75 at 95 (Lord Diplock).

[525] See, e.g. R. Scott, "Procedures at Inquiries: The Duty to be Fair" (1995) 111 L.Q.R. 596; B. Hadfield, "R. v Lord Saville of Newdigate Ex p. Anonymous Soldiers: What is the Purpose of a Tribunal of Inquiry?" [2003] P.L. 663; L. Blom-Cooper, "Tribunals under Inquiry" [1999] P.L. 1; L. Blom-Cooper, "Public Interest in Public Inquiries" [2003] P.L. 578.

[526] Hadfield [2003] P.L. 663, 667. In general also, inquiries should not discuss matters of national policy: Bushell v Secretary of State for the Environment [1981] A.C. 75. This is a difficult distinction to maintain in practice: R. v Secretary of State for Transport Ex p. Gwent CC [1988] Q.B. 429 at 437 (Woolf L.J.).

Strangeways and other prison riots, only those persons whose actions were at risk of being criticised were allowed to be represented, witnesses were normally only called by counsel to the inquiry, who exercised his discretion as to whom should be called, and cross-examination was strictly limited. Different techniques were used for different classes of evidence, only part was given orally (not all in public), other evidence was written and in the case of the Prison Inquiry even seminars were employed to canvass issues of wide-ranging nature. This departure from the usual common law adversarial nature of resolving issues of fact was used to save both time and resources and to avoid the inquiries being overwhelmed by material. It meant that reports were able to be produced within reasonable time limits, which was very much in the public interest, without any complaints of lack of fairness.[527]

An even more restricted approach to the representation of witnesses was **7–118** adopted in the case of the inquiry conducted by Scott L.J. into the Matrix Churchill, Arms to Iraq affair.[528] Meanwhile, the Budd inquiry into the circumstances surrounding the resignation of David Blunkett, was primarily inquisitorial without formal hearings or the questioning of witnesses by lawyers.[529] However, as just noted, much will depend on the nature of the inquiry; and in the unique circumstances of the Bloody Sunday inquiry, where the right to life of witnesses may have been at risk, questions regarding anonymity of witnesses and the location in which evidence would be given, were of paramount importance.[530]

ECHR ART.6: CONTENT

A number of rights are contained within ECHR Art.6.[531] The right to a fair **7–119** hearing, the right to a public hearing, and the right to a hearing within a reasonable time are separate and distinct rights from the right to a hearing before an independent and impartial tribunal established by law.[532]

---

[527] As to techniques used at the Woolf Inquiry, see *Prison Disturbances*, section 2 (Cm. 1456, 1991); R. Morgan "Woolf: In Retrospect and Prospect" (1991) M.L.R. 713.
[528] L. Blom-Cooper, "Witnesses and the Scott Inquiry" [1994] P.L. 1.
[529] *An Inquiry into an Application for Indefinite Leave to Remain*. HC Paper No.175 (Session 2004/05). *cf.* the Hutton Inquiry, which combined inquisitorial and adversarial elements in a two-stage process: *Report of the Inquiry into the Circumstances Surrounding the Death of Dr David Kelly CMG*. HC Paper No.247 (Session 2004/05) paras 4–8. For discussion, see N. Bamforth, "Political Accountability in Play: The Budd Inquiry and David Blunkett's Resignation" [2005] P.L. 229.
[530] Hadfield [2003] P.L. 663; see also *R. v Lord Saville of Newdigate Ex p. B (No.2)* [2000] 1 W.L.R. 1855, CA; *R. (on the application of A) v Lord Saville of Newdigate (Bloody Sunday Inquiry)* [2001] EWCA Civ 2048; [2002] 1 W.L.R. 1249, CA.
[531] On Convention rights generally, see Ch.13.
[532] *Magill v Porter* [2001] UKHL 6; [2002] 2 A.C. 357 at [87] (Lord Hope of Craighead). For discussion, see Ovey and White (2006), pp.175–188.

Fair hearing

7-120 The right to a fair hearing in Art.6 requires access to "equality of arms", which means that it is necessary to strike a "fair balance" between the parties.[533] Thus, each party must be afforded a reasonable opportunity to present his case, including his evidence, under conditions that do not place him at a substantial disadvantage in relation to his opponent.[534] Absolute equality of arms is not required however, and there is, for instance, no duty on the State to provide legal aid to a indigent litigant to such a level as to ensure total parity with a wealthy opponent.[535] This may include the right to legal representation, although there is no absolute right to legal representation.[536] The right to a fair hearing will be violated where the defendant, without good cause, prevents an applicant from gaining access to, or falsely denies the existence of, documents in its possession which are of assistance to the applicant's case.[537] The right also means that in certain circumstances, parties to civil proceedings should be entitled to cross-examine witnesses.

7-121 There is no express requirement to provide reasoning in Art.6. The ECtHR has, however, regarded this requirement as implicit in the obligation to provide a fair hearing and Art.6 includes an obligation to give a reasoned judgment to enable the decision to decide whether to appeal.[538] Whether this requirement adds anything to the common law position has

---

[533] *R. v Secretary of State for the Environment Ex p. Challenger* [2001] Env. L.R. 209 at [48]–[51] (the court was not persuaded that there was "inequality of arms" where the claimant did not have financial resources for representation at a rail public inquiry given that the claimant had applied for and been rejected funding; given that the Inspector at the public inquiry would ensure the proper presentation of Challener's case; and the local authority had a role in adducing evidence which would support Challener's case). The concept of "equality of arms" was first mentioned in the case of *Neumeister v Austria* (1979–80) 1 E.H.R.R. 91.

[534] *Dombo Beheer BV v The Netherlands* (1994) 18 E.H.R.R. 213, para.33. *Ruiz-Mateos v Spain* (1993) 16 E.H.R.R. 505; *Lilly France v France* (2003) ECtHR (violation of Art.6(1) where party had not received a copy of the report submitted by the reporting judge to the Court of Cassation, whereas the advocate-general had); *Willams v Cowell* [2000] 1 W.L.R. 187, CA (no violation of Art.6 where Employment Appeal Tribunal sitting in London refused to conduct proceedings in Welsh, given that the appellant could speak and understand English): *MB v Secretary of State for the Home Department: AF v Secretary of State for the Home Department* [2007] UKHL 46 (Art 6 meant that defendants in control order proceedings had the right to know the key evidence against them and that defendants were entitled to "such measure of procedural protection as is commensurate with the gravity of the potential consequences": [24]–[90]).

[535] *Steel and Morris v UK* (2005) 41 E.H.R.R. 403 at para.59.

[536] *X v Austria* 42 C.D. 145 (1972) E. Com. H.R.; *cf. Financial Services Authority v Rourke* [2002] C.P. Rep. 14 (cross-examination may not be allowed in cases suitable for summary disposal, without breach of Art.6(1)). Legal representative includes lawyers from other EU Member States: *R. (on the application of Van Hoogstraten) v Governor of Belmarsh Prison* [2002] EWHC 1965; [2003] 1 W.L.R. 263; and *Ezeh and Connors v UK* (2002) 35 E.H.R.R. 691.

[537] *McGinley and Egan v UK* (1998) 27 E.H.R.R. 1, para.86.

[538] *Hadjianastassiou v Greece* (1992) 16 E.H.R.R. 219; *Garcia Ruiz v Spain* (1999) 31 E.H.R.R. 589; *Ruiz Jorija v Spain* (1994) 19 E.H.R.R. 553; *Anya v University of Oxford* [2001] E.L.R. 711 at [12]; *English v Reimbold and Strick* [2002] 1 W.L.R. 2409 at [8]–[14], CA.

been questioned.[539] The ECtHR will hold that Art.6(1) has been violated if a judgment leaves it unclear whether the court in question has addressed a contention advanced by a party that is fundamental to the resolution of the litigation.[540] In relation to the standard of reasons, Art.6 requires that a decision contains reasons that are sufficient to demonstrate that the core issues raised by the parties have been addressed by the domestic court and how those issues have been resolved. It does not, however, seem to go further and require a judgment to explain why one contention, or piece of evidence, has been preferred to another.[541] Moreover, reasons do not have to be given on every point, but they must enable the party to understand the essence of the decision in order to be able to exercise appeal rights.[542] In certain situations, fairness does not require that the parties should be informed of the reasoning: interlocutory decisions in the course of case management provide an obvious example.[543] By contrast, a failure to give reasons on costs decisions can only comply with Art.6 if the reason for the decision in respect of costs is clearly implicit from the circumstances in which the award is made.[544]

Public hearing and public pronouncement of judgment

ECHR Art.6 confers a general right to an oral hearing, deriving from the right to a public hearing and the public pronouncement of judgment.[545] The failure to provide an oral hearing before an administrative or other tribunal determining "civil rights and obligation" may not however constitute a violation of Art.6, if the case is considered on appeal or reviewed by a court sitting in public.[546] Similarly, while Art.6 normally requires that a criminal sentence is determined at a public hearing,[547] the right is qualified and a hearing in private may be justified in certain circumstances, including in the interests of public order.[548] Thus, it has

7–122

---

[539] *English v Reimbold and Strick* [2002] 1 W.L.R. 2409 at [12], CA.
[540] See, e.g. *Ruiz Torija v Spain* 19 E.H.R.R. 553; *Hiro Balani v Spain* (1994) 19 E.H.R.R. 566.
[541] *English v Reimbold and Strick* [2002] 1 W.L.R. 2409 at [12]
[542] *Helle v Finland* (1998) 26 E.H.R.R. 505.
[543] *English v Reimbold and Strick* [2002] 1 W.L.R. 2409 at [13].
[544] [2002] 1 W.L.R. 2409 at [14].
[545] The right to a public hearing implies a right to an oral hearing at the trial court level unless there are exceptional circumstances which justify excluding a hearing: *Fischer v Austria* (1995) 20 E.H.R.R. 349 at para.44; *Allan Jacobsson v Sweden (No.2)* (2001) 32 E.H.R.R. 463.
[546] *Schuler-Zgraggen v Switzerland* (1993) 16 E.H.R.R. 405 at para.5 (court recognised that there were technical areas of decision-making where there are good reasons for avoiding oral hearings); *R. (on the application of Adlard) v Secretary of State for the Environment, Transport and the Regions* [2002] EWCA Civ 735; [2002] 1 W.L.R. 2515 (upholding refusal to grant oral hearing to objectors to a planning application).
[547] *R. (on the application of Smith) v Secretary of State for the Home Department* [2004] EWCA Civ 99 at [91]; *R. (on the application of Hammond) v Secretary of State for the Home Department* [2005] UKHL 69; [2006] 1 A.C. 603 at [16]–[17], HL (statutory provision which precluded the possibility of an oral hearing to determine the minimum term of a mandatory life prisoner violated Art.6).
[548] *R. (on the application of Bannatyne) v Secretary of State for the Home Department, The Independent Adjudicator* [2004] EWHC 1921 at [66].

been considered contrary to public interest, given the public order problems of moving prisoners out of prisons to judges, to require all disciplinary prison matters to be determined in public hearings.[549] Similarly, the interests of justice have necessitated a private hearing where the trustees of a charity applied for the directions of the court in relation to legal proceedings to which the charity was a party,[550] or where the interests of children are at issue.[551] It is also the case that categories of cases may be designated as not requiring an oral hearing, without infringing Art.6.[552]

7–123   In criminal cases, Art.6 confers a right to a hearing in the presence of the accused.[553] In civil cases, however, the right of a party to be present at the hearing has been held to extend only to certain kinds of cases, such as cases which involve an assessment of a party's personal conduct,[554] including proceedings relating to the exercise of a profession.[555] Where the professional has been given proper notice however, but fails to attend without good reason, the tribunal may proceed in his absence.[556]

7–124   As for public pronouncement of judgment, when deciding whether a judgment in the context of a High Court challenge to arbitration should be public, although the court could start with the parties' wish for confidentiality and privacy, it should hear representations from either party for the hearing to continue in public, or even, if appropriate, raise the possibility itself of having the hearing in public. It is for the court to ensure the hearing is in compliance with Art.6 and to determine if the public interest in a public hearing outweighed the parties' wishes for continuing privacy.[557] Even if the hearing has been in private however, the court must take into account that stricter standards have to be imposed in relation to the public pronouncement of the judgment than to the public hearing of the underlying proceedings and that where judgment could be given without disclosing significant confidential information, the public interest in ensuring appropriate standards of fairness in the conduct of arbitrations militated in favour of a public judgment.[558] Generally, it is not necessary for the judgment to be pronounced at a public hearing where it is available to the public.[559]

---

[549] *Bannatyne* [2004] EWHC 1921.
[550] *In re Trusts of X Charity* [2003] EWHC 257, Ch; [2003] 1 W.L.R. 2751.
[551] *P and B v UK* (2002) 34 E.H.R.R. 529 (hearing to determine the residence of children).
[552] *R. (on the application of Ewing) v Department for Constitutional Affairs* [2006] EWHC 504, [2006] 2 All E.R. 993 at [42]–[43] (no violation of Art.6 where there was no entitlement to an oral hearing for those seeking to have a civil proceedings order set aside, given that the court had an unfettered discretion to order an oral hearing).
[553] *Ekbatini v Sweden* (1988) 13 E.H.R.R. 504, para.25.
[554] *Muyldermans v Belgium* (1991) 15 E.H.R.R. 204, para.64.
[555] *Bakker v Austria* (2004) 39 E.H.R.R. 26.
[556] *Dhirendra Nath Das v General Medical Council* [2003] UKPC 75 at [8]; also *Komanický v Slovakia* June 4, 2002 at paras 50–55 (violation of Art.6(1) where adjournment not granted despite applicant's good medical reason for non-attendance and the importance of his presence at the appeal hearing).
[557] *Department for Economics, Policy and Development of City of Moscow v Bankers Trust Co* [2004] EWCA Civ 314; [2005] Q.B. 207.
[558] *City of Moscow* [2004] EWCA Civ 314; [2005] Q.B. 207 [39].
[559] *Pretto v Italy* (1984) 6 E.H.R.R. 182; *P and B v UK* (2002) 34 E.H.R.R. 529.

Hearing within a reasonable time

ECHR Art.6 requires that a hearing take place within a reasonable time. **7–125** This right is not an aspect of overall fairness, but is an independent right which must be considered separately.[560] An accused is not required to show that prejudice has been, or is likely to be, caused, as a result of delay. It is simply necessary to determine whether, having regard to all the circumstances of the case, the time taken to determine the person's rights and obligations was unreasonable.[561] The threshold for proving a breach of the "reasonable time" requirement has been held to be a high one. If the period of delay was one which, on its face and without more, gave grounds for real concern it was almost certainly unnecessary to go further. This was because the concern in such a case was that there were infringements of basic human rights and not departures from the ideal.[562]

Relevant circumstances to be considered include complexity of the **7–126** factual or legal issues raised by the case; the conduct of the applicant and the competent administrative and judicial authorities; and what is "at stake" for the applicant.[563] For example, "special diligence" was required where an applicant dying of AIDS sought compensation from the State for having negligently infected him with HIV.[564] An overall assessment may be made though, without considering each of these specific criteria.[565] In general, the threshold of proving a breach of the reasonable time requirement is high.[566]

The reasonable time requirement applies to all stages of criminal **7–127** proceedings, including sentencing, confiscation orders and appeals.[567] Where there has been an unreasonable delay, the appropriate remedy depends on the nature of the breach and all the circumstances, including particularly the stage of the proceedings at which the breach was established. It would be appropriate to stay or dismiss the proceedings only if either a fair hearing was no longer possible or it would be, for any compelling reason, unfair to try the defendant. The public interest in the final determination of criminal charges require that such a charge should not be stayed or dismissed if any lesser remedy would be just and proportionate in all the circumstances. Where the breach is discovered retrospectively, it is only appropriate to quash the conviction where the hearing was unfair or it was unfair to try the defendant at all.[568] Where

[560] *Magill v Porter* [2002] 2 A.C. 357 at [108]–[109].
[561] *Magill* [2002] 2 A.C. 357 at [108]–[109].
[562] *Dyer v Watson* [2002] UKPC D 1; [2004] 1 A.C. 379 at [52] (Lord Bingham of Cornhill).
[563] *Zimmerman and Steiner v Switzerland* (1983) E.H.R.R. 587; *Davies v UK* (2002) 35 E.H.R.R. 720.
[564] *A v Denmark* (1996) 22 E.H.R.R. 458.
[565] *Ferrantelli and Santangelo v Italy* (1996) 23 E.H.R.R. 288.
[566] *Lloyd v Bow Street Magistrates Court* (2003) EWHC 2294.
[567] *R. (on the application of Lloyd) v Bow Street Magistrates Court* [2003] EWHC 2294 at [14], [18], [27], [29] (breach of Art.6.1 due to delay in having enforcement proceedings in respect of a confiscation order determined within a reasonable time).
[568] *Attorney General's Reference No.2 of 2001* [2003] UKHL 68; [2004] 2 A.C. 72 at [24]. See further *HM Advocate v R.* [2002] UKPC D 3; [2004] 1 A.C. 462 (unreasonable delay rendered the continuance of a prosecution incompatible with Art.6).

there has been an unreasonable delay between the conviction and the hearing of an appeal, if the conviction is upheld as sound, it may not be necessary to quash the conviction. Instead it may be sufficient to compensate the individual by reducing his sentence.[569]

ECHR ART.2: CONTENT

The requirements of Art.2

7–128 ECHR Art.2 protects the right to life.[570] Where a death has occurred, the State may have a positive obligation to conduct an investigation.[571] To constitute an "effective" investigation, it is generally necessary for the person carrying out the investigation to be independent from those implicated in the events.[572] This means not only a lack of hierarchical or institutional connection but also a practical independence.[573] The investigation should be capable of leading to the determination of whether the force used in the case was or was not justified and to the identification and punishment of those responsible.[574] There is an implicit requirement of promptness and reasonable expedition,[575] and there must be a sufficient element of public scrutiny of the investigation or its results to secure accountability in practice as well as in theory; and the investigation must involve the next of kin in the investigative procedure to the extent necessary to protect their legitimate interests.[576] The types of procedural failures which will violate Art.2 include: failing to exercise proper control over the scene of the investigation;[577] failure to seek follow-up information from those present at the scene of the incident;[578] failure to interview military personnel or police officers immediately after the incident;[579] and a failure to give reasons for refusing to prosecute police officers for collusion in an incident.[580] Lack of independence has been found where the investigation is conducted by officers who are part of the police force suspected of issuing threats against the victim.[581] The minimum standards

---

[569] *Mills v Her Majesty's Advocate* [2002] UKPC D 2; [2004] 1 A.C. 441 at [52]–[56].
[570] See 13–001.
[571] See 13–001.
[572] *Jordan v UK* (2003) 37 E.H.R.R. 52 at para.106.
[573] *Jordan v UK* (2003) 37 E.H.R.R. 52 at para.106; *Finucane v UK* (2003) 37 E.H.R.R. 29.
[574] *Jordan* (2003) 37 E.H.R.R. 52 at para.107. Also: *Middleton* [2004] UKHL 10; [2004] 2 A.C. 182 at [20]; R. (*on the application of Hurst*) *v Commissioner of Police of the Metropolis* [2007] UKHL 13; [2007] 2 W.L.R. 726 at [19].
[575] *Jordan* (2003) 37 E.H.R.R. 52 at para.108.
[576] *Jordan* (2003) 37 E.H.R.R. 52 at para.109.
[577] *Jordan* (2003) 37 E.H.R.R. 52 at para.118 (although on the facts in *Jordan*, there was no such failure).
[578] *Jordan* (2003) 37 E.H.R.R. 52.
[579] *Kelly v UK* App. No.30054/96 (May 4, 2001); *McKerr v UK* (2002) 34 E.H.R.R. 20.
[580] *Shanaghan v UK* App. No.377115/97 (May 4, 2001), *The Times*, May 18, 2001; *Finucane* (2003) 37 E.H.R.R. 29 at paras 77–78.
[581] *Finucane* (2003) 37 E.H.R.R. 29 at para.76.

for an effective investigation will also not be met where the inquiry is held in private and without participation of the family of the victim;[582] although it may be necessary to grant anonymity to a witness if the life of that witness is at risk.[583]

Inquests

The mere fact that an inquest has been held will not mean that the requirements of Art.2 are satisfied; whether Art.2 is satisfied will depend on how the inquest is conducted.[584] The inquest should involve participation of the family of the deceased,[585] and Art.2 may require that the deceased's family is given funding for legal representation,[586] however usually this will only be where the case falls into the "exceptional category where legal representation is needed in order to ensure effective participation by the deceased's family and an effective investigation".[587] An inquest must also, at the very least, "culminate in an expression, however brief, of the jury's conclusion on the disputed factual issues at the heart of the case".[588]

7–129

[582] R. (on the application of Amin) v Secretary of State for the Home Department [2003] UKHL 51; [2004] 1 A.C. 653.
[583] R. (on the application of A) v HM Coroner for Inner South London [2004] EWCA Civ 1439; [2005] U.K.H.R.R. 44 See Re Officer L [2007] UKHL 36; [2007] 1 W.L.R. 2135 (the test is whether the risk of injury or death would be materially increased if evidence was given without anonymity).
[584] R. (on the application of Wright) v Secretary of State for the Home Department [2001] EWHC Admin 520; [2002] H.R.L.R. 1; R. v DPP Ex p. Manning [2001] Q.B. 330.
[585] R. (on the application of Khan) v Secretary of State for Health [2003] EWCA Civ 1129; [2004] 1 W.L.R. 971 at [69].
[586] Khan [2003] EWCA Civ 1129; [2004] 1 W.L.R. 971 at [74]–[75].
[587] R. (on the application of Challender) v Legal Services Commission [2004] EWHC 925; [2004] A.C.D. 57, [68]; Khan [2003] EWCA Civ 1129; [2004] 1 W.L.R. 971 at [74]–[75].
[588] R. (on the application of Middleton) v West Somerset Coroner [2004] UKHL 10; [2004] 2 A.C. 182.

CHAPTER 8

PROCEDURAL FAIRNESS: EXCEPTIONS

SCOPE

We have seen in Chapter 7 that decision-makers performing public 8–001
functions are generally required to adopt fair procedures; and in relation to
a variety of different circumstances, we considered the content of the
requirements of procedural fairness. As we noted, a person may also have a
legitimate expectation of fair treatment, and that will be considered in
Chapter 12.

This Chapter examines the situations where, although the requirements 8–002
of procedural fairness are on first appearance applicable, the decision-
maker may be exempt from all or some of the procedural safeguards that
would otherwise be required.[1] Several factors may be identified as capable
of excluding the normal procedural fairness requirements: (a) express
statutory exclusion;[2] (b) legislation expressly requires fairness in some
situations, but is silent about others;[3] (c) fairness in the form of disclosure
would be prejudicial to the public interest;[4] (d) prompt action is needed;[5]
(e) it is impractical to comply with fairness requirements;[6] (f) a procedurally flawed decision has been followed by a hearing or appeal that is
fair;[7] (g) the procedurally flawed decision is merely a preliminary one;[8] (h)
the procedural defect would have made no difference to the outcome;[9] and
(i) the failure to provide a fair procedure is no fault of the decision-
maker.[10] We examine these in turn.

---

[1] The situations examined in the Chapter are where there is no entitlement to procedural
fairness. The courts may also hold that there has been a breach of procedural fairness
requirements but nonetheless exercise discretion at the conclusion of a claim for judicial
review to withhold a remedy: see 18–048. The distinction between these two ways of denying
an enforceable right to procedural fairness have not always been articulated with clarity: see
8–043.
[2] See 8–003.
[3] See 8–005.
[4] See 8–006.
[5] See 8–015.
[6] See 8–020.
[7] See 8–023.
[8] See 8–032.
[9] See 8–043.
[10] See 8–053.

EXPRESS STATUTORY EXCLUSION

8–003   Provided it does so "clearly and expressly",[11] an Act of Parliament may dispense with the requirements of fair procedures where they would otherwise be required.[12] A statute may, for example, permit the exercise of powers without notice.[13] In the interests of administrative efficiency and expedition, the requirements of fairness have been excluded by statutory provisions which, for example, enable decision makers to decline to conduct an oral hearing,[14] or to entertain particular kinds of representations and objections.[15]

8–004   Any statutory exclusion of procedural fairness will be construed strictly. Thus, where a statutory provision did not expressly or by necessary implication exclude the right to legal professional privilege, the provision was interpreted not to do so.[16] Subordinate legislation purporting to exclude a hearing should also be strictly construed.[17] Indeed, even when a discretion to hold a hearing or conduct an inquiry is conferred by a statute,

[11] *Wiseman v Borneman* [1971] A.C. 297 at 318.
[12] See 7–011; For an Australian case, see *Haoucher v Minister for Immigration and Ethnic Affairs* (1990) 169 C.L.R. 648 at 652–653 (Dean J.).
[13] See, e.g. Crime and Disorder Act 1998 s.1D; *R. (on the application of M) v Secretary of State for Constitutional Affairs* [2004] EWCA Civ 312; [2004] 1 W.L.R. 2298 at [39]; *R.(on the application of X) v Chief Constable of the West Midlands* [2004] EWCA Civ 1068; [2005] 1 W.L.R. 65 at [37] (no duty on a chief constable to permit representations pursuant to a statutory power to disclose details of discontinued criminal charges to a prospective employer, since disclosure was the "policy of the legislation in order to serve a pressing social need"); *Cheetham v Mayor of Manchester* (1875) L.R. 10 C.T. 249.
[14] See, e.g. Criminal Procedure Rules 2005 (SI 2005/384) r.67.2, considered in *Re A* [2006] EWCA Crim 4; [2006] 1 W.L.R. 1361.
[15] See, e.g. *R. (on the application of WB and KA) v Leeds Organisation Committee* [2002] EWHC 1927; [2003] E.L.R. 67; Highways Act 1980 s.258 (objections to compulsory purchase order excluded where objections are based on urging alternative route and are not made in accordance with the specified procedure); *Re Berkhamsted Grammar School* [1908] 2 Ch. 25; and for a more equivocal formula which was held to exclude any duty to act judicially, *Patterson v District Commissioner for Accra* [1948] A.C. 341; for a Canadian case, see *British Columbia Wildlife Federation v Debeck* (1976) 1 B.C.L.R. 244 at [17]–[19] (no duty to act in accordance with procedural fairness where there was no requirement to hear objections). On situations in which courts will supplement the statutory procedure, see 7–013 and 7–041.
[16] *R. (on the application of Morgan Grenfell & Co Ltd) v Inland Revenue Commissioners* [2002] UKHL 21; [2003] 1 A.C. 563; and *R. (on the application of Singh) v Chief Constable of the West Midlands Police* [2006] EWCA Civ 1118; [2006] 1 W.L.R. 3374 at [79]–[83]; in Canada see *R. v British Columbia Pollution Control Board* (1967) 61 D.L.R. (2nd) 221 (objector had no right to be "heard", but his right to lodge objections imposed certain implied procedural duties on the deciding body).
[17] *R. v Housing Appeal Tribunal* [1920] 3 K.B. 334; *R. v Local Government Board* [1911] 2 I.R. 331 at 342–343; in New Zealand see *Tauhara Properties Ltd v Mercantile Developments Ltd* [1974] 1 N.Z.L.R. 584 at 590; *Drew v Attorney-General* [2002] 1 N.Z.L.R. 58 (prison regulation' that would lead to some disciplinary hearings being conducted in breach of natural justice held ultra vires). Cf. decisions in which procedural rules contained in regulations have been held directory only in the absence of a specific statutory power to impose formal requirements by regulation: *Francis Jackson Developments Ltd v Hall* [1951] 2 K.B. 488; *R. v Devon and Cornwall Rent Tribunal Ex p. West* (1975) 29 P. & C.R. 316. On directory and mandatory requirements, see 5–049.

a refusal to hold the inquiry may constitute a denial of natural justice if fairness plainly demands that a hearing be held.[18] And an express statutory power to proceed without a hearing will not necessarily exclude the right to make informal or written representations.[19] Similarly, an express statutory provision excluding a duty to give reasons has been held not to exclude a duty to disclose the substance of the case so that an applicant for citizenship could make representations.[20] Finally, where the statute purporting to limit or exclude procedural fairness engages a Convention right, the limitation must be compatible with the Convention.[21]

LEGISLATION REQUIRES FAIRNESS FOR SOME BUT NOT OTHER PURPOSES

There are circumstances in which the requirements of procedural fairness 8–005 may be invoked to supplement statutory procedures.[22] The obverse circumstances can exist and a statutory procedural framework may impliedly exclude the more extensive protection provided by common law by means of application of the maxim *expressio unius est exclusio alterius* (the expression of one thing implies the exclusion of another), although on occasion, the courts have expressed reservations about the application of this maxim.[23] The common law requirements of fair procedures should not be excluded unless the statute represents a settled legislative intent that the procedural safeguard should be excluded, rather than a case of a "mere omission" which may be filled by the courts.[24] For example, where the

[18] *Binney v Secretary of State for the Environment* [1984] J.P.L. 871; *R. v Secretary of State for Transport Ex p. Ellison* (1995) 70 P. & C.R. 161, QBD; in New Zealand see *Fraser v State Services Commission* [1984] 1 N.Z.L.R. 116 at 122, 125. Fairness will not require a public inquiry where, without an inquiry, the two or more conflicting issues can be properly weighed and those with a right to make representations can have their representations properly taken into account: *R. (on the application of Little) v Secretary of State for Trade and Industry* [2002] EWHC 3001 at [25]; and *Decra Plastics Ltd v Waltham Forest LBC* [2002] EWHC 2718; *R. (on the application of Persimmon Homes (South East) Ltd) v Secretary of State for Transport* [2005] EWHC 96; [2005] 2 P. & C.R. 24.
[19] *Ex p Guardian Newspapers Ltd (Written Submissions), The Times*, October 26, 1993, CA; *Re A* [2006] EWHC Crim 4; [2006] 1 W.L.R. 1361 at [28]; in Canada see *Hundal v Superintendent of Motor Vehicles* (1985) 20 D.L.R. (4th) 592; cf. *Nicholson v Haldimand-Norfolk Regional Board of Commissioners of Police* [1979] 1 S.C.R. 311, [22]-[27].
[20] *R. v Secretary of State for the Home Department Ex p. Fayed* [1998] 1 W.L.R. 763.
[21] See, e.g. *R. (on the application of G) v Immigration Appeal Tribunal* [2004] EWCA Civ 1731; [2005] 1 W.L.R. 1445 (even though the Nationality, Immigration and Asylum Act 2002 did not provide for an oral hearing in its statutory review of refusal of permission to appeal against the decision of an immigration officer, the statutory procedure provided adequate and proportionate protection of the rights of asylum seekers and judicial review remained available in respect of errors not susceptible to statutory review); see 8–029; 17–004.
[22] See 7–013 and 7–041.
[23] *R. (on the application of West) v Parole Board* [2005] UKHL 1; [2005] 1 W.L.R. 350 at [29] (Lord Bingham noting that "the maxim *expressio unius exclusio alterius* can rarely, if ever, be enough to exclude the common law rules of natural justice").
[24] *R. v Secretary of State for the Home Department Ex p. Abdi* [1996] 1 W.L.R. 298; *R. v Secretary of State for Education and Employment Ex p. M* [1996] E.L.R. 162; *R. v Secretary of State for Wales Ex p. Emery* [1996] 4 All E.R. 1; and see 7–012.

statute provides for certain documents to be disclosed, it may exclude an obligation to disclose all relevant documents;[25] or an obligation to communicate may be excluded where other forms of communication are expressly envisaged by the legislation.[26] Similarly, where regulations specifically provide for reasons to be given with respect to certain circumstances and not others, a common law duty to give reasons may not arise in respect of the circumstances not listed in the regulations.[27]

RISK TO THE PUBLIC INTEREST

Disclosure: the need for balancing

8–006   In Chapter 16 we examine the statutory right to disclosure of certain information under the Freedom of Information Act 2000, the Data Protection Act 1998 and other legislation—and the limits of the rights to access to information.[28] Here we consider the limits to common law rights to disclosure.[29] In the past, the courts of England and Wales readily accepted the argument that to require ministers to reveal to interested parties materials prepared or obtained in the course of departmental duties might unduly interfere with the administrative process by destroying the anonymity of the civil service, discouraging frank comment in official reports and undermining the principle of ministerial responsibility to Parliament.[30] Likewise, in housing and town planning cases, courts often refused to require the disclosure of inspectors' reports on inquiries and other relevant materials, even where the minister's functions were recognised as including a judicial element.[31] In general, the climate of opinion has changed; and the administrative process has become less opaque.[32]

---

[25] *Abdi* [1996] 1 W.L.R. 289 at 314 (holding that an implied obligation to disclose all relevant documents would be wholly inconsistent with the express obligation to disclose specific documents set out in the Asylum Appeals (Procedure) Rules 1993).

[26] *Furnell v Whangarei High Schools Board* [1973] A.C. 660 at 681 (Lord Morris concluding that an omission "must have been deliberate since the regulations proceed with great particularity to specify when and how communication should be made to him and when and how he should make response").

[27] *R. (on the application of Venture Projects Ltd) v Secretary of State for the Home Department,* October 20, 2000 unreported at [3], [4] and [13] (Schiemann L.J. noting that "statutory provisions echoed a choice which had to be made"); and *R. v Birmingham City Council Ex p. Ferrero Ltd* [1993] 1 All E.R. 530; *R. v Secretary of State for Education and Employment and the North East London Education Authority Ex p. M* [1996] E.L.R. 162 at 208.

[28] See 16–026.

[29] On the duty to disclose, see 7–057.

[30] *R. v Local Government Board Ex p. Arlidge* [1915] A.C. 120; *Laffer v Gillen* [1927] A.C. 886 at 895–896.

[31] See 6–035.

[32] *cf.* Town and Country Planning (Inquiries Procedure) Rules 1974 (SI 1974/419) r.10(4), which allowed an inspector of a planning appeal "not to require or permit the giving or production of any evidence . . . which would be contrary to the public interest". This

What is required is a balance between the need for confidentiality and the need for disclosure and, as Simon Brown L.J. has summarised it, the question to be asked is:

"Does the public interest in making the limited further disclosure now sought outweigh the remaining confidentiality in the report? That in turn seems to me to depend upon whether disclosure to the requesting states is required in the interests of fairness. If fairness demands disclosure, then to my mind disclosure clearly becomes the overriding public interest."[33]

National security and terrorism

One justification for a departure from the requirements of procedural fairness is the requirements of national security. In the current era of global terrorism, Parliament has enacted legislation which in various ways excludes the ordinary entitlements to fairness of those suspected of terrorist-related activities.[34] The common law has also for many years recognised the exigencies of national security.[35] In so doing, the courts 8–007

provision has been removed from the Rules (now Town and Country Planning (Inquiries Procedure) (England) Rules 2000 (SI 2000/1624). But Town and Country Planning Act 1990 s.321 enables the Secretary of State to give directions limiting public access to information regarding national security, information regarding the measures taken or to be taken to ensure the security of any premises or property, or information the disclosure of which would be contrary to the national interest; also Planning (National Security Directions and Appointed Representatives) (England) Rules 2006 (SI 2006/1284); *R. v Secretary of State for Defence Ex p. Camden LBC* [1995] J.PL. 403; H. McCoubrey, "Security Planning Regulations and Defence Establishments" [1994] J.P.L. 1075; "National Security—Application of Circular 18/94 Pt IV—Car Park Building at Regent's Park Barracks" [1995] J.P.L. 403; "Applying the Planning Acts to the Crown" [2005] J.P.L. B23–24.

[33] *R. v Secretary of State for the Home Department Ex p. King of Belgium*, February 15, 2000 (unrep.); *R. (on the application of Gunn-Russo) v Nugent Care Society* [2001] EWHC Admin 566; [2002] 1 F.L.R. 1 (holding that the care society should have considered each document to balance confidentiality against disclosure).

[34] D. Feldman, "Human Rights, Terrorism and Risk: the Roles of Politicians and Judges" [2006] P.L. 364; D. Dyzenhaus, *The Constitution of Law Legality in a Time of Emergency* (2006); L. Lustgarten and I. Leigh, *In from the Cold; National Security and Parliamentary Democracy* (1994); J. Strawson, *Law after Ground Zero* (2002); in Australia, national security has been less readily employed as a basis for excluding procedural fairness: P. Hanks, "National Security-A Political Concept" (1988) 14 Monash Univ. L. Rev. 114. *cf.* M. Aronson, B. Dyer and M. Groves, *Judicial Review of Administrative Action*, 3rd edn. (2004), p.387.

[35] See, e.g. *Council of Civil Service Unions v Minister for the Civil Service* [1985] A.C. 374; *Hutton v Attorney-General* [1927] 1 Ch. 427 at 439 (defence policy); *R. v Secretary of State for the Home Office Ex p. Stitt*, The Times, February 3, 1987, DC (Secretary of State did not have to give reasons for his conclusion that a person was "concerned in the commission, preparation, or instigation of acts of terrorism" where there was bona fide evidence that security was involved, and the court would not examine the strength of that justification); *R. v Secretary of State for the Home Department Ex p. H*, The Times, August 5, 1987, DC; *R. v Director, Government Communications Headquarters Ex p. Hodges*, The Times, July 26, 1988, DC (question of whether an individual's positive vetting clearance should be removed was a matter to be decided with reference to national security considerations and as such could not

have often been unwilling to examine the strength of a public authority's defence that national security justifies departure from the entitlement to procedural fairness that would otherwise exist.[36] Increasingly though, the courts require that a balancing exercise be undertaken between, on the one hand the requirements of national security, and on the other the interests of the individual in the fairness of the decision. As a general principle, issues of national security "do not fall beyond the competence of the courts"; however, it is "self-evidently right that national courts must give great weight to the views of the executive on matters of national security".[37] Moreover, it is "clearly established that, where there are real concerns about national security, the obligations of fairness may have to be modified or excluded".[38] Even the requirements of Art.6 may be qualified where national security interests are at stake, provided that appropriate procedural safeguards remain in place.[39]

be examined by the courts); *R. v Secretary of State for the Home Department Ex p. Cheblak* [1991] 1 W.L.R. 890 (immigrant not entitled to full particulars of the case against him or legal representation where the deportation was stated to be for reasons of national security); *R. v Secretary of State for the Home Department Ex p. Chahal* [1995] 1 W.L.R. 526 and *Chahal v UK* (1997) 23 E.H.R.R. 413 (violations of ECHR Art.13, read with Art.3, and Art.5(4)).

[36] See, e.g. *R. v Secretary of State for Home Affairs Ex p. Hosenball* [1977] 1 W.L.R. 766 at 783–4 (Lord Lane noting in the context of a deportation order that, if disclosure of information to an alien might have an adverse effect on national security, "[t]he choice is regrettably clear: the alien must suffer, if suffering there be, and this is so on whichever basis of argument one chooses"); *Cheblak* [1991] 1 W.L.R. 809 at 902 (Lord Donaldson describing national security as "the exclusive responsibility of the executive"); *Council of Civil Service Unions* [1985] A.C. 374 at 412 (Lord Diplock describing national security as "par excellence a non justiciable question").

[37] *Secretary of State for the Home Department v Rehman* [2001] UKHL 47; [2003] 1 A.C. 153, [31] (Lord Steyn); and *A, X and Y v Secretary of State for the Home Department* [2002] EWCA Civ 2 1502; [2004] Q.B. 335, [40] (Lord Woolf C.J.: "Decisions as to what is required in the interest of national security are self-evidently within the category of decisions in relation to which the court is required to show considerable deference when it comes to judging those actions").

[38] *R. (on the application of Tucker) v Director-General of the National Crime Squad* [2003] EWCA Civ at [43] (Scott Baker L.J. citing *R. v Secretary of State for the Home DepartmentEx p. Hosenball* [1977] 1 W.L.R. 766 at 773, 786); and e.g. *R. v Secretary of State for the Home Department Ex p. Mr and Mrs B, The Independent,* January 29, 1991 (deportation); *R. v Secretary of State for the Home Department Ex p. Al-Harbi* (Otton J., March 21, 1991) (asylum); *Hussain v Secretary of State for the Home Department* [1993] Imm. A.R. 353, CA (asylum); *Balfour v Foreign and Commonwealth Office* [1994] 1 W.L.R. 681 at 688 (dismissal of employee); *R. v Secretary of State for the Home Department Ex p. Gallagher* [1994] 3 C.M.L.R. 295 at [12]–[18], CA (when making an exclusion order on the grounds of national security, the Secretary of State was permitted to withhold allegations and the identity of the statutory adviser); *R. v Secretary of State for the Home Department Ex p. Adams* [1995] All E.R. (EC) 177; [1995] 3 C.M.L.R. 476 (exclusion order); *R. v Secretary of State forthe Home Department Ex p. McQuillan* [1995] 4 All E.R. 400 (Sedley J.) (exclusion order).

[39] The House of Lords has held that although a judge in control order proceedings may pursuant to para.4(3)(b) of the Schedule of the prevention of Terrorism Act 2005, refuse to disclose evidence to the defendant the power of non-disclosure does not apply "where to do so would be incomplete with the right of the controlled person to a fair trial"; *MB(FC) v Secretary of State for the Home Department: AF v Secretary of State for the Home Department* [2007] UKHL 46 at [72]: see also [84]. *On the modification of procedural fairness requirements in the interests of national security, see [32], [63], [80] and [91]. See also 8–013.*

A balancing exercise will be especially important where the individual's 8–008
fundamental rights are in issue, such as the right to life, to freedom,[40] or
other rights protected by the ECHR.[41] In *Chahal v United Kingdom*,[42] the
ECtHR held unanimously that the failure of the English courts to carry out
or supervise effectively a balancing test (weighing national security considerations) was a breach of Art.5(4), since Mr Chahal's deprivation of liberty
had not been subject to any effective judicial control. The Court considered
that it must be possible to employ techniques which both accommodate
legitimate security concerns about the nature and sources of intelligence
information and yet accord the individual a substantial measure of
procedural justice. In the Belmarsh detainees case,[43] a majority of the
House of Lords made it clear that although the response necessary to
protect national security was a matter of political judgement for the
executive and Parliament, where Convention rights were in issue national
courts were required to afford them effective protection by adopting an
intensive review of whether such a right had been impugned, and the
courts were not precluded by any doctrine of deference from examining
the proportionality of a measure taken to restrict such a right.[44]

Additionally, if "the decision is successfully challenged, on the ground 8–009
that it has been reached by a process which is unfair, then the Government
is under an obligation to produce evidence that the decision was in fact
based on grounds of national security".[45] The difficulty, though, is that
such a requirement may be easily satisfied. The courts do not require
evidence that the deposed risk to national security is proved to any
particular standard of proof;[46] they are in practice satisfied with evidence
which, while more than "mere assertion", simply indicates in very broad
terms the grounds upon which the Secretary of State considers that matters
of national security have been raised.[47] Once this factual basis has been

---

[40] *Chahal v Secretary of State for the Home Department* [1995] 1 W.L.R. 526; *Chahal v UK* (1997) 23 E.H.R.R. 413.
[41] *Johnston v Constable of the Royal Ulster Constabulary* [1986] 3 C.M.L.R. 240 at 262 (decision of ECJ that provision of Northern Ireland Sex Discrimination Order requiring Tribunals to treat a national security certificate as conclusive evidence that conditions for derogating from the principle of equal treatment were fulfilled were contrary to the provision of effective judicial control laid down in Art.6 of the Equal Treatment Directive; the Court relying upon principles of the ECHR).
[42] *Chahal v UK* (1997) 23 E.H.R.R. 413.
[43] *X v Secretary of State for the Home Department* [2004] UKHL 56; [2005] 2 A.C. 68.
[44] See, e.g. *Secretary of State for the Home Department v MB* [2006] EWCA Civ 1140; [2006] 3 W.L.R. 839; (for HL, see [2007] UKHL 46 and 8–013) *Fitt v UK* (2000) 30 E.H.R.R. 480, ECtHR. On proportionality and deference, see 11–004.
[45] *Council of Civil Service Unions* [1985] A.C. 374 at 402 (Lord Fraser, citing *The Zamora* [1916] 2 A.C. 77), 421 (Lord Roskill: "evidence, and not mere assertion, must be forthcoming"); cf. *R. v Secretary of State for the Home Department Ex p. Mr B. and Mrs B, The Independent*, January 29, 1991 (Mann L.J.: "Of course the Court requires more than mere assertion. Evidence is required"); *Balfour v Foreign and Commonwealth Office* [1994] 1 W.L.R. 681 at 688 (Russell L.J.).
[46] *Rehman* [2001] UKHL 47; [2003] 1 A.C. 153 at [29], [55].
[47] See, e.g. *Hussain* [1993] Imm. A.R. 353 at 357, CA *McQuillan* [1995] 4 All E.R. 400 at

established, so that the court is satisfied that the interest of national security is a relevant factor to be considered in the determination of the case, and was in fact so considered, then "the court will accept the opinion of the Crown or its responsible officer as to what is required to meet it, unless it is possible to show that the opinion was one which no reasonable minister advising the Crown could in the circumstances reasonably have held".[48] Such a safeguard will usually be nugatory, since the court will not have before it the evidence upon which the minister has come to his decision;[49] it will be very difficult for the court to come to the conclusion that the minister's decision was not within the band of rational decisions.[50]

Counter-terrorism measures

8–010 Just as the First and Second World Wars resulted in the detention of individuals in circumstances where their rights were not properly protected,[51] so have recent terrorist incidents in London and elsewhere created similar situations. They are situations which can be particularly challenging for courts and tribunals. On the one hand it is of critical importance that the courts and tribunals are vigilant in protecting individuals who are detained or subjected to other restrictions on their activities in connection with suspected terrorist activities who have not been charged with any offence. On the other hand the courts have to be sensitive to the responsibility that the security services have for protecting the public at large from what can be deadly incidents.

8–011 Here we are only concerned with the steps taken by the government in the national interest to limit what would be, in normal circumstances, the undoubted right of the suspects to have a fair hearing into the issue of whether their detention is lawful. We have already indicated that procedural fairness can be limited by interest of national security, but we have not described how courts and tribunals should approach their responsibility to hold the balance between the rights of the individual suspect and the needs of national security.

8–012 Having regard to the issue at the stake, namely the right of the suspect to challenge the justification for his detention, the possible inroads on his rights to procedural fairness could not be more basic; neither he nor his

423; for even weaker formulations, see *Cheblak* [1991] 1 W.L.R. 890 and *Al-Harbi* Otton J., March 21, 1991; cf. *R. v Secretary of State for the Home Department Ex p. Ruddock* [1987] 1 W.L.R. 1482, 1491–2 (Taylor L.J.); *Rehman* [2001] UKHL 47; [2003] 1 A.C. 153 at [24], [54].

[48] *ibid.*, at 406, 412, 420 (Lords Scarman, Diplock and Roskill). In Israel it has been held that the right to be heard is not automatically excluded under emergency regulations which allow a military commander to demolish a house without judicial proceedings: B. Bracha, "Judicial Review of Security Powers in Israel: A New Policy of the Courts" (1991) 28 Stanford J. of Int. Law 39, 75–80. The fair hearing may however be excluded when "urgent action is necessary to avoid serious consequences", *ibid.*, p.77.

[49] *Rehman* [2001] UKHL 47; [2003] 1 A.C. 153 at [26].

[50] *McQuillan* [1995] 4 All E.R. 400 at 423 (Sedley J.).

[51] See 6–020.

legal advisers may be aware of the nature of the evidence relied on as justifying his detention and they may have no opportunity to challenge that evidence. Instead he would be allocated a special advocate to appear on his behalf who would know what was relied on by the security services but could not take instructions from the suspect in relation to the matters of which he was aware.[52] The special advocate could, however, cross examine the witnesses relied on by the security services.

Although the availability of a special advocate is certainly better than no protection and there have been cases where they have secured the release of those who are detained, they clearly act under a significant disadvantage. So great is the disadvantage, the question arises whether that process is so flawed that it cannot amount even to the restricted form of hearing that Parliament intended. There is a minimum degree of fairness that must exist if the whole process is not to be regarded as so fundamentally flawed that it contravenes the rule of law. The hearing does however take place before a tribunal of three members one of whom is a High Court judge and now the detention is not in an institution but under a control order. We regard this situation as being very much at the boundary of an infringement of procedural rights that can be tolerated. In *Roberts v Parole Board*, the House of Lords decided by a majority in a parallel situation that the special advocate provided just sufficient protection to avoid it being necessary to prevent the Parole Board adopting a similar process when determining whether a murderer who had served his tariff should be refused parole.[53] By contrast, more recently, the House of Lords has held that the special advocate procedure will not in all cases constitute a sufficient safeguard against the unfairness which results from the non-disclosure of key evidence in control order proceedings; and consequently, the judge's powers of non-disclosure could not extend "to witholding particulars of reasons or evidence where to do so would deprive the controlee of a fair trial". [53a] Overall, the circumstances of an individual case will be closely scrutinised and the tribunal will want to be satisfied that there are not circumstances which would justify greater protection being provided to the suspect the balance is a fine one.

8–013

---

[52] The role of special advocate was created by the Special Immigration Appeals Commission Act 1997, which established SIAC (a superior court of record). See *A v Secretary of State for the Home Department* [2005] UKHL 71; [2006] 2 A.C. 221 and House of Commons Constitutional Affairs Committee, *The Operation of the Special Immigration Appeals Commission (SIAC) and the use of Special Advocates.* HC Paper No. 323–I (Session 2004/05).
[53] [2005] UKHL 45; [2005] 2 A.C. 738.
[53a] *MB v Secretary of State for the Home Department: AF v Secretary of the Home Department* [2007] UKHL 46, at [34]–[35](Lord Bingham): [65]–[67], [72](Baroness Hale): [81]–[85] (Lord Carswell); [90] (Lord Brown).

Other public interests

8–014   Modifications of the requirements of procedural fairness have been deemed
acceptable for the protection of other facets of the public interest,
including: the internal workings of the decision-maker;[54] the sources of
information leading to the detection of crime or other wrongdoing;[55]
sensitive intelligence information;[56] and other information supplied in
confidence for the purposes of government,[57] or the discharge of certain
public functions.[58] The conception that secrecy may be in the public
interest has not been confined to matters of administration, and for
example, the welfare of children[59] and of psychiatric patients[60] has arisen in

[54] *R. (on the application of Edwards) v Environment Agency (No.2)* [2006] EWCA Civ 877;
[2007] Env. L.R. 9 at [91]; *Bushell v Secretary of State for the Environment* [1981] A.C. 75.
[55] *R. v Gaming Board for Great Britain Ex p. Benaim and Khaida* [1970] 2 Q.B. 417; *R. v
Lewes Justices Ex p. Home Secretary* [1973] A.C. 388 (names of informants, details of
information supplied to police and content of police reports in respect of applicants for
gaming club consents). *Cf. R. v Chief Constable of the West Midland Police Ex p. Wiley* [1995]
1 A.C. 274, HL (no justification for imposing general class public interest immunity on all
documents generated by police complaints procedure).
[56] *R. (on the application of Tucker) v Director General of the National Crime Squad* [2003]
EWCA Civ 2; [2003] I.C.R. 599; (although the decision to terminate the appellant's
secondment to the NCS did not involve sufficient public law elements to justify susceptibility
to judicial review (see 3–066), the CA added that fairness did not require that reasons should
be given for the termination given the sensitivity of the work of the NSC); and *R. v Secretary
of State for the Home Department Ex p. Hosenball* [1977] 1 W.L.R. 766 (intelligence
information).
[57] *Collymore v Attorney-General* [1970] A.C. 538 (confidential information about industrial
disputes and relations); *Crompton (Alfred) Amusement Machines Ltd v Customs and Excise
Commissioners (No.2)* [1974] A.C. 405 (non-disclosure of documents which would have
disclosed the commissioners' methods and information obtained from third parties both
voluntarily and under statute); *Cf. Norwich Pharmacal Co v Customs and Excise Commissioners* [1974] A.C. 133 (confidential information supplied by traders to commissioners
making inquiries). Confidential particulars relating to an informant's commercial or financial
affairs supplied in connection with air transport licences must normally be withheld by the
Civil Aviation Authority: Civil Aviation Act 1982 ss.23, 64–72; and *R. v Board of Visitors of
Wandsworth Prison Ex p. Raymond, The Times* June 17, 1987, DC (circumstances which
could justify withholding a welfare report made on prisoner for disciplinary hearing, although
normally to ensure that "justice . . . be seen to be done", it should be disclosed); *R. v
Secretary of State for Health Ex p. US Tobacco International Ltd* [1992] 1 Q.B. 353 at 371
(Taylor L.J.: disclosure of scientific advice given to Secretary of State by independent experts
in relation to proposed ban on oral snuff).
[58] *Cf. D v NSPCC* [1978] A.C. 171; *Science Research Council v Nasse* [1980] A.C. 1028.
[59] *Re K (Infants)* [1965] A.C. 201; *Re D (Infants)* [1970] 1 W.L.R. 599 (local authority case
records on children under care); *Re B (Disclosure to Others)* [2001] 2 F.L.R. 1017 (father of
child had Art.6 rights, but not entitled to see police and psychiatric reports on other children
of same mother where that would interfere with Art.8 rights of children); *C v C* [2005]
EWHC 2741 at [20]–[21]. See also *Re PA (an Infant)* [1971] 1 W.L.R. 1530 (report to court
on adoption issue), though *Re M* [1973] Q.B. 108; *Re B (A Minor)* [1975] Fam. 127 (report to
court on adoption issue); *Re F (D) (A Minor)* (1977) 76 L.G.R. 133 at 142–143; *R. v Norfolk
CC Ex p. M* [1989] Q.B. 619 (entry of H on the council's child abuse register judicially
reviewable and could be struck down for breach of natural justice or fairness, although the
courts would be reluctant to do so, given the confidential nature of the list, and the
paramountcy of the child's interests); approved *R. v Harrow LBC Ex p. D* [1990] Fam. 133;
[1991] 1 W.L.R. 395 (on these cases, see 3–026); *H v H* [1974] 1 W.L.R. 595 (information
supplied to judge in confidence by a child during custody proceedings); cf. *B v W* [1979] 1

a number of cases. In one child custody case, the House of Lords refused disclosure of confidential reports made to the court by the Official Solicitor because their disclosure to the parents concerned might damage children whose welfare it was the paramount duty of the court to protect. It was reasoned that common-law duties to abide by the rules of natural justice were not ends in themselves, and where they did not serve the ends of justice, they could not be allowed to "become the master instead of the servant of justice".[61]

FAIR PROCEDURES WOULD HINDER PROMPT ACTION

Statutory relaxation of procedural propriety

Desirable though it may be to allow a hearing or an opportunity to make **8–015** representations, or simply to give prior notice, before a decision is taken, summary action may be alleged to be justifiable when an urgent need for protecting the interests of other persons arises.[62] There are in fact remarkably few situations in which the enforcement powers of public authorities are exercisable without notice;[63] but examples exist. For example, interim anti-social behaviour orders made without notice are not unlawful where it is necessary for the court to act urgently to protect the interests of a third party or to ensure that the order of the court is effective.[64]

There are numerous illustrations of statutory provisions which for **8–016** reasons of public safety or public health permit public authorities to interfere with property or other rights. For example: the destruction of infected crops;[65] the cancellation of a residential care or nursing home's registration;[66] the prevention of the business of a bank being carried on in a manner detrimental to the interests of the public or of depositors or other creditors;[67] prohibition on entry to an airport;[68] suspension of the licence

---

W.L.R. 1041 (breach of natural justice not to disclose social workers report used by court to assess character of party in wardship proceedings).

[60] *Re W.L.W.* [1972] Ch. 456 (report on condition of psychiatric patient); *R. v Kent Police Authority Ex p. Godden* [1971] 2 Q.B. 662 (disclosure of medical report to be restricted to applicant's own doctor). Outside the context of cases involving children and psychiatric patients, see: *Re Murjani (A Bankrupt)* [1996] 1 W.L.R. 1498 (non-adversarial bankruptcy proceedings); *R. v Canterbury (Archbishop) Ex p. Morant* [1944] K.B. 282 at 292 (non-disclosure in the interests of the "peace of the parish").

[61] *Re K* [1965] A.C. 201 at 238 (Lord Devlin).

[62] See 7–043; and 7–062 *Kioa v West* (1985) 159 C.L.R. 550 at 586 (Mason J.), 626 (Brennan J.), 633 (Deane J.).

[63] See, e.g. the notices required for planning enforcement: Town and Country Planning Act 1990 s.172; and the relatively recent "Planning Contravention Notice", Town and Country Planning Act 1990 s.171C.

[64] *R. (on the application of M) v Secretary of State for Constitutional Affairs* [2004] EWCA Civ 312; [2004] 1 W.L.R. 2298 at [24].

[65] Plant Health Act 1967 ss.3, 4 (as amended).

[66] Care Standards Act 2000 s.14.

[67] *Suisse Security Bank & Trust Ltd v Governor of the Central Bank of the Bahamas* [2006] UKPC 11; [2006] 1 W.L.R. 1660 at [35]–[36].

[68] *R. (on the application of Scott) v Heathrow Airport Ltd* [2005] EWHC 2669.

of a public service vehicle;[69] seizure of obscene works;[70] seizure of food suspected of not complying with food safety requirements;[71] local authorities may examine and test sewers, drains and sanitary conveniences that it believes to be defective; to remedy stopped-up drains; to order the cleansing or destruction of filthy or verminous articles; and to remove to hospital an inmate of a common lodging house who is suffering from a notifiable disease giving rise to a serious risk of infection. Public health officers may also destroy or infest verminous articles offered for sale.[72] A different kind of public interest is protected when the owner of a building is not entitled to prior notice of its intended listing as being of architectural or historic interest,[73] but should he wish to alter the building, he is entitled to a hearing against a refusal of listed building consent.[74]

8–017   In some of these examples in which summary action needs to be taken without prior notice, a range of safeguards after the action is provided by statute law. For example, although interim anti-social behaviour orders can be made without notice, they are subject to the safeguards of early review or discharge hearings, which are compliant with procedural fairness.[75] Moreover, the application for an interim order can only be made when a justices' clerk is satisfied that it is necessary for the application to be made without notice and the order can only be made for a limited period when the court considered it just to make it.[76]

8–018   Even where a statutory power to give prior notice exists, legislation may permit prior notice to be dispensed with if it is impracticable to give it, for example where direct action has to be taken to make a dangerous building safe.[77] Alternatively, powers of direct enforcement may become exercisable only by virtue of an order made by a magistrate upon an application made by a competent authority.

---

[69] Road Traffic Act 1988 ss.69, 70, 72.

[70] Customs Consolidation Act 1876 s.42; Customs and Excise Management Act 1979 s.139 Sch. 3; Obscene Publications Act 1959 s.3(3).

[71] Food Safety Act 1990 s.9.

[72] Public Health (Control of Disease) Act 1984 s.41 (cf. s.37); Public Health Act 1961 ss.17, 37. Other direct enforcement powers conferred by public health legislation are exercisable only when notice has been served on the persons affected, e.g. powers to cleanse and disinfect premises and articles in order to prevent the spread of infectious disease, and to destroy rodents which are overrunning premises: Public Health (Control of Disease) Act 1984 ss.31–32; Prevention of Damage by Pests Act 1949 s.6.

[73] Planning (Listed Buildings and Conservation Areas) Act 1990 ss.1–2.

[74] Planning (Listed Buildings and Conservation Areas) Act 1990 s.20.

[75] R. (on the application of M) v Secretary of State for Constitutional Affairs [2004] EWCA Civ 312; [2004] 1 W.L.R. 2298 at [39].

[76] M [2004] EWCA Civ 312; [2004] 1 W.L.R. 2298 at [39].

[77] Building Act 1984 ss.77, 78(1) and (2). The question whether it would have been more reasonable to apply to a magistrates' court for an order to be made against the owners can be determined in proceedings in which the recovery of expenses for the work executed is claimed (Building Act 1984, s.78(3) and (5)).

Common law exclusion of procedural propriety for urgency

Urgency may warrant relaxing the requirements of fairness even where **8–019** there is no legislation under which this is expressly permitted.[78] Thus a local authority could, without any consultation, withdraw children from a special school after allegations of persistent cruelty and abuse without this involving any procedural impropriety. In such circumstances there exists an emergency in which the primary concern is as to the safety and welfare of the children.[79] The suspension without first affording an opportunity to be heard, of a Romanian Airline's flight permit, following the failure by five of its pilots of Civil Aviation Authority examinations in aviation law, flight rules, and procedures, was not unfair where an immediate threat to air safety was apprehended.[80] Similarly where a self-regulatory organisation acted urgently to protect investors, it was not required to consider whether there was sufficient time to receive representations.[81] Likewise, a local authority was entitled to prohibit allegedly dangerous toys as an "emergency holding operation".[82] In general, whether the need for urgent action outweighs the importance of notifying or consulting an affected party depends on an assessment of the circumstances of each case on which opinions can differ.

IMPRACTICABLE TO PROVIDE FAIR PROCEDURE

In the past the duty to act fairly did not normally apply to decisions **8–020** containing a substantial "policy" content or regarded as essentially "allocative".[83] Even after the demise of the old distinction between "judicial" and "administrative" decisions, the category of "legislative" decision has tended to survive in other jurisdictions;[84] and has also been affirmed in this

---

[78] *De Verteuil v Knaggs* [1918] A.C. 557 at 560–561. Thus a magistrate is under no obligation to hear a person other than the informant before issuing a search warrant: *R. v Peterborough Justices Ex p. Hicks* [1977] 1 W.L.R. 1371. For a broad statement, restricting the application of the requirements of procedural fairness in the interests of public health, see *R. v Davey* 305–306.

[79] *R. v Powys CC Ex p. Horner* [1989] Fam. Law 320.

[80] *R. v Secretary of State for Transport Ex p. Pegasus Holdings (London) Ltd* [1988] 1 W.L.R. 990. Cf. in Australia, *Coutts v Commonwealth* (1985) 157 C.L.R. 91 (no requirement of natural justice where air force pilot, whose appointment was held at the pleasure of the Crown, was compulsorily retired on medical grounds).

[81] *R. v Life Assurance Unit Trust Regulatory Organisation Ex p. Ross* [1993] Q.B. 17, CA; also *R. v Birmingham City Council Ex p. Ferrero Ltd* [1993] 1 All E.R. 530, CA. The rules of natural justice do not apply to the making a Notice of Intervention in a solicitor's practice on the ground of suspected dishonesty under the Solicitors Act 1974, so that there is no requirement to give particulars of the reasons for intervention in the Notice: *Giles v Law Society* (1996) 8 Admin. L.R. 105, CA. However, the Act does afford a right of judicial consideration after the event.

[82] *R. v Birmingham CC Ex p. Ferrero Ltd* [1991] 3 Admin. L.R. 613.

[83] See 6–029.

[84] For example, in Canada *Inuit Tapirisat of Canada v Attorney-General of Canada* [1980] 2 S.C.R. 735; *Cardinal v Kent Institution* [1985] 2 S.C.R. 643 at para.14; cf. in New Zealand *Fowler & Roderique Ltd v Attorney General* [1987] 2 N.Z.L.R. 56.

jurisdiction on occasion, at least in respect of the making of delegated legislation.[85] As we have contended however[86] "policy" or "legislative" decisions should not on the ground of being classified as such be excused from the duty to act fairly. Indeed, in a number of cases that duty has been imposed in a policy setting,[87] although the content of the duty may be relaxed.[88]

8–021   There may however, in a particular case, be good reasons why the duty to act fairly should not apply where the decision involves policy formulation or rule-making. The most convincing reason will be that the number of persons affected by a particular order, act or decision is so great as to make it manifestly impracticable for them all to be given an opportunity of being heard by the competent authority beforehand.[89] This is the reason why representations may not be required for the making of regulations of a legislative character.[90] But a statute may impliedly require an opportunity to be given for representations to be made against local authority byelaws before they are confirmed by a minister,[91] and an Act can provide for notice and opportunity to be heard prior to statutory instruments being

---

[85] *Bates v Lord Hailsham* [1972] 1 W.L.R. 1373 (affirmed in *BAPIO Action Ltd v the Secretary of State for the Home Department and another* [2007] EWHC 199 at [47]; R. *(on the application of the British Casino Association Ltd v Secretary of State for Culture Media & Sport* [2007] EWHC 1312 at [82]; cf. *R. v Secretary of State for Health Ex p. US Tobacco International Inc* [1992] Q.B. 353.

[86] See 7–026.

[87] See, e.g. *US Tobacco International* [1997] Q.B. 353 (although a statutory duty to consult applied here); *R. (on the application of Capenhurst) v Leicester City Council* [2004] EWHC 2124; (2004) 7 C.C.L. Rep. 557 (since the local authority had accepted that voluntary organisations should be consulted, the consultation should be fair); *R. (on the application of Newsum) v Welsh Assembly (No.2)* [2005] EWHC 538; [2006] Env. L.R. 1; *R. v Secretary of State for the Environment Ex p. Brent LBC* [1982] Q.B. 593, DC; *R. v Secretary of State for Transport Ex. p. Greater London Council* [1986] Q.B. 556. The existence of a legitimate expectation may also result in requirements of procedural fairness even in a policy or legislative context: see 12–00; *R. v British Coal Corp & Secretary of State for Trade & Industry Ex p. Vardy* [1993] I.C.R. 720, DC; *R. v Lord Chancellor Ex p. The Law Society* (1994) 6 Admin L.R. 833.

[88] See, e.g. in respect of the right to cross examination *Bushell v Secretary of State for the Environment* [1981] A.C. 75.

[89] Cf. *BAPIO Action Ltd v the Secretary of State for the Home Department and another* [2007] EWHC 199 at [47] (Stanley Burnton J. noting that "the remedy is political rather than judicial"); *R. v Secretary of State for Social Services Ex p. Child Poverty Action Group, The Times*, August 8, 1985, CA; in New Zealand see *Waitemata County v Local Government Commission* [1964] N.Z.L.R. 689 at 698–699; *White v Ryde Municipal Council* [1977] 2 N.S.W.L.R. 909 at 921.

[90] See n.87; in Australia see *Kioa v West* (1985) 159 C.L.R. 550 at 584 (Mason J. would exclude from the right to procedural fairness decisions having a quasi-legislative or 'policy' or 'political' character—in other words cases where an individual is not directly affected by the decision, but rather indirectly affected as a member of the public or a class of the public); cf. *Bread Manufacturers of New South Wales v Evans* (1981) 180 C.L.R. 404. In Canada, the fact that a decision is contained in an instrument normally associated with legislative powers (e.g. a byelaw or regulation) is not determinative of the characterisation of the power as being exempt from a fair hearing. The legislative nature of a board's powers was however given as reason for keeping to a minimum the procedural content of an express statutory duty to conduct a hearing: *Manitoba League of the Physically Handicapped Inc v Manitoba (Taxicab Board)* (1988) 56 D.L.R. (4th) 191.

[91] Local Government Act 1972 s.236 (as amended).

made.[92] We noted in Chapters 6 and 7, the contrast with the well-established American experience, where extensive "rulemaking" procedures are required for all subordinate law-making, and also with the more recent similar South African experience.[93] Another reason for excluding the fair hearing in such cases may be that the decision maker is responsible to Parliament for the decision.[94]

The large number of applicants competing for scarce resources may 8–022 make it impracticable to offer each applicant a hearing. If, for example, there are 1,000 applicants for 100 places available in a university law department (or a corresponding ratio of applicants to available licences, permits or grants) it may be impossible to afford interviews (or hearings) to many of those who, from the particulars supplied with their written applications, appear sufficiently meritorious or suitable to warrant fuller personal consideration.[95] Criteria for selection should however be evolved and applied in an attempt to do justice as far as this is possible; but there will inevitably be persons who will reasonably feel aggrieved at having been denied an adequate opportunity of presenting their case. Where a hearing can be provided, considerations of administrative practicality may influence or determine the content of the procedure which is capable of being adopted.[96] Even if the court finds that a breach of procedural fairness has occurred, administrative impracticability may still be relied upon as a reason for refusing a remedy in its discretion.[97]

SUBSEQUENT FAIR HEARING OR APPEAL

The common law and the ECHR both permit a public authority to make 8–023 decisions which do not comply fully with procedural fairness requirements if the person affected has recourse to a further hearing or appeal which itself provides fairness.

[92] See 7–026.

[93] See 6–052, 6–057 and 7–026.

[94] See, e.g. *Essex CC v Ministry of Housing & Local Government* (1967) 66 L.G.R. 23.cf. *CREEDNZ V Governor General* [1981] 1 N.Z.L.R. 172 at 189.

[95] *R. v Aston University Senate Ex p. Roffey* [1969] 2 Q.B. 538 at 554; and *Central Council for Education and Training in Social Work v Edwards*, The Times, May 5, 1978 (supports the propositions contained in the text, but where a refusal to admit was declared invalid on the ground that the interview was conducted unfairly; in the context of licences); *McInnes v Onslow Fane* [1978] 1 W.L.R. 1520 (Megarry V.-C.'s distinction between "application" and "revocation" cases may be explained as resting upon this basis; see 7–019).

[96] See, e.g. *R. v Birmingham CC Ex p. Darshan Kaur* [1991] C.O.D. 21, DC (lack of translator at public meeting not improper because it was administratively impossible to provide translators for every language spoken at the meeting); *R. v Secretary of State for Wales Ex p. Williams* [1996] C.O.D. 127 (Secretary of State, having consulted in relation to a proposal to close special schools, was not required to consult further in relation to representations of local authority made during consultation process; it was undesirable so to prolong the consultation process); *WWF UK Ltd v Scottish Natural Heritage* [1999] 1 C.M.L.R. 1021 (when consulting the public on prevention of adverse environmental effects, a planning authority was not in principle obliged to submit the final terms of proposed measures for such consultation, since that would make the process unduly protracted).

[97] See 18–048.

Common law and subsequent hearings

8–024 There are situations where the absence of procedural fairness before a decision is made can subsequently be adequately "cured", for example on appeal.[98] A prior hearing may be better than a subsequent hearing, but a subsequent hearing is better than no hearing at all;[99] and in some cases the courts have held that statutory provisions for an administrative appeal[100] or even full judicial review on the merits[101] are sufficient to negative the existence of any implied duty to have a hearing before the original decision is made.[102] This approach may be acceptable where the original decision does not cause significant detriment to the person affected,[103] or where there is also a paramount need for prompt action, or where it is otherwise impracticable to afford antecedent hearings.

8–025 The question of whether a decision vitiated by a breach of the rules of fairness can be made good by a subsequent hearing does not admit of a single answer applicable to all situations in which the issue may arise. Whilst it is difficult to reconcile all the relevant cases, case law indicates that the courts are increasingly favouring an approach based in large part upon an assessment of whether, in all the circumstances of the hearing and appeal, the procedure as a whole satisfied the requirements of fairness. Of particular importance are (a) the gravity of the error committed at first instance,[104] (b) the likelihood that the prejudicial effects of the error may also have permeated the rehearing, (c) the seriousness of the consequences for the individual, (iv) the width of the powers of the appellate body and (d) whether the appellate decision is reached only on the basis of the material before the original tribunal or by way of fresh hearing, or

---

[98] On a claim for judicial review under CPR Pt 54, the person will in any event normally be expected to use such an alternative method of challenging the legality of the initial decision: see 16–014.

[99] Cf. *Cinnamond v British Airports Authority* [1980] 1 W.L.R. 582.

[100] *Calvin v Carr* [1980] A.C. 574 at 593–593; *Pearlberg v Varty* [1972] 1 W.L.R. 534 (tax assessments); *Furnell v Whangarei High Schools Board* [1973] A.C. 660 (suspension of teacher pending full hearing); *Maynard v Osmond* [1977] Q.B. 240 at 253 (right of legal representation on appeal a reason for not implying the same right in original proceedings). In Australia see *Twist v Randwick MC* (1976) 136 C.L.R. 106 at 116; *Marine Hull & Liability Insurance Co v Hurford* (1985) 67 A.L.R. 77.

[101] In Australia see *Literature Board of Review v HMH Publishing Co Inc* [1964] Qd.R. 261; *Twist v Randwick MC* (1976) 136 C.L.R. 106; and on enforcement powers 8–015.

[102] Similarly, a fair hearing may not be required at the second hearing of a two-stage process where the person affected had an adequate hearing at the first stage, in Australia see: *South Australia v O'Shea* (1987) 163 C.L.R. 378. Cf. *Haoucher v Minister for Immigration and Ethnic Affairs* (1990) 169 C.L.R. 648.

[103] Although detriment may not be immediately obvious; it may be less easy to convince a decision maker that a decision already taken is wrong than to persuade the body initially of the merits of one's case. Cf. *R. v Portsmouth CC Ex p. Gregory* (1990) 89 L.G.R. 478, DC, where the determinations of a special council committee set up to investigate two councillors were irremediably flawed by the earlier investigations of a council subcommittee.

[104] Thus an original decision vitiated by bias will normally not be allowed to stand: in New Zealand, see *Anderton v Auckland CC* [1978] 1 N.Z.L.R. 657 at 700.

rehearing *de novo*.[105] In India it has been held that a post-decisional hearing cannot normally cure an act that is a nullity for want of natural justice.[106] On occasion, the United States courts have also upheld the principle of a "post-decisional hearing".[107]

In general, it is increasingly the case that the courts will not intervene on   **8–026** grounds of procedural unfairness where the procedurally unfair decision is subject to correction by a procedure which has proper procedural safeguards.[108] In *Calvin v Carr*[109] the Privy Council doubted that there was a general rule[110] that a failure of fairness at the initial hearing is not to be cured by procedurally correct appeal; in particular, it was suggested, a more latitudinarian attitude should be taken towards the proceedings of domestic tribunals whose authority is derived from the consensual rules of a voluntary association. Thus, in that case, an appeal to the Committee of the Australian Jockey Club was held, for this reason, to cure a defective decision of race stewards who had disqualified the owner of a horse alleged to have been raced improperly. In *Lloyd v McMahon*,[111] the House of Lords confirmed this trend outside the context of domestic tribunals. It was held that the decision of a district auditor to surcharge councillors for failure to set a valid rate, without according them oral hearings would, had it been procedurally defective, have been cured by the statutory appeal from the auditor's decision to the High Court. It should be noted, however, with reference to the criteria set out above, that the scope of the

---

[105] See, e.g. *Pillai v Singapore CC* [1968] 1 W.L.R. 1278 at 1286; *Calvin v Carr* [1980] A.C. 574; *Lloyd v McMahon* [1987] A.C. 625; *Twist v Randwick MC* (1976) 136 C.L.R. 106; *R. v LAUTRO Ex p. Tee* (1995) 7 Admin. L.R. 289; *R. v Legal Aid Board Ex p. Donn & Co (A Firm)* [1996] 3 All E.R. 1 (Area Committee's unfairness in failing to consider full representations of solicitors seeking legal aid contract not cured by chairman subsequently confirming individually with six of seven members of committee that full representations made no difference to their decision).

[106] *State of Orissa v Bina Pani* A.I.R. 1967 S.C. 1269 at 1271; S. Sorabjee, "Obliging Government to Control Itself: Recent Developments in Indian Administrative Law" [1994] P.L. 39, 41. However in some cases a post-decisional hearing has been applied; but in *KI Shepherd v Union of India* 1987 (4) S.C.C. 431 the court said that "It is common experience that once a decision has been taken, there is a tendency to uphold it and a representation may not yield any fruitful purpose".

[107] See, e.g. *Philips v Commissioner of Internal Revenue* 283 U.S. 589 (1931). However, in general, due process requires that individuals must receive notice and an opportunity to be heard *before* the government deprives them of property: *US v James Daniel Good Real Property* 510 U.S. 43 (1993). The legislation at issue in *Phillips* has since been amended to provide a pre-deprivation hearing: see *Kindred v Commissioner of Internal Revenue* 454 F.3d 688 at 695 (7th Cir. 2006).

[108] If a claimant commences judicial review before the completion of a hearing, or fails to use an appeal route or other alternative remedy, permission may be refused: see 16–014.

[109] [1980] A.C. 574; cf. *Rees v Crane* [1994] 2 A.C. 173 at 192, where Lord Slynn, having referred to the 4th edition of this book, went on to say "the courts should not be bound by rigid rules" and to stress in that case the respondent could not rely on urgency or administrative inconvenience.

[110] As proposed by Megarry J. in *Leary v National Union of Vehicle Builders* [1971] Ch. 34 (trade union expulsion case).

[111] [1987] A.C. 625.

appeal was very wide, all the evidence being susceptible of re-examination, including the merits of the decision.[112]

8–027   Where there is an option for rapidly seeking annulment or amendment of the order made, the initial procedurally unfair proceeding will not be reviewed.[113] Thus, where interim anti-social behaviour orders were made without notice, there was no breach of procedural fairness since the orders were subject to the safeguards of early review or discharge hearings, which were compliant with procedural fairness.[114] Similarly, where a re-categorisation decision is being made in respect of a determinate sentence prisoner, there is no need to permit the prisoner to make representations in advance of the re-categorisation decision; all that fairness requires is that the prisoner have an opportunity to appeal the re-categorisation decision.[115] It has also been held that unfairness in the context of school exclusion decisions are capable of being cured by means of statutory appeal, provided that the independent appeal body is entrusted with the task of dealing with the merits of the case fully and *de novo*, and that it does so in a way that is not open to challenge on normal judicial review grounds and the appeal process is not contaminated in some real sense by the defect in the earlier decision-making process.[116] The curative principle also applies in the immigration context[117] and in the context of care proceedings.[118] It is not just appeal procedures which can cure an initial defective decision and defective decisions have been cured by a minister's lawful approval[119] and later fair and open-minded reconsideration of the decision.[120]

---

[112] It was expressly suggested that the situation might be different if the appellate body was bound by findings of fact, or restricted to questions of law (Lord Templeman at 891); this suggests that a rehearing by way of judicial review would not be sufficient (Lord Bridge at 884).

[113] *Wiseman v Borneman* [1971] A.C. 297 at 318F–G.

[114] *R. (on the application of M) v Secretary of State for Constitutional Affairs* [2004] EWCA Civ 312; [2004] 1 W.L.R. 2298 at [39].

[115] *R. (on the application of Palmer) v Secretary of State for the Home Department* [2004] EWHC 1817 at [27]–[28].

[116] *R. (on the application of DR) v Head Teacher of St George's Catholic School* [2002] EWCA Civ 1822 at [55] (Keene L.J.); and *R. v Visitors of the Inns of Court Ex p. Calder & Persaud* [1994] Q.B. 1 at 59C (noting that an appeal to visitors, entailing a full re-hearing on the merits, should cure any procedural defect on the part of the initial tribunal); *R. (on the application of A) v Enfield LBC* [2002] EWHC 395 at [18] (Mitchell J., even at the first level, decision-makers must "act in the knowledge that their decisions are amenable to judicial review", although it will be "rare" that recourse to judicial review will be appropriate).

[117] *R. v Secretary of State for the Home Department Ex p. Sesay* [1995] Imm AR 521 at 522–523 (Sedley J.).

[118] *Re C (Care Proceedings: disclosure of local authority's decision-making process)* [2002] EWHC 1379 (Fam) [2002] 2 FCR 673 at [240] (although there had been unfairness and incompatibility with the ECHR Art.6 in the earlier stages of the care proceedings, nevertheless the trial had been fair overall).

[119] *R. v Secretary of State for Education Ex p. Cumbria CC* [1994] E.L.R. 220 at 228.

[120] *R. (on the application of Martin) v Secretary of State for the Home Department* [2003] EWHC 1512; *The Times*, May 15, 2003. Cf. *R. (on the application of Banks) v Secretary of State for the Environment, Food and Rural Affairs* [2004] EWHC 416; [2004] N.P.C. 43 at [107] where there was no evidence of a "fair, open-minded and comprehensive" reconsidera-

Limits

There are however limits to the extent to which procedural unfairness can **8–028** be "cured". There may be situations in which, although the provision of a right of appeal is not required, a court will be satisfied that nothing short of compliance with the requirements of procedural fairness at both stages will afford to the individual the standards of fairness demanded in the particular context.[121] For example, trial on indictment is not an adequate alternative to judicial review for committal on inadmissible evidence given the importance of providing a right to cross-examine at a preliminary stage.[122] Similarly, inadequate consultation was not corrected by appeal where a budgetary decision was easier to overturn before it was firmly made;[123] while a procedurally defective decision will not be cured by the decision-maker communicating with the aggrieved party after the decision, in defence of the decision.[124] A right of individual petition to the ECtHR is also not a right of appeal to an appeal court capable of curing the national authorities' failure to provide a fair trial.[125]

ECHR Art.6 and subsequent hearings

It is well-established in the case law of the ECtHR that the requirements of **8–029** Art.6 are satisfied if either (a) the initial decision-maker is independent and impartial or (b) there is control by a judicial body with full jurisdiction, which does satisfy the Art.6 requirements.[126] In other words, the question is whether the composite procedure satisfies Art.6.[127] The expression, "'full jurisdiction' does not mean full decision-making power. It means full jurisdiction to deal with the case as the nature of the decision requires".[128] In assessing compatibility with Art.6, it is necessary to have regard to matters such as the subject matter of the decision appealed against, the manner in which that decision was arrived at, and the content of the dispute, including the desired and actual grounds of appeal.[129]

---

[121] *Leary v National Union of Vehicle Builders* [1971] Ch. 34; in New Zealand, see *Denton v Auckland City* [1969] N.Z.L.R. 256; *Chalmers v Disciplinary Committee of the Pharmaceutical Society of New Zealand* (1991) 9 N.Z.A.R. 529 (provision for full appeal on the merits did not cure the defects because what was said at the initial stages had permeated the proceedings and influenced the appellate body). These cases should not now be regarded as authority for the wider proposition that defects may never be cured by a fair hearing at an appeal: *Calvin v Carr* [1980] A.C. 574.

[122] *R. v Bedwellty Justices Ex p. Williams* [1997] A.C. 225 at 235–236.

[123] *R. (on the application of Haringey Consortium of Disabled People and Carers Association) v Haringey LBC* (2002) 5 C.C.L. Rep. 422 at [49].

[124] *R. v P Borough Council Ex p. S* [1999] Fam 188 at 221–222.

[125] *R. (on the application of Ramda) v Secretary of State for the Home Department* [2002] EWHC 1278 at [27].

[126] *Albert and Le Compte v Belgium* (1983) 5 E.H.R.R. 533.

[127] See, e.g. *Magill v Porter* [2001] UKHL 67; [2002] 2 A.C. 357 (no breach of Art.6 when the procedure of district auditor and the Divisional Court on appeal were considered as a whole); see 10–017.

[128] *R. v Secretary of State for the Environment, Transport and the Regions Ex p. Holdings & Barnes Plc* (the *Alconbury* case) [2001] UKHL 23; [2003] 2 A.C. 295 at [87].

[129] *Bryan v UK* (1995) 21 E.H.R.R. 342; *Tower Hamlets LBC v Begum (Runa)* [2003] UKHL 5; [2003] 2 A.C. 430 at [51].

8–030   Given that judicial review does not involve a fresh hearing on the merits and has traditionally involved limited review of factual errors,[130] the question has often arisen as to whether judicial review is sufficient to remedy any shortcomings in an initial decision-making procedure. In most cases, courts in England and Wales have been satisfied that the availability of judicial review can remedy an initial decision-making process which has not been compliant with Art.6.[131] Generally, the more administrative and less judicial the decision-making process established by Parliament, the less intensive will be the judicial review required to ensure compliance with Art.6;[132] but the overriding requirement is that the overall procedure must be lawful and fair.[133] In the planning context, judicial review sufficed where the minister has power to call in applications for planning permission or to hear a recovered appeal against a refusal of planning permission.[134] In relation to the latter, the House of Lords concluded that the procedural rules applying to the minister's decision[135] combined with the rules on judicial review meant that the procedure as a whole complied with Art.6.[136]

---

[130] See 11–041; 11–00.

[131] Cf. R. (on the application of Chief Constable of Lancashire) v Preston Crown Court [2001] EWHC Admin 928; [2002] 1 W.L.R. 1332 at [40] (since Crown Court's "appreciation of local conditions is not something which, on its merits, can sensibly be second guessed in judicial review proceedings", the lack of independence and impartiality "is, in reality, beyond the scope of judicial review securely to cure or amend") and R. (on the application of Kehoe) v Secretary of State for Work and Pensions [2004] EWCA Civ 225; [2004] Q.B. 1378 (judicial review could not overcome the shortcomings in the system for taking enforcement proceedings for child maintenance payments against the absent parent, as established by the Child Support Act 1991).

[132] See, e.g. Begum [2003] UKHL 5; [2003] 2 A.C. 430 at [5] (Lord Bingham, noting the intensity of review required to cure non-compliance at first instance that "the narrower the interpretation given to 'civil rights', the greater the need to insist upon review by a judicial tribunal exercising full powers. Conversely, the more elastic the interpretation given to 'civil right', the more flexible must be the approach to the requirement of independent and impartial review if the emasculation (by over judicialisation) of administrative welfare schemes is to be avoided."); R. (on the application of Beeson) v Dorset CC [2002] EWCA Civ 1812; [2003] H.R.L.R. 11 at [22] (in general a statutory scheme involving administrative-type decisions albeit by a non-independent decision-maker will satisfy Art.6 where judicial review is available).

[133] Begum [2003] UKHL 5; [2003] 2 A.C. 430.

[134] Holding & Barnes Plc [2001] UKHL 23; [2003] 2 A.C. 295.

[135] The rules included where the minister differed from the inspector on a matter of fact, or took into account new evidence or was disposed to disagree with the inspector, notifying persons entitled to appear at the inquiry, allowing written representation and giving reasons for any difference with the inspector: Town and Country Planning (Inquiries Procedure) (England) Rules 2000 r.17(5).

[136] Holding & Barnes Plc [2001] UKHL 23; [2003] 2 A.C. 295 at [16]–[19], [49]–[56] (Lord Slynn); [155]–[160] (Lord Clyde); [188]–[189] (Lord Hutton); in the planning context, R. (on the application of Adlard) v Secretary of State for the Environment, Transport and the Regions [2002] EWCA Civ 735; [2002] 1 W.L.R. 2515; Adan v Newham LBC [2001] EWCA Civ 1916; [2002] 1 W.L.R. 2120 (although council's internal review not "independent and impartial" appeal to the county court ensured compatibility with Art.6); R. (on the application of Q) v Secretary of State for the Home Department [2003] EWCA Civ 364; [2004] Q.B. 36 at [116]–[117] (provided that fair system of questioning of asylum-seekers in relation to welfare benefits, availability of judicial review would ensure compliance with Art.6); Friends Provident Life and Pensions Ltd v Secretary of State for Transport, Local Government and the Regions

Judicial review has also been deemed adequate in relation to decisions on compensation for miscarriages of justice;[137] decision-making on welfare benefits,[138] including benefits for asylum-seekers;[139] and in disciplinary proceedings,[140] although if the disciplinary proceedings are determining a civil right or obligation, it will be necessary to provide an appeal on the merits, rather than merely an appeal on point of law.[141] It is also open to a court in judicial review to adopt a more intensive scrutiny of the rationality of the initial decision, by considering whether it had been made on a misunderstanding or ignorance of an established and relevant fact, or where rights were at stake, by using proportionality.[142]

Limits of curative effect

However, every decision-making procedure must be reviewed in its entirety, and judicial review will not always be considered to have curative effect. This point was emphasised in the decision of the ECtHR in *Tsfayo v United Kingdom*,[143] in which it was held that judicial review could not provide sufficient remedy for a decision taken on the basis of "a simple question of fact", and without the need for professional knowledge or experience and exercise of administrative discretion.[144] The applicant in *Tsfayo*, an Ethiopian national seeking asylum in the United Kingdom, had been successful in her application to Hammersmith and Fulham LBC (the council) for housing and council tax benefit, but had failed to renew her application the following year, as was required by law.[145] On realising that

8–031

[2001] EWHC Admin 820, [2002] 1 W.L.R. 1450 (planning authority not independent and impartial but judicial review Court having full jurisdiction in relation to a matter of planning judgment).

[137] *R. (on the application of Mullen) v Secretary of State for the Home Department* [2002] EWHC 230; [2002] 1 W.L.R. 1857 (although Secretary of State not an independent and impartial tribunal in relation to compensation for miscarriages of justice, Art.6 compliance because of supervisory jurisdiction of the Court, if necessary including questions of fact).

[138] *R. (on the application of Bono) v Harlow DC* [2002] EWHC 423; [2002] 1 W.L.R. 2475 (council's housing benefit decision not independent and impartial but judicial review remedying the deficiency where sufficient control in respect of issues of primary fact).

[139] *R. (on the application of Q) v Secretary of State for the Home Department* [2003] EWCA Civ 364; [2004] Q.B. 36 at [116]–[117] (provided that fair system of questioning of asylum-seekers in relation to welfare benefits, availability of judicial review would ensure compliance with Art.6).

[140] *R. (on the application of Thompson) v Law Society* [2004] EWCA Civ 167; [2004] 1 W.L.R. 2522 at [100] (if Office for Supervision of Solicitors had been determining a civil right or obligation, availability of judicial review would have secured Art.6 compatibility).

[141] *Albert and Le Compte v Belgium* (1983) 5 E.H.R.R. 533 at para.36, ECtHR (in a case involving disciplinary decisions relating to doctors taken by professional associations not complying with Art.6(1), an appeal to a Belgian Court of Cassation only on a point of law was a violation of Art.6); *Ghosh v General Medical Council* [2001] UKPC 29, [2001] 1 W.L.R. 1915 (GMC proceedings as a whole complying with Art.6 given availability of rehearing on appeal to PC).

[142] *Holding & Barnes* [2001] UKHL 23; [2003] 2 A.C. 295 at [49]–[54] (Lord Slynn); see 11–073.

[143] App. No.60860/00, [2007] H.L.R. 19.

[144] *Tsfayo* App. No.60860/00, [2007] H.L.R. 19 at para.45.

[145] *Tsfayo* App. No.60860/00, [2007] H.L.R. 19 at para.9–10.

her benefits had ceased, she applied to the council for both prospective and backdated benefits.[146] Although her application for prospective benefits was successful, her application for back-dated benefits was rejected on the basis that she did not have "good cause" for failing to renew her claim for benefits earlier.[147] The council upheld its decision,[148] and on appeal, the council's decision was upheld by Hammersmith and Fulham LBC Housing Benefit and Council Tax Benefit Review Board (the HBRB), on the basis that the applicant did not have "good cause" for failing to renew earlier and was not a credible witness.[149] With three councillors from the council in its membership and advised by a barrister from the council's legal department, the HBRB clearly did not satisfy the "independence" requirement of Art.6, and the issue arose as to whether judicial review could provide curative effect in this situation.[150] The ECtHR reasoned that, while the Administrative Court had the power to quash the decision if it considered, inter alia, that there was no evidence to support the HBRB's factual findings, that its findings were plainly untenable, or that the HBRB had misunderstood or been ignorant of an established and relevant fact,[151] it did not have jurisdiction to rehear the evidence or substitute its own views as to the applicant's credibility.[152] This meant that there was never a possibility that the central issue would be determined by a tribunal that was independent of one of the parties to the dispute, and consequently, a violation of Art.6 was found.[153]

PRELIMINARY DECISIONS

8–032 In what circumstances must the rules of procedural fairness be observed by persons entrusted with the conduct of an investigation but having no power to give a binding decision? This is one of the most troublesome problems in relation to procedural fairness. The authorities often appear to be, and sometimes are, in conflict with one another. When one comes across a judicial formulation of general legal principle it is not infrequently misleading because the court has in mind only a limited range of contexts in which the problem arises. Again, some of the best-known dicta have been uttered in cases where no allegation of unfairness was made, and one can never be certain that the same words would have been used if that issue had been before the court. Nor is it always possible to assess how far the form of the proceedings has influenced the approach adopted by the court.

[146] *Tsfayo* App. No.60860/00, [2007] H.L.R. 19 at para.10.
[147] *Tsfayo* App. No.60860/00, [2007] H.L.R. 19 at para.11.
[148] *Tsfayo* App. No.60860/00, [2007] H.L.R. 19 at para.13.
[149] *Tsfayo* App. No.60860/00, [2007] H.L.R. 19 at paras 14, 47.
[150] *Tsfayo* App. No.60860/00, [2007] H.L.R. 19 at paras 35, 40, 46.
[151] See 11–041.
[152] *Tsfayo* App. No.60860/00, [2007] H.L.R. 19 at para.47.
[153] *Tsfayo* App. No.60860/00, [2007] H.L.R. 19 at para.48.

If a quashing order is sought in relation to a non-binding report, the court may well look askance;[154] although this will not be the case if the report has "potentially wide implications"[155] and it is in the public interest to withdraw it.[156] If a prohibiting order is sought to prevent an investigation from going further, the court is also likely to be more easily persuaded.[157] Many of the considerations relevant in this context are also in play where the court is invited to refuse permission to apply for judicial review because an applicant has failed to pursue an alternative remedy.[158] However, the case law considered here is distinctive because the courts are considering a prior question; namely, are the procedural framework and effects of the preliminary decision such that it would be unfair to the affected person to hold that his entitlement to be heard at a later stage, or his entitlement to challenge the preliminary decision, means that no hearing or other procedural protection is required in respect of the preliminary decision?

Even if we ignored the existing authorities altogether, and the problem is 8–033 examined entirely in the light of the need for fairness to be shown to individuals and for efficiency to be displayed in the conduct of public affairs, it is unlikely that any neat set of answers will emerge. It may not be very difficult to give the best available answer to a problem set in a given legislative and factual context; it is very difficult to supply satisfactory answers couched in general terms. However, the following tentative observations, based on principle as well as authority, are offered.

Proximity between investigation and act or decision

The degree of proximity between the investigation in question and an act 8–034 or decision directly adverse to the interests of the claimant may be important. Thus, a person conducting a preliminary investigation with a view to recommending or deciding whether a formal inquiry or hearing (which may lead to a binding and adverse decision) should take place is not normally under any obligation to comply with the rules of fairness.[159] But

---

[154] See, e.g. *R. v St Lawrence's Hospital, Caterham, Statutory Visitors Ex p. Pritchard* [1953] 1 W.L.R. 1158; *R. (on the application of United Cooperatives Ltd) v Manchester City Council* [2005] EWHC 364 at [21] (Elias J. noting that. "the courts are in principle reluctant to permit mere advice to be the subject of review"). Cf. 3–025.

[155] *United Cooperatives Ltd* [2005] EWHC 364 at [22].

[156] See, e.g. *Gillick v West Norfolk and Wisbech Area Health Authority* [1986] A.C. 112; *R. v Secretary of State for the Environment Ex p. Greenwich LBC* [1989] C.O.D. 530, DC; *R. (on the application of Association of British Travel Agents Ltd (ABTA)) v Civil Aviation Authority* [2006] EWCA Civ 1356 at [65].

[157] See 8–034 et seq; 7–034.

[158] See 16–014.

[159] See, e.g. *Beetham v Trinidad Cement Co* [1960] A.C. 132, PC; *Parry-Jones v Law Society* [1969] 1 Ch. 1; *Moran v Lloyd's* [1981] 1 Lloyd's Rep. 423 at 427; *Giles v Law Society* (1996) 8 Admin. L.R. 105 at 114; in Australia, see *Medical Board of Queensland v Byrne* (1958) 100 C.L.R. 582; *Ex p. Tange; Re Drummoyne MC* (1962) 62 S.R. (N.S.W) 193; in Canada, see *R. v Saskatchewan College of Physicians and Surgeons Ex p. Samuels* (1966) 58 D.L.R. (2d) 622; *R. v Ministry of Education Ex p. Southampton School District* (1967) 59 D.L.R. (2nd) 587; *R. v British Columbia College of Dental Surgeons Ex p. Schumacher* (1970) 8 D.L.R. (3rd) 473 at para.20; cf. *Hammond v Association of British Columbia Professional Foresters* [1991] B.C.W.L.D. 639 (distinguishing *Schumacher* where the investigating committee exercised significant influence).

such a person may be placed under such an obligation if the investigation is an integral and necessary part of a process which may terminate in action adverse to the interests of a person claiming to be heard before him.[160]

8–035   For instance, the principles of fairness must be observed by magistrates conducting a preliminary investigation in respect of a charge of an indictable offence.[161] A further reason for requiring observance of natural justice in a preliminary investigation by magistrates is that the investigation may end with a remand in custody or a requirement that bail be furnished; but because of the limited purpose of the hearing the accused is not entitled to confront and cross-examine all the witnesses who may be called by the prosecution at trial.[162] Although "prosecuting" decisions, whether in the criminal or disciplinary sphere, may be reviewable,[163] it would only be in a wholly exceptional case that the prosecutor might come under a duty to hear or consult the prospective accused, the complainant, or any other party, before coming to a decision as to whether or not to prosecute.[164]

[160] *Wiseman v Borneman* [1971] A.C. 297 at 317 (Lord Wilberforce) (preliminary steps towards tax assessment; requirements of fairness satisfied by statutory procedure); *cf. Pearlberg v Varty* [1972] 1 W.L.R. 534 (no duty to observe natural justice). See also *Balen v Inland Revenue Commissioners* [1978] 2 All E.R. 1033; *cf. Rees v Cranel* [1994] 2 A.C. 173. In Canada, see *Re Attorney-General Canada and Canadian Tobacco Manufacturers' Council* (1986) 26 D.L.R. (4th) 677 (duty of fairness applied to a power to recommend if, as a result of the recommendation, adverse consequences for the applicant are "probable or close to probable"). In Ireland suspensions do not require a fair hearing when made not as a way of punishment but by way of a holding operation pending full investigation of the complaint: *Morgan v The Provost Fellows and Scholars of the College of the Most Holy and Undivided Trinity of Queen Elizabeth near Dublin* (2004) 15 E.L.R. 235 (however person who is being suspended pending a full inquiry must be informed of the reason for his suspension and the full hearing must be heard within a reasonable time).
[161] *R. v Coleshill Justices Ex p. Davies* [1971] 1 W.L.R. 1684; *R. v Colchester Magistrates Ex p. Beck* [1979] 2 W.L.R. 637 at 645, DC; *cf.* in Australia *Sankey v Whitlam* (1978) 142 C.L.R. 1 at 83–84 (Mason J.).
[162] *R. v Epping and Harlow Justices Ex p. Massaro* [1973] Q.B. 433; *cf.* the duty of fairness imposed upon the prosecution in a trial to call or to reveal to the accused beforehand the identity of material witnesses: *R. v Leyland Justices Ex p. Hawthorn* [1979] Q.B. 283 (although quaere whether this decision should properly be seen as resting upon a duty of fairness: *R. v Secretary of State for the Home Department Ex p. Al Mehdawi* [1990] 1 A.C. 876). However, the defendant has the right to give evidence after the magistrates have rejected his submission of no case to answer: *R. v Horseferry Road Stipendiary Magistrate Ex p. Adams* [1977] 1 W.L.R. 1197, DC. Courts may also be reluctant to intervene in the conduct of preliminary examinations before their conclusion: *R. v Wells Street Stipendiary Magistrate Ex p. Seillon* [1978] 1 W.L.R. 1002 (refusal of cross-examination); *R. v Wells Street Stipendiary Magistrate Ex p. Deakin* [1980] A.C. 477.
[163] See 3–006; *R. v Metropolitan Police Commissioner Ex p. Blackburn* [1968] 2 Q.B. 118; *R. v General Council of the Bar Ex p. Percival* [1991] 1 Q.B. 212. In the Canadian case of *Re Peel Board of Education and B* (1987) 59 O.R. (2nd) 654, it was held that a school principal must give a pupil an opportunity to be heard before suspending for misconduct; *Knight v Indian Head School Division No.19* (1990) 69 D.L.R. (4th) 489 (education director entitled to notice and fair opportunity to respond before being dismissed, even though dismissible without cause and the opportunity of subsequent review by a board).
[164] *Wiseman* [1971] A.C. 297 In *Selvarajan v Race Relations Board* [1975] 1 W.L.R. 1686 at 1696, Lawton L.J. suggested that the courts might be entitled to interfere with the DPP's discretion to initiate a prosecution if he acted "unfairly" but there was no suggestion that fairness might require consultation: *Blackburn* [1968] 2 Q.B. 118; *R. v Police Complaints Board Ex p. Madden* [1983] 1 W.L.R. 447 (where it was accepted that the Board was under a

Preliminary investigations subject to procedural fairness

Principles of procedural fairness may also apply to the conduct of an inquiry or investigation, the holding of which is not a prerequisite of further proceedings or action. 8–036

Public inquiries

For instance, since the hearings and report of an inquiry set up to investigate an alleged public scandal attract a great deal of publicity, it may be unfair to deny a person against whom damaging allegations may be made before the tribunal the procedural protection accorded to a defendant in legal proceedings.[165] But even where the report of such an inquiry may be expected to contain criticism of particular persons, it may be that the efficient conduct of the inquiry requires that rights to legal representation and particularly cross-examination be dispensed with.[166] 8–037

Investigations under the Companies Act

The case for requiring a Department of Trade inspector conducting a formal investigation into a company's affairs[167] to observe the detailed rules of fairness has been thought to be perhaps less strong: here again the report may lead to judicial proceedings, but is not a prerequisite of the institution of such proceedings; the inspector's report may at the discretion of the Secretary of State be published,[168] but the investigation is carried out in private. The balance is still a fine one: the investigation (to which 8–038

---

duty to act "fairly" in considering complaints); *Percival* [1991] 1 Q.B. 212; *Brooks v DPP of Jamaica* [1994] 1 A.C. 568 (decision of DPP to prefer indictment, or of judge to consent to preferral, was a purely procedural step and neither principles of fairness nor Jamaican Constitution entitled person indicted to be given prior notice of DPP's decision, or to attend before Judge).

[165] See Inquiries Act 2005 s.9 (requirement of impartiality), s.17 (evidence and procedure). Procedural irregularities in a report may be raised collaterally in proceedings to declare invalid an instrument for the making of which a valid report was a prerequisite: *Hoffmann-La Roche (F) & Co AG v Secretary of State for Trade and Industry* [1975] A.C. 295 at 354, 365. In Canada, in *Syndicat des employés de production du Québec et de l'Acadie v Canada* (Canadian Human Rights Commission) (1989) 62 D.L.R. (4th) 385, the Supreme Court stated, obiter, that complainants are entitled to know the substance of evidence contained in the investigative report and to comment on it before their complaint of discrimination is dismissed. And in *Federation of Women's Teachers' Association of Ontario v Ontario* (Human Rights Commission) (1988) 67 Q.R. (2nd) 492 it was held that the Commission, before deciding whether to refer a complaint of discrimination for adjudication, was required to inform those under investigation of the substance of the case against them.

[166] See Sir Louis Blom-Cooper, "Witnesses and the Scott Inquiry" [1994] P.L. 1 (on the Arms to Iraq inquiry); and 7–116. In New Zealand natural justice has been held to apply to preliminary decisions: *Birss v Secretary for Justice* [1984] 1 N.Z.L.R. 513; *Fraser v State Services Commission* [1984] 1 N.Z.L.R. 116; and when reporting and making recommendations affecting private interests Royal Commissions and Commissions of Inquiry in New Zealand must observe natural justice principles: *Re Erebus Royal Commission; Air New Zealand Ltd v Mahon* [1984] A.C. 808, PC; *Peters v Davison* [1999] 3 N.Z.L.R. 164.

[167] Companies Act 1985 ss.431–434; 436–437, 439, 441, 442–446A–E.

[168] Companies Act 1985 s.437(3)(c).

officers or agents of the company, or any other person whom the inspectors believe may be in possession of information relating to any matter which they believe is relevant to the investigation may be compelled to attend and to answer questions and produce documents[169]) and report expose persons to a legal hazard[170] as well as potentially damaging publicity. It has accordingly been held that the rudiments of procedural fairness must be observed. The inspector must, before publishing a report containing serious criticisms and allegations against a person, put to that person the substance of them and give him an opportunity of rebutting them.[171]

8-039   However, it has been held that the inspector is not required to allow the cross-examination of witnesses, nor is he required to recall the person to rebut allegations subsequently made by other witnesses, nor to submit his tentative conclusions to the "accused" before sending his report to the minister (although it is in fact the usual practice of inspectors to submit draft conclusions to affected individuals).[172] The minister is under no implied procedural duty to entertain representations or to disclose the information that he has acquired before exercising his discretion to appoint inspectors to conduct an inquiry.[173] Judicial authority on investigations of the kind conducted under the Companies Act has often laid emphasis on their non-judicial character, the importance of an expeditious conclusion and the difficulty of the investigative task.[174] This view has also been taken by the ECtHR, on a challenge to an inspectors' report on the ground that it violated the applicants' rights to honour and reputation under Art.6(1) of the Convention, and denied them effective court access.[175] The ECtHR held that the functions performed by the inspectors were essentially investigative, in that they did not adjudicate either in form or in substance,

---

[169] Companies Act 1985 s.434.

[170] Cf. *Testro Bros Pty Ltd v Tait* (1963) 109 C.L.R. 353 at 370 (Kitto J., concurring with the proposition in the text); *Wiseman v Borneman* [1971] A.C. 297 at 317; *R. v Cheltenham Justices Ex p. Secretary of State for Trade* [1977] 1 W.L.R. 95; *London and County Securities Ltd v Nicholson* [1980] 1 W.L.R. 948; *Savings and Investment Bank Ltd v Gasco Investments (Netherlands) BV* [1984] 1 W.L.R. 271. As to the effect of the privilege against self-incrimination, see *McClelland, Pope & Langley Ltd v Howard* [1968] 1 All E.R. 549, HL. In *Re London United Investments Plc* [1992] Ch. D. 578 (privilege is impliedly excluded by 1985 Act); see now *Saunders v UK* (1997) 23 E.H.R.R. 313.

[171] *Re Pergamon Press Ltd* [1971] Ch. 388.

[172] *Maxwell v Department of Trade and Industry* [1974] Q.B. 523; *R. v Chettenham Justices Ex p. Secretary of State for Trade* [1977] 1 W.L.R. 95, DC (witness summons, issued to inspector to reveal evidence given in confidence at an inquiry, quashed); but below for the position under the European Convention. As was done by the Scott Inquiry (n. 166); *R. (on the application of Clegg) v Secretary of State for Trade and Industry* [2002] EWCA Civ 519; [2003] B.C.C. 128.

[173] *Norwest Holst Ltd v Department of Trade* [1978] Ch. 201.

[174] See, e.g. *Re Grosvenor & West-End Ry. Terminus Hotel Co* (1897) 76 L.T. 337: *Hearts of Oak Assurance Co v Attorney General* [1932] A.C. 392; *O'Connor v Waldron* [1935] A.C. 76. See also s.236 of the Insolvency Act 1986, under which a person may be compelled to answer questions without the benefit of the privilege against self-incrimination: In *British & Commonwealth Holdings Plc (Joint Administrators) v Spicer and Oppenheim* [1993] A.C. 426 [1992] 3 W.L.R. 854; *Bishopsgate Investment Management v Maxwell* [1993] 1 Ch. 1.

[175] *Fayed v UK* (1994) 18 E.H.R.R. 393.

nor make a civil or criminal adjudication concerning the applicants' rights. Even though the report may have led to uncompensated damage to the applicants' reputations, it was held that the potential remedy of judicial review, while limited, provided sufficient guarantees for the persons affected.[176]

Binding nature of preliminary decision

In a number of cases in which the proceedings of investigating bodies have been impugned (mainly on grounds other than non-compliance with the principles of fairness), the courts have refused to intervene unless the investigation does or can culminate in a determination or order which has binding force or will itself acquire binding force upon confirmation or promulgation by another body or which otherwise controls the decision of that other body.[177] To put the matter in another way, an investigating body is under no duty to act fairly if it cannot do more than recommend or advise on action which another body may take in its own name and in its own discretion.[178] This proposition cannot be accepted without qualification. Whilst it would be absurd to impose judicial standards on every body who advises a government department as to the exercise of its executive functions, justice will sometimes demand, as the courts are increasingly recognising, that an investigation preceding a discretionary administrative decision be conducted in accordance with the requirements of procedural fairness.[179]   8–040

Illustrations

- Inspectors holding inquiries in respect of compulsory purchase orders are undoubtedly obliged to act fairly,[180] although their findings and recommendations are in no way binding on the minister when he decides whether or not to confirm the order.   8–041

---

[176] R. (on the application of Harrison) v Secretary of State for the Home Department [2003] EWCA Civ 432; [2003] I.N.L.R. 284 (Minister of State's letter refusing Harrison's claim for citizenship and inviting him to make a fresh application for naturalisation was at its highest a provisional determination of the claimant's application); R. v Secretary of State for Health Ex p. C [2000] 1 F.L.R. 627.

[177] See 3–025.

[178] For example, in Canada: R. v Macfarlane Ex p. O'Flanagan and O'Kelly (1923) 32 C.L.R. 518 (not a natural justice case); R. v St Lawrence's Hospital, Caterham, Statutory Visitors [1953] 1 W.L.R. 1158; Guay v Lafleur [1965] S.C.R. 12; de Freitas v Benny [1976] A.C. 239. Cf. Rees v Crane [1994] 2 A.C. 173; R v Wokingham DC Ex p. J [1999] 2 F.L.R. 1136, QBD.

[179] Whether or not the function may be characterised as "judicial": Re Pergamon Press Ltd [1971] 1 Ch. 388; R. v Race Relations Board Ex p. Selvarajan [1975] 1 W.L.R. 1686; R. v Commission for Racial Equality Ex p. Cottrell and Rothon [1980] 1 W.L.R. 1580 at 1587; R. v Secretary of State for the Home Department Ex p. Hosenball [1977] 1 W.L.R. 766 (hearing before advisory committee pending deportation on national security grounds); R. v Secretary of State for the Home Department Ex p. Cheblak [1991] 1 W.L.R. 890.

[180] See 7–017.

- If express procedural duties are cast upon an investigating authority this in itself may support the view that a common-law duty to observe the requirements of fairness attaches to the investigations.[181]

- Even where statute expressly accords a great degree of procedural latitude to the Parliamentary Ombudsman, the courts recognise that a report containing criticisms of a government department should be sent in draft to the department for comments.[182] However, it has been held that a person whose complaint initiated the Ombudsman's investigation—and who may be offered financial recompense as a consequence of his report—is not entitled to a copy of the draft report, because although the complainant's rights are affected by the decision, it is the department and not the complainant who is being investigated and who is liable to face public criticism for its acts.[183]

- A duty of procedural fairness is imposed upon the proceedings of the Parole Board both by statute and by the common law, inasmuch as a decision by the Home Secretary to revoke the licence of a released prisoner and recall him to jail may be contingent upon the receipt of a recommendation by the Board to that effect.[184]

Duty to observe principles of fairness

8–042 In special situations, persons conducting an inquiry limited to the purpose of collecting information may be obliged to observe the principles of procedural fairness, although they are not even entitled to make recom-

[181] For example, in Canada: *Saulnier v Quebec Police Commission* [1976] 1 S.C.R. 572; and *Moumdjian v Canada (Security Intelligence Review Committee)* (1999) 177 D.L.R. (4th) 192.
[182] The obligation to give the official against whom a complaint is made and his departmental head an opportunity of commenting on the allegations may be regarded as importing a more general duty to act fairly with respect to those officials; but, this apart, the ombudsmen enjoy the widest freedom of action in relation to matters within his competence (Parliamentary Commissioner Act 1967 s.7; Health Service Commissioner Act 1993 s.11; Local Government Act 1974 ss.28, 29); *Grunwick Processing Laboratories Ltd v ACAS* [1978] A.C. 655 where an express statutory duty to ascertain workers' opinions was construed as mandatory; although it is virtually inconceivable that this would ever require a formal hearing to be held, some of the judgments referred to the body's function as judicial and to its procedural duty to comply with the rules of natural justice. On Ombudsmen generally, see 1–066.
[183] *R. v Parliamentary Commissioner for Administration Ex p. Dyer* [1994] 1 W.L.R. 621, DC; Cf. *R. v Commissioner for Local Administration Ex p. Eastleigh BC* [1988] Q.B. 855; *R. v Commissioner for Local Administration Ex p. Croydon LBC* [1989] 1 All E.R. 1033.
[184] Crime (Sentences) Act 1997 ss.28, 32; *Thynne, Wilson and Gunnell v UK* (1990) 13 E.H.R.R. 666; *R. v Parole Board Ex p. Wilson* [1992] 1 Q.B. 740. However, where the Parole Board merely reviewed (as an extra-statutory practice) and confirmed the decision of the Secretary of State to recall to prison a discretionary life sentence prisoner who had been released on licence, prior to a full statutory review, the CA held that the requirements of full hearing do not apply, because that review was only intended to be "tentative and provisional": *R. v Parole Board Ex p. Watson* [1996] 1 W.L.R. 906 (Sir Thomas Bingham M.R.); *cf. R. v Secretary of State for the Home Department Ex p. Seton* (April 25, 1996, unrep.). Moreover, in an emergency situation, the Secretary of State has the power pursuant to s.32(2) to revoke the licence without consulting the Board: *Re Cummings* [2001] EWCA Civ 45; [2001] 1 W.L.R. 822.

mendations to the deciding body.[185] Such a situation can arise because the type of inquiry conducted is one in which members of the public have come to expect certain minimum procedural standards to be maintained. In this situation, as in some of the others reviewed in this Chapter, the observance of the *audi alteram partem* principle (hear both sides) may be called for because non-observance would give the appearance of injustice. This was the position with the preliminary investigation into the conduct of a judge: the suspension of a judge, even temporarily, was a matter of such significance that he should be given the opportunity of making representations before it happened.[186]

LACK OF FAIR PROCEDURE MADE NO DIFFERENCE OR CAUSED NO HARM

The contention that a procedural flaw "made no difference"—in so far as 8–043 the defendant public authority would have made the same decision even if different procedures had been followed—can be made in two distinct ways. (a) The court may hold that there is no *entitlement* to fair procedure. (b) The court may accept that there is an entitlement to fair procedure but exercise *discretion to withhold a remedy*.[187] In each situation, the court is in some measure invited to look beyond the narrow question of whether the decision was taken in a procedurally improper manner, to the wider question of whether a decision properly taken would or could have benefited the applicant.

This Chapter is concerned with situation (a), though a sharp distinction 8–044 is not always drawn in the judgments. The response of the courts to this argument, in its many forms, is still uncertain.[188] In some cases the courts have refused to grant relief when satisfied that the outcome could not have been different had natural justice been fully observed.[189] These decisions

[185] *Wednesbury Corp v Ministry of Housing and Local Government (No. 2)* [1966] 2 Q.B. 275 at 302–303 (Diplock L.J.).
[186] *Rees v Crane* [1994] 2 A.C. 173. *cf.* the majority decision in *Furnell v Whangerei High School Board* [1973] A.C. 660 (suspension of school teacher). On suspension of a judge, see now Constitutional Reform Act 2005 ss.108–121 and Sch.14.
[187] See 18–048.
[188] For comparative perspectives, see the Australian case *Re Refugee Review Tribunal; Ex p. Aala* (2000) 204 C.L.R. 802 (where constitutional writs are sought at least, exception for relief to be refused on basis that breach of procedural fairness made no difference); and in Canada, *Mobil Oil Canada Ltd v Canada Newfoundland Offshore Petroleum Board* (1994) 111 D.L.R. (4th) 1.
[189] *Glynn v Keele University* [1971] 1 W.L.R. 487 at 496; *Cinnamond v BAA* [1980] 1 W.L.R. 582; *R. v Chief National Insurance Commissioner Ex p. Connor* [1981] Q.B. 758; *R. v Monopolies and Mergers Commission Ex p. Argyll* [1986] 1 W.L.R. 763; *R. v Bristol CC Ex p. Pearce* (1984) 83 L.G.R. 711; *R. v Criminal Injuries Compensation Board Ex p. Aston* [1994] C.O.D. 500; *Davis v Carew-Pole* [1956] 1 W.L.R. 833 at 840; *Byrne v Kinematograph Renters Society Ltd* [1958] 1 W.L.R. 762 at 785; *Durayappah v Fernando* [1967] 2 A.C. 337 at 350. *Fulop (Imre) v Secretary of State for the Home Department* [1995] Imm. A.R. 323, CA ("no

have been sought to be explained on the ground that the relief sought was discretionary,[190] or on the ground that breach makes an order voidable rather than void.[191] It is submitted that neither explanation is sufficient. As to the former, it is right to note that a refusal of relief on the ground that it would make "no difference" may be explained either as an exercise of the courts' discretion as to the grant of relief,[192] or as a part of the consideration of whether the principles of fairness have in fact been infringed at all. However, this in itself goes no way towards an identification of those cases in which the courts are prepared to refuse relief, as a matter of discretion or otherwise. As to the latter, it is clear that the court may still have discretion to refuse the statutory remedy even though the decision is void.[193] There are also cases, arising in various contexts, in which it has been assumed that the inadequacy of the hearing is in itself sufficient for the decision to be set aside: in those instances the courts have declined to embark upon a speculative inquiry about the possible impact of the procedural irregularity upon the decision.[194]

Statutory applications to quash

8–045 Whether a person who has been denied an adequate hearing must also establish that this affected the ultimate decision is particularly relevant when proceedings are brought for the statutory remedy to quash, for example, a planning appeal or a compulsory purchase order.[195] Relief may

possibility" of a different decision since missing documents unhelpful to applicant); *R. v Camden LBC Ex p. Paddock* [1995] C.O.D. 130 (case "falls within the narrow margin of cases in which the court can say with confidence that the [unfairness] has caused no actual injustice"; *R. v Islington LBC, Ex p. Degnan* [1998] C.O.D. 46, CA ("exceptional case"; judge "near to certainty" that the flawed decision made no difference to the result); *R. (on the application of Ghadami) v Harlow DC* [2004] EWHC 1883 at [73]; *Aston v Nursing & Midwifery Council* [2004] EWHC 2368 at [73]; *R. (on the application of Varma) v Duke of Kent* [2004] EWHC 1705 at [27]; *R. (on the application of Wainwright) v Richmond upon Thames LBC* [2001] EWHC Civ 2062; *Mousaka Inc v Golden Seagull Maritime Inc* [2002] 1 W.L.R. 395 at [35].
[190] *Glynn* [1971] 1 W.L.R. 487; *R. v Aston University Senate Ex p. Roffey* [1969] 2 Q.B. 538 (certiorari; undue delay); *Fullbrook v Berkshire Magistrates' Courts Committee* (1970) 69 L.G.R. 75 (declaration; unreasonable conduct of plaintiff). See 18–048.
[191] In *Stevenson v United Road Transport Union* [1977] I.C.R. 893, the characterisation of the decision as void or voidable was stated to be relevant only to the court's approach to its exercise of discretion to grant relief, in that case a declaration. On the void/voidable distinction, see 4–056.
[192] See 18–048.
[193] *Miller v Weymouth and Melcombe Regis Corp* (1974) 27 P. & C.R. 46 at 480–481 (not a natural justice case, but where the court declined to quash a void decision for lack of prejudice to the applicant); *Kent CC v Secretary of State for the Environment* (1977) 75 L.G.R. 452 at 460–461. Cf. *Goddard v Minister of Housing and Local Government* [1958] 1 W.L.R. 1151 at 1153; *Savoury v Secretary of State for Wales* (1976) 31 P. & C.R. 344 at 347.
[194] *R. v Registrar of Building Societies* [1960] 1 W.L.R. 669 at 684; *Annamunthodo v Oilfield Workers' Trade Union* [1961] A.C. 945 at 956; *Kanda v Government of Malaya* [1962] A.C. 322, 327; *John v Rees* [1970] Ch. 345, 402; *R. v Thames Magistratres' Court Ex p. Polemis* [1974] 1 W.L.R. 1371 at 1375–1376; *R. v Devon and Cornwall Rent Tribunal Ex p. West* (1975) 29 P. & C.R. 316 at 320–332; *Fairmount*, above, and the cautionary dicta of Lord Hailsham in *London & Clydeside Estates Ltd v Aberdeen DC* [1980] 1 W.L.R. 182 at 189.
[195] See 17–025.

be granted either, if there has been a failure to comply with statutory requirements and the applicant has been substantially prejudiced thereby, or if the decision or order in question was not one that the authority was empowered to make.[196]

In some cases where it has been assumed that a breach of the rules of **8-046** natural justice falls under the first limb, the claimant has been granted relief upon showing that had he been afforded the hearing to which he was entitled, the decision might have been different.[197] In other cases, however the courts have treated the defect as falling under the second limb, but have defined a breach of natural justice to include the risk that the irregularity might have affected the outcome, although no clear guidance has emerged on the closeness with which a court should scrutinise the facts.[198] Once again, it may be questioned, however, whether such categorisation does more than mask the principles upon which the courts act. It appears clear that in planning cases, where a failure to comply with a statutory requirement is alleged, substantial prejudice must be shown.[199] In other circumstances, however, the position is less clear although courts are unlikely to interfere with decisions where the results, however irregular, are of trivial importance, or wholly speculative,[200] or remote.

Caution required in relation to the "no difference" argument

The courts have rightly cautioned against the suggestion that no prejudice **8-047** has been caused to the applicant because the flawed decision would inevitably have been the same and as a general principle, a court will be slow to rule that no harm has been done.[201] It is not for the courts to

---

[196] See, e.g. Town and Country Planning Act 1990 s.288.

[197] See, e.g. *Wilson v Secretary of State for the Environment* [1973] 1 W.L.R. 1083 at 1095–1096 (if adequate notice had been given, representations might have been made and an inquiry might have been held); *Leighton and Newman Car Sales Ltd v Secretary of State for the Environment* (1976) 32 P. & C.R. 1; *Davies v Secretary of State for Wales* [1977] J.P.L. 102; and *George v Secretary of State for the Environment* (1979) 250 E.G. 339 (relief denied); *R. v Mayor of Greenwich LBC Ex p. Patel* (1985) 51 P. & C.R. 282 (real as opposed to remote or fanciful loss or prejudice must be shown) *R. v Canterbury City Council Ex p. Springimage Ltd* (1994) 68 P. & C.R. 171 (relief denied because "no real possibility" of different decision).

[198] *Hibernian Property Co Ltd v Secretary of State for the Environment* (1974) 27 P. & C.R. 197 at 212, 214; *Lake District Special Planning Board v Secretary of State for the Environment* [1975] J.P.L. 220; *Performance Cars Ltd v Secretary of State for the Environment* (1977) 34 P. & C.R. 92; *General Accident Fire & Life Assurance Corp Ltd v Secretary of State for the Environment, ibid.* at 588; *R. v Visiting Justice at Her Majesty's Prison, Pentridge Ex p. Walker* [1975] V.R. 883 (magistrate's failure to realise that he had a discretion to allow legal representation did not prejudice applicant); *George v Secretary of State for the Environment* (1976) 32 P. & C.R. 1.

[199] *R. v Mayor of Greenwich LBC Ex p. Patel* (1985) 51 P. & C.R. 282.

[200] Although in such cases the claimant for judicial review is unlikely to be regarded as having "sufficient interest" for the grant of permission (see Ch.2). In India it has been held that a prior hearing is required when an administrative action is "prejudicial to the citizen": *The Scheduled Caste and Weaker Sections Welfare Assoc v State of Karnataka* A.I.R. 1991 S.C. 1117.

[201] *R. v Tandridge District Council Ex p. Ali Fayed* [2000] 1 P.R.L. 58.

substitute their opinion for that of the authority constituted by law to decide the matters in question.[202] As it has been put, in a case involving a destruction order under the Dangerous Dogs Act 1991,[203]

> "the notion that when the rules of natural justice have not been observed, one can still uphold the result because it would not have made any difference, is to be treated with great caution. Down that slippery slope lies the way to dictatorship. On the other hand, if it is a case where it is demonstrable beyond doubt that it would have made no difference, the court may, if it thinks fit, uphold a conviction even if natural justice had not been done."

8–048　Further, "natural justice is not always or entirely about the fact or substance of fairness. It has also something to do with the appearance of fairness. In the hallowed phrase, 'Justice must not only be done, it must also be seen to be done'".[204] These cases support the view that the fundamental principle at stake is that public confidence in the fairness of adjudication or hearing procedures may be undermined if decisions are allowed to stand despite the absence of what a reasonable observer might regard as an adequate hearing, rather than that injustice lies only in holding an individual bound by a decision whose substantive reliability is cast in doubt by the existence of procedural irregularities.[205]

8–049　But on the whole judges have declined to commit themselves une-quivocally to the proposition that intervention will never be withheld when they are satisfied that no amount of procedural propriety would have affected the outcome.[206]

---

[202] *Chief Constable of the North Wales Police v Evans* [1982] 1 W.L.R. 1155, 1160 (Lord Hailsham), 1173 (Lord Brightman); *John v Rees* [1970] Ch. D 345, 582; *R. v Secretary of State for the Environment Ex p. Brent LBC* [1982] Q.B. 593 at 734; *R. v Secretary of State for Education Ex p. Prior* [1994] I.C.R. 877 (Brooke J.).

[203] *R. v Ealing Magistrates Court Ex p. Fanneran* (1996) 160 J.P. 409 (Staughton L.J.).

[204] *R. v Ealing Magistrates' Court Ex p. Fanneran* (1996) 8 Admin. L.R. 351, 358 (Staughton L.J.). A possibly more extreme formulation was set out by Rougier J. in the same case (at 359): "...no one can ever say for certain what must have happened in the circumstances which have not, in fact, arisen. The robing rooms up and down this land are full of strange tales of seemingly impregnable cases foundering on some unforeseen forensic reef. It is not, in my opinion, for this court to employ its imagination to postulate facts which might or might not have occurred or arguments which might or might not have succeeded had the rules of natural justice been followed".

[205] *Cheall v Association of Professional Executive, Clerical and Computer Staff* [1983] Q.B. 126 (Donaldson L.J.). On the facts, relief was refused on the ground that although the applicant had been denied a fair hearing, the Court held that he could not "feel unfairly treated", effectively because the decision maker did not have a discretion to decide in his favour. *cf. R. v Inner West London Coroner Ex p. Dallaglio* [1994] 4 All E.R. 139; *Harada Ltd (t/a Chequepoint UK Ltd) v Turner (No.1)* [2001] EWCA Civ 599; *R. (on the application of Takoushis) v HM Coroner for Inner North London* [2005] EWCA Civ 1440; [2006] 1 W.L.R. 461.

[206] See, e.g. *Ridge v Baldwin* [1964] A.C. 40 at 68; *Maradana Mosque Trustees v Mahmud* [1967] 1 A.C. 13 at 24–25; *Malloch v Aberdeen Corp* [1971] 1 W.L.R. 1578 at 1582–1583, 1600; *Re B (Minors)* [1973] Fam. 179 at 189; *Wislang v Medical Practitioners Disciplinary*

Illustrations

- A decision by school governors refusing to correct an inaccurate **8–050** statement in a consultation paper, and refusing to extend the consultation period was not unfair because the error in question could not have led a person reading the pamphlet to have reached a different conclusion.[207]

- A decision by the chairman of the Monopolies and Mergers Commission to recommend to the Secretary of State that a take-over reference be laid aside, while beyond his powers, should not, in the discretion of the court, be quashed because there was little doubt that a properly constituted committee would have reached the same decision.[208]

- Moreover, it has been held that there was no procedural unfairness caused by refusing to permit a prisoner to make further submissions on the basis of a report and the failure to do so had not been procedurally unfair as the report did not contain any new information and was based entirely on evidence placed before the parole board.[209]

- There was no procedural unfairness where notices of a planning application were served by post and one person had not been served notice as that person clearly knew of the planning application and was not denied the opportunity to make representations.[210]

- Although the claimant should have seen the evidence put to the university visitor in respect of a decision to terminate his registration

---

Committee [1974] 1 N.Z.L.R. 29 at 42, 45; *Scott v Aberdeen Corp* 1976 S.L.T. 141; *Hickmott v Dorset CC* (1977) 35 P. & C.R. 195; *R. v Hull Prison Board of Visitors Ex p. St Germain* [1979] Q.B. 425 at 450–451; *Stininato v Auckland Boxing Association (Inc)* [1978] 1 N.Z.L.R. 1 at 29 (but see the dissenting view of Woodhouse J, at 15–16). *cf. Bhardwaj v Post Office* [1978] I.C.R. 144 (appeal from industrial tribunal dismissed because no real likelihood that chairman's overly strict attitude towards the appellant would have affected the result: but the tribunal's order of costs against appellant was allowed). An employee who alleges that he was dismissed unfairly because he was given no opportunity to be heard may recover less statutory compensation if the industrial tribunal decides that he contributed to his own dismissal by his conduct, but the tribunal should not consider whether he would have been dismissed, absent the unfair treatment, in any event: *Polkey v AE Dayton Services Ltd* [1987] 1 W.L.R. 1147.

[207] *R. v Haberdashers' Aske's Hatcham School Governors Ex p. ILEA, The Times*, March 9, 1989.

[208] *R. v Monopolies and Mergers Commission Ex p. Argyll* [1985] 1 W.L.R. 763 (the CA also took into account the needs of good public administration); *cf. R. v Secretary of State for Education and Science Ex p. ILEA* [1990] C.O.D. 319; *R. v Bristol CC Ex p. Pearce* (1984) 83 L.G.R. 711 (food hawkers not shown objections; but those objections could not possibly have motivated decision).

[209] *R. (on the application of Faulkner) v Secretary of State for the Home Department* [2006] EWHC 563.

[210] *R. (on the application of Ghadami) v Harlow DC* [2004] EWHC 1883 at [73] (Moreover, although the notice was defective for want of a closing date for representations, the court would refuse relief as the defect had not frustrated the relevant object of giving the public an opportunity to make representations about the proposed development and neither the applicant nor the public had suffered any prejudice).

as a student, he could not have made any representations which would have affected the result and consequently, leave for judicial review was refused.[211]

- Similarly, although a local authority had breached its statutory duty to consult by failing sufficiently to notify individual local residents of plans to construct a toucan crossing, the decision to approve the crossing could stand because there was no real possibility that the local authority would have reached a different decision had it complied with the duty to consult.[212]

8–051 Whether the requisite flexibility is to be found in the definition of a breach of the *audi alteram partem* (hear both sides) principle, in the statutory requirement of substantial prejudice" or in the court's discretion over the remedy will generally be immaterial (except where the relief sought is non-discretionary, for example, an appeal[213] or a claim for damages).

Undeserving claimants

8–052 In some cases it has been suggested that a claimant who is for some reason undeserving may forfeit the right to procedural fairness.[214] The forfeiture may be based upon a prejudgement of their merit as claimants, or a prejudgment of the likelihood of their wining the sympathy of the decision maker. We suggest below[215] that a legitimate expectation which is derived from the representation of the decision-maker should not be forfeited by the conduct of the claimant, however unmeritorious. It is also wrong for a hearing to be conditional upon the good behaviour of the claimant, and

---

[211] *R. (on the application of Varma) v Duke of Kent* [2004] EWHC 1705; [2004] E.L.R. 616 at [27].
[212] *R. (on the application of Wainwright) v Richmond upon Thames LBC* [2001] EWCA Civ 2062 at para.55; *Mousaka Inc v Golden Seagull Maritime Inc* [2002] 1 W.L.R. 395 at [35] (since there was no effective right of appeal from the decision of the High Court on an application for appeal of an arbitrator's award, a requirement on the judge to provide reasons in full for refusing the application would be "completely worthless"); *Aston v Nursing & Midwifery Council* [2004] EWHC 2368 at [73] (although a defendant's legal representative had been incompetent during the conduct of a trial, the legal adviser and, save for one exception, the solicitor appearing for the Council were astute to prevent the representative from damaging the presentation of the claimant's case: he did have a full opportunity to put his side, his version of the facts, and there was a full opportunity for the committee to judge the Council's witnesses when tested in cross-examination).
[213] *cf. Ottley v Morris* [1979] 1 All E.R. 65 (whether refusal of adjournment constituted ground of appeal on point of law depended on whether appellant might thereby have suffered a substantial injustice). *Hickmott v Dorset CC* (1977) 35 P. & C.R. 195 (evidence improperly received in breach of *audi alteram partem* rule could not have affected the result: appeal dismissed in absence of miscarriage of justice).
[214] See, e.g. *Cinnamond v British Airports Authority* [1980] 1 W.L.R. 582 (minicab drivers at Heathrow Airport previously prosecuted frequently for breach of byelaw thus not entitled to fair hearing because no legitimate expectation (Lord Denning) or because it would have "availed them nothing" (Lord Brandon); *R. (on the application of Scott) v Heathrow Airport Ltd* [2005] EWHC 2669 at [25]–[28].
[215] See 12–042.

risky to prejudge the merits of the claimant's present case upon his previous wrongdoing.

DECISION-MAKER NOT AT FAULT

Where alleged procedural unfairness is not the fault of the tribunal or other decision-maker, is a claimant still entitled to have the decision quashed on the basis that he has not been accorded procedural fairness? Where, at a hearing on notice, the absence of procedural fairness is due to the conduct of, or a failure by, the other party to the hearing, it was at one time thought that the courts had discretion to quash the decision.[216] Thus, where prison authorities failed to make known to a prisoner charged with an offence against discipline the existence of a witness to the alleged offence, the determination of the prison board of visitors was quashed on the grounds of unfairness, albeit that this was not caused by the tribunal itself.[217] Where an important prosecution witness on a charge of shoplifting deceived the court as to his reason for resigning from the Metropolitan Police (being in fact required to resign following disgraceful conduct including a conviction), it was held that his deliberate concealment constituted unfairness, so that the conviction should be quashed.[218]

8–053

It has been suggested, however, that these decisions should be viewed not as resting on principles of fairness, but as based upon the alternative principle that "fraud unravels everything", or because the "process leading to conviction" has been distorted and vitiated as a result of a breach of duty owed to the court and to the defence by a prosecutor.[219] The principles of fairness, in contrast, are "concerned solely with the propriety of the procedure adopted by the decision-maker".[220] But this approach, it is submitted, risks leaving uncorrected procedural errors which are the responsibility of the prosecution or respondent, but which cannot be

8–054

---

[216] *R. v Blundeston Prison Board of Visitors Ex p. Fox-Taylor* [1982] 1 All E.R. 646; *R. v Leyland J. Ex p. Hawthorn* [1979] Q.B. 283; *R. v Bolton Justices Ex p. Scally* [1991] 1 Q.B. 537; *Al Mehdawi v Secretary of State for the Home Department* [1990] 1 A.C. 876.

[217] *R. v Blundeston Prison Board of Visitors Ex p. Fox-Taylor* [1982] 1 All E.R. 646.

[218] *R. v Knightsbridge Crown Court Ex p. Goonatilleke* [1986] Q.B. 1 (since the witness in question had presented the defendant for prosecution, and had ensured that he was prosecuted, it is suggested that he was effectively in the position of a prosecutor or respondent rather than a true third party).

[219] Lord Bridge in *Al Mehdawi v Secretary of State for the Home Department* [1990] A.C. 876 at 895–896, Lord Bridge's reinterpretation of the earlier decisions is not entirely satisfactory, because it is not clear that in all such cases there has been anything approaching a breach of duty owed to the Court or to the defence, let alone fraud. For example, in *R. v Bolton Justices Ex p. Scally* [1991] 1 Q.B. 537, evidence led by the Crown Prosecution Service of blood alcohol levels in a drink-driving case was held to be unreliable due to 'an ordinary lack of care'. The Court held that certiorari would lie, because the prosecution's error had 'corrupted the process leading to conviction in a manner which was unfair' (Watkins L.J.), but it would not appear that anything approaching fraud or breach of duty was established. See J. Herberg, "The Right to a Hearing: Breach without Fault" [1990] P.L. 467.

[220] *Al Mehdawi* [1991] A.C. 876 at 894c.

characterised as fraud or breach of duty. As Bingham L.J. has said, "If a procedural mishap occurs as a result of misunderstanding, confusion, failure of communication, or perhaps even inefficiency, and the result is to deny justice to the applicant, I should be very sorry to hold that the remedy of judicial review was not available".[221] Moreover, recent cases have found decisions of authorities to be unfair notwithstanding lack of fault by the decision-maker;[222] and where there has been blameless unfairness, not caused by unfairness or malpractice by any party, a conviction will be quashed in judicial review.[223]

8–055   As a general rule, a person who has himself impeded or frustrated the service of notice of impending action cannot afterwards be heard to complain that he did not receive actual notice.[224] But where the mistake is due to the conduct of the applicant's legal representatives, the position is not entirely clear. The question was expressly left open in *R. v. Immigration Appeal Tribunal, Ex p. Enwia*.[225] In *R. v. Immigration Appeal Tribunal, Ex p. Rahmani*,[226] the Court of Appeal held that where an immigrant applicant's solicitors had negligently failed to proceed with an appeal from a refusal of an application for an extension of stay, the applicant was entitled to judicial review of the dismissal of her appeal, since she had been denied a basic opportunity to be heard, and the applicant herself was wholly innocent of responsibility for this. Although the House of Lords in *Rahmani* upheld the decision of the Court of Appeal, it did so on different grounds and did not approve or reject the Court of Appeal's view.[227]

8–056   However, in *R. v Secretary of State for the Home Department Ex p. Al Mehdawi*,[228] the House of Lords did directly consider the Court of Appeal's decision in *Rahmani*, and came to a very different conclusion. In *Al*

---

[221] *Bagga Khan v Secretary of State for the Home Department* [1987] Imm. A.R. 543–555.

[222] *R. (on the application of Maqsood) v Special Adjudicator* [2001] EWHC Admin 1003; [2002] Imm. A.R. 268.

[223] *R. (on the application of Pownall) v Flintshire Magistrates Court* [2004] EWHC 1289 at [13]–[14].

[224] *De Verteuil v Knaggs* [1918] A.C. 557 at 560–561; *James v Institute of Chartered Accountants* (1907) 98 L.T. 225; *Glynn v Keele University* [1971] 1 W.L.R. 487 at 495 (failure to notify change of address); *R. v Newport Justices Ex p. Carey* (1996) 160 J.P 613, DC (applicant's absence from hearing his own fault); *R. v Secretary of State for the Home Department Ex p. Kikaka* [1996] Imm. A.R. 340 (applicant had chosen to represent herself); *Pine v Law Society* [2001] EWCA Civ 1574; [2002] U.K.H.R.R. 81 at [42]–[43] (when the claimant could not afford the fare to attend a hearing he could have sought an adjournment, sought admission of evidence by affidavit or some more informal means, sought a hearing closer to where he lived, or asked the tribunal to re-open the hearing).

[225] [1984] 1 W.L.R. 117, CA. At first instance, Comyn J. held that the court could grant relief in such circumstances, although his judgment was reversed on the facts by the CA.

[226] [1985] Q.B. 1109, CA; [1986] A.C. 475, HL (*sub nom. Rahmani v Diggiues*).

[227] *cf. Rahmani* holding on claimant's lack of fault has been applied in other cases: *R. (on the application of Tataw) v Immigration Appeal Tribunal* [2003] EWCA Civ 925; [2003] I.N.L.R. 585 at [20].

[228] [1990] 1 A.C. 876; *Hassan v Secretary of State for the Home Department* [1994] Imm. A.R. 482, CA; all following *Al Mehdawi* [1990] A.C. 876: *Secretary of State for the Home Department v Mohammed Yasin* [1995] Imm. A.R. 118 at 121–122 (failure of applicant's advisors to draw Tribunal's attention to brother's case); *Samuel Dele Adeniyi v Secretary of State for the Home Department* [1995] Imm. A.R. 101 (failure of solicitors to send notice of

Mehdawi, the applicant had lodged an appeal against the Home Secretary's decision to make a deportation order against him. Notice of the appeal was sent to his solicitors, who misaddressed the letter when sending it on to the applicant, who consequently never received notice of the appeal. The appeal was therefore dismissed in his absence. On an application for judicial review of the decision to dismiss the appeal, on the ground that the applicant had been denied a fair (or any) hearing, the House of Lords held that a party cannot complain of a denial of a fair hearing where he has failed to make use of an opportunity to be heard through the fault of his own advisers, even if he himself is not responsible in any way for that failure. Lord Bridge drew an analogy with the position in private law, where a party who lost the opportunity to have his case heard through the negligence of his legal advisers would be left with no remedy except against those advisers. Their Lordships were clearly influenced by the fear that to allow review in such circumstances could open the way for manipulation of hearings, and would hinder the dismissal of abandoned appeals by administrative bodies.[229] However, the *Al-Mehdawi* rule is not absolute. In the case of *R. v The Criminal Injuries Compensation Board Ex p. A*, Lord Slynn, noting that the failure of the board and the police to acquire and consider a medical report of which they were aware constituted procedural unfairness, added that it did not seem to be "necessary to find that anyone was at fault in order to arrive at this result. It is sufficient if objectively there is unfairness".[230] It has also been suggested in *Haile v Immigration Appeal Tribunal* that *Al Mehdawi* did not preclude a court from considering "the wider interests of justice".[231]

appeal to correct address); *R. v Governors of Sheffield Hallam University Ex p. R* [1995] E.L.R. 267 (failure of applicant's solicitor to seek sufficient adjournment to consider new material); *R. v Secretary of State for the Home Department Ex p. Osei Yaw Yeboah* [1995] Imm. A.R. 393 (applicant not represented at appeal through fault of solicitor); *R. v Monopolies and Mergers Commission Ex p. Stagecoach Holdings Plc, The Times,* July 23, 1996.
[229] *R. (on the application of Mathialagan) v Southwark LBC* [2004] EWCA Civ 1689; [2005] R.A. 43; *R. (on the application of R) v Secretary of State for the Home Department* [2005] EWHC 520; *Maqsood v the Special Adjudicator and the Secretary of State* [2001] EWHC Admin 1003; *Parmar (t/a Ace Knitwear) v Woods (Inspector of Taxes) (No.1)* [2002] EWHC 1085. On the other hand, fault by an applicant's legal advisers may be a "good reason" for delay in bringing an application for judicial review; *R. v Secretary of State for the Home Department Ex p. Oyeleye* [1994] Imm. A.R. 268; *R. v Newham LBC Ex p. Gentle* (1994) 26 H.L.R. 466.
[230] [1999] 2 A.C. 330 at 345.
[231] *Haile v Immigration Appeal Tribunal* [2001] EWCA Civ 663; [2002] Imm. A.R. 170 at [26] (Simon Brown L.J.). See also *FP (Iran) v Secretary of State for the Home Department* [2007] EWCA Civ 13 at [45] (distinguishing *Al-Mehdawi*).

CHAPTER 9

PROCEDURAL FAIRNESS: FETTERING OF DISCRETION

SCOPE

This chapter examines two ways in which a discretion conferred on a 9–001
public authority may be "fettered" unlawfully: (a) by the over-rigid
application of a self-created rule or policy; and (b) by giving an undertaking to exercise its discretion in a particular manner.

FETTERING OF DISCRETION BY SELF-CREATED RULES OR POLICY

A decision-making body exercising public functions which is entrusted with 9–002
discretion must not, by the adoption of a fixed rule or policy, disable itself
from exercising its discretion in individual cases. It may not "fetter" its
discretion. A public authority that does fetter its discretion in that way may
offend against either or both of two grounds of judicial review: the ground
of legality and the ground of procedural propriety. The public authority
offends against legality by failing to use its powers in the way they were
intended, namely, to employ and to utilise the discretion conferred upon
it.[1] It offends against procedural propriety by failing to permit affected
persons to influence the use of that discretion. By failing to "keep its mind
ajar", by "shutting its ears" to an application, the body in question
effectively forecloses participation in the decision-making process.

Because the "no fettering" prinicple is mostly employed as a means of 9–003
keeping open the possibility of meaningful participation in the decision-
making process, we deal with it in this section of the book as a species of
the genus procedural fairness. Other treatments of the no-fettering doctrine see it as part of a more general head of review, namely, the "retention
of discretion".[2] This includes the requirement that the exercise of discretion should not be delegated to another—a matter we consider under the
ground of "illegality" in Chapter 5.[3] As we have said, the so-called grounds
of review are by no means entirely self-contained and aspects of the no-
fettering doctrine could also fit within the ground of "irrationality".[4]

[1] See Ch.5.
[2] See, e.g. H.W.R. Wade and C. Forsyth, *Administrative Law*, 9th edn (2004), Ch.10.
[3] See 5–135 et seq.
[4] See Ch.11.

9–004   The principle against fettering discretion does not prevent public authorities upon which a discretionary power has been conferred guiding the implementation of that discretion by means of a policy or a rule that is within the scope of its conferred powers. The principle directs attention to the *attitude* of the decision-maker, preventing him from rigidly excluding the possibility of any exception to that rule or policy in a deserving case. Nor does the principle focus upon the content of the hearing or other means of communication which must be afforded to persons interested in changing the decision-maker's mind. The decision-maker must allow interested individuals the opportunity to persuade him to amend or deviate from the rule or policy, but, unlike the principle of natural justice or fair hearing, the principle against fettering is not concerned with any particular form of hearing or with any particular technique of making or receiving representations.[5]

Underlying rationale

9–005   The underlying rationale of the principle against fettering discretion is to ensure that two perfectly legitimate values of public law, those of legal certainty and consistency (qualities at the heart of the principle of the rule of law), may be balanced by another equally legitimate public law value, namely, that of responsiveness.[6] While allowing rules and policies to promote the former values, it insists that the full rigour of certainty and consistency be tempered by the willingness to make exceptions, to respond flexibly to unusual situations, and to apply justice in the individual case.[7] There are also other background values in play, namely, accountability (public bodies could be held to account (politically if not legally) if they do not fulfil their announced policies) and efficiency—it is clearly more efficient for a housing authority to set out its criteria for admission through a "points system" than to assess each application afresh. For similar reasons, university departments normally publish their admissions criteria

[5] *R. v Secretary of State for the Environment Ex p. Brent LBC* [1982] Q.B. 593 (decision of the Secretary of State was held unlawful both for fettering of discretion and for failing to provide a fair hearing).
[6] *R. v Ministry for Agriculture, Fisheries and Food Ex p. Hamble Fisheries (Offshore) Ltd* [1995] 2 All ER 714 at 722 (Sedley J. described the "two conflicting imperatives of public law"—rigidity and certainty as against individual consideration).
[7] C. Hilson, "Judicial Review, Policies and the Fettering of Discretion" [2002] P.L. 111; D. Galligan, "The Nature and Functions of Policy Within Discretionary Power" [1976] P.L. 332. For an analysis of the advantages and disadvantages of creation by various administrative techniques, criteria to regulate the exercise of discretion, see J. Jowell, "The Legal Control of Administrative Discretion" [1973] P.L. 178; *Law and Bureaucracy* (1975); D. Galligan, *Discretionary Powers, A Legal Study of Official Discretion* (1986); K.C. Davis, *Discretionary Justice* (1969). On the distinction between rules and objectives, see *Oddy v Transport Salaried Staff's Association* [1973] I.C.R. 524; H. Molot, "The Self-Created Rule of Policy and Other Ways of Exercising Administrative Discretion" (1972) 18 McGill L.J. 310; *R. v Secretary of State for the Home Department Ex p. Venables* [1998] A.C. 407 at 494 (Lord Browne-Wilkinson restated the distinction between a proper policy and an over-rigid or inflexible one, and referred to the passage in the text).

which not only assist the admissions tutor to make decisions with despatch, but also help prospective applicants by discouraging applications that, in the absence of exceptional circumstances, are unlikely to succeed.

Application of the no-fettering principle

The no-fettering principle does not necessarily frown on the articulation of **9–006** policies (provided, as we shall see, that they are lawful and rational) but it does not permit them to be rigidly applied. Many of the cases illustrating the no-fettering principles have been concerned with the discretionary grant of licences and permits; but the ambit of these principles is by no means confined to this class of function.[8] In 1858 the Court of Appeal in Chancery sternly reproved a sanitary authority for having laid down a general rule that all cesspits and privies in its area should be replaced by water-closets, instead of having dealt with each case individually on its merits.[9] There the authority was treated as a body analogous to a tribunal exercising a judicial discretion. But similar principles have been applied to a huge range of functions of public authorities, without drawing artificial analogies with tribunals, or resorting to the obsolete distinction between judicial, quasi-judicial and administrative bodies.[10]

Illustrations

- In the planning context, the Secretary of State for the Environment **9–007** was held to have fettered his discretion in adopting a policy of disallowing all purely local objections to the allocation of land for gypsy sites.[11]

- In the award of costs, a tribunal which has power to award costs fails to exercise its discretion if it fixes specific amounts to be applied indiscriminately to all cases before it.[12] However, a tribunal's statutory discretion may be wide enough to justify the adoption of a rule not to award any costs save in exceptional circumstances,[13] as distinct from a rule never to award any costs at all.

---

[8] This statement of the law was approved by the Divisional Court in *Ex p. Brent* [1982[Q.B. 593; and see *Lavender (H) & Son Ltd v Minister of Housing and Local Government* [1970] 1 W.L.R. 1231; compare *Stringer v Minister of Housing and Local Government* [1970] 1 W.L.R. 1281 (local authority fettered its planning policy by agreement but Secretary of State on appeal not so fettered).
[9] *Tinkler v Wandsworth Board of Works* (1858) 27 L.J.Ch. 342; *Wood v Widnes Corp* [1898] 1 Q.B. 463.
[10] See Appendix B.
[11] *R. v Secretary of State for the Environment Ex p. Halton DC* (1983) 82 L.G.R. 662.
[12] *R. v Merioneth Justices* (1844) 6 Q.B. 153; *R. v Glamorganshire Justices* (1850) 19 L.J.M.C. 172.
[13] *Re Wood's Application* (1952) 3 P. & C.R. 238; *R. v Secretary of State for the Environment Ex p. Reinisch* (1971) 70 L.G.R. 126. Indeed, when a tribunal departs from its normal rule it may be required to give clear reasons for its decision: *Pepys v London Transport Executive* [1975] 1 W.L.R. 234; *R. v Wreck Commissioner Ex p. Knight* [1976] 3 All E.R. 8.

- In exercising discretion to award grants or benefits, generally, any policies adopted should be applied flexibly. The Supplementary Benefits Commission was entitled to assess an applicant's resources on the assumption that if he was a university student he was in receipt of a parental contribution bringing his grant up to the maximum awarded by local authorities; however, it was not permitted to calculate the applicant's resources on this basis when the facts of the particular case showed that the assumed contribution had not been made.[14]

- The Law Society was entitled to have policies governing claims against the Compensation Fund (including a policy excluding compensation for consequential loss) provided that such policy admitted of exceptions in appropriate cases, and that any special reasons put forward were considered.[15]

- The House of Lords has even applied the non-fettering principles to the discretionary award of investment allowances to industrialists by a government department.[16]

- There have also been many cases where local authorities policies prohibiting discretionary grants to students have in practice amounted to an unlawful fetter on their discretion, despite an apparent willingness to consider exceptional cases.[17]

- In the context of appointments, in a Scottish case it was assumed that the Secretary of State, in deciding whether to approve an appointment to the office of chief constable, was not entitled to adopt a rigid rule never to approve the appointment of an officer who was already a member of the local police force in question.[18]

- Educational policies should be flexible; and local authorities must be prepared, at least when an objection is expressly raised,[19] to make exceptions, after considering the merits of individual cases, to their general rules about allocating children to denominational schools,[20] abolishing secondary schools that admit children on the basis of ability,[21] or refusing applications for requests for assessments of a child's special educational needs.[22]

[14] R. v Barnsley Supplementary Benefits Appeal Tribunal Ex p. Atkinson [1977] 1 W.L.R. 917; R. v Greater Birmingham Appeal Tribunal Ex p. Simper [1974] Q.B. 543.
[15] R. v Law Society Ex p. Reigate Projects Ltd [1993] 1 W.L.R. 1531.
[16] British Oxygen Co Ltd v Board of Trade [1971] A.C. 610; compare R. v Secretary of State for Transport Ex p. Sheriff & Sons Ltd, The Times, December 18, 1986.
[17] See, e.g. R. v Warwickshire CC Ex p. Collymore [1995] E.L.R. 217; R. v Warwickshire CC Ex p. Williams [1995] E.L.R. 326; R. v Bexley LBC Ex p. Jones [1995] E.L.R. 42. See also R. v Secretary of State for the Home Department Ex p. Bennett, The Times, August 18, 1986 (Home Secretary's criteria for approval of police rent allowance was over-rigid).
[18] Kilmarnock Magistrates v Secretary of State for Scotland, 1961 S.C. 350 (entitled to adopt a general policy to that effect, subject to willingness to make exceptions in special cases).
[19] Smith v Inner London Education Authority [1978] 1 All E.R. 411.
[20] Cumings v Birkenhead Corp [1972] Ch. 12.
[21] Smith [1978] 1 All E.R. 411.
[22] R. v Hampshire CC Ex p. W [1994] E.L.R. 460.

- Housing policies of local authorities should be open to flexible application, as has been held in respect of policies on eviction of tenants of council houses who are in arrears with their rent,[23] on payment for the provision of temporary housing accommodation,[24] on refusal of applications for housing by children of those "intentionally homeless",[25] on requiring a homeless individual who had rejected accommodation as unsuitable to first move into the accommodation before being permitted to appeal,[26] on suspending a person who had unreasonably refused accommodation from the housing register for two years,[27] and on referral of tenancies to a rent tribunal.[28]

- In the context of prosecutions and disciplinary decisions, a chief constable ought not to adopt a rigid rule not to institute any prosecution at all for an anti-social class of criminal offence[29] nor should he fetter his discretion by treating the decision of the Director of Public Prosecutions that there was insufficient evidence to justify the prosecution of an officer, as determinative of the

---

[23] *Bristol DC v Clark* [1975] 1 W.L.R. 1443 at 1448 (dicta); *R. v Tower Hamlets LBC Ex p. Khalique* (1994) 26 H.L.R. 517 (rule that cases where rent arrears greater than £500 would be rendered "non-active" went well beyond the bounds of a lawful policy since it permitted no flexibility whatsoever); *R. v Lambeth LBC Ex p. Njomo* (1996) 28 H.L.R. 737; compare *Elliott v Brighton BC* (1980) 79 L.G.R. 506 (fettering of discretion to recondition substandard houses after failure to comply with improvement notice).
[24] *Roberts v Dorset CC* (1977) 75 L.G.R. 462.
[25] *Attorney General ex rel. Tilley v Wandsworth LBC* [1981] 1 W.L.R. 854 at 858 (Templeman L.J. went further in suggesting that even a policy resolution hedged around with exceptions might not be entirely free from attack).
[26] *R. v Newham LBC Ex p. Dada* [1996] Q.B.507 at 516A.
[27] *R. v Westminster City Council, Ex p Hussain* (1999) 31 HLR 645.
[28] *R. v Barnet & Camden Rent Tribunal Ex p. Frey Investments Ltd* [1972] 2 Q.B. 342 (explaining *R. v Paddington & St Marylebone Rent Tribunal Ex p. Bell London & Provincial Properties Ltd* [1949] 1 K.B. 666 as a case of a capricious reference made without consideration of relevant matters).
[29] *R. v Metropolitan Police Commissioner Ex p. Blackburn* [1968] 2 Q.B. 118 (gaming offences in clubs); but a large measure of discretion must be conceded to the police as prosecutors: *Buckoke v GLC* [1971] Ch. 655; *R. v Metropolitan Police Commissioner Ex p. Blackburn (No.3)* [1973] Q.B. 241. See also *R. v Race Relations Board Ex p. Selvarajan* [1975] 1 W.L.R. 1686 at 1697 (dicta that exercise of discretion by DPP is reviewable in the courts); *R. v General Council of the Bar Ex p. Percival* [1991] 1 Q.B. 212; *R. v DPP Ex p. Langlands-Pearse* [1991] C.O.D. 92; *R. v IRC Ex p. Mead* [1993] 1 All E.R. 772; *R. v Chief Constable of Kent Ex p. L* [1993] 1 All E.R. 756; *R. v DPP Ex p. C* [1995] 1 Cr. App. R. 136. The effect of these decisions is that the power to review a decision of the CPS or DPP not to prosecute is only to be exercised sparingly; only (Kennedy L.J. in *Ex p. C* [1995] 1 Cr.App.R.136 where the decision has been taken (a) because of some unlawful policy; or (b) because of a failure to act in accordance with a settled policy; or (c) perversely. A prosecution unreasonably or unfairly instituted may be struck out as an abuse of process or may result in an absolute discharge or a reduced sentence (*Buckoke v GLC* [1971] Ch. 655 at 668, 670–671; *Smedleys Ltd v Breed* [1974] A.C. 839 at 856–857, 861; *R. v Arrowsmith* [1975] Q.B. 678 at 689–691); and see *DPP v Humphrys* [1977] A.C. 1; compare *Johnson v Phillips* [1976] 1 W.L.R. 65 (limited discretion of police officer to commit technical offences in the execution of duty to protect life and property); see also *Donnelly v Jackman* [1970] 1 W.L.R. 562; *Squires v Botwright* [1972] R.T.R. 462 (apparent extensions of the powers of police officers to stop suspects).

question of whether to dismiss for unfairness disciplinary charges against that officer based on substantially the same facts.[30]

- In the conduct of hearings, domestic tribunals have been said to act improperly in refusing to allow a party to appear at a disciplinary hearing with a legal representative solely because it has never been their practice to permit it.[31] It has also been held that the Army Board of the Defence Council cannot have an inflexible policy not to hold an oral hearing where allegations of race discrimination are made.[32]

- Policies on the imposition of penalties or sentences should not be so rigid as to exclude consideration of the proportionality of the penalty in particular circumstances.[33] For example, in *R. v Secretary of State for the Home Department Ex p. Venables*,[34] the Secretary of State for the Home Office was held to have fettered his discretion in setting a "tariff" period of 15 years for a person sentenced to be detained at Her Majesty's Pleasure, because the "tariff" period did not permit review on grounds other than those relating to the circumstances of the commission of the crime and the applicant's state of mind, contrary to the Secretary of State's statutory power which was not fettered in this way.[35]

- In the realm of politics, the courts have required that a manifesto commitment is not blindly implemented following an election victory.[36] It has also been held that a local council's resolution could be quashed if councillors voted for it on orders from their political party, although not if they conscientiously decided to prefer the party's policy to their own opinions.[37]

[30] *R. v Chief Constable Thames Valley Police Ex p. Police Complaints Authority* [1996] C.O.D. 324.
[31] See, e.g. *Pett v Greyhound Racing Association (Ltd) (No.1)* [1969] 1 Q.B. 125; *Enderby Town Football Club Ltd v Football Association Ltd* [1971] Ch. 591 at 605–606.
[32] *R. v Army Board of the Defence Council, Ex p. Anderson* [1992] Q.B.169 at 188.
[33] *Lindsay v Commissioners of Customs and Excise* [2002] EWCA Civ 267; [2002] 1 W.L.R. 1766; *Gascoyne v Commissioners of Customs and Excise* [2003] EWCA Civ 892 at [19].
[34] [1998] A.C. 407.
[35] *ibid.* 45e–50g (Lord Browne-Wilkinson), 69c–73d (Lord Steyn, although his Lordship did not use the language of fettering of discretion) and 80c–f, 82d–84f (Lord Hope); compare CA [1997] 2 W.L.R. 67 at 90b–e (Lord Woolf M.R.); the Home Secretary no longer has a role in setting tariff periods; and *R. v Secretary of State for the Home Department, Ex p. Hindley* [2001] 1 A.C. 410; *R. (on the application of Smith) v Secretary of State for the Home Department* [2005] UKHL 51; [2006] 1 A.C. 159 (no unlawfulness where regular review of sentence in place).
[36] *R. v GLC Ex p. Bromley LBC* [1983] 1 A.C. 768 (the "Fares Fair" case). Lords Diplock and Brandon, in particular, criticised the G.L.C. for implementing its manifesto commitment to introduce a subsidy policy automatically after the election. compare *R. v Merseyside CC Ex p. Great Universal Stores Limited* (1982) 80 L.G.R. 639, where the Fares Fair case was distinguished on the ground, inter alia, that the Merseyside had considered its manifesto commitment afresh after the election, before implementing the policy; compare *R. v Waltham Forest LBC Ex p. Baxter* [1988] Q.B. 419 (councillors entitled to regard manifesto as very important factor in reaching decision).
[37] *R. v Waltham Forest LBC Ex p. Baxter* [1988] Q.B. 419 (on the evidence, the councillors had exercised their discretion).

- In the operation of prisons, policies should usually be applied flexibly and a policy of the Prison Service requiring incarcerated mothers to be separated from their children after 18 months was held to be applied too inflexibly and therefore unlawful.[38]

- Finally, non-fettering principles have also been applied in diverse circumstances ranging from deportation decisions[39] to the disclosure of information by voluntary adoption agencies.[40]

Power to articulate rules or policy

It is obvious that a rule or policy must not be based on considerations **9–008** extraneous to those contemplated by the enabling Act; otherwise the body will have exercised its discretion invalidly by taking irrelevant considerations into account or exceeding the statutory purpose.[41] Even a factor that may properly be taken into account in exercising a discretion may become an unlawful fetter upon discretion if it is elevated to the status of a general rule that distorts the purpose of the statutory scheme by pursuing that one factor in preference to others or by creating rigidity when flexibility was intended.[42] Thus the policy of the Prison Service to remove children over the age of 18 months from mother and baby units in prison, although permitting the occasional exception, nevertheless contradicted the aim of the relevant provision, which was to further the welfare of the child.[43]

A public authority to which discretion has been entrusted may also, of **9–009** course, have been expressly authorised to make regulations or issue a code of practice etc. in order to confine its discretion and to provide guidance about how it is likely to be exercised. For example, licensing authorities are

---

[38] *R. v Secretary of State for the Home Department Ex p. Q* [2001] EWCA Civ 1151; [2001] 1 W.L.R. 2002; and *R. (on the application of P) v Secretary of State for the Home Department,* May 17, 2002; *R. v Secretary of State for the Home Department Ex p. Simms* [2000] A.C. 115. compare *R. v Secretary of State for the Home Department Ex p. Zulfikar* [1996] C.O.D. 256 (blanket policy of strip-searching prisoners after every visit not unlawful).
[39] *R. v Secretary of State for the Home Department Ex p. Hastrup* [1996] Imm. A.R. 616 (Minister's discretion as to whether to deport a person married to a British citizen with a British child not fettered by Home Office policy document).
[40] *R. (on the application of Gunn-Russo) v Nugent Care Society* [2001] EHWC Admin 566; [2001] U.K.H.R.R. 1320 at [39]–[43].
[41] See 5–110–134.
[42] *R. v Flintshire CC County Licensing (Stage Plays) Committee Ex p. Barrett* [1957] 1 Q.B. 350 (committee adopted general rule that no alcoholic liquor or tobacco be sold in a theatre if adequate drinking facilities were available near by, irrespective of the past record of the theatre, and having imposed this condition on one theatre imposed it on the applicants in the interests of consistency).
[43] *Ex p. Q* [2001] EWCA Civ 1151; [2001] 1 W.L.R. 2002: the principal argument was based upon Convention rights and the restriction was held to be disproportionate, but the same result is achieved under fettering principles in domestic law; for further examples, see C. Hilson, "Judicial Review, Policies and the Fettering of Discretion" [2002] P.L. 111. compare *Attorney General ex rel. Tilley v Wandsworth LBC* [1981] 1 W.L.R. 854 (a policy not to house families with children whose parents had become "intentionally homeless" was declared both an unlawful fetter on the authority's discretion and contrary to the purpose of the legislation).

required by statute to determine and publish three-year policies.[44] Planning authorities possess the power to make plans to guide their decisions on development and the Department of Communities and Local Government has power to issue regulations about the scope of those plans.[45] As we have discussed above,[46] regulations must of course be within the scope of the powers conferred.[47] However, when the purpose of the function is not expressly defined in the statute (and nowhere in the Planning Acts is "planning" defined) it may be elaborated in the process of regulation-making, within limits that are not always easy to discover. Over the years planning functions have been extended to take into account economic and social functions, such as the provision of affordable housing[48]—a function not contemplated when land-use planning was initially introduced and concerned primarily with the physical features of development.

9–010   Even, however, where there is no specific power to make regulations or issue guidelines, the courts have recognised such a power as implicit. Lord Clyde has said that the provision of guidance of a discretion is "perfectly proper" and that policies are "an essential element in securing the coherent and consistent performance of administrative functions".[49] It is obviously desirable that a public authority should openly state any general principles by which it intends to be guided in the exercise of its discretion and the courts have encouraged licensing decision-makers to follow this practice.[50] When a decision-maker is required to give an individual an opportunity to be heard, it may be a denial of natural justice not to disclose the principles upon which the decision-maker proposes to exercise its discretion.[51] In

[44] Licensing Act 2003 s.5(1). The policy must however be kept under review during the three-year period and revisions made as appropriate: s.5(4).
[45] Planning and Compulsory Purchase Act 2004 ss.36, 38 (note that s.38(6) states that if "regard is to be had to the development plan for the purpose of any determination to be made under the planning Acts the determination must be made in accordance with the plan unless material considerations indicate otherwise".
[46] See 5–020–048.
[47] As must a code of practice: R. (on the application of Munjaz) v Mersey Care NHS Trust [2005] UKHL 58; [2006] 2 A.C. 148.
[48] See, e.g. Local Government Act 2000 s.4, which requires every local authority to prepare a "community strategy" "for promoting or improving the economic, social and environmental well-being of their area and contributing to the achievement of sustainable development in the United Kingdom". By s.62(5) of the Planning and Compulsory Purchase Act 2004, local planning authorities must have regard to the "community strategy".
[49] R. v Secretary of State for the Environment, Transport and the Regions Ex p. Holdings & Barnes Plc (the Alconbury case) [2001] UKHL 23; [2003] 2 A.C. 295 at [143]; R. v Secretary of State for the Home Department Ex p. Venables [1998] A.C. 407 at 432 (the area of prisoner release "calls out" for the development of policy to provide consistency, certainty and fairness).
[50] See, e.g. R. (on the application of Quark Fishing Ltd) v Secretary of State for Foreign and Commonwealth Affairs [2001] EWHC Admin 1174; [2002] A.C.D. 197 at [67]–[68] and [2002] EWCA Civ 1409; R. v Holborn Licensing Justices Ex p. Stratford Catering Co (1926) 136 L.T. 278 at 281; R. v Torquay Licensing Justices Ex p. Brockman [1951] 2 K.B. 784 at 788.
[51] R. v Criminal Injuries Compensation Board Ex p. Ince [1973] 1 W.L.R. 1334 at 1345. In Canada, it has been held that precise standards may be required: see Re Garden Gulf Court & Motel Inc v Island Telephone Co (1981) 126 D.L.R. (3rd) 281; Re Irving Oil Ltd v Public Utilities Commission (1986) 34 D.L.R. (4th) 448.

some cases the courts have come close to saying that there is not only a power but a duty to articulate policies and that the lack of a policy to guide the public may amount to irrationality.[52]

Yet in other cases where specific statutory criteria are provided, it has **9–011** been held that the power to supplement those criteria by others may be limited.[53] Overall, therefore, whether the policy itself constitutes a fetter on the exercise of discretion will largely depend on the function performed and on how the policy is phrased. In a case involving an application for a discretionary grant for the Legal Practice Course, the policy was expressed in terms that first, provided that no discretionary awards would be provided, then went on to admit applications in exceptional circumstances and, finally, provided a list of criteria that would count as exceptional circumstances. The court made it clear that, had there not been a category of "other" criteria in the list, the effect of the policy would have been to provide exhaustive criteria which would have fettered the discretion.[54] Some policies have the effect of predetermining the issue, as by resolving to refuse all applications,[55] or all applications of a certain class,[56] or all applications except those of a certain class,[57] thus inevitably leading to the refusal of an application in pursuance of the policy.[58] A policy that permits applications to depart from it only in circumstances that are "most extraordinary" may also fall foul of the no-fetter principle as amounting in practice to a blanket policy.[59] Likewise, a blanket policy that forbade prisoners access to the press, apart from "exceptionally", was held to be unlawful.[60]

[52] *R. v North West Lancashire Health Authority Ex p. A* [2000] 1 W.L.R. 977 at 991 (Auld L.J.).
[53] In Australia, see *Green v Daniels* (1977) 13 A.L.R. 1 (executive officer had no discretion in the interests of administrative efficiency to add to the statutory conditions of eligibility for benefit).
[54] *R. v Warwickshire CC Ex p. Williams* [1995] E.L.R. 326.
[55] *R. v Walsall Justices* (1854) 3 W.R. 69.
[56] *R. v LCC Ex p. Corrie* [1918] 1 K.B. 68 (local authority resolved to refuse all further permits, without exception, to distribute literature in public parks); compare *Sharp v Hughes* (1893) 57 J.P 104; and *Sagnata Investments Ltd v Norwich Corp* [1971] 2 Q.B. 614; *R. v Tower Hamlets LBC Ex p. Kayne-Levenson* [1975] Q.B. 431; *R. v Wakefield Crown Court Ex p. Oldfield* [1978] Crim.L.R. 164; *R. v Rochdale MBC Ex p. Cromer Ring Mill Ltd* [1982] 3 All E.R. 761.
[57] Also *R. v Sylvester* (1862) 31 L.J.M.C. 93 (refusal to issue any beer house licences except to applicants who agreed to take out an excise licence for sale of spirits also); *R. v Barry DC Ex p. Jones* (1900) 16 T.L.R. 556 (refusal to issue any new taxicab licences except to two proprietors and their drivers).
[58] Ordinarily, any challenge to a resolution will occur, the stage of the application of that resolution to a particular case, rather than in the form of a general challenge to the making of the resolution itself. Nevertheless, in an appropriate case, where the difficulties of establishing locus standi can be overcome, the resolution itself may be challenged by way of an application for declaratory relief or otherwise; see *Re Findlay* [1985] A.C. 318.
[59] *R. v Warwickshire Ex p. Collymore* [1995] E.L.R. 217 (Judge J.); compare *R. v Warwickshire CC Ex p. Williams* [1995] E.L.R. 326 (Schiemann J., the council was entitled to have a policy to make no discretionary education grants save in "exceptional circumstances").
[60] *R. v Secretary of State for the Home Department Ex p. Simms* [2000] 2 A.C. 115.

9-012   It will, however, be a rare case where a policy is not permitted, as policies and guidance are normally advisory rather than mandatory (as opposed to statutory instruments which do have the force of law).[61] That is not to say, however, as we have seen,[62] that guidance is wholly without legal effect. Depending upon the statutory scheme it will normally be a relevant consideration that must be taken into account. In one case[63] this issue was complicated by the fact that the scheme allowed two sets of guidance to be issued which were not compatible. Under the terms of the Mental Health Act 1983 the Secretary of State for Health was required to prepare a code of practice for the guidance of mental health practitioners and hospitals in relation to "the admission and medical treatment of patients suffering from mental disorder". The Secretary of State published the code, which included a chapter on the procedures to be adopted for the confinement of patients. The chapter provided that hospitals should themselves have clear written guidelines on the subject. The Mersey Care Trust drew up such guidelines which provided for less frequent reviews of patients than the Secretary of State's code and one of the questions was which code should prevail. By majority, the House of Lords held that the Secretary of State's code did not have the binding effect of a statute or statutory instrument and was "guidance" rather than "instruction". As such, the hospital was at liberty to depart from it, but only if such a departure was supported by "cogent reasoned justification".[64]

Do exceptions have to be specified in the rule or policy?

9-013   It is clear that a policy will usually be valid if it provides, for example, that unless "exceptional circumstances" are present, it will not grant any further licences to enable residential hotels to serve liquor to non-residents.[65] Another permitted formulation is that the body will "normally" give priority to those applicants for licences, for which demand exceeds supply, who do not already have one.[66] However, as just discussed, a general rule or policy that does not on its face admit of exceptions will be permitted in most circumstances.[67] There may be a number of

---

[61] For comparative perspectives on the acceptability of a flexible policy, see in Canada, *Halfway River First Nation v British Columbia* (1999) 178 D.L.R. (4th) 666; in Australia, *R. v Queensland Fish Management Authority Ex p. Hewitt Holdings Pty Ltd* (1993) 2 Qd.R 201 at 204.

[62] See 5–073–074; 5–120–22.

[63] *R. (on the application of Munjaz) v Mersey Care NHS Trust* [2005] UKHL 58; [2006] 2 A.C. 148.

[64] But see the dissents of Lords Steyn and Brown.

[65] *R. v Torquay Licensing Justices Ex p. Brockman* [1951] 2 K.B. 784; *R. v Holborn Licensing Justices Ex p. Stratford Catering Co* (1926) 136 L.T. 278.

[66] *R. v Tower Hamlets LBC Ex p. Kayne-Levenson* [1975] Q.B. 431 at 446, 452; *Perilly v Tower Hamlets LBC* [1973] Q.B. 9 (rule that licences granted in order of application upheld).

[67] But see *Attorney General ex rel. Tilley v Wandsworth LBC* [1981] 1 W.L.R. 854 (a policy which stated that the council would not house families with young children where the parents of those children had become intentionally homeless was held to be unlawful).

circumstances where the authority will want to emphasise its policy, such as that "no discretionary awards [for student grants] will be made"[68] but the proof of the fettering will be in the willingness to entertain exceptions to the policy, rather than in the words of the policy itself. Thus, where a policy not to fund a particular medical treatment listed unspecified "exceptional personal or clinical circumstances" as an exception to the policy, it was necessary for the decision-maker to be able to envisage what such exceptional circumstances might be: if it was not possible to envisage any such circumstances, the policy would be in practice a complete refusal of assistance, and unlawful.[69]

Tribunals

The role of precedent in tribunal decisions requires special mention.[70] **9–014** Formerly, the courts have expressed strong disapproval of the use of precedent in tribunal decision-making, and in the past, the Court of Appeal has warned the Transport Tribunal (in its capacity as a transport licensing appellate authority) against developing a body of rigidly binding precedent.[71] More recently, however, courts have placed greater emphasis on fairness and consistency.[72] For example, in immigration decisions, while immigration judges must examine the facts of individual cases, it has been held that there is no public interest in multiple examinations of the political backdrop of a particular state and that a system of "factual precedent",[73] or "judicial policy (with the flexibility that the word implies) needs to be adopted on the effect of the in-country data in recurrent classes of case".[74] Thus, failure by an adjudicator without good reason, to follow such a "country guidance" decision of the Asylum and Immigration Tribunal, which is intended to be authoritative as to the situation for the time being in the country in question, may give rise to error of law.[75] Of course, this is all subject to the proviso that "each case, whether or not such guidance is available, must depend on an objective and fair assessment of its own facts".[76]

---

[68] *Collymore* [1995] E.L.R. 217; and see the examples of the regulation of taxis provided by C. Hilson, "Judicial Review, Policies and the Fettering of Discretion" [2002] P.L. 111, 117–120.
[69] *R. (on the application of Rogers) v Swindon NHS Primary Care Trust* [2006] EWCA Civ 392; [2006] 1 W.L.R. 2649.
[70] T. Buck "Precedent in Tribunals and the Development of Principles" (2006) 25 C.J.Q. 458.
[71] *Merchandise Transport Ltd v British Transport Commission* [1962] 2 Q.B. 173 at 186, 192–193.
[72] See, e.g. *Shirazi v Secretary of State for the Home Department* [2003] EWCA Civ 1562 at [29]; *Januzi v Secretary of State for the Home Department* [2006] UKHL 5 at [50].
[73] *S v Secretary of State for the Home Department* [2002] EWCA Civ 539; [2002] I.N.L.R. 416 at [28].
[74] *Shirazi* [2003] EWCA Civ 1562 at [29].
[75] *R. (Iran) v Secretary of State for the Home Department* [2005] EWCA Civ 982 at [90].
[76] *Januzi* [2006] UKHL 5 at [50].

9–015   Similarly, in the employment context, the Employment Appeal Tribunal has also considered, as part of its function, the development of guidance as to the general approach to what constitutes reasonable conduct by an employer.[77]

Evidence of a fetter on discretion

9–016   How do the courts ensure that the authority is genuine in its professed willingness to depart from a fixed rule or policy? It should be remembered here that the authority is not obliged to consider every application before it afresh, but must at least keep its mind ajar in the interest of fairness and the achievement of its statutory purpose. In *British Oxygen* Lord Reid upheld the claim of a fetter on the Department's discretion, but emphasized that the principle did not require the Department to listen to "a multitude of similar applications" but simply be prepared to listen to someone with "something new to say".[78] The relevant principles were well stated by Bankes L.J. in a case in which the Port of London Authority had refused an application for a licence to construct certain works, on the ground that it had itself been charged with the provision of accommodation of that character.

> "There are on the one hand cases where a tribunal in the honest exercise of its discretion has adopted a policy, and, without refusing to hear an applicant, intimates to him what its policy is, and that after hearing him it will in accordance with its policy decide against him, *unless there is something exceptional in his case* . . . if the policy has been adopted for reasons which the tribunal may legitimately entertain, no objection could be taken to such a course. On the other hand there are cases where a tribunal has passed a rule, or come to a determination, not to hear any application of a particular character by whosoever made. There is a wide distinction to be drawn between these two classes."[79]

Conduct of the decision-maker

9–017   The courts will therefore scrutinise closely the conduct of a decision-maker in assessing whether or not he has unlawfully fettered his discretion. A course of conduct involving the consistent rejection of applications belonging to a particular class may justify an inference that the competent

---

[77] *Grundy (Teddington) Ltd v Plummer and Salt* [1983] I.C.R. 367 at 375; and *Buck*, 481.
[78] *British Oxygen Co Ltd v Board of Trade* [1971] A.C. 610 at 625; adopted in *R. v Secretary of State for the Environment Ex p. Brent LBC* [1982] Q.B. 593.
[79] *R. v PLA Ex p. Kynoch Ltd* [1919] 1 K.B. 176 at 184 (Bankes L.J.'s emphasis). The vital words here italicised (by the author of the first edition of this work) are omitted from the report of Bankes L.J.'s judgment in other series of reports: 88 L.J.K.B. 559; 120 L.T. 179; 83 J.P 43. The judgment appears to have been substantially rewritten for the purpose of publication in the *Law Reports*.

authority has adopted an unavowed rule to refuse all.[80] In cases involving discretionary grants for students it was held that although the policy admitted of exceptions, in practice there was no evidence of any procedures to allow applications in exceptional circumstances.[81] Where a departmental handbook on its face fettered the discretion of the Ministry, the courts were prepared to go behind a claim that the handbook was not in fact relied upon in reaching the impugned decision, and held that the handbook was so much a "part of the Department's thinking" that its influence could not be dismissed.[82] On the other hand, where a policy to ban taxi drivers who had been found guilty of plying for hire without a licence was enforced with very few exceptions, it was held that to hold the line on the policy in that way was necessary in order to provide an effective deterrent.[83]

A blanket policy may also be acceptable where it is 'unrealistic and   9–018
impractical' to consider each case individually.[84] The courts should, however, be sufficiently alert to spot a charade. Where a health authority's policy was to refuse surgical treatment of transsexualism, and the policy on its face provided for an exception in cases of "overriding clinical need", it was held that the authority was in practice operating a "blanket policy" of refusing surgery under any circumstance.[85] In addition, it should be noted that the duty not to fetter a discretion continues after representations have been entertained, up to the time that the final decision is taken, and accordingly, it may well be an unlawful fetter for a decision-maker to refuse to entertain a delegation who have already been heard, if the decision-maker does not ascertain whether they have any new representations to make.[86]

---

[80] cf. *Macbeth v Ashley* (1874) L.R. 2 H.L.Sc. 352 at 357. This passage was expressly approved in *Collymore* [1995] E.L.R. 217 where Judge J. held that where, over a period of three years, 300 appeals from decisions of the council to refuse discretionary student grants had all failed, it could be inferred that the policy to refuse to award discretionary grants save in "most extraordinary" circumstances had been applied far too rigidly. See also *R. v Newham LBC Ex p. Dada* [1996] Q.B. 507; *R. (on the application of Kelly) v Liverpool Crown Court* [2006] EWCA Civ 11 (taxi licence applications).
[81] *R. v Bexley LBC Ex p. Jones* [1995] E.L.R. 42.
[82] *R. v Secretary of State for Transport Ex p. Sheriff & Sons, The Times*, December 18, 1986. compare *R. v Southwark LBC Ex p. Udu* (1996) 8 Admin. L.R. 25 (local authority entitled to have general policy of not funding courses at private colleges and postgraduate courses, subject to "exceptional cases").
[83] *R. v Nottingham CC Ex p. Howitt* [1999] C.O.D. 530.
[84] *R. (on the application of S) v Chief Constable of South Yorkshire* [2004] UKHL 39; [2004] 1 W.L.R. 2196 at [60] (blanket policy to retain DNA and fingerprint samples; was considered "unrealistic and impracticable" to consider each case individually); *R. v Secretary of State for the Home Department Ex p. Hepworth* [1998] C.O.D. 146 (Laws J. regarded a system of incentives in prisons as no fetter as "in a mileu such as this there cannot be black-and-white rules").
[85] *R. v North West Lancashire Health Authority Ex p. A* [2000] 1 W.L.R. 977.
[86] *Brent* [1982] Q.B. 593 (Secretary of State fettered discretion in refusing to entertain new representations from affected local authorities).

Prior opportunity to make representations

9–019 In determining the validity of the exercise of discretion particular importance may be attached to the fact that before the agency applied its rules or
policy an opportunity was afforded the individual affected to make
representations. It will be rare that the repository of discretion will be held
to have fettered its exercise unlawfully if it has been addressed on the
applicability of the non-statutory criterion to the particular case, on
whether an exception to the rules or policy should be made in that instance
and on the soundness of the standard that has been adopted.[87] One reason
why the courts have rarely impugned decisions for fettering ministerial
dispositions of planning appeals, proposals for compulsory acquisition of
land and other matters that are decided after a public inquiry has been
held, is that individuals affected by these decisions will have had an
opportunity to bring to the Minister's attention considerations that may
mitigate against a mechanical application of some rule of thumb.[88] Another
reason for judicial reluctance to intervene is the wide range of policy
considerations relevant to the exercise of the statutory powers in question.
It will require a decision letter worded with particular infelicity or the
adoption by the court of an unduly narrow construction of it.[89]

Duty to hear the applicant?

9–020 In order to ensure that the authority genuinely takes into account
representations to apply its policy flexibly, the courts may require the
applicant to have a hearing, although there is little authority on the point.
A hearing of some sort might be thought to be appropriate in these
circumstances to guard against any improper fettering of discretion,[90] and
because the adoption of more specific criteria may give rise to disputes for
the resolution of which a hearing would be appropriate.[91] Normally,

---

[87] See, e.g. *Boyle v Wilson* [1907] A.C. 45; *British Oxygen* [1971] A.C. 610 at 625, 631;
Malloch v Aberdeen Corp (No.2) 1974 S.L.T. 253; *Smith v ILEA* [1978] 1 All E.R. 411.
compare *R. v Rotherham Licensing Justices Ex p. Chapman* [1939] 2 All E.R. 710.
[88] *Stringer v Minister of Housing and Local Government* [1970] 1 W.L.R. 1281.
[89] See, e.g. *Lavender (H) & Son Ltd v Minister of Housing and Local Government* [1970] 1
W.L.R. 1231 to lead the court to the conclusion that the Minister, in effect, viewed the
inquiry and the inspector's report with the utmost cynicism. It may also be noted that there
are dicta in the majority judgments in *Sagnata Investments Ltd v Norwich Corp* [1971] 2 Q.B.
614 at 632, 633, 639 that lend support to the view that even after a hearing, an
administrative discretion may not be exercised solely on the basis of a policy decision to grant
no more licences of specified types. However, in that case the court was primarily considering
the legality of a decision of Quarter Sessions, to which an appeal lay by way of rehearing from
the licensing authority, rather than whether the original decision to refuse the licence was
ultra vires the local authority. Moreover, an unimpeachable finding of fact by the Recorder
was treated as virtually amounting to an assertion that the hearing had been treated by the
council as a mere formality.
[90] See e.g. *British Oxygen* [1971] A.C. 610.
[91] See, e.g. *R. v Holborn Licensing Justices Ex p. Stratford Catering Co Ltd* (1926) 42 T.L.R.
778 at 781; *R. v Criminal Injuries Compensation Board Ex p. Ince* [1973] 1 W.L.R. 1334 at
1345 (tribunals that are in any event required to conduct a hearing should disclose the

however, the courts seek a system or procedure for making representations, rather than any specific form of hearing.[92] An inflexible policy *not* to hold an oral hearing may, itself constitute an unlawfully fettering of its discretion.[93]

Policies engendering legitimate expectations

When a public authority openly prescribes the criteria upon which it proposes to decide may thereby create a legitimate expectation create an interest that in fairness should be given some procedural, or even substantive, protection. Thus there are circumstances in which an authority will not be permitted to depart from its previously announced policy without affording a hearing to those adversely affected by it. This question is examined in Chapter 12, but here we should note a subtle change in the argument and in the interests and values advanced. Up to now we have seen the public authority seeking, in the interest of legal certainty (and perhaps also of efficiency) to operate a known and certain rule or policy. The claimant wishes to persuade the authority to depart from the rule or policy in the interest of responsive administration, so as to provide justice in the individual case. Where a legitimate expectation is claimed, it is the claimant who, in the interest of legal certainty, wishes the public body to abide by its policy and to fulfil expectations engendered by its representations. And it can be the public authority that wishes to be free to depart from its previous announcements in the interest of responsive administration and in order to fulfil its public duties.

9–021

UNDERTAKING NOT TO EXERCISE A DISCRETION

A public authority cannot effectively bind itself not to exercise a discretion if to do so would be to disable itself from fulfilling the primary purposes for which it was created. It has been said that "if a person or public body is entrusted by the Legislature with certain powers and duties expressly or impliedly for public purposes, those persons or bodies cannot divest themselves of these powers and duties. They cannot enter into any contract

9–022

principles upon which they propose to make their decision). See also *Salemi v MacKellar (No.2)* (1977) 137 C.L.R. 396, for conflicting dicta on whether, before deciding to deport an alien on the ground that he did not fall within the terms of an amnesty for certain classes of prohibited immigrants, the Minister must allow representation to be made. compare *Birdi v Home Secretary* (1975) 119 S.J. 322. In *Brent* [1982] Q.B. 593 it was held that the failure of the Secretary of State to hear London councils which were pleading against a reduction of their grants for overspending amounted both to an unlawful fetter on the Secretary of State's discretion and a breach of the duty to provide a fair hearing.

[92] *Ex p. Jones* [1995] E.L.R. 42 (Leggatt L.J. required "an exceptions procedure worthy of the name" and which would provide evidence of "genuine willingness" to hear the case).
[93] *R. v Army Board of the Defence Council Ex p. Anderson* [1992] Q.B. 169 at 188.

or take any action incompatible with the due exercise of their powers or duties".[94] So to act would be "to renounce a part of their statutory birthright".[95] Clearly this cannot be understood to mean that a public authority is never competent to limit its discretion by entering into commercial contracts[96] or restrictive covenants;[97] the principle must be stated more conservatively. Breaking it down into a series of neat propositions presents problems: formulations are not uniform, the decided cases have arisen in a variety of contexts and not all are reconcilable with one another. However, some generalisations are possible.

General principle

9–023 A public authority cannot effectively disable itself by contractual or other undertakings from making[98] or enforcing[99] a byelaw, refusing or revoking a grant of planning permission,[100] or exercising any other statutory power of primary importance,[101] such as a power of compulsory purchase,[102] nor can

[94] *Birkdale District Electricity Supply Co v Southport Corp* [1926] A.C. 355 at 364.
[95] *Birkdale* [1926] A.C. 355 at 371; and *Ayr Harbour Trustees v Oswald* (1883) 8 App.Cas. 623, 634. For discussion, see P. Hogg, *Liability of the Crown*, 3rd edn (2000) Ch.9; A. Davies, "*Ultra Vires* Problems in Government Contracts" (2006) 122 L.Q.R. 98; C. Turpin, *Government Procurement Contracts* (1989); P. Rogerson, "On the Fettering of Public Powers" [1971] P.L. 288; J. Evans, "Governmental Factors in Contracts of Public Authorities" (1972) 35 M.L.R. 88.
[96] See, e.g. *Birkdale* [1926] A.C. 355; compare *York Corp v Henry Leetham & Son* [1924] 1 Ch. 557; *R. v GLC Ex p. Burgess* [1978] I.C.R. 991 (Local Government Act 1972 s.111 wide enough to enable local authority to enter into a closed shop agreement).
[97] See, e.g. *Stourcliffe Estates Co v Bournemouth Corp* [1910] 2 Ch. 12.
[98] *Cory (William) & Son Ltd v City of London Corp* [1951] 2 K.B. 475; compare Case 81/72 *Commission of the European Communities v Council of the European Communities* [1973] E.C.R. 575.
[99] *Bean (William) & Sons Ltd v Flaxton RDC* [1929] 1 K.B. 450.
[100] *Ransom & Luck Ltd v Surbiton BC* [1949] Ch. 180 at 195, 198; *Stringer* (though in this case the planning authority did not purport to fetter itself absolutely); *Windsor and Maidenhead RBC v Brandrose Investments Ltd* [1983] 1 W.L.R. 509 (planning authority cannot bind itself by contract to grant planning permission; relief refused in court's discretion). compare *R. v Sevenoaks DC Ex p. Terry* [1985] 3 All E.R. 226 (council which granted planning permission to developer did not act unlawfully in resolving previously to sell site to developers, since formal sale agreement not entered into until after grant of planning permission, *Steeples v Derbyshire CC* [1985] 1 W.L.R. 256 not followed). Decisions such as *Terry* are susceptible to an analysis in terms of bias; see *Terry*, *R. v St Edmundsbury BC Ex p. Investors in Industry Commercial Properties Ltd* [1985] 1 W.L.R. 1168. On the use of planning agreements between local authorities and developers, see M. Grant, "Planning by Agreement" [1975] J.P.L. 501; J. Jowell, "Bargaining in Development Control" [1977] J.P.L. 414; J. Alder, "Planning Agreements and Planning Powers" [1990] J.P.L. 880.
[101] *Ayr Harbour Trustees v Oswald* (1883) 8 App.Cas. 623; in New Zealand, *Ski Enterprises Ltd v Tongariro National Park Board* [1964] N.Z.L.R. 884; compare *Stourcliffe* [1910] 2 ch.12 where the power restricted was of a subsidiary nature; and *R. v Secretary of State for the Home Department Ex p. Fire Brigades Union* [1995] 2 A.C. 513 (Home Secretary could not disable himself from ability to bring statutory scheme into effect by adopting alternative scheme having consequence that statutory scheme "will not now be implemented").
[102] *Triggs v Staines UDC* [1969] 1 Ch. 10; compare *Sovmots Investments Ltd v Secretary of State for the Environment* [1977] Q.B. 411 at 420–421, 479–480; [1979] A.C. 144 at 185–186 (local authority did not unlawfully fetter its discretion when, on its compulsory

it effectively bind itself to exercise such a power in any particular way. Similarly, it cannot be estopped by its inertia or acquiescence from fulfilling a duty to exercise a power when the occasion arises for it to be exercised.[103] These principles apply a fortiori to fettering the effective discharge of public duties.[104]

Discretion in relation to land

More specifically, a public authority endowed with statutory powers and duties exercisable for public purposes in relation to land cannot disable itself from fulfilling those purposes by dedicating or granting the land or interests therein in a manner or for a purpose incompatible with the fulfilment of the primary purposes.[105] Whether a proposed new purpose is compatible with the primary purposes may raise questions of interpretation, fact and reasonably foreseeable probability; incompatibility cannot be established by mere conjecture.[106] Contracts for the sale of council houses have been specifically enforced even after the local authority has changed its policy on this matter;[107] similarly, a resolution by a Conservative-dominated local authority authorising the sale of a council-owned block of flats on terms including a restrictive covenant preventing the authority from letting vacant flats in council-retained neighbouring blocks was held (by a majority of the Court of Appeal) to be a lawful resolution not

9–024

acquisition of leasehold interest, it undertook to obey the covenants and not to seek unilaterally to acquire the freehold).

[103] *Yabbicom v R* [1899] 1 Q.B. 444 (power to prosecute for breach of byelaw). For the circumstances in which assurances (including assurances given by officials) may possibly operate as an estoppel, see Ch. 12.

[104] *Sunderland Corp v Priestman* [1927] 2 Ch. 107 at 116; *Maritime Electric Co v General Dairies Ltd* [1937] A.C. 610; *Customs and Excise Commissioners v Hebson Ltd* [1953] 2 Lloyd's Rep. 382; *Society of Medical Officers of Health v Hope* [1960] A.C. 551 at 568, 569; in New Zealand see *Union Steam Ship Company of New Zealand Ltd v Commissioner of Inland Revenue* [1962] N.Z.L.R. 656; *Smith v Attorney General* [1973] 2 N.Z.L.R. 393 at 397; in Australia see *Northwest County DC v Case (JI) (Australia) Pty Ltd* [1974] 2 N.S.W.L.R 511.

[105] *Ayr Harbour Trustees* (1883) 8 App.Cas. 623; *Patterson v Provost of St Andrews* (1881) 6 App.Cas. 833; *R. v Leake (Inhabitants)* (1833) 5 B. & Ad. 469, 478; *R. (on the application of Kilby) v Basildon DC* [2007] EWCA Civ 479 CA; *British Transport Commission v Westmorland CC* [1958] A.C. 126; *Dowty Boulton Paul Ltd v Wolverhampton Corp (No.2)* [1976] Ch. 13 (com *cf. Dowty Boulton Paul Ltd v Wolverhampton Corp* [1971] 1 W.L.R. 204); *R. v Hammersmith and Fulham LBC Ex p. Beddowes* [1987] Q.B. 1050; *Stourcliffe* [1910] 2 Ch.12 restriction upon discretion to use land for a subordinate purpose held binding where there were two conflicting statutory provisions); *Blake v Hendon Corp* [1962] 1 Q.B. 283 at 301–303 (statutory power to let was subordinate to primary power to make land available as a public park and would not therefore be lawfully exercisable unless compatible with that power).

[106] *Westmorland* [1958] A.C. 126; compare *British Railways Board v Glass* [1965] Ch. 538 (a curious case in which CA held BRB to be bound by a right of way across the lines conferred by a predecessor in title, although there was evidence that the right of way gave rise to danger and inconvenience); P. Rogerson, "On the Fettering of Public Powers" [1971] P.L. 288.

[107] *Storer v Manchester CC* [1974] 1 W.L.R. 1403; *Gibson v Manchester CC* [1978] 1 W.L.R. 520 (rev'd. [1979] 1 W.L.R. 294 on other grounds).

fettering the exercise by the council of its housing powers, because the policy was consistent with the purposes of the housing legislation.[108]

Discretion and contract

9–025 Contracts and covenants entered into by the Crown are not to be construed as being subject to implied terms that would exclude the exercise of general discretionary powers for the public good; on the contrary, they are to be construed as incorporating an implied term that such powers remain exercisable.[109] This is broadly true of other public authorities also, but the status and functions of the Crown in this regard are of a higher order. Indeed, the principle that the Crown's general power to dismiss its servants cannot be ousted even by the express terms of a contract has never been over-ruled[110] albeit that it has been significantly eroded by statute, the civil service disciplinary scheme and the courts' acceptance that civil servants may be engaged under contract of employment.[111]

9–026 Assertions such as that the Crown is incapable of so contracting as to fetter its future executive action in any way, or that in all contracts entered into by the Crown there is an implied term that the Crown may repudiate its obligations whenever in its opinion executive necessity so demands, must be viewed with reserve today.[112] The Crown cannot be allowed to tie its hands completely by prior undertakings, but the courts will not allow the Crown to evade compliance with ostensibly binding obligations

---

[108] *R. v Hammersmith and Fulham LBC Ex p. Beddowes* [1987] Q.B. 1050. However, as the dissent of Kerr L.J. suggests, it should not of itself be sufficient answer to a charge of unlawful fettering to establish that the policy implemented is within the four corners of the empowering legislation; where the legislation leaves open a choice of policy alternatives it may, it is submitted, be an unlawful fetter to resolve in advance of the decision to adopt a particular policy approach, e.g. *R. v Legal Aid Board Ex p. RM Broudie & Co (A Firm)* [1994] C.O.D. 435 (guidance to taxing officer as to choice of circumstances which could be regarded as "exceptional" in determining uplift to solicitor's costs was unlawful as restricting taxing officer's discretion where words of legislation—"all the relevant circumstances"—were unlimited).

[109] *Crown Lands Commissioners v Page* [1960] 2 Q.B. 274 (no covenant for quiet enjoyment to be implied in Crown lease so as to preclude Crown from exercising statutory requisitioning powers); *Molton Builders Ltd v City of Westminster* (1975) 30 P. & C.R. 182 at 188 (applicability of the doctrine of derogation from grant to exercise by Crown Estate Commissioners of their statutory power to consent to enforcement notice left open); *Cudgen Rutile (No.2) Ltd v Chalk* [1975] A.C. 520 (contract to lease Crown land other than in accordance with statutory provisions invalid). On contracts and judicial review generally, see 3–056.

[110] *Riordan v War Office* [1959] 1 W.L.R. 1046 at 1053–1054.

[111] Employment Rights Act 1996 s.191 (protection against unfair dismissal); Civil Service Order in Council 1992 on civil service discipline; on civil servant contracts, see *R. v Lord Chancellor's Department Ex p. Nangle* [1992] 1 All E.R. 897; P. Wallington, "Discretion and Duty: the Limits of Legality" in M. Supperstone, J. Goudie and P. Walker (eds), *Judicial Review*, 3rd edn (2005), para.7.24.5.

[112] The rule ambiguously formulated in *Rederiaktiebolaget Amphitrite v R.* [1921] 3 K.B. 500 is one of open texture. For a critical discussion, see *Ansett Transport Industries (Operations) Pty Ltd v Commonwealth* (1977) 17 A.L.R. 513. Specific relief in civil proceedings is in any event not available directly against the Crown.

whenever it thinks fit.[113] How and where the line is to be drawn is anything but clear.

As noted above in the context of the exercise of discretion in relation to land, the court will consider statutory interpretation, fact and reasonably foreseeable probability: and where it is contended that a contract is incompatible with a statutory discretion, the relevant factors will not only be whether the contract is incompatible with the public body's statutory purpose, but also whether the public body is likely to exercise the relevant statutory discretion and whether there are good reasons to preserve its ability to do so.[114] Where a public authority, rather than the Crown, wishes to exercise a statutory discretion which is incompatible with a contract which it has entered into, the statutory discretion will almost always be prioritised with the result that the contract will be found to be ultra vires.[115] However, this will not always be the case[116] and again, the line is difficult to draw.[117]

9–027

If a public authority lawfully repudiates or departs from the terms of a binding contract in order to exercise its overriding discretionary powers, or if it is held never to have been bound in law by an ostensibly binding contract because the undertakings would improperly fetter its general discretionary powers, at common law, the other party to the agreement has no right whatsoever to damages or compensation under the general law, no matter how serious the damage that party may have suffered.[118] There is a case for providing an appropriate remedy by way of an award of compensation determinable by a judicial body.[119] In the case of the local authority certified private finance contracts, the Local Government (Contracts) Act 1997 modifies the common law position and provides protection for private contractors in the event of a finding of ultra vires:[120] the

9–028

---

[113] *Crown Lands Commissioners v Page* [1960] 2 Q.B. 274 at 291–294 (Devlin L.J.); *HTV Ltd v Price Commission* [1976] I.C.R. 170 at 185G–H (Lord Denning M.R.); *R. v IRC Ex . p. Preston* [1985] A.C. 835 at 865 (Lord Templeman) and *R. v Secretary of State for Home Department Ex p. Doody* [1994] 1 A.C. 531.
[114] Davies [2006] 122 L.Q.R. 98, 106; and *R. v Leake (Inhabitants)* (1833) 5 B. & Ad. 469; *Westmoreland* [1958] A.C. 126 at 144; *Blake v Hendon Corp* [1962] 1 Q.B. 283.
[115] *Cory (William) & Son Ltd v City of London Corp* [1951] 2 K.B. 475.
[116] *Dowty Boulton Paul Ltd v Wolverhampton Corp* [1971] 1 W.L.R. 204.
[117] Davies (2006) 122 L.Q.R. 98.
[118] For two well-known examples of the common law position on ultra vires government contracts, see: *Crédit Suisse v Allerdale BC* [1997] Q.B. 306; *Hazell v Hammersmith and Fulham LBC* [1992] 2 A.C. 1.
[119] Such provisions exist in French administrative law: Davies (2006) 122 L.Q.R. 98, 112, citing the *"fait du prince"* remedy, which applies where the public authority upsets the economic equilibrium of the contract by exercising its public powers, and enables the contractor to either seek an indemnity from the public authority or, where appropriate, increase its charges to consumers. The only exception is for changes in the law "affecting all citizens equally". See L. Brown and J. Bell, *French Administrative Law*, 5th edn (1998), pp.206–210; P. Craig, *Administrative Law*, 5th edn (2003), pp.547–548; H.W.R. Wade and C. Forsyth, *Administrative Law*, 9th edn (2004), pp.332–333; Hogg (2000), arguing against the validity of the *Amphitrite* principle and urging that there should be a remedy in damages; compare Campbell pointing out objections of principle to the latter view. We suspect that to day a court faced with thios problem would find a method of awarding compensation, as justice so clearly requires this.
[120] Local Government (Contracts) Act 1997, ss.2 and 4.

contract may be continued,[121] discharged on terms set out in the contract,[122] or discharged on the basis that the private contractor is entitled to whatever payments would have been due up to the date of the court's order and in addition to damages as for a repudiatory breach by the local authority.[123]

---

[121] Local Government (Contracts) Act 1997 s.5(3).
[122] Local Government (Contracts) Act 1997 s.6(2)(b).
[123] Local Government (Contracts) Act 1997 s.7(2).

CHAPTER 10

PROCEDURAL FAIRNESS: BIAS AND CONFLICT OF INTEREST

SCOPE

This chapter considers: 10–001

- The history of the concept of bias in judicial and administrative settings.

- The test of bias.

- Situations which will normally disqualify a decision-maker for bias.

- Situations which will not normally disqualify a decision-maker for bias.

- The requirements of Art.6 ECHR.

- Comparative perspectives.

INTRODUCTION

Procedural fairness demands not only that those whose interests may be   10–002
affected by an act or decision should be given prior notice and an adequate
opportunity to be heard. It also requires that the decision-maker should
not be biased or prejudiced in a way that precludes fair and genuine
consideration being given to the arguments advanced by the parties.[1]
Although perfect objectivity may be an unrealisable objective, the rule
against bias thus aims at preventing a hearing from being a sham or a ritual
or a mere exercise in "symbolic reassurance",[2] due to the fact that the
decision-maker was not in practice persuadable. An adjudicator may indeed
seldom achieve "the icy impartiality of a Rhadamanthus",[3] and the idea

---

[1] Bias has been defined as "an operative prejudice, whether conscious or unconscious": *R. v Queen's County Justices* [1908] 1 I.R. 285 at 294 (Lord O'Brien C.J.); and see more recently *Flaherty v National Greyhound Racing Club Ltd* [2005] EWCA Civ 1117; (2005) 102(37) L.S.G. 31 at [28] (Scott-Baker L.J.: "a predisposition or prejudice against one party's case or evidence on an issue for reasons unconcerned with the merits of the issue).

[2] M. Edelman, *The Symbolic Uses of Politics* (1967).

[3] Coke, *Institutes* iii 35: Rhadamanthus, the cruel judge of Hell, punished before he heard; *cf. Jackson v Barry Railway Company* [1893] 1 Ch. 238 at 248 (Bowen J.). But even Rhadamanthus was not, apparently, conversant with the *audi alteram partem* principle.

that "by taking the oath of office as a judge, a man ceases to be human and strips himself of all predilections, becomes a passionless thinking machine",[4] is doubtless beyond achievement.

10–003   Nevertheless, the common law (and sometimes statute) disqualifies a decision-maker from adjudicating whenever circumstances point to a real possibility that his decision may be predetermined in favour of one of the parties. This may arise from: (a) personal connections or predispositions which raise real doubts about the decision-maker's *impartiality*; or (b) the institutional setting of the decision-making process which throws doubt upon its *independence*.[5]

10–004   Since the 5th edition of this work in 1995, as we have seen, most of the provisions of the ECHR have been incorporated into our law.[6] Article 6(1) states (with emphasis added):

"In the determination of his civil rights and obligations or of any criminal charge against him, everyone is entitled to a fair and public hearing within a reasonable time *by an independent and impartial tribunal* established by law".

10–005   Insofar as the common law test of bias previously differed from the ECHR test, necessary adjustments have in most respects been made and it has been claimed that nowadays there is "no difference between the common law test of bias and the requirement under Art.6 of the Convention of an independent and impartial tribunal".[7]

10–006   The principle expressed in the maxim *nemo iudex in sua causa* (no one should be a judge in his own cause) refers not only to the fact that no one shall adjudicate his own case; it also refers to the fact that no one should adjudicate a matter in which he has a conflicting interest.[8] In order to give effect to those two aspects of the principle, the concern is not only to prevent the distorting influence of *actual bias*, but also to protect the integrity of the decision-making process by ensuring that, however

---

[4] *Re JP Linahan* 138 F 2d 650 (1942) (Jerome Frank J.); and *R. v Barnsley Licensing Justices* [1960] 2 Q.B. 167 (Devlin L.J.) on unconscious bias; and see generally, for a sophisticated analysis with special reference to international adjudication. T. Franck, "The Structure of Impartiality" (1967) 19 Stanford L.R. 1217.

[5] *Gillies v Secretary of State for Work and Pensions* [2006] UKHL 2; [2006] 1 W.L.R. 781 at [38] (Baroness Hale of Richmond draws a distinction between independence which she defines as "the tribunal's approach to deciding the cases before it" and independence, which she defines as the "structural or institutional framework which secures this impartiality"—a structure which should be viewed as unbiased not only by members of the tribunal but also by members of the public, now referred to as "the fair-minded and informed observer").

[6] Ch.13; and on Art.6 in particular, see 7–119 on the "threshold" issues that determine whether Art.6 applies.

[7] *Lawal v Northern Spirit Ltd* [2003] UKHL 35; [2004] 1 All E.R. 187 at [14] (Lord Steyn). On the extent to which the requirement of an unbiased decision applies in a situation outside of a judicial setting or when interests are being considered which fall short of what Art.6 calls "civil rights and obligations", see 10–65.

[8] In Israel the test of bias is named "conflict of interest": I. Zamir and A. Zysblat, *Public Law in Israel* (1997), p.96.

disinterested the decision-maker is in fact, the circumstances should not give rise to the *appearance of bias*. As has been famously said: "justice should not only be done, but should manifestly and undoubtedly be seen to be done".[9]

In defining the scope of the rule against bias and its content, at least two **10-007** requirements of public law are in play. The first seeks accuracy in public decision-making. If a person is influenced in a decision by his private interests or personal predilections, he will not follow, or may be tempted not to follow, the required standards and considerations which ought to guide the decision.[10] An accurate decision is more likely to be achieved by a decision-maker who is in fact impartial or disinterested in the outcome of the decision and who puts aside any personal prejudices. The second requirement is for public confidence in the decision-making process.[11] Even though the decision-maker may in fact be scrupulously impartial, the appearance of bias can itself call into question the legitimacy of the courts and other decision-making bodies.

Historical Development

Early background

Bracton wrote that a judge was not to hear a case if he was suspected of **10-008** partiality because of consanguinity, affinity, friendship or enmity with a party or because of his subordinate status towards a party or because he was or had been a party's advocate.[12] These principles, which Bracton set out as if they were already part of the common law, were in fact the canon law rules for recusation of suspected judges,[13] which were applied in the

---

[9] *R. v Sussex Justices Ex p. McCarthy* [1924] 1 K.B. 256 at 259 (Lord Hewart C.J.). The Franks Report (Report on Administrative Tribunals and Inquiries (Cmnd. 218, 1957) which considered that the tribunal system should be based upon "openness, fairness and impartiality" (para.24). Impartiality required both "an open mind" (para.4) and "freedom . . . from the influence, real or apparent, of Departments concerned with the subject-matter of their decisions" (para.42). See also the Council on Tribunals, *Framework of Standards of Tribunals* (November 2002) which states that tribunals should be free to decide "without influence (actual or perceived) from the body or person whose decision is being challenged or appealed, or from anyone else" (para.1(a)). The Tribunals, Court and Enforcement Act 2007 s.1 now provides an express statutory guarantee of judicial independence for certain tribunal judges.

[10] D. Galligan, *Due Process and Fair Procedures* (1996). Lord Steyn considers that procedural fairness "plays an instrumental role in promoting just decisions" *Rajiv General Medical Council* [2003] UKPC 24; [2003] 1 W.L.R. 1052 at [13].

[11] *Belilos v Switzerland* (1998) 10 E.H.R.R. 466 at para.67 (ECtHR based the rule against bias under Art.6 on the need for "the confidence which must be inspired by the courts in a democratic society").

[12] *De Legibus*, p.412.

[13] For the grounds of exception to the suspectus judex in canon law (pecuniary interest, advocacy, kinship, friendship, great enmity), see *Codex Juris Canonici*, canons 16131614; R. Naz (ed.), *Traité de Droit Canonique* (1955), iv, pp.95–98. There is a legend that a Pope (subsequently canonised) once condemned himself to be burned to death for his sins ((1430) YB. 8 Hen. 6, Hill. pl. 6).

English ecclesiastical courts[14] and also, it seems, in medieval Scottish courts.[15] They bear a close resemblance to the grounds for disqualification of judges for likelihood of bias in modern English law. It might well be supposed, therefore, that they were imported into the common law in its early formative period by Bracton himself, or by his contemporaries or predecessors. Indirect support for an opinion that they were received into the common law might be derived from the fact that the grounds of exception for interest and bias to the competency of witnesses in courts Christian had been applied from the earliest times to the challenge of jurors of the grand assize[16] and the possessory assizes.[17] Moreover, at least as early as the 14th century, common law judges were held to be incompetent to hear cases in which they were themselves parties.[18] Yet there seems to be no evidence that Bracton's broad statement of canon law doctrine as common law was accepted and acted upon by his successors. On the contrary, it was laid down that favour was not to be presumed in a judge.[19]

10–009   The principle that a judge was disqualified from adjudicating whenever there was a real likelihood that he might be biased was not unequivocally established until the 1860s.[20] Bracton is not cited in any of the leading English cases on the matter. One must conclude that the balance of probability is titled against the view that the canon law rules were ever directly incorporated in the common law. The common law judges came to adopt principles substantially the same as those of the canon lawyers, not by way of conscious imitation, but by moving independently towards a just and reasonable solution.

10–010   The reluctance of the common lawyers to recognise the concept of disqualification of judges for interest or bias is illustrated by Coke's bald assertion[21] that judges and justices, unlike jurors, could not be challenged, an assertion reiterated by Blackstone, who thought it a salutary rule of

---

[14] F.W. Maitland, *Roman Canon Law in the Church of England* (1898), p.114.

[15] Lord Cooper (ed.), *Regiam Majestatem and Quoniam Attachiamenta* (1947), pp.324–325.

[16] Glanvill, *De Legibus*, Bk. 11, c.12 (transl. Pound and Plucknett, *Readings on the History and System of the Common Law*, 3rd edn, p.143). For the canon law rules, see *Wigmore on Evidence*, 3rd edn (1940), ii, p.678, n.14; R. Naz, (ed.), *Dictionaire de droit Canonique* (1935–65), Vol. iv, 483–484.

[17] Bracton, *De Legibus*, pp.143b, 185. See (1354) 28 Lib.Ass. 18 (juror challengeable because member of commonalty that was party to suit); (1481) YB. 21 Edw. 4, Mich. pl. 3 (juror challengeable in assize brought by dean and chapter of Lincoln, because he was brother of a prebendary of the chapter). The King could judge his own causes, with the exception that he could not be both actor and judex in cases of high treason: Bracton, *De Legibus*, p.119; L. Ehrlich, *Proceedings Against the Crown 1216–1377* (1921), pp.47–49.

[18] See, e.g. (1371) 45 Lib.Ass. 3, where a party in a case at assizes that had to be heard before two judges was himself appointed judge upon the death of one of the two justices of assize: held, he could not judge his own cause. References to early Yearbook cases are collected by S. Thorne (ed.), *Egerton's Discourse upon the Statutes*, 73n. See also 2 Roll Abr. 92–93.

[19] *Brooks v Earl of Rivers* (1668) Hardres 503 (Chamberlain of Chester not disqualified from hearing an action in which his brother-in-law was a party).

[20] Blackburn J.'s judgment in *R. v Rand* (1866) L.R. 1 Q.B. 230 is regarded as the *locus classicus*.

[21] Co.Litt. 294a.

public *policy*.[22] Long before Blackstone's day, however, Sir Nicholas Bacon,[23] the Earl of Derby[24] and the Mayor of Hereford (who was laid by the heels by the Court of King's Bench)[25] had discovered that the common law did not permit a judge to determine a matter in which he had a direct pecuniary or proprietary interest.[26] And it was Coke himself who had elevated to a fundamental principle of the common law the proposition that no man should be a judge in his own cause. In *Dr Bonham's* case, when examining the claim of the College of Physicians to fine its members for malpractice, he said that the censors of the College "cannot be judges, ministers, and parties . . . *quia aliquis non debet esse judex in propria causa* . . . and one cannot be judge and attorney for any of the parties". Moreover, "when an Act of Parliament is against common right or reason, or repugnant, or impossible to be performed, the common law will controul it, and adjudge such Act to be void". So "if any Act of Parliament gives to any to hold, or to have conusans of all manner of pleas arising before him within his manor . . . yet he shall have no plea, to which he himself is party; for, as hath been said, *iniquum est aliquem suae rei esse judicem*".[27] Similar views were expressed by Hobart[28] and Holt.[29] It is doubtful whether a court ever held a statute to be void solely because it made a man a judge in his own cause[30] and it has been argued that Coke was merely laying down that statutes framed in such terms were to be strictly construed to avoid what would appear to be an obvious absurdity.[31] That Parliament is competent to make a person a judge in his own cause has long been indisputable[32] but the courts continue to uphold the common

---

[22] Comm., iii, p.361 ("For the law will not suppose the possibility of bias or favour in a judge, who is already sworn to administer impartial justice, and whose authority greatly depends upon that presumption and idea").

[23] *Sir Nicholas Bacon's case* (1563) 2 Dyer 220b.

[24] *Earl of Derby's case* (1613) 12 Co.Rep. 114.

[25] *Anon.* (1697) 1 Salk, 396 (facts given in *Wright v Crump* (1702) 2 Ld.Raym. 766).

[26] For other early reported cases, see the *Foxham Tithing case* (1705) 2 Salk. 607 (surveyor adjudicated as justice in matter concerning his office); Company of Mercers and Ironmongers of *Chester v Bowker* (1725) 1 Str. 639 (member of company became mayor and member of court before judgment). cf. *Markwick v City of London* (1707) 2 Bro. PC. 409: *Great Charte v Kennington* (1742) 2 Str. 1173 (justices in removal case interested as local ratepayers).

[27] (1610) 8 Co.Rep. 113b, 118. See also Co.Litt. 141a.

[28] *Day v Savadge* (1614) Hob. 85 at 86, 87.

[29] *London (City of) v Wood* (1701) 12 Mod. 669 at 686–688.

[30] T. Plucknett, "Bonham's Case and Judicial Review" (1926) 40 Harv.L.R. 30.

[31] R. MacKay, "Coke: Parliamentary Sovereignty or the Supremacy of Law" (1924) 22 Mich. L.R. 215; S. Thorne, "Dr Bonham's Case" (1938) 54 L.Q.R. 543; J. Gough, *Fundamental Law in English Constitutional History* (1955), pp.31–39.

[32] *Great Charte v Kennington* [1742] 2 Str. 1173 (dictum); *Lee v Bude & Torrington Junction Ry.* (1871) L.R. 6 C.P 576, 582 (Willes J. describes Hobart C.J.'s dicta in *Day v Savadge* (1614) Hob. 85 as "a warning, rather than an authority to be followed"); *Rich v Christchurch Girls' High School Board of Governors (No.1)* [1974] 1 N.Z.L.R. 1 at 9, 18–20. Subject now to the requirements of European Community law (Ch.14) and the Human Rights Act 1998 (Ch.13).

law tradition by declining to adopt such a construction of a statute if its wording is open to another construction.[33]

Later developments

10–011 In developing the modern law relating to disqualification of judicial officers for interest and bias, the superior courts have striven to apply the principle enumerated by Lord Hewart C.J. that it "is of fundamental importance that justice should not only be done, but should manifestly and undoubtedly be seen to be done",[34] without giving currency to "the erroneous impression that it is more important that justice should appear to be done than that it should in fact be done".[35] The emphasis thus shifted from the simple precepts of the law of nature to the need to maintain public confidence in the administration of justice.[36] In some cases, such as when the person was a party to proceedings or who had any direct pecuniary or proprietary interest in the result it was held that the person was automatically disqualified at common law to adjudicate in those proceedings. If, however, it was alleged that the adjudicator has made himself partisan, by reason of his words or deeds or his association with a party who was instituting or defending the proceedings before him, the courts would not hold him automatically to be disqualified.

THE TEST OF BIAS

10–012 A decision may always be invalidated if actual bias on the part of a decision-maker was proved.[37] In some situations, however, especially with regard to criminal justice, the court will not be concerned to investigate

[33] Bl.Comm. i, 91; *Mersey Docks & Harbour Board Trustees v Gibbs* (1866) L.R. 1 H.L 93, 110; *Wingrove v Morgan* [1934] Ch. 423 at 430; *Rice v Commissioner of Stamp Duties* [1954] A.C. 216, 234; *University of Edinburgh v Craik* 1954 S.C. 190 at 195; *cf. R. v Minister of Agriculture & Fisheries Ex p. Graham* [1955] 2 Q.B. 140; *Wilkinson v Barking Corp* [1948] 1 K.B. 721; and *Jeffs v New Zealand Dairy Production and Marketing Board* [1967] 1 A.C. 551. See the discussion of the "principle of legality" at 5–036 *et seq.*
[34] *R. v Sussex Justices Ex p. McCarthy* [1924] 1 K.B. 256 at 259; *R. v Essex Justices Ex p. Perkins* [1927] 2 K.B. 475 at 488 (Avory J. suggests that "be seen" must be a misprint for "seem").
[35] *R. v Camborne Justices Ex p. Pearce* [1955] 1 Q.B. 41 at 52. *cf. R. v Byles* (1912) 77 J.P, 40 (Avory J.: "It is as important (if not more important) that justice should seem to be done, as that it should be done"); *cf. Shrager v Basil Dighton Ltd* [1924] 1 K.B. 274 at 284 (Atkin L.J.: "Next to the tribunal being in fact impartial is the importance of its appearing so"); *cf. R. v Atkinson* [1978] 1 W.L.R. 425 at 428 (Lord Scarman: "in this sensitive area, the appearance of justice is part of the substance of justice"; sentence quashed on appeal on the ground that comments made by the judge could have given rise to a reasonable suspicion that he had discussed with counsel during a pre-trial review the possibility that a plea-bargain should be struck).
[36] *Serjeant v Dale* (1877) 2 Q.B.D. 558 at 567.
[37] See, e.g. *R. v Burton Ex p. Young* [1897] 2 Q.B. 468 at 471; *R. v Tempest* (1902) 86 L.T. 585 at 587.

evidence of actual bias. It is no doubt desirable that all adjudicators, like Caesar's wife, should be above suspicion,[38] but it would not be desirable to inquire into the mental state of a judge, a member of a jury or justices or their clerk because of the confidential nature of the judicial decision-making process. Nor would it be useful to do so because in many cases bias may be unconscious (as it is said—subconscious may be a more accurate description) in its effect.[39] For those reasons, the courts look at the circumstances of the particular case to see if there is an appearance of bias.

Various tests developed

Various tests have been applied to establish the limits of apparent bias. At **10–013** the one extreme, the courts disallow any decision where there has been a "reasonable suspicion of bias".[40] At the other extreme, a decision-maker will only be disqualified where there is a "real likelihood of bias".[41] "Real likelihood" can refer to either the possibility or the probability of bias. In respect of either test, there are two variants. Under the first, the suspicion or likelihood of bias is derived in the circumstances of the case from the point of view of the "reasonable man".[42] Under the second variant, the courts themselves decide the matter, based upon the impression they have of bias in the light of their own knowledge of the circumstances of the case. In cases where there has been pre-trial publicity which may have influenced the jury or members of the tribunal the test is "whether the risk of

[38] *Lesson v General Medical Council* (1889) 43 Ch.D 366 at 385.
[39] The courts have frequently laid down that they are not concerned with the question whether an adjudicator was in fact biased. *Allinson v General Medical Council* [1894] 1 Q.B. 750 at 758; *R. v Queen's County Justices* [1908] 2 I.R. 285 at 306; *R. v Halifax Justices Ex p. Robinson* (1912) 76 J.P 233 at 234–235; *R. v Caernarvon Licensing Justices Ex p. Benson* (1948) 113 J.P 23, 24; *R. v Barnsley Licensing Justices* [1960] 2 Q.B. 167 at 187.
[40] *R. v Sussex Justices Ex p. McCarthy* [1924] 1 K.B. 256 at 259 (Hewart C.J.: "Nothing is to be done which creates even a suspicion that there has been an improper interference with the course of justice"); *R. v Huggins* [1895] 1 Q.B. 563; *Cottle v Cottle* [1939] 2 All E.R. 535. *Metropolitan Properties Co (FGC) Ltd v Lannon* [1969] 1 Q.B. 577 at 599 (Lord Denning: "The court does not look to see if there was a real likelihood that he would, or did, in fact favour one side at the expense of the other. The court looks at the impression which would be given to other people"), 606 (Edmund Davies L.J.: it was enough if there is "reasonable suspicion of bias"), 601–602 (Danckwerts L.J.). After Lannon the reasonable suspicion test was applied by Lord Widgery C.J. in *R. v Uxbridge Justices Ex p. Burbridge, The Times,* June 21, 1972, and *R. v McLean Ex p. Aikens* (1974) 139 J.P 261. But he was more uncertain in *R. v Altrincham Justices Ex p. N. Pennington* [1975] Q.B. 549. See also *R. v Liverpool City Justices Ex p. Topping* [1983] 1 W.L.R. 119; *R. v Morris* (1990) 93 Cr. App. R. 102.
[41] *R. v Barnsley Licensing Justices Ex p. Barnsley & District Licensed Victuallers' Association* [1960] 2 Q.B. 167 at 187 (Devlin L.J.); and *R. v Rand* (1866) L.R. 1 Q.B. 230 (Blackburn J.); *Frome United Breweries Co Ltd v Bath Justices* [1926] A.C. 586, 591; *R. v Camborne Justices Ex p. Pearce* [1955] 1 Q.B. 41.
[42] Lord Denning M.R. in *Metropolitan Properties Co v Lannon* [1969] 1 Q.B. 577; and *R. v Sunderland Justices* [1901] 2 K.B. 357 at 373; *Hannam v Bradford Corp* [1970] 1 W.L.R. 937 at 942 (Sachs L.J.), 949 (Cross L.J.). See also *Ardahalian v Unifert International SA (The Elissar)* [1994] 2 Lloyd's Rep. 84; *Bremer Handelsgesellschaft mbH v Ets. Soules et Cie* [1985] 1 Lloyd's Rep. 160; [1985] 2 Lloyd's Rep. 199.

prejudice is so grave that no direction by a trial judge, however careful, could reasonably be expected to remove it".[43]

10–014　The various tests of bias thus range along a spectrum (see Figure 1). At the one end a court will require that, before a decision is invalidated, bias must be shown to have been present. At the other end of the spectrum, the court will strike at the decision where a reasonable person would have a reasonable suspicion from the circumstances of the case that bias might have infected the decision. In between these extremes is the "probability of bias" (this being closer to the "actual bias" test), and the "possibility of bias" (this test being closer to that of reasonable suspicion).

Figure 1

| Bias must be shown to be present | Probability of bias | Possibility of bias | Reasonable suspicion that bias might have infected decision |

Gough: "real danger" of bias

10–015　In *R. v Gough*, the House of Lords considered these various tests in relation to an allegation of bias on the part of a juror in a criminal trial.[44] Having carefully considered the authorities, it was held that direct pecuniary or proprietary interest always disqualified the decision-maker.[45] Outside of that category, it was held that the correct test is whether, in the circumstances of the case, the court considers that there appeared to be a "real danger of bias". In such a case, the decision should not stand. This test is similar to that of the "real likelihood of bias" and it was made clear that it refers to the *possibility*—not probability—of bias.[46] The "reasonable suspicion test" was thus rejected. It was also held that the same test should be applied in all cases of apparent bias (whether concerning justices, members of tribunals, arbitrators, justices' clerks or jurors). It was held too that the "real danger" test should be applied from the point of view of the court, not from that of the "reasonable man", however slim the difference between the two points of view in practice. As Lord Goff said:

---

[43] *Montgomery v HM Advocate* [2003] 1 A.C. 641 at 667 (Lord Hope); *R. (on the application of Mahfouz) v General Medical Council* [2004] EWCA Civ 233; [2004] Lloyd's Rep. Med. 377 at [33] (Carnwath L.J.: "knowledge of prejudicial material need not be fatal: its effects must be considered in the context of the proceedings as a whole, including the likely impact of the oral evidence and the legal advice available").

[44] [1993] A.C. 646. The appellant was indicted on a single count of conspiring with his brother to commit robbery. The brother had been discharged, but after conviction it was discovered that the brother's neighbour had served on the jury.

[45] See 10–019 *et seq.*

[46] The expression "real danger" of bias had been adopted by Lord Ackner in *R. v Spencer* [1987] A.C. 128, approving *R. v Sawyer* (1980) 71 Cr. App. R. 283, 285. See also *R. v Puttnam* (1991) Cr. App. R. 281. The Gough test was followed in *R. v Secretary of State for the Environment Ex p. Kirkstall Valley Campaign* [1996] 3 All E.R. 304.

"Since however the court investigates the actual circumstances, knowledge of such circumstances as are found by the court must be imputed to the reasonable man; and in the results it is difficult to see what difference there is between the impression derived by a reasonable man to whom such knowledge has been imputed, and the impression derived by the court, here personifying the reasonable man".[47]

Gough reconsidered

In *Pinochet*[48] Lord Browne-Wilkinson indicated that the test in *Gough* may need to be reconsidered, and it was then questioned, on the ground that it does not evaluate the interest of the decision-maker by the standard of the perception of appearance of bias on the part of the public (whose confidence is necessary in such cases). Instead, it requires a consideration by the court of whether the context of the case establishes the possibility that there was bias.[49] Much Commonwealth authority prefers a test under which the court considers "whether a fair-minded and informed person might apprehend or suspect that bias existed (the "reasonable apprehension" test).[50] In *Re Medicaments and Related Classes of Goods (No.2)*[51] the Court of Appeal considered the test of bias under ECHR Art.6 where the European Court of Human Rights asks whether there is a risk of bias "objectively" in the light of the circumstances which the court has identified.[52] Lord Phillips of Worth Matravers M.R. felt that both because the test in *Gough* did not command universal approval and because it was at odds with the test under Art.6, it should be modified[53] and that, in order

10–016

---

[47] Gough [1993] A.C. 646 at 667–668. In *Auckland Casino Ltd v Casino Control Authority* [1995] 1 N.Z.L.R. 142, the New Zealand Court of Appeal noted that since *R. v Gough and Webb v R.* (1994) 122 A.L.R. 41 there was, as to the test for apparent bias, a conflict of approach between the HL and the High Court of Australia, but said that once it is accepted that the hypothetical reasonable observer must be informed, the distinction between the real danger and reasonable suspicion tests becomes very thin. In the South African case *BTR Industries v Metal & Allied Workers Union* 1992 (3) S.A. 673(A) it was held that for "judicial" situations a "reasonable suspicion" test applies while "real likelihood" of bias applies to all other cases. In *R. v Bow Street Metropolitan Stipendiary Magistrate Ex p. Pinochet Ugarte (No.2)* [2000] 1 A.C. 119 the majority of the HL seemed to prefer the Australian approach to Gough, although that matter was not directly decided.

[48] *Pinochet (No.2)* [2000] 1 A.C. 119, discussed at 10–023 *et seq.*

[49] See, e.g. *Locobail (UK) Ltd v Bayfield Properties Ltd* [2000] Q.B. 451 at [16] (Lord Bingham M.R. and Simon Brown L.J.).

[50] See e.g. the Australian case of *Webb v The Queen* (1994) 181 C.L.R. 41 referred to in *R. v Central Criminal Court Ex p. Bright* [2001] 1 W.L.R. 662. A similar test has been applied over the years in Scotland. See *Law v Chartered Institute of Patent Agents* [1919] 2 Ch. 276; *Doherty v McGlennan* 1997 S.L.T. 444; *Bradford v McLeod* 1986 S.L.T. 244; *Millar v Dickson* 2001 S.L.T. 988 at 1002–1003; for comparative perspectives, see 10–085 *et seq.*

[51] [2001] 1 W.L.R. 700.

[52] See, e.g. *Piersack v Belgium* (1982) 5 E.H.R.R. 169 at 179–80; *De Cubber v Belgium* (1984) 7 E.H.R.R. 236 at 246; *Pullar v United Kingdom* (1996) 22 E.H.R.R. 391 at 402–403. In *Hauschildt v Denmark* (1989) 12 E.H.R.R. 266 at 279 the ECtHR observed that in considering whether a judge was biased the standpoint of the accused is important, but not decisive: "what is decisive is whether this fear can be held objectively justified".

[53] [2001] 1 W.L.R. 700 at [67].

to fulfil the confidence of the public, the court should consider the question of bias through the eyes of an "objective onlooker".[54]

Gough adjusted: "real possibility"

10–017 The matter was then resolved by the House of Lords in *Porter v Magill*,[55] where Lord Hope suggested a "modest adjustment" to the test in *Gough*. The reference to "real danger" should be deleted and the test should be whether "the fair-minded and informed observer, having considered the facts, would conclude that there was a real possibility of bias".[56] The emphasis thus shifts from the view of the court to that of an objective and informed observer.[57] The observer, however, should not be regarded as unduly neurotic or, as put by Kirby J. in an Australian case, "neither complacent nor unduly sensitive or suspicious".[58] As Lord Hope said:

> "The fair-minded and informed observer can be assumed to have access to all the facts that are capable of being known by members of the public generally, bearing in mind that it is the appearance that these facts give rise to that matters, not what is in the mind of the particular judge or tribunal member who is under scrutiny."[59]

10–018 Despite the alteration in the test of bias, it will not always be clear whether the perspective of the judge or that of the "fair-minded observer" will differ. Neither test can be mechanically applied to a particular case and it is now necessary to consider some particular situations in which a decision-maker may be disqualified for bias.

---

[54] [2001] 1 W.L.R. 700 at [87] ("the court must first ascertain all the circumstances which have a bearing on the suggestion that the judge was biased. It must then ask whether those circumstances would lead a fair-minded and informed observer to conclude that there was a real possibility . . . that the tribunal was biased").

[55] [2001] UKHL 67; [2002] 2 A.C. 357; see S. Atrill, "Who is the 'Fair-Minded Observer'? Bias after *Magill*" [2003] C.L.J. 279.

[56] [2001] UKHL 67; [2002] 2 A.C. 357 at [103].

[57] This approach was endorsed by the HL in *Lawal v Northern Spirit Ltd* [2003] UKHL 35; [2004] 1 All E.R. 187 at [19] (Lord Steyn), citing in support *Belilos v Switzerland* (1988) 10 E.H.R.R. 466 at para.67. See also *Davidson v Scottish Ministers* [2004] UKHL 34; 2005 1 S.C. (H.L.) 7 where it was held that a former Lord Advocate (the Law Officer of the Scottish Executive) was disqualified from sitting in the Court of Session when he was called upon to interpret legislation the meaning of which he had previously advised. Lord Bingham at [17] said that the fair-minded and informed observer "would conclude that there was a real possibility that [the judge] . . .would subconsciously strive to avoid reaching a conclusion which would undermine the very clear assurances he had given to Parliament".

[58] *Johnson v Johnson* (2000) 200 C.L.R. 488; cited with approval in *Gillies v Secretary of State for Work and Pensions* [2006] UKHL 2; [2006] 1 W.L.R. 781 at [17] (Lord Hope), [39] (Baroness Hale).

[59] *Gillies* [2006] UKHL 2; [2006] 1 W.L.R. 781 at [17]. In India, the former principle of "real likelihood of bias" has now shifted to "real danger of bias": *MP Special Police Establishment v State of MP* 2004 (8) S.C.C. 788 at 800, following *Kunaon Mandal Vikas Nigam v Girja Shankar Pant* 2001 (1) S.C.C. 182.

Automatic Disqualification for Bias

There are some interests which have been held to be so clearly indicative of   **10–019**
bias that the courts have automatically disqualified the decision-maker
from taking part in the decision on the ground that public confidence
would inevitably be shaken if the decision were allowed to stand.

Direct pecuniary or proprietary interest

Such are cases where the decision-maker has a *direct pecuniary or*   **10–020**
proprietary interest in the outcome of the proceedings. These cases clearly
breach the maxim that nobody may be judge in his own cause[60] and
"attract the full force [of the requirement that] justice must not only be
done but manifestly be seen to be done".[61] The rule of automatic
disqualification was held to apply in the case of *Dimes v Grand Junction
Canal Co Proprietors*[62] where the decision-maker was no less exalted than
the Lord Chancellor with respect to a company in which he was a
shareholder The application of this rule has been strictly applied, whether
or not the judge could reasonably be suspected of having allowed himself
to be influenced by his pecuniary interest.[63] In other words, the interest is
regarded as so obviously requiring disclosure that it is not even necessary
to conduct an investigation into whether there was any likelihood or
suspicion of bias, The mere fact of the interest is sufficient to suggest
disqualification, unless sufficient disclosure has been made. The rule applies
to members of magistrates' courts[64] and arbitrators.[65] The application of
the rule extends beyond judicial appointments and was well brought out by
a case in which the unanimous decision of a local authority to grant
permission for the development of land as a roadhouse in the face of

---

[60] See, e.g. *R. v Rand* (1866) L.R. 1 Q.B. 230 at 232 (Blackburn J.: "Any pecuniary interest,
however small, in the subject matter of the inquiry, does disqualify a person from acting as a
judge in the matter"); *Dimes v Proprietors of Grand Junction Canal* (1852) 3 H.L. Cas. 759 at
793 (Lord Campbell).

[61] *R. v Gough* [1993] A.C. 646 at 661 (Lord Goff). The above passage was approved in *R. v
Bow Street Metropolitan Stipendiary Magistrate Ex p. Pinochet Ugarte (No.2)* [2000] 1 A.C.
119 where it was held by the HL that a Law Lords was automatically disqualified from
hearing a matter in a case where his decision could lead to the promotion of a cause in which
the judge was involved with one of the parties (in this case the Law Lord was a director of a
charity closely associated to a party and sharing its objectives).

[62] (1852) 3 H.L. Cas. 759. *cf.* Sir Nicholas Bacon's case (1563) 2 Dyer 220b; Earl of Derby's
case (1613) 12 Co.Rep. 114. There can be no real doubt that interest as a creditor will
normally disqualify: *Jeffs v New Zealand Dairy Production and Marketing Board* [1967] 1 A.C.
551; *Barker v Westmorland CC* (1958) 56 L.G.R. 267 (dicta).

[63] *Dimes* (1852) 3 H.L. Cas. 759; *R. v Cambridge Recorder* (1857) 8 E. & B. 637 at 643.

[64] *R. v Cheltenham Commissioners* (1841) 1 Q.B. 466; *Ex p. Steeple Morden Overseers* (1855)
19 J.P 292, (justices hearing rating appeals concerning premises in which they had a
proprietary interest); and *R. v O'Grady* (1857) 7 Cox C.C. 247 for presence of proprietary
interest in another context.

[65] *Blanchard v Sun Fire Office* (1890) 6 T.L.R. 365; *cf. Re Elliott and South Devon Ry* (1848)
12 Jur. (O.S.) 445 and *Ranger v Great Western Ry* (1854) 5 H.L.C. 72.

objections by other ratepayers was quashed because one of the councillors was acting as agent for the existing owner of the land in negotiations for sale to the prospective developer.[66]

10–021   In a number of cases, reaching into the second half of the 19th century, justices who were ratepayers were held to be disqualified from making orders for the removal of paupers from their own parishes,[67] and from performing other duties in which they had had pecuniary interests by virtue of their membership of a local community.[68] If the pecuniary interest of a justice was in no way personal but arose solely from his capacity as a trustee for the general body of ratepayers, he was not disqualified.[69] With the disappearance of the conditions that had called for its adoption, the ratepayers' disqualification was abolished by statute.[70] Where a councillor retired with a subcommittee for part of the decision-making process about whether to renew the licence to operate a sex establishment, it was held that the councillor should have been disqualified, even though he did not take part in the debate, because he was a director of the co-operative society which owned the premises next to the shop.[71] Where members of a tribunal are disqualified for pecuniary interest but the invalidating effect of that interest upon their decisions is removed by statute, the nature and effect of their pecuniary interest may still have to be examined in order to determine whether it gives rise to a real possibility of bias on their part.[72]

10–022   Statutory disqualifications for pecuniary interest may add to those of the common law. For example, officers and members of local authorities are disqualified from participating in any question on which they have more than an insignificant interest.[73]

---

[66] *R. v Hendon RDC Ex p. Chorley* [1933] 2 K.B. 696; cf. *R. v Holderness DC Ex p. James Roberts Developments Ltd* (1993) 157 L.G.R. 643 (rival developer not disqualified from sitting on local authority planning committee).

[67] *Great Charte v Kennington* (1742) 2 Str. 1173; *R. v Yarpole Inhabitants* (1790) 4 T.R. 71; *R. v Rishton* (1813) 1 Q.B. 479n.; *R. v Suffolk Justices* (1852) 18 Q.B. 416; *R. v Breconshire Justices* (1873) 37 J.P. 404. On the changing role of Justices of the Peace, see Ch.15.

[68] *R. v Gudridge* (1826) 5 B. & C. 459; *R. v Cambridge Recorder* (1857) 8 E. & B. 637 (where the rule was applied extremely strictly); *R. v Gaisford* [1892] 1 Q.B. 381.

[69] *R. v Middlesex Justices* (1908) 72 J.P 251. A similar principle was applied in another context in *R. v Rand* (1866) L.R. 1 Q.B. 230. Such an interest may still give rise to a likelihood of bias.

[70] Effect was given to statutes removing disqualifications in *R. v Essex Justices* (1816) 5 M. & S. 513; *R. v Bolingbroke* [1893] 2 Q.B. 347; *Ex p. Workington Overseers* [1894] 1 Q.B. 416.

[71] *R. v Chesterfield BC Ex p. Darker Enterprises Ltd* [1991] C.O.D. 466.

[72] *R. v Barnsley Licensing Justices Ex p. Barnsley & District Licensed Victuallers' Association* [1960] 2 Q.B. 167; *R. v Tempest* (1902) 86 L.T. 585.

[73] Local Government Act 1972 ss.94–98; and see Local Government Act 2000 (permitting Council's to establish Codes of Conduct); Local Authorities (Model Code of Conduct) Order 2007 (SI 2007/1159) Pt.2.

Pinochet: extension of automatic disqualification to "promotion of a cause"

The events surrounding the arrest in London of the former Chilean **10–023** dictator Augusto Pinochet led the House of Lords to clarify and then to extend the rule of automatic disqualification.[74] The Lords had held that Pinochet was not immune from arrest and extradition proceedings in respect of his conduct during the time he was in office. At the hearing Amnesty International, a charitable organisation which promotes human rights, was granted permission to appear as an intervener. After the decision was handed down it was revealed that one of the Law Lords in the majority in the case was a director and chairman of Amnesty International Charity Ltd, a charity which was closely linked to Amnesty International. It should be stressed that he was unpaid and that there was never any suggestion that he was in any way actually biased. However, his interest was not declared to the parties during the hearing and it was therefore held, on petition of the matter to the House of Lords, that the decision was vitiated by bias.[75] Lord Browne-Wilkinson made the following distinction between two ways in which a person could judge in their "own cause".

"First, it may be applied literally: if a judge is in fact a party to the litigation or has a financial or proprietary interest in its outcome then he is indeed sitting as a judge in his own cause . . . and that . . . is sufficient to cause his automatic disqualification. The second application of the principle is where a judge is not a party to the suit and does not have a financial interest in its outcome, but in some other way his conduct or behaviour may give rise to a suspicion that he is not impartial, for example because of his friendship with a party. This second type of case is not strictly speaking an application of the principle that a man must not be a judge in his own cause, since the judge will not normally be himself benefiting, put providing a benefit to another by failing to be impartial."[76]

Lord Brown-Wilkinson in the above passage appears to confine the rule of **10–024** automatic disqualification to cases of financial or proprietary interest alone, but it was unanimously held that, despite the fact that interest in this case was not pecuniary or proprietary—since the Law Lord would have had nothing financially to gain by the decision—automatic disqualification

---

[74] D. Woodhouse (ed.), *The Pinochet Case: A Legal and Constitutional Analysis* (2000).
[75] *R. v Bow Street Metropolitan Stipendiary Magistrate Ex p. Pinochet Ugarte (No.2)* [2000] 1 A.C. 119.
[76] *Pinochet (No.2)* [2000] 1 A.C. 119 at 132–133.

extends, particularly in a case involving criminal litigation, to the "promotion of a cause".[77]

Further extension of automatic disqualification

10–025 In some cases it seems that the automatic disqualification test is being extended even beyond *Pinochet*. In *AWG Group Ltd (formerly Anglian Water Plc) v Morrison*,[78] the judge designated to hear the trial informed the parties that a witness the claimants proposed to call was a long-standing family acquaintance. The defendants sought the judge's recusal but the judge instead accepted the claimant's suggestion that they would call other witnesses instead, as the case was complex and postponement would not be in the interest of the parties. Mummery L.J. stressed that the prejudicial effect that the judge's withdrawal from the trial would have had on the parties and the administration of justice was irrelevant as "efficiency and convenience" were not the "determinative values" in this situation,[79] and it was held that because of the depth of the connection between the judge and the witness, and the fact that the withdrawal of the witness would not practically remove him from the events, the judge ought to have recused himself under the rule of automatic disqualification.

10–026 The automatic disqualification rule was also invoked to invalidate the composition of a disciplinary tribunal of the Council of the Inns of Court since one of the members of the tribunal had been a member of the Professional Conduct and Complaints Committee of the Bar Council (PCCC) which was the body responsible for the decision to prosecute the member of the Bar. It was held by the Visitors to the Inns of Court that each member of the PCCC had a common interest in the prosecution and therefore was acting as a judge in his or her own cause.[80]

Exceptions to automatic disqualification

10–027 The automatic disqualification rule has always been subject to a number of exceptions.

[77] *Pinochet* (No.2) [2000] 1 A.C. 119 at 132–133 (Lord Browne-Wilkinson: "If the absolute impartiality of the judiciary is to be maintained, there must be a rule which automatically disqualifies a judge who is involved, whether personally or as a director of a company, in promoting the same causes in the same organisation as is a party to the suit. There is no room for fine distinctions"). Following the Pinochet case the Lord Chancellor, Lord Irvine, suggested that future decisions on potential bias in the House of Lords should be a collectively taken, with the panel of judges addressing the issue of bias before the hearing, with the Law Lord in the chair taking the final decision: K. Malleson, "Judicial Bias and Disqualification after *Pinochet* (No.2)" (2000) 63 M.L.R. 119.
[78] [2006] EWCA Civ 6; [2006] 1 W.L.R. 1163.
[79] [2006] EWCA Civ 6; [2006] 1 W.L.R. 1163 at [29].
[80] *P (A Barrister) v General Council of the Bar* [2005] 1 W.L.R. 3019; *cf. Preiss v General Dental Council* [2001] UKPC 36; [2001] 1 W.L.R. 1926 (lack of independence and impartiality but no automatic disqualification); *Tehrani v United Kingdom Central Council for Nursing Midwifery and Health Visiting* [2001] I.R.L.R. 20 (no bias).

Trivial interests

Although some cases have held that the rule of automatic disqualification 10–028
applies however trivial the interest,[81] disqualification will not attach if the
connection between the pecuniary interests of the decision-makers and the
issue before them is very tenuous,[82] or if their pecuniary interest will arise
only upon the occurrence of an improbable sequence of events.[83] A judge
who had a shareholding in a bank robbed by the appellant was not
disqualified from trying his case.[84]

Interests of spouses

In Australian cases it has been held that the pecuniary interest of a judge's 10–029
spouse in an issue does not automatically disqualify the judge from
adjudicating, though it will be a different matter if the circumstances give
rise to a real likelihood of bias.[85] In *Pinochet* Lord Browne-Wilkinson said,
obiter, that the fact that the Law Lord's wife was employed by Amnesty
International would not lead to automatic disqualification. And the Court
of Appeal have held that the fact that the husband of the judge was a
barrister in chambers that undertook work for one of the parties neither
led to automatic disqualification or, in the circumstances, to any implication of bias.[86]

Great degree of flexibility in application of automatic disqualification

Five cases, heard together, on the subject of judicial bias have indicated a 10–030
greater degree of flexibility on the question of automatic bias. In *Locabail
(UK) Ltd v Bayfield Properties Ltd*,[87] the deputy judge in the case became
aware that the law firm in which he was a senior partner was acting against
one of the parties to the litigation before him on another matter. It was

---

[81] Justices who were shareholders in a railway company were held to be disqualified from
hearing charges against persons accused of travelling on the railway without a proper ticket:
Re Hopkins (1858) E.B. & E. 100; *R. v Hammond* (1863) 9 L.T. (N.S.) 423 (Blackburn J.:
"The interest to each shareholder may be less than 1/4d but it is still an interest"); *cf.*
Auckland Casino Ltd v Casino Control Authority [1995] 1 N.Z.L.R. 142 at 148 (New Zealand
Court of Appeal was prepared to accept that the *de minimis* rule could apply).
[82] *R. v Mckenzie* [1892] 2 Q.B. 519 (shipping official prosecuted union leader for disorderly
picketing held, justices not disqualified because of shareholdings in shipping companies); and
R. v Manchester, Sheffield & Lincolnshire Ry (1867) L.R. 2 Q.B. 336; *cf. Auten v Rayner*
[1958] 1 W.L.R. 1300.
[83] *R. v Burton Ex p. Young* [1897] 2 Q.B. 468 (X, a justice who was a member of the
Incorporated Law Society, held qualified to hear charge brought by Society against Y for
falsely pretending to be a solicitor; no pecuniary interest could arise unless costs were
awarded against the Society and the society was dissolved, making X personally liable).
[84] *R. v Mulvihill* [1990] 1 W.L.R. 438.
[85] *R. v Industrial Court* [1966] Qd.R. 245 (citing unreported passage in *Bank of New South
Wales v Commonwealth* (1948) 76 C.L.R. 1).
[86] *Jones v Das Legal Expenses Insurance Co Ltd* [2003] EWCA Civ 1071; [2004] I.R.L.R. 218.
[87] [2000] Q.B. 451, CA (constituted by the Lord Chief Justice, Master of the Rolls and Vice-
Chancellor).

held that automatic disqualification would not be necessary as the connection between the firm's success in the case and its profits was "tenuous".[88] It was also held that the complaining party had effectively waived her right to challenge an adverse decision.[89] In a joined appeal, a challenge was mounted to the judge who, as was revealed by a newspaper, was a director of a family property company whose tenants included the defendant in the case. It was held that the judge's "nominal and indirect interest" did not establish a bar to the judge sitting in the case.[90]

10–031   In an appeal from New Zealand, the Privy Council held that an association between a judge and a witness as solicitor and client 8 years previously did not amount to bias.[91] In a later case, the fact that the judge was a client of the claimant's solicitor was held not to constitute bias, even though the solicitor had not charged for amending the judge's will. Lord Woolf felt that the "fair-minded and informed observer" could be expected to understand the legal traditions and culture of this jurisdiction. He regarded these to be sufficient safeguards of high standards of integrity and not to require the judiciary to isolate itself from contact with the legal profession.[92] Atrill warns that to impute this kind of specialised knowledge of the cultural traditions of the legal profession risks divorcing the test of bias from the interests it is meant to advance, namely, the confidence of the non-specialised public.[93] When the issue is complex the view of the "fair-minded observer" is bound to become the view of the court.[94]

Can automatic disqualification be justified?

10–032   In some respects the rule of automatic disqualification for pecuniary or proprietary interests is a misnomer, and might be more accurately considered a rule of automatic disclosure.[95] This is because the parties may waive the offer of the decision-maker to recuse himself.[96] In addition, some financial or proprietary interests have been held to be subject to the *de minimis* rule and not invoke automatic disqualification where the interest is "so small as to be incapable of affecting the decision one way or another".[97] The *Pinochet* case was in any event held to be exceptional on its facts.

[88] Note Lord Bingham C.J.'s warning at [14] that an extension of the automatic disqualification rule could lead to cost and delay.
[89] On waiver, see 10–055 *et seq.*
[90] *R v Bristol Betting and Gaming Licensing Committee Ex p. O'Callaghan* [2000] Q.B. 451 (CA).
[91] *Man O'War Station Ltd v Oakland City Council (No.1)* [2002] UKPC 28.
[92] *Taylor v Lawrence (Appeal: Jurisdiction to Reopen)* [2002] EWCA Civ 90; [2003] Q.B. 528.
[93] Atrill, "Who is the 'Fiar-Minded and Informed Observer'? Bias after Magill" [2003] P.L. 279.
[94] As in relation to the technicalities of trade mark law in *Hart v Relentless Records* [2002] EWHC 1984; [2003] F.S.R. 36; a point made by S. Hanif, "The Use of the Bystander Test for Apparent Bias"[2005] J.R. 78, 81.
[95] T. Jones, "Judical Bias and disqualification in the Pinochet case" [1999] P.L. 391, 399.
[96] On waiver, see 10–055 *et seq.* In addition, a situation of "necessity" may exist (where there is no other qualified decision-maker). 10–059 *et seq.*
[97] See 10–00; *Locabail (UK) Ltd v Bayfield Properties Ltd* [2000] Q.B. 451 at [10].

However, should the automatic disqualification rule extend beyond **10–033** financial and proprietary interests, and should the rule apply irrespective of the context of the decision? Do the circumstances of financial interest in themselves indicate an impression of bias without even the need to carry out an evaluation as to whether there is any "danger", or "likelihood", or "apprehension" of bias? Some commentators believe that automatic disqualification is "mechanistic", "smacks of abdication", and is "draconian, disproportionate and unnecessary".[98] It has also been argued that in *Pinochet* the same result could have been reached by assessing the context of the decision by the standards of the appropriate test, and that the result will deter judges from involving themselves with the activities of the growing list of parties who may become interveners in cases before them.[99] It may also be that if automatic disqualification is applied without discrimination the "public confidence"[100] that the rule seeks to inspire will be compromised by an appearance of technicality,[101] exacerbated by the additional cost and delay that a change of judge may entail.[102]

The state of the law on automatic disqualification is uncertain. It is not **10–034** always applied to purely financial or proprietal interests and it is not clear how far beyond that it may extend. Perhaps the most sensible approach is to require in each case a realistic assessment of the possibility of bias on the part of the "fair-minded observer". Some situations will then raise a presumption of bias and others not; the presumptions in either case would be open to rebuttal. In *Locabail* Lord Bingham C.J. suggested some of the factors which would and would not raise the presumption of bias. In most cases, he thought, "the answer, one way or the other, will be obvious. But if in any case there is real ground for doubt, that doubt should be removed in favour of recusal".[103]

Factors which *will*, on their face, raise a presumption of bias include: **10–035** personal friendship or animosity; close acquaintance and other "real ground for doubting the ability of the judge to ignore extraneous consid-

[98] A. Olowofoyeku, "The Nemo Judex Rule: The Case Against Automatic Disqualification" [2000] P.L. 456; B. Raiment, "Bias: Recent Developments" [2001] J.R. 93; P. Havers and O. Thomas, "Bias Post-*Pinochet* and Under the ECHR" [1999] J.R. 111.
[99] K. Malleson, "Judicial Bias and Disqualification after *Pinochet* (No.2)" (2000) 63 M.L.R. 119; Malleson "Safeguarding Judicial Impartiality" (2002) 22 L.S. 53; D. Williams, "Bias, the Judges and the Separation of Powers" [2000] P.L. 45.
[100] *Metropolitan Properties Ltd v Lannon* [1969] 1 Q.B. 577 at 599 (Lord Denning justified the *nemo iudex* rule by the fact that "justice is rooted in confidence").
[101] Olowofoyeku [2000] P.L. 456; and M. Elliott (ed.), *Beatson, Matthews, and Elliott's Administrative Law: Text and Materials* (2005), Ch.10.
[102] *Ebner v Official Trustee in Bankruptcy* [1999] F.C.A. 110 at [37] (Finn, Kenny and Sackville JJ.): criticism of the automatic disqualification rule has been voiced by the Australian Federal Court of Appeal in a case where it was held that a judge's shareholding in a corporate party to litigation should not lead to automatic disqualification where the shares were worth so little that no reasonable person could suggest any suspicion of bias (the test of bias applied in Australia). It was doubted whether the "confidence of fair-minded people in the administration of justice would be shaken by the existence of a direct pecuniary interest of no tangible value" and suggested that confidence was more likely to be shaken "by the waste of resources and the delays brought about by setting aside a judgment on the ground that the judge is disqualified for having such an interest".
[103] *Locabail* [2000] Q.B. 451 at [25].

erations, prejudices and predilections and bring an objective judgment to bear on the issues before him".[104]

10–036   Factors which *will not* give rise to a real danger of bias include: religion; ethnic or national origin; gender; class; means; or sexual orientation of the judge. Nor "at any rate ordinarily" will the following factors indicate bias:

> "social or educational or service or employment background or history, nor that of any member of the judge's family; or previous political associations; or membership of social or sporting or charitable bodies; or Masonic associations; or previous judicial decisions; or extra-curricular utterances (whether in text books, lectures, speeches, articles, interviews, reports or responses to consultation papers); or previous receipt of instructions to act for or against any party, solicitor or advocate engaged in a case before him; or membership of the same Inn, circuit, local Law Society or chambers".[105]

OTHER SITUATIONS IN WHICH BIAS MAY OCCUR

10–037   The existence of bias depends entirely on the context of the relevant relationships between the decision-maker and a party with an interest in, or influence upon, the decision. The Parole Board, previously regarded as independent of government, has now been held to be too closely related to the Department of Justice to avoid the appearance of bias.[106] We now examine: (a) situations where a decision-maker participates in a subsequent decision (for example, an appeal against his original decision); (b) relationships; and (c) attitudes towards an issue.

Participation in subsequent decisions

10–038   Normally a decision will be invalid for bias if the decision-maker takes part in a determination or appeal against one of his own decisions, or one in which he has participated, unless he is expressly authorised to do so by statute.[107] At best he is likely to incline towards affirming his earlier decision; at worst he can be depicted as a judge in his own cause. In general, a decision-maker must not participate or indeed give the impression of participating in such an appeal.

---

[104] [2000] Q.B. 451 at [25].
[105] [2000] Q.B. 451 at [25].
[106] *R. (Brooke) v Parole Board* [2007] EWHC 2036 (Admin).
[107] Authorisation by rules of a voluntary association may be inadequate, for these can be declared to be contrary to natural justice. No question of invalidity was raised in *Herring v Templeman* [1973] 3 All E.R. 569 about the terms of a trust deed establishing a teacher-training college which authorised the principal to recommend a student's dismissal and nominated him chairman of the academic board which assessed the student's record.

Illustrations

- A clerk to a statutory tribunal ought not to act as clerk to a tribunal **10–039** hearing an appeal against that decision if he takes part in the appellate tribunal's deliberations.[108]

- Similarly, a lay representative who served on a disciplinary panel conducting a hearing into a disciplinary matter concerning a barrister, was held to be disqualified by reason of the fact that she had attended a meeting of the Professional Conduct Committee which had decided to prosecute the barrister.[109]

- A magistrate who had convicted a defendant of threatening to kill his wife was disqualified from sitting on the bench which a month later tried the defendant for a separate offence.[110]

- The president of a mental health review tribunal who had previously sat on the case of an applicant seeking discharge from an institution was not disqualified from sitting on a later application by the same patient.[111]

- But a licensing justice was not disqualified from sitting on an appeal against a refusal of a wine bar licence when he had sat on the decision to refuse a previous application by the applicant; licensing justices were bound to and entitled to bring to bear their local knowledge on licensing matters.[112]

- In *Gillies*,[113] the House of Lords held that the fact that a member of a tribunal has in the past been employed as an expert by the

[108] *R. v Salford Asst Cttee Ex p. Ogden* [1937] 2 K.B. 1 (where a strict rule was applied). *cf. Re Lawson* (1941) 57 T.L.R. 315; *R. v Architects' Registration Tribunal Ex p. Jaggar* [1945] 2 All E.R. 131; *R. v Liverpool Dock Labour Board Ex p. Brandon* [1954] 2 Lloyd's Rep. 186; and *R. v Minister of Agriculture and Fisheries Ex p. Graham* [1955] 2 Q.B. 140. *R. v South Worcestershire Magistrates Ex p. Lilley* [1995] 1 W.L.R. 1595 (lay justices heard and rejected public interest immunity application and then went on to hear prosecution. The procedure was such that "a reasonable and fair-minded person could reasonably have suspected the applicant could not have a fair trial"); *R. v Parole Board Ex p. Watson* [1996] 1 W.L.R. 906, CA (no bias in extra-statutory practice).
[109] *P (A Barrister) v General Council of the Bar* [2005] 1 W.L.R. 3019; and see also *Preiss v General Dental Council* [2001] UKPC 36; [2001] 1 W.L.R. 1926 and *Tehrani v UK Central Council for Nursing, Midwifery and Health Visiting* [2001] I.R.L.R. 20.
[110] *R. v Downham Market Magistrates' Court Ex p. Nudd* [1989] R.T.R. 169 (it was made clear, however, that in such a case the mere knowledge of the defendant's previous convictions did not necessarily preclude a fair trial); *cf. Huchard v DPP* [1994] C.O.D. 451 show the bench details of a previous conviction of the same offence (drink driving) but application refused as the applicant had pleaded guilty and the previous conviction was only relevant to sentence and in addition the bench had itself concluded the knowledge was not prejudicial.
[111] *R. v Oxford Regional Mental Health Review Tribunal Ex p. Mackman, The Times*, June 2, 1986.
[112] *R. v Crown Court at Bristol Ex p. Cooper* [1990] W.L.R. 1031, CA; and *R. v Secretary of State for Trade Ex p. Perestrello* [1981] 1 Q.B.19; *R. v Board of Visitors of Frankland Prison Ex p. Lewis* [1986] 1 W.L.R. 130. On the doctrine of necessity, see 10–059 *et seq.*
[113] *Gillies v Secretary of State for Work and Pensions* [2006] UKHL 2; [2006] 1 W.L.R. 781.

defendant authority does not in itself raise an implication that she would lean in favour of accepting reports of other doctors in that class. In that and other cases, the local experience of tribunal members has been favoured and not regarded as tainting the integrity of the tribunal.[114]

Superior courts

10–040 However, it has been held that the superior judges may not apply such a principle to the exercise of their own appellate functions,[115] and judges who, in the Administrative Court have refused permission to a claimant on a paper hearing, have heard the oral application for permission to appeal.[116] It was also held that the "practical realities" in a London council housing department permit a housing officer to sit twice on a determination of whether a person is homeless (at least when the matter is thereafter open to appeal in the county court).[117]

Sub-committees

10–041 Practical problems are liable to arise where a body exercising licensing or disciplinary functions refers a particular case to a committee or sub-committee of its members for hearing and report, and the report is then considered and the issue decided by the parent body. Are the members who made the report disqualified from sitting on the parent body when it makes its decision?[118] Disqualification normally attaches if members of the sub-committee show active partisanship as members of the parent body.[119] However, in one such case it was held that a president of a mental health review tribunal, who had sat on the case of a patient seeking discharge from a mental health institution, was not disqualified by statute from sitting on a later application by the same patient.[120]

---

[114] See, e.g. *R v Hereford and Worcester Council Ex p. Wellington DC* [1996] J.P.L. 573; *M and J Gleeson and Co v Competition Authority* [1999] 1 I.L.R.M. 401.
[115] *R. v Lovegrove* [1951] 1 All E.R. 804.
[116] See, e.g. *R. (on the application of Holmes) v General Medical Council* [2002] EWCA Civ 1838.
[117] *Feld v Barnet LBC* [2004] EWCA Civ 1307; [2005] H.L.R. 9 at [49] (Ward L.J.); See 1–061.
[118] *Osgood v Nelson* (1872) L.R. 5 H.L. 636 was decided on the assumption that participation in the final decision by the members concerned was unexceptionable; and *Jeffs v New Zealand Dairy Production and Marketing Board* [1967] 1 A.C. 551.
[119] *R. v LCC Ex p. Akkersdyk* [1892] 1 Q.B. 190.
[120] *R. v Oxford Regional Mental Health Review Tribunal Ex p. Mackman*, *The Times*, June 2, 1986.

Relationships

Friendship[121]

Normally close personal friendship will give rise to a real possibility of bias.[122] The Court of Appeal has held that a judge was wrong not to recuse himself from a trial when he discovered that one of the potential witnesses in the case was a longstanding friend whose role in the trial was not predictable. The agreement not to call the witness was not held relevant as substitute witness would not remove him from the case.[122a] In Australia the decision of a tribunal was set aside because a member of the tribunal was a personal friend of an applicant's husband.[123]   **10–042**

Members of local tribunals are, of course, often acquainted with the parties who appear before them. A member who is a close friend of a party will normally think it proper not to sit if a quorum can be formed without him. In *Gough*[124] the fact that a juror was a neighbour of the defendant's brother was held, on the facts of that case, not to have been indicative of bias.   **10–043**

Family and kinship

Kinship has always been recognised as a ground for challenging a juror, and in 1572 a court went so far as to uphold an objection to proceedings in which the sheriff who had summoned the jury was related in the ninth degree to one of the parties.[125] Despite a 17th century decision that kinship did not operate as a disqualification for a judge,[126] it was later well established that it does disqualify wherever it is close enough to cause a likelihood of bias.[127] Family relationship between judge and counsel does not appear to be exceptionable, but it has been suggested that judges are disqualified from sitting in cases where near relatives are witnesses.[128] There is no reason for differentiating between the courts and administrative tribunals in these matters. In a Canadian case the decision of a tribunal was set aside because the chairman was the husband of an executive officer of a body which was a party to proceedings before the tribunal.[129] As we   **10–044**

---

[121] See A. Olwofoyeku, "Subjective Objectivity, Judicial Impartiality and Social Intercourse in the US Supreme Court" [2006] P.L.15.

[122] Personal friendship is listed in Lord Bingham's list of matters likely to give rise to a real possibility of bias in Locobail: see 10–035.

[122a] *Feld v Barnett LBC* [2004] EWCA Civ 1307.

[123] *Ex p. Blume, re Osborn* (1958) 58 S.R. (N.S.W.) 334.

[124] *R. v Gough* [1993] A.C. 646.

[125] *Vernon v Manners* (1572) 2 Plowd. 425.

[126] *Brookes v Earl of Rivers* (1668) Hardres 503. *cf. Bridgman v Holt* (1693) 1 ShowPC. 111, where Holt C.J. withdrew from a case in which his brother was a party.

[127] *R. v Rand* (1866) L.R. 1 Q.B. 230, 232–233; *R. (Murray and Wortley) v Armagh County Justices* (1915) 49 I.L.T. 56; and *Becquet v Lempriere* (1830) 1 Knapp 376 (Jurat of Royal Court of Jersey held by PC to be disqualified from hearing case in which deceased wife's nephew a party); *cf. Auten v Rayner* [1958] 1 W.L.R. 1300.

[128] Sir Alfred Denning "The Independence and Impartiality of the Judges" (1954) 71 S.A.L.J. 345, 355.

[129] *Ladies of the Sacred Heart of Jesus v Armstrong's Point Association* (1961) 29 D.L.R. (2d) 373. *R. v Wilson and Sprason* (1996) 8 Admin. L.R. 1 (wife of prison officer on jury); *R. v Salt* (1996) 8 Admin. L.R. 429 (son of usher on jury).

have discussed, in *Pinochet*[130] Lord Browne-Wilkinson said, *obiter*, that the fact that the Law Lord's wife was employed by Amnesty International could have led to the implication of appearance of bias. However, the Court of Appeal have held that the fact that the husband of the judge was a barrister in chambers that undertook work for one of the parties did not, in the circumstances of that case, lead to any implication of bias.[131] The fact that a lay member of a professional conduct committee had worked in Wales was not held to disqualify her from considering cases from Wales.[132]

Professional and vocational relationships

10–045 Possibility of bias may arise because of the professional[133] business[134] or other vocational relationship of an adjudicator with a party before him. It is unlikely that proceedings could be successfully impugned on this ground unless the community of interest between judge and party (or the conflict of interest between them)[135] was directly related to the subject matter of the proceedings.[136] The courts have refused to hold that a person is disqualified from sitting to hear a case merely on the ground that he is a member of the public authority, or a member of or subscriber to the voluntary association, that is a party to the proceedings.[137]

---

[130] [2000] 1 A.C. 119.

[131] *Jones v Das Legal Expenses Insurance Co Ltd* [2003] EWCA Civ 1071; [2004] I.R.L.R. 218.

[132] *Nwabueze v General Medical Council* [2000] 1 W.L.R. 1760; and *Modahl v British Athletic Federation Ltd (No.2)* [2001] EWCA Civ 1447; [2002] 1 W.L.R. 1192.

[133] On the competence of a barrister to rule as arbitrator on the misconduct of solicitors with whom he had had close professional relations, see *Bright v River Plate Construction Co* [1900] 2 Ch. 835.

[134] *Veritas Shipping Co v Anglo-Canadian Cement Ltd* [1966] 1 Lloyd's Rep. 76.

[135] *R. v Huggins* [1895] 1 Q.B. 563 (one member of bench belonged to small class of licensed river pilots; defendant charged with infringement of their privileges; conviction of defendant quashed, despite no finding that there had been real likelihood of bias); cf. *R. v Burton Ex p. Young* [1897] 2 Q.B. 468.

[136] *Stevens v Stevens* (1929) 93 J.P. 120 (validity of matrimonial proceedings unaffected by fact that one of the justices was member of husband's trade union); cf. *R. v Barnsley Licensing Justices* [1960] 2 Q.B. 167 (decision to grant an off-licence to a co-operative society was upheld although all but one of the justices were members of the society); cf. *Metropolitan Properties Co (FGC) Ltd v Lannon* [1969] 1 Q.B. 577; *Man O'War Station Ltd v Oakland City Council (No.1)* [2002] UKPC 28 (professional association between witness and judge as solicitor and client 8 years ago gave no rise to danger of partiality); and M. Taggart, "Judicial Review in the Grove of Academe" [1999] N.Z.L.J. 171.

[137] *R. v Handsley* (1882) 8 Q.B.D. 383 (member of local authority not disqualified for likelihood of bias from adjudicating in proceedings brought by the authority); *Allinson v General Medical Council* [1894] 1 Q.B. 750 (members of GMC hearing charges of professional misconduct against doctors were members of the Medical Defence Union which had initiated the proceedings, but they had themselves taken no part in initiating them); *R. v Pwllheli Justices Ex p. Soane* [1948] 2 All E.R. 815 (justice member of fishery board who were prosecutors; he had taken no part in resolution to prosecute); *R. v Altrincham Justices Ex p. Pennington* [1975] Q.B. 549 (magistrate not disqualified by her membership of local authority from hearing case in which an officer of the authority was the prosecutor); *Hanson v Church Commissioners for England* [1978] Q.B. 823 (Lord Chief Justice and Master of the Rolls not disqualified from hearing appeal from rent assessment committee by virtue of their *ex officio* status as Commissioners, the landlords of the appellant).

Professional relationships between magistrates' clerks (who may still be **10–046** solicitors in private practice) and parties before the magistrates' court may render the proceedings vulnerable. Just as it is improper for the one person to act as judge and advocate,[138] so is it improper for the clerk of the court to act as solicitor for a party.[139] In one case the clerk was a member of a firm of solicitors which was acting for a party in civil proceedings arising out of a motoring accident in connection with which the other party was convicted of a criminal offence by the justices;[140] in another case the clerk's own firm had (unknown to him) given advice on matrimonial matters to a party, who, some years later, instituted matrimonial proceedings before the justices.[141] Although in each case the clerk had retired with the justices while they considered their decision but he had not actually influenced the decision, the decisions of the magistrates were quashed by the Divisional Court for apparent bias.[142]

We have seen above that the relationships between barristers, judges and **10–047** their clients must be seen in the context of the facts of each case and also of the prevailing culture.[143] In a case from Belize the Privy Council held that mere membership of a professional organization such as the Bar Association did not automatically disqualify the chairman of a body considering whether a judge had misbehaved while in office. The situation might have been otherwise if the chairman has actively participated in the decision to take proceedings against the judge.[144]

Membership of particular organisations which adopt well-known atti- **10–048** tudes towards particular issues may or may not disqualify a decision-maker for bias. In *R. (on the application of Port Regis School Ltd) v North Dorset DC*[145] it was held that members of the Society of Freemasons were not barred on the ground of bias from participating in local government decisions whenever another Freemason had an interest in the decision's outcome.

---

[138] Though conceptions of judicial propriety were still fluid in the 19th century: *Thellusson v Rendlesham* (1859) 7 H.L.C. 429.
[139] *R. v Brekenridge* (1884) 48 J.P 293.
[140] *R. v Sussex Justices Ex p. McCarthy* [192411 K.B. 256.
[141] *R. v Essex Justices Ex p. Perkins* [1927] 2 K.B. 475; *cf. R. v Lower Munslow Justices Ex p. Pudge* [1950] 2 All E.R. 756 (clerk had acted for previous owner of property that was subject of proceedings).
[142] See also *R. v Legal Aid Board Ex p. Donne and Co (A Firm)* [1996] 3 All E.R. 1 (presence of territorial officer at application to Legal Aid Board for action arising out of claim for Gulf War Syndrome).
[143] See 10–031.
[144] *Meerabux v Attorney General of Belize* [2005] UKPC 12; [2005] 2 A.C. 513. See S. Shetreet, *Judges on Trial* (1976) p.310; S. Bailey in D. Feldman (ed.), *English Public Law* (2004), para.15.76, citing *Leeson v General Council of Medical Education and Registration* (1889) 43 Ch. D. 366 and *Allison v General Council of Medical Education and Registration* [1894] 1 Q.B. 750.
[145] [2006] EWHC 742 (Admin); [2006] B.L.G.R. 696.

Employer and employee

10–049 Possibility of bias may arise from the fact that an adjudicator is the employer or employee of one of the parties, if their personal relationship is a close one or if their respective interests are directly involved in the subject matter of the proceedings.[146] Public authorities are often empowered by statute to determine questions affecting the rights of their own employees.

10–050 In a number of cases it has been held that a former employee of an authority is not necessarily infected with bias in favour of that organisation when making subsequent decisions on a contractual basis. The Court of Appeal held that a consultant psychiatrist member of a review tribunal to which the appellant had applied for his discharge from detention under s.3 of the Mental Health Act 1983 was not disqualified from considering the appellant's case because he was employed by the Mersey Care National Health Service Trust.[147] In *Gillies*,[148] it was held that a doctor who had previously been employed by the Benefits Agency was not necessarily to be seen by a fair-minded observer as a "Benefits Agency doctor" and thereby partial in his assessments in the role of independent adviser. The distinction should be made of the decision-maker's knowledge or the particular facts of the relevant case, and his knowledge of the subject matter in general.[149]

Personal hostility

10–051 Personal animosity towards a party disqualifies a judge from adjudicating on the ground of bias. Thus, a conviction by an Irish magistrate was quashed when it was shown, by an uncontradicted affidavit, that very bad feeling (originating in a trespass by a fowl) existed between him and the defendant's family, and that shortly after the conviction he had used words indicative of enmity towards the defendant.[150] In Canada a magistrate was held to be disqualified from hearing a charge against a person with whom he had recently come to blows.[151] But the evidence must be compelling; the

---

[146] *cf. R. v Hoseason* (1811) 14 East 605 (magistrate convicted own farm employee for breach of contract on complaint brought by own bailiff: criminal information against magistrate dismissed, but clearly application for certiorari to quash conviction would have been granted); and *R. v Altrincham Justices Ex p. Pennington* [1975] Q.B. 549 at 556 (dicta that a magistrate should regard himself as automatically disqualified from determining the guilt of a person accused of shoplifting from a chain store, on the ground that he was the manager of a store owned by the same company, but located a hundred miles away).

[147] *R. (on the application of PD) v West Midlands and North West Mental Health Review Tribunal* [2004] EWCA Civ 311; (2004) 148 S.J.L.B. 384.

[148] *Gillies v Secretary of State for Work and Pensions* [2006] UKHL 2; [2006] 1 W.L.R. 781.

[149] Baroness Hale at [45]. See also *R v Spear* [2002] UKHL 13; [2003] 1 A.C. 734.

[150] *R. (Donoghue) v Cork County Justices* [1910] 2 I.R. 271; and *R. (Kingston) v Cork County Justices* [1910] 2 I.R. 658; *R. (Harrington) v Clare County Justices* [1918] 2 I.R. 116 (X, a participant in a political procession, charged Y, a police officer, with assault arising out of a clash with the procession; Z, also a participant in the procession, held disqualified from hearing the summons against Y).

[151] *R. v Handley* (1921) 61 D.L.R. 656.

courts are reluctant to conclude that any judicial officer's judgment is likely to be warped by personal feeling.[152] General expressions of hostility towards a group to which a party belongs (e.g. poachers or motorists[153] or indeed, more recently, judges in general[154]) have not acted as a disqualification. A teetotaller was competent to sit as a licensing justice; the courts declined to accept the view that his principles were likely to prevent him from dealing fairly with applications before him.[155] Where, however, an adjudicator expressed his general sentiments so vehemently as to make it likely that he would be incapable of dealing with an individual case in a judicial spirit (as where a licensing justice who was a proselytising teetotaller wrote that he would have been a traitor to his principles if he had voted for the granting of a particular licence,[156] or where an arbitrator said that in his experience all persons of the nationality of one of the parties before him were untruthful witnesses),[157] the courts have held him to be disqualified. Again, where an adjudicator manifested open hostility to a party or his advocate[158] at the hearing, the only reasonable conclusion may be that a fair hearing has not been granted. When the chair of the bench of magistrates produced a note to be used as a basis for passing sentence of the defendants before all the evidence had been called, it was held that the note had promoted the appearance of bias.[159] In one case it was held that when a coroner used the terms "unhinged" and "mentally unwell" to describe relatives of the deceased, these expressions indicated a

---

[152] See, however, *R. v Abingdon Justices Ex p. Cousins* (1964) 108 S.J. 840, where the court, applying a test of suspicion of bias, set aside the conviction of an unsatisfactory former pupil of the chairman of the Bench (who was a headmaster).

[153] *Ex p. Wilder* (1902) 66 J.P 761.

[154] *Triodos Bank NV v Dobbs (Application for Stay of Appeal)* [2005] EWCA Civ 468; [2006] C.P. Rep. 1 (Neuberger L.J. held that he and others on the bench need not recuse themselves on the ground the ground of prejudice towards one of the parties who had previously made trenchant criticism of the judges in general, and Neuberger L.J. in particular).

[155] *R. v Dublin Justices* [1904] 2 I.R. 75; *Goodall v Bilsland* 1909 S.C. 1152; *M'Geehen v Knox* 1913 S.C. 688 (members of and subscribers to bodies that include opposition to grant of new licences among their objects are not disqualified); *R. v Nailsworth Licensing Justices Ex p. Bird* [1953] 1 W.L.R. 1046 at 1048.

[156] *R. v Halifax Justices Ex p. Robinson* (1912) 76 J.P 233. See also *R. v Rand* (1913) 15 D.L.R. 69 for prejudgment of a case.

[157] *Re "Catalina" v "Norman"* (1938) 61 Ll.Rep. 360 (actual bias shown); and *Ex p. Schofield, re Austin* (1953) 53 S.R. (N.S.W) 163 (magistrate, in convicting X and Y for obstructing Z in the course of his duty, called X and Y perjurers; he immediately heard and dismissed summonses brought by X and Y against Z for assault; held, disqualified from adjudicating in second case). *R. v Horseferry Magistrates' Court Ex p. Bilhar Chima* [1995] C.O.D. 317 (clerk made racist remark).

[158] *R. v Magistrate Taylor Ex p. Ruud* (1965) 50 D.L.R. (2nd) 444; *Re Elliott* (1959) 29 W.W.R. (N.S.) 579; *Re Golomb and College of Physicians and Surgeons of Ontario* (1976) 68 D.L.R. (3rd) 25; *cf. Re College of Physicians and Surgeons of Ontario and Casullo* [1977] 2 S.C.R. 2 (vigorous questioning of an evasive witness justifiable); and see *R. v Watson Ex p. Armstrong* (1976) 136 C.L.R. 248 (statement by judge in the course of proceedings that he did not believe the evidence of either party held to be vitiating bias).

[159] *R. v Romsey Justices Ex p. Gale* [1992] Crim. L.R. 451; and *Ellis v Ministry of Defence* [1985] I.C.R. 257 (a preliminary or tentative indication of the decision-maker's view is permissible, provided that it does not give the impression of being a concluded decision at a stage when evidence is still to be received and arguments heard).

real possibility that he had unconsciously allowed himself to be influenced against the applicant's argument that the inquest should be reopened.[160] On the other hand, robust questioning of a party at a hearing of a domestic tribunal has held not to amount to an indication of either actual or apparent bias, particularly where an inquisitorial approach to the testing of evidence is adopted.[161] The House of Lords held that the fair-minded and informed observer would not consider that there was an appearance of bias arising out of a press conference attended by an auditor who gave his provisional views as to the culpability of the respondents.[162]

10–052   If members of a tribunal have formed an unfavourable impression of a party in previous proceedings before them, it may be unrealistic to insist that they should not sit in judgment on that party again.[163] Thus a number of cases have held that the appearance of bias did not exist when there had been previous exposure to one of the parties in the role of company inspector,[164] member of a board of prison visitors,[165] member of a health tribunal,[166] and a licensing justice.[167]

10–053   Knowledge of prejudicial material about a party may disqualify a decision-maker, depending on the circumstances. The test is the same as the common law test when applied to pre-trial publicity, namely, "whether the risk of prejudice is so grave that no direction by a trial judge however careful could reasonably be expected to remove it".[168] In disciplinary hearings what will be relevant to the issue of prejudice is the directions received on the matter by the judge or chair or independent legal adviser, the length of time since the publication of the material, and the impact of any witnesses on the proceedings.[169]

[160] *R. v Inner West London Coroner Ex p. Dallaglio* [1994] 4 All E.R. 139. *Dallaglio* was applied in *R. v Highgate Magistrate's Court Ex p. Riley* [1996] C.O.D. 12.
[161] *Flaherty v National Greyhound Racing Club Ltd* [2005] EWCA Civ 1117; (2005) 102(37) L.S.G. 31; and *Connor v Chief Constable of Merseyside Police* [2006] EWCA Civ 1549; [2007] H.R.L.R. 6 ("inappropriate" or "inavisable" comments in a lengthy trial not prejudicial in the circumstances).
[162] *Porter v Magill* [2001] UKHL 67; [2002] 2 A.C. 357.
[163] *Re B (TA) (an Infant)* [1971] Ch. 270 at 277–278; *Ewert v Lonie* [1972] V.R. 308. But extreme cases may arise, creating a likelihood of bias or prejudice: *Munday v Munday* [1954] 1 W.L.R. 1078 at 1082; *R. v Grimsby Borough QS Ex p. Fuller* [1956] 1 Q.B. 36; *R. v Board of Visitors of Frankland Prison Ex p. Lewis* [1986] 1 W.L.R. 130 (no bias where Chairman of Board of Visitors trying prisoner for drug offence had previously been a member of the local review committee considering his application for release on licence).
[164] *R. v Secretary of State for Trade Ex p. Perestrello* [1981] 1 Q.B. 19. This and the following cases are considered in greater detail under the doctrine of necessity in Ch.11.
[165] *R. v Board of Visitors of Frankland Prison Ex p. Lewis* [1986]1 W.L.R. 130.
[166] *R. v Oxford Regional Mental Health Review Tribunal Ex p. Mackman, The Times*, June 2, 1986.
[167] *R. v Crown Court at Bristol Ex p. Cooper* [1990] 2 All E.R. 193, CA; and *CREEDNZ v Governor-General (NZ)* (1981) N.Z.L.R. 172 (no "predetermination" when decision taken by Executive Council).
[168] *Montgomery v HM Advocate* [2003] 1 A.C. 641 at 667 (Lord Hope).
[169] *Subramanian v General Medical Council* [2002] UKPC 64; [2003] Lloyd's Rep. Med. 69 (appellant's conduct 20 years ago unlikely to affect credibility); *R. (on the application of Mahfouz) v General Medical Council* [2004] EWCA Civ 233; [2004] Lloyd's Rep. Med. 377.

Partisan views on a particular issue

Another situation in which attitudes may amount to bias concerns the **10–054**
expression of partisan views on a particular issue. Thus a judge's comments
on the ECHR may disqualify him from hearing a case on that subject
again.[170] Extra-judicial writings, depending of course on how expressed,
may also raise an implication of bias.[171]

SITUATIONS WHERE BIAS WILL NOT APPLY

Waiver

A party may waive his objections to a decision-maker who would otherwise **10–055**
be disqualified on the ground of bias.[172] Objection is generally deemed to
have been waived if the party or his legal representative knew of the
disqualification and acquiesced in the proceedings by failing to take
objection at the earliest practicable opportunity.[173] But there is no presumption of waiver if the disqualified adjudicator failed to make a
complete disclosure of his interest,[174] or if the party affected was prevented
by surprise from taking the objection at the appropriate time[175] or if he was
unrepresented by counsel and did not know of his right to object at the
time.[176]

Since one of the objectives of the principle against bias is that public **10–056**
confidence should be preserved in the administration of justice, caution
must be exercised in resting the decision in one of the parties, especially if
the case affects the broader public. This fundamental point was observed in
New Zealand.[177]

Sometimes the declaration of interest by the decision-maker is done in an **10–057**
informal way at the beginning of the hearing and counsel to the claimant
may put informal pressure on him not to seek a replacement. The question

---

[170] *Hoekstra v HM Advocate (No.3)* 2000 J.C. 391.
[171] *Timmins v Gormley* (one of the Locabail appeals) [2000] Q.B. 451; [2000] 2 W.L.R. 870.
[172] *R. (Giant's Causeway, etc. Tramway Co) v Antrim Justices* [1895] 2 I.R. 603.
[173] *R. v Byles* (1912) 77 J.P 40. In *R. v Richmond Justices* (1860) 24 J.P 422 and *Ex p. Ilchester Parish* (1861) 25 J.P 56 it was held that an applicant for certiorari had to specify in his affidavits that neither he nor his advocate knew of the objection at the time of the hearing or acquiesced in it. But should such an omission ought to be so seriously regarded? *cf. R. v Essex Justices* [1927] 2 K.B. 475. See also *R. v Lilydale Magistrates' Court Ex p. Ciccone* [1973] V.R. 122 at 131–136 where the authorities are reviewed.
[174] *R. v Cumberland Justices* (1882) 52 J.P 502.
[175] *R. (Harrington) v Clare County Justices* [191812 I.R. 116.
[176] *R. v Essex Justices Ex p. Perkins* [1927] 2 K.B. 475.
[177] *Auckland Casino Ltd v Casino Control Authority* [1995] 1 N.Z.L.R. 142 (although confronted with an agonising choice, the party ultimately complaining in that case had waived the objection by delaying until the decision was known. It was accepted, however, that displays of blatant bias, likely to undermine public confidence in the justice system, should not necessarily be capable of private waiver; while in criminal cases private waiver should not normally be possible at all); B. Toy-Cronin, "Waiver of the Rule Against Bias" (2002) 9 Auckland U. L. Rev. 850.

in such a case is whether the claimant acted freely and in full knowledge of the facts relevant to the decision whether or not to waive. In *Jones v Das Legal Expenses* Ward L.J., for the Court of Appeal, laid down a five-point check list for the guidance of the court in such situations,[178] the "vital requirements" of which were summarised in a subsequent case by Lord Phillips of Matravers C.J. as "that the party waiving should be aware of all material facts, of the consequences of the choice open to him, and given a fair opportunity to reach an un-pressured decision".[179] In *Jones* it was held that, in all the circumstances, the claimant had waived his right but in *Smith*[180] it was held that the appellant had not waived his rights as he was not told when the trial could take place before another judge (and was wrongly urged by his counsel not to object on the ground of costs).

10–058   Cases have raised the question of the proper behaviour expected of an inspector following a planning inquiry.[181] There is little doubt that an inspector who accepts hospitality or a lift to the site visit from one party in the absence of the other would be disqualified for bias, but this would not be the case where the inspector had asked sought and obtained the consent of the parties.[182]

Necessity

10–059   There are two ways in which the doctrine of "necessity" has been held to apply. First, if the person who makes the decision is biased, but cannot effectively be replaced, e.g. if a quorum cannot be formed without him.[183] Secondly, where the administrative structure makes it inevitable that there is an appearance of bias.

---

[178] *Jones v Das Legal Expenses Insurance Co Ltd* [2003] EWCA Civ 1071; [2004] I.R.L.R. 218 at [35]:(i) the first step involves the judge seeking a replacement if possible. If this is not possible then (ii) time should be taken to prepare a full explanation of the extent of bias that will be explained to the parties; (iii) to avoid controversy and the matter becoming a "festering sore" the explanation should be carefully recorded; (iv) a full explanation should be given to the parties as to matters which might give rise to possible conflict of interest and the possibilities of moving the case; (v) the options should be explained to the parties, including seeking the judge's recusal; (vi) the time for reflection should be established, if necessary providing help to the claimant to seek advice.
[179] *Smith v Kvaerner Cementation Foundations Ltd* [2006] EWCA Civ 242; [2007] 1 W.L.R. 370 at [29].
[180] *Smith* [2006] EWCA Civ 242; [2007] 1 W.L.R. 370 at [35]–[38].
[181] *Fox v Secretary of State for the Environment and Dover DC* [1993] J.P.L. 448; *Cottrell v Secretary of State for the Environment* [1991] J.P.L. 1155; *Halifax Building Society v Secretary of State for the Environment* [1983] J.PL. 816.
[182] *Fox* [1993] J.P.L. 448 and *Cottrell* [1991] J.P.L. 1155.
[183] *cf.* Lamond, "Of Interest as a Disqualification in Judges" (1907) 23 S.L.R. 152–153, citing a Scottish case of 1744 where withdrawal of the interested judges would have left the court without a quorum; and R. Tracey, "Disqualified Adjudicators: The Doctrine of Necessity in Public Law" [1982] P.L. 628.

Illustrations

- If proceedings were brought against all the superior judges, they **10–060** would have to sit as judges in their own cause.[184] In such a situation, a judge may even, in theory, be obliged to hear a case in which he has a pecuniary interest.[185]

- Similarly, a colonial governor could validly assent in the Queen's name to a Bill indemnifying him against the legal consequences of his own conduct, since there was no other officer who could have done so.[186] In such cases it is not possible for the matter to be delegated to another or others, or the tribunal to be reconstituted. The doctrine of necessity therefore applies to prevent a failure of justice overall.

- What if a minister were called upon to decide whether or not to confirm an order made by a local authority affecting his own property? As we have seen in Chapter 5, he could not lawfully transfer or delegate to another minister his duty to decide.[187] He might depute one of his own officials to make the decision, but the decision would nevertheless be made in the minister's name. If it were possible to show that the minister had taken into account his own interests, then the decision could be challenged for the taking into account of an irrelevant consideration, or for bad faith,[188] but otherwise it might be difficult to assert that the minister was judge in his own cause; for the legal duty to decide the matter had been cast upon him, and upon him alone.[189]

- The doctrine of necessity was applied in a case where inspectors authorised by the Secretary of State for Trade investigated the affairs of a company of which the applicant was chairman, and some of the same inspectors had previously investigated another company of which he was chairman. It was held that the terms of the inspectors' powers inevitably permitted them to have "suspicions" about the applicant's conduct.[190]

[184] 2 Roll.Abr. 93, pl.6; and 16 Vin.Abr. (2nd edn), 573 *et seq.*, citing 15th-century cases.
[185] *Great Charte v Kennington* (1742) 2 Str. 1173; *R. v Essex Justices* (1816) 5 M. & S. 513; *Grand Junction Canal Co v Dimes* (1849) 12 Beav. 63; *Dimes v Grand Junction Canal Proprietors* (1852) 3 H.L.C. 759 at 778–779, *Ranger v Great Western Ry* (1854) 5 H.L.C. 72, 88.
[186] *Phillips v Eyre* (1870) L.R. 6 Q.B. 1; and *The Judges v Attorney General for Saskatchewan* (1937) 53 T.L.R. 464 (judges required to rule on the constitutionality of legislation rendering them liable to pay more income tax); *Willing v Hollobone (No.2)* (1975) 11 S.A.S.R. 118 (magistrates not disqualified for bias, inter alia, because the ground applied to all magistrates); *Re Caccamo and Minister of Manpower and Immigration* (1977) 75 D.L.R. (3rd) 720 (disqualification applicable to all immigration officers).
[187] See 5–135 *et seq.* But most legislation nowadays avoids specifying which minister should exercise powers, referring instead to the "Secretary of State", which is a single office (see 3–003); presumably in such circumstances another Secretary of State could exercise the power for his colleague.
[188] See 5–110 *et seq.* (irrelevant considerations); 5–080 *et seq.* (bad faith).
[189] *cf. Auten v Rayner* [1958] 1 W.L.R. 1300.
[190] *R. v Secretary of State for Trade Ex p. Perestrello* [1981] 1 Q.B. 19.

- On the other hand, where a board of prison visitors found a prisoner guilty of having a controlled drug in his cell, and the prisoner alleged the presence of bias because the chairman of the board had been a member of a local review committee which had earlier considered the prisoner's release on licence under the parole system, the application was dismissed because the functions of the board of visitors were such that they would inevitably have considerable knowledge of a prisoner charged with a disciplinary offence.[191]

10–061 The doctrine of necessity has been sparingly employed, and if possible the decision-making body should remove that part of it which is infected with bias (for example, by the recusal of those members of a disciplinary committee who had been a part of a previous sub-committee which decided to institute proceedings against the claimant).[192] Alternatively, where possible the body should be reconstituted (e.g. by constituting a separate panel). However, as we have seen, this is not always possible.

10–062 Since the Human Rights Act 1998, the doctrine of necessity may become difficult to assert in the face of a *right* to an independent and impartial tribunal under Art.6(1) ECHR.[193] In *Kingsley v United Kingdom*[194] it was argued that the Gaming Board could not be impartial in its decision to revoke the applicant's certificate of approval for a management position, having already previously taken the view that the claimant was not a "fit and proper person" to be director of a casino company. Although it was held that there was not unconscious bias in that case, it was stated that had there been such bias the doctrine of necessity would apply as the decision could only be taken by the Gaming Board and delegation to any other body would be unlawful.

10–063 When *Kingsley* was argued before the ECtHR[195] it is noteworthy that counsel for the government argued that the doctrine of necessity was not applicable to a case where the allegation was one of actual bias. The argument that the doctrine did apply to cases of apparent bias, however, failed. The Court was critical of the fact that English courts did not have the power ("full jurisdiction")[196] either to remit the matter for a fresh decision by a differently composed decision-making tribunal, or to decide the matter themselves.

10–064 Since the government has already conceded, in Kingsley, that necessity should not excuse actual bias, it would not be a far step to concede that apparent bias should similarly not be condoned. In order to do this, they would have to employ radical means to avoid apparent bias, at least where an individual's right to an independent and impartial tribunal is in issue.[197]

---

[191] *R. v Board of Visitors of Frankland Prison Ex p. Lewis* [1986]1 W.L.R. 130.
[192] As in *P (A Barrister) v General Council of the Bar* [2005] 1 W.L.R. 3019.
[193] See 10–082 *et seq.*
[194] [1996] C.O.D. 178.
[195] (2001) 33 E.R.H.H. 288.
[196] For the ECtHR's position to the procedures of judicial review, see 10–082 *et seq.*
[197] This may not apply to some of the examples mentioned above, e.g. where judicial salaries are the subject of litigation.

Where there is no possibility of removing the bias by lawfully constituting another tribunal under the relevant statutory scheme, the courts may now have to declare the scheme itself incompatible[198] with Art. 6(1), or perhaps even exercise their power to decide the matter themselves.[199]

Policy and bias

Closely related to the doctrine of necessity is that which permits decision- **10–065** makers to exhibit certain kinds of bias in the exercise of their judgment or discretion on matters of public policy. Ordinary members of legislative bodies are entitled, and sometimes expected, to show political bias. They ought not to show personal bias, or to participate in deliberations on a matter in respect of which they have a private pecuniary or a proprietary interest, but their participation in such circumstances may not in itself affect the validity of a legislative instrument.[200]

Where a councillor had previously indicated his opposition in general to **10–066** the existence of sex establishments, he was not disqualified from sitting on a panel to license sex establishments,[201] provided he gave genuine consideration to the decision.[202] Nor was a minister disqualified from determining a planning application on a site where he had previously (as a Member of Parliament) supported an opponent of planning permission.[203]

However, if the personal interests of members participating in a decision **10–067** affecting individual rights or interests (such as a decision to grant planning permission) preclude them from acting fairly, the decision can be declared to be invalid.[204] It has been held, however, that a builder was not disqualified from sitting on a local authority planning committee on the ground of his being a commercial rival of the applicant for planning permission.[205]

When an authority is expressly empowered to make a provisional **10–068** decision, and is then empowered to entertain representations or consider objections against it with a view to deciding whether or not to give it final

---

[198] HRA, s.4; see 13–045.
[199] Under the CPR r.54.19(3), discussed at 18–03 (suggested by I. Leigh, "Bias, Necessity and Convention Rights" [2002] P.L. 407). Such an innovation may now be more difficult since the amendment of Supreme Court Act (Senior Court Act) 1981 s.31(5)—see Appendix D.
[200] If a member of the House of Commons votes on a matter on which he has a private pecuniary interest, his vote may be disallowed; but the rule is not at all exacting, and no vote has been disallowed on such a ground since the 19th century: Erskine May, *Parliamentary Practice* (23rd edn), pp.492. For the duties of local authority members and officers to declare pecuniary interests, see 10–022.
[201] *R. v Reading BC Ex p. Quietlynn Ltd* (1987) 85 L.G.R. 387; *R. v Tower Hamlets LBC Ex p. Khatun* (1995) 27 H.L.R. 465, CA (an interview regarding intentional homelessness not flawed as conducted by council employee aware of local housing conditions.)
[202] See also *R. v Chesterfield BC Ex p. Darker Enterprises Ltd* [1992] C.O.D. 466.
[203] *London and Clydeside Estates Ltd v Secretary of State for Scotland* 1987 S.L.T. 459; see also *CREED N.Z.* (1981) N.Z.L.R. 172.
[204] *R. v Hendon RDC Ex p. Chorley* [1933] 2 K.B. 696 (certiorari issued to quash a grant of planning permission vitiated by a councillor's pecuniary interest).
[205] *R. v Holderness DC Ex p. James Roberts Developments Ltd* (1993) 157 L.G.R. 643 (Butler-Sloss L.J. considered that architects or surveyors would also not be disqualified in these circumstances).

effect, it is absurd to expect that authority to be totally impartial between itself and the objectors; the authority is naturally likely to be biased in favour of the proposal that it has initiated.[206]

10–069   Members of tribunals exercising discretionary regulatory powers, such as planning inspectors, will normally be entitled, indeed expected, to adopt and follow general policy guidelines. These guidelines will influence their decisions in individual cases. But by announcing their intention to follow those guidelines they ought not, in general, to be regarded as disqualified for bias unless they have committed themselves so firmly to the implementation of those policies as to make it impracticable for them to deal fairly with subsequent cases on their merits.[207]

10–070   In some situations those who have to make decisions can hardly insulate themselves from the general ethos of their organisation or institution; they are likely to have firm views about the proper regulation of its affairs, and they will often be familiar with the issues and the conduct of the parties before they assume their role as adjudicators. Licensing justices have been held entitled to bring their local knowledge to bear on their decisions, including information they may have obtained about an applicant during a previous hearing.[208] Applications of the rules against interest and bias must be tempered with realism; educational institutions, trades unions, clubs and even professional associations are apt to present special problems and it may be right to require evidence of actual bias, rather than mere danger of bias, before a decision is set aside by a court in these settings.[209]

10–071   The normal standards of impartiality applied in an adjudicative setting cannot meaningfully be applied to a body entitled to initiate a proposal and then to decide whether to proceed with it in the face of objections. What standards should be imposed on the Secretary of State for the Environment when he has to decide whether or not to confirm a compulsory purchase order or clearance order made by a local authority or to approve a local planning authority's structure plan or to allow an appeal against refusal of planning permission? It would be inappropriate for the courts to insist on his maintaining the lofty detachment required of a judicial officer determining a dispute between the parties.[210] The Secretary of State's decisions

[206] As in *Franklin v Minister of Town and Country Planning* [1948] A.C. 87.
[207] On fettering of discretion, see Ch.9; on government policy as a material or relevant consideration, see 5–073 *et seq.*
[208] *R. v Crown Court at Bristol Ex p. Cooper* [1990] 1 W.L.R. 1031.
[209] But see a case where latitudinariasm was carried too far: *Ward v Bradford Corp* (1971) 70 L.G.R. Cf. *Hannam v Bradford Corp* [1970] 1 W.L.R. 937, CA (three out of 10 members of Education Authority Committee governors of school from which applicant dismissed. Held: disqualification because of real likelihood of bias); *Rees v Crane* [1994] 2 A.C. 173 (PC thought it right to take into account the distinguished nature of the members of the Judicial and Legal Service Commission and say of them that "their professional backgrounds are such that an assumption of bias should not be lightly made").
[210] A point conceded by implication by the report of the Franks Committee on Administrative Tribunals and Enquiries (Cmnd. 218 (1957)), pp.5, 59–61, 88–83; *cf.* views of the Committee on Ministers' Powers (Cmd. 4060 (1932)), p.78 on disqualification for "departmental bias".

can seldom be wrenched entirely from their context and viewed in isolation from his governmental responsibilities.[211]

In some situations it will even be perfectly proper for a public body to **10–072** make a particular decision for its own pecuniary advantage (as distinct from the pecuniary advantage of individual members or officers). It has been held to be a "material" planning consideration that the developer will contribute some of the profits of the development to a benefit or advantage for the local community.[212] However, in *Steeples v Derbyshire CC*[213] a local planning authority had entered into an agreement with a developer which provided that the authority would be liable for liquidated damages if it failed to use its "best endeavours" to procure planning permissions. The decision was invalidated on the ground of bias.[214] Later cases, however, have made it clear that the courts will not lightly interfere with a planning decision made on the basis of a predetermined policy so long as the authority gives genuine consideration to the application. Thus where the majority party group had met and decided in advance to support an application for a development, it was held that the members of the group were not disqualified from subsequently sitting on the committee which determined the application. Politics was held to play so large a part in local government that, if disqualification was to be avoided, the planning committee would have had to adopt impractical standards.[215] Other cases have held that a local authority was not disqualified from granting a planning permission on a site in which the authority had an interest where the decision was properly considered, was by no means a foregone

---

[211] *Re Manchester (Ringway Airport) Compulsory Purchase Order* (1935) 153 L.T. 219. For the apparent bias of a minister confirming an enforcement of planning law following a hearing at a public inquiry see the discussion below of *R. v Secretary of State for the Environment, Transport and the Regions Ex p. Holdings & Barnes Plc* [2001] UKHL 23; [2003] 2 A.C. 295 ("the Alconbury case").

[212] See, e.g. *R. v Westminster City Council Ex p. Monahan* [1990] 1 Q.B. 87; see 5–084 *et seq.* on the limits of "planning gain".

[213] [1984] 3 All E.R. 468.

[214] *cf. Lower Hutt City Council v Bank* [1974] 1 N.Z.L.R. 545 (council had precluded itself from fairly considering objections to its own proposed scheme by entering into a contract to carry out the work contemplated by the scheme).

[215] *R. v Amber Valley DC Ex p. Jackson* [1985] 1 W.L.R. 298; and *R. v Waltham Forest LBC Ex p. Baxter* [1988] Q.B. 419 (local authority councillor entitled to give weight to views of party colleagues and party whip but could not abdicate responsibility by voting blindly in support of party policy. On the evidence, discretion not fettered by party whip). In *R. v Secretary of State for the Environment Ex p. Kirkstall Valley Campaign Ltd* [1996] 3 All E.R. 304 Sedley J. carefully considered to what extent participation in proceedings would amount to bias. He concluded that the person need not necessarily withdraw from discussion, but it would be "wise advice" to do so. See also *R. v Buckinghamshire CC Ex p. Milton Keynes BC* (1997) 9 Admin. L.R. 159 (Conservative party members had not been "instructed" to vote, on proposals for the establishment of a grammar school, in a manner inconsistent with what was lawfully allowed in the interest of party unity as set out in *Baxter*); and *R. (on the application of Island Farm Development Ltd) v Bridgend CBC* [2006] EWHC 2189.

conclusion[216] and the council had not acted in such a way that it "could not exercise proper discretion".[217]

10–073   Despite the latitude given to policy decisions, it should be remembered that four other principles of public law remain in play. First, the person or tribunal holding an inquiry into the matter may not ignore the other part of procedural fairness, namely, the granting of a fair hearing. Thus the procedural protections considered above[218] would still apply in an appropriate case. Secondly, the "no fettering doctrine" would apply.[219] The policy could therefore not be applied rigidly, and the decision-maker will still be required not to shut his ears to someone with something new to say. Any inquiry must genuinely take into account the argument presented.[220] On the other hand, where a previous commitment to a development was reversed when a new party gained control of the council, their previous opposition to the proposal was held to be a legitimate "predisposition" rather than an unlawful "predetermination".[221]

10–074   Thirdly, the body will not be able to pursue powers outside of the statutory purposes conferred upon it. In *Magill v Porter*,[222] the Conservative party leaders of Westminster City Council pursued a policy of increasing the number of owner-occupiers. The policy was directed to marginal wards and its purpose was to encourage votes for the Conservative Party in future elections—a purpose which was held to unlawful.

10–075   Fourthly, it is no longer the case that the full rigours of procedural safeguards are reserved only for decisions that are "judicial". Although this distinction was firmly scotched in the 1960s[223] in relation to the *audi alteram partem* (hear both sides) principle, it rears its head from time to time in relation to bias.[224] However, as Sedley J. has pointed out, "in the modern state the interests of individuals or of the public may be more radically affected by administrative decisions than by the decisions of courts of law and judicial tribunals".[225] The fact that the body is "admin-

---

[216] *R. v Sevenoaks DC Ex p. Terry* [1985] 3 All E.R. 226; *R. v St Edmundsbury BC Ex p. Investors in Industry Commercial Properties Ltd* [1985] 3 All E.R. 234; *R. v Carlisle City Council Ex p. Cumbrian Co-operative Society Ltd* (1985) 276 E.G. 1161; [19861 J.PL. 206; *R. v Merton LBC Ex p. Burnett* [19901 P.L.R. 72; [19901 J.P.L. 354; *R. v Canterbury CC Ex p. Springimage Ltd* [1995] J.P.L. 20.

[217] *Terry* [1985] 3 All E.R. 226 at 233 (Glidewell J.). This test was followed in *R. v City of Wakefield MDC and British Coal Corp Ex p. Warmfield Co Ltd* [1994] J.P.L. 341.

[218] See Chs 7–8.

[219] See Ch.9.

[220] Cases where the matter was held unlawfully predetermined by closed minds include: *Bovis Homes Ltd v New Forest Plc* [2002] EWCH 483 (Admin); *R. (on the application of Partingdale Residents Association) v Barnet LBC* [2005] EWHC 947 (Admin), citing *Lower Hutt* [1974] 1 N.Z.L.R. 545; *Georgiu v Enfield LBC* [2004] EWHC 779 (Richards J.'s statements in *Georgiu* on bias at [35]–[36] doubted by Collins J. in at [30]).

[221] *R. (on the application of Island Farm Development Ltd) v Bridgend CBC* [2006] EWHC 2189; [2007] B.L.G.R. 60.

[222] [2001] UKHL 67; [2002] 2 A.C. 357.

[223] *Ridge v Baldwin* [1964] A.C. 40; and see Appendix B.

[224] See, e.g. *R. v Reading BC Ex p. Quietlynn Ltd* (1986) 85 L.G.R. 387.

[225] *R. v Secretary of State for the Environment Ex p. Kirkstall Valley Campaign Ltd* [1996] 3 All E.R. 304, at 323.

istrative" rather than judicial or quasi-judicial has therefore been rejected in favour of one that looks at the "particular nature and function of the body whose decision is impugned".[226] Even in a situation, therefore, where the application of policy is being decided in a non-judicial setting, the decision will be struck down if, in the circumstances of the case, its outcome has been "predetermined whether by adoption of an inflexible policy or by the effective surrender of the body's independent judgment".[227]

Finally, it should be noted that many decisions require a consideration of **10–076** fact, judgement and policy. For example, a decision whether to enforce against a breach of planning law may require the decision-maker to determine whether a building's use has been changed to another (a question of fact); whether that use is suitable to be carried out in that area (a question of planning judgment) and whether wider questions of public policy dictate the need to enforce the law against the change of use (a question of policy). As we shall see in the section below, it has been an article of faith in this country that ministers accountable to Parliament should ultimately be charged with deciding matters of policy, despite the fact that they are predisposed in favour of their policies. A wholly independent and judicialised tribunal would therefore be wanting in terms both of expertise and democratic accountability. To what extent that approach can be sustained under ECHR Art.6 of the ECHR will now be considered.

ARTICLE 6 ECHR

We have seen that fair procedures in the United Kingdom are now **10–077** governed not only by the common law but also by the provisions of Art.6 ECHR under the Human Rights Act 1998. Chapter 13 deals more fully with Convention rights, but a short summary is necessary here of the way that Art.6 requirements relate to the common law and, in turn, how the common law has been, and may in the future be influenced by Art.6.[228] Article 6(1) requires "a fair and public hearing" only in circumstances where there has been "determination of [a person's] civil rights and obligations, or any criminal charge", a matter considered in Chapter 7.[229] Questions arise therefore of what is meant by "civil rights and obligations", and whether, or to what extent decisions of a policy nature (the issue discussed in the previous section) come within that definition. If so, what are the ingredients of independence and impartiality required by the ECHR? If the requirement is a judicial-style tribunal, then this causes

---

[226] At 320.
[227] At 321.
[228] P. Craig, "The Human Rights Act, Art.6 and Procedural Rights" [2003] P.L. 753.
[229] On which, see 7–032.

problems for the many decision-making bodies to make decisions involving policy, from the Minister deciding whether to grant or refuse planning permission to other decisions taken by committees of local authority politicians, discussed above.

10–078   This issue came before the House of Lords in the Alconbury litigation.[230] The decision in question was that of the minister, considering an appeal against a decision of a local authority to enforce a breach of planning law. The Minister would act on the advice of a planning inspector (an official), who had heard the appeal in accordance with fair procedures, but two local groups objected to the Minister deciding the matter as he was not considered by them to be "independent or impartial" because of his prior commitment to policies which were predisposed to enforcement in that case.

10–079   It was held that since this decision involved substantial considerations of "policy" and "public interest" (or, in the words of the ECtHR, "expediency") it did not need to be taken by a judicial-style tribunal—indeed it was desirable that the decision be made by a public official responsible to Parliament. As Lord Nolan put it, to hand over those policy functions to an "independent and impartial body with no central electoral accountability would not only be a recipe for chaos: it would be profoundly undemocratic".[231] However, in accordance both with common law principles about bias, and Art.6, the overall decision-making process (including the prior investigation of the facts by a departmental Inspector) had provided adequate procedural safeguards (particularly as the facts found by the Inspector must be accepted by the Minister unless he had notified the objectors and given them an opportunity to make representations[232]). In addition, it was held that, as had been accepted by the ECtHR in the *Bryan* case,[233] the fact-finding procedures of any subsequent judicial review of the Minister's decision provided a "sufficiency of review", especially as they permitted review for lack of evidence or ignorance of an established and relevant fact.[234]

10–080   In a subsequent case, *Tower Hamlets LBC v Begum (Runa)*[235] the House of Lords considered a decision by a local authority as to whether accommodation offered to the appellant was "suitable". The decision was reviewed by a rehousing officer in the same local authority. This issue was held to involve a determination of "civil rights and obligations" but it was also held that the reviewing officer need not be an independent tribunal exercising full judicial powers.[236] This was because questions of fact were

---

[230] *R. v Secretary of State for the Environment, Transport and the Regions Ex p. Holdings & Barnes Plc* [2001] UKHL 23; [2003] 2 A.C. 295.
[231] At [60]; see also Lord Hoffmann at [128]: "The Human Rights Act 1998 no doubt intended to strengthen the rule of law but not to inaugurate the rule of lawyers."
[232] Town and Country Planning (Inquiries Procedure) (England) Rules 2000 r.17(5).
[233] In *Bryan v UK* (1996) 21 E.H.R.R. 342 holding that judicial review provides "full jurisdiction" and thus has a curative effect on any procedural defects of the primary decision.
[234] See 11–041 *et seq.*
[235] [2003] UKHL 5; [2003] 2 A.C. 430.
[236] Lord Bingham, at [5] considered that a flexible approach ought to be taken in such a case "if emasculation (by over-judicialisation) of administrative welfare schemes is to be avoided".

only part of broader considerations concerning local conditions and requiring specialist knowledge and experience. In addition, the review process contained adequate procedural safeguards that the applicant's representations would be taken into account. Finally, it was held that an appeal to a county court of the reviewing officer's decision would provide sufficiency of review, as accepted in *Bryan*. Lord Hoffmann also considered that in schemes of social welfare the values of "efficient administration and the sovereignty of Parliament" entitled Parliament to take the view "that it is not in the public interest that an excessive proportion of the funds available for a welfare scheme should be consumed in administration and legal disputes".

Neither the utilitarian considerations raised by Lord Hoffmann in **10–081** *Begum*, nor the arguments accepted there and in *Alconbury* in favour of the non-judicialisation of the respective decision-making schemes was held by the High Court to apply to a scheme to review challenges to decisions by a local authority on the entitlement of housing and other benefit.[237] The decision in question was reviewed by a Board known as the Housing Benefit and Council Tax Benefit Review Board consisting of three councillors from the same council which had made the initial decision, advised by a lawyer from the council's legal department.[238] Moses J. held that the situation was different from that of *Alconbury*, as the judgment was not largely based upon matters of policy but upon a finding of fact.[239] In addition, in such a case the court on judicial review exercised "only limited control" as it could not substitute its views as to the weight of evidence. The "curative" effect of judicial review was thus inadequate and could not "replenish the want of independence in the Review Board, caused by its connection to a party in the dispute".

In *Tsfayo v United Kingdom*,[240] the ECtHR considered the proceedings **10–082** of the same Board's decision as to whether the appellant had "good cause" for delay in submitting an application for benefit. It was held that the Board's lack of structural independence (on the ground that it was directly connected to one of the parties to the dispute) amounted to a violation of Art.6(1). *Bryan* was distinguished both by the fact that it did not involve a determination of civil rights and by the fact that, although it did involve

---

[237] *R. (on the application of Bewry) v Norwich CC* [2001] EWHC Admin 657; [2002] H.R.L.R. 2.

[238] The Board, criticised by the Council on Tribunals, has now been replaced. *Bewry* was followed, even after the HL judgment in *Begum* in *R. (on the application of Bono) v Harlow DC* [2002] EWHC 423; [2002] 1 W.L.R. 2475.

[239] In *Begum* [2003] UKHL 5; [2003] 2 A.C. 430, Lord Bingham at [7]–[8] similarly said that although judicial review allows review for lack of evidence or for a misunderstanding or ignorance of an established fact, the "judge may not make fresh findings of fact and must accept apparently tenable conclusions on credibility made on behalf of the authority". Lord Hoffmann however suggested that a full appeal is no different from review in that respect, as "it is not easy for an appellate tribunal which has not itself seen the witnesses to differ from the decision-maker on questions of primary fact, and more especially . . . on questions of credibility" (at 47).

[240] [2007] B.L.G.R. 1; see 8–031.

some fact-finding, the Inspector was called upon "to exercise his discretion on a wide range of policy matters"[241] and it was those policy judgments, rather than the findings of primary fact, that were challenged in that case. In contrast, in *Tsfayo* the Board "was deciding a simple question of fact", unlike both *Bryan* and *Begum* where "the issues to be determined required a measure of professional knowledge or experience and the exercise of administrative discretion pursuant to wider policy aims".[242] It was also held that the central issue of fact was not open to a "sufficiency of review" because, despite the power of the High Court to quash the decision if its findings were plainly untenable, or if it had misunderstood or been ignorant of an established and relevant fact, "it did not have jurisdiction to rehear the evidence or substitute its own views as to the applicant's credibility".[243]

10–083 　As we have seen, it has been suggested that our common law standards relating to bias and those under Art.6 are the same.[244] There certainly is no significant difference between them and they are likely in any event to converge. In situations where what is being decided is an entitlement or right[245] or matter of factual determination,[246] it is clear that both standards require the absence of apparent bias. In the area of policy-making,[247] or decisions which require special expertise or professional knowledge, it seems that the lack of structural independence will still be tolerated in English law for reasons that these qualities are necessary to determine questions of the public interest, provided of course that other public law principles are observed.

10–084 　After *Tsfayo*, however, we can be less sure that utilitarian arguments (e.g. about the cost of providing appeal mechanisms)[248] against the establishment of judicial-style tribunals will, or ought any longer to prevail in respect of many decisions so far regarded as involving at least a substantial element of policy-making. Similar doubts apply to the doctrine of necessity.[249] Clearly the greater the element of fact-finding, the more judicialised should the tribunal be. However, when the relevant decision depends for its outcome upon a finding of fact, then the availability of judicial review may no longer prove sufficient to "cure" any defects in the structure of the primary decision-making process—at least so long as our judicial review does not permit the rehearing of evidence or the substitution of its own view of the facts.[250]

[241] At para.42.
[242] At para.44.
[243] At [47].
[244] See n.7 above and *Kataria v Essex Strategic Health Authority* [2004] EWHC 641; [2004] 3 All E.R. 572 at [46] (Stanley Burnton J.).
[245] See 10–079–10–080.
[246] As in *Tsfayo* [2007] B.L.G.R. 1.
[247] As in *R. (on the application of Cummins) v Camden LBC* [2001] EWHC (Admin) 1116.
[248] As suggested by Lord Hoffmann in *Begum* [2003] UKHL 5; [2003] 2 A.C. 430.
[249] J. Howell, "Alconbury Crumbles" [2007] J.R. 9.
[250] For a further discussion of inadequate factual basis of decisions see 11–041 *et seq*.

COMPARATIVE PERSPECTIVES

Australia

Both at common law and under the Administrative Decisions (Judicial **10–085**
Review) Act 1977,[251] the test is not whether there is actual bias but
whether there is an *appearance* of bias. Following *Webb v The Queen*,[252] in
Ebner v Official Trustee in Bankruptcy the High Court of Australia stated
that the test was whether a "fair-minded lay observer might reasonably
apprehend that the judge might not bring an impartial mind to the
resolution of the question the judge is required to decide".[253] This test is to
be applied to bias whether arising from interest, conduct, association,
extraneous information or some other circumstance.[254] The court elaborated on the application of the test and articulated a two step application:
(a) the identification of what it is said might lead a judge (or juror) to
decide a case other than on its legal and factual merits; and (b) there must
be an articulation of the logical connection between the matter and the
feared deviation from the course of deciding the case on its merits.[255] In
Smits v Roach[256] the High Court affirmed the basic principles of
apprehended bias as articulated in *Ebner* with particular emphasis on the
importance of the second limb of the test. The court also considered
whether waiver had occurred and held that, having regard to counsel's role
in the conduct of litigation, there was no distinction between the
knowledge of counsel and their clients.[257] The test has been modified for
administrative proceedings held in private to a "hypothetical fair-minded
lay person who is properly informed as to the nature of proceedings . . .
and the conduct which is said to give rise to the . . . bias" rather than by
reference to the "fair-minded lay observer".[258]

Automatic disqualification

Until the decision in *Ebner*, an automatic disqualification rule applied, **10–086**
irrespective of an appearance of bias, if the decision-maker was a member
of the judiciary with a direct *pecuniary interest* in the outcome of the
decision. However, *Ebner* held that there is no free-standing automatic
disqualification rule and each case will depend upon the application of the
fair-minded lay observer test.[259]

---

[251] ss.5(1)(a) and 6(1)(a).
[252] (1994) 181 C.L.R. 41, discussed at 10–016.
[253] *Ebner v Official Trustee in Bankruptcy* (2000) 205 C.L.R. 337 at 345.
[254] *Ebner* (2000) 205 C.L.R. 337 at 350.
[255] *Ebner* (2000) 205 C.L.R. 337 at [8].
[256] (2006) 228 A.L.R. 262.
[257] *Smits v Roach* (2006) 228 A.L.R. 262 at [45]–[49].
[258] *Re Refugee Tribunal; Ex p. H* (2001) 179 A.L.R. 425.
[259] *Ebner* (2000) 205 C.L.R. 337 at 351. Kirby J. dissented and has reaffirmed his position in
Hot Holdings Pty Ltd v Creasy (2002) 210 C.L.R. 438 at 474.

Canada

10–087 The standard test in Canada for bias remains that articulated by de Grandpré J. in his dissenting judgment in *Committee for Justice and Liberty v National Energy Board*:[260]

> "[T]he apprehension must be a reasonable one, held by reasonable and right-minded people, applying themselves to the question and obtaining thereon the required information. In the words of the Court of Appeal, that test is "what would an informed person, viewing the matter realistically and practically—and having thought the matter through—conclude.""

10–088 However, as a consequence of the lowering of the procedural fairness threshold, the Supreme Court has recognised that the standard is a contextual one and more difficult to establish in the case of members of regulatory bodies with broad policy-making functions,[261] and municipal councillors even when exercising functions subject to a duty of procedural fairness.[262] In these contexts, the test is that of whether the person subject to challenge is "amenable to persuasion" in the sense of not having "a closed mind".

Lack of independence

10–089 Fuelled by the use of the term in both the Canadian Bill of Rights and the Charter of Rights and Freedoms, Canadian case law now recognises a lack of independence both in an institutional and personal sense as a ground of challenge.[263] The test for a lack of independence is a variant on the standard *National Committee for Justice and Liberty* test for bias. The key elements of institutional independence are security of tenure, financial security, and day to day administrative distance from the government or other parties. Once again, the extent to which these elements must be present is contextual.[264] Attacks based on a lack of institutional independence have surfaced in the context of the way in which a tribunal operates in practice or the terms of their rules of procedure.[265] However, they can

---

[260] [1978] 1 S.C.R. 369 at 394–395; and *Canadian Pacific Ltd v Matsqui Indian Band*, [1995] 1 S.C.R. 3; *Wewaykum Indian Band v Canada* [2003] 2 S.C.R. 259 (involving an allegation of bias against a judge of the Supreme Court). It remains unclear whether pecuniary bias has been subsumed within the general test or remains an automatic basis for disqualification provided the interest is non-trivial.

[261] *Newfoundland Telephone Co v Newfoundland (Board of Commissioners of Public Utilities)* [1992] 1 S.C.R. 623.

[262] *Old St Boniface Residents Assn Inc v Winnipeg (City)* [1990] 3 S.C.R. 1170; *Save Richmond Farmland Society v Richmond (Township)* [1990] 3 S.C.R. 1213.

[263] *2734–3174 Québec Inc v Québec (Régie des permis d'alcool)* [1996] 3 S.C.R. 919.

[264] *Ocean Port Hotel Ltd v British Columbia (General Manager, Liquor Control and Licensing Branch)* [2001] 2 S.C.R. 781.

[265] *Matsqui Indian Band* [1995] 1 S.C.R. 3; *Katz v Vancouver Stock Exchange* [1996] 3 S.C.R. 405; *Régie de permis d'alcool* [1996[3 S.C.R. 919.

also arise in the context of an attack on the tribunal's primary legislation by reference to the Charter of Rights and Freedoms ss.7 and 11, the Canadian Bill of Rights 1960 s.2(e)[266] and underlying constitutional principles.[267] It remains to be seen, however, the extent to which, if at all, the underlying constitutional principle of judicial independence applies to tribunals and provides a basis for an attack on their constitutive legislation.[268]

Automatic disqualification

In *Newfoundland Telephone* Co the Supreme Court accepted that bias was **10–090** automatically disqualifying and could not be cured by the tribunal's subsequent decision.[269] The hearing and any subsequent decision is void. Whether there are any kinds of interest that are automatically disqualifying without more is unclear.[270]

New Zealand

The test for bias in New Zealand is objective: "viewed through the eyes of **10–091** the reasonable observer aware of all the relevant circumstances".[271] In *Man O'War Station Ltd v Auckland City Council (No.1)*[272] the Privy Council was invited by counsel "to adopt for New Zealand the adjustment of the test in *Gough*" made in *Porter v Magill.*[273] The Privy Council did not think it right to accede to that request without the benefit of the view of the Court of Appeal on whether the New Zealand law should be so altered. Lord Steyn went on to say that the distinction between the tests is "a fine one". And, in any event, on the facts of this case, "the difference between the two tests cannot arguably influence the outcome". The unsuccessful appellants sought to overturn a Court of Appeal judgment on the ground that one of the judges who had decided the appeal should have disqualified himself for apparent bias. The basis for this claim was that the judge had been a very close friend and former partner of G, and G's son whom the judge knew but not very well was an important witness in the action. In addition, there had some business contact between their respective law and engineering firms over the years. The Court of Appeal, held that none of the factors put forward could seriously show a "real danger that the judge unfairly regarded the case of the [unsuccessful] appellant with disfavour when he participated as a member of the Court on appeal".[274] This judgment was

[266] *Bell Canada v Canadian Telephone Employees Association* [2003] 1 S.C.R. 884.
[267] *Charkaoui v Canada (Citizenship and Immigration)* 2007 S.C.C. 9.
[268] *Ocean Port* [2001] 2 S.C.R. 781; *Bell Canada* [2003] 1 S.C.R. 884.
[269] [1992] 1 S.C.R. 623.
[270] In *Wewaykum* [2003] 2 S.C.R. 259 at paras 70–71, the Court discusses *Locobail* and *Pinochet* but does not come to any definite conclusion.
[271] *Collier v Attorney General* [2002] N.Z.A.R. 257 at [22], CA.
[272] [2002] UKPC 28; [2002] 3 N.Z.L.R. 577.
[273] See n.162 above.
[274] [2000] 2 N.Z.L.R. 267 at [19].

upheld on appeal to the Privy Council. Lord Steyn concluded by saying "their Lordships are satisfied that no fair-minded observer could possibly have doubted the neutrality and objectivity" of the judge.[275]

10–092   In *Erris Promotions Ltd v Commissioner of Inland Revenue* the Court of Appeal pointed out the different vantage points adopted in the *Gough/Auckland Casino*[276] and *Webb/Porter*[277] tests and said in a case where this difference mattered it would be necessary to choose.[278] Anderson J. on behalf of the Court went on to suggest that when that time came a revised test might be: "Would the reasonably informed observer think that the impartiality of the adjudicator might be/might have been affected?" It was not necessary to decide in that case because even on the stricter *Gough/Auckland Casino* test the decision-maker should have recused himself.[279] In the only Supreme Court decision to address this matter, it was said "[w]hatever test of appearance of bias is appropriate in New Zealand", the bias argument had no chance of success on either test in that case.[280]

Automatic disqualification

10–093   While New Zealand law is moving closer to Australian law on the test for apparent bias, on the separate aspect of automatic disqualification for pecuniary interest the two jurisdictions now are poles apart. The dissent of Kirby J. in the High Court of Australia's decision in *Ebner*[281]—supporting continuation of automatic disqualification for financial interest where it is "direct" and not saved by the *de minimis* principle, is in line with the New Zealand position.[282]

South Africa

10–094   The test for bias in South African law has now authoritatively been set as a "reasonable suspicion" of bias.[283] The confusion at common law prior to this decision was whether the appropriate test was "a real likelihood" or a "reasonable suspicion" of bias.[284] The Promotion of Administrative Justice Act 2000 however, subsumes both of these approaches. Section 6(2)(a)(iii)

---

275 See n.272 above, at [11].
276 *Auckland Casino Ltd v Casino Control Authority* [1995] 1 N.Z.L.R. 142, CA.
277 See 10–016.
278 (2003) 16 P.R.N.Z. 1014 at [32].
279 See further Justice Noel Anderson, "The Appearance of Bias" (2005) 12 Waikato L.R. 1.
280 *Taunoa v Attorney General* [2006] N.Z.S.C. 94 at [5].
281 (2000) 205 C.L.R. 337.
282 *Auckland Casino Ltd v Casino Control Authority* [1995] 1 N.Z.L.R. 142, CA.
283 *BTR Industries South Africa v Metal and Allied Workers' Union* 1992 (3) S.A. 673 (A). This has since been confirmed by the Constitutional Court in *President of the Republic of South Africa v South African Rugby Football Union* 1999 (4) S.A. 147, CC and *S v Basson* 2005 (12) B.C.L.R. 1192, CC. Although this later case law deals with recusal of judges, the courts have noted that the factors relevant to the determination of bias in an administrative law setting are the same. See *Gold Fields Ltd v Connellan NO* [2005] 3 All S.A. 142 (W).
284 *City and Suburban Transport (Pty) Ltd v Local Board Road Transportation, Johannesburg* 1932 W.L.D. 100.

allows review of administrative decisions if the administrator taking the decision was "biased or reasonably suspected of bias". In the constitutional era the test has been formulated as follows:

"(1) There must be a suspicion that the judicial officer might, not would, be biased.
(2) The suspicion must be that of a reasonable person in the position of the accused or litigant.
(3) The suspicion must be based on reasonable grounds.
(4) The suspicion is one which the reasonable person referred to would, not might, have".[285]

Hoexter considers that the preference of the Constitutional Court for the term "apprehension" of bias over " "suspicion" is not significant.[286] There does not seem, therefore, to be any basis for "automatic disqualification" in South African law. Whatever interests or connections an adjudicator has to a particular case will be relevant to the crucial inquiry as to whether the administrator is in fact biased, or can be said to be reasonably suspected of bias. The inquiry will have to be performed whatever the circumstances and whatever the allegation of bias, and it will have to be established in each case that the administrator was in fact biased or that a reasonable person would have had a reasonable suspicion of bias. South African courts have held, though, that the "smallest pecuniary interest" will usually be enough to raise a reasonable suspicion of bias.[287] **10–095**

---

[285] *S v Roberts* 1999 (4) S.A. 915 at paras 32–34.
[286] C. Hoexter, *Administrative Law in South Africa* (2007), pp.406–407.
[287] *Rose v Johannesburg Local Road Transportation Board* 1947 (4) S.A. 272 (W); *Barnard v Jockey Club of South Africa* 1984 (2) S.A. 35 (W), 46; Hoexter (2007), pp.407–412.

CHAPTER 11

SUBSTANTIVE REVIEW AND JUSTIFICATION

SCOPE

This chapter considers the following matters.   11–001

- The constitutional context in which the courts carry out judicial review of the substance of decisions.[1]

- The *Wednesbury* formulation of unreasonableness as a ground of review, and its subsequent development.[2]

- The use of unreasonable process or justification by public authorities (including failures properly to balance relevant considerations, flaws in logic and reasoning, and decisions which rest on inadequate evidence or a mistake of fact.[3]

- The violation of the constitutional principles of the rule of law or equality.[4]

- Decisions which are oppressive.[5]

- The use of proportionality as a ground of review—as a test of fair balance and in its more sophisticated form as a structured test of justifiability.[6]

- The intensity of substantive review by the court, which ranges from "correctness review" for abuse of power, to "structured proportionality", and a variable intensity of unreasonableness review.[7]

- Comparative perspectives.[8]

INTRODUCTION

We now turn to the ground of review normally referred to as "unrea- 11–002
sonableness" or, under Lord Diplock's redefinition, as "irrationality".[9]
This chapter is called "substantive review and justification" for a number

[1] See 11–012.
[2] See 11–018.
[3] See 11–032.
[4] See 11–057.
[5] See 11–070.
[6] See 11–073.
[7] See 11–086.
[8] See 11–103.
[9] *Council of Civil Service Unions v Minister for the Civil Service* [1985] A.C. 374 at 410–411.

543

of reasons. First, both the terms "unreasonableness" and "irrationality" are notoriously imprecise. Secondly, the tautological formula of unreasonableness set by the famous *Wednesbury* case[10] ("so unreasonable that no reasonable decision-maker could come to it") has been substantially reformulated in recent years. Thirdly, the concept of "proportionality" has been adopted as the appropriate test for review of European Community law[11] and Convention rights (under the Human Rights Act 1998).[12] Fourthly, there is overlap between proportionality and unreasonableness. Finally, even in respect of purely domestic law, the deeper justification required of decision-makers under the test of proportionality has infiltrated all public decision-making.

11–003   The issue under this ground of review is not whether the decision-maker strayed outside the terms or authorised purposes of the governing statute (the test of "illegality").[13] It is whether the power under which the decision-maker acts, a power normally conferring a broad discretion, has been improperly exercised or insufficiently justified. The court therefore engages in the review of *the substance* of the decision or its *justification*.

11–004   The question of the appropriate measure of deference, respect, restraint, latitude or discretionary area of judgment[14] (to use some of the terms variously employed) which the courts should grant the primary decision-maker under this head of review is one of the most complex in all of public law and goes to the heart of the principle of the separation of powers. This is because there is often a fine line between assessment of the *merits* of the decision (evaluation of fact and policy) and the assessment of whether the principles of "just administrative action"[15] have been met. The former questions are normally matters for the primary decision-maker, but the latter are within the appropriate capacity of the courts to decide. As we shall see, however, this does not mean that the courts may not consider whether the facts or judgment of the authority are properly determined. As public law develops, we are increasingly adopting a "culture of justification"[16] in English public decision-making.

11–005   We shall shortly turn to a discussion of the "unreasonable" decision (used interchangeably, albeit imprecisely, with the term "irrationality" these days) and then consider the "disproportionate" decision. However, it

---

[10] *Associated Provincial Picture Houses v Wednesbury Corp* [1948] 1 K.B. 223.

[11] See Ch.14.

[12] See Ch.13.

[13] Seee Ch.5.

[14] On intensity of review, see 11–086.

[15] The term used in s.33 of the Constitution of South Africa and includes the right to administrative action that is "lawful, reasonable and procedurally fair"; *cf.* Art.41 the Charter of Fundamental Rights of the European Union, which establishes a right to "good administration".

[16] The late Professor Etienne Mureinik wrote about the shift in South Africa after the end of apartheid in 1994 from "a culture of authority" to a "culture of justification": E. Mureinik, "A Bridge to Where? Introducing the Interim Bill of Rights" (1994) S.A.J.H.R. 31, 32. See further D. Dyzenhaus, "Law as Justification: Etienne Mureinik's Conception of Legal Culture" (1998) 13 S.A.J.H.R. 11; M. Taggart, "Reinventing Administrative Law" in N. Bamforth and P. Leyland (ed.), *Public Law in a Multi-Layered Constitution* (2004), p.311.

should be noted that there are two senses in which both unreasonableness and proportionality are employed as follows.

Unreasonableness review

Various formulations of the test have been devised and applied by the courts over the years,[17] although the most common contemporary formulation asks whether the decision falls "within the range of reasonable responses open to the decision-maker".[18] Where broad discretionary power has been conferred on the decision-maker there is a presumption that the decision is within the range of that discretion and the burden is therefore on the claimant to demonstrate the contrary.   **11–006**

Anxious scrutiny unreasonableness review

Where human or fundamental rights are in issue,[19] the courts engage in deeper scrutiny of the decision, and the burden shifts towards the public authority to justify its decision to invade those rights.[20]   **11–007**

Proportionality as a test of fair balance

Here the court considers whether the public authority has struck a "fair balance" between competing considerations or between means and ends.[21] Courts will normally not interfere with the balance of relevant considerations or with the impact of a decision unless it is *manifestly* disproportionate, so here too the burden of argument of rests on the claimant.   **11–008**

Proportionality as a structured test of justification

This form of review is most developed in the context of the adjudication of the qualified Convention rights contained in Arts 8–11 ECHR, and in relation to European Community law rights.[22] Here the court assesses lawfulness by applying a structured set of questions relating to the balance, necessity and suitability of the public authority's action. Although the English courts have yet to embrace this form of review outside the fields of European Community law and Convention rights, there are signs that this approach is having a growing influence on the common law in purely domestic cases. The burden of argument falls squarely in these cases on the   **11–009**

---

[17] See 11–018.
[18] See 11–024.
[19] On rights recognised by common law, see 5–036.
[20] See 11–093.
[21] See 11–075.
[22] See 11–077 and 13–079.

authority to justify its decision to depart from a fundamental norm, although the degree of deference accorded the decision depends upon its context.

Overlap between unreasonableness and proportionality

11–010 To identify these different approaches to proportionality does not, however, mean that there is not overlap between them. Proportionality in the sense of achieving a "fair balance" has always been an aspect of unreasonableness. There are also aspects of the structured test of proportionality which are inherent in traditional notions of unreasonableness (such as the requirement that there be a "rational connection" between the means of a decision and its ends). There may also be aspects of proportionality it its sense of structured justification that could profitably be incorporated into the notion of an "unreasonable" decision (such as the requirement that the decision-maker take into account less restrictive means to achieve a given end). Indeed it may be in the interest of English law to collapse the distinction between unreasonableness and proportionality. Flexibility has its advantages, but different standards for different issues may not serve the needs of a coherent, accessible and comprehensible system of judicial review.

Abuse of power

11–011 To those four categories a further should be added: abuse of power.[23] There are some areas of substantive review where the courts do not accord the pubic authority any discretionary latitude. The term "abuse of power" was first employed in the context of a failure of a decision-maker to fulfil a substantive legitimate expectation derived from an express or implied promise.[24] Its use is intended less to break free from the uncertainties attached to the notion of unreasonableness (the notion of "abuse" is no less sure than that of "unreasonableness")[25] than to evade its connotation of extreme deference by the courts to the decision-maker. Another general term that is gaining currency is that of simple "unfairness".[26]

THE CONSTITUTIONAL CONTEXT OF SUBSTANTIVE REVIEW

11–012 The courts have on occasion regarded it as relevant to the reasonableness of a decision of a Minister that the decision had by resolution been approved by one or both Houses of Parliament.[27] While these resolutions

---

[23] See 11–087.
[24] *R. v Inland Revenue Commissioners Ex p. Preston* [1985] A.C. 835 at 866–867 (and on legitimate expectations generally see see Ch.12).
[25] *R. (on the application of Nadarajah) v Secretary of State for the Home Department* [2005] EWCA Civ 1363 at [67]–[68]; *The Times*, December 14, 2005 (Laws L.J.).
[26] *R. (Iran) v Secretary of State for the Home Department* [2005] EWCA Civ 982; [2005] Imm. A.R. 535; *E v Secretary of State for the Home Department* [2004] EWCA Civ 49; [2004] Q.B. 1044.
[27] *R. v Secretary of State for the Environment Ex p. Nottinghamshire CC* [1986] A.C. 240 at 247 (Lord Scarman); *R. v Secretary of State for the Environment Ex p. Hammersmith & Fulham LBC* [1991] 1 A.C. 521 at 597 (Lord Bridge).

of course fall short of statutory authority, they may constitute strong evidence of the reasonableness of a decision. But such evidence should not be regarded by the courts as conclusive proof of unreasonableness.[28] The resolutions cannot make what is unreasonable, reasonable. The resolutions do not have the imprimatur of statutes and so do not excuse the courts from performing their proper role. Subordinate legislation has recently been held unreasonable despite the fact it was approved in Parliament and supported by ministerial statements. As Lord Phillips of Matravers M.R. put it,

> "the 'wider principle' of common law must accommodate the right and the duty of the Court to review the legality of subordinate legislation. The fact that, in the course of debate, the Secretary of State or others make statements of fact that support the legitimacy of the subordinate legislation, and that the House thereafter approves the subordinate legislation, cannot render it unconstitutional for the Court to review the material facts and form its own judgment, even if the result is discordant with statements made in parliamentary debate".[29]

In *Huang v Secretary of State for the Home Department*, the House of 11–013 Lords found unpersuasive the submission of the Secretary of State that the decision-maker and the court should assume that the immigration rules adopted by the responsible Minister and laid before Parliament "had the imprimatur of democratic approval and should be taken to strike the right balance between the interests of the individual and those of the community".[30] In other cases the courts have deferred to the judgement of public authorities on the ground that they were elected and are politically accountable for their actions.[31] However, political and legal authority should be distinguished, and the courts should not automatically defer to the legislature as they would thus be abdicating their own fundamental responsibility to determine whether the matter in question is lawful.[32]

---

[28] In *R. v Secretary of State for the Home Department Ex p. Brind* [1991] 2 A.C. 696, the Home Secretary's directions were also approved by both Houses of Parliament. Yet the directives that were held partially invalid in *R. v Immigration Appeal Tribunal Ex p. Begum Manshoora* [1986] Imm. A.R. 385 had also been laid before Parliament.

[29] *R. (on the application of Javed) v Secretary of State for the Home Department* [2001] EWCA Civ 789; [2002] Q.B. 129 at [37] (holding a statutory instrument, approved by resolution of both Houses of Parliament, was unreasonable).

[30] *Huang v Secretary of State for the Home Department* [2007] UKHL 11; [2007] 2 W.L.R. 581 at [17]; *cf. Kay v Lambeth LBC* [2006] UKHL 10; [2006] 2 A.C. 465, where such an assumption was made in relation to housing policy.

[31] *Secretary of State for Home Affairs v Rehman* [2001] UKHL 47; [2003] 1 A.C. 153 at [62] (Lord Hoffmann); *International Transport Roth GmbH v Secretary of State for the Home Department* [2002] EWCA Civ 158; [2003] Q.B. 728 at [27] (Laws L.J.).

[32] D. Dyzenhaus, "The Politics of Deference: Judicial Review and Democracy" in M. Taggart (ed.), *The Province of Administrative Law* (1997); J. Jowell, "Judicial Deference and Human Rights: A Question of Competence" in P. Craig and R. Rawlings (ed.), *Law and Administration in Europe; Essays in Honour of Carol Harlow* (2003), p.67; J. Jowell, "Judicial

Constitutional and institutional limitations on the court's role

11–014 Asserting the constitutional capacity of the courts in these situations does not, however, mean that the courts should not recognise both their own constitutional and relative institutional limitations. As we have already discussed in relation to the question of "justiciability",[33] decisions involving "policy"—the utilitarian calculation of the public good—such as decisions about the levels of taxation or public expenditure are, constitutionally, in the realm of the legislature.[34] In respect of other decisions, the relative institutional capacity of courts and the legislature, executive and other bodies will be relevant to the extent and degree of judicial intervention. Decisions that are polycentric, involving the allocation of scarce resources[35] (for example, whether a hospital should provide very expensive treatments) are similarly not normally suited to decision by courts.[36]

Deference: Servility, Civility or Institutional Capacity?" [2003] P.L. 592; R. Clayton, "Judicial Deference and the Democratic Dialogue: The Legitimacy of Judicial Intervention Under the HRA 1998" [2004] P.L. 33.; R. Clayton, "Principles for Due Deference" [2006] J.R. 109; Lord Justice Dyson, "Some Thoughts on Judicial Deference" [2006] J.R. 103; R. Edwards, "Judicial Deference under the HRA" (2002) 65 M.L.R. 859; Lord Steyn, "Deference: a Tangled Story" [2005] P.L. 346 and "2000–2005: Laying the Foundations of Human Rights Law in the United Kingdom" [2005] E.H.R.L.R. 349, 359; *et seq.* M. Hunt, "Why Public Law Needs 'Due Deference'", in N. Bamforth and P. Leyland (eds), *Public Law in a Multi-Layered Constitution* (2003), p.351; T.R.S. Allan, "Human Rights and Judicial Review: A Critique of "Due Deference"' [2006] C.L.J. 671; A. Barak, *The Judge in a Democracy* (2006), pp.251–252.

[33] See 1–025–1–043; and see further on deference 5–124–5–134.

[34] *Wilson v First County Trust Ltd* [2003] UKHL 40; [2004] 1 A.C. 816 at [70] (Lord Nicholls: "The more the legislation concerns matters of broad social policy the less ready will be a court to intervene"); *R. (on the application of Hooper) v Secretary of State for Work and Pensions* [2003] EWCA Civ 813; [2003] 1 W.L.R. 2623 at [63]–[64] (Laws L.J.: "A very considerable margin of discretion must be accorded to the Secretary of State. Difficult questions of economic and social policy were involved, the resolution of which fell within the province of the executive and the legislature rather than the courts"; appeal allowed by the HL in *Hooper v Secretary of State for Work and Pensions* [2005] UKHL 29; [2005] 1 W.L.R. 1681).

[35] See 1–033 *et seq*; and see, e.g. *Michalak v Wandsworth LBC* [2002] EWCA Civ 271; [2003] 1 W.L.R. 617 at [41] (Brooke L.J.: "this is pre-eminently a field in which the courts should defer to the decisions taken by a democratically elected Parliament, which has determined the manner in which public resources should be allocated for local authority housing").

[36] This point has been made most forcefully by Lord Hoffmann, "Separation of Powers" [2002] J.R. 137 and his statement in *R. v Secretary of State for the Environment, Transport and the Regions Ex p. Holdings & Barnes Plc* (the Alconbury case) [2001] UKHL 23; [2003] 2 A.C. 295 at [75]–[76], where he distinguished "policy decisions" from a "determination of right". Policy decisions should be made not by the courts, he said, but, in a democracy by "democratically elected bodies or persons accountable to them". In *Grape Bay Ltd v Attorney General of Bermuda* [2000] 1 W.L.R. 574 at 585 (Lord Hoffmann, for the PCI, held that a restriction on the expansion of a US restaurant chain in Bermuda was a "pure question of policy, raising no issue of human rights or fundamental principle" and the matter was therefore "pre-eminently one for democratic decision by the elected branch of government").

Decisions taken by experts,[37] and those best able to calculate risk,[38] indicate some measure of institutional respect.

Courts' secondary function of testing quality of reasoning and justification

We do not have any carefully calibrated theory of institutional capacity, **11–015** but even where the courts recognise their lack of relative capacity or expertise to make the primary decision, they should nevertheless not easily relinquish their secondary function of probing the quality of the reasoning and ensuring that assertions are properly justified.[39] And even policy decisions may contain within them a legal or constitutional principle (the decision of the hospital might, for example, engage a Convention right or fundamental right recognised by the common law) which is the court's to safeguard (for example, where the policy was applied in a discriminatory fashion or offended the right to life). As Lord Nicholls said in *Ghaidan v Godin-Mendoza*[40] in respect of national housing policy:

"Parliament has to hold a fair balance between the competing interests of tenants and landlords, taking into account broad issues of social and economic policy. But, even in such a field, where the alleged violation comprises differential treatment based upon grounds such as race or sex or sexual orientation the court will scrutinize with intensity any reasons said to constitute justification".

In addition, as was reflected in *Huang*,[41] there are some matters in which **11–016** the determination of policy by the legislative or executive branch is deficient. Lord Bingham distinguished between a case which concerns established housing policy[42]—where the result represented "a considered democratic compromise", and where all parties were represented in the debate and where the issue involved the allocation of finite resources—and the situation in immigration policy where those elements were not present.

---

[37] See, e.g. *R. v Secretary of State for the Home Department Ex p. Swati* [1986] 1 W.L.R. 477; *R. v Chief Constable of the Merseyside Police Ex p. Calveley* [1986] 1 Q.B. 424; *Pulhofer v Hillingdon LBC* [1986] A.C. 484; *R. v Secretary of State for Social Services Ex p. Stitt* [1990] C.O.D. 288; *R. (on the application of W) v Thetford Youth Justices* [2002] EWHC 1252; (2002) 166 J.P. 453 at [40] (Sedley L.J.: "A youth court has expertise which a higher court lacks"); *R. (on the application of Legal Remedy UK Ltd) v Secretary of State for Health* [2007] EWHC 1252 (court wary of "donning the garb of policy maker" in challenge to restructuring of postgraduate medical training).
[38] See, e.g. *R. (on the application of Farrakhan) v Secretary of State for the Home Department* [2002] EWCA Civ 606; [2002] Q.B. 1391; *R. v Secretary of State for the Home Department Ex p. Turgut* [2001] 1 All E.R. 719 at 729 (Simon Brown L.J.: "The court is hardly less well placed than the Secretary of State himself to evaluate the risk once the relevant material is placed before it").
[39] Allan [2006] C.I.J. 671, 693.
[40] [2004] 2 A.C. 557 at [19].
[41] [2007] UKHL 11; [2007] 2 W.L.R. 581.
[42] As in *Kay v Lambeth LBC* [2006] UKHL 10; [2006] 2 A.C. 465.

In cases, therefore, where relevant interests have not been well represented, and where there are other reasons for confidence in the relative institutional capacity of the courts to decide the matter, courts can quite properly review the substance or justification of the matter in question.

Political mandate

11–017 Sometimes local authorities have asserted that their mandate from the electorate permits them to implement a policy without legal restraint. In *Bromley*[43] the Greater London Council justified a 25 per cent reduction in transport fares partly on the basis that the recent election had given them a "mandate" to lower the fares in the way the successful majority party had promised in its electoral manifesto. The House of Lords disagreed; those elected had to consider the interests of all the inhabitants of the area, in the light of their legal duties.[44] In the *Tameside* case[45] the local authority introduced a scheme, promised at a recent local election, to abolish certain recently established comprehensive schools and to reintroduce grammar schools by a process of selection, all in a period of four months. The Secretary of State sought to intervene under s.68 of the Education Act 1944 which permitted him to do so when "he was satisfied" that a local authority were acting "unreasonably". The House of Lords held that the Secretary of State did not in those circumstances have the power to intervene because the council had not acted unreasonably in the *Wednesbury* sense. This decision was considerably influenced by the fact that the local authority was recently elected, with a mandate to reintroduce grammar schools. While superficially contradictory, these two cases were decided on different grounds. The *Bromley* case was decided on the basis of the council exceeding the particular powers established in the governing statute. It is therefore authority for the correct proposition that no "mandate" from the electorate can serve as a justification for an illegal act.[46] In *Tameside*, although the scope of the governing statute was in issue, the case turned on the unreasonableness of the local authority's behaviour. A manifesto commitment may be relevant evidence of the unreasonableness

---

[43] *Bromley LBC v GLC* [1983] 1 A.C. 768.
[44] Cited with approval in *R. (on the application of Island Farm Developments Ltd) v Bridgend County BC* [2006] EWHC 2189; [2007] B.L.G.R. 60 at [23] (Collins J.); and *R. v Secretary of State for Employment Ex p. Begbie* [2001] 1 W.L.R. 1115 (pre-election promise does not create a legitimate expectation).
[45] *Secretary of State for Education and Science v Tameside MBC* [1977] A.C. 1014.
[46] In *Bromley*, Lord Denning, in the CA, [1982] 2 W.L.R. 62 said that a manifesto should "not be taken as gospel. . . When a party gets into power, it should consider any proposal or promise afresh, and on its merits. . .". And see his reservations about the doctrine of the mandate in The Changing Law (1953) where he wrote: "Some people vote for [a member] because they approve of some of the proposals in his party's manifesto, others because they approve of others of the proposals. Yet others because, while they do not really approve of the proposals, they disapprove still more of the counter-proposals of the rival party, and so forth. It is impossible to say therefore that the majority of the people approve of any particular proposal, let alone every proposal in the manifesto" (at 8–10).

of a decision which permits a range of lawful courses of action. It should never, however, be taken as conclusive proof of reasonableness, as other factors may be weighed against it.[47]

THE WEDNESBURY FORMULATION AND ITS SUBSEQUENT DEVELOPMENT

Substantive review in English law has been dominated by the concept of 11-018 unreasonableness closely identified with the famous formulation by Lord Greene M.R. in the *Wednesbury* case,[48] that the courts can only interfere if a decision "is so unreasonable that no reasonable authority could ever come to it".[49] That formulation attempts, albeit imperfectly, to convey the point that judges should not lightly interfere with official decisions on this ground. In exercising their powers of review, judges ought not to imagine themselves as being in the position of the competent authority when the decision was taken and then test the reasonableness of the decision against the decision they would have taken. To do that would involve the courts in a review of the merits of the decision, as if they were themselves the recipients of the power. For that reason Lord Greene in *Wednesbury*[50] thought that an unreasonable decision under his definition "would require something overwhelming" (such as a teacher being dismissed on the ground of her red hair).[51]

Wednesbury is tautological

One of the difficulties with the *Wednesbury* test is its tautological defini- 11-019 tion,[52] which fails to guide us with any degree of certitude.[53] Lord Greene did attempt to provide a list of administrative sins which he thought were

---

[47] See also *R. v Somerset CC Ex p. Fewings* [1995] 1 All E.R. 513 where (in relation to the council's ban on stag-hunting over its own land) Laws J. held that the fact that the council were an elected body would not influence the court to interpret "benevolently" whether the decision was within the permissible scope of the statute, "as may be the approach in the case of an assessment of the reasonableness of the exercise of a discretionary power".

[48] *Associated Provincial Picture Houses Ltd v Wednesbury Corp* [1948] 1 K.B. 223. For a history of that case see M. Taggart "Reinventing Administrative Law", in N. Bamforth and P. Leyland (eds), *Public Law in a Multi-Layered Constitution* (2004) at 312; for discussion of scope of *Wednesbury* review see: Lord Irvine, "Judges and Decision-Makers: the theory and practice of *Wednesbury* review" [1996] P.L. 59; P. Walker, "What's Wrong with Irrationality?" [1995] P.L. 556; A. Le Sueur, "The Rise and Ruin of Unreasonableness" [2005] J.R. 32.

[49] [1948] 1 K.B. 223 at 229–230.

[50] [1948] 1 K.B. 223.

[51] [1948] 1 K.B. 223 at 229. The illustration is from *Short v Poole Corp* [1926] Ch. 66. Previous editions of this work considered that cases in the 1960s had shorn the *Wednesbury* formula of its unnecessary reference to "overwhelming" proof.

[52] Because it defines the negative term unreasonableness by both a negative and positive reference to itself: an unreasonable decision is "so unreasonable that no reasonable body should so act".

[53] *R. v IRC Ex p. Taylor (No.2)* [1989] 3 All E.R. 353 at 357 (Glidewell L.J.: ". . .we still adhere to [the *Wednesbury* definition of unreasonableness] out of usage if not affection"); for a criticism of *Wednesbury* see J. Jowell and A. Lester, "Beyond Wednesbury: Towards Substantive Standards of Judicial Review" [1987] P.L. 368.

covered by his notion of unreasonableness, all of which he considered to "overlap to a very great extent" and "run into one another".[54] These included: bad faith, dishonesty, attention given to extraneous circumstances, disregard of public policy, wrong attention given to irrelevant considerations, and failure to take into account matters which are bound to be considered. Some of these instances, particularly those referring to the taking into account of irrelevant considerations (or failing to take them into account) we have seen in Chapter 5 are today more appropriately considered as instances of illegality rather than unreasonableness, because they are extraneous to the objects or purposes of the statute under which the power is being exercised, thus taking the decision outside the "four corners" of the governing statute.

11–020   In contrast, in 1898 a relatively specific account of unreasonableness in the context of a review of local authority byelaws was provided in the case of *Kruse v Johnson*.[55] Lord Russell of Killowen C.J. expressed the view there that byelaws should be benevolently interpreted by the courts, but could be struck down for unreasonableness: "If, for instance, they were found to be partial and unequal in their operation between different classes; if they were manifestly unjust; if they disclosed bad faith; if they involved such oppressive or gratuitous interference with the rights of those subject to them such as could find no justification in the minds of reasonable men".

11–021   Although this formulation includes the indeterminate notion of "manifest injustice", it has the advantage of specifying aspects of unreasonableness such as unequal treatment, bad faith and decisions which constitute an unjustified interference with rights. Over the years some decisions which unduly curtail rights have been held unreasonable, although the specification of the right has not always been articulated. In more recent years, as we shall shortly see,[56] the courts have identified human rights as deserving of particularly anxious scrutiny. Since the HRA 1998 has incorporated into domestic law most of the rights specified in the ECHR, infringement of these statutory rights falls under the ground of review of illegality rather than unreasonableness.[57] Nevertheless, it is still open to the courts to identify fundamental rights inherent in the common law,[58] and the methods of reasoning adopted by the courts in deciding whether a breach of a right is justifiable is still informed by some of the approaches learned through unreasonableness review about the appropriate role of courts and other branches of government.

[54] *Wednesbury* [1948] 1 K.B. 223 at 229.
[55] [1889] 2 Q.B. 291.
[56] See 11–086.
[57] See Ch.13.
[58] See 5–036; 1–015.

Wednesbury associated with extreme behaviour

Apart from its vagueness, the *Wednesbury* formulation has been challenged **11–022** in recent years for the reason that it depicts "unreasonableness" as particularly extreme behaviour, such as acting in bad faith, or a decision which is "perverse",[59] or "absurd"—implying that the decision-maker has "taken leave of his senses".[60] In the *GCHQ* case,[61] in the famous passage where he formulated the "grounds" of judicial review, Lord Diplock preferred to use the term "irrational", which he described as applying to "a decision which is so outrageous in its defiance of logic or accepted moral standards that no sensible person who had applied his mind to the question to be decided could have arrived at it".[62] This definition is at least candid in its acknowledgement that courts can employ both logic and accepted moral standards as criteria by which to assess official decisions, but it does not assist in elucidating any more specific categories of legally unacceptable substantive decisions. In addition, as has been pointed out, the term irrationality has the drawback that it casts doubt on the mental capacity of the decision-maker,[63] whereas many decisions which fall foul of this ground of review have been coldly rational. In addition, Lord Diplock's precondition of decisions which are "outrageous" denotes a very low level of judicial scrutiny.[64] Lord Bingham has noted that the threshold of irrationality is "notoriously high", and that a claimant making a challenge under that head has "a mountain to climb".[65] Lord Cooke opined that *Wednesbury* was "an unfortunately retrogressive decision in English administrative law, insofar as it suggested that there are degrees of unreasonableness and that only a very extreme degree can bring an administrative decision within the legitimate scope of judicial invalidation".[66]

[59] *Pulhofer v Hillingdon LBC* [1986] A.C. 484 at 518 (Lord Brightman).
[60] *R. v Secretary of State for the Environment Ex p. Notts CC* [1986] A.C. 240 at 247–248 (Lord Scarman).
[61] *Council of Civil Service Unions v Minister for the Civil Service* [1985] A.C. 374.
[62] [1985] A.C. 374 at 410; *cf. Luby v Newcastle-under-Lyme Corp* [1964] 2 Q.B. 64 at 72.
[63] *R. v Devon CC Ex p. George* [1988] 3 W.L.R. 49 at 51 (Lord Donaldson M.R.: "I eschew the synonym of 'irrational', because, although it is attractive as being shorter than Wednesbury unreasonable, and has the imprimatur of Lord Diplock . . . it is widely misunderstood by politicians, both local and national, and even more by their constituents, as casting doubt on the mental capacity of the decision-maker, a matter which in practice is seldom, if ever, in issue"); reversed in HL [1989] A.C. 573.
[64] Lord Diplock's other attempts at definitions of unreasonableness were based on the notion of "justifiability": *Bromley LBC v Greater London Council* [1983] A.C. 768 at 821 ("decisions that, looked at objectively, are so devoid of any plausible justification that no reasonable body of persons could have reached them"); *Luby v Newcastle-under-Lyme Corp* [1964] 2 Q.B. 64 at 72 (whether the decision was "exercised in a manner which no reasonable man could consider justifiable"). Under the 1994 Interim Constitution of South Africa where "just administrative action" was enshrined as a fundamental right, it was provided that every person shall have the right to "administrative action which is justifiable in relation to the reasons given for it where any of his or her rights is affected or threatened". Compare s.33 of the current South African Constitution.
[65] *R. v Lord Chancellor Ex p. Maxwell* [1997] 1 W.L.R. 104 at 109.
[66] *R. v Secretary of State for the Home Department Ex p. Daly* [2001] UKHL 26; [2001] 2 A.C. 532 at [32].

Attempts to reformulate Wednesbury

11–023 For that reason, there have been various attempts to reformulate the *Wednesbury* test, such as: "a decision so unreasonable that no person acting reasonably could have come to it",[67] or a decision which elicits the exclamation: "My goodness, that is certainly wrong!"[68]

11–024   These tests perhaps help to give an indication of the flavour of the conduct which qualifies as being within the concept of unreasonableness, but are no more helpful as guides to its precise parameters. Lord Cooke regretted the fact that the *Wednesbury* formula had become "established incantations in the courts of the United Kingdom and beyond".[69] He thought that judges had no need for "admonitory circumlocutions", and preferred the simple test of "whether the decision in question was one which a reasonable authority could reach".[70] He considered that such an "unexaggerated" criterion would "give the administrator ample and rightful rein, consistently with the constitutional separation of powers".[71] Under criticisms such as these, the test is being increasingly rephrased to a decision which is "within the range of reasonable responses".[72] We shall consider below whether this formulation accords more appropriately with the respective roles of judges and administrators.

Statutory unreasonableness

11–025 What standard is implied when a statute requires a public authority not to act "unreasonably"? In *Tameside*[73] the Secretary of State had the power, under the Education Act 1944, to issue directions to the local authority "if he is satisfied" that the local authority is "acting unreasonably". Despite this seemingly subjective formulation, the House of Lords read the term "unreasonably" as expressing the *Wednesbury* formulation. The Secretary of State could therefore issue directions only where the local authority were acting so unreasonably that no reasonable authority could so act.[74]

---

[67] *Champion v Chief Constable of the Gwent Constabulary* [1990] 1 W.L.R. 1 at 16 (Lord Lowry).

[68] *Neale v Hereford & Worcester CC* [1986] I.C.R. 471 at 483 (May L.J., not in the context of judicial review, but employed by the Lord Donaldson M.R. in *R. v Devon CC Ex p. George* [1998] 3 W.L.R. 49 and in *Piggott Brothers & Co Ltd v Jackson* [1992] I.C.R. 85.

[69] *R. v Chief Constable of Sussex Ex p. International Trader's Ferry Ltd* [1999] 2 A.C. 418.

[70] cf. *Boddington v British Transport Police* [1999] 2 A.C. 143 at 175 (Lord Steyn, asking whether the decision is "within the range of reasonable decisions open to the decision maker").

[71] *International Trader's Ferry* [1999] 2 A.C. 418 at 452.

[72] See, e.g. *Ala v Secretary of State for the Home Department* [2003] EWHC 521 at [44]–[45] (Moses J.); *Edore v Secretary of State for the Home Department* [2003] EWCA Civ 716; [2003] 1 W.L.R. 2979 at [20] (Simon Brown L.J.); *R. (on the application of Razgar) v Secretary of State for the Home Department (No.2)* [2003] EWCA Civ 840; [2003] Imm. A.R. 529 at [40]–[41](Dyson L.J.); *Huang v Secretary of State for the Home Department* [2005] EWCA Civ 105 (Laws L.J.).

[73] *Secretary of State for Education and Science v Tameside MBC* [1977] A.C. 1014 (for a critical account, see D. Bull, "Tameside Revisited: Prospectively 'Reasonable'; Retrospective 'Maladministration'" (1987) 50 M.L.R. 307).

[74] A second aspect of *Tameside* was the possible mistake of material fact: see 11–041–11–057.

Should the extreme reserve of *Wednesbury*, which was devised to inhibit **11–026** the powers of *courts* to intervene in the merits of an administrative decision, apply so as similarly to inhibit the actions of a *Minister*, whose constitutional position is entirely different? The matter surely depends upon the administrative scheme established by a particular statute. It could be argued that the Education Act 1944 pursued the purpose the placing of education policy primarily with the local authority, with the Minister having power to intervene only in extreme cases. In the case of other administrative schemes, however, the statute may pose the Minister with fewer obstacles to intervention.[75] For example, s.9 of the Education Act 1981 placed a local authority under a duty to comply with a request from a parent for an assessment of their child's special needs unless the request is in the opinion of the authority "unreasonable". It was held that the "public law test" of reasonableness which was "intended to protect the local authority . . . against interference by the Secretary of State" was not applicable to s.9, which required a "straightforward factual test" of unreasonableness, "based on all the material before the authority".[76] This clearly implies that the *Wednesbury* formulation may be appropriately applied in cases such as that of *Tameside*, but is not appropriate to all statutes where the term unreasonable is employed.[77] Similarly, it was held that a statutory provision of "reasonableness" in relation to the Secretary of State's reviewing of harbour licences should be interpreted in accordance with "common sense" and not technically.[78]

A similar approach must be taken to any reviewing body. For example, **11–027** in *Huang* it was held that the task of the immigration appellate authority, on an appeal on a Convention right ground against a decision of the primary decision-maker refusing leave to enter or remain in this country, is to decide itself whether the matter is compatible with a Convention right. It was not a secondary, reviewing function confined to the grounds of judicial review, including unreasonableness.[79] The term "unreasonable", in

[75] Sometimes by permitting the Minister to exercise default powers even in the absence of unreasonable behaviour on the part of a local authority, e.g. the formulation under the Housing Act 1980 which empowered the Secretary of State to intervene to exercise the local authority's powers to sell council housing "where it appears to the Secretary of State that tenants . . . have or may have difficulty in exercising their right to buy effectively and expeditiously": *R. v Secretary of State for the Environment Ex p. Norwich CC* [1982] Q.B. 808.
[76] *R. v Hampshire CC Ex p. W, The Times*, June 9, 1994 (Sedley J.).
[77] For example, the wide discretion of a legal aid committee to refuse legal aid "if it appears unreasonable in the particular circumstances of the case": *R. v Legal Aid Committee No.1 (London) Ex p. Rondel* [1967] 2 Q.B. 482.
[78] *R. (on the application of Dart Harbour and Navigation Authority) v Secretary of State for Transport, Local Government and the Regions* [2003] EWHC 1494; [2003] 2 Lloyd's Rep. 607; *R. v Secretary of State for the Environment Ex p. North Norfolk DC* [1994] 2 P.L.R. 78; *R. v Hampshire County Council ex p. W, The Times*, June 9, 1995; *R. v Devon CC Ex p. S* [1995] C.O.D. 181.
[79] *Huang v Secretary of State for the Home Department* [2007] UKHL 11; [2007] 2 W.L.R. 581 at [11] affirming the CA [2005] EWCA Civ 105; [2006] Q.B. 1, and overruling *Edore v Secretary of State for the Home Department* [2003] EWCA Civ 716; [2003] 1 W.L.R. 2979 and *M (Croatia) v Secretary of State for the Home Department* [2004] UKIAT 24; [2004] Imm. A.R. 211.

its *Wednesbury* or any other sense, is no magic formula; everything must depend upon the context.

Categories of unreasonableness

11–028 The great many cases held unlawful on the ground of unreasonableness may be divided into the following broad categories (recognising of course that there will always be decisions which do not easily fall into any of them, or that overlap between them).

Unreasonable process

11–029 First, is the case where there has been material a defect in the decision-making *process*.[80] The assessment here focuses upon the quality of reasoning underlying or supporting the decision; upon the weight placed upon the factors taken into account on the way to reaching the decision; upon the way the decision is justified. We shall examine here: (a) decisions based on considerations which have been accorded manifestly inappropriate weight; and (b) strictly "irrational" decisions, namely, decisions which are apparently illogical or arbitrary (c) uncertain decisions, (d) decisions supported by inadequate or incomprehensible reasons or (e) by inadequate evidence or which are made on the basis of a mistake of fact.

Violations of common law or constitutional principles

11–030 Secondly, there are situations in which it is alleged that decisions taken violate common law or constitutional principles governing the exercise of official power.[81] These principles include: (a) the rule of law (under which a number of different values are protected, such as access to justice); and (b) equality, which requires decisions to be consistently applied and prohibits measures which make unjustifiable or unfair distinctions between individuals. Another value underlying the rule of law, that of legal certainty, which requires the protection of a person's legitimate expectations, is considered in the next chapter (only because it has developed so many different facets over the past few years, and thus merits separate treatment).[82]

Oppressive decisions

11–031 A third category contains what might be called oppressive decisions.[83] The focus here is upon the end-product of the decision; upon its affect on individuals (and not upon the process by which the decision was reached). Decisions may be impugned under this head because of the unnecessarily

---

[80] See 11–032–11–056.
[81] See 11–057–11–069.
[82] See Ch.12.
[83] See 11–070–11–072.

onerous impact they have on the rights or interest of persons affected by them. While this category is more pragmatically grounded, it too is not unaffected by constitutional principle, which requires a person's liberties not to be unreasonably infringed.

We examine each of these categories in turn.

UNREASONABLE PROCESS

The first category of decision to be considered involves some defect in the **11–032** process of arriving at the decision; in the way the decision was reached or in the manner by which it has been justified. The focus here is thus upon the factors taken into account by the decision-maker on the way to making the decision; the evidence by which the decision was influenced or the quality of it justification. We shall first look at decisions where the considerations taken into account are wrongly balanced, and then at strictly "irrational" decisions, for instance those that are based upon the lack of ostensible logic or inadequate evidence.

Balance of relevant considerations

Up to now, the English courts—where no European Community law or **11–033** Convention rights are in issue—have approached allegations of misbalance as a question of unreasonableness, i.e. a decision is unreasonable, and therefore unlawful, because manifestly excessive or manifestly inadequate weight has been accorded to a relevant consideration.[84] As we shall see below, English law stands at the brink of a development that would allow a more direct question to be asked, namely whether a decision is unlawful because it is disproportionate (without needing to have regard to the concept of unreasonableness).[85]

Planning cases

The law reports contain countless examples of the unreasonableness **11–034** approach to balance. In the context of town and country planning, for instance, a local authority, or the Secretary of State on appeal, may, in considering whether to grant a permission for the change of use of a building, have regard not only to the proposed new use but also to the existing use of the building and weigh the one against the other. The courts are concerned normally to leave the balancing of these considerations to the planning authority.[86] However, where the refusal of planning permis-

---

[84] This passage was approved by Silber J. in *Secretary of State for Trade and Industry Ex p. BT3G Ltd* [2001] Eu.L.R. 325 at [187] (see subsequently [2001] EWCA Civ 1448).
[85] See 11–077–11–083.
[86] *Tesco Stores v Secretary of State for the Environment* [1995] 1 W.L.R. 759, HL.

sion is based on the preference for the preservation of the building's existing use, the refusal may be struck down in the extreme case where there is in practice "no reasonable prospect" of that use being preserved.[87] In effect, in such a case the courts are holding that the existing use is being accorded excessive weight in the balancing exercise involved. Although planning authorities are required, in deciding whether to grant or refuse planning permission, to have regard to government circulars, or to development plans,[88] a "slavish" adherence to those (relevant and material) considerations may render a decision invalid.[89] The courts have also interfered with the balancing of "material" planning considerations, by holding that excessive weight had been accorded to a planning permission that had long since expired.[90] Although these are all matters of "planning judgment" which is normally for the authority to decide, courts are not "shy in an appropriate case of concluding that it would have been irrational of a decision-maker to have had regard to an alternative proposal as a material consideration or that, even if possibly he should have done so, to have given it any or any sufficient weight".[91]

Other cases

11–035 In licensing cases it has also been held that too much weight had been placed by an authority upon recent precedent refusing refreshment licences and too little on the 50–year previous enjoyment of the licence by the claimant.[92] Similarly, an adjudicator on an asylum appeal, who had reversed the Secretary of State's decision to deport an asylum seeker who had served a prison sentence in the United Kingdom, had placed excessive weight upon the risk of the appellant re-offending, and insufficient weight upon the character of the offence.[93] And where the police, in the face of disruptive demonstrations by animal welfare groups, withdrew protection

---

[87] *London Residuary Body v Lambeth LBC* [1990] 1 W.L.R. 744; *Westminster City Council v British Waterways Board* [1985] A.C. 676 at 683 (Bridge L.J.: "In a contest between the planning merits of two competing uses, to justify refusal of permission for use B on the sole ground that use A ought to be preserved, it must, in my view, be necessary at least to show a balance of probability that, if permission is refused for use B, the land in dispute will be effectively put to use A"); *Nottinghamshire CC v Secretary of State for the Environment, Transport and the Regions* [2001] EWHC Admin 293; [2002] 1 P. & C.R. 30.
[88] See 5–073–5–074.
[89] *Simpson v Edinburgh Corp* 1960 S.C. 313; *Niarchos (London) Ltd v Secretary of State for the Environment* (1977) 35 P. & C.R. 259; *R. v Derbyshire CC Ex p. Woods* [1997] J.P.L. 958.
[90] *South Oxfordshire DC v Secretary of State for the Environment* [1981] 1 W.L.R. 1092.
[91] *R. (on the application of Mount Cook Land Ltd) v Westminster CC* [2003] EWCA Civ 1346; [2004] C.P. Rep. 12 at [33] (Auld L.J.).
[92] *R. v Flintshire County Licensing Committee Ex p. Barrett* [1957] 1 Q.B. 350.
[93] *R. (Kenya) v Secretary of State for the Home Department* [2004] EWCA Civ 1094; *The Times*, September 13, 2004 (May and Judge L.JJ., Sedley L.J. dissenting); also *R. (on the application of Harris) v Secretary of State for the Home Department* [2001] EWHC Admin 225; [2001] I.N.L.R. 584 (unreasonable to refuse leave to re-enter the UK to a person who had made a brief visit to a dying relative abroad, on the ground of a previous conviction which itself would not have been a ground for deportation).

from the exporters of animals for certain days of the week, it was held by the House of Lords that the considerations taken into account (e.g. pressures on police protection elsewhere in the county) had been fairly balanced against the danger to the rule of law that the withdrawal of protection would entail.[94]

Rationality: logic and reasoning

Although the terms irrationality and unreasonableness are these days often used interchangeably, irrationality is only one facet of unreasonableness.[95] A decision is irrational in the strict sense of that term if it is unreasoned; if it is lacking ostensible logic or comprehensible justification. Instances of irrational decisions include those made in an arbitrary fashion, perhaps "by spinning a coin or consulting an astrologer",[96] or where the decision simply fails to "add up—in which, in other words, there is an error of reasoning which robs the decision of logic".[97]   **11–036**

"Absurd" or "perverse" decisions may be presumed to have been decided in that fashion, as may decisions where the given reasons are simply unintelligible. Less extreme examples of the irrational decision include those in which there is an absence of logical connection between the evidence and the ostensible reasons for the decision, where the reasons display no adequate justification for the decision, or where there is absence of evidence in support of the decision. Mistake of material fact may also, according to recent cases, render a decision unlawful.   **11–037**

We have seen that the absence of reasons for a decision may constitute a breach of a fair hearing.[98] Irrationality may also sometimes be inferred from the absence of reasons.[99] When reasons are required, either by statute or by the growing common law requirements, or where they are provided,   **11–038**

---

[94] R. v Chief Constable of Sussex Ex p. International Trader's Ferry Ltd [1999] 2 A.C. 418; Lord Hoffmann, "A Sense of Proportion" (1997) The Irish Jurist 49. But substantial withdrawal of police protection was held to be unlawful and a violation of the rule of law: R. v Coventry City Council Ex p. Phoenix Aviation [1995] 3 All E.R. 37.
[95] R. v Secretary of State for the Home Department Ex p. Omibiyo [1996] 2 All E.R. 901 at 912 (Sir Thomas Bingham M.R.: "I would accordingly incline to accept the Secretary of State's argument on this point, while observing that decisions reached by him are susceptible to challenge on any Wednesbury ground, of which irrationality is only one").
[96] R. v Deputy Industrial Injuries Commissioner Ex p. Moore [1965] 1 Q.B. 456 at 488 (Diplock L.J.); R. v Lambeth LBC Ex p. Ashley (1997) 29 H.L.R. 385 (points scheme for the allocation of housing was plainly "illogical and irrational"); R. v Islington LBC Ex p. Hassan (1995) 27 H.L.R. 485 (finding of intentional homelessness illogical).
[97] R. v Parliamentary Commissioner for Administration Ex p. Balchin [1998] 1 P.L.R. 1, 13, cited in R. (on the application of Norwich and Peterborough Building Society) v Financial Ombudsman Service Ltd [2002] EWHC 2379; [2003] 1 All E.R. (Comm) 65 at [59].
[98] See Ch.7.
[99] Padfield v Minister of Agriculture Fisheries and Food [1968] A.C. 997 at 1932 1049 1053, 1054, 1061–1062; Lonrho Plc v Secretary of State for Trade and Industry [1989] 1 W.L.R. 525 at 539; R. v Civil Service Appeal Board Ex p. Cunningham [1991] 4 All E.R. 310. But it may not be possible for the court to infer unreasonableness from the lack of reasons, see e.g. R. v Secretary of State for the Home Department Ex p. Adams [1995] E.C.R. 177 (Steyn L.J. and Kay J.).

even though not strictly required, those reasons must be both "adequate and intelligible".[100] They must therefore both rationally relate to the evidence in the case,[101] and be comprehensible in themselves.[102] The reasons for a decision must not be "self contradictory".[103]

11-039   As we shall see, one of the ingredients of proportionality as applied under European Community law, and under the HRA when applying Convention rights, is that the objectives of a decision or policy must bear a "rational connection" to the measures designed to further the objectives.[104] A similar approach is taken to the notion of unreasonableness or irrationality in domestic law, as shown in a recent case where a non-statutory scheme was introduced to provide compensation for British civilians interned during World War II by the Japanese. The scheme excluded individuals whose parents or grandparents were not born in the United Kingdom. The Court of Appeal examined carefully whether the exclusion bore a rational connection to the "foundation" and "essential character" of the scheme, but held in the circumstances that the scheme did not fail the *Wednesbury* test.[105] The House of Lords had adopted a similar approach in a case where, under an *ex-gratia* compensation scheme, British soldiers injured in Bosnia were accorded treatment different from those injured in Northern Ireland.[106]

Uncertainty

11-040   Substantial doubt over what is intended may result in a decision being held invalid for uncertainty. A byelaw or statutory instrument may be pronounced invalid for uncertainty where it fails to indicate adequately what it

---

[100] See Ch.7.

[101] *Re Poyser and Mills' Arbitration* [1964] 2 Q.B. 467 at 478 (Megaw J., speaking of the duty to give reasons imposed by the Tribunals and Inquiries Act 1958 s.12 said that the required reasons "must be read as meaning that proper adequate reasons must be given . . . which deal with the substantial points that have been raised").

[102] In *R. v Hammersmith and Fulham LBC Ex p. Earls Court Ltd*, The Times, September 7, 1993, it was held that a condition imposed upon an entertainment licence which was so obscure that it necessitated the issue of a construction summons was "unreasonable in the Wednesbury sense" (Kennedy L.J.).

[103] *Mahon v Air New Zealand Ltd* [1984] A.C. 808 at 835 PC (Lord Diplock required the finding to be based on some material that tends logically to show the existence of facts consistent with the finding).

[104] See 11–080 for the test propounded in *De Freitas v Permanent Secretary of the Ministry of Agriculture, Fisheries, Land and Housing* [1999] 1 A.C. 69, 80 (Lord Clyde), applied by Lord Steyn in *R. (on the application of Daly) v Secretary of State for the Home Department* [2001] UKHL 26; [2001] 2 A.C. 532 at [27].

[105] *R. (on the application of Association of British Civilian Internees (Far East Region)) v Secretary of State for Defence* [2003] EWCA Civ 473; [2003] Q.B. 1397 at [40].

[106] *R. v Ministry of Defence Ex p. Walker* [2000] 1 W.L.R. 806 at 812 (Lord Slynn: "It is not for the courts to consider whether the scheme . . . is a good scheme or a bad scheme, unless it can be said that the exclusion is irrational or unreasonable that no reasonable Minister could have adopted it"); Lord Hoffmann considered the distinction to be "fine" but not irrational: "That is too high a hurdle to surmount".

is prohibiting.[107] However, a byelaw will be treated as valid unless it was so uncertain in its language as to have no ascertainable meaning or was so unclear in its effect as to be incapable of certain application.[108] Mere "ambiguity" would not suffice.[109] Uncertainty is a ground for invalidating conditions annexed to grants of planning permission and site licences. Such conditions may be void for uncertainty if they can be given no meaning at all, or no sensible or ascertainable meaning.[110] An uncertain decision could also be described as arbitrary, in the sense that "it is incapable of providing any meaningful answer",[111] or indeed as failing to comply with the rule of law.[112]

Inadequate Evidence and Mistake of Fact

Since courts in judicial review are concerned with the law and not the merits of a case, they will not normally interfere with a public authority's assessment of the evidence or the facts.[113] Sometimes there is a double limitation on review for fact, for the courts may be reviewing the decision of an appeal tribunal which itself had jurisdiction only to review the **11–041**

---

[107] *Staden v Tarjanyi* (1980) 78 L.G.R. 614 at 623 at 624; D. Williams, "Criminal Law and Administrative Law: Problems of Procedure and Reasonableness", in P. Smith (ed.), *Criminal Law: Essays in Honour of J.C. Smith* (1987), p.170. In *McEldowney v Forde* [1971] A.C. 632, the majority of their Lordships assumed that the test of uncertainty applied to statutory instruments as well as byelaws.
[108] *Percy v Hall* [1997] Q.B. 924 at 941 (Simon Brown L.J.).
[109] *cf. Kruse v Johnson* [1898] 2 Q.B. 473.
[110] *cf. Fawcett Properties Ltd v Buckingham CC* [1961] A.C. 636; *Hall v Shoreham-by-Sea UDC* [1964] 1 W.L.R. 240; *Mixnam's Properties Ltd v Chertsey UDC* [1964] 1 Q.B. 214; [1965] A.C. 735; *David Lowe and Sons Ltd v Musselburgh Corp* 1974 S.L.T. 5 (condition incapable of any certain or intelligible interpretation); *Bizony v Secretary of State for the Environment* (1976) 239 E.G. 281 at 284 (test of uncertainty applied to a planning condition was limited to linguistic ambiguity or uncertainty in meaning: mere difficulty in determining whether the condition had been breached on particular facts was not enough); *Shanley M.J. Ltd (In liquidation) v Secretary of State for the Environment* [1982] J.P.L. 380 (condition favouring local people was void for uncertainty); *cf. Alderson v Secretary of State for the Environment* [1984] J.P.L. 429, CA (condition limiting occupation of premises to persons "employed locally in agriculture" was not uncertain); *Bromsgrove DC v Secretary of State for the Environment* [1988] J.P.L. 257 (difficulty of enforcement does not invalidate for uncertainty); *R. v Barnett LBC Ex p. Johnson* [1989] C.O.D. 538 (conditions attached to grant-aid for a community festival prohibiting "political activity" were held "meaningless").
[111] *R. v Bradford Metropolitan Council Ex p. Sikander Ali* [1994] E.L.R. 299 at 308.
[112] *R. v Hammersmith and Fulham LBC Ex p. Earls Court Ltd*, The Times, July 15, 1993; *R. (on the application of Z L) v Secretary of State for the Home Department* [2003] EWCA 25 at [17].
[113] See generally: I. Yeats, "Findings of Fact: The Role of the Courts", in G. Richardson and H. Genn (eds), *Administrative Law and Government Action* (1994), Ch.6; T. Jones, "Mistake of Fact in Administrative Law" [1990] P.L. 507; M. Kent, "Widening the Scope of Review for Error of Fact" [1999] J.R. 239; M. Demetriou and S. Houseman, "Review for Error of Fact: a Brief Guide [1997] J.R. 27 (comparison of mistake of fact with the notion of "manifest error" as applied by the ECJ).

primary decision for errors of "law".[114] The complexity intensifies in the light of the notorious difficulty of making a clear distinction between law and fact.[115] These days the prohibition on the court's assessment of fact is being blurred by the requirement that the decision-maker justify all aspects of a decision—be it law, fact, judgement or policy. Authorities acting on behalf of the public ought to be accountable for the overall quality of the decision-making process. Nevertheless, in general courts in judicial review, which is not appeal, should leave assessment of evidence and fact to the primary decision-maker, who is in any event often in a better position than the court accurately to evaluate the facts of a case and to decide their merits. We should therefore briefly consider the difference between law and fact and then go on to consider under what circumstances the courts may interfere on the ground of inadequate evidence or mistake of fact.

Fact and law distinguished

11–042 There is often no difficulty in distinguishing a question of law from one of fact. A finding of fact may be defined as an assertion that a phenomenon exists, has existed or will exist, independently of any assertion as to its legal effect.[116] The meaning that a lawyer should attribute to the terms of a policy of insurance is a question of law; the question whether the holder of a policy has renewed the policy before its expiry is one of fact.

11–043 Perplexing problems may, however, arise in analysing the nature of the process by which a public authority determines whether a factual situation falls within or without the limits of standard prescribed by a statute or other legal instrument. Every finding by a public authority postulates a process of abstraction and inference. At what point does an inference drawn from facts become an inference or law? Scrutton L.J. suggested that if a judge agrees with a decision of the primary decision-maker he calls it one of fact, but "if he disagrees with them then that is one of law, in order that he may express his own opinion the opposite way".[117] Although this statement may appear cynical, it expresses the view that the purpose of

---

[114] See, e.g. Tribunals, Courts and Enforcement Act 2007 s.11 (right of appeal "on any point of law" from First-tier Tribunal to Upper Tribunal); an appeal on point of law lies from decisions of housing authorities to the county courts.

[115] *Moyna v Secretary of State for Work and Pensions* [2003] UKHL 44; [2003] 1 W.L.R. 1929 at [22] (test set out in the Social Security Contributions and Benefits Act 1972 s.72 is a notional test to be construed in a general sense, and a person's ability to cook a meal is not to be assessed on a day-to-day basis but rather with regard to a whole period). In *Gillies v Secretary of State for Work and Pensions* [2006] UKHL 2; [2006] 1 W.L.R. 781 at [4]–[7] (Lord Hope: question of whether a person was biased was a question of law); on bias, see Ch.10.

[116] The 5th edition of this work contained a fuller account of the distinction between law and fact in Ch.5 ("Jurisdiction, Law and Fact"), most of which was written by de Smith.

[117] *Currie v Commissioners of Inland Revenue* [1921] 2 K.B. 332 at 339.

distinguishing law and fact is to delineate a limit on the autonomy of the primary decision-maker.[118]

Matters of degree

What has been called a question of a matter of degree, is a matter of fact **11–044** but one on which reasonable persons may arrive at different conclusions on the evidence before them.[119] Examples of such questions are: whether a house is "unfit for human habitation" or whether a "substantial part" of premises is to be reconstructed;[120] whether a house has changed its character because of structural alteration;[121] whether operations on land involve a "material change of use" constituting development for which planning permission is required.[122]

Questions of "mixed law and fact"

A further concept is that questions of "mixed law and fact". Thus, whether **11–045** the facts in issue are capable of falling within a category prescribed by statute may be treated as a question of law, since it entails a determination of the legal ambit of that category; whether they do fall within that category may be treated as a question of fact.[123] But the latter question can also be treated as a question of law; the factual part of a question of "mixed law and fact" is then confined to the ascertainment of the primary facts and perhaps the drawing of certain inferences from the facts.[124]

Distinction between fact, judgment and policy

Finally, mention might be made of the distinction between fact, judgment **11–046** and policy. In English planning law there is a distinction between facts (which are suitable for rigorous examination at public inquiries—such as

---

[118] T. Endicott, "Questions of Law" (1998) 114 L.Q.R. 292 (in a subtle analysis, Endicott employs the example of *Couzens v Brutus* [1973] A.C. 854 on disruption of Wimbledon tennis court held not to be "insulting" behaviour, and supports the approach of *Edwards (Inspector of Taxes) v Bairstow* [1956] A.C. 14, concluding that a question of application of fact to law is a question of law when the law requires one answer to the question of application).

[119] W. Wilson, "Questions of Degree" (1969) 32 M.L.R. 361. Endicott (1998) 114 L.Q.R. 292 does not approve of this distinction.

[120] *Re Bowman* [1932] 2 K.B. 621; *Daly v Elstree RDC* [1949] 2 All E.R. 13; *Hall v Manchester Corp* (1915) 84 L.J.Ch. 732; *Atkinson v Bettinson* [1955] 1 W.L.R. 1127; *Bewlay (Tobacconists) Ltd v British Bata Shoe Co* [1959] 1 W.L.R. 45; and *Scurlock v Secretary of State for Wales* (1977) 33 P. & C.R. 202 (whether a building is a "dwelling-house" is a question of fact).

[121] *Mitchell v Barnes* [1950] 1 K.B. 448; *Solle v Butcher* [1950] 1 K.B. 671; cf. *Pearlman v Keepers and Governors of Harrow School* [1979] Q.B. 56.

[122] Town and Country Planning Act, 1990 s.70.

[123] See, e.g. *White v St Marylebone BC* [1915] 3 K.B. 249; *Re Butler* [1939] 1 K.B. 570 at 579; *R. v Supplementary Benefits Commission Ex p. Singer* [1973] 1 W.L.R. 713; *Brooks and Burton Ltd v Secretary of State for the Environment* [1977] 1 W.L.R. 1294; *Clarks of Hove Ltd v Bakers' Union* [1978] 1 W.L.R. 1207 at 1217; *Bocking v Roberts* [1974] Q.B. 307; *Burton v Field & Sons Ltd* [1977] I.C.R. 106; *R. v West London Supplementary Benefits Appeal Tribunal Ex p. Wyatt* [1978] 1 W.L.R. 240.

[124] See, e.g. *Felix v General Dental Council* [1960] A.C. 704 at 717; *Bhattacharya v General Medical Council* [1967] 2 A.C. 259 at 265; *Faridian v General Medical Council* [1971] A.C. 995.

whether a building will obscure a particular view), planning judgment (the question whether the tall building will nevertheless overall improve the environment) and policy (the question whether buildings over a certain height should be allowed at all).[125]

Situations where review of fact permitted

11–047 Despite dicta attempting to restrict judicial review on questions of fact to situations where the public authority is acting "perversely",[126] review of fact has been permitted in the following situations: (a) where the existence of a set of facts is a condition precedent to the exercise of a power—a matter dealt with in Chapter 4;[127] (b) where there has been a misdirection or mistake of material fact; and (c) where the decision is unsupported by substantial evidence

Misdirection or mistake of material fact

11–048 Lord Denning contended on at least three occasions that a misdirection in fact or law could form the basis of review.[128] In the *Tameside* case,[129] judgments in both the Court of Appeal[130] and the House of Lords made similar suggestions. In particular, Lord Wilberforce said:

> "In many statutes a minister or other authority is given a discretionary power and in these cases the court's power to review any exercise of the discretion, though still real is limited. In these cases it is said that the courts cannot substitute their opinion for that of the minister: they can interfere on such grounds as that the minister has acted right outside his powers or outside the purpose of the Act, or unfairly, or upon an incorrect basis of fact."

[125] See in particular Lord Diplock's attempt to draw that distinction in *Bushell v Secretary of State for the Environment* [1981] A.C. 75 (Lord Edmund-Davies dissenting); *R. v Secretary of State for the Environment, Transport and the Regions Ex p. Holdings & Barnes Plc* (the Alconbury case) [2001] UKHL 23; [2003] 2 A.C. 295 (distinction made between "policy decisions" and "determinations of rights").

[126] *Pulhofer v Hillingdon LBC* [1986] A.C. 484 at 518 (Lord Brightman: "it is the duty of the court to leave the decision [of the existence or non-existence] of a fact to the public body to whom Parliament has entrusted the decision-making power save in a case where it is obvious that the public body, consciously or unconsciously, are acting perversely").

[127] See 4–047 *et seq*; see, e.g. *R. v Secretary of State for the Home Department Ex p. Khawajah* [1984] A.C. 74.

[128] *Secretary of State for Employment v ASLEF (No.2)* [1972] 2 Q.B. 455 at 493; *Laker Airways v Department of Trade* [1977] 1 Q.B. 643 at 705–706; *Smith v Inner London Education Authority* [1978] 1 All E.R. 411 at 415 ("It is clear that, if the education authority or the Secretary of State have exceeded their powers or misused them, the courts can say: 'Stop'. Likewise, if they have misdirected themselves in fact or in law. I go further. If they have exercised their discretion wrongly, or for no good reason, then too the courts can interfere").

[129] *Secretary of State for Education and Science v Tameside MBC* [1977] A.C. 1014.

[130] See, e.g. *Tameside* [1977] A.C. 1014 at 1047 (Lord Scarman: "misunderstanding or ignorance of an established and relevant fact" was within the "scope of judicial review").

A number of English planning decisions have assumed that a material **11–049**
mistake of fact is a proper ground for the courts to quash the decision of a
planning inspector.[131] Where the decision-maker has taken into account as
a fact something which is wrong or where he has misunderstood the facts
upon which the decision depends, such a decision is clearly an affront to
justice on the ground, we would argue, that it is strictly "irrational".
However, the courts have been slow to recognise mistake of material fact
as a ground of judicial review, because it appears to involve the judges in
assessing the merits of a decision. However, there have been instances
where the courts have intervened on that basis.[132]

In *R. v Criminal Injuries Compensation Board Ex p. A* Lord Slynn **11–050**
considered that a decision could be quashed on the basis of a mistake (in
relation to material which was or ought to have been within the knowledge
of the decision-maker).[133] In *Alconbury* Lord Slynn again confirmed that
view, in support of the view that the jurisdiction of the courts in the United
Kingdom meet the requirements of the ECHR[134] in that respect.[135] Lord
Nolan considered that the matter was settled in *Edwards v Bairstow*,[136]
where the House of Lords had upheld the right and duty of an appellate
court to reverse a finding which had "no justifiable basis".[137] Lord Clyde
held that a reviewing court could penetrate the factual areas of a decision
which "are irrelevant or even mistaken".[138]

[131] See, e.g. *Mason v Secretary of State for the Environment and Bromsgrove* DC [1984] J.P.L.
332 (inspector based decision on miscalculation of distance between two properties; but not
material); *Jagendorf v Secretary of State* [1985] J.P.L. 771 (material error that extension would
not obstruct premises when clearly would do so); *Hollis v Secretary of State for the
Environment* (1984) 47 P. & C.R. 351 (Glidewell J. assumes incorrect conclusion by
inspector that land never had green belt status a ground for quashing the decision); and T.
Jones, "Mistake of fact in Administrative Law" [1990] P.L. 507. *cf. R. v Independent
Television Commission Ex p. TSW Broadcasting Ltd* [1996] E.M.L.R. 291, HL (Lord
Templeman: "Judicial review does not issue merely because a decision-maker has made a
mistake").
[132] See, e.g. *Hollis v Secretary of State for the Environment* (1984) 47 P. & C.R. 351 (incorrect
conclusion by inspector that land never had green belt status a ground for quashing the
decision); *Simplex GE Holdings Ltd v Secretary of State for the Environment* (1989) 57 P. &
C.R. 306 (decision quashed because the Minister mistaken in a "material" or "significant"
fact—that council had carried out a study); *Secretary of State for Education and Science v
Tameside MBC* [1977] A.C. 1014 at 1030 (Lord Scarman: "misunderstanding of ignorance of
an established and relevant fact" could ground a claim in judicial review), 1047 (Lord
Wilberforce: need for "proper self-direction on the facts"); *Pulhofer v Hillingdon LBC* [1986]
AC 484 at 518 (Lord Brightman: duty of a court to leave the decision as to the existence of a
fact "to the public body to whom Parliament has entrusted the decision-making power, save
in a case were it is obvious that the public body, consciously or unconsciously, are acting
perversely"); *Wandsworth LBC v A* [2000] 1 W.L.R. 1246; *R. v Legal Aid Committee No.10
(E. Midlands) Ex p. McKenna* (1990) 2 Admin. L.R. 585 (refusal of legal aid quashed where
the decision was based upon a "demonstrably mistaken view of the facts").
[133] [1999] 2 A.C. 330 at 344–445 (citing in support of that proposition the 5th edition of this
work, at p.288 and H.W.R. Wade and C. Forsyth, *Administrative Law*, 7th edn (1994),
pp.316–318).
[134] Art.6(1) ECHR.
[135] *R. (on the application of Holding & Barnes Plc) v Secretary of State for the Environment,
Transport and the Regions* [2001] UKHL 23; [2003] 2 A.C. 295 at [54].
[136] [1956] A.C. 14.
[137] [1956] A.C. 14 at [61].
[138] [1956] A.C. 14 at [62].

11–051   The matter of mistake or ignorance of fact was considered by the Court of Appeal in *E v Secretary of State for the Home Department*.[139] The issue concerned two asylum seekers, both of whom resisted deportation on the ground that they would risk persecution in the country to which they would be deported. The Home Secretary based his decision to deport them on the ground they would not be subject to persecution, in ignorance of other "objective evidence" to the contrary. On appeal, the Immigration Appeal Tribunal acknowledged the mistake, but refused to reopen the matter in the interest of finality. Faced with conflicting authority as to whether "misunderstanding or ignorance of an established and relevant fact"[140] could be a cause of legal invalidity, Carnwath L.J., for the Court, held that mistake of fact "giving rise to unfairness" was indeed a ground on which to quash a decision on judicial review, provided that, first, there was a mistake as to an existing fact (including as to the availability of evidence on the matter). Secondly, the fact must be "established" (and thus "objective" and not "contentious"). Thirdly, the applicant or his advisers must not have been responsible for the mistake and fourthly, the mistake must have played a material (although not necessarily a decisive) part in the decision-maker's reasoning.[141] In so deciding, the Court of Appeal held that mistake of fact under those circumstances could not be absorbed into the traditional grounds of review but that it was a separate and new such ground.[142]

Decisions unsupported by substantial evidence

11–052   This encompasses situations where there is "no evidence" for a finding upon which a decision depends[143] or where the evidence, taken as a whole, is not reasonably capable of supporting a finding of fact. Such decisions may be

---

[139] [2004] EWCA Civ 49; [2004] Q.B. 1044 (discussed by P. Craig, "Judicial Review, Appeal and Factual Error" [2004] P.L. 788).

[140] The words used by Lord Scarman in *Tameside* [1977] A.C. 1014.

[141] The reasoning in the E case has been endorsed in *R. (Iran) v Secretary of State for the Home Department* [2005] EWCA Civ 982; [2005] Imm. A.R. 535; and *MT (Algeria) v Secretary of State for the Home Department* [2007] EWCA Civ 808 at [112].

[142] At [62], [63] and [66]. Thus siding with Wade and Forsyth, n.133 above, and not with Lord Slynn who in *R. v Criminal Injuries Compensation Board Ex p. A* [2007] 1 W.L.R. 977 rooted mistake of fact in a breach of natural justice. Carnwath L.J. also disagreed with the 5th edition of this work (at p.288) that mistake of fact could be absorbed into other traditional grounds of review, such as taking into account an irrelevant consideration.

[143] *Ashbridge Investments Ltd v Minister of Housing and Local Government* [1965] 1 W.L.R. 1320; *Coleen Properties Ltd v Minister of Housing and Local Government* [1971] 1 W.L.R. 433; *Archer and Thompson v Secretary of State for the Environment and Penwith DC* [1991] J.P.L. 1027; *Hertsmere BC v Secretary of State for the Environment and Percy* [1991] J.P.L. 552; *R. v Secretary of State for Home Affairs ex p. Zakrocki* [1996] C.O.D. 304; *R. v Newbury DC Ex p. Blackwell* [1988] C.O.D. 155 (planning committee's failure to obtain evidence of likely increase in road use on safety "unreasonable in the *Wednesbury* sense").

impugned[144] as "irrational"[145] or "perverse", providing that this was a finding as to a material matter.[146] Should we now go further and adopt a general rule empowering the courts to set aside findings of fact by public authorities if "unsupported by substantial evidence"?[147] If such a rule were to become meaningful, it would require bodies which at present conduct their proceedings informally to have verbatim transcripts or to keep detailed notes of evidence.[148] In some contexts the substantive evidence rule has much to commend it; and, as we have noted, some judges have already asserted jurisdiction to set aside decisions based on clearly erroneous inferences of fact either by classifying this type of error as an error of law or merely by proceeding on the assumption that manifest error of fact makes a decision unlawful.

---

[144] See, e.g. *Allinson v General Council of Medical Education and Registration* [1894] 1 Q.B. 750 at 760, 763; *American Thread Co v Joyce* (1913) 108 L.T. 353; *Smith v General Motor Cab Co* [1911] A.C. 188; *Doggett v Waterloo Taxi Cab Co* [1910] 2 K.B. 336; *Jones v Minister of Health* (1950) 84 Ll. L.Rep. 416; *Cababe v Walton-on-Thames UDC* [1914] A.C. 102 at 114; *Rowell v Minister of Pensions* [1946] 1 All E.R. 664 at 666; *Davies v Price* [1958] 1 W.L.R. 434 at 441–442; *R. v Birmingham Compensation Appeal Tribunal Ex p. Road Haulage Executive* [1952] 2 All E.R. 100; *Maradana Mosque Trustees v Mahmud* [1967] 1 A.C. 13; *Global Plant Ltd v Secretary of State for Social Services* [1972] 1 Q.B. 139 at 155. In India it has been held that facts may be reviewed in judicial review: *Bombay Dying v Bombay Environment Action Group* 2006 (3) S.C.C. 434 at 490 (Sinha J.).
[145] Decisions unsupported by evidence have been held to be unreasonable in: *Osgood v Nelson* (1872) L.R. 5 H.L. 636; *R. v Attorney General Ex p. Imperial Chemical Industries Plc* (1986) 60 Tax Cas. 1; *R. v Birmingham City Council Ex p. Sheptonhurst Ltd* [1990] 1 All E.R. 1026 (no evidence in licensing decision on sex establishment "irrational"); *R. v Housing Benefit Review Board of Sutton LBC Ex p. Keegan* (1995) 27 H.L.R. 92 (lack of evidence of failure to pay rent rendered decision "unreasonable"); *Piggott Bros and Co Ltd v Jackson* [1992] I.C.R. 85 (Lord Donaldson M.R., in the context of employment law, held that, to find a decision "perverse", the appeal tribunal had to be able to identify a finding of fact unsupported by any evidence); *Peak Park Joint Planning Board v Secretary of State for the Environment* [1991] J.P.L. 744 (a conclusion which "flew in the face of the evidence" and was "based on a view of the facts which could not reasonably be entertained" was held to be "perverse"). Sometimes such decisions have been held to involve excess of jurisdiction, e.g. *Ashbridge Investments* [1965] 1 W.L.R. 1320. Lord Diplock occasionally held that the principles of natural justice required a decision to be based on "evidential material of probative value", e.g. *Attorney General v Ryan* [19801 A.C. 718; *R. v Deputy Industrial Injuries Commissioner Ex p. Moore* [1965] 1 Q.B. 456 (reached a verdict that "no reasonable coroner could have reached").
[146] *Miftari v Secretary of State for the Home Department* [2005] EWCA Civ 481.
[147] As in the federal administrative law of the USA (Administrative Procedure Act of 1946 s.10(e)) and Canada (Federal Court Act 1970 s.28)).
[148] See, e.g. *Savoury v Secretary of State for Wales* (1976) 31 P. & C.R. 344 (challenge to a clearance order failed in because of the difficulty in establishing upon what evidence, if any, the local authority decided that there was "suitable accommodation available" for those displaced); *cf. Sabey (H) & Co Ltd v Secretary of State for the Environment* [1978] 1 All E.R. 586 (written evidence admissible to show that there was no evidence upon which the inspector or the Minister could base a finding of fact). For more recent cases where new evidence has been submitted: *R. v Secretary of State for the Home Department Ex p. Turgut* [2001] 1 All E.R. 719; *A v Secretary of State for the Home Department* [2003] EWCA Civ 175; [2003] I.N.L.R. 249; *Khan v Secretary of State for the Home Department* [2003] EWCA Civ 530; *Polat v Secretary of State for the Home Department* [2003] EWCA Civ 1059.

Evidence not before the decision-maker

11–053 One of the difficulties for the courts in permitting mistake of fact in judicial review proceedings is the extent to which they should permit evidence to be submitted which was not before the primary decision-maker. The principles for new evidence were set out clearly by Denning L.J. in *Ladd v Marshall*[149] as follows: (a) when the new evidence could not with reasonable diligence have been obtained for use at the trial (or hearing); (b) the new evidence should probably have had an important (thought not necessarily decisive) influence on the result of the case;, and (c) the new evidence was apparently credible although it need not be incontrovertible.

11–054 In the *E* case, Carnwath L.J. said that the admission of new evidence in a case where mistake of material fact was pleaded was subject to the *Marshall* principles, which might be departed from "in exceptional circumstances where the interests of justice required".[150] It should not, however, be assumed that in the English legal system the failure of a party to adduce evidence will lead the court necessarily to infer that the silence should be converted into proof against that party. As was said by Lord Lowry, "if the silent party's failure to give evidence . . . can be explained . . . the effect of his silence in favour of the other party may be either reduced or nullified".[151]

11–055 The wrongful rejection of evidence by a decision-maker may also amount either to a failure to take into account a relevant consideration and thus render the decision unlawful[152] or to a failure to afford procedural propriety.[153]

General principles summarised

11–056 Our view is that mistake of fact in and of itself renders a decision irrational or unreasonable. In general it is right that courts do leave the assessment of fact to public authorities which are primarily suited to gathering and

---

[149] [1954] 1 W.L.R. 1489 at 1491.

[150] [2004] EWCA Civ 49 at [91]; *Iran* [2005] EWCH Civ 982; [2005] Imm. A.R. 535 (Brooke L.J. carefully considers under what circumstances new evidence may be admitted by the reviewing court where there has been a change of circumstances since the original decision).

[151] *R. v Inland Revenue Commissioners Ex p. TC Coombs and Co* [1991] 2 A.C. 283 at 300; and *Gouriet v Union of Post Office Workers* [1978] A.C. 435 at 486 (Lord Dilhorne). Expert evidence may be rejected without evidence to contradict it where the matter is within the professional experience of a planning inspector: see *Kentucky Fried Chicken (GB) Ltd v Secretary of State for the Environment* (1978) 245 E.G. 839; *Ainley v Secretary of State for the Environment* [1987] J.P.L. 33. Lack of reasons may, however, permit an interference of irrationality: see the cases cited at n.99 above.

[152] See 5–110–5–134.

[153] See Ch.7. See e.g. *R. v Wood* (1855) 5 E. & B. 49 (conviction after refusal to hear submission that byelaw contravened was ultra vires); *GMC v Spackman* [1943] A.C. 627 (doctor struck off register after GMC had refused to receive evidence by him to disprove adultery with patient); *R. v Kingston-upon-Hull Rent Tribunal Ex p. Black* (1949) 65 T.L.R. 209 (tribunal reduced rent after failing to give landlady opportunity to be heard on the substantial issue); *R. v Birkenhead Justices Ex p. Fisher* [1962] 1 W.L.R. 1410; *Bond v Bond* [1967] P. 39.

assessing the evidence. Review must not become appeal. On the other hand it should be presumed that Parliament intended public authorities rationally to relate the evidence and their reasoning to the decision which they are charged with making. The taking into account of a mistaken fact can just as easily be absorbed into a traditional legal ground of review by referring to the taking into account of an irrelevant consideration; or the failure to provide reasons that are adequate or intelligible, or the failure to base the decision upon any evidence. In this limited context material error of fact has always been a recognised ground for judicial intervention. Since *E*, however, the circumstances in which a decision of the primary decision-maker may be impugned on fact has been somewhat curtailed. In *Shaheen v Secretary of State for the Home Department*,[154] Brooke L.J., for the Court of Appeal, was unwilling to reopen the decision of the primary decision-maker taken on a mistaken belief that there was no evidence to refute a material fact. He suggested the following possible summary of the situation to date:

> "(i) Proof or admission that the tribunal of fact misapprehended a potentially decisive element of the evidence before it discloses an error of law (as held in the *E case*)[155]
> (ii) Proof or admission of a subsequently discovered fact permits an appellate court to set aside a decision for fraud, provided that it was potentially decisive and it can be shown that the defendant was responsible for its concealment.
> (iii) The emergence of any other class of new fact, whether contested or not, has either to be processed (within the Immigration Rules in that case) or simply lived with, as Lord Wilberforce explained in the *Ampthill Peerage* case[156]. . . In any other case, finality prevails".

VIOLATION OF CONSTITUTIONAL PRINCIPLE

We have seen in a number of situations how the scope of an official power **11–057** cannot be interpreted in isolation from general principles governing the exercise of power in a constitutional democracy.[157] The English courts have relatively recently explicitly referred to the notion of constitutional rights and principles, even in the absence of any written constitution. In the mid-1990s, even before the Human Rights Act 1998 incorporated Convention rights into domestic law, the courts adopted an approach which, instead of seeking to apply the ungrounded unreasonableness standard, based their assessment upon the rule of law and other necessary condition of a

[154] [2005] EWCA Civ 1294; [2006] Imm. A.R. 57; and *Verde v Secretary of State for the Home Department* [2004] EWCA Civ 1726.
[155] [2004] EWCH Civ 49; [2004] Q.B. 1044.
[156] [1977] A.C. 547 at 569.
[157] See 1–015; 5–036.

constitutional democracy. Thus the absence of a prisoner's access to a lawyer,[158] or to the press[159] was struck down not on the ground of unreasonableness (however strictly scrutinised), but on the ground that a fundamental constitutional principle (access to justice and free expression respectively) had been infringed. These principles were implied from the fact that public officials ought to maintain the standards of a modern European democracy.[160] An orthogonal principle of "legality" provided that the courts would apply the rule of law and any other constitutional principles (such as free expression) unless Parliament expressly and clearly excluded them. Ambiguity was not enough to exclude those principles. In practice, any departure from these "home grown" constitutional principles was assessed under the structured proportionality test that we shall consider below[161] under which these rights may be curtailed only to the extent necessary to meet the ends which justify their curtailment.

11–058   In Chapter 5 we considered how a number of rights of the individual have been recognised in the common law.[162] To these we may add the *principles* of respect for the rule of law and equality.[163] The courts presume that these principles apply to the exercise of all public functions. Even where the decision-maker is invested with wide discretion, that discretion is to be exercised in accordance with those principles. However, as long as parliamentary sovereignty endures as the prime constitutional principle (subject to European Community law), other constitutional principles will ultimately give way to Parliament's clear expression of intent to override them.

The rule of law

11–059   The rule of law has proved itself to be elastic enough to be able, particularly in recent years, to act as a significant constraint upon the exercise of administrative discretion in different circumstances. It received statutory recognition in s.1 of the Constitutional Reform Act 2005.[164] The rule of law has been a resilient and effective force behind the general development of judicial review.[165] Dicey's view of the rule of law[166] has been contested,[167] but as a general principle it has provided the major justification for constraining the exercise of official power, promoting the core institutional

---

[158] *R. v Secretary of State for the Home Department Ex p. Leech (No.2)* [1994] Q.B. 198.
[159] *R. v Secretary of State for the Home Department Ex p. Simms* [2000] 2 A.C. 115.
[160] *R. v Secretary of State for the Home Department Ex p. Pierson* [1998] A.C. 539.
[161] See 11–077–11–083.
[162] See 5–036–5–040.
[163] See 1–015–1–021.
[164] "This Act does not adversely affect—(a) the existing constitutional principle of the rule of law, or (b) the Lord Chancellor's existing constitutional role in relation to that principle".
[165] J. Jowell, "The Rule of Law Today" Ch.1 in J. Jowell and D. Oliver (eds), *The Changing Constitution*, 6th edn (2007); Lord Bingham, "The Rule of Law" [2007] C.L.J. 67; P. Craig, Appendix 6 to the House of Lords Select Committee on the Constitution, *Relations between the executive, the judiciary and Parliament* HL Paper No.151 (Session 2006/07).
[166] A.V. Dicey, *The Law of the Constitution*, 10th edn. (1959).
[167] See, e.g. Sir Ivor Jennings, *The Law and the Constitution* (1933).

values of legality, certainty, consistency, due process and access to justice. Being a principle and not a clear rule, the precise content of the rule of law has been articulated on a case-by-case basis, particularly in recent years.

In practice, many of the decisions held unreasonable are so held because **11–060** they offend the values of the rule of law. The concept of "unreasonable-ness", or "irrationality" in itself imputes the arbitrariness that Dicey considered was the antithesis of the rule of law. A local authority which withdrew the licence of a rugby club whose members had visited South Africa during the apartheid regime fell foul of the rule of law on the ground that there should be no punishment where there was no law (since sporting contacts with South Africa were not then prohibited).[168] A Minister's rules allowing a prison governor to prevent a prisoner corresponding with his lawyer, even when no litigation was contemplated, was held to violate the prisoner's "constitutional right" of access to justice.[169] Access to Justice as a value of the rule of law was again held to have been violated by the imposition of court fees which an impecunious litigant was unable to afford.[170] The courts will not lightly sanction the withdrawal of policing in the face of protesters if do so offends the rule of law.[171]

The richness of the rule of law's underlying values was demonstrated **11–061** when a decision had not been communicated to the person affected.[172] The appellant could not easily invoke the normal requirements of the rule of law in her favour as the decision did not take effect retrospectively; ignorance of the law does not normally excuse its application, and the doctrine of prior notice normally applies only to permit the appellant to make representations on the case to the primary decision-maker (here the Home Secretary). Nevertheless, the House of Lords, by majority, held that the decision violated "the constitutional principle requiring the rule of law to be observed".[173] Lord Steyn, with whom the majority of their Lordships concurred, based his argument both upon legal certainty ("surprise is the enemy of justice") and upon accountability: the individual must be informed of the outcome of her case so "she can decide what to do" and "be in a position to challenge the decision in the courts" (this being an aspect of the principle of the right of access to justice).[174] Similarly, the Court of Appeal

---

[168] *Wheeler v Leicester City Council* [1985] A.C. 1054.

[169] *Ex p. Leech (No.2)* [1994] Q.B. 198.

[170] *R. v Lord Chancellor Ex p. Witham* [1997] 1 W.L.R. 104.

[171] *R v Coventry City Council Ex p. Phoenix Aviation Ltd* [1995] 3 All E.R. 37; *cf. R. v Chief Constable of Sussex Ex p. International Trader's Ferry Ltd* [1999] 2 A.C. 418.

[172] *R. (on the application of Anufrijeva) v Secretary of State for the Home Department* [2003] UKHL 36; [2004] 1 A.C. 604 (legislation permitted asylum-seekers' right to income support to be terminated once their application for asylum had been refused by a "determination" of the Home Secretary. The refusal in this case was recorded only in an internal file note in the Home Office and communicated to the Benefits Agency, which promptly denied the appellant future income support. The determination was not, however, communicated to the appellant).

[173] Lord Steyn at [28].

[174] Lord Steyn at [26]–[38] (who had no truck with the notion that the Home Secretary's determination had formally and strictly been made. This was "legalism and conceptualism run riot", which is reminiscent of the state described by Kafka "where the rights of an individual are overridden by hole in the corner decisions or knocks on the doors in the early hours").

held that the Home Secretary could not follow unpublished guidelines on detention of asylum seekers, and that in the case of interference with the liberty of the subject, publication of the policy was necessary to afford it legality.[175]

The principle of equality

11–062　Baroness Hale has observed that

> "Democracy is founded on the principle that each individual has equal value. Treating some as automatically having less value than others not only causes pain and distress to that person but also violates his or her dignity as a human being."[176]

There are two senses of equality: formal equality and substantive equality.

Formal equality (consistency)

11–063　Formal equality requires officials to apply or enforce the law consistently and even-handedly, without bias. Dicey considered this to be fundamental to his notion of the rule of law: "With us, every official, from the Prime Minister down to a constable or collector of taxes, is under the same responsibility for every act done without legal justification".[177] This kind of consistency was fundamental to Dicey primarily because of its value in furthering the central feature for him of the rule of law, namely, legal certainty and predictability.[178] Consistent application of the law also, however, possesses another value in its own right—that of ensuring that all persons similarly situated will be treated equally by those who apply the law. It is this notion of the equal (rather than the certain or predictable) application of the law which is the central aim of formal equality.

11–064　　A number of cases have considered the question as to whether selective enforcement or selective concessions (e.g. concessions to individuals or groups of taxpayers by the HM Revenue and Customs) violates equal treatment, or whether to cease a previously unfair practice is unfair to those who were previously unfairly treated. In general, selective enforcement of the law has been held not to breach the principle of equal treatment in view

---

[175] R. (on the application of Nadarajah) v Secretary of State for the Home Department [2003] EWCA Civ 1768; [2004] I.N.L.R. 139 at [68]; and R. v North West Lancashire Health Authority Ex p. A [2000] 1 W.L.R. 977 (suggested that it might be irrational for a health authority not to draft a policy for the allocation of different medical treatments); on legitimate expectations, see Ch.12; on the principle of consistency, see 11–00.
[176] Ghaidan v Godin-Mendoza [2004] UKHL 30; [2004] 2 A.C. 557 at [132].
[177] A.V. Dicey, The Law of the Constitution, 10th edn (1959), p.193.
[178] This aim is connected with Dicey's view that discretionary power inevitably leads to its arbitrary exercise. Equal application of the law also formed the basis of Dicey's dubious claim that, unlike what he saw as the French position, in "England" officials were subject to the same law as ordinary individuals.

of the limited resources available to the prosecuting officials and the legitimacy of exemplary prosecutions.[179] However, the principle of consistency has been applied in a number of cases.[180] In holding that the test of whether an applicant for a student grant was "ordinarily resident in the United Kingdom" should be consistently applied, the Master of the Rolls said that "it is a cardinal principle of good public administration that all persons in a similar position should be treated similarly".[181] Where mushroom pickers were excluded from a reduced minimum wage for harvesters, the decision was held to be unreasonable and unlawful.[182] It is well established that planning permission may be refused on the ground that a grant of permission would create a precedent from which, as a practical matter, it would be difficult for the authority to depart without creating an impression of unfairness,[183] thus upholding the notion of consistency and equality of treatment as a "material consideration" in planning. And it is material to the grant of planning permission that permission was granted in other similarly situated cases.[184]

Although in the past the decisions of planning inspectors were not considered "material considerations" which should be followed in like cases, they have now been accorded the status of precedent in the interest of consistency and equality of treatment.[185] Where a London council devolved its powers to allocate housing to the homeless to seven neighbourhoods, and where this arrangement resulted in the application of variable standards for letting housing to the homeless, this was held to be "unfair and irrational".[186] The preferential allocation of council housing to a councillor, in

11–065

---

[179] On prosecutorial discretion, see 5–071 and Y. Dotan, "Should Prosecutorial Discretion Enjoy Special Treatment in Judicial Review? A Comparative Analysis of the Law in England and Israel" [1997] P.L. 513; e.g. *Vestey v IRC* [1980] A.C. 1148; *R. v IRC Ex p. National Federation of Self-Employed and Small Businesses Ltd* [1982] A.C. 617; *R. v IRC Ex p. Mead* [1993] 1 All E.R. 772; *Woods v Secretary of State for Scotland* 1991 S.L.T. 197; cf. dicta indicating equality of treatment may be applied in the tax field: *J Rothschild Holdings v IRC* [1988] S.T.C. 435; *R. v IRC Ex p. Warburg* [1994] S.T.C. 518 at 541.

[180] K. Steyn, "Consistency—A Principle of Public Law?" [1997] J.R. 22; *R. (on the application of Munjaz) v Mersey Care NHS Trust* [2005] UKHL 58; [2006] 2 A.C. 148 at [122] (Lord Brown of Eaton-under-Heywood: requirement of the ECtHR that the "quality of the law"— in the context of the expression "in accordance with the law"—requires compatibility with the rule of law (*Hewitt v UK* (1992) 14 E.H.R.R. 657) and regarded the "quality of the law" "to encompass notions of transparency, accessibility, predictability and consistency, features of a legal regime designed to guard against the arbitrary use of power and to afford sufficient legal protection to those at risk of its abuse").

[181] *R. v Hertfordshire CC Ex p. Cheung, The Times*, April 4, 1986 (Lord Donaldson M.R.).

[182] *R. (on the application of Middlebrook Mushrooms Ltd) v Agricultural Wages Board of England and Wales* [2004] EWHC (Admin) 1635 at [74] (citing the 5th edition of this work with approval).

[183] See, e.g. *Collis Radio v Secretary of State for the Environment* (1975) P. & C.R. 390; *Tempo Discount v Secretary of State for the Environment* [1979] J.P.L. 97; *Poundstretcher Ltd v Secretary of State for the Environment & Liverpool Council* [1989] J.P.L. 90. *Rumsey v Secretary of State for the Environment, Transport and the Regions* (2001) 81 P.& C.R. 32.

[184] *Ynys Mon Isle of Anglesey BC v Secretary of State for Wales and Parry Bros* [1984] J.P.L. 646.

[185] *North Wiltshire DC v Secretary of State for the Environment* [1992] J.P.L. 955, CA; *Aylesbury Vale DC v Secretary of State for the Environment and Woodruff* [1995] J.P.L. 26.

[186] *R. v Tower Hamlets LBC Ex p. Ali* (1992) 25 H.L.R. 158 at 314.

order to put her in a better position to fight a local election in her own constituency, was held to be an "abuse of power" because it was unfair to others on the housing list.[187] It has been held that a decision to renew a licence should not disregard the fact that licences were recently granted in other like cases.[188] The Home Secretary was bound to apply an existing policy to the claimant (where no good reason had been advanced for not doing so) in the interest of consistency and fairness.[189]

11–066   The principle of consistency is linked to other aspects of the rule of law, such as that law should be predictable and known in advance so that people are not in ignorance of the way that the law is applied. For that reason, in cases where a policy is insufficiently specified, there may be a legal obligation to provide precise rules to affected parties so that they can be reasonably certain how to plan their actions.[190] An "overbroad" policy may also be held incompatible with the requirement in a number of Convention rights that interference with a right, to be lawful, must be "prescribed by law" (Arts 10 and 11 ECHR) or "in accordance with the law" (Art.8 ECHR). In *R. (on the application of S) v Secretary of State for the Home Department*[191] it was held that a policy document conferring very wide discretion on a Minister to depart from its terms was incompatible with the Convention requirements because it failed to "give any protection against arbitrary interference by Ministers" and because its open-ended nature was not "foreseeable".[192]

Substantive equality

11–067   The second type of equality, substantive equality, does not refer to the enforcement of law but to its content. It seeks equal laws—laws which themselves do not discriminate between individuals on invidious grounds. There are a number of different philosophical theories of substantive

---

[187] *R. v Port Talbot BC Ex p. Jones* [1988] 2 All E.R. 207, QBD.
[188] *R. v Birmingham City Council Ex p. Steptonhurst Ltd* [1990] 1 All E.R. 1026.
[189] *R (on the application of Rashid) v Secretary of State for the Home Department* [2005] EWCA Civ 744; [2005] Imm. A.R. 608 at [34] (Pill L.J.). See N. Blake, "Judicial Interpretation of Policies Promulgated by the Executive" [2006] J.R. 298; R. Clayton, "Legitimate Expectations, Policy and the Principle of Consistency" [2003] C.L.J. 93 (emphasising that the rationale of the case was not legitimate expectation but the free-standing principle of consistency); M. Elliott, "Legitimate Expectations, Consistency and Abuse of Power: The Rashid case" [2005] J.R. 281. *R. (on the application of O'Brien) v Independent Assessor* [2007] UKHL 10; [2007] 2 W.L.R. 544 at [30] (concerning the calculation of compensation for miscarriages of justice, "It is generally desirable that decision-makers, whether administrative or judicial, should act in a broadly consistent manner. If they do, reasonable hopes will not be disappointed").
[190] See, e.g. *R. (on the application of Quark Fishing Ltd) v Secretary of State for Foreign and Commonwealth Affairs* [2001] EWHC 1174; [2002] EWCA Civ 1409 (applicants for valuable fishing licence entitled to be in no doubt about circumstances in which it would be granted); cf. rule against fettering of discretion discussed in Ch.9.
[191] [2006] EWCA Civ 1157; [2006] I.N.L.R. 575.
[192] At [113].

equality[193] which obviously have not formed the basis for any judicial application of the principle in English law. However, a particular restricted formulation of substantive equality is applied as a "general principle of law" in European Community law[194] and in the law relating to the ECHR, in particular in relation to Art.14.[195] Principles of substantive equality are given effect in several provisions of domestic legislation.[196]

This formulation has also justified a number of decisions in English **11–068** administrative law sometimes expressly, but mostly under the guise of unreasonableness. We have already seen that in the 19th century Lord Russell considered that byelaws could be held unreasonable because of "partial and unequal treatment in their operation as between different classes".[197] Although subsequent cases did not articulate the principle with equivalent clarity, unequal treatment has justified a number of instances where the courts have struck down a decision or provision which infringes equality in either its formal or its substantive sense. English common law has traditionally placed ancient duties, requiring equality of treatment, upon common carriers, inn-keepers and some monopoly enterprises such as ports and harbours, obliging them to accept all travellers.[198] In addition the courts have occasionally invoked notions of "public policy" to strike down discriminatory provisions. In *Nagle v Fielden*[199] the Jockey Club's refusal of a horse trainer's licence to a woman was held to be against public policy, and in *Edwards v SOGAT*,[200] a case involving a challenge to the withdrawal of collective bargaining rights, Lord Denning said that our courts "will not allow a power to be exercised arbitrarily or capriciously or with unfair discrimination, neither in the making of rules or in the enforcement of them" (a statement which addresses itself to both substantive and formal equality). In *Ghaidan v Godin Mendoza* (a case under the HRA), holding that unmarried same sex partners were entitled to same inheritance rights to

---

[193] J. Jowell, "Is Equality a Constitutional Principle?" (1994) C.L.P Pt 2, 1; R. Singh, "Equality: The Neglected Virtue" [2004] E.H.R.L.R. 141; D. Feldman, *Civil Liberties and Human Rights in England and Wales*, 2nd edn. (2002), Ch.3; T.R.S. Allan, *Law, Liberty and Justice* (1993); C. McCrudden, "Equality and Non-Discrimination", Ch.11 in D. Feldman (ed.), *English Public Law* (2004); Baroness Hale of Richmond, "The Quest for Equality and Non-Discrimination" [2005] P.L. 571; S. Fredman, "From Deference to Democracy: the Role of Equality under the Human Rights Act 1998" (2006) 112 L.Q.R. 53.
[194] See Ch.14.
[195] See Ch.13.
[196] See, e.g. Sex Discrimination Act 1975; Race Relations Act 1976; Disability Discrimination Act 1995; Employment Equality (Religion or Belief) Regulations 2003 (SI 2003/1660); Employment Equality (Sexual Orientation) Regulations 2003 (SI 2003/1661); Employment Equality (Age) Regulations 2006 (SI 2006/1031).
[197] *Kruse v Johnson* [1889] 2 Q.B. 291.
[198] *Rothfield v NB Railway* 1920 S.C. 805 ("and others who are in a reasonable fit condition to be received"); *Pidgeon v Legge* (1857) 21 J.P 743. Similar principles have applied to the providers of some utilities, e.g. *South of Scotland Electricity Board v British Oxygen Ltd* [1959] 1 W.L.R. 587.
[199] [1966] 2 Q.B. 633.
[200] [1971] Ch. 354. The reach of public policy was not sufficient to prohibit certain forms of discrimination which were thus made unlawful through legislation first passed in the 1960s and now consolidated in the Equality Act 2006.

tenancies as unmarried heterosexual partners, Baroness Hale of Richmond said that unequal treatment

"is the reverse of the rational behaviour we now expect from government and the state. Power must not be exercised arbitrarily. If distinctions are to be drawn, particularly upon a group basis, it is an important discipline to look for a rational basis for those distinctions."[201]

Illustrations of application of substantive inequality principle in common law

11–069   Independently of European Community law and the ECHR, equality of treatment has shown itself to be a principle of lawful administration in English law.

- *Religion.* In *Board of Education v Rice*, a case noted for its application of natural justice, the substantive issue was the authority's power to fund church schools less favourably than other schools. Lord Halsbury, who felt that the differential treatment was based upon hostility to the church schools said: "it is clear that the local education authority ought to be as impartial as the rate collector who demands the rate without reference to the peculiar views of the ratepayer".[202]

- *Age.* In *Prescott v Birmingham Corp*[203] the corporation, which had power to charge "such fares as they may think fit" on their public transport services introduced a scheme for free bus travel for the elderly. The decision was declared to be an improper exercise of discretion because it conferred out of rates "a special benefit on some particular class of inhabitants [and] would amount simply to the making of a gift or present in money's worth to a particular section of the local community at the expense of the general body of ratepayers".[204] The House of Lords has held (in advance of statutory or European Community law requirements on the matter) that the adoption by a local authority of the statutory criterion of pensionable age (65 for men and 60 for women) as the qualification for free admittance to a leisure centre is a breach of the statutory prohibition against sex discrimination.[205]

---

[201] [2004] UKHL 30; [2004] 2 A.C. 557, [132].
[202] [1911] A.C. 179, 186.
[203] [1955] 1 Ch. 210.
[204] Clearly the notion of equality applied in *Prescott* would not suit all theories of equality. Local authorities were given power ultimately to allow certain classes of free travel by the Travel Concessions Act 1964. In *Roberts v Hopwood* [1925] A.C. 578 the HL confirmed the view of the district auditor that the attempt of Poplar BC to raise the level of wages of both men and women employees to an equal level was unlawful. Lord Atkinson considered that the council was guided by "eccentric principles of socialistic philanthropy, or feminist ambition to secure the equality of the sexes". Despite its headnote, the case was not decided on unreasonableness but on the ground of illegality, there being no "rational proportion" between the rates paid to women employees and the going market rate; *Pickwell v Camden LBC* [1993] Q.B. 962 at 999–1000 (Ormrod L.J.).
[205] *James v Eastleigh BC* [1990] 2 A.C. 751.

- *Location-related factors.* Conditions in planning policies that favour "locals only" in the allocation of housing or office space have been held unlawful, although if the provision is placed in a development plan, it may thus be considered a material consideration.[206] Questions of place of residence have also arisen in relation to the admissions criteria for schools.[207] The courts have held that admissions policies must treat children both within and outside a local authority boundary in the same way,[208] though proximity to a school may be a valid consideration in determining a school admissions policy,[209] as may religious affiliation even where the school in question was not a church school.[210] The Court of Appeal considered whether the policy to exclude from compensation to former internees (of British nationality) by the Japanese in the Second World War those whose parents or grandparents were not born in the United Kingdom offended the principle of equality. While subscribing to the general acceptance of equality as a constitutional principle, Dyson L.J. held that the birth-related criteria in that case were "not unreasonable in the *Wednesbury* sense".[211] A similar conclusion was reached by the House of Lords in rejecting an argument that differential treatment under an ex gratia compensation scheme of British soldiers injured in Bosnia as compared with those injured in Northern Ireland should be regarded as an irrational distinction.[212]

- *Financial circumstances.* Regulations which restricted the admission of dependent relatives to those having a standard of living "substantially below [their] own country", which would benefit immigrants from affluent countries, were held to be "manifestly unjust and unreasonable".[213] But the court refused to intervene in arrangements under

---

[206] *Slough Industrial Estates Ltd v Secretary of State for the Environment* [1987] J.P.L. 353; *Kember v Secretary of State for the Environment* [1982] J.P.L. 383. Such conditions may be void for uncertainty, see 11–040. For unreasonably discriminatory taxi licence conditions (giving advantages to Hackney cabs) see *R. v Blackpool BC Ex p. Red Cab Taxis, The Times,* May 13, 1995.

[207] See now Department for Education and Skills, *School Admissions Code* (2007).

[208] *R. v Greenwich LBC Ex p. Governors of the John Ball Primary School* (1989) 88 L.G.R. 589; *R. v Kingston-on-Thames LBC Ex p. Kingwell* [1992] 1 F.L.R. 182; *R. v Bromley LBC Ex p. C* [1992] 1 F.L.R. 174; *R. v Rochdale MBC Ex p. Schemet* (1993) 91 L.G.R. 425; *R. v Devon CC Ex p. George* [1989] A.C. 573.

[209] *R. v Rotherham MBC Ex p. LT* [2000] B.L.G.R. 338, CA.

[210] *R. v Governors of Bishop Challoner Roman Catholic School Ex p. Choudhury* [1992] 2 A.C. 182.

[211] *R. (on the application of Association of British Civilian Internees (Far East Region)) v Secretary of State for Defence* [2003] EWCA Civ 473; [2003] Q.B. 1397.

[212] *R. v Ministry of Defence Ex p. Walker* [2000] 1 W.L.R. 806 at 812 (Lord Slynn: "It is not for the courts to consider whether the scheme with its exclusion is a good scheme or a bad scheme, unless it can be said that the exclusion is irrational or so unreasonable that no reasonable Minister could have adopted it").

[213] *R. v Immigration Appeal Tribunal Ex p. Manshoora Bugum* [1986] Imm.A.R. 385 (the offending provision was severed from the rest of the regulations).

which prisoners, granted legal aid for legal representation, could represent themselves in civil proceedings or judicial review claims only if able to meet the costs of travel and a security escort, or make a formal request to the Home Secretary for a direction (which the claimant in this case refused to do).[214]

- *Sexual orientation.* Prior to the HRA, the Court of Appeal accepted the principle of equality as being applicable to the question of the exclusion of homosexual men and women from the armed forces; the policy was not, however, held to be irrational.[215]

- *Nationality.* Rules excluding from employment at GCHQ people whose parents were foreign nationals were held to be made in the interests of national security and non-justiciable.[216]

- *Language.* In a Privy Council appeal, where a challenge was made to a new policy which added Oriental languages to the list of subjects be taken as part of the school-leaving curriculum, the appellants claimed that the policy favoured children from homes where those languages were spoken. Lord Hoffmann did not doubt that equality before the law was a principle which is "one of the building blocks of democracy and necessarily permeates any democratic constitution", as well as "a general axiom of rational behaviour".[217] However, he also acknowledged that the reason for different treatment may involve "questions of social policy, on which views may differ".

OPPRESSIVE DECISIONS

11–070   Official decisions may be held unreasonable when they are unduly oppressive because they subject the complainant to an excessive hardship or an unnecessarily onerous infringement of his rights or interests. As we shall see, the principle of proportionality directs itself to the evaluation of the permitted degree of infringement of rights or interests.[218] However,

---

[214] *R. v Secretary of State for the Home Department Ex p. Wynne* [1993] 1 W.L.R. 115, HL.
[215] *R. v Ministry of Defence Ex p. Smith* [1996] Q.B. 517, CA: *Smith and Grady v UK* (1999) 29 E.H.R.R. 493 (ECtHR held that the exclusion offended Convention rights under Arts 8 and 13, but did not base their decision upon equality).
[216] *R. v Secretary of State for Foreign and Commonwealth Affairs Ex p. Manelfi* [1996] 12 C.L. 65.
[217] *Matadeen v Pointu* [1999] A.C. 98 at 109, citing paras 13–036 to 13–045 of the 5th edn of this work with approval. In *Matadeen*, the appellants failed in their claim that the new policy offended the limited prohibition of unequal treatment under the constitution of Mauritius.
[218] See 11–073 *et seq.*

whether or not proportionality is expressly applied, this aspect of substantive review is well known to English law. As Laws L.J. has said:

"Clearly a public body may choose to deploy powers it enjoys under statute in so draconian a fashion that the hardship suffered by affected individuals in consequence will justify the court in condemning the exercise as irrational and perverse".[219]

The focus of attention in these cases will be principally the *impact* of the decision upon the affected person. The outcome or end-product of the decision-making process will thus be assessed, rather than the way the decision was reached (although the factors taken into account in reaching the decision may also be—or may be assumed to be—incorrectly weighed). Since the claim is essentially abuse of power, in the sense of excessive use of power, each case must be considered in the context of the nature of the decision, the function of the particular power and the nature of the interests or rights affected. **11–071**

Illustrations of oppressive decisions

- *Imposing an uneven burden.* A very early case involved the Commissioner of Sewers imposing on one landowner alone charges for repairs to a river bank from which other riparian owners had also benefited. This decision was held to be contrary to the law and reason.[220] The actions of a local authority were held *Wednesbury* unreasonable when, in order to avoid raising rents generally as required by legislation, they charged the whole of required rent increases upon a single unoccupied and unfit property.[221] **11–072**

- *When implementation is impossible.* A byelaw requiring the annual cleaning of lodging houses when access was not always possible.[222]

- Where delegated legislation deviates materially from the general law of the land in imposing "burdensome prohibitions".[223]

---

[219] R. (on the application of Khatun) v Newham LBC [2004] EWCA Civ 55; [2005] Q.B. 37 at [41] (neither oppressive, perverse or disproportionate for the council to require an claimant who had not viewed an offered property to accept it on pain of his existing accommodation being cancelled if he did not).

[220] Rooke's case (1598) 5 Co.Rep. 99b.

[221] Backhouse v Lambeth LBC, The Times, October 14, 1972.

[222] Arlidge v Mayor etc. of Islington [1909] 2 K.B. 127. Cf. Dr Bonham's case (1610) 8 Co.Rep. 107(a) (Coke C.J. said that an Act of Parliament could be controlled by the common law if the Act "is against common right or reason, or repugnant, or impossible to be performed"); in Germany a provision which is impossible of implementation falls foul of the principle of proportionality.

[223] See, e.g. London Passenger Transport Board v Sumner (1935) 154 L.T. 108; Powell v May [1946] K.B. 330; R. v Brighton Corp. Ex p. Tilling (Thomas) Ltd (1916) 85 L.J.K.B. 1552; R. v Customs and Excise Commissioners Ex p. Hedges & Butler Ltd [1986] 2 All E.R. 164 (regulation unlawful because it gave power to officials to inspect all the records of a business, and not only those records pertaining to dutiable goods).

- Regulations have been held unreasonable where their effect is to prevent access to the courts.[224]

- Town and country planning provides countless examples where planning conditions have been held unreasonable because of their unnecessarily onerous impact. Although the legislation permits the local authority, or the Secretary of State on appeal, to attach conditions to planning permissions as they "think fit",[225] conditions have been held unreasonable which, in effect, require the developer to dedicate part of his land for public use[226] or otherwise require the developer to provide the off-site physical infrastructure necessary to unlock the development.[227] Similarly, a planning condition was held unreasonable which, in effect, required the developer to construct housing to local authority standards and rents, and to take tenants from the council's waiting list.[228] Conditions attached to similar broad powers to license caravan sites were held by the House of Lords to be unreasonable because they were "a gratuitous interference with the rights of the occupier".[229] A condition attached to the reopening of a public inquiry by the Secretary of State was held to be unreasonable because it resulted in "considerable expense, inconvenience and risk to the applicant".[230] The Secretary of State's refusal to renew a temporary planning permission was struck down because it would be "unreasonably burdensome" on the applicant.[231]

- The exercise of compulsory purchase powers has similarly been held unreasonable when the authority already possessed, or was able to

[224] *Commissioner of Customs and Excise v Cure and Deeley Ltd* [1962] 1 Q.B. 340; *R. v Secretary of State for the Home Department Ex p. Leech (No.2)* [1994] Q.B. 198.

[225] Town & Country Planning Act 1990 s.70(1).

[226] *Hall & Co. Ltd v Shoreham-by-Sea UDC* [1964] 1 W.L.R. 240. The purpose of the condition was to ensure safe access to the site—a purpose well within the "four corners" of the legislation.

[227] *City of Bradford MC v Secretary of State for the Environment* [1986] J.P.L. 598. But such a condition may survive if framed in negative terms: Grampian RC v Aberdeen CC 1984 S.C. (H.L.) 58. A negative condition may survive even if there is no "reasonable prospect" of the development being carried out: *British Railways Board v Secretary of State for the Environment* [1993] 3 P.L.R. 125, HL.

[228] *R. v Hillingdon LBC Ex p. Royco Homes Ltd* [1974] 1 Q.B. 720. For an older case holding it unlawful to seek developers' contributions, see *R. v Bowman* [1898] 1 Q.B. 663. But where these contributions are provided by means of what are now called "planning obligations" (and used to be called planning agreements or "planning gain") under s.106 of the Town and Country Planning Act 1990, developers' contributions may be upheld.

[229] *Mixnam's Properties Ltd v Chertsey UDC* [1965] A.C. 735 (the conditions provided, inter alia, for security of tenure, no premium charged, and no restrictions on commercial or political activity); *R. v North Hertfordshire DC Ex p. Cobbold* [1985] 3 All E.R. 486 (oppressive condition attached to licence for pop concert); *R. v Barnett LBC Johnson* (1989) 89 L.G.R. 581 (condition prohibiting political parties and activities at community festival held unreasonable).

[230] *R. v Secretary of State for the Environment Ex p. Fielder Estates (Canvey) Ltd* (1989) 57 P. & C.R. 424; *Niarchos (London) Ltd v Secretary of State for the Environment* (1980) 79 L.G.R. 264.

[231] *Niarchos Ltd v Secretary of State for the Environment* (1977) 35 P. & C.R. 259.

acquire voluntarily, other equally suitable land.[232] Where a local authority acquired land for one purpose (such as a wall to protect the coast), it was held unreasonable for it to acquire more land than it needed.[233]

- *Delay*: A long delay before the Home Secretary's review of a life prisoner's sentence (a power now abolished) was held to be unreasonable and "excessive beyond belief".[234] Excessive delay in giving notice of pending police disciplinary proceedings has invalidated those proceedings[235] and the courts ordered an end to delay in admitting a British "patrial" into the country.[236] When the primary decision-maker seeks to excuse delay on the ground of indadequate resources in the past the courts have not readily intervened, as has been discussed in previous chapters.[237] However, it should be noted that the ECHR now requires a "speedy" trial under Art.5(4)[238] and a hearing within a "reasonable time" under Art.6(1).[239] In *Noorkoiv*[240] the Court of Appeal considered the parole board's decision to

---

[232] *Brown v Secretary of State for the Environment* (1978) 40 P. & C.R. 285; *Prest v Secretary of State for Wales* (1982) 81 L.G.R. 193; cf. *R. v Secretary of State for Transport Ex p. de Rothschild* [1989] 1 All E.R. 933; *R. v Rochdale MBC Ex p. Tew* [1999] 3 P.L.R. 74; *R. v Bristol City Council Ex p. Anderson* (1999) 79 P. & C.R. 358.

[233] *Webb v Minister of Housing and Local Government* [1965] 1 W.L.R. 755. See also *Gard v Commissioners of Sewers of City of London* (1885) 28 Ch.D. 486; *Leader v Moxon* (1773) 3 Wils.K.B. 461 (Paving Commissioners empowered to execute street works in such a manner "as they shall think fit". Held, action for trespass lay where they had exercised their discretion "oppressively"); and cases where byelaws were invalidated for imposing burdensome prohibitions: *Munro v Watson* (1887) 57 L.T. 366; *Johnson v Croydon Corp* (1886) 16 Q.B.D. 708 (prohibition of musical instruments). But see *R. v Powell* (1884) 51 L.T. 92; *Slee v Meadows* (1911) 75 J.P. 246; cf. Williams, "Criminal Law and Administrative Law: Problems of Procedure and Reasonableness"; (n.107 above) *London Passenger Transport Board v Summer* (1935) 154 L.T. 108; *R. v Brighton Corp Ex p. Tilling (Thomas) Ltd* (1916) 85 L.J.K.B. 1552 at 1555 (Sankey J.).

[234] *R. v Secretary of State for the Home Department Ex p. Handscombe* (1987) 86 Cr.App.R. 59; *Doody v Secretary of State for the Home Department* [1994] 1 A.C. 531 (Lord Mustill). The Home Secretary no longer has a role in setting tariffs for life prisoners. *R. v Secretary of State for the Home Department Ex p. Zulfikar* [1996] C.O.D. 256 (policy of strip-searching prisoners not unreasonable).

[235] *R. v Merseyside Chief Constable Ex p. Calvaley* [1986] Q.B. 424.

[236] *R. v Home Secretary Ex p. Phansopokar* [1976] Q.B. 606; citing the Magna Carta 1215, c.29: "to no one will we delay right or justice." See also *Re Preston* [1985] A.C. 835 at 870 (Lord Templeman); *R. v Glamorgan CC Ex p. Gheissary*, *The Times*, December 18, 1985 (decisions to refuse student grants irrational when the delay in the students' applications was caused by misleading advice from the authority's officials); *R. (on the application of M) v Criminal Injuries Compensation Authority* [2002] EWHC 2646; (2003) 100(2) L.S.G. 31 (delay in dealing with compensation claim held unreasonable); *R. v Secretary of State for the Home Department Ex p. Mersin* [2000] Imm. A.R. 645 (unreasonable delay in granting refugee status following asylum claim); *R. (on the application of J) v Newham LBC* [2001] EWHC Admin 992; (2002) 5 C.C.L. Rep. 302 (irrational to postpone assessments under Children Act).

[237] On justiciability, see 1–025; on implementation of duties, see 5–064.

[238] See 13–070.

[239] See 7–125.

[240] *R. (on the application of Noorkoiv) v Secretary of State for the Home Department (No.2)* [2002] EWCA Civ 770; [2002] 1 W.L.R. 3284.

postpone the claimant's review at the end of the quarter following the end of his tariff period. It was held that the delays were unacceptable because they treated every case alike, and Burnton J. held that if the delay is inconsistent with a speedy hearing then the onus was on the authority to justify its excuse of lack of resources and the court would assess carefully whether it had taken sufficient measures to rectify the problem.[241]

- It was perverse for magistrates to have imposed the same sanction on a poll tax defaulter who could not afford to pay because destitute as one who simply refused to pay.[242] The award of excessively low compensation was held, in the absence of justifying reasons, to be irrational,[243] as had been the award to a retiring civil servant of a derisory gratuity.[244] The initiation of an investigation by the Commission for Racial Equality has also been struck down as being oppressive.[245]

- In the 1980s, some local authorities were held unlawfully to have imposed excessive penalties on bodies with associations with South Africa during the apartheid regime. In *Wheeler v Leicester City Council*[246] the council withdrew the licence of a local rugby club to use the council-owned recreation ground. The reason was that the club had refused sufficiently to press four of its members, who had been selected for the English rugby footballers' tour of South Africa, to withdraw from that tour. Although it was not unlawful for the members to travel to South Africa, the council acted under its broad statutory power (to grant licences on their own land) and also in pursuance of its general statutory duty under the Race Relations Act 1976 s.61 to "promote good relations between persons of different racial or ethnic groups". The House of Lords held the council's action unlawful, Lord Templeman considering it to be a "misuse of power", "punishing the club where it had done no wrong". Lord Roskill referred to the "unfair manner in which the council set about attaining its objective".[247] The reasoning in *Wheeler* was supported

---

[241] At [47]; and *R. (on the application of C) v Mental Health Review Tribunal* [2001] EWCA Civ 1110; [2002] 1 W.L.R. 176; *R. (on the application of Murray) v Parole Board* [2003] EWCA Civ 1561; (2004) 101(1) L.S.G. 21; S. Lambert and A. Strugo, "Delay as a Ground of Review" [2005] J.R. 253.

[242] *R. v Mid-Hertfordshire Justices Ex p. Cox* (1996) Admin. L.R. 409.

[243] *R. v Civil Service Appeal Board Ex p. Cunningham* [1991] 4 All E.R. 310, CA; cf. *R. v Investors Compensation Scheme Ltd Ex p. Bowden* [1996] 1 A.C. 261, HL (refusal to provide full compensation not unreasonable).

[244] *Williams v Giddy* [1911] A.C. 381.

[245] *R. v Commission for Racial Equality Ex p. Hillingdon LBC* [1982] Q.B. 276; *R. v Hackney LBC Ex p. Evenbray Ltd* (1987) 19 H.L.R. 557 (unreasonable for authority to seek to invoke statutory powers or to complain about standards in hotels in which the authority had housed homeless families as an interim measure.)

[246] [1985] 1 A.C. 1054.

[247] None of their Lordships expressly considered the ban unreasonable, although Lord Roskill would have been prepared so to hold, but instead, unusually, used the term "procedural impropriety" to describe the lack of relation between the penalty and the council's legitimate objectives.

by reference to the earlier case of *Congreve v Home Office*,[248] where the Home Secretary's decision to withdraw television licences from those who had failed to pay a higher fee (but were nevertheless within their rights so to do) was held by the Court of Appeal to be unlawful because it imposed a punishment which related to no wrong. In both cases, the courts refused to countenance the achievement of a legitimate end (the raising of revenue in *Congreve* and the promotion of good race relations in *Wheeler*) by means which were excessive (punishing, in each case, where the individual had done no legal wrong).[249]

- Similar reasoning was employed in a case where some London local authorities decided to withdraw their subscriptions to all publications in their public libraries published by the Times Newspapers group. Following an acrimonious labour dispute, the action was taken in an attempt to impose sanctions on the newspaper proprietors. This consideration was held to be extraneous to the statutory duty of providing a comprehensive and efficient library service".[250] The imposition of the sanctions was also held to be unreasonable and an abuse of the councils' powers.[251]

- When the Secretary of State for Social Security made a regulation which sought to discourage asylum claims by economic migrants by effectively excluded a large class of such migrants from income support, the Court of Appeal invalidated the regulations on the ground that they were so draconian that they rendered the rights of the migrants to remain in the country nugatory. Simon Brown L.J.

[248] [1976] 1 Q.B. 629.
[249] There may be different explanations of the grounds on which both Congreve and Wheeler were decided. One ground may be the infringement of the principle of legal certainty (see 11–040). Another may be that the decisions were "illegal" in that both the council in Wheeler and the Home Secretary in Congreve acted for an improper purpose (namely, the imposition of a punishment): see Ch.5; *cf*. Browne-Wilkinson L.J. in his dissenting judgment in the CA (see n.246) at 1064–1065, where he raised the conflict between "two basic principles of a democratic society", one that allowed a "democratically elected body to conduct its affairs in accordance with its own views" and the other "the right to freedom of speech and conscience enjoyed by each individual". Basing his decision on illegality rather than on unreasonableness (the council having taken a "legally irrelevant factor" into account), he came close to deciding the matter on the ground of the council's acting inconsistently with "fundamental freedoms of speech and conscience". *R. v Lewisham LBC Ex p. Shell UK Ltd* [1988] 1 All E.R. 938 (boycott of the products of the Shell company in order to bring pressure on one of its subsidiary companies to withdraw its (lawful) business from South Africa held illegal).
[250] Public Libraries and Museums Act 1964 s.7(1).
[251] *R. v Ealing LBC Ex p. Times Newspapers* (1986) 85 L.G.R. 316 (not explicitly stated that the decision amounted to an excessive and unnecessary infringement on freedom of expression). The case raises interesting questions as to the reasonableness of decisions to cease subscriptions to, or remove books from the library of "politically incorrect" material. In *R. v Liverpool CC Ex p. Secretary of State for Employment* (1988) 154 L.G.R. 118, the council sought to boycott the Government's Employment Training Scheme, despite the fact that it was voluntary. The council did this outside of any statutory framework, by imposing a standard condition on all grant aid that the organisation to be aided took no part in the scheme. The purpose, punishment of the organisations, was held to be unlawful.

held that the regulations contemplated for some migrants "a life so destitute that, to my mind no civilisation can tolerate it".[252]

DISPROPORTIONATE DECISIONS

11–073 Proportionality was suggested by Lord Diplock in the *GCHQ* case in the mid-1980sas a possible fourth ground of judicial review in English law.[253] Yet it has been said that the adoption of proportionality into domestic law would lower the threshold of judicial intervention and involve the courts in considering the merits and facts of administrative decisions.[254] Originating in Prussia[255] in the 19th century, proportionality has assumed a specific form under the case law of the European Court of Justice, where it is regarded as a "general principle of law"[256] and it is similarly employed by the European Court of Human Rights as a standard by which to assess a State's compliance with aspects of the ECHR.[257] British courts now explicitly apply proportionality in respect of directly effective European Community law[258] and, under the HRA 1998, as a structured test to evaluate compatibility with Convention rights, particularly the qualified rights under Arts 8–11.[259] Proportionality is also applied in the domestic

[252] *R. v Secretary of State for Social Security Ex p. Joint Council for the Welfare of Immigrants* [1997] 1 W.L.R. 275, 292 (Simon Brown L.J., duty to maintain foreigners was held to emanate from the common law, citing Lord Ellenborough C.J. in *R v Eastbourne (Inhabitants)* 1803 4 (East) 103 at 107, who said "As to there being no obligation for maintaining poor foreigners . . . the law of humanity, which is anterior to all positive laws, obliges us to afford them relief, to save them from starving"); *R. v Secretary of State for Social Security Ex p. Tamenene* [1997] C.O.D. 480 (judicial response to legislation that sought to reinstate provisions held unlawful in the *JCWI* case).

[253] *Council for Civil Service Unions v Minister of State for the Civil Service* [1985]1 A.C. 374, 410.

[254] *R. v Secretary of State for the Home Department Ex p. Brind* [1991] A.C. 696 at 766–767 (Lord Lowry), 762 (Lord Ackner)—argument on proportionality. See also S. Boyron, "Proportionality in English Administrative Law: A Faulty Translation?" (1992) 12 O.J.L.S. 237; R. Thomas, *Legitimate Expectations and Proportionality in Administrative Law* (2000), pp.77 ff; G. Wong, "Towards the Nutcracker Principle: reconsidering the Objections to Proportionality" [2000] P.L. 92.

[255] The principle of Verhaltnismassigkeit was invoked by the Prussian Supreme Administrative Court to check the discretionary powers of police authorities. See M. Singh, *German Administrative Law: A Common Lawyer's View* (1985), pp.88–101; J. Jowell and A. Lester, "Proportionality: Neither Novel nor Dangerous" in J. Jowell and D. Oliver (eds), *New Directions in Judicial Review* (1989), p.5; J. Schwartze, *European Administrative Law* (revised edn. 2006), Ch.5.

[256] See 14–089.

[257] See 13–083. See D. Feldman, "Proportionality and the Human Rights Act 1998" in E. Ellis (ed.), *The Principle of Proportionality in the Laws of Europe* (1999); P. Craig, *Administrative Law*, 5th edn. (2003), pp.617 ff.; P. Sales and B. Hooper, "Proportionality and the Form of Law" (2003) 119 L.Q.R. 426; M. Fordham and T. de la Mare, "Proportionality and the Margin of Appreciation" in J. Jowell and J. Cooper (eds), *Understanding Human Rights Principles* (2000).

[258] See 11–058.

[259] See 11–059. I. Leigh, "Taking Rights Proportionately: Judicial Review, the Human Rights Act and Strasbourg" [2002] P.L.265; R. Clayton and H. Tomlinson, *The Law of Human Rights* (2000), para.6–78.

law of some European countries, and was recommended for adoption in all the Contracting States of the Council of Europe by its Committee of Ministers.[260] It was defined there as requiring an administrative authority, when exercising a discretionary power, to "maintain a proper balance between any adverse effects which its decision may have on the rights, liberties, or interests of persons and the purpose which it pursues".

English law is faced with the decision whether proportionality should **11–074** now become a separate ground of review, or whether it should supplant unreasonableness as a ground of review. In *British Civilian Internees* Dyson L.J. said that "the result that follows will often be the same whether the test that is applied is proportionality or *Wednesbury* unreasonableness". However, he felt that he was unable, without the sanction of the House of Lords, yet "to perform its [unreasonableness'] burial rights". [261] As we have set out above, there are in fact two different ways in which proportionality is applied: (a) a test of fair balance; and (b) a structured test to examine whether interference by a public authority with a fundamental norm can be justified.

Proportionality as a test of fair balance

Insofar as the general concept of proportionality is a test requiring the **11–075** decision-maker to achieve a fair balance, it provides an implicit explanation for some of the existing judicial interventions on the ground of unreasonableness, particularly under two of the categories of unreasonableness we have identified above, namely, those held invalid because they manifestly failed to balance one or more (relevant) consideration,[262] and those where the decision was held to be unreasonably onerous or oppressive.[263] Under the first of these, the courts evaluate whether manifestly disproportionate *weight* has been attached to one or other considerations relevant to the decision. Under the second, the courts consider whether there has been a disproportionate *interference* with the claimant's rights or interests. There will of course always be an examination of rationality in its narrow sense of logical connection between ends and means. In both of these instances, it makes little difference whether the term employed to describe the administrative wrong is "unreasonable" or "disproportionate" although the latter describes more accurately why the decision is unacceptable. The principal difference between this kind of proportionality and the structured

---

[260] Adopted March 11, 1980.
[261] *R. (on the application of the Association of British Civilian Internees (Far East Region)) v Secretary of State for Defence* [2003] EWCA Civ 473; [2003] Q.B. 1397 at [33]–[35]; *R. v Secretary of State for the Environment, Transport and the Regions Ex p. Holdings & Barnes Plc* (the Alconbury case) [2001] UKHL 23; [2003] 2 A.C. 295 at [50]–[51] (Lord Slynn); *R. (on the application of Daly) v Secretary of State for the Home Department* [2001] UKHL 26; [2001] 2 A.C. 532 at [32] (Lord Cooke).
[262] See 11–033—11–036.
[263] See 11–070—11–072.

test is that the burden of asserting the disproportion is on the claimant rather than the decision-maker.

11-076   As a mere test of "fair balance", proportionality is not therefore alien to English law. Article 20 of Magna Carta provides that "For a trivial offence, a free man will be fined only in proportion to the degree of his offence, and for a serious offence correspondingly, but not so heavily as to deprive him of his livelihood". Proportionality therefore fits well within the ambit of unreasonableness as fair balance and, although recent dicta almost suggests that proportionality might found the basis of all judicial review,[264] its name has sometimes been explicitly invoked. For example, Lord Denning would have struck down a decision suspending a stallholder's licence on the ground that "the punishment is altogether excessive and out of proportion to the occasion".[265] A resolution of a local authority banning a member of the public from local authority property was held to be "out of proportion to what the applicant had done",[266] and proportionality was expressly used to test the government's suspension of the permits of Romanian pilots.[267] Laws J. held that when justices were determining what sentence to impose upon a person who had failed to pay his non-domestic rates, sufficient regard should be had to the principle of proportionality".[268] He also refused to prohibit the publication of a report critical of the claimant by the Advertising Standards Authority pending a judicial review unless there was a "pressing ground (in the language of the ECtHR, a "pressing social need") to restrain the public body from carrying out its functions in the ordinary way".[269]

Proportionality as a structured test of justifiability

11-077   A more sophisticated version of proportionality provides a structured test—a series of questions for the court to address in assessing whether the impugned decision is justifiable.

[264] R. v Secretary of State for Education and Employment Ex p. Begbie [2001] 1 W.L.R. 1115 at [68]; Nadarajah and Abdi v Secretary of State for the Home Department [2005] EWCA Civ 1363; The Times, December 14, 2005, [68]–[69] (Laws L.J.).
[265] R. v Barnsley MBC Ex p. Hook [1976] 1 W.L.R. 1052 at 1057 (offence was urinating in the street and using offensive language; CA struck down the suspension on the ground of the lack of a fair hearing); R. v Secretary of State for the Home Department Ex p. Benwell [1984] I.C.R. 723 at 736 (Hodson J.: "in an extreme case an administrative or quasi-administrative penalty can be attacked on the ground that it was so disproportionate to the offence as to be perverse"); J. Beatson, "Proportionality" (1988) 104 L.Q.R. 180.
[266] R. v Brent LBC Ex p. Assegai (1987) 151 L.G.R. 891 (reason for the ban was the claimant's unruly behaviour at previous meetings).
[267] R. v Secretary of State for Transport Pegasus Holidays (London) Ltd and Airbro (UK) Ltd [1988] 1 W.L.R. 990.
[268] R. v Highbury Corner Justices Ex p. Uchendu [1994] R.A. 51; Commissioner of Customs and Excise v Peninsular & Oriental Steam Navigation Company [1994] S.T.C. 259 (in relation to a penalty imposed for a serious misdeclaration of VAT, only in the most limited circumstances will the doctrine of proportionality be applied to penalties provided for by national law).
[269] R. v Advertising Standards Authority Ltd Ex p. Vernon Organisation [1992] 1 W.L.R. 1289.

Structured proportionality in European Community Law

Proportionality is applied by the European Court of Justice and the Court **11–078** of First Instance to test the lawfulness of Community action or the action of Member States where Community law applies.[270] It applies in domestic courts where European Community law is engaged.[271] Here the courts ask first whether the measure which is being challenged is suitable to attaining the identified ends (the test of *suitability*). Suitability here includes the notion of 'rational connection' between the means and ends. The next step asks whether the measure is necessary and whether a less restrictive or onerous method could have been adopted (the test of *necessity*, requiring *minimum impairment* of the right or interest in question). If the measure passes both tests the court may then go on to ask whether it attains a *fair balance* of means and ends.[272] It is important to note here that the burden of justification in such cases falls on the public authority which has apparently infringed the rights of the claimant or offended a norm of European Community law.

Structured proportionality in Convention rights

Although the ECHR does not specify proportionality as a standard of **11–079** review, proportionality is employed in a similar way to European Community law as a structured test, in particular to assess the conformity of a measure with one of the rights which may be limited—the "qualified rights" under Arts 8–12.[273] Here too the burden is on the public authority to justify the departure from the right in question. The authority will normally be required to demonstrate that the measures are "prescribed by the law"; that they pursue a legitimate end or an end specified in the relevant Article (ends such as national security or public safety); that they are rationally connected to that end; that no less restrictive alternative could have been adopted, and that they are necessary (and not merely desirable). Some of the Articles specify the concept of necessity as being "necessary in a democratic society". This requirement engages the courts in an exercise of constitutional review. This is because it seeks not merely a 'fair balance' between the measure and the social end, but because it requires the court to assess the measures by the standards of a constitutional democracy.[274] This point is well illustrated by the difference of

[270] See 14–089; proportionality is now expressly recognised in Art.5 of the EC Treaty and fundamental rights recognised in Art.6 of the Treaty on European Union; P. Craig, *EU Administrative Law* (2006), Chs 17 and 18; J. Schwartze, *European Administrative Law* (2006), Pt II.
[271] See 11–058.
[272] Referred to by Craig as "proportionality strictu senso" (2006), p.657.
[273] See 13–023; I. Leigh, "Taking Rights Proportionately: Judicial Review, the Human Rights Act and Judicial Review" [2002] P.L. 265; P. Craig, "The Courts, the Human Rights Act and Judicial Review" (2001) 117 L.Q.R. 589; M.Elliott, "The HRA 1998 and the Standard of Substantive Review" (2001) 60 C.L.J. 301.
[274] J. Jowell, "Beyond the Rule of Law: Towards Constitutional Judicial Review" [2000] P.L. 671.

approach between the Court of Appeal and the ECtHR in *Smith*,[275] where, despite applying the test of "anxious scrutiny",[276] the Court of Appeal upheld the ban on homosexuals in the armed forces. The ECtHR not only required more convincing justification for the ban, but also tested it by the democratic requirements of "pluralism, tolerance and broadmindedness".[277]

Structured proportionality in English law

11–080 In *Daly*,[278] a case which came to be decided before the HRA came into force, the House of Lords adopted the test of proportionality adopted by the Privy Council in *de Freitas v Permanent Secretary of Ministry of Agriculture, Fisheries, Land and Housing*.[279] Drawing on South African, Canadian and Zimbabwean authority, it was said that:

> "When determining whether a limitation (by an act, rule or decision) is arbitrary or excessive the court should ask itself: "whether: (i) the legislative objective is sufficiently important to justify limiting a fundamental right; (ii) the measures designed to meet the legislative objective are rationally connected to it; and (iii) the means used to impair the right or freedom are no more than is necessary to accomplish the objective".

11–081 Clearly this test is, as Lord Steyn said in *Daly*, "more sophisticated than the traditional (i.e. unreasonableness) ground of judicial review".[280] It is much more than the "fair balance" test.[281] It requires the court to seek first whether the action pursues a legitimate aim (i.e. one of the designated reasons to depart from a Convention right, such as national security). It then asks whether the measure employed is capable of achieving that aim, namely, whether there is a "rational connection" between the measures and the aim. Thirdly it asks whether a less restrictive alternative could have been employed. Even if these three hurdles are achieved, however (and the tripartite *de Frietas* test ignores this) there is a fourth step which the decision-maker has to climb, namely, to demonstrate that the measure must be "necessary" which requires the courts to insist that the measure genuinely addresses a "pressing social need", and is not just desirable or reasonable, by the standards of a democratic society.[282] In *Huang*, Lord

[275] *R. v Ministry of Defence Ex p. Smith* [1996] Q.B. 517.
[276] See 11–086 *et seq.*
[277] *Smith and Grady v United Kingdom* (1999) 29 E.H.R.R. 493, paras 138–139.
[278] *R. v Secretary of State for the Home Department Ex p. Daly* [2001] UKHL 26; [2001] 2 A.C. 532.
[279] [1999] 1 A.C. 69, 80 (Lord Clyde).
[280] At [27].
[281] *Brown v Stott* [2003] 1 A.C. 681, 728 (Lord Hope alluded to it as a "fair balance" test).
[282] *Sunday Times v UK* (1979) 2 E.H.R.R. 245 at 275, 277–278; *R. v Secretary of State for the Home Department Ex p. Daly* [2001] UKHL 26; [2001] 2 A.C. 532 at [28] (a point elaborated by Lord Steyn in *Daly* when dealing with the intensity of review, which he said was determined by "the twin requirements that the limitation of the right was necessary in a democratic society, in the sense of meeting a pressing social need, and the question whether the interference was really proportionate to the legitimate aim being pursued").

Bingham acknowledged that that fourth step, which featured in the judgment of Dickson C.J. in the Canadian case *R. v Oakes*,[283] "should never be overlooked or discounted" and the failure to consider that final step "should be made good".[284]

Proportionality was pleaded in *Brind*, and, although not there applied, **11–082** future application was not ruled out.[285] However, in *Attorney General v Guardian Newspapers Ltd (No.2)*, Lord Goff had said that "It is established in the jurisprudence of the European Court of Human Rights that . . . interference with freedom of expression should be no more than is proportionate to the legitimate aim pursued. I have no reason to believe that English law, as applied in the courts, leads to any different conclusion".[286]

The reserve expressed towards proportionality in *Brind* was not shared **11–083** in *Leech*, in which the Court of Appeal upheld the constitutional right of a prisoner to access to the courts.[287] The question was whether the interference with a prisoner's mail permitted by the regulations was broad enough to infringe that right. The test adopted by Steyn L.J. to decide that question was whether there was a "self-evident and pressing need" for such a power.[288] None was demonstrated. The language of proportionality was thus explicit and the Court of Appeal even went so far as to consider the case law of ECtHR on the matter which, although not directly applicable in this pre-HRA case, "reinforces a conclusion that we have arrived at in the light of the principles of our domestic jurisprudence".[289] In *Daly*,[290] although Lord Steyn held that proportionality is "applicable in respect of review where Convention rights are at stake",[291] Lord Bingham made it clear that proportionality was also the test under common law constitutional rights. He said that

---

[283] [1986] 1 S.C.R. 103 at 139.

[284] *Huang v Secretary of State for the Home Department* [2007] UKHL 11; [2007] 2 W.L.R. 581 at [19]—as it had been overlooked in *R. (on the application of Razgar) v Secretary of State for the Home Department (No.2)* [2004] UKHL 27; [2004] 2 A.C. 368 at [20]. Lord Bingham described the *Oakes* test as requiring "the striking of a fair balance between the rights of the individual and the interests of the community". This is indeed described in *Oakes* as a general objective of the proportionality test, however the actual words used in Oakes require a proportionality between "the effects of a measure [responsible for limiting the Canadian Charter's rights]" and the "objective which has been identified as of 'sufficient importance'". This in effect imports the 'necessity' test in the context of the Canadian Charter of Rights and Freedoms, s.1 which requires the rights and freedoms set out in it to be subject only to "such reasonable limits prescribed by law as can be demonstrably justified in a free and democratic society".

[285] [1991] 1 A.C. 696 (Lords Bridge, Roskill and Templeman); *R. v Independent Television Commission TSW Broadcasting Ltd* [1996] E.M.L.R. 291 (Lord Templeman was willing to apply proportionality if appropriate, which it was not).

[286] [1990] 1 A.C. 109 at 283; Lord Griffiths at 273.

[287] *R. v Secretary of State for the Home Department Ex p. Leech* [1994] Q.B. 198.

[288] At 211; also referred to as "objective need" (at 212) or "demonstrable need" (at 213).

[289] At 212 (Steyn L.J); the case referred to was *Campbell v UK* (1993) 15 E.H.R.R. 137.

[290] [2001] UKHL 26; [2001] 2 A.C. 532 (where the approach in *Leech* ([1994] Q.B. 198)) was confirmed.

[291] At [24].

"the policy provides for a degree of intrusion into the privileged legal correspondence of prisoners which is greater than is justified by the objectives the policy is intended to serve, and so violates the common law rights of prisoners".[292]

The overlap between proportionality and unreasonableness

11–084   We have seen that the standards of proportionality—in both its senses—and unreasonableness are inextricably intertwined. Unreasonableness contains two elements of proportionality when it requires the weight of relevant considerations to be fairly balanced, and when it forbids unduly oppressive decisions. The notion of "rational connection" between means and ends is another. As we have noted above, such a test was applied, for example in a recent case where a non-statutory scheme was introduced to provide compensation for British civilians interned during World War II by the Japanese. The scheme excluded individuals whose parents or grandparents were not born in the United Kingdom. The Court of Appeal examined carefully whether the exclusion bore a rational connection to the "foundation" and "essential character" of the scheme, but held in the circumstances that the scheme did not fail the *Wednesbury* test.[293] The House of Lords had adopted a similar approach in a case where, under an *ex gratia* compensation scheme, British soldiers injured in Bosnia were accorded treatment different from those injured in Northern Ireland.[294] The Canadian Supreme Court defined the notion of "rational connection" under their test of structured proportionality in terms which show strikingly how the notion of reasonableness lies deep within proportionality: "The measures must be carefully designed to meet the objective in question. They must not be arbitrary, unfair or based on irrational considerations".[295]

11–085   In addition, the notion in proportionality of "minimal impairment" (that a less restrictive alternative be pursued) has been applied in a number of cases based overtly on unreasonableness. As we have seen, planning conditions have been struck down because a less restrictive or less onerous alternative could be provided—such as would permit compensation to be paid to the owner of the land.[296] Compulsory purchase of land has been invalidated because the authority was able voluntarily to acquire other

---

[292] At [21].

[293] *R. (on the application of Association of British Civilian Internees (Far East Region)) v Secretary of State for Defence* [2003] EWCA Civ 473; [2003] Q.B. 1397 at [40].

[294] *R. v Ministry of Defence Ex p. Walker* [2000] 1 W.L.R . 806 at 812 (Lord Slynn: "It is not for the courts to consider whether the scheme . . . is a good scheme or a bad scheme, unless it can be said that the exclusion is so irrational or unreasonable that no reasonable Minister could have adopted it"), 816 (Lord Hoffmann: the distinction was "fine" but not irrational: "That is too high a hurdle to surmount").

[295] *R. v Chaulk* [1990] 3 S.C.R. 1303 at 1335–1336 (Lamer C.J.). The test was first established in *R. v Oakes* [1988] 1 S,C.R. 103 at 137–138.

[296] *Hall and Co v Shoreham-by-Sea UDC* [1964] 1 W.L.R. 240.

equally suitable land.[297] It has been held that the decision to delist a company, as opposed to "lesser measures" (such as the continuation of the suspension of the shares) was, in the circumstances, and having taken into account the interests of the shareholders, "not disproportionate to the damage which it was designed to prevent either at common law or under Community law".[298]

INTENSITY OF REVIEW

Whether a court carries out substantive review of a decision by reference to the concept of unreasonableness or proportionality, two questions arise: To what extent should the courts allow a degree of latitude or leeway to the decision-maker?[299] And to what extent should it be uniform?[300] The answers to these questions depend in large part on the respective constitutional roles of the court and the primary decision-maker (the impugned public authority),[301] but also on practical considerations. The willingness of the courts to invalidate a decision on the ground that it is unreasonable or disproportionate will be influenced in part by the administrative scheme under review; the subject matter of the decision; the importance of the countervailing rights or interests and the extent of the interference with the right or interest. Indeed the intensity of review will differ, for the reason that "in public law, context is all".[302] The threshold of intervention is particularly influenced by the respective institutional competence of the decision-maker and the court.

11–086

---

[297] *Brown v Secretary of State for the Environment* (1978) 40 P.& C.R. 285.

[298] R. v International Stock Exchange of the United Kingdom and the *Republic of Ireland Ex p. Else (1982) Ltd* [1993] Q.B. 534 (proportionality was applied here as an aspect of rationality); *R. v Tamworth Justices Ex p. Walsh* [1994] C.O.D. 277 (Justices acted unreasonably in committing to custody a solicitor who criticised the listing system in court. Three alternative measures were available: ordering his removal; reporting him to the Law Society, or adjourning the matter. They had used "a sledgehammer to crack a nut"); *R. v Camden LBC Ex p. Cran* [1995] R.T.R. 346 (consultation with residents about car-parking scheme deficient because "there had been no recognition of the possibility let alone the fact that a number of the beneficial results of introducing full controls might have been well achieved by other means").

[299] On the "discretionary area of judgement", see D. Pannick, "Principles of Interpretation of Convention Rights Under the HRA and the Discretionary Area of Judgment" [1998] P.L. 545; A. Lester and D. Pannick, *Human Rights Law and Practice*, 2nd edn (2004), paras 3.18–3.21.

[300] J. Rivers, "Proportionality and variable intensity of review" [2006] C.L.J. 174; Y. Arai-Takahashi, *The Margin of Appreciation Doctrine and the Principle of Proportionality in the Jurisprudence of the ECHR* (2000); M. Elliott, "The Human Rights Act and the Standard of Substantive Review" [2001] C.L.J. 301; A. Le Sueur, "The Rise and Ruin of Unreasonableness" [2005] J.R.32.

[301] See 11–014.

[302] *Daly* [2001] UKHL 26; [2001] 2 A.C. 532 at [28] (Lord Steyn).

Figure 1

FULL INTESITY REVIEW	STRUCTURED PROPORTIONALITY REVIEW	VARIABLE INTENSITY UNREASONABLENESS REVIEW Depending on the nature of the subject matter			NON-JUSTICIABLE
Court decides "correctness" and whether power abused	Intensity of review may vary according to the context	←		→	But adequacy of justification still required
	Burden of justification on public authority	Anxious scrutiny unreasonableness review	Standard *Wednesbury* unreasonableness review	"Light touch" unreasonableness review	
		Burden on public authority	Burden on claimant	Burden on claimant	

Full intensity "correctness" review for abuse of power

11–087 There are situations in which there is no constitutional reason, or reason based upon institutional capacity,[303] for the court to allow any margin of discretion to the public authority. The court is in as good a position as the primary decision-maker to assess the relevant factors and may indeed have a duty to do so. When the court intervenes in this way it sometimes refers to the ground of review as "abuse of power" rather than unreasonableness or proportionality. Three main fields may be identified.

- First, as we have seen above there are cases where no evidence for the decision exists, or where a decision is taken in ignorance of an established or relevant fact.[304]

- Secondly, are decisions offending against consistency.[304a]

- Thirdly, are some (but not all) decisions where the decision-maker seeks to disappoint a legitimate expectation, which will be discussed in Chapter 12.

11–088 In many cases of legitimate expectation the courts will show deference to the decision-maker who wishes to alter his policy in the public interest, but when the class of promisee is limited and the promise is in the "nature of a contract", the court itself will determine whether the breach of promise is unlawful.

Structured proportionality review

11–089 As we have seen, structured proportionality requires the public authority to justify its actions by satisfying the court that it fulfils a series of stepped standards. It is more searching than unreasonableness review because the

[303] See 11–014.
[304] See 11–041.
[304a] See 11–059.

burden is on the public authority to justify a departure from a fundamental norm. This involves a more sophisticated scrutiny than mere unreasonableness review because it erects more barriers for the decision-maker to hurdle (some of which overlap with ordinary unreasonableness review, such as those which require a "rational connection" and "fair balance" between ends and means). As Lord Hope said in R. v Shayler, proportionality (under the HRA) requires "a close and penetrating examination of the factual justification of the restriction"[305] and Lord Bingham said the "the court will now conduct a much more rigorous review than was once thought to be permissible".[306] The requirement under proportionality of "minimum impairment" of rights, requires decision-makers to consider less onerous means to achieve their ends. Although, as we have seen,[307] the English courts have sometimes required the decision-maker to have considered less onerous alternatives, they have not generally gone that far.[308] This process of justification will therefore require more attention from the courts to the process of reasoning of the decision-maker, and the relationship between the facts and the inferences drawn from them, than the default position of unreasonableness review normally concedes. In Tweed v Parades Commission for Northern Ireland it was held that "the proportionality of a public authority's interference with a protected Convention right is likely to call for a careful and accurate evaluation of the facts"[309] and therefore in order to assess the issues of proportionality the court should have access to documents from which the Commission received information and advice.

However, structured proportionality does not herald the end of defer- **11–090** ence. In European Community law, even in the context of structured proportionality, the ECJ requires "manifest" disproportionality before interfering with certain decisions.[310] Varying levels of the intensity of review will be appropriate in different categories of case. For example, in respect of measures involving the European Commission in "complex economic assessment", such as in the implementation of anti-dumping

---

[305] [2003] 1 A.C. 247 at [61].
[306] At [33].
[307] See 11–070—11–072.
[308] Indeed it is not clear that the English courts are pursuing this requirement even in respect of Convention rights as much as they might. T. Hickman, "Proportionality: Comparative Law Lessons" [2007] J.R. 31. Minimum impairment has been applied in Israeli law: I. Zamir and Z. Zysblat, Public Law in Israel (1996), Pts 2, 3 and 11, see e.g. Laor v Board of Censorship for Films and Plays (1987) 41(1) P.D. 421 (total ban on a film causing "near certainty of substantial damage" to public order was held disproportionate where less restrictive measures, such as the cutting out of certain scenes, could have dealt with the problem); I. Zamir, "Unreasonableness, Balance of Interests and Proportionality" (1993) Tel-Aviv Studies in Law 131; A. Barak, The Judge in a Democracy (2006), pp.254–260. For an application of the least restrictive alternative approach (under a test of unreasonableness) in Hong Kong, see Society for the Protection of the Harbour Ltd v Town Planning Board (Ct of First Instance No.19 of 2003, Chu J. (upheld for different reasons by the Court of Final Appeal of the Hong Kong Special Administrative Region No.14 of 2003 (Civil)).
[309] [2006] UKHL 53; [2007] 1 A.C. 650 at 655 (Lord Bingham).
[310] See Ch.14; e.g. R. v Ministry of Agriculture, Fisheries and Food Ex p. Astonquest [2000] Eu L.R. 371 (Robert Walker L.J.) using the test of "manifest inappropriateness".

measures, the ECJ will display "extreme self restraint"[311] and only substitute its own discretion for that of the Commission if it can be shown that the conclusions of the Commission were "manifestly" or "patently" wrong.[312]

11–091   Similarly, in relation to Convention rights, the courts tend to defer to the legislature or administration in decisions involving "broad social policy"[313] or the allocation of finite financial resources[314] (although, as we shall consider below,[315] these categories do not wholly relieve the authority from judicial scrutiny, particularly in order to determine whether the decision was otherwise properly justified).[316]

Variable intensity unreasonableness review

11–092 The broadest spectrum of intensity of review consists of those cases in which the court acknowledges that the public authority is to be allowed a degree of latitude. It has been suggested in a number of cases that we now have a "sliding scale of review".[317] Over the past 20 years or so, the courts carrying out substantive review under the head of unreasonableness have sought to develop a series of categories to explain the intensity or lack of intensity of review that should be used in particular contexts.

Heightened scrutiny unreasonableness review

11–093 There was a growing realisation that the traditional *Wednesbury* standard was inappropriate where a decision interfered with a fundamental right or important interest. Such decisions should be subject to the "most anxious

---

[311] A. Egger, "'The Principle of Proportionality in Community Anti-dumping Law" (1993) 18 E.L. Rev. 367.

[312] See 14–00; Case 57/72 *Westzucker v EVS Zucher* [1973] E.C.R. 321; Case 136/77 *Rache v HZA Mainz* [1978] E.C.R. 1245.

[313] This point has been made most forcefully by Lord Hoffmann: "Separation of Powers" [2002] J.R. 137 and his statement in *R. v Secretary of State for the Environment, Transport and the Regions Ex p. Holdings & Barnes Plc* (the Alconbury case) [2001] UKHL 23; [2003] 2 A.C. 295 at [75]–[76], where he distinguished a "policy decisions" from a "determination of right". Policy decisions should be made not by the courts, he said, but, in a democracy by "democratically elected bodies or persons accountable to them". Wilson v Secretary of State for Trade and Industry [2003] UKHL 40; [2004] 1 A.C. 816 at [70] (Lord Nicholls: "The more the legislation concerns matters of broad social policy the less ready will be a court to intervene"); *Hooper v Secretary of State for Work and Pensions* [2003] EWCA Civ 813; [2003] 1 W.L.R. 2623 at [63]–[64] (Laws L.J.: "A very considerable margin of discretion must be accorded to the Secretary of State. Difficult questions of economic and social policy were involved, the resolution of which fell within the province of the executive and the legislature rather than the courts"); *R. v Secretary of State for Education and Employment Ex p. Begbie* [2000] 1 W.L.R. 1115 at 1131 (Laws L.J.: less intrusive judicial review should apply to decisions in the "macro-political field").

[314] *Michaelek v Wandsworth LBC* [2002] EWCA Civ 271; [2003] 1 W.L.R. 617 at [41] (Brooke L.J.: "this is pre-eminently a field in which the courts should defer to the decisions taken by a democratically elected Parliament, which has determined the manner in which public resources should be allocated for local authority housing").

[315] See 11–098—11–102.

[316] A point well made by T.R.S. Allan, "Human Rights and Judicial Review: A Critique of Due Deference" [2006] C.L.J. 671.

[317] *Begbie* [2000] 1 W.L.R. 1115 at 1130.

scrutiny of the courts".[318] In *Brind*, the majority indicated that a decision-maker who exercises broad discretion must show that an infringement of the right to expression can only be justified by an "important competing public interest".[319] Perhaps the clearest indication of this approach is to be found in the Court of Appeal's decision in *R. v Ministry of Defence Ex p. Smith*. In this challenge to the exclusion of homosexuals from the armed forces, Sir Thomas Bingham M.R. accepted that "the more substantial the interference with human rights, the more the court will require by justification before it is satisfied that the decision is reasonable"[320]—a formulation which goes some way towards asking not the claimant to demonstrate unreasonableness, but the decision-maker to justify that the decision was "reasonable".[321] In *Saville*, the Court of Appeal said that "it is not open to the decision-maker to risk interfering with fundamental rights in the absence of compelling justification".[322]

This notion of "anxious" or "heightened" scrutiny is difficult to define   **11–094** with any precision, but it does indicate that the full rigour of *Wednesbury* is softened. Two fundamentals govern the court's role. First, the court's function remains one of review for error of law.[323] The court is not a fact-finder (though, as we have seen,[324] it may evaluate the fact-finding process of the primary decision-maker).[325] Secondly, the burden of argument shifts from the claimant to the defendant public authority, which needs to produce a justification for the decision. The court will be less inclined to accept ex post facto justifications from the public authority, compared to traditional unreasonableness review.[326]

---

[318] *Bugdaycay v Secretary of State for the Home Department* [1987] A.C. 514 at 531 (Lord Bridge, speaking of the right to life in a deportation case); and *National and Local Government Officers Association v Secretary of State for the Environment* (1993) Admin. L.R. 785 (applying the test to the restriction on the political activities on local government officers); In *Prest v Secretary of State for Wales* (1982) 81 L.G.R. 193 (Watkins L.J. said that compulsory purchase decisions must be "carefully scrutinised", and Lord Denning M.R. said the Secretary of State must in such cases show that the public interest "decisively demands" the compulsory purchase order); *R. v Secretary of State for the Home Department Ex p. Launder* [1997] 1 W.L.R. 839 (it was normally open to the court to review the exercise of the Home Secretary's discretion under the Extradition Act 1989 s.12. The fact that a decision was taken on policy grounds of an important or sensitive nature and involving delicate relations between foreign states did not affect the court's duty to ensure the claimant was afforded proper protection, although the court would be mindful of both the limitations of its constitutional role and the need in such a case for "anxious scrutiny").
[319] *R. v Secretary of State for the Home Department Ex p. Brind* [1991] A.C. 696 at 749–751.
[320] A similar approach has been taken in India towards interference with fundamental rights: *Om Kumar v Union of India* 2001 (2) S.C.C. 386 at 399, 405 (Rao J.).
[321] [1996] Q.B. 517.
[322] *R v Lord Saville of Newdigate Ex p. A* [2000] 1 W.L.R. 1855 at [37].
[323] *R. (on the application of Davila-Puga) v Immigration Appeal Tribunal* [2001] EWCA Civ 931 at [31] (Laws L.J.: "As is well known, in 1987 Lord Bridge said in the case of Musisi [1987] 1 A.C. 514 that these cases need to be approached with anxious scrutiny, given what may be involved. And so they must. But as a reading of his Lordship's speech in that case readily demonstrates, the court's role remains one of review for error of law. There is no error of law here").
[324] See 11–042.
[325] See 11–041.
[326] *R. (on the application of Leung) v Imperial College of Science, Technology and Medicine* [2002] EWHC 1358; [2002] E.L.R. 653.

11–095   That is not to say that there should be no deference. Heightened scrutiny is not merits or "correctness" review[327] any more than is structured proportionality and the courts have urged a "common sense" approach. Anxious scrutiny "does not mean that the court should strive by tortuous mental gymnastics to find error in the decision under review when in truth there has been none".[328] Moreover, "the concern of the court ought to be substance not semantics", so it is inappropriate to focus "on particular sentences" in a decision-maker's determination "and to subject them to the kind of legalistic scrutiny that might perhaps be appropriate in the case of a statutory instrument, charter party or trust deed".[329] But while it would be wrong to interpret the decision of a decision maker "in a minute textual fashion . . . it must be right in every case to see whether substantial and proper reasons are given".[330]

11–096   The scope for application of anxious scrutiny approaches to unreasonableness has changed since the coming into force of the HRA. Many of the leading statements explaining the need for anxious scrutiny were made before English courts could directly apply Convention rights. Today, assessment of the lawfulness of decisions in many of these cases would fall to be determined by the structured proportionality test.

Wednesbury, light-touch review and non-justiciability[331]

11–097   The default position is still, at the time of writing, that of the *Wednesbury* formulation,[332] although it has been reformulated to a standard that requires the decision-maker to act within the "range of reasonable responses".[333] Beyond that, however, recent cases, even those where human rights are engaged, have sometimes reverted to what we have called light-touch review, allowing considerable latitude to public authorities and interfering only when the decision is "outrageous",[334] or "arbitrary".[335] Beyond that there may be cases which are not easily amenable to judicial review (sometimes called non-justiciable decisions). These decisions include those in which the court is constitutionally disabled from entering on

---

[327] *Daly* [2001] UKHL 26; [2001] 2 A.C. 532 at [27]–[28] (Lord Slynn).
[328] *R. (on the application of Sarkisian) v Immigration Appeal Tribunal* [2001] EWHC Admin 486 (Mumby J.).
[329] *R. (on the application of Puspalatha) v Immigration Appeal Tribunal [2001] EWHC Admin 333, [43] (Sullivan J.).*
[330] *R. (on the application of Kurecaj) v Secretary of State for the Home Department* [2002] EWHC 1199 (Gibbs J.).
[331] On justiciability, see 1–025—1–043.
[332] See T. Hickman, "The Reasonableness Princple" [2004] C.L.J. 166.
[333] See 11–023—11–024.
[334] CCSU v Minister for the Civil Service [1985] AC 374 at 410 (Lord Diplock).
[335] See, e.g. *Pro-Life Alliance v BBC* [2003] UKHL 23; [2004] 1 A.C. 185, where the HL held that the prohibition of the showing of aborted foetuses in a party election broadcast could not be interfered with unless the decision was "arbitrary". Lord Scott, dissenting, held that since free expression was engaged a structured proportionality test ought to be employed. See E. Barendt, "Free Speech and Abortion" [2003] P.L. 580; J. Jowell, "Judicial Deference: Servility, Civility or Institutional Capacity?" [2003] P.L. 592.

review, because the matter concerns policy—such as setting the level of taxation or to undertake a space programme.[336] Other decisions are not justiciable, or require due deference from the court because of their lack of relative institutional capacity to enter into a review of the decision. This issue is discussed in Chapter 1[337] and need not be repeated now.

A culture of justification

A sensitive appreciation of relative institutional capacity must however be qualified in two respects. First, as has been discussed above,[338] institutional deference does not mean constitutional deference. The courts ought not automatically to kowtow to Parliament (when legislation is being reviewed under the Human Rights Act or European Community law) or to the executive or other officials, on the ground that they are accountable to the electorate and the courts are not.

11–098

Secondly, the acceptance of institutional imperfection on the part of the courts, or of a superior institutional capacity on the part of the primary decision-maker (for example, on the ground that he had access to "special sources of knowledge and advice")[339] should not inevitably signal a low level of scrutiny of the decision. As was said in *Huang*,[340] although the public authority may be better placed to investigate the facts and test the evidence, the court cannot abdicate its responsibility of ensuring that the facts are properly "explored and summarized in the decision, with care".[341] Even where the courts recognise their lack of relative capacity or expertise to make the primary decision, they should nevertheless not easily relinquish their secondary function of probing the quality of the reasoning and ensuring that assertions are properly justified. The proper approach to this issue was taken by O'Regan J. in *Bato Star Fishing Ltd v The Chief Director: Marine and Coastal Management*[342] that a decision on the allocation of fishing quotas and requiring "an equilibrium to be struck between a range of competing interests or considerations and which is to be taken by a person or institution with special expertise in that area must be shown respect by the Courts". Nevertheless, she said that:

11–099

"this does not mean, however, that where the decision is one which will not reasonably result in the achievement of the goal, or which is not reasonably supported on the facts, or is not reasonable in the light of the reasons given for it, a Court may not review that decision . . . a court

[336] See 1–026; *R. (on the application of Gentle) v Prime Minister* [2006] EWCA Civ 1690 (invasion of Iraq); *R. (on the application of Marchiori) v Environment Agency* [2002] EWCA Civ 3; [2002] Eu. L.R. 225 (national defence policy).
[337] See 1–025; 5–00; 11–014.
[338] See 11–014.
[339] *Huang* [2007] UKHL 11; [2007] 2 W.L.R. 581.
[340] [2007] UKHL 11; [2007] 2 W.L.R. 581 at [16].
[341] [2007] UKHL 11; [2007] 2 W.L.R. 581 at [15].
[342] (2004) (4) S.A. 490 at para.48, CC.

should not rubber-stamp an unreasonable decision simply because of the complexity of the decision or the identity of the decision-maker".

11–100 The Chief Justice of Canada made a similar point when she warned against judicial deference "simply on the basis that the problem is serious and the solution difficult".[343]

11–101 Although it is too early to pronounce the demise of unreasonableness, the increased use of structured proportionality has changed our expectations of how decision-makers ought to behave. It has introduced what has been called a "culture of justification",[344] which requires decision-makers not only to act in accordance with bare rationality, but also to consider carefully the relationship between the means of a decision and its ends, to insist upon the consideration of less oppressive alternatives in appropriate cases and to ask for more cogent justification than bare *Wednesbury* permits when decisions interfere with established rights and significant interests.

11–102 If these expectations are confirmed in the case law of the future, the abandonment of the test of unreasonableness will not have breached the line between judicial review and appeal. We shall still not have adopted merits review. The courts will simply require more fulsome justification of a decision, the merits of which still lie within the scope of the primary decision-maker. However, instead of getting away with simply stating that he has carried out a proper balancing exercise, decision-makers will be required positively to "identify the factors he has weighed and explain why he has given weight to some factors and not to others".[345] The function of the courts in ensuring adequate justification of decisions is always within their institutional capacity and is indeed the task they are best qualified to perform.[346]

COMPARATIVE PERSPECTIVES[347]

Australia

11–103 Unlike England and Wales and New Zealand, in Australia judicial review remains firmly based upon a traditional ultra vires view of jurisdiction. It is not influenced by more substantive rights-based principles such as rule of

---

[343] *RJR-MacDonald v Canada (Attorney General)* [1995] 3 S.C.R. 119 (McLauglan C.J.). The former President of Israel's Supreme Court, Aharon Barak, considers that the term "deference" does not serve a useful purpose because if a court does not invalidate a decision as unreasonable it is lawful and if it exceeds the zone of unreasonableness then it must be invalidated and there is no room for deference: The Judge in a Democracy (2006), pp.251–252.

[344] See the works of Mureinik cited in n.16, above.

[345] *R. (on the application of X) v Chief Constable of the West Midlands* [2004] EWCA Civ 1068; [2005] 1 W.L.R. 65 at [101].

[346] Account will also have to be taken of the possible need to engage in a more intensive fact-finding review following the decision of the ECtHR in *Tsfayo v United Kingdom* [2007] B.L.G.R. 1.

[347] See also T. Hickman, "Proportionality: Comparative Law Lessons" [2007] J.R. 31.

law, consistency, equality, rationality and mistake of fact. The unreasonableness ground of review in Australia is applied cautiously, which is explained because of the close relationship between unreasonableness and merits review.[348] The English practice of adopting a lower standard of unreasonableness in cases involving fundamental human rights has been rejected by the Federal Court.[349]

The strict dichotomy between judicial and merits review is normally **11–104** justified by the principle of the separation of powers provided for in the Constitution.[350] In *Minister for Immigration and Multicultural Affairs v Eshetu*[351] for example, there was a substantial narrowing of the application of the test. Gleeson and McHugh JJ. held that if there was no more than strong disagreement with the decision maker's process of reasoning on an issue of fact this is not sufficient to make out the ground for review.[352] The extent of justification required for a decision and the court's duty to inquire in relation to obtaining information relevant to a decision as a factor in determining unreasonableness has been recently considered and any duty to check facts and to make inquiries as to further information appears to be very limited.[353] Insofar as it applies it is considered as part of unreasonableness or the duty to take into account all relevant considerations.[354]

At the federal level in Australia there is no equivalent to the HRA. As **11–105** such, there is no statutory procedural requirement to "justify" legislative measures that contravene fundamental rights and freedoms.[355] However, in both the Australian Capital Territory and Victoria human rights legislation has been introduced, based predominantly on the model of the HRA and requires the production of statements of compatibility with the chartered rights for all bills introduced to Parliament.[356] In Queensland, there is a

---

[348] *Minister for Aboriginal Affairs v Peko-Wallsend* (1985) 162 C.L.R. 24 at 42; E. Carroll, "Scope of Wednesbury Unreasonableness: In Need of Reform?" (2007) 14 *Australian Journal of Administrative Law* 86, pp.91–92.

[349] *STKB v Minister for Immigration and Multicultural and Indigenous Affairs* [2004] F.C.A. 546 at [8]–[10] (Selway J.), affirmed on appeal *STKB v Minister for Immigration and Multicultural and Indigenous Affairs* [2004] FCAFC 251 at [19]. Although note the conflicting comments of Kirby and Hayne JJ. in *Re Minister for Immigration and Multicultural Affairs; Ex Parte Applicant S20/2002.*

[350] B. Selway, "The Principle Behind Common Law Judicial Review of Administrative Action—the Search Continues" (2002) 30 *Federal Law Review* 217; S. Kneebone, "What is the Basis of Judicial Review" (2001) 12 *Public Law Review* 95.

[351] (1999) 197 C.L.R. 611.

[352] *Minister for Immigration and Multicultural and Indigenous Affairs v Eshetu* (1999) 197 C.L.R. 611 at 626.

[353] *Foster v Minister for Customs and Justice* (2000) 200 C.L.R. 442; *Abebe v Commonwealth* (1999) 197 C.L.R. 510 at 578; *Minister for Immigration and Ethnic Affairs v Ah Hin Teoh* (1995) 183 C.L.R. 273 although note the criticism in *Re Minister for Immigration and Multicultural Affairs; Ex parte Lam* (2003) 214 C.L.R. 1; see further Ch.12.

[354] M. Aronson, B. Dyer and M. Groves, *Judicial Review of Administrative Action*, 3rd edn. (2004), p.268 referring to *Re Minister for Immigration and Multicultural Affairs; Ex p. Application S20/2002* (2003) 198 A.L.R. 59.

[355] M. Aronson, B Dyer and M. Groves, *Judicial Review of Administrative Action* (2004) p.359.

[356] Gleeson C.J. and McHugh J. at 626; Charter of Human Rights and Responsibilities Act 2006 (Vic) and Human Rights Act 2004 (ACT).

statutory regime that requires justification for newly introduced bills that infringe upon individual rights and liberties.[357] Similarly in New South Wales, a Legislative Review Committee reports to Parliament on all bills that trespass on personal rights and liberties.[358]

Review of fact

11–106   In relation to review for mistake of fact, the High Court of Australia has not yet ruled as to whether a "material error of fact" is reviewable,[359] However, it is generally accepted that review does not lie for error of fact except in two circumstances, first, where an error as to a jurisdictional fact has been made.[360] Secondly, *Re Minister for Immigration & Multicultural Affairs; Ex parte Applicant S20/2002*[361] confirmed that review is available where the decision is irrational, illogical and not based upon findings or inferences of fact supported by logical grounds.

Canada

11–107   As has been discussed above, the Supreme Court of Canada has pioneered the principle of proportionality as a tool for assessing Charter rights.[362]

11–108   The Supreme Court of Canada has held that, in the absence of statutory specification of the standard of review, for every case of substantive (though not procedural) review and appeal from statutory authorities, including challenges for abuse of discretion, the first step is to establish a standard of review by reference to various "pragmatic and functional" factors.[363] The Court has also accepted that there are three and no more possible such standards of review:[364] correctness, unreasonableness, and patent unreasonableness. In practice, in the face of mounting criticism of the difficulty in articulating the differences between the latter two standards,[365] the Court may be moving in the direction of combining them.[366]

11–109   At present, the most deferential standard of review (patent unreasonableness) is most clearly indicated in the case of expert adjudicative tribunals, decisions of which are protected by a strong privative clause, and also in the case of broad discretion with polycentric dimensions typically involving a Cabinet Minister or specialised administrative agencies. In contrast,

[357] Legislative Standards Act 1992 (Qld).
[358] Legislative Review Committee Act 1987 (NSW).
[359] *Re Minister for Immigration and Multicultural and Indigenous Affairs; Ex parte Applicants S134/2002* (2003) 211 C.L.R. 441 at [35]–[42].
[360] M. Aronson, "The Resurgence of Jurisdictional Facts" (2001) 12 *Public Law Review* 17.
[361] (2003) 198 A.L.R. 59.
[362] D. Beattie, *The Ultimate Rule of Law* (2003), Ch.5.
[363] See, e.g. *Dr Q v College of Physicians and Surgeons of British Columbia* [2003] 1 S.C.R. 226.
[364] *Law Society of New Brunswick v Ryan* [2003] 1 S.C.R. 247.
[365] *Toronto (City) v CUPE, Local 79* [2003] 3 S.C.R. 77, concurring judgment of Le Bel J. (Deschamps J. concurring).
[366] *Council of Canadians with Disabilities v Via Rail Canada* 2007 S.C.C. 17.

correctness is most clearly indicated in the case of a tribunal or other statutory authority without the protection of a privative clause and perhaps subject to a right of appeal when deciding questions of law that are collateral to their mandate or otherwise involve issues of general law on which the regular courts will have as much, if not greater expertise as the agency itself.

Despite the admonition that a standard of review analysis is always a **11–110** necessary prelude to the exercise of the judicial review function, the Supreme Court itself has carved out one overly broad exception: when a statutory or prerogative authority is determining questions of Constitutional Law in the exercise of its authority (including questions pertaining to the Canadian Charter of Rights and Freedoms), the standard of review is automatically that of correctness.[367] The Court has also, by reference to traditional conceptions of ultra vires suggested that there are certain situations (such as the validity of municipal byelaws or action taken under byelaws) where there is little or no need for a pragmatic and functional analysis; correctness will almost inevitably be the standard of review.[368]

In an effort to forestall litigation over the standard of review and **11–111** perhaps as an implicit criticism of the courts' standard of review jurisprudence, British Columbia in its 2005 Administrative Tribunals Act (SBC) 2004 has attempted both to specify the standard of review applicable to tribunals coming within the reach of that Act and to define what each of the standards embraces. While there is legislation in other jurisdictions, such as the Federal Courts Act, specifying the grounds of judicial review, British Columbia is the only jurisdiction to attempt a partial legislative codification of the actual standards of review.

In Canada, the common law grounds of judicial review and much of the **11–112** legislative codification of the grounds of review and conferral of a right of appeal continue to be expressed in terms of the traditional common law grounds: jurisdiction, error of law (though not requiring the error to appear on the face of the record), a decision based on a complete lack of evidence, and the usual abuse of discretion grounds: bad faith, taking account of irrelevant factors, failure to take account of relevant factors, acting for an improper purpose, unlawful fettering of discretion, acting under dictation, and, occasionally, *Wednesbury* unreasonableness. However, the standard of review jurisprudence has had some impact on the grounds of review. Error of fact review is now more commonly considered in terms of whether there has been a "patently unreasonable finding of fact".[369] Similarly, *Wednesbury* unreasonableness has been subsumed by the term patent unreasonableness when that is the chosen standard of review. Also, in cases where the chosen standard is that of unreasonableness, exercises of discretionary power may now be subject to a

---

[367] *Multani v Marguerite-Bourgeoys (Commission Scolaire)* [2006] 1 S.C.R. 256.
[368] See, e.g. *United Taxi Drivers' Fellowship of Southern Alberta v Calgary (City)* [2004] 1 S.C.R. 425.
[369] See, e.g. *Toronto (City) Board of Education v OSSTF, Local 15* [1997] 1 S.C.R. 487.

more searching review than was the case under *Wednesbury*. It is, however, the case that the courts have yet to come to terms with the detail of the impact of applying a standard of review to abuse of discretion challenges not only in this context but also in relation to the discrete grounds of abuse of discretion. Thus, for example, in *Baker*,[370] the Court seemed to suggest that unreasonableness review might appropriately involve judicial reweighing of the various considerations that the decision-maker took into account. However, the Court retreated from that in *Suresh*.[371]

11–113   To this point, the Supreme Court has shown no disposition to move with the courts of England and Wales and to adopt or adapt other grounds of review such as proportionality, substantive legitimate expectation, and inconsistency. Indeed, the Court has explicitly rejected a doctrine of legitimate expectation with substantive consequences and review for inconsistency.[372] However, substantive review does from time to time involves the courts bringing to bear underlying "constitutional principles" as a supplement or context to the review exercise.

New Zealand

Proportionality and unreasonableness

11–114   Proportionality is a central element in deciding the reasonable limits of right under the New Zealand Bill of Rights Act 1990 (BORA). The doctrine requires that the legislative measures designed to give effect to certain objectives must be rationally connected to those objectives and impair rights no more than is necessary to accomplish the objectives. In New Zealand proportionality is known as the *Oakes* test,[373] it having been having imported from Canada[374] and modified subsequently.[375] It is assumed that any challenge to the exercise of administrative power on the ground that it unreasonably limits rights in the BORA will go through the three or four steps in this proportionality analysis.[376]

Intensity of review

11–115   In the last decade the New Zealand Courts, following UK developments, overtly have adopted a variable approach to the intensity of review: that is, the graver the impact of the decision upon the individual affected by it, the

---

[370] *Baker v Canada (Minister of Citizenship & Immigration)* [1999] 2 S.C.R. 817.
[371] *Suresh v Canada (Minister of Citizenship & Immigration)* [2002] 1 S.C.R. 3. But see *Singh Multani v Commissioner Scolaire* 2006, S.C.C. 6.
[372] *Domtar Inc v Québec (Commission d'appel en matière de lesions professionnelles)* [1993] 2 S.C.R. 756; *National Steel Car Ltd v United Steelworkers of America, Local 7135* (2006) 218 O.A.C. 207 (CA).
[373] See 11–00.
[374] *Ministry of Transport v Noort* [1992] 3 N.Z.L.R. 260 at 283, CA (Richardson J.).
[375] *Moonen v Film & Literature Board of Review* [2000] 2 N.Z.L.R. 9 CA.
[376] P. Rishworth, G. Huscroft, S. Optican and R. Mahoney, *The New Zealand Bill of Rights* (2003), pp.176–186.

more substantial the justification that will be required to assure the court of its legality. The emphasis on justification is all-important, and it is not coincidental that the common law is increasingly requiring reasons and putting great emphasis on transparency. It is now generally recognised that judicial review of discretionary decision-making involves a sliding scale, with non-justiciability at one end and close scrutiny at the other.[377] This recognition of the need to intensify review when fundamental human rights and interests are threatened is of a piece with the principle of legality.

Outside the "human rights" arena of administrative law (either affirmed **11–116** in BORA or fundamental common law rights), New Zealand has yet to embrace the doctrine of proportionality and so far have stuck with *Wednesbury* unreasonableness (albeit of variable intensity). New Zealand courts remain wary of a stand-alone doctrine of proportionality in the "non-rights" part of administrative law.[378] This was confirmed more recently in *Wolf v Minister of Immigration*,[379] where Wild J. refused to accept proportionality as a stand-alone principle in the absence of any infringement of BORA rights, and opted instead to apply *Wednesbury* unreasonableness. Wild J. accepted, however, the view that *Wednesbury* was not a monolithic test and that the intensity of review varied depending on the context, and that the most important factor pointing in the direction of the most intense scrutiny was the presence of human or fundamental rights. He applied a more intensive or searching scrutiny in that case because the decision "involve[d] the deportation of the appellant, and the consequent break up of a New Zealand family unit" and implicated New Zealand's international obligations under the ICCPR and the Convention on the Rights of the Child (although the rights of the child or the right to family life do not find expression in the BORA, but the BORA only affirms existing rights, and is not intended to affect other existing but unenumerated rights).[380] Wild J. was wary of the "Europeanisation" of UK public law which rendered its importation in New

---

[377] *Pharmaceutical Management Agency Ltd v Roussel Uclaf Australia Pty Ltd* [1998] N.Z.A.R. 58 at 66, CA; *Ports of Auckland Ltd v Auckland City Council* [1999] 1 N.Z.L.R. 601, HC; *Wolf v Minister of Immigration* [2004] N.Z.A.R. 414, HC; *Progressive Enterprises Ltd v North Shore City Council* [2006] N.Z.R.M.A. 72, HC; *Hamilton City Council v Fairweather* [2002] N.Z.A.R. 477 at [45], HC.

[378] In 2002, the CA held a professional disciplinary sanction "altogether excessive and out of proportion" and quashed the orders made: *The Institute of Chartered Accountants of New Zealand v Bevan* [2003] 1 N.Z.L.R.154. This is the principle described by Tipping J. as "[a] sledgehammer should not be used to crack a nut" (*Moonen v Film & Literature Board of Review* [2000] 2 N.Z.L.R.9 16). The CA in *Bevan's* case stressed that it was not entering into the "broader question. . . whether proportionality is a distinct head of review", noting that the disproportionate penalty case it was following (*R. v Barnsley MBC Ex p. Hook* [1976] 1 W.L.R. 1052 were accepted by commentators as well established (at [55]). That left the law as laid down by Tipping J. in *Isaac v Minister of Consumer Affairs* [1990] 2 N.Z.L.R.606 at 636, HC that disproportionality goes to Wednesbury unreasonableness. See also *Waitakere City Council v Lovelock* [1997] 2 N.Z.L.R. 385 at 408, CA (Thomas J.).

[379] [2004] N.Z.A.R. 414 at [32], HC.

[380] BORA s.28.

Zealand inapt. He held that proportionality should remain within the traditional fold of (*Wednesbury*) unreasonableness, and not stand-alone.

11–117   New Zealand's constitutional and administrative law is evolving in ways quite different to that of the United Kingdom.[381] The Supreme Court has made it clear recently in *Hansen v The Queen*[382] that parliamentary sovereignty holds greater sway in New Zealand than amongst many of the higher judiciary in the United Kingdom. Now that appeal to the Privy Council has been abandoned, New Zealand courts can chart an indigenous course. There are voices advocating adoption of proportionality in New Zealand.[383] However, where BORA rights are engaged, proportionality applies; in all other case variable intensity (*Wednesbury*) unreasonableness applies, with the possibility of a grey area of fundamental common law rights or interests somewhere in the middle.

11–118   However, it is becoming common for New Zealand judges on review to invoke the American terminology of "hard look" to describe a more intensive scrutiny of the reasonableness of administrative action. In the Court of Appeal in *Pharmaceutical Management Agency Ltd v Roussel Uclaf Australia Pty Ltd* it was said "in some cases, such as those involving human rights, a less restricted approach, even perhaps, to use the expression commonly adopted in the United States, a "hard look" may be required".[384] In *Thompson v Treaty of Waitangi Fisheries Commission*,[385] one of the prime judicial movers behind the introduction of this terminology—Hammond J.—attempted to rebadge the "hard look" doctrine as an "adequate consideration doctrine". This doctrine, he said, would go further than taking into account, or failing to take into account, relevant considerations. Presumably it would go further, too, than reasonableness review for giving manifestly too much or too little weigh to relevant factors.[386] The notion of adequate consideration, said Hammond J., would "check poor public administration and inadequate, cursory and ill-considered decisions". Professor Taggart has argued that in the New Zealand context "hard look" is an unnecessary transplant and should be rejected[387] as it is no more precise than unreasonableness and does not tell a judge how hard to look in any particular case.[388]

[381] G. Beresford, "The Processes of Constitutionalism in New Zealand and the UK" (2005) 2 *New Zealand Postgraduate Law e-Journal*.
[382] [2007] N.Z.S.C. 7 (February 20, 2007).
[383] J. Varuhas, "Keeping Things in Proportion: The Judiciary, Executive Action and Human Rights" (2006) 22 N.Z.U.L.R. 300.
[384] [1998] N.Z.A.R. 58 at 66; and see, e.g. Dame Sian Elias, "'Hard Look' and the Judicial Function" (1996) 4 *Waikato Law Review* 1; P. Joseph, *Constitutional and Administrative Law in New Zealand*, 2nd edn. (2001), p.831.
[385] [2005] 2 N.Z.L.R. 9 at [214]–[219], CA.
[386] *New Zealand Fishing Industry Association Inc v Minister of Agriculture and Fisheries* [1988] 1 N.Z.L.R. 546 at 552,CA (Cooke P.); and *Minister for Aboriginal Affairs v Peko-Wallsend Ltd* (1986) 66 A.L.R. 229 at 309–310, HCA (Mason J.).
[387] M. Taggart, "Review of Developments in Administrative Law" [2006] New Zealand Law Rev. 75, 85–87.
[388] *New Zealand Public Service Association Inc v Hamilton City Council* [1997] 1 N.Z.L.R. 30 at 34–35 HC.

Consistency

The New Zealand courts have yet to firmly establish this as a ground of **11–119** review for essentially the same reasons they are hesitant about substantive legitimate expectations (indeed expectations based on past practice or decisions often support the claim of inconsistency): it may unduly fetter discretion and hence be contrary to the public interest. The strongest statement in New Zealand law for review for inconsistency is in the dissenting judgment of Thomas J. in *Pharmaceutical Management Agency Ltd v Roussel Uclaf Australia Pty Ltd.*[389] where he was of the view that the agency "failed to act even-handedly between two companies in direct competition".[390]

Review for mistake of fact

It was in a New Zealand appeal to the Privy Council[391] that gave Lord **11–120** Diplock (as he had by then become) the opportunity to confirm at the highest Commonwealth level what he had said as a puisne judge 20 years earlier in *R v Deputy Industrial Injuries Commissioner, ex p. Moore*;[392] namely, it is a breach of natural justice to base a finding of fact upon material which does not logically support it. Despite the binding nature of Privy Council decisions in New Zealand law (until 2003) this procedural approach to "no evidence" review has not really taken hold. The courts have preferred to see error of fact as an error going to substance or outcome. In a series of dicta, emanating in the beginning from Sir Robin Cooke when on the New Zealand Court of Appeal and for some time not decided by other members of the court, review was permitted if decision-makers proceeded upon an incorrect basis of fact or misunderstood an established and relevant fact or decided on no evidence.[393] In *S & D v M & Board of Trustees of Auckland Grammar School*,[394] Smellie J. noted the continuing division of view at the Court of Appeal level but pointed out that there are "numerous [High Court] decisions where mistake of fact has been held to be a ground of review", naming nine High Court judges who had done so between 1987–97. Smellie J. went on to invalidate a school's

---

[389] [1998] N.Z.A.R. 58, CA.

[390] Citing the 5th edition of this work at pp.576–582, Thomas J. invoked the principles of equality, and of equal and consistent treatment (at 72). The majority decision was upheld on further appeal to the Privy Council: *Roussel UCLAF Australia Pty Ltd v Pharmaceutical Management Agency Ltd* [2001] N.Z.A.R. 476 for substantially the reasons given by the majority below.

[391] *Re Erebus Royal Commission; Air New Zealand v Mahon* [1983] N.Z.L.R. 662 at 671.

[392] [1965] 1 Q.B. 456 at 488.

[393] *Daganayasi v Minister of Immigration* [1980] 2 N.Z.L.R. 130 at 145–148 (note reservations of other judges, [1980] 2 N.Z.L.R. 130 at 132, 149); *New Zealand Fisheries Association Inc v Minister of Agriculture & Fisheries* [1988] 1 N.Z.L.R. 544 at 552 CA (Cooke P.) (note reservation of Richardson J., [1988] 1 N.Z.L.R. 544 at 564); *Devonport v Local Government Commission* [1989] 2 N.Z.L.R. 203 at 208 CA; *Auckland City Council v Minister of Transport* [1990] 1 N.Z.L.R.264 at 293, CA (Cooke P.); *Southern Ocean Trawlers v Director-General of Agriculture & Fisheries* [1993] 2 N.Z.L.R. 53 61, CA (Cooke P.).

[394] High Court, Auckland, M. 477/97, June 11, 1998.

suspension of a student as based on a "significantly incorrect factual basis". By the mid-1990s, mistake of fact had became accepted as a ground of review at High Court level and is now orthodoxy in New Zealand administrative law. To succeed on this ground, however, the "fact" must be clearly established or "an established and recognised opinion" and "it cannot be said to be a mistake to adopt one of two different points of view of the facts, each of which may be reasonably held".[395]

South Africa

11–121 The South African Constitution 1996 s.33 enshrines the notion of "just administrative action", which is defined as administrative action which is "lawful, reasonable and procedurally fair". It required a statute to fill in the detail of those requirements, and in 2000 Parliament enacted the Promotion of Administrative Justice Act (PAJA). In *Pharmaceutical Manufacturers Association of South Africa*[396] the Constitutional Court held that exercise of public power, and therefore its regulation by the courts, is always a constitutional matter, and exercises of public power are rooted in and gain their force from the Constitution.[397] The rule of law, Chaskalson P. concluded, requires exercises of public power to be rational:

"It is a requirement of the rule of law that the exercise of public power by the Executive and other functionaries should not be arbitrary. Decisions must be rationally related to the purpose for which the power was given, otherwise they are in effect arbitrary and inconsistent with this requirement."[398]

Standard of review

11–122 The Constitution thus envisages two standards of review, or two standards of judicial scrutiny of exercises of public power. First, "administrative action" must be lawful, reasonable and procedurally fair. Secondly, all acts must be lawful and non-arbitrary. The Constitutional Court has on a number of occasions since *Pharmaceutical Manufacturers* used this second,

---

[395] *New Zealand Fisheries Association Inc v Minister of Agriculture & Fisheries*. 1988] 1 N.Z.L.R. 544 at 552, CA (Cooke P.).
[396] 2000 (2) S.A. 674, CC.
[397] 2000 (2) S.A. 674 at [33].
[398] 2000 (2) S.A. 674 at [85] (footnotes, including to the 5th edition of this work, excluded).

broader and less exacting standard of scrutiny to review decisions.[399] However, where a decision infringes a right held by a member of the public, that decision would expose the decision to the higher standards of scrutiny imposed by the Promotion of Administrative Justice Act s.33.

Statutory unreasonableness

The PAJA sets out a comprehensive list of grounds of judicial review, one of which is the *Wednesbury* formulation. PAJA s.6(2)(h) reads:

11–123

"A court or tribunal has the power to judicially review an administrative action if the exercise of the power or the performance of the function authorised by the empowering provision, in pursuance of which the administrative action was purportedly taken, is so unreasonable that no reasonable person could have so exercised the power or performed the function".

As has been discussed above,[400] in *Bato Star Fishing (Pty) Ltd v Minister of Environmental Affairs*, O'Regan J. held for a unanimous Constitutional Court that this formulation was not consistent with the right enshrined in the South African Constitution to administrative action which is "reasonable". Reading the PAJA provision down, she held:[401]

11–124

"Even if it may be thought that the language of s.6(2)(h), if taken literally, might set a standard such that a decision would rarely if ever be found unreasonable, that is not the proper constitutional meaning which should be attached to the subsection. The subsection must be construed consistently with the Constitution and in particular s 33 which requires administrative action to be "reasonable". Section 6(2)(h) should then be understood to require a simple test, namely that an administrative decision will be reviewable if, in Lord Cooke's words, it is one that a reasonable decision-maker could not reach".

---

[399] See, e.g. *AAA Investments (Pty) Ltd v Micro Finance Regulatory Council* 2006 (11) B.C.L.R. 1255, CC; *Affordable Medicines Trust v Minister of Health* 2006 (3) S.A. 247, CC; *Dawood v Minister of Home Affairs* 2000 (3) S.A. 936, CC; *Janse van Rensburg NO v Minister of Trade and Industry* 2001 (1) S.A. 29, CC. The lower courts have also reviewed actions against the standards of the doctrine of legality, see e.g. *Nala Local Municipality v Lejweleputswa District Municipality* [2005] 3 All S.A. 571 (O); *Van Zyl v Government of RSA* [2005] 4 All S.A. 96 (T); *Mgoqi v City of Cape Town* 2006 (4) S.A. 355 (C). In a number of similar decisions courts have held that it is unnecessary to decide if the action or decision complained against amounts to administrative action, since the action or decision fails to discharge the requirements of the doctrine of legality and falls to be set aside on that basis alone: *Chairperson: Standing Tender Committee v JFE Sapela Electronics (Pty) Ltd* [2005] 4 All S.A. 487, SCA; *Sebenza Forwarding & Shipping Consultancy (Pty) Ltd v Petroleum Oil and Gas Corporation of SA (Pty) Ltd t/a Petro* 2006 (2) S.A. 52 (C), *Reed v Master of the High Court of SA* [2005] 2 All S.A. 429 (E).
[400] See Ch.11.
[401] 2004 (4) S.A. 490, CC, paras 42–45 (footnotes omitted). The reference to Lord Cooke is to *R. v Chief Constable of Sussex Ex parte International Trader's Ferry Ltd* [1999] 2 A.C. 418.

11–125 As to the substance of reasonableness review, the Court in *Bato Star* adopted an approach based on "reasonable equilibrium". Where an administrator is enjoined by legislation to have regard to a range of considerations in making a decision, and has to strike a balance between often-competing considerations, the court's role "is merely to determine whether the decision made is one which achieves a reasonable equilibrium in the circumstances". This is consistent with the view of one of the leading works, where Hoexter suggests that reasonableness as a standard of review connotes "an area of "legitimate diversity", a space within which "various reasonable decisions may be made".[402] O'Regan J. therefore set out a range of factors that courts must consider when investigating whether the administrative action concerned is reasonable or not. These include:

> "the nature of the decision, the identity and expertise of the decision-maker, the range of factors relevant to the decision, the reasons given for the decision, the nature of the competing interests involved and the impact of the decision on the lives and well-being of those affected".

11–126 O'Regan J. also considered the notion of deference, and although willing to concede to the expertise of the primary decision-maker in a complex case of resource allocation, was not willing to "rubber stamp" such a decision. She was anxious to emphasise that

> "The use of the word 'deference' may give rise to misunderstanding as to the true function of a review Court. This can be avoided if it is realised that the need for Courts to treat decision-makers with appropriate deference or respect flows not from judicial courtesy or etiquette but from the fundamental constitutional principle of the separation of powers itself".[403]

Mistake of fact

11–127 In respect of mistake of fact, if such mistake leads to an unreasonable decision it will be reviewable on that ground. A court of review would clearly not engage with an administrator's findings of facts, since to do so would be to engage in the merits in a manner that *Bato Star* does not allow. The only facts that are relevant to review courts are "jurisdictional facts": facts that must exist in order to ground an administrator's authority to make a decision in the first place. The PAJA recognises review on this basis in s.6(2)(b), which allows review if "a mandatory and material procedure or condition prescribed by an empowering provision was not complied with".

---

[402] C. Hoexter, *Administrative Law in South Africa* (2007), p.313; see also "The Future of Judicial review in South African Administrative Law" (2000) 117 S.A.L.J. 484, 509–510.
[403] *Bato Star* (2004) (4) S.A. 490 at para.46.

CHAPTER 12

LEGITIMATE EXPECTATIONS

INTRODUCTION

Since the early 1970s one of the principles justifying the imposition of both **12–001** procedural and substantive protection has been the legitimate expectation. Such an expectation arises where a decision-maker has led someone affected by the decision to believe that he will receive or retain a benefit or advantage (including that a hearing will be held before a decision is taken). It is a basic principle of fairness that legitimate expectations ought not to be thwarted.[1] The protection of legitimate expectations is at the root of the constitutional principle of the rule of law, which requires regularity, predictability, and certainty in government's dealings with the public.[2] "Legal certainty" is also a basic principle of European Community law.[3] For these reasons the existence of a legitimate expectation may, even in the absence of a right in private law, justify recognition in public law.

Initially, the legitimate expectation was employed to require a fair **12–002** hearing: a person's legitimate expectations (to a benefit or advantage, including the expectation of a hearing) could not be terminated without giving the person the opportunity to advocate its retention. In Chapter 7 we merely noted the extension of the scope of the fair hearing so as to encompass the legitimate expectation. We now return to consider that aspect of the legitimate expectation in more detail, together with a consideration of the more recent expansion of the legitimate expectation to the protection of substantive rights (thus adding to the armoury of substantive principles considered in Chapter 11).

---

[1] J. Rawls, *A Theory of Justice* (1972), pp.235–243; Blackstone, *Commentaries of the Laws of England* (1765) Vol.1, p.44; F. Maitland, *Collected Papers*, Vol.1 (1911), p.81 ("Known general laws, however bad, interfere less with freedom than decisions based on no previous known rule"; Maitland equated arbitrary power with power that is "uncertain" or "incalculable"); note the Roman Law principle that the Praetor could not depart from the published terms of his edict (Asconius, in Comelianum, 52 and Dio Cassius 36.40; A. Watson, *Law Making in the Later Roman Republic* (1974), pp.93–94); and Bentham's "disappointment-prevention principle" as an element of his greatest happiness principle. This requires more than "regret", but the loss of an "expectation". See P. Schofield (ed.), *Official Aptitude Maximised; Expense Minimised* (1993), Appendix B "On Retrenchment".
[2] See generally J. Raz, *The Authority of Law* (1979), Ch.11.
[3] See 14–093 Schwarze, *European Administrative Law* (2006). The European law is based upon the concept of "vertrauensschutz" (the honouring of a trust or confidence).

Legitimate expectations of procedural fairness

12–003   The term "legitimate expectation" first made an appearance in the context of procedural fairness in *Schmidt v Secretary of State for Home Affairs.*[4] A foreign student sought review of the Home Secretary's decision to refuse an extension of his temporary permit to stay in the United Kingdom. In rejecting the student's contention that he ought to have been afforded a hearing, Lord Denning M.R. said *obiter* that the question of a hearing "all depends on whether he has some right or interest, or, I would add, some *legitimate expectation*, of which it would not be fair to deprive him without hearing what he has to say".[5]

12–004   *Schmidt* and the cases which followed it referred to the legitimate expectation without analysing its scope or basis, and in particular without distinguishing it from the right to a hearing arising from the existence of a protectable interest.[6] The distinction between the legitimate expectation and protectable interest may not always be clear, particularly if the two overlap.[7] However, the underlying principles justifying one or the other are distinct. The legitimate expectation derives its justification from the principle of allowing the individual to rely on assurances given, and to promote certainty and consistent administration. Such a justification is distinct from that which permits a person to participate in the process of reaching a decision which may threaten his rights or interests.

12–005   In *R. v Liverpool Corporation Ex p. Liverpool Taxi Fleet Operators' Association* it was held that the Corporation's decision to increase the number of taxi licences without consulting the Operator's Association was unfair because the decision was in breach of an assurance to the contrary.[8]

---

[4] [1969] 2 Ch. 149.

[5] [1969]2 Ch. 149 at 170 (emphasis added). Lord Denning's dicta were not supported by the other members of the CA. Russell L.J., dissenting, simply thought that the case was not sufficiently clear to warrant an order to strike out the action; Widgery J. classified a situation where the renewal of a licence might "reasonably be expected" as being "tantamount to the withdrawal of a right" (at 353).

[6] In *Schmidt*, Lord Denning suggested that a revocation of an existing permit would have given the applicant "an opportunity of making representations: for he would have a legitimate expectation of being allowed to stay for the permitted time". See also *Breen v Amalgamated Engineering Union* [1971] 2 Q.B. 175; *McInnes v Onslow Fane* [1978] 1 W.L.R. 1520; *O'Reilly v Mackman* [1983] 2 A.C. 237 (Lord Diplock).

[7] See e.g. *R. v Assistant Commissioner of Police of the Metropolis Ex p. Howell* [1985] R.T.R. 52, CA: Assistant Commissioner refused to renew the taxi licence of H, a cab driver, without first having given him an indication of the objections to renewal and without having given him a fair chance to meet the objections. In holding that the action of the Assistant Commissioner was unfair, and that the decision should be set aside, the CA used both strands of reasoning. On the one hand, a protectable interest was taken away without consultation: "I think natural justice required that the Assistant Commissioner, before reaching a final decision on a matter of such momentous importance to [H], should at the very least have given him the opportunity to comment. . ." (Slade L.J. at 61); on the other hand, "given the doctor's view [that] he was fit to drive taxi cabs, and having been told [in the regulations] by the Assistant Commissioner that before he could grant him a further licence he would need a certificate to that effect, [H] had a reasonable expectation that the licence would be granted to him on the provision by his doctor of that certificate" (Ackner L.J. at 60).

[8] [1972] 2 Q.B. 299.

Although the duty to hear was not expressly justified by the doctrine of legitimate expectation in that case, later cases adopted and explained the decision on that basis.[9] In 1983 the Privy Council quashed an order of the Hong Kong government to deport an immigrant in breach of a promise to give immigrants a fair opportunity to present their case in advance of deportation. The failure to implement the promise was held not to be in the "interest of good administration".[10]

GCHQ case defines legitimate expectation

The first attempt at a comprehensive definition of the principle of legitimate expectation was provided by the House of Lords in *Council of Civil Service Unions v Minister for the Civil Service* ("the GCHQ case"). [11] A bare majority of their Lordships rested their conclusion on the fact that, but for national security, there would have been a duty on the Minister to consult with the Union, on the ground that the civil servants had a legitimate expectation that they would be consulted before their trade union rights were taken away.[12] Lord Diplock stated that, for a legitimate expectation to arise, the decision: **12–006**

> "must affect [the] other person . . . by depriving him of some benefit or advantage which either (i) he had in the past been permitted by the decision-maker to enjoy and which he can legitimately expect to be permitted to continue to do until there has been communicated to him some rational grounds for withdrawing it on which he has been given an opportunity to comment; or (ii) he has received assurance from the decision-maker will not be withdrawn without giving him first an opportunity of advancing reasons for contending that they should not be withdrawn."[13]

This definition indicates the two ways in which the expectation may found the right to a hearing. First, the expectation may be based upon an assurance that a past benefit (such as the right to trade union membership   **12–007**

---

[9] Lord Denning M.R. did not refer to the nascent doctrine, but to the "private law" principle of equitable estoppel. For other cases which then adopted the doctrine of legitimate expectation as the basis for a duty to be heard, see: *Salemi v MacKellar (No.2)* (1977) 137 C.L.R. 396 (Stephen J., dissenting) and *R. v Secretary of State for the Home Department Ex p. Asif Mahmood Khan* [1984] 1 W.L.R. 1337.

[10] *Attorney General of Hong Kong v Ng Yuen Shiu* [1983] 2 A.C. 629.

[11] [1985] A.C. 374. This was not the first time that the HL had considered the doctrine; see *O'Reilly v Mackman* [1983] 2 A.C. 237 at 275 (Lord Diplock, *obiter*), a prisoner has a legitimate expectation that he will not be awarded a forfeiture of remission by board of visitors without being heard in accordance with the procedures of natural justice); *Re Findlay* [1985] A.C. 318 (prisoner has no legitimate expectation that he will be granted parole under policy which has been superseded by a more restrictive one).

[12] Lords Diplock (at 408–409), Fraser (at 401B) and Roskill (at 1204H) all expressed a preference for the term "legitimate" over the term "reasonable" expectation. Lords Scarman and Brightman affirmed the duty to consult without resting on the doctrine of legitimate expectation (ibid. at 1193G and 1208E).

[13] [1965] A.C. 374 at 408–409.

in *GCHQ*) will continue. In such a case the benefit may not be denied without a hearing. However, the reference by Lord Diplock to *past* advantage or benefit is unduly restrictive. The expectation may also surely extend to a benefit in the future which has not yet been enjoyed but which has been promised.

12–008   Second, the expectation may be based upon an assurance of a hearing itself, which should not be denied. In the GCHQ case Lord Fraser held that the civil servants enjoyed a legitimate expectation that they would be consulted before their trade union membership was withdrawn. The expectation was in his view grounded on the fact that prior consultation had in the past been the standard practice when conditions of service were significantly altered.[14]

Voluntary compliance with fair procedures

12–009   If a body which is entitled to reach a decision without any prior hearing elects to give a hearing before coming to its decision, can that decision be impugned on the ground that the hearing did not conform to the standards of fairness? Some older authority suggests that it cannot.[15] In other areas of the law the volunteer is at times burdened with the same duties as the conscript. I am under no obligation to give a hitchhiker a lift in my car, but if I choose to give him a lift I owe him the same duty of care as I would if he were a fare-paying passenger and I were a common carrier or bound by contract to convey him. Whatever the position may have been in the past,[16] it seems clear today that by providing a voluntary hearing the decision-maker will have induced a legitimate expectation of fairness and the hearing will therefore have to conform to the standards appropriate to the decision being made.

Statutory fair procedure requirements

12–010   A statutory scheme requiring a hearing or specifying particular procedures may have the effect of preventing a legitimate expectation from arising.[17]

Legitimate expectations of substantive benefit

12–011   When considering the procedural, as opposed to substantive aspects of the legitimate expectation, the promise or representation or conduct which creates the expectation will only require that the person receive a fair

---

[14] [1985] A.C. 374 at 401–403.
[15] *Ex p. Death* (1852) 18 Q.B. 647 at 659; *Green v Blake* [1948] I.R. 242 at 267; *Russell v Duke of Norfolk* [1948] 1 All E.R. 488 at 491; [1949] 1 All E.R. 109 at 115; *Nakkuda Ali v Jayaratne* [1951] A.C. 66 at 77; in Canada, *R. v Bird* (1963) 38 D.L.R. (2nd) 354. Cf. *R. v Minister of Labour Ex p. General Supplies Ltd* (1965) 47 D.L.R. (2nd) 189, applying a dictum in *R. v Metropolitan Police Commissioner Ex p. Parker* [1953] 1 W.L.R. 1150 at 1157.
[16] See the 4th edition of this work at pp.237–238.
[17] *R. v DPP Ex p. Kebiline* [2000] 2 A.C. 326.

hearing. The expectation therefore extends only to the opportunity to make representations or to any other component of a fair hearing, for example, the duty to give reasons.[18] Once the duty to give the hearing has been fulfilled there is not necessarily any further duty to provide the actual substance of the expectation. From the mid 1980s the English courts began to uphold the protection of substantive expectations under limited conditions.[19] In what circumstances may a decision which disappoints an expectation of a substantive benefit or advantage be held invalid on that account?

The answer to this question engages a number of public law values.[20] In **12–012** particular, the relative virtues and defects of certainty and flexibility must be kept in mind. A stubborn concern for internal consistency[21] may fetter an authority's discretion.[22] Yet flexibility can lead to inconsistency and unequal treatment. Fairness to the disappointed individual (who might also have suffered financial loss in reliance upon the expectation) may conflict with the authority's duty to the public. And what will be the practical effect of the principle? Will the assiduous fulfilment of legitimate expectations deter public bodies from articulating their policies?[23] Policies must not be treated as a set of rules, yet, as Sedley L.J. put it: "a policy has virtues of flexibility which rules lack and virtues of consistency which discretion lacks".[24] Underlying these questions is the fundamental issue of the degree of scrutiny *(Wednesbury* or more intrusive) which the courts should employ when judging whether the non-application or alteration of a policy in the public interest outweighs the unfairness to the individual who legitimately expected the policy to be applied.

---

[18] *R. v Secretary of State for the Home Department Ex p. Duggan* [1994] 3 All E.R. 277.
[19] See e.g. *R. v Secretary of State for the Home Department Ex p. Ruddock* [1987] 1 W.L.R. 1482 (legitimate expectation that circular establishing procedures for telephone tapping should be fulfilled but held that it was); *R. v Board of Inland Revenue Ex p. MFK Underwriting Agencies Ltd* [1990] 1 W.L.R. 1545 (ruling on tax consequences of scheme could create expectation of fulfilment, but not on the facts of this case); *R. v Secretary of State for Health Ex p. U.S. Tobacco International Inc* [1992] 1 Q.B. 353 (change of policy led to manufacture of "oral snuff" being banned. Held no substantive-but only procedural-legitimate expectation in the circumstances); *Olonilvyi v Secretary of State for Home Affairs* [1989] Imm.A.R. 135 (representation that applicant would be able to re-enter UK must be fulfilled). But see *R. v Secretary of State for Home Affairs Ex p. Patel* [1990] 3 Imm. A.R. 89; *R. v Croydon Justices Ex p. Dean* [1993] Q.B. 769 (expectation that would not be prosecuted); *R. v Lord Chancellor Ex p. Hibbit and Saunders* [1993] C.O.D. 326 (unfair to fulfil a legitimate expectation where applicants who had previous long-standing contracts as court shorthand writers not given opportunity to submit lower tender in new tender procedure. But not amenable to judicial review as "private law"); *R. v Walsall MBC Ex p. Yapp* [1994] I.C.R. 528 (council able to seek fresh tenders for building works and no legitimate expectation that own workforce would be favoured).
[20] P. Craig, *Administrative Law*, 5th edn (2003) p.641.
[21] Decisions of public authorities "may not be internally inconsistent": *R. v IRC Ex p. MFK Underwriting Agencies Ltd* [1990] 1 W.L.R. 1545 at 1569, DC (Bingham L.J.). On consistency and equality, see 11–062–069.
[22] On fettering of discretion, see ch.9.
[23] On tort liability for erroneous statements, see 19–046.
[24] *R. v Department of Education and Employment Ex p. Begbie* [2000] 1 W.L.R. 1115.

12–013   The complexity of weighing these often contradictory values may be the reason why a number of common law jurisdictions have avoided or rejected at least the substantive legitimate expectation, preferring to allow public decision-makers to keep their options open and to retain the freedom to change their minds.[25] The liberty of a public body to change its policies is an important constitutional principle. Yet in this country we have not only endorsed the legitimate expectation as a value worth protecting, but have even sometimes flirted with its application even when the expectation is induced by a representation that the authority has no legal power to fulfil. Of course the protection of the legitimate expectation is hedged with qualifications and is contingent upon a number of different factors, to which we shall shortly turn, after first considering the essential features of the legitimate expectation (which are common to expectations which induce both procedural and substantive rights).

Illustrations

12–014   • British Coal and the Secretary of State were held in breach of their duty to consult with the unions on the question of pit closures. The expectation was in that case based upon an agreement establishing review procedures (known as the Modified Colliery Review Procedure) and procedures to refer pit closures to an independent tribunal.[26]

• Gypsies have had a legitimate expectation that a council would not evict them without finding an alternative site.[27]

• Contractors on a council's list of approved contractors had a legitimate expectation that they would not be removed from the list without a hearing.[28]

• An applicant submitting a tender for council land enjoyed a legitimate expectation that he would be given a further opportunity to tender following the failure of the favoured bid, since he had been "left with that impression".[29]

• A prisoner serving his sentence in Scotland where remission was one half of the sentence had a legitimate expectation when transferred to

---

[25] On fettering of discretion, see ch.9.

[26] *R. v British Coal Corp and Secretary of State for Trade and Industry Ex p. Vardy* (1994) 6 Admin. L.R. 1.

[27] *R. v Brent LBC Ex p. MacDonagh* (1990) 21 H.L.R. 494. The legitimate expectation arose both from an express promise of the council, and because of a past practice of letting the gypsies stay on the land, providing services, etc. Today, Art.8 ECHR may be relevant.

[28] *R. v Enfield LBC Ex p. T.F. Unwin (Roydon) Ltd* (1989) 1 Admin. L.R. 51. The legitimate expectation would seem to be as a result of past practice: the contractors had been on the council's list "for many years". But see *R. v Lord Chancellor Ex p. Hibbit and Saunders* [1993] C.O.D. 326 (shorthand writers on list of Lord Chancellor's Department). On judicial review of contracting decisions, see 3–056.

[29] *R. v Barnet LBC Ex p. Pardes House School* [1989] C.O.D. 512.

England, where remission was only one third of sentence, that the earlier release date would be applied.[30]

- The Commission for the New Towns had a legitimate expectation (based on a representation more than 15 years earlier) that if a local council constructed a highway, it would do so without charge.[31]

- Residents in a home for the elderly had a legitimate expectation to be consulted about its closure.[32-33]

- Detainees had a legitimate expectation that the Secretary of State would consider a British National's request that representations be made on his behalf.[34]

- Yet when the Secretary of State decided to abolish a discretionary ex gratia scheme under which compensation was paid to those who had suffered a miscarriage of justice, and did so without consultation, it was held that there had been no representation or promise that the scheme would continue indefinitely, or that the Secretary of State would consult or give notice before withdrawing it.[35]

THE SOURCE OF A LEGITIMATE EXPECTATION

In *GCHQ*, Lord Fraser indicated the two ways in which a legitimate **12–015** expectation may arise: "either from an express promise given on behalf of a public authority or from the existence of a regular practice which the claimant can reasonably expect to continue".[36] The representations which induce a legitimate expectation can thus be express or implied.

Express representation

An obvious example is where an express undertaking is given which **12–016** induces an expectation of a specific benefit or advantage. The form of the express representation is unimportant as long as it appears to be a considered assurance, undertaking or promise of a benefit, advantage or course of action which the authority will follow.[37] The promise may relate

[30] *Walsh v Secretary of State for Scotland* 1990 S.L.T. 526.
[31] *R. v Northamptonshire CC Ex p. Commission for the New Towns* [1992] C.O.D. 123.
[32-33] *R v Devon CC Ex p. Baker* [1995] 1 All E.R. 73; *R. v Wandsworth LBC Ex p. Beckith* (1995) 159 L.G.Rev. 929 (duty to consult extends to residents of other homes only indirectly affected by closure).
[34] *R. (on the application of Al Rawi) v Secretary of State for Foreign and Commonwealth Affairs* [2006] EWCA Civ 1270; [2006] H.R.L.R. 42
[35] *R. (on the application of Noorullah Niazii) v Secretary of State for the Home Department* [2007] EWHC 1495 (Admin).
[36] [1985] A.C. 374 at 401B.
[37] Where the Revenue have entered into an agreement under s.54(1) of the Taxes Management Act 1970 with a taxpayer in relation to a scheme, it has been held that they are precluded from litigating the subject-matter of the agreement, even if it is based upon an error of law. *Cenlon Finance Co Ltd v Elwood* [1962] A.C. 782; *Olin Energy Systems Ltd v Scorer* [1985] A.C. 645 at 658 (Lord Keith).

to an existing situation which will continue, or to a future benefit. In the case an expectation inducing a right to procedural fairness, rather than the substance of the expectation, the promise, as we have seen, may be either to the benefit itself or to a fair hearing (or any aspect of a fair hearing).

12–017   The representation may be directed at a single individual, or a number of individuals,[38] or a class.[39] An example of a personally-directed representation occurred in one of the earliest cases on the substantive expectation (although those words were not used). In *Preston v Inland Revenue Commissioners*,[40] the applicant taxpayer claimed that the Revenue should honour an agreement with him not to pursue certain tax claims. It was held on the facts that the agreement did not bind the Revenue, but Lord Templeman made it clear that, in principle, conduct equivalent to a breach of contract or breach of representation could amount to an "abuse of power" on the part of the tax authorities.[41] Later, the House of Lords unanimously accepted that it may be an abuse of power for the Revenue to seek to extract tax contrary to an advance clearance given to the taxpayer by the Revenue.[42]

12–018   The analogy of the express representation giving rise to a legitimate expectation with the law of contract and the private law principle of estoppel is obvious and probably encouraged the acceptance by the courts that creating a legitimate expectation can have consequences in public law. However, the House of Lords recently indicated that to have effect a substantive legitimate expectation does not depend upon being able to identify a private law analogy. In *R. (on the application of Reprotech Ltd) v*

---

[38] As in *R. v North and East Devon HA Ex p. Coughlan* [2001] Q.B. 213, where residents of a home for severely disabled people had been promised a "home for life".

[39] Racehorse owners in *R. v Jockey Club Ex p. RAM Racecourses Ltd* [1993] All E.R. 225; and *R. v IRC Ex p. Camcq Corp* [1993] 1 W.L.R. 191.

[40] [1985] A.C. 835. For discussion of the substantive legitimate expectation: G. Ganz, "Legitimate Expectation: A Confusion of Concepts" in C. Harlow (ed.), *Public Law and Politics* (1986), Ch.8; R. Baldwin and D. Home, "Expectations in a Joyless Landscape" (1986) 49 M.L.R. 685; P. Elias, "Legitimate Expectation and Judicial Review" in J. Jowell and D. Oliver (eds), *New Directions in Judicial Review* (1988), pp.37–50; C. Forsyth, "The Provenance and Protection of Legitimate Expectations" [1988] C.L.J. 238; B. Hadfield, "Judicial Review and the Concept of Legitimate Expectation" (1988) 39 N.I.L.Q. 103; P. Craig, "Legitimate Expectations: a Conceptual Analysis" (1992) 108 L.Q.R. 79; P. Craig, "Substantive Legitimate Expectations in Domestic and Community Law" [1996] C.L.J. 289; A. Lester, "Government Compliance with International Human Rights Law: A New Year's Legitimate Expectation" [1996] P.L. 187; R. Singh and K. Steyn, "Legitimate Expectation in 1996: Where Now?" [1996] J.R. 17; C. Himsworth, "Legitimately Expecting Proportionality?" [1996] P.L. 46; Y. Dotan, "Why Administrators should be Bound by Their Policies" (1997) 17 O.J.L.S. 23; S. Schonberg, *Legitimate Expectations in Administrative Law* (2000); P. Craig and S. Schonberg, "Substantive Legitimate Expectations after *Coughlan*" [2000] P.L. 684; R. Clayton, "Legitimate Expectations, Policy, and the Principle of Consistency" [2003] C.L.J. 93; P. Sales and K. Steyn, "Legitimate Expectations in English Public Law: An Analysis" [2004] P.L. 564; I. Steele, "Substantive Legitimate Expectations: Striking the Right Balance?" (2005) 121 L.Q.R. 300; M. Elliott, "Legitimate Expectations and the Search for Principle: Reflections on *Abdi and Nadarajah*" [2006] J.R. 281.

[41] *Preston* [1985] A.C. 835 at 867. See also Lord Scarman at 851–852 and his speech extolling the virtues of consistency in *HTV Ltd v Price Commission* [1976] I.C.R. 170.

[42] *Matrix Securities Ltd v IRC* [1994] 1 W.L.R. 334 (Lord Browne-Wilkinson).

East Sussex CC, Lord Hoffmann said that ". . . in this area, public law has already absorbed whatever is useful from the moral values which underlie the private law concept of estoppel and the time has come for it to stand on its own two feet".[43]

Implied representation

The promise or representation on which the expectation is based may be implied, e.g. from past conduct or a practice which the claimant may reasonably expect will be continued—as in another tax case where the Court of Appeal held that the Revenue could not resile from a long practice of accepting a claim for a tax refund despite the fact that the statutory time limit had expired.[44]   **12–019**

Not all past practice however may justify a legitimate expectation that the practice will continue. For example, a general, though informal, practice of notification of applications for planning permission to neighbours on adjacent sites was held not to create a legitimate expectation of consultation in a case where an individual had not been notified because of the council's oversight.[45] An alien with leave to remain in the United Kingdom for a limited period who, within that period, temporarily left the country in reliance upon first, the leave and a stamp stating that the holder was exempt from having to obtain a visa[46] and secondly, an oral assurance by a Home Office official that she would have "no trouble returning", had a legitimate expectation that she would be allowed to re-enter the United Kingdom.[47] However, another alien who relied on the effect of the stamp alone could not establish a legitimate expectation that he was allowed to re-enter even though the use of the stamp appeared "almost calculated to mislead".[48] However, a legitimate expectation was held to arise from government practice that consideration would be given to diplomatic intervention,[49] and to regular and consistent private use of a stretch of water on the river Thames.[50]   **12–020**

---

[43] [2002] UKHL 8; [2003] 1 W.L.R. 348 at [35], with which Lord Mackay agreed (at [6]); S. Atrill, "The End of Estoppel in Public Law?" [2003] C.L.J. 3.
[44] *R. v Inland Revenue Commisisoners Ex p. Unilever* [1996] S.T.C. 681.
[45] *R. v Secretary of State for the Environment Ex p. Kent* [1988] J.P.L. 706: affirmed [1990] J.P.L. 124, CA (individual affected by planning application who was not notified either of council hearing of application, or of appeal to Secretary of State, could not challenge the decision since jurisdiction was ousted by a six-week limitation clause and there was no legitimate expectation of notification, nor a protectable interest in consultation).
[46] And a stamp imposed pursuant to s.3(3)(b) Immigration Act 1971, stating that the leave granted would apply unless superseded by any subsequent leave obtained by the holder.
[47] *R. v Secretary of State for the Home Department Ex p. Oloniluyi* [1989] Imm. A.R. 135.
[48] *R. v Secretary of State for the Home Department Ex p. Islam* [1990] Imm. A.R. 220; and *R. v Secretary of State for the Home Department Ex p. Patel* (1990) 3 Admin. L.R. 89.
[49] *R. (on the application of Abbasi) v Secretary of State for Foreign and Commonwealth Affairs* [2002] EWCA Civ 1598; [2003] U.K.H.R.R. 76.
[50] *Rowland v Environment Agency* [2002] EWHC 2785; [2003] Ch. 581 (discussed further below, 12–071 *et seq.*

To whom directed—personal or general?

12–021 As the examples above make clear, where the legitimate expectation derives from an express representation, that representation need not be made to the applicant personally or directly; a general policy which affects the applicant as a member of a class is sufficient.[51] Similarly, a regular past practice not previously affecting the applicant and not directed at him personally could provide the basis for a legitimate expectation. It is of course necessary that the applicant is a member of the class of persons who are the subject of the representation while that representation is operative.[52]

12–022 If a representation is made generally, directed to the world at large, this normally means that a public body has adopted a *policy*.[53] However, policies can also be directed at a class, for example, those who chose to read published decisions of the Revenue about extra-statutory concessions.[54]

12–023 When the expectation arises from a policy, its assertion may have different consequences reflecting different (albeit overlapping) values. First, the claimant may require the policy to be *implemented* and not departed from in his particular case. In one of the earliest cases where a substantive legitimate expectation was recognised, the Court of Appeal held that the Home Office could not disappoint an expectation raised by the terms of a Home Office circular, setting out the conditions for the adoption of children from abroad.[55] In such a situation the claim is based less on the

---

[51] See *Attorney General for Hong Kong v Ng Yuen Shiu* [1983] 2 A.C. 629 and *R. v Secretary of State for the Home Department Ex p. Asif Mahmood Khan* [1983] 1 W.L.R. 1337 Of course, an individual personally in receipt of a representation may be in a better position factually to establish a legitimate expectation than a member of a class: this explains the decision in *R. v Secretary of State for the Home Department Ex p. Islam* [1990] Imm. A.R. 220, Div Ct (lack of a personal assurance from the Home Office led to the conclusion that no legitimate expectation could arise, distinguishing *R. v Secretary of State for the Home Department Ex p. Oloniluyi* [1989] Imm. A.R. 135).

[52] *R. v IRC Ex p. Camacq Corp* [1990] 1 W.L.R. 191, CA (where the revenue operates a practice to benefit one class of taxpayer, only someone within that class may have a legitimate expectation that it will continue). See also *R. v Jockey Club Ex p. RAM Racecourses* [1993] 2 All E.R. 225 at 238–39.

[53] On policies, see 5–073 and 9–008 *et seq.* and 12–031.

[54] The Revenue may give advice through official published statements and unofficial private "rulings" and advance clearances. They also have discretion to disapply the law by means of extra-statutory concessions under its powers of "wide managerial discretion". See e.g. *R. v IRC Ex p. National Federation of Self-Employed and Small Businesses Ltd* [1982] A.C. 617; *Vestey v IRC (Nos 1 & 2)* [1980] A.C. 1148; *R. v Inspector of Taxes Ex p. Fulford Dobson* [1987] 1 Q.B. 978 at 988.

[55] *R. v Secretary of State for the Home Department Ex p. Asif Mohammed Khan* [1984] 1 W.L.R. 1337. Parker L.J. considered, following the *Hong Kong* case, that the Secretary of State having induced a reasonable expectation that the circular advice would be followed, could not "resile from that undertaking without affording interested persons a hearing and then only if the overriding public interest demanded it". Dunn L.J. held that, although the circular letter did not create an estoppel, the Home Secretary reached his decision on irrelevant considerations, having failed to take into account his own rules, and had therefore acted unreasonably.

principle of legal certainty than that of *consistency*, which is an element of the rational decision that we have discussed in the previous chapter.[56] This claim is of course subject to the policy fitting the claim—a matter of interpretation, discussed above.[57] The claim will also be subject to the fact that policies may differ in their determinacy. Some are regarded as mere guidance for the exercise of an authority's discretion, while others are intended to apply unless exceptional circumstances indicate otherwise.

In a second case of a legitimate expectation arising from a policy the **12–024** consequences of the claim is more radical: it seeks not only that the policy be implemented, but that the recipient of the expectation should *not be subject to a new policy*. The claimant here asserts that that the expectation carries such weight that it can not be altered or replaced where to do so would unfairly disappoint the expectation that is raised. Such a claim engages the principles of certainty and fairness but also raises a fundamental constitutional question about the freedom of public bodies to alter their policies in the public interest, which will be discussed below.[58]

International treaties

In some cases a legitimate expectation has arisen in relation to an **12–025** international treaty which has not been incorporated in domestic law.[59] In the Australian case of *Minister for Immigration and Ethnic Affairs v Teoh*,[60] the High Court of Australia held in relation to the International Covenant on the Rights of the Child, that:[61]

". . . ratification of a convention is a positive statement by the executive government of this country to the world and to the Australian people that the executive government and its agencies will act in accordance with the Convention. That positive statement is an adequate foundation for a legitimate expectation, absent statutory or executive indications to the contrary, that administrative decision-makers will act in conformity with the Convention".

Recognition that legitimate expectations may arise in this way is not (as **12–026** some critics have suggested) tantamount to incorporating a treaty into domestic law "by the back door"—that is, without parliamentary

---

[56] *R. v Secretary of State for the Home Department Ex p. Gangadeen* [1998] 1 F.L.R. 762; *R v Secretary of State for the Home Department Ex p. Urmaza* [1996] C.O.D. 479; *R. (on the application of Rashid) v Secretary of State for the Home Department* [2005] EWCA Civ 744; [2005] Imm. A.R. 608.

[57] See 5–020–048.

[58] See 12–042 *et seq.*

[59] See also: unincorporated treaties as relevant considerations (See 5–123) and as an aid to statutory interpretation (See 5–043–048).

[60] (1995) 183 C.L.R. 273; M. Taggart, "Legitimate expectation and Treaties in the High Court of Australia" (1996) 112 L.Q.R. 50; R. Piotrowicz, "Unincorporated Treaties in Australian Law" [1996] P.L. 190; E. Handsley, "Legal Fictions and Confusions as Strategies for Protecting Human Rights: A Dissenting View on Teoh's Case" (1997) 2 Newcastle L.J. 56; M. Hunt, *Using Human Rights Law in English Courts* (1997), pp.242–47. See 12–080 *et seq.*

[61] At para.34 (Mason C.J. and Deane J.).

legislation—because there is no suggestion that the courts are enforcing the provisions of a treaty directly or treating them as binding legal rules. If the government makes it clear that the action of ratification is not intended to create a legitimate expectation, then none will be created. *Teoh* has been followed in England and Wales in *R. v Secretary of State for the Home Department Ex p. Ahmed*[62] and in *R. v Uxbridge Magistrates' Court Ex p. Adimi*;[63] in Scotland in *Musaj v Secretary of State for the Home Department*;[64] and in Northern Ireland.[65] The majority and minority judgments in the Privy Council death penalty case *Thomas v Baptiste* accepted that, in principle, a legitimate expectation may arise in relation to a government's acceptance of treaty obligations.[66]

12–027   While in Australia doubt has been cast upon the authority of *Teoh*[67] and the Canadian Supreme Court has held that no legitimate expectation arose from the ratification of the UN Convention on the Rights of the Child,[68] there is now little doubt in the United Kingdom that as a matter of general principle, ratification of a treaty may be regarded as part of the conduct of government. Things said and done by government in relation to the nation's treaty obligations should not—by reason only of the action being on the international plane—be excluded from the wide range of governmental assurances and practices that may from time to time give rise to a legitimate expectation. A court will need to assess the whole context; it is a matter of evidence.[69] In seeking to identify what if any express or implied representations the government may have made in relation to an unincorporated treaty, account may be had of (among other factors) the fact of

---

[62] [1999] Imm. A.R. 22, CA (Lord Woolf describing *Teoh* as "wholly convincing"). On the facts, the UK Government had not created a legitimate expectation because policy statements has been lawfully adopted which made clear how officials should take into account the international convention in question.

[63] [2001] Q.B. 667 at [56] (Simon Brown L.J.), Div Ct. The applicants argued that they were entitled to be protected from prosecution for travelling on false papers by Art.31(1) of the UN Convention relating to the Status of Refugees 1951. *cf. R. (on the application of European Roma Rights Centre) v Immigration Officer, Prague Airport* [2003] EWCA Civ 666; [2004] Q.B. 811 at [101] (Laws L.J., expressing "some unease in relation to [this] particular line of authority").

[64] [2004] ScotCS 119; 2004 S.L.T. 623N at [23] (Court of Session (Outer House), Lady Smith: "the nature of the Dublin Convention is not such that ratification would of itself give rise to any legitimate expectation on the part of the individual applicant for asylum. Nor was there anything about the circumstances of its ratification which did so. It is clear that its purpose was not that of affording benefit to such individuals"). See also *Khairandish v Secretary of State for the Home Department* 2003 S.L.T. 1358.

[65] *In the Matter of Phillips (A Minor)* [2000] NIQB 38 (Carswell L.J., obiter); *Re T* [2000] N.I. 516.

[66] [1999] UKPC 13; [2000] 2 A.C. 1 at [34]–[37] (Lord Browne-Wilkinson, Lord Steyn and Lord Millett; at [58] (Lord Goff of Chieveley and Lord Hobhouse of Woodborough, dissenting on other points: "We accept that treaty obligations assumed by the Executive are capable of giving rise to legitimate expectations which the Executive will not under the municipal law be at liberty to disregard"); *cf. Higgs v Minister of National Security* [2000] A.C. 228.

[67] *R. v Minister for Immigration Ex p. Lam* (2003) 195 A.L.R. 502.

[68] *Baker v Minister of Citizenship and Immigration* [1999] 2 S.C.R. 817.

[69] *Musaj*, n.64 above, [21]–[22].

ratification, things said[70] or done by the government in relation to ratification, the nature of the treaty rights in issue—particularly whether they are of such a nature as to define individual rights[71]—and any steps that the government may have made in giving practical effect to the treaty. If a statutory provision is part of the background to the claim, that must be taken into account as well.[72] Each case must be judged in the round.

There is some uncertainty as to whether the expectation is limited to **12–028** procedural fairness or whether it may extend to substantive benefit. In *Ex p. Ahmed*, the Court of Appeal implied that it extended to substantive benefit,[73] something accepted in *Musaj*,[74] but in *Thomas v Baptiste* the Privy Council appears to take the view that only procedural protection is available.[75]

LEGITIMACY

To qualify as "legitimate" the expectation must possess the following **12–029** qualities.

---

[70] *R. v Secretary of State for the Home Department Ex p. Behluli* [1998] Imm. A.R. 407 CA (Beldam L.J.: "The extent to which statements can found such an expectation must depend upon the circumstances in which they are made, whether reasonably construed they can be taken as propounding a policy or are merely statements applicable to particular cases or classes of case").

[71] See e.g. *R. v Secretary of State for the Home Department Ex p. Senkoy* [2001] EWCA Civ 328; [2001] Imm. A.R. 399.

[72] *Behluli* [1998] Imm. A.R. 407.

[73] [1999] Imm. A.R. 22. (Lord Woolf M.R.: "This legitimate expectation could give rise to a right to relief, as well as additional obligations of fairness, if the Secretary of State, without reason, acted inconsistently with the obligations which this country had undertaken").

[74] *Musaj* n.64 above, [21] ("it is simply a matter of assessing whether, in the whole circumstances, the act of ratification gives rise to an inference that the government thereafter intends to afford to individuals, the benefit of its terms").

[75] [2000] 2 A.C. 1 at [37] ("Even if a legitimate expectation founded on the provisions of an unincorporated treaty may give procedural protection, it cannot by itself, that is to say unsupported by other constitutional safeguards, give substantive protection, for this would be tantamount to the indirect enforcement of the treaty").

Clear unambiguous and devoid of relevant qualification

12–030   The representation must be "clear unambiguous and devoid of relevant qualification".[76] Whether or not the representation fulfils these qualities is a matter of construction as to which the intention of the promissor and the understanding of the promisee may be relevant but not determinative.[77] The context of the representation is therefore important. As was said in *Zeqiri*,[78] "while it might be appropriate in the case of dealings between the Revenue and sophisticated tax advisers to insist upon a high degree of clarity in the alleged representation, this need not necessarily be required in other cases".[79] The Secretary of State had not acted in breach of a legitimate expectation in deciding to abolish a discretionary *ex gratia* scheme under which compensation was paid to those who had suffered a miscarriage of justice. There was nothing that amounted to a representation or promise that the scheme would continue indefinitely.[80]

12–031   The expected benefit or advantage must be more than a "mere hope".[81] For example, a departmental circular letter setting out the criteria for the adoption of children from abroad may induce a legitimate expectation that its details will be followed.[82] But other circulars, as we have just noted, may be more in the nature of advisory documents, purporting to interpret the law[83] or the likely implementation of government policy and therefore not intended or understood as inducing binding expectations (for example, Planning Policy Guidance notes issued by the Department for Communities and Local Government on diverse matters, including policy in relation to affordable housing, or to permissible conditions attached to planning permissions). Answers or representations made in Parliament, however,

---

[76] *Ex p. MFK Underwriters* [1990] 1 W.L.R. 1545 1570 (Bingham L.J.); and *R. v Shropshire County Council Ex p. Jones* (1997) 9 Admin. L.R. 625 (applicant for student grant given to understand he has a very good chance of securing an award does not acquire a legitimate expectation); *R. v IRC Ex p. Unilever Plc* [1996] S.T.C. 681, CA; *R. v Gaming Board of Great Britain Ex p. Kingsley (No.2)*[1996] C.O.D. 241.

[77] *R. v Ministry of Agriculture Fisheries and Food Ex p. Hambles Fisheries (Offshore) Ltd* [1995] 2 All E.R. 714 (Sedley J.); *R. v Secretary of State for the Home Department Ex p. Ahmed* [1999] Imm. A.R. 22 at 40 (Hobhouse L.J.: the principle of legitimate expectation was a "wholly objective concept and not based on any actual state of knowledge of individual immigrants").

[78] *R. v Secretary of State for the Home Department Ex p. Zeqiri* [2002] UKHL 3; [2002] Imm. A.R. 296.

[79] Lord Hoffmann at [44].

[80] *R. (on the application of Noorullah Niazii) v Secretary of State for the Home Department* [2007] EWHC 1495 (Admin).

[81] See Sedley L.J. in *Begbie*.

[82] *R. v Secretary of State for the Home Department Ex p. Asif Mohammed Khan* [1984] 1 W.L.R. 1337; and *R. v Secretary of State for Defence Ex p. Camden LBC* [1995] J.P.L. 403.

[83] *R. (on the application of Beale) v Camden LBC* [2004] EWHC 6; [2004] H.L.R. 48 at [22] (Munby J.: "Statements by ministers as to what the law are no more determinative of the citizen's rights than similar statements by anyone else . . . if correct it adds nothing: if it is incorrect, it is for present purposes irrelevant").

have been held not to give rise to legitimate expectations.[84] Nor have after-dinner speeches given by government Ministers.[85] Nevertheless, it is often difficult to determine the precise source of a policy. They emerge from ministerial statements, White Papers, appeal decisions, and draft circulars or codes. A genuinely consultative document cannot be regarded as a policy from which any obligations flow.[86]

Induced by the conduct of the decision-maker

A legitimate expectation must be induced by the conduct of the decision-maker. The representation by a different person or authority will therefore not found the expectation. Thus representations by the police will not create a legitimate expectation about the actions of the prison service.[87]   **12-032**

It is important to note that we are not here dealing with an expectation of fairness in general, or to the reasonable exercise of the decision-maker's discretion.[88] The legitimate expectation does not flow from any generalised anticipation of being treated justly, based upon the scale or context of the decision.[89] In the context of the legitimate expectation which induces a procedural right, this distinction marks the difference between an   **12-033**

---

[84] R. v Secretary of State for the Home Department Ex p. Sakala [1994] Imm. A.R. 227; R. v DPP Ex p. Kebilene [2000] 2 A.C. 326 at 329 (Lord Bingham was "hesitant to hold that a legitimate expectation could be founded on answers given in Parliament to often very general questions; to do so is to invest assertions by the executive with a quasi-legislative authority, which could involve an undesirable blurring of the distinct functions of the legislature and the executive").

[85] Dinsdale Developers Ltd v Secretary of State for the Environment [1986] J.P.L. 276.

[86] Pye (JA) (Oxford) Estates Ltd v Secretary of State for the Environment and West Oxford DC [1982] J.P.L. 577; cf. Richmond upon Thames LBC v Secretary of State for the Environment [1984] J.P.L. 24 and Westminster City Council v Secretary of State for the Environment [1984] J.P.L. 27 (account may be taken of advice to Secretary of State, although not yet formally policy).

[87] R. (on the application of Bloggs 61) v Secretary of State for the Home Department [2003] EWCA Civ 686; [2003] 1 W.L.R. 2724; R. v Secretary of State for the Home Department Ex p. Mapere [2001] Imm .A.R. 89 at [36] ("wrong in principle for courts to rule that a decision-maker's discretion should be limited by an assurance given by another person").

[88] R. (on the application of Rashid) v Secretary of State for the Home Department [2005] EWCA Civ 744; [2005] Imm. A.R. 608 it was suggested that the expectation was that public officials will implement their own policies on asylum—see 13–00 and the criticism of I. Steele, "Substantive Legitimate Expectations: Striking the Right Balance?" (2005) 121 L.Q.R. 300, who regards such an approach as "denuding the concept of any utility".

[89] As was insisted by Lords Diplock and Fraser in the GCHQ case [1985] A.C. 374 thus indorsing the PC decision in Shiu [1983] 2 A.C. 629 and impliedly rejecting, insofar as it conflicted, the approach of earlier cases such as Schmidt, Breen, and McInnes [1978] 1 W.L.R. 1520 Ganz [1965] P.L. 321 criticises the "confusion" which GCHQ imports into the law, but it is contended that GCHQ in fact resolves the confusion which previously existed. For criticism of the analysis of the legitimate expectation as resting on the conduct of the decision-maker, see the Australian cases of Kioa v Minister for Immigration and Ethnic Affairs (1986) 62 A.L.R. 321 at 370–375 (Brennan J., arguing that since the principles of judicial review have their basis in the presumed intentions of Parliament, therefore "legitimate expectation" could not be based on expectations engendered by decision-makers, which would be irrelevant to the construction of the statutory framework); cf. Salemi v Mackellar (No. 2) (1977) 137 C.L.R. 396, 404 (Barwick CJ.). But for criticism of this view see Elias n.40 above.

entitlement to a hearing based upon the legitimate expectation and that based upon other interests.[90] It is therefore misleading to classify under the head of legitimate expectation interests which may require procedural protection irrespective of the conduct of the decision-maker.[91] For example, while the Court of Appeal in *R. v Liverpool Corporation Ex p. Liverpool Taxi Fleet Operators' Association*[92] rightly held that the express assurance of consultation by the Corporation created a legitimate expectation, the *obiter* view of Lord Denning M.R. that even in the absence of an assurance the applicants' interest in maintaining the value of their licences would have entitled them to a hearing before the number of licences was increased, identifies a protectable interest quite separate from that derived from the legitimate expectation.[93] It has also been held that objectors to an application for planning permission had no legitimate expectation of being able to make representations because no conduct of the planning authority had induced such an expectation. Nevertheless, the objectors were entitled to be heard in order to defend their interests[94] as the proposed action would affect them adversely.[95] Further, in *R. v Secretary of State for Health Ex p. US Tobacco International Inc,*[96] while it was held that the applicants could have no (substantive) legitimate expectation that the Minister would not change his policy regarding the production and sale of oral snuff, it was held that the Minister was in breach of his (statutory) duty to consult

---

[90] e.g. the view of Lord Bridge in *Re Westminster CC* [1986] A.C. 668. Rejecting an argument that "the scale of [the] decisions [in respect of which natural justice was sought] and the context in which they were taken were such that the [affected] bodies would clearly have a legitimate expectation to be consulted", he warned that "if the courts were to extend the doctrine of legitimate expectation [beyond the foundation of "either a promise or a practice of consultation"] to embrace expectations arising from the "scale" or "context" of particular decisions, the duty of consultation would be entirely open-ended and no public authority could tell with any confidence in what circumstances a duty of consultation was cast upon them [and] the suggested development of the law would, in my opinion, be wholly lamentable". Lord Bridge clearly sought to limit the doctrine to situations arising out of representations of the decision-maker and argues against its expansion to take in a class of interests (of a certain "scale" or "context") independent of this basis. See also the clear distinction between legitimate expectations and protectable interests made by Taylor J. in *R. v Secretary of State for the Environment Ex p. GLC* [1985] J.PL. 543 (Secretary of State's exercise of discretion to delay consideration of the GLC's proposed amendments to the Greater London Development Plan not vitiated by lack of natural justice: not requirement to consult either on basis of a legitimate expectation, or under the audi alterem partem rule or because of a duty to act fairly, considering *Durayappah v Fernando* [1967] 2 A.C. 337).

[91] A view taken by commentators such as Ganz; but see Elias n.40 above.

[92] [1972] 2 Q.B. 299.

[93] Of course, it is possible that a requirement of procedural fairness may flow from both causes, e.g. the revocation of a licence without a hearing may well infringe the interest protectable in itself and disappoint a legitimate expectation derived from the past conduct of the body which granted the licence.

[94] *R. v Great Yarmouth BC Ex p. Botton Brothers Arcades Ltd* [1988] J.P.L. 18.

[95] It was held that the circumstances of this case were however unique because the council had reversed its previously declared policy as to the amusement arcades in coming to the decision complained of. There was at that time no general duty on councils to consult or notify those affected by a grant of planning permission; see also *R. v Secretary of State for the Environment Ex p. Kent* [1968] J.P.L. 706; [1990] J.P.L. 124.

[96] [1992] 1 All E.R. 212.

by refusing to reveal the contents of an independent report. The "high degree of fairness and candour" to the applicants was based upon the "catastrophic" effect of the ban on the applicants' financial interests.

Made by a person with actual or ostensible authority

The representation must be made by a person with actual or ostensible **12–034** authority to make the representation.[97] The authority will not be bound if the promisee knew, or ought to have known, that the person making the representation had no power to bind the authority.[98] A manifesto commitment made by a political party or a pre-election promise by a politician seeking election, would therefore not qualify as an enforceable representation, as that party or person had no right at that point to speak on behalf of the government of which it or he was not yet part.[99] When a Minister piloting a bill through Parliament makes a statement about its intended implementation, that statement, as we have seen, may be relevant to the subsequent interpretation of the statute's purpose.[100] Being relevant to the manner in which the way discretion under the statute will be exercised, the statement could be said to give rise to a legitimate expectation, but such an expectation should always be subject to the overall statutory scheme and purpose. In *Sakala*[101]the claimant contended that the Home Secretary should be bound by a statement made in Parliament during the passage of the Immigration Bill 1988— that he would, in a decision about political asylum, "invariably accept the recommendations of a special adjudicator", unless the decision was perverse or unlawful. It was held that he was not so bound.

One of the class to whom it may reasonably be expected to apply

A person who seeks to rely upon a representation must be one of the class **12–035** to whom it may reasonably be expected to apply. Thus a report from the Jockey Club announcing the intended availability of new licensed racecourses, which was sent to existing racecourse owners, was held not to apply to prospective new racecourse owners who spent money on a new site in reliance upon the report.[102]

---

[97] *South Buckinghamshire DC v Flanagan* [2002] EWCA Civ 690; [2002] 1 W.L.R. 2601 (Keene L.J.).

[98] See e.g. *Ex p. Matrix Securities* (1994) 1 W.L.R. 334 where the assurance was given by a local inspector of taxes, but should have been given by the Financial Division of the Revenue. But see 11–00 on unlawful or unauthorised representations.

[99] *R. v Secretary of State for Education and Employment Ex p. Begbie* [2000] 1 W.L.R. 1115. On the question of the mandate, see 11–017.

[100] In the case of an ambiguity under *Pepper v Hart* [1993] A.C. 593; see 5–026–31.

[101] *R. v Secretary of State for the Home Department Ex p. Sakala* [1994] Imm. A.R. 227.

[102] *R. v Jockey Club Ex p. RAM Racecourses Ltd* [1993] 2 All E.R. 225; and *R. v IRC Ex p. Camacq Corp* [1990] 1 W.L.R. 191 (applicant not within the class of intended beneficiaries of tax clearance).

Full disclosure

12–036 The representation must be preceded by full disclosure. Thus where a person is seeking advance clearance for a scheme from the tax authorities he must be frank about what is being sought and put "all his cards face up on the table", giving full details of the specific transaction on which a ruling is required, the ruling that is sought, and the use intended to be made of it.[103]

Is knowledge of the representation necessary?

12–037 Is knowledge of the representation necessary to found a legitimate expectation? How can an expectation be claimed when the claimant has been unaware of the representation upon which it is supposedly based? Yet should a person in the class to which the representation is directed be deprived of the benefits of that representation simply because they were ignorant of it?

12–038 As Lord Hoffmann has said, "Kosavar refugees cannot be expected to check the small print".[104] There is surely merit in encouraging good administration which requires decision-makers to bear the normal consequences of their representations. But is this rationale based less upon the existence of a legitimate expectation than upon a general expectation of fairness, good governance, or consistency in public administration? In *Rashid* the claimant asylum seeker was denied asylum in the United Kingdom contrary to a settled policy.[105] The claimant was ignorant of the policy. Yet it was held that the Secretary of State had breached the claimant's legitimate expectation "that the Secretary of State will apply his policy on asylum to the claim".[106] Knowledge on the part of the claimant of the policy was held not to be "relevant" or "material" to that expectation.[107]

12–039 Clearly there should be an expectation that public officials will implement their own policies, but the use of the term "expectation" in that context may not add anything to these general public law duties and indeed may dilute their essence. In any event, as has been discussed in Chapter 11, there is an independent duty of consistent application of policies,[108] which is based on the principle of equal implementation of laws, non-discrimination and the lack of arbitrariness. Although in some

---

[103] *MFK Underwriters* [1990] 1 W.L.R. 1545 1569–1570 (Bingham L.J.). Lack of full disclosure also vitiated the expectation in *Matrix Securities* [1994] 1 W.L.R. 334.
[104] *R. v Secretary of State for the Home Department Ex p. Zeqiri* [2002] UKHL 3; [2002] Imm. A.R. 296 at [44].
[105] *R. (on the application of Rashid) v Secretary of State for the Home Department* [2005] EWCA Civ 744; [2005] Imm. A.R. 608.
[106] Pill L.J. at [25].
[107] Pill L.J. at [25]; and see Dyson L.J. at [47].
[108] See R. Clayton, "Legitimate Expectations, Policy and the Principle of Consistency" [2003] C.L.J. 93.

cases lack of knowledge of an assurance or practice has defeated a legitimate expectation,[109] it is surely right that reliance should not be a "necessary precondition" of a legitimate expectation "where statements are made to the public at large".[110]

Detrimental reliance not essential

Despite dicta to the contrary,[111] it is not normally necessary for a person to have changed his position or to have acted to his detriment in order to qualify as the holder of a legitimate expectation.[112] In a number of leading cases it has been held that a legitimate expectation should have been fulfilled in a situation where detrimental reliance had not taken place or was not appropriate or required in the circumstances.[113] For example, the applicant may legitimately seek the promised benefits of a tax scheme without having expended funds on promoting the scheme,[114] and individuals might legitimately seek the enforcement of a policy about the tapping of telephones[115] or the criteria for the adoption of children from abroad,[116] without incurring expenditure or otherwise acting to their detriment. Private law analogies from the field of estoppel are, we have seen, of limited relevance where a public law principle requires public officials to honour their undertakings and respect legal certainty, irrespective of whether the loss has been incurred by the individual concerned.[117] In addition, as pointed out by Schiemann L.J., "to disregard the legitimate expectation because no concrete detriment can be shown would be to place the weakest in society at a particular disadvantage. It would mean that

12–040

---

[109] See e.g. *R. v Secretary of State for the Home Department Ex p. Hindley* [2001] 1 A.C. 410 (Myra Hindley's lack of knowledge of a 30-year tariff which was not communicated to her defeated a legitimate expectation); *R. v Minister of Defence Ex p. Walker* [2000] 1 W.L.R. 806.

[110] *R. v Department for Education and Employment Ex p. Begbie* [2000] 1 W.L.R. 1115 at 1133 (Sedley L.J.).

[111] *Rootkin v Kent CC* [1981] W.L.R. 1186; *R. v Jockey Club Ex p. RAM Racecourses Ltd* [1993] 1 All E.R. 225; *R. v IRC Ex p. Camacq Corp* [1990] 1 W.L.R. 191.

[112] This statement does not apply to the legitimate expectation in European Community law: see *Milk Marketing Board of England and Wales v Tom Parker Farms Ltd* [1998] 2 C.M.L.R. 721.

[113] *R. v Ministry for Agriculture, Fisheries and Foods Ex p. Hambles Fisheries (Offshore) Ltd* [1995] 2 All E.R. 714 at 725 (Sedley J.: "the decision-maker's knowledge or ignorance of the extent of reliance placed by the applicant upon the factors upon which the expectation is founded has no bearing upon the existence or legitimacy of the expectation"); and *R. (on the application of Bibi) v Newham LBC (No.1)* [2001] EWCA Civ 607; [2002] 1 W.L.R. 237 at [31] (Schiemann L.J.).

[114] *MFK Underwriters* [1990] 1 W.L.R. 1545 at 1569–1570 (Bingham L.J. did not require detrimental reliance but said that "if a public authority so conducts itself so as to create a legitimate expectation that a certain course will be followed it would often be unfair if the authority were permitted to follow a different course to the detriment of one who entertained the expectation *particularly if he relied on it*").

[115] *R. v Secretary of State for the Home Department Ex p. Ruddock* [1989] 1 W.L.R. 1982

[116] *Ex p. Asif Khan* n.9 above.

[117] S. Atrill, "The End of Estoppel in Public Law?" [2003] C.L.J. 3.

those who have a choice and the means to exercise it in reliance on some official practice or promise would gain a legal toehold inaccessible to those who, lacking any means of escape, are compelled simply to place their trust in what has been represented to them".[118]

12–041   Although detrimental reliance should not therefore be a condition precedent to the protection of a substantive legitimate expectation, it may be relevant in two situations: first, it might provide *evidence* of the existence or extent of an expectation. In that sense it can be a consideration to be taken into account in deciding whether a person was in fact led to believe that the authority would be bound by the representations. Secondly, detrimental reliance may affect the *weight of the expectation* and the issue of the fairness of disappointing the expectation.[119] This is particularly relevant to the decision of the authority whether to disappoint a legitimate expectation—an issue which we now consider.

WHEN IS THE DISAPPOINTMENT OF A SUBSTANTIVE LEGITIMATE EXPECTATION UNLAWFUL?

12–042   Given the duty of a public body not to fetter its discretion,[120] and to act in the public interest, under what circumstances will the courts require a body not to deviate from a representation or policy? Clearly the deviation must involve a lawful exercise of discretion,[121] taking into account relevant considerations, ignoring the irrelevant and pursuing authorised and not extraneous purposes.[122] These considerations and purposes can include matters such as the need to maintain national security[123] and matters of public policy.[124] However, although it may be free to depart from its representation or policy, the authority is by no means free to ignore the existence of a legitimate expectation. Now that the legitimate expectation has been accepted in law as an interest worthy of protection, its existence itself becomes a relevant consideration which must be taken into account in

[118] *R. v Newham LBC Ex p. Bibi* [2001] EWCA Civ 607; [2002] 1 W.L.R. 237 at [31].
[119] See 12–058.
[120] See Ch.9.
[121] Scarman L.J. in *Re Findlay* [1985] A.C. 318; *R. v Criminal Injuries Compensation Board Ex p. M (A Minor)* [1988] P.I.Q.R. P107; [1998] C.O.D. 128, affirmed by CA [2000] R.T.R. 21; [1999] P.I.Q.R. Q195 (suggestions that the prerogative power cannot be extended by the representation of an authority in ways which might create a legitimate expectation). On prerogative powers, see 3–032. We doubt whether, these days, the prerogative should be treated any differently in this respect from any other power.
[122] The conduct of the person to whom the representation was made should not be regarded as a relevant consideration to disappointing the expectation, as it was held to be in *Cinnamond v British Airport Authority* [1980] 1 W.L.R. 582 (Lord Denning M.R.). However, appropriate conduct could be implied as a condition of the fulfilment of the expectation. The conduct could of course be taken into account in the decision of the court as to whether, in its discretion, to award the applicant a remedy.
[123] As in *GCHQ* [1985] A.C. 374.
[124] As in *US Tobacco International Inc* [1992] 1 All E.R. 212 where the expectation was disappointed in the interest of protecting public health.

the exercise of discretion. It is placed upon the scale and must therefore be properly weighed.

In this exercise, on the one side of the scale is the unfairness to an **12–043** individual of the disappointment of the expectation induced by the decision-maker. Other things being equal, fairness dictates that a public authority ought to abide by the important principle of legal certainty which is, as we have seen, a cornerstone of the rule of law. On the other side of the scale, however, is the duty of the authority to pursue the public interest which is never static and may conflict with the interest of the recipient of the legitimate expectation. In the days when judicial review was driven by the need to fulfil the public interest, rather than to respect private rights and interests, the courts would have been inclined to permit the authority wide freedom to override an individual's expectation in favour of its public duty. These days, however, as we have seen, public power must be exercised with due respect for those for whose benefit the power exists. Therefore there is still a balancing exercise to be performed, both by the authority and then by the courts, who have to decide what discretionary leeway to permit the authority on the matter.

A number of cases have emphasised that, by declaring a policy, a **12–044** decision maker "cannot preclude any possible need to change it".[125] In one such case two life-sentence prisoners claimed that they should have been released under the terms of a policy in relation to parole announced by the Home Secretary but which had since been suddenly changed. Lord Scarman, with whom the other members of the House of Lords agreed, said that:

"Given the substance and purpose of the legislative provisions governing parole, the most that a convicted prisoner can legitimately expect is that his case will be examined individually in the light of whatever policy the Secretary of State sees fit to adopt provided always that the adopted policy is a lawful exercise of discretion conferred upon him by statute. Any other view would entail the conclusions that the unfettered discretion conferred by the statute on the minister can in some cases be restricted so as to hamper, or even prevent, changes of policy."[126]

A similar view was expressed in a case where the applicants had been **12–045** encouraged through a government grant to manufacture their product, "oral snuff", in the United Kingdom. Shortly after their factory opened the Minister was advised to ban the product on the ground of its danger to health. The applicants claimed that the decision infringed their legitimate

---

[125] Ex p. *Ruddock* [1987] 1 W.L.R. 1982 at 1497 (Taylor L.J.). Although a hearing may have to be provided before changing it.

[126] *Re Findlay* [1985] A.C. 318 at 338; and *Hughes v Department of Health and Social Security* [1985] A.C. 776 at 788 (Lord Diplock: "The liberty to make such change [of administrative policy] is something which is inherent in our form of constitutional government", in relation to compulsory retirement of civil servants at 65 changed to 60).

expectation to continue to manufacture their product. It was held, however, that the Minister's" moral obligations" to the applicants could not fetter his discretion and could not therefore "prevail over the public interest".[127]

12–046   However, in *Pierson*, Lord Steyn made it clear that a decision of the Home Secretary to raise the minimum "tariff" period after which a life prisoner could expect parole offended the rule of law because it breached the prisoners' substantive legitimate expectation[128] and, as we have seen, the unfairness of disappointing a legitimate expectation has succeeded in a number of other cases in recent years.[129] In *Coughlin*, the Court of Appeal held that the authority was not free to disappoint its promise of a "home for life" to the appellant, who was seriously ill and disabled, in a residential care home providing specialist care.[130]

THE STANDARD OF JUDICIAL REVIEW

12–047 We now come to one of the liveliest questions about the legitimate expectation—the standard by which the courts, on judicial review, should scrutinise the authority's decision to disappoint a legitimate expectation. Ought it to be on a mere *Wednesbury* basis,[131] or a more intrusive standard? Two contrasting views on this matter were put forward in the High Court in the 1990s. Laws J. proposed that the courts should only second-guess the authority's view of the overriding public interest under the *Wednesbury* standard of review.[132] Sedley J., in line with his interpretation of the approach to the issue under European Community law, preferred the standard of full review, under which it is for the courts to judge the fairness of the disappointment of the legitimate expectation.[133] Sedley J.'s view was then held to be a "heresy"[134] and "wrong in principle"[135] by the Court of Appeal. A few years later, however, in *Coughlan*, the Court of Appeal was asked to decide whether the authority could disappoint its promise to the appellant (who was seriously ill and disabled) of a "home for life" in a residential care home providing specialist care.[136] Lord Woolf, for the Court (which included Sedley L.J.), posed three ways in which the matter could be decided:[137]

---

[127] *US Tobacco International Inc.* [1992] 1 All E.R. 212 368 (Taylor L.J.); and 372 (Moreland J.). The legitimate expectation did, however, found a right on the part of the applicants to a fair hearing.
[128] *R. v Secretary of State for the Home Department Ex p. Pierson* [1998] A.C. 539.
[129] See Ch.12.
[130] *R. v North and East Devon HA Ex p. Coughlan* [2001] Q.B. 213.
[131] See Ch.11.
[132] *R. v Secretary of State for Transport Ex p. Richmond-upon-Thames LBC* [1994] 1 W.L.R. 74.
[133] *R. v Minister of Agriculture, Fisheries and Food Ex p. Hamble (Offshore) Fisheries Ltd* [1995] 2 All E.R. 714 at 731–35.
[134] *R. v Secretary of State for the Home Department Ex p. Hargreaves* [1997] 1 W.L.R. 906 at 921, with whom Peter Gibson L.J. agreed.
[135] [1997] 1 W.L.R. 906 at 924 (Pill L.J.).
[136] *R. v North and East Devon Health Authority Ex p. Coughlan* [2001] Q.B. 213.
[137] [2001] Q.B. 213 at [57].

"(a) the court may decide that the public authority is only required to bear in mind its previous policy or other representation, giving it the weight it thinks right, but no more, before deciding whether to change course. Here the court is confined to reviewing the decision on *Wednesbury* grounds. . .

(b) . . . the court may decide that the promise or practice induces a legitimate expectation of . . . being consulted before a particular decision is taken. Here, it is uncontentious that the court will require the *opportunity for consultation* to be given unless there is an overriding reason to resile from it, in which case the court itself will judge the adequacy of the reason advanced for the change in policy, taking into account what fairness requires.

(c) Where the court considers that a lawful promise or practice has induced a legitimate expectation of a *benefit which is substantive*, not simply procedural, authority now establishes that here too the court will in a proper case decide whether to frustrate the expectation is so unfair that to take a new and different course will amount to an abuse of power. Here, once the legitimacy of the expectation is established, the court will have the task of weighing the requirements of fairness against any overriding interest relied upon for the change in policy".

It was held that, in the circumstances of that case, the question whether the disappointment of the expectation was unfair or an abuse of power should be decided under the third of the above approaches. As would be the case in the second approach, where purely procedural matters were in issue, the court would weigh the various issues relevant to the question as to whether the expectation was unfairly disappointed and whether the authority's power was abused. In other words, the courts would decide the "correctness" of the matter themselves. **12–048**

Coughlan, however, by no means requires that the deference associated with the *Wednesbury* standard is to be abandoned in all cases involving the disappointment of a legitimate expectation in the future. In particular, as the Court was careful to point out, this is a developing area of law, and the representation in that case had "the character of a contract" (in the sense that it was expressly made to a small group of people on more than one occasion in unambiguous terms). In addition, this case was driven by (i) the importance of the promise (the fact that the appellant's human right to respect for her home were in issue—as we have seen, the *Wednesbury* approach is softened where human rights are engaged), (ii) the fact that the promise was limited to a few individuals, and not to the world at large, and (iii) the fact that the consequences to the authority of requiring it to honour its promise were likely to be financial only (and not of very great financial consequence at that). **12–049**

12–050   Subsequent cases have emphasised both that the three approaches set out in *Coughlan* are not "hermetically sealed",[138] and that the judicial reserve associated with the *Wednesbury* test has by no means been abandoned in all cases involving a legitimate expectation. In *Begbie*, even Sedley L.J., who was a member of the unanimous Court of Appeal in *Coughlan*, felt that the distinctions between the first and third approaches in *Coughlan* "deserves further examination" and that a policy "must not be treated by its custodians as a set of rules".[139] In *Mullen*,[140] the House of Lords considered whether the Home Secretary needed to apply his policy to provide compensation to persons wrongfully convicted. The claimant was given a fair opportunity to make representations on the matter but was refused compensation on the ground that he had been involved in terrorist activity. The House applied a test of rationality in upholding the Home Secretary's decision.[141]

12–051   It seems therefore as if there will now be a "sliding scale of review, more or less intrusive according to the nature and gravity of what is at stake".[142] Such an approach would be in accord with the tendency of the courts to provide stricter scrutiny to decisions engaging human rights[143] (as in Coughlan, which involved the right to a home). In *Begbie* the newly-elected Labour government had passed legislation which was at variance with various undertakings (issued both before and after the election of 1997) to honour a commitment to provide assisted places at certain schools to pupils who had already been offered them.[144] In that case the expectation yielded to the contrary terms of an amending statute. However, it was also made clear that the *Coughlan* approach, under which the court is the judge of whether the overriding public interest justifies disappointing a legitimate expectation, was not necessarily appropriate in cases involving "wide-ranging issues of social policy".[145] In such cases the courts should respect the fact that the decision maker is obliged to take into account a number of different interests in addition to those of the disappointed claimant, including, as Laws L.J. put it "interests not represented before the court".[146]

12–052   In *Begbie*, Laws L.J. considered that the test of "abuse of power" was not sufficiently precise to act as a standard of review to guide the issue of whether a legitimate expectation ought to be protected. Instead he offered

---

[138] *R. v Secretary of State for Education and Employment Ex p. Begbie* [2001] 1 W.L.R. 1115 (Laws J.).
[139] *Begbie* [2001] 1 W.L.R. 1115.
[140] *R. (on the application of Mullen) v Secretary of State for the Home Department* [2004] UKHL 18; [2005] 1 A.C. 1.
[141] *Mullen* [2004] UKHL 18, [2005] 1 A.C. 1 [58]–[62] (Lord Steyn).
[142] *Begbie* [2001] 1 W.L.R. 1115 (Laws L.J.).
[143] See Ch.11; Ch.5.
[144] See Ch.11; Ch.5.
[145] *Begbie* [2001] 1 W.L.R. 1115 For a further discussion of the kinds of powers which are more or less amenable to judicial review, or to more or less intrusive review.
[146] *Begbie* [2001] 1 W.L.R. 1115.

the test of proportionality.[147] In some ways the approach of proportionality is apposite as a standard in these cases. This is because the disappointment of the legitimate expectation requires positive justification. As we saw in the last chapter, the standard of structured proportionality differs from that of domestic rationality in that it places the burden on the authority to justify its decision, which involves a departure from a fundamental norm.[148] The breach of legal certainty as an integral requirement of the rule of law similarly requires such justification. Proportionality is not however a complete answer to the difficult balancing issues involved in these questions.[149] For a start, as we have just noted, and as Laws L.J. asserted in *Begbie*, in decisions involving what he called "macro-political" issues of policy,[150] the rationality test was considered more appropriate. In other cases, the courts have simply required the authority to take the legitimate expectation into account as a relevant consideration.[151] Finally, in some instances the courts have only permitted the substantive expectation to ground a fair hearing, rather than the benefit itself.[152]

On the whole, however, where a legitimate expectation has been **12-053** disappointed the onus should be on the authority to justify its frustration. No magic formula can reach the right answer as to whether the expectation should be honoured, but in considering whether the disappointment of an expectation is deserving of protection, the following factors may be relevant:

The subject matter of the representation

The distinction between a mere "hope" and an expectation has already **12-054** been made. However, some expectations are more secure than others. Most secure will be those where the claimant already possesses a benefit or advantage, such as a home,[153] or a tax advantage,[154] which the alteration of policy is seeking to take away. In these "forfeiture", or "deprivation" cases the authority will be seeking to deprive the claimant of a right or interest which is already vested and therefore may be more deserving of protection[155] than a promise of some benefit in the future (such as an assisted

---

[147] *Begbie* [2001] 1 W.L.R. 1115 [68], requiring any disappointed expectation to be "objectively justified as a proportionate response in the circumstances".
[148] See Ch.11.
[149] M. Elliott, "Legitimate Expectations and the Search for Principle: reflections on *Abdi and Nadarajah*" [2006] J.R. 281.
[150] *Begbie* [2001] 1 W.L.R. 1115 at [69].
[151] See e.g. *R. (on the application of Ibrahim) v Redbridge LBC* [2002] EWHC 2756; [2003] A.C.D. 25 at [12] (proper account had been taken of the expectation of permanent accommodation and therefore it was for the authority to "balance the legitimate aspirations of those on the housing waiting list and the legitimate expectations of the Claimant and others in like position"). See D. Pievsky, "Legitimate Expectations as a Relevancy" [2003] J.R.147.
[152] As in *US Tobacco* [1992] 1 All E.R. 212.
[153] *Coughlan* [2001] Q.B. 213.
[154] *Unilever* [1996] S.T.C. 681.
[155] cf. *McInnes R. v TRC Exp.*

633

place at a school[156]). In addition, more weight might be placed on expectations of a fundamental human right, such as, in *Coughlan*, the right to a home or, as in cases involving deportation, the right to life. On the other hand, as Lord Hoffmann pointed out in *Reprotech*, some rights are entitled to greater protection than others.[157] He contrasted the right to a home (as engaged in *Coughlan*), with property rights which "are in general far more limited by considerations of public interest".

Particular or general

12–055 It is more likely that the legitimate expectation should be respected where it arises from a representation to an individual or a class rather than the world at large. The numbers in the class may not be relevant. In one case the Hong Kong Court of Final Appeal protected a legitimate expectation made by over 1,000 claimants who had been led to believe that they could postpone their own claims in deference to a particular test case.[158] However, as was shown in *Coughlan*, representations which have "the character of a contract" (and therefore not likely to affect a broader section of the public) are specially deserving of protection. This is because the impact of the case in such cases is likely to be "discrete and limited".[159]

Degree of reassurance

12–056 Another factor which affects the strength or weight of the expectation is the extent to which the promisee has been reassured by the promissor that the expectation will not be dashed. Clearly a representation which is implied (e.g. from repeated past conduct) is unlikely to carry as much weight as an express oral or written representation. Few cases of implied representations founding legitimate expectations exist.[160] In some cases it has been suggested that the weight of a representation is diminished where the claimant had the opportunity to seek reassurance about the expectation (e.g. where he was legally represented), but failed to do so.[161]

Nature of the decision

12–057 A body should be less willing to yield to a legitimate expectation where it is duty bound to make policies which lie in what has been described as "the macro-political field".[162] In these cases the authority might rightly give

---

[156] *Begbie* [2001] 1 W.L.R. 1115.
[157] *R. (on the application of Reprotech (Pebsham) Ltd v East Sussex CC* [2002] UKHL 8; [2003] 1 W.L.R. 348 at [34].
[158] *Ng Siu Tong v Director of Immigration* [2002] 1 HKLRD 561.
[159] *Begbie* [2001] 1 W.L.R. 1115.
[160] *Unilever* [1996] S.T.C. 681.
[161] See e.g. *Henry Boot Homes Ltd v Bassetlaw DC* [2002] EWCA Civ 983; [2003] 1 P. & C.R. 23 at [58] (Keene L.J.: "it is relevant that the appellant . . . had access to legal advice. . . . It was as capable as the Local Planning Authority of informing itself as to the legal consequences of commencing development in breach of a condition"); and *Rowland v Environment Agency* [2003] EWCA Civ 1885, [2005] Ch [157]–[159] (Mance L.J.).
[162] *Begbie* [2001] 1 W.L.R. 1115 (Laws L.J.).

priority to decisions that affect the public at large, or a significant section of it. On the other hand, the fact that the authority would need to engage in expenditure in order to meet a legitimate expectation may not be decisive. For example, in *Coughlan*, the local authority would be inconvenienced and caused expense in relation to its plans to close a nursing home if it was decided that the representation was binding. However, the court in that case preferred the claim of the occupants' health which could be very adversely affected by an enforced move.

Detrimental reliance

We have seen that in *Reprotech*, Lord Hoffmann stated that the legitimate **12–058** expectation should separate itself from private law estoppel and "stand on its own two feet".[163] That statement strongly suggests that to the extent that detrimental reliance may be a condition precedent to estoppel in private law, it need not be a condition precedent to the existence of a legitimate expectation in public law. Nevertheless, detrimental reliance is a factor to be placed on the scales of the fairness and will add to the weight of the legitimate expectation. It may be overridden by a competing public interest, but the greater the evident detriment to the promisee, the greater the countervailing weight of the public interest must be in order to override an expectation that is held to be legitimate.[164]

Mitigation of the effects of a disappointed expectation

Short of implementing the legitimate expectation, a body may instead **12–059** mitigate the effects of its disappointment. In *Matrix Securities*, Lord Griffiths said that if the person relying on a clearance from the Inland Revenue were entitled to do so, and spent money promoting a scheme before the clearance was withdrawn, then "fairness demands that the applicant should be reimbursed for out-of-pocket expense and it could be regarded as an abuse for the Revenue to refuse to do so".[165] This statement makes the valuable point that a change of policy resulting in a disappointed expectation is more likely to be held unlawful where it is within the capacity of the authority to compensate the claimant but failed to do so. In so far, however, as the dictum may suggest that compensation will *always* release the authority from the duty to satisfy the full expectation (in *Matrix Securities*, the expectation of the tax-free benefit for the scheme), then it is of more doubtful validity.[166] In *Rowland v Environmental Agency*, a case

---

[163] See n.43 above, and 12–018.
[164] P. Sales and K. Steyn, "Legitimate Expectations in English Administrative Law" [2004] P.L. 564, 72.
[165] [1994] 1 W.L.R. 334 782.
[166] In *R. (on the application of Bibi) v Newham LBC (No.1)* [2001] EWCA Civ 607; [2002] 1 W.L.R. 237 1 W.L.R. 237 the matter was remitted to the body for consideration of whether the effect of the (unlawful) disappointment of the expectation might be reconsidered.

involving an unlawful representation which nevertheless created a legitimate expectation, Mance L.J. said that where it would be unfair to disappoint such an expectation, the unfairness could be mitigated by compensation, or by "smoothing the position as far possible, consistent with the authority's other duties".[167] Sedley L.J. has also said that "the unfairness which a change of policy may work on those who have relied on the earlier policy can often be adequately mitigated by . . . compensating them in money. The point, however, is that such a payment of money is not an anticipatory payment of damages: it is a practical means of eliminating unfairness".[168]

12–060   There may also be other ways than monetary compensation of mitigating the effect of the frustrated expectation, for example, in *Jones v Environment Agency*, it was held that an expectation that a licence would not be required could be disappointed, but only if the claimant was given at least a year's notice of that fact.[169]

CAN UNLAWFUL REPRESENTATIONS CREATE LEGITIMATE EXPECTATIONS

12–061 To what extent can a public body with limited powers bind itself by an undertaking to act outside of its authorised powers? And if it purports to repudiate that undertaking can it be bound to it by the person to whom it was made? There is a great deal of authority that answers both those questions in the negative,[170] and goes further to assert that a body entrusted with duties or with discretionary powers for the public benefit may not avoid its duties or fetter itself in the discharge of its powers (including

---

[167] [2001] EWCA Civ 607, [2002] 1 W.L.R. 237 [153].

[168] *R v Commissioners of Customs and Excise Ex p. F&I Services Ltd* [2001] EWCA Civ 762; [2001] S.T.C. 939, [72]; see also *Bibi* [2001] EWCA Civ 607, [2002] at [56] where it was suggested that monetary compensation or assistance could mitigate the breach of a legitimate expectation. For monetary compensation see Ch.19. An official's statement, if untrue and given in response to a specific request could also found a tort claim for damages for negligent misstatement, see e.g. *Davy v Spelthorne DC* [1984] A.C. 262. *cf.* In *R. (on the application of Nurse Prescribers Ltd) v Secretary of State for Health* [2004] EWHC 403 (claimant sought damages for expenditure wasted as result of the Department of Health's change of policy on prescribing saline solution, which had not been communicated to the claimant. The court found that a legitimate expectation had been disappointed but considered there was no basis to award damages).

[169] [2005] EWHC 2270.

[170] *Fairtitle v Gilbert* (1787) 2 T.R. 169 (invalid mortgage), *Rhyl UDC v Rhyl Amusements Ltd* [1959] 1 W.L.R. 465 (invalid lease); *Cudgen Rutile (No.2) Pty Ltd v Chalk* [1975] A.C. 520, PC (invalid contract to lease); *Co-operative Retail Services Ltd v Taff-Ely BC* (1980) 39 P. & C.R. 223 (unauthorised communication of void planning permission cannot estop local authority from denying the permission); *Rootkin v Kent CC* [1981] 1 W.L.R. 1186 (council not estopped from denying factual error which would have prevented it from exercising its statutory discretion); *R. v West Oxfordshire DC Ex p. Pearce Homes Ltd* [1986] J.PL. 522 (council not estopped from resiling from previous resolution granting permission because notification of that permission had been qualified by a condition not yet accepted); *R. v Yeovil BC Ex p. Trustees of Elim Pentacostal Church* (1972) 23 P. & C.R. 39.

duties to exercise its powers free from extraneous impediments).[171] In *R. v Ministry of Agriculture, Fisheries and Food Ex p. Hamble (Offshore) Fisheries Ltd*, Sedley J. said that to bind public bodies to an unlawful representation would have the "dual effect of unlawfully extending the[ir] statutory power and destroying the *ultra vires* doctrine by permitting public bodies arbitrarily to extend their powers".[172] On the other hand, to bind bodies to a promise to act outside their powers would in effect endorse an unlawful act. It must, on this view, be doubtful whether the expectation that a body will exceed its powers can be legitimate.[173]

There may, however, be situations where fairness requires an expecta-   12–062
tion to be fulfilled, even where the public body exceeds its authority. In such a situation should the principle of legality yield to those of legal certainty and fairness, especially where there has been no significant harm to third parties? To what extent should the law permit this to happen without posing a real threat to the rule of law's fundamental requirement that public bodies should always act within the scope of their conferred powers?

Principles of agency

In the law of agency an agent (a) cannot bind his principal to do what is   12–063
ultra vires and probably (b) cannot bind his principal by exceeding his own authority if that authority is circumscribed by statute.[174] Nor do purported authorisation, waiver, acquiescence and delay preclude a public body from reasserting its legal rights or powers against another party if it has no power to sanction the conduct in question or to endow that party with the legal right or immunity that he claims.[175]

---

[171] *Customs and Excise Commissioners v Hebson Ltd* [1953] 2 Lloyd's Rep. 382 at 396–397; *Sovmots Investments Ltd v Secretary of State for the Environment* [1977] Q.B. 411 at 437, 479–480, reversed on other grounds [1979] A.C. 144; *Laker Airways Ltd v Department of Trade* [1977] Q.B. 643 at 708, 728 (*cf.* the somewhat ambiguous formulation on Lord Denning M.R. at 707); *Turner v DPP* (1978) 68 Cr.App.R. 70; *Hughes v Department of Health and Social Security* [1985] A.C. 776 at 788 (Lord Diplock: "The liberty to make such changes [in policy] is inherent in our constitutional form of government"); *Re Findlay* [1985] A.C. 318, 338 (Lord Scarman); *US Tobacco International Inc* [1992] 1 All E.R. 212 369 (Taylor L.J.).

[172] [1995] 2 All E.R. 714 731; and M. Elliott, "Legitimate Representations and Unlawful Representations" [2004] C.L.J. 261.

[173] *Re Findlay* [1985] A.C. 318 at 338 (Lord Scarman, emphasis supplied: "It is said that the refusal to except [the appellants] from the new policy was an unlawful act on the part of the Secretary of State in that his decision frustrated their expectation. But what was their *legitimate* expectation?"); *Flanagan and Flanagan v South Bucks DC* [2002] J.P.L. 1465 (no legitimate expectation arose from the a representation from the council's solicitor that planning enforcement notices would be withdrawn as the solicitor lacked the authority to withdraw the notices; Keene L.J. (at [18]) held that unless the representor had actual or ostensible authority to make the representation, although the representee might have "subjectively acquired the expectation", it was not "legitimate").

[174] Se e.g. G. Ganz, "Estoppel and Res Judicata in Administrative Law" [1965] P.L. 321; P. Craig, "Representations by Public Bodies" (1977) 73 L.Q.R. 398.

[175] A. Bradley, "Administrative Justice and the Binding Effect of Official Acts" (1981) 34 C.L.P. 1.

12–064   There are, however, dicta to the effect that planning authorities may waive certain defects in formal procedural requirements,[176] at least so long as third parties are not adversely affected. And in respect of unauthorised and erroneous assurances or advice given by officials upon whom members of the public rely to their detriment, there have been two approaches.

12–065   At one time it could be safely said that such assurances were simply nugatory (unless they fell within the scope of agency in contract), although a negligent misstatement or course of conduct causing economic loss might give rise to liability in tort.[177] Thus if a local government officer to whom the necessary powers have not been delegated assures a builder that planning permission is not required for what he proposes to do, this assertion, though acted upon by the builder, does not affect the power of the local authority to arrive at and act on an opposite decision.[178]

12–066   Another line of cases, attributable in large part to the efforts of Lord Denning, held that in some circumstances when public bodies and officers, in their dealings with a citizen, take it upon themselves to assume authority on a matter concerning him, the citizen is entitled to rely on their having the authority that they have asserted if he cannot reasonably be expected to know the limits of that authority; and he should not be required to suffer for his reliance if they lack the necessary authority.[179] Thus, public authorities have been held bound by assurances given in disregard of a formal statutory requirement, upon which an individual relied to his detriment.[180] The Court of Appeal in *Lever Finance* applied this principle to a determination by a planning official, even though the power to decide had not been delegated to him in proper form.[181]

---

[176] *Wells v Minister of Housing and Local Government* [1967] 1 W.L.R. 1000 at 1007 (Lord Denning); *Lever Finance Ltd v Westminster CC* [1971] Q.B. 222. This aspect of *Lever Finance* was approved in *Western Fish*.

[177] See 19–046.

[178] *Southend-on-Sea Corp v Hodgson (Wickford) Ltd* [1962] 1 Q.B. 416; *Western Fish*.

[179] *Robertson v Minister of Pensions* [1949] 1 K.B. 227 at 223 (Denning J.); *Falmouth Boat Construction Co. v Howell* [1950] 1 K.B. 16 at 26 (Lord Denning); *Re L (AC) (an Infant)* [1971] 3 All E.R. 743 (local authority, having misled mother into believing that she need not lodge a second formal objection to the authority's application for parental rights, not entitled to rely on her failure to lodge the second objection in due time); cf. *Hanson v Church Commissioners for England* [1978] Q.B. 823 (tenant denied a hearing before rent assessment committee as a result, in part, of misleading advice given to him by the clerk to the committee); and *R. v Tower Hamlets LBC Ex p. Kayne-Levenson* [1975] Q.B. 431 at 441 (Lord Denning: local authority misled licensee into thinking that she could not nominate the applicant to be her successor; Lord Denning appeared to think that the local authority was not bound to treat the applicant as though he had been nominated). cf. *Suthendran v Immigration Appeal Tribunal* [1977] A.C. 359 (erroneous intimation by Home Office that appellant had a right of appeal caused no prejudice); *R. v Melton and Belvoir Justices Ex p. Tynan* (1977) 75 L.G.R. 544. For an example of the estoppel where no question of vires was raised, see *Crabb v Arun DC* [1976] Ch. 179.

[180] *Wells* [1967] 1 W.L.R. 1000 (informal determination that planning permission not required); cf. *Western Fish* where *Wells* was narrowly distinguished; *Re L (AC) (an Infant)* [1971] 3 All E.R. 743 (*Wells* followed in different context); *English-Speaking Union of the Commonwealth v Westminster (City) LBC* (1973) 26 P. & C.R. 575.

[181] *Lever Finance* (oral assurance by borough architect that planning permission not required).

The general principle remains, however, that a public authority may not **12–067** vary the scope of its statutory powers and duties as a result of its own errors or the conduct of others. Judicial resort to estoppel in these circumstances may prejudice the interests of third parties.[182] For example, the neighbouring property owners in *Lever Finance*, who found that houses had been built closer to their boundary line than had been allowed under the original planning permission, might well feel aggrieved that they had had no opportunity to object to the form of the permission that ultimately bound the planning authority.[183] Despite the cases to the contrary, it seems today that, in general, authority that is unlawfully assumed will not bind a public authority. Even Lord Denning appeared to have relented when he said in respect of a purported grant of a planning permission by a town clerk unauthorised to grant the permission, that: "The protection of the public interest is entrusted to the representative bodies and to the ministers. It would be quite wrong that it should be pre-empted by a mistaken issue by a clerk of a printed form—without any authority in that behalf . . . when the result would be to damage the interests of the public at large".[184]

The two lines of authority are not easily reconciled. However, in **12–068** general, both authority and principle assert that a public authority cannot be estopped from denying its lawful duties and powers.[185] Nor can estoppel be pleaded by a public authority against an individual who has apparently accepted the benefits of an unlawful act or provision.[186]

This decision, applying *Robertson* [1949] 1 K.B. 227, and *Wells* [1971] 3 All E.R. 743 cannot be reconciled with *Southend-on-Sea Corp* [1962] 1 Q.B. 416, or with the observations in *Howell* [1950] 1 K.B. at 845 and 847. Delegation to officials by local authority members was authorised by the Local Government Act 1972 as amended.

[182] And may curtail the willingness of public officials to give informal advice: *Brooks and Burton Ltd v Secretary of State for the Environment* (1976) 75 L.G.R. 285 at 296 (*Lever* was described as "the most advanced case of the application of the estoppel doctrine, and one not to be repeated"); on appeal, the CA stated that an estoppel could not be established on the facts: [1977] 1 W.L.R. 1294 at 1300.

[183] Could they have recovered damages from the local authority by establishing that the officer was careless and that the permission would not have been granted had it been originally applied for in its subsequently amended form? See 19–046.

[184] *Co-operative Retail Services Ltd v Taff-Ely* BC (1980) 39 P. & C.R. 223 at 239–240; and *R. v Yeovil BC Ex p. Trustees of Elim Pentacostal Church*; *R. v W. Oxfordshire DC Ex p. Pearce Homes Ltd* [1986] J.P.L. 523 (formal notification of a decision has no effect if the notification is contrary to the terms of the decision); *R. v Secretary of State for Education & Science Ex p. Hardy* [1989] C.O.D. 186 (decision to approve scheme could be revoked because it was not a "formal precise and published" decision). *cf. Costain Homes Ltd v Secretary of State for the Environment* [1988] J.P.L. 701; *R. v Southwark LBC Ex p. Bannerman* (1990) 2 Admin. L.R. 381 (despite lack of formal delegation to official it is "to be assumed that those who write letters on behalf of their superiors have the authority to do so").

[185] *Western Fish Tandridge DC v Telecom Securicor Cellular Radio* [1996] J.P.L. 128 (refusal to grant planning permission to erect a multi-antenna mast for mobile telephone service); *Lever*; *Camden LBC v Secretary of State for the Environment and Barker* (1994) 67 P. & C.R. 59 (considered on question of whether estoppel arose; no evidence of detrimental reliance); *R. v Criminal Injury Compensation Board Ex p. Keane & Marsden* [1988] C.O.D. 128.

[186] *City of Bradford MC v Secretary of State for the Environment* [1986] J.P.L. 598, CA. *cf. Hidenborough Village Preservation Society v Secretary of State for the Environment* [1978] J.P.L. 708.

12–069   There have however, been two exceptions to these rules. The first exception has arisen when the authority has power to delegate authority to an official and there are special circumstances justifying the applicant in believing that the officer concerned had power to bind the authority (e.g. where there was evidence of a widespread practice of delegation of powers to officers, to authorise immaterial modifications of approved plans).[187] The second exception has arisen where the authority has waived a formal procedural requirement. In such a case it has been estopped from relying on its absence.[188]

12–070   In recent years, however, the courts appear to have become reluctant to permit a public official or body to extend their authority by way of an unlawful representation, especially in areas where the interests of third parties or the public might be compromised. In *Henry Boot Homes Ltd v Bassetlaw DC*, the Court of Appeal considered whether a developer possessed a legitimate expectation that works carried out in breach of the conditions under a planning permission would be treated as a "commencement" of the works within five years (thus preserving the permission).[189] The council had indicated that the works would be treated in that way, having misinterpreted the law.[190] Keene L.J. said that "the interests of third parties and the public . . . greatly reduce the potential for a legitimate expectation . . . to arise".[191] Although not prepared to adopt an absolute position that the legitimate expectation could never arise in similar circumstances, he agreed with the court below, that "the public nature of Town and Country Planning . . . is not a matter for private agreement between developers and Local Planning Authorities".[192] The House of Lords took a similar view in *R. v East Sussex CC Ex p. Reprotech (Pebsham) Ltd*, where Lord Hoffmann held that a determination by a planning subcommittee did not amount to a binding representation with juridical effect. He said that:[193]

---

[187] *Lever* was followed, despite the qualifications of *Western Fish*, presumably under this exception, in *Camden* [1994] 67 P. & C.R. 59 (authority held to the terms of a letter written by officer representing that a proposed roof extension did not require planning permission; officer had actual or ostensible authority); *Gowa v Attorney General* [1985] 1 W.L.R. 1003 (Crown estopped, by letter from colonial governor 30 years earlier, from denying registration of British citizenship).

[188] *Camden* [1994] 67 P. & C.R. 59; A. Bradley, "Administrative Justice and the Binding Effects of Official Acts" (1981) 34 C.L.P 1; M. Akehurst, "Revocation of Administrative Decisions" [1982] P.L. 613; N. Bamforth, "Legitimate Expectation and Estoppel" [1998] J.R. 196.

[189] [2002] EWCA Civ 983; [2003] 1 P. & C.R. 23.

[190] Under the *Whitley* principle (*Whitley and Sons v Secretary of State for the Environment* [1992] 64 P. & C.R. 296), where Woolf J. held that operations carried out in breach of a condition to a planning permission cannot be relied on as a material consideration capable of "commencing" the development.

[191] *Henry Boot Homes*, [55].

[192] *Henry Boot Homes*, [52] (Sullivan J.); *R v Leicester CC Ex p. Powergen United Kingdom Plc* [1994] 4 P.L.R. 91 at 101G–H (Dyson J.).

[193] [2002] UKHL 8; [2003] 1 W.L.R. 348 at [29]. *Reprotech* was followed in *South Bucks DC v Flanagan* [2002] EWCA Civ 690; [2002] 1 W.L.R. 2601. See S. Atrill, "The End of Estoppel in Public Law" [2003] C.L.J. 3.

"[A] determination is not simply a matter between the applicant and the planning authority in which they are free to agree on whatever procedure they please. It is also a matter which concerns the general public interest and which requires other planning authorities, the Secretary of State on behalf of the national public interest and the public itself to be able to participate."

A changing approach?

The decision of the Court of Appeal in *Rowland v Environment Agency* **12–071** does contain suggestions, albeit obiter, that an unlawful promise may give rise to a legitimate expectation.[194] The case concerned the ancient public rights of navigation on the river Thames. The agency had made a cut in the river in order to bypass a stretch of water difficult to navigate and put up signs to the effect that there was no thoroughfare on that part of the river and that it was private. The claimant owned land abutting on that part of the river, including the river bed, which she had always treated as private, and objected when the authority sought to reopen it to public navigation. She claimed that the initial representation had given rise to a legitimate expectation,[195] the disappointment of which was an abuse of power. The Court of Appeal held that the authority's representation to the appellant was beyond their statutory power and that they were not bound by it in the circumstances of the case.

In *Rowland* the principle of lawfulness prevailed over that of fairness **12–072** and certainty, but interest was taken in the proposition of Professor Craig that in some circumstances fairness should prevail, even in the case of an *ultra vires* representation.[196] Craig's argument had to some extent been endorsed in two cases of the European Court of Human Rights, *Pine Valley Developments v Ireland*,[197] and *Stretch v UK*.[198] In *Pine Valley* it was held that a legitimate expectation may constitute a "possession" under Article 1 of Protocol 1 of the Convention and may be protected "notwithstanding the fact that it was beyond the powers of the public body which fostered the expectation to realize the expectation". In such circumstances, however, the expectation did not automatically entitle the person to a "realisation" of the *ultra* vires expectation, but may entitle him to other discretionary relief, such as compensation, "which it is within the powers of the public body to afford".[199]

---

[194] [2003] EWCA Civ 1885; [2005] Ch. 1; S. Hannett and L. Busch, "Ultra Vires Representations and Illegitimate Expectations" [2005] P.L. 729.
[195] As well as a possession under ECHR Art. 8 and Art.1, Protocol 1.
[196] P. Craig, *Administrative* Law, 5th edn. (2003), pp.665 *et seq.*
[197] (1992) 14 E.H.R.R. 319.
[198] (2004) 38 E.H.R.R. 12.
[199] *Pine Valley*, para.80.

12–073   The Court in *Pine Valley*, while allowing an unlawful representation to give rise to a legitimate expectation, limited the circumstances in which the expectation was required to be fulfilled. The Court went on to say that the fact that that the representation was unlawful "may be a reason, and indeed a strong reason, going to the justification for the interference [with the person's "possession"] and its proportionality".[200]

12–074   In *Stretch* the Court considered whether a representation, that the authority had power to grant an option to renew a lease, which was mistakenly thought to be lawful, could bind the authority. It was held that the unlawful representation could give rise to a legitimate expectation and a "possession" under Article 1 of the First Protocol. In this case the authority was held to be bound by the expectation as the transaction was essentially of a private law nature and not against any "public interest or prejudicial to third party interests.[201]

12–075   As a result of those two cases, as Mance L.J. said in *Rowlands*: "Whatever the previous position . . . [the lack of the Agency's power] can no longer be an automatic answer under English law to a case of legitimate expectation".[202] In *Rowland* itself, it was unanimously held that, despite the fact that the representation of the kind contended for by the appellant would have been unlawful, it nevertheless gave rise to a "legitimate" expectation. This much was new. However, despite the fact that the expectation was legitimate, it was held that the authority was not required to fulfil its substance, for different reasons. May L.J. considered that the unfairness in this case "illustrates a defect in the law", but nevertheless held that the Court of Appeal was "obliged to uphold an unjust outcome". Mance L.J. noted the distinction between the *existence* of a legitimate expectation and its *strength*, as discussed above.[203] He held that, despite the legitimacy of an expectation (albeit based upon an unlawful expectation), it lacked the weight to justify its protection. As opposed to *Pine Valley* and *Stretch*, the representation in *Rowlands* was not based upon any "direct commercial relationship" between the parties, nor did they obtain any assurances as to the nature of the interest. In the circumstances, therefore, it was right that the appellant should bear the risk of the transaction.[204]

12–076   What is the point of calling an expectation "legitimate" if it can be overridden for lack of "strength" or cannot be upheld in law? Mance L.J. considered that even though an unlawful legitimate expectation need not bind the authority, the expectation which it created was legitimate at least to the extent that it could " still survive and require recognition".[205] In his view the expectation is a factor that must be taken into account by the

---

[200] However, since other developers in a similar position had been granted relief, there was held to be a violation of ECHR Art.14 for which substantial compensation was later awarded against the Irish State: (1993) 16 E.C.H.R. 379.
[201] [2003] EWCA Civ 1885; [2005] Ch. 1 at paras 38 and 39.
[202] *Rowland* [2003] EWCA Civ 1885; [2005] Ch. 1 at [152].
[203] [2003] EWCA Civ 1885; [2005] Ch. 1 at 156.
[204] [2003] EWCA Civ 1885; [2005] Ch. 1 at [157] and [162].
[205] [2003] EWCA Civ 1885; [2005] Ch. 1 at [155].

decision-maker although it will not, at least in the present state of the law, bind the authority. In cases where it would be unfair to disappoint such an expectation, the unfairness could be mitigated by compensation, or by "smoothing the position as far possible, consistent with the authority's other duties".[206] However, the court will not reserve jurisdiction over the performance of the authority by continuous supervision of any assurances that may have been offered.[207]

Clear principles do not obviously or easily emerge from the present state 12–077 of the case law on unlawful expectations. In our view the law should be slow to weaken the principle of legality, which is the fundamental ingredient of the rule of law. Yet there is growing authority to suggest that an unlawful expectation can at least be "legitimate". If that is so, its legitimacy is conferred under the principles of legal certainty (which is, after all, another important ingredient of the rule of law) and fairness.

If an authority is to be held to the terms of its unlawful representation 12–078 (and we are not convinced that it should), then the balance of fairness in favour of the claimant should be overwhelming and the following conditions at least should apply:

(a) Although, as we have seen,[208] both knowledge of the representation and detrimental reliance are not always required to support an expectation based upon an *intra vires* representation, both those requirements are surely necessary to bind an *ultra vires* representation. In the absence of those requirements, unfairness is unlikely to weigh very much, especially if the claimant has had access to legal advice on the lawfulness of the representation.

(b) As in *Pine Valley* and *Stretch*,[209] where the breach of the expectation would lead to the recipient being deprived of a human right (such as a "possession" under Art.1 of the First Protocol) the deprivation of the right needs to be balanced against the public interest.

(c) An unlawful representation should not prevail where third party interests were or might have been compromised.

In general the courts, as suggested in *Rowland*, should prefer to require 12–079 compensation to be given to the claimant, rather than permitting the expectation to be upheld and thereby sanctioning an unlawful act by a public body with limited powers. However, administrative redress will in any event often be a more appropriate remedy than judicial review, and complaints may be investigated by the appropriate Ombudsman as allegations of injustice caused by maladministration.[210]

---

[206] [2003] EWCA Civ 1885; [2005] Ch. 1 at [153].
[207] [2003] EWCA Civ 1885; [2005] Ch. 1 at [155] (Peter Gibson L.J. and Mance L.J.); *cf. R. (on the application of Bibi) v Newhom LBC* [2001] EWCA Civ 607; [2002] 1 W.L.R. 23 at [42]. But the claimant may be able to raise the matter by way of separate claim.
[208] See 12–037–041.
[209] See 12–072.
[210] See 1–066.

COMPARATIVE PERSPECTIVES

Australia

12–080 The High Court of Australia has recognised a principle of legitimate expectation as an aspect of the requirement to accord procedural fairness.[211] However, it has more recently queried the basis and breadth of the doctrine. Gleeson C.J. has stated that a departure from a legitimate expectation will not be enough to import procedural fairness requirements; what must be shown is unfairness.[212] McHugh, Gummow and Callinan JJ. referred to the limited scope of the doctrine if procedural fairness was implied in the absence of clear legislative intent to the contrary.[213] The English position protecting substantive expectations was rejected in Australia in *Re Minister for Immigration and Multicultural Affairs; Ex parte Lam*.[214] The court has referred to the separation of powers entrenched in the Constitution as the basis for the strict separation between merits and judicial review.[215]

12–081 In relation to international agreements, in *Minister for Immigration and Ethnic Affairs v Ah Hin Teoh*,[216] the court found a legitimate expectation had been created by the ratification of an international convention. In the absence of anything to the contrary, it was a positive statement that the executive intended to act in accordance with the convention. This meant that an administrator could not depart from the principles in the convention without giving the person affected by the departure a hearing. Further, the court also held that the finding of a legitimate expectation was objectively determined and not dependent upon the knowledge of the ratification of the convention by the individual.[217] Following *Teoh*, the government and opposition issued an executive statement that Australia,

---

[211] *Haoucher v Minister for Immigration and Ethnic Affairs* (1990) 169 C.L.R. 648, *Annetts v McCann* (1990) 170 C.L.R. 596, *Minister for Immigration and Ethnic Affairs v Teoh* (1995) 183 C.L.R 273.

[212] *Re Minister for Immigration and Multicultural Affairs; Ex parte Lam* (2003) 214 C.L.R. 1, [35].

[213] *Re Minister for Immigration and Multicultural Affairs; Ex parte Lam* (2003) 214 C.L.R. 1 at [81]–[83] (McHugh and Gummow JJ.) [150] (Callinan J.) referring to *Minister for Immigration and Ethnic Affairs v Teoh* (1995) 183 C.L.R. 273 at 311–312 (McHugh J.).

[214] (2003) 214 C.L.R. 1 at [28] (Gleeson C.J.), [68]–[70] (McHugh and Gummow JJ.), [148] (Callinan J.).

[215] *Re Minister for Immigration and Multicultural Affairs; Ex parte Lam* (2003) 214 C.L.R. 1 at [76]–[77] (McHugh and Gummow JJ.). See also A. Mason, "Procedural Fairness: Its development and continuing role of legitimate expectation" (2005) 12 *Australian Journal of Administrative Law* 103, 108–110.

[216] (1995) 183 C.L.R. 273. For criticism, see M. Taggart, "Legitimate Expectations and Treaties in the High Court of Australia" (1996) 112 L.Q.R. 50; M. Hunt, *Using Human Rights Law in English Courts* (1997), pp.242–247; E. Handsley, "Legal Fictions and Confusion as Strategies for Protecting Human Rights: A Dissenting View on *Teoh's* Case" (1997) 2 Newcastle L.J. 56.

[217] *Minister for Immigration and Ethnic Affairs v Ah Hin Teoh* (1995) 183 C.L.R. 273 at 291 (Mason C.J. and Deane J.), 301 (Toohey J.).

being a party to an international convention, or domestic legislation that reproduced or referred to international instruments, did not give rise to a legitimate expectation of a kind that might provide a basis at law for invalidating or in any way changing the effect of an administrative decision. Proposed legislation to this effect was also introduced to Parliament but was not successful; South Australia successfully introduced similar legislation with respect to administrative actions by the State executive.[218] The ratio in *Teoh* has been queried in *Re Minister for Immigration and Multicultural Affairs; Ex parte Lam* by McHugh, Gummow, Hayne and Callinan JJ. Doubts were expressed whether the ratification of a treaty could amount to a positive statement of the type found in *Teoh*.[219]

Canada

The Supreme Court of Canada has recognized legitimate expectation as a **12–082** ground of review on a number of occasions, though in none of those cases was the argument successful.[220] The Supreme Court has explicitly rejected the argument that the doctrine can give rise to legally enforceable substantive rights in *Mount Sinai Hospital*,[221] a case in which the Court (contrary to the holding of the Quebec Court of Appeal) also rejected the possibility of reaching the same result through the agency of public law estoppel, though not in such a way as to preclude entirely the use of the latter doctrine to achieve substantive outcomes. Subsequently, in *Canadian Pacific Railway Co v Vancouver (City)*,[222] the Court did accept that a decision-maker, while not bound to give effect to a legitimate expectation of a substantive outcome, might have to treat that as a factor that had to be taken into account in the exercise of a discretionary power. Earlier in *Baker*,[223] the Court accepted that a legitimate expectation of a substantive outcome could give rise to a procedural or a heightened procedural entitlement. Also relevant is the Court's acceptance in *Lévis (City) v Tétrault*,[224] of the availability of the defence of 'officially induced error'.

In relation to international agreements, in *Baker*,[225] on the facts of that **12–083** case, the Court held that a ratified but unincorporated treaty did not give rise to a legitimate expectation of enhanced procedural protections but

---

[218] Administrative Decisions (Effect of International Instruments) Act 1995 (SA).

[219] *Re Minister for Immigration and Multicultural Affairs; Ex parte Lam* (2003) 214 C.L.R. 1 at [95]–[96] (McHugh and Gummow JJ.), [122(Hayne J.)], [147] (Callinan J.).

[220] *Old St. Boniface Residents Assn Inc v Winnipeg (City)* [1990] 3 S.C.R. 1170; *Reference re Canada Assistance Plan* [1991] 2 S.C.R. 525; *Baker v Canada (Minister of Citizenship and Immigration)* [1999] 2 S.C.R. 817; *Mount Sinai Hospital v Quebec (Minister of Health and Social Services)* [2001] 2 S.C.R. 281; *Canadian Union of Public Employees (CUPE) v Ontario (Minister of Labour)* [2003] 1 S.C.R. 539; though it was one of the factors leading to review on procedural grounds in *Congrégation des témoins de Jéhovah de St.-Jérôme v Lafontaine (Village)* [2004] 2 S.C.R. 650.

[221] [2001] 2 S.C.R. 281.

[222] [2006] 1 S.C.R. 227.

[223] [1994] 2 S.C.R. 817.

[224] [2006] 1 S.C.R. 420.

[225] [1994] 2 S.C.R. 817.

explicitly left open the question whether in other circumstances that could be the case. Thereafter, however, the Court held that, in any event, the provisions of the ratified but unincorporated treaty were, nonetheless, relevant considerations that the decision-maker was obliged to take into account.

India

12-084   The doctrine of legitimate expectations in the substantive sense has been accepted as part of the law of India and the decision-maker can normally be compelled to give effect to his representation in regard to the expectation based on previous practice or past conduct in the absence of some overriding public interest.[226] The doctrine of legitimate expectation operates to protect both procedural and substantive rights.[227]

New Zealand

12-085   The concept of legitimate expectation as an aspect of procedural fairness has been well established in New Zealand administrative law since the late 1970s. There is, however, no clear adoption of the doctrine of substantive legitimate expectation by the higher judiciary.

12-086   In *Brierley Investments Ltd v Bouzaid*,[228] the Court of Appeal split over the place of legitimate expectation in the tax context. There a company attempted to stop the Commissioner conducting a broad investigation into its tax affairs on the ground that the Commissioner had agreed previously to the use of the formula employed by the company (and now questioned by the Revenue). It was alleged this action was an abuse of power, and relied on *R v Inland Revenue Commissioners Ex p. MFK Underwriting Agents Ltd.*[229] The Court of Appeal was unanimous in rejecting the challenge on the ground that no "agreement" had been reached or representation made, but the three judges each took a different position on the law. Richardson J. distinguished the English cases on the ground that the New Zealand tax legislation put the Commissioner under a duty to collect all tax due, and there could be no estoppel as it would be incompatible with the Commissioner's statutory duty. "As a public authority," Richardson J. said, "the commissioner cannot by contract or conduct abdicate or fetter the future exercise of his audit functions in particular cases". Casey J. took the exact opposite view on the law, applying *Re Preston* and the later English legitimate expectation cases. He was disposed to accept that "in an appropriate case a decision by the commissioner to

---

[226] *Punjab Communications Ltd v Union of India* 1999 (4) S.C.C. 727 at 747.
[227] *MP Oil Extraction v State of M.P.* 1997 (7) S.C.C. 592 at 612, followed in *National Building Construction v S Raghunathan* 1998 (7) S.C.C. 66 at 77.
[228] [1993] 3 N.Z.L.R. 655.
[229] [1990] 1 W.L.R. 1545.

act inconsistently with a taxpayer's legitimate expectation in the process leading up to an assessment could constitute unfairness amounting to an abuse of power, so as to justify intervention by way of judicial review". McKay J. disposed of the case on the facts and left the resolution of the difference of opinion for another day.

Shortly after that decision the New Zealand tax legislation was changed, **12–087** adopting the British legislative model of "care and management".[230] Consequently, the British tax cases that provided the platform for the judiciary to develop the law of substantive legitimate expectation.[231] However, in 1994 a regime was introduced allowing taxpayers to seek and receive rulings that bind the Revenue, even if they later turn out to be incorrect in law.[232] There is an argument that the provision of this statutory avenue for providing certainty and protecting detrimental reliance might be seen as inconsistent with a wider acceptance of legitimate expectation doctrine in the tax area based on less formal advice, practices and representations. Moreover, although there has been significant use of judicial review in tax cases in New Zealand administrative law in the last 15 years, the impact of this case law on broader administrative law is less evident. In a recent tax case, where the Inland Revenue had proffered a (subsequently held) erroneous interpretation of a statute in publications that misled the claimant initially as to his rights, the Court of Appeal and Supreme Court simply remarked that this could not affect the correct interpretation of the statute.[233]

In other case appellate courts have often been critical of High Court **12–088** judges invoking the doctrine of legitimate expectation instead of grappling with the basic issues of statutory interpretation that, if correctly decided, would obviate the need to rely on the doctrine.[234] Early cases were mixed. Some rejected the substantive version out of hand,[235] whereas *Northern Roller Milling Co Ltd v Commerce Commission*[236] was accepting of the concept. More recently, the High Court has been cautious.[237] In *Challis v Destination Marlborough Trust Board Inc*[238] the alleged substantive legitimate expectation was not made out on the facts so it was unnecessary to decide whether New Zealand public law recognized such a doctrine. Wild J denied that estoppel had any part to play in New Zealand public law, in

---

[230] Tax Administration Act 1994 (NZ) s.6A.
[231] *Miller v Commissioner of Inland Revenue* [1995] 3 N.Z.L.R. 664, CA; *Golden Bay Cement Co Ltd v Commissioner of Inland Revenue* [1996] 3 N.Z.L.R. 665, CA.
[232] Tax Administration Act 1994 Pt VA.
[233] *Allen v Commissioner of Inland Revenue* [2006] 3 N.Z.L.R. 1 at [38], SCNZ.
[234] *Attorney General v Unitec Institute of Technology* [2007] 1 N.Z.L.R. 750 at [54]–[59], CA; *Attorney General v E* [2000] 3 N.Z.L.R. 257, CA.
[235] *Tay v Attorney General* [1992] 2 N.Z.L.R. 693, HC, Hillyer J.
[236] [1994] 2 N.Z.L.R. 747, HC, Gallen J.; strongly criticised by M. Poole, "Legitimate Expectation and Substantive Fairness: Beyond the Limits of Procedural Propriety" [1995] N.Z.L.Rev. 426.
[237] *Lumber Specialties Ltd v Hodgson* [2000] 2 N.Z.L.R. 347 at [125]–[139], HC, Hammond J.
[238] [2003] 2 N.Z.L.R. 107, HC, Wild J.

part because it "is analogous to legitimate expectation, overlapping and essentially duplicating it, and adding nothing but confusion" More ambiguous is the stance in *Staunton Ltd v Chief Executive Ministry of Fisheries*,[239] where the contesting views were briefly surveyed and the judge said "abuse of power" had to be the basis of the doctrine of legitimate expectation "as it would be unfair to permit a [p]ublic [a]uthority to depart from its promulgated policy or promise".

Substantive unfairness

12–089   Legitimate expectation language is sometimes mixed with the notion of substantive unfairness.[240] The doctrine of substantive unfairness is part of New Zealand law primarily due to the Court of Appeal decision in *Thames Valley Electric Power Board v NZFP Pulp & Paper Ltd*[241] (one of the last judgments given by Sir Robin Cooke prior to his life peerage)

International treaties

12–090   *Teoh's* case[242] is seldom relied upon in New Zealand.[243] The current New Zealand approach, stemming from dicta in *Tavita v Minister of Immigration*,[244] is that ratified but unincorporated treaty obligations are mandatory relevant obligations and must be taken into account. Although the Court of Appeal in subsequent cases has been careful not to endorse *Tavita* enthusiastically,[245] numerous High Court judges have thus been encouraged to apply ratified but unincorporated human rights treaty obligations as mandatory relevant considerations.[246] Now that New Zealand is no longer bound by precedents from the Privy Council, there is no longer any danger that the flirtation with *Teoh* in the Caribbean death penalty Privy Council cases will endanger the well-settled mandatory relevant consideration approach in New Zealand.

---

[239] [2004] N.Z.A.R. 68, HC Gendal J.
[240] *Northern Roller Milling Co Ltd v Commerce Commission* [1994] 2 N.Z.L.R. 747, HC, Gallen J..
[241] [1994] 2 N.Z.L.R. 641, CA.
[242] (1995) 183 C.L.R. 273.
[243] An exception is Thomas J.'s part-concurring, part-dissenting judgment in *New Zealand Maori Council v Attorney General* [1996] 3 N.Z.L.R. 140 at 184–185, CA, founding an expectation on the Treaty of Waitangi. Cf. *Nga Tahu Maori Trust Board v Director General of Conservation* [1995] 3 N.Z.L.R. 553, CA.
[244] [1994] 2 N.Z.L.R. 257, CA.
[245] *Puli'uvea Removal Review Authority* (1996) 2 H.R.N.Z. 510; *Rajan v Minister of Immigration* [1996] 3 N.Z.L.R. 543; Justice Ken Keith, "Sources of Law, Especially Statutory Interpretation, With Suggestions about Distinctiveness" in R. Bigwood (ed.), *Legal Method in New Zealand: Essays & Commentaries* (2001), pp.77, 90.
[246] See e.g., *Elika v Minister of Immigration* [1996] 1 N.Z.L.R. 741; *Mil Mohammud v Minister of Immigration* [1997] N.Z.A.R. 223; *Patel v Minister of Immigration* [1997] 1 N.Z.L.R. 252.

South Africa

The Promotion of Administrative Justice Act[247] (PAJA) requires that all **12–091** administrative actions that affect rights *or legitimate expectations* must be procedurally fair (s.3(1)). Administrative action is defined in s.1 of PAJA, however, as a decision that affects 'rights'. So although review on the grounds listed in s.6(2) is limited to administrative actions, or decisions that affect rights, all decisions that affect legitimate expectations must be procedurally fair.[248]

There are instances of courts affording varying degrees of substantive **12–092** protection to legitimate expectations,[249] but the Constitutional Court has been careful not to decide the issue. In *Premier, Mpumalanga v Executive Committee, Association of State-Aided Schools Eastern Transvaal*[250] O'Regan J. raised but did not answer the question of substantive protection of legitimate expectation, while in *Bel Porto* Chaskalson P. said the question of substantive protection was a contentious issue that has no clear authority in our law.[251]

At first glance, the scheme of PAJA seems to establish different standards **12–093** of review: administrative actions affecting legitimate expectations must be lawful and procedurally fair, while administrative actions affecting rights must be lawful, procedurally fair, and reasonable. PAJA seems to contemplate the protection of only procedural interests where legitimate expectations are concerned, as questions about the substantive lawfulness or reasonableness of a decision affecting a legitimate expectation cannot be investigated. There are, however, significant problems that arise from the inconsistency between the definition of administrative action in s.1 as decisions affecting rights and the formulation in s.3 of administrative actions 'affecting rights or legitimate expectations'. These difficulties have led courts in some cases to adopt an approach that abolishes the distinction between procedural review for legitimate expectations and substantive review for rights. In *Tirfu Raiders Rugby Club v SA Rugby Union*[252] Yekiso J. found that the applicant's legitimate expectation constituted a right for the purposes of s.1 of PAJA, and held the impugned decision reviewable against substantive as well as procedural grounds of review listed in PAJA. Stacey has suggested that this is the correct approach, on the argument that the Constitution does not contemplate differing ambits of application of

---

[247] 3 of 2000.
[248] C. Hoexter, *Administrative Law in South Africa* (2007), pp.355–362.
[249] See e.g. *Ampofo v MEC for Education, Arts, Culture, Sports and Recreation, Northern Province* 2002 (2) S.A. 215 (T), *Coetzer v Minister of Safety and Security* 2003 (3) S.A. 368, LC and in the Constitutional Court *Bel Porto School Governing Body v Premier, Western Cape* 2002 (3) S.A. 265.
[250] 1999 (2) S.A. 91, CC.
[251] For academic analysis see. Quinot, "The Developing Doctrine of Substantive Legitimate Expectations in South African Administrative Law" (2004) 19 *South African Public Law* 543; Campbell, "Legitimate Expectations: the Potential and Limits of Substantive Protection in South Africa" (2003) 12 *South African Law Journal* 292.
[252] [2006] 2 All S.A. 549 (C).

the right to lawful and reasonable administrative action on the one hand and the right to procedurally fair administrative action on the other.[253]

12–094   Where courts have substantively protected legitimate expectation, they have done so by extending the rights to lawful and reasonable administrative action to them. The test, where this extension has been made, is thus no different to the test for substantive protection of an affected right. Given the way that PAJA has forced courts to extend substantive protection of legitimate expectations, the treatment of legitimate expectations has been no different to the substantive protection of rights affected by administrative action. PAJA has thus created an "all or nothing" approach: either legitimate expectations fit through the definition of administrative action in s.1 and thus into the realm of substantive protection of the whole of PAJA, or they do not, and enjoy only procedural protection.

12–095   An unlawful promise or representation is unlikely to found a legitimate expectation in South African law.[254]

---

[253] Stacey, "Substantive Protection of Legitimate Expectations in the Promotion of Administrative Justice Act" (2006) 22 *South African Journal on Human Rights*.
[254] Hoexter, *Administrative Law in South Africa*, (2007) pp.387–392.

CHAPTER 13

CONVENTION RIGHTS AS GROUNDS FOR JUDICIAL REVIEW

SCOPE

This chapter analyses the use of the rights set out in the European 13–001 Convention on Human Rights (ECHR) as grounds for judicial review. Since Convention rights have been incorporated into United Kingdom law under the Human Rights Act 1998 (HRA), their infringement by public authorities has become a ground of illegality.[1] In addition, the courts may review legislation for conformity with Convention rights.[2] Some of the Convention rights are absolute, but others may be limited and in those circumstances the courts have to decide whether the infringement of the right has been adequately justified under the test of proportionality considered in Chapter 11.[3] We start by setting out the background to the protection of fundamental rights in international law and then consider the approach to the ECHR by the European Court of Human Rights (ECtHR). The chapter then proceeds to consider the provisions of the HRA and the approach of domestic courts to Convention rights, both when reviewing official action and legislation. Finally, the Convention rights themselves are briefly considered, so as to give a flavour of the judicial approach in the first few years of the existence of the HRA.

PROTECTION OF FUNDAMENTAL RIGHTS IN DOMESTIC AND INTERNATIONAL LAW

The protection of fundamental rights recognised by the common law is 13–002 addressed in Chapter 1.[4] It is sufficient to say here that in the past the concept of parliamentary sovereignty and the residual nature of common law rights combined to make fundamental rights vulnerable to interference, especially at times of actual or perceived national emergency.[5] In addition,

---

[1] On illegality as a ground of review generally, see Ch.5.
[2] On review of legislation generally, see 3–011.
[3] See 11–079.
[4] See 1–039.
[5] For example habeas corpus was liable to be suspended by Parliament. The last occasion for the then UK was 1866–69 in Ireland, although it was also suspended in British colonies in the

the development of independent common law rights protection was, ironically, hampered by the existence of the ECHR. Since Parliament had decided not to incorporate the ECHR into domestic law, the courts felt constrained not to achieve the same effect through the common law for fear of being accused of circumventing Parliament's decision.[6]

13–003   The development of the notion of binding international human rights took significant hold with the adoption of the Universal Declaration on Human Rights by the then recently-formed General Assembly of the United Nations in 1948. The limits and even dangers of unrestrained popularism, without any protection for fundamental rights, had been highlighted by the tyrannies in Germany, Italy and Spain which had precipitated the Second World War. The Universal Declaration did not have the status of an enforceable international treaty but was, nonetheless, one of the principal signs of a shift in the understanding of the nature of international law which had previously been known as the law of nations.[7] For the first time, individuals (rather than states) were seen as the holders of international legal rights.

The Council of Europe

13–004 The results of two World Wars on European soil and the disregard for human rights in some of its own nations led to the foundation of the Council of Europe in 1949. The 10 founding members of the Council committed themselves to upholding the rule of law and the protection of fundamental freedoms.[8] The greatest monument to the Council is the ECHR which came into force on September 3, 1953.[9]

13–005   However, even within Europe, there were divisions about the content of the ECHR and how it would be enforced. Largely at the insistence of the United Kingdom government, the jurisdiction of the ECtHR and the right of individual petition were initially optional.[10] The ECHR in its present form was substantially drafted in Whitehall by a former senior legal adviser

20th century. Executive detention was introduced in 1915 by delegated legislation (not having been mentioned in the parent legislation: the Defence of the Realm Consolidation Act 1914). Such detention was upheld (with only one dissent: Lord Shaw of Dumfermline) in *R. v Halliday Ex p. Zadig* [1917] A.C. 260. See A. Simpson, *In the Highest Degree Odious: Detention Without Trial in Wartime Britain* (1994); K. Ewing and C. Gearty, *The Struggle for Civil Liberties: Political Freedom and the Rule of Law in Britain, 1914–1945* (2000); D. Foxton, "*R. v Halliday ex parte Zadig* in Retrospect" (2003) 119 L.Q.R. 455.

[6] *R. v Secretary of State for the Home Department Ex p. Brind* [1991] 1 A.C. 690 at 748, 761–762.

[7] The Declaration was given legal content by the International Covenant on Civil and Political Rights and the International Covenant on Economic, Social and Cultural Rights (1966) (Cmnd 6702); see Lord Steyn, "Human Rights: The Legacy of Mrs. Roosevelt" [2002] P.L. 473.

[8] The founding members were Belgium, Denmark, France, Ireland, Italy, Luxembourg, the Netherlands, Norway, Sweden and the UK.

[9] The ECHR required to be ratified by 10 members before it entered into force. The UK was the first State Party to do so in March 1951.

[10] Discussed in Simpson, *Human Rights*, pp.655–65 and 523–525.

to the Home Office and contained 15 Articles.[11] However, three of those (the rights to property, education and free and secret elections) were not considered compatible with the policy of the UK government at the time which was committed to the widespread nationalisation of industry, the abolition of fee-paying schools and maintenance of often undemocratic forms of government in parts of the Commonwealth (to which the application of the ECHR was to be extended). For this reason, the ECHR initially contained 12 Articles and the other three were hived off into the First Protocol.[12]

The institutional structure of the Council of Europe was established at **13–006** Strasbourg and was threefold: the Committee of Ministers, the European Commission on Human Rights and the ECtHR.[13] However, the increasing popularity of petitioning Strasbourg and the expansion of the Council of Europe (to some 46 members in 2007) created an unacceptable back log of cases. The response was to streamline the procedure by eliminating the role of the Commission and replacing it with a single full-time Court.[14] The ECtHR now comes in four incarnations: the Plenary Court, Committees, Chambers and the Grand Chamber. The Plenary Court does not decide cases, but has overall procedural control in adopting rules of the ECtHR and setting up Chambers and electing their Presidents.[15] To hear cases, the ECtHR may sit in a Committee of three judges, in Chambers of seven or in a Grand Chamber of 17 judges.[16] The judge from the State Party concerned is always a member of the Chamber or Grand Chamber. Upon the introduction of these reforms in 1998, the right of individual petition and the acceptance of the jurisdiction of the ECtHR were made compulsory.

[11] G. Marston, "The United Kingdom's Part in the Preparation of the European Convention on Human Rights, 1950" (1993) 42 I.C.L.Q. 796; Lord Lester, "UK Acceptance of the Strasbourg Jurisdiction: What Really Went on in Whitehall in 1965" [1998] P.L. 237; E. Wicks, "The United Kingdom Government's Perception of the ECHR at the Time of Entry" [2000] P.L. 438.

[12] Simpson, *Human Rights*, Ch.15.

[13] In 1990 the Council of Europe set up another body, the Commission for Democracy Through Law (the Venice Commission), to assist the countries of the former Soviet Union with their new democratic constitutions, institutions of democracy and the rule of law.

[14] The new procedure is set out in Protocol 11 to the ECHR which came into force on November 1, 1998. The Commission in fact continued to function until October 31, 1999 to deal with cases which had already been declared admissible. The role of the Committee of Ministers was also limited to supervising the execution of judgments (Art.46(2)): P. Leach, "The Effectiveness of the Committee of Ministers in Supervising the Enforcement of Judgments of the European Court of Human Rights" [2006] P.L. 443. In light of the continued backlog of cases, Protocol 14 was opened for signature in May 2004. Protocol 14 introduces three new mechanisms for limiting the ECtHR's caseload: permitting single judges to determine the admissibility of unmeritorious cases; introducing a new admissibility criterion that the applicant has suffered significant disadvantage; and introducing new measures to deal with repetitive cases: S. Greer, "Reforming the European Convention on Human Rights: towards Protocol 14" [2003] P.L. 663; and Lord Woolf, *Review of the Working Methods of the European Court of Human Rights* (2005).

[15] ECHR Art.26.

[16] ECHR Art.27; A. Mowbray, "An Examination of the Work of the Grand Chamber of the European Court of Human Rights" [2007] P.L. 507.

13–007   There are two mechanisms provided by the ECHR for its enforcement: complaints brought by other State Parties and individual petition.[17] Inter-state complaints have been very rare although some of them have proved to be highly significant.[18] Individual petitions are much more common and it is these which have seen the greatest growth: from 138 in 1955 to over 45,000 in 2005.[19] Article 34, in fact, confers standing not just on individuals, but also non-governmental organisations and groups of individuals.[20] The right to freedom of association (Art.11) can as easily be violated against a trade union as against an individual. However, certain other Convention rights can only be enforced by natural persons: the rights not to be subject to degrading treatment and punishment (Art.3), to freedom of conscience (Art.9), and to education (Art.2 of the First Protocol).[21] However, unlike in domestic judicial review, there is no concept of the pure public interest application and individuals are required to demonstrate that they are (or may be) the victim of the any alleged violation.[22]

THE EUROPEAN CONVENTION ON HUMAN RIGHTS

13–008   Before we turn to examine how the United Kingdom has given effect to the ECHR by the HRA, it is necessary to understand something of how the ECHR operates as an international legal instrument.[23]

13–009   The ECHR protects the following rights: to life (Art.2), to be free from inhuman and degrading treatment or punishment (Art.3), to be free from slavery and forced labour (Art.4), to liberty and security of the person

---

[17] ECHR Arts 33 and 34 respectively. The UK delayed accepting the right of individual petition until it was thought too late for the Burmah Oil Company to impugn the War Damage Act 1965 (which retrospectively deprived the company of its legal victory in *Burmah Oil Co v Lord Advocate* [1965] A.C. 75).

[18] See e.g. the case brought by the Republic of Ireland against the UK relating to alleged violations of Art.3 in the treatment of terrorist suspects in Northern Ireland (*Ireland v UK* (1978) 2 E.H.R.R. 25). Cyprus has brought a series of cases against Turkey relating to the situation in Northern Cyprus. The very first case brought under the ECHR in 1956 was by Greece against the UK and concerned action taken to suppress an insurrection in the then Crown Colony of Cyprus (Simpson, *Human Rights*, Chs 18–19).

[19] Of the applications pending before the ECtHR in 2006, some 20% are against Russia, 12% concern Romania and 10% are against Turkey. The number of judgments delivered by the ECtHR has also increased dramatically: from 56 in 1995 to 1,560 in 2006. The following eight States accounted for 70% of these judgments (in descending order): Turkey, Slovenia, Ukraine, Poland, Italy, Russia, France and Romania. The ECtHR produces an informative annual survey of its activities which is available on its website *http://www.echr.coe.int/*.

[20] *Air Canada v UK* (1995) 20 E.H.R.R. 150 involved a non-European based corporate entity complaining of a breach of Art.6.

[21] P. Van Dijk, F. van Hoof, A. van Rijn and L. Zwaak, *Theory and Practice of the European Convention on Human Rights*, 4th edn (2006), para.1.13.2.

[22] See 2–042.

[23] See further Van Dijk et al. (2006); C. Ovey and R. White, *Jacobs and White: The European Convention on Human Rights*, 4th edn (2006); K. Starmer, *European Human Rights Law*, 2nd edn (2007).

(Art.5), to a fair trial (Art.6), to be free from retrospective criminal legislation (Art.7), to respect for one's private and family life, home and correspondence (Art.8), to freedom of thought, conscience and religion (Art.9), to freedom of expression (Art.10), to freedom of assembly and peaceful association (Art.11), and to freedom to marry and found a family (Art.12). The First Protocol contains the right to the enjoyment of possessions (Art.1), the right to education (Art.2) and the right to free elections (Art.3). The Sixth Protocol (Arts 1 and 2) abolishes the death penalty.

The ECHR also contains the right to an effective remedy before a   13–010
national authority for breach of the ECHR (Art.13). Article 13 is therefore a further illustration of the general principle that national authorities bear the primary responsibility for implementing and enforcing Convention rights.[24] It is also consistent with the requirement that individuals should exhaust their domestic remedies before petitioning the ECtHR (Art.35(1)). Article 13 is not a free-standing right and must be linked to at least an alleged violation of another Convention right.

The relevant national enforcement need not be judicial in nature but it   13–011
must be sufficiently independent of the body which is challenged and it must be able to provide effective redress. For example, the power of the UK courts to exclude evidence obtained through covert surveillance was held not to be an effective remedy since the court could not address the substance of the complaint that the interference with Art.8 was not in accordance with law or provide that the individual could obtain a suitable remedy for a violation of Art.8.[25] As with other areas of the ECHR, the more serious the interference and the more fundamental the right concerned, the more that is required to comply with Art.13.[26] This gives rise to the question of whether pre-HRA judicial review provided an adequate remedy. In some cases, it has been held to. However, in other cases, the inability of the domestic courts to address the substance of the question of justification (i.e. whether the restriction fulfils a pressing social need and is proportionate) has been found to breach Art.13.[27] Since 2000, such matters are now properly before a domestic court.[28] The ECHR also contains a right not to be discriminated against in the exercise of Convention rights.[29]

In addition to these express rights, the ECtHR has developed implied   13–012
rights in certain limited circumstances. The most striking example is the right of access to the courts which the ECtHR found to be inherent in the right to a fair hearing protected by Art.6(1).[30]

---

[24] *Kudla v Poland* (2002) 35 E.H.R.R. 198, paras 152–155.
[25] *Khan v UK* (2001) 31 E.H.R.R. 1016, para.44. The power to exclude is contained in s.78 of the Police and Criminal Evidence Act 1984.
[26] *Z v UK* (2002) 34 E.H.R.R. 97, paras 109–11 (violations of Arts 2 and 3 may require investigation by the state as well as compensation).
[27] See 11–079
[28] See 13–083.
[29] On Art.14, see 13–089.
[30] *Golder v UK* (1975) 1 E.H.R.R. 524 para.36. On Art.6, see 7–032.

ABSOLUTE, LIMITED AND QUALIFIED RIGHTS

13–013 Convention rights may be grouped in a number of different ways. One distinction is between qualified and unqualified rights.

Unqualified rights

13–014 An example of an unqualified right is provided by Art.3 which states: "No one shall be subjected to torture or to inhuman or degrading treatment or punishment".[31] If the claimant establishes on the balance of probabilities that his Art.3 rights have been interfered with, that is the end of the ECtHR's inquiry and the State is not permitted to seek to justify the interference by reference to overriding State interests. The ECtHR has held that:

> "79. Art.3 enshrines one of the most fundamental values of democratic society . . . The Court is well aware of the immense difficulties faced by States in modern times in protecting their communities from terrorist violence. However, even in these circumstances, the ECHR prohibits in absolute terms torture or inhuman or degrading treatment or punishment, irrespective of the victim's conduct. Unlike most of the substantive clauses of the ECHR and of Protocols Nos. 1 and 4, Art.3 makes no provision for exceptions and no derogation from it is permissible under Art.15 even in the event of a public emergency threatening the life of the nation . . .

> 80. The prohibition provided by Art.3 against ill-treatment is equally absolute in expulsion cases. Thus, whenever substantial grounds have been shown for believing that an individual would face a real risk of being subjected to treatment contrary to Art.3 if removed to another State, the responsibility of the Contracting State to safeguard him or her against such treatment is engaged in the event of expulsion . . . In these circumstances, the activities of the individual in question, however undesirable or dangerous, cannot be a material consideration. . .

> 82. It follows from the above that it is not necessary for the Court to enter into a consideration of the Government's untested, but no doubt bona fide, allegations about the first applicant's terrorist activities and the threat posed by him to national security."[32]

[31] The other unqualified rights are in Arts 2 (right to life), 4 (prohibition on slavery and forced labour), 5 (right to liberty and security), 6 (right to a fair trial), 7 (no punishment without law), 12 (right to marry), 14 (prohibition on discrimination), (the right to education and (Art.2 of the First Protocol), and (the right to free elections) (Art.3 of the First Protocol).
[32] *Chahal v UK* (1996) 23 E.H.R.R. 413. The case concerned a challenge to the Home Secretary's decision to deport Mr Chahal on national security grounds even though he faced the risk of ill-treatment if returned to his native India.

As this passage indicates, Art.3 is an example of an absolute right in the **13–015**
sense that the State cannot derogate from it even in times of emergency.[33]
Other examples of absolute rights are the right to life, the prohibition on
slavery and the ban on punishment without law.[34]

General limitations on Convention rights

However, there are several general limitations on the exercise of Conven- **13–016**
tion rights. Art.16 permits to state to impose restrictions on the political
activities of aliens notwithstanding Arts 10, 11 and 14.[35] Art.18 limits the
restrictions permitted in the ECHR to the purposes for which they have
been prescribed. More importantly, Art.17 provides that: "Nothing in this
Convention may be interpreted as implying for any state, group or person
any right to engage in any activity or perform any act aimed at the
destruction of any of the rights and freedoms set forth herein or at their
limitation to any greater extent than is provided for in the Convention".[36]
On occasion, the ECtHR does not make express reference to Art.17, but
nonetheless qualifies the protection of Convention rights by reference to
the principle it enshrines.[37] The scope of this broad and troublesome
provision is tempered somewhat by the requirement that there be a link
between the right abused and that which the state seeks to limit.[38]

---

[33] The concept of derogation is explained at 13–020.

[34] See 13–059.

[35] This limitation is to be strictly construed (*Piermont v France* (1995) 20 E.H.R.R. 301, paras 59–64). This restriction is likely to become of still less relevance if European citizenship is introduced. The Fourth and Seventh Protocols (neither of which has been ratified by the UK) provide a number of protections for aliens including freedom of movement within a state and freedom to leave it, freedom from collective expulsion and restrictions on individual expulsion. They are described in greater detail in A. Lester and D. Pannick, paras 4.16.3–4, 16.14.

[36] Under this provision, the ECtHR has upheld against a challenge based on Art.10 (freedom of expression) by a defendant fined for placing a poster in the window of his house depicting the World Trade Centre in flames with a prohibition sign across it and the words "Islam out of Britain" (*Norwood v UK* (2005) 40 E.H.R.R. SE111). The ECtHR relied on Art.17 to hold that: "Such a general, vehement attack against a religious group, linking the group as a whole with a grave act of terrorism, is incompatible with the values proclaimed and guaranteed by the ECHR, notably tolerance, social peace and non-discrimination." See also *Jersild v Denmark* (1995) 19 E.H.R.R. 1.

[37] See e.g. *Refah Partisi (The Welfare Party) v Turkey* (2003) 37 E.H.R.R. 1 (rejection of Art.11 (freedom of association) challenge to the decision of the Turkish Constitutional Court to dissolve the political party, Refah, which was committed to the introduction of Sharia contrary to the express commitment to secularism in the Turkish Constitution. The ECtHR subsumed consideration of Art.17 within its analysis of Art.11(2) and stated: "In view of the very clear link between the Convention and democracy, no one must be authorised to rely on the Convention's provisions in order to weaken or destroy the ideals and values of a democratic society. Pluralism and democracy are based on a compromise that requires various concessions by individuals or groups of individuals, who must sometimes agree to limit some of the freedoms they enjoy in order to guarantee greater stability of the country as a whole", para.99). See further *United Communist Party of Turkey v Turkey* (1998) 26 E.H.R.R. 121.

[38] Thus, the Irish government could not rely on Art.17 to limit the Art.5 and 6 rights of members of the IRA where there was no suggestion that the IRA had abused Arts *it* 5 and 6 in the course of its activities (*Lawless v Ireland (No. 3)* (1970) 1 E.H.R.R. 15, para.7).

13–017   The ECtHR has accepted that certain Convention rights can be waived
in certain circumstances. The issue has arisen most often in two contexts:
whether an individual can waive his right to a fair hearing under Art.6 and
whether public authorities can lawfully persuade their employees to waive
certain Convention rights such as freedom of expression and privacy. The
ECtHR has acknowledged that advantages may flow from a waiver for the
individual, but has sought to ensure that the individual is safeguarded by
insisting on a clear and unequivocal waiver that has been entered into in
circumstances where the individual was not under undue pressure to do
so.[39]

13–018   The ECtHR has also developed the concept of implied limitations on
unqualified Convention rights. For example, in relation to the implied right
of access to the Court:

"The Court considers . . . that the right of access to the courts is not
absolute. As this is a right which the Convention sets forth . . . without,
in the narrower sense of the term, defining it, there is room, apart from
the bounds delimiting the very content of any right, for limitations
permitted by implication. . . . The Court and the Commission have cited
examples of regulations and especially of limitations which are to be
found in the national law of states in matters of access to the courts, for
instance regulations relating to minors and persons of unsound mind.
Although it is of a less frequent kind, the restriction complained of by
Golder constitutes a further example of such a limitation."[40]

13–019   The ECtHR still requires that the restriction should pursue a legitimate aim
and that there is a reasonable relationship of proportionality between that
aim and the means used to achieve it.[41]

Derogations

13–020   Article 15(1) defines the circumstances in which Member States may
derogate from certain Convention rights:[42] "In time of war or national
emergency threatening the life of the nation, any High Contracting Party
may take measures derogating from its obligations under this Convention
to the extent strictly required by the exigencies of the situation, provided

[39] *Deweer v Belgium* (1980) 2 E.H.R.R. 439, para.49.
[40] *Golder* (1995) 1 E.H.R.R. 524 para.38. Here, the Home Secretary had introduced a
requirement that prisoners should obtain his permission before consulting a solicitor. On the
facts, the ECtHR held that this restriction did violate the right of access to the court.
[41] Restrictions have been upheld in a number of cases: e.g. the immunity of police
investigations from negligence claims in tort was held to serve the legitimate aim of
maintaining an effective police force and thereby preventing disorder and crime, but the
blanket nature of the immunity was held to breach ECHR rights in *Osman v UK* (1998) 29
E.H.R.R. 245, para.150. The right to vote and stand for election in Art.3 of the First Protocol
has also been held to be subject to implied limitations (*Mathieu-Mohin and Clerfayt v Belgium*
(1987) 10 E.H.R.R. 1, para.52).
[42] As stated above, no derogation is permitted from Arts 2, 3, 4(1) and 7.

that such measures are not inconsistent with its other obligations under international law".[43]

Reservations

The ECHR also permits reservations to the extent set out in Art.57:   13–021

"Any State may, when signing this Convention or when depositing its instrument of ratification, make a reservation in respect of any particular provision of the Convention to the extent that any law then in force in its territory is not in conformity with this provision. Reservations of a general character shall not be permitted under this Art."[44]

Limited rights

Limited Convention rights are those which contain express limitations 13–022 which authorise interferences with the right in certain circumstances. An example is the right to liberty and freedom of the person under Art.5.[45] The permitted limitations on this right are described at 13.070.

Qualified rights

By contrast, Art.10 provides an example of a qualified right since it makes 13–023 provision for interferences to be justified by the State:

"1. Everyone has the right to freedom of expression. This right shall include freedom to hold opinions and to receive and impart information and ideas without interference by public authority and regardless of frontiers. This Article shall not prevent States from requiring the licensing of broadcasting, television or cinema enterprises.

2. The exercise of these freedoms, since it carries with it duties and responsibilities, may be subject to such formalities, conditions, restrictions or penalties as are prescribed by law and are necessary in a democratic society, in the interests of national security, territorial

[43] The UK derogated from the obligation under Art.5(3) to bring arrested or detained persons "promptly before a judge or other officer authorised by law to exercise judicial power" after the detention of terrorist suspects for periods of four to six days in Northern Ireland was found to be in breach of the ECHR (*Brogan v UK* (1988) 11 E.H.R.R. 117, paras 58–62). The ECtHR upheld the UK's derogation in *Brannigan and McBride v UK* (1993) 17 E.H.R.R. 539, paras 58–60. The UK's more recent derogation in response to the threat of terrorism after the 11 September attacks in the USA was held to violate the ECHR by domestic courts in *X v Secretary of State for the Home Department* [2004] UKHL 56; [2005] 2 A.C. 68.
[44] The UK has entered a reservation in relation to the right to education under Art.2 of the First Protocol which provides that "the right of parents to ensure teaching and instruction in conformity with their own religious and philosophical convictions" is subject to the extent to which this is compatible with the provision of efficient instruction and the avoidance of unreasonable public expenditure.
[45] Other examples of limited rights are the prohibition on force labour (Art.4(2) and (3)), the right to marry (Art.12) and to education (Art.2 of the First Protocol).

integrity or public safety, for the prevention of disorder or crime, for the protection of health or morals, for the protection of the reputation or rights of others, for preventing the disclosure of information received in confidence, or for maintaining the authority and impartiality of the judiciary."[46]

13–024 Under Art.10, therefore, a finding of interference does not exhaust the inquiry and States have frequently successfully argued that an interference is nonetheless justified. In order to justify an interference with a qualified Convention right, a State Party has to demonstrate on the balance of probabilities that it has acted in a manner which is prescribed by law, for one of the reasons identified as legitimate in the relevant Article and that the interference was necessary in a democratic society.[47]

Positive obligations

13–025 Article 1 requires the high contracting parties to secure Convention rights to everyone within their jurisdiction. There is no requirement that the victim should be a national of the relevant State or indeed of any Contracting State to the ECHR. The State's responsibilities may also extend to areas of foreign states where it exercises effective control as a consequence of lawful or unlawful military action.[48] By Art.56(1) and by declaration, the United Kingdom has extended its protection of Convention rights to those non-self-governing territories which belong to the Commonwealth. Article 1 has been held to contain positive obligations on the State Parties which can lead to liability even where the act which gave rise to the violation was performed by a private party.[49] Other manifestations of the State's obligation to provide positive protection for Conven-

---

[46] The other qualified rights are in Arts 8 (right to private and family life), 9 (right to freedom of thought, conscience and religion), 11 (freedom of assembly and association) and the right to the enjoyment of possessions (Art.1 of the First Protocol).

[47] See 13–079; other examples of qualified rights are the right to private life (Art.8), the right to manifest one's religious belief (Art.9), freedom of assembly and association (Art.11) and the right to property (Art.1 of the First Protocol).

[48] *Loizidou v Turkey* (1995) 20 E.H.R.R. 99, para.62 (in which Turkey was found to be responsible for Northern Cyprus which it occupied). On the territorial reach of the HRA, Ch.3.

[49] For example, the State cannot avoid its obligations to protect school pupils from inhuman and degrading treatment and to protect their privacy by arguing that the disciplinary regime in private, fee-paying schools is a matter for the school and does not engage the State's ECHR obligations (*Costello-Roberts v UK* (1993) 19 E.H.R.R. 112, paras 26–28). In fact, there was found to be no violation of Arts 3 and 8 in this case by the headmaster's administration of three blows with a slipper on a pupil's clothed buttocks. The limits of the State's liability for private acts is illustrated by *Appleby v UK* (2003) 37 E.H.R.R. 783, paras 41–50 in which the ECtHR rejected the claim that a ban on the distribution of leaflets in a privately owned shopping mall engaged the State's obligation to protect Art.10. The ECtHR emphasised the need to balance the competing rights of the owners of the mall under Art.1 of the First Protocol and the fact that there remained other outlets for the claimant's message. See further, A. Mowbray, *The Development of Positive Obligations under the European Convention on Human Rights by the European Court of Human Rights* (2004); S. Fredman, "Human Rights Transformed: Positive Duties and Positive Rights" [2006] P.L. 498.

tion rights include the duty to change the law or administrative practice or to provide financial assistance to protect Convention rights.[50]

Interpreting the ECHR

One of the most important characteristics of the application of the ECHR   **13–026**
is the doctrine of the margin of appreciation.[51] In essence, this doctrine permits the ECtHR to accord some latitude to the State in how Convention rights are protected. This reflects the fact that the ECtHR's role is subsidiary to that of the States in ensuring the protection of Convention rights. The doctrine is most often invoked in fields where there is no consensus across the Council of Europe about how a matter should be addressed or where a matter lends itself to having local circumstances taken into account. In the context of an obscenity prosecution and freedom of expression, the ECtHR has stated:

> "[I]t is not possible to find in the domestic law of the various Contracting States a uniform European conception of morals. The view taken by their respective laws of the requirements of morals varies from time to time and from place to place, especially in our era which is characterised by a rapid and far-reaching evolution of opinions on the subject. By reason of their direct and continuous contact with the vital forces of their countries, State authorities are in principle in a better position than the international judge to give an opinion on the exact content of these requirements as well as on the 'necessity' of a 'restriction' or 'penalty' intended to meet them".[52]

The doctrine of the margin of appreciation is not confined to cases arising under Art.10.[53]

The ECtHR adopts a number of additional principles when interpreting   **13–027**
Convention rights. As an international treaty, it is accepted that the ECHR should be interpreted in accordance with the general principles of international law as set out in the Vienna Convention on the Law of Treaties 1969. The overriding principle established by the Vienna Convention is

---

[50] *Gaskin v UK* (1989) 12 E.H.R.R. 36, para.49 (the UK was required to amend the administrative practice which prevented transsexuals from altering their gender on their birth certificates in order to protect the right to private life) and *Steel and Morris v UK* (2005) 41 E.H.R.R. 403, paras 59–72 (the UK had failed to ensure equality of arms as required by Art.6 between the indigent defendants in libel proceedings and the claimant corporation (Macdonalds)).

[51] Its origins are discussed in Simpson, *Human Rights*, p.1003.

[52] The doctrine was first set out by the ECtHR in *Handyside v UK* (1976) 1 E.H.R.R. 737, para.48. The ECtHR has identified the following factors as relevant to the breadth of the margin of appreciation in relation to Art.8: the importance of the individual right at stake, whether there is a consensus across the Council of Europe on how to address the matter, whether the case involves sensitive moral or ethical issues and whether there is a balance between private and public interests (*Evans v UK* (2008) 49 E.H.R.R. 21 (para.77).

[53] For the application of a margin of discretion under the HRA, see 11–014.

that treaties should be interpreted in good faith in accordance with the ordinary meaning to be given to the terms of the document in their context and in light of the treaty's object and purpose.[54] The ECtHR may also have regard to other international legal instruments in interpreting the Convention.[55]

13–028   An example of the ECtHR's contextual approach is its dynamic interpretation of the ECHR. The ECHR is to be read as a living instrument and its interpretation can therefore change over time to keep pace with changes in the approach to social issues within the Contracting States.[56] A further principle is that of effectiveness. This principle is intended to ensure that practical protection is provided for Convention rights and not safeguards which are merely theoretical or illusory.[57] The final general characteristic of the interpretation of the ECHR is that the Strasbourg court adopts an autonomous definition of the concepts which appear in it.[58]

13–029   The Council of Europe has adopted a total of 14 Protocols. Of these, Protocols 1, 4, 6, 7, 12 and 13 added further rights or liberties to those guaranteed in the main body of the ECHR. The United Kingdom has ratified the First Protocol[59] and the Sixth Protocol (which abolishes death penalty in most circumstances) and, more recently, the Thirteenth (which abolished it in all circumstances). The Fourth Protocol is described above.[60] The Seventh Protocol provides additional rights in criminal cases: to review of a criminal conviction or sentence and to compensation after a

[54] Art.31(1) of the Vienna Convention 1980, Cmnd 7964.
[55] For example in *T and V v UK* (2000) 30 E.H.R.R. 121, para.44, the ECtHR relied on the United Nations Convention on the Rights of the Child in determining the scope of the Art.6 rights of children accused of murder.
[56] The treatment of transsexuals under the ECHR provides an excellent example. The ECtHR held in a series of cases up to 1986 that the state did not breach the right to respect for private life in failing to recognise the individual's change of gender on the birth registration system (*Rees v UK* (1986) 9 E.H.R.R. 56, paras 42–3). However, by 2002, the ECtHR changed its mind on this issue after taking account of "the clear and uncontested evidence of a continuing international trend in favour not only of increased social acceptance of transsexuals but of legal recognition of the new sexual identity of post-operative transsexuals". *Goodwin v UK* (2002) 35 E.H.R.R. 18, para.85. The HL applied this decision in the domestic context in *Bellinger v Bellinger* [2003] UKHL 21; [2003] 2 A.C. 467 in which it granted a declaration of incompatibility in relation to the Matrimonial Causes Act 1973 which made no provision for the recognition of gender reassignment (at [68]–[70], Lord Hope). The violation was remedied by the Gender Recognition Act 2004.
[57] For example Art.6(1) was found to contain a right to civil legal aid in *Airey v Ireland* (1979) 2 E.H.R.R. 305, paras 26–28. Mrs Airey could not afford a lawyer and required a judicial decree of separation. The effective protection of her right of access to the courts required that she be provided with public funding in the circumstances. *Steel and Morris* (2005) 41 E.H.R.R. 403.
[58] For example the concepts of "civil rights and obligations" or "criminal charge" in Art.6 and of "possessions" in Art.1 of the First Protocol are entirely independent of the meanings which may be attached to them in domestic law (*Engel v Netherlands* (1976) 1 E.H.R.R. 647, para.82: domestic classification of proceedings as civil is no more than a starting point for the ECtHR in determining whether the matter relates to a criminal charge). On the autonomous definition of possessions, see *Tre Taktorer Aktiebolag v Sweden* (1989) 13 E.H.R.R. 209, para.53.
[59] See 13–077, 094 and 097.
[60] See n–35.

miscarriage of justice. It also prohibits double jeopardy. The UK Government has indicated that it intends to ratify these provisions. The UK Government has indicated that it does not intend to sign or ratify the Twelfth Protocol on the ground that it is "too general and open-ended".[61]

THE HUMAN RIGHTS ACT 1998[62]

The campaign for the incorporation of the ECHR into domestic law has a   13–030
long history.[63] It bore fruit with the election of the Labour government on May 1, 1997 which had committed itself to incorporation. In October of the same year, a White Paper, *Rights Brought Home: The Human Rights Bill*, was produced together with the draft Bill.[64] The HRA was passed in 1998 and entered into force on October 2, 2000.[65] The Long Title to the HRA states that it is designed to "give further effect to" Convention rights.[66] Convention rights for the purposes of the HRA are those set out in Arts 2–12 and 14 of the ECHR, Arts 1 to 3 of the First Protocol and Arts 1 and 2 of the Sixth Protocol.[67]

Constitutional status of the HRA

The HRA is not an entrenched provision in the sense that it is not   13–031
protected substantively or procedurally from express amendment or repeal. Indeed, as explained below, Parliament has provided that its sovereignty is preserved so that it can legislate inconsistently with Convention rights.[68]

---

[61] *Hansard*, HL, Vol.617, col.WA37, October 11, 2000.
[62] On the HRA generally: Lester and Pannick (2004), R. Clayton and H. Tomlinson, *Human Rights Law* (2000); S. Grosz, J. Beatson and P. Duffy, *Human Rights: the 1998 Act and the European Convention* (2000); J. Wadham, H. Mountfield, A. Edmundson and C. Gallagher, *Blackstone's Guide to the Human Rights Act 1998*, 4th edn (2007).
[63] The campaign is described by one of its principal participants (Lord Lester of Herne Hill) in Lester and Pannick (2004), paras 1.34–1.44. For many years, the campaign ran with a parallel one for a domestic Bill of Rights as either a free-standing document or as part of a written constitution. This issue has continued to be debated since the HRA:see 13–102.
[64] Cm. 3782.
[65] The delay was substantially in order to ensure that there was sufficient time to train the judges and other who would have to apply the HRA in Convention principles.
[66] Lord Irvine of Lairg L.C. explained this in Parliament: the HRA "does not create new human rights or take any existing human rights away. It provides better and easier access to rights which already exist" (*Hansard*, HL, col.755, February 5, 1998).
[67] HRA s.1(1). Convention rights take effect subject to any reservation that the UK has made to the Convention or any derogation that it has made or may make from Convention rights (HRA ss.14, 15).
[68] Some have questioned whether the HRA actually incorporates the ECHR at all: G. Marshall, "Patriating Rights—With Reservations: The Human Rights Act 1998" in J. Beatson, C. Forsyth and I. Hare (eds), *Constitutional Reform in the United Kingdom: Practice and Principles* (1998), p.73. The HRA is weaker than an ordinary Act of Parliament in that it does not impliedly repeal earlier inconsistent legislation. Lord Hoffmann described it as "misleading" to refer to the HRA as incorporating Convention rights: the HRA creates domestic rights in the same terms as those contained in the Convention, but they are domestic rights, not international rights (*In re McKerr* [2004] UKHL 12; [2004] 1 W.L.R. 807 at [63]).

However, it has also been argued that the HRA has a constitutional status.[69] It certainly marks a shift in both practice and expectations by making it possible for courts to adjudicate upon the compatibility of legislation with Convention Rights. In addition, the requirement that all legislation whenever passed must be read and given effect so far as possible in a way consistent with Convention rights does modify the doctrine of implied repeal as far as the HRA is concerned. Thus a later Act of Parliament will not be read as impliedly repealing any Convention rights.[70]

The omission of Arts 1 and 13

13–032 Parliament did not include Arts 1 (obligation to respect human rights) and 13 (right to an effective remedy) in the list of incorporated Convention rights. The ostensible justification was that this was unnecessary since the HRA itself was securing Convention rights and providing adequate domestic remedies. Whatever the merits of that argument, the consequences of Parliament's failure have been much mitigated by judicial decision:

> "The domestic counterpart to Art.13 is sections 7 and 8 of the Human Rights Act, read in conjunction with section 6. This domestic counterpart to Art.13 takes a different form from Art.13 itself. Unlike Art.13, which declares a right ("Everyone whose rights . . . are violated shall have an effective remedy"), sections 7 and 8 provide a remedy. Art.13 guarantees the availability at the national level of an effective remedy to enforce the substance of Convention rights. Sections 7 and 8 seek to provide that remedy in this country. The object of these sections is to provide in English law the very remedy Art.13 declares is the entitlement of everyone whose rights are violated."[71]

13–033 As stated above, judicial review will generally provide adequate protection for Convention rights since the enactment of the HRA. The ECtHR has also acknowledged that the Home Office's general practice of not seeking to enforce a decision in relation to which permission to seek judicial review has been granted does provide sufficient protection despite the difficulties

---

[69] *Thoburn v City of Sunderland* [2002] EWHC 195 (Admin); [2003] 1 Q.B. 151 at [62] (Laws L.J. described the HRA as falling into the category of constitutional measures along with, for example, Magna Carta, the Act of Union 1706 and the European Communities Act on the ground that they condition the relationship between the individual and the State in a general, overarching manner or enlarge or diminish the scope of fundamental rights). See also J. Jowell, "Parliamentary Sovereignty under the New Constitutional Hypothesis" [2006] P.L. 562.
[70] *Thoburn* [2002] EWHC 195 (Admin), [2003] 1 Q.B. 151.
[71] *Re S (Children) (Care Order: Implementation of Care Plan)* [2002] UKHL 10; [2002] 2 A.C. 291 at [61] (Lord Nicholls of Birkenhead).

of obtaining interim relief against the Crown.[72] Further, the discretionary nature of judicial review remedies does not breach Art.13.[73]

The authority of Strasbourg decisions

In interpreting Convention rights, domestic courts are required to "take **13–034** into account" (but not to follow) any relevant decision of the Strasbourg organs.[74] This gives rise to two interesting questions. First, when would it be appropriate for a domestic court to depart from the Strasbourg jurisprudence? More particularly, is it only possible for the domestic court to do so where it adopts a more "protective" interpretation of the relevant right than Strasbourg? Secondly, may a domestic court refuse to give effect to domestic authority which would normally be binding upon it where there is conflicting Strasbourg jurisprudence? These questions are addressed below. So far, United Kingdom courts have identified two situations where it may be appropriate to depart from the Strasbourg jurisprudence. The first is where the domestic court is unable to identify a clear and constant line of authority.[75] The second arises where the ECtHR has reached an erroneous view on a matter particularly within the knowledge of the domestic court.[76] The scope of these exceptions to the general rule (and whether they are the only ones) remains uncertain.

---

[72] *Soering v UK* (1989) 11 E.H.R.R. 433, para.123.
[73] *Vilvarajah v UK* (1991) 14 E.H.R.R. 248, para.126. One matter which is not satisfactorily resolved concerns the status of Art.13 in relation to primary domestic legislation which violates Convention rights. Art.13 has never been held to require that the Convention itself be incorporated into domestic law and does not require that primary legislation which requires a particular result be set aside. (The answer is different if the domestic legislation is merely facilitative (*Peck v UK* (2003) 36 E.H.R.R. 719, para.101.) However, this result appears to be inconsistent with post-HRA decisions of the ECtHR in which it has held that the declaration of incompatibility does not constitute an effective remedy which needs to be exhausted before an application to Strasbourg could be made (*Hobbs v UK* (App No. 63684/00, June 18, 2002)). The ECtHR based the decision on the fact that the declaration does not bind the parties to the litigation and does not require the Minister to introduce amending legislation.
[74] HRA s.2(1). As a result of the procedural reforms described at 13–006, this is likely to mean principally decisions of the ECtHR in future.
[75] See e.g *N v Secretary of State for the Home Department* [2005] UKHL 31; [2005] 2 A.C. 296 (concerning) (Art.3 and the interpretation of the ECtHR's earlier ruling in *D v UK* (1997) 24 E.H.R.R. 425). In the very exceptional circumstances of that case, it was found to be a breach of Art.3 to expel D to St Kitts where the treatment available for his HIV/AIDS was very limited. Since D, the ECtHR had sought to limit the effect of this decision but without establishing clear principles distinguishing the case from others. Lord Nicholls described the doctrine as "not in an altogether satisfactory state" ([11]), but held that D should not be extended further. Lord Hope of Craighead at [26]–[50] and Lord Brown at [78]–[94] carried out extensive reviews of the ECtHR jurisprudence without being able to identify any clear principles. The HL therefore felt constrained to reject the application in *N* on the basis that N's advanced HIV/AIDS did not prevent her compulsory return to Uganda despite the prospect that her life expectancy would be reduced to a year or two in the absence of the treatment she had received since arriving in the UK.
[76] The HL felt able to depart from a decision of the ECtHR in *R. v Spear* [2002] UKHL 31; [2003] 1 A.C. 734 (an Art.6 challenge to the independence and impartiality of the junior officers who sit on courts-martial). In that case, Lord Bingham of Cornhill suggested that in the earlier case of *Morris v UK* (2002) 34 E.H.R.R. 1253, the ECtHR had "not receive[d] all

13-035   As a matter of general principle, though, domestic courts should not
expand the scope of Convention rights beyond their interpretation in
Strasbourg. This obligation is said to flow from the fact that the ECHR is
an international instrument and its authoritative interpretation should be
consistent throughout the countries covered by it. Since the domestic court
is also bound by s.6 of the HRA to act consistently with Convention rights,
there should be no departure which reduces the scope of protection for
Convention rights either.[77] This is consistent with other judicial statements
that the purpose of the HRA was not to enlarge the Convention rights or
remedies of those in the UK, but to enable those rights and remedies to be
asserted and enforced by the domestic courts and not only by recourse to
Strasbourg.[78]

13-036   The answer to the second question (whether the HRA has had an impact
on the doctrine of precedent) has been clearly answered in the negative. In
the case of a conflict between binding domestic authority and Strasbourg
jurisprudence, the United Kingdom court should follow the domestic
authority and expedite an appeal rather than following the Strasbourg
jurisprudence.[79]

Giving effect to Convention rights

13-037 The HRA seeks to give further effect to Convention rights through four
principal mechanisms which are addressed in turn below.

- Public authorities (which include courts and tribunals) are required
  to act in a way which is compatible with Convention rights.[80]

the help which was needed to form a conclusion" and had therefore reached an erroneous
view on a matter particularly within the knowledge of the domestic courts (at [12]). Lord
Rodger expressed a similar view (at [92]). The challenge was rejected.
[77] *R. v Special Adjudicator Ex p. Ullah* [2004] UKHL 26; [2004] 2 A.C. 323 (HL declined to
extend the ECtHR jurisprudence to cover the case where an individual facing expulsion from
the UK sought to rely on potential violations of his Art.9 right to freedom of thought,
conscience and religion). The ECtHR has previously held that individuals may only rely on
alleged breaches of rights overseas (other than Art.3) in the most exceptional circumstances.
Lord Bingham of Cornhill concluded that the domestic court's duty was to keep pace with the
developing doctrine: "no more, but certainly no less" [20]).
[78] *R. (on the application of SB) v Governors of Denbigh High School* [2006] UKHL 15; [2007]
1 A.C. 100 at [29] (Lord Bingham of Cornhill). The case concerned an unsuccessful challenge
to the ban on wearing the jilbab on Art.9 and Art.2 of the First Protocol grounds.
[79] *Kay v Lambeth LBC* [2006] UKHL 10; [2006] 2 A.C. 465 at [33] (Lord Bingham of
Cornhill). This is subject to the most limited exception arising in the circumstances of *D v
East Berkshire Community NHS Trust* [2003] EWCA Civ 1151; [2004] Q.B. 558 where the
CA held that the decision of the HL in *X (Minors) v Bedfordshire County Council* [1995] 2
A.C. 633 could not survive the introduction of the HRA since its policy basis had been
completed removed. *Kay* concerned possession proceedings in domestic courts where the
defendant seeks to raise an argument based on their Art.8 right to respect for their home and/
or family life. Earlier HL authority stated that the court did not need to take account of
Convention rights, but this conclusion appeared to be inconsistent with subsequent ECtHR
case law saying that Art.8 rights would have to be weighed (*Harrow LBC v Qazi* [2003]
UKHL 43; [2004] 1 A.C. 983 and *Connors v UK* (2004) 40 E.H.R.R. 189 respectively).
[80] HRA s.6(1).

- Legislation (whenever passed) is to be interpreted so far as possible in a manner which is consistent with Convention rights.[81]

- Where it is not possible to interpret primary legislation compatibly with a Convention right, the court may make a declaration of incompatibility.[82] The declaration does not affect the result in the individual case or the validity of the primary legislation, but it does trigger a ministerial power to take remedial action to remove the incompatibility through a streamlined legislative process.[83]

- A minister in charge of a Bill before Parliament must make a statement of compatibility to the effect that the Bill is consistent with Convention rights or must explain why he wishes to proceed despite any incompatibility.[84]

Although compatible with the doctrine of parliamentary sovereignty, the HRA is far more than an ordinary Act of Parliament. Lord Hope of Craighead stated: "the incorporation of the European Convention on Human Rights into our domestic law will subject the entire legal system to a fundamental process of review and, where necessary, reform by the judiciary".[85]   13–038

Public authorities

The definitions of "public authority" and "function of a public nature" are examined in Chapter 3.[86] It is important to note the limits on the duty contained in s.6 of the HRA which relate to the preservation of parliamentary sovereignty. First, just as a national court cannot set aside primary legislation, a public authority is not required to act compatibly with Convention rights where primary legislation requires it to act differently or where the authority is acting to give effect to or enforce primary or secondary legislation which cannot be read compatibly with Convention rights.[87] Secondly, an act is defined to include a failure to act, but does not include a failure to introduce in, or lay before, Parliament a proposal for legislation or a failure to make any primary legislation or remedial order.[88]   13–039

---

[81] HRA s.3(1).
[82] HRA s.4.
[83] HRA s.10.
[84] HRA s.19.
[85] *R. v DPP Ex p. Kebilene* [2000] 2 A.C. 326 at 374–375.
[86] See 3–069.
[87] *Aston Cantlow and Wilmcote with Billesley Parochial Church Council v Wallbank* [2003] UKHL 37; [2004] 1 A.C. 546 at [19] (Lord Nicholls of Birkenhead).
[88] HRA s.6(6). On the balancing of rights protection and parliamentary sovereignty, see F. Klug, "The Human Rights Act—A 'Third Way' or 'Third Wave' Bill of Rights" (2001) 4 E.H.R.L.R. 361 and C. Gearty, *Principles of Human Rights Adjudication* (2004).

The duty to interpret legislation compatibly with Convention rights[89]

13-040 The obligation to read and give effect to all legislation in a way which is compatible with Convention rights so far as it is possible to do so applies to all courts and tribunals and in all proceedings whether or not a public authority is a party to the proceedings. This obligation is deliberately stronger than its equivalent in the New Zealand Bill of Rights Act 1990 which was one of the models for the HRA.[90] The obligation has been described as creating a rebuttable presumption in favour of a meaning which is compatible with Convention rights.[91] Moreover, the obligation does not depend on any finding of ambiguity and is retrospective in operation. Lord Steyn has described s.3 as the HRA's "principal remedial measure".[92] The following illustrations reveal the extent of the obligation.

13-041 In *R. v A (No.2)*,[93] the House of Lords had to consider the provisions of the Youth Justice and Criminal Evidence Act 1999 which were introduced drastically to reduce the use of evidence of a complainant's prior sexual history in rape trials. The plain words of s. 41 of the 1999 Act would have led to the exclusion of certain evidence which would prejudice the defendant's right to a fair trial under Art.6 of the ECHR. The House held that this section should be read subject to the implied proviso that evidence or questioning which is required to ensure a fair trial under Art.6 should be admitted.[94]

13-042 Perhaps an even more striking example is provided by the House's decision in *Ghaidan v Goden-Mendoza*.[95] This concerned the interpretation of the 1977 Rent Act's provisions on succession to a protected tenancy. The 1977 Act draws a clear distinction between spouses and those living together as husband and wife on the one hand and other members of the tenant's family on the other. In an earlier decision, the House had decided that same sex partners could not be considered as living together as husband and wife.[96] After the HRA entered into force, Mr Goden-Mendoza alleged

---

[89] On statutory interpretation generally, see 5–020.

[90] M. Taggart, "Tugging on Superman's Cape: Lessons from the Experience with the New Zealand Bill of Rights Act 1990" [1998] P.L. 266. Other comparisons are discussed by S. Kentridge, "Parliamentary Supremacy and the Judiciary under a Bill of Rights: Some Lessons from the Commonwealth" [1997] P.L. 96.

[91] Lord Steyn, "Incorporation and Devolution: A Few Reflections on the Changing Scene" [1998] E.H.R.L.R. 153 at 155. Lord Steyn states that, given the inherent ambiguity of language, the presumption is likely to be a strong one.

[92] *Ghaidan v Goden—Mendoza* [2004] UKHL 30; [2004] 2 A.C. 557 at [39]. Lord Steyn also drew an analogy (at [45]) between s.3 and the obligation under European Community law on national courts, as far as possible, to interpret national legislation in the light of the wording and purpose of directives (on which, see *Marleasing SA v La Comercial Internacional de Alimentación* SA (Case C–106/89) [1990] ECR I–4135 at 4159). See C. Gearty, "Reconciling Parliamentary Democracy and Human Rights" (2002) 118 L.Q.R. 248.

[93] [2001] UKHL 25; [2002] 1 A.C. 45.

[94] Lord Steyn accepted that s.3 required the court to adopt on occasion "an interpretation which linguistically may appear strained" (*R. v A*, [2001] UKHL 25, [2002] 1 A.C. 45 at [44]).

[95] [2004] UKHL 30; [2004] 2 A.C. 557.

[96] *Fitzpatrick v Sterling Housing Association Ltd* [2001] 1 A.C. 27.

that the 1977 Act violated his right not to be discriminated against under Art.14 when read with Art.8. Art.8 creates no right to be provided with a home by the State. However, if the State does provide such resources, it must not do so in a way which discriminates contrary to Art.14. The clear distinction on grounds of sexuality in the present case was found not to pursue any legitimate aim: the Rent Act could not be justified as being in support of the traditional family because it extended beyond married couples and to those with no children and no prospect of having any. As such, it could only be based on an assumption that the relationship between heterosexual couples is somehow closer. Lord Nicholls rejected this: "A homosexual couple, as much as a heterosexual couple, share each other's life and make their home together. They have an equivalent relationship. There is no rational or fair ground for distinguishing the one couple from the other in this context".[97] The 1977 Act was therefore read as extending to same sex couples and Mr Goden-Mendoza was entitled to succeed to the tenancy.

However, the obligation has limits.[98] Parliament expressly preserved the **13–043** principle of parliamentary sovereignty in the HRA[99] and the procedures for making a declaration of incompatibility and taking remedial action would be otiose unless there were some matters of incompatibility which could not be interpreted away. Two such limits have been established in the cases: where the proposed interpretation is contrary to a fundamental feature of the legislation or where the impact of the interpretation is not predictable within the judicial process. An example of the first limitation is

[97] *Goden-Mendoza* [2001] UKHL 25, [2002] 1 A.C. 45 at [17]. Lord Nicholls of Birkenhead also rejected the argument that the interpretation should be subject to the discretionary area of judgment. While accepting that housing policy did involve a balancing of social concerns which required some judicial reticence, distinctions drawn on grounds of race, sex or sexual orientation will be scrutinised "with intensity" (at [19]). Lord Millett disagreed forcefully ([at 100]).

[98] For example *Goden-Mendoza* was distinguished in *R. (on the application of Wilkinson) v IRC* [2005] UKHL 30; [2005] 1 W.L.R. 1718 a widower argued that s.262(1) of the Income and Corporation Taxes Act 1988 which conferred a tax allowance on "his widow [where] a married man whose wife is living with him dies" should be read as entitling him to the allowance to avoid gender discrimination contrary to Art.14; HL rejected the argument and distinguished *Goden-Mendoza* on the basis that the presence of the phrase "as his or her wife or husband" was a general concept which gave the court greater interpretative discretion than the more specific words of the 1988 Act, [at 18]). See further: Lord Lester, "The Art of the Possible: Interpreting Statutes under the Human Rights Act" [1998] E.H.R.L.R. 665; Justice Bertha Wilson, "The Making of a Constitution: Approaches to Judicial Interpretation" [1988] P.L. 370; D. Feldman, "Proportionality and The Human Rights Act 1998" in E. Ellis (ed.), *The Principle of Proportionality in the Laws of Europe* (1999); D. Nicol, "Statutory Interpretation and Human Rights after Anderson" [2004] P.L. 273; and the work of A. Kavanagh: "The Role of Parliamentary Intention in Adjudication under the Human Rights Act 1998" (2006) 26 O.J.L.S. 179; "Unlocking the Human Rights Act: The 'Radical' Approach to Section 3(1) Revisited" [2005] E.H.R.L.R. 259; "Statutory Interpretation and Human Rights after Anderson: a more contextual approach" [2004] P.L. 537.

[99] HRA s.3(2)(b) and (c) provide that s.3 does not affect the validity, continuing operation or enforcement of any incompatible primary legislation or subordinate legislation if primary legislation prevents the removal of the incompatibility. Of course, a legislator will be acting in breach of s.6 and therefore ultra vires if he adopts subordinate legislation in breach of Convention rights (unless required by the parent Act).

Re S (Care Order: Implementation of Care Plan).[100] The case concerned final care orders made under the Children Act 1998. The Court of Appeal held that the manner in which the care orders were made and implemented breached the parents' Convention rights under Arts 6(1) and 8 and therefore introduced a new system whereby stages in the implementation of the care plan would be "starred". The local authority's failure to implement the starred aspects of a care plan would trigger the right to come back to court for further directions. The House of Lords overturned this result on the basis that s.3 of the HRA could not be used to produce a result which departed substantially from a fundamental feature of an Act of Parliament. In this case, it was a cardinal principle of the Children Act that the courts would not intervene in the manner in which local authorities discharged their responsibilities under final care orders. In an important passage, Lord Nicholls acknowledged the importance of s.3 and the forthright and uncompromising language in which it is expressed. However, his Lordship emphasised that s.3 is a tool of interpretation and not amendment and the difficulty for the courts lay in determining where the legitimate judicial task of interpretation ended and impermissible amendment began. Lord Nicholls stated that this line is likely to be crossed where the interpretation involves a departure from a fundamental feature of the legislation, especially where, as here, the departure would have practical repercussions which the court is not equipped to evaluate.[101]

13–044   The second limitation is illustrated by *Bellinger v Bellinger*.[102] In this case, the question was whether the parties were lawfully married. It was not disputed that the petitioner was born male, but underwent gender reassignment treatment and had gone through a ceremony of marriage in 1981 with Michael Bellinger. Section 11(c) of the Matrimonial Causes Act 1973, provides that a marriage is void unless the parties are "respectively male and female". The House held that it was unable to resolve this matter through interpretation and so issued a declaration of incompatibility. Lord Nicholls explained the judicial reason for not relying on s.3 of the HRA on the ground that such an interpretation would represent a major change in the law with far-reaching ramifications. His Lordship referred to the extensive research and consultation into the issues which would be required and which went beyond the judicial capacity of enquiry. Such matters were especially suited to determination by Parliament where the legislature had indicated that it intended to introduce comprehensive primary legislation on the subject.[103]

---

[100] [2002] UKHL 10; [2002] 2 A.C. 291.
[101] [2002] UKHL 10; [2001] 2 A.C. 291 at [37]–[40].
[102] [2003] UKHL 21; [2003] 2 A.C. 467.
[103] [2003] UKHL 21; [2003] 2 A.C. 467 at [37]. Lord Nicholls gave examples of the breadth of the issues raised in [38]–[49].

Declaration of incompatibility[104]

Only the higher courts listed in s.4(5) of the HRA have the power to make **13–045** a declaration of incompatibility. These are the House of Lords, the Judicial Committee of the Privy Council, the Courts Martial Appeal Court, the Court of Appeal and the High Court (in England, Wales and Northern Ireland) and the Court of Session and the High Court of Justiciary sitting otherwise than as a trial court (in Scotland). This list indicates the importance of the declaration of incompatibility and the government's reluctance to have criminal trials in the Crown Court or before magistrates disrupted by declarations of incompatibility. These higher courts are under no obligation to make a declaration of incompatibility and have a discretion. This fits with the general discretionary nature of the declaration as a common law remedy (and, indeed, with all other public law remedies). However, it is difficult to envisage circumstances in which a court would find there to be incompatibility and yet would not issue a declaration to that effect.[105]

Again, Parliament was careful to state that the declaration has no effect **13–046** on the validity, continuing operation or enforcement of legislation.[106] The effect of the declaration of incompatibility is therefore to place the onus back on Parliament to decide whether or not to amend the offending provision. Judges have therefore emphasised that in making a declaration of incompatibility, the courts are not in conflict with the will of the legislature, but are simply performing the task which Parliament assigned to them by s.4 of the HRA.[107]

Moreover, a declaration of incompatibility is not even binding on the **13–047** parties to the proceedings in which it is made.[108] A declaration may trigger remedial action under s.10 of the HRA. This is not the only trigger. The other arises where it appears to a Minister or Her Majesty in Council that

---

[104] See Tables 1 and 2 at the end of this Chapter for a summary of the declarations of incompatibility made up to the end of July 2007.

[105] In Parliament, Lord Irvine L.C. gave the example of where there was an alternative remedy by way of statutory appeal which could be used rather than the declaration of incompatibility which would place pressure on Parliament to take remedial action (*Hansard* HL, col.546, November 18, 1997). As David Pannick points out, this explanation does not really make sense since it is only after a declaration has been made that Parliament can take remedial action as envisaged by the Act and such a declaration does not place pressure on Parliament since Parliament has an unreviewable discretion to ignore a declaration (Lester and Pannick (2004) para.2.4.2, fn.3).

[106] HRA s.4(6)(a).

[107] *R. (on the application of Anderson) v Secretary of State for the Home Department* [2002] UKHL 46; [2003] 1 A.C. 837 at [63] (Lord Hutton). In this case, the HL decided that the Home Secretary's power to set the tariff period for mandatory life prisoners was incompatible with the Art.6(1) right to a fair hearing by an independent and impartial tribunal. However, the Minister's power was expressly confirmed by s.29 of the Crime (Sentences) Act 1997 and this could not be read compatibly with the ECHR. Therefore the HL was required to issue a declaration of incompatibility.

[108] HRA s.4(6)(b). This has the effect that damages will not be available against a defendant who has been found to have acted in breach of Convention rights where a declaration has been made.

a provision of UK legislation is incompatible with Convention rights as a result of a decision of the ECtHR involving the UK after the HRA came into force.[109] In either case, or where "he considers that there are compelling reasons" for doing so, the Minister then has a discretion make such amendments by order to the legislation as he considers necessary to remove the incompatibility.[110] As is clear from this, the minister is under no obligation to act on a declaration of incompatibility.[111] Up to the end of July 2007, there have been 24 such declarations, six of which were overturned on appeal.[112] Amending legislation has usually been by way of primary legislation rather than remedial order.

13–048   The HRA gives the Crown the right to intervene in any proceedings where the court is considering making a declaration of incompatibility.[113] The court will give notice to the Crown in any case where it is considering whether or not to make a declaration of incompatibility. In response, the relevant representative of the Crown is entitled to be joined to the proceedings.[114]

Ministerial statement of compatibility

13–049   The requirement that the minister in charge of a Bill in either House of Parliament shall make a statement of compatibility before the second reading of the Bill is designed to ensure that adequate consideration is given to the impact the Bill may have on Convention rights.[115] The statement must be in writing and published in whatever manner the minister considers appropriate.[116] A court is, of course, not bound by any such statement.[117] Equally, there can be no liability under the HRA or

[109] HRA s.10(1)(b).
[110] HRA s.10(2). Schedule 2 to the HRA makes further provision about remedial orders. Remedial orders are thus a fast-track procedure for removing incompatibilities in legislation by means of the affirmative resolution procedure without having to introduce amending primary legislation.
[111] Lord Irvine L.C. indicated that where a Minister has made a statement of compatibility under s.19 and a declaration of incompatibility is subsequently granted "it is hard to see how the Minister could withhold remedial action" ("Keynote Address" in Beatson, Forsyth and Hare, *Constitutional Reform* (1998), p.4).
[112] See Tables 1 and 2 below.
[113] HRA s.5.
[114] HRA s.5(1) and (2).
[115] HRA s.19. This provision is similar to the requirement under s.7 of the New Zealand Bill of Rights Act 1990 to bring to the attention of the House of Representatives any provision of a Bill which appears to be inconsistent with the rights and freedoms contained in the Bill. The statement has been referred to as a "strong spur to the courts to find a means of construing statutes compatibly with the Convention" (Lord Irvine of Lairg, "The Development of Human Rights in Britain under an Incorporated Convention on Human Rights" [1998] P.L. 221, 228).
[116] The Statement will usually be referred to in the Explanatory Notes which have accompanied all Government Bills since 1998. They are available at *http://www.parliament.uk* (Bills) and *http://www.legislation.hmso.gov.uk* (Acts). Since they do not form part of the Act, the Notes are admissible in legal proceedings: *Wilson v First County Trust Ltd (No.2)* [2003] UKHL 40; [2004] 1 A.C. 816 at [64] (Lord Nicholls).
[117] *R. v A* [2001] UKHL 25; [2002] 1 A.C. 45 at [69](Lord Hope).

otherwise arising out of the nature of such a statement.[118] Parliamentary scrutiny is further informed by the work of the Joint Committee on Human Rights.[119]

Standing under the HRA

The HRA repeats the formulation of the test for standing under the ECHR itself. That is, an individual may only rely on the ECHR if he is or would be a victim of the unlawful act in question.[120] Section 7 of the HRA also makes clear that a victim so defined may rely on their Convention rights either in proceedings they institute in the appropriate court or tribunal[121] or in any legal proceedings. This latter formula covers proceedings which are instituted by a public authority where the defendant may bring a collateral challenge to the lawfulness of the statute under which he is charged[122] or where a Convention point is taken on appeal.[123] There is authority from other legal systems that the court may modify the ordinary costs rules in order not to deter individuals from asserting their Convention rights.[124]

13–050

Time limits

Proceedings brought against a public authority under s.7(1)(a) of the HRA must be before the end of the period of one year beginning with the date on which the act complained of took place or for such longer period as the court considers equitable having regard to all the circumstances.[125] This provision is subject to any rule imposing a stricter time limit. Given the shorter and less flexible three-month time limit for judicial review generally, there is a risk of inconsistency.[126]

13–051

Damages

Where the court finds that an act of the public authority is unlawful by virtue of s.6(1) of the HRA, it may grant such relief or remedy (or make such order) within its powers as it considers to be just and equitable.[127]

13–052

---

[118] The making of the statement will fall within the immunity for those "exercising functions in connection with proceedings in Parliament" in s.6(3).

[119] The JCHR was established in 2001 to consider matters relating to human rights generally, proposals for remedial orders and whether attention should be drawn to them. The Committee's reports are available at *http://www.parliament.uk*. See D. Feldman, "The Impact of Human Rights on the UK Legislative Process" (2004) 25 Statute L.R. 91.

[120] See 2–042.

[121] CPR r.7.11 states that proceedings under s.7(1)(a) concerning a judicial act must be brought in the High Court, but that any other claim under this sub-section may be brought in any appropriate court.

[122] On collateral challenge in judicial review proceedings generally, see 4–064.

[123] HRA s.7(6).

[124] See Ch.16.

[125] HRA s.7(5).

[126] See 16–050.

[127] HRA s.8(1).

Only those courts or tribunals which have the power to award damages or order the payment of compensation in civil proceedings may do so.[128] As such, the Crown Court would not be able to award damages for a breach of Convention rights. Further, awards of damages are only to be made where, taking account of all the circumstances, the award is necessary to afford just satisfaction to the person in whose favour it is made.[129] In deciding where to award damages and the amount of such damages, the court must take into account the principles applied by the ECtHR when deciding whether to award compensation under Art.41 ECHR. The principles governing the award of damages under the HRA are considered in Chapter 19.[130]

13–053   Applications for damages in relation to judicial acts must be brought by way of appeal or a claim for judicial review.[131] In any event, no award of damages may be made in relation to a judicial act where the act was done in good faith. The exception is for compensation required by Art.5(5) (the right to compensation for arrest or detention in breach of the ECHR).[132] In relation to compensation under Art.5(5), an award can only be made against the Crown and then only if the responsible Minister is joined to the proceedings.[133]

Safeguarding existing rights

13–054   Section 11 of the HRA makes clear that reliance on a Convention right does not restrict any other right conferred upon an individual under United Kingdom law or his right to bring any proceedings independently of the terms of the HRA.[134]

Special regard to the freedoms of expression and of thought, conscience and religion

13–055   Sections 12 and 13 of the HRA contain provisions which make no significant difference to the scope of Convention rights and were inserted in the course of the parliamentary debates as a result of lobbying by the Press Complaints Commission and various religious bodies.[135] They require the courts to pay particular regard to the rights contained in Arts 10 (freedom of expression) and 9 (freedom of thought, conscience and religion) where the matter before them raises issues under these Articles. It

---

[128] HRA s.8(2).
[129] HRA s.8(3).
[130] See 19–081.
[131] HRA s.9(1). This does not expand the availability of judicial review in relation to court decisions (s.9(2)). On the availability of judicial review of court decisions, see 3–008.
[132] HRA s.9(3).
[133] HRA s.9(4) and (5).
[134] The provision fulfils a similar purpose to Art.53 ECHR.
[135] *Cream Holdings v Banerjee* [2004] UKHL 44; [2005] 1 A.C. 253.

is doubtful whether those sections confer any special preferred status on those rights.

The domestic effect of derogations and reservations

Section 1(2) of the HRA provides that Convention rights should have **13–056** effect subject to any designated derogations or reservations.[136] A designated derogation is defined as any derogation designated for the purposes of the HRA in an order made by the Secretary of State for Justice.[137] A designated reservation means the existing reservation to Art.2 of the First Protocol (the right to education) or any other reservation designated by the Secretary of State by Order.[138] The aim is to ensure that the liability of public authorities under the HRA reflects that of the United Kingdom before the ECtHR. The HRA expressly reserves the right of the Secretary of State to make a fresh designation or reservation order (which may be done in anticipation of a proposed derogation by the United Kingdom).[139] Derogations are intended to be temporary in nature and a designation order will lapse within five years of it being made unless renewed by order under the affirmative resolution procedure.[140] The Secretary of State shall also review any designated reservation on a five-yearly basis.[141]

Territorial and temporal scope of the HRA

One matter not addressed in the HRA is its territorial scope.[142] This matter **13–057** is considered more fully in Chapter 3.[143] Where proceedings are brought against him by a public authority, an individual may rely on Convention rights whenever the act in question took place. Otherwise, an individual may only rely on their Convention rights in relation to an act occurring after October 2, 2000.[144]

---

[136] See 13–020.
[137] HRA s.14(1).
[138] HRA s.15(1).
[139] HRA s.14(4) and (6) and 15(4).
[140] HRA s.16(1) and 20(4).
[141] HRA s.17.
[142] HRA s.22(6) provides that the HRA applies to Northern Ireland. It does not apply to Jersey, Guernsey or the Isle of Man (which have adopted legislation broadly similar to the HRA).
[143] See 3–095.
[144] HRA s.22(4). The most extensive discussion of the (limited) retrospective effect of the HRA is in *Wilson* [2003] UKHL 40; 1 A.C. 616 at [19]–[21], [98]–[99], [160] and [212]. The HL there held that there was no indication that the HRA was intended to have retrospective effect and so the interpretative obligation under s.3 was not relevant to the application of the Consumer Credit Act 1974 to an agreement entered into before the HRA came into force. The question of retrospective effect was stated to be one of degree: the greater the unfairness or effect on vested rights, the clearer an expression of Parliament's intention which will be required. See further, *R. (on the application of Hurst) v London Northern District Coroner* [2007] UKHL 13; [2007] 2 W.L.R. 726 at [53]–[59] (Lord Brown of Eaton-under-Heywood), in which the HL declined to require a coroner to exercise his discretion in accordance with Art.2 in relation to an inquest into a death occurring before the HRA came into force.

THE CONTENT OF CONVENTION RIGHTS UNDER THE HRA

13-058   As stated above, Convention rights under the HRA fall into three groups: absolute, limited and qualified rights. These are addressed in turn.

Absolute rights

13-059   As stated above, absolute rights are those which are not qualified and from which the State cannot derogate. They include the right to life, the right to be free from torture, inhuman and degrading treatment or punishment, the prohibition on slavery and the ban on punishment without law.

The right to life

13-060   Article 2(1) provides that everyone's life shall be protected by law.[145] Despite its status as an absolute right, Art.2(2) provides exceptions where the use of force is strictly necessary in defence of any person from unlawful violence, in order to effect a lawful arrest or prevent escape from lawful detention or in action taken to quell a riot or insurrection. Recent controversy has arisen in relation to the beginning and the end of life. For some time, it appeared clear that Art.2 could not be invoked to protect the interests of a foetus.[146] However, as a result of more recent decisions, it may be that the Strasbourg court will extend some protection to the unborn in certain circumstances.[147] On the other hand, it is now established that Art.2 does not protect the right to die.[148]

13-061   The right to life imposes a number of positive obligations on State Parties which go beyond a requirement to refrain from action which may cause death. These obligations have both substantive and procedural elements. Substantively, the State may be required to take steps to protect an individual from the criminal acts of another private individual.[149] This

---

[145] Art.2(1) provides an exception for the death penalty which is no longer relevant given the Sixth and Thirteenth Protocols.

[146] *Paton v UK* (1981) 3 E.H.R.R. 408, paras 22–23.

[147] In a much criticised decision, the Grand Chamber refused to decide the matter in *Vo v France* (2005) 40 E.H.R.R. 12, para.82. The ECtHR has emphasised that the question of when life begins for the purposes of Art.2 is a matter for domestic law (*Evans v UK* (2006) E.H.R.R. 21, paras 54–56). In *Evans*, the Grand Chamber held that the provisions of the Human Fertilisation and Embryology Act 1990 which required that embryos should be destroyed on withdrawal of consent by either potential parent did not violate Art.2 since the embryos did not have the right to life under domestic law.

[148] In *Pretty v UK* (2002) 35 E.H.R.R. 1, paras 38–40 the ECtHR followed the reasoning of the HL in rejecting a challenge by the victim of a degenerative disease to the Director Public Prosecution's decision not to offer an assurance not to prosecute the victim's husband if he assisted her suicide. The HL decision is *R. (on the application of Pretty) v DPP* [2001] UKHL 61; [2002] 1 A.C. 800.

[149] *Osman v UK* (2000) 29 E.H.R.R. 245, paras 115–116. The CA has held that the state may breach Art.2 by failing to protect vulnerable witnesses from threats by a criminal defendant (*Van Colle v Chief Constable of Hertfordshire Police* [2007] EWCA Civ 325; [2007] 1 W.L.R. 1821 at [71]–[75]).

obligation may extend to the prevention of accidental deaths in some situations.[150] The State may also be required to provide life-sustaining treatment.[151] Procedurally, Art.2 requires that there should be an adequate official investigation into deaths which occur as a result of force used by the State or when an individual is in the State's custody.[152] The state retains a certain degree of flexibility in the nature of the investigation, but it must be independent, permit some participation by the victim's relatives, identify and allow for the punishment of those found to have caused unlawful death and be prompt.[153]

The circumstances in which the State may use lethal force are limited by 13–062 the requirements of strict necessity. Thus, it will not be justified to use lethal force to effect an arrest just because the individual may otherwise escape apprehension if the fugitive poses no threat to life or limb and is not suspected of committing a violent offence.[154] Art.2 also requires the court to examine the circumstances surrounding the use of force and to enquire whether better intelligence or earlier intervention could have averted the situation in which force had to be used.[155] However, Art.2 does not require the court to substitute its judgment for that of the officer on the scene.[156]

The right to be free from torture, inhuman and degrading treatment or punishment

Art.3 provides that no one shall be subjected to torture or to inhuman or 13–063 degrading treatment or punishment. Art.3 is (like Art.2) one of the fundamental provisions of the ECHR and also contains negative and positive obligations and has a procedural aspect. Treatment must attain a minimum level of severity to fall within Art.3 and there is a hierarchy of treatment within the Article. Torture is the most severe form and requires deliberate inhuman treatment causing very serious and cruel suffering. Inhuman treatment causes intense physical and mental suffering. Degrading treatment arouses feelings of fear, anguish and inferiority in the victim

[150] For example, Turkey was held to have breached Art.2 in failing to take adequate measures of waste storage or to provide suitable information to slum dwellers about the dangers they faced in inhabiting a rubbish tip when a landslide caused the death of the applicant's relatives (*Oneryildiz v Turkey* (2005) 41 E.H.R.R. 20, para.75).

[151] *NHS Trust A v M* [2001] Fam 348 at [37] (Dame Elizabeth Butler-Sloss P.), concerning a hospital's obligations towards a patient in a permanent vegetative state.

[152] *R. (on the application of Amin) v Secretary of State for the Home Department* [2003] UKHL 51; [2004] 1 A.C. 653 at [30]–[33] (Lord Bingham of Cornhill) (concerning the liability of a prison for a death in custody caused by a fellow prisoner of known racist tendencies) and *R. (on the application of Middleton) v HM Coroner for Western District of Somerset* [2004] UKHL 10; [2004] 2 A.C. 182 at [30]–[35] (Lord Bingham of Cornhill) (a prisoner who hanged himself while in custody).

[153] *Edwards v UK* (2002) 35 E.H.R.R. 487, paras 69–73.

[154] *Nachova v Bulgaria* (2006) 42 E.H.R.R. 43, paras 93–109.

[155] *McCann v UK* (1995) 21 E.H.R.R. 97, paras 202–214 concerning the deaths of three IRA members who were shot by British soldiers on Gibraltar.

[156] In *Bubbins v UK* (2005) 41 E.H.R.R. 24, paras 138–140, the ECtHR found that there was no violation of Art.2 where a police officer shot dead an individual who had pulled a replica gun.

which are capable to humiliating and debasing the victim and possibly of breaking his physical or moral resistance. Treatment may also be regarded as inhuman or degrading where, to a seriously detrimental extent, it denies the most basic needs of any human being.[157] The court will also consider the duration of any such treatment and the effect on the particular victim (for example, in relation to their age and health).[158] Conditions of detention may be found to constitute degrading treatment.[159] Because of its particular associations, race discrimination may also constitute degrading treatment in some situations.[160]

13–064   The risk of treatment in breach of Art.3 will also engage the State's responsibility where it may occur abroad if an individual is removed from the United Kingdom.[161] Where the source of harm is a non-state actor, the individual will also be required to demonstrate that the foreign state has failed to provide a reasonable level of protection against such harm.[162] A breach of Art.3 may arise from the suffering inherent in certain forms of illness where the treatment afforded by the State exacerbates it.[163] There is also a procedural obligation on the State to carry out an effective official investigation into plausible allegations of a breach of Art.3 by State actors.[164] Domestic courts have drawn on Art.3 in determining whether evidence which may have been obtained by torture should be admissible in legal proceedings.[165]

---

[157] *R. (on the application Limbuela) v Secretary of State for the Home Department* [2005] UKHL 66; [2006] 1 A.C. 396 at [7] (Lord Bingham of Cornhill). In that case, the HL held that statutory provisions which prevented the state from providing welfare benefits to asylum seekers in certain circumstances could breach Art.3. In cases where the individual is reduced to sleeping in the street, lacks nourishment or is unable to maintain basic requirements of hygiene, there is likely to be a violation of Art.3. See S. Fredman, "Human Rights Transformed: Positive Duties and Positive Rights" [2006] P.L. 498.

[158] *Pretty*, [2001] UKHL 61; [2002]1 A.C. 800 at, [52]. *Ireland v UK* [1978] 2 E.H.R.R. 25 para.162 concerned the use of interrogation techniques by the UK security forces against suspected terrorists. The techniques included wall-standing, hooding, subjection to continuous noise and food and sleep deprivation. In the circumstances, these were found to constitute degrading treatment, but not torture. Since the ECHR is a living instrument, a more serious view may be taken of such treatment today. In *Selmouni v France* (2000) 29 E.H.R.R. 403, paras 101–104, the victim was found to have been tortured where he was severely beaten, threatened with a blowtorch and urinated on by police.

[159] For example, the detention of a severely disabled person in extremely cold and insanitary conditions (which carried a risk of physical harm) was held to breach Art.3 in *Price v UK* (2002) 34 E.H.R.R. 53, para.30.

[160] *East African Asians v UK* (1981) 3 E.H.R.R. 76, paras 207–208.

[161] *Chahal* (1996) 23 E.H.R.R. 413 and *D* (1974) 24 E.H.R.R. 425.

[162] *R. (Bagdanavicius) v Secretary of State for the Home Department* [2005] UKHL 38; [2005] 2 A.C. 668 at [22]–[24] (Lord Brown).

[163] *Pretty* [2001] UKHL 61; [2002] 1 A.C. 800 at [52].

[164] *Assenov v Bulgaria* (1999) 28 E.H.R.R. 652, para.95.

[165] In *A v Secretary of State for the Home Department* [2005] UKHL 71; [2006] 2 A.C. 221, the HL decided that the Special Immigration Appeals Commission (which had been established in part to determine appeals of those foreign nationals detained on suspicion of involvement in international terrorism) should exclude evidence where it was established on the balance of probabilities that it had been obtained by torture.

The prohibition on slavery and forced labour

Article 4 expressly prohibits slavery and servitude and any requirement to **13–065** perform forced or compulsory labour. The prohibition on forced labour is more accurately described as a limited right as Art.4(3) excludes the following from the definition of forced or compulsory labour: work required to be done in the ordinary course of detention imposed according to Art.5 or during conditional release from such detention; military service (or service exacted instead of military service in countries where conscientious objection to military service is recognised); service exacted in case of emergency or calamity threatening the life or well-being of a community; and work which forms part of normal civic obligations.[166] Strictly speaking, only the right to be free from slavery or servitude is non-derogable under Art.15.

Perhaps unsurprisingly, there have been very few cases under Art.4. **13–066** Slavery has been defined as "the status or condition of a person over whom any or all of the powers attaching to the right of ownership are exercised".[167] Servitude carries the obligation to provide one's services to another and to live on the other's property without the chance to alter one's condition, but is regarded as less serious since it does not carry the concept of ownership.[168] Forced or compulsory labour arises where work is compelled by the threat of a penalty or is otherwise involuntary.[169]

The ban on punishment without lawful authority

Article 7 contains two prohibitions: first, no one may be found guilty for **13–067** any act or omission which did not constitute a criminal offence under national or international law at the time it was committed; and, secondly, no one shall have a heavier penalty imposed than was applicable at the time the offence was committed.[170] Article 7 is subject to the exception in Art.7(2) which permits the trial and punishment of an individual for an act

---

[166] The last category has been held to cover compulsory fire service (*Schmidt v Germany* (1994) 18 E.H.R.R. 513, para.23) and, domestically, filling in a balance sheet on a tax return (*Murat v Ornoch (Inspector of Taxes)* [2004] EWHC 3123; [2005] S.T.C. 184 at [20]–[21], Moses J.).

[167] Art.1 of the Slavery Convention 1926, cited in *Siliadin v France* [2006] 43 E.H.R.R. 16, para.122. In this case, a child without immigration status was required to work for private individuals without pay. The ECtHR held that this constituted forced labour and servitude, but not slavery.

[168] *Van Droogenbroeck*, Case B 44 (1977) 17 D.R. 59 at 72.

[169] In *Van der Mussele v Belgium* (1983) 6 E.H.R.R. 163, paras 32–34, the ECtHR rejected a claim that the professional requirement on pupil advocates to represent indigent litigants without payment violated the prohibition on forced labour. The ECtHR held that the burden imposed was not disproportionate to the advantages attached to the future exercise of the profession (which the applicant had chosen voluntarily to enter). The HL has rejected the claim that Art.4 protects a right to refuse to participate in military operations on grounds of conscience: *Sepet v Secretary of State for the Home Department* [2003] UKHL 15; [2003] 1 W.L.R. 856 at [21]–[23] (Lord Bingham).

[170] The prohibition on retrospective criminalisation is an established principle of English common law, although the exceptions to this principle may offend Art.7 (*C v DPP* [1996] 1 A.C. 1).

or omission which was criminal according to the general principles of law recognised by civilised nations at the time it was committed.[171]

13–068   Article 7 only applies to criminal proceedings. However, the scope of what is treated as criminal is an autonomous concept and the ECtHR is not bound by the domestic classification of a norm as civil. In deciding whether a penalty is criminal in nature, the ECtHR has regard to whether it was imposed following conviction of a criminal offence, the classification in domestic law, its nature and purpose, the procedures involved in its creation and implementation and its severity.[172] Article 7 only applies to proceedings which result in a conviction or the imposition of a penalty. As such, it does not apply where a prosecution is abandoned or to extradition, preventative detention or to changes in the parole rules.[173] Most cases involve a challenge to the decision to apply the existing criminal law to a new situation rather than new laws which impose retrospective sanctions. The ECtHR has accepted that the laws of the State in question may be expressed with some uncertainty where a concept is very broad or difficult to define and that the law must be permitted to develop. The ECtHR has also upheld convictions for conduct not previously considered to be criminal where it falls within the original concept of the offence.[174] In such cases, the crucial requirement is that the law must be reasonably foreseeable with the help of legal advice, if necessary.[175] The ECtHR also draws a distinction between the imposition of a retrospective penalty and laws on recidivism which may impose a more serious penalty for a later offence on the ground that the offender has committed a similar offence in the past.[176]

Limited rights

13–069   Limited rights contain express exceptions and include the right to liberty and security of the person (Art.5), the prohibition on forced labour (Art.4(2) and (3)), the right to marry (Art.12) and to education (Art.2 of the First Protocol).

---

[171] The so-called Nuremberg exception.

[172] *Welch v UK* (1995) 20 E.H.R.R. 247, paras 27–36. In *Welch*, the ECtHR held that the application of a new law (which involved the forfeiture of the proceeds of crime and potential imprisonment for refusal to pay them over) to the applicant who had been convicted of drug dealing the year before did involve the retrospective imposition of a heavier penalty and breached Art.7. By contrast, the imposition of a requirement that a convicted sex offender should register with the police was found not to be a penalty (*Adamson v UK* (App No.44293/98, January 26, 1999).

[173] *X v Netherlands* (1976) 6 D.R. 184 (extradition); *De Wilde Ooms and Versyp v Belgium* (1971) 1 E.H.R.R. 373, para.87 (preventative detention); and *Hogben v UK* (1986) 46 D.R. 231 (parole rules).

[174] The ECtHR rejected a challenge to the change in the common law (*R. v R.* [1992] 1 A.C. 599) which removed the previous exemption of husbands from criminal prosecution for rape of their wives (*SW v UK* (1995) 21 E.H.R.R. 363). This development of the criminal law was sufficiently foreseeable given the progressive narrowing of the exemption which had occurred over previous years.

[175] paras 33–36.

[176] The ECtHR upheld a 1994 law which doubled the applicant's sentence for a later offence because of his previous conviction for a similar crime some 10 years earlier (*Achour v France* (2007) 45 E.H.R.R. 2, paras 51–55).

The right to liberty and security of the person

Article 5(1) protects the right to liberty and security of the person and only **13–070** permits exceptions which are in accordance with a procedure established by law and in the following circumstances.[177]

(a) The lawful detention after conviction by a competent court. A competent court is one with jurisdiction to determine the case and there must be lawful procedures in place to carry out the detention. However, the court is not concerned with the validity or the fairness of the conviction or the conditions of detention under this Article.

(b) The lawful arrest or detention of a person for non-compliance with the lawful order of a court or in order to secure the fulfilment of any obligation prescribed by law. Under this provision, the obligation or order must be sufficiently clear, the individual must have the opportunity to comply and detention must be the only reasonable way to secure compliance.

(c) The lawful arrest or detention of a person effected for the purpose of bringing him before the competent legal authority on reasonable suspicion of having committed an offence or when it is reasonably considered necessary to prevent his committing an offence or fleeing after having done so. This clearly requires that there should an objective basis for the suspicion and an honest belief will not suffice.

(d) The detention of a minor by lawful order for the purpose of educational supervision or his lawful detention for the purpose of bringing him before the competent legal authority. A minor is a person under the age of 18.

(e) The lawful detention of persons for the prevention of the spreading of infectious diseases, of persons of unsound mind, alcoholics or drug addicts or vagrants. This provision is potentially very broad and the Court has emphasised that detention must be proportionate. As such, it will not be sufficient that a person is simply, say, of unsound mind. It will also be necessary to demonstrate that their condition justifies compulsory detention.[178]

(f) The lawful arrest or detention of a person to prevent his effecting an unauthorised entry into the country or of a person against whom action is being taken with a view to deportation or extradition. The ECtHR has held that detention in a reception centre as part of a process of fast-tracking certain asylum claims was in order to prevent an unauthorized entry even though the individual had

---

[177] See further, J. Murdoch, *Art.5 of the European Convention on Human Rights: The Protection of Liberty and Security of Persons*, 2nd edn. (2002).
[178] *Johnson v UK* (1999) 27 E.H.R.R. 296, paras 59–60.

already been in the country for some time under temporary leave and the detention was not necessary.[179] The court will also not examine the merits of the decision to deport under this provision, but merely require that there be a legal basis for it and a genuine intention to effect deportation.[180]

13–071 The aim of these permitted exceptions is to prevent arbitrary detention. However, Art.5 is only concerned with the deprivation of liberty rather then restrictions on freedom of movement.[181] The dividing line between the two is a question of degree and the court will take into account the type, duration, effects and manner of implementation of the measure in question.[182]

13–072 Article 5 also confers a number of procedural rights on those subject to detention. Art.5(2) provides that everyone who is arrested shall be informed promptly, in a language which he understands, of the reasons for his arrest and of any charge against him. The obvious aim of this right is to permit a challenge to be made to the lawfulness of a detention. Art.5(3) grants everyone arrested or detained in accordance with the provisions of Art.5(1)(c) the right to be brought promptly before a judge or other officer authorised by law to exercise judicial power. This is designed to prevent prolonged detention before charge.[183] Art.5(3) also requires that an individual once charged shall be entitled to trial within a reasonable time or to release on bail.[184] Release may be conditioned by guarantees to appear for trial.

13–073 Article 5(4) provides that everyone who is deprived of his liberty by arrest or detention shall be entitled to take proceedings by which the lawfulness of his detention shall be decided speedily by a court and his release ordered if the detention is not lawful. Although the reference to a court does not necessarily require a traditional judicial body, any

[179] *Saadi v UK* (2007) 44 E.H.R.R. 50, paras 39–47. This decision is presently before the Grand Chamber.
[180] In *Chahal* (1996) 23 E.H.R.R. 413, para.112, the ECtHR held that detention is only justified if deportation proceedings are in progress.
[181] In *R. (on the application of Gillan) v Commissioner of Police of the Metropolis* [2006] UKHL 12; [2006] 2 A.C. 307, the HL held that the stop and search provisions of the Terrorism Act 2000 did not constitute a deprivation of liberty. On the other hand, the system of control orders under the Prevention of Terrorism Act 2005 was found (by a majority) to amount to a deprivation of liberty in *Secretary of State for the Home Department v JJ* [2007] UKHL 45 at [20]–[24] (Lord Bingham). The orders confined the claimants to their one-bedroom flats (which were subject to spot searches by the police) for 18 hours a day, required any visitors to be authorised by the Home Office and restricted them in the remaining six hours of the day to a limited urban area.
[182] *Guzzardi v Italy* (1980) 3 E.H.R.R. 333, paras 91–94. The presence of an informal patient at a mental hospital (*HL v UK (Bournewood)* (2004) 40 E.H.R.R. 761, paras 91–94) was held to be a deprivation of liberty.
[183] *Brogan* (1998) 11 E.H.R.R. 117.
[184] The refusal of bail must be justified by reasons such as preventing absconding, interference with the course of justice, further offending or a risk to public order.

decision-maker must be independent of the executive.[185] What constitutes a speedy determination will depend on the circumstances. A prolonged period of detention will require a process to determine the lawfulness of the detention at reasonable intervals.[186] Art.5(5) entitles everyone who has been the victim of arrest or detention in contravention of Art.5 to an enforceable right to compensation.[187]

The right to a fair hearing

This right is considered in Chapters 6 and 7[188] and Chapter 10.[189]   **13–074**

The right to be free from forced labour

This right is considered at 13–065.   **13–075**

The right to marry and found a family

Article 12 provides that men and women of marriageable age shall have the   **13–076** right to marry and found a family according to the national laws governing the exercise of this right. Art.12 does not concern interferences with the relations between parent and child which are covered by Art.8.[190] Art.12 clearly provides the State with substantial leeway to determine, for example, what is marriageable age and any formalities necessary for a valid marriage.[191] However, restrictions must serve some legitimate State purpose.[192] There is no right to a dissolution of marriage. As regards founding a family, the ECtHR has not accepted that there is a right to adopt or that the failure to provide artificial insemination was a breach of Art.12.[193]

---

[185] *Benjamin and Wilson v UK* (2003) 36 E.H.R.R. 1, para.33. The Mental Health Review Tribunal has been held to be sufficiently independent for Art.5(4) and the Parole Board has not *(R. (a the application of Brooke) v. Parole Board* [2007] EWHC 2036 (Admin)). The use of special advocate procedure was narrowly held to be justified to prevent a prisoner from discovering the source of information about him in *Roberts v Parole Board* [[2005] UKHL 45; [2005] 2 A.C. 738 at [19] (Lord Bingham).

[186] See e.g. *T and V v UK* (1999) 30 E.H.R.R. 121, paras 119–121 concerning the imprisonment of the juvenile murderers of Jamie Bulger and *R. (on the application of MH) v Secretary of State for Health* [2005] UKHL 60; [2006] 1 A.C. 441 at [17] (Baroness Hale) in which the inherent changeability of mental disorders made it essential that reviews of detention should take place at reasonable intervals.

[187] HRA s.9(3) makes a limited exception to the principle that damages are not available against the decision of a court to accommodate this requirement.

[188] See 6–048, 7–119.

[189] See 10–077.

[190] *P, C and S v UK* (2002) 35 E.H.R.R. 31.

[191] In *X v Y (Overseas Same-Sex Relationship)* [2006] EWHC 2022 (Fam) at [55]–[67], Sir Mark Potter P. found no violation of Art.12 in the UK's refusal to recognise a same-sex marriage as a marriage, but to classify it instead as a civil partnership.

[192] The bans on all prisoners *(Hamer v UK* (1982) 4 E.H.R.R. 139, paras 70–74) and transsexuals *(Goodwin,* (2002) 35 E.H.R.R. 18 marrying were found to violate Art.12. A requirement for persons subject to immigration control to obtain a certificate of approval if not marrying in accordance with the rites of the Church of England was found to be a disproportionate means of preventing sham marriages and to be in violation of Art.12 *(Secretary of State for the Home Department v Baiai* [2007] EWCA Civ 478 at [48]–[57] (Buxton LJ).

[193] The latter case was brought by a life prisoner whose wife would be too old to conceive at the earliest date of his release *(Dickson v UK* (2007) 44 E.H.R.R. 21, paras 34–40).

The right to education

13–077 Art.2 of the First Protocol states that no person shall be deprived of the right to education. This Article is unusual in that it protects a social or cultural right, rather than a civil or political right like all the other Convention rights.[194] The right breaks down into the following elements: a right to effective education; a right of access to existing educational institutions; a right to be educated in the (or one of the) national language(s); and a right to obtain official recognition of completed studies.[195] The negative formulation of the right does not require the State to establish or fund education of any particular type. The State also retains its right to insist that children attend school or are adequately taught at home.[196] Although the focus of Art.2 is on primary and secondary education, it has been held to extend to higher education.[197]

13–078 Article 2 also requires the state to respect the right of parents to ensure that their children's education is in conformity with their own religious and philosophical convictions. This does not prevent the State from teaching religious or philosophical matters so long as the instruction is objective, critical and pluralistic and does not constitute indoctrination.[198] The obligation extends beyond the curriculum to organisation and finance and school discipline.[199]

Qualified rights

13–079 As stated above, the qualified Convention rights are contained in Arts 8 (right to private and family life), 9 (right to freedom of thought, conscience and religion), 10 (freedom of expression), 11 (freedom of assembly and association) and the right to the enjoyment of possessions (Art.1 of the First Protocol). Interference with a qualified right may be justified if the public authority can fulfil three conditions. These are: (i) that the limitation is prescribed (or required for Art.8) by law; (ii) that it is done to secure a legitimate aim under the relevant Article; and (iii) that it is necessary in a democratic society, that is, it fulfils a pressing social need and goes no further than is strictly necessary to secure that need. This latter is the principle of proportionality. Since this structure is common to all qualified rights, it is addressed before the individual rights themselves.

---

[194] The UK's reservation to this right is described at 13–021.

[195] *The Belgian Linguistics Case (No. 2)* (1968) 1 E.H.R.R. 252, paras 3–7, 021 and 42.

[196] *Family H v UK* (1984) 37 D.R. 105.

[197] *Sahin v Turkey* (2007) 44 E.H.R.R. 5, paras 134–142.

[198] *Kjeldsen v Denmark* (1976) 1 E.H.R.R. 711, para.54 where the ECtHR rejected a parental objection to sex education.

[199] The ECtHR upheld a parent's objection to corporal punishment in *Campbell and Cosans v UK* (1982) 4 E.H.R.R. 293, para.37. The HL has held that the ban on corporal punishment may interfere with a parental belief in its virtues, but the interference is justified (*R. (Williamson) v Secretary of State for Education and Employment* [2005] UKHL 15; [2005] 2 A.C. 246 at [49]–[52] (Lord Nicholls).

Prescribed by law

The requirement that a limitation is prescribed by law is a fundamental **13–080** aspect of the rule of law or the principle of legality. It has three main elements: that the public authority should be able to point to legal authority for any interference, that the legal authority must be reasonably accessible to the individual and be sufficiently certain that the individual can foresee the likelihood of State intervention.[200] Where there is no legal basis for an interference, the claimant will necessarily succeed under the ECHR.[201] However, such challenges are relatively rare since if there is no domestic law justifying the public authority's actions, the individual will normally have a remedy without relying on their Convention rights. Where a public authority relies on guidance which does not itself have the status of law, such guidance must be adequately supported by statutory authority.[202]

In order to be foreseeable, a limitation must be accessible to the **13–081** individual and be sufficiently clearly expressed that the individual can predict its application with a reasonable degree of certainty. Such a challenge arose in *R. (on the application of Gillan) v Commissioner of Police for the Metropolis* concerning the stop-and-search powers under Pt 5 of the Terrorism Act 2000.[203] This broad new power permits the police to stop and search individuals without any ground in reasonable suspicion that they are terrorists, but merely because they are within a specified area.[204]

---

[200] *Sunday Times v UK* (1979) 2 E.H.R.R. 245, paras 46–53 (where the common law of contempt of court passed the test) and *Malone v UK* (1984) 7 E.H.R.R. 14, paras 68–80 (where the informal system for authorising telephone tapping did not). These requirements were satisfied domestically by the law on official secrets: *R. v Shayler* [2002] UKHL 11; [2003] 1 A.C. 247 at [56] (Lord Hope).

[201] *Halford v UK* (1997) 24 E.H.R.R. 523, paras 61–63.

[202] See e.g. *R. (on the application of Munjaz) v Mersey Care NHS Trust* [2005] UKHL 58; [2006] 2 A.C. 148 at [127] (the dissent of Lord Brown concerning the use of a code of practice to regulate the seclusion of mental patients).

[203] [2006] UKHL 12; [2006] 2 A.C. 307.

[204] There is no requirement to publicise the authorisation and confirmation of the powers. Despite this, the House rejected the challenge based on foreseeability on a number of different bases. Lord Bingham (with whom the other Lords of Appeal agreed) held that there was a sufficiently foreseeable basis in the 2000 Act itself and that publication of the authorisation could defeat the purpose of the legislation (at [35]). Lord Hope held that the interference with Convention rights in stop and search powers was not very great and that the authorisation was therefore adequate in this context ([56]). Lord Bingham of Cornhill did, however, provide the following description of the requirement of legality: "The lawfulness requirement in the Convention addresses supremely important features of the rule of law. The exercise of power by public officials, as it affects members of the public, must be governed by clear and publicly accessible rules of law. The public must not be vulnerable to interference by public officials acting on any personal whim, caprice, malice, predilection or purpose other than that for which the power was conferred. This is what is, in this context, meant by arbitrariness, which is the antithesis of legality. This is the test which any interference with or derogation from a Convention right must meet if a violation is to be avoided" (at [34]).

The legitimate aim

13–082　The existence or otherwise of a legitimate aim is determined by the text of the qualified Convention right in question and not all the lists of legitimate interests in second parts of Arts 8–11 are identical. However, they are generally expressed in broad terms and it is rare for challenges to succeed on the basis that a limitation was not in pursuit of a legitimate aim. The reference to the "rights of others" in these Articles is not limited to Convention rights.[205]

Necessary in a democratic society: proportionality

13–083　The ECtHR has held that the term necessary requires something more than reasonable, desirable or useful, but less than indispensable. The best definition is that it requires that the measure should fulfil a "pressing social need" and a powerful justification is required to limit Convention rights.[206] The ECtHR has also emphasised the link between the terms "necessary" and "democratic society". The characteristics of the latter include pluralism, tolerance and broadmindedness and the test of necessity must be set against this background.[207] The ECtHR then applies the test of proportionality proper.[208] In applying the test of proportionality, the ECtHR will consider whether the interference affects the essence of the right or is more peripheral to it, whether there exist effective safeguards over the interference as a matter of domestic law and whether there is a less restrictive alternative which would achieve the State's legitimate aims but involve less interference with Convention rights. Finally, the ECtHR considers whether the State has advanced relevant and sufficient reasons to justify the interference.[209] We have seen in Chapter 11[210] how our domestic courts apply the concept of proportionality by the standards set out in *R. v Secretary of State for the Home Department Ex p. Daly*[211] and *de Freitas v Permanent Secretary of Ministry of Agriculture, Fisheries, Land and Housing*.[212] In the following paragraphs, we consider the application of this test to the actual scope of qualified Convention rights.

The right to respect for private and family life

13–084　Article 8 protects a number of rights which fall within the broad scope of privacy: the rights to respect for one's private life, family life, one's home and one's correspondence. It is therefore potentially of a very broad nature. The ECtHR has adopted an inclusive definition of it:

---

[205] *VgT Verein Gegen Tierfabriken v Switzerland* (2001) 34 E.H.R.R. 159, paras 59–62.
[206] *Sunday Times*, (1979) 2 E.H.R.R. 245, para.59.
[207] *Lustig-Prean and Beckett v UK* (2000) 29 E.H.R.R. 548, para.80.
[208] *Soering v UK* (1989) 11 E.H.R.R. 433, para.89.
[209] In *Hirst v UK* (2006) 42 E.H.R.R. 41, paras 78–79, the ECtHR found that the UK had failed to provide evidence of any considered debate in the legislature before the imposition of the blanket ban on prisoners voting.
[210] See 11–00.
[211] [2001] UKHL 26; [2001] 2 A.C. 532.
[212] [1999] 1 A.C. 69 at 80 (Lord Clyde).

"As the Court has had previous occasion to remark, the concept of 'private life' is a broad term not susceptible to exhaustive definition. It covers the physical and psychological integrity of a person. It can sometimes embrace aspects of an individual's physical and social identity. Elements such as, for example, gender identification, name and sexual orientation and sexual life fall within the personal sphere protected by Art.8. Art.8 also protects a right to personal development, and the right to establish and develop relationships with other human beings and the outside world. Although no previous case has established as such any right to self-determination as being contained in Art.8 of the ECHR, the Court considers that the notion of personal autonomy is an important principle underlying the interpretation of its guarantees."[213]

Private life has been held to extend to business relationships and environ- **13–085** mental issues such as noise or pollution may give rise to a claim.[214] Article 8 may even provide some protection in what may appear to be public places if the individual has a reasonable expectation of privacy there.[215] Family life is also broadly defined and extends beyond formal relationships and covers de facto couples, illegitimate or adopted children and the extended family.[216] The definition of home is broad, but requires the existence of sufficient and continuous links. There is no right to a choice of a particular home.[217] Correspondence extends beyond more traditional written forms of communication. Article 8 also imposes positive obligations on the State which may give rise to liability arising from the acts of private individuals.[218]

---

[213] *Pretty v UK* (2002) 35 E.H.R.R. 1, para.61.
[214] *Niemietz v Germany* (1993) 16 E.H.R.R. 97, paras 29–33 (a search of a lawyer's offices) and *Hatton v UK* (2002) 34 E.H.R.R. 1, para.107 (noise pollution from night flights over houses). The CA rejected an Art.8 challenge to the hunting ban based on its alleged impact on the use of the claimants' land and ability to make their living from hunting (*R. (on the application of Countryside Alliance) v Attorney General* [2006] EWCA Civ 817; [2007] 1 Q.B. 305 at [100]–[105]). The rules on payments of financial support by non-resident parents do not interfere with Art.8 (*Secretary of State for Work and Pensions v M* [2006] UKHL 11; [2006] 2 A.C. 91 at [85], (Lord Walker).
[215] A public figure may therefore be protected from press intrusion while engaged in everyday activities (such as shopping or fetching their children from school): *Von Hannover v Germany* (2005) 40 E.H.R.R. 1, paras 61–69. Art.8 was breached by the release of CCTV footage taken in the street of a man attempting suicide (*Peck v UK* (2003) 36 E.H.R.R. 41, paras 62–87). See further, M. Tugendhat and I. Christie, *The Law of Privacy and the Media* (2002) and, for a comparative perspective, M. Colvin (ed.), *Developing Key Privacy Rights: The Impact of the Human Rights Act 1998* (2002).
[216] *Kroon v Netherlands* (1994) 19 E.H.R.R. 263, para.30 (de facto relationships) and *Marckx v Belgium* (1979) 2 E.H.R.R. 330, para.31 (illegitimate children). The ECtHR has traditionally been less willing to acknowledge homosexual relationships as constituting family (as opposed to private) life. This may be changing (see *Goodwin*, (2002) 35 E.H.R.R. 18).
[217] *Buckley v UK* (1996) 23 E.H.R.R. 101, para.84.
[218] In *Von Hannover* (2005) 40 E.H.R.R. 1, the state was liable because its law provided insufficient protection from intrusion by the media.

13–086   The breadth of this definition means that most cases are resolved at the second stage of justification. Since domestic law contained no right to privacy before the HRA,[219] Article 8 has been a focus of litigation since 2000.[220] Domestic courts have used Art.8 to develop a right not to be subject to offensive disclosures and to replace the protective jurisdiction of the Family Division over children's right to privacy.[221]

The right to freedom of thought, conscience and religion

13–087   Article 9 protects the right freedom of thought, conscience and religion which includes the right to change one's religion or belief and to manifest those beliefs in worship, teaching, practice and observance either alone or with others and in public or private.[222] Freedom of thought, conscience and religion is a fundamental Convention right and may be regarded as absolute, in contrast to the right to manifest such beliefs which may be subject to legitimate interference. There is no qualitative restriction on which beliefs fall within Art.9. However, the ECtHR has required that a belief must go beyond mere opinions or ideas and achieve a certain level of cogency, seriousness, cohesion and importance.[223] In order to qualify for protection under Art.9, a manifestation must be required by the religion or belief and must relate directly to it (rather than merely being associated with it).[224]

13–088   The existence of an established church does not violate Art.9, but the State's responsibility is generally to hold the ring and permit a variety of religions to be practised. The State should not impose severe disadvantage

---

[219] *Wainwright v Home Office* [2003] UKHL 53; [2004] 2 A.C. 406 (a strip search in breach of the Prison Rules on two visitors gave rise to no cause of action in English law). The ECtHR unsurprisingly found a violation of Art.8 (*Wainwright v UK* (2007) 44 E.H.R.R. 40, paras 46–49).

[220] It has been invoked in relation to decisions to dismiss employees for sexual activity outside the workplace (*X v Y (Unfair Dismissal)* [2004] EWCA Civ 662; [2004] I.C.R. 1634 at [51] (Mummery L.J., no interference since the activity was found to take place in public)) and police retention of DNA evidence after acquittal (*R. (on the application of S) v Chief Constable of South Yorkshire Police* [2004] UKHL 39; [2004] 1 W.L.R. 2196 at [31] (Lord Steyn, no interference with Art.8)).

[221] The model Naomi Campbell's Art.8 rights were violated by photographs of her leaving a meeting of Narcotics Anonymous: *Campbell v MGN Ltd* [2004] UKHL 22; [2004] 2 A.C. 457 at [116]–[118] (Lord Hope) and [149]–[157] (Baroness Hale). N. Moreham, "Privacy in Public Places" [2006] C.L.J. 606. See further, *Re S (A Child)* [2004] UKHL 47; [2005] 1 A.C. 593.

[222] See further, S. Knights, *Freedom of Religion, Minorities and the Law* (2006) and C. Evans, *Freedom of Religion Under the European Convention on Human Rights* (2001).

[223] *Campbell and Cosans* (1982) 4 E.H.R.R. 243. This covers beliefs as diverse as pacifism or veganism. Domestic courts have applied the same approach (*Williamson* [2005] UKHL 15; [2005] 2 A.C. [23]–[24] (Lord Nicholls). The High Court of Australia adopted a similar approach in *Church of the New Faith v Commissioner of Pay-Roll Tax (Victoria)* (1983) 154 C.L.R. 120 at 129–130 and 174. The belief in the right to hunt with hounds does not reach the level of importance to qualify (*R. (on the application of Countryside Alliance) v Attorney General* [2006] EWCA Civ 817; [2007] 1 Q.B. 305 [176]–[179]).

[224] As such, the distribution of leaflets to soldiers encouraging them not to serve in Northern Ireland was an attempt to challenge British policy in that province rather than an expression of pacifist beliefs (*Arrowsmith v UK* (1978) 3 E.H.R.R. 218, para.71).

on the individual in order to encourage support for a particular belief.[225] Restrictions on this right must fulfil the standard criteria for limiting qualified Convention rights and generally require evidence that the State has sought to strike a fair balance between the competing interests.[226]

Freedom of expression

Article 10 protects the right to freedom of expression and the right to hold **13–089** opinions and receive and impart information without interference by a public authority.[227] Freedom of expression is regarded as one of the cornerstones of any democratic society. Expression is broadly defined and includes artistic and commercial expression as well as the political and journalistic.[228] It also protects speech which shocks, offends or disturbs.[229] Article 10 imposes positive obligations on the State.[230]

As regards limitations, the legitimacy of the licensing of broadcasting, **13–090** television and cinema is expressly preserved and Art.10(2) states that the exercise of the right to freedom of expression carries with it duties and responsibilities.[231] The ECtHR is particularly sceptical of prior restraints and criminal sanctions on expression.[232] However, the ECtHR has

---

[225] Requiring a member of parliament to swear on the gospel in order to retain his seat was a breach of Art.9 (*Buscarini v San Marino* (2000) 30 E.H.R.R. 208, paras 34–41). This level of severity was not reached by requiring lower test scores for Catholics than Protestants in order to enter the Northern Ireland Police Service (*Re Parson's Application for Judicial Review* [2004] N.I. 38).

[226] For example between a Muslim teacher's desire for time off to attend Friday prayers and the state's need to organise the school curriculum efficiently (*Ahmed v UK* (1981) 4 E.H.R.R. 126, paras 11–19). Restrictions on wearing headscarves for university students to support the secular nature of the State have been upheld (*Sahin v Turkey*, (2007) 44 E.H.R.R. 5). See further, D. McGoldrick, *Human Rights and Religion: The Islamic Headscarf Debate in Europe* (2006). The domestic cases of *Williamson* and *SB* are described at n.199 and 202. In *SB*, the majority of the HL decided that the school's prohibition on the jilbab was not an interference with SB's Art.9 rights since she could have attended another school in the area which permitted it. Restrictions must, of course, be proportionate and a criminal ban on door-to-door proselytising exceeded the state's margin of appreciation (*Kokkinakis v Greece* (1993) 17 E.H.R.R. 397, paras 47–50).

[227] See further, E. Barendt, *Freedom of Speech*, 2nd edn (2007).

[228] *Wingrove v UK* (1996) 24 E.H.R.R. 1, paras 47–50 (film) and *Barthold v Germany* (1985) 7 E.H.R.R. 383, paras 42–43 (advertising). Political expression is entitled to the highest level of protection. The ECtHR has acknowledged the importance of journalists being able to protect their sources (*Roeman and Schmit v Luxembourg* (App No. 51772/99, February 25, 2003), para.46).

[229] *Lingens v Austria* (1986) 8 E.H.R.R. 407, paras 41–42.

[230] These did not go so far as to require that an individual be given access to a particular forum which was on private property (a shopping centre) where there existed other avenues for such expression (*Appleby v UK* (2003) 37 E.H.R.R. 783, para.47).

[231] The licensing of broadcasting is not therefore subject to Art.10(2), but the ECtHR has held that any interference with broadcasting should be minimal and consistent with the broad aims of Art.10(2) (*Autotronic AG v Switzerland* (1990) 12 E.H.R.R. 485, paras 49–52).

[232] *Observer v UK* (1991) 14 E.H.R.R. 153 (the *Spycatcher* case) and *Varh v Turkey* (App No. 57299/00, April 27, 2006). Domestic courts have upheld criminal restrictions on speech in the Official Secrets Act 1989 (*R. v Shayler* [2002] UKHL 11; [2003] 1 A.C. 247) a ban on a party political broadcast on grounds of offensiveness (*R. (on the application of ProLife Alliance) v British Broadcasting Corporation* [2003] UKHL 23; [2004] 1 A.C. 185 at [12]–[16] (Lord Nicholls), [78]–[81] (Lord Hoffmann), cf. Lord Scott's dissent, at [94]–[100]); and a ban on tobacco advertising (*R. (on the application of British American Tobacco UK Ltd) v Secretary of State for Health* [2004] EWHC 2493; [2005] A.C.D. 27).

provided limited protection for free speech against restrictions on hate speech or holocaust denial.[233]

Freedom of assembly and association

13-091   Article 11 confers the right to freedom of peaceful assembly and to association with others and includes the right to join trade unions for the protection of one's interests. As with Art.10, the ECtHR will require particularly compelling justifications for restrictions on political assemblies. However, the ECtHR is more willing to accept the imposition of conditions rather than complete bans. The right to freedom of association does not necessarily mean that an individual can join a particular trade union[234] and does not extend to the regulatory bodies of liberal professions.[235] The right not to associate is also implicitly protected by Art.11.[236]

13-092   Article 11 also carries positive obligations which may require the State to take steps to ensure that other individuals or groups do not interfere with the right of peaceful assembly by violent counter-demonstrations or to prohibit private employers from imposing financial penalties on employees who belong to a trade union.[237] However, the ECtHR has not gone so far as to protect other trade union activities such as calling a strike, collective bargaining or the right to be consulted.[238]

13-093   Limitations must be justified according to the usual requirements.[239] General bans on organisations or on membership of them will rarely be justified.[240] However, Art.11(2) expressly legitimises the imposition of

---

[233] *Jersild v Denmark* (1995) 19 E.H.R.R. 1 paras 31–37. I. Hare: "Crosses, Crescents and Sacred Cows: Criminalising Incitement to Religious Hatred" [2006] P.L. 521.

[234] The ECtHR upheld a complaint by the union ASLEF that its Art.11 rights had been violated by a UK law which prevented it from excluding a member on the grounds of membership of a political party (in that case, the British National Party) where there was no effect on the individual's livelihood and the union was not a state body (*ASLEF v UK* (2007) 45 E.H.R.R. 34, paras 50–53). Domestic courts upheld the right of the RSPCA to exclude individuals from membership who wished to oppose the Society's position on hunting (*Royal Society for the Prevention of Cruelty to Animals v Attorney General* [2002] 1 W.L.R. 448 at [37] (Lightman J.)).

[235] *Le Compte v Belgium* (1981) 4 E.H.R.R. 1, paras 64–65.

[236] As such, a requirement that all employees should belong to a trade union upon pain of dismissal was a breach (*Young, James and Webster v UK* (1981) 4 E.H.R.R. 38, paras 62–65).

[237] *Plattform "Artze fur das Leben" v Austria* (1988) 13 E.H.R.R. 204, para.32 and *Wilson v UK* (2002) 35 E.H.R.R. 20, paras 47–48 respectively.

[238] *Schmidt v Sweden* (1976) 1 E.H.R.R. 632, paras 35–36.

[239] The ECtHR held a ban on a peaceful demonstration in opposition to a ceremony by surviving members of the SS at a cemetery was in violation of Art.11 where there was little evidence of a likelihood of interference with the Art.9 rights of other cemetery users: *Ollinger v Austria* (App No. 76900/01, June 29, 2006), paras 43–51. The HL held that the decision to escort buses of protestors back to London to prevent them from protesting at an airbase where there was no imminent breach of the peace was a wholly disproportionate interference with Art.11 (and Art.10): *R. (on the application of Laporte) v Chief constable of Gloucestershire* [2006] UKHL 58; [2007] 2 W.L.R. 46.

[240] A ban on a political party which is committed to the implementation of a manifesto which is contrary to the democratic structure of the state and in conflict with Convention rights was upheld in *Refah Partisi v Turkey*, (2003) 37 E.H.R.R. 1, paras 93–136.

lawful restrictions on the exercise of Art.11 rights by members of the armed forces, the police or the administration of the state.[241]

The right to the enjoyment of possessions

Article 1 of the First Protocol provides that every natural or legal person is **13–094** entitled to the peaceful enjoyment of his possessions and that no one shall be deprived of his possessions except in the public interest and subject to the conditions provided for by law and by the general principles of international law.[242] The ECtHR has adopted a broad definition of possessions (which is an autonomous concept under the ECHR) which may include intellectual property rights, shares, licences, rights to compensation and legitimate expectations.[243] After a long period of controversy, it is now also established that there is no need for a statutory benefit to be contributory before it can constitute a possession under the ECHR.[244] The protection of the right may involve positive obligations on the State.[245]

Article 1 has been held to contain three distinct prima facie rights: that **13–095** the peaceful enjoyment of one's possessions will not be interfered with by the State; that the State will not deprive an individual of his possessions; and that the State will not subject possessions to control.[246] An interference with peaceful enjoyment is generally less intrusive than the exercise of control over it or, of course, a deprivation. The ECtHR will look at the substance of the right in determining whether there has been a deprivation and may find there to be one even if the applicant retains legal owner- ship.[247] Examples of State control over the use of property include the imposition of taxes, restrictions on evicting tenants and planning

---

[241] Staff at the UK General Communications Headquarters were held to be covered by this (*Council of Civil Service Unions v UK* (1987) 50 D.R. 228), but German schoolteachers were not (*Vogt v Germany* (1995) 21 E.H.R.R. 205, paras 66–67). Even these general restrictions must justified by convincing and compelling reasons (*Tum Haber Sen and Cinar v Turkey* (App No. 28602/95, February 21, 2006), paras 135–140).

[242] The background to the provision is described in T. Allen, *Property and the Human Rights Act 1998* (2005).

[243] A legitimate expectation must be more than a mere hope, but can arise from an ultra vires act: *Stretch v UK* (2004) 38 E.H.R.R. 12, paras 32–41, where the local authority was held to have violated Mr Stretch's legitimate expectation that a lease would be renewed even though the original grant was unlawful. See the domestic case of *Rowland v Environment Agency* [2003] EWCA Civ 1885; [2005] Ch. 1 discussed at 12–020.

[244] *Stec v UK* (2006) 43 E.H.R.R. 47, para.53. This does not mean that the individual can claim a right that a benefit shall continue, but just that their claim to it must be determined in accordance with the law in force at the relevant time.

[245] A failure to take steps to protect the applicants' property from destruction by a landslide at a municipal tip breached Art.1 (*Oneryildiz v Turkey*, (2005) 41 E.H.R.R., 20 paras 134–136). See the domestic case of *Marcic v Thames Water Utilities Ltd* [2003] UKHL 66; [2004] 2 A.C. 42 at [36] (Lord Nicholls) (repeated failure to prevent flooding could violate Art.1).

[246] *Sporrong and Lonnroth v Sweden* (1982) 5 E.H.R.R. 35, para.61.

[247] The law on adverse possession was found not to violate Art.1 in *JA Pye (Oxford) Ltd v UK* (App No. 44302/02, August 30, 2007, paras 75.85.

controls.[248] The importance of the distinctions is that the ECtHR requires a stronger State justification for deprivations than for control or interferences.

13–096   The limitation clause provides that Art.1 is subject to the right of a State to enforce such laws as it deems necessary to control the use of property in accordance with the general interest or to secure the payment of taxes or other contributions or penalties. The interference must be lawful and must strike a fair balance between the public interest and the rights of the individual. The public interest is broadly defined and may be pursued by measures which do not benefit the public as a whole.[249] The requirement that there should be a fair balance essentially requires that the individual should not be excessively prejudiced by the pursuit of the general interest.[250] There is no right to receive the full value of appropriated property under the ECHR, but the level of compensation will plainly be relevant to the fairness of the treatment.[251]

The right to free elections

13–097   Article 3 of the First Protocol appears merely to impose an obligation on the State to hold free elections at reasonable intervals.[252] However, the ECtHR has held that Art.3 of the First Protocol does confer individual rights to vote and to stand for election. Although not subject to express limitation, the State may impose conditions which pursue a legitimate aim, are not disproportionate and do not frustrate the aim of the Article.[253] The legislature may include some regional bodies, but the term election is not apt to cover referenda. The State retains a broad discretion concerning the electoral system.[254]

---

[248] *Mellacher v Austria* (1989) 12 E.H.R.R. 391, paras 41–44 (rent control). The dividing line between control and a deprivation is not always easy to draw. In *Air Canada v UK* (1995) 20 E.H.R.R. 150, the airline argued that the state had deprived it of one of its aircraft which was seized after drugs were found onboard and would only be returned on payment of £50,000. The ECtHR found that this amounted to control only (paras 33–34).

[249] In *James v UK* (1986) 8 E.H.R.R. 123, paras 45–52 the ECtHR rejected a challenge to the leasehold enfranchisement laws by a number of landlords. The interference was justified by the general public interest in property distribution even though only particular leaseholders benefited from it.

[250] For example it was not fair to require small landowners opposed to hunting to transfer their hunting rights to another (*Chassagnou v France* (1999) 29 E.H.R.R. 615, paras 74–85). There is no requirement that the State should chose the course of action which involves the least possible impairment of the property owner's rights (*Countryside Alliance*, [2006] EWCA Civ 817; [2007] 1 Q.B. 305 at [121]–[125] (Sir Anthony Clarke M.R.).

[251] *Holy Monasteries v Greece* (1994) 20 E.H.R.R. 1, para.71.

[252] The elections must be by secret ballot and under conditions which will ensure the free expression of the opinion of the people in the choice of the legislature.

[253] *Mathieu-Mohin v Belgium* (1987) 10 E.H.R.R. 1, paras 52–57. The ECtHR found the automatic statutory bar on convicted prisoners voting to be disproportionate (*Hirst v UK* (2006) 42 E.H.R.R. 41, paras 78–85). Age and residence requirements have been upheld.

[254] A challenge to the UK's electoral system was rejected in *Liberal Party v UK* (1980) 3 E.H.R.R. 106, paras 8–9.

The prohibition on discrimination

Article 14 guarantees that the rights and freedoms set forth in the 13–098
Convention shall be secured without discrimination on grounds such as
sex, race, colour, language, religion, political or other opinion, national or
social origin, association with a national minority, property birth or other
status.[255] Article 14 therefore only applies to discrimination in the enjoyment of other substantive Convention rights and requires that a prohibition
at least falls within the ambit of another Convention right before it can be
invoked.[256] In effect, Art.14 is treated as if it is incorporated in each of the
other Convention rights. Article 14 is not however limited to the State's
acts in fulfilling its other obligations under the ECHR. Thus, if the State
provides a benefit, it must comply with Art.14 even if under no ECHR
obligation to provide the benefit in the first place.[257]

The prohibited grounds of discrimination under Art.14 are broadly 13–099
defined and non-exhaustive.[258] It is for the applicant to prove that he has
been treated differently from those who are in an analogous or relevantly
similar situation and the burden then shifts to the respondent to justify the
difference in treatment.[259] Justification is the familiar two-stage process:
does the distinction fulfil a legitimate aim and is there a reasonable
relationship of proportionality between the means employed and the aim

[255] Equality is also recognised by the common law (see 11–062) and in European Community
law (see 14–134). S. Fredman, "From Deference to Democracy: The Role of Equality under
the Human Rights Act 1998" (2006) 122 L.Q.R. 53.
[256] Indeed, the ECtHR will not usually proceed to consider the merits of an Art.14 complaint
at all if it finds the breach of a substantive right to be made out (*Dudgeon v UK* (1981) 4
E.H.R.R. 149, para.69). By contrast, the unratified Protocol 12 would provide a general
requirement of equal treatment. The narrowness of the court's focus has been criticised: A.
Baker, "The Enjoyment of Rights and Freedoms: A New Conception of the 'Ambit' under
Art.14 ECHR" (2006) 69 M.L.R. 714.
[257] For example the State may be under no duty to provide a particular welfare benefit, but
will be subject to Art.14 scrutiny if the manner in which it does so is discriminatory (*Stec v
UK*, (2006) 43 E.H.R.R. 47). See further, *Goden-Mendoza* [2004] UKHL 30; [2004] 2 A.C.
557) discussed at 13–042.
[258] The "other status" must relate to a personal characteristic of the applicant, but is not
otherwise limited and has been applied to marital status (*Sahin v Germany* (2003) 36
E.H.R.R. 43, paras 55–61), conscientious objection (*Thlimmenos v Greece* (2000) 31
E.H.R.R. 411, para.42) or residence (*Darby v Sweden* (1990) 13 E.H.R.R. 774, paras 29–34).
The HL did not accept that the historical fact that a person's fingerprints and DNA sample
had been taken and retained by the police constitutes a personal characteristic or status for
the purposes of Art.14 (and therefore they could not complain of discrimination compared to
those whose samples had not been taken and retained by the police) (*R. (on the application of
S) v Chief Constable of South Yorkshire Police* [2004] UKHL 39; [2004] 1 W.L.R. 2196 at
[53] (Lord Steyn)). Similarly, in *Stubbings v UK* (1996) 23 E.H.R.R. 213, paras 68–71 the
victims of child sexual abuse failed in their attempt to compare themselves to the victims of
negligently inflicted harm who benefited from a more generous limitation period.
[259] The burden on the applicant is the heavier criminal standard where he complains about
indirect discrimination (that is, that an apparently non-discriminatory practice has a disproportionate impact on members of his group) (*Jordan v UK* (2003) 37 E.H.R.R. 2, paras
154–155 (statistics which showed that members of the nationalist or Roman Catholic
communities were disproportionately targeted by the security forces was insufficient to
demonstrate a breach of Art.14)).

sought to be achieved.[260] The House of Lords has described the correct approach in the following terms:[261]

"Article 14 does not apply unless the alleged discrimination is in connection with a Convention right and on a ground stated in Art.14. If this prerequisite is satisfied, the essential question for the court is whether the alleged discrimination, that is, the difference in treatment of which complaint is made, can withstand scrutiny. Sometimes the answer to this question will be plain. There may be such an obvious, relevant difference between the claimant and those with whom he seeks to compare himself that their situations cannot be regarded as analogous. Sometimes, where the position is not so clear, a different approach is called for. Then the court's scrutiny may best be directed at considering whether the differentiation has a legitimate aim and whether the means chosen to achieve the aim is appropriate and not disproportionate in its adverse impact."

THE IMPACT OF THE HRA

13–100 In July 2006 the Department of Constitutional Affairs published its *Review of the Implementation of the Human Rights Act*.[262] This Review concluded that the HRA had no significant impact on the Government's ability to protect the public from crime or on government policy on immigration and asylum. The Review did find that the HRA has had an impact on counter-terrorism legislation which was said to arise principally from the decision in *Chahal v United Kingdom*.[263] The Review did not rule out the prospect

[260] There is no list of legitimate aims for the purposes of Art.14 and a broad range of such interests have been recognised, including, for example, supporting the traditional family (*Marckx v Belgium* (1979) 2 E.H.R.R. 330, para.32). The ECtHR will scrutinise distinctions based on nationality, religion, gender, race, sexual orientation, marital status and birth particularly closely.

[261] *R. (on the application of Carson) v Secretary of State for Work and Pensions* [2005] UKHL 37; [2006] 1 A.C. 173 at [3] (Lord Nicholls). In *Carson*, the HL cast doubt on the more structured series of questions set out by the CA in *Wandsworth LBC v Michalak* [2002] EWCA Civ 271; [2003] 1 W.L.R. 617 at [20] (Brooke L.J.) which were: (i) Do the facts fall within the ambit of one or more Convention rights? (ii) Was there a difference in treatment in respect of that right between the complainant and others put forward for comparison? (iii) Were those others in an analogous situation? (iv) Was the difference in treatment objectively justifiable? (v) Was the difference in treatment based on one or more of the grounds proscribed by Art.14? These questions are likely still to prove a valuable analytical tool if not applied rigidly. For the ECtHR's approach (which is similar to that of the HL) see *Belgian Linguistics Case (No. 2)* (1968) 1 E.H.R.R. 252, para.10. HL found the differential treatment of prisoners who were liable to removal from the country to be unjustified in the present day and hence in breach of Art.14 as discriminatory on grounds of national origins in *R (Clift) v Secretary of State for the Home Department* [2006] UKHL 54; [2007] 2 W.L.R. 24.

[262] DCA 38/06. The Review was triggered by the reporting of a number of high-profile cases decided (or thought to have been decided) under the HRA, in particular, the cases of the Afghani aircraft hijackers, the unreturned foreign prisoners and that of Anthony Rae.

[263] (1996) 23 E.H.R.R. 413

of amending the HRA by requiring particular regard to be had to the right to life in Art.2.[264] Overall, the Review concluded that the HRA had a beneficial impact on UK law by increasing the influence of human rights considerations on policy making and prompting a dialogue between UK judges and those in Strasbourg.[265] The Government has since repeated its commitment to maintaining the HRA in force and remaining part of the ECHR system.

A more empirical enquiry into the impact of the HRA was carried out by the Public Law Project. Their study provided a detailed breakdown of the civil judicial review claims issued and granted permission in various categories of subject matter in the first half of 2002. The conclusion was that the HRA did not appear to have contributed materially to the number of cases before the Administrative Court. Moreover, although cited in around half of the claims issues, in the majority of cases the HRA made little difference to the claimant's prospects of success.[266] **13–101**

The HRA has also reinvigorated the debate about whether the United Kingdom should adopt its own domestically drafted Bill of Rights either to supplement or replace the ECHR. Some commentators have criticised the ECHR as out-dated for lacking direct protection for economic social and cultural rights, freedom of information or a free-standing right not to be discriminated against.[267] This is part of the wider debate about a new constitutional settlement for the United Kingdom which may include entrenchment of the devolution settlements in Scotland, Wales and Northern Ireland and further reform of the structure and working of Parliament.[268] **13–102**

---

[264] In the same way as ss.12 and 13 draw particular attention to the rights to free speech and religion.

[265] Similar conclusions were reached by the Joint Committee on Human Rights, *The Human Rights Act: the DCA and Home Office Reviews*. HL Paper No.278/AC Paper No.1716 (Session 2006/07).

[266] The Public Law Project, *The Impact of the Human Rights Act on Judicial Review: An Empirical Research Study* (2003).

[267] I. Hare, "Social Rights as Fundamental Rights" in B. Hepple (ed.), *Social and Labour Rights in a Global Context: International and Comparative Perspectives* (2002) and J. Wadham and R. Taylor, "Bringing More Rights Home" [2002] E.H.R.L.R. 713.

[268] The Northern Ireland Human Rights Commission has a statutory duty to consult and advise the Secretary of State on the scope of defining fundamental rights beyond those protected by the Convention. Its preliminary report is available at *http://www.nihrc.org*.

Table 1 Declarations of incompatibility under HRA s.4 up to end of July 2007 which have not been overturned on appeal

Source: information derived from table prepared by Ministry of Justice reproduced on House of Lords Selected Committee on the Constitution, 6th Report of Session 2006–07 (HL Paper 151), Appendix 6; updated.

	Judgment	Right	Legislation	Response
1	R. (on the application of H) v Mental Health Review Tribunal for the North and East London Region [2001] EWCH Civ 415; [2002] Q.B.1	Art.5(1), 5(2)	Mental Health Act 1983 s.73: did not require tribunal to discharge a patient where it could not be shown that he suffered from a mental disorder warranting detention	Mental Health Act 1983 (Remedial) Order 2001 (SI 2001/3712)
2	McR's Application for Judicial Review [2003] NI 1	Art.8	Offences Against the Person Act 1861 s.62: offence of attempted buggery continued to apply in Northern Ireland to consenting adults	Sexual Offences Act 2003 repealed s.62 of the 1861 Act
3	International Transport Roth GmbH v Secretary of State for the Home Department [2002] EWCH Civ 158; [2003] Q.B. 728	Art.6 Art.1 of First Protocol	Immigration and Aslum Act 1999 Pt II: penalty system for carriers who unknowingly transported clandestine entrants to the UK	Nationally Immigration and Aslum Act 2002 s.125 modified the system
4	R. (on the application of Anderson) v Secretary of State for the Home Department [2002] UKHL 46; [2003] 1 A.C. 837	Art.6	Crime (Sentences) Act 1997 s.29: Home Secretary set minimum period to be served by a mandatory life sentence prisoner before he could be considered for release on licence	Criminal Justice Act 2003 ss 303 and 332 repealed s.29 of the 1997 Act
5	R v Secretary of State for the Home Department, ex p. D [2002] EWHC 2805; [2003] 1 W.L.R. 1315	Art.5(4)	Mental Health Act 1983 s.74 gave discretion to Home Secretary whether or not to refer a discretionary life prisoner's case to Parole Board where a mental health review tribunal concluded that prisoner no longer liable to be detained under 1983 Act	Criminal Justice Act 2003 s.295 amended s.74 of the 1983 Act

6	*Blood v Secretary of State for the Health* (Sullivan J., unreported, February 28, 2003.)	Art.8, Art.14	Human Fertilisation and Embryology Act 1990 s.28(6)(b): prevented deceased father's name being entered on his child's birth certificate	Human Fertilisation and Embryology (Deceased Fathers) Act 2003
7	*Bellinger v Bellinger* [2003] UKHL 21; [2003] 2 A.C. 467	Art.8, Art.12	Matrimonial Causes Act 1973 s.11(c) no provision for recognition to valid marrige	Gender Recognition Act 2004
8	*R. (on the application of M) v Secretary of State for Health* [2003] EWCH 1094; [2003] U.K.H.R.R. 746	Art.8	Mental Health Act 1983 ss 26 and 29 patient liable to be detained under the Act had no choice over appointment of "nearest relative" or legal means of challenge	Mental Health Act 2007
9	*R. (on the application of Hooper) v Secretary of State for Work and Pensions* [2003] EWCA Civ 875 (unaffected by judgment [2005] UKHL 29; [2005] 1 W.L.R. 1681)	Art.14, Art.8, Art 1 of Protocol 1	Social Security Contributions and Benefit Act 1992 ss.36–37: Widowed Mothers Allowance payable to woman but not men	Welfare Reform and Pension act 1999 s.54(1) had already altered law prospectively
10	*R. (on the application of Wilkinson) v Inland Revenue Commissioners* [2003] EWCA Civ 814 (unaffected by subsequent House of Lords' judgment [2005] UKHL 30; [2005] 1 W.L.R. 1718)	Art.14, Art 1 of Protocol 1	Income and Corporation Taxes Act 1988 s.262; payment of Widows but not widowers	Finance Act 1999 ss.34(1) and 139 had already repealed s.262 prospectively
11	*X v Secretary of State for the Home Department* (Belmarsh detainees case) [2004] UKHL 56; [2005] 2 A.C. 68	Art.5, Art.14	Anti-terrorism, Crime and Security Act 2001 s.23: Home Secretary empowered to order detention of foreign nationals living in the UK suspected of terrorism who could not be deported without breaching Art.3	Prevention of Terrorism Act 2005 repealed detention order system (and created new system of control order)

	Judgment	Right	Legislation	Response
12 & 13	*R. (on the application of Morris) v Westminster City Council (No.3)* [2005] EWCA Civ 1184; [2006] 1 W.L.R. 505 Similar point in *R. (on the application of Gabaj) v First Secretary of State* (unreported), relating to claimant's pregnant wife who was not a British citizen	Art.14	Housing Act 1996 s.185(4): requiring dependent child who is subject to immigration control to be disregarded when determining whether a British citizen has priority need for accommodation	Not yet remedied
14	*R. (on the application of Baiai and others) v Secretary of State for the Home Department* [2007] EWCA Civ 478	Art.12	Asylum and Immigration (Treatment of Claimants, etc.) Act 2004 s.19(3): procedures designed to stop sham marriages must be completed before any persons subject to immigration control may marry in the UK	Not yet remedied
15	*R. (on the application of Wright) v Secretary of State for Health* [2006] EWHC 2886; [2007] 1 All E.R. 825	Art.6, Art.8	Care Standards Act 2000 s.82(4)(b): list of persons unsuitable to work with vulnerable adults	Subject to appeal
16	*R. (on the application of Clift) v Secretary of State for the Home Department; Hindawi v Secretary of State for the Home Department* [2006] UKHL 54; [2007] 2 W.L.R. 24	Art.14, Art.5	Criminal Justice Act 1991, ss 46(1) and 50(2): early release from prison provisions applied differently to British and foreign nationals	Criminal Justice Act 2003 repealed provision, save that they continued to apply on a transitional basis to offences committed before April 4, 2005. Home Office considering remedy for transitional category

17	Smith v Scott, 2007, CSIH 9; 2007 S.L.T. 137	Art.3 of First Protocol	Representation of the People Act 1983 s.3(1): incapacity of convicted prisoners to vote in general elections	Government considering the implications of this ruling in light of ECtHR ruling to similar effect in Hirst v UK (2006) 42 E.H.R.R. 41
18	R. (on the application of Nasseri) v Secretary of State for the Home Department [2007] EWHC 1548; The Times, August 3, 2007	Art.3	Asylum and Immigration ('Treatment of Claimants, etc.) Act 2004 s.33, Sch.3, para.3: provisions "deeming" it safe to remove asylum seeker to a third country	Not yet known

Table 2: Declarations of incompatibility under HRA, s.4. subsequently overturned on appeal up to end of July 2007.

Source: information derived from table prepared by Ministry of Justice, reproduced in House of Lords Select Committee on the Constitution, 6th Report of Session 2006–07 (HL Paper 151), Appendix 6.

	Final decision	Court making declaration	Right	Legislation
1	R. v Secretary of State for the Environment, Transport and the Regions Ex p. Holdings & Barnes Plc (the Alconbury case) [2001] UKHL 23; [2003] 2 A.C. 295	Divisional Court [2001] H.R.L.R. 2	Art.6	Town and Country Planning Act 1990 ss.77, 78 and 79 and similar provisions relating to compulsory purchase orders (in which minister and officials had appellate roles)
2	Wilson v First County Trust Ltd (No.2) [2003] UKHL 40; [2004] 1 A.C. 816	[2001] EWCA Civ 633; [2002] Q.B. 74	Art.6; Art.1 of 1st Protocol	Consumer Credit Act 1974 s.127(3) (restriction on creditors' contractual rights in regulated loans that had not been properly executed)

	Final decision	Court making declaration	Right	Legislation
3	*Matthews v Ministry of Defence* [2003] UKHL 4; [2003] 1 A.C. 1163	[2002] EWCA Civ 773; [2002] 1 W.L.R. 2621	Art.6	Crown Proceedings Act 1947 s.10 (certificate issued by minister that personal injury attributable to service, accompanied by no-fault compensation, precluded ordinary civil claim)
4	*R. (on the application of Uttley) v Secretary of State for the Home Department* [2004] UKHL 38; [2004] 1 W.L.R. 2278	[2003] EWCA Civ 1130; [2003] 1 W.L.R. 2590	Art.7	Criminal Justice Act 1991 ss.33(2), 37(4)(a) and 39 (prisoners released on licence, subject to conditions and recall, after serving two-thirds of sentence)
5	*R. (on the application of MH) v Secretary of State for Health* [2005] UKHL 60; [2006] 1 A.C. 441	[2004] EWCA Civ 1609; [2005] 1 W.L.R. 1209	Art.5(4)	Mental Health Act 1983 s.2 (extension of detention of patient who was incompetent to apply for discharge)
6	*Re MB* [2006] EWCA Civ 1140; [2006] 3 W.L.R. 839	[2006] EWHC 1000, [2006] H.R.L.R. 29	Art.6	Prevention of Terrorism Act 2005 s.2 (non-derogating control order)

CHAPTER 14

REVIEW UNDER EUROPEAN COMMUNITY LAW

SCOPE

This chapter examines the principal ways in which Community law may be   **14–001**
utilised in claims for judicial review in the Administrative Court, including:

- the principle of "conforming interpretation";[1]

- the requirement of effective protection of Community law rights,[2]
  including effective judicial review[3] and state liability for breaches of
  Community law;[4]

- and the grounds of review under Community law, including: non-
  discrimination;[5] proportionality;[6] legal certainty and legitimate expectations;[7] fundamental rights;[8] the right to be heard;[9] and requirements
  to state reasons.[10]

INTRODUCTION

The United Kingdom's membership of the European Union (EU) has brought   **14–002**
with it significant changes to the English legal system and the UK constitution.[11] This Chapter has the narrower focus of examining the use of

---

[1] See 14–044.
[2] See 14–052.
[3] See 14–060.
[4] See 14–066.
[5] See 14–087.
[6] See 14–089 and 14–124.
[7] See 14–093 and 14–137.
[8] See 14–096 and 14–119.
[9] See 14–101.
[10] See 14–107 and 14–117.
[11] See generally: D. Chalmers, C. Hadjiemmanuil, G. Monti and A. Tomkins, *European Union
Law* (2006); S. Weatherill, *Cases & Materials on EU Law*, 8th edn (2007); P. Craig and G. de
Búrca, *EU Law*, 4th edn (2007); T.C. Hartley, *The Foundations of European Community
Law*, 6th edn (2007); A. Arnull, A. Dashwood, M. Dougan, M. Ross, E. Spaventa and D.
Wyatt, *Wyatt and Dashwood"'s European Union Law*, 5th edn (2006); A. Arnull *The European
Union and its Court of Justice* 2nd edn (2006); P. Craig, *EU Administrative Law* (2006). For a
comprehensive treatment of the role of Community law in judicial review: R. Gordon, *EC
Law in Judicial Review* (2007).

European Community[12] law in judicial review claims in England and Wales, though that needs to be set in general context of the EU legal system. In the Administrative Court:

- claimants may challenge actions and omissions by English public authorities, and even provisions of an Act of Parliament, on the ground of breach of Community law;[13]

- less commonly, claims for judicial review may also raise questions about the validity of administrative decisions and legislation made by the institutions of the EU.[14]

14–003   Moreover, Community law has had an impact on the basic methods of work of national courts, including their approach to interpreting legislation,[15] the procedures to be followed by litigants and the nature of the remedies available to protect individuals' rights under Community law.[16]

14–004   The two courts of the EU—the European Court of Justice (ECJ)[17] and the Court of First Instance (CFI)[18]—have important roles. When a national court or tribunal requests it to do so, the ECJ gives authoritative rulings on questions of interpretation of Community law.[19] Both courts also have powers to determine actions brought directly to them alleging that Member States or institutions of the EU have breached Community law, though consideration of this aspect of their work falls outside the scope of this chapter.[20]

---

[12] On the distinction between European Union and European Community law, see 14–005. In this Chapter the abbreviation EC or EC Treaty refers to the Treaties establishing the European Communities; TEU refers to the Treaty on European Union. Revision of the EC by the Treaty of Amsterdam (signed in 1997 and coming into force in 1999) led to a renumbering of treaty provisions; where useful, we therefore supply the previous number of the Article in square brackets, e.g. Art.234 [177] EC.

[13] See 14–112.

[14] See 14–041.

[15] See 14–044.

[16] See 14–051.

[17] The ECJ was established in 1952 and its jurisdiction includes jurisdiction to hear actions brought against Member States for failure to fulfil Community obligations (Art.226 [169] EC and Art.227 [170] EC); to hear actions brought by individuals against Community institutions (Art 230); to hear actions against the Parliament, Council or Commission for failure to act (Art 232 [175] EC), and to give rulings on preliminary references (Art.234 [177] EC).

[18] The CFI was created in 1988 (Art.225 [168a] EC) to determine certain types of case. The CFI hears cases brought by individuals against Community institutions. It does not give preliminary rulings under Art.234 [177] EC, on which see 14–075. For a detailed comment on the jurisdictional divide between the ECJ and the CFI, see Craig (2006), Ch 9.

[19] 14–075.

[20] See n.11; and A. Ward, *Judicial Review and the Rights of Private Parties in EU Law*, 2nd edn (2007), Chs 6 and 8.

OVERVIEW OF THE EU LEGAL SYSTEM

Three pillars of the EU

The EU legal system stems from the treaties which establish the European **14–005**
Union and the European Community—principally the Treaties establishing
the European Communities (EC)[21] and the Treaty on European Union
(TEU).[22] The TEU, as amended, sets out the broad decision-taking framework for the EU in which there are three broad "pillars", or spheres of
public policy: (a) pillar 1 is the European Community; (b) pillar 2 is
Common Foreign and Security Policy;[23] (c) pillar 3 is Police and Judicial Co-
operation in Criminal Matters.[24] At intergovernmental conferences, the
Member States have from time to time revised these treaties to adapt the
basic institutional framework and decision-making processes.[25] In the United
Kingdom, the treaties have been incorporated into national law by successive
Acts of Parliament.[26]

Policy areas within the field of the European Community

Some indication of the broad range of policy areas which fall within the **14–006**
ambit of Community law can be seen from Art.3 EC:[27]

"1. For the purposes set out in Art.2, the activities of the Community shall
include, as provided in this Treaty and in accordance with the timetable
set out therein:

(a) the prohibition, as between Member States, of customs duties and
quantitative restrictions on the import and export of goods, and of
all other measures having equivalent effect;

(b) a common commercial policy;

(c) an internal market characterised by the abolition, as between
Member States, of obstacles to the free movement of goods,
persons, services and capital;

(d) measures concerning the entry and movement of persons as provided for in Title IV;

(e) a common policy in the sphere of agriculture and fisheries;

(f) a common policy in the sphere of transport;

(g) a system ensuring that competition in the internal market is not
distorted;

---

[21] Also known as the Treaty of Rome.
[22] Also known as the Maastricht Treaty.
[23] TEU, Title V.
[24] TEU, Title VI.
[25] The most recent revision was by the Treaty of Nice (Cm. 3780), signed in 2001 and coming
into force in 2003.
[26] European Communities Act 1972, as amended.
[27] These Community policies are spelt out in more detail in Pt 3 of EC.

703

(h) the approximation of the laws of Member States to the extent required for the functioning of the common market;

(i) the promotion of co-ordination between employment policies of the Member States with a view to enhancing their effectiveness by developing a co-ordinated strategy for employment;

(j) a policy in the social sphere comprising a European Social Fund;

(k) the strengthening of economic and social cohesion;

(l) a policy in the sphere of the environment;

(m) the strengthening of the competitiveness of Community industry;

(n) the promotion of research and technological development;

(o) encouragement for the establishment and development of trans-European networks;

(p) a contribution to the attainment of a high level of health protection;

(q) a contribution to education and training of quality and to the flowering of the cultures of the Member States;

(r) a policy in the sphere of development co-operation;

(s) the association of the overseas countries and territories in order to increase trade and promote jointly economic and social development;

(t) a contribution to the strengthening of consumer protection;

(u) measures in the spheres of energy, civil protection and tourism.

14-007 In some of these areas of governance, the Community has exclusive policy-making and legislative competence.[28] Where this is so and the Community makes regulations, Member States are prohibited from passing national legislation on the same subject matter.[29] Where the EU has such sole competence, schemes will nevertheless normally be given practical implementation by national institutions such as HM Customs and Revenue and the Department for Environment, Food and Rural Affairs in England and so claimants may challenge the legality of the steps taken to administer EU policy and law. This is known as "shared or decentralised management";[30] "centralised" management,[31] whereby EU institutions implement

[28] For example, regulation of imports into the EU of goods from non-Member States and compliance with international conservation and management measures by fishing vessels on the high seas. On exclusive and non-exclusive competences, see A. Bogdandy and J. Bast, "The European Union's Vertical Order of Competences: the Current Law and Proposals for its Reform" (2002) 39 C.M.L. Rev. 227.

[29] See, e.g. Case 74/69 *Hauptzollamt Bremen-Freihafen v Waren-Import-Gesellschaft Krohn & Co* [1970] E.C.R. 451 (to the extent that Member States have assigned legislative powers in tariff matters to the Community in order to ensure the proper operation of the common agricultural market, they no longer have the power to make autonomous provisions in this field).

[30] Council Regulation (EC) 1605/2002 on the Financial Regulation Applicable to the General Budget of the European Communities [2002] O.J. L248/1, Art. 53(b); P Craig "The Constitutionalisation of Community Administration" (2003) 28 E.L. Rev. 840; Craig (2006), Ch 3.

[31] Council Regulation (EC) 1605/2002 on the Financial Regulation Applicable to the General Budget of the European Communities [2002] OJ L248/1, Arts 53(a), 53a, and 54–57. See Craig (2006)) Ch 2.

programmes either themselves, by outsourcing to a private party or delegating to an executive agency, is less common, although has been increasing.[32] In many other areas of policy-making and legislation, Member States and the EU share competence—both are permitted, within limits, to pursue their own goals.[33] Some spheres of governance remain matters wholly internal to Member States and Community law has no application. However, even in areas of government where Member States retain competence, such as for foreign and security policy, they have to respect common EU policies which touch upon that area.[34]

Community law as "a new legal order"

Community law (in distinction to the law governing the other two pillars of the EU) is "a new legal order"[35] with distinctive characteristics, including direct effect and primacy over inconsistent national law of Members States. It is with the Community that this Chapter is mainly concerned.[36] Rules of Community law have their main sources in the treaties which establish the European Community and the EU, in secondary legislation made by the institutions of the EU, and in the general principles of law developed by the ECJ. The Charter of Fundamental Rights of the EU (Charter) is not legally binding yet, but has had important influential impact. It is also important to note developments surrounding the draft Treaty Establishing a Constitution of Europe (Constitutional Treaty), which was not adopted, and its proposed replacement, the Reform Treaty.   14–008

Primacy of Community law

Early on, the ECJ propounded the doctrine that any rule of Community law, whatever its source, prevails over inconsistent rules of national law in Member States.[37] The primacy of Community law is absolute. It applies whether the national rule came into being before or after the rule of Community law; it precludes the adoption of new legislative measures to the extent that they would be incompatible with Community law; it also applies to all forms of national law, including constitutional norms.[38] Where a   14–009

[32] J Schwarze, "Judicial Review of European Administrative Procedure" [2004] P.L. 146, 147.
[33] For example, the regulation of competition and the imposition of value added tax.
[34] C-124/95 R. v HM Treasury Ex p. Centro-Com Sri [1997] E.C.R. I–81, para.30 (Member States retained competence in the area of foreign and security policy, but had to respect the Community's common commercial policy in whatever foreign and security measures were taken).
[35] Case 26/62 Van Gend en Loos NV v Nederlandse Tariefcommissie [1963] E.C.R. 1 at 12.
[36] The ECJ is only minimally associated with the second and third pillars: Case C-160/03 Spain v Eurojust [2005] E.C.R. I–2077, paras 37–38.
[37] Case 6/64 Costa v ENEL [1964] E.C.R. 585; 14–113.
[38] Case 106/77 Simmenthal [1978] E.C.R. 629, paras 17–22. There is one narrow exception to the principle of supremacy where the national provision is necessary to give effect to obligations under an international agreement entered into by the Member State before it became a party to the relevant Community Treaty: Case C-158/91 Levy [1993] E.C.R. I–4287, para.22.

person before an inferior court or tribunal seeks to rely upon a rule of Community law which is irreconcilable with national law, that court or tribunal is obliged immediately to disregard the national law: under Community law, it has "the power to do everything necessary at the moment of its application to set aside national legislative provisions which might prevent Community rules from having full force and effect".[39] In England and Wales, primacy therefore means that all courts and tribunals must, in a case where Community rights are in issue, "disapply" any provision in an Act of Parliament or statutory instrument, and depart from any common law precedent, that is irreconcilable with Community law.[40] Thus, while English law generally requires public law issues to be dealt with by the CPR Pt 54 claim for judicial review procedure,[41] Community law requires that questions of compatibility of national laws with Community law be dealt with by the court or tribunal in which they first arise during the ordinary course of legal proceedings. This may result in a bench of lay magistrates or the First-tier Tribunal adjudicating on the applicability of an Act of Parliament. Claims for judicial review are only one of many types of legal proceedings in which the primacy principle operates; civil claims, criminal proceedings and tribunal appeals, for example, may all provide the forum for raising arguments about compatibility of domestic law with Community law.

Direct effect of Community law measures

14–010   Early on in the development of the Community law, the ECJ held that certain provisions of the treaties may be relied upon directly by litigants in national courts (the doctrine of "direct effect") even though they may not have been specifically incorporated into a Member State's domestic legal system.[42] It can now be said that direct effect extends to all provisions in the EC Treaty which create rights and obligations which are sufficiently complete, clear and precise.[43] These requirements are not applied strictly[44]

---

[39] *Simmenthal* [1978] E.C.R. 629, para 22.

[40] See 14–039.

[41] On procedural exclusivity see Ch.3. The Human Rights Act 1998 restricts declarations of incompatibility of legislation with Convention rights (s.4) to the higher courts, though all courts and tribunals are obliged to read and give effect legislation so far as possible in ways which are compatible (s.3).

[42] *Van Gend en Loos* [1963] E.C.R. 1. The relationship between national law and treaty obligations varies between the Member States according to the constitution of each.

[43] *Van Gend en Loos* [1963] E.C.R. 1 at 13 (only those provisions which were clear, negative, unconditional, containing no reservation on the part of the Member State, and not dependent on a national implementing measure can be directly effective); and C-62/00 *Marks & Spencer Plc v Customs and Excise Commissioners* [2002] E.C.R. I–6325, para.25 (provisions of directives can be directly effective if they are "unconditional and sufficiently precise").

[44] Through subsequent case law, these criteria have evolved to a looser requirement of justiciability: P. Pescatore, "The Doctrine of 'direct effect': an Infant Disease of Community Law" (1983) 8 E.L. Rev. 155, pp.176–177; Ward (2007) Ch.2; e.g. Case 43/75 *Defrenne v Société Anonyme Belge de Navigation Aérienne* [1976] E.C.R. 455, para.16 (which found directly effective the obligation in Art.141 [119] EC on States to ensure "the application of the principle that men and women should receive equal pay for equal work", at least in so far as it related to direct discrimination).

and generally, only very open-ended provisions will not be found to be directly effective.[45] A provision can also be found to be partially directly effective, where it is capable of application in certain areas, but where further implementing measures are necessary for the provision to be enforceable over the whole of its range of intended application.[46] The provisions which are directly effective may be relied upon by litigants in national courts and tribunals both "vertically" against state institutions[47] and also "horizontally" against other citizens and business enterprises.[48] The enforceability of measures adopted under the second and third pillars of the EU is notably weaker than is the case with the EC and, for example, the direct effect of Framework Decisions and Decisions adopted under the third pillar is expressly excluded by force of Art.34(2) TEU.

REFORM

The unratified Constitutional Treaty

The Constitutional Treaty, signed by heads of state and government in 2004, 14–011
was a historic step forward in consolidating and revising the treaty framework—but it was not ratified following failures to secure affirmative votes in referendums in some Member States.[49] The Constitutional Treaty, which, as already noted, has been abandoned, sought to replace the current three-pillar structure of the EU by a single Treaty establishing a single Constitution for Europe, such that there would no longer be an EC within the wider EU.[50] There were four parts to the Treaty: the first established fundamental principles, containing provisions on the objectives, law-making powers and the finances of the EU, fundamental rights, citizenship and

---

[45] See, Case 126/86 *Zaera v Institutio Nacionale de la Seguridad Social* [1987] E.C.R. 3697(EC Art.2 was not directly effective), paras 10–11; Case T–191/99 *Petrie v Commission* [2001] E.C.R. II–3677, paras 34–35 (principle of access to documents in Art.255 [191a] was not unconditional and required further implementation and so could not be directly effective); Case C-9/99 *Echirolles Distribution SA v Association du Dauphine* [2000] E.C.R. I–8207, para.25 (EC Arts 3a, 102a and 103, which refer to economic policy, the implementation of which must comply with the principle of an open-market economy with free competition, were not capable of direct effect).
[46] C. Lewis, *Judicial Remedies in Public Law*, 3rd edn (2004), para.15–011. In *Defrenne* [1976] E.C.R. 455 Art.141 [119] was not found to be directly effective in relation to indirect discrimination.
[47] See, e.g. *Van Gend en Loos* [1963] E.C.R. 1.
[48] Case 36/74 *Walrave & Koch v Association Union Cycliste Internationale* [1974] E.C.R. 1405, paras 15–17; Case 43/75 *Defrenne v Sabena* [1976] E.C.R. 455, para.39; Case C-415/93 *Union Royale Belge des Sociétés de Football Association v Bosman* [1995] E.C.R. I–4921, paras 82–84; C-281/98 *Angonese v Cassa di Risparmio di Bolzano SpA* [2000] E.C.R. I–4139, para.31.
[49] Art.IV–443(4) of the Constitutional Treaty provided that if there were difficulties in ratification in one or more Member States two years after the signature of the Treaty, it should be referred to the European Council.
[50] Although the distinctions in law-making powers between the three areas of policy would have been maintained: see, e.g. Arts I–33 and Art.I–40.

democracy and on the EU's institutional framework;[51] the Charter of Fundamental Rights was found in the second part;[52] the EU's common policies were found in the third part;[53] and final provisions were found in the fourth part.[54] The role performed by the Treaty was primarily the enhancement of transparency, rather than making radical changes:[55] thus, competence provisions which are currently scattered throughout the EC treaty were consolidated[56] and the principle of primacy of Community law over national law was articulated in treaty text for the first time.[57] Certain novel features of the Treaty included stating that the EU, and not just the EC as at present, would have a legal personality;[58] a procedure for voluntary withdrawal from the Union;[59] the creation of a Union Minister of Foreign Affairs;[60] and making the Charter legally binding. Protocols 1 and 2 of the Constitutional Treaty would have engaged national parliaments in the policing of the principle of subsidiarity.[61]

The proposed Reform Treaty

14–012   Following negative results in the French and Dutch referendums, the European Council concluded that the date initially planned for a report on ratification of the Treaty, November 1, 2006 was no longer realistic and in June 2005, a "period of reflection" was declared. In June 2007 the European Council agreed not to proceed with the Constitutional Treaty, and instead issued a mandate for a new treaty, the Reform Treaty, which, at the time of writing, is in the process of being drafted by an intergovernmental conference, in the hope of ensuring ratification by June 2009.[62]

14–013   It appears that the Reform Treaty will seek to achieve similar amendments to those proposed in the Constitutional Treaty, albeit that all references to "constitution" or "constitutional" are to be removed.[63] The TEU and EC Treaty will remain separate; however the EC Treaty will be re-named Treaty on the Functioning of the Union, and the word "Community" throughout both treaties will be replaced by "Union".[64] The TEU will be divided into six

[51] Constitutional Treaty Arts I–1 to I–60.
[52] Constitutional Treaty Arts II–61 to II–114.
[53] Constitutional Treaty Arts III–115 to III–436.
[54] Constitutional Treaty Arts IV–437 to IV–448.
[55] On the Constitutional Treaty, see further J. Shaw, "Europe's Constitutional Future" [2005] P.L. 132; P. Craig, "Competence: Clarity, Conferral, Containment and Consideration" (2004) 29 E.L. Rev. 323; A. Dashwood, "The EU Constitution: What Will Really Change?" (2004/2005) 7 C.Y.E.L.S. 33.
[56] Constitutional Treaty Arts I–11 to I–18.
[57] Constitutional Treaty Art.I–6.
[58] Constitutional Treaty Art.I–7.
[59] Constitutional Treaty Art.I–60.
[60] Constitutional Treaty Art.I–28.
[61] See further S. Weatherill, "Better Competence Monitoring" (2005) 30 E.L. Rev. 23.
[62] Council of the European Union, Presidency Conclusions, June 21/22, 2007, paras 8–14 and Annex 1.
[63] Presidency Conclusions, June 21/22, 2007, Annex I, para.I–3.
[64] Presidency Conclusions, June 21/22, 2007, Annex I, para.I–2; Draft Treaty amending the Treaty on European Union and the Treaty establishing the European Community ("Draft Reform Treaty") Art.1(2).

titles, the first of which, common provisions, will outline the Union's values and objectives. The Article on fundamental rights will contain a cross-reference to the Charter, giving it legally binding effect and setting out the scope of its application.[65] The second title will contain provisions on democratic principles, including provisions aimed at strengthening the role of national parliaments in the policing of subsidiarity from the proposal contained in the Constitutional Treaty.[66] The remaining titles (provisions on institutions; provisions on enhanced cooperation; general provisions on the Union's external action and specific provisions on the common foreign and security policy; and final provisions) will integrate many of the institutional changes proposed in the Constitutional Treaty.[67] The mandate also sets out a detailed list of amendments to be made to the EC Treaty;[68] and the provision on primacy of Union law which was proposed for the Constitutional Treaty, will not be reproduced in the TEU, but will be contained in a Declaration of the intergovernmental conference and will be annexed to the Final Act of the Conference.[69]

SECONDARY LEGISLATION

An unusual feature of the first pillar of EU, the Community, in comparison with other international organisations, is that legislative powers have been conferred on its institutions by the Treaties. Art.249 EC provides: 14–014

"In order to carry out their task and in accordance with the provisions of this Treaty, the European Parliament acting jointly with the Council, the Council and the Commission shall make regulations and issue directives, take decisions, make recommendations or deliver opinions.

A regulation shall have general application. It shall be binding in its entirety and directly applicable in all Member States.

A directive shall be binding, as to the result to be achieved, upon each Member State to which it is addressed, but shall leave to the national authorities the choice of form and methods.

A decision shall be binding in its entirety upon those to whom it is addressed.

[65] Presidency Conclusions, June 21/22, 2007, Annex I, para.I–9; Draft Reform Treaty, Art.1(8).
[66] Presidency Conclusions, June 21/22, 2007, Annex I, para. II–11; Draft Reform Treaty Art.1(12).
[67] Presidency Conclusions, June 21/22, 2007, Annex I, paras II–12–II–16; see Draft Reform Treaty, (n. 64) Art.1(13)–(21) (institutions); Art.1(22) (cooperation); Art.1(23)–(24) (external action); Art.1(25)–(52) (common foreign and security policy); Art.1(53)–(63) (final provisions).
[68] Presidency Conclusions June 21/22, 2007, Annex I, paras III–17–III–20; Draft Reform Treaty, Art.2.
[69] Presidency Conclusions June 21/22, 2007, n.1.

Recommendations and opinions shall have no binding force."[70]

14–015 These forms of legal instruments were devised at the inception of the Community. The practical distinction between regulations and directives has lost some of its significance. This is in part because of a legislative practice of often drafting regulations and directives with a similar degree of detail; in part because of the development in the case law of the ECJ of the notion of direct effect of directives.[71] Nevertheless, important differences remain.

Regulations

14–016 All regulations are "directly applicable". Regulations thus become part of national law without any need for the Member State to adopt implementing measures. Indeed it will often be unlawful for Member States to transpose regulations into national law. This is so in particular where such transposition may obscure or distort the Community provisions, or have the effect of concealing their Community character.[72] Moreover, in some fields the Community will be regarded as having exclusive legislative competence, so that the adoption of EC regulations will preclude Member States from adopting any legislative measures in the field occupied by the regulations.[73]

14–017 Regulations may however sometimes be incomplete in that they do not specify, for example, the administrative measures necessary for their application or the penalties to be imposed in the event of non-compliance. Thus, it is settled case law that Member States may adopt rules for the application of a regulation if they do not obstruct its direct applicability, do not conceal its Community nature and specify that a discretion granted by the regulation is being exercised; provided that they adhere to the parameters laid down under it.[74] In such cases, Member States, far from being prohibited from acting, are under a duty to adopt the legislative measures necessary to make the regulations fully effective.[75]

14–018 Since regulations are, by virtue of Art.249 [189] EC, directly applicable, it is not usually necessary to consider separately the question of their direct effect. But direct effect is distinct from direct applicability. Not all provisions

---

[70] See further Art.34 TEU (providing power to the Council to adopt a common position, a framework decision, a decision or a convention in the area of Police and Judicial Co-operation in Criminal Matters); and Art.12 TEU (enabling the Council and European Council to adopt principles and guidelines; decide on common strategies; adopt joint actions; adopt common positions; and strengthen systematic co-operation between Member States in the conduct of policy in the area of Common Foreign and Security Policy).

[71] See 14–022.

[72] Case 39/72 *Commission v Italy* [1973] E.C.R. 101, para.17; Case 34/73 *Variola* [1973] E.C.R. 981 at 991; *cf. Case 272/83 Commission v Italy* [1985] E.C.R. 1057, para.27.

[73] See, e.g. Case 74/69 *Hauptzollamt Bremen v Krohn* [1970] E.C.R. 451 at 458. *Cf. Case 40/69 Bollman* [1970] E.C.R. 69 at 79. This is reminiscent of the notion of pre-emption in US constitutional law, where the expression "occupying the field" is used of US federal legislation, see, e.g. *Sprietsma v Mercury Marine* 537 U.S. 51 (2002) at 69.

[74] C-113/02 *Commission v Netherlands* [2004] E.C.R. I–9707, para.16.

[75] Case 128/78 *Commission v United Kingdom (Tachographs)* [1979] E.C.R. 419; Case 72/85 *Commission v Netherlands* [1986] E.C.R. 1219.

of regulations have direct effect, just as not all provisions of Acts of Parliament create rights and duties. However, the ECJ has ruled that regulations are "capable of creating individual rights which national courts must protect"[76] and where the provisions of regulations are by their nature and wording directly enforceable, they will readily be held to have direct effect.[77] The ECJ has also deemed regulations to be "horizontally" directly effective, and capable of being enforced by one private litigant against another.[78]

Directives

Directives, as has been seen, are binding on Member States as to the result to be achieved, but leave to the national authorities the choice of forms and methods. Directives, therefore, in contrast to regulations,[79] require that national measures should be adopted to give effect to them.   **14–019**

Implementation of directives

In principle, a directive must be implemented by legislation, not by mere   **14–020** changes in administrative practice or by the adoption of administrative circulars. Implementation must fully satisfy the requirement of legal certainty; Member States must therefore transpose their terms into national law as binding provisions.[80] Moreover it is a general requirement of Community law, following from the principles of legal certainty and legal protection of the individual, that Member States' laws "should be worded unequivocally so as to give the persons concerned a clear and precise understanding of their rights and obligations and enable national courts to ensure that those rights and obligations are observed."[81] Legislative action may not be necessary where the existence of general principles of constitutional or administrative law renders implementation by specific legislation superfluous:

"provided . . . that those principles guarantee that the national authorities will in fact apply the directive fully and that, where the directive is intended to create rights for individuals, the legal position arising from those principles is sufficiently precise and clear and the persons concerned are made fully aware of their rights and, where appropriate, afforded the possibility of relying on them before the national courts. That last condition is of particular importance where the directive in question is

---

[76] Case 43/71 *Politi SAS v Italian Ministry for Finance* [1971] E.C.R. 1039, para.9.
[77] Case 93/71 *Leonesio v Ministero dell' Agricoltura e Foreste* [1972] E.C.R. 287, para.22.
[78] Case C-253/00 *Muñoz y Cia SA and Superior Fruiticola SA v Frumar Ltd, Redbridge Produce Marketing Ltd* [2002] E.C.R. I–7289; see also Opinion of AG Geelhoed, para.41.
[79] See 14–016.
[80] Case 239/85 *Commission v Belgium* [1986] E.C.R. 3645, para.7; on the limits of the Member State's discretion, see Case 143/83 *Commission v Denmark* [1985] E.C.R. 427, paras 8–9; Case C-262/95 *Commission v Germany* [1996] E.C.R. I–5729.
[81] Case 257/86 *Commission v Italy* [1988] E.C.R. 3249, para.12; see 14–093.

intended to accord rights to nationals of other Member States because those nationals are not normally aware of such principles."[82]

14–021 The ECJ has frequently held that "a Member State may not plead provisions, practices or circumstances existing in its internal legal system in order to justify a failure to comply with the obligations and time-limits laid down in a directive".[83] Failure to implement a directive may render the Member State liable in damages, giving those affected a Community right to sue in the national courts.[84]

Direct effect of directives

14–022 Although directives are not "directly applicable" (in the sense that they are not intended to have the force of law in the absence of national implementing measures), nevertheless they may—like some treaty provisions[85]—have "direct effect".[86] This means that litigants before national courts and tribunals may rely directly on provisions contained in a directive if certain conditions are satisfied. First, the time limit set for Member States to implement the directive must have expired. Secondly, the Member State must have failed to implement the directive into national law properly or at all. Thirdly, the directive must create justiciable rights or obligations (this criterion is similar to that for the direct effect of treaty provisions): the provision relied upon must be unconditional and sufficiently precise.[87] Once a directive has been correctly transposed into national law, an individual is confined to his remedies under the domestic legislation and no longer has an individually enforceable Community right under the directive.[88] However, where a directive has been correctly implemented, but is not being correctly *applied* by national administrative authorities, an individual may still rely on the directive before national courts.[89]

14–023 There is an important difference between the operation of the principle of direct effect in relation to treaty provisions and directives. Treaty provisions which are directly effective may be relied upon by a litigant against any other litigant, including fellow citizens and business enterprises. The principle of direct effect allows directives, in contrast, to be relied upon only "vertically" against "emanations of the state".[90]

---

[82] Case 29/84 *Commission v Germany* [1985] E.C.R. 1661, para.23; and Case C-456/03 *Commission of the European Communities v Italy* [2005] E.C.R. I–5335, para.51.
[83] Case C-298/95 *Commission v Germany* [1996] E.C.R. I–6747.
[84] Joined Cases C-6/90 and C-9/90 *Francovich* [1991] E.C.R. I–5357; and see 14–066.
[85] On direct effect of treaty provisions, see 14–010.
[86] Case 41/74 *Van Duyn v Home Office* [1974] E.C.R. 1337.
[87] Case C-246/94 *Cooperativa Agricola Zootecna S Antonio v Amministrazione delle finanze dello Stato* [1996] E.C.R. I–4373, paras 17–19; *Marks & Spencer* [2002] E.C.R. I–6325, para.25.
[88] *R. v Hammersmith and Fulham LBC Ex p. CPRE London Branch* [2000] Env. L.R. 565, paras 32–35.
[89] *Marks & Spencer* [2002] E.C.R. I–6325.
[90] Case 148/78 *Tullio Ratti* [1979] E.C.R. 1629, para.22; Case 152/84 *Marshall v Southampton and South West Hampshire Area Health Authority (Teaching)* [1986] E.C.R. 723 para.48.

This limitation on the direct effect of directives in mitigated in three ways **14–024** however.[91] First, the notion of the state is broadly defined for this purpose; a body is an emanation of the state, "whatever its legal form", if it is "subject to the authority or control of the state or had special powers beyond those which result from the normal rules applicable to relations between individuals".[92] Thus, the obligation to give effect to directives is one incumbent on all authorities of the Member States, including local authorities,[93] public authorities providing health services;[94] the governing body of a profession where "entrusted with a public duty";[95] and the governing body of a voluntary aided school.[96] Most bodies which are subject to judicial review in the English courts would therefore be regarded as a manifestation of the state for the purpose of permitting an individual to invoke a directive against them. The obligation to comply with a Directive applies regardless of the capacity in which the organ of the state is acting.[97] A public corporation will also be deemed to be "an organ of the state" if, whatever its legal form, it has been made responsible pursuant to a measure adopted by the state for providing a public service under the control of the state and has special powers over and above those powers enjoyed by ordinary individuals.[98] Thus, it has been held that, prior to privatisation, British Gas was an organ of the state.[99]

Secondly, there is a requirement that national legislation must be con- **14–025** strued wherever possible so as to conform to directives:[100] this is known as the indirect effect of directives and applies in litigation between private parties.[101] Indirect effect will be discussed in further detail below.[102]

---

[91] See further Ward (2007), pp.31–35.
[92] Case C-188/89 *Foster v British Gas Plc* [1990] E.C.R. I–3313, paras 18, 22; and Cases C-253–258/97 *Helmut Kampelmann* [1997] E.C.R. I–6907, para.47; on "public functions" as a test of amenability to judicial review in England, see 3–041; on "functions of a public nature" in HRA s.6, see 3–069.
[93] Case 103/88 *Costanzo v Comune di Milano* [1989] E.C.R. 1839.
[94] *Marshall* [1986] E.C.R. 723.
[95] Case 56/83 *Rienks* [1983] E.C.R. 4233.
[96] *NUT v St Mary's School* [1997] 3 C.M.L.R. 630, CA.
[97] Public bodies have had directives relating to equality in employment matters enforced against them, see, e.g. Case 222/84 *Johnston v Chief Constable of the Royal Ulster Constabulary* [1986] E.C.R. 1651.
[98] *Foster* [1990] E.C.R. 1–3313, para.20.
[99] *Foster* [1990] E.C.R. 1–3313; HL in [1991] 2 A.C. 306; cf. *Doughty v Rolls Royce* [1992] I.C.R. 538, CA; *Griffin v South West Water Services Ltd* [1995] I.R.L.R. 15 (applying *Foster*, a privatised water company is a State authority against which directives can be enforced directly; the material criterion for the purposes of direct effect is not whether the body in question is under the control of the State but whether the public service which it performs is under State control).
[100] Case 14/83 *Von Colson and Kamann v Land Nordrhein-Westfalen* [1984] E.C.R. 1891.
[101] Case 169/80 *Administration des Douanes v Gondrand Freres* [1981] E.C.R. 1931, para.17; Joined Cases 212–217/80 *Salumi* [1981] E.C.R. 2735, para.10; Case 70/83 *Kloppenburg* [1984] E.C.R. 1075, para.11.
[102] See 14–044.

14–026   Thirdly, directives may be invoked in so-called "triangular" situations,[103] even if the application of the directive would result in what the ECJ has described as "mere adverse repercussions on the rights of third parties, even if the repercussions are certain."[104] This is known as the "incidental effect" of directives. Thus, the ECJ has held that directives which require certain actions on the part of the Member State, such as notification to the Commission of technical standards likely to impede the free movement of goods[105] or the undertaking of an environmental impact assessment,[106] may be relied upon by individuals in national courts, even where this may have negative consequences for third parties. In the case of *Wells*, the claimant sought to rely on Directive 85/337 in judicial review proceedings against the Mineral Planning Authority in respect of its grant of permission to the owner of a long dormant quarry to resume mining in the quarry without having conducted an environmental impact assessment. The ECJ approved reliance on the directive, even though its application had the potential to result in the loss of mining permission for the owner of the quarry.[107] Similarly, the earlier *Medicines Control Agency* case involved judicial review of the Medicines Control Agency for granting a market authorisation to a company in respect of a proprietary medicinal product. The review proceedings were taken by a competing undertaking which held an original market authorisation for a product with the same name on the basis that the subsequent authorisation had been granted by the Agency contrary to the provisions of the relevant directive.[108] The ECJ held that the competitor was entitled to rely on the directive for the purposes of challenging the validity of the authorisation.[109]

---

[103] K. Lackhoff and H. Nyssens, "Direct effect of directives in triangular situations" (1998) 23 E.L. Rev. 397; and S. Weatherill, "Breach of Directives and Breach of Contract" (2001) 26 E.L. Rev. 177; D. Colgan, "Triangular Situations: the Coup de Grâce for the Denial of Horizontal Effect of Community Directives" (2002) 8 E.P.L. 545.

[104] Case C-201/02 *Wells v Secretary of State for Transport, Local Government and the Regions* [2004] E.C.R. I–723, para.57. See also *R. v Durham C Cl Ex p. Huddleston* [2000] 1 W.L.R. 1484, CA at para.18 ("enforcement of a Directive by an individual against the state is not rendered inadmissible solely by its consequential effect on other individuals").

[105] Council Directive 83/189 [1983] O.J. L109/8, as amended; see Case C-194/94 *CIA Security International SA v Signalson SA and Securitel SPRL* [1996] E.C.R. I–2201; Case C-159/2000 *Sapod Audic v Eco-Emballages SA* [2002] E.C.R. I–5031; Case C-443/98 *Unilever Italia SpA v Central Food SpA* [2000] E.C.R. I–7535; C-212/04 *Adeneler* [2006] E.C.R. I–6057; Case C-13/05 *Sonia Chacon Navas v Eurest Cole* [2006] 3 C.M.L.R. 40. The scope of the principle has been limited to those cases where application of national regulations would hinder the use or marketing of a product not in conformity with them: Case C-226/97 *Lemmens* [1998] E.C.R. I–3711.

[106] See, e.g. *Wells* [2004] E.C.R. I–723.

[107] [2004] E.C.R. I–723 paras 57–58, 69–70.

[108] Council Directive 65/65 as amended by Council Directive 87/21 [1987] O.J. L15/36.

[109] Case C-201/94 *R. v The Medicines Control Agency Ex p. Smith & Nephew Pharmaceuticals Ltd* [1996] E.C.R. I–5819, para.39. Whether the third parties who are negatively affected may be able to claim the protection of legitimate expectations in this context is unclear: see Wyatt and Dashwood (2006), para.5–037, n.45.

Decisions

Under provisions of the EC Treaty and of EU legislation, the Council or the **14-027** Commission are empowered to adopt binding decisions, addressed to Member States or to individuals. In accordance with Art.249 of the EC Treaty, decisions are binding in their entirety upon those to whom they are addressed. A decision addressed to a Member State may often impose obligations on it: such a decision might require it, for example, to abolish an unlawful tax or an unlawful state aid. Such decisions may have direct effect where their terms are clear and precise, and so confer rights on individuals enforceable in the national courts.[110]

THE CHARTER OF FUNDAMENTAL RIGHTS OF THE EU

At present, the Charter is a text, solemnly proclaimed at Nice on December **14-028** 7, 2000, by the European Parliament, the Council and the Commission and has been published as such in the Official Journal.[111] In terms of content, the Charter is often said not provide any new rights that were not already protected by Community law, and that its purpose is merely declaratory.[112] However it is clear that the Charter reformulates existing rights, with potential for different interpretations;[113] while it also recognises as fundamental, rights which would not previously have been described as such.[114] It provides a combination of classic civil and political rights, in addition to economic and social rights, which are found in six chapters: dignity;[115] freedoms;[116] equality;[117] solidarity;[118] citizen's rights;[119] justice.[120] The rights were derived from a number of sources: rights recognised in the TEU, the EC Treaty, the ECHR, the Social Charters adopted by the Community and

---

[110] Case 9/70 *Grad v Finanzamt* [1970] E.C.R. 825.

[111] OJ 2000, C364/1; see Craig (2006) Ch.14; P. Eeckhout, "The EU Charter of Fundamental Rights and the Federal Question" (2002) 39 C.M.L. Rev. 945; L. Besselink, "The Member States, the National Constitutions and the Scope of the Charter" (2000) 8 M.J. 68; J. Morijn, *Judicial Reference to the EU Fundamental Rights Charter: First Experiences and Possible Prospects*, Working Paper I, Coimbra Human Rights Centre; A. Menéndez, *Chartering Europe: the Charter of Fundamental Rights of the European Union* Lucas Pires Working Papers on European Constitutionalism, WP 2001/03; C. McCrudden, *The Future of the EU Charter of Fundamental Rights* Jean Monnet Working Paper 13/01.

[112] Lord Goldsmith, "The Charter of Rights—A Brake not an Accelerator" (2004) 5 E.H.R.L.R. 473. Other commentators have disputed this: P. Eeckhout, (2002) 39 C.M.L. Rev. 945.

[113] For example, while Art.8(1) ECHR refers to the right to "respect . . . for correspondence"; Art.7 of the Charter refers to right to "respect . . . for communications" which takes into account the growth of electronic communications.

[114] Eeckhout, (2002) 39 C.M.L. Rev. 945 p.951.

[115] Chapter Arts 1–5.

[116] Chapter Arts 6–19.

[117] Chapter Arts 20–26.

[118] Chapter Arts 27–38.

[119] Chapter Arts 39–46.

[120] Chapter Arts 47–50.

by the Council of Europe, and the case law of the ECJ and European Court of Human Rights; rights recognised in the constitutions of the Member States; and international human rights treaties concluded by the Member States.[121] A distinction is drawn between rights and principles;[122] although the impact of the distinction and the categorisation of provisions as rights or principles is unclear.[123] Any Charter provisions based on existing Community law rights have the same meaning and scope as their corresponding provisions in Community law;[124] and likewise, notwithstanding any difference of language, the rule is that those Charter provisions which correspond to a provision in the ECHR have the same meaning and scope as the Convention rights.[125] In so far as Charter provisions draw upon the constitutional traditions common to the Member States, they should be interpreted "in harmony" with those constitutional traditions.[126]

Limited legal effect of the Charter

14–029 The Charter has not been proclaimed by the Member States and was not included in the Treaty of Nice: accordingly, the provisions of the Charter do not have founding treaty status. The fact that the Charter has not been adopted however, does not mean that the proclamation is devoid of all legal effect and it is generally accepted that the solemn proclamation of the Charter expresses a level of voluntary commitment which may produce legal effects.[127] In particular, although the Charter is not legally binding, "it is worthwhile referring to it given that it constitutes the expression at the highest level, of a democratically established political consensus on what must today be considered as the catalogue of fundamental rights guaranteed by the Community legal order".[128]

14–030 The ECJ has referred to the Charter on a number of occasions, beginning with a case in which the Community legislation in question, Council Directive 2003/86/EC of September 22, 2003 on the right to family

---

[121] Charter, Preamble.

[122] Art.I–9 of the Constitutional Treaty stated that "[t]he Union shall recognise the rights, freedoms and principles set out in the Charter of Fundamental Rights which constitutes Part II"; see also Art.52(1) Charter (referring to "rights and freedoms") and Art.23 Charter, which refers to the "principle" of equality between men and women and Art.21 which sets out the right to non-discrimination on grounds of sex.

[123] The word "principle" sometimes appears in the wording of the provision, but frequently its special character must be inferred from other aspects of the drafting method, e.g. the formula "the Union recognises and respects" is used to signal that a provision is a principle rather than a right. An example of this, in relation to social security benefits and social services, is found in Art.34 of the Charter.

[124] Charter Art.52(2).

[125] Charter Art.52(3).

[126] Charter Art.52(4) as amended by Constitutional Treaty Art.II–112(4).

[127] Eeckhout (2002) 39 C.M.L. Rev. 945, 947; and Opinion of AG Kokott in Case C-105/04 *Nederlandse Federatieve Vereniging voor de Groothandel op Elektrotechnisch Gebied v Commission* [2006] E.C.R. 8425, para.107, n.59 (noting that "it must be taken into account" in cartel proceedings that the Commission has made a solemn commitment to comply with the Charter of Fundamental Rights).

[128] Opinion of AG Mischo in Joined Cases C-20/00 and C-64/00 *Booker Aquaculture and Hydro Seafood* [2003] E.C.R. I–7411, para.126.

reunification, had invoked the Charter in its Preamble.[129] The Court noted that the Community legislature had acknowledged the importance of the Charter by stating, in the second recital in the preamble to Directive, that the Directive observes the principles recognised not only by Article 8 of the ECHR but also in the Charter. The Court observed that

> "the principal aim of the Charter, as is apparent from its preamble, is to reaffirm 'rights as they result, in particular, from the constitutional traditions and international obligations common to the Member States, the Treaty on European Union, the Community Treaties, the [ECHR], the Social Charters adopted by the Community and by the Council of Europe and the case-law of the Court . . . and of the European Court of Human Rights'".

The Charter is regularly cited by parties in making applications to the ECJ[130] **14–031** and by national courts in preliminary references.[131] It is cited regularly in opinions of Advocates General[132] and in judgments of the CFI. In the CFI's *Jégo-Quéré* judgment, where the right to an effective remedy enshrined in Art.47 of the Charter was relied on, alongside Arts 6 and 13 ECHR, to justify a broadening of the scope of standing to challenge an EC Regulation.[133] For the most part, the Charter has been used to bolster arguments that could be made on other grounds, most notably European Convention grounds,[134] rather than as a self-standing ground of judicial review; and

---

[129] Case C-540/03 *Parliament v Council* [2006] E.C.R. I–5769, para.38. See also Cases C-411/04 *Salzgitter Mannesmann GmbH v Commission* [2007] 4 C.M.L.R. 17; Case C-432/05 *Unibet (London) Ltd v Justitiekanslern* [2007] 2 C.M.I.R. 30, para.37; Case C-303/05 *Advocaten voor de Wereld VZW v Leden van de Ministerraad* [2007] 3 C.M.L.R. 1, para.46 (noting that the principle of the legality of criminal offences and penalties and the principle of equality and non-discrimination are "reaffirmed" in the Charter).

[130] See, e.g. Case C-547/03P *AIT v Commission* [2006] 2 C.M.L.R. 29, para.26.

[131] See, e.g. C-453/03 *R. (on the application of ABNA) Ltd v Secretary of State for Health* [2006] 1 C.M.L.R. 48, para.27. On preliminary references, see 14–075.

[132] See Opinion of AG Tizzano in Case C-173/99 *BECTU* [2001] E.C.R. I–4881, para.28; Opinion of AG Leger in Case C-353/99 *P Council v Hautala* [2001] E.C.R. I–9565, para.80 (noting that the Charter is not a "mere list of purely moral principles without any consequences"); Opinion of AG Kokott in Case C-105/04 *Nederlandse Federatieve Vereniging voor de Groothandel op Elektrotechnisch Gebied v Commission* [2006] E.C.R. 8725, para.107. (noting that the Charter does "as a legal reference, provide information on the fundamental rights guaranteed by the Community legal order"); Opinion of AG Case C-208/00 *Überseering BV v Nordic Construction Company Baumanagement GmbH* (NCC) [2005] 1 C.M.L.R. 1, para.59 (describing the Charter as "an invaluable reflection of the common denominator of the legal values paramount in Member States, from which emanate, in their turn, the general principles of Community law"); Opinion of AG Tizzano in *R. (Broadcasting, Entertainment, Cinematographic and Theatre Union) v Secretary of State for Trade and Industry* [2001] E.C.R. I152, para.28 (noting that "the relevant statements of the Charter cannot be ignored"); Opinion of AG Mengozzi in Case C-354/04 P *Gestoras Pro Amnistia v Council* [2007] 2 C.M.L.R. 22, para.76.

[133] Case T–177/01 *Jégo-Quéré* [2002] ECR II–2365, para.42. The ECJ did not follow the CFI's approach: see Case C-263/02P [2004] E.C.R. I–3425.

[134] See, e.g. Opinion of AG Kokott in Case C-10/05 *Mattern v Ministre du Travail et de l'Emploi*, [2006] E.C.R. I–3145 (referring to the "right to a family life, as expressed in Art.8 of the European Convention on Human Rights and now also in Art.7 of the Charter of fundamental rights of the European Union").

rights are often said to be "restated",[135] "repeated"[136] or "reaffirmed"[137] by the Charter. The English courts have also cited the Charter to bolster arguments made on other grounds;[138] or on occasion to assist in interpretation of rights found elsewhere.[139]

14–032   The Charter is to be binding on EU institutions and on Member States "only when they are implementing Union law".[140] The current position of the ECJ is that Member States must abide by the fundamental rights jurisprudence of the ECJ when acting "within the scope of Community law"[141] and it is widely accepted that the horizontal provisions of the Charter will not be interpreted more narrowly than the ECJ's current formulation.[142] Any limitation on the exercise of the rights and freedoms recognised by the Charter must be provided for by law and respect the essence of those rights and freedoms. Subject to the principle of proportionality, limitations may be made only if they necessarily and genuinely meet objectives of general interest recognised by the Union or the need to protect the rights and freedoms of others.[143]

GENERAL PRINCIPLES OF LAW

14–033   An important source of Community law is the general principles of law applied by the ECJ. These principles stem from the legal systems of the Member States and have been used by the ECJ, by a process analogous with the development of the common law by the English courts, to supplement

---

[135] See, e.g. *ABNA* [2006] 1 C.M.L.R. 48, para.27.
[136] Opinion of AG Tizzano C-465/00 *Rechnungshof v Österreichischer Rundfunk* [2003] E.C.R. I–4989, para.2, n.5.
[137] *Advocaten voor de Wereld* [2007] 3 C.M.L.R. 1; Case T–38/02 *Groupe Danone t Commission of the European Communities* [2006] 4 C.M.L.R. 25, para.216.
[138] See, e.g. *White v Paul Davidson & Taylor* [2004] EWCA Civ 1511; [2005] P.N.L.R. 15 a [41].
[139] *R. (on the application of Hooper) v Secretary of State for Work and Pensions* [2005] UKHL 29; [2005] 1 W.L.R. 1681 at [88] (Lord Hope referring to a contrast between the Charter and ECHR Art.14 to help elucidate the meaning of the latter. Thus, while Art.21 of the Charter and Art.II–81 of the Treaty "expressed a free-standing anti-discrimination prohibition. Art.14 does not" with the result that "Article 14 cannot be transformed by the jurisprudence of the Strasbourg court into a simple prohibition, along the lines of its Charter counterpart") *Bellinger v Bellinger* [2003] UKHL 21; [2003] 2 A.C. 467 at [69] (Lord Hope contrasting ECHR Art.12 which protects the right to marry of "men and women of marriageable age" with Art.9 of the Charter which "states simply that the 'right to marry' shall be guaranteed")
[140] Art.51(1) Charter.
[141] Case C-260/89 *ERT v DEP & Sotirious Kouvelas* [1991] E.C.R. 2925; and 14–121.
[142] Art.II–112(7) of the Constitutional Treaty noted that "[t]he explanation drawn up by way of providing guidance in the interpretation of the Charter of Fundamental Rights shall be given due regard to by the courts of the Union and the Member States". The Declaration concerning the Explanations relating to the Charter of Fundamental Rights interpret Art.51(1) to mean that the Charter is binding on Member States when they "act in the context of Community law" and refers specifically to the existing ECJ case law, see, e.g. Case 5/88 *Wachauf v Germany* [1989] E.C.R. 2609; Case C-260/89 *ERT v DEP & Sotiriou Kouvelas* [1991] E.C.R. 2925. See further 14–119.
[143] Art.52(1).

and refine the EU Treaties and secondary legislation. In order for the ECJ to apply such a principle, it is not necessary that it is recognised in the domestic law of all Member States; and even where it is so recognised, its scope in Community law may be different from its scope in national law. Where a Community measure infringes a general principle, such as the principle of non-discrimination (or equality), it may be annulled by the ECJ;[144] it may also give rise to an action in the ECJ for damages against the EU under Art.288(2)[215(2)] EC. Further, the ECJ uses the general principles as an aid for the interpretation of EU acts. The general principles of law are binding not only on the EU institutions but also, within the scope of Community law, on the Member States and a national measure may be held invalid on the ground that it is incompatible with such a principle.[145]

European Communities Act 1972

So far as the courts and tribunals of England and Wales are concerned, the 14–034 sources of Community law are incorporated into English law by virtue of the European Communities Act 1972 and its subsequent amendments. The Act has been described as a "constitutional" statute.[146]

The European Communities Act 1972 seeks to give legal effect in the 14–035 United Kingdom to the principles of primacy and direct effect. The scheme of the Act is straightforward; apart from limited amendments to the law, it contains in s.2, two principal provisions, s.2(1) and s.2(2), which enable the entire corpus of Community law to be given effect in the United Kingdom. Section 2(1) provides in substance that all directly effective Community law should have such effect in the United Kingdom:

> "All such rights, powers, liabilities, obligations and restrictions from time to time created or arising by or under the Treaties, and all such remedies and procedures from time to time provided for by or under the Treaties, as in accordance with the Treaties are without further enactment to be given legal effect or used in the United Kingdom shall be recognised and available in law, and be enforced, allowed and followed accordingly; and the expression 'enforceable Community right' and similar expressions shall be read as referring to one to which this subsection applies."

The wording makes it clear that the question whether a particular provision has direct effect[147] is determined by Community law.

---

[144] See 14–087.
[145] See 14–119.
[146] *Thoburn v Sunderland City Council* [2002] EWHC 195 (Admin) [2003] Q.B. 151 at [62]–[64], [69].
[147] Elegantly rendered by s. 2(1) as: to be given legal effect, etc. without further enactment.

14-036   Section 2(2) makes provision for the implementation of Community law in the United Kingdom by means of subordinate legislation.[148] This part of the Act has been amended by Pt III of the Legislative and Regulatory Reform Act 2006. Implementation of Community law may be by Order in Council or by order, rules, regulations or schemes made by a minister or department designated for the purpose by Order in Council.[149] Implementing measures will take the form of a statutory instrument.[150] If not approved by each House, they will be subject to annulment by negative resolution of either House.[151] Paragraph 1A of Sch.2 to the 1972 Act, as inserted by s.28 of the Legislative and Regulatory Reform Act 2006, provides for ambulatory references to be made to Community legislation in the implementing statutory instrument. Detailed provisions is also made for statutory instruments containing provisions made in exercise of the power conferred by s.2(2) of the 1972 Act to be laid before Parliament for approval by resolution of each House of Parliament and the instrument also contains provision made in exercise of a power conferred by any other enactment and various conditions apply.[152]

14-037   Section 2(4) of the Act provides that implementing measures made under s.2(2) may include 'any such provision (of any such extent) as might be made by Act of Parliament'. It would seem therefore that such measures are not subject to the limitations normally applicable to delegated legislation and that they may override Acts of Parliament.[153]

14-038   Section 3(1) of the Act provides as follows:

"For the purposes of all legal proceedings any question as to the meaning or effect of any of the Treaties, or as to the validity, meaning or effect o

---

[148] For the interpretation of s.2(2), see *R. v Secretary of State for Trade and Industry Ex p Unison* [1997] 1 C.M.L.R. 459; *Oakley Inc v Animal Ltd* [2005] EWCA Civ 1191; [2006 Ch. 337 at [28] and [39] (Waller L.J.: s.2(2)(a) is concerned primarily with the bringing into force of Community obligations arising from the Treaty and implementing regulations should be construed by reference to the directive being introduced; since a line by line approach to the directive was not required, it was not logical to confine the power to make regulations to the new aspects of the law and to suggest that transitional provisions which the UK had a choice to take advantage of and which retained old law for a period needed primary legislation whereas the rest of the directive did not; while s.2(2)(b) "is a subsection to enable further measures to be taken which naturally arise from or closely relate to the primary purpose being achieved"). See also *Department of the Environment, Food and Rural Affairs Asda Ltd* [2003] UKHL 71; [2004] 1 W.L.R. 105, para.26 (subordinate legislation may implement not only existing EC obligations, but also embrace future amendments to the obligations).

[149] S.2(2) ECA as amended by Legislative and Regulatory Reform Act 2006 s.27(1)(a).

[150] Sch. 2 para.2(1) and s.1(1) of the Statutory Instruments Act 1946.

[151] Sch. 2 para.2(2).

[152] Sch.2 paras 2A–2C as inserted by the Legislative and Regulatory Reform Act 2006, s.29.

[153] *R. v Secretary of State for Transport Ex p. Factortame Ltd (No.1)* [1990] A.C. 85 at 14 (Lord Bridge); P. Craig, "Sovereignty of the UK Parliament after Factortame" (1991) Y.E.L 221. Implementing measures made under s. 2(2) may not, however, by Sch.2: (a) impose or increase taxation: (b) enact retroactive legislation: (c) sub-delegate legislative power (except to make rules of procedure for any court or tribunal); (d) create any new criminal offence punishable with imprisonment for more than two years or punishable on summary conviction with imprisonment for more than the prescribed term (see Sch.2, para.3) or with a fine of more than, £5000 (if not calculated on a daily basis) or with a fine of more than £100 per day.

any Community instrument, shall be treated as a question of law (and, if not referred to the European Court, be for determination as such in accordance with the principles laid down by and any relevant decision of the European Court)."

Thus the case law of the ECJ is expressed to be binding on United Kingdom courts and tribunals.

CHALLENGING A NATIONAL MEASURE IN A NATIONAL COURT

In judicial review as in other types of litigation, national courts and the ECJ **14–039** and CFI have separate and different roles in adjudicating on issues of Community law. In England and Wales, a claimant for judicial review in the Administrative Court may seek to utilise rules of Community law in various ways. A claimant for judicial review may argue that an act or omission by a public authority in England and Wales is in breach of Community law.[154] By virtue of the principle of supremacy, all national measures—including Acts of Parliament—may be challenged as being contrary to any rule of Community law.[155] Community law is thus a broad "chapter head" of judicial review in addition to those of illegality, procedural impropriety and irrationality propounded by Lord Diplock.[156] Alternatively, like a breach of Convention rights, a breach of Community law may be held to offend the ground of illegality. The constituent parts of this chapter head will be considered in more detail below.[157] Where a Member State makes delegated legislation or takes administrative action to implement EU provisions, such national measures may also be open to challenge on the ground that the EU provisions are themselves invalid.[158] Even the "intention or obligation" of the government to implement a directive, without further implementing measures, is open to challenge on the ground that the directive is invalid.[159] A statutory instrument made pursuant to s.2(2) of the European Commu-

[54] On what constitutes a public authority (or a body exercising public functions), see Ch.3 above. Note that the Community law concept of "emanation of the state", used to determine against whom directives may be directly effective, is formulated in different terms: see para.14–024, above.
[55] See 14–113; *R. v Secretary of State for Transport Ex p. Factortame Ltd (No.2)* [1991] 1 A.C. 603, HL; *R. v Secretary of State for Employment Ex p. Equal Opportunities Commission* [1995] 1 A.C. 1 at 28; *A v Chief Constable of West Yorkshire* [2004] UKHL 21; [2005] 1 A.C. 51.
[56] *Council of Civil Service Unions v Minister for the Civil Service* [1985] A.C. 374 at 410.
[57] See 14–112.
[58] See, e.g. *R. v Minister of Agriculture, Fisheries and Food Ex p. FEDESA* [1988] 3 C.M.L.R. 61, HC. This ground of challenge presumably does not apply to Acts of Parliament. Note that a national court has no power to determine that a Community measure is invalid (though it may declare that it is valid): see 14–043.
[59] Case C-491/01, *R. v Secretary of State Ex p. British American Tobacco (Investments) Ltd and Imperial Tobacco Ltd* [2002] E.C.R. I–11453, paras 2, 24–25, 28–41 (this challenge was also permitted although the time limit for implementing the directive had not expired).

nities Act 1972 may also be challenged on the ground that it is contrary to *English* law if it goes beyond the enabling provision by purporting to do more than is required to implement the Community measure.[160]

14–040   Arguments based on Community law cannot be used in all cases. A claimant for judicial review needs to show that the act or omission of the public authority which is complained about is required or permitted by Community law. If the impugned decision is authorised solely by national law—that is, it is wholly internal to a Member State—then Community law has no application.[161] It is difficult to describe succinctly what fields of government decision-making will be open to challenge on Community grounds and the range of government actions which can be deemed to be purely internal is constantly decreasing.[162]

CHALLENGING A COMMUNITY MEASURE IN A NATIONAL COURT

14–041   Most claims for judicial review in which issues of Community law arise are concerned with attempts to argue that a public authority in the United Kingdom has acted contrary to Community law, as outlined in the previous sections. Occasionally, however, the intent is different and the claimant seeks to argue that a Community regulation,[163] directive[164] or a decision,[165] or a rule contained within it, is itself invalid. This may be a necessary step in an attempt to challenge a national measure (e.g. an argument that a statutory instrument is ineffective because the directive which it purports to transpose into English law is, as a matter of Community law, invalid) or the aim may

---

[160] *Hayward v Cammell Laird Shipbuilders (No. 2)* [1988] A.C. 894, HL; see also n.148.

[161] See, e.g. *R. v Ministry of Agriculture, Fisheries and Food Ex p. First City Trading Ltd* [1997] 1 C.M.L.R. 250 (general principles of Community law could not be used as ground of review of UK's Beef Transfer Scheme, which granted emergency aid to slaughterhouses in the wake of the BSE crisis, because the Scheme was not adopted pursuant to Community law and the UK government did not have to rely upon any Community law permission in order to implement it): *Krasniqi v Chief Adjudication Officer* [1999] C.O.D. 154 (entitlement to welfare benefits of Kosovan refugee in UK a matter wholly internal to UK so, despite its literal wording, Community Regulation on Application of Social Security Schemes 1408/71 did not apply). However, the number of areas untouched by Community law is shrinking: see 14–006.

[162] See, e.g. Case C-60/00 *Carpenter v Secretary of State for the Home Department* [2002] E.C.R. I-6279 (upholding a challenge to a UK deportation order in respect of a third country national on the ground that it violated the third country national's husband's freedom to provide services pursuant to Art.49 EC, as read in the light of Art.8 ECHR). This case is discussed in further detail at 14–122. *cf. W(China) v Secretary of State for the Home Department* [2006] EWCA Civ 1494; [2007] 1 C.M.L.R. 17 (distinguishing *Carpenter*). See further Case C-186/01 *Dory v Germany* [2003] E.C.R. I-2479, para.35 (ECJ considered Germany's practice of reserving compulsory military service to men to be outside the scope of Community law but commented that "decisions of the Member States concerning the organisation of their armed forces cannot be completely excluded from the application of Community law, particularly where observance of the principle of equal treatment of men and women in connection with employment, access to military posts, is concerned").

[163] See 14–016.

[164] See 14–019.

[165] See 14–027.

bluntly be the Community measure in and of itself.[166] The grounds for arguing that Community measures are invalid are considered below.

There are obvious problems in allowing national courts to adjudicate upon the efficacy of rules of Community law—not least the practical ones that courts in Member States may reach different conclusions and the judgments of the courts in one Member State have no binding precedent in others. To avoid these difficulties, the following arrangements have been devised. National courts are allowed to examine the validity of a Community measure and, if they decide that the arguments advanced to challenge its validity are unfounded, they may conclude that the Community measure is valid.[167] **14–042**

National courts are not, however, permitted to declare measures adopted by EU institutions invalid: if the national court is minded to do this, it must refer the question to the ECJ for a preliminary ruling on the correct interpretation of Community law.[168] The ECJ has sole jurisdiction to rule definitively on the validity of actions and omissions of the EU institutions.[169] Pending the ECJ's ruling, a national court may grant interim remedies. Where the contested Community measure has been incorporated into national law by national legislation, for example, measures implementing a directive or furthering the implementation of a regulation,[170] the national court may grant interim remedies to suspend the operation of the national measure.[171] National courts are not however permitted to grant interim relief where the Community fails to act since in such cases, they cannot make a reference to the ECJ.[172] **14–043**

---

[56] See, e.g. *Ex p. British American Tobacco (Investments) Ltd* [2002] E.C.R. 11453.

[57] Case 314/85 *Firma Foto-Frost v Hauptzollamt Lübeck-Ost* [1987] E.C.R. 4199, para.14.

[58] *Firma Foto-Frost* [1987] E.C.R. 4199, para.20. On the procedure by which national courts obtain preliminary rulings, see 14–075. Case C-344/04 *R. (International Air Transport Association) v Department of Transport* [2006] ECR I–403.

[59] *Firma Foto-Frost* (n.167), para.17.

[0] Case C-143/88 *Zuckerfabrik Süderdithmarschen AG v Hauptzollant Itzehoc* [1991] E.C.R. I-415, paras 23–31.

[1] Three conditions were set out in Case C-143/88 *Zuckerfabrik Süderdithmarschen AG v Hauptzollant Itzehoc* [1991] E.C.R. I-415, para.33 and a fourth was added in C-465/93 *Atlanta Fruchthandelsgesellschaft mbH v Bundesamt fur Ernahrung and Forstwirtschaft* [1995] E.C.R. I–3761, para.51. Interim relief can only be granted (i) if the national court entertains serious doubts as to the validity of the Community measure and, should the question of the validity of the contested measure not already have been brought before the ECJ, itself refers that question to the ECJ; (ii) if there is urgency and a threat of serious and irreparable damage to the applicant; (iii) if the national court takes due account of the Community's interests; and (iv) in its assessment of all those conditions, the national court respects any decisions of the ECJ or the CFI ruling on the lawfulness of the regulation or on an application for interim measures seeking similar interim relief at Community level. For an example of interim relief being granted, see *R. (on the application of ABNA) v Secretary of State for Health* [2003] EWHC 2420 (Admin).

[2] Case C-68/95 *T Port GmbH v Bundesanstalt fürLandwirtschaft und Ernährung* [1996] E.C.R. I–6065, para.53.

INTERPRETATION BY NATIONAL COURTS

14–044 In the course of a claim for judicial review, as in other forms of legal proceedings, national courts may have the task of interpreting national legislation which deals with the same subject matter as Community law. They have an obligation to interpret national legislation in a manner which is consistent with and gives effect to the rules of Community law.[173] This "principle of conforming interpretation"[174] or "indirect effect", is an incident of the general Art.10[5] EC duty placed on all national institutions in Member States to:

> "take all appropriate measures, whether general or particular, to ensure fulfilment of the obligations arising out of this Treaty or resulting from action taken by the institutions of the Community. They shall facilitate the achievement of the Community's tasks.
>
> They shall abstain from any measure which could jeopardise the attainment of the objectives of this Treaty."[175]

14–045 More recently, the ECJ has stated that the obligation is "inherent in the system of the Treaty" since it permits the national courts to ensure the full effectiveness of Community law when it determines the dispute before it.[17] Thus, national legislation must be construed in the light of the wording and aims of any relevant Community measures, including provisions of the EC Treaty;[177] directives;[178] recommendations of institutions, although they have no binding force;[179] and even a Framework Decision adopted under Art.3-

---

[173] This obligation is sometimes referred to as the obligation of "conform interpretation": S Weatherill, *Cases and Materials on EU Law* (2007), p.148.

[174] Case C-105/03 *Criminal Proceedings against Pupino* [2005] E.C.R. I–5285, para.43; an *Dabas v High Court of Justice in Madrid* [2007] UKHL 6; [2007] 2 W.L.R. 254 at [76].

[175] See, e.g. Case 14/83 *Von Colson and Kamann v Land Nordrhein-Westfalen* [1984] E.C.F 189, para.26.

[176] Case C-397/01 *Pfeiffer v Deutsches Rotes Kreuz* [2004] E.C.R. I–8835, para.114.

[177] See, e.g. Case C-165/91 *Van Munster v Rijksdienst voor Pensioenen* [1994] E.C.R. I–466 (where a national court has to characterise a social security benefit awarded under th statutory scheme of another Member State, for the purpose of applying a provision of i domestic law, it should interpret its own legislation in the light of the aims of Arts 48–51 E and, as far as is at all possible, prevent its interpretation from being such as to discourage migrant worker from actually exercising his Community law right of freedom of movement

[178] Case 14/83 *Von Colson and Kamann v Land Nordrhein-Westfalen* [1984] E.C.R. 18 para.26; Case C-106/89 *Marleasing SA v La Comercial Internacional de Alimentacion S* [1990] E.C.R. I–4135 (Spanish Civil Code had to be interpreted in the light of Directiv 68/151). Leading House of Lords cases involving interpretation of directives include *Litster Forth Dry Dock & Engineering Co Ltd* [1990] 1 A.C. 546 (the UK's Transfer of Undertakin (Protection of Employment) Regulations 1981 were made in order to implement Directiv 77/187 and had to be construed to give effect to the purpose of the directive); *Pickstone Freemans* [1989] A.C. 66 (employee's claim to be doing work of equal value to a more high paid employee of the opposite sex not barred by the fact that other employees of the opposi sex are employed on the same terms as the claimant). See further *Ghaidan v Godin-Mendoz* [2004] UKHL 30; [2004] 2 A.C. 557 at [45]–[48] (Lord Steyn, discussing the principle *Marleasing, Litster, Pickstone*).

[179] Case 322/88 *Grimaldi* [1989] E.C.R. 4407, para.18 (national courts are bound to tak recommendations into consideration in order to decide disputes submitted to them, particular where they cast light on the interpretation of national measures adopted in order implement them or where they are designed to supplement binding Community provisions

TEU, which falls under the third pillar and not the Community pillar of the EU.[180] In respect of this last measure, while there is no counterpart to Art.10 EC in the non-EC parts of the EU Treaty, the ECJ has invoked Art.1 TEU and the need for the Union to carry out its task effectively and to the system being based on co-operation between Member States and EU institutions.[181]

Most of the case law in this area has focused on the obligation to interpret national law in the light of the wording and purpose of any pertinent directives and indirect effect is the primary method of ensuring the effectiveness of directives.[182] The obligation of conforming interpretation applies even if a Member State has failed to transpose a directive into national law by the due date, or it has failed to do so fully.[183] The interpretative obligation also applies whether the national legislation was passed before or after the directive in question and whether or not the national legislation was passed specifically to implement the directive.[184] After some uncertainty,[185] it has been settled that the date on which the interpretative obligation arises is the date on which the period for transposition of the directive has expired,[186] albeit that, from the date upon which a directive has entered into force, the courts of the Member State must refrain as far as possible from interpreting domestic law in a manner which might seriously compromise, after the period for transposition has expired, attainment of the objective pursued by that directive.[187] 14–046

In so far as the extent of the interpretative obligation is concerned, in 1990, the ECJ stated that:[188] 14–047

> "in applying national law, whether the provisions were adopted before or after the directive, the national court is called upon to interpret it is required to do so, as far as possible, in the light of the wording and

---

[180] *Pupino* [2005] E.C.R. I–5285, paras 41–43. On the pillar structure, see 14–005.

[181] *Pupino* [2005] E.C.R. I–5285, paras 41–43. The judgment is also significant due to the decoupling of direct effect from indirect effect as Art.34 TEU makes it clear that Framework Decisions under the third pillar cannot entail direct effect: see D. Chalmers *et al*, *European Union Law* (2006), pp.389–390.

[182] G. Betlem, "The Doctrine of Consistent Interpretation: Managing Legal Uncertainty" (2002) 22 O.J.L.S. 397, p.399.

[183] *Von Colson* [1984] E.C.R. 189.

[184] *Marleasing* [1990] E.C.R. I–4135; Case C-144/04 *Mangold v Helm* [2006] 1 C.M.L.R. 43, para.68.

[185] See Case 80/86 *Kolpinghuis Nijmegen* [1987] E.C.R. 3979, para.15 and Case C-456/98 *Centrosteel v Adipol* [2000] E.C.R. I–6007, para.17 (interpretative duty arose in relation to "facts postdating the expiry of the period for transposing the Directive"); and *cf.* Case C-212/04 *Adeneler v Ellinikos Organismos Galaktos* [2006] E.C.R. 6057, paras 47–54, AG Kokott indicated a preference for the duty of interpretation to begin from the moment of publication, arguing that direct effect of Directives derives from Art.249 EC which binds Member States at the moment of transposition, while by contrast indirect effect is based on Art.10 EC which imposes a positive obligation on all national bodies, including courts, to take all appropriate measures to ensure compliance with Community law.

[186] *Adeneler* [2006] E.C.R. 6057, para.115.

[187] [2006] E.C.R. 6057, para.123.

[188] *Marleasing* [1990] E.C.R. I–4135, para.8. See also Case C-91/02 *Dori v Recreb Srl* [1994] E.C.R. I–3325, para.26. Art.249 EC is at 14–014.

purpose of the directive in order to achieve the result pursued by the latter and thereby comply with the third paragraph of Art.189 [now Art.249] of the Treaty".[189]

14–048 Since then questions have arisen as to what this requires—does "as far as possible" require a national court to distort the clear meaning of national legislation? It is clear that no ambiguity in the national legislation is required and the court must first establish the meaning of the EU obligation and conclude whether it is possible to achieve the necessary reconciliation with national law.[190] English courts have stated that although a construction which departs boldly from the ordinary meaning of the language can be adopted, "the exercise must still be one of construction and it should not exceed the limits of what is reasonable".[191] The ECJ has also indicated in the past that a *contra legem* interpretation is not required; and that, where it is not possible to interpret national legislation in conformity with the Directive, a damages remedy against the relevant Member State is the only option.[192]

14–049 Recently, however, the ECJ has articulated the obligation on the national court in more robust terms, as being "to do whatever lies within its jurisdiction, having regard to the whole body of national law, to ensure" that the directive is fully effective.[193] In the *Pfeiffer* case, the ECJ considered the appropriate interpretation of the German implementation of Directive 93/104, the Working Time Directive, which permitted derogation from the 48–hour weekly limit found in the Directive. The ECJ described the interpretative obligation as requiring the national court to do whatever lay within its jurisdiction to ensure that the maximum period of weekly working time, which is set at 48 hours by Art.6(2) of Directive 93/104, was not exceeded.[194] This effectively required the national court to search for interpretative methods which would enable it to interpret national legislation permitting derogation from the 48–hour limit, to preclude derogation from the 48–hour limit.[195]

14–050 The ECJ has stated repeatedly that the interpretative duty should not result in an imposition on an individual of an obligation laid down in a directive which has not been transposed.[196] This statement must also be

---

[189] See also Case C-456/98 *Centrosteel v Adipol* [2000] E.C.R. I–6007, para.19.

[190] *Pickstone* [1989] A.C. 66; *Litster* [1990] 1 A.C. 546; C. Docksey and B. Fitzpatrick, "The Duty of National Courts to Interpret Provisions of National Law in accordance with Community Law" (1991) 20 I.L.J. 113, p.119.

[191] *Clarke v Kato* [1998] 1 W.L.R. 1647 at 1656 (Lord Clyde); and *Durham CC Ex p. Huddleston* [2000] 1 W.L.R. 1484 at para.10 (primary legislation incompatible with EC Directive and "convergent construction" solution not possible).

[192] Case C-334/92 *Wagner-Miret v Fondo de Garnantia Salarial* [1993] E.C.R. I–6911, para.22.

[193] Cases C-397–403/01 *Pfeiffer v Deutsches Rotes Kreuz* [2004] E.C.R. I–8835, para.118.

[194] *Pfeiffer* [2004] E.C.R. I–8835, para.119.

[195] See further Case C-185/97 *Coote v Granada Hospitality* [1998] E.C.R. I–5199; Joined Cases C-240–244/98 *Océano Grupo Editorial v Rocio Murciano Quintero* [2000] E.C.R. I–4491; S. Drake, "Twenty Years after *Von Colson*: the Impact of 'Indirect Effect' on the Protection of the Individual's Community Rights" (2005) 30 E.L. Rev. 329.

[196] Case C-168/95 *Criminal Proceedings against Arcaro* [1996] E.C.R. I–4705, para.42.

qualified however. It is clear that a directive cannot, of itself and independently of a national law adopted by a Member State for its implementation, have the effect of determining or aggravating the liability in criminal law of persons who act in contravention of the provisions of that directive.[197] However, outside of the criminal law context, the obligation of conforming interpretation may result in civil law obligations for private individuals.[198]

EFFECTIVE PROCEDURES AND REMEDIES[199]

While occasionally Community law provides procedural rules for the enforcement of Community rights,[200] Community law more often than not vests rights in individuals without prescribing explicitly the procedural rules applicable in national courts or tribunals or the remedies for the infringement of the rights. The question then arises to what extent Community law governs the procedural rules applicable and the remedies available. The issue has frequently been put before the ECJ in references from national courts themselves; and a number of different phases in the ECJ's approach can be detected. The cases are often difficult to reconcile and the outcome seems to depend on the particular facts and the complex rule at issue.[201]

14–051

---

[197] Case 80/86 *Officier van Justitie v Kolpinghuis Nijmegen* [1987] E.C.R. 3969, para.13; Case C-60/02 *Criminal Proceedings against X* [2004] E.C.R. I–651 para.64; and Joined Cases C-387/02 *Silvio Berlusconi* [2005] E.C.R. I–3565, para.74.

[198] In Case C-456/98 *Centrosteel v Adipol* [2000] E.C.R. I–6007, AG Jacobs (at paras 33–34) expressly rejected the proposition that the *Arcaro* case (n.196) placed a limit on the interpretive obligation outside the criminal law context. In the *Pfeiffer* case, if the national judge succeeded in interpreting national law to give full effect to the Directive, it would have resulted in an obligation on the German Red Cross to pay overtime to ambulance workers who had previously been exempted in the German legislation from the 48–hour limit. Even in the criminal law context, although, as already noted, criminal liability cannot be exacerbated by a conforming interpretation; the procedure by which the criminal trial is conducted can be affected, provided it does not render the trial unfair: *Pupino* [2005] E.C.R. I–5285 (Italian law, which did not provide for special procedures for cross-examining vulnerable witnesses, had to be interpreted in light of the Framework Decision which did provide such special procedures). But see Case C-235/03 *QDQ Media SA v Omedas Lecha* [2005] ECR 1937 paras 14–16 (where it was clear from the explanation given by the national court that national law could not be interpreted in conformity with the directive, the directive could not of itself impose obligations on an individual).

[199] For a more detailed account, see T. Tridimas, *The General Principles of EU Law*, 2nd edn. (2006) Ch.9; M. Dougan, *National Remedies before the Court of Justice* (2004); C. Kilpatrick, T. Novitz and P. Skidmore (eds), *The Future of Remedies in Europe* (2000).

[200] See, e.g. Council Regulation (EEC) 729/70 on the financing of the common agricultural policy [1970] O.J. L94/13 (Art.8 obliges Member States to require the repayment of wrongly paid premiums in the context of the implementation of the Common Agricultural Policy, which overrides any different administrative rules on revocation of administrative acts in national administrative procedure). See also Council Directive 89/665/EEC of December 21, 1989 on the coordination of the laws, regulations and administrative provisions relating to the application of review procedures to the award of public supply and public works contracts [1989] O.J. L395/33. See now also COM (2006) 195.

[201] Chalmers *et al.* (2006), p.394

Principle of national procedural autonomy

14–052 In principle it is the national law which applies, for Community law and national law are independent systems of law, each operating autonomously in its own sphere. This is known as the principle of national procedural autonomy and provides that "it is for the domestic legal system of each Member State to designate the courts having jurisdiction and to determine the procedural conditions governing actions at law intended to ensure the protection of the rights which citizens have from the direct effect of Community law".[202] The principle has always been subject to two conditions, namely, equivalence and practical possibility or effectiveness. The condition of equivalence requires that national rules governing the exercise of Community law rights must not be less favourable than those governing the same right of action on an internal matter; while the condition of effectiveness requires that the rules must not make it impossible or excessively difficult in practice to exercise the Community law rights.[203] The criteria of effective protection of Community law rights and equivalence are cumulative.[204]

Principle of effective protection

14–053 Initially, the ECJ emphasised the principle of national procedural autonomy and indicated, in strong terms, that the EC Treaty was not intended to create new remedies in the national courts.[205] On other occasions, however, the principle of the effective protection has been given precedence[206] and the ECJ has required the displacement of all procedural and other obstacles to the protection of Community law rights, with the result that national courts have been required not to apply any rule of national law whose effect is to preclude immediate enforcement of a Community law right.[207] One of the

---

[202] Case 45/76 *Comet BV v Produktschap voor Siergewassen* [1976] E.C.R. 2043, para.13. See also Case C-432/05 *Unibet (London) Ltd v Justitiekanslern* [2007] 2 C.M.L.R. 30, para.39.

[203] See, e.g. Case 158/80 *Rewe-Handelsgesllschaft Nord mbH v Hauptzollamt Kiel* [1981] E.C.R. 1805, para.5; Case C-473/00 *Cofidis SA v Jean Louis Fredout* [2002] E.C.R. I–10875, paras 36–37.

[204] Case 199/82 *Amministrzione delle finanze dello Stato v San Giorgio* [1983] E.C.R. 3595.

[205] *Rewe-Handelsgesllschaft Nord* (n.203), para.44; and Case 6/60 *Humblet v Belgium* [1960] E.C.R. 559; Case 26/74 *Société Roquettes Fréres v Commission* [1976] E.C.R. 677 (it was for Member States to decide whether to award interest on the reimbursement of sums wrongly levied under Community law).

[206] *Autologic Holdings Plc v Inland Revenue Commissioners* [2004] EWCA Civ 690; [2005] 1 W.L.R. 52, para.25 (Peter Gibson L.J. noting that "[t]he importance of the principle of effectiveness in Community law cannot be overstated.")

[207] The first clear statement of this principle was in *Simmenthal* [1978] E.C.R. 629; see para.14–009. In Case C-208/90 *Emmott v Minister for Social Welfare* [1991] E.C.R. I–4269, para.23 it was held that until such time as a directive has been properly transposed, a defaulting Member State could not rely on an individual's delay in initiating the proceedings against it in order to protect rights conferred upon him by the provisions of the directive and that a period laid down by national law within which proceedings must be initiated could not

most striking examples of the application of the effectiveness requirement is found in the *Factortame* case, in which the ECJ did not even refer to its case law on national procedural autonomy, but required that national courts have "the power to do everything necessary" at the moment of application of Community law "to set aside national legislative provisions which might prevent, even temporarily Community rules from having full force and effect".[208] This resulted in the novel grant of interim relief to suspend the operation of a Westminster statute. The principle of effectiveness has also led the ECJ to hold that a party to a contract which violates EC competition law can nonetheless receive damages, provided that the party seeking the damages did not bear significant responsibility for the distortion of competition caused by the contract.[209] The Court has also held that it is not necessary for a national legal order to create a free-standing action to examine the compatibility of national provisions with the EC Treaty, provided that other effective legal remedies, no less favourable than those governing domestic actions, make it possible to determine the question of compatibility.[210] However, interim relief should be available until compatibility is determined, if necessary to ensure effectiveness of the judgment;[211] and even if it is uncertain under national law whether an action to safeguard respect for an individual's rights under Community law is admissible, the principle of effective judicial protection still requires the national court to be able, at that stage, to grant the interim relief necessary to ensure those rights are respected.[212]

---

begin to run before that time. See also Case 271/91 *Marshall v Southampton and South West Area Health Authority II* [1991] E.C.R. I–4367 (two national rules governing remedies, one imposing a ceiling on damages and the other removing the power to award interest, had to be overridden or disapplied by the national court). See further M. Hoskins, "Tilting the Balance: Supremacy and National Procedural Rules" (1996) 21 E.L. Rev. 365; A. Ward, "Effective Sanctions in EC Law: A Moving Boundary in the Division of Competence" (1995) 1 E.L.J. 205.

[208] Case C-213/89 *R. v Secretary of State for Transport Ex p. Factortame Ltd* [1990] E.C.R. I–2433, para.20. Another striking example is found in the ECJ's case law on state liability in damages, as to which see 14–066.

[209] Case C-453/99 *Courage v Crehan* [2001] E.C.R. I–6297, paras 30–31 (the ECJ also indicated that, in awarding damages, the national court could act to prevent any unjust enrichment of the party seeking damages). See further G. Cumming, "*Courage Ltd v Crehan*" (2002) 23 European Competition L. Rev. 199; G Monti "Anticompetitive Agreements: The innocent party's right to damages" (2002) 27 E.L. Rev. 282; O. Odudu and J. Edelman, "Compensatory Damages for Breach of Article 81" (2002) 27 E.L. Rev. 327. See now also Commission Green Paper: Damages actions for breach of the EC antitrust rules, COM (2005) 672; Commission Staff Working Paper—Annex to the Green Paper; Damages actions for breach of the Antitrust rules; SEC (2005) 1732.

[210] *Unibet* [2007] 2 C.M.L.R. 30, para.47.

[211] *Unibet* [2007] 2 C.M.L.R. 30, para.67

[212] *Unibet* [2007] 2 C.M.L.R. 30, para.73. If the application is admissible in national law, and Community law does not call into question that inadmissibility, interim relief need not be available: para.73. The criteria governing the grant of interim relief are those applicable to equivalent domestic actions, provided they comply with the principles of equivalence and effectiveness: para.82.

Balancing procedural autonomy and effective protection

14–054 At present, the ECJ tends to apply what has been described as a "more complex and nuanced balance"[213] which determines whether a national procedural rule renders application of Community law impossible or excessively difficult:

> "by reference to the role of that provision in the procedure, its progress and its special features, viewed as a whole, before the various national instances. In the light of that analysis the basic principles of the domestic judicial system, such as protection of the rights of the defence, the principle of legal certainty and the proper conduct of procedure, must, where appropriate, be taken into consideration."[214]

14–055 The national rule must be examined not in the abstract, but in the specific circumstances of each case:[215] on a case-by-case basis, taking account of each case's own factual and legal context as a whole, which cannot be applied mechanically in fields other than those in which they were made.[216] Thus, the ECJ has found that a Dutch rule preventing a party from raising a new point of law involving questions of fact on appeal did not render the exercise of the Community right impossible or excessively difficult since "it safeguards the right of the defence; and it ensures proper conduct of proceedings".[217] By contrast, a rule preventing a tax payer from raising a new point of law on appeal to the Court of Appeal from the decision of an administrative tax official; after the lapse of a period of 60 days, where the Court of Appeal could not raise the issue of its own motion, was found to violate the requirement of effective protection, given that the administrative official could not himself make a reference to the ECJ; the Court of Appeal could not raise the issue of its own motion; no other court or tribunal was entitled to raise the issue.[218]

Requirement of equivalence

14–056 The condition of equivalence requires that the national rule at issue be applied without distinction, whether the infringement alleged is of Community law or national law, where the purpose and cause of action are

---

[213] Craig and de Búrca, (2007), p.320.
[214] Case C-312/93 *Peterbroeck, Van Campenhout & Cie v Belgian State* [1995] E.C.R. I–4599, para.14; Cases C-430–431/93 *Van Schijndel & Van Veen v Stichting Pensioenfonds voor Fysiotherapeuten* [1995] E.C.R. I–4705, para.19; C-327/00 *Santex SpA v Unita Socio Sanitaria Locale No.42 di Pavia* [2003] E.C.R. I–1877, para.56.
[215] Craig and de Búrca (2007), p.321.
[216] *Cofidis* [2002] E.C.R. I–10875, para.37.
[217] *Van Schijndel* [1995] E.C.R. I–4075, para.21.
[218] *Peterbroeck* [1995] E.C.R. I–4599. Another difference in the two cases was that in the first, the ability of the national court to make an Art.234 preliminary reference was preserved whereas it was precluded in the latter case.

similar.[219] In determining whether the requirement of equivalence has been satisfied, it is necessary to take into account the role played by the relevant provision in the procedure as a whole, as well as the operation and any special features of that procedure before the different national courts.[220] This analysis must not be carried out subjectively by reference to circumstances of fact, but must involve an objective comparison in the abstract, of the procedural rules at issue.[221] The national court must also scrutinise the domestic procedures to determine not only whether they are comparable but also whether there is any inherent discrimination in their application in favour of domestic claims.[222] The principle does not mean that a Member State must extend its most favourable national rule to the Community action,[223] but the national court must consider both the purpose and the essential characteristics of allegedly similar domestic actions in order to reach its conclusions.[224]

Limitation periods

In numerous cases, national courts in Member States have had to consider the criteria of equivalence and effectiveness in relation to limitation periods for bringing legal action, and there have been references to the ECJ for preliminary rulings. As a general principle, reasonable national time limits are consistent with the principle of effective judicial protection since such time limits are an application of the principle of legal certainty protecting both individuals and administration;[225] and the decision as to whether a limitation period is reasonable is one for the national court, following the guidance of the ECJ.[226] Similarly, it is for the national court to determine whether the time limit complies with the requirement of equivalence, although it may receive extensive guidance as to the outcome from the ECJ.[227] Where a temporal restriction is imposed on the right to obtain a

14–057

---

[219] Case C-326/96 BS Levez v TH Jennings (Harlow Pools) Ltd [1998] E.C.R. I–7835, para.39. See also i-21 Germany GmbH and Arcor AG & Co KG (formerly, ISIS Multimedia Net GmbH & Co KG) v Germany [2007] 1 C.M.L.R. 10 at [69] ECJ.

[220] Levez [1998] E.C.R. I–7835, paras 43–44.

[221] Case C-78/98 Preston v Wolverhampton Healthcare NHS Trust [2000] E.C.R. I–3201.

[222] Case C-228/98 Douanias v Ypourgio Oikonomikon [2000] E.C.R. I–577, para.65.

[223] See Case C-260/96 Ministero delle Finanze v Spac [1998] E.C.R. I–4997; Case C-229/96 Aprile v Amminstrazione delle Finanze dello Stato [1998] E.C.R. I–7141; Case C-343/96 Dilexport v Amministrazione delle Finanze dello Stato [1999] E.C.R. I–579 and Case C-88/99 Roquette Fréres v Direction des Services Fiscaux du Pas-de-Calais [2000] E.C.R. I–10465. cf. Emmott [1991] E.C.R. I–4269.

[224] Levez [1998] E.C.R. I–7835, para.43. See further Case C-231/96 Edis v Ministero delle Finanze [1998] E.C.R. I–4951, para.36 (time limits).

[225] Case 45/76 Comet v Produktschap voor Siergewassem [1976] E.C.R. 2043; see also Case 33/76 Rewe v Landwinschaftskammer Saarland [1976] E.C.R. 1989; Case 2/94 Denkavit Internationaal BV v Kamer van Koophandel en Fabrieken voor Midden-gelderland [1996] E.C.R. I–2827 (AG Jacobs, para.64); Marks & Spencer [2002] E.C.R. I–6325, para.35.

[226] Comet [1976] E.C.R. I–2043 (ECJ expressed no view as to whether a 30–day time limit constituted a reasonable period of limitation, leaving the issue to be decided by the national court).

[227] Levez [1998] E.C.R. I–7035, paras 29–53.

refund of charges levied in breach of Community law, the general rule regarding reasonable time limits is subject to the additional principles, first, that the time limit not be specifically intended to limit the consequences of a judgment of the Court and second, that the time set for the application of the time limit must be sufficient to ensure that the right to repayment is effective.[228]

14–058   On occasion, the requirements of Community law have been applied very strictly, with the result that national provisions may have to be applied *more* favourably to a claimant where a Community law right is in issue than in a case of a purely internal character:[229] this principle has been limited however to the situation where a time bar has the result of depriving the applicant of any opportunity whatever to rely on her Community right;[230] or where the delay in exercising the remedy is due in some way to the conduct of the national authorities.[231] Moreover, an otherwise reasonable time limit may be displaced by the particular circumstances. The ECJ has held that a national rule applicable in an equal pay claim under which entitlement to arrears of remuneration is restricted to the two years preceding the date on which the proceedings were instituted was not in itself open to criticism; however given that the claimant in the national proceedings was late in bringing her claim because of inaccurate information provided by her employer, to allow the employer to rely on the time limit in such circumstances would be "manifestly incompatible with the principle of effectiveness".[232]

14–059   In principle, it might in appropriate circumstances be possible for a claimant for judicial review in England and Wales to seek to argue that the requirement in CPR Pt 54.5 that applications for permission to apply for judicial review be made "promptly and in any event within three months from the date when grounds for the application first arose"[233] is an unreasonable impediment to exercising Community law rights. Such an argument is unlikely to succeed, however: first, the court has discretion which it would surely exercise to extend the period for applying for permission if it "considers there is good reason"; and secondly the ECJ's own limitation period for receiving direct actions challenging the legality of EU measures is only two months.[234]

---

[228] *Marks & Spencer* [2002] E.C.R. I–6325, para.36.
[229] See, e.g. Case 208/90 *Emmott v Minister for Social Welfare* [1991] E.C.R. I–4269 (until such time as a directive had been properly transposed, a defaulting Member State might not rely on an individual's delay in initiating proceedings against it in order to protect rights conferred on her by the directive; a period laid down by national law within which proceedings had to be initiated could not begin to run before that time).
[230] Case C-188/95 *Fantask A/S v Indus triministeriet (Erhvervsministeriet)* [1997] E.C.R. I–6783.
[231] *Edis* [1998] E.C.R. I–4951, para.48; Joined Cases C-279/96, C-280/96 and C-281/96 *Ansaldo Energia SpA v Amministrazione delle Stato* [1998] E.C.R. I–5025, para.22; *Ministero delle Finanze v Spac SpA* [1998] E.C.R. I–4997, para.31; *Santex* [2003] E.C.R. I–1877, para.62.
[232] *Levez* [1998] E.C.R. I–7835 paras 20, 27–34.
[233] See 16–050.
[234] See 14–082.

Effective judicial review

The ECJ lays considerable stress on the requirement that Member States **14–060** provide effective means of judicial review. In *Les Verts*,[235] it emphasised that the EU "is a Community based on the rule of law, inasmuch as neither its Member States nor its institutions can avoid a review of the question whether the measures adopted by them are in conformity with the basic constitutional charter, the Treaty". The national courts may be required to ensure the effective protection of rights created by the Treaty or by secondary legislation. In *Johnston v Chief Constable of the Royal Ulster Constabulary*[236] in 1986, the ECJ spelt out the requirements of effective judicial review under Community law. On a reference from the Industrial Tribunal, the ECJ ruled that the principle of effective judicial review laid down in Art.6 of the directive reflected a general principle of law which underlay the constitutional traditions common to the Member States and was also laid down in Arts 6 and 13 ECHR (right to a fair trial of civil rights and obligations and effective remedies for breach of Convention rights). That principle did not allow a certificate issued by a national authority stating that the conditions for derogating from the principle of equal treatment for men and women for the purposes of protecting public safety were satisfied to be treated as conclusive evidence so as to exclude the exercise of any power of review by the courts. The ECJ has also held that review for arbitrariness will not suffice in the context of EC procurement rules.[237] Similarly, in *UNECTEF v Heylens*, the ECJ ruled that a decision by a national authority rejecting a claim under Community law must be reasoned and subject to judicial review in the national courts even if this is not normally the case under the relevant national legal system.[238] Furthermore, where the decision of a national authority not to recommend granting aid from an EU fund is binding on the Commission, the national court must review the national authority's decision for lawfulness, and regard an action brought for that purpose as admissible even if domestic rules of procedure do not provide for this.[239]

However, where a Directive required that individuals be able to pursue **14–061** their claims under it "by judicial process", it was sufficient that a general claim before civil courts for compensation against the State was available.[240] The principle of effective judicial protection will also not require a

---

[235] Case 294/83 *Partie Ecologiste (Les Verts) v European Parliament* [1986] E.C.R. 1339, para.23.
[236] Case 222/84, [1987] Q.B. 129.
[237] Case C-92/00 *Hospital Ingenieure Krankenhaustechnik Planungs GmbH (HI) v Stadt Wien* [2002] ECR I–5553, para.63: holding that review of a local authority's withdrawal of its invitation to tender for a public service contract, limited to whether the decision was arbitrary, did not satisfy the requirement in Directive 89/665 to ensure effective review of contracting authorities to ensure compliance with the Community public procurement rules).
[238] Case 222/86 *UNECTEF v Heylens* [1987] E.C.R. 4097. See further Case C-340/89 *Irène Vlassopoulou v Ministerium für Justiz, Bundes-und Europaangelegenheiten Baden-Württemberg* [1991] E.C.R. I–2357.
[239] Case C-97/91 *Oleificio Borelli SpA v Commission* [1992] E.C.R. I–6313, paras 12–13.
[240] Case C-380/01 *Schneider v Bundesminister der Justiz* [2004] E.C.R. I–1389 paras 26–28.

national court to substitute its own judgment for that of a national authority where the national authority applying Community law is called upon to make complex assessments or has a wide measure of discretion. In such a case, judicial review may be restricted to verifying that the action taken by the national authority is not vitiated by manifest error or a misuse of powers and that the authority has not clearly exceeded the bounds of its discretion.[241] The ECJ has also ruled that it is permissible to provide only a remedy by way of judicial review to an EU national who has been refused entry on grounds of public policy, even where there was a more substantial remedy by way of appeal for nationals whose immigration status was in question, because it considered that the two situations were not comparable.[242]

Repayment

14-062 Where a charge is imposed contrary to Community law, the question arises of the extent to which an action for recovery is governed by national law or Community law.[243] The ECJ has insisted that entitlement to repayment of charges levied contrary to Community law is a consequence of and an adjunct to the rights conferred on individuals by the Community provisions prohibiting such charges.[244] Provided that the conditions of equivalence and effective protection are satisfied, recovery may be made conditional on the claimant's proving that the charges had not been passed on to third parties.[245] The Member State can only plead the defence, however, where "it is established that the charge has been borne in its entirety by another person and that reimbursement of the trader would constitute unjust enrichment".[246] The ECJ has dismissed an argument that an excusable error by the authorities, such as imposing charges over a long period of time while unaware that the charges were in breach of Community law, could constitute a defence to a claim for repayment.[247] It is not necessary for interest to be paid on arrears of social security benefits; however,

---

[241] Case C-120/97 *Upjohn Ltd v The Licensing Authority established by the Medicines Act 1968* [1999] E.C.R. I–223 (noting that there is no need for national courts to engage in more extensive review than that in which the ECJ engages in similar circumstances).

[242] Cases C-65/95 and C-111/95 *R. v Secretary of State for the Home Department Ex p. Shingara and Ex p. Radiom* [1997] E.C.R. I–3341.

[243] On rights to restitution under English law, see 19–075.

[244] Case 199/82 *Amministrazione delle Finanze dello Stato v San Giorgio* [1983] E.C.R. 3595; C-192/95 *Comateb v Directeur Général des Douanes et Droits Indirects* [1997] E.C.R. I–165. See further M. Dougan, "Cutting your Losses in the Enforcement Deficit: A Community Right to the Recovery of Unlawfully Levied Charges" (1998) 1 C.Y.E.L.S. 233.

[245] Case 199/82 *Amministrazione delle Finanze dello Stato v SpA San Giorgio* [1983] E.C.R. 3595. In Case 104/86 *Commission v Italy* [1988] E.C.R. 1799, a national rule providing that recovery is only possible if the taxpayer proves, by documentary evidence alone, that the taxes were not passed on to others, was regarded to make recovery impossible or excessively difficult. See further Joined Cases 331, 376 and 378/85 *Bianco and Girard v Directeur Générales Douanes et droits indirects* [1988] E.C.R. 1099.

[246] *Comateb* [1997] E.C.R. I–165.

[247] *Fantask* [1997] E.C.R. I–6783.

interest payments are required on compensation for loss or damage caused by national authorities.[248] Limits on damages, even in respect of compensation, may be permissible.[249]

No general obligation to reopen final judicial and administrative decisions

The ECJ held in *Kapferer v Schlank & Schick* that Art.10 EC[250] does not **14–063** require a national court to disapply its internal rules of procedure in order to re-open and set aside a judicial decision which has become final, even if that decision should be contrary to Community law.[251] This is because of the importance, both for the Community legal order and national legal systems, of the principle of *res judicata*, and because it is important, in order to ensure both stability of the law and legal relations and the sound administration of justice, that judicial decisions which have become definitive after all rights of appeal have been exhausted or after expiry of the time limits provided for in that connection can no longer be called into question.[252]

Similarly, in principle, administrative bodies are not under an obligation **14–064** to reopen an administrative decision which has become final.[253] In relation to administrative decisions, the principle is subject to an exception. This is where under national law the administrative body (a) has the power to re-open the relevant decision, (b) the administrative decision in question has become final as a result of the judgment of a national court ruling at final instance, (c) that judgment is, in the light of a decision given by the ECJ subsequent to it, based on a misinterpretation of Community law which was adopted without a question being referred to the ECJ for a preliminary ruling under Art.234(3) EC, and (d) the person concerned complained to the administrative body concerned immediately after becoming aware of that decision of the ECJ.[254]

In *Kapferer*, the ECJ did not decide the question of whether a similar **14–065** exception applied in respect of final judicial decisions, but noted that, even assuming that the principles laid down in that judgment could be transposed into a context which, like that of the main proceedings, relates to a final judicial decision, the obligation of the body concerned to review a

[248] Case C-66/95 *R. v Secretary of State for Social Security Ex p. Eunice Sutton* [1997] E.C.R. I–2163, paras 23–24.
[249] Case C-180/95 *Draehmpaehl v Urania Immobilienservice* [1997] E.C.R. I–2195 (a maximum compensatory award of three months' salary could be adequate in the case of a candidate who had been deemed ineligible for a job on grounds of sex where that candidate would not have obtained the job because the person appointed had superior qualifications and where the loss sustained was therefore more limited).
[250] The text of Art.10 EC is set out at 14–044 above.
[251] Case C-234/04 [2006] E.C.R. I–2585, paras 21, 24.
[252] Case C-234/04 [2006] E.C.R. I–2585, para.21.
[253] Case C-453/00 *Kühne & Heitz NV v Productschap voor Pluimvee en Eieren* [2004] E.C.R. I–837, para.24; Joined Cases C-392/04 and C-422 *i-21 Germany GmbH and Arcor AG & Co KG v Bundesrepublik Deutschland* [2007] 1 C.M.L.R. 10, para.51.
[254] *Kühne & Heitz* [2004] E.C.R. I–837, para. 28; *i-21* [2007] 1 C.M.L.R. 10, para. 52.

final decision, is subject to the condition, among other things, that that body should be empowered under national law to reopen that decision.[255]

State liability in damages for breach of Community law

14–066 The requirement to provide effective remedies for the protection of Community law rights may also include the obligation to provide adequate compensation.[256] It is a principle of Community law that Member States are obliged to pay compensation for harm caused to individuals by breaches of Community law for which they are held responsible. Where there is a dispute over payment of such compensation, it is national courts which adjudicate on the issues.[257] The harm in question may be caused in many ways for instance, by the failure to transpose a directive into national law within the required period;[258] by incorrectly transposing a directive;[259] by enacting primary legislation contrary to the provisions of the EC Treaty;[260] or by officials taking administrative action such as refusing an export licence in breach of Community law.[261] In *Francovich v Italy*, the ECJ (giving a preliminary ruling to an Italian court) held that the full effectiveness of Community rules would be impaired and the protection of rights which they granted would be weakened if individuals were unable to obtain compensation when their rights were infringed by breach of Community law for which a Member State was responsible.[262] The possibility of compensation by the Member State was particularly indispensable where (as on the facts of the case) the full effectiveness of Community rules was subject to prior action on the part of the state and,

[255] *Kapferer* [2004] E.C.R. I–2585, para 23.
[256] On rights to damages under English law, see 19–025; on the approach to damages under HRA, s.8, see 19–081.
[257] Only those courts in the UK which have power to award damages generally may grant damages for breach of Community law; where a statutory tribunal, such as an employment tribunal, lacks that power, a claimant will have to pursue a claim in the county courts or the High Court in the ordinary way: *Potter v Secretary of State for Employment* [1998] Eu L.R. 388. A claim for judicial review made under CPR Pt 54 may include a claim for damages: see 19–005.
[258] Joined Cases C-6 and 9/90 *Francovich v Italy* [1991] E.C.R. I–5357. Italy had failed to transpose Directive 80/987, guaranteeing employees a minimum level of protection in the event of an employer's insolvency, into national law. Member States were required to set up institutions which would provide specific guarantees of payment of unpaid wage claims. The ECJ held that provisions in the Directive were not sufficiently precise and unconditional to be directly effective: (see 14–010).
[259] See, e.g. Case C-392/93 *R. v HM Treasury Ex p. British Telecommunications Plc* [1996] Q.B. 615 (incorrect transposition of Directive 90/531 on procurement procedures of enterprises operating in the water, energy, transport and telecommunications sector).
[260] See, e.g. Case C-48/93 *R. v Secretary of State for Transport Ex p. Factortame Ltd* [1996] Q.B. 404 (enactment by UK Parliament of Merchant Shipping Act 1988, Pt II contrary to provisions in the EC Treaty).
[261] See, e.g. Case C-5/94 *R. v Ministry of Agriculture, Fisheries and Food ex p. Hedley Lomas (Ireland) Ltd* [1997] Q.B. 139 (refusal, contrary to EC Treaty, of export licence for live sheep destined for Spanish slaughterhouse).
[262] *Francovich* [1991] E.C.R. I–5357, para.33.

consequently, individuals could not, in the absence of such action, enforce the rights granted to them before the national courts.[263] Further foundation for the Member States' obligation to pay compensation for such harm was to be found in Art.10[5] EC, which requires Member States to take all appropriate measures, whether general or particular, to ensure fulfilment of their obligations under Community law.[264]

In *Francovich* and subsequent cases in which national courts have **14-067** requested preliminary rulings, the ECJ has laid down the broad principles for liability, although in the absence of Community legislation, it is a matter for the internal legal order of each Member State to develop more specific conditions.[265] It is for the internal legal order of each Member State to designate the competent courts and lay down the detailed procedural rules governing the new damages remedy.[266] Synthesising the pronouncements of the ECJ, it may now be said that there is an entitlement to compensation where three conditions are met by the claimant.[267]

Right-conferring provision

First, the rule of Community law which has been infringed (i) must be **14-068** intended to confer rights on individuals and (ii) where the complaint is that a directive has not been transposed, the content of those rights must be able to be identified on the basis of the provisions of the directive itself.[268] The right conferred by Community law may or may not be directly effective.[269]

[263] [1991] E.C.R. I–5357, para.34.

[264] [1991] E.C.R. I–5357, para.36; see 14–044.

[265] *Francovich* [1991] E.C.R. I–5357, para.42. Art.10 EC provides: "Member States shall take all appropriate measures, whether general or particular, to ensure fulfilment of the obligations arising out of this Treaty or resulting from action taken by the institutions of the Community. They shall facilitate the achievement of the Community's tasks. They shall abstain from any measure which could jeopardise the attainment of the objectives of this Treaty".

[266] *Francovich* [1991] E.C.R. I–5357, para.42.

[267] See further M. Dougan, "The Francovich Right to Reparation: Reshaping the Contours of Community Remedial Competence" (2000) 6 E.P.L. 103; T. Tridimas, "Liability for Breach of Community Law: Growing Up or Mellowing Down?" (2001) 38 C.M.L. Rev. 301.

[268] These conditions were specified in *Francovich* [1991] E.C.R. I–5357 In *Bowden v South West Water Services Ltd* [1998] Env L.R. 445 a fisherman claimed that the United Kingdom had breached Directive 91/492 (on the health conditions for the production and the placing on the market of live bivalve molluscs) by making a statutory instrument prohibiting the harvesting of shellfish from a certain part of the coastline. The High Court held that the claimant had failed to demonstrate that the Directive involved the "grant of rights to individuals". Likewise, in Case C-222/02 *Paul v Germany* [2004] E.C.R. I–9425 (para.51), the ECJ held that directives imposing supervisory obligations on Member States over credit institutions did not confer rights on depositors in the event that their deposits were unavailable due to defective supervision, even though the objectives pursued by the directives included protection of depositors. See also *Three Rivers DC v Governor and Company of the Bank of England* [2000] 2 A.C. 1 at 196, 219.

[269] In C-48/93 *R. v Secretary of State for Transport Ex p. Factortame (No.4)* [1996] Q.B. 404 the successful claim against the United Kingdom was that the Merchant Shipping Act 1988 breached a directly effective provision in the EC Treaty prohibiting discrimination on the ground of nationality. The ECJ rejected an argument that *Francovich* was concerned only "to fill a lacuna in the system for safeguarding the rights of individuals" and so limited to situations were the Community law right was not directly effective.

Sufficiently serious breach

14–069   Secondly, the breach of Community law must be "sufficiently serious", which means that the Member State had "manifestly and gravely disregarded the limits on its discretion".[270] As already noted, in principle it is for the national court to determine whether the conditions for state liability are met, although the ECJ "may indicate certain circumstances which the national courts may take into account in their evaluation".[271] As a general matter, the following factors will be material in determining whether an infringement passes the threshold of seriousness:[272] (i) the clarity and precision of the rule breached;[273] (ii) the measure of discretion left by that rule to the national authorities;[274] (iii) whether the infringement and damage caused was intentional or involuntary; (iv) whether any error of law was excusable or inexcusable;[275] (v) the fact that the position taken by a EU institution may have contributed towards the omission; and (vi) the adoption or retention of national measures or practices contrary to Community law. More specifically, a failure by a Member State to transpose a directive within the prescribed period is *per se* a serious breach of Community law and the circumstances of the failure are not relevant to

---

[270] Case C-46/93 *Brasserie du Pêcheur SA v Germany* [1996] E.C.R. I–1029, para.55. See further A. Cygan, "Defining a Sufficiently Serious Breach of Community Law: The House of Lords casts its nets into the Waters" (2000) 25 E.L. Rev. 452.

[271] Case C-150/99 *Sweden v Stockholm Lindöpark Aktiebolag et al* [2001] E.C.R. I–493, para.38.

[272] *Brasserie du Pêcheur* [1996] E.C.R. I–1024, para.56; *R. v Secretary of State for Transport, ex p. Factortame Ltd (No.4)* [1996] Q.B. 404.

[273] In the *British Telecommunications* case [1996] Q.B. 615 the ECJ held that incorrect transposition of part of Directive 90/531 on procurement did not amount to a serious breach because the Article in question was imprecisely worked and was reasonably capable of bearing the interpretation given to it by the United Kingdom in good faith. The interpretation was shared by other Member States and was not manifestly contrary to the wording of the Directive and the objectives pursued by it. Also, no guidance had been available from the ECJ. Finally, the Commission did not raise the matter when the implementing legislation was adopted. *cf.* Case C-140/97 *Rechberger v Austria* [1999] ECR I–3499, paras 50–51 (where Art.7 of Directive 90/314 on package travel, package holidays and package tours gave no discretion to the Member State and as such, the attempt of Austria to limits its application constituted a sufficiently serious breach of Community law to give rise to a damages action).

[274] For example, in C-5/94 *R. v Ministry of Agriculture, Fisheries and Food Ex p. Hedley Lomas (Ireland) Ltd* [1997] Q.B. 139 the United Kingdom imposed a general ban on the export of live animals to Spain for slaughter, contrary to EC Treaty, Art.28 [30] on the free movement of goods. The ECJ held that here the national authorities had not been called upon to make any legislative choices and had only reduced discretion, or even no discretion. In such a situation the mere infringement of Community law may be sufficient to establish the existence of a sufficiently serious breach.

[275] For example, in *R. v Secretary of State for Transport Ex p. Factortame Ltd (No.5)* [1998] 1 All E.R. 736 (Note), the High Court held that the damage caused by the enactment of the Merchant Shipping Act 1988 Pt II was sufficiently serious because: (1) discrimination on the ground of nationality contrary to the EC Treaty was the intended effect of the criteria; (2) the government was aware that those criteria would necessarily injure the applicants who would be unable to fish against the British quota; (3) the Act was constructed to ensure it would not be delayed by legal challenges and this made it impossible for the applicants to obtain interim relief without the ECJ's intervention; and (4) the Commission had been consistently hostile to the proposed legislation.

determining liability,[276] although this principle is subject to slight modification where an administrative authority has attempted to give the provisions of the Directive immediate effect despite its non-implementation by the national legislature.[277] Where the Member State concerned is not in a position to make any legislative choices and has only a considerably reduced, or even no, discretion, the mere infringement of Community law may be sufficient to establish the existence of a sufficiently serious breach.[278] Where the breach, whether intentional or otherwise, is of a fundamental principle of the EC Treaty, such as the prohibition on discrimination on the grounds of nationality, this will almost invariably give rise to liability in damages.[279] Furthermore, "on any view", a breach of Community law will be sufficiently serious if it has persisted despite a judgment finding the infringement in question to be established or a preliminary ruling or settled case law of the ECJ on the matter from which it is clear that the conduct in question constituted an infringement.[280] Failing to adopt measures necessary to comply with an interim order of the ECJ will also constitute a sufficiently serious breach.[281] By contrast, if a decision by an official would have been the same even if no breach of Community law had occurred, this may be insufficiently serious to warrant compensation.[282] Where there has been a bona fide misinterpretation of an unclear provision that is also unlikely to constitute a "sufficiently serious breach".[283] In assessing whether or not a national court has committed a sufficiently serious breach, the Court has rejected an attempt to limit liability to situations of intentional fault or serious misconduct on the part of the court; and liability must be available in respect of both interpretation of provisions of law and assessment of facts or evidence.[284]

---

[276] See, Case C-178, C-179, C-188–190/94 *Dillenkofer v Germany* [1997] Q.B. 259 (Germany had failed within the prescribed time to transpose the Package Travel Directive 90/314/EEC which sought to protect tourists in the event of the insolvency of the travel operator). The ECJ noted, at para.26, that where a Member State fails "to take any of the measures necessary to achieve the result prescribed by a directive within the period it lays down, that Member State manifestly and gravely disregards the limits on its discretion".
[277] See 14–074.
[278] *Hedley Lomas* [1997] Q.B. 139, para.28; *Dillenkofer* [1997] Q.B. 259 at para.25.
[279] *R. v Secretary of State for Transport Ex p. Factortame Ltd (No.5)* [1998] C.O.D. 381, CA.
[280] *Brasserie du Pêcheur* [1996] E.C.R. I–1029, para.56.
[281] [1996] E.C.R. I–1029, para.64.
[282] *R. v Secretary of State for the Home Department Ex p. Gallagher* [1996] 2 C.M.L.R. 951, CA (order excluding applicant from entering Great Britain was made under the Prevention of Terrorism (Temporary Provisions) Act 1989 without following the rules of procedural fairness set out in Directive 64/221, but the breach was not sufficiently serious to merit an award of compensation as there was no evidence to suggest that the Secretary of State would have reached a different conclusion had he received the applicant's representations at an earlier stage).
[283] *R. v Ministry of Agriculture, Fisheries and Food Ex p. Lay and Gage* [1998] C.O.D. 387.
[284] Case C-173/03 *Traghetti del Mediterraneo SpA (In Liquidation) v Italy* [2006] E.C.R. 5177, para.46.

Causal link

14-070 Thirdly, causal link must exist between the breach of the Member State's obligation and the harm sustained by the injured party.[285] This condition is to be decided in accordance with national rules on liability, provided that national law is not less favourable than those relating to a similar purely domestic claim and they are not such, as in practice to make it impossible or excessively difficult to obtain effective reparation for loss or damage resulting from breach of Community law.

Quantum

14-071 Where these three conditions are satisfied, the quantum awarded must be "commensurate with the loss or damage sustained".[286] Thus, in the absence of Community provisions, it is for the domestic legal system of each Member State to set the criteria for determining the extent of reparation, subject to the Community principles of equivalence and effectiveness. Thus, for example, the ECJ has held that English rules, which restrict liability to cases where the tort of misfeasance in public office is established, make it impossible in practice to enforce liability where the national legislature is responsible for the breach.[287] A national court may not totally exclude loss of profit as a head of damage.[288] If exemplary damages are available in domestic claims, these may be awarded in similar situations for breach of Community law.[289] A national court may however enquire whether the injured person showed reasonable diligence in order to avoid the loss or damage or limit its extent and whether "he availed himself in time of all the legal remedies available to him".[290]

14-072   Where liability is established, Member States must compensate for the loss or damage caused by the breach, in accordance with national laws on liability, provided that national laws do not treat the Community law claim less favourably than a similar domestic claim and do not make it impossible or excessively difficult in practice to obtain compensation.[291] The ECJ has held that English rules, which restrict liability to cases where the tort of misfeasance in public office is established, make it impossible in practice to

---

[285] See further G. Anagnostaras, "Not as Unproblematic as You Might Think: The Establishment of Causation in Governmental Liability Actions" (2002) 27 E.L. Rev. 663.

[286] *Brasserie du Pêcheur* [1996] E.C.R. I-1029, para 82.

[287] Lewis (2004), para.15–069; *Factotame*, para.73. On misfeasance in public office, see 19–048.

[288] Lewis (2004), para.15–070; *Factortame* paras 87–88.

[289] In *R. v Secretary of State for Transport Ex p. Factortame Ltd (No.5)* [1998] 1 C.M.L.R. 1353, the High Court held that liability for a breach of Community law could best be compared with breach of statutory duty (on which see para.16–052), as it was not possible to compare the UK's actions with the tort of misfeasance in public office (see para.16–048). Under English law, a breach of statutory duty only gave rise to exemplary damages if there was express statutory provision for them and no such provision existed in this case.

[290] *Brasserie du Pêcheur* [1996] E.C.R. I-1029, para.84.

[291] Lewis (2004), para.15–069; *Factortame*, paras 67–74.

enforce liability where the national legislature is responsible for the breach.[292] The national court is also not permitted to completely exclude loss of profit as a head of damages.[293]

Identifying the defendant

In identifying the defendant to a damages action, a "unitary" or indivisible **14–073** concept of the state has been adopted by the ECJ and the obligation to pay compensation arises without the state being allowed to "plead the distribution of powers and responsibilities between the bodies that exist in its national legal order to free itself from liability on this basis".[294] Thus damages actions can be brought in respect of the actions of administrative authorities,[295] the legislature[296] and even against the highest court for a "manifest breach" of Community law.[297] Moreover, damages actions can be brought against territorial bodies and public law entities enjoying a degree of institutional and functional autonomy from the central government.[298] In short,

> "[i]t is for each Member State to ensure that individuals obtain reparation for damage caused to them by non-compliance with Community law, whichever public authority is responsible for the breach and whichever public authority is in principle, under the law of the Member State concerned, responsible for making reparation".[299]

[292] Lewis (2004), para.15–069; *Factortame*, para.73
[293] Lewis (2004), para.15–070; *Factortame*, paras 87–88.
[294] Case C-302/97 *Konle v Austria* [1999] E.C.R. I–3099, para.62. See further Case C-118/00 *Gervais Larsy v Institut national d'assurances sociales pour travailleurs independents ("INASTI") (No.2)* [2001] E.C.R. I–5063, para.35; Case C-424/97 *Haim v Kassenzahnärztliche Vereinigung Nordrhein* [2000] E.C.R. I–5123, para.27. See further R.W. Davis, "Liability in Damages for a Breach of Community Law: Some Reflections on the Question of Who to Sue and the Concept of 'the State'" (2006) 31 E.L. Rev. 69.
[295] See, e.g. *Hedley Lomas* [1997] Q.B. 139; Case C-127/95 *Norbrook Laboratories Ltd v Ministry of Agriculture, Fisheries and Food* [1998] E.C.R. I–1531; Case C-319/96 *Brinkmann Tabakfabriken GmbH v Skatteministeriet* [1998] E.C.R. I–5255.
[296] *Francovich* [1991] E.C.R. I–5357; *Brasserie du Pêcheur* [1996] E.C.R.I–1029; *Factortame*; *British Telecom*; *Dillenkofer*; Cases C-283, 291 and 292/94 *Denkavit Internationaal BVs v Bundesampt für Finanzen* [1996] E.C.R. I–5063; *Konle* (n.294); C-140/97 *Rechberger v Austria* [1999] ECR I–3499.
[297] In Case C-224/01 *Köbler v Republik Österrich*, para.53 (*Francovich* reparation is available in principle where there has been default by a domestic court, although this will be "only in the exceptional case where the court has manifestly infringed the applicable law"). Furthermore, *Köbler* suggested that liability could only arise in respect of national courts of last instance rather than more generally. In *Köbler* itself, the ECJ found that the Austrian court had interpreted ECJ case law incorrectly and had wrongfully withdrawn a preliminary reference, but found neither act to constitute a manifest infringement since the ECJ considered that Community law did not provide an obvious answer to the question: paras 120–126. See H. Scott and N. Barber, "State Liability under *Francovich* for Decisions of National Courts" (2004) 120 L.Q.R. 403. For a comment on the consequences of the relationship between national courts and the Court of Justice under the preliminary reference procedure, see P. Wattel, "*Köbler, CILFIT* and *Welthgrove*: We Can't Go on Meeting Like This" (2004) 42 C.M.L. Rev. 177.
[298] *Haim* [2000] E.C.R. I–5123; *Brinkmann* (n.295); *Konle* [1999] E.C.R. I–3099.
[299] *Larsy II* [2000] E.C.R. I–5063.

14–074 That said, it is possible for the named defendant to be the autonomous public body, and the named defendant will not always be "the state".[300] Indeed, the choice of defendant may be of crucial importance in determining liability. Thus, in *Brinkmann*,[301] the autonomous actions of a Danish tax authority, given administrative effect to the Second Tax Directive as if the Directive had actually been implemented, were held to have severed the necessary link between the government's clear failure to implement the Directive by executive order and the harm suffered by the claimant. While the failure of the Danish Government to implement the Directive would have constituted a sufficiently serious breach of Community law, the tax authority's failure to correctly interpret the Directive was not a sufficiently serious breach, since its interpretation of the Directive was reasonable.

PRELIMINARY RULINGS

14–075 Any national court or tribunal is empowered to refer questions on the interpretation of Community law to the ECJ. In relation to claims for judicial review in England and Wales, this means the Administrative Court, Court of Appeal and House of Lords may, and in some situations must, refer questions of law to the ECJ. Art.234 states:[302]

> "The Court of Justice shall have jurisdiction to give preliminary rulings concerning:
>
> (a) the interpretation of this Treaty;
> (b) the validity and interpretation of acts of the institutions of the Community and of the ECB;
> (c) the interpretation of the statutes of bodies established by an act of the Council, where those statutes so provide.
>
> Where such a question is raised before any court or tribunal of a Member State, that court or tribunal may, if it considers that a decision on the question is necessary to enable it to give judgment, request the Court of justice to give a ruling thereon.
>
> Where any such question is raised in a case pending before a court or tribunal of a Member State against whose decisions there is no judicial remedy under national law, that court or tribunal shall bring the matter before the Court of Justice."

[300] *Larsy II* [2000] E.C.R. I–5063.
[301] [1998] E.C.R. I–5255 above.
[302] See also Note for Guidance on References by National Courts for Preliminary Rulings [1997] All E.R. (EC) 1 (issued by the ECJ) and Practice Direction (Supreme Court: References to the Court of Justice of the European Communities) [1999] 1 W.L.R. 260 (issued in England and Wales). See further D. Anderson and M. Demetriou, *References to the European Court*, 2nd edn (2002); M. Hoskins, "Preliminary References to the ECJ: Some Practical Pointers" [2002] J.R. 162; B. Lang (ed.) *Administrative Court: Practice and Procedure* (2006), Ch.14.

The ECJ cannot therefore rule on the applicability or interpretation of **14–076**
provisions of purely national or international law:[303] this applies even
where the national law has been introduced to implement EU obligations,[304] although the ECJ may accept a preliminary reference in a purely
internal situation where domestic legislation adopts a solution which is
consistent with Community law on the basis that accepting the reference
will promote uniformity in the interpretation of Community law.[305] The
ECJ has no jurisdiction to apply Community law to particular facts in the
main proceedings,[306] although it may rule on the legal consequences of
given primary facts.[307] The ECJ will not accept preliminary references
where there is no legal dispute,[308] the factual and legal context has not
been provided in sufficient detail for the ECJ to be able to give an
answer,[309] or the question is not relevant to the dispute.[310] Whether the
doctrine of precedent applies to rulings of the ECJ for preliminary
references was unresolved for some time[311]; but it is now clear that rulings
given by the ECJ bind all courts and administrative authorities in the
EU[312]—unless the national court seeks to obtain a fresh ruling from the
ECJ in which the question can be reconsidered.Where a court, not under
an obligation to make a preliminary reference, is faced with an Art.234 EC
issue the determination of which is critical to the court's final decision, the
appropriate course is ordinarily to refer the issue to the ECJ unless the
national court can with complete confidence resolve the issue itself.[313] In
addition, however, when deciding whether to make a reference, "the court
must observe some measure of self-restraint; lest the Court of Justice

---

[303] Case C-37/98 *R. v Secretary of State for the Home Department Ex p. Abdulnasir Savas*
[2000] E.C.R. I–2927, para.71. This includes "mixed agreements" where both the Community and the Member States are parties: Case 12/86 *Demirel* [1987] E.C.R. 3719; Joined
Cases C-300/98 and C-392/98 *Dior* [2000] E.C.R. I–11307.
[304] Case 23/75 *Rey Soda v Cassa Conguaglio Zucchero* [1975] E.C.R. 1279, paras 50–51.
[305] Joined Cases C-297/88 and C-197/89 *Dzodzi* [1990] E.C.R. I–3763, para.37; Case
C-300/01 *Salzmann* [2003] E.C.R. I–4899, para.34; Case C-222/01 *British American Tobacco
Manufacturing BV v Hauptzollamt Krefeld* [2004] E.C.R. I–4683, paras 40–41.
[306] European Communities Act 1972 s. 3(1); Case C-421/01 *Traunfellner* [2003] E.C.R. I–
11941, paras 21–24; *British Horseracing Board Ltd v William Hill Organisation Ltd* [2005]
EWCA Civ 863; [2006] E.C.C. 16 at [22] (Jacobs L.J.).
[307] Case C-206/01 *Arsenal Football Club Plc v Reed* [2003] Ch. 454.
[308] The ECJ does not provide advisory opinions: Case 244/80 *Foglia v Novello* [1981] E.C.R.
3045, paras 18, 20–31.
[309] Case C-320/90 *Telemarsicabruzzo SpA v Circostel* [1993] E.C.R. I–393, para.5.
[310] Case C-379/98 *PreussenElektra v Schleswag* [2001] E.C.R. I–2099; Case C-144/04
Mangold v Helm [2005] E.C.R. I–9981, paras 36–38; Case C-390/99 *Canal Satélite Digital*
[2002] E.C.R. I–607, paras 18 and 19; Case C-373/00 *Adolf Truley* [2003] E.C.R. I–1931,
paras 21 and 22; *Schneider* [2004] E.C.R. I–1389, paras 21 and 22; Case C-83/91 *Meilicke v
ADV/ORGA FA Meyer AG* [1992] ECR I–4971; Opinion of AG Kokott, Case C-225/02 *Rosa
Garcia Blanco* [2005] E.C.R. I–523, para.28 (noting that the justification for a reference for a
preliminary ruling is not that it enables advisory opinions on general or hypothetical questions
to be delivered but rather that it is necessary for the effective resolution of a dispute).
[311] Chalmers *et al., European Union Law* (2006) pp.295–297.
[312] *Kühne & Heitz* [2004] E.C.R. I–837, paras 21–27.
[313] *R. v International Stock Exchange of the United Kingdom and the Republic of Ireland Ltd
Ex p. Else Ltd* [1993] Q.B. 534 at 545 (Sir Thomas Bingham M.R.).

become overwhelmed".[314] A further justification for the exercise of caution can be found in the increasing familiarity of English courts with Community law.[315] In particular, the court should be cautious when asked to make a reference for a preliminary ruling in a case where it may turn out, after the facts have been established, that the point does not, in the event, arise.[316] Caution should also be exercised where there is an established body of case law; or where the question turns on a narrow point considered in the light of a very specific set of facts and the ruling is unlikely to have any application beyond the instant case.[317] By contrast, it will be appropriate to make a reference "where the question is one of general importance and where the ruling is likely to promote the uniform application of the law throughout the European Union".[318]

14–077   Pursuant to Art.234 EC, it would normally be compulsory for the House of Lords as the final court of appeal on the judicial review claim to make a reference for a preliminary ruling. The fact that leave must be sought to bring an appeal before the House of Lords means that if a question arises as to the interpretation or validity of a rule of Community law, Art.234 EC imposes an obligation on the House to refer the question to the ECJ either at the stage of the examination of the admissibility of the appeal or at a later stage.[319] However, where the question of Community law is "so obvious as to leave no scope for any reasonable doubt as to the manner in which the question raised is to be resolved",[320] a reference will not be necessary. This doctrine is referred to as the *acte clair* doctrine and it only applies to courts of last instance, within the meaning of Art.234(3) EC.[321] The conditions to satisfy the doctrine are extremely stringent;[322] although

---

[314] *Prudential Assurance Co Ltd v Prudential Insurance Co of America (No.1)* [2003] EWCA Civ 327; [2003] 1 W.L.R. 2295 at [50] (Chadwick L.J., declining to make a reference where determination of the point would not have been decisive); *Trinity Mirror Plc (formerly Mirror Group Newspapers Ltd) v Customs and Excise Commissioners* [2001] EWCA Civ 65; [2001] S.T.C. 192 at [51]–[55]; *Professional Contractors Group v Commissioners for Inland Revenue* [2001] EWCA Civ 1945; [2002] S.T.C. 165 at [91] (Walker L.J.).

[315] *Professional Contractors' Group* [2001] EWCA Civ 1945; [2002] S.T.C. 165 at [91]

[316] *Prudential Assurance* [2003] EWCA Civ 327; [2003] 1 W.L.R. 2295 at [50].

[317] Case C-338/95 *Wiener v SI GmbH v Hauptzollamt Emmerich* [1997] E.C.R. I–6495, Opinion of AG Jacobs, para.20; *Trinity Mirror* [2001] EWCA Civ 65; [2001] S.T.C. 192 at [52].

[318] *Wiener* [1997] E.C.R. I–6495, para.20.

[319] Case C-99/00 *Lyckeskog* [2002] E.C.R. I–4839, para.18. This confirmed the "concrete" understanding of Art.234 EC which understood a reference to be obligatory for the highest court in the case; as opposed to the "abstract" understanding of Art.234 which considered a reference obligatory for only the highest court in the land.

[320] Case C-283/81 *CILFIT Srl v Ministry of Health* [1982] E.C.R. 3415, para.16.

[321] As was presumably the case in *Equal Opportunities Commission v Secretary of State for Employment* [1995] 1 A.C. 1, HL (statutory provisions on rights of part-time workers declared to be inconsistent with Community law).

[322] In determining whether the Community law point is so obvious as to leave no scope for reasonable doubt, it is also necessary for the national court to consider "the characteristic features of Community law and the particular difficulties to which its interpretation gives rise", including (a) the need to compare the different language versions of Community legislation, each of which is equally authentic; (b) the use of terminology which is peculiar to

the practice of national courts has often been to misapply or even disregard them.[323] The ECJ has been invited to relax the requirements of the *acte clair* doctrine, but has declined to do so.[324]

It will always be compulsory for a national court to seek a preliminary **14–078** ruling where it is intending to question the validity of an EC act (for example a Regulation or Directive).[325] Indeed, the ECJ has stated that "all national courts *must* therefore refer a question to the court when they have doubts about the validity of a Community act, stating the reasons for which they consider that the Community act might be invalid".[326] In such cases, the caution of self-restraint noted above does not apply.[327]

DIRECT ACTIONS IN THE ECJ AND CFI

The ECJ and CFI have their own powers to adjudicate directly on **14–079** challenges to the legal validity of legal instruments, acts and omissions of the EU institutions, but not national measures.[328] Detailed consideration of the work of the ECJ and CFI in determining actions made directly to them fall outside the scope of this book, except insofar as it has an impact on the manner in which the Administrative Court in England and Wales exercises its own function of judicial review. Two main types of proceedings are relevant.

Enforcement actions

The Commission, or under certain conditions a Member State, may bring **14–080** an action directly before the ECJ against a Member State for failure of the latter to fulfil an obligation under the treaty.[329] The ECJ has no power to

---

Community law, or which has a different meaning in Community law from its meaning in the law of the various Member States; and (c) the need to place every provision of Community law in its context and to interpret it in the light of the provisions of Community law as a whole, regard being had to the objectives of Community law and to its state of evolution at the date on which the provision in question is to be applied: see *CILFIT* [1982] E.C.R. 3415, paras 17–20.

[323] Chalmers *et al., European Union Law* (2006) p.301; D. Anderson and M. Demetriou, *References to the European Court* (2002), paras 6–051–6–058; M. Brealey and M. Hoskins, *Remedies in EC Law* 2nd edn. (1998), pp.227–228;

[324] *Lyckeskog* [2002] E.C.R. I–4839, paras 9, 20–21.

[325] See 14–043.

[326] ECJ emphasis in ECJ Information Note on references from national courts for a preliminary ruling, [2005] O.J. C143/1, paras 15–16.

[327] Case C-338/95 *Wiener* [1997] E.C.R. I–6495, Opinion of AG Jacobs, para.25; *R. (on the application of Unitymark Ltd) v Secretary of State for the Environment, Food and Rural Affairs* [2003] EWHC 2748; [2004] Eu. L.R. 338 at [28]–[31] (Evans-Lombe J.).

[328] The ECJ has full jurisdiction to consider any matter falling within the EC pillar; it has no jurisdiction in respect of the second pillar; with regard to the third pillar, it can interpret and rule on the validity of framework decisions and decisions, but only has the power to interpret conventions and cannot rule these invalid: Arts. 46(a)-(b) and 35(1) TEU. As to the different pillars, see 14–005.

[329] Arts 226–228 [169–171] EC.

adjudicate on complaints from individuals against Member States.[330] If the ECJ finds that the defendant Member State has infringed Community law, it must take the necessary measures to comply with the judgment of the ECJ. The ECJ may impose a financial penalty on a Member State. In England and Wales, claims for judicial review by a person against a public authority, alleging breach of Community law, are sometimes conducted at the same time as the Commission brings an enforcement action before the ECJ. Thus in relation to provisions of the Merchant Shipping Act 1988, the Spanish trawler owners commenced judicial review against the Secretary of State for Transport in the High Court and the Commission brought proceedings against the United Kingdom in the ECJ.[331] Attempts of the United Kingdom Government to comply with a ruling of the ECJ in enforcement proceedings may themselves be subject to judicial review[332] though the Commission also monitors compliance by Member States.

Review of legality

14–081 One the main functions of the ECJ and CFI is to review the legality of secondary legislation and actions[333] and failures to act[334] of the EU institutions. The courts may annul a measure adopted by an EU institution or require an EU institution to adopt a measure. Where the applicant in such an action is an institution of the EU or a Member State, the action is dealt with by the ECJ.

14–082 Where the applicant is an individual, business enterprise or pressure group (known as non-privileged applicants) the CFI also has jurisdiction.[335] The standing requirements for a non-privileged applicant are strict: a non-privileged applicant can challenge the validity of decisions addressed to that person;[336] and where the decision is not addressed directly to the particular applicant or where the measure challenged is a regulation, the applicant will have standing only to the extent that the decision is "of direct and individual concern" to that person.[337] The ECJ has interpreted the requirement of "individual concern" narrowly to require that the decision affect the applicant "by reason of certain attributes which are peculiar to them or by reason of circumstances in which they are differentiated from all other persons and by virtue of these factors

---

[330] It is however open to an aggrieved person to lodge a complaint with the Commission inviting the Commission to institute proceedings under Art.226 [169] EC; but the individual cannot compel the Commission to institute such proceedings and cannot challenge any failure or refusal by the Commission.

[331] [1991] 1 A.C. 603 and [1992] Q.B. 680, ECJ.

[332] *R. v Secretary of State for the Environment Ex p. Friends of the Earth Ltd* (1995) 7 Admin. L.R. 793.

[333] Art.230 [173] EC.

[334] Art.232 [175] EC.

[335] Art.225(1) EC.

[336] For the definition of a "decision", see 14–027.

[337] Art.230 [173] EC.

distinguishes them individually just as in the case of the person addressed".[338] The ECJ has persisted with this test for standing, in spite of calls to relax the requirements from both the CFI and Advocates-General.[339] Individuals have no right to bring proceedings questioning the legality of a directive.[340] The time limit for bringing actions is only two months. The grounds upon which actions may be brought are "lack of competence, infringement of an essential procedural requirement, infringement of this Treaty or of any rule of law relating to its application, or misuse of powers".[341] These are considered further below.[342] A person with standing to challenge the legality of a decision or regulation, but who fails to do so within the two-month time limit, is precluded from questioning the validity of that decision before a national court.[343]

GROUNDS OF JUDICIAL REVIEW AGAINST COMMUNITY MEASURES:
OVERVIEW

Community law provides grounds for challenging both the legality of **14–083** Community measures and of national measures. The next two sections of the Chapter consider each of these situations in turn. As we have already noted, Community measures may be challenged either directly in the ECJ and CFI,[344] or (with restrictions) in proceedings before a national court.[345] The grounds of review are broadly the same in each situation and in outline they are the following:

(i) lack of adequate reasoning;

(ii) failure to state, or state correctly, the provisions of the treaty under which the measure was adopted;

---

[338] Case 25/62 *Plaumann v Commission* [1963] E.C.R. 95.
[339] Case T–177/01 *Jégo-Quéré v Commission* [2002] E.C.R. II–2365 (CFI proposed that the "individual concern" requirement be satisfied by an individual if the measure "affects his legal position, in a manner which is both definite and immediate, by restricting his rights or by imposing obligations on him"); cf. response of ECJ in Case C-263/02 P *Commission v Jégo-Quéré* [2004] E.C.R. I–3425, para.45; and Case C-50/00 P *Unión de Pequeños Agricultores v Council* [2002] E.C.R. I–6677. See also C-113/05 *European Federation for Cosmetic Ingredients (EFFCI) v Council of the European Union* [2006] E.C.R. I–46, para.37.
[340] Art.230[173] EC. The only option is to challenge the directive in a national court: see 14–113. The ECJ has held that the fact that the measure is a directive will not in itself render the action inadmissible, but it will be extremely difficult to satisfy the standing requirement: Case C-298/89 *Gibraltar v Council* [1993] E.C.R. I–3605.
[341] Art.230 [173] EC.
[342] See 14–083.
[343] Case C-188/92 *TWD Textilwerke Deggendorf GmbH v Germany* [1994] E.C.R. I–833; Case C-178/95 *Wiljo NV v Belgium* [1997] All E.R. (E.C.) 226. However, where a person would not "undoubtedly" have satisfied the "individual concern" requirement, it will be possible for that person to plead the illegality of the Community provisions in proceedings in national courts: *Textilwerke*; see also Case C-441/05 *Roquette Frères v Ministre de l'Agriculture, de l'Alimentation, de la Pêche et de la Ruralité* [2007] 2 C.M.L.R. 29, para.48.
[344] See 14–081.
[345] See 14–078.

    (iii) failure to hear a person affected before adopting the measure;

    (iv) failure to consult other bodies where consultation is required;

    (v) breach of the general principles of law developed by the European Court including proportionality, non-discrimination, respect for fundamental rights, legal certainty, and protection of legitimate expectations.

14–084 So extensive are the grounds of review that it is now probably more helpful to indicate the grounds on which the ECJ will *not* annul a measure. These include:

    (a) A minor procedural irregularity which is not regarded as sufficiently serious to justify annulment of the measure,[346] or which has not prejudiced the applicant.[347]

    (b) An alleged misjudgment by the Council or Commission in an area where the institution concerned enjoys a wide power of appraisal in assessing a complex economic situation.[348]

14–085 The grounds of review are thus wider than those under English law. A ground of challenge recognised under English law will probably be available under Community law; while some grounds available in Community law, for example lack of adequate reasoning, are not yet generally available under English law.[349] In any case in which the validity of a Community measure is in issue in the English courts, the court may have to consider whether the question of validity should be referred to the ECJ under Art.234 [177] EC. The English court will thus have to give preliminary consideration to a challenge based on any of the grounds indicated above, in order to decide whether a reference is justified.

GENERAL PRINCIPLES OF LAW[350]

14–086 The general principles of Community law constitute a considerable limitation on the policy-making powers of the EU institutions.[351] They also govern the interpretation of provisions of Community law and on occasion

---

[346] See, e.g. Joined Cases 156/79 and 51/80 *Gratreau v Commission* [1980] E.C.R. 3943, paras 23–24.
[347] See, e.g. Joined Cases 209 to 215, 218/78 *Van Landewyck v Commission* [1980] E.C.R. 3215, para.47. For a similar point in English law see *R. v Commissioners of Customs and Excise Ex p. Cooke and Stevenson* [1970] 1 All E.R. 1068.
[348] Case 331/88 *FEDESA* [1990] E.C.R. I–4203, para.14.
[349] See 7–087.
[350] See Tridimas (2006); J. Usher, *General Principles of EC Law* (1998); H. Nehl, *Principles of Administrative Procedure in EC Law* (1999).
[351] See, e.g. Case 162/82 *Cousin* [1983] E.C.R. 1101 (ECJ invalidated a Regulation which provided substantially more severe criteria for the determination of the origin of cotton yarn than for the determination of the origin of cloth and fabrics).

the ECJ may adopt a strained interpretation of a measure in order to avoid conflict with one of the general principles.[352] Most of the principles are wholly or mainly the product of judicial development, although the principle of proportionality is now expressly recognised in the Treaty as a constitutional principle of the Community legal order in Art.5 EC. Similarly, fundamental rights were first recognised by the ECJ's case law, then endorsed by declarations of the institutions and finally written into the fundamental law of the EU.[353]

Non-discrimination

Although certain provisions of the EC Treaty provide for the principle of equal treatment with regard to specific matters,[354] the ECJ has held that the principle of equality is a general principle of law of which those provisions are merely specific expressions and which precludes comparable situations from being treated differently unless the difference in treatment is objectively justified.[355] It also prohibits different situations from being treated in the same way unless such treatment is objectively justified.[356] Whether objective justification exists depends on the particular circumstances of each case, account being taken of the objectives of the measure in question. In general, the ECJ has interpreted the notion of "objective justification" broadly.[357]

14–087

---

[352] Case 78/74 *Deuka v EVGF* [1975] E.C.R. 421 (legitimate expectations); Joined Cases C-465/00, C-138/01 and C-139/01 *Rechnungshof v Österreichischer Rundfunk* [2003] E.C.R. I–4989 paras 68–72, 91 (fundamental rights); Case T–214/95 *Vlaams Gewest v Commission* [1998] E.C.R. II–717 (CFI held that guidelines adopted by the Commission had to be applied in accordance with the principle of equal treatment with the implication that like cases, as defined in the guidelines, had to be treated alike).

[353] Art.6 TEU.

[354] See, e.g. Art 12 [6] EC (prohibition of discrimination on the grounds of nationality); Art. 34(3) [40(3)] EC (prohibition of discrimination between producers and consumers in the common agricultural policy); Art.141 [119] EC (equal pay for equal work for men and women); Art.13 EC (conferring positive competence on the Community to take action to combat discrimination based on sex, racial or ethnic origin, religion or belief, disability, age or sexual orientation).

[355] See, e.g. Case 810/79 *Uberschar v Bundesversichorungsanstalt fur Angestellte* [1980] E.C.R. 2747, para.16; Joined Cases 117/76 and 16/77 *Ruckdeschel v Hauptzollamt Hamburg St Annen* [1977] E.C.R. 1753, para.7; Case 84/87 *Erpelding v Secretaine d'Etat d l'Agriculture et d la Viticulture* [1988] E.C.R. 2647, para.29; Case 152/73 *Sotgiu v Deutsche Bundespost* [1974] E.C.R. 153, para.11; Case 114/76 *Bela-Mühle Josef Bergman v Grows-Farm* [1977] E.C.R. 1211 (the effect of a policy making animal feed producers use skimmed-milk powder was to increase the price of animal feed and this harmed all livestock breeders and the benefits of the policy were felt only by dairy farmers; thus the policy operated in a discriminatory manner between different categories of farmers); and Case C-144/04 *Mangold v Helm* [2005] E.C.R. I–9981, para.75 (ECJ asserted that the principle of non-discrimination on grounds of age must be regarded as a general principle of Community law).

[356] Case 106/83 *Sermide v Cassa Conguaglio Zucchero* [1984] E.C.R. 4209, para. 28; Case C-106/01 *R. (on the application of Novartis Pharmaceuticals UK Ltd) v Licensing Authority* [2004] E.C.R. I–4403, para.69.

[357] Thus, it has been held that the discrimination which arises from the fact that a Council Regulation grants aid for sugar in transit between two approved warehouses situated in a single Member State but refuses such aid for sugar in transit between two approved warehouses situated in different Member States is objectively justified on the ground of the difference in the supervisory measures required: Case 8/82 *Wagner* [1983] E.C.R. 371.

14-088   In order to determine whether two products or two undertakings are in a comparable situation, the ECJ may have recourse to the criterion of competition. Thus, in the case of products, the ECJ will consider whether the one can be substituted for the other in the specific use to which the latter is traditionally put. Where two products are interchangeable they are in a comparable competitive position and, in principle, should be treated in the same manner.[358] By contrast, products which have different applications are not in a comparable situation and a difference in their treatment will not normally amount to prohibited discrimination.[359] In the case of undertakings, the ECJ may have regard to their production or to their legal structure[360] with a view to determining whether their competitive positions are comparable. The ECJ has held that differences in treatment which are based on objective differences arising from the underlying economic situations of Member States cannot be considered discriminatory.[361]

Proportionality

14-089   Action taken by the EU must be proportionate to its objectives.[362] It requires, in particular, that "the individual should not have his freedom of action limited beyond the degree necessary in the public interest to attain the purpose of the measure".[363] The assessment of proportionality is carried out by what we have described in Chapter 11 as a structured test, involving a series of stepped questions. Thus, in order to establish whether a provision of Community law is consonant with the principle of proportionality, it is necessary to establish, first, whether the means it employs to achieve the aim correspond to the importance of the aim and, secondly,

---

[358] See, e.g. Joined Cases 117/76 and 16/77 *Ruckdesche* l; Joined Cases 124/76 and 20/77 *Moulins Pont-a-Mousson v Office Interprofessionnel des Cereales* [1977] E.C.R. 1795.

[359] See, e.g. Case 125/77 *Koninklijke Scholten-Honig v Hoofdproduktschap voor Akkerbouwprodukten* [1978] E.C.R. 1991, paras 30–31; Case C-18/89 *Maizena* [1990] E.C.R. I–2587.

[360] Joined Cases 17 and 20/61 *Klockner v High Authority* [1962] E.C.R. 325 at 345; C280/99 *Moccia Irme SpA v Commission of the European Communities* [1999] E.C.R. II–1477, paras 189–210.

[361] Case 230/78 *Eridania v Minister for Agriculture and Forestry* [1979] E.C.R. 2749, para.19; Joined Cases C-181, C-182 and C-218/88 *Deschamps and Others v Ofival* [1989] E.C.R. 4381.

[362] The principle was initiated in 19th Century Prussia and developed in German law as *Verhältnismässigkeit*, a principle which in the case law of the *Bundesverfassungsgericht* (Federal Constitutional Court) has been held to underlie certain provisions of the German Grundgesetz (Basic Law). Cf. the scope of the principle in areas of English law where Community law does not apply; J. Schwarze, *European Administrative Law* (revised edn 2006), Ch. 5; J. Jowell and A. Lester, "Proportionality: Neither Novel nor Dangerous" in J. Jowell and D. Oliver (eds), *New Directions in Judicial Review* (1988), p.51; G de Búrca, "The Principle of Proportionality and its Application in EC Law" (1993) 13 Y.E.L. 105; N. Emiliou, *The Principle of Proportionality in European Law* (1996).

[363] Case 11/70 *Internationale Handelsgesellschaft v Einfuhr-und Vorratsstelle Getreide* [1970] E.C.R. 1125 at 1147 (AG de Lamothe).

whether they are necessary for its achievement.[364] In other words, there is a test of suitability and a test of necessity.[365] Where there is a choice between several appropriate measures, recourse must be had to the least onerous, and the disadvantages caused must not be disproportionate to the aims pursued.[366]

The principle of proportionality enables the ECJ to review not only the legality but, to some extent, also the merits of legislative and administrative measures taken by the EU institutions.[367] However, the intensity with which the principle is applied will range from extremely deferential to rigorous and searching depending on such factors as the interest of the individual at stake, the importance of the objective alleged to be served by the measure and by the expertise and competence of the ECJ as against the decision-making authority.[368] In the field of economic law, the principle is particularly important and often applied rigorously, since this field "frequently involves imposing taxes, levies, charges or duties on businessmen in the hope of achieving economic objectives".[369] In this context, the ECJ has

14–090

---

[364] Case 66/82 *Fromancais v Forma* [1983] E.C.R. 395, para.8; Case 15/83 *Denkavit Nederland v Hoofdproduktschap voor Akkerbouwprodukten* [1984] E.C.R. 2171, para.25; Case 21/85 *Mass v Bundesantalt fur Landwirtschaftliche Marktordnung* [1986] E.C.R. 3537; Case 181/84 *Man (Sugar) v IBAP* [1985] E.C.R. 2889; Case 240/78 *Atalanta v Produktschap voor Vee en Vless* [1979] E.C.R. 2137 (ECJ held that Art.5(2) of Commission Regulation (EEC) 1889/76 laying down detailed rules for granting private storage aid for pig-meat, which provides that "[t]he security shall be wholly forfeit if the obligations imposed by the contract are not fulfilled" was disproportionate as it did not permit the penalty to be made commensurate with the degree of failure to implement the contractual obligations or with the seriousness of the breach of those obligations); cf. Case C-104/94 *Cereol Italia v Azienda Agricola Castello* [1995] E.C.R. I–2983 (ECJ found that penalties which went as far as forfeiture of entitlement to aid for two marketing years, where a producer deliberately or by reason of serious negligence failed to notify the Commission of changes in the area sown, were proportionate in view of the importance of the obligation of notification for the operation of the aid system). For further successful challenges on the ground of proportionality: Case C-296/94 *Pietsch v Hauptzollamt Hamburg-Waltershof* [1996] E.C.R. I–3409 (ECJ annulled a Commission regulation, which imposed a charge on the import of mushrooms from third world countries equal to 90% of their value, on the ground that the level of the charges was disproportionate and amounted effectively to a prohibition of imports); Case C-295/94 *Hupeden & Co KG v Hauptzollamt Hamburg-Jonas* [1996] E.C.R. I–3375 (ECJ annulled a Council regulation holding that a flat-rate charge set at a very high level, 150% of the value of the goods, and levied on all traders who exceeded the import quota regardless of whether they did so inadvertently or fraudulently, was excessive).

[365] Tridimas (2006), p.139. This has been debated: de Búrca has suggested that there is a three part test, namely: (1) is the measure suitable to achieve a legitimate aim; (2) is the measure necessary to achieve that aim and (3) does the measure have an excessive effect on the applicant's interests: G de Búrca, "The Principle of Proportionality and its Application in EC Law" (1993) Y.E.L. 105, 113. Tridimas notes however that, while the tripartite test has received "some judicial support", "in practice the Court does not distinguish in its analysis between the second and third test": p.139.

[366] Case C-157/96 *R. v Minister of Agriculture, Fisheries and Food Ex p National Farmers' Union* [1998] E.C.R. I–2211, para.60; Case C-375/96 *Galileo Zaninotto v Ispettorato Central Repressione Frodi-Ufficio di Conegliano—Ministero delle Risorse Agricole, Alimentari e Forestali* [1998] E.C.R. I–6629, para.63.

[367] Tridimas (2006), p.140; Case C-84/94 *UK v Council Case* [1996] E.C.R. I–5755, para.58; *Ex p. British American Tobacco* [2002] E.C.R. I–11453, para.123.

[368] de Búrca (n.365) 111–112.

[369] Hartley (2007), p.152; e.g. Case 240/78 *Atalanta* [1979] E.C.R. 2137 at 2151; Case 181/84 *Man Sugar* [1985] E.C.R. 2889; see 14–006.

also held that although, in exercising their powers, the EU institutions must ensure that the amounts which commercial operators are charged are no greater than is required to achieve the aim which the authorities seek to accomplish,[370] it does not necessarily follow that that obligation must be measured in relation to the individual situation of any one particular group of operators since, given the multiplicity and complexity of economic circumstances, such an evaluation would not only be impossible to achieve but would also create perpetual uncertainty in the law.[371]

14-091   The ECJ applies the principle of proportionality less stringently in cases where the institution has a wide margin of appraisal or where it must make political, economic and social policy choices which require complex assessments. In such cases, which include the common agricultural policy,[372] and health,[373] judicial review of the exercise of discretion is usually limited to "examining whether it has been vitiated by manifest error or misuse of powers, or whether the institution concerned has manifestly exceeded the limits of its discretion".[374]

14-092   In summary, although the principle of proportionality permits the ECJ to substitute its own evaluation of the exercise of discretion there are cases where the margin of appraisal allowed to the decision-making institution is wider than others. The test of "manifest" error is not far from that of the *Wednesbury* approach described in Chapter 11[375] as it accords a measure of discretion to the decision-maker, with the difference that in the context of breach of Community law the authority (rather than the claimant) bears the burden of justifying the breach of the relevant provision.

---

[370] See, e.g. Case C-26/90 *Hauptzollamt Hamburg-Jonas v Wunscher* [1991] E.C.R. I–4961.

[371] See, e.g. Case 5/73 *Balkan-Import-Export v Hauptzollamt Berlin-Packhof* [1973] E.C.R. 1091, para.22; Case C-189/01 *Jippes v Minister van Landbouw, Natuurbeheer en Visserij* [2001] E.C.R. I–5689, para.99.

[372] *FEDESA* [1990] E.C.R. I–4203, para.14.

[373] *Ex p. British American Tobacco* [2002] E.C.R. I–11453 (ECJ applied a "manifestly inappropriate" standard in its review of Directive 2001/37, which amended and extended common rules governing tar yields and warnings on tobacco product packaging); and Case C-210/03 *R. v Secretary of State for Health Ex p. Swedish Match AB* [2004] E.C.R. I–11893, para.58 ("manifestly inappropriate" standard applied in the context of public health where the issue was a ban on marketing of tobacco for oral use).

[374] C-84/94 *UK v Council Case* [1996] E.C.R. I–5755, para.58. Alternatively, the ECJ has stated that the legality of a measure in such a sphere "can be affected only if the measure is manifestly inappropriate having regard to the objective which the competent institution is seeking to pursue": *FEDESA* [1990] E.C.R. I–4203. See further Case 265/87 *Schrader v Hazptzollamt Gonau* [1989] E.C.R. 2237, paras 21 and 22; *Ex p. British American Tobacco* (n.373), para.123. Even in this context however, the ECJ has on occasion engaged in quite considered review: Case C-189/01 *Jippes v Minister van Landbouw, Natuurbeheer en Visserij* [2001] E.C.R. I–5689, paras 85–100 (a proportionality challenge to the Community policy to tackle foot-and-mouth disease was found unsuccessful but only after careful scrutiny by the ECJ).

[375] See 11–018.

Legal certainty and legitimate expectations

The principles of legal certainty and of the protection of legitimate 14–093
expectations require that the effect of Community legislation must be clear
and predictable for those who are subject to it.[376] One of the most
important manifestations of the principle of legal certainty is the principle
of non-retroactivity. According to the established case law of the ECJ, a
Community measure, other than a criminal measure, may "exceptionally"
take effect from a point in time before its publication provided that two
conditions are fulfilled: the purpose to be achieved by the measure so
demands and the legitimate expectations of those concerned are duly
respected.[377] With regard to criminal provisions, however, the prohibition
of retroactive application is absolute.[378] The principle of legal certainty also
requires that sufficient information is made public to enable parties to
know clearly what the law is so that they may comply with it; it is applied
particularly strictly in the case of measures liable to have financial
consequences in order that those concerned may know precisely the extent
of the obligations which are imposed on them.[379] It also means that the
Commission cannot depart from the ordinary meaning of words used in
secondary legislation when it implements the legislation.[380]

The concept of legitimate expectation has been described as "the 14–094
corollary of the principle of legal certainty".[381] Legitimate expectations
may arise out of conduct of the EU institutions[382] or out of previous
legislation.[383] A legitimate expectation can arise in respect of representations of EU institutions, such as in guidelines, notices and so on, as
opposed to just formal decisions.[384] One of the most notable examples of
the application of the principle is provided by the milk quota cases. With a

---

[376] Opinion of AG Jacobs in Case C-168/91 *Konstantinidis* [1993] E.C.R. I–1191; and Case
C-233/96 *Kingdom of Denmark v Commission* [1988] E.C.R. I–5759, para.38 (Community
rules must enable those concerned to know precisely the extent of the obligations imposed on
them); Case 169/80 *Grondrand Frères* [1981] E.C.R. 1931 at 1942; Case C-245/97 *Germany
v Commission* [2000] E.C.R. I–11261, para.72. See further S. Schonberg *Legitimate Expectations in Administrative Law* (2000).
[377] See, e.g. Case 98/78 *Racke* [1979] E.C.R. 69, para.20; Case 99/78 *Decker* [1979] E.C.R.
101, para.8; Case 108/81 *Amylum v Council* [1982] E.C.R. 3107, paras 4–17; Case C-368/89
Crispoltoni [1991] E.C.R. I–3695, para.17.
[378] Case 63/83 *R. v Kirk* [1984] E.C.R. 2689, paras 21–22.
[379] Case T–115/94 *Opel Austria v Council* [1997] E.C.R. II–39, para.124.
[380] Case C-245/97 *Germany v Commission* [2000] E.C.R. I–11261, para.72.
[381] Case C-63/93 *Duff v Minister for Agriculture and Food, Ireland and the Attorney General*
[1996] E.C.R. I–569, para.20; Case C-83/99 *Commission v Spain* [2001] E.C.R. I–445,
para.24.
[382] See, e.g. Case 81/72 *Commission v Council* [1973] E.C.R. 575; Case 127/80 *Grogan v
Commission* [1982] E.C.R. 869; Case T–203/96 *Embassy Limousines & Services v European
Parliament* [1998] E.C.R. II–4239 (there could be a breach of legitimate expectations where a
company submitting a tender was encouraged to make irreversible investments in advance of
the contract being awarded and thereby to go beyond the risks inherent in making a bid).
[383] See, e.g. Case C-152/88 *Sofrimport v Commission* [1990] E.C.R. I–2477.
[384] Case C-313/90 *CIRFS v Commission* [1993] E.C.R. I–1125, paras 34–36 (ECJ accepted
that the Commission was bound by the terms of a policy framework); and Case 148/73
Louwage v Commission [1974] E.C.R. 81, para.12.

view to curbing excess milk production, the Council enacted Regulation No.1078/77 offering a premium to producers who undertook not to market milk products for a period of five years and those who undertook to convert their dairy farms to meat production for a period of four years. Subsequently, Council Regulation 857/84 introduced a levy payable on quantities of milk delivered beyond a guaranteed threshold known as reference quantity. It did not provide, however, for the allocation of a reference quantity to producers who, pursuant to an undertaking under Regulation 1078/77, had not delivered milk and who, upon the termination of their undertaking, were willing to resume milk production. The Court held that the total exclusion of those producers from the allocation of a reference quantity ran counter to the principle of legitimate expectations.[385] Regulation 857/84 was subsequently amended so as to provide that those producers were entitled to a reference quantity equal to 60 per cent of the quantity of milk delivered by the producer during the 12 calendar months preceding the month in which his application for the non-marketing or conversion premium under Regulation 1078/77 was made. The Court held, however, that the ceiling of 60 per cent was also contrary to the principle of legitimate expectations and therefore invalid:

"It must be made clear . . . that where a reduction . . . is applied, the principle of the protection of legitimate expectations precludes the rate of reduction from being fixed at such a high level, by comparison with those applicable to producers whose reference quantities are fixed pursuant to . . . Regulation No. 857/84, that its application amounts to a restriction which specifically affects them by very reason of the undertaking given by them under Regulation No. 1078/77."[386]

14-095　A legitimate expectation will not be protected, however, unless it is reasonable: the question is whether a "prudent and discriminating" person would have had the expectation.[387] Thus, the ECJ has emphasised that traders cannot have an expectation that an existing situation which is capable of being altered by the EU institutions in the exercise of their discretionary power will be maintained.[388] A trader cannot have a legitimate expectation to derive an advantage from a particular measure if that measure was never intended to bestow that advantage;[389] similarly, an

---

[385] Case 120/86 *Mulder v Minister van Landbouw en Visserij* [1988] E.C.R. 2321; Case 170/86 *Von Deetzen v Hauptzollamt Hamburg-Jonas* [1988] E.C.R. 2355.
[386] Case C-189/89 *Spagl* [1990] E.C.R. I–4539, para.22; Case C-217/89 *Pastatter* [1990] E.C.R. I–4585, para.13.
[387] Case C-22/94 *Irish Farmers Association v Minister for Agriculture, Food and Forestry* [1997] ECR I–1809, para.25.
[388] Case C-350/88 *Delacre v Commission* [1990] E.C.R. I–395; Case C-375/96 *Galileo Zaninotto v Ispettorato Centrale Repressione Frodi-Ufficio di Conegliano-Ministero delle risorse agricole, alimentare e forestali* [1998] E.C.R. I–6629, para.50 (CAP); Case C-284/94 *Kingdom of Spain v Council* [1998] E.C.R. I–7309, para.43.
[389] Case 2/75 *Mackprang v Commission* [1975] E.C.R. 607.

undertaking to which aid is granted cannot entertain a legitimate expectation that the aid is lawful unless it has been granted in accordance with proper procedure, and a diligent businessman should be able to determine whether the procedure has been followed.[390] In addition, a legitimate expectation cannot be relied upon against "a *precise* provision of Community law, or an *unambiguous* provision of Community law"; or against an overriding public interest.[391] Furthermore, a legitimate expectation may not be relied upon by an undertaking which has committed a manifest infringement of the rules in force.[392]

Human rights[393]

Although the EC Treaty does not provide for a catalogue of fundamental rights, the principle of respect of fundamental rights has been endorsed in subsequent texts, notably in the preamble to the Single European Act,[394] in the TEU,[395] and the Treaty of Amsterdam.[396] **14–096**

After initially refusing to countenance arguments that EU institutions had violated human rights,[397] the ECJ acknowledged the importance of human rights[398] and then in its seminal judgment in *Internationale Handelsgesellschaft,* went further with the pronouncement that:[399] "respect for **14–097**

---

[390] Case C-183/02 P *Daewoo Electronics Manufacturing Espana SA (DEMESA) v Commission* [2004] ECR I–10609, para.44.

[391] Case 316/86 *Firma P Krücken* [1988] E.C.R. 2213 at 2239; Joined Cases C–31/91 to C-44/91 *SpA Lois Lageder and others v Amministrazione delle Finanze dello Stato* [1993] E.C.R. I–1761, para.34; Case C 94/05 *Emsland-Starke GmbH v Landwirtschaftskammer Hannover* [2006] E.C.R. I–2619. On overriding public interest, see Case 74/74 *CNTA v Commission* [1975] E.C.R. 533, para.43 and Case T–155/99 *Dieckmann & Hansen GmbH v Commission* [2001] E.C.R. II–3143, para.80.

[392] Case 67/84 *Sideradria v Commission* [1985] E.C.R. 3983, para.21; Joined Cases T–551/93, 231/94 233–234/94 *Industria Pesdquera Campos v Commission* [1996] E.C.R. II–247, para.76; Case T–125/01 *José Martí Peix SA v Commission of the European Communities* [2003] E.C.R. II–865, para.107.

[393] L. Betten and N. Grief, *EU Law and Human Rights* (1998); P. Alston (ed.), *The EU and Human Rights* (1999). For human rights as a ground of challenge to national measures in the scope of application of Community law, see 14–119.

[394] [1987] O.J. L/169.

[395] Art.6 [F].

[396] Arts 6, 7 and 11 TEU as amended by the Treaty of Amsterdam; Reference to Human Rights in the Common Foreign and Security Policy Art.11(1) [J.1(1)] TEU); Provisions on Police and Judicial Co-operation in Criminal Matters state that one of the objectives of the EU is the combating of racism and xenophobia (Art.29 [K.1] TEU). Amendments brought in by Treaty of Amsterdam specify that respect for human rights is a precondition for joining the Community (Art.49 and Art.6(1) [F(1)] TEU) and that a Member State which persistently disregards them may have some of its rights under the Treaties suspended: Arts 7 TEU, and 309 EC.

[397] Case 1/58 *Stork v High Authority* [1959] E.C.R. 17; Joined Cases 36, 37, 38 and 40/59 *Geitling v High Authority* [1980] E.C.R. 423; Case 40/64 *Sgarlata v Commission* [1965] E.C.R. 215.

[398] Case 29/69 *Stauder v City of Ulm* [1969] E.C.R. 419 (referring to the "fundamental rights enshrined in the general principles of Community law and protected by the Court").

[399] Case 11/70 *Internationale Handelsgesellschaft v Einfuhr-und Vorrarsstelle Getreide* [1970] E.C.R. 1125, para.4.

fundamental rights forms an integral part of the general principles of law protected by the ECJ. The protection of such rights, whilst inspired by the constitutional traditions common to the Member States, must be ensured within the framework of the structure and objectives of the Community".

14–098   In *Nold*[400] the ECJ stated that it cannot uphold measures which are incompatible with fundamental rights recognised and protected by the Constitutions of the Member States.[401] It also identified as a source of human rights international treaties for the protection of human rights on which the Member States have collaborated or of which they are signatories. In subsequent cases, the ECJ has indicated that the ECHR has special significance in this respect.[402] However, even though the ECHR is a special source for the ECJ's jurisprudence, if a right does not form part of the ECHR jurisprudence, the ECJ can deem it to be a right.[403] The ECJ also refers regularly to the International Covenant on Civil and Political Rights of the United Nations;[404] to the 1989 Community Charter of Fundamental Social Rights of Workers and the 1962 European Social Charter.[405]

14–099   The rights recognised by the ECJ can be broadly categorised[406] as civil, economic and rights of the defence (in French, *droits de la défense*).[407] Civil rights include freedom of trade union activity,[408] prohibition of discrimination based on sex,[409] protection from discrimination on grounds of sexual orientation,[410] religious equality,[411] freedom of expression,[412] the right to respect private life and medical secrecy,[413] the protection of the privacy of business premises,[414] the right to fair legal process within a reasonable

---

[400] Case 4/73 *Nold v Commission* [1974] E.C.R. 491.
[401] See also Case 44/79 *Hauer v Land Rheinland- Pfalz* [1979] E.C.R. 3727 (ECJ reviewed the property provisions in the constitutions of Germany, Italy and Ireland and also analysed in some detail the relevant provisions of the ECHR); and see also constitutional rights recognised by the common law.
[402] Case 222/84 *Johnston v Chief Constable of the Royal Ulster Constabulary* [1986] E.C.R. 1651; *ERT* [1991] E.C.R. 2925, Case C-94/00 *Roquette Frères SA v Directeur Général de la concurrence, de la consummation et de la repression des fraudes* [2002] E.C.R. I–9011 (ECJ) para.23; Case C-299/95 *Kremzow v Austria* [1997] E.C.R. I–2629.
[403] In Case 155/79 *AM&S v Commission* [1982] E.C.R. 1575, AG Warner noted that the ECHR made no mention of a principle of lawyer/client confidentiality, yet the ECJ held that it was part of Community law, at 290–291.
[404] Case 374/87 *Orkem v Commission* [1989] E.C.R. 3283.
[405] Case 24/86 *Blaizot v Belgium* [1988] E.C.R. 379.
[406] Chalmers *et al.* (2006), pp.238–241.
[407] O. Due, "Le respect des droits de la défense dans le droit administratif communautaire" in *Cahiers de Droit Européen* (1987), p.383. For an extensive treatment, see J. Schwarze, *European Administrative Law* pp.1243–1371; Joined Cases 46/87 and 227/88 *Hoechst AG v Commission* [1989] E.C.R. 2859, para.14 (referring to "the rights of the defence").
[408] Case 175/73 *Union Syndicate v Council* [1974] E.C.R. 917.
[409] Case 149/77 *Defrenne v Sabena* [1978] E.C.R. 1365.
[410] Case C-117/01 *KB v National Health Service Pensions Agency* [2004] E.C.R. I–541
[411] Case 130/75 *Prais v Council* [1976] E.C.R. 1589.
[412] *ERT* [1991] E.C.R. 2925; Case C-219/91 *Ter Voon* [1992] E.C.R. I–5485.
[413] Case 136/79 *National Panasonic v Commission* [1980] E.C.R. 2033; Case C-62/90 *Commission v Germany* [1992] E.C.R. I–2575; Case C-404/92P *X v Commission* [1994] E.C.R. I–4737.
[414] *Roquette Frères* [2002] E.C.R. I–9011, para.29.

period,[415] protection of personal data,[416] the right to free and informed consent before any medical procedure,[417] and human dignity.[418] The economic rights include the right to property,[419] the right freely to choose and practise a trade or profession,[420] and freedom of trade.[421] The rights of the defence include, in particular, the right to an effective legal remedy before the national courts,[422] the right to be heard,[423] the right in certain circumstances to be assisted by a lawyer,[424] legal professional privilege,[425] the right not to be compelled to provide the Commission with answers which might involve an admission on the undertaking's part of the existence of an infringement which it is incumbent upon the Commission to prove and the right of access to the file.[426]

It is not easy to identify in the abstract the exact content of a right 14–100 recognised by the ECJ as forming part of the EU legal order. The Court has held, for example, that the right to property and the individual's right freely to choose and practise a trade or profession do not constitute unfettered rights but must be viewed in the light of their social function.[427] On this basis, the ECJ has held that those rights may be restricted, for example, in the context of a common organisation of the market, provided that those restrictions correspond to objectives of general interest pursued by the EU and that they do not constitute a disproportionate and intolerable interference which infringes upon the very substance of the rights guaranteed.[428] In general, therefore, provided that the substance of a right is respected, certain aspects of it may have to give way to the attainment of EU objectives or may be sacrificed in order to safeguard an overriding interest.[429] The Court has held however, that fundamental

---

[415] Case C-185/95P *Baustahlgewebe GmbH v Commission* [1998] E.C.R. I–8417, paras 20–22
[416] Case C-101/01 *Lindqvist* [2003] E.C.R. I–12971; Joined Cases C-465/00, C-138/01 and C-139/01 *Rechnungshof v Österreichisches Rundfunk* [2003] E.C.R. I–4989.
[417] Case C-377/98 *Netherlands v Parliament and Council* [2001] E.C.R. I–7079.
[418] Case C-36/02 *Omega Spielhallen-und-Automatenaufstellungs v Oberbügermeisterin der Bundesstadt Bonn* [2004] E.C.R. I–9609.
[419] *Hauer* [1979] E.C.R. 3727.
[420] *Nold* [1974] E.C.R. 491; *Hauer* [1979] E.C.R. 3727.
[421] Case 19/92 *Dieter Kraus v Land Baden-Wurttemberg* [1993] E.C.R. I–1663.
[422] Case 222/84 *Johnston v Chief Constable of the Royal Ulster Constabulary* [1986] E.C.R. 1651.
[423] Case 17/74 *Transocean Marine Paint v Commission* [1974] E.C.R. 1063.
[424] See, e.g. Case 115/80 *Demont v Commission* [1981] E.C.R. 3147.
[425] Case 155/79 *AM & S v Commission* [1982] E.C.R. 1575.
[426] Case C-219/00 P *Aalborg Portland v Commission ("Cement")*[2004] E.C.R. I–123, paras 65 and 68.
[427] *Nold* [1974] E.C.R. 491; *Hauer* [1979] E.C.R. 3727.
[428] Hartley (2007) Ch.5. The Treaty of Amsterdam introduced a special preliminary reference procedure in relation to Title IV of the EC Treaty (Arts 61–69) on Visas, Asylum, Immigration and other policies related to the Free Movement of Persons.
[429] See, e.g. Case 204/86 *Procureur de la Republique v ADBHU,*[1988] E.C.R. 5323, para.12 (freedom of trade); Case C-219/91 *Ter Voort* [1992] E.C.R. I–5485, para.38 (freedom of expression); L. Besselink, "Entrapped by the Maximum Standard: On Fundamental Rights, Pluralism and Subsidiarity in the European Union" (1998) 35 C.M.L. Rev. 629; J. Weiler, "Fundamental Rights and Fundamental Boundaries: On Standards and Values in the Protection of Human Rights" in N. Neuwahl and A. Rosas (eds), *The European Union and Human Rights* (1995).

rights, such as freedom of expression, may take precedence over the EC Treaty free movement rights, provided the interference with free movement is proportionate.[430] In general, challenges to specific administrative acts rather than legislative measures are likely to be more successful in the context of breach of fundamental rights.[431]

The right to be heard[432]

14–101 Among the rights of the defence recognised by the ECJ is a person's right to be heard before a decision affecting him is taken. The ECJ appears to have first considered the importance of procedural protection in the context of the staff of EU institutions;[433] however, the right to be heard has subsequently been extended to all proceedings which are initiated against a person and which are liable to culminate in a measure adversely affecting that person.[434] The right is a fundamental principle of Community law which must be guaranteed even in the absence of any specific rules.[435] It is in the context of competition cases that much of the law on the right to be heard has been developed: the right has been recognised as an inherent right of undertakings in competition proceedings and of Member States in proceedings relating to Art.86 [90] EC and in proceedings under Art.88 [93] EC on state aids. However, the right has also been extended to parties to, and to persons liable to be affected by, many other types of proceedings.

Right to be heard in competition proceedings[436]

14–102 In competition law, the ECJ examined the right to a fair hearing in the *Transocean Marine Paint* case.[437] There, the Commission exempted from the prohibition provided for in Art.81(1) [85] of the Treaty an agreement concluded between the members of the Transocean Marine Paint Associa-

---

[430] This was in the context of review of national rather than Community measures, but is an indication of the growing importance of fundamental rights in the EC legal order: Case C-112/00 *Schmidberger v Austria* [2003] E.C.R. I–5659.

[431] Craig and de Búrca (2007), p.390. Challenges in the field of competition and staff cases have been more readily entertained by the CFI and on occasion by the ECJ, e.g. Case C-404/92P *X v Commission* [1994] E.C.R. I–4737; Case C-122 & 125/99P *D v Council* [2001] E.C.R. I–4319; C-191/98P *Tzoans v Commission* [1999] E.C.R. I–8223; C-252/97 *N v Commission* [1998] E.C.R. I–4871.

[432] For procedural propriety as a general challenge to purely domestic situations in English law, see Chs 6–10 above.

[433] Case 35/67 *Van Eick v Commission* [1968] E.C.R. 329 at 342 (ECJ noting that EC institutions, when acting in the context of staff disciplinary procedures, were "bound in the exercise of [their] powers to observe the fundamental principles of the law of procedure").

[434] See 14–102 *et seq*.

[435] Case 234/84 *Belgium v Commission* [1986] E.C.R. 2263, para.27; Case C-301/87 *France v Commission* [1990] E.C.R. I–307, para.29: Joined Cases C-48/90; C-66/90 *Netherlands v Commission* [1992] E.C.R. 1–565, paras 37, 44; *Cement* [2004] E.C.R. I–123.

[436] C. Kerse and N. Khan, *EC Antitrust Procedure*, 5th edn (2005).

[437] Case 17/74 *Transocean Marine Paint v Commission* [1974] E.C.R. 1063.

tion but made the exemption subject to a condition, in relation to which the Association considered that the Commission had not given it the opportunity to make its views known in advance. The Commission argued that Regulation 99/63, which required the Commission to inform undertakings and associations of undertakings of the objections raised against them, did not relate to the conditions which the Commission intended to attach to a decision granting exemption. The Court accepted that argument but continued:[438]

> "It is clear, however, both from the nature and objective of the procedure for hearings, and from Articles 5, 6 and 7 of Regulation No. 99/63, that this Regulation . . . applies the general rule that a person whose interests are perceptibly affected by a decision taken by a public authority must be given the opportunity to make his point of view known. This rule requires that an undertaking be clearly informed, in good time, of the essence of conditions to which the Commission intends to subject an exemption and it must have the opportunity to submit its observations to the Commission. This is especially so in the case of conditions which, as in this case, impose considerable obligations having far reaching effects."

Because this had not been done, the condition was annulled.

In competition proceedings, the right to a hearing requires the Commission to inform the undertaking concerned of the facts upon which the Commission's adverse decision is based. However, the requirement to disclose the necessary information may come into conflict with the obligation of "professional secrecy"[439] incumbent upon EU officials. Consequently, the Commission may not use to the detriment of an undertaking facts or documents which it is under an obligation not to disclose, where the failure to make such disclosure adversely affects the undertaking's opportunity to be heard.[440] In *Orkem*[441] the ECJ was confronted with the question whether, in the absence of any right to remain silent expressly embodied in the relevant provisions of Community law, the general principles of Community law included the right of an undertaking not to supply information capable of being used in order to establish against it an infringement of EU competition law the privilege against self-incrimination. The Court held that the Commission is entitled to compel an undertaking to provide all necessary information concerning such facts as may be known to it and to disclose to the Commission all relevant documents which are in its possession, even if the latter may be used to establish, against it or another undertaking, the existence of anti-competitive conduct. However, the Commission may not, by means of a 14–103

---

[438] [1974] E.C.R. 1063, para.15 of the judgment.
[439] Art.287 [214] EC; Art.20 of Reg.17 [1962] O.J. L13/204.
[440] Case 85/76 *Hoffmann-La Roche v Commission* [1979] E.C.R. 461, para.14.
[441] Case 374/87 *Orkem v Commission* [1989] E.C.R. 3283.

decision calling for information, undermine the rights of defence of the undertaking concerned and therefore it may not compel an undertaking to provide it with answers which might involve an admission on its part of the existence of an infringement, which it is incumbent upon the Commission to prove. On that basis, the ECJ annulled certain questions contained in the contested decision addressed by the Commission to the undertaking concerned. The Court thus took an extensive view of the privilege against self-incrimination, although that privilege is generally recognised by the laws of the Member States only for natural persons and only in the context of criminal proceedings.[442]

Right to be heard in anti-dumping proceedings

14–104 In *Al-Jubail*,[443] the ECJ held that the right to a fair hearing must be respected in anti-dumping proceedings before anti-dumping measures are adopted, even though such measures are adopted by way of regulation rather than decision, as in the competition context. The basic anti-dumping legislation must therefore be interpreted so as to take account of the requirements stemming from the right to a fair hearing. In performing their duty to provide information, the EU institutions must act with all due diligence by seeking—

"to provide the undertakings concerned, as far as is compatible with the obligation not to disclose business secrets, with information relevant to the defence of their interests, choosing, if necessary on their own initiative, the appropriate means of providing such information. In any event, the undertakings concerned should have been placed in a position during the administrative procedure in which they could effectively make known their views on the correctness and relevance of the facts and circumstances alleged and on the evidence presented by the Commission in support of its allegation concerning the existence of dumping and the resultant injury."

14–105 However, the right does not apply to all aspects of the anti-dumping proceedings. The Court has held that it is within the discretion of the Council to choose any one of the methods provided for by the EU rules for the purposes of calculating the export price and therefore the Council is under no obligation to give the undertaking concerned the opportunity to present its observations in advance on the method selected.[444]

The right to be heard in other proceedings

14–106 Although in *Transocean Marine Paint*, the ECJ referred to the right to be heard as a "general rule", its language in subsequent cases was more guarded.[445] However, the rights of the defence generally now appear to be

---

[442] *cf. Westinghouse Uranium Contract* [1978] A.C. 547, HL.
[443] Case C-49/88 *Al-Jubail Fertilizer Company v Council* [1991] E.C.R. I–3187, para.17.
[444] Case C-178/87 *Minolta v Council* [1992] E.C.R. I–15.
[445] See, e.g. Case 85/76 *Hoffmann-La Roche v Commission* [1979] E.C.R. 461 (the right to be heard was to be observed "in proceedings in which sanctions, in particular fines or penalty payments, may be imposed").

considered to be a "fundamental principle of Community law", which applies in all administrative proceedings which are initiated against a person and are liable to culminate in a measure adversely affecting that person, regardless of whether or not there are rules governing the procedure.[446] This includes investigative proceedings which despite their general scope, may directly and individually affect the undertakings concerned and entail adverse consequences for them.[447] The right also applies in the context of customs law;[448] administration of the European Social Fund;[449] and in the context of remission of import duties.[450] Moreover, the Commission must be all the more scrupulous where the rules in question do not provide all the procedural guarantees for the protection of the individual which may exist in certain national legal systems.[451] The principle is not however limitless, and in the state aid context, the ECJ has held that interested third parties, including the recipient of the aid, other than the Member State responsible for granting the aid cannot claim a right to debate the issues with the Commission in the same way as the Member State.[452]

The requirement to state reasons[453]

Art.253 [190] EC requires that binding acts of the European Parliament, **14–107** the Council and the Commission must state the reasons on which they are based and that they must refer to any proposals or opinions which were required to be obtained pursuant to the Treaty. Insufficient reasoning constitutes a breach of an essential procedural requirement. The require-

---

[446] Case C-32/95P *Lisrestal* [1996] E.C.R. I–5377; Case C-135/92 *Fiskano v Commission* [1994] E.C.R. 1–2885, para.39 (the right was recognised in proceedings relating to an alleged infringement by a Swedish vessel of a Fisheries Agreement between the EU and Sweden). See also Case T–102/00 *Yleams Fonds voor de Sociale Integratie van Personen met een Handicap v Commission* [2003] E.C.R. I–2433, para.59.

[447] *Al-Jubail* [1994] E.C.R. I–3187, para.15. On the exemption of preliminary inquiries from procedural fairness in English law, see 8–032.

[448] Case C-269/90 *Technische Universität München* [1991] E.C.R. 1–5469, para.25 (ECJ departed from its previous case law. Undertakings which seek duty-free import of scientific instruments have the right to be heard on objections to their application before the Commission takes a decision: in such an administrative procedure the person concerned should be able, during the actual procedure before the Commission, to put his own case and properly make his views known on the relevant circumstances, and where necessary, on the documents taken into account by the Community institution).

[449] Case T–450/93 *Lisrestal v Commission* [2994] E.C.R. II–1177, para.42.

[450] Case T–42/96 *Eyckeler & Malt AG* [1998] E.C.R. II–401, paras 76–80 (ECJ noted rights of the defence required not only that the person concerned should be placed in a position in which he may effectively make known his views on the relevant circumstances, but also that he should at least be able to put his own case on the documents taken into account by the decision-making authority).

[451] *Al-Jubail* [1991] E.C.R. I–3187, para.16.

[452] Case T–198/01R *Technische Glaswerke Ilmenau v Commission* [2004] 3 C.M.L.R. 7, paras 192–193 (on appeal to the ECJ as C-404/04).

[453] For reasons as a ground of challenge to national measures in Community law, see 14–117; and in purely domestic situations, see 7–087.

ment of reasoning has a threefold objective:[454] it seeks to give an opportunity to the parties involved of defending their rights, to the ECJ of exercising its supervisory functions and to the Member States and third persons of ascertaining the circumstances in which the enacting institution has applied the EC Treaty.

14–108   As a general rule, the statement of reasons must disclose in a clear and unequivocal fashion the reasoning of the authority which adopted the measure in such a way as to enable the persons concerned to ascertain the reasons for the measure and to enable the competent Community Court to exercise its power of review.[455] A distinction is drawn between acts of general application and decisions.[456] With regard to general acts, especially regulations, it is sufficient if the reasons given explain in essence the measures taken without need for a specific statement of reasons in support of all the details which might be contained in such a measure, provided that such details fall within the general scheme of the measure as a whole.[457] In principle, an act must state in its preamble the legal basis on which it was adopted. Failure to refer to a precise provision of the Treaty need not constitute an infringement of an essential procedural requirement, however, when the legal basis of the measure can be determined from other parts of that measure.[458]

14–109   With regard to individual decisions, the ECJ has stated that the purpose of the requirement of reasoning is to enable the ECJ to review the legality of the decision and to provide the person concerned with details sufficient to allow him to ascertain whether the decision is well founded or is vitiated by a defect which will allow its legality to be contested.[459] A decision must therefore refer to the matters of fact and law on which the legal justification for the measure is based.[460] The extent of reasoning required

---

[454] Case 24/62 *Germany v Commission* [1963] E.C.R. 63 at 69; Case 294/81 *Control Data v Commission* [1983] E.C.R. 911, para.14.

[455] Case 108/81 *Amylum v Council* [1982] E.C.R. 3107, para.37; Case C-350/88 *Delacre v Commission* [1990] E.C.R. I–395, para.13.

[456] Opinion of AG Van Gerven in Case C-137/92 *Commission v BASF* [1994] E.C.R. I–2555 at 2571.

[457] Case 166/78 *Italy v Commission* [1979] E.C.R. 2575, para.8.

[458] Case 45/86 *Commission v Council* [1987] E.C.R. 1493, para.9.

[459] See, e.g. Case 32/86 *Sisina v Commission* [1987] E.C.R. 1645, para.8; *Technische Universität* [1991] E.C.R. I 5469, para.26 and Opinion of AG Jacobs at 5492–5493.

[460] See, e.g. Case 322/81 *Michelin v Commission* [1983] E.C.R. 3461, para.14; Case 41/69 *ACF Chemiefarma v Commission* [1970] E.C.R. 661, para.78; Case C-358/90 *Compagnia Italiana Alcool v Commission* [1992] E.C.R. I–2457. For a case where ECJ annulled a Commission decision on State aid, see Joined Cases C-329/93, 62/95, 63/95 *Germany, Hanseatische Industrie-Beteiligungen GmbH and Bremer Vulkan Verbund AG v Commission* [1996] E.C.R. 1–5151. See also Case T–95/94 *Sytraval and Brink's France SARL v Commission* [1995] E.C.R. II–2651. Cf. Case C-166/95 P *Commission v Daffix* [1997] E.C.R. I–983 (ECJ found that on the circumstances of the case the decision of the Commission to remove an official from office on grounds of misconduct was sufficiently reasoned and quashed the judgment of the CFI (Case T–12/94 [1995] E.C.R. II–233)); Case C-254/95 *Parliament v Innamorati* [1996] E.C.R. I–3423, reversing the decision of the CFI in Case T–289/94 [1995] E.C.R. II–393 (in a competition for recruitment of Community officials, the criteria for marking adopted by the selection board are secret so that failure to communicate those criteria to an unsuccessful candidate does not breach the requirement to give reasons).

depends on the content of the measure, the nature of the reasons given and the interest which the addressees of the measure or other parties to whom it is of direct and individual concern may have in obtaining explanations. It is not necessary for the reasoning to go into all the relevant facts and points of law, since the question whether the statement or reasons meets the requirements of Art.253 EC must be assessed with regard not only to its wording but also to its context and to all the legal rules governing the matter in question.[461] The degree of precision of the statement of the reasons must also be weighed against practical realities and the time and technical facilities available for making the decision.[462]

A few concrete examples are illustrative. When the Council decides not to adopt a proposal for a regulation imposing definitive anti-dumping duties, it should provide an adequate statement of reasons which shows clearly and unambiguously why, in the light of the provisions of the basic regulation, there is no need to adopt the proposal.[463] Although the reasons on which a decision following a well-established line of decisions is based may be given in a summary manner, for example by a reference to those decisions, the enacting authority must give an explicit account of its reasoning if the decision goes appreciably further than the previous decisions.[464] This does not, however, mean that the Commission must, in addition to stating the reasons for its decision by reference to the case-file to which the decision relates, specifically set out its reasons for reaching a different conclusion than in a previous case concerning similar or identical situations or the same market participants.[465] **14–110**

When a decision is addressed to a Member State and that State has been closely involved in the process by which the decision was made and is therefore aware of the reasons which led the enacting institution to adopt the decision, there is no need for extensive reasoning.[466] For instance, when the Commission issues a decision rejecting an application for assistance from the European Social Fund for a vocational training course it is sufficient for that decision to contain a concise statement of reasons. That is an unavoidable consequence of the processing of a large number of applications for assistance upon which the Commission must adjudicate within a short period.[467] By contrast, where an application for assistance **14–111**

---

[461] Case C-76/01 P *Eurocoton v Council* [2003] E.C.R. I–10091, para.87.
[462] Case 16/65 *Schwarze v Einfuhr- und Vorratsstelle Getreide* [1965] E.C.R. 877, 888; *Delacre v Commission* [1990] E.C.R. I–395, para.16.
[463] *Eurocoton* [2003] E.C.R. I–10091, para.89.
[464] Case 73/74 *Papiers Peints v Commission* [1975] E.C.R. 1491, para.31; T–64/02 *Hans Heubach GmbH & Co KG v Commission of the European Communities* [2006] 4 C.M.L.R. 21, para.221 (finding that the Commission had adequately stated its reasons for imposing a fine that was much higher than the fine imposed in previous comparable situations).
[465] Case T–210/01 *General Electric Co v Commission of the European Communities* [2006] 4 C.M.L.R. 15, CFI.
[466] Case 13/72 *Netherlands v Commission* [1973] E.C.R. 27, para.11; Case 819/72 *Germany v Commission* [1981] E.C.R. 31, para.19.
[467] Case C-213/87 *Gemeente Amsterdam and VIA v Commission* [1990] E.C.R. I–221.

from the European Social Fund has been accepted, a decision of the Commission which reduces the amount of the assistance initially granted has more grave adverse consequences for the person concerned and must state clearly the reasons which justify that reduction.[468]

GROUNDS FOR JUDICIAL REVIEW OF NATIONAL MEASURES

14–112 Since in most fields EU measures are implemented by the authorities of the Member States, issues of legality will usually arise between the individual and those authorities, rather than between the individual and the EU institutions themselves. The standard case is that in which the individual claims a right under Community law, contending that the national measures fail to give effect to that right. The failure alleged may be either non-implementation or implementation which purports to give effect to Community law rights but does so incorrectly. Because of the direct effect of many provisions of Community law the individual will often be able to rely on EU provisions notwithstanding the absence of implementing measures and indeed even in the presence of conflicting national provisions.[469] Such cases will be brought in the national court, and although the national court has no jurisdiction to declare EU measures invalid[470] it can of course declare a national measure unlawful and grant appropriate remedies.[471] It may do so, if the Community law is clear, without a reference to the ECJ.[472]

14–113 By relying upon the direct effect of Community law, the individual may be able to challenge national measures and have them declared unlawful.[473] All national measures can be subject to review on grounds of compatibility with Community law: primary legislation;[474] secondary regulations;[475]

---

[468] Case C-181/90 *Consorgan v Commission* [1992] E.C.R. I–3557.
[469] See 14–009 and 14–010.
[470] See 14–043.
[471] On remedies, see Ch.18.
[472] See 14–077.
[473] On direct effect of treaty provisions, see 14–010; on direct effect of directives, see 14–022.
[474] *R. v Secretary of State for Employment Ex p. Equal Opportunities Commission* [1995] 1 A.C. 1; *R. v Secretary of State for Transport Ex p. Factortame* [1990] 2 A.C. 85; *Stoke-on-Trent City Council v B&Q Plc* [1991] Ch. 48 at 69 (Hoffmann J.); *R. v Secretary of State for the Home Department Ex p. Hoverspeed* [1999] Eu. L.R. 596, QBD; *Gough v Chief Constable of Derbyshire* [2002] EWCA Civ 351; [2002] Q.B. 1213. For an argument that the English courts have shown excessive deference when reviewing legislative acts, see R. Thompson, "Community Law and the Limits of Deference" (2005) 3 E.H.R.L.R. 243.
[475] *R. v Secretary of State for Social Services Ex p. Urbanek* (1995) 7 Admin. L.R. 781 (income support regulations introducing 'habitual residence' precondition consistent with Art 39 EC); *R. (on the application of Compassion in World Farming Ltd) v Secretary of State for the Environment, Food and Rural Affairs* [2003] EWHC 2850; [2004] Eu. L.R. 382 (animal welfare regulations and enforcement policy not constituting an inadequate transposition or failure properly to implement an EC Directive) (CA at [2004] EWCA Civ 1009; [2004] Eu. L.R. 1021); *R. (on the application of Amicus) v Secretary of State for Trade and Industry* [2004] EWHC 860; [2004] I.R.L.R. 430 (employment regulations not incompatible with EC Directive).

administrative decisions;[476] and the failure to enact primary legislation.[477] A deportation order will be quashed if it is found contrary to Community law.[478] Even the "intention or obligation" of the Government to implement a directive, without further implementing measures, is open to challenge on the ground that the Directive is invalid.[479] There are frequent examples of challenge to measures imposing restrictions on imports from other Member States contrary to Art 28–30 [30–36] EC.[480] Such cases may arise whether or not the individual has a directly enforceable right under Community law. In other cases, an individual may not rely on the direct effect of Community law provisions, but simply contend that the national authorities have acted unlawfully, independently of the question whether the Community law provisions have direct effect.[481]

In terms of the intensity of review, it has been doubted whether   14–114

"distinctions between primary and secondary legislation . . . are of much assistance in determining the margin of appreciation available to a national decision-maker. To give weight to the formal distinction between primary and secondary legislation would be inappropriate, particularly in view of the very wide power to amend primary legislation by order in council conferred by s.2 of the European Communities Act 1972."[482]

---

[476] R. v Ministry of Agriculture Fisheries and Food, Ex p. Hedley Lomas (Ireland) Ltd [1997] Q.B. 139 (refusal of licence for live exports based on belief that Spain would not comply with EC Directive was an unjustified restriction on exports); R. v Chief Constable of Sussex Ex p. International Trader's Ferry Ltd [1999] 2 A.C. 418 (decision restricting policy protection for live calf exporters justified and so not a breach of Art.29); R. v Westminster City Council Ex p. Dinev, unreported, October 24, 2000 (licensing scheme not infringement of Art.43); R. (on the application of Watts) v Secretary of State for Health [2003] EWHC 2228; [2003] 3 C.M.L.R. 23 at [110] (medical and hospital services falling within Art.49, so non-reimbursement a barrier to freedom to receive services and Art.49 breached unless NHS treatment available without undue delay).

[477] R. v Ministry of Agriculture Fisheries & Food Ex p. Bostock [1994] E.C.R. I–955 (application for declaration that failure to enact primary legislation incompatible with EC law); R. v Commissioners of Customs and Excise Ex p. Lunn Poly Ltd [1999] Eu.L.R. 653 at 660 (declaration granted that Finance Act 1987 s.21 incompatible with EC law and not capable of being lawfully applied); R. (on the application of Association fo Pharmaceutical Importers) v Secretary of State for Health [2001] EWCA Civ 1986, [2002] Eu.L.R. 197, CA (challenge to pharmaceutical price regulations scheme as breach of Art.28); R. (on the application of International Transport Roth GmbH) v Secretary of State for the Home Department [2003] Q.B. 728, CA (immigration carrier penalty scheme not interfering with Art.28 rights).

[478] R. v Secretary of State for the Home Department Ex p. Dannenberg [1984] Q.B. 766.

[479] Ex p. British American Tobacco [2002] E.C.R. I–11453, paras 2, 24–25, 28–41 (this challenge was also permitted although the time limit for implementing the directive had not expired).

[480] R. v Secretary of State for Social Services Ex p. Bomore Medical Supplies Ltd [1986] 1 C.M.L.R. 228 (decision of minister on reimbursement of pharmacists).

[481] See, e.g. Twyford Parish Council v Secretary of State for the Environment [1992] 1 C.M.L.R. 276; R. v H.M. Treasury Ex p. Smedley [1985] Q.B. 657.

[482] R. v Ministry of Agriculture Fisheries and Food, Ex p. Astonquest [2000] Eu.L.R. 371 at 384.

14–115 As a result of developments in the case law of the ECJ, the grounds on which national measures may be challenged as being unlawful under Community law correspond closely (although not exactly) with the grounds on which EU measures may be challenged.[483] Thus national measures may be challenged not only as infringing the Treaty or EU legislation, but also, where giving effect to Community law provisions, as infringing the general principles of law recognised in Community law: for example the principle of proportionality, the principle of non-discrimination, the principle of respect for fundamental rights, and the principle of protection of legitimate expectations. It is now clearly established that where Community law is applicable, the grounds on which national measures may be challenged in the national courts are not the same as those on which national measures may be challenged in English law. The situations in which Community law may arise are so varied that no definitive general statement is possible; the following points should be treated as illustrative only.

Review of discretion

14–116 Where there is an apparent breach of Community law, the courts will require the decision-maker to justify the breach.[484] This will require a more intrusive scrutiny and closer investigation of the facts of the case than the *Wednesbury* approach would follow.[485]

Failure to state reasons

14–117 Where a decision of the national authorities has the effect of denying a fundamental Community law right, such a decision must be open to challenge by judicial proceedings so that its legality under Community law can be reviewed; accordingly the person concerned must be able to ascertain the reasons for the decision so that he can decide whether to take proceedings with full knowledge of the relevant facts.[486] It is therefore not sufficient for him to be informed of the reasons for a decision only after legal proceedings have been commenced. The obligation to state reasons however applies only to individual decisions of national authorities which have adverse legal effects on individuals and not to national rules of general application.[487]

[483] See 14–083.
[484] *R. v Minister of Agriculture, Fisheries and Food Ex p. Bell Lines* [1984] 2 C.M.L.R. 502 at 509–511.
[485] *R. v Secretary of State for Social Services Ex p. Schering Chemicals Ltd* [1987] 1 C.M.L.R. 277; *R. v Minister of Agriculture, Fisheries and Food Ex p. Roberts* [1991] 1 C.M.L.R. 555.
[486] Case 222/86 *UNECTEF v Heylens* [1987] E.C.R. 4097; Case C-340/89 *Vlassopoulou v Ministerium für Justiz, Bundes- und Europaangelegenheiten Baden-Wurttemberg* [1991] E.C.R. I-2357; Case C-104/91 *Colegio Oficial de agentes de la Propiedad Inmobiliaria v Aguirre Borrell* [1992] E.C.R. I-3003; Case C-19/92 *Kraus v Land BadenWurttemberg* [1993] E.C.R. I-1663.
[487] Case C-70//95 *Sodemare SA v Fédération de Maisons de Repos Privés de Belgique (Femarbel) ASBL and Regione Lombardia* [1997] ECR I-3395.

General principles of law

A national measure may be struck down on the ground that it runs counter **14–118** to a general principle of law. Examples will be given here by reference to the principle of protection of fundamental rights, the principle of proportionality, the principle of equality, and the principle of protection of legitimate expectations.

Fundamental rights

In the context of review of national measures[488] the principle of protection **14–119** of fundamental rights has been applied in two distinct situations: first, in reviewing measures taken by the Member States when implementing Community law; secondly, in reviewing measures taken by the Member States not directly acting within the field of Community law, but where such measures fall within the scope of the Treaty.

Implementation of Community law

The first category may be illustrated by cases in the field of agriculture, **14–120** where the Member States implement EU legislation. Since the EU institutions are bound by the principle of respect for fundamental rights and their legislation must be interpreted accordingly, it follows that the national authorities, in implementing that legislation, are also so bound.[489] Thus, in *Wachauf*,[490] Mr Wachauf was a tenant farmer who had received a milk quota under the applicable EU rules. Upon the expiry of his tenancy, he requested compensation for the definite discontinuance of milk production but his request was refused on the ground that the lessor had not given his consent as required by Community law. It was argued that if the EU rules in question were interpreted as meaning that, upon the expiry of the lease, the lessee's milk quota must be returned to the lessor, they could have the effect of precluding the lessee from benefiting from the system of compensation for discontinuance of milk production if the lessor were opposed to it. That is because in so far as the milk quota corresponding to the farm in question returns to the lessor, it cannot be taken into account for the purposes of granting compensation. It was argued that such a consequence would be unacceptable if the lessor had never engaged in milk production since the lessee, who would have acquired the milk quota by his own labour, would then be deprived, without compensation, of the fruits of that labour. After recalling its judgment in *Hauer,* the ECJ stated:[491]

---

[488] For human rights in the context of review of Community measures, see 14–096; for constitutional rights in English law, see 5–039; and on Convention rights, see 6–048, 7–032 *et seq.*, 7–119 *et seq.*, 10–00 and Ch.13.
[489] Joined Cases 201 and 202/85 *Klensch v Secretaire d'Etat d l'Agriculture et a la Viticulture* [1986] E.C.R. 3477.
[490] Case 5/88 *Wachauf v Germany* [1989] E.C.R. 2609; cf. Case C-2/92 *Bostock* [1994] E.C.R. I–955.
[491] *Wachauf* [1989] E.C.R. 2609, para.19.

"Community rules which, upon the expiry of the lease, had the effect of depriving the lessee, without compensation, of the fruits of his labour and of his investments in the tenanted holding would be incompatible with the requirements of the protection of fundamental rights in the Community legal order. Since those requirements are also binding on the Member States when they implement Community rules, the Member States must, as far as possible, apply those rules in accordance with those requirements."

In the circumstances of the case, the ECJ found that the EU rules left the competent national authorities a sufficiently wide margin of discretion to enable them to apply those rules in a manner consistent with the requirements of the protection of fundamental rights.

Where the Member State is not directly implementing EU measures

14–121 Even where Member States are not implementing EU measures, similar principles may apply. The effect of the ECHR on the review of national measures is demonstrated by the ECJ's judgment in *ERT,* which concerned certain exclusive television rights under Greek law. The Court considered the issue of restrictions on the freedom to provide services and the justification for such restrictions under Art.46 [Art.56] and Art.55 [66] EC, and devoted a section of its judgment to the issue raised under ECHR Art.10 (freedom of expression). It stated that where national legislation falls within the scope of Community law, the ECJ must supply all the elements of interpretation necessary for the national court to assess the conformity of that legislation with the fundamental rights protected by the ECJ, as they derive, in particular, from the ECHR. Where a Member State invokes the combined provisions of Arts 46 and 55 EC to justify legislation liable to impede the exercise of the freedom to provide services, that justification, provided for by Community law, must be interpreted in the light of the general principles of law and in particular of fundamental rights; thus the national legislation in question may only benefit from the exceptions provided for by the combined provisions of Articles 46 and 55 if it is in conformity with fundamental rights.[492] It followed, the ECJ concluded, that in such a case it was the duty of the national court and, where appropriate, the ECJ to assess the application of those provisions having regard to all the rules of Community law, including the freedom of expression enshrined in Art.10 of the ECHR, as a general principle of law protected by the ECJ.[493]

14–122 More recently, the ECJ has reviewed for compliance with ECHR Art.8 (right to respect for family and private life), a UK deportation order in respect of a Filipino national, Mrs Carpenter, who had violated UK

[492] *ERT v Pliroflorisis* [1991] E.C.R. 2925, paras 42–43; and Case 159/90 *SPUC v Grogan* [1991] ECR I–4685.
[493] *ERT* [1991] E.C.R. 2925, para.44.

immigration laws by not leaving the country prior to the expiry of her leave to remain as a visitor.[494] Mr Carpenter was a UK national, living in the UK and running a business selling advertising space, which was established in the UK. A significant proportion of the business however was conducted with advertisers established in other Member States and Mr Carpenter travelled to other Member States to pursue his business. It was argued that the deportation order would interfere with his Art.49 freedom to provide services. The Court accepted that the separation of Mr and Mrs Carpenter would be detrimental to their family life and, therefore, to the conditions under which Mr Carpenter exercised a fundamental freedom.[495] As such, the deportation order could only be upheld if the measure was compatible with the fundamental rights.[496] The Court however considered that the deportation order was a disproportionate interference with Art.8.[497]

Thus, the Court's case law has developed from a review of EU measures adopted by the EU institutions themselves, to a review of measures adopted by Member States in implementing EU measures, and more recently to a review of measures adopted by Member States which, in one way or another and, even if tenuously, fall within the scope of Community law.[498] It is also expected that, should it become legally effective, the Charter of Fundamental Rights will bind Member States in the same way as they are currently bound by the fundamental rights case law of the ECJ.[499]   **14–123**

The principle of proportionality

The principle of proportionality[500] can be used as the basis for challenging   **14–124** national measures and for claiming rights in the national courts. It applies across the whole field of Community law, but its precise effect will depend upon the context. The assessment of proportionality will again here be of a structured kind,[501] asking a series of questions starting with the requirement of a legitimate aim, and proceeding to ask whether the obligation is strictly necessary to attain the aim. The measure must apply the least restrictive alternative and there must be a rational connection between the ends and means.

Many of the applications of the principle to national measures concern   **14–125** the scope of exceptions to the basic freedoms of movement of goods and persons under the Treaty. For example, restrictions on the free movement

---

[494] See n.161.
[495] *ERT* [1991] E.C.R. 2925, para.39.
[496] *ERT* [1991] E.C.R. 2925, para.40.
[497] *ERT* [1991] E.C.R. 2925, paras 42–45.
[498] Advocate General's Opinion of December 9, 1992 in Case C-168/91, *Konstantinidis* [1993] E.C.R. I–1191.
[499] See 14–032.
[500] In relation to Community measures, see 14–089; for proportionality as a ground in English law, see 11–073; and in relation to Convention rights, see 11–077.
[501] 11–077.

of goods are permitted on such grounds as public health under Art.30 EC, but such grounds must not result in restrictions. Where the national measure is tested against a basic Treaty freedom, such as the free movement of goods, strict scrutiny will be applied to the national restriction. Thus the ECJ has struck down measures which enable pharmaceutical companies to limit imports from other Member States to their own main distributors and to exclude "parallel imports" from other Member States, in the absence of a compelling public health justification.[502] The Court has also held that a Member State may not impose on nationals of other Member States, exercising their right to freedom of movement, the obligation to make a declaration of residence within three days of entering the State's territory, subject to a penal sanction for failure to comply, since the time limit of three days cannot be regarded as reasonable.[503] Where fundamental rights, such as freedom of association, are asserted by Member States to justify interference with Treaty free movement rights, they may take precedence, but again, only if the interference with free movement is proportionate.[504]

14–126   In the citizenship context, the principle of proportionality has had particularly interesting effect. Given the direct effect of Art.18 EC, limitations placed on the right to reside and move of non-economically active Union citizens are scrutinised for proportionality, and in the *Baumbast* case, it was held that national rules may be questioned—even if they are consistent with secondary Community legislation—if they produce results which are disproportionate to the objective pursued.[505] Thus, in *Baumbast*, depriving a Union citizen, who had resided for several years in another Member State of his right to reside, because he lacked emergency health insurance, was disproportionate to the aim of preventing him from becoming an "unreasonable burden" on that State's welfare system.[506]

14–127   Criminal penalties imposed by national law are also strictly subject to the test of proportionality. As the ECJ stated in *Casati*:[507]

> "In principle, criminal legislation and the rules of criminal procedure are matters for which the Member States are still responsible. However, it is clear from a consistent line of cases decided by the Court, that Community law also sets certain limits in that area as regards the control measures which it permits the Member States to maintain in connection with the free movement of goods and persons. The administrative measures or penalties must not go beyond what is strictly necessary, the

[502] Case 104/75 *De Peijper v The Netherlands (Ministere Public)* [1976] E.C.R. 613.
[503] C-265/88 *Criminal Proceedings against Messner* [1989] E.C.R. 4209.
[504] *Schmidberger* [2003] E.C.R. I–5659.
[505] Case C-413/99 *Baumbast and R v Secretary of State for the Home Department* [2003] E.C.R. I–7091.
[506] See Wyatt and Dashwood (2006) para.7–009 (describing the principle in this context as operating "as an hermeneutic principle"). See also M. Dougan, "The Constitutional Dimension to the Case Law on Union Citizenship" (2006) 31 E.L. Rev. 613.
[507] Case 203/80 E.C.R. 2595, para.27.

control procedures must not be conceived in such a way as to restrict the freedom required by the Treaty and they must not be accompanied by a penalty which is so disproportionate to the gravity of the infringement that it becomes an obstacle to the exercise of that freedom."

Thus, the ECJ has held that national legislation which penalises offences **14–128** concerning the payment of value added tax on importation from another Member State more severely than those concerning the payment of value added tax on domestic transactions is incompatible with Art.90 [95] of the Treaty in so far as that difference is disproportionate to the dissimilarity between the two categories of offences.[508] The Court has also held that seizure or confiscation of a product imported illegally could be considered disproportionate, and therefore incompatible with Art.28 [30], to the extent to which the return of the product to the Member State of origin would be sufficient.[509]

Similarly, derogations from directives providing for equal treatment **14–129** must be strictly construed. *Thomas*[510] concerned the scope of the derogation under Art.7(1)(a) of Directive 79/7 from the principle of equal treatment for men and women in matters of social security. According to Art.7(1)(a) the directive was to be without prejudice to the right of the Member States to exclude from its scope the determination of pensionable age for the purposes of granting old-age and retirement pensions and "the possible consequences thereof for other benefits". The Court held that that derogation was limited to the forms of discrimination existing under the other benefit schemes which are *necessarily* and objectively linked to the difference in retirement ages.

The test of proportionality is clearly a stringent one, especially when the **14–130** need for the national measure falls to be weighed against a fundamental Treaty freedom, and it has been suggested that there will be circumstances in which a higher standard of justification will be required for interference with EC law than with an ECHR right.[511] However, the application of the principle is far from straightforward, and on occasion, the ECJ has been willing to interpret the principle flexibly, in light of particular values applicable within Member States.[512] Moreover, the fact that a Member

---

[508] Case 299/86 *Drexl* [1988] E.C.R. 1213.
[509] Case C-367/89 *Aime Richardt* [1991] E.C.R. I–4621; see further Case 41/76 *Donckvn-wolcke v Procureur de la Republique* [1976] E.C.R. 1921; Case 179/78 *Procureur de la Republique v Rivoira* [1979] E.C.R. 1147. On confiscation, see also Case C-83/94 *Leifer* [1995] E.C.R. I–3231; Case C-84/95 *Bosphorus Hava Yollari Turizm ve Ticaret AS v Minister for Transport and the Attorney General* [1996] E.C.R. I–3953; Case C-177/95 *Ebony Maritime SA v Prefetto della Provincia di Brindisi* [1997] E.C.R. I–1111.
[510] Case C-328/91 *Secretary of State for Social Security v Thomas* [1993] E.C.R. I–1247.
[511] *R. (Countryside Alliance) v Attorney General* [2006] EWCA Civ 817; [2007] Q.B. 305, paras 158–159. On the standard of proportionality review for Convention rights, see Ch.13.
[512] See, e.g. Case C-36/02 *Omega Spielhallen- und Automatenaufstellunsgs-GmbH v Oberbürger-meisterin der Bundesstadt Bonn* [2004] ECR I–9609: it was held that the public policy justification of the Bonn police for fobidding laser games involving simulated killing, on

State introduces measures which are more restrictive of a particular freedom than subsequent Community measures will not in itself justify the conclusion that the Member State legislation is disproportionate.[513]

14-131   In some cases the answer seems quite obvious; yet in other cases, it may be more subjective, or in other ways not suited to judicial determination.[514] For example; the question whether the measure is reasonably likely to attain its objective may be a matter in which expertise is required and expert evidence may conflict; but when in addition the question is asked whether other less restrictive measures might be used to achieve the same objective, a court may find it not merely difficult, but impossible, to answer.[515] The difficulties are compounded where the issue is not resolved by the ECJ itself but is in effect referred back to the national court. For example in *De Peijper*,[516] a case concerning the marketing of pharmaceutical products, the ECJ held that a particular national rule or practice (which had the effect of impeding parallel imports and so raised the issue of restricting trade between Member States contrary to Articles 28 to 30 [30 to 36] of the Treaty) could not be maintained "unless it is clearly proved that any other rule or practice [presumably, less restrictive of trade between Member States but achieving the same public health objectives] would obviously be beyond the means which can reasonably be expected of an administration operating in a normal manner". The difficulties in leaving to national courts the application of the principle of proportionality were clearly illustrated in the protracted Sunday trading litigation, in which English supermarket chains sought to evade the prohibition on Sunday trading by relying on Art.28 [30] of the Treaty.[517]

14-132   It should also be noted that even if the difficulties could be resolved in the national courts, such an approach would scarcely serve the purpose of securing the uniform interpretation and application of Community law in

the basis that it infringed the right to dignity in the German Constitution, was proportionate; and it was not necessary for the restrictive measure to be chosen by all Member States. See also Case C-124/97 *Läärä, Cotswold Microsystems Ltd and Oy Transatlantic Software Ltd v Finland* [1999] E.C.R. I-6067 (granting a public body the exclusive right to operate slot machines in infringement of the freedom to provide services could potentially be justified on grounds of consumer protection). See also Craig (2006), pp.708-710.

[513] Case C-510/99 *Tridon* [2001] E.C.R. I-7777, para.59.

[514] For a readiness to apply the principle, *Thomas* (CA); on appeal, referred by HL, [1993] E.C.R. I-1247.

[515] Although in order to determine whether a national measure complies with the principle of proportionality the ECJ will take into account whether other less restrictive measures exists, a restriction imposed by a Member State on a fundamental freedom will not necessarily fail the test of proportionality merely because another Member State imposes a less severe restriction. If that were so, Member States would need to align their legislation with the Member State which imposes the least onerous requirements. See Case C-384/93 *Alpine Investments* [1995] E.C.R. I-1141; Case C-3/95 *Reiseburo Broede v Gerd Sandker* [1996] E.C.R. I-6511.

[516] Case 15/74 *De Peijper v Sterling Drug Inc* [1974] E.C.R. 1147.

[517] *Stoke-on-Trent CC and Norwich CC v B & Q* [1991] Ch. 48 (Hoffmann J.); Opinion of AG Van Gerven in Case C-169/91 *B & Q* [1992] E.C.R. I-6635; R. Rawlings, "The Eurolaw Game: Some Deductions from a Saga" (1993) J.L. & Soc. 309. The scope of Art.30 was reconsidered by the Court in Joined Cases C-267/91 and C-268/91 *Keck and Mithouard* [1993] E.C.R. I-6097. For a Sunday trading case decided subsequently, see Joined Cases C-69/93 and C-258/93 *Punto Casa Spa v Sindaco del Comune di Capena* [1994] E.C.R. 1-2355. See also Craig (2006), pp.711-714.

all the Member States. The difficulties are not confined to the application of the principle of proportionality; similar difficulties may arise in applying human rights principles.[518]

In conclusion, the application of proportionality can go beyond the 14–133 English ground of unreasonableness or irrationality and is most strictly applied when the need for a national measure falls to be weighed against a Treaty freedom. However, its application and the margin of appraisal permitted to the decision making authority may vary, in accordance with different situations.

Equality[519]

The principle of equality, like the principle of proportionality, is binding 14–134 not only on the EU institutions but also, within the field of Community law, on the Member States. Thus where EU rules leave Member States free to choose between various methods of implementation, a Member State may not choose an option whose implementation in its territory would be liable to create, directly or indirectly, discrimination prohibited by Community law.[520] One of the most fundamental principles of the Treaty is the prohibition of discrimination on the grounds of nationality.[521] That prohibition covers indirect discrimination, that is to say, discrimination which although it is ostensibly made by the application of other criteria leads effectively to the same result.[522] Thus, depending on the circumstances, discrimination on the ground of residence may result in indirect discrimination.[523]

There is a close affinity between the principle of equal treatment and the 14–135 protection of fundamental rights. In *P v S and Cornwall County Council*[524] the applicant in the main proceedings was dismissed from his employment

---

[518] A. Clapham, "A human rights policy for the European Community" (1990) Y.E.L. 309, pp.328–332.
[519] On equality as a ground of challenge in relation to Community measures, see 14–087; as a principle of English law, see Ch.11; on Art.14 ECHR, see Ch.13.
[520] *Klensch v Secretaire d'Etat* [1986] E.C.R. 3477.
[521] The general prohibition is contained in Art.12 [6] EC. It is implemented in relation to specific domains by other provisions of the Treaty, e.g. Art.39 [48] EC (free movement of workers), Art.43 [52] EC (freedom of establishment) and Art.49 [59] EC (freedom of services). Art.6 EC applies independently only to situations with regard to which there is no specific prohibition: Case 9/73 *Schluter* [1973] E.C.R. 1135; Case C-357/ 89 *Raulin* [1992] E.C.R. I–1027; Case C-295/90 *European Parliament v Council* [1992] E.C.R. I–5299; Case C-92/92 *Phil Collins v Imtrat Handelsgesellschaft* [1993] E.C.R. I–5145. The Court has also relied heavily on Art.12 [6] EC in the application of the citizen provisions (Arts 17–22 EC) to undermine the distinction between economic and non-economic Union migrants: Case C-85/96 *Martinez Sala v Freistaat Bayern* [1998] E.C.R. I–2691; Case C-184/99 *Grzelczyk v Centre Public d'Aide Sociale d'Ottignes-Louvain-la-Neuve (CPAS)* [2001] E.C.R. I–6193; and Case C-138/02 *Collins v Secretary of State for Work and Pensions* [2004] E.C.R. I–2703.
[522] Case 152/73 *Sotgiu v Deutsche Bundespost* [1974] E.C.R. 153; Case 71/76 *Thieffry* [1977] E.C.R. 765; Case 15/69 *Sudmilch v Ugliola* [1969] E.C.R. 363.
[523] Case 52/84, *Commission v Belgium* [1986] 1 E.C.R. 89.
[524] Case C-13/91 [1996] E.C.R. I–2143.

following his decision to undergo gender reassignment by surgical operation. The question was referred to the ECJ whether the Equal Treatment Directive precludes dismissal of a transsexual for reasons related to a gender reassignment. The Court held that, in view of sex equality as a fundamental human right, the scope of the directive cannot be confined to discrimination based on the fact that a person is of one or other sex. It stated that discrimination arising from gender reassignment is based essentially, if not exclusively, on the sex of the person concerned. Where a person is dismissed on the ground that he or she has undergone gender reassignment, he or she is treated unfavourably by comparison with persons of the sex to which he or she was deemed to belong before undergoing gender reassignment. The Court concluded (at para. 22) that: "To tolerate such discrimination would be tantamount, as regards such a person, to a failure to respect the dignity and freedom to which he or she is entitled, and which the Court has a duty to safeguard".

14-136   The case provides a prime example of the way the ECJ views the principle of equality as a general principle of Community law transcending the provisions of EU legislation. In effect, the ECJ applied a general principle of unwritten EU human rights law, according to which discrimination on arbitrary criteria is prohibited, rather than the provisions of the Equal Treatment Directive, a literal interpretation of which does not seem to support the ECJ's finding. The Court has also held that Art.141 [119] EC in principle, precludes legislation which, in breach of the ECHR, prevents a heterosexual couple, where the sexual identity of one of the partners is the result of gender reassignment surgery, from fulfilling a marriage requirement which must be met for one of them to be able to benefit from part of the pay of the other.[525] By contrast, in *Kalanke v Freir Hansestadt Bremen*,[526] the ECJ found that the Bremen Law on Equal Treatment which provided for positive discrimination in favour of women was incompatible with Art.2(4) of the Equal Treatment Directive.

Protection of legitimate expectations[527]

14-137   National authorities responsible for applying Community law are bound to observe the principle of protection of legitimate expectations. The principle is best illustrated in the context of the recovery by national authorities of aid paid by Member States in breach of EU rules. Where for example the Commission finds that aid which has been granted by a state to an undertaking is incompatible with the common market, and thus

[525] Case C-117/01 *KB v National Health Service Pensions Agency and Secretary of State for Health* [2004] E.C.R. I–541.
[526] Case C-450/93 [1995] E.C.R. I–3051. See also *D v Council* [2001] E.C.R. I–4319 for a more deferential judicial position on equality.
[527] Case 5/82 *Hauptzollamt Krefeld v Maizena* [1982] E.C.R. 4601, para.22. For legitimate expectations as a ground for challenging Community measures, see 14–093; as a ground in English law, see Ch.12.

unlawful under Art.87 [92] of the Treaty, it may require the national authorities to recover that aid.[528] In general, the ECJ has been reluctant to accept that the principle provides a good defence against an order to recover unlawfully paid state aid. In one case,[529] the undertaking concerned claimed that the Commission's order to the national authorities to recover the aid was incompatible with the principle of protection of legitimate expectations on the ground that it had received the aid on the basis of definitive decisions and on the ground that it had used it in relation to a product which was not subject to the guidelines notified to the Member States by the Commission. The Court rejected those arguments stating that failure to include that specific product in the guidelines could not justify a legitimate expectation on the part of the undertaking, since the guidelines could not derogate from Articles 87 [92] and 88 [93] of the Treaty which prohibited the granting of the aid. In another case, however, the ECJ accepted that the Commission's unreasonable delay in requiring the recovery of state aid gave rise to a legitimate expectation on the part of the undertaking which prevented the Commission from requiring the national authorities to order the refund of the aid.[530]

In the context of agricultural aids, the ECJ has held that Community law **14–138** does not prevent national law from having regard, in excluding recovery of unduly paid aids, to the need to protect legitimate expectations, provided that the same procedural rules are applied to the recovery of purely national financial benefits and that the interests of the EU are taken fully into account.[531]

A practice of a Member State which infringes Community law may never **14–139** give rise to legitimate expectations on the part of an economic operator;[532] and that is so even where a EU institution has failed to take the necessary action to ensure that the state in question correctly applies the EU rules.[533] It should also be noted that, the concept of legitimate expectations in Community law requires detrimental reliance,[534] unlike, it appears, the domestic equivalent.[535]

---

[528] See, e.g. Case C-5/89 *Commission v Germany* [1990] E.C.R. I–3437.
[529] Case 310/85 *Deufil v Commission* [1987] E.C.R. 901.
[530] Case 223/85 *RSV v Commission* [1987] E.C.R. 4617; *cf.* Case C-301/87 *France v Commission* [1990] E.C.R. I–307.
[531] Joined Cases 205–215/82 *Deutsche Milchkontor v Germany* [1983] E.C.R. 2633, para.33.
[532] Case 316/86 *Hauptzollamt Hamburg-Jonas v Krucken* [1988] E.C.R. 2213, para.23.
[533] Case 5/82 *Hauptzollamt Krefeld v Maizena* [1982] E.C.R. 4601, para.22.
[534] *Milk Marketing Board of England and Wales v Tom Parker Farms Ltd* [1998] 2 C.M.L.R. 721, at [39] QBD (Comm) ("In approaching the issue of Community law in this case it is necessary to remember that the purpose of the principle of protection of legitimate expectations is the avoidance of prejudice to a party who has justifiably changed that anterior position to the detriment of the other. The protection afforded by the principle is only to those who, because of their circumstances and their reliance, have been prejudiced. Its conceptual function is not the furtherance of consistency of conduct by public bodies but avoidance of prejudice by inconsistency of conduct.").
[535] See 12–040.

Part III
PROCEDURES AND REMEDIES

CHAPTER 15

THE HISTORICAL DEVELOPMENT OF JUDICIAL REVIEW REMEDIES AND PROCEDURES

SCOPE

Professor S.A. de Smith was acutely conscious of the importance of history, **15–001** yet aware that no more than a brief survey could be given in a book of this kind when he prepared the first three editions of this work.[1] This chapter is a synthesis of the historical accounts which, up to the 4th edition of this book, were been distributed throughout the text. These have been brought together, and brought up to date, in an attempt to provide a more accessible narrative.

INTRODUCTION

The importance of an historical perspective

An understanding of the historical development of the remedies and **15–002** procedures of judicial review[2] is necessary for several reasons. First, whilst many Commonwealth countries have undertaken root and branch reform to the supervisory jurisdiction of their courts,[3] modernisation of the judicial review procedures and remedies in England and Wales has been more superficial. The Supreme Court Act 1981 (renamed the Senior Courts Act 1981 by the Constitutional Reform Act 1981), which puts the High Court's general power of judicial review on a statutory footing, does so by

---

[1] For reasons of space, it has been necessary to abridge the account of the historical origins of the prerogative writs given in Appendix 1 of the 3rd and 4th editions, and to omit some of the footnotes to de Smith's sources. Readers with a special interest will continue to find that appendix a useful point of reference; so too de Smith's journal publications, especially "The Prerogative Writs" (1951) 11 C.L.P. 40 and "Wrongs and Remedies in Administrative Law" (1952) 15 M.L.R. 189.

[2] The distinction between the terms "procedures" and "remedies" is often blurred; some, for example, speak of the "remedy of judicial review". Here, procedure is used to refer to those steps—stipulated in the Civil Procedure Rules and formerly in the Rules of the Supreme Court—which must be followed in order to bring a matter before the court. Remedies refer to the formal orders, both interlocutory and final, which may be granted by the court. The study of such adjectival aspects of administrative law is often as-or more-revealing of the underlying values of the legal system as is the study of the rules of substantive law. *cf.* Sir Henry Maine's well-known remark that ". . . substantive law has at first the look of being gradually secreted in the interstices of procedure" (*Early Law and Custom* (1891), p.389).

[3] See 1–001.

779

reference to the pre-existing common law powers of the court: s.29(1), before its amendment in 2004,[4] provided that "The High Court shall have jurisdiction to make orders of mandamus, prohibition and certiorari in those classes of cases in which it had power to do so immediately before the commencement of this Act".[5] The jurisdiction exercised by the Queen's Bench Division today is thus directly linked to that of the Court of King's Bench in the 17th century and earlier.

15–003   Secondly, a further consequence of piecemeal reform is that the High Court continues to exercise its review powers through a hotchpotch of procedures.[6] In addition to judicial review under CPR 54 (formerly RSC Ord.53), aggrieved citizens may make, where appropriate, an application for the writ of habeas corpus (RSC Ord.54) or make a statutory application to quash a decision or order under a variety of specific enactments (governed by RSC Ord.94). There is also a diverse range of appeals to the High Court, some of which resemble judicial review in the role that they perform. The lack of system can only be satisfactorily explained by reference to the historical development of the separate procedures.

15–004   Thirdly, the historical sketch that follows is a salutary reminder that many of the central preoccupations of today, for example, the questions of which bodies are susceptible to judicial review and who has standing to make such challenges, are not new.[7]

The writ system

15–005 One of the central characteristics of the English common law is the writ. In the earliest times, the royal writs were sealed governmental documents, drafted in a crisp, business-like manner, by which the King conveyed notifications or orders.[8] Certiorari[9] was essentially a royal demand for information; the King, wishing to be certified of some matter, orders that the necessary information be provided for him. Thus, the King wishes to be more fully informed of allegations of extortion made by his subjects in Lincoln, and therefore appoints commissioners to inquire into them.[10] The Calendar of Inquisitions mentions numerous writs of certiorari, addressed

---

[4] See 3–016.
[5] This is a re-enactment of Administration of Justice (Miscellaneous Provisions) Act 1938, s.7 which turned the prerogative "writs" of mandamus, certiorari and prohibition into "Orders".
[6] See 16–001.
[7] Other useful work includes: L.J. Jaffe and E.G. Henderson "Judicial Review and the Rule of Law: Historical Origins" (1956) 72 L.Q.R. 345; E.G.Henderson, *Foundations of English Administrative Law* (1963); H.W. Arthurs, *"Without the Law": Administrative Justice and Legal Pluralism in 19th century England* (1985); G.Drewry, Ch.2, in M. Supperstone, J. Goudie and P. Walker (eds), *Judicial Review*, 3rd edn (2005); and M. Loughlin, *Public Law and Political Theory* (1992).
[8] R.C. Van Caenegem, *Royal Writs in England from the Conquest to Glanville: Studies in the Early History of the Common Law* (Seldon Society, 1959), p.v and Pt 2.
[9] The word is not, apparently, of classical origin: Du Cange, *Glossarium Mediae et Infimae Latinitatis*, Vol.2.
[10] *Placitorum Abbreviatio* 155 (49 Hen. 3).

to the escheator[11] or the sheriff, to make inquisitions; the earliest are for the year 1260.[12] When Parliament grants Edward II one foot-soldier for every township, the writ addressed to the sheriffs to send in returns of their townships to the Exchequer is a writ of certiorari.[13] It was, in fact, one of the King's own writs, used for general governmental purposes.

In early times, the King also issued countless innominate writs that included the word "mandamus"—"the autocratic head of a vast administrative system will have occasion to 'mandamus' his subjects many times in the course of a day[14]—but it seems probable that the connection between most of these royal mandates and the modern judicial writ was verbal only. Moreover, the writs called mandamus that appear in the early law books are concerned not with private grievances at all, but with steps to be taken by the escheator or the sheriff in connection with possible accretions to the royal revenues.

15–006

Subjects unattracted to the justice dispensed by the "antiquated and archaic process" of the local courts came in increasing numbers to seek a remedy from the King himself, in the form of a royal writ. In this way, it has been noted, "arbitrary, even irresponsible interventions in law suits" took place.[15] By the middle of the 12th century, such royal interventions became judicialised and redress was obtained through the King's Court rather than from the King himself. Eventually, writs came to be issued in certain standard forms, collected in the Register of Writs. Each was designed to deal with a particular type of grievance. New forms of writs were capable of creation only by the Chancellor. By the time of Bracton,[16] it could be said that a remedy from the King's Courts could be obtained only if an appropriate writ existed. The development of the writ system, therefore, has about it a hint of paradox for modern administrative law: what began as *executive* commands aimed at *avoiding* judicial proceedings became in turn the central mechanism for the judicial *control* of executive action.

15–007

The term "prerogative writs"

When and why did some of these judicialised writs come to be called, individually and then later collectively, "prerogative" writs? Although this term for the writs of certiorari, mandamus, prohibition and habeas corpus

15–008

---

[11] *cf.* Register of Original Writs, *et seq.*, 293, 296; for history of the escheator, see W.A. Morris and J.R. Strayer, *The English Government at Work, 1327–36* (1947), Vol.ii, pp.109–167.

[12] *Calendar of Inquisitions*, Vol.i, pp.30, 131.

[13] *Inquisitions and Assessments Relating to Feudal Aids*, Vol.i, p.16; see also Introduction, p. xxiii.

[14] E. Jenks, "The Prerogative Writs in English law" (1923) 32 Yale L.J. 523.

[15] See, generally, R.C. Van Caenegem, *The Birth of the English Common Law*, 2nd edn (1988), p.30.

[16] Henry de Bracton (d. 1268). His *De Legibus et Consuetudinibus Angliae* (hereinafter *De Legibus*) was the first systematic treatise on English law.

is well known wherever the language of the common law is spoken, there is no entirely satisfactory answer to these questions. The use of the phrase prerogative writs to refer *collectively* to these four writs emerges only surprisingly late in the history of writs generally, in the time of Blackstone and Mansfield in the mid-18th century. The origins of the term can, however, be traced to the political inclinations of certain Royalist judges in the 17th century who were keen to associate the beneficent remedy of habeas corpus with the King's personal solicititude for the welfare of his subjects.[17]

15–009   Few judges were more ardently Royalist than Montagu, who succeeded Coke[18] as Chief Justice of the King's Bench after Coke had been removed by the King in 1617. It is in a case decided by Montagu and three brethren not noted for their independence of the Crown that habeas corpus is for the first time reported as being called a prerogative writ. In Montagu's words it is "a prerogative writ, which concerns the King's justice to be administered to his subjects; for the King ought to have an account why any of his subjects are imprisoned".[19] His primary purpose was to emphasise that the writ would run to the Cinque Ports in spite of the fact that they were an exempt jurisdiction to which writs relating to ordinary suits between subjects would not run. Even so, it is reasonable to ascribe his use of the word "prerogative" to his political inclinations. Habeas corpus was a beneficent remedy, and it was sound politics to associate its award with the King's concern for his subjects. Its value became enhanced during the constitutional struggles of the 17th century—albeit, paradoxically, as a safeguard of the liberty of the King's political opponents and it came to be regarded, with Magna Carta,[20] as the greatest bastion of individual liberty.

15–010   Though the four writs had acquired their "prerogative" characteristics by the middle of the 17th century, strangely it was not until a century later, in 1759, that anybody (Mansfield) seems to have thought of classifying the writs as a group.[21] Those shared characteristics included the following:

---

[17] The theory that the prerogative writs were in origin peculiar to the King himself is valid only with respect to certain obsolete and obsolescent writs. The earliest appearances of certiorari and mandamus in judicial proceedings were often as the result of applications made by subjects.

[18] Sir Edward Coke (1552–1634). He was successively Solicitor General, Speaker of the House of Commons, Attorney General, Chief Justice of Common Pleas and Chief Justice of the King's Bench. He was removed from the last named post by the King in 1617. To the displeasure of the King, he asserted the jurisdiction of the common law courts over royal power: he held that a royal proclamation could not change the law and doubted the King's prerogative to control the conduct of litigation which involved royal interests. His Institutes (hereinafter "Co. Inst.") were the first treatise on the modern common law.

[19] *Richard Bourn's Case* (1620) Cro. Jac. 543. See also the judgments of his brethren reported in Palm. 54 for like language. Similar reasoning was used in two slightly earlier cases in 2 Roll.Abr. 69; but the word "prerogative" is not mentioned there.

[20] Habeas Corpus was often said to be founded on Magna Carta: Holdsworth, *The History of English Law*, Vol.i, p.228. So, too, was mandamus: *R. v Heathcote* (1712) 10 Mod. 48, 53; *Tapping on Mandamus* (1848) pp.2, 5.

[21] *R. v Cowle* (1759) 2 Burr. 834 at 855–856, per Mansfield. This seems to be the first reference to certiorari as a prerogative writ.

- They were not writs of course which could be purchased by or on behalf of any applicant[22] from the Royal Chancery; they could not be had for the asking, but proper cause had to be shown to the satisfaction of the court why they should issue.

- The award of the prerogative writs usually lay within the discretion of the court. The court was entitled to refuse certiorari and mandamus to applicants if they had been guilty of unreasonable delay or misconduct or if an adequate alternative remedy existed, notwithstanding that they have proved a usurpation of jurisdiction by the inferior tribunal or an omission to perform a public duty. But although none of the prerogative writs was a writ of course, not all were discretionary. Prohibition, for example, issued as of right in certain cases; and habeas corpus *ad subjiciendum*, the most famous of them all, was a writ of right which issued *ex debito justitiae* when the applicant had satisfied the court that his detention was unlawful. These two writs, therefore, were not in the fullest sense writs of grace.

- The prerogative writs were awarded pre-eminently out of the Court of King's Bench.[23] Bracton described the emergent court as "*aula regia* where the King's justices *proprias causas regis terminant.*"[24] This jurisdiction belonged peculiarly to the King's Bench; the court held—at one time in reality, later only in theory[25]—*coram rege ipso*.[26] It comprised the hearing of pleas of the Crown and the examination and correction of the errors of other courts.

- At common law they would go to exempt jurisdictions (e.g. the Counties Palatine, the Cinque Ports), to which the King's writs did not normally run.

Today, the prerogative remedies remain at the centre of judicial review and they continue to manifest their early characteristics. Aggrieved citizens still cannot initiate judicial review proceedings as of right; they must first seek the permission of the court. The grant or refusal of a remedy is still in the discretion of the courts. And judicial review remains within the jurisdiction of the Queen's Bench Division, of which the Administrative Court is part.[27]   **15–011**

The late recognition that the prerogative writs formed a group distinct from other writs is perhaps the oddest feature of their history. Although a relationship between the writs was assumed to exist, its nature was not defined; there was no Bracton to undertake the task of systematic analysis and rationalisation. After Coke and until Mansfield and Blackstone no   **15–012**

---

[22] G.O. Sayles, Introduction to Vol.57, Selden Soc., p.lxxvii.
[23] Proceedings upon the writ *ne exeat regno* were confined to the Court of Chancery.
[24] *De Legibus*, f.150b.
[25] *Prohibitions del Roy* (1607) 12 Co.Rep. 63.
[26] Holdsworth, *History of English Law*, Vol. i, pp.204–206.
[27] See Ch. 16.

common lawyer except Hale[28] was able to survey the whole field of the law with scholarship and insight. And by the time that Mansfield had perceived the close relationship between the writs and had chosen to link them verbally with the rights of the Crown, each writ had developed piecemeal its own special characteristics, so that to define the class with precision in terms of characteristics common to all its members had become virtually impossible. But it is easy enough to explain why Mansfield[29] and Blackstone,[30] who were good King's men, should have insisted on the prerogative character of habeas corpus. And if these were the qualities which in their eyes entitled habeas corpus to classification as a prerogative writ, they were shared in large measure by mandamus, "a command issuing in the King's name from the court of King's Bench" and "a writ of a most extensively remedial nature".[31] The writ of mandamus, moreover, expressly alleged a contempt of the Crown[32] consisting in the neglect of a public duty; and it was a writ of grace. The "prerogative" characteristics of prohibition and certiorari were still more obvious. Prohibition had always been associated with the maintenance of the rights of the Crown. Certiorari was historically linked with the King's person as well as with the King's Bench; it was of high importance for the control of inferior tribunals, particularly with respect to the administration of criminal justice; it was a writ of course for the King but not for the subject.

15–013   Mansfield and Blackstone, then, were responsible, if not for the invention of the term "prerogative writ", at least for its acceptance as part of the lawyer's vocabulary. We may now turn to examine in more detail the separate development of each of the prerogative writs.

CERTIORARI AND PROHIBITION[33]

The origins of the writ of certiorari

15–014   From about 1280, the judicial forms of the writ of certiorari were in common use, issuing on the application of ordinary litigants. Sometimes it was in the nature of a writ of error;[34] sometimes the proceedings at

[28] Sir Matthew Hale (1609–76) wrote prolifically. Perhaps most important is his *History of the Common Law* (1713).
[29] Earl Mansfield (William Murray), 1705–93 was Chief Justice of the King's Bench from 1756.
[30] Sir William Blackstone, 1723–80, first Vinerian Professor of English law in the University of Oxford. His *Commentaries on the Law of England* (hereinafter *Commentaries*) were published between 1756–69.
[31] Blackstone, Commentaries, Vol. iii, p. 110.
[32] See the form of the writ in *Bagg's Case* (1615) 11 Co. Rep. 93b. The phrase also appeared in some modern forms of the writ: F.H. Short and F.H. Mellor, *Practice on the Crown Side*, 2nd edn. (1908), pp.518, 591 *et passim*.
[33] The writs of certiorari and prohibition shared so many characteristics that they can well be discussed together.
[34] See S.F.C. Milsom, *Historical Foundations of the Common Law*, 2nd edn (1981) pp.55–58, on certiorari as the progenitor of the writ of error.

Westminster were in effect general appellate proceedings. The breadth of the issues that could be thus raised is amply illustrated in the edited volumes of King's Bench cases for the reigns of Edward I and his six successors.[35] The conception then prevailing was well expressed in a modern Canadian case:

> "The theory is that the Sovereign has been appealed to by some one of his subjects who complains of an injustice done him by an inferior court; whereupon the Sovereign, saying that he wishes to be certified certiorari-of the matter, orders that the record, etc., be transmitted into a court in which he is sitting."[36]

Much of this very broad remedial jurisdiction passed from the courts of common law to the Court of Chancery, and in the Tudor and early Stuart periods the writ of certiorari frequently issued to bring the proceedings of inferior courts of common law before the Chancellor.[37] Later, however, the Chancery confined its supervisory functions to inferior courts of equity. 15–015

From the 14th century until the middle of the 17th century the following seem to have been the main purposes served by certiorari: 15–016

(a) To supervise the proceedings of inferior courts of specialised jurisdiction—for example, the Commissioners of Sewers, the Courts Merchant, the Court of Admiralty, the Courts of the Forests—by bringing up cases to Westminster for trial or, if necessary, retrial or review.

(b) To obtain information for administrative purposes; for example, the sheriff is told to find out whether one who has been granted the King's protection is tarrying in the city instead of journeying forth in the King's service; the escheator must certify into the Chancery the value of knights' fees and advowsons which have escheatod to the King.

(c) To bring into the Chancery or before the common-law courts judicial records and other formal documents for a wide diversity of purposes. The Register of Writs gives many examples.

(d) To remove coroners' inquisitions and indictments into the King's Bench.

The origins of the writ of prohibition

Prohibition is one of the oldest writs known to the law. From the first its primary function seems to have been to limit the jurisdiction of the ecclesiastical courts.[38] The examples given by Glanvill show that it would 15–017

---

[35] Seldon Soc., Vols 55, 57, 58, 74, 76, 82, 88, edited by G.O. Sayles.
[36] *R. v Titchmarsh* (1915) 22 D.L.R. 272 at 277–278.
[37] Cowell, *Interpreter*, M2; Spence, *Equitable jurisdiction*, Vol.i, pp.686, 687.
[38] N. Adams, "The Writ of Prohibition to Court Christian" (1936) 20 Minn.L.R. 272.

issue at the suggestion of a subject, and the prohibitory clause recites that the suits in question "*ad coronam et dignitatem meam pertinent*". It later came to be used as a weapon by the common law courts in their conflicts with the Courts of Chancery and Admiralty. The early history of the writ and its verbal identification with the rights of the Crown help to explain the extravagant language in which later lawyers were wont to describe its qualities. Thus, in *Warner v Suckerman*[39] Croke J., holding that it would issue to the courts of the County Palatine of Lancaster, said: "It is *breve regium* and jus *coronae*, and if this writ shall be denied in such cases, this would be *in laesionem, exhereditationem, et derogationem coronae*." The matter was expressed more soberly in another case: "The King is the indifferent arbitrator in all jurisdictions, as well spiritual and temporal, and [it] is a right of his Crown to . . . declare their bounds" by prohibitions.

15–018   Disobedience to a prohibition was conceived of as a contempt of the Crown. Since it was "the proper power and honour of the King's Bench to limit the jurisdiction of all other courts"[40] the writ usually issued out of that court; but it could also be awarded by the Chancery and the Common Pleas.

15–019   The "prerogative" character of the writ has been repeatedly stressed. Fitzherbert says that "the King for himself may sue forth this writ, although the plea in the spiritual court be betwixt two common persons, because the suit is in derogation of his Crown",[41] That the protection of private interests is only a secondary function of the writ is brought out in the comparatively modern case of *Worthington v Jeffries*, where it was said that:

> "the ground of decision in considering whether prohibition is or is not to be granted, is not whether the individual suitor has or has not suffered damage, but is whether the royal prerogative has been encroached upon by reason of the prescribed order of the administration of justice having been disobeyed."[42]

Hence it has been said that even a complete stranger to the proceeding in the other court could have the writ.[43]

The expansion of government

15–020 Before elected borough and county councils were established by the Municipal Corporations Acts 1835 and 1882, local government functions were carried out by the justices of the Peace. JPs were drawn almost

[39] (1615) 3 Bulst. 119; see also Skin. 626.
[40] *Case of the Company of Homers in London* (1642) 2 Roll.R. 471.
[41] Fitzherbert, *Natura Brevium*, p.40 E.
[42] (1875) L.R. 10 C.P. 379, 382; see also R.T. Walker, "Is the Writ of Prohibition a Prerogative Writ?" (1939) 37 Mich. L.R. 789; and Note (1923) 36 Harv.L.R. 863.
[43] *Worthington v Jeffries* (1875) L.R. 10 C.P. 379.

exclusively from the ranks of the landed gentry and their duties included the regulation of wages and prices, the implementation of the Poor Law as well as the administration of petty justice. With the vast increase in the non judicial duties of the JPs after 1660, certiorari acquired a new importance. By whom and by what means were the decisions of JPs to be subjected to judicial review? The conciliar courts had gone, and no new governmental organ had arisen to take their place. The Court of King's Bench, which had always been associated with the work of government and which had retained a supervisory jurisdiction over the work of the justices in sessions and of other local bodies during the heyday of the Council and the Star Chamber, was manifestly the proper superintending authority. But it could not exercise its authority by means of the writ of error, for although error lay to impeach the record of a judgment given on an indictment it would not he to quash convictions and orders made in summary proceedings. Persons aggrieved by summary convictions and orders might bring applications for habeas corpus or civil actions for trespass or replevin in order to obtain redress; but these modes of proceeding were not always appropriate, and in any event collateral attack was available only for acts done without jurisdiction.[44] After a period of doubt and vacillation, the court ultimately committed itself to the proposition that the appropriate remedy in all cases where an inferior statutory tribunal had exceeded its jurisdiction or drawn up a conviction or order that was bad on its face was a writ of certiorari to quash the conviction or order. The process by which this proposition came to be established is still not free from obscurity; but by 1700 it was possible for Holt C .J., in the famous case of *Groenvelt v Burwell*,[45] to proclaim the grand generalisation that: "It is a consequence of all jurisdictions to have their proceedings returned here by certiorari to be examined here . . . Where any court is erected by statute, a certiorari lies to it . . .".

Thereafter the King's Bench became inundated with motions for cer- **15–021** tiorari to quash rates and orders made by justices and other bodies exercising administrative functions under semi judicial forms. It became what Gneist has called an *Oberverwaltungsgericht*,[46] a superior administrative court, supervising much of the business of local government by keeping subordinate bodies within their legal limitations by writs of certiorari and prohibition, and ordering them to perform their duties by writs of mandamus. The modern High Court has succeeded to much of this jurisdiction, and there can be no doubt that the absence in the common law systems of a distinct body of public law, whereby proceedings against public authorities are instituted only before special administrative courts and are governed by a special body of rules, is directly traceable to the extensive use of prerogative writs by the Court of King's Bench.

[44] A. Rubinstein, "On the Origins of Judicial Review" (1964) 1 U. of B.C.Law Rev 1, 3–7.
[45] (1700) 1 Ld.Raym. 454 at 459 (certiorari to review disciplinary decisions of the censors of the College of Physicians).
[46] R. von Greist, *Englishe Verfassungsgeschichte* (1882) p.574.

15–022   Certiorari and prohibition established themselves as the most important remedies in administrative law because in the latter part of the 17th century local administration was free from effective supervision by the central government. The role of supervisor was assumed by the Court of King's Bench, which had declared that it would "examine the proceedings of all jurisdictions erected by Act of Parliament . . . to the end that . . . they keep themselves within their jurisdictions".[47] Apart from their formal ministerial duties, whatever the justices had to do was "the exercise of a jurisdiction".[48] It was assumed that the writs of certiorari and prohibition, by which they were controlled in their capacity as courts of summary jurisdiction, were equally appropriate devices for superintending the exercise of their multifarious governmental functions. All those functions of the justices which were not purely ministerial were regarded for this purpose as being judicial: no separate category of discretionary "administrative" acts, immune from the reach of certiorari and prohibition, was yet recognised.[49] A no less broad conception of "judicial" functions governed review of orders made by the Commissioners of Sewers, who presided over a court of record which performed administrative duties under judicial forms.

15–023   Thus, whilst certiorari would not lie to bring up a warrant in issuing which a justice had no statutory discretion,[50] it would lie to bring up and quash discretionary orders for fixing rates for the repair of bridges[51] for the production of poor rate books,[52] and for prohibiting the clerk of the peace from taking certain court fees,[53] and an order by Commissioners of Sewers for the removal of their clerk.[54] The general rule that the discretionary acts of justices were to be treated as judicial was unaffected by a few isolated decisions that went the other way.[55] It was not seriously challenged until it was held in a group of cases in the 1890s that the functions of licensing justices in deciding upon the granting and renewal of licences were not judicial but "administrative" and were not controllable by certiorari.[56] After 1906, however, they were regarded as judicial for this purpose.[57] The distinction is no longer very important in modern law.

---

[47] R. v Glamorganshire Inhabitants (Cardiff Bridge Case) (1700) 1 Ld.Raym. 580.
[48] F.W. Maitland, "The Shallows and Silences of Real Life," Collected Papers, Vol.i, p.478.
[49] See Ferguson v Earl of Kinnoul (1842) 9 Cl. & F. 251 at 290 for an early recognition of a third category of function.
[50] R. v Lediard (1751) Say. 6; Ex p. Taunton (1831) 1 Dowl. 55.
[51] Cardiff Bridge Case (1700) 1 Ld.Raym. 580.
[52] Case of the Borough of Warwick (1734) 2 Str. 991.
[53] R. v Coles (1845) 8 Q.B. 75.
[54] Arthur v Commissioners of Sewers for Yorkshire (1724) 8 Mod. 331.
[55] R. v Lloyd (1783) Cald. 309; R. v Hatfield Peverel (Inhabitants) (1849) 14 Q.B. 298 (order for removal of pauper lunatic to asylum), with which contrast R. v Boycott Ex p. Keasley [1939] 2 K.B. 651; R. v Drummond Ex p. Saunders (1903) 88 L.T. 833 (appointment of justices' clerk), with which contrast dictum in Re Constables of Hipperholme (1847) 5 D. & L. 79 at 81.
[56] See, e.g. R. v Sharman [1898] 1 Q.B. 578.
[57] R. v Woodhouse [1906] 2 K.B. 501.

With the coming of industrialisation, urbanisation and democratic 15–024
reform, the JPs shed many of their general local government functions.[58] A
new phase opened in the history of certiorari and prohibition during the
1830s. Two legal issues (still a source of controversy in judicial review
proceedings today) engaged the courts during this period. The first was the
question of which of the newly created government bodies were amenable
to certiorari and prohibition. Ad hoc bodies and elected local government
authorities, clothed with extensive regulatory powers over persons and
property, were set up to administer the expanding functions of government. Auditors were invested with statutory powers to disallow illegal
payments made out of public funds.[59] Parliament not infrequently provided
a statutory method of challenging the decisions of these authorities by way
of certiorari.[60] It was natural that the courts should take the view that
common law certiorari and prohibition could properly issue to other
authorities discharging similar functions where Parliament had made no
express provision for a method of challenge.[61]

With the accumulation of precedents, the courts took a step further and 15–025
held (after some vacillation) that the orders of central government departments and ministers[62] (but not of the Crown as such) were amenable to
certiorari and prohibition. No longer was the availability of the writs
limited to courts *stricto sensu*, or even to bodies that closely resembled the
courts.

The question whether the writs would issue in any particular case had 15–026
come to be determined by reference to the character of the act or decision
that was impugned and not merely by reference to the general character of
the body that had acted or decided. If the act or decision was of a judicial
character, its validity could be challenged by certiorari or prohibition.
Doubts about the propriety of issuing the writs to administrative bodies
had been so far dispelled by 1882 that it could be said, in a case where a
local authority sought a prohibition against a central government department, that wherever the legislature entrusts to any body of persons other

[58] See W.R. Cornish and G. de N. Clark, *Law and Society in England 1750–1950* (1989),
p.21.
[59] See W.A. Robson, *The Development of Local Government* (1954) for an account of the
development of the office of District Auditor.
[60] See, e.g. Poor Law Amendment Act 1834 ss.105, 106; Municipal Corporations (General)
Act 1837 s.44; Tithe Act 1837 s.3; Poor Law Amendment Act 1844 s.35. In some instances
statutory certiorari was apparently intended to take the place of an appeal to the courts and to
enable the courts to review the merits of the order impugned: *Re Dent Tithe Commutation*
(1845) 8 Q.B. 43 at 59; *R. v Roberts* [1908] 1 K.B. 407. See also *The State (Raftis and
Dowling) v Leonard* [1960] I.R. 381. *cf.* statutory applications to quash, below, Ch.12.
[61] See, e.g. *R. v Arkwright* (1848) 12 Q.B. 960 (certiorari to church building commissioners
for order stopping up churchyard paths); *R. v Aberdare Canal Co* (1850) 14 Q.B. 854
(certiorari to ad hoc commissioners for sanction given to building of a bridge); *Re Crosby-
upon-Eden Tithes* (1849) 13 Q.B. 761 (prohibition to tithe commissioners); *Church v
Inclosure Commissioners* (1862) 11 C.B. (N.S.) 664 (prohibition to inclosure commissioners).
[62] For a useful judicial survey of the development of remedies against Ministers, see *M. v
Home Office* [1994] 1 A.C. 377.

than to the superior courts the power of imposing an obligation upon individuals, the courts ought to exercise as widely as they can the power of controlling those bodies if they attempted to exceed their statutory powers.[63]

15–027   By the early 1900s, it was well settled that certiorari would issue to a body which "would not ordinarily be called a court, nor would its act ordinarily be termed 'judicial acts'"; that in this context "the term 'judicial act' is used in contrast with purely ministerial acts"; and that in general a judicial act was one which involved "the exercise of some right or duty to decide" a question affecting individual rights.[64] It did not follow, however, that every act affecting individual rights was necessarily "judicial" because it was not ministerial.

Certiorari, prohibition and the problem of locus standi

15–028   Apart from these difficulties over which decisions were amenable to challenge by way of certiorari and prohibition, the courts came to be beset with another problem: who could apply for these prerogative writs?[65] The courts developed a restrictive and highly technical approach to locus standi. As we shall see later, the problem was not confined to the writs of certiorari and prohibition, but also afflicted applications for mandamus and, later, the declaration. The old law in relation to the standing of an applicant for certiorari and prohibition must be stated tentatively. This is because of a series of conflicting 19th century decisions,[66] in which the expressions "clear want of jurisdiction", "discretionary", "as of right" and "*ex debito justitiae*" were used with a singular disregard for consistency. They enveloped the right of access to the courts in a fog that is not easily penetrated. The perplexity of the 19th century author who doubted "whether any legal question has ever given rise to so great a conflict of judicial opinion"[67] is more readily understandable than the confident assertion by another authority that the question "has now been set at rest".[68]

[63] *R. v Local Government Board* (1882) 10 Q.B.D. 309 at 321 (Brett L J.) a much-quoted dictum.
[64] *R. v Woodhouse* [1906] 2 K.B. 501 at 535 (Fletcher Moulton L.J.) See also *R. v Dublin Corp* (1878) 2 L.R.Ir. 371 at 376.
[65] For an account of the modern law on standing, see Ch.2.
[66] See, on the one side, *Worthington v Jeffries* (1875) L.R. 10 C.P. 379 and *Ellis v Fleming* (1876) 1 C.P.D. 23; on other side, *Foster v Foster and Berridge* (1863) 32 L.J. Q.B. 312; *R, v Twiss* (1869) L.R. 4 Q.B. 407 at 413–414 and *Chambers v Green* (1875) L.R. 20 Eq. 552. The judgment of Willes J. in *London Corp v Cox* is authoritative but contains elements of ambiguity. The law is most clearly stated in *Farquharson v Morgan* [1894] 1 Q.B. 552, CA.
[67] J. Shortt, *Informations, Mandamus and Prohibition* (1887), p.441.
[68] F.H. Short and F.H. Mellor, *The Practices on the Crown Side of the Kings Bench Division*, 2nd edn (1908), p.254.

Prohibition and locus standi

The rules that governed *locus standi* in relation to prohibition may be 15–029 stated as follows. If a defect of jurisdiction was apparent on the face of the proceedings, in other words was patent, the application for prohibition might be brought not only by a party aggrieved but also by a "stranger" to the proceedings,[69] and the court was obliged to allow the application and was not entitled to have regard to the conduct of the applicant.[70] If the defect of jurisdiction was not patent,[71] the court had a discretion to refuse to award prohibition to the applicant, but whereas it would incline towards exercising its discretion in favour of a party aggrieved,[72] it would refuse an application made by a "stranger" unless he made out a very strong case.[73]

The rule that a stranger[74] had *locus standi* to apply for prohibition was 15–030 explained by the old idea that a usurpation of jurisdiction was a contempt of the Crown and an encroachment upon the royal prerogative. Consequently it was immaterial by what means and by whom the court was informed of the usurpation.[75] But this was a shaky foundation for such a rule, and it seems unlikely that in administrative law a court would ever award prohibition to an applicant (other than the Crown) who lacked any personal interest at all in the proceedings impugned.[76]

Still more anomalous was the sharp distinction drawn between patent 15–031 defects of jurisdiction and the other grounds for prohibition. Two reasons were put forward to support the rule that the court had no discretion if want of jurisdiction appeared on the face of the proceedings: "that the case

---

[69] Co.Inst., ii, 607; *De Haber v Queen of Portugal* (1851) 17 Q.B. 171 at 214; *London Corp v Cox* (1867) L.R. 2 H.L. 239 at 279; *Worthington v Jeffries* (1875) L.R. 10 C.P. 379.
[70] *Buggin v Bennett* (1767) 4 Burr. 2037; *Farquharson v Morgan* [1894] 1 Q.B. 552; *R. v Comptroller General of Patents and Designs Ex p. Parke, Davis & Co* [1953] 2 W.L.R. 760 at 764.
[71] The rule concerning latent defects of jurisdiction doubtless applied where breach of the rules of natural justice was alleged.
[72] *Farquharson v Morgan* [1894] 1 Q.B. 552. In *Foster v Foster and Berridge* (1863) 32 L J.Q.B. 312, 314, *London Corp v Cox* (1867) L.R. 2 H.L. 239 at 283, and *Broad v Perkins* (1888) 21 Q.B.D. 533, prohibition is spoken of as issuing as of right or ex debito justitiae on the application of a party aggrieved, but in each case the court recognised its discretion to refuse the writ if the circumstances so warranted.
[73] *Foster v Foster and Berridge* (1863) 32 L.J.Q.B. 312 at 314; Short & Mellor (1908), p.265.
[74] In the various assertions that a "stranger" had locus standi it is not always clear who is understood to be a stranger. Sometimes the term seemed to mean merely a person who was not a party to the proceedings sought to be prohibited; it did not necessarily follow that the court would have been prepared to accord standing to someone who had no personal interest whatsoever to protect in moving for a prohibition. See S. Thio, *Locus Standi and Judicial Review* (1971), Ch.4. And compare the judgments of Lord Denning M.R. and Bridge L.J. in *R. v GLC Ex p. Blackburn* [1976] 1 W.L.R. 550 at 559, 567.
[75] *Worthington v Jeffries* (1875) L.R. 10 C.P. 379, 382; *Farquharson v Morgan* (1894) 1 Q.B. 552 at 556.
[76] It may be remarked that the public interest in securing the release of persons from unlawful detention is more obvious than in preventing the usurpation of jurisdiction by administrative tribunals; yet a stranger cannot bring an application for habeas corpus without the authority of the prisoner, unless access to the prisoner is denied so that no instructions can be received from him.

might become a precedent if allowed to stand without impeachment"[77] and that the defect was one of which the court itself ought to take notice.[78] The first proposition applied with almost equal force to cases where the defect of jurisdiction was not patent; the second meant no more than that it would often be unseemly for the court to refuse to interfere.

Certiorari and locus standi

15–032 Whereas most of the cases on prohibition resulted from proceedings originally instituted before courts *stricto sensu*,[79] the *locus standi* required of an applicant for certiorari often arose in the general field of administrative law. But most of the decisions failed to provide a full exposition of the relevant principles and many of the dicta were ambiguous. It was not even clear how far the rules relating to prohibition were applicable to certiorari. There were numerous dicta to the effect that a "stranger" might be awarded certiorari.[80] On the other hand, Lord Denning observed that the court "would not listen, of course, to a mere busybody who was interfering in things which did not concern him".[81] and in no reported English case was an application brought by such a person successful. Certiorari is a discretionary remedy, and the discretion of the court extended to permitting an application to be made by any member of the public. A person aggrieved, i.e. one whose legal rights had been infringed or who had any other substantial interest in impugning an order, might be awarded a certiorari *ex debito justitiae*[82] if he could establish any of the recognised grounds for quashing; but the court retained a discretion to refuse his application if his conduct was such as to disentitle him to relief[83] Only in highly exceptional circumstances did the court exercise its discretion in favour of an applicant who was not a person aggrieved. It may be assumed that it would hardly ever exercise its discretion in favour of an applicant who had himself instituted the proceedings[84] or benefited from the order[85]

[77] *Ricketts v Bodenham* (1836) 4 Ad. & E. 433 at 441; *Marsden v Wardle* (1854) 5 E. & B. 695, 701.
[78] *Farquharson v Morgan* (1894) 1 Q.B. 552 at 559.
[79] *R. v Minister of Health Ex p. Villiers* [1936] 2 K.B. 29; *R. v Liverpool Corp* [1972] 2 Q.B. 299 and *R. v GLC Ex p. Blackburn* [1976] 1 W.L.R. 550 are among the more notable exceptions.
[80] See, e.g. *R. v Surrey JJ.* (1870) L.R. 5 Q.B. 466 at 472–473 (where Blackburn J. mentions the "very analogous case of prohibition").
[81] *R. v Paddington Valuation Officer Ex p. Peachey Property Corp Ltd* [1966] 1 Q.B. 380 at 401.
[82] Understood by Denning L.J. in *R. v Thames Magistrates' Court Ex p. Greenbaum* (1957) 55 L.G.R. 129 to mean "injustice to the applicant".
[83] See, generally, *Greenbaum* (1957) 55 L.G.R. 129 and *R. v Stafford JJ. Ex p. Stafford Corp* [1940] 2 K.B. 33 at 43–44 (Lord Greene M.R.) explaining the judgment of the court in *R. v Surrey JJ.* (1870) L.R. 5 Q.B. 466.
[84] See *Permanent Trustee Co of NSW v Campbelltown Corp* (1960) 105 C.L.R. 401 at 413, per Menzies J.
[85] See *R. v Denbighshire JJ.* (1853) 17 J.P. 312. But see *R. v Assessment Appeal Board Ex p. Cornwall* (1965) 49 D.L.R. (2nd) 769 (certiorari lay to quash severable part of an order although the applicant had benefited from another part).

that he impugned. Whether the court retained any discretion where want of jurisdiction appeared on the face of the proceedings was never clearly settled. Since the primary purpose of both certiorari and prohibition was to prevent the usurpation of jurisdiction, it was argued that the same rule ought to apply as for prohibition; on the other hand, there was something to be said against the extension of anomalous doctrines by analogy.

As has been indicated, a court was in practice unlikely to allow an **15–033** application for certiorari unless it had been made by someone whom it regarded as a person aggrieved. For this purpose, persons aggrieved were defined as those who "have a peculiar grievance of their own beyond some grievance suffered by them in common with the rest of the public".[86] Persons who had been deprived of their offices or proprietary rights, or who had been denied or deprived of an occupational licence, clearly fell within this category. But the category was drawn very widely, and included trade rivals objecting to the grant or renewal of a liquor licence[87] an adjoining landowner objecting (under now repealed planning legislation) to a grant of interim development permission,[88] a local user of a highway that justices had ordered to be stopped up,[89] a prospective defendant in proceedings to be brought by a party to whom a civil legal aid certificate had been granted by a legal aid committee,[90] newspaper proprietors affected by a magistrates' order to restrict reporting of committal proceedings,[91] and local ratepayers objecting to the validity of a valuation list[92] and to decisions by a minister,[93] a local authority[94] and a district auditor[95] that would potentially have increased their fiscal liability. It could not be said that the additional burdens, actual or contingent, that were to be borne by the ratepayers who applied for certiorari fell more heavily on them than on other members of the local community; yet they were treated as persons aggrieved. To this extent the definition of "persons aggrieved" quoted above was therefore too narrow, and should be broadened to include members of a local community who have a special grievance of their own by virtue of their membership of that community.[96] Indeed, by the 1960s,

---

[86] *R. v Nicholson* [1899] 2 Q.B. 455 at 471. See also *Greenbaum* (1957) 55 L.G.R. 129, 134 (Parker L.J.).
[87] *R. v Groom Ex p. Cobbold* [1901] 2 K.B. 157.
[88] *R. v Hendon R.D.C. Ex p. Chorley* [1933] 2 K.B. 696.
[89] *R. v Surrey JJ* (1870) L.R. 5 Q.B. 466.
[90] *R. v Manchester Legal Aid Committee Ex p. Brand (RA) & Co* [1952] 2 Q.B. 413.
[91] *R. v Russell Ex p. Beaverbrook Newspapers Ltd* [1969] 1 Q.B. 342; *R. v Blackpool JJ. Ex p. Beaverbrook Newspapers Ltd* [1972] 1 W.L.R. 95.
[92] *R. v Paddington Valuation Officer Ex p. Peachey Property Corp Ltd* [1966] 1 Q.B. 380. The application was dismissed on the merits.
[93] *R. v Minister of Health Ex p. Dore* [1927] 1 K.B. 765 (remission of surcharge imposed by district auditor on borough councillors for unlawful expenditure).
[94] *R. v Hendon RDC Ex p. Chorley* [1933] 2 K.B. 696 (grant of development permission gave applicant a contingent right to compensation that would be payable by ratepayers).
[95] *R. (Bridgeman) v Drury* [1894] 2 I.R. 489 (unlawful expenditure allowed by auditor). Certiorari is not now the appropriate means of challenging an auditor's decision.
[96] cf. *R. v Taunton St. Mary* (1815) 3 M. & S. 465 at 472. And see *R. v GLC Ex p. Blackburn* [1976] 1 W.L.R. 550.

the courts were still more liberal, according locus standi to the Crown and the Gaming Board who objected to the production of a police report for the purpose of a private prosecution for libel,[97] and to trades unions applying for certiorari on behalf of members.[98]

15–034   A narrower view of locus standi was, however, taken by the courts when the ground upon which the decision was challenged was that some person other than the applicant was denied a fair opportunity to be heard.[99] To this extent the rules of natural justice seem to confer rights that are personal to those entitled to be heard by the decision-maker. But it may be possible to satisfy a court that an applicant's interests have been prejudiced by a failure on the part of the authority to give proper notice to others who would have lent weight to the representations of the applicant.[100] A person who had a right to be heard before an administrative tribunal had locus standi to challenge a decision of the tribunal on the ground that the hearing that he was afforded was inadequate, and, frequently, on other grounds as well.

THE WRIT OF MANDAMUS

Origins: restoration to office

15–035   Today the main role of the order of mandamus, now obtainable only in CPR Pt 54 judicial review proceedings, is to compel inferior tribunals to exercise jurisdiction that they have wrongfully declined, and to enforce the exercise of statutory duties and discretion in accordance with the law. The origins of the writ are rather later than those of certiorari and prohibition. Although the history and qualities of certiorari and prohibition well qualified them for inclusion in a "prerogative" group of writs, the claims of mandamus were less obvious. Not until 1573 do we find a reported case that centres around a judicial writ of mandamus serving purposes substantially similar to those of the modern writ[101]—it was issued to restore a

---

[97] *R. v Lewes JJ. Ex p. Home Secretary* [1973] A.C. 388; see also *R. v Cheltenham JJ. Ex p. Secretary of State for Trade* [1977] 1 W.L.R. 95 (witness summons issued to department inspector quashed on application of Minister and the inspector).

[98] *R. v Deputy Industrial Injuries Commissioner Ex p. Amalgamated Engineering Union* [1967] 1 A.C. 725.

[99] This would seem to be the explanation of a curious decision of the Privy Council in *Durayappah v Fernando* [1967] 2 A.C. 337. Relief was denied to the mayor of a municipal council which had been dissolved by a Minister without first according the council a hearing. The Board may have proceeded on the assumption that the restrictive rules governing *locus standi* for injunctions—the appellant was seeking a multiplicity of remedies—were also applicable to certiorari. The mayor was held to have no independent right to be heard. The case may be criticised for taking too restrictive a view of the interests deserving procedural safeguards.

[100] *Wilson v Secretary of State for the Environment* [1973] 1 W.L.R. 1083.

[101] *Middleton's case*, 3 Dyer 332b. The writ in this case was modelled after one issued in an earlier unreported case of a similar character: *Anable's* case, temp. Henry VI. Miss Henderson has observed (*Foundations of English Administrative Law*, pp.49, 53–54) that the writ in Middleton's case was analogous to a writ of privilege. In the 17th century mandamus lost its connection with privilege (*Foundations of English Administrative Law*, pp.75–76).

citizen of London to his franchise of which he had been illegally deprived. The modern writ of mandamus did not, however, begin to emerge till the early years of the 17th century; and for practical purposes its history can be said to have begun with *Bagg's* case.[102] The writ in this case is shown to have issued out of the King's Bench and to have been attested by Coke as Chief Justice; it recited that Bagg, a capital burgess of Plymouth, had been unjustly removed from his office by the mayor and commonalty, and commanded them to restore him unless they showed to the court good cause for their conduct. They failed to satisfy the court and a peremptory mandamus was issued to restore Bagg. From then onward many such writs issued to compel restitution[103] to offices and liberties. By the early years of the 18th century it had become—thanks largely to the work of Holt—something more comprehensive than a writ of restitution. It would go, on the application of a party aggrieved, to compel the performance of a wide range of public or quasi-public duties, performance of which had been wrongfully refused. It would issue, for example, to compel the admission (as well as the restoration) of a duly qualified alderman to a corporation,[104] or to compel the holding of an election to the office,[105] and it became a valuable device to prevent the unlawful packing of corporations.[106] More important still, it would issue to inferior tribunals that wrongfully declined jurisdiction.[107] Through the writ of mandamus, the King's Bench compelled the carrying-out of ministerial duties incumbent upon both administrative and judicial bodies.

Lord Mansfield's contribution

The rules governing the issue of the writ gradually took shape until they were fully stated by Lord Mansfield in a series of cases.[108] What is particularly interesting about Mansfield's judgments is that he persistently refers to mandamus as a "prerogative" writ.[109] Thus, in a typical passage, he calls it "a prerogative writ flowing from the King himself, sitting in his court, superintending the police and preserving the peace of this country".[110] Speaking in 1762, Mansfield observed that within the past century mandamus had been: 15–036

---

[102] (1615) 11 Co. Rep. 93b.
[103] In the 17th century the writ was often called a writ of restitution: see e.g. 1 Bulst. 174; Poph. 133 at 176; Style 32; 3 Salk. 231; Hale, *Analysis of the Law*, p.60.
[104] *R. v Norwich (Mayor)* 2 Ld.Raym. 1244.
[105] *R. v Evesham (Mayor)* 7 Mod. 166.
[106] It was regularly used after 1688 by the Whigs to secure admission to the Tory-packed borough corporations.
[107] See, e.g. *Groenvelt v Burwell*, 1 Ld.Raym. 454; *R. v Montague*, Sess.Cas. 106.
[108] See, esp. *R. v Blooer* (1760) 2 Burr. 1043; *R. v Barker* (1762) 3 Burr. 1265; *R. v Askew* (1768) 4 Burr. 2186.
[109] For example, in *R. v Cowle* (1759) 2 Burr. 834, 855; *R. v Barker* (1762) 1 Wm.B1. 352; *R. v Vice-Chancellor (of Cambridge University)* (1765) 3 Burr. 1647 at 1659. For a similar early reference to mandamus, see *Knipe v Edwin* (1694) 4 Mod. 281; *cf. R. v Patrick*, 1 Keb. 610.
[110] *R. v Barker* (1762) 3 Burr. 1265.

"liberally interposed for the benefit of the subject and advancement of justice. . . . It was introduced, to prevent disorder from a failure of justice, and defect of police. Therefore it ought to be used upon all occasions where the law has established no specific remedy, and where in justice and good government there ought to be one."[111]

15–037 Already by that time the primary function of the writ was to compel inferior tribunals to exercise jurisdiction and discretion according to law. But it issued also for what Blackstone called "an infinite variety of other purposes"[112] large and small to compel the town of Derby to fulfil its obligations under the Militia Acts,[113] to order the election, admission or restoration of a party aggrieved "to any *office* or franchise of a public nature whether spiritual or temporal",[114] to secure the use of a meeting-house, to obtain production, delivery and inspection of public documents, to compel local officials to pay over sums due and to perform a variety of other public duties, to compel justices of the peace to issue warrants, make rates, appoint overseers and pass accounts, to compel a body corporate to surrender its regalia or to affix its common seal.

15–038   By the middle of the 19th century the body of case law had swollen to grotesque proportions. In 1848 Thomas Tapping incorporated in his exhaustive and unreadable treatise on the writ,[115] an analysis of all the cases, arranged alphabetically according to subject matter. The list, which ranged from Abbot through Bastards, Corpse, Scavenger and Swordbearer down to Yeoman of Wood Wharf, ran to 252 pages. But the heyday of mandamus was by then nearly over, and its significance was to dwindle almost as swiftly as it had risen.

The decline of mandamus

15–039 After 1835 the corrupt oligarchies which had controlled the boroughs were superseded by local councils elected on broad franchise. Half a century later the broom of reform swept through the counties, and for most administrative purposes elected local authorities replaced the county justices and the parish vestries. The new regime made for a more orderly system of local government, in which the delays and irregularities which had evoked so many applications for mandamus were less likely to occur. Central administrative control, exercised by means of district audit of accounts, inspection of services, powers to act in default, and a host of other regulatory devices, became the normal agency for securing the proper discharge of local duties. In respect of acts and decisions by local

---

[111] *R. v Barker* (1762) 3 Burr. 1265 at 1267.
[112] Blackstone, *Commentaries*, Vol.iii, p.110.
[113] Holdsworth, *The History of English Law*, Vol.x, p.156.
[114] Blackstone, *Commentaries*, Vol.iii, p.110.
[115] Entitled "The Law and Practice of the High Prerogative Writ of Mandamus, as it obtains both in England, and in Ireland".

authorities affecting individual rights, Parliament adopted the practice of providing persons aggrieved with a right of complaint, objection or appeal to a central government department; and by supplying these efficacious alternative remedies it indirectly took away the right of the individual to obtain a mandamus. The decline of mandamus was also expedited by such factors as reform in the administration of other classes of corporations, and the gradual disappearance of the concept of freehold office in which the holder was quasi-proprietary rights enforceable by mandamus.[116] For these and other reasons[117] the area of public activity and inactivity within which mandamus can play an effective part has diminished. So, while reform of local government leads to an increasing role for certiorari and prohibition, it spelt a diminishing importance for mandamus.

Mandamus and locus standi

As with certiorari and prohibition, the nature of the interest required to support an application for mandamus was always difficult to state with any degree of confidence. It was often said that the applicant had to have a specific legal right to enforce, or a specific legal right to the enforcement of the duty, and in one case a court applied this principle when refusing an application by a local sanitary authority for an order to compel the responsible officers to implement the provisions of the Vaccination Acts in their district.[118] Again, in cases where the courts refused applications for mandamus against Crown servants the decisions were sometimes explained on the ground that the respondent owed no legal duty to the applicant.[119] But in these cases the references to the absence of any legal duty owed towards the applicants were designed to bring out the point that the duties cast upon the respondents were owed by them to the Crown alone; they are not to be understood as purporting to lay down propositions about the nature of the legal interest needed for applications for mandamus in general. 15–040

What meaning, then, can be attributed to the broader assertions that a legal right-duty relationship had to be present between the applicant and the respondent? Sometimes, one suspects, they were nothing but 15–041

---

[116] The holder of a freehold office was removable only for misbehaviour, and had the right to be heard in his own defence before removal.

[117] Some of which are referred to in J. Shortt, *Informations, Mandamus and Prohibitions* (1887), pp.271–272.

[118] *R. v Lewisham Union Guardians* [1897] 1 Q.B. 498 (one of two reasons for the decision). *cf.*, however, *R. v Keighley Union Guardians* (1876) 40 J.P. 70; and see *R. v Leicester Guardians* [1899] 2 Q.B. 632 (Local Government Board has *locus standi* to enforce such a duty). The test formulated in the Lewisham Union case has been adopted to some more recent decisions: see, e.g. *R. v Customs and Excise Commissioners Ex p. Cook* [1970] 1 W.L.R. 450 at 455; *Environmental Defence Society Inc v Agricultural Chemicals Board* [1973] 2 N.Z.L.R. 758.

[119] See *R. v Lords Commissioners of the Treasury* (1872) L.R. 7 Q.B. 387 at 395, 398–400, 402; *R. v Inland Revenue Commissioners, re Nathan* (1884) 12 Q.B.D. 461; *R. v Secretary of State for War* [1891] 2 Q.B. 326; *R. v Arndel* (1906) 3 C.L.R. 557; *R. v Governor of South Australia* (1907) 4 C.L.R. 1497 at 1512; *Kariapper v Wijesinha* [1968] A.C. 717 at 745.

tautologies: mandamus would be to secure the enforcement of a legal duty on the application of one who was recognised by law as being entitled to apply for its enforcement by this method. In some contexts they may be understood to mean merely that the "duty" imposed on the respondent must be one recognised by law if it is to be enforceable in the courts[120] or that it is not enough for the applicant to rely upon a private equitable right.[121] If they are to be understood to mean that no application for mandamus for the enforcement of a legal duty may be brought except by one who has a right to bring an action for damages for breach of duty, they are manifestly wrong.[122]

15–042 Perhaps the most reasonable construction to place on the proposition that the applicant had to show a legal right to the performance of the duty is that he had to have a substantial personal interest in its performance. There is, indeed, a good deal of judicial support for the view that a mere stranger had no locus standi, and that an applicant had to establish that he was specially aggrieved by the non-performance of the duty or had an immediate interest[123] in its performance greater than that of members of the public generally.[124]

15–043 It is possible to explain some of these decisions on the basis that the court was not disclaiming jurisdiction because of the insufficiency of the applicant's locus standi but was merely exercising its discretion not to award him the relief he sought. The view has in fact been advanced that in applications for mandamus, as in applications for certiorari, *locus standi* was not restricted by any rule of common law and that the courts could in their discretion grant an application made by any member of the public.[125] Certainly the courts on occasion showed the utmost liberality in granting

---

[120] *cf. Ex p. Napier* (1852) 18 Q.B. 692; *R. v Secretary of State for War* [1891] 2 Q.B. 326.

[121] *R. v Stafford (Marquis)* (1790) 3 T.R. 646. See, however, *R. v Registrar of Titles Ex p. Moss* [1928] V.L.R. 411; Thio, pp.114–115; *Stafford*'s case was overtaken by the judicature Acts.

[122] In *R. v Inland Revenue Commissioners, re Nathan* (1884) 12 Q.B.D. 461 Brett M.R. confused the issue still further by assuming that no duty was owed to the applicant unless he could bring an action and that if an action would lie, mandamus would not.

[123] For a case where mandamus was refused because the applicant's interest was only indirect, see *R. v Frost* (1838) 8 A. & E. 822. See also *R. v Orton Vicarage Trustees* (1849) 14 Q.B. 139; and *cf. R. v Industrial Court Ex p. ASSET* [1965] 1 Q.B. 377 at 389–390 (dictum). The authorities are reviewed in *R. v Whiteway Ex p. Stephenson* [1961] V.R. 168.

[124] Thus, a rating authority was held not to have a sufficient legal interest to obtain a mandamus to compel an assessment committee to perform its statutory duties properly: *R. v City of London Union Assessment Committee* [1907] 2 K.B. 764. In cases in which writs of mandamus were awarded against local authorities to carry out duties to make a byelaw and prepare a town planning scheme in conformity with statute, the courts examined the interests of the applicants at some length on the assumption that unless they were substantial the court would have no jurisdiction to grant the relief sought. In the one case the applicants had a financial interest in the making of the byelaw and had, moreover, secured the insertion of the clause in the Private Bill requiring the byelaw to be made: *R. v Manchester Corp* [1911] 1 K.B. 560. In the other, a modern Irish case in which the English authorities were considered, the applicants were builders who had suffered financial and other detriment because of the corporation's failure to adopt a scheme: *The State (Modern Homes (Ireland) Ltd) v Dublin Corp* [1953] I.R. 202.

[125] See D.C.M. Yardley, "Prohibition and Mandamus and the Problem of Locus Standi" (1957) 73 L.Q.R. 534, 539.

applications made by persons whose interest in the performance of the duty in question was tenuous.[126] Although the preponderance of authority is opposed to the view that the courts were entitled to exercise a free discretion in determining questions of *locus standi* in applications for mandamus, and indicates that an applicant had to have a direct interest of his own in the performance of the duty, the courts did in practice exercise a wide discretion in deciding the degree of interest required for the purpose of a particular application.

THE WRIT OF HABEAS CORPUS[127]

Finally, we turn to the prerogative writ of habeas corpus *ad subjicien-* **15–044** *dum*.[128] Though it is the most renowned contribution of the English common law to the protection of human liberty, its origins were modest.[129] The earliest writs of habeas corpus were used in mesne process; they were commands addressed to royal officials to bring before one of the King's courts the body of a person whose presence was required for the purpose of a judicial proceeding. In this form habeas corpus preceded Magna Carta. The connection, readily discerned by 17th century writers, between the text of the Charter and the development of the writ owes less to historical fact than to partisan imagination and wishful legend.

In the 14th century there emerged the writ of habeas corpus *cum causa,* **15–045** requiring the person who already had custody of a prisoner to produce him before the court, together with the ground for the detention. A means of testing the legality of the detention, this was the immediate ancestor of the modern writ.[130] It was used by the common law courts at Westminster to protect, assert and extend their own jurisdiction against their various rivals by securing the release of litigants and others from custody.[131] It was also used by private litigants to procure an order for release from wrongful imprisonment; and in this way it came to assume high constitutional importance as a device for impugning the validity of arbitrary imprisonment by the Executive. The decision in *Darnel's* case,[132] that a warrant certifying a committal to be "by the special command of the King"

---

[126] Thus, in one case a local vicar, who had unsuccessfully objected to the transfer of a liquor licence obtained a mandamus to order the justices to hear and determine the application for transfer according to law: *R. v Cotliam* [1898] 1 Q.B. 802 (the court did not discuss the applicant's *locus standi*).

[127] See 17–010.

[128] Other forms of habeas corpus are now practically obsolete.

[129] M. Cohen, "The Immigration Act and Limitations upon Judicial Power: Bail" (1938) 16 Can.B.R. 92; A.D.R. Zellick and R.J. Sharpe, *The Law of Habeas Corpus*, 3rd edn (2005), Ch.1.

[130] M. Cohen, "Some Considerations on the Origins of Habeas Corpus" (1940) 18 Can.B.R. 10, 172. See also Holdsworth, *The History of English Law*, Vol.ix, pp.24–51; E. Jenks, "The Story of Habeas Corpus" (1902) 18 L.Q.R. 64.

[131] In some situations its effect was analogous to that of a writ of prohibition.

[132] (1627) 3 St.Tr. 1.

disclosed a sufficient ground for imprisonment, was overruled by the Petition of Right in the following year. But the machinery for removing the abuse of lengthy imprisonment without trial was still defective. Reforms were introduced by the Habeas Corpus Act 1679: if a person was held on a serious criminal charge, he was to be given release on bail or a speedy trial in pursuance of an application for habeas corpus.[133] Severe financial penalties (which are still in force) were imposed on judges wrongfully refusing to issue the writ, on gaolers evading service of or compliance with the writ and on persons recommitting a prisoner who had already been discharged on a habeas corpus.

15–046   In 1816 the Act was extended to cases of civil detention and the judges were empowered to inquire into the truth of the facts set out in the gaoler's return to the writ in such cases. Given a relatively temperate political climate, with an alert body of informed opinion and an independent judiciary, habeas corpus flourished while liberty in many lands languished. Efficiency was its virtue: habeas corpus really worked. "When Dicey declared that the Habeas Corpus Acts were 'for practical purposes worth a hundred constitutional articles guaranteeing individual liberty'[134] he spoke for the mass of English constitutional lawyers".[135] Substantive guarantees unaccompanied by any effective procedural technique for enforcing them are, indeed, often worthless. But a number of modern constitutional bills of rights incorporate not only entrenched substantive guarantees (which Britain lacks) but also entrenched procedures for enforcement in the courts.[136] This new emphasis on the importance of judicial remedies can be regarded as an indirect recognition of English experience.[137] It has, however, been doubted whether habeas corpus serves any useful purpose today, given the expansion in the scope of judicial review.[138]

EQUITABLE REMEDIES: INJUNCTIONS[139]

15–047   After the labyrinthine by-ways of the common law prerogative writs one has a sense of greater freedom in the fields of equity. The injunction and the declaratory order were more flexible and adaptable instruments of

[133] Habeas Corpus Act 1679 s.6. This section was repealed by the Courts Act 1971 s. 56(4) Sch.11 Pt iv.
[134] *Introduction to the Study of the Constitution*, 10th edn (1959), p.199.
[135] S.A. de Smith, *The New Commonwealth and its Constitutions* (1964), p.167.
[136] See, e.g. Constitution of India, Arts 19, 21, 22, 32, 226; Constitution of Jamaica (SI 1962/1550 Sch.2) ss.15, 20, 25, 49, 50.
[137] England was not the only country to devise an effective judicial remedy for obtaining release from wrongful imprisonment. Thus, similar remedies were evolved in Scots law, Roman-Dutch law and some Latin American systems. But habeas corpus has attracted special attention overseas. See, e.g. L. Kutner, *World Habeas Corpus; and Seminar on Amparo, Habeas Corpus and other Similar Remedies* (United Nations, 1962).
[138] A. Le Sueur, "Should we Abolish the Writ of Habeas Corpus" [1992] P.L. 13; cf. M. Shrimpton, "In Defence of Habeas Corpus" [1993] P.L. 24 and Law Com No.226, Pt XI.
[139] On modern law and practice see 18–034.

judicial control than the common law remedies. They were less burdened by precedent. They were comparatively free from the abstruse technicalities and hair-splitting distinctions besetting certiorari, prohibition and mandamus. They could be awarded against bodies whose functions contained no judicial element. However, historically the intrusions of equity upon the domain of public law were desultory and selective. The injunction, still pre-eminently a private law remedy, did not come to play a significant part in public law until the 19th century. And although declarations have equitable roots, the remedy is better seen as a statutory one. By the time the equitable remedies had begun to extend their reach, the prerogative writs were recognised as the principle methods of obtaining judicial review of administrative action, and they were too securely entrenched to be readily ousted by newcomers. The expectations of those who looked for a dramatic increase in the part played by equitable remedies in administrative law have not been fulfilled.

Nevertheless, the equitable sector, which until recently was little more   **15–048** than a miscellany of loosely connected topics, has acquired cohesion and substance through the creative activity of individual judges; and the creative impulse is by no means spent.[140] Moreover, a consequence of the procedural reforms of 1977 that enable an applicant for judicial review to request a declaration or an injunction (or both), alone or combined with one or more of the prerogative orders, is that these remedies have moved closer to the mainstream of administrative law.

The origins of equitable intervention and much of the subsequent course   **15–049** of its evolution are shrouded in obscurity. Three topics in particular are important: the constant interplay between matters of public right and matters of private right; the influence of the Crown's prerogative capacity as *parens patriae;* and the significant role of the Court of Exchequer.

The Court of Exchequer

The Court of Exchequer assumed a general equitable jurisdiction during   **15–050** the course of the 16th century.[141] In addition, it exercised equitable powers incidentally to its capacity as a court of revenue.[142] In the exercise of this ancillary jurisdiction it entertained English informations filed by the Attorney-General to secure the protection and enforcement of the proprietary and fiscal rights of the Crown against subjects.[143] The relief awarded

---

[140] See Lord Denning's own dicta in *Lee v Showmen's Guild of Great Britain* [1952] 2 Q.B. 329 at 346; *Barnard v National Dock Labour Board* [1953] 2 Q.B. 18 at 41–44; *Taylor v National Assistance Board* [1957] P. 101 at 111, and *Pyx Granite Co v Ministry of Housing and Local Government* [1958] 1 Q.B. 554 at 571.
[141] Holdsworth, *History of the Laws of England*, Vol.i, p.241. It was described as "an ancient though originally usurped jurisdiction" in *Attorney General v Halling* (1846) 15 M. & W. 687 at 694, where the history of the several sides to the court's equitable jurisdiction is traced. See also Holdsworth, *History of the Laws of England*, Vol.xii, pp.456–458.
[142] See *Attorney General v Halling* (1846) 15 M. & W. 687 at 694.
[143] G. Robertson, *Civil Proceedings by and against the Crown* (1908), pp.234 *et seq.*

included injunctions and declaratory orders. The English information may well have been the earliest form of equitable proceeding lying predominantly within the field of public law. Its procedural rules were unwarrantably favourable to the Crown, and a belated recognition of this injustice was one reason why it had fallen into desuetude some years before it was abolished by Parliament in 1947.[144]

15–051   A more beneficent and important contribution made by the Court of Exchequer to public law was its practice of awarding equitable relief against the Crown, represented by the Attorney General.[145] For this purpose it does not seem that the court differentiated between cases where the interests of the Crown were indirectly affected and cases where the interests of the Crown were directly affected.[146] Judgment in favour of the subject usually took the form of a declaratory order. After 1841 the practice of suing the Attorney General in an action for a declaration (except under special statutory provisions or upon a petition of right) fell temporarily into abeyance.[147] But this dormant jurisdiction of the Court of Exchequer passed to the High Court of Justice of 1873; and, as we shall see, it was revived in 1911 in a notable case[148] which gave a new impetus to the action for a declaration in public law.

The Court of Chancery

15–052 In its early days the Court of Chancery appears to have had little concern with matters of public law, save in so far as its jurisdiction to issue common injunctions to restrain persons from proceeding in the courts of common law and enforcing judgments obtained at common law[149] incidentally raise questions of constitutional importance. The chronology of its interventions in the field of public law cannot be traced with assurance. One can say that the blurred outlines of its jurisdiction were taking shape soon after the Restoration, that they had become more distinct by the middle of the 18th century and that the process of clarification did not end with the judicature Acts; but much must be left to conjecture. Blackstone's account of equitable jurisdiction was inadequate, but it would appear that by his time the Court of Chancery was entertaining at least four classes of proceedings that have a bearing on our inquiry. First, the Crown could sue in Chancery as an alternative to bringing an English information in the Exchequer.[150]

---

[144] Crown Proceedings Act 1947 s.13 Sch.1 para.1.
[145] Preceding the award of such relief by the Court of Chancery: Holdsworth, "History of Remedies against the Crown" (1922) 38 L.Q.R., 280–281. See also H.G. Hanbury, *Essays in Equity* (1934), pp.114–120.
[146] G. E. Robinson, *Public Authorities and Legal Liability* (1925), pp.xxxvii–xxxix (introductory chapter on remedies against the Crown by J.H. Morgan).
[147] See Court of Chancery Act 1841.
[148] *Dyson v Attorney General* [1911] 1 K.B. 410.
[149] Substantially abolished with respect to proceedings in the superior courts by the Supreme Court of Judicature Act 1873 s.24(5). See Supreme Court of Judicature (Consolidation) Act 1925 s. 41.
[150] Robertson pp.237, 238.

Secondly, a Crown grantee or other person claiming rights under the **15–053** Crown was permitted to sue in the King's name in order to take advantage of the prerogative. If he sued in his own name in a proceeding that touched the rights of the Crown he had to join the Attorney General as co-plaintiff.[151] From these beginnings there emerged a general principle that in matters of equitable jurisdiction in which the King's interest were involved the Attorney General was competent to sue at the relation of a private plaintiff, the relator bearing the costs and receiving the benefit of the court's award.[152]

Thirdly, the court would issue injunctions to restrain the commission or **15–054** continuance of public nuisances,[153] though this was a power more frequently exercised by the Court of Exchequer.[154] Such an injunction could be addressed even to the members of an inferior court whose order had been responsible for creating the nuisance.[155] In Hardwicke's time it was established that an information by the Attorney General was the proper mode of proceeding,[156] unless an individual had suffered particular damage by reason of the nuisance, in which case the intervention of the Attorney General was unnecessary.

Fourthly, during the 17th century the Attorney General was bringing **15–055** information in the Court of Chancery to secure the establishment and due administration of charitable or public trusts.[157] This class of proceeding was of major historical importance; it was the commonest, and possibly the first, of the early forms of relator actions in equity.[158] It was founded on

---

[151] Robertson p.464.

[152] *Attorney General of Duchy of Lancaster v Heath* (1690) Prec.Ch. 13; *Attorney General v Oglender* (1740) 1 Ves Jun. 246, 1 Ves.Jun.Supp. 105.

[153] The general jurisdiction of the Court of Chancery to restrain nuisances goes back to Elizabethan times; *Attorney General v Richards* (1788) 2 Anst. 608; *Story on Equity* (2nd English edn), para.921. See generally W.J. Jones, *The Elizabethan Court of Chancery* (1967).

[154] *Attorney General v Cleaver* (1811) 18 Ves. 211, 217.

[155] *Box v Allen* (1727) Dick. 49 (injunction to Commissioners of Sewers); *Attorney General v Forbes* (1836) 2 My. & Cr. 123 (injunction to magistrates at quarter sessions).

[156] *Baines v Baker* (1752) Amb. 158 at 159.

[157] The view that the Attorney General's intervention preceded the Statute 43 Eliz. c.4 seems to be erroneous. His intervention is traceable to the time of Charles I and became common in the second half of Charles II's reign: G. Jones, *History of the Law of Charity, 1532–1827*, pp.21–22, 34 *et seq.*

[158] It was the only form of equitable relator action mentioned by Blackstone, *Commentaries*, Vol.iii, p.427. An early example of a proceeding by way of Attorney General's information and private bill with respect to a charity was *Attorney General v Newman* (1670) 1 Ch.Cas. 157, where the appropriateness of the bill was doubted. For early examples of the settled form of relator action, see *Attorney General v Hart* (1703) Prec.Ch. 225; *Attorney General v Bains* (1708) Prec.Ch. 270. For the limits of the court's intervention, see J. Fonblanque, *Treatise of Equity*, 3rd edn. Vol.ii, pp.205–206; *Attorney General v Smart* (1748) 1 Ves.Sen. 72. At common law the informer who was permitted to bring a civil action upon a penal statute (see Holdsworth, *The History of English Law*, Vol.ii, pp.453–454; Vol.iv, pp.355–359), or a *qui tam* information for a penalty to be shared by himself and the Crown, was also called a relator (see 21 Jac. 1, c.4). In the 18th century a criminal information could be exhibited either by the Attorney General *ex officio* or by the Master of the Crown Office at the relation of an informer (*The History of English Law*, Vol.ix, pp.237–246). In civil proceedings at common law the only class of relator action corresponding with the relator action in equity was the information in the nature of a *quo warranto*; see, e.g. 9 Anne c.20 s.4.

the status of the Crown as *parens patriae;* and it was the progenitor of new types of proceedings brought by the Attorney General as the Crown's representative in matters especially appertaining to the public welfare.

15–056   The Sovereign, as *parens patriae, is* responsible for the superintendence of infants, idiots, lunatics and charities.[159] The Chancellor, as the keeper of the King's conscience, was the appropriate officer to dispense this prerogative jurisdiction, and the Attorney General, as the King's forensic representative, was the appropriate officer to appear for the Crown in the Chancellor's court. If the funds of a public body were deemed to be impressed with a charitable trust, it was clearly appropriate for the Attorney General to go to the Court of Chancery to seek an injunction against their misapplication. Thus the Attorney General came to bring information to restrain unlawful expenditure of borough funds.[160]

15–057   The concept of a *parens patriae* had still larger implications. The Crown, as *parens patriae,* had a visitatorial authority over those charitable and ecclesiastical corporations which lacked founders or visitors. A municipal corporation had no visitor; then let the Crown be its visitor and supervisor.[161] At common law the visitatorial power was exercised by bringing *quo warranto* informations and applications for writs of mandamus and *scire facias* in the King's Bench. Most of these proceedings arose out of defaults other than the misuse of corporate funds. Since the Crown was empowered, in a proper case, to sue in such of its courts as it thought fit, it could and did elect to take proceedings in equity generally to secure the observance of the law by municipal corporations.[162] This trend of development could well end with a broad proposition that the Attorney General, representing the Crown, could properly apply to the Court of Chancery to restrain the execution of illegal acts commuted not merely by corporations which held property on trust for public purposes but also by other bodies, of statutory as well as of non-statutory origin, where such illegalities tended to injure the public welfare. So, indeed, it did end, but not without a long period of judicial hesitation.[163]

15–058   Gradually, during the course of the 19th century, a group of general principles crystallised. The Attorney General could proceed *ex proprio motu* (of his own motion) in any action in which he might appear at the instance of a relator;[164] the relator need not show any personal interest in the subject-matter of the suit, for the proceedings were the Attorney General's;[165] the right of the Attorney General to intervene depended upon

[159] *Chitty on Prerogative*, Ch.IX. Lord Nottingham referred to the King as *pater patriae*: Reports of Cases by Lord Nottingham, Vol. 1 (Selden Soc., Vol.73, edn D.E.C. Yale), 209. The prerogative jurisdiction has been partly superseded by statute.
[160] *Attorney General v Aspinall* (1837) 2 My. & Cr. 613.
[161] *cf.* Roscoe Pound, "Visitatorial Jurisdiction over Corporations in Equity" (1936) 49 Harv.L.R. 369.
[162] As in *Attorney General v Galway Corp* (1828) 1 Molloy 95.
[163] See H.A. Street and S. Brice, *Ultra Vires* (1930), pp.265–266.
[164] *Attorney General v Dublin Corp* (1827) 1 Bli.(N.S.) 312 at 337–338.
[165] *Attorney General v Vivian* (1825) 1 Russ. 236.

the public consequences of the act complained of, not on the intrinsic characteristics of the defendant body;[166] the right of an individual to sue without joining the Attorney General depended on whether his own legal interests were more particularly affected than those of the public in general. In essence, the general right of the Attorney General to seek the repression of ultra vires acts tending to injure the public grew out of a broad conception of the prerogative of protection, and the details of the rules governing locus standi were substantially borrowed from the law of public nuisance.

There was then only the most tentative relaxation of the rules governing **15–059** locus standi in relation to injunctions,[167] and the function of the Attorney General as protector of the public interest, enabling him to obtain an injunction to restrain breaches of the criminal law, was extended.[168] But the main factor conducive to an expansion of the role of the injunction in public law has been its close association with the declaratory judgment. It is quite common for injunctive and declaratory relief to be claimed in the same proceedings, and in such cases the courts tend to refrain from drawing fine distinctions between the permissible scope of the two remedies.

DECLARATIONS[169]

The potentialities of the declaration in public law have been realised only **15–060** during the 20th century. But a great authority on the action for a declaration has said that "All that is new about declaratory judgments is the name—the phenomenon itself is as ancient as the administration of justice by courts" and that "Anglo-American statutes have from time immemorial authorised and courts have rendered judgments purely declaratory in form and effect".[170] To question these assertions with reference to English law may be presumptuous, especially as the development of

---

[166] See, e.g. *Attorney General v Oxford, Worcester & Wolverhampton Ry* (1854) 2 W.R. 330; *Attorney General v Cockermouth Local Board* (1874) L.R. 18 Eq. 172.
[167] In *Gouriet v Union of Post Office Workers* [1978] A.C. 435, the House of Lords reaffirmed the requirements that an injunction to restrain a breach of the criminal law will only be granted to an individual who can establish that the defendant's conduct either endangers a private legal right or may occasion him special loss not suffered by members of the public at large.
[168] In a number of recent cases local authorities have been accorded a similar role as guardians of the public interest in their locality by virtue of the Local Government Act 1972 s.222. In *Gouriet* [1978] A.C. 435, however, a warning was sounded about the dangers of a regular resort to injunctions for this purpose.
[169] On the modern law and practice relating to declarations in judicial review proceedings, see 18–038.
[170] E.M. Borchard, *Declaratory Judgments*, 1st edn (1934), pp.62, 73. The author fails to cite any relevant English authority in support of his assertions. In the second edition the former passage is reworded to read: "All that is new about the declaratory judgment is its name and its broad scope-the phenomenon itself is as old as judicial history" (p.137).

declaratory orders in English legal history has never been thoroughly investigated; yet it would seem that in England the purely declaratory judgment is a comparatively modern institution.

Judicial resistance to declaratory relief

15–061 From its earliest days the Court of Chancery did indeed issue declaratory orders.[171] But the books on Chancery practice are silent on the matter of purely declaratory judgments. And if a general practice of rendering purely declaratory judgments had ever existed, it had certainly been abandoned by the 1840s. Thus, Bruce V.C. observed in 1847:[172] "Nakedly to declare a right, without doing or directing anything else relating to the right, does not, I conceive, belong to the functions of this Court." This view is supported by many other judicial dicta[173] and the contrary view would make nonsense of Lord Brougham's prolonged agitation for importing the main features of the Scots action of declarator into English law.[174]

15–062 The practice of the Court of Chancery not to make declaratory orders unaccompanied by other relief was subject to a limited exception introduced after 1830. The court would permit a suppliant to bring a petition of right to obtain the consent of the Crown to permit itself to be sued through the Attorney General for equitable relief including a declaration,[175] and in one such case the court awarded the suppliant a pure declaration against the Attorney General.[176]

15–063 After the Petitions of Right Act 1860 (under which the judgment of the court was always declaratory in form,[177] although it would normally declare that the suppliant was entitled to damages or other specific relief), a number of petitions claiming equitable relief were directed against the Crown and in some cases the judgment of the court was purely declaratory in substance as well as in form.[178]

15–064 More significant for the development of the action for a declaration in public law was the practice of the Court of Exchequer, which, uninhibited by the restraints that the Court of Chancery had imposed upon itself, had long awarded equitable relief against the Crown, represented by the

[171] G. Spence, *Equitable Jurisdiction of the Court of Chancery* (1846), Vol.i, p.390. See also Comment, "Developments in the Law Declaratory judgments, 1941–1949" (1949) 62 Harv.L.R. 787.
[172] *Clough v Ratcliffe* (1847) 1 De G. & S. 164 at 178–179.
[173] See, e.g. *Elliotson v Knowles* (1842) 11 L.J. Ch. 399 at 400.
[174] See Borchard (1941), pp.125–128, for an account of the rules of Scots law and Brougham's campaign.
[175] *Clayton v Attorney General* (1834) 1 Coop.t.Cott. 97
[176] *Taylor v Attorney General* (1837) 8 Sim. 413.
[177] Petitions of Right Act 1860 s.9; W.B. Clode, *Petition of Right* (1887), p.183.
[178] As in *P & O Steam Navigation Co v R.* [1901] 2 K.B. 686 (declaration as to the amount of crewspace shipowners were required by statute to provide for Lascars); but all the relevant decisions appear to have been given after the introduction of RSC, Ord.25 r.5, in 1883.

Attorney General, on bills filed by subjects.[179] Its jurisdiction to grant relief against the Crown was derived from a statute of 1841,[180] its judgments were usually declaratory in form. Whether its jurisdiction extended to declaring that the Crown was under an obligation (e.g. to pay money) to the plaintiff is very dubious.[181] In 1841 its general equitable jurisdiction passed to the Court of Chancery,[182] but it seems probable that its jurisdiction to give equitable relief against the Crown was incidental to its capacity as a court of revenue and did not, therefore, pass to the Court of Chancery.[183] But whatever may be the correct view, it appears to have ceased to exercise this jurisdiction after 1841 and the Court of Chancery was never called upon to determine whether it had succeeded to it. Not until 1911 was its jurisdiction to award declaratory judgments in ordinary civil actions against the Crown, represented by the Attorney General, rediscovered and revived[184] and all the precedents cited on that occasion were Exchequer precedents.

Legislative reforms

The aversion of the Court of Chancery to awarding purely declaratory judgments could be cured only by legislative action. Parliament, however, was to find its prescriptions received without enthusiasm. An Act of 1850 empowered persons interested in the construction of written instruments to state a special case for the opinion of the court, which was authorised to declare its opinion thereon without proceeding to administer consequential relief.[185] In 1852 a further step was taken, and it was enacted that no suit should be open to objection on the ground that a merely declaratory decree 15–065

---

[179] The view taken by the Chancery has been that since equity acts in personam it would be indecent to command the Crown and, moreover, the court's command would be nugatory, since it could not be enforced by attachment or sequestration (Clode (1887), pp.142–143). This does not sufficiently explain the refusal to make purely declaratory orders against the Crown. The explanation is to be found in the general practice of the court not to make such orders against any person.

[180] Crown Debts Act 1541 (33 Hen. 8, c.39); see esp. s.79 (repealed). The leading cases on equitable relief against the Crown in the Exchequer include *Sir Thomas Cecil's Case* (1598) 7 Co.Rep. 18b; *Pawlett v Attorney General* (1668) Hardres 465; *Casberd v Attorney General* (1819) 6 Price 411; *Deare v Attorney General* (1835) 1 Y. & C.Ex. 197; *Hodge v Attorney General* (1839) 3 Y. & C.Ex. 342.

[181] See *Tito v Waddell (No.2)* [1977] Ch. 106 at 256–259, where the plaintiffs were unable to proceed under the Crown Proceedings Act 1947 in so far as their claim against the Crown was held not to arise "in respect of His Majesty's Government in the United Kingdom" (s.40(2)(b)). It was further stated that even if jurisdiction to grant declaratory relief in such circumstances did exist, this statutory exemption of the Crown from liability should normally lead the court in its discretion to refuse relief.

[182] Court of Chancery Act 1841.

[183] See *Attorney General v Halling* (1846) 15 M. & W. 687 at 698–699. No clear finding on this point was made in *Dyson v Attorney General* [1911] 1 K.B. 410. If the revenue jurisdiction passed to the High Court under s.10 of the Judicature Act 1873 and was exercised by the Queen's Bench Division after 1881, the point is an academic one.

[184] *Dyson v Attorney General* [1911] 1 K.B. 410.

[185] Court of Chancery, England, Act 1850 ss.1, 14.

or order was sought thereby, and that it would be lawful for the court to make binding declarations of right without granting consequential relief.[186] These valuable accessions of authority (which were especially useful for the determination of disputed points arising in the administration of estates and trusts) were construed more restrictively than had seemed possible. The court not only maintained its traditional reluctance to declare future rights, but held that the classes of cases in respect of which declarations could be made had not been enlarged;[187] a declaration could now be made unaccompanied by any consequential relief, but only in cases where the plaintiff would have been entitled to other relief had he but chosen to ask for it.[188] More explicit directions were needed to bestir the court from the torpor of unimaginative conservatism.

15–066 The Judicature Acts of 1873–75 transferred the jurisdiction of the superior courts of common law and equity to the High Court, and empowered the Rule Committee to make rules regulating the practice and procedure of the court. RSC, Ord.25 r.5, made in 1853 provided:

> "No action or proceeding shall be open to objection, on the ground that a merely declaratory judgment or order is sought thereby, and the Court may make binding declarations of right whether any consequential relief is or could be claimed, or not."

15–067 The concluding words of the rule were designed to rectify the unsatisfactory state of affairs that had arisen through the restrictive interpretation given to the 1852 Act. But the courts, while recognising that RSC, Ord.25 r.5, had introduced an innovation of a very important kind",[189] still showed a curious reluctance to award declarations save in cases where other relief might have been claimed for a legal wrong, and they insisted that the jurisdiction should be exercised with great caution.

The turning point

15–068 The turning-point came in 1911. The Inland Revenue Commissioners issued to Dyson, a taxpayer, a form and notice requiring him under penalty to submit certain particulars. Relying on the pre-1842 Exchequer precedents and RSC Ord.25 r.5, he sued the Attorney General for declarations

---

[186] Court of Chancery Procedure Act 1852 s.50. See also the Legitimacy Declaration Act 1858, enabling a person to obtain a declaration of legitimacy in an action in which the Attorney General would appear as respondent.

[187] *Langdale (Lady) v Briggs* (1856) 2 De G.M. & G. 391 at 427–428. See also *Garlick v Lawson* (1853) 10 Hare App.xiv; *Bright v Tyndall* (1876) 4 Ch.D. 189 at 196; *Hampton v Holman* (1877) 5 Ch.D. 183. cf. *Jenner v Jenner* (1866) L.R. 1 Eq. 364 for an illustration of judicial conservatism in making declarations of right in another context.

[188] *Jackson v Turnley* (1853) 1 Dr. 617 at 628; *Rooke v Lord Kensington* (1856) 2 K & J 753 at 760–762. See also *Dyson v Attorney General* [1911] 1 K.B. 410, 422.

[189] *Ellis v Duke of Bedford* [1899] 1 Ch. 494 at 515; *Chapman v Michaelson* [1909] 1 Ch. 238 at 243.

that the requisition was unauthorised and that he was under no obligation to comply with it inasmuch as it was ultra vires the Finance Act. The Court of Appeal held that this form of proceeding was a proper one,[190] and subsequently granted the declarations sought.[191] The judgments in the first *Dyson* case were founded partly on a misreading of legal history;[192] the court failed, moreover, to consider the question whether RSC, Ord.25 r.5, bound the Crown[193] and the decision raised the difficult problem whether, and if so, how far, the action for a declaration against the Attorney-General could be employed, when a petition of right against the Crown would have been an appropriate remedy.[194] But the decision was of the highest importance in the development of the action for a declaration. In the first place, the members of the court not merely upheld the propriety of the form of proceeding adopted but gave it their warm approval.[195]

Secondly, this was a case in which the plaintiff had no "cause of action" **15–069**
that would have entitled him to any other form of judicial relief, the threat to his interests created by the unlawful demand that had been made upon him could be directly averted only by the award of a binding declaration.[196]

Thirdly, the plaintiff could have waited until he was sued for penalties **15–070**
for non-compliance with the requisition and then set up its invalidity by way of defence; nevertheless, the court declined to regard that procedure as the only permissible method of determining the issue.

---

[190] *Dyson v Attorney General* [1911] 1 K.B. 410.
[191] *Dyson v Attorney General* [1912] 1 Ch. 159. The Dyson principle was applied in *Burghes v Attorney General* [1911] 2 Ch. 139 (affirmed [1912] 1 Ch. 173).
[192] The court erroneously assumed (see also *Esquimalt & Nanaimo Railway Co v Wilson* [1920] A.C. 358 at 365–368) that the Exchequer precedents were equally applicable to the Court of Chancery. For an attempt to explain away this aberration, see *Bombay & Persia Steam Navigation Co v Maclay* [1920] 3 K.B. 402 at 407. But Cozens-Hardy M.R. observed ([1911] 1 K.B. 410 at 417): "The absence of any precedent does not trouble me".
[193] See H. Street, *Governmental Liability* (1953), p.134, pointing out that as the rule was not expressed to bind the Crown the decision can be defended only on the assumption that the Exchequer precedents alone were being relied on; the Chancery practice had been to refuse to award declarations against the Crown except on a petition of right.
[194] Semble, where the rights of the Crown were directly affected and a petition of right was a proper remedy, an action for a declaration against the Attorney General as the representative of the Crown would not lie: *Attorney General for Ontario v MacLean Gold Mines Ltd* [1927] A.C. 185. The controversy surrounding this question (for which see Street pp.132–133; Glanville Williams, *Crown Proceedings* (1948), p.90) has become largely irrelevant since the Crown Proceedings Act 1947, which abolished the petition of right procedure for almost all purposes; though cf. Colonial Stock Act 1877 s.20; *Franklin v Attorney General* [1974] Q.B. 185. And see *Tito v Waddell (No.2)* [1977] Ch. 106 at 259, 260 (declaratory relief should not be granted when an action under the Crown Proceedings Act 1947 could be instituted).
[195] See Farwell L.J. [1911] 1 K.B. 410 at 420; Fletcher Moulton L.J. [1912] 1 Ch. 158 at 168.
[196] It would seem that the legal right asserted by Dyson was his privilege to decide what information to supply to the Commissioners in the absence of any legally enforceable duty of the kind alleged by them. In *Gouriet v Union of Post Office Workers* [1978] A.C. 435 at 502, Lord Diplock suggested that the relevant interest of Dyson was that an unlawful demand had been made for a penalty payable for non-compliance, which, had the plaintiff succumbed, he could have sued to recover; cf. his Lordship's analysis of the applicant's rights affected in *R. v Criminal Injuries Compensation Board Ex p. Lain* [1967] 2 Q.B. 864 at 888–889. See now *Woolwich Equitable Building Society v Inland Revenue Commissioners* [1993] 1 A.C. 70.

15–071   In 1915 the principle laid down in *Dyson's* case was buttressed by a further decision of the Court of Appeal in which it affirmed its power to make a declaration that plaintiffs were not under a legal obligation (to repay money paid to them in respect of certain bills of exchange) to which the defendants (who had instituted proceedings against the plaintiffs in the United States) claimed them to be subject.[197] In this case the defendant had contended that RSC, Ord.25 r.5, was not ultra vires. The Rule Committee had statutory power to make rules for practice and procedure with respect to all matters over which the Supreme Court had jurisdiction;[198] it had admittedly no power to extend the jurisdiction of the court. The Court of Appeal held, however, that the rule had not conferred any new jurisdiction upon the court and was, therefore, ultra vires. Jurisdiction to give purely declaratory judgments, even in cases where there was no independent cause of action and no possibility of granting consequential relief, had (so the court held) always resided in the Court of Chancery although the court had adopted a settled practice of refusing to render such judgments.[199] Seldom has the elastic concept of jurisdiction been more judiciously stretched. And Bankes L.J. expressed the view that the rule "should receive as liberal a construction as possible".[200]

The growth in use of the declaration

15–072   During the 20th century the action declaration has become one of the most popular forms of proceedings in the High Court. As early as 1917 an American authority was able to write that the practice of making declarations of right had completely revolutionised English remedial law.[201] Most of the declaratory judgments to which he referred were given in proceedings instituted by originating summons in the Chancery Division for the determination of questions arising out of the administration of estates and trusts or for the construction of various classes of written instruments. Proceedings instituted by writ under RSC, Ord.25 r.5, were not frequent until after the *Dyson* case. In those areas of administrative law where statutory tribunals and inquiries do not operate, it has come to be more widely used against public authorities than the older and less flexible non-statutory remedies. Flexibility is, indeed, the greatest merit of the declaratory judgment.

[197] *Guaranty Trust Co of New York v Hannay & Co* [1915] 2 K.B. 536 (Pickford and Bankes L.JJ. Buckley L.J. dissenting). The plaintiffs were eventually successful in obtaining the declarations they had sought: see [1918] 2 K.B. 623. See also *Russian Commercial & Industrial Bank v British Bank for Foreign Trade Ltd* [1921] 2 A.C. 438.
[198] Judicature Act 1873 ss.16, 23; Judicature Act 1925 s.17.
[199] [1915] 2 K.B. 563–564. This interpretation of the effect of r.5 is not easily reconcilable with the observations on its effect referred to above, n.189.
[200] At 572.
[201] E.R. Sunderland, "Modern Education in Remedial Rights; the Declaratory Judgment" (1917) 16 Mich. L.R. 69, 77.

Locus standi and declarations

Prior to the reforms of 1978, the rules of locus standi in relation to declaratory relief were as difficult to formulate as those relating to the prerogative orders. The plaintiff in an action for a declaration had to establish that he had an immediate personal interest in the subject matter of the proceedings. In a matter affecting the public at large, a plaintiff had normally to show that his own interests were in some way "peculiarly affected"[202] by the defendant's conduct, but in determining whether the plaintiff's interests were sufficiently affected to give him title to sue, the courts exercised a wide and not always consistent discretion. There were decisions founded on the assumption that a plaintiff had title to sue although he was threatened with no greater injury than other members of the section of the community to which he belonged.[203] On the other hand, a plaintiff whose interests were directly and substantially impaired by an invalid grant of planning permission to a third party was held to be lacking in locus standi to impugn the decision because it did not encroach on any legal "right" vested in him.[204] But it was clearly sufficient that the plaintiff had a direct and substantial interest in the proceedings, even though he had no independent cause of action.

15-073

LEGISLATIVE REFORM OF PROCEDURES

So far this historical survey has focused on the development of remedies rather than procedures.[205] As we have seen, the fundamental characteristics of the remedies available to challenge governmental action in the High Court were largely settled by the early years of the 20th century; the major concerns since then have been with the search for effective, efficient and flexible procedures.

15-074

Procedural goals in public law proceedings

In the context of public law, the procedural rules and practices of the Administrative Court and its forerunners can be seen as attempting to achieve a number of goals.[206] First, they may seek to assist the court in

15-075

---

[202] The phrase used by Porter J. in *Stockwell v Southgate Corp* [1936] 2 All E.R. 1343 at 1351.

[203] See, e.g. *Nicholls v Tavistock UDC* [1923] 2 Ch. 18; *Prescott v Birmingham Corp* [1955] Ch. 210; and see *R. v GLC Ex p. Blackburn* [1976] 1 W.L.R. 550, 559, weakened by *Gouriet v Union of Post Office Workers* [1978] A.C. 435.

[204] *Gregory v Camden LBC* [1966] 1 W.L.R. 899. This case may be contrasted with *Prescott v Birmingham Corp* [1955] Ch. 210 as illustrating the two extreme positions adopted by the court.

[205] For the distinction between procedures and remedies, see 15–002.

[206] For a more detailed analysis of these procedural goals in relation to the requirement of leave (now called permission), see A.P. Le Sueur and M. Sunkin "Applications for Judicial Review: the Requirement of Leave" [1992] P.L. 102, 104–107.

achieving the efficient flow of cases through what is today called the Administrative Court (formerly the Crown Office List).[207] The concerns about how best to cope with growing numbers of applications are not new, but stretch back at least as far as the 1930s.[208] Secondly, the form of procedures may seek to protect the interests of the respondents (usually, of course, governmental bodies) and third parties from unmeritorious or tardy challenge. Thirdly, the procedures may seek to promote access for applicants, for example, by having relatively relaxed rules as to who has standing to apply for judicial review and ensuring that the procedural regime is as simple as possible.

The complex array of public law procedures that exist today can be seen as an attempt to accommodate all these goals in differing degrees.[209]

Statutory applications to quash[210]

15–076   Statutory review clauses in statutes provide that within a strict time limit, usually six weeks, any person aggrieved by a specified administrative order, notice, scheme, action or other decision made may challenge its legality in the High Court. The procedural regime for so doing is entirely distinct from that of CPR Pt 54; for example, in addition to the different time limits, there is no general requirement that the applicant obtain the permission of the court.[211]

15–077   The first statutory review clause was enacted by s.11 of the Housing Act 1930 which dealt with challenges to slum clearance orders. The innovatory new procedure was prompted by a series of cases during the preceding years in which successful applications for certiorari had been made to quash orders of local authorities when the schemes had been almost brought into operation and after great expense had been incurred. The clause was presented by the government during its passage through Parliament as "a most important and valuable provision. It is the greatest safeguard you can afford to the individual and at the same time provides a method by which questions of right can be determined at the earliest possible moment".[212]

---

[207] On the Administrative Court, see Ch.17.

[208] See, e.g. the review by The Business of the Courts Committee chaired by Viscount Hanworth M.R. established in 1933. See further, A.P. Le Sueur and M. Sunkin "Applications for Judicial Review: the Requirement of Leave" [1992] P.L.102, 103, n.5 and pp.107–109; A.P. Le Sueur "Should we Abolish the Writ of Habeas Corpus?" [1992] P.L. 13.

[209] Some have argued that the third goal at facilitating access to the courts has been given insufficient weight: see Lord Scarman, "The Development of Administrative law: Obstacles and Opportunities" [1990] P.L. 490, 492; Le Sueur and Sunkin, above [1992] P.L. 102, 127.

[210] For an account of the modern practice and procedure, see Ch.17.

[211] But s.289 of the Town and Country Planning Act 1990 provides an appeal to the High Court against an enforcement notice upheld by the Secretary of State for the Environment on appeal. The Planning and Compensation Act 1991 introduced a requirement (now the new s.289(6)) that an appeal may only be brought under that section with the leave of the court. This limitation was proposed by Robert Carnwath Q.C. in his report, *Enforcing Planning Control* (1989).

[212] *Hansard* HL, cols 461–463 (July 15, 1930). See also *Hansard* HL, cols 582–583 (July 21, 1930).

There has been an expansion in the subject areas in which statutory **15–078** review is used. At first confined to compulsory purchase and land use planning,[213] clauses have come to be used increasingly in the field of regulation of industry.[214] The introduction of the statutory review procedure can clearly be seen as instigated by dissatisfaction with the operation of the common law prerogative orders. From the perspective of the respondents—particularly local authorities—the prerogative writs and procedures had failed to provide sufficient safeguards, particularly from tardy challenges.[215] Typically, however, the reforms implemented were piecemeal and designed to deal with one particular context only, namely slum clearance orders. It was to be another three years before the general inadequacies of the prerogative writ procedures were tackled.

Procedures for applying for prerogative writs[216]

Throughout the 1930s, the courts and government continued to be **15–079** concerned that the procedures for obtaining the prerogative writs were unacceptably inefficient; they were wasteful of court time and the delays that ensued had a capacity to frustrate administrative action.

Introduction of the leave requirement[217]

Until 1933, an applicant for any of the prerogative writs applied first for an **15–080** order (or rule) nisi. At this hearing, before a Divisional Court of three judges, the court considered the applicant's case in full and determined whether the writ sought should issue. If the applicant satisfied the court that his case had merit, the order nisi was granted. The onus then lay on the *respondent* to show cause, at a second hearing before a Divisional Court, why the order should *not* be made absolute. Both government and the courts became dissatisfied with this procedure. From the Government's perspective, it was seen as inappropriate that at the second hearing applicants could "sit back" and watch the respondent try to get the order nisi discharged. The court's dissatisfaction lay in what was seen as a duplication of efforts at the nisi and absolute hearings; at both stages a Divisional Court considered the merits of the application.

Following recommendations of the Hanworth Business of the Court **15–081** Committee,[218] legislation was introduced to modernise procedures on the Crown Side of the King's Bench Division, though leaving the writ of

---

[213] See, e.g. the modern provisions in the Town and Country Planning Act 1990 ss.287, 288; Local Government and Planning Act 1980 Sch.32, Pt.I (designation of Enterprise Zones); Ancient Monuments and Archaeological Areas Act 1979 s.55; Highways Act 1980 Sch.2.

[214] See, e.g. Petroleum Act 1987 s.4; Airport Act 1986 s.49; Telecommunications Act 1984 s.18; Medicines Act 1968 s.107.

[215] The Association of Municipal Councils played an important role in advocating introduction of the new review procedure.

[216] For an account of the modern practice and procedure, see Ch.18.

[217] For a more detailed account of the history of the leave requirement, see Le Sueur and Sunkin, [1992] P.L. 102.

[218] The Business of the Courts Committee: Interim Report, Cmnd 4265 (1933).

habeas corpus, and the procedure for obtaining it, untouched; it was apparently thought that to meddle with it might be construed as subversive activity.[219] The Administration of Justice (Miscellaneous Provisions) Act 1933 abolished the two stage nisi and absolute procedure and introduced a requirement that an applicant first obtain the leave of the court before an application for a prerogative writ be made. The leave hearing continued to be an ex parte (without notice) hearing before a Divisional Court. The real significance of the reform was that, leave having been granted, the burden remained on the applicant at the second hearing to prove his case. The 1938 Act of the same name replaced the writs of certiorari, prohibition and mandamus by orders of the same names. The change of designation reflected only a simplification of procedure.

Reform agendas

15–082 Thirty years later, dissatisfaction with the public law procedures and remedies of the High Court persisted. During the intervening period, branches of administrative law other than judicial review had undergone important reforms: the Crown Proceedings Act 1947 had more or less put the Crown in the same position as that of the ordinary defendant in private law litigation; the Tribunals and Inquiries Act 1958 had implemented many of the recommendations of the landmark Franks Committee Report; and the office of Parliamentary Commissioner for Administration had been created. In contrast, High Court procedure for judicial review-despite the limited reforms of the 1930s were little different to those that had operated a century before.

15–083   In 1966 the Law Commission[220] began to take soundings on administrative law reform, with special reference to the role of the courts. In 1967 it published an exploratory working paper, and after extensive consultations it formally recommended to the Lord Chancellor in May 1969 that a wide-ranging inquiry be conducted by a Royal Commission or a body of similar status into the following questions: (1) whether the form and procedure of existing judicial remedies in administrative law needed to be altered; (2) whether changes in the scope of judicial review were required; (3) how far remedies in respect of administrative acts and omissions should include the right to damages; (4) whether special principles should govern administrative contracts and torts; and (5) how far changes should be made in the organisation and personnel of the courts for the purposes of administrative law.[221]

15–084   At this time the civil service was beginning to receive the impact of the Parliamentary Commissioner for Administration and was also about to undergo reconstruction in the light of the recommendations of the Fulton

---

[219] See R.M. Jackson, *Machinery of Justice in England*, 6th edn (1972), pp.45–46.
[220] Constituted as a permanent advisory body on law reform in pursuance of the Law Commissions Act 1965.
[221] Cmnd 4059 (1969).

Committee.[222] Many prominent civil servants, moreover, were uneasy at the spontaneous revival of judicial activism. And some lawyers thought that procedural reform was too urgent to be deferred till the conclusion of a large-scale inquiry.

In December 1969 the Lord Chancellor rejected the Law Commission's 15–085 recommendations and requested it to undertake its own inquiry into question (1), the form and procedure of judicial remedies; changes in the scope of review were to be outside the Commission's terms of reference.[223]

In 1971, whilst the Law Commission was carrying out its investigation, 15–086 the organisation Justice (the British Section of the International Commission of Jurists) published its own report entitled *Administration under Law*, in which it examined some of the basic issues shelved by the Government. Among its proposals were the extension of duties to provide official information and reasons for decisions, the creation of new machinery to enable a court to ascertain the facts on which administrative decisions were based, and the conferment of power to award damages to persons aggrieved by decisions tainted with procedural or substantive irregularity in circumstances where there is no cause of action for damages under the law as it now stands. The detailed recommendations were open to criticism on various grounds,[224] particularly in view of the burden they would impose on the public service, but the suggestions for compensation and damages pinpointed an important weakness inherent in the present scope and effect of judicial review. Since this was a report by an unofficial body, it could be and was conveniently ignored by the Government.

The creation of the new RSC, Ord.53 application for judicial review

The Law Commission, impeded by the unfortunately restrictive nature of 15–087 its brief, produced its final report in 1976,[225] some four and a half years after the publication of a detailed working paper.[226] The principal proposal of the Commission was that all the existing non-statutory administrative law remedies should be capable of being claimed in a unified application for judicial review. Again, as in the reforms of the 1930s, no consideration was given to the status of the writ of habeas corpus. The Commission's main recommendation was implemented, with an expedition which was previously absent, by amendments to the Rules of the Supreme Court that took effect in January 1978.[227] The new RSC, Ord.53 provided for a single

---

[222] Report of the Committee on the Civil Service, Cmnd 3638 (1968).
[223] *Hansard* HL, Vol.306, cols 189–190 (December 4, 1969).
[224] See, e.g. (1972) 12 J.S.P.T.L. (N.S.) 72.
[225] Cmnd 6407 (1976).
[226] Remedies in Administrative Law (Law Com No.40). A similar working paper on the corresponding remedies in Scots law was issued by the Scottish Law Commission (Memorandum No.14). The working paper's modest proposals evoked a surprising amount of criticism both on technical grounds and because they would indirectly expand the scope of judicial review, which would be undesirable.
[227] RSC (Amendment No.3) 1977 SI 1977/1955) (L.30). *cf.* Judicature (Northern Ireland) Act 1978 ss.18–25.

procedure for obtaining the prerogative orders, injunctions, declarations and damages in public law proceedings. The leave requirement was retained. The Divisional Court of the Queen's Bench continued to hear both applications for leave[228] and substantive hearings. The limited nature of the reforms is revealed by the fact that they were implemented by means of a series of amendments to the Rules of Court. Only several years later, after questions were raised as to the vires under which the Rule Committee had acted, was the application for judicial review put on a statutory footing.[229] The aspects of the Commission's proposals (in particular that interim declaratory relief be available against the Crown) which clearly required to be introduced by statute remained unimplemented.[230]

Problems with the new RSC, Ord.53

15–088 The new RSC, Ord.53 was to some extent a victim of its own success: the availability of a streamlined procedure was one reason for the rapid growth in the number of applications for judicial review. Soon there were considerable delays in determining cases on the Crown Office List. In 1980, two years after the major reform, a number of further extensive and fundamental changes were made to RSC, Ord.53. Provision was made for both leave and substantive applications to be heard by single judges rather than the Divisional Court[231] and applications for leave could now be made "on paper" without the need for any hearing.

15–089 In 1985, the Government attempted to take a further step to make RSC, Ord.53 more efficient. By clause 43 of the Administration of Justice Bill, it sought to abolish the applicant's right to renew a leave application to the Court of Appeal. Judges of the Court of Appeal took the unprecedented step of speaking against this proposal while giving judgment[232] and during the committee stage of the Bill in the House of Lords, Lord Denning described the proposal as a "constitutional monstrosity". The clause was defeated, reintroduced in an amended form (allowing renewal to a Divisional Court including a Lord Justice of Appeal), but that too was defeated. For a period, the modified RSC, Ord.53 enabled applications for judicial review to be determined with acceptable dispatch. By the close of the 1980s, however, the Crown Court List was again beset with delays.

Justice/All Souls Review

15–090 Undeterred by the lack of government interest in its earlier report, justice again picked up the gauntlet of administrative law reform. In 1978, a committee was established in conjunction with All Souls College, Oxford

---

[228] Except during Vacation, when the application was to a judge in chambers.

[229] Supreme Court Act 1981 s.31.

[230] For comments, see H.W.R. Wade "Reform of Remedies in Administration Law" (1978) 94 L.Q.R. 179; C. Harlow "Comment" [1978] P.L. 1; J. Beatson and M.H. Matthews, "Reform of Administrative Law Remedies: The First Step" (1978) 41 M.L.R. 437.

[231] A Divisional Court continues to hear applications for leave (permission) and substantive applications in "criminal causes or matters": see 16–073.

[232] *R. v Income Tax Special Commissioner Ex p. Stipplechoice Ltd* [1985] 2 All E.R. 465 at 467 (Ackner L.J.). See also A.W. Bradley, "Comment" [1986] P.L. 361.

charged with devising practical proposals for reform with the aim of giving administrative law clarity, coherence, comprehensibility and accessibility.[233] Ten years later, it published its report.[234] It made several recommendations in relation to judicial review remedies and procedures. First, that the leave requirement in RSC, Ord.53 proceedings should be abandoned. In its place there should be a procedure for striking out hopeless or bogus applications or, alternatively, a two-stage procedure similar to that in Scotland should be introduced.[235] Secondly, the three-month limitation period should be repealed and undue delay should be a barrier only in so far as it causes substantial prejudice or hardship to others or would be detrimental to good administration.[236] Thirdly, discovery and cross-examination should be permitted more liberally; the general rule should be that documents which are relevant to contested issues between the parties should be disclosed. Fourthly, the Committee supported the increasingly liberal grant of locus standi.[237]

The Committee's report attracted considerable interest and no less criticism. Given its commitment to promoting access to justice rather than the safeguarding of respondents or to efficiency, it never looked likely to find favour with government. **15–091**

Reconsideration by the Law Commission

During the early 1990s the Law Commission once again turned its attention to judicial review procedures and remedies.[238] Its recommendations were cautious. The liberal interpretation of *O'Reilly v. Mackman*[239] and its principle of procedural exclusivity, already accepted by the House of Lords,[240] was approved. The report recommended that the leave stage in RSC, Ord.53 proceedings ought to be retained, though renamed the "preliminary consideration" and that the test be whether the application discloses a serious issue which ought to be determined. The Law Commission endorsed the continued existence of a requirement of standing, but argued that the court should have a discretion to allow applications where the applicant was not directly affected by the impugned decision but it was nevertheless in the public interest that the application proceed.[241] In **15–092**

---

[233] For a critique of the Committee's methodology, see D.Oliver and R. Austin [1991] P.L. 441, C. Harlow (1990) 10 J.L.S. 85.
[234] Report of the Committee of the Justice/All Souls Review of Administrative Law in the United Kingdom, *Administrative Justice-Some Necessary Reforms*, 1988.
[235] Justice/All Souls Review, Ch.6.
[236] Justice/All Souls Review.
[237] Justice/All Souls Review, para.8–050.
[238] See: Law Commission Fifth Programme of Law Reform, Law Com. No.200 (1991); Law Commission Consultation Paper No.126 (1993); Administrative Law: Judicial Review and Statutory Appeals, Law Com No.226 (October 1994); R. Gordon [1995] P.L. 11.
[239] See further Ch.3.
[240] *Roy v Kensington and Chelsea and Westminster Family Practitioner Committee* [1992] 1 A.C. 624.
[241] The continuing liberalisation of the standing rules by the court has in effect achieved this without the need for any change to the procedural rules: see Ch.2.

relation to the forms of relief, the report recommended that the Latin names for the prerogative writs (certiorari, prohibition and mandamus) be replaced with plain English ones. Interim and advisory declarations should be available to the court.[242] The report recommended that there be no reform of habeas corpus as a distinct remedy with its own procedural route, though it argued against the narrow approach to the scope of review adopted by the Court of Appeal in recent applications for habeas corpus.[243]

Recent reforms

15–093 The Law Commission's 1994 recommendations were soon eclipsed by initiatives on two other fronts—the fundamental reforms to the whole civil litigation system in England and Wales and preparations for implementing the Human Rights Act 1998.

15–094 The Civil Procedure Rules (CPR) sought to create a new approach to litigation, to ensure that the civil justice system is "accessible, fair and efficient".[244] The CPR provided, for the first time, a unified procedural code for the county courts, High Court and Court of Appeal (replacing the Rules of the Supreme Court 1965 and County Court Rules 1981). The reforms put in place the approach recommended by Lord Woolf's inquiry into Access to Justice, commissioned by the Lord Chancellor in 1994 amidst growing concerns that court processes were disproportionately costly and unduly slow.[245] Among the overarching recommendations was that court-based litigation should be a last resort, with aggrieved parties encouraged to use alternative dispute resolution whenever possible. Where there was no alternative to litigation, judges were to assume far greater powers to manage the conduct of the litigation to ensure timeliness and costs in proportion to the importance of the issues at stake. In relation to judicial review, the *Access to Justice* report endorsed most, though not all of the Law Commission's 1994 proposals.[246] At the time one of the largest categories in the judicial review caseload was challenges to the lawfulness of decisions by local housing authorities in relation to rights and duties and the homelessness legislation. The report recommended that an appeal on point of law to the county court should replace judicial review; local courts were more accessible and less costly than the High Court. This recommendation was speedily implemented.[247]

15–095 The CPR came into force in April 1999. There was not, however, time to revise the judicial review procedures and integrate them into the CPR. So for some 18 months the RSC, Ord.53 judicial review procedure

---

[242] See now 18–043.
[243] See 17–010.
[244] Civil Procedure Act 1997 s.1(3). The CPR is subordinate legislation made under powers conferred by that Act.
[245] *Access to Justice: a final report to the Lord Chancellor* (1996).
[246] *Access to Justice* did not support the suggestion that the remedies of mandamus, prohibition and certiorari be renamed; it also proposed including habeas corpus as one of the remedial orders available in a claim for judicial review, while also retaining it as a separate procedure.
[247] Housing Act 1996 ss.202, 204; and see 17–045.

continued in force, re-enacted as a schedule to the CPR. As it happened, the delay was fortunate because it enabled thought to be given to the impact of the Human Rights Act 1998, which was due to come into force in October 2000. A small committee, chaired by a distinguished accountant Sir Jeffery Bowman, was commissioned by the Lord Chancellor to review the Crown Office list—looking at the pressures thought likely to result from the Human Rights Act, as well as the backlog of immigration and asylum cases and the relationship between the *Access to Justice* report and the Law Commission's 1994 recommendations.[248] The task of the committee was "to put forward costed recommendations for improving the efficiency of the Crown Office List" that did not "compromise the fairness or probity of the proceedings, the quality of decisions, or the independence of the judiciary".[249]

The Bowman committee concluded that there was a continuing need for a specialised court as part of the High Court to deal with public and administrative law cases and recommended that the Crown Office List should be renamed "The Administrative Court" and given additional judicial and administrative resources. Greater specialism among the judiciary was also urged, with judges sitting in the new court for longer periods. In relation to immigration and asylum cases, the committee said that they should remain in the Administrative Court, arguing that it was not possible to "fast track" them when they represented such a large proportion of the overall judicial review caseload. The committee pointed out that without longer term reforms in the immigration and asylum tribunal system as a whole there was little opportunity to reduce recourse to judicial review in this area.[250] Moreover, there needed to be a comprehensive study of the structure, jurisdiction, procedures, remedies and routes of appeal of tribunals.[251]   **15–096**

The committee concluded that special procedures, in addition to the standard ways of initiating and conducting civil proceedings set out in the CPR, were needed.[252] The committee agreed with the conclusions of the Law Commission and *Access to Justice* report that leave stage requirement   **15–097**

---

[248] Other members of the committee were Lord Justice Simon Brown, Alan Cogbill (Director of Civil Justice and Legal Aid Reform in the Lord Chancellor's Department, Professor Jeffrey Jowell Q.C., Mr Justice Keene, Bernadette Kenny (Director of Operational Policy, LCD) and Anne Owers (Director of the organisation Justice). Sir Jefferey Bowman had in 1996–97 conducted an efficiency review of the Court of Appeal Civil Divison.

[249] *Review of the Crown Office List* (LCD, London, 2000), p.ii.

[250] Wide-ranging reforms were eventually introduced by the Asylum and Immigration (Treatment of Claimants etc) Act 2004, which created the Asylum and Immigration Tribunal as the successor to the previous two-tier system (the Immigration Appellate Authority and the Immigration Appeals Tribunal). Government proposals to oust the jurisdiction of the courts in relation to the new tribunal were withdrawn following sustained criticism of them as a threat to the rule of law: see R. Rawlings, "Review, Revenge and Retreat" (2005) 68 M.L.R. 378.

[251] Something achieved in 2001 with the publication of the Report of the Review of Tribunals by Sir Andrew Leggatt: *Tribunals for Users—One System, One Service*, discussed at 1–084; substantially implemented by the Tribunals, Courts and Enforcement Act 2007.

[252] *cf.* D. Oliver, "Public Law Remedies and Procedures—Do We Need Them?" [2002] P.L. 91.

(to be called "permission") should be retained in the new procedure, but recommended that in future the applications for permission should be served on defendant public authorities, which should have the opportunity at that point to set out their objections to the grant of permission. One aim of defendant involvement at this stage was to encourage the earlier settlement of disputes. The permission procedure should initially be carried out on paper applications, whereas previously applicants had the choice of whether to make an oral or written application. Significantly, the committee recommended that the criteria for obtaining permission should be made explicit in the new rules and that there should be a presumption in favour of permission being granted. The permission requirement was regarded by the committee as an important tool of case management, allowing the Administrative Court to dispose of cases efficiently.[253] The committee urged a "blitz" on the backlog of cases, in preparation for the coming into force of the Human Rights Act.

15–098   With considerable speed, the Lord Chancellor's Department drafted the new judicial review rules (which were to become CPR Pt 54) and a practice direction. Following a short period of consultation, they come into force on October 2, 2000, the same day as the Human Rights Act.[254] In most respects, the new rules reflected the recommendations of the Bowman committee (though the rules did not set out any express criteria for the permission stage and nor was there a presumption in favour of its grant). A pre-action protocol on judicial review followed in 2001.[255] Some recommendations of the Law Commission report and the Bowman committee required amendments to primary legislation. Although consultees has overwhelming supported reform of habeas corpus, the Government decided not to proceed with this due to the declining recourse to the remedy.[256] Changes to the Latin names of mandamus, prohibition and certiorari were made in 2004.[257] Several procedural routes, including that for statutory applications to quash certain decisions, still require integration into the CPR.[258]

15–099   The current rules—examined in Chapters 17 and 18—are merely the latest episode in the long history of the remedies and procedures which provide the practical processes for the often small scale, day-to-day vindication of the rule of law.

---

[253] For a critique of the committee's assumptions, see T. Cornford and M. Sunkin, "The Bowman Report, Access and the Recent Reforms of the Judicial Review Procedure" [2001] P.L. 11.
[254] For further commentary, see M. Fordham, "Judicial Review: The New Rules" [2001] P.L. 4.
[255] See Appendix I.
[256] DCA, CP(R) 10/01 (October 2003).
[257] Civil Procedure (Modification of the Supreme Court Act 1981) Order 2004 (SI 2004/1033), amending Supreme Court Act 1981 ss.29, 31.
[258] See 17–001.

CHAPTER 16

CPR PT 54 CLAIMS FOR JUDICIAL REVIEW

SCOPE

There are several procedures by which the lawfulness of a public author- **16–001** ity's decision may be challenged in the Administrative Court.

- A claim for judicial review under CPR Pt 54.[1]

- A modified CPR Pt 54 procedure in the case of some immigration and asylum decisions.[2]

- An application for the writ of habeas corpus.[3]

- A statutory application to quash specific orders and decisions of Ministers, tribunals and other bodies made under particular statutes and statutory instruments.[4]

- By a complex array of appeals from magistrates, tribunals, Ministers and other decision-making bodies.[5]

- In addition, bodies other than the Administrative Court apply judicial review principles in determining cases—including the county courts dealing with appeals against homelessness decisions of local authorities,[6] and the Upper Tribunal in supervising the determinations of the First-tier Tribunal.[7]

This chapter describes and evaluates the first of these procedures.[8] The **16–002** procedural regime is set out in a "somewhat cumbrous and confusing . . . hierarchy of rules and guidance",[9] comprising: statutory provisions;[10] the

---

[1] Introduced in October 2000 to replace RSC, Ord.53, dealt with in this Chapter.
[2] See 17–004.
[3] See 17–010.
[4] See 17–025.
[5] See 17–036.
[6] See 17–037.
[7] See 1–084, under Supreme Court Act (Senior Courts Act) 1981 s.31A.
[8] For practical guidance, see also: B. Lang (ed.), *Administrative Court: Practice and Procedure* (2006); C. Lewis, *Judicial Remedies in Public Law*, 3rd edn. (2004), Ch.9; M. Supperstone and L. Knapman et al (eds), *Administrative Court Practice Judicial Review* (2002); J. Halford, "Strategy in Judicial Review: Using the Procedure to the Claimant's Advantage" [2006] J.R. 153; A. Lidbetter, "Strategy in Judicial Review for Defendants" [2007] J.R. 99.
[9] *Mount Cook Ltd v Westminster City Council* [2003] EWCA Civ 1346 at [67] (Auld L.J.)
[10] Supreme Court Act (Senior Courts Act) 1981 ss.29, 31 and 43. These provisions were amended on May 1, 2004 by the Civil Procedure (Modification of the Supreme Court Act 1981) Order 2004 (SI 2004/1033), renaming the remedies of mandamus, prohibition and certiorari as mandatory, prohibition and quashing orders respectively. See Appendix D.

Civil Procedure Rules (which are statutory instruments made pursuant to ss.1 and 2 of the Civil Procedure Act 1997);[11] Practice Directions made by the Lord Chief Justice in exercise of his inherent jurisdiction;[12] various Practice Statements; a Pre-Action Protocol on Judicial Review;[13] and Administrative Court Office Notes for Guidance on Applying for Judicial Review.[14] The Practice Directions provide general guidance, but do not have binding effect, and yield to the CPR in the event of a clear conflict between them.[15]

The Administrative Court

16–003 The Administrative Court, created in October 2000 to replace the Crown Office List, is part of the Queen's Bench Division of the High Court. It has jurisdiction over a wide range of matters, several of which fall outside the scope of this book.[16] The Administrative Court sits mainly in London, where it has the regular use of six courtrooms in the Royal Courts of Justice. Most claims for judicial review are now heard by a single judge, though some (notably those in a "criminal cause or matter") continue to be heard by a divisional court of two or occasionally three judges.[17] Hearings

[11] See Appendix G.
[12] See Appendix H. *R. (on the application of Ewing) v Department for Constitutional Affairs* [2006] EWHC 504; [2006] 2 All E.R. 993 at [13].
[13] See Appendix I. This sets out "a code of good practice and contains the steps which parties should generally follow before making a claim for judicial review" (para.5). Failure to comply with the Pre-Action Protocol may result in a successful party's order for costs being reduced, see e.g. *Aegis Group Plc v Inland Revenue Commissioners* [2005] EWHC 1468; [2005] S.T.C. 989. The Pre-action Protocol is reissued from time to time; the version in force at the time of writing is October 2006.
[14] Available from HM Court Service website (*http://www.hmcourts-service.gov.uk/*).
[15] *Mount Cook Ltd* [2003] EWCA Civ 1346 at [68]; *Godwin v Swindon BC* [2001] EWCA Civ 1478; [2002] 1 W.L.R. 997 at [11] (May L.J., "They are, in my view, at best a weak aid to the interpretation of the rules themselves"); *Re C (Legal Aid: Preparation of a Bill of Costs)* [2001] 1 F.L.R. 602 at [21] (Hale L.J.: "the Practice Directions are not made by Statutory Instrument. They are not laid before Parliament or subject to either the negative or positive resolution procedures in Parliament. They go though no democratic process at all, although if approved by the Lord Chancellor he will bear ministerial responsibility for them to Parliament. But there is a difference in principle between delegated legislation which may be scrutinised by Parliament and ministerial executive action. There is no ministerial responsibility for Practice Directions made for the Supreme Court by the Heads of Division. As Professor Jolowicz says 'It is right that the court should retain its power to regulate its own procedure within the limits set by statutory rules, and to fill in gaps left by those rules; it is wrong that it should have power actually to legislate'").
[16] Including vexatious litigant proceedings, applications relating to contempt of court, extradition matters, the Proceeds of Crime Act 2002, appeals (formerly made to the Privy Council) relating to the striking off of health care professionals under the National Health Service Reform and Health Care Professions Act 2002; applications under s.13 of the Coroners Act 1988; appeals from the Law Society Disciplinary Tribunal; and applications relating to parliamentary and local government elections under the Representation of the People Acts. See further Lang (2006).
[17] Supreme Court Act (Senior Courts Act) 1981, ss.19, 66 and 151(4). See Lang (2006), para.1–04.

may also take place in major centres around England. Specific provision is made for the Administrative Court to sit in Wales where a claim for judicial review relates to a devolution issue arising out of the Government of Wales Act 2006 or an issue concerning the National Assembly for Wales, the Welsh Assembly Government, or any Welsh public body (including a Welsh local authority) whether or not it involves a devolution issue.[18] Proceedings in Wales may take place in Welsh.[19]

The judges of the Administrative Court are those Justices of the High **16–004** Court nominated by the Lord Chief Justice to deal with Administrative Court business.[20] Their number has grown from four in 1981 to 37 in 2007. They are mainly judges of the Queen's Bench Division, but also include judges of the Family Division and the Chancery Division. Deputy High Court judges (experienced circuit judges and practitioners appointed to sit on a part-time basis) may also be authorised to deal with Administrative Court matters, though by convention they do not hear cases relating to central government and they have limited powers to hear cases involving the Human Rights Act 1998.[21] The Master of the Administrative Court[22] has no general jurisdiction to make orders in claims for judicial review, except for interim applications (such as orders for expedition or orders and stand out of the list pending determination of a test case).[23]

A Lead Judge of the Administrative Court is appointed by the Lord Chief **16–005** Justice. The nominated judges spend only some of their time on Administrative Court business (typically there are eight single judges and one divisional court sitting, the constitutions changing after periods of three weeks); like other High Court judges they also hear other civil and criminal cases on circuit and in London.[24] These arrangements reflect a compromise: while recognising the need for expert judges in the field of public law, it maintains the English tradition that everyone, including public bodies and office-holders, ought to be subject to justice in the ordinary courts.[25]

The work of the Administrative Court is supported by the legal and **16–006** administrative staff of the Administrative Court Office[26] (part of the Courts Service), under the direction of the Master of the Administrative Court

---

[18] Practice Direction 54, para.3. On devolution issues, see 1–113.

[19] Welsh Language Act 1993 s.22.

[20] Hence the term "nominated judges" to refer to the judges who determine judicial review claims.

[21] Practice Direction 2b para.7A. They may not hear a "claim made in respect of a judicial act" or where there is a claim for a declaration of incompatibility.

[22] An office combined with that of Registrar of Criminal Appeals: Courts and Legal Services Act 1990 s.78.

[23] Practice Direction 2b para.3.1(c).

[24] The Bowman committee reviewing judicial review procedures before the coming into force of the Human Rights Act recommended that it should become a more specialised court with the nominated judges spending a greater proportion of their time on its work (para.23).

[25] A.V Dicey, *Introduction to the Study of the Law of the Constitution*, 10th edn (1959), p.193: a second meaning of the "rule of law" was that "every man, whatever his rank or condition, is subject to the ordinary law of the realm and amenable to the jurisdiction of the ordinary tribunals".

[26] Known as the Crown Office until 2000.

(formally still the Master of the Crown Office) and the Head of the Administrative Court Office. A team of 10 lawyers assist in the management of cases, each one specialising in a range of subject areas. Claims for judicial review received by the Administrative Court Office are examined by one of the lawyers. The lawyer to whom the case is assigned produces a note, summarising the issues (without expressing an opinion on the merits of the claim), drawing the court's attention to relevant authorities (especially unreported ones) and alerting the court to any similar cases that may be pending.[27]

16–007   The Administrative Court provides commendable transparency and accountability for its work though the publication of an annual statement by the Lead Judge, the existence of a "court users' group" which meets at least three times a year "for those who wish to voice their opinions on the running of, or issues relating to the Administrative Court and the Administrative Court Office", a clear system for dealing with complaints by court users about administrative failures and regular newsletters.[28]

CPR PT 54

16–008   Of the various procedures for review,[29] it is the claim for judicial review under CPR Pt 54 that is of prime importance both in terms of the number of claims made and the effect it has had as a stimulus to the development of the principles of administrative law.[30] Although some flexibility now exists, where public law issues are at the heart of a claim, claimants are expected to use the CPR Pt 54 claim form and procedure (a signficantly modified varient of the CPR Pt 8 arrangments for litigation) rather than the general procedure and form for commencing civil proceedings laid down by CPR Pt 7, or the alternative procedure in CPR Pt 8.[31]

16–009   Two main features distinguish the judicial review procedure from these other types of civil claims. First, a claimant may not pursue a claim for judicial review to a full hearing without obtaining the permission (formerly "leave") of the Administrative Court to do so.[32] Secondly, there is a requirement that permission be sought promptly, and in any event within

---

[27] *R. v Lord Chancellor's Department Ex p. O'Toole* [1998] C.O.D. 269 (claimants have no right at common law to disclosure of such notes, though any unreported judgment mentioned in the note should be disclosed to the claimant to avoid apparent unfairness).

[28] See *http://www.courtservice.gov.uk.*

[29] See 16–044.

[30] See 1–097.

[31] See 3–00.

[32] Since the coming into force of the CPR, the differences between CPR Pt 54 and other proceedings are less pronounced as judges in all cases now have responsibility to manage the conduct of the litigation more closely than once was the case. See 3–103 and see M. Fordham, "Judicial review: the new rules" [2001] P.L. 4 and T. Cornford and M. Sunkin, "The Bowman Report, Access and the Recent Reforms of the Judicial Review Procedure" [2001] P.L. 11.

three months from the date when grounds for the claim first arose.[33] The time periods for commencing civil claims in tort and breach of contract, laid down in the Limitation Act 1980, are typically six years from the date on which the cause of action arose.

Between 1978 (when judicial review procedures were modernised) and **16–010** October 2000 (when CPR Pt 54 came into force) judicial review litigation was regulated by Order 53 of the Rules of the Supreme Court. Today, reference to cases about the RSC Ord.53 procedure must therefore be made with caution.[34] The importance now attached to the "overriding objective" of the CPR may require re-evaluation of practices and principles adopted in the past. So too with the Human Rights Act 1998: it should not be assumed that approaches adopted to the judicial review process prior to October 2000 are always complient with Convention rights. As a public authority, the Administrative Court must itself avoid acting in a way which is inconsistent with Convention rights.[35] The CPR must be read and given effect in a manner which is compatible with Convention rights so far as it is possible to do so.[36]

The overriding objective

CPR Pt 54 must be interpreted and applied in the light of the CPR's **16–011** "overriding objective of enabling the court to deal with cases justly".[37] This "provides a compass to guide courts and litigants and legal advisers as to their general course".[38] More particularly[39]:

"Dealing with a case justly includes, so far as practicable—

   (a) ensuring that the parties are on an equal footing;
   (b) saving expense;
   (c) dealing with the case in ways which are proportionate—

       (i) to the amount of money involved;
       (ii) to the importance of the case;

---

[33] See 16–050.
[34] *Biguzzi v Rank Leisure Plc* [1999] 1 W.L.R. 1926 (Lord Woolf M.R.: "The whole purpose of making the CPR a self-contained code was to send the message that it now generally applies. Earlier authorities are no longer generally of any relevance once the CPR applies"); this does not mean that in all cases the old authorities "should be completely thrown overboard" (*UCB Corporate Services Ltd (formerly UCB Bank Plc) v Halifax (SW) Ltd (Striking Out: Breach of Rules and Orders)* [1999] C.P.L.R. 691, Ward L.J.) but it does mean that pre-CPR authorities must always be re-evaluated in the light of the overriding objective.
[35] Human Rights Act 1998 s.6.
[36] Human Rights Act 1998 s.3. If it is impossible to give the CPR a compatible interpretation they will be ultra vires unless the incompatibility is specifically required by the Civil Procedure Act 1997 (*General Mediterranean Holdings SA v Patel* [2000] 1 W.L.R. 272). See generally, J. Jacob, *Civil Litigation in the Age of Human Rights* (2007).
[37] CPR r.1.1(1).
[38] *Access to Justice: Final Report*, p.275.
[39] CPR r.1.1(2).

(iii) to the complexity of the issues; and

(iv) to the financial position of each party;

(d) ensuring that it is dealt with expeditiously and fairly; and

(e) allotting to it an appropriate share of the court's resources, while taking into account the need to allot the resources to other cases."

16–012 CPR Pt 3 confers on the court general powers of case management. Except where the CPR provide otherwise, the court may (among other things) "extend or shorten the time for compliance with any rule, practice direction or court order (even if an application for extension is made after the time for compliance has expired)",[40] "exclude an issue from consideration" and "take any other step or make any other order for the purpose of managing the case and furthering the overriding objective". Generally, purely technical breaches of the rules should not hinder access to the court,[41] though other sanctions (such as costs) may be imposed. The overriding objective requires that parties be dealt with "on an even footing".[42] Equality of arms is also an aspect of ECHR Art.6(1).[43]

The procedural stages

16–013 A claim for judicia review may encompass several stages, each of which will be examined below.

- The exhaustion of other remedies and use of ADR.

- Gathering of information, including use of the Freedom of Information Act 2000 and Data Protection Act 1998.

[40] See, e.g. *R. v Vale of Glamorgan Council Ex p. Clements*, *The Times*, August 22, 2000 (CA allowed a renewed application for permission for judicial review in exceptional circumstances, even though the application for permission to appeal had not been made within the prescribed seven day period and the documents normally expected to accompany the application had not been lodged with the court).

[41] See, e.g. *Cala Homes (South) Ltd v Chichester DC (Time Limits)* [2000] C.P.Rep. 28 (claimant mistakenly filed a claim form in the wrong court office and used the wrong claim form but court declined to strike out the claim); *R. v Secretary of State for the Environment, Transport and the Regions Ex p. National Farmers Union*, November 24, 1999 (unreported, Keene J.) (NFU applied for judicial review rather than made a statutory application to quash but the court allowed the claim to be amended and to proceed).

[42] See, e.g. *Maltez v Lewis* (1999) 96(21) L.S.G. 39 (the overriding objective could not interfere with a party's right to choose a legal representative, but: "if it were to transpire, for instance, that one party could afford very experienced, large and expensive solicitors, whereas the other party could only afford a small and relatively inexperienced firm, then the court can—indeed, I suggest the court should—make orders to ensure that the level playing field envisaged by r.1(2)(a) is, so far as possible, achieved. It might be appropriate, for instance, when ordering disclosure, to give the party with the smaller firm of solicitors more time than the party with the larger firm. On preparing bundles, it might be right to direct the party instructing the larger firm to take on the duty of preparing and copying bundles" (Neuberger J.).

[43] See, 6–048, 7–119, 10–077; see, e.g. *Dombo Beheer BV v Netherlands* (1994) 18 E.H.R.R. 213 (each party in a civil proceeding must have a reasonable opportunity to present his case under conditions which do not disadvantage him in relation to his opponent).

- The exchange of letters between the would-be claimant and defendant before starting the claim.

- The preparation of the claim form.

- The application for permission to make a claim for judicial review and any appeal against the refusal of permission.

- An interlocutory stage.

- The hearing of the substantive claim;

- Finally, any appeal against the substantive claim.

EXHAUSTION OF OTHER REMEDIES AND ADR

In numerous cases in recent decades, the Administrative Court and its **16–014** precursor have made plain that (in the absense of exceptional circumstances) permission to proceed with a judicial review claim will be refused where a claimant has failed to exhaust other possible remedies.[44] A claiment will not be required to resort to some other procedure if that other procedure is "less satisfactory" or otherwise inappropriate.[45] In each case the question is whether the court should exericise its discretion; "it would be both foolish and impossible to seek to anticipate" all the factors that may properly influence the court's discretion.[46]

Added impetetus to the older case law on the need to exhaust alternative **16–015** remedies has been given by the growing recognition of the importance of alternative dispute resoluton (ADR) in civil litigation generally and, more recently, the Ministry of Justice's policy on "proportionate dispute resolution".[47]

Alternative (or substitute) remedies

Claimants are refused permission to proceed with judicial review where the **16–016** court forms the view that some other form of legal proceedings or avenue of challenge is available and should be used. Questions as to whether a

[44] Pre-Action Protocol for Judicial Review (October 2006), para.2 ("Judicial review may be used where there is no right of appeal or where all avenues of appeal have been exhausted"); *R. (on the application of Sivasubramaniam) v Wandsworth County Court* [2002] EWCA Civ 1738; [2003] 1 W.L.R. 475. For surveys of the voluminous case law, see M. Fordham, *Judicial Review Handbook*, 4th edn (2004), pp.699–720 and C. Lewis, *Judicial Remedies in Public Law*, 3rd edn (2004), paras 11–042—11–074. See also R. Moules, "The exhaustion of alternative remedies: re-emphasising the courts' discretion" [2005] J.R. 350.
[45] *R. v Hillingdon LBC Ex p. Royco Homes Ltd* [1974] Q.B. 720; *R. v Chief Immigration Officer Ex p. Kharrazi* [1980] W.L.R. 1396 (not practicable to use the machinery under s.13 Immigration Act 1971 as claimant would have to return to Iran to exercise his right of appeal and would be caught in a war); *cf. R. (on the application of George) v General Medical Council* [2003] EWHC 1124; [2004] Lloyd's Rep. Med. 33.
[46] *R. v Hereford Magistrates Court Ex p. Rowlands* [1998] Q.B. 110.
[47] See 1–057.

claimant should have used another type of redress process should arise on the application for permission and not at or after the substantive hearing of the judicial review claim. Once the court has heard arguments on the grounds of review, there is little purpose in requiring the parties to resort to some other remedy;[48] indeed, to do so may be contrary to the overriding objective of the CPR. But a failure to pursue other remedies may influence how the court exercises its discretion to award costs.[49]

16–017   The most obvious type of substitute remedy is an avenue of appeal or review created by statute.[50] A range of other forms of challenge have also been held to be acceptable substitutes for judicial review.[51] There are various reasons why legislation may create an avenue of redress into which the Administrative Court may seek to divert challenges, including: a desire to make access to justice available more locally; a wish to prevent the Administrative Court becoming overburdened with cases; the fact that a tribunal or other specialist body may have more expertise in the subject of the claim than the Administrative Court; and that substitutes for judicial review may be provided at lesser cost.

Avenues of appeal or review created by statute

16–018 The most straightforward substitute remedy is where legislation provides an appeal. Judicial review is essentially a mechanism to be used where there is no statutory right of appeal. In almost all cases the Administrative Court will regard a statutory appeal, whether to a court or a tribunal, as a proper substitute for judicial review,[52] though exceptional circumstances may dictate otherwise.[53]

16–019   There are numerous examples of appeal and review systems other than judicial review.[54] The new tribunal system created by the Tribunals, Courts and Enforcement Act 2007 creates one such appeal route: first to the First-tier Tribunal, from there to the Upper Tribunal, and then to the Court of Appeal.[55] There is an appeal from decisions of local authorities relating to homelessness to the county courts.[56] In many circumstances, an appeal lies from decisions of magistrates' courts either to the Crown Court or ("by

[48] R. v Chief Constable of Merseyside Police Ex p. Calveley [1986] 1 Q.B. 424.
[49] See 16–087.
[50] See 16–018.
[51] See 16–021.
[52] R. v Birmingham City Council Ex p. Ferrero Ltd [1993] 1 All E.R. 530; Farley v Secretary of State for Work and Pensions (No.2) [2006] UKHL 31; [2006] 1 W.L.R. 1817.
[53] R. v Secretary of State for the Home Department Ex p. Capti-Mehmet [1997] C.O.D. 61 (error or incompetence of the claimant's legal representatives will not of itself constitute an exceptional circumstance).
[54] It is arguable that in some contexts appeals (or indeed, judicial review) limited to issues of law are insufficient: this has been the subject of criticisms over several years by the House of Lords Constitution Committee, which has taken the view that "appeals should provide an opportunity for the regulated to have their objections reviewed on the merits of the case": The Regulatory State: Ensuring its Accountability. HL Paper No.68 (Session 2004/05) Ch.11.
[55] See 1–090.
[56] Housing Act 1996; see 17–045.

way of case stated") to the Administrative Court.[57] Some appeals may enable the appellate tribunal or court to reconsider the merits of the case, but often appeals are limited to "points of law", which encompasses all the grounds of judicial review.

The powers of a tribunal or court hearing an appeal will often be at least **16–020** as extensive as those in judicial review (and perhaps greater). In most situations there can be no constitutional or practical objection to the Administrative Court routinely refusing permission to proceed with a judicial review claim where there is a statutory appeal to a tribunal[58] or a court.[59] To hold otherwise would risk subverting Parliament's intention in creating such appeals.[60] The one appeal system the Administrative Court was called upon to supervise frequently was refusals of permission to appeal from Immigration Adjudicators to the Immigration Appeal Tribunal; this appellate system has now been superceded.[61] The desirability of an authoritative ruling on a point of law may point towards judicial review being the appropriate remedy in some contexts, if the appeal or review procedure is incapable of making such a ruling.[62]

Other avenues of legal challenge

In addition to statutory appeals, the Administrative Court has regarded a **16–021** range of other grievance redressing mechanisms as substitutes for judicial review. These include: a statutory complaints procedure;[63] an express right to give notice of objection to a government Minister proposing to impose a penalty;[64] the possibility of bringing a private prosecution,[65] remedies under the Public Supply Contracts Regulations 1995 and other public

---

[57] See 1–009.
[58] *R. v Secretary of State for the Home Department Ex p. Swati* [1986] 1 W.L.R. 722; *R. v Ministry of Defence Ex p. Sweeney* [1999] C.O.D. 122; *R. (on the application of M) v Bromley LBC* [2002] EWCA Civ 1113; [2002] 2 F.L.R. 802 (Care Standards Tribunal established under the Protection of Children Act 1999).
[59] *R. v Mansfield DC Ex p. Ashfield Nominees Ltd* [1999] E.H.L.R. 290 (appeal to county court against repairs notices issued under the Housing Act 1985); *R. v Merton LBC Ex p. Sembi* (2000) 32 H.L.R. 439 (appeal to county court under Housing Act 1996); *R. v Blackpool BC Ex p. Red Cab Taxis Ltd* [1994] R.T.R. 402 (private hire vehicles licensing, appeal to justices). Cf. *R. v Hereford Magistrates Court Ex p. Rowlands* [1998] Q.B. 110 (stressing that it was always a question of discretion whether to allow judicial review where a defendant in criminal proceedings had not pursued an appeal to the Crown Court).
[60] See, e.g. *R. (on the application of Sivasubramaniam) v Wandsworth County Court* [2002] EWCA Civ 1738, [2003] 1 W.L.R. 475.
[61] See 1–094; on the new system, see 17–004.
[62] *Falmouth and Truro Port HA v South West Water Ltd* [2001] Q.B. 445.
[63] *R. v East Sussex CC Ex p. W (A Minor)* [1998] 2 F.L.R. 1082 (care order and Children Act 1989).
[64] *R. (on the application of Balbo B&C Auto Transporti Internazionali) v Secretary of State for the Home Department* [2001] EWHC Admin 195; [2001] 1 W.L.R. 1556 (relating to a civil penalty issued under the Immigration and Asylum Act 1999 s.35 on lorry owner), considered in *International Transport Roth GmbH v Secretary of State for the Home Department* [2002] EWCA Civ 158; [2003] Q.B. 728.
[65] *R. v DPP Ex p. Camelot Group Plc* (1998) 10 Admin.L.R. 93; *cf. R. v Commissioner of Police for the Metropolis Ex p. Blackburn* [1968] 2 Q.B. 118.

procurement regulations;[66] proceedings in the Chancery Division questioning the compatibility of a statutory provision with European Community law;[67] and a request to a Secretary of State to exercise default powers (conferred under various Acts of Parliament) to intervene to prevent the unreasonable exercise of power by a public authority.[68] In this category of case, a more searching inquiry may be needed than in the case of a straightforward statutory appeal; the question ought to be whether the substitute for judicial review adequately protects the rights and interests of the claimant. The other body may for example lack the power to deal with the issue.[69] If the claimant is seeking to raise questions about the lawfulness of a broad question of policy, the Adminsitrative Court may be a more appropriate forum than a criminal court.[70] The other procedure may be less expeditious and if a matter is urgent the court may allow the application to proceed.[71] Among the factors to be considered are "the comparative speed, expense and finality of the alternative processes, the need and scope for fact finding, the desirability of an authoritative ruling on any point of law arising, and (perhaps) the apparent strength of the claimant's substantive challenge".[72] Recourse to one of the ombudsmen[73] may also, in some cases, provide a substitute for judicial review. As discussed in Chapter 1, the potential problem here is that the ombudsmen may also regard judicial review as appropriate and refuse to conduct an inquiry into what otherwise might be maladministration causing injustice.[74]

[66] *Cookson & Clegg Ltd v Ministry of Defence* [2005] EWHC 38; [2005] Eu. L.R. 517; S.H. Bailey, "Judicial Review and the Public Procurement Regulations" (2005) 6 P.P.L.R. 291. Note that each of the various public procurement regulations has their own provision for enforcement.

[67] *Aegis Group Plc v Inland Revenue Commissioners* [2005] EWHC 1468; [2005] S.T.C. 989.

[68] See, e.g. *R (on the application of Baker) v Devon County Council* [1995] 1 All E.R. 73 at 92. *cf. R. v Inner London Education Authority Ex p. Ali* (1990) 2 Admin. L.R. 822 (the fact that the Secretary of State had power to give directions under the Education Act 1944 s.99, and can do so on complaint, creates no inference that the ordinary jurisdiction of the court is ousted, though it is very relevant to the exercise of the court's discretion). For examples of default powers, see Education Act 1996 Pt 9.

[69] See, e.g. *Leech v Deputy Governor of Parkhurst Prison* [1988] A.C. 533 (at that time the Home Secretary lacked the power to remove a disciplinary finding in relation to a prisoner from his record); *Smith v North Eastern Derbyshire Primary Care Trust* [2006] EWCA Civ 1291; [2006] 1 W.L.R. 3315 (a patients' forum, a body established under the National Health Service Reform and Health Care Professions Act 2002 s.15 lacked the power to require a primary care trust to reverse a decision).

[70] *R. (on the application of A) v South Yorkshire Police* [2007] EWHC 1261 (Admin) (judicial review preferable to raising issues on an application to the Youth Court to dismiss or stay the criminal proceedings on the ground that they are an abuse of the process).

[71] *Ex p. Royco Homes Ltd* [1974] Q.B. 720.

[72] *Falmouth and Truro Port HA v South West Water Ltd* [2001] Q.B. 445.

[73] The Parliamentary Commissioner for Administration, the Commission for Local Administration, the Health Services Commissioner and (in Wales) Public Services Ombudsman for Wales: see 1–066.

[74] See 1–083.

Alternative Dispute Resolution (ADR)[75]

An important aspect of the new approach to civil litigation embraced by **16–022** the CPR is that all courts must futher the overriding objective by "actively managing cases". This includes "encouraging the parties to use an alternative dispute resolution procedure if the court considers that appropriate and facilitating the use of such procedure".[76] The requirement for practitioners to use—or at least consider the use of—ADR instead of resorting too early to judicial review claims was set down by the Court of Appeal in *Cowl v Plymouth CC.*[77] The Court of Appeal spoke of "the paramount importance of avoiding litigation whereever possible" in disputes with public authorities and said that the LSC should co-operate with the Administrative Court "to scrutinise extremely carefully" judicial review claims so as to ensure that parties tried "to resolve the dispute with the minimum involvement of the courts". The Pre-action Protocol on Judicial Review identifies "some of the options" as: discussion and negotiaton; ombudsmen; early neutral evaluation; and mediation.[78] To this should be added the use of internal complaints procedures and an offer of a rehearing by the original decision-maker.[79] All of these techniques are encouraged by the Ministry of Justice's policy of "proportionate dispute resolution" (which extends beyond ADR to include, among other things, steps to avoid disputes arising in the first place).[80] In encouraging ADR, it needs to be "recognised that no party can or should be forced to mediate or enter into any form of ADR"[81]—an important respect in which ADR differs from the court's approach to insisting upon the use of formal rights of appeal in place of judicial review.

In the years immediately following *Cowl* there has been relatively slow **16–023** progress towards establishing a principled basis on which ADR can be used in public law disputes (clearly not all disputes are suitable for ADR),[82] establishing a suitable funding regime to pay for ADR and making practical arrangements for its delivery. A particular problem relates to timing. The

---

[75] See also 1–065.
[76] CPR r.1.4(2)(d).
[77] [2001] EWCA Civ 1935; [2002] 1 W.L.R. 803; see A. Le Sueur, "How to Resolve Disputes with Public Authorities" [2002] P.L. 203; S. Boyron, "The Rise of Mediation in Administrative Law Disputes: Experiences from England, France and Germany" [2006] P.L. 320.
[78] Para 3.2 (October 2006 issue). A list of agencies offering mediation and other services can be found on the Community Legal Service Direct website (*http://www.clsdirect.org.uk*). The Public Law Project, funded by the Nuffield Foundation, is carrying out a study of mediation and judicial review in 2007.
[79] *R. v London Beth Din Ex p. Bloom* [1998] C.O.D. 131.
[80] See 1–057.
[81] Pre-action Protocol for Judicial Review (October 2006), para.34. If however a party unreasonably refuses to engage in mediation, the court may subsequently refuse to make a costs order in its favour, see e.g. *Dunnett v Railtrack Plc* [2002] EWHC 9020 (Costs), available at *http://www.bailii.org*.
[82] For example, where important legal principles are at stake or it is necessary to establish a precedent; *cf.* M. Supperstone, D. Stilitz and C. Sheldon, "ADR in Public Law" [2006] P.L. 299.

fact that a claimant has been pursing alternative remedies or using ADR does not, as the rules now stand, operate to suspend the requirement that claims for judicial review are to be made promptly and in any event within three months. It may therefore be prudent to commence a claim and then stay proceedings pending the outcome of the other remedy—a precaution that somewhat undermines the policy goal of saving cost.

ECHR Arts 6(1) and 13

16–024 In deciding whether to steer a would-be claimant away from judicial review, the court needs now to consider ECHR Art.6(1) which, in relation to "civil rights and obligations or of any criminal charge", guarantees a right to "a fair and public hearing within a reasonable time by an independent and impartial tribunal established by law" and which implicitly protects the right of access to a court.[83] Not all claims for judicial review raise "civil rights or obligation", or a criminal charge, but where they do weight needs to be given protecting access to a court. Where other Convention rights are in issue, the court should attach important to the need for an "effective remedy".[84]

Exchange of letters before claim

16–025 As in other types of litigation, a claimant who proposes to seek permission to make a judicial review claim is generally expected to give full notice in writing to the defendant before doing so.[85] The purpose of the letter is "is to identify the issues in dispute and establish whether litigation can be avoided".[86] The public authority is exected to respond in writing within 14 days of a letter before claim, using a standard format letter. Interested parties should be sent copies of both letters.[87] Compliance with the good practices set out in the Pre-Action Protocol for Judicial Review does not affect the requirement that permission be sought promptly and in any event within three months.[88]

GATHERING EVIDENCE AND INFORMATION

16–026 Although it is often said that claims for judicial review do not (or should not) deal with matters of fact, information in the hands of a public authority is often vital to establishing whether a decision is wrong in law—

[83] See 6–048, 7–119.
[84] See 13–010.
[85] Except in urgent cases: see Pre-action Protocol, para.6.
[86] PD58, para.8. A standard form letter is provided, which claimants "should normally use": Pre-action Protocol.
[87] See 2–063.
[88] See 16–050. R. (on the application of McCallion) v Kennet DC [2001] EWHC Admin 575; [2002] P.L.C.R. 9.

for instance: that an irrelevant consideration was taken into account or a relevant consideration was not taken into account;[89] or that reasoning processes were so illogical as to amount to irrationality.[90] Where breach of a Convention right is in issue, the court's engagement with the factual background of the case will often be even more intensive than under ordinary domestic review and the court may be required to make findings of fact (not merely assess whether the public authority made reasonable findings of fact).[91] Review on the basis of proportionality requires the court to assess evidence of impact and alternative ways of achieving the public authority's policy goals.[92] The absence in English law of a general duty under common law to give reasons for decisions does not assist the claimant.[93] Once a claim for judicial review is afoot, the defendant public authority is expected to proceed with "all the cards face upwards on the table"[94] and the court may order disclosure.[95] Before that point, claimants may consider exercising statutory rights to rights of access to information, an overview of which we provide in the following paragraphs.

Freedom of Information Act 2000

The Freedom of Information Act 2000 introduced a statutory regime for **16–027** obtaining information from public authorities.[96] Section 1 provides that "Any person making a request for information to a public authority is entitled—(a) to be informed in writing by the public authority whether it holds information of the description specified in the request, and (b) if that is the case, to have that information communicated to him". Public authorities have a duty "to provide advice and assistance, so far as it would be reasonable to expect the authority to do so, to persons who propose to make, or have made, requests for information to it".[97]

"Public authority" for the purposes of the 2000 Act has a somewhat **16–028** different meaning than it does in relation to claims for judicial review and the Human Rights Act 1998.[98] Rather than stipulate a test, the 2000 Act simply lists those office-holders and bodies that constitute a "public authority".[99] Public authorities are required to comply with requests for information "promptly and in any event not later than the twentieth

---

[89] See 5–110.
[90] See 11–036.
[91] See 11–079.
[92] See 11–079.
[93] See 7–087.
[94] R. v Lancashire CC Ex p. Huddleston [1986] 2 All E.R. 941 at 945.
[95] See 16–065.
[96] For an assessment, see R. Austin, "The Freedom of Information Act 2000—A Sheep in Wolf's Clothes?", Ch.16 in J. Jowell and D. Oliver, The Changing Constitution, 6th edn (2007).
[97] Freedom of Information Act 2000 s.16.
[98] See Ch.3.
[99] Freedom of Information Act 2000 s.3 and Sch.1 (as amended by Order from time to time).

working day following the date of receipt".[100] A public authority may refuse to comply if the cost of obtaining the information would exceed a stipulated limit (at the time of writing, £600 for central government and Parliament; £450 for other public authorities.). If a request under the 2000 Act is not complied with, an application may be made to the Information Commissioner who will adjudicate on the matter. An appeal from the Information Commissioner lies to the Information Tribunal.

16–029   The right to obtain information is subject to three main kinds of exemptions. First, where a public authority is not listed in Sch.1 to the Act (such as the Security Service and the Secret Intelligence Service), any information kept by that body is wholly outside the statutory right to request information. Secondly, the 2000 Act bars access to information by exempting from disclosure whole categories of information or record, such as: information accessible to applicant by other means; information intended for future publication; information supplied by, or relating to, bodies dealing with security matters; other information required for the purpose of safeguarding national security. Thirdly, the Act creates "contents-based" exemptions in relation to which the public authority must assess each item of information requested and apply a public interest test by assessing whether disclosure "would, or would be likely to, prejudice" the specified interests in question, which include: defence; international relations; relations between any administration in the United Kingdom and any other such administration; the economy; information relating to criminal investigations and proceedings conducted by public authorities.

Environmental Information Regulations 2004

16–030   European Union Council Directive 2003/4/EC on public access to environmental information required Member States to legislate to provide rights of access in this field. In England and Wales, the relevant legislation is the Environmental Information Regulations 2004 (SI 2004/3391) (EIR). Public authorities covered by the Freedom of Information Act 2000 are subject to the EIR, but regulations also extend further to cover "any other body or other person, that carries out functions of public administration" and any other body or other person, "that is under the control" of a public authority and "(i) has public responsibilities relating to the environment; (ii) exercises functions of a public nature relating to the environment; or (iii) provides public services relating to the environment".[101] There are a number of exemptions and limits on the right to information under the EIR.

[100] Freedom of Information Act 2000 s.10.
[101] SI 2004/3391 reg.2(2).

Access requests under the Data Protection Act 1998

The Data Protection Act 1998 (which came into force in March 2000) **16–031** regulates the processing of information about individuals.[102] Sections 7–9 create a right for a "data subject" (or his authorised agent) to request a copy of certain kinds of data held by any "data controller" (which may be a public or private sector body or person); the 1998 Act binds the Crown. This is known as a "data subject access request". A data controller may charge a fee of up to £10. A response must be made promptly and in any event within 40 working days, describing the personal data held, the purposes for which they are being processed, and those to whom they are or may be disclosed. The data subject is entitled to have communicated to him in an intelligible form the information constituting any personal data of which he is the data subject (generally as a copy of the information in permanent form) and any information available to the data controller as to the source of those data.

The data in respect of which a subject access request may be made can be **16–032** a computerised record or manual data in a paper-based filing system. "Data" means information "being processed by means of equipment operating automatically in response to instructions given for that purpose" or "is recorded with the intention that it should be processed by means of such equipment" or "is recorded as part of a relevant filing system or with the intention that it should form part of a relevant filing system"[103] or "forms part of an accessible record"[104] (which means a "health record",[105] an "educational record",[106] or an "an accessible public record as defined by Schedule 12", in relation to which the general rules governing subject access requests are modified).[107] Expressions of opinion and intention fall within the definition of data.

Certain data are party or wholly exempt from subject access requests by **16–033** Pt 4 of the Act, including data processed in relation to: national security; crime and taxation; information as to the physical or mental health or condition of the data subject; certain regulatory activities; literature, journalism and art; research, history and statistics; information available to the public by or under enactment; domestic purposes; and miscellaneous matters set out in Sch.7 to the Act.

---

[102] The 1998 Act gives effect to EC Directive 95/46/EC; it repeals the Data Protection Act 1984. See also Access to Medical Reports Act 1988.
[103] Freedom of Information Act 2000 s.1(1).
[104] Freedom of Information Act 2000 s.68.
[105] Freedom of Information Act 2000 s.68(2); and Data Protection (Subject Access Modification)(Health) Order 2000 (SI 2000/413).
[106] Freedom of Information Act 2000 Sch.11; Data Protection (Subject Access Modification) (Education) Order 2000 (SI 2000/414).
[107] Sch.12 (which deals with housing and social services records); Data Protection (Subject Access Modification) (Social Work) Order 2000 (SI 2000/415).

16–034   If a data controller unlawfully fails to comply with a data subject access request, a court may make an order requiring compliance.[108] County courts and the High Court have jurisdiction.[109] Where the data controller is a public authority and the issue arises in a public law context, a claim for judicial review will normally be appropriate.[110]

PREPARING THE CLAIM FORM

16–035 A claim for judicial review is commenced by serving claim form N461 on the defendant and any interested parties and filing it at the Administrative Court Office,[111] along with notice of issue of a Community Legal Service Order funding certificate (if appropriate), witness statements[112] and the prescribed fee. The claim form acts as both the basis for seeking permission to proceed[113] and, if permission is granted, the basis on which the claimant's case will be put at the full hearing of the claim.[114] Clearly the claim form is a document of great importance in the conduct of the litigation.

16–036   The claim form must identify and give details[115] of the decision, etc. which is challenged, set out a detailed statement of the grounds for bring the review, and a statement of the facts relied upon. There is an obligation on the claimant to set out fully and fairly all material facts as he knows them or ought to have known them following inquiries.[116] If relevant, an application to extend the time limit for filing the claim form may be made.[117] The claim form must also set out the remedies sought including

[108] Freedom of Information Act 2000 s.7(9);
[109] Freedom of Information Act 2000 s.15(1).
[110] In *R. (on the application of Lord) v Secretary of State for the Home Department* [2003] EWHC 2073 Munby J. ordered disclosure, in full and without redactions, of reports prepared by the Prison Service in relation to a decision to refuse to reclassify the claimant from Category A to B.
[111] CPR rr.8.2, 54.6, PD 54, para.5.6. See Appendix J. On filing a document by fax, see CPR 5PD.6. The postal address is: The Administrative Court Office, Room C315, Royal Courts of Justice, Strand, London WC2A 2LL.
[112] Witness statements must comply with CPR Pts 22 and 32. Generally the claimant and the claimant's solicitor will both make witness statements. The claimant may explain the importance and impact of the defendant's action or inaction. The solicitor's statement may explain what steps have been taken to resolve the dispute.
[113] See 16–041.
[114] See 17–072.
[115] "There is good reason why all this information is required and why, although no doubt prolixity is to be discouraged, it is important that the claimant does actually provide, properly particularised, the 'detail' called for by Form N461": *R (on the application of W) v Essex CC* [2004] EWHC 2027 (ADMIN), [2004] All ER (D) 103 (Aug), [35] (Munby J.).
[116] *R. v Lloyd's of London Ex p. Briggs* [1993] 1 Lloyd's Rep. 176. There the obligation was said to arise because (following the practice of the time) applications for leave were made ex parte. Under the CPR, defendants and interested parties now have the right through their acknowledgment of service to put to the court a summary of their reasons for opposing the grant of permission.
[117] See 16–055.

any interim remedies. It should also indicate that the pre-action protocol has been complied with or reasons for non-compliance.[118]The claim must be verified by a statement of truth.[119] If a protective costs order is sought (limiting liability to pay the defendant's legal costs in the event of the claim failing),[120] the claimant should normally do so at the permission stage.[121]

The claim form must be accompanied by: all relevant written evidence in **16–037** support of the claim (and any extension of time that is sought); a copy of the order that the claimant challenges; where the decision being challenged is that of a court or tribunal, an approved copy of their reasons; copies of any documents on which the claimant proposes to rely; copies of any relevant legislation; and a list of essential documents for advance reading by the court (with page reference to the passages relied on).

If a claimant seeks to raise an issue or claim a remedy under the Human **16–038** Rights Act 1998,[122] the claim form must additionally:[123] give precise details of the Convention right which it is alleged has been infringed and details of the alleged infringement; specify the relief sought; state if the relief includes a claim for a declaration of incompatibility under s.4 or damages under s.9(3) of the HRA; and precise details of the legislative provision alleged to be incompatible and details of the alleged incompatibility.

If a "devolution issue" is at stake,[124] the claim form must specify that the **16–039** claimant wishes to raise such an issue and identify the relevant provisions of the Government of Wales Act 2006, the Scotland Act 1998 or the Northern Ireland Act 1998 and contain a summary of the facts, circumstances and points of law on the basis of which it is alleged that the devolution issue arises.

If circumstances change, or the basic legal arguments rethought, between **16–040** the time permission is granted and the full hearing, in order to avoid "litigation creep" the claim form should be amended "promptly and properly . . . to keep pace with what may be the rapidly changing dynamics of a case".[125] The guiding principle is that the "court will normally permit such amendments as may be required to ensure that the real dispute between the parties can be adjudicated upon".[126] Permission is required to amend the claim form, and such an application should normally be accompanied by a draft of the proposed amendment. The decision, etc. under challenge must be identified with precision and if in the light of changing circumstance or evidence it changes, the claim form should reflect

---

[118] *Practice Statement (Administrative Court: Listing and Urgent Cases)* [2002] 1 W.L.R. 810.
[119] CPR r.22.1.
[120] On PCOs, see 16–089.
[121] *R. (on the application of Corner House Research) v Secretary of State for Trade and Industry* [2005] EWCA Civ 192; [2005] 1 W.L.R. 2600.
[122] See Ch.13.
[123] PD 16, para.15.
[124] See 1–113.
[125] *R (on the application of W) v Essex CC* [2004] EWHC 2027 (Admin); [2004] All E.R. (D) 103 (Aug) at [39].
[126] W [2004] EWHC 2027 (Admin); [2004] All E.R. (D) 103 (Aug) at [35].

this.[127] Similarly with changes to the legal basis of the challenge. While minor changes may be permitted by the court exercising its inherent jurisdiction, a claimant seeking to rely at the full hearing on a ground other than those for which he was initially given permission must seek permission to do so in advance of the hearing.[128]

PERMISSION

16–041   A requirement that a would-be litigant wishing to challenge the legality of a public authority's decision first obtain the permission (formerly called "leave") of the court has been a feature of judicial review since 1933.[129] Permission must be sought even if a claim is transferred to the Administrative Court having been commenced elsewhere.[130] Permission must also be sought subsequently if a claimant seeks to rely on grounds other than those for which he has been given permission to proceed.[131]

16–042   The permission stage procedure was modified in significant ways in 2000. Previously permission (leave) was determined in most cases solely on the basis of the claimant's case whereas now the defendant (and any interested parties) are able to provide the court with an acknowledgment of service setting out in summary their reasons for contesting the claim before permission is granted or refused.[132] This provides defendants with an early opportuinty to reassess the strength of their case and aims to encourage early settlement of some or all issues. The "summary"required is different from the "detailed grounds for contesting the claim" and the supporting "written evidence" which are required following the grant of permission.[133] Defendants should avoid drafting an elaborate document at this stage. In most cases, all that is necessary is in effect that the defendant copies, for the benefit of the court, the gist of matters in the exchange of correspodence with the claimant.

---

[127] W [2004] EWHC 2027 (Admin); [2004] All E.R. (D) 103 (Avg) at [35].
[128] CPR r.54.15; PD 54, para.11 (notice of seven clear days before the full hearing must be given to the court and all parties).
[129] Now Supreme Court Act (Superior Courts Act) 1981 s.31(3). M. Fordham, "Permission Principles" [2006] J.R. 176.
[130] CPR r.52.4.
[131] CPR r.54.15.
[132] Within 21 days of service on them of the claim form. CPR r.54.8; if permission is granted, the defendant has an opportunity to provide more detailed grounds for resisting the claim: CPR r.54.14.
[133] CPR r.54.14. *Ewing v Office of the Deputy Prime Minister* [2005] EWCA Civ 1583; [2006] 1 W.L.R. 1260 at [43] (Carnwath L.J., offering guidance about the "summary": "If a party's position is sufficiently apparent from the Protocol response, it may be appropriate simply to refer to that letter in the Acknowledgement of Service. In other cases it will be helpful to draw attention to any 'knock-out points' or procedural bars, or the practical or financial consequences for other parties (which may, for example, be relevant to directions for expedition). As the Bowman report advised, it should be possible to do what is required without incurring 'substantial expense at this stage'").

In almost all cases permission is intially determined without a hearing.[134] **16–043**
Brief written reasons for granting or refusing permission are given.[135]
Where an oral hearing takes place, a written judgment may be produced
but there is a general prohibition on the citation of such judgments in later
cases if the reported point is relates merely to whether the claim is
arguable.[136]

An application for permission is a "proceeding" for the purpose of **16–044**
Supreme Court Act (Senior Courts Act) 1981 s.42 regulating the access to
the courts by vexatious litigants, and so a person subject to a civil
proceedings order under s.42 must make a separate prior application for
permission to institute the proceedings.[137]

The purpose of the permission stage

The permission stage proceedings serves a number of purposes. First, it **16–045**
may safeguard public authorities by deterring or eliminating clearly ill-
founded claims without the need for a full hearing of the matter. The
requirement may also prevent administrative action being paralysed by a
pending, but possibly spurious, legal challenge.[138] Secondly, for the Administrative Court, the permission procedure provides a mechanism for the
efficient management of the ever growing judicial review caseload. A large
proportion of claims can be disposed of at the permission stage with the
minimum use of the court's limited resources.[139] By granting permission to
proceed on some but not all grounds of a claim, the court is able to stop
hopeless aspects of a case in their tracks. Thirdly, for the claimant the
permission stage, far from being an impediment to access to justice, may
actually be advantageous since it enables the litigant expeditiously and
cheaply to obtain the views of a High Court judge on the merits of his
application.[140]

---

[134] In urgent cases, claimants may contact the Admin Ct Office by telephone to seek guidance
prior to filing the claim form (telephone 020 7947 6205): see PD54, para.2.4. Urgent cases
include decisions of a Crown Court judge to withdraw bail (*R. (on the application of Allwin) v
Snaresbrook Crown Court* [2005] All E.R. (D) 40 (Apr)). Especially where Convention rights
are in issue, such as where a person's liberty (Art.5), judicial authorities must ensure that
appropriate provision is made for speedy applications regardless of vacation times (*E v
Norway* (1994) 17 E.H.R.R. 30). An application for urgent consideration is referred to a
judge within the timeframe set out in the urgency application form—form N463.
[135] CPR r.54.12(2).
[136] *Practice Direction (Citation of Authorities)* [2001] 1 W.L.R. 1001 at [6]. A court handing
down such a judgment may release it from the general prohibition where the court seeks to
lay down general guidance (see, e.g. *R. (on the application of Pharis) v Secretary of State for
the Home Department* [2004] EWCA Civ 654; [2004] 1 W.L.R. 2590). Judgments given at
the permission stage are in any event of only persuasive authority: *Clark v University of
Lincolnshire and Humberside* [2000] 1 W.L.R. 1988 at [43].
[137] *Ex p. Ewing (No.2)* [1994] 1 W.L.R. 1553; CPR rr.3.3(7), 3.11; *Ewing v Office of the
Deputy Prime Minister* [2005] EWCA Civ 1583; *Bhamjee v Forsdick* [2003] EWCA Civ 1113;
[2004] 1 W.L.R. 88.
[138] *Inland Revenue Commissioners v National Federation of Self-Employed and Small Businesses* [1982] A.C. 617 at 643 (Lord Diplock).
[139] In 2003, 27% of applications were granted; in 2002, 21%.
[140] H. Woolf, *Protection of the Public—A New Challenge* (1990), p.21.

Criteria on which permission is granted or refused

16–046   No comprehensive statement of the criteria for determining applications for permission exists. During the mid-1990s, concerns were expressed that the arrangements then in place led to unacceptable disparities of approach in the ways different nominated judges dealt with applications for leave (now "permission") to commence judicial review claims.[141] In 2000, the Bowman committee recommended that there be a statutory presumption that permission should be given if the claim discloses an arguable case,[142] but this was not implemented. Supreme Court Act 1981 (Senior Courts Act 1981) s.31 and CPR Pt 54 refer expressly to only two grounds on which permission should be refused: where there has been delay in applying to the court;[143] or where the claimant does not have a sufficient interest in the matter to which the claim relates.[144] It has been held, however, that these issues of delay[145] and standing[146] should ordinarily be left to be dealt with at the full hearing; in practice, only in the clearest cases will permission be refused on either of these grounds alone.[147]

16–047   As previously discussed, the failure to use a substitute remedy (especially to exercise a right of appeal) will normally lead to the refusal of permission.[148] The most commonly given reason for refusing permission is that the claim is unarguable. The test ought to be broadly similar to that governing applications for summary judgment in other types of claim, namely that there "no real prospect of succeeding on the claim or issue".[149] If permission is granted, it may be subject to conditions or on some grounds only.[150] If a claimant at the substantive hearing seeks to rely on grounds not previously granted permission, permission must be sought from the trial judge.[151]

16–048   Permission has sometimes been refused on grounds of policy, notably that to subject certain sorts of decision to judicial review challenge would hamper decision-making in some contexts.[152] It has been suggested that it is wrong for such a broad discretion to be exercised at this preliminary stage of the litigation process, if only because important issues of principle may often emerge only late in the litigation process.[153]

[141] L. Bridges *et al.*, *Judicial Review in Perspective*, 2nd edn (1995) and Law Com. 226, p.163 (which called the then arrangements "too much of a lottery").
[142] Bowman, recommendation 33.
[143] Supreme Court Act (Senior Courts Act) 1981 s.31(6),(7) and CPR r.54.5. See 16–050.
[144] Supreme Court Act (Senior Courts Act) 1981 s.31(3). See 2–007.
[145] *Caswell v Dairy Produce Quota Tribunal for England and Wales* [1990] 2 A.C. 738; *cf. R. v Secretary of State for Trade and Industry Ex p. Greenpeace Ltd* [1998] Env. L.R. 415.
[146] *Inland Revenue Commissioners v National Federation of Self-Employed and Small Businesses* [1982] A.C. 617; *R. v Somerset County Council Ex p. Dixon* (1998) 75 P. & C.R. 175.
[147] Le Sueur and Sunkin [1992] P.L. 102, 120–121.
[148] See 16–014.
[149] CPR r.24.2.
[150] CPR r.54.12.
[151] CPR r.54.15.
[152] See e.g. *R. v Hillingdon LBC Ex p. Puhlhofer* [1986] A.C. 484 (homeless persons); *R. v Secretary of State for the Home Department Ex p. Swati* [1986] 1 W.L.R. 772 (genuine visitor cases); *R. v Harrow LBC Ex p. D* [1990] Fam. 133 (child protection register).
[153] See Le Sueur and Sunkin [1992] P.L. 102, 125.

Permission may be granted on only some of a claimant's grounds, and **16–049** refused on the others.[154] At the susequent full hearing of the claim the judge would require a "significant justification before taking a different view", but does have discretion to allow submissions on the grounds refused permission if there is a good reason to do so.[155] Permission may also be refused to pursue a particular remedy, while granting it in relation to other remedies.[156] Permission may be granted in relation to one impugned decision and refused in relation to others.[157]

The timing of the application for permission

An application for permission may be refused if it is made tardily or if it is **16–050** premature.[158] The claim form must be filed (a) "promptly" and (b) in any event not later than three months after the grounds to make the claim first arose.[159] The time limit cannot be extended by agreement between the parties,[160] but the court has a discretion to extend the time limit if there is a good reason to do so.[161] Under the Inquiries Act 2005, judicial review challenges to decisions of a Minster or member of an inquiry panel must be

---

[154] CPR r.54.12(1)(ii).
[155] *Smith v Parole Board* [2003] EWCA Civ 1014; [2003] 1 W.L.R. 2548.
[156] *R. (on the application of Anufrijeva) v Southwark LBC* [2003] EWCA Civ 1406; [2004] Q.B. 1124 the CA held in relation to claims for judicial review seeking damages under the Human Rights Act 1998: ". . . (iii) Before giving permission to apply for judicial review, the Admin Ct judge should require the claimant to explain why it would not be more appropriate to use any available internal complaint procedure or proceed by making a claim to the [Ombudsmen] at least in the first instance. The complaint procedures of the [Ombudsmen] are designed to deal economically (the claimant pays no costs and does not require a lawyer) and expeditiously with claims for compensation for maladministration. (From inquiries the court has made it is apparent that the time scale of resolving complaints compares favourably with that of litigation. (iv) If there is a legitimate claim for other relief, permission should if appropriate be limited to that relief and consideration given to deferring permission for the damages claim, adjourning or staying that claim until use has been made of ADR, whether by a reference to a mediator or an ombudsman or otherwise, or remitting that claim to a district judge or master if it cannot be dismissed summarily on grounds that in any event an award of damages is not required to achieve just satisfaction".
[157] *R. v Hammersmith and Fulham LBC Ex p. CPRE* [2000] Env.L.R. 534.
[158] Supreme Court Act (Senior Courts Act) 1981 s.31(6)–(7); CPR r.54.5; PD 54, para.4.1. Questions of delay may also be relevant to withholding a remedy after the full hearing: see Ch.18.
[159] CPR r.2.8 stipulates that "(2) A period of time expressed as a number of days shall be computed as clear days. (3) In this rule 'clear days' means that in computing the number of days—(a) the day on which the period begins; and (b) if the end of the period is defined by reference to an event, the day on which that event occurs are not included"—but this probably does not apply to the three *month* limit for judicial review: see *Crichton v Wellingborough BC* [2002] EWHC 2988; [2004] Env. L.R. 11 at [56]. "Where 'month' occurs in any judgment, order, direction or other document, it means a calendar month": CPR r.2.10. The Human Rights Act 1998 s.7(5) allows a year for claims in relation to s.6, "but that is subject to any rule imposing a stricter time limit in relation to the procedure in question".
[160] CPR r.54.4.
[161] CPR r.3.1; PD 54, para.5.6(3); see, e.g. *R. (on the application of Harrison) v Flintshire Magistrates Court* [2004] EWHC 2456; (2004) 168 J.P. 653 (permission granted 17 months after conviction when it came to light that the speed limit on a road was 60 mph, not 30 mph, as the police, claimant and magistrates had believed).

brought within 14 days after the day on which the applicant became aware of the decisions unless that time limit is extended by the court.[162]

16–051   Generally "grounds to make the claim" arise when the public authority does an act with legal effect, rather than something preliminary to such an act. So in the context of town and country planning, time runs from when planning permission is actually granted rather than from when a local authority adopts a resolution to grant consent.[163] Where a quashing order is sought in respect of any judgment, order, conviction or other proceedings, time begins to run from the date of that judgment, etc.[164] The subjective experience and state of knowledge of the claimant are not relevant in determining the start date,[165] though those facts may be relevant to whether time should be extended.

16–052   The primary requirement is always one of promptness and permission may be refused on the ground of undue delay even if the claim form is filed within three months.[166] The fact that a breach of a public law duty is a continuing one does not necessarily make it irrelevant to take into account the date at which the breach began in considering any question of delay.[167]

16–053   There is no general legislative formula to guide the court on issues of delay. Factors taken into account include: whether the claimant had prior warning of the decision complained of;[168] and whether there has been a period of time between the taking of the decision impugned and its communication to the claimant.[169]

---

[162] Inquiries Act 2005 s.38.

[163] R. v Hammersmith and Fulham LBC Ex p. Burkett [2002] UKHL 23; [2002] 1 W.L.R. 1593 at [36]–[51]. "In law the resolution is not a juristic act giving rise to rights and obligations. It is not inevitable that it will ripen into an actual grant of planning permission". ([at 42], Lord Steyn). This is not to say that a planning resolution cannot be the subject of a judicial review claim.

[164] PD54, para.4.1.

[165] R. v Department of Transport Ex p. Presvac Engineering Ltd (1992) 4 Admin. L.R. 121.

[166] See, e.g. R. v Secretary of State for Health Ex p. Alcohol Recovery Project [1993] C.O.D. 344; R. v Swale B. C. Ex p. Royal Society for the Protection of Birds (1990) 2 Admin. L.R. 790. The courts have warned of the need for especial promptness in the context of challenges to planning permission; in evaluating this, regard will be had to the fact that in statutory applications to quash the time limit is fixed at six weeks: R. (on the application of McCallion) v Kennet DC [2001] EWHC Admin 575; [2002] P.L.C.R. 9.

[167] R. v Essex CC Ex p. C [1993] C.O.D. 398; and on renewed decisions, see 3–028. It was open to question whether the requirement of promptness provided sufficient legal certainty to be compatible with Convention rights and EU law: see R. v Hammersmith and Fulham LBC Ex p. Burkett [2002] UKHL 23; [2002] 1 W.L.R. 1593 at [53] (Lord Steyn), [59] (Lord Hope); cf. Lam v United Kingdom (App No.41671/89), not cited in Burkett, in which the ECtHR held this argument to be manifestly ill-founded. In Hardy v Pembrokeshire CC (Permission to Appeal) [2006] EWCA Civ 240; [2006] Env. L.R. 28 the CA dismissed the idea that there was any conflict between a requirement of promptness (a term used in the ECHR itself) and the requirements of legal certainty; R. (on the application of Western International Campaign Group) v Hounslow LBC [2003] EWHC 3112; [2004] B.L.G.R. 536.

[168] R. v Secretary of State for Transport Ex p. Presvac Engineering Ltd (1992) 4 Admin.L.R. 121.

[169] R. v Redbridge LBC Ex p. Gurmit Ram [1992] 1 Q.B. 384.

The following have been held to be good reasons for undue delay: time **16–054** taken to obtain legal aid;[170] the importance of the point of law at stake;[171] the pursuit of alternative legal remedies.[172] The following have been held not to be good reasons: tardiness on the part of a claimant's non-legal advisor;[173] time taken pursuing avenues of political redress, such as organising a lobby of Parliament, before applying for permission.[174]

The mere fact that permission is granted does not mean that an **16–055** extension of time for making the application is given; an express application for extension of time must be made.[175] If at the permission stage the court extends time under CPR 3.1(2)(a), the correctness of granting that extension cannot be raised subsequently at the full hearing.[176]

Section 31(6) SCA 1981 requires the court to consider whether the **16–056** granting of relief would "be likely to cause substantial hardship to, or substantially prejudice the rights of, any person or would be detrimental to good administration".[177] In all but the clearest cases, the court will, however, normally postpone consideration of hardship, prejudice and detriment to good administration until the full hearing,[178] though only if the judge granting permission has indicated that this should be so, or if fresh and relevant material relating to delay has arisen in the mean time.[179]

Seeking permission prematurely is almost as common a ground for **16–057** refusing permission as delay.[180] Judicial review may be premature for several reasons: the decision-taker may not yet have determined the facts;[181] or completed assessment of relevant factors[182] (though in cases involving deprivation of liberty the court will be cautious in rejecting a claim as precipitate);[183] or the impugned decision is merely preliminary to a

---

[170] *R. v Stratford on Avon DC Ex p. Jackson* [1985] 1 W.L.R. 1319.
[171] *R. v Secretary of State for the Home Office Ex p. Ruddock* [1987] 1 W.L.R. 1482.
[172] See e.g. *R. v Stratford on Avon DC Ex p. Jackson* [1985] 1 W.L.R. 1319; *R. v Rochdale MBC Ex p. Cromer Ring Mill Ltd* [1982] 2 All E. R. 761; *R. v Secretary of State for the Environment Ex p. West Oxfordshire DC* [1994] C.O.D. 134.
[173] *R. v Tavistock General Commissioners Ex p. Worth* [1985] S.T.C. 564.
[174] See, e.g. *R. v Secretary of State for Health Ex p. Alcohol Recovery Project* [1993] C.O.D. 344; *R. v Redbridge LBC Ex p. G* [1991] C.O.D. 398.
[175] *R. v Lloyd's of London Ex p. Briggs* [1993] 1 Lloyd's Rep. 176. This should be included in the claim form.
[176] *R. v Criminal Injuries Compensation Board Ex p. A* [1999] 2 A.C. 330.
[177] See 18–051.
[178] *Caswell v Dairy Produce Quota Tribunal for England and Wales* [1990] 2 A.C. 738. On remedies and discretion to withhold remedies, see Ch.18.
[179] *R. v Lichfield DC Ex p. Lichfield Securities Ltd* [2001] EWCA Civ 304; (2001) 3 L.G.L.R. 35.
[180] Le Sueur and Sunkin [1992] P.L. 102, 123; and J. Beatson, "Prematurity and Ripeness for Review", in C. Forsyth and I. Hare (eds), *The Golden Metwand and the Crooked Cord* (1998). On situations where the matter is "hypothetical" or "academic", see 3–025 and 18–043.
[181] See, e.g. *R. (on the application of Paul Rackham Ltd) v Swaffham Magistrates Court* [2004] EWHC 1417; [2005] J.P.L. 224; *Draper v British Optical Association* [1938] 1 All E.R. 115.
[182] See, e.g. *R. (on the application of A) v East Sussex CC (No.2)* [2003] EWHC 167; (2003) 6 C.C.L. Rep. 194.
[183] See, e.g. *R. (on the application of Secretary of State for the Home Department) v Mental Health Review Tribunal* [2004] EWHC 2194.

final decision.[184] The court's general approach is to reject challenges made before the conclusion of a hearing in formal proceedings.[185] Importance must also be attached to the fact that judicial review is intended to be an expeditious process and that some decisions taken by public authorities need to be taken quickly.

Challenging the grant of permission

16–058   It is generally no longer possible for a defendant or interested party to seek to overturn the grant of permission to proceed with a claim for judicial review.[186] The rationale for the change is that defendants and interested parties are now routinely able to provide the court with a summary of their reasons for contesting the claim before permission is determined.[187] If through error a defendant has not been served with the claim, or the court wrongly grants permission before the time for serving the acknowledgement of service has elapsed, the court still retains jurisdiction to set aside the grant of permission.[188]

Challenging the refusal of permission

16–059   A claimant who is refused permission without an oral hearing has at that point no right of appeal, but "may request the decision to be reconsidered at a hearing".[189] Studies in the past suggest that a significant proportion of renewed applications for permission are successful.[190]

16–060   The options open to a claimant whose application for permission has been refused after renewal of an oral hearing depends on whether the claim for judicial review is "in a criminal cause or matter". The category of criminal judicial review—typically but not exclusively against magistrates' courts—consists of those proceedings "the outcome of which may be the trial of the applicant and his punishment for an alleged offence by a court claiming jurisdiction to do so".[191] The Court of Appeal has no jurisdiction

---

[184] See, e.g. R. (on the application of St John) v Governor of Brixton Prison [2001] EWHC Admin 543; [2002] Q.B. 613; R. (on the application of The Garden and Leisure Group Ltd) v North Somerset Council [2003] EWHC 1605; [2004] 1 P. & C.R. 39.

[185] See, e.g. R. v Association of Futures Brokers and Dealers Ltd Ex p Mordens Ltd (1991) 3 Admin.L.R. 254 at 263; R. (Hoar-Stevens) v Richmond-upon-Thames Magistrates' Court [2003] EWHC 2660; [2004] Crim. L.R. 474 at [18]; cf. R. (on the application of Widgery Soldiers) v Lord Saville of Newdigate [2001] EWCA Civ 2048; [2002] 1 W.L.R. 1249 at [43] (CA stresses that "the concern of the courts is whether what has happened has resulted in real injustice", giving as examples the unfair refusal of an interpreter or an adjournment).

[186] CPR r.54.13.

[187] See 16–063.

[188] R. (on the application of Webb) v Bristol City Council [2001] EWHC Civ 696.

[189] CPR r.54.12(3)–(5).

[190] M. Sunkin, "What is happening to judicial review?" (1987) 50 M.L.R. 432, 456. In 2005 approx 18% of renewed applications were granted.

[191] Supreme Court Act (Senior Courts Act) 1981 s.18(1)(a); "matters relating to trial on indictment" are not amenable to judicial review: Supreme Court Act (Senior Courts Act) 1981 s.29(3); see 3–009.

to hear appeals in criminal judicial review, so for practical purposes the refusal of permission by the Administrative Court is final and conclusive.[192]

In other, non-criminal, cases a claimant who is unsuccessful following **16–061** the renewed application has three main options. First, to give up. Secondly, to seek permission to appeal to the Court of Appeal against the refusal of permission to proceed. Permission to appeal should be sought from the Administrative Court and, if unsuccessful, thereafter to the Court of Appeal within seven days. In order to prevent unnecessary hearings, the Court of Appeal has jurisdiction to grant permission to proceed with the judicial review not merely permission to appeal.[193] The Court of Appeal may deal with an application for permission to appeal without a hearing. If refused on the papers, "the person seeking permission may request that the decision be reconsidered at a hearing".[194] If it seems likely that the claimant will be able to demonstrate that the claim for judicial review should proceed to a full hearing, the Court of Appeal may hold the hearing on notice, to allow the defendant to be represented, and then to grant permission to proceed with the claim for judicial review rather than merely permission to appeal.[195] (The full hearing of the claim will normally be directed to be heard by the Administrative Court, or the Court of Appeal itself may hear the claim).[196] The possibility of further appeals to the House of Lords against Court of Appeal's determination depends on the order that was made. If the Court of Appeal refuses only permission *to appeal* against the Administrative Court's refusal to grant permission for judicial review, there is no possibility of an appeal to the House of Lords. Such a decision of the Court of Appeal is final and conclusive.[197] If however the Court of Appeal grants permission to appeal, hears the appeal, and goes on to refuse the application for permission *to proceed* with the judicial review, the House of Lords does have jurisdiction to consider a petition for appeal against that decision.[198]

[192] The HL may have jurisdiction to receive a petition for leave to appeal from the Admin Ct's refusal of permission, but the Admin Ct would first have to certify that the case involves a point of law of general public importance ("Red Book", House of Lords Practice Directions and Standing Orders Relating to Criminal Appeals, para.2); it is difficult to image circumstances in which the Admin Ct would refuse permission to proceed with a judicial review claim when such a point of law is raised.
[193] CPR r.52.15(3). There is little point in determining permission to appeal, then hearing the substantive appeal and then remitting the claim back to the Admin Ct for it to be granted permission to proceed with the judicial review claim.
[194] CPR r.52.3(4); PD 52, para.4.13.
[195] *R. (on the application of Werner) v Inland Revenue Commissioners* [2002] EWCA Civ 979; [2002] S.T.C. 1213.
[196] CPR r.52.15(3); PD 52, para.15.3. This will be the preferable course of events were an appeal to the CA seems inevitable, for example because the Admin Ct is bound by a CA precedent that has been called into question.
[197] *R. v Secretary of State for Trade and Industry Ex p. Eastaway* [2000] 1 W.L.R. 2222. Note that *Eastaway* "is only authority for the proposition that when the Court of Appeal has refused permission to appeal in the face of a first instance refusal of permission to seek judicial review the House [of Lords] has no jurisdiction to give leave to appeal" (*R. v Hammersmith and Fulham LBC Ex p. Burkett* [2002] UKHL 23; [2002] 1 W.L.R. 1593 at [12] (Lord Steyn).
[198] *R. v Hammersmith and Fulham LBC Ex p. Burkett* [2002] UKHL 23; [2002] 1 W.L.R. 1593.

16–062   Thirdly, but only in exceptional cases, a claimant may make a fresh application to the Administrative Court for permission to proceed if there has been a significant change of circumstances, or if the claimant has become aware of significant new facts, or if a proposition of law is now maintainable which was not previously open to the claimant.[199] As the refusal of permission is an interlocutory judgment, the doctrine of *res judicata* does not preclude a fresh application, though that may constitute an abuse of process in the absence of new material or circumstances.

INTERLOCUTORY STAGE

16–063   Within seven days of receiving permission to proceed, the claimant must pay the court fee.[200] The defendant and any interested parties who wish to contest the claim must file and serve detailed grounds and any relevant written evidence within 35 days.[201]

Applications by interveners

16–064   There is a growing incidence of interventions in judicial review claims, by campaign groups, public authorities and other bodies concerned about the outcome of a claim.[202] A person wishing to intervene by making written submissions or be represented at the hearing must seek permission to do so at "at the earliest reasonable opportunity".[203]

Disclosure

16–065   Until the 1978 judicial review reforms,[204] the court had no power to order disclosure of documents (formerly "discovery"). RSC, Ord.53 did not introduce an automatic right to disclosure but did allow a party to apply to the court for orders for disclosure of documents. The court was sparing in

---

[199] *R. (on the application of Opoku) v Southwark College Principal* [2002] EWHC 2092; [2003] 1 W.L.R. 234. Note that in *Smith v Parole Board* [2003] EWCA Civ 1014; [2003] 1 W.L.R. 2548, the CA doubted the limitations set out by Lightman J. in relation to opening up grounds, previously refused permission, at the full hearing; but those are not doubts about the jurisdiction of the court to hear fresh applications for permission when the previously the claimant has been refused permission in toto.

[200] £180 (in October 2007).

[201] For details of the other steps to be taken, reference should be made to Appendices H and I below.

[202] See 2–064.

[203] PD 54, para.13.5. The application is made by a letter to the Admin Ct Office (rather than filing an application notice) "identifying the claim, explaining who the applicant is and indicating why and in what form the applicant wants to participate in the hearing"; "If the applicant is seeking a prospective order as to costs, the letter should say what kind of order and on what grounds"; see 16–089.

[204] See Ch.15.

its use of disclosure orders. One rationale for limiting rights to disclosure is that defendant public authorities are expected, and generally do, approach judicial review litigation in an open-handed manner.[205] This general arrangement continued under CPR Pt 54, with any application for specific disclosure determined in accordance with CPR 31.

Opinion has been divided as to whether discovery should become more **16–066** routinely available in judicial review proceedings or whether a strict (or stricter) approach should be maintained.[206] A new, "more flexible and less prescriptive principle, which judges the need for disclosure in accordance with the requirements of the particular case, taking into account the facts and circumstances", and having regard to the overriding objective of the CPR, was signalled by the House of Lords in December 2006.[207] Even where Convention rights and proportionality are in issue, disclosure should be limited to the issues which require it in the interests of justice and, where possible, claimants should specify particular documents or classes of documents rather than seeking an order for general disclosure. Parties should exhibit documents referred to in their witness statements.[208]

Where Convention rights are in issue, facts may be more important to **16–067** the resolution of the dispute than in ordinary domestic law judicial review "since human rights decisions under the Convention tend to be very fact-specific and any judgment on the proportionality of a public authority's interference with a protected Convention right is likely to call for a careful and accurate evaluation of the facts".[209]

In practice, unless the claimant can show a prima facie breach of public **16–068** duty, disclosure will not usually be granted.[210] Where the challenge is on the ground of *Wednesbury* irrationality,[211] standard disclosure of the type which is a matter of routine in private law proceedings will seldom be ordered.[212] Applications for disclosure "in the hope that something might turn up" are regarded as an illegitimate exercise, at least in the absence of a prima facie reason to suppose that the deponent's evidence is untruthful.[213]

---

[205] *Huddleston* [1986] 2 All E.R. 941; this general approach is reflected today in the CPR requirement that parties co-operate with each other in the conduct of the proceedings (CPR r.1.4(2)(a)).
[206] See Law Commission Consultation Paper No.126, Administrative Law: Judicial Review and Statutory Appeals, para.8.10. In its 1994 report, the Law Commission made no recommendations for amendments of the Rules dealing with discovery: see Law Com. No.226, para.7.12.
[207] *Tweed v Parades Commission for Northern Ireland* [2006] UKHL 53; [2007] 2 W.L.R. 1 at [32]–[33] (Lord Carswell).
[208] *Tweed* [2006] UKHL 53; [2007] 2 W.L.R. 1 at [33] (Lord Carswell).
[209] *Tweed* [2006] UKHL 53; [2007] 2 W.L.R. 1 at [3] (Lord Bingham).
[210] *R. v Inland Revenue Commissioners Ex p. National Federation of Self Employed and Small Business Ltd* [1982] A.C. 617 at 654E (Lord Scarman).
[211] Ch.11.
[212] *R. v Secretary of State for the Environment Ex p. Smith* [1988] C.O.D. 3; *cf. R. v Secretary of State for Transport Ex p. APH Road Safety Ltd* [1993] C.O.D. 150.
[213] See, e.g. *R. v Secretary of State for the Environment Ex p. Doncaster BC* [1990] C.O.D. 441; *R. v Secretary of State for the Environment Ex p. Islington LBC and London Lesbian and Gay Centre* [1992] C.O.D. 67; *R. v Secretary of State for Foreign and Commonwealth Affairs Ex p. World Development Movement Ltd* [1995] 1 W.L.R. 386.

Generally, discovery to go behind the contents of a statement of truth will be ordered only if there is some material before the court which suggests that the claim form is not accurate.[214] Even reports referred to in a claim, routinely inspected in private law proceedings, will not be the subject of discovery in judicial review unless the claimant shows that the production of the documents is necessary for fairly disposing of the matter before the court.[215]

Interim remedies

16–069　Pending the full hearing of the claim, the claimant may apply to the court for one or more interim remedies.[216] These include an interim injunction, interim declaration and stay of proceedings. The term "stay of proceedings" is not confined to proceedings of a judicial nature, but encompasses the process by which any decision challenged has been reached, including the decision itself.[217] Although a stay of proceedings and an interim injunction perform the same function of preserving the status quo until the full hearing, there are conceptual and practical differences between the two forms of relief. While the injunction protects the interest of the litigant in dispute with another, the stay is not addressed to an "opposing" party but rather is directed at suspending the operation of a particular decision. The Administrative Court and Court of Appeal may order that a claimant be temporarily released.[218]

Preparation of skeleton arguments

16–070　The claimant must submit the skeleton 21 working days before the date of the hearing; the defendant and interested parties must do so 14 working days before the hearing.[219] Practice Direction 54 sets out the minimum requirements for a skeleton argument.

Discontinuing and orders by consent

16–071　A significant proportion of claims, given permission to proceed, are withdrawn before the full hearing.[220] If the parties agree about the final order to be made, the court may make the order without a hearing if it is

[214] *R. v Secretary of State for the Home Department Ex p. BH* [1990] C.O.D. 445; *Brien v Secretary of State for the Environment and Bromley LBC* [1995] J.P.L. 528; *World Development Movement Ltd* [1996] 1 W.L.R. 386. In its 1994 report, the Law Commission considered that this approach was unduly restrictive and undermined the basic test of relevance and necessity laid down in *O'Reilly v Mackman*: see Law Com. No.226, para. 7.12.
[215] *R. v Inland Revenue Commissioners Ex p. Taylor* [1989] 1 All E.R. 906.
[216] CPR r.25.1; see further Ch.18.
[217] *R. v Secretary of State for Education and Science Ex p. Avon CC* [1991] 1 Q.B. 558.
[218] PD 54, para.17.
[219] PD 54, para.15.
[220] M. Sunkin, "Withdrawing: A Problem in Judicial Review" in P. Leyland and T. Wood (eds), *Administrative Law Facing the Future* (1997), pp.221–241.

satisfied that the order should be made. Because of the public interest involved in many judicial review claims, the parties cannot determine for themselves what order should be made. The court will not make an order if it is not in the public interest to do so. In addition, if a decision of a court or tribunal is the subject of the claim, it would be wrong for that decision to be altered merely by agreement of the parties. The Court must be satisfied that this is appropriate.

THE FULL HEARING

Where an application for permission has been granted on the papers, a full **16–072** hearing of the claim for judicial review will take place some weeks or months later (unless there is urgency and an order for expedition is made). In practice, the grant of permission often acts as a spur to negotiations between the parties and in many cases where permission is granted the claimant does not set the claim down for full hearing. Where an application for permission is to be decided at an oral hearing, the court may direct that the permission application and the full hearing be "rolled up" into a single hearing.

In a criminal cause or matter,[221] the full hearing of the claim normally **16–073** takes place before a Divisional Court (of two or three judges) rather than a single judge. The rationale for this is that it is the last effective appeal.[222] In other claims, the hearing is normally before a single judge, though a claim may be listed for hearing by a Divisional Court for other reasons (for example, it raises a new point of law of wide application).

CPR r.8.6(2), which applies to claims for judicial review, provides that **16–074** "The court may require or permit a party to give oral evidence at the hearing, and cross examination may be permitted". In practice oral testimony and cross examination are rare. Cross examination should take place only when justice so demands,[223] for example where there is a conflict of evidence, where the claimant alleges that a precedent fact to the making of a decision did not exist, or where the court must reach its own view on the merits.[224]

---

[221] See 3–090.
[222] See 16–078; the only appeal lies to the HL.
[223] *R. v Secretary of State for the Home Department Ex p. Khawaja* [1984] A.C. 74 at 125 (Lord Bridge: "oral evidence and discovery, although catered for by the rules, are not part of the ordinary stock in trade of the prerogative jurisdiction"); *Roy v Kensington and Chelsea and Westminster FPC* [1992] 1 A.C. 624 (Lord Lowry).
[224] See, e.g. *R. (on the application of Wilkinson) v Broadmoor Special Hospital Authority* [2001] EWCA Civ 1545; [2002] 1 W.L.R. 419 (medical witnesses ordered to attend and be cross-examined so that court could reach its own view as to the merits of a medical decision and whether it infringed the patient's human rights); *R. (on the application of B) v Haddock (Responsible Medical Officer)* [2006] EWCA Civ 961; [2006] H.R.L.R. 40 (oral evidence would not have assisted the court); *R. (on the application of N) v M* [2002] EWCA Civ 1789;

16–075   Written evidence is regulated by CPR r.54.16, and may be relied upon only if it has been served in accordance with any rule in Pt 54, or a direction of the court, or the court gives permission. The court is generally wary of allowing the claimant to introduce fresh evidence which the defendant was unable to address before the claim was commenced.[225] Where the claimant's ground of challenge is that the defendant failed to give adequate reasons the court will be cautious about allowing the defendant to explain or amplify the reasons originally given to the claimant.[226]

16–076   An innovation introduced by the CPR is that in the court may decide a claim for judicial review on the basis of the papers without a hearing where all the parties agree,[227] though there has not been extensive use of this provision in practice. Where a claim turns on a discrete point of law, especially one going to the jurisdiction of the court to deal with the claim, the court may order that that be tried as a preliminary issue.[228]

APPEALS AFTER THE FULL HEARING

16–077   As *Access to Justice: Final Report* noted: "Appeals serve two purposes: the private purpose, which is to do justice in particular cases by correcting wrong decisions, and the public purpose, which is to ensure public confidence in the administration of justice by making such corrections and to clarify and develop the law and to set precedents".[229] The appeal routes from judgments in judicial review claims vary according to whether or not the claim is in a criminal cause or matter.[230]

[2003] 1 W.L.R. 562 (it should not often be necessary to adduce oral evidence with cross-examination where there are disputed issues of fact and opinion in cases where the need for forcible medical treatment of a patient is being challenged on human rights grounds. Nor do we consider that the decision in *Wilkinson* should be regarded as a charter for routine applications to the court for oral evidence in human rights cases generally. Much will depend on the nature of the right that has allegedly been breached, and the nature of the alleged breach. Furthermore, although in some cases (such as the present) the nature of the challenge may be such that the court cannot decide the ultimate question without determining for itself the disputed facts, it should not be overlooked that the court's role is essentially one of review").

[225] *R. v Secretary of State for the Environment Ex p. Powis* [1981] 1 W.L.R. 584; *R. (on the application of Dwr Cymru Cyfyngedig) v Environment Agency of Wales* [2003] EWHC 336; (2003) 100 L.S.G. 27.

[226] *R. v Westminster City Council Ex p. Ermakov* [1996] 2 All E.R. 302.

[227] CPR r.54.18.

[228] See, e.g. *R. (on the application of Heather) v Leonard Cheshire Foundation* [2001] EWHC Admin 429; (2001) 4 C.C.L. Rep. 211 at [9].

[229] Lord Woolf, *Access to Justice: Final Report* (1996), Ch.14, para.2.

[230] On which see 3–090.

Appeals in a criminal cause or matter

If the claim for judicial review constitutes a "criminal cause or matter", the **16–078** appeal route is directly to the House of Lords (the Court of Appeal having no jurisdiction).[231] The Administrative Court must first certify that the proposed appeal involves a point of law of general public importance.[232] In recent years, there has been a decline in the number of appeals in claims for judicial review from the Administrative Court to the Court of Appeal, from 109 to 60 in the five years since October 2000.[233]

Appeals in civil judicial review claims

In non-criminal claims, appeal lies to the Court of Appeal and is governed **16–079** by CPR Pt 52.[234] Permission to appeal is required. Permission should first be sought orally at the hearing at which the decision to be appealed against is handed down. If permission is refused, permission may be sought from the Court of Appeal in writing. In exceptional cases, an appeal may "leapfrog" directly from the Administrative Court to the House of Lords, bypassing the Court of Appeal. For this to happen, there must be agreement from all parties and a certificate from the Administrative Court that the appeal involves a point of law of general public importance which relates "wholly or mainly to the construction of an enactment or of a statutory instrument" or is "one in respect of which the judge is bound by the decision of the Court of Appeal or the House of Lords in previous proceedings".[235]

FUNDING JUDICIAL REVIEW

The cost of bringing a claim for judicial review, the limited availability of **16–080** legal aid, and the practice that "costs follow the event"[236] are all serious barriers to access to justice. In 2005, the typical cost of making a claim for

---

[231] Supreme Court Act (Senior Courts Act) 1981 s.18(1)(a); e.g. R. *(on the application of South West Yorkshire Mental Health NHS Trust) v Bradford Crown Court* [2003] EWCA Civ 1857; [2004] 1 W.L.R. 1664.
[232] Administration of Justice Act 1960 s.1(1)(a).
[233] Lord Justice Brooke, "Access to Justice and Judicial Review" [2006] J.R. 1, n.1.
[234] Supreme Court Act (Senior Courts Act) 1981) s.16(1); CPR r.52.3.
[235] Administration of Justice Act 1968 s.12. One such appeal was *R. v Secretary of State for the Environment, Transport and the Regions Ex p. Holdings & Barnes Plc* (the Alconbury case) [2001] UKHL 23; [2003] 2 A.C. 295, which decided issues of major importance about the compatibility of the planning system in England and Wales with Convention rights; see also *R. (on the application of Jones) v Ceredigion CC (Permission to Appeal)* [2005] EWCA Civ 986; [2005] 1 W.L.R. 3626 (refusal of the HL to entertain an appeal on a particular issue from the High Court under the leapfrog procedure did not preclude an appellant from appealing to the CA on that particular issue where the High Court judge had granted the appellant contingent permission to appeal to the CA in relation to that issue).
[236] See 16–087; a successful claimant will normally recover his legal costs from the defendant public authority; an unsuccessful claimant will normally be ordered to pay the legal costs of the public authority.

judicial review was in the region of £9,600.[237] Court fees in a typical claim for judicial review amount to £230.[238] In October 2004, the Court of Appeal gave the following figures as illustrative of the legal costs (excluding VAT) in one case in which there were appeals to the Court of Appeal and House of Lords.[239]

	Party	Solicitors' bill	Counsel's fees	Other disbursements	Total
High Court	Claimant	£9,482	£17,275	£969	£27,726
(Four days)	Defendant	£8–10,000	£24,300		£32–34,300
Court of Appeal (One day)	Claimant	£18,487	£5,100	£1,247	£25,834
	Defendant	£3,000	£4,000		£7,000
House of Lords (Leave hearing & two days) two days)	Claimant	£39,946	£83,450	£11,945	£135,341
	Defendant	£5,500	£23,800		£29,300

16–081　For most claimants, this expense is prohibitive and judicial review litigation cannot be pursued without financial assistance from the Community Legal Service (CLS) Fund[240] administered by the Legal Services Commission (LSC).[241] Public funding of judicial review, together with the court's approach to awarding costs to successful parties, seek to strike a balance between on the one hand facilitating access to the court and, on the other, discouraging unnecessary litigation.[242] Funding is available for various levels of service, including initial advice ("Legal Help") and assistance and

[237] This is the average summary assessment of costs in claims where there was a full hearing lasting half a day.
[238] Lang (2006): application for permission to apply for judicial review is £50; application for judicial review after permission is granted £180.
[239] R. (on the application of Burkett) v Hammersmith and Fulham LBC (Costs) [2004] EWCA Civ 1342; [2005] C.P. Rep. 11 at [10].
[240] At the time of writing, the legal aid system is undergoing radical reform: see Department of Constitutional Affairs, A Fairer Deal for Legal Aid, Cm. 6993 (2005); Lord Carter of Coles, Legal Aid: a market-based approach to reform (2006); Department for Constitutional Affairs/ Legal Services Commission, Legal Aid Reform: the Way Ahead, Cm. 6993 (2006); House of Commons Constitutional Affairs Committee Implementation of the Carter Review of Legal Aid. HC Paper No.223–I (Session 2006/07). Many involved in the provision of legal advice in public law cases have expressed concern or opposition to the proposed changes, which will introduce a system of fixed fees in October 2007 and transitional arrangements towards a system of competitive tendering for legal services by 2009.
[241] Established by the Access to Justice Act 1999 to replace the civil legal aid system, the Community Legal Service Fund is administered by the Legal Services Commission (which replaced the Legal Aid Board), an executive agency of the Ministry of Justice. Some claimants may be fortunate enough to secure pro bono legal advice and representation.
[242] On alternatives to judicial review, see 1–057 and 16–014).

for legal representation in court ("Investigative Help" or "Full Representation").[243]

The criteria applied by the LSC in deciding whether to fund legal representation are set out in a Funding Code, made under powers conferred by the Access to Justice Act 1999 and approved by the Lord Chancellor and Parliament.[244] For the large proportion of would-be claimants who cannot afford to fund a judicial review claim themselves, these criteria, and the manner in which they are applied, will for practical purposes determine whether a claim may be taken forward. Access to the court is often, in effect, regulated by public officials in the LSC rather than the Administrative Court.[245]   **16–082**

Funding where permission has not yet been granted

Where permission has not yet been sought by the claimant[246] and granted by the Administrative Court, applications for funding for legal representation may be refused "if the act or decision complained of in the proposed proceedings does not appear to be susceptible to challenge", "if there are administrative appeals or other procedures which should be pursued before proceedings are considered", and if the proposed defendant has not been "given a reasonable opportunity to respond to the challenge or deal with the claimant's complaint, save where this is impracticable in the circumstances".[247] Significant weight will be attached to the claimant's prospects of successfully obtaining the remedial order sought in the proceedings. Funding will be refused if prospects of success appear to be poor or unclear. Where it is borderline, funding will also be refused if the case does not appear to have significant wider public interest, to be of overwhelming importance to the client or to raise significant human rights issues. A cost benefit assessment is made and funding "may be refused unless the likely benefits of the proceedings, having regard to the costs, are proportionate to the benefits of the proceedings, having regard to prospects of success and all other circumstances".[248]   **16–083**

In some contexts, the court has been asked to consider whether a claim for judicial review amounts to an "abuse of process" where it is brought by a person entitled to public funding in circumstances where the claim might have been made by another, perhaps more obvious, person who is not so entitled.[249] The question is one that ought to be left to the LSC, or at least   **16–084**

---

[243] See generally R. Weekes, "Public Funding", Ch.4 in Lang (2006).
[244] Published at *http://www.legalservices.gov.uk*. Revisions to the Funding Code were approved by Parliament in July 2007 and apply from October 2007.
[245] On the permission requirement for judicial review claims, see 17–00.
[246] The claimant in judicial review proceedings and the proper claimant for LSC funding will not always be the same where children are involved: see 2–151.
[247] Funding Code Criteria, Section 7.4.4 (2005).
[248] Funding Code Criteria, Section 7.4.6.
[249] This is distinct from the question of whether a person has sufficient interest in the matter to which the claim relates, on which see Ch.2.

significant respect ought to be accorded to the LSC's decision. Indeed, in the field of education the LSC has issued guidance on the situations in which it will regard claims brought in the name of a child, rather than a parent, as legitimate.[250] In other circumstances, the Administrative Court may consider whether to exercise discretion to refuse permission to proceed with a claim if there is "clear evidence" that the LSC may have decided to grant funding without being fully informed of the facts.[251]

Funding after permission has been granted

16–085 The statutory requirement to make an application for permission promptly[252] may necessitate a claim for judicial review to be commenced before the LSC has determined an application for funding. The Funding Code establishes a presumption in favour of funding after permission has been granted by the Administrative Court if the following conditions are met: (a) the case has a significant wider public interest; (b) is of overwhelming importance to the client; or (c) raises significant human rights issues. In the absence of these factors, the LSC may refuse funding if the "prospects of success are borderline or poor" or "the likely costs do not appear to be proportionate to the likely benefits of the proceedings, having regard to the prospects of success and all the circumstances".[253]

The "wider public interest"

16–086 Guidance about the criterion of "wider public interest", relevant to funding decisions before and after the court has granted permission have been issued.[254] "Wider public interest" means, for the purposes of Section 2 of the Funding Code Criteria, the potential to produce real benefits for individuals other thab the applicant in question. Those benefits fall into four categories: (a) the protection of life or other basic human rights; (b) direct financial benefit; (c) potential financial benefit; or (d) cases concerning tangible benefits, such as health, safety or quality of life. Establishing a new legal precedent may also establish wider public interest. The Funding Code Criteria requires wider public interest to be "significant". The LSC may seek guidance from the Public Interest Advisory Panel on decisions in cases raising public interest issues.

[250] See funding Code Criteria, Decision-making Guidance—Gernal Principles.
[251] *R. (on the application of Edwards) v The Environment Agency* [2004] EWHC 736 (Admin) at [19] (Keith J.).
[252] See 16–050.
[253] Funding Code, Criteria Section 7.5.3.
[254] See funding Code Decision-making Guidance—Gernal Principles, Section 5.

COSTS

For claimants who are not publicly funded, a significant disincentive to **16–087** starting litigation is the prospect that if they fail in their claim, they are likely to have to pay the public authority's legal costs in defending the claim, as well as their own. Court fees are payable at various points in a claim for judicial review, unless the claimant makes an application for exemption or remission of those fees.[255] The costs of litigation are substantial and can pose a threat to the constitutional right of access to the courts.[256]

The court has a broad discretion in making orders as to costs.[257] The **16–088** general rule guiding the exercise of that discretion is that "the unsuccessful party will be ordered to pay the costs of the successful party".[258] The court will decide whether to apply the general rule that costs follow the event, or award costs on an issue by issue basis.[259] In making costs awards, the court must have regard to the CPR's overriding objective[260] though, in several respects, a different costs regime is required in the context of public law proceedings compared to other civil claims.[261] In exceptional circumstances, a costs order may be made against a person who is not a party to the proceedings.[262] In many judicial review claims, the defendant is an inferior court, tribunal or coroner which (though making the decision that is challenged) has no real interest in resisting the claim. Where such a party does not participate in the proceedings, or only "in order to assist the court neutrally on questions of jurisdiction, procedure, specialist case law and such like", the court's general approach will be to make no order for costs; costs may, however, be ordered if they appear and actively resist the claim or if there was "a flagrant instance of improper behaviour or when the inferior court or tribunal unreasonably declined or neglected to sign a consent order disposing of the proceedings".[263] In its discretion, the court

---

[255] See n.238.

[256] See, e.g. *R. v Lord Chancellor Ex p. Witham* [1998] Q.B. 575; the UNECE (Aarhus) Convention on Access to Information, Public Participation in Decision-making and Access to Justice in Environmental Matters (ratified by the UK in 2005), Art.9 includes the requirement that court procedures must fair, equitable, timely and not prohibitively expensive.

[257] Supreme Court Act 1981 (Senior Courts Act 1981) s.51 (as substituted by Courts and Legal Services Act 1990 s.4); CPR r.44.3. Although the discretion is broad, it is "by no means untrammelled" and "must be exercised in accordance with the rules of court and established principles": *R. (on the application of Corner House Research) v Secretary of State for Trade and Industry* [2005] EWCA Civ 192; [2005] 1 W.L.R. 2600 at [8] (Lord Philips M.R.)

[258] CPR r.44.3(1). *Boxhall v Waltham Forest LBC* (2001) 4 C.C.L.R. 258 (Scott Baker J.), cited with approval in *R. (on the application of Kuzeva) v Southwark LBC* [2002] EWCA Civ 781.

[259] Z. Leventhal, "Costs Principles on Taking Judgment in a Judicial Review Case" [2005] J.R. 139.

[260] See 16–011.

[261] *Mount Cooke Land Ltd* [2003] EWCA Civ 1346 at [76].

[262] *Dymocks Franchise Systems (NSW) Pty Ltd v Todd (Costs)* [2004] UKPC 39; [2004] 1 W.L.R. 2807.

[263] *R. (on the application of Davies) v Birmingham Deputy Coroner (Costs)* [2004] EWCA Civ 207; [2004] 1 W.L.R. 2739.

may decide to make no costs order against an unsuccessful claimant if the defendant unreasonably refuses to consider the alternative remedy of mediation following a suggestion of the judge.[264]

Protective costs orders in public interest cases

16–089   A protective costs order (PCO)[265]—"cost capping"—fixes in advance the maximum sum in costs that may be awarded to a party, or determines that whatever the outcome of the claim there should be no order as to costs (with the consequence that the claimant bears only its own costs).[266] The courts have developed this mechanism to facilitate access to justice in "pure public interest" cases, where the claimant has no private interest in the matter.[267] Claimants will typically be pressure groups or public spirited individuals.[268] The overriding purpose of a PCO is to enable a claimant to "to present its case to the court with a reasonably competent advocate without being exposed to such serious financial risks that would deter it from advancing a case of general public importance at all, where the court considers that it is in the public interest that an order should be made".[269] This potentially beneficial approach has so far been restricted to cases where the issues at stake involve the public interest and the court has been reluctant to make PCOs where the case involves a private interest. PCOs will most commonly benefit claimants[270]—whether a campaign group or a public spirited individual—though they may also be made in favour of an individual defendant (such as a coroner) who would otherwise have to bear the costs himself.[271]

16–090   The Court of Appeal has set out the following guidance which ought to govern the court's discretion to make a PCO:[272]

---

[264] *Dunnett v Railtrack Plc* [2002] EWHC 9020 (Costs), available at *http://www.bailii.org.* (not a judicial review claim); *cf.* Pre-action Protocol for Judicial Review (October 2006), para.34.

[265] *R. v Lord Chancellor Ex p. Child Poverty Action Group* [1999] 1 W.L.R. 347 (Dyson J.: "I think that the adjective 'pre-emptive' is more apt").

[266] R. Clayton, "Public Interest Litigation, Costs and the Role of Legal Aid" [2006] P.L. 429; B. Jaffey, "Protective Costs Orders in Judicial Review" [2006] J.R. 171; P. Brown, "Procedural Update" [2006] J.R. 325, 327–336.

[267] *Goodson v HM Coroner for Bedfordshire and Luton* [2005] EWCA Civ 1172; [2006] C.P. Rep. 6 (daughter seeking fuller coroner's inquiry into her father's death had only a private interest); *cf.* the more liberal approach adopted by the Scottish court in *McArthur v Lord Advocate* 2006 S.L.T. 170 (although the petitioners were relatives of the deceased victims of Hepatitis C caught from blood transfusions, they had no financial interest in pursuing the challenge to Scottish Minister's refusal to hold an inquiry and the "no private interest" test was therefore satisfied). The restriction on private interests probably has the effect of excluding most claims sought to be brought relying on Convention rights, as HRA s.7 confers standing only on those who are victims.

[268] On standing, see 2–035.

[269] *Corner House Research* [2005] EWCA Civ 192; [2005] 1 W.L.R. 2600 at [74].

[270] See Ch.2.

[271] *R. (on the application of Ministry of Defence) v Wiltshire and Swindon Coroner* [2005] EWHC 889, *The Times*, May 5, 2005.

[272] *Corner House Research* [2005] EWCA Civ 192; [2005] 1 W.L.R. 2600 at [74].

"1. A protective costs order may be made at any stage of the proceedings, on such conditions as the court thinks fit, provided that the court is satisfied that:

   (i) The issues raised are of general public importance;

   (ii) The public interest requires that those issues should be resolved;

   (iii) The claimant has no private interest in the outcome of the case;[273]

   (iv) Having regard to the financial resources of the claimant and the respondent(s) and to the amount of costs that are likely to be involved it is fair and just to make the order;

   (v) If the order is not made the claimant will probably discontinue the proceedings and will be acting reasonably in so doing.[274]

2. If those acting for the claimant are doing so pro bono this will be likely to enhance the merits of the application for a PCO.

3. It is for the court, in its discretion, to decide whether it is fair and just to make the order in the light of the considerations set out above."

These principles apply equally where a PCO is sought for the first time at the appeal stage[275] as they do to the more normal method for requesting a PCO, which is on the claim form at the permission stage (to which the would-be defendant may respond in its acknowledgment of service). If a PCO is refused, the claimant may request that the matter be reconsidered at an oral hearing (lasting no more than an hour), though if the renewed application is unsuccessful the claimant may have to bear not insignificant costs.[276] The precise scope of the PCO order is a matter for the court's discretion.[277]   **16–091**

---

[273] A criterion criticised in *Wilkinson v Kitzinger* [2006] EWHC 835; [2006] 2 F.L.R. 397 at [54] (in which the petitioners sought HRA declarations whether the Civil Partnership Act 2004 was compatible with Convention rights). Sir Mark Potter P. found it a "somewhat elusive concept to apply in any case in which the applicant, either in private or public law proceedings is pursuing a personal remedy, albeit his or her purpose is essentially representative of a number of persons with a similar interest"; so "in such a case, it is difficult to see why, if a PCO is otherwise appropriate, the existence of the applicant's private or personal interest should disqualify him or her from the benefit of such an order. I consider that, the nature and extent of the 'private interest' and its weight or importance in the overall context should be treated as a flexible element in the court's consideration of the question whether it is fair and just to make the order". This is surely correct.

[274] In *Wilkinson* [2006] EWHC 835; [2006] 2 F.L.R. 397 at [58] a CPO was granted even though it was probable that the litigation would continue.

[275] *Goodson* [2005] EWCA Civ 1172; [2006] C.P. Rep.6.

[276] *Corner House Research* [2005] EWCA Civ 192; [2005] 1 W.L.R. 2600 at [79].

[277] For example, in *Corner House* [2005] EWCA Civ 192; [2005] 1 W.L.R. 2600 at [79] the claimant was protected from any adverse costs order but was permitted to recover costs if it won; in *R. (on the application of Campaign for Nuclear Disarmament (Costs)) v Prime Minister (Costs)* [2002] EWHC 2712; [2003] C.P. Rep. 28, CND's liability for adverse costs was capped at £25,000 in respect of its attempt to obtain declarations as to UN Security Council Resolution 1441 and the war in Iraq; in *R. (on the application of the British Union for the Abolition of Vivisection) v Secretary of State for the Home Department* [2006] EWHC 250 (Admin) a cap of £40,000 was imposed; in *Wilkinson* [2006] EWHC 835; [2006] 2 F.L.R. 397, the cap was £25,000 (inclusive of VAT).

Costs before and at the permission stage

16–092 Where a claim for judicial review is withdrawn before the court considers whether or not to grant permission,[278] the court may make a costs order against the defendant, though only where a "plain and obvious case" was set out in the letter before action and the defendant failed to take that opportunity properly to assessed the merits of the proposed claim and avoid a unnecessary proceedings.[279] Where the response of the defendant to an unanswerable claim has been tardy, costs may be awarded to the claimant on an indemnity basis.[280]

16–093 A defendant is entitled (but not obliged) to respond to a claim for judicial review at the permission stage by filing an acknowledgement of service *summarising* the grounds on which the claim is contested.[281] The general approach is that a successful defendant who does prepare and file such an acknowledgement of service is entitled to recover the costs of doing so from the unsuccessful claimant.[282] Where, however, permission is refused after a hearing at which the defendant chose to be represented, PD 54 discourages the court from making a costs order against the unsuccessful claimant in relation to attendance at the hearing, except in exceptional circumstances.[283] The court should make a summary assessment of costs at the conclusion of the permission hearing.[284] The rationale for this approach is that to require claimants who fail at a hearing to bear the entire defendant's cost would risk discouraging claimants from seeking justice.

16–094 Where the claimant is granted permission, the costs will be costs in the case unless the judge granting permission makes a different order.[285]

---

[278] On permission, see 16–041.

[279] *R. v Kensington & Chelsea Royal LBC Ex p. Ghrebregiosis* (1994) 27 H.L.R. 602; *R. v Hackney LBC Ex p. Rowe* [1996] C.O.D. 155; *R. (on the application of Kemp) v Denbighshire Local Health Board* [2006] EWHC 181; [2006] 3 All E.R. 141(no order for costs because "the chance of obtaining permission to apply for judicial review would have been less than evens" (at [74]) as the claimant had not complied with the Pre-action Protocol and an alternative remedy was available).

[280] *R. (on the application of Taha) v Lambeth LBC*, unreported, February 7, 2002.

[281] See 16–063.

[282] *R. (on the application of Leach) v Commissioner for Local Administration* [2001] EWHC Admin 445, as explained in *Mount Cook Land Ltd v Westminster City Council* [2003] EWCA Civ 1346; [2004] C.P. Rep. 12.

[283] PD 54, para.8.6; in *Mount Cook Land Ltd* [2003] EWCA Civ 1346; [2004] C.P. Rep. 12 a "non-exhaustive list" of exceptional circumstances was provided at [76]: (a) the hopelessness of the claim; (b) the persistence in it by the claimant after having been alerted to facts and/or of the law demonstrating its hopelessness; (c) the extent to which the court considers that the claimant, in the pursuit of his application, has sought to abuse the process of judicial review for collateral ends—a relevant consideration as to costs at the permission stage, as well as when considering discretionary refusal of relief at the stage of substantive hearing, if there is one; and (d) whether, as a result of the deployment of full argument and documentary evidence by both sides at the hearing of a contested application [for permission], the unsuccessful claimant has had, in effect, the advantage of an early substantive hearing of the claim.

[284] *Payne v Caerphilly CBC (Costs)* [2004] EWCA Civ 433.

[285] *Practice Statement (QBD (Admin Ct): Judicial Review: Costs)* [2004] 1 W.L.R. 1760.

The Court of Appeal has twice urged the Rules Committee to provide **16–095** specific rule or practice direction governing the procedure for applications for costs at the permission stage, and the principles to be applied—and in the mean time suggested a practice to be followed.[286]

Costs when a claim is discontinued after permission

A significant number of claims are withdrawn between the grant of **16–096** permission and the full hearing.[287] Where the claim has been resolved without a hearing, but the parties cannot agree about costs, the following principles apply:[288]

> "It will ordinarily be irrelevant that the claimant is legally aided. The overriding objective is to do justice between the parties without incurring unnecessary court time and consequently additional costs. At each end of the spectrum there will be cases where it is obvious which side would have won had the substantive issues been fought to a conclusion. In between, the position will, in differing degrees, be less clear. How far the court will be prepared to look into the previously unresolved substantive issues will depend on the circumstances of the particular case, not least the amount of costs at stake and the conduct of the parties. In the absence of a good reason to make any other order the fallback is to make no order as to costs. The court should take care to ensure that it does not discourage parties from settling judicial review proceedings for example by a local authority making a concession at an early stage."

In most cases, the claimant will be awarded costs only where it is "overwhelmingly probable" that the claim would have been successful.[289]

Costs after the full hearing

Costs following a full hearing of a claim for judicial review will generally **16–097** be awarded to the successful party. In some circumstances, however, it may be inappropriate for the unsuccessful claimant to be ordered to meet the

---

[286] In *Mount Cook* [2003] EWCA Civ 1346; [2004] C.P. Rep. 12 and *R. (on the application of Ewing) v Office of the Deputy Prime Minister* [2005] EWCA Civ 1583; [2006] 1 W.L.R. 1260 at [47] (Carnwath L.J.): "(i) Where a proposed defendant or interested party wishes to seek costs at the permission stage, the Acknowledgement of Service should include an application for costs and should be accompanied by a Schedule setting out the amount claimed; (ii) The judge refusing permission should include in the refusal a decision whether to award costs in principle, and (if so) an indication of the amount which he proposes to assess summarily; (iii) The claimant should be given 14 days to respond in writing and should serve a copy on the defendant. (iv) The defendant will have 7 days to reply in writing to any such response, and to the amount proposed by the judge; (v) The judge will then decide and make an award on the papers".
[287] See 16–071.
[288] *R. (on the application of Kuzeva) v Southwark LBC* [2002] EWCA Civ 781, approving *R. v Liverpool City Council Ex p. Newman* (1992) 5 Admin. L.R. 669 (Simon Brown J.).
[289] *R. v (on the application of DG) v Worcestershire CC* 2005 WL 2996844 at [20].

defendant's costs, where the claim was brought not with view to personal gain and there was a wider public interest involved.[290] Costs of the successful party may be limited to some of the issues argued. In claims were there is more than one defendant or interested party, an unsuccessful claimant will normally be ordered to pay only one set of costs.[291] Neither the Administrative Court nor the Court of Appeal has jurisdiction to award costs out of public funds to the successful party.[292]

[290] See, e.g. R. v Secretary of State for the Environment, Transport and the Regions Ex p. Challenger [2001] Env. L.R. 12; cf. R. (on the application of Smeaton) v Secretary of State for Health (Costs) [2002] EWHC 886; [2002] 2 F.L.R. 146 (Society for the Protection of Unborn Children, represented by Smeaton, ordered to pay costs of challenge to legality of the "morning after pill"—this was not a matter of public concern until the proceedings were commenced by the Society).
[291] Corner House Research [2005] EWCA Civ 192; [2005] 1 W.L.R. 2600 [24].
[292] Holden & Co v Crown Prosecution Service (No.2) [1994] 1 A.C. 22.

CHAPTER 17

OTHER JUDICIAL REVIEW PROCEEDINGS

SCOPE

In addition to claims for judicial review under CPR Pt 54,[1] several other **17–001** procedures exist though which the Administrative Court exercises its supervisory jurisdiction, including the following:[2]

- A modified CPR Pt 54 procedure to deal with some immigration and asylum decisions.[3]

- Applications for the writ of habeas corpus *ad subjiciendum* under RSC, Ord.54, part of the old Rules of the Supreme Court preserved in Sch.1 to the CPR;[4]

- Applications under CPR Pt 8 to quash certain orders, etc. of ministers, tribunals and other bodies made under particular statutes and statutory instruments;[5]

- Appeals to the High Court from criminal courts;[6]

- Applications to quash certain decisions of coroners, under the Coroners Act 1988, s.13.[7]

Beyond the Administrative Court, a number of other courts apply judicial **17–002** review principles, including county courts in relation to decisions of local authorities relating to homelessness under the Housing Act 1996[8] and the Upper Tribunal (which is a superior court of record).[9] Except for a much-criticised anomaly in relation to habeas corpus,[10] the grounds of review or appeal in each of these proceedings are essentially the same as those

---

[1] See Ch.16.
[2] See also C. Lewis, *Judicial Remedies in Public Law*, 3rd edn (2004), Ch.12 (habeas corpus) and Ch.13 (appeals and statutory applications); B. Lang (ed.), *Administrative Court: Practice and Procedure* (2006).
[3] See 17–004, dealing with Pt III of CPR Pt 54, as required by the Nationality, Immigration and Asylum act 2002 s.103A.
[4] See 17–010.
[5] See 17–025.
[6] See 17–036.
[7] See 17–043.
[8] See 17–043.
[9] See 17–037 and 1–087.
[10] See 17–017.

available in CPR Pt 54 judicial review claims.[11] Where one of these procedures is relevant to an aggrieved person's circumstances, he is expected to use that procedure rather than make a CPR Pt 54 judicial review claim. This is so even if the governing legislation does not expressly oust the jurisidiction of the court to hear a CPR Pt 54 claim because the court is likely to exercise its discretion and apply the general principle that judicial review is a matter of last resort and cannot be used were a reasonably satisfactory alternative remedy exists.[12]

17–003   The justifications for having a range of judicial review and appeal procedures in addition to CPR Pt 54 is explained in two main ways. First, by the forces of inertia. There is no doubt that several of the procedures could usefully be assimilated into CPR Pt 54 and indeed this has been proposed in relation to some of them. As things stand, several of the procedures languish in the backwaters of Sch.1 to the CPR, where a handful of former Rules of the Supreme Court (RSC)[13] still remain awaiting attention. A second explanation is a functional one. The standard judicial review procedure has been found to be inadequate for dealing with the needs of claimants and defendants in some contexts. In relation to immigration and asylum matters, the perceived need for expedition and finality of litigation has been given priority by modifications to the standard procedure. In relation to some planning, compulsory purchase and regulatory decisions, the need for a speedy resolution to doubts about legality has been accommodated in a special procedure. In relation to homelessness decesions, the need for cheaper, more accessible local justice has prevailed over preserving the High Court's monopoly over the grounds and remedies of judicial review.

SPECIAL PROCEDURE FOR REVIEW OF ASYLUM AND IMMIGRATION DECISIONS

17–004   For many years, the largest category of judicial review claims has been decisions in the asylum and immigration context.[14] Frustration on the part of government that such challenges were too often used as a tactic to delay

---

[11] On the assimilation of the grounds of review irrespective of the procedure by which they reach the High Court, see *E v Secretary of State for the Home Department* [2004] EWCA Civ 49; [2004] Q.B. 1044 at [42] (Carnwath L.J.: ". . . in spite of the differences in history and wording, the various procedures have evolved to the point where it has become a generally safe working rule that the substantive grounds for intervention are identical"); *R. v Inland Revenue Commissioners Ex p. Preston* [1985] A.C. 835; *Chief Adjudication Officer v Foster* [1993] A.C. 754.

[12] See 16–014.

[13] The procedural code that governed practice in the High Court and the Court of Appeal before the introduction of the CPR in 1998.

[14] In 2005, 58% of applications for permission to proceed with a claim for judicial review were "immigration decisions" (*(Judicial Statistics (Revised) England and Wales for the year 2005*, Cm. 6903), p.23). For a more detailed account of the law and practice in this field, see I. Macdonald and F. Webber (eds), *Macdonald's Immigration Law and Practice* (2001).

removal from the United Kingdom of claimants with unmeritorious cases (something not universally accepted as true) has led to the standard judicial review procedure being modified,[15] as well as wide-ranging restructuring of the tribunal system (separate from the reforms introduced by the Tribunals, Courts and Enforcement Act 2007).

Before April 2005, a person dissatisfied with a determinition of an **17–005** immigration officer, entry clearance officer or the Home Secretary could appeal first to an immigration adjudictor. There was then the possibility of a further appeal to a second tier tribunal, the Immigration Appeal Tribunal (IAT), with permission from the IAT.[16] In most cases permission was refused. An unsuccessful appellant could then resort to judicial review to challenge the lawfulness of such refusals of permisson. The normal approach of the Administrative Court is to be wary of such challenges to the appellate process, for fear of undermining the principle of finality of litigation and distorting the appellate system.[17] A different approach was however adopted in relation to the IAT, in part because the court recognised that fundamental rights were often at stake (including the right to life and the right not to be subjected to torture) and also because the practical realities were that the IAT had to work under intense pressure of time and the consequences of error were considerable.[18] The Nationality, Immigration and Asylum Act 2002 s.101 introduced modifications to the standard CPR Pt 54 claim for judicial review procedure in respect of challenges to the refusal of permission by the IAT. the government stressed that "this was not a strategy to try to get rid of judicial review", rather the aim was to create a paper-based, fast and final review of IAT decisions.[19] The normal requirement that permission for judicial review be sought promptly and in any event within three months was replaced for these cases with a 14-day time limit. Criteria for granting permission to bring judicial review were specified and imposed a higher threshold than in other cases:[20] it was granted only if the appeal sought by the claimant had "a real prospect of success" or there was "some other compelling reason why the appeal should be heard" by the IAT (a test more akin to permission to appeal to the Court of Appeal).

Despite the apparent success of the modified CPR Pt 54 procedure, the **17–006** government remained dissatisfied with the arrangements and during 2004 included a clause in the Asylum and Immigration (Treatment of Claimants,

---

[15] A. Le Sueur, "Three strikes and it's out? The UK government's strategy to oust judicial review from immigration and asylum decision-making" [2004] P.L. 225.

[16] On the approach to be adopted, see *Huang v Secretary of State for the Home Department* [2007] UKHL 11; [2007] 2 W.L.R. 581 (in relation to Convention rights, the task of the appellate authority was to decide for itself whether the impugned decision was unlawful).

[17] See, e.g. *R. (on the application of Sivasubramaniam) v Wandsworth County Court* [2002] EWCA Civ 1738; [2003] 1 W.L.R. 475; R. Kellar, "Judicial review of refusals to grant permission to appeal" [2005] J.R. 244.

[18] *Sivasubramaniam* [2002] EWCA Civ 1738; [2003] 1 W.L.R. 475 at [52].

[19] *Hansard*, HL col.722 (July 29, 2002), Baroness Scotland.

[20] See 16–046.

etc.) Bill to oust the jurisdiction of the Administrative Court over immigration and asylum decisions altogether.[21] Following intense and sustained criticism of the proposals, which were regarded by many as a threat to the rule of law, they were withdrawn, but CPR Pt 54 was nevertheless further modified in the context of wider reforms to the tribunal system.[22]

17–007   In April 2004 a new single-tier appellate tribunal called the Asylum and Immigration Tribunal (AIT) was formed and this led to further modifications to CPR Pt 54.[23] Persons challenging initial decisions may appeal to the AIT on grounds of both fact and law. Most appeals are heard by single immigration judges, but in novel or complex cases panels of three immigration judges may determine the appeal. From decisions of a single judge,[24] a party to the appeal may apply to the Administrative Court for an order requiring the AIT to reconsider its decision.[25] The function of the Administrative Court, and the procedures to be followed, are far removed from those in a standard claim for judicial review. The time limits for making an application are short: five days for claimants living in England or Wales; 28 days if they are resident in another country; and two days if the case has been dealt with by the AIT "fast-track procedure". Generally, the Administrative Court considers only the papers lodged by the claimant and decision of the Administrative Court is final.[26] The remedies at the disposal of the Administrative Court are limited: (a) it may dismiss the application; (b) if the Administrative Court believes that the AIT has made an error of law, the case will be sent back to the AIT for the appeal to be reconsidered; the Administrative Court cannot itself quash the decision; or (c) if the Administrative Court believes that the case involves an important point of law, it may send the case directly to the Court of Appeal (Civil Division). The Court of Appeal has accepted that this modified form of judicial review process provides "adequate and proportionate protection" of asylum seekers' rights: these arrangements therefore provide an acceptable alternative remedy and the court exercise its discretion to refuse permission if a claimant uses the ordinary judicial review procedure.[27]

17–008   For an unspecified transitional period a "filter provision" is in place. Under this arrangement, immigration judges review applications made to the Administrative Court and may order the AIT to reconsider the appeal if there is an error of law. If the immigration judge refuses to make such an

---

[21] See 1–051 and Appendix C.

[22] CPR rr.54.28–36. R. Thomas, "After the ouster: review and reconsideration in a single tier tribunal" [2006] P.L. 674.

[23] See 1–097.

[24] There is no right to make an application to the Administrative Court where the case has been determined by three or more legally qualified immigration judges.

[25] Immigration and Asylum Act 2002 s.103A (inserted by the Asylum and Immigration (Treatment of Claimants, etc.) Act 2004.

[26] In contrast to the standard CPR Pt 54 procedure, where the court normally has a summary of the other party's reasons for contesting the claim and there is a possibility of appeal to the Court of Appeal.

[27] R. (on the application of G) v Immigration Appeal Tribunal [2004] EWCA Civ 1731; [2005] 1 W.L.R. 1445.

order, claimants seeking a review may then "opt in" and have their application considered by the Administrative Court.[28] The Administrative Court will only order that the AIT reconsiders its decision if the tribunal has made an error of law and there is a real possibility that the AIT would make different decision on reconsidering the appeal.

Special arrangements also apply where the judicial review is to a decision 17–009 of the Immigration and Nationality Directorate of the Home Office to remove a person from the United Kingdom before that removal takes place.[29]

HABEAS CORPUS

The unlawful deprivation or significant curtailments[30] of a person's liberty 17–010 by a public authority has long been recognised as a constitutional as well as a legal wrong. In modern times, this fundamental right is given expression in ECHR Art.5 which guarantees the right to liberty and security of the person.[31] In the past in England and Wales the prerogative writ of habeas corpus *ad subjiciendum* was one of the principal means for securing the release of a person unlawfully detained.[32] Indeed, earlier editions of this book described habeas corpus as "the most renowned contribution of the English common law to the protection of human liberty".[33] Today, however, its potency has diminished. The procedure for obtaining habeas corpus has been left largely untouched by reforms to judicial review and in languishes in the backwater of Sch.1 to the CPR.[34] Perhaps in part because of this, the number of applications for habeas corpus has declined.[35] There is doubt about the scope of review.[36] Moreover, habeas corpus has more

[28] CPR r.54.31.
[29] Practice Direction 52, Section II.
[30] Total incarceration is not necessary: *Re SA (Vulnerable Adult with Capacity: Marriage)* [2005] EWHC 2942 (Fam), [2006] 1 F.L.R. 867 at [54], [71] (Munby J.: "a means of ascertaining whether someone is in fact being kept confined, controlled, coerced or under restraint").
[31] See 13–070.
[32] D. Clark and G. McCoy, *The Most Fundamental Legal Rights: Habeas Corpus in the Commonwealth* (2000); A.D.R. Zellick and R. J. Sharpe, *The Law of Habeas Corpus*, 3rd edn (2005); A.P. Le Sueur, "Should the Writ of Habeas Corpus be Abolished?" [1992] P.L. 13; M. Shrimpton, "In Defence of Habeas Corpus" [1993] P.L. 24; Law Com. No.226 (1994), Part XI.
[33] J. Evans, *De Smith: Judicial Review of Administrative Action*, 4th edn (1980), p.596. And see *A v Secretary of State for the Home Department* [2005] UKHL 71, [2006] 2 A.C. 221 at [83] (Lord Hoffmann: "the writ of habeas corpus is not only a special (and nowadays infrequent) remedy for challenging unlawful detention but also carries a symbolic significance as a touchstone of English liberty which influences the rest of our law").
[34] See 15–074.
[35] In 2005 the High Court received 13 applications for habeas corpus, of which only three was determined, one of which was allowed (*Judicial Statistics (Revised) England and Wales for the year 2005*, Cm.6903), p.32. In 1998 there were 66 applications, of which 54 were determined. This may, at least in part, have been the result of the introduction of the new appeal procedures in the Extradition Act 2003.
[36] See 17–017.

than once been found by the European Court of Human Rights to be an inadequate remedy because it fails to provide the court with sufficiently intensive powers to review the factual basis or judgments upon which detention has been ordered.[37]

17–011   There are, however, still situations where habeas corpus provides an appropriate procedure for dealing with unlawful confinement (though in almost all circumstances comparable relief could be obtained by means of a claim for judicial review under CPR Pt 54). The Extradition Act 2003 provides for an appeal from decisions of district judges to the High Court, but this does not oust the jurisdiction of the Administrative Court to hear habeas corpus applications.[38] The other main areas are immigration, asylum and mental health.[39]

17–012   It is not appropriate to apply for habeas corpus: in relation to children placed into the care of a local authority;[40] to challenge a committal order in contempt of court proceedings, whether civil or criminal;[41] or as a way of appealing against conviction or sentence passed by a court of competent jurisdiction.[42] The general rule is that habeas corpus does not issue as a penalty for unlawful detention which has been discontinued.[43]

17–013   The need, now as in the past, is for a fast and effective method for challenging cases of alleged unlawful detention. Applications for habeas corpus are sometimes said to have the advantage that they take priority over all other court business—though there is provision for handling urgent claims for judicial review under CPR Pt 54.[44] There have been calls for habeas corpus to be incorporated into the standard judicial review procedure, so that it would become a remedy at the disposal of the court on CPR Pt 54 judicial review claim without the need for a separate set of court procedures.[45] The Law Commission rejected this idea in 1994[46] and

[37] X v United Kingdom (1981) 4 E.H.R.R. 188, para.58 (Home Secretary released X, sent to Broadmoor Hospital following an act of violence, on conditional discharge and later recalled him. Habeas corpus did not enable "a court to examine whether the patient's disorder still persisted and whether the Home Secretary was entitled to think that a continuation of the compulsory confinement was necessary in the interest of public safety"); L v United Kingdom (2005) 40 E.H.R.R. 32 (L, an autistic man incapable of consenting to medical treatment, was detained in hospital outside the statutory powers of compulsory detention; held that habeas corpus was not an adequate remedy as it did not allow for the resolution of complaints on the basis of incorrect diagnoses and judgments).
[38] Nikonovs v Governor of Brixton Prison [2005] EWHC 2405; [2006] 1 W.L.R. 1518.
[39] See, e.g. R. (on the application of T–T) v Royal Park Centre Hospital Managers [2003] EWCA Civ 330; [2003] 1 W.L.R. 1272.
[40] S v Haringey LBC (Habeas Corpus) [2003] EWHC 2734; [2004] 1 F.L.R. 590. Note that where an application is made involving a child in custody it should be made to the Family Division not the Administrative Court: Ord.54 r.11.
[41] See Linnett v Coles [1987] Q.B. 555; Re Sriven [2004] EWCA Civ 543; (2004) 148 S.J.L.B. 511. The person should instead appeal.
[42] Re Wring [1960] 1 W.L.R. 138; Re Corke [1954] 1 W.L.R. 899.
[43] Barnardo v Ford [1892] A.C. 336 (where a writ was nevertheless issued so that further inquiries could be pursued).
[44] See 16–043; PD 54, para.2.4.
[45] Le Sueur [1992] P.L. 13; Sir Simon Brown, "Habeas Corpus: a New Chapter" [2000] P.L. 31; B v Barking, Havering and Brentwood Community Healthcare NHS Trust [1999] 1 F.L.R. 106 at 117 (Lord Woolf M.R.).
[46] Law Com. No.126, paras 11.5–11.9.

following consultation in 2003 the Lord Chancellor decided reform was not needed,[47] partly because of the dwindling number of applications.

Standing and capacity

The application must be made by or with the concurrence of the detainee, **17-014** unless he is held incommunicado[48] or is incapable in law or in fact of consenting to the institution of the proceedings. In child custody cases the claimant may be a parent, guardian, next friend, local authority or possibly the Official Solicitor. Habeas corpus is not limited to British nationals; every person within the jurisdiction is entitled to equal protection.[49] In the past, prisoners of war and enemy aliens were thought to be unable to make applications for habeas corpus,[50] but this was not because of any lack of standing to do so but because the legality of their detection could not be challenged as they were detained under the royal prerogative; this will no longer give rise to difficulties as prerogative actions are now reviewable.[51] It can be expected that the court will usually be much more concerned with the merits of the application than technical questions of standing. It is suggested that the approach should be at least as flexible and liberal as the current approach to standing in claims for judicial review.[52]

Defendants

The defendant will normally be the person having actual custody of the **17-015** person detained, for example, a prison governor. In special cases the person who had custody of the detainee but has lost it temporarily in circumstances where he may be able to resume control may be the only proper defendant.[53] Although, if possible, notice should always be served on the custodian there is no reason of principle why it should not also be served on a minister who has ordered the detention and is competent to countermand it.[54] Nor is there any rule of law precluding the award of the

---

[47] LCD, "Response to the Consultation Paper 'The Administrative Court: Proposed Changes to the Primary Legislation following Sir Jeffrey Bowman's *Review of the Crown Office List*" (Oct. 2003).

[48] *Ex p. Child* (1854) 15 C.B. 238; *Re SA (Vulnerable Adult with Capacity: Marriage)* [2005] EWHC 2942 (Fam), [2006] 1 F.L.R. 867 at [51].

[49] *R. v Secretary of State for the Home Department Ex p. Khawaja* [1984] A.C. 74 at 111.

[50] *R. v Vine Street Police Station Supt Ex p. Liebmann* [1916] 1 K.B. 268; *R. v Knockaloe Camp Commandant Ex p. Foreman* (1917) 87 L J.K.B. 43; *R. v Bottrill Ex p. Kuelchenmeister* [1947] K.B. 41.

[51] See 3–034.

[52] See Ch.2.

[53] As in *R. v Home Secretary Ex p. O'Brien* [1923] 2 K.B. 361; affirmed sub nom. *Home Secretary v O'Brien* [1923] A.C. 603.

[54] *O'Brien* [1923] 2 K.B. 361. Quaere whether a minister who has not ordered the detention and has never had custody of the prisoner but who may have power to direct his release can properly be made defendant if the custodian is overseas; see discussion of the authorities on "constructive custody" in *Ex p. Mwenya* [1960] 1 Q.B. 241 at 277–280, DC.

writ against a minister acting in his capacity as a Crown servant.[55] Though in practice rarely issued, there is no reason of principle why the writ cannot he against detention based upon a decision of a superior court of record.[56] The writ may lie against private individuals as well as public authorities.[57]

Territorial ambit

17–016 Habeas corpus will not issue to a custodian on foreign soil nor, in general, in respect of detention on foreign soil.[58] Nor will it issue from the High Court to Scotland[59] or Northern Ireland;[60] but it may issue to the Isle of Man.[61] Before 1862 it could issue from London to any dependent territory within Her Majesty's dominions. The Habeas Corpus Act of that year provided that no such writ was to issue into any colony or "foreign dominion of the Crown", where there was a court having authority to issue and enforce the execution of the writ.

Scope of review

17–017 It is very difficult to present a coherent and concise account of the extent of judicial review in habeas corpus applications, for the case law is riddled with contradictions. In particular, it is not clear whether the scope is more limited than in CPR Pt 54 claims for judicial review—and confined to "jurisdictional errors" in the narrow sense.[62] There is high judicial and academic authority for the proposition that the approach of the courts in both forms of judicial review proceedings should be the same.[63] In both

[55] O'Brien [1923] 2 K.B. 361; R. v Secretary of State for the Home Department Ex p. Muboyayi [1992] Q.B. 244.
[56] See, e.g. Linnett v Coles [1987] Q.B. 555 and R v Governor of Spring Hill Prison Ex p. Sohi [1988] 1 W.L.R. 596.
[57] Re SA (Vulnerable Adult with Capacity: Marriage) [2005] EWHC 2942 (Fam), [2006] 1 F.L.R. 867.
[58] R. v Pinckney [1904] 2 K.B. 84 (private detention in France); Re Ning Yi-Chin (1939) 56 T.L.R. 3 (imprisonment of Chinese nationals in British leased territory in China). But exceptional cases may warrant deviations from the general rule (cf. O'Brien [1923] 2 K.B. 361; and possibly the High Court might be prepared to award habeas corpus in respect of the wrongful detention of a British subject at a British leased base in foreign territory, if service of the writ on an appropriate defendant within the jurisdiction were feasible.
[59] R. v Cowle (1759) 2 Burr. 834.
[60] Re Keenan [1972] 1 Q.B. 533.
[61] Ex p. Brown (1864) 5 B. & S. 280.
[62] See 4–037 for further discussion of this point.
[63] R. v Secretary of State for the Home Department Ex p. Khawaja [1984] A.C. 74 at 111 (Lord Scarman): "There are of course procedural differences between habeas corpus and modern . . . judicial review . . . But the nature of the remedy sought cannot affect the principle of the law." And, per Lord Wilberforce, at 99: "In practice many claimants seek both remedies. The court considers both any detention which may be in force and the order for removal: the one is normally ancillary to the other. I do not think that it would be appropriate unless unavoidable to make a distinction between the two remedies . . ." Beldam L.J. in R. v Secretary of State for the Home Department Ex p. Cheblak [1991] 1 W.L.R. 890 at 10 adopted a similar view.

habeas corpus and judicial review, the extent of review of questions of fact is the same[64]—and since the coming into force of the Human Rights Act 1998, more extensive than in the past if the nature of the case requires it.[65] Not only errors of law and defects of form but also erroneous findings of material facts (which may be controverted by affidavit[66]) may be grounds for the award of habeas corpus if the existence of those facts affects the legality of the restraint. The onus of proving that the factual conditions precedent to a lawful detention existed rests on the administrative authority.[67]

Procedure: RSC, Ord.54

Applications for habeas corpus are made under RSC, Ord.54, found in Sch.1 to the CPR. This is quite separate from the procedure for claims for judicial review procedure made under CPR Pt 54. In principle, claimants may commence both forms of proceedings simultaneously though there will normally be no practical need to do so and this should be avoided if it will increase costs unnecessarily. Where a CPR Pt 54 claim and an application for habeas corpus are commenced, "every effort should be made to harmonise the proceedings".[68] In practice this means that the same affidavit and witness statements should be used for both proceedings, both cases should come at the same time before a court for interlocutory and full hearings and in the event of an appeal, the same notice of appeal should suffice. Applications for habeas corpus involve a two stage procedure: an application without notice to the other party (formerly called "ex parte"); and a hearing on notice.   **17–018**

Application without notice

At this stage, the court has power either to issue the writ forthwith (that is, order the claimant's release) or to adjourn the application so that notice may be given to the defendant.[69] The modern practice almost invariably dictates an adjournment, except perhaps in cases where there is no possible defence to the application when the claimant's release can be ordered forthwith. The application for the writ must be supported by a witness   **17–019**

---

[64] *R. v Secretary of State for the Home Department Ex p. Khawaja* [1984] A.C. 74.
[65] See 1–110.
[66] Habeas Corpus Act 1816 ss.3, 4. See, however, *Re Shahid Iqbal* [1979] Q.B. 264, affirmed. [1979] 1 W.L.R. 425, where habeas corpus was refused even though affidavit evidence established that the ground given for the detention had no support in fact: it was held that the existence of another valid ground for detention and the absence of any prejudice to the claimant from the error justified refusal of the writ. While it might be thought that this reasoning obliquely introduces a discretionary element to the grant of habeas corpus, it does not do so since if there is another ground for the restraint it is not unlawful.
[67] *Khawaja* [1984] A.C. 74.
[68] *B v Barking, Havering and Brentwood Community Healthcare NHS Trust* [1999] 1 F.L.R. 106 at 117 (Lord Woolf M.R.).
[69] Ord.54 r.2.

statement or affidavit.[70] Generally this is made by the person who is subject to the restraint, setting out the nature of the restraint. If he is unable to make a witness statement or affidavit, it may be made by another person on his behalf but must then explain the special circumstances which prevent the claimant making his own witness statement or affidavit.[71] Copies of the witness statement or affidavit to be relied on at the subsequent hearing must be served on all the parties concerned.

Without notice applications in criminal causes or matters[72] are in practice heard by a Divisional Court; and in civil cases by a single judge sitting in open court. Applications for habeas corpus have priority over all other court business.

17–020   There is no statutory or common law statement of the criteria to be applied by the court at the without notice stage in deciding whether the application should proceed (or indeed whether the writ should be issued then). The court will generally adopt an approach similar to that at the permission stage of CPR Pt 54 claims for judicial review,[73] though questions of delay will not usually be relevant and there is no statutory time limit within which the writ must be sought. The claimant may be granted bail pending the full hearing, subject now to s.17 of the Criminal Justice Act 2003.[74]

On notice hearing

17–021   Where the usual practice is followed—i.e. that after a successful without notice hearing no order is made for the writ to issue, but the application is adjourned—notice is served on the defendant to appear at a hearing. At a hearing on the date named, oral argument takes place, although disputed questions of fact are normally dealt with on the basis of witness statements or affidavits upon which deponents are only exceptionally subject to cross-examination.[75] If the application is allowed, the court will order that the person restrained is released.[76] Occasionally, as a formality, the court will order the writ to issue—somewhat incongruously after the release of the claimant.

17–022   In contrast to the other prerogative remedies available on a claim for judicial review,[77] habeas corpus is a writ of right. If the claimant establishes that his detention is unlawful, the court has no discretion to refuse the writ.[78] The court may, however, have power to refuse the writ where the

---

[70] Ord.54 r.1(2).
[71] Ord.54 r.1(3).
[72] Most applications for habeas corpus are in criminal matters. Cases involving the return of fugitive offenders or extradition are criminal (see *R. v Governor of HM Prison Brixton Ex p. Savakar* [1910] 2 K.B. 1056) and most cases of detention under the Mental Health Act 1983 are expressly criminal causes (see ss.35–55).
[73] See 16–046.
[74] See 18–022.
[75] *R. v Secretary of State for the Home Department Ex p. Khawaja* [1984] A.C. 74, 124–125.
[76] Ord.54 r.4(1).
[77] See Ch.18.
[78] *Greene v Secretary of State for Home Affairs* [1942] A.C. 284 at 302.

error is merely a technical flaw in the process leading to the claimant's detention.[79] An application may also be struck out as an abuse of the process of the court where it was apparent, looking at the application in the context of a series of other applications, that the machinery of the court was not being used for its proper purposes.[80]

Repeat applications and appeals

For many years it was thought that an unsuccessful claimant for habeas corpus could renew his application before each superior court and each superior judge in turn.[81] Section 14(2) of the Administration of Justice Act 1960 now provides that no application for habeas corpus shall be made on the same grounds to the same court or judge or any other court or judge, unless fresh evidence is adduced. To come within the exception, the fresh evidence must be relevant and admissible.[82] A claimant who is unsuccessful obtaining permission to proceed with a CPR Pt 54 claim for judicial review can expect to have a subsequent application for habeas corpus, in relation to the same matter, refused as an abuse of process.[83]   **17–023**

Appeal routes from a refusal or grant of an application for habeas corpus depend on whether it is a criminal matter[84] or a non-criminal matter. In criminal applications the appeal is to the House of Lords, with permission of either the High Court or the House of Lords.[85] Unlike appeals in criminal claims for judicial review under CPR Pt 54,[86] there is no need for the High Court to certify that the appeal involves a point of law of general public importance. In non-criminal applications, appeal lies to the Court of Appeal. Where the appeal is against the refusal to grant habeas corpus the appeal to the Court of Appeal is as of right: the claimant does not require permission.[87]   **17–024**

---

[79] *R. v Governor of Pentonville Prison Ex p. Osman (No.3)* [1990] 1 W.L.R. 878.

[80] *Re Osman, The Independent*, November 26, 1991, DC.

[81] See, e.g. *Re Hastings (No.1)* [1958] 1 W.L.R. 372; *Re Hastings (No.2)* [1959] 1 Q.B. 358; *Re Hastings (No.3)* [1959] Ch. 368.

[82] *Ex p. Schtraks* [1964] 1 Q.B. 191. Evidence is only "fresh" for this purpose if the claimant could not, or could not reasonably have been expected to produce it on the first application: *R. v Governor of Pentonville Prison Ex p. Tarling* [1979] 1 W.L.R. 1417. Administration of Justice Act 1960 s.14(2) has not stopped the phenomenon of successive applications for habeas corpus. During the late 1980s and early 1990s, Mr Lorrain Osman, committed into custody under the Fugitive Offenders Act 1967 s.7(5) awaiting return to Hong Kong, made nine unsuccessful applications for the writ: see, e.g. *R. v Governor of Pentonville Prison Ex p. Osman* [1990] 1 W.L.R. 277 and *Re Osman* [1991] C.O.D. 459.

[83] *R. v Secretary of State for the Home Department Ex p. Sheikh, The Times*, September 7, 2000.

[84] On the distinction see Ch.16; and see Administration of Justice Act 1960 s.14(3).

[85] Administration of Justice Act 1960 ss.1, 15; Supreme Court Act 1981 (Senior Courts Act 1981) s.18(1).

[86] See 16–078.

[87] CPR r.52.3.

APPLICATIONS TO QUASH CERTAIN ORDERS, ETC.

17–025 A significant number of statutes and statutory instruments make provision for persons aggrieved by certain specified orders, decisions, etc. to make applications to the High Court to quash them. The term "appeal" is sometimes used in relation to these applications but they are more akin to judicial review. They are most commonly found in the context of town and country planning, compulsory land acquisition and regulation of commercial activity (especially of former state-owned enterprises).[88] The grounds of review are broadly comparable to those used in CPR Pt 54 claims for judicial review. There are two main features to applications to quash. First, they must be sought using a procedure distinct and different from the standard judicial review regime under CPR Pt 54. Secondly, applications to quash almost invariably contain a preclusive clause, ousting the jurisdiction of the court to hear challenges to the lawfulness of the order in question except by means of the application to quash procedure.[89]

17–026 Where the claimant's challenge is directed not at the order, etc. itself, but a matter antecedent or collateral to it, standard proceedings under CPR Pt 54 may be appropriate.[90] In cases where the claimant is not a person aggrieved by the order, etc. or he does not seek actually to quash the order, CPR Pt 54 proceedings may also be used.[91]

Procedure

17–027 The procedure for applications to quash is now governed principally by CPR Pt 8.

[88] Examples include: Town and County Planning Act 1990 ss.287–288 (formerly, ss.245 and 246 of the 1971 Act); Clean Neighbourhoods and Environment Act 2005 s.129D ("gating orders"); Planning and Compulsory Purchase Act 2004 s.113 (spatial strategies and development plans); Regional Development Agencies Act 1998 Sch.6 para.14(8) (acquisition of land); Water Industry Act 1991 ss.21, 22E (enforcement orders and financial penalties on water companies); Postal Services Act 2000 ss.28, 36 (enforcement of orders relating to licences for postal services); Electricity Act 1989 s.27A (penalties on electricity providers); Gas Act 1986 s.30E; Transport Act 2000 s.57F; New Roads and Street Works Act 1991 Sch.2 para.10; Wildlife and Countryside Act 1981 Sch.15 (footpath modification); Highways Act 1980 Sch.2 (orders concerning classification, construction and stopping up of roads); Road Traffic Regulations Act 1984 Sch.9. For an account of the historical development of statutory applications to quash, see 15–076.

[89] On ouster clauses, see 4–014.

[90] For example, in *R. v Camden LBC Ex p. Comyn Ching and Co (London) Ltd* (1984) 47 P. & C.R. 1417 it was held that a resolution by the local authority to make a compulsory purchase order could properly be challenged under the standard judicial review procedure (then RSC, Ord.53); but once the order had been made, Acquisition of Land Act 1981 s.25 required any challenge to be made by statutory review.

[91] In *Greater London Council v Secretary of State for the Environment* [1985] J.P.L. 868, Woolf J. held RSC, Ord.53 proceedings were appropriate where a claimant sought to challenge the reasoning of a planning inspector who had found in its favour. The statutory review provisions of the Town and Country Planning Act were inapplicable because the claimant was not a person aggrieved and it did not provide an appropriate remedy (i.e. a declaration).

The time period within which proceedings must be made is in most cases **17–028** six weeks (or 42 days). Often the Act in question states that time begins to run from some specific occurrence (such as the publication of an order) and so creates a "window" rather than just an end date. Accordingly, a claimant who commences an application before the start date does so prematurely and is as much out of time as one who is late.[92] In contrast to the requirement of promptness and in any event three months on a claim for judicial review under CPR Pt 54, this limitation period gives the court no discretion to extend the time for lodging the application,[93] as the court's jurisdiction is defined by the window of time allowed.

A different form of words ("any person aggrieved") usually defines the **17–029** standing of potential claimants for statutory review in contrast to the requirement of "a sufficient interest in the matter to which the application relates" for CPR Pt 54 claims. There is, however, a tendency for the courts to equate the forms of standing.[94]

The remedial powers of the court on an application to quash are **17–030** normally more limited in scope than CPR Pt 54. In each instance the precise powers are derived from the Act under which the application is made. The court is invariably given power to quash the order generally or in so far as it affects the claimant and is usually given power to make an interim order suspending the operation of the decision challenged until the court determines the application.[95] There are, for example, no powers to make declarations or orders equivalent to the remedy of prohibition or mandamus. In some instances, the court has express powers to remit the decision back to the decision-maker for reconsideration;[96] though even in the absence of such a provision reconsideration will be the normal course of events. Where the application relates to the imposition of the penalty, the court may have a power to substitute a penalty of a lesser amount.[97]

Proceedings are commenced by claim form, which must be filed in the **17–031** Administrative Court Office and served on the defendant minister and other parties within the time limit specified by the legislation under which the application is made.[98] In contrast to CPR Pt 54 claims for judicial review there is no permission stage though it has been suggested that there ought to be.[99] Evidence at the hearing is by witness statement.[100] The

---

[92] *Enterprise Inns Plc v Secretary of State for the Environment, Transport and the Regions* (2001) 81 P. & C.R. 18.
[93] *Smith v East Elloe RDC* [1956] A.C. 736; *R. v Secretary of State for the Environment Ex p. Ostler* [1977] Q.B. 177; *R. v Cornwall CC Ex p. Huntingdon* [1994] 1 All E. R. 694.
[94] See 2–055.
[95] See, e.g. Town and Country Planning Act 1990 s.288(5).
[96] *Botton v Secretary of State for the Environment* [1992] 1 P.L.R. 1.
[97] See, e.g. Water Industry Act 1991 s.22E. The power to make or vary a substantive decision is unusual in a court with principally supervisory jurisdiction; *cf.* the little-used power of the court in CPR Pt 54 claims for judicial review: 18–031.
[98] PD 8, para.22.
[99] *Enforcing Planning Control*, Report by R. Carnwath Q.C. for the Secretary of State for the Environment (1989), para.6. Cf. Town and Country Planning Act 1990 s.289(6), which in relation to appeals on point of law and case stated against enforcement notices requires permission to be obtained.
[100] PD 8, para.22.

hearing is before a single judge. Given the rationale for the procedure—expedition in the disposal of legal challenges—time is of the essence in prosecuting applications.

Grounds of review

17–032 The various Acts usually provide for the validity of an order, decision, action, etc. to be questioned on two alternative grounds, that:[101] (a) it is not within the powers conferred by the statute; or (b) any of the requirements of the statute[102] have not been complied with. The first challenge is based upon the criteria laid down by the Court of Appeal in *Ashbridge Investments Ltd v Minister of Housing and Local Government* where Lord Denning M.R. said that the court could interfere if the minister:[103]

> "... has acted on no evidence; or if he has come to a conclusion to which on the evidence he could not reasonably come; or if he has given a wrong interpretation to the words of the statute; or if he has taken into consideration matters which he ought not to have taken into account, or vice versa. It is identical with the position where the court has power to interfere with the decision of a lower tribunal which has erred in point of law."[104]

17–033 These criteria cannot today be distinguished from the grounds of judicial review known as illegality and unreasonableness.[105] Indeed, the language of judicial review is sometimes employed to assess the validity of decisions challenged under applications to quash. For example, the House of Lords in *Newbury District Council v Secretary of State for the Environment*[106] held that planning conditions may be quashed if they exceed the scope of the Town and Country Planning Act or if they are unreasonable in the *Wednesbury* sense.[107] Yet tests of the validity of individual statutes may be peculiar to their own contexts. Planning conditions, for example, may also be quashed, if they do not "fairly and reasonably relate" to the development.[108] This test is not directly employed in relation to any other statutory function.[109]

---

[101] See, e.g. Town and Country Planning Act 1990 ss.277–288. Some Acts make express reference to unreasonableness as a ground of challenge (e.g. Postal Services Act 2000 s.36(6), Railways Act 1993 s.57(1)(c)), though in any event an unreasonable decision will not be "within the powers conferred by the Act". On unreasonableness generally, see Ch. 11.
[102] Or other relevant requirements, e.g. of the Tribunals and Inquiries Act 1992.
[103] [1965] 1 W.L.R. 1320.
[104] [1965] 1 W.L.R. 1320 at 1326. This formula was adopted in, e.g. *Seddon Properties Ltd v Secretary of State for the Environment* [1978] J.P.L. 835; *Eckersley v Secretary of State for the Environment* (1977) 34 P. & C.R. 124. For similar tests in relation to compulsory purchase orders see *de Rothschild v Secretary of State for Transport* [1989] J.P.L. 173.
[105] See Ch.5 (illegality) and Ch.13 (unreasonableness).
[106] [1981] A.C. 578.
[107] See Ch.11.
[108] The condition in *Newbury DC v Secretary of State for the Environment* [1981] A.C. 578 that the buildings be demolished after a period of time was held invalid on this ground as that condition did not fairly and reasonably relate to the application for a mere change of use.
[109] But compare the test of proportionality: see 11–073.

The second ground of challenge above relates to procedural require- **17–034**
ments. This ground is close to the ground of judicial review of "procedural
propriety", which was defined by Lord Diplock in *GCHQ* as including
both the common law rules of natural justice and the breach of statutorily
required procedures.[110] In applications to quash, the procedural requirements specified in the statute may be supplemented by common law
principles of natural justice.[111]

Normally in applications to quash, for the claimant to succeed in **17–035**
quashing the decision he must have been "substantially prejudiced" by the
failure to comply with the statute's procedural conditions.[112] Under both
substantive and procedural grounds of review the courts possess a residual
discretion not to quash a decision where there has been no prejudice or
detriment to the claimant[113] and to refuse relief in exceptional
circumstances.[114]

APPEALS FROM THE MAGISTRATES' COURTS AND THE CROWN COURT

Detailed consideration of criminal appeals falls outside the scope of a book **17–036**
on judicial review.[115] The High Court does, however, continue to carry out
its historic role of overseeing the work of magistrates' courts and the
Crown Court in relation summary criminal cases, by means of appeals by
way of case stated (as well as judicial review in some situations).[116] In 2001
Sir Robin Auld's review of the criminal courts of England and Wales
recommended that the Adminsitrative Court's supervisory jurisdiction over
criminal courts be replaced with new routes of appeal to the Court of
Appeal (Criminal Appeal).[117] The Government accepted this and the Law
Commission is currently (in 2007) considering how this may best be
achieved.[118]

---

[110] *Council of Civil Service Unions v Minister for the Civil Service* [1985] A.C. 374; see Ch.6.
[111] See Chs 7–9.
[112] Town and Country Planning Act 1990 s.288(5)(b).
[113] *Miller v Weymouth & Melcombe Regis Corp* (1974) 27 P. & C.R. 468; *Kent CC v Secretary
of State for the Environment* (1976) 33 P. & C.R. 70; *Peak Park Joint Planning Board v
Secretary of State for the Environment* (1979) 39 P. & C.R. 361 at 385; *Richmond-upon-
Thames LBC v Secretary of State for the Environment* [1984] J.P.L. 24; *Tameside MBC v
Secretary of State for the Environment* [1984] J.P.L. 180.
[114] *Bolton MBC v Secretary of State for the Environment* (1990) 61 P. & C.R. 343 (Glidewell
L.J., obiter).
[115] P. Taylor, *Taylor on Appeals* (2000).
[116] See 3–005.
[117] Review of the Criminal Courts of England and Wales, Ch.12.
[118] Law Commission, *Judicial Review of Decisions of the Crown Court* (July 2005).

APPEALS FROM TRIBUNALS[119]

Prior to the Tribunals, Courts and Enforcement Act 2007

17–037 This section describes the appeal regime up to the time when the Tribunals, Courts and Enforcement Act 2007 is brought fully into force. The Leggatt review of tribunals commented, dismally, that the "structure of appeal routes is haphazard, having developed alongside the unstructured growth of the tribunals themselves".[120] Section 11 of the Tribunals and Inquiries Act 1992 provided for appeals by parties dissatisfied in point of law from tribunals falling within its ambit. These appeals were regulated by RSC, Ord.94 in Sch.1 to the CPR. There were two distinct avenues of appeal depending on whether the proceedings were still in course or whether the point of law relates to the tribunal's final determination.

17–038   Under s.11(3) of the 1992 Act, where a point of law arose during the course of a tribunal's proceedings,[121] either the parties or the tribunal of its own motion may state a "special case" for the decision of the High Court. This does not include the final decision of the tribunal.[122] Such appeals are governed by Ord.94 r.9 and, with modifications, CPR Pt 54.[123] There is no limitation period for these appeals, other than the fact that it must be before the tribunal reaches its final determination.

17–039   Section 11(1) provided an avenue of appeal from final decisions, which is governed by Ord.94 r.8. CPR Pt 52 governed appeals generally, and applied with modifications to these statutory appeals.[124] Appellants must file notice of appeal in the Administrative Court Office within 28 days.

Under the Tribunals Courts and Enforcement Act 2007

17–040 The 2007 Act establishes the First-tier Tribunal and the Upper Tribunal, each organised in "chambers", to which jurisdiction of most (but not all) previously existing tribunals will be transferred.[125] In order to avoid the need for an appeal when it seems clear something has gone wrong, both the First-tier Tribunal and Upper Tribunal have discretion to review their own decisions (either on their own motion or on the application of a party), subject to the Tribunal Procedure Rules.[126] There are two additional ways of challenging a decision: appeal and judicial review.

---

[119] On tribunals, see 1–084.

[120] Sir Andrew Leggatt, *Tribunals for Users: One System, One Service* (2001), para.6.68.

[121] Points of law are similar in scope to the grounds of judicial review. Thus, a tribunal's refusal to grant an adjournment which was unfair constitutes a point of law: *S v Hounslow LBC* [2001] E.L.R. 88.

[122] *Altan-Evans v Leicester LEA* [1998] E.L.R. 237.

[123] PD 54, paras 18.7–18.20.

[124] PD 52, para.17.

[125] See 1–087. The Asylum and Immigration Tribunal remains outside this new structure.

[126] Tribunal, Courts and Enforcement Act 2007 ss.9–10.

The new regime provides a uniform system for appeals, all subject to a **17–041** permission requirement. An appellant may appeal on point of law from the First-tier Tribunal to the Upper Tribunal (which is a superior court of record) except from an "excluded decision".[127] If an appeal is successful, the Upper Tribunal may set aside the decision of the First-tier Tribunal and either remit the matter back for reconsideration or re-make the decision itself. From the Upper Tribunal (except in relation to "excluded decisions"), an appeal on point of law will lie, with permission, to the Court of Appeal.[128]

The Upper Tribunal will also have limited jurisdiction to deal with **17–042** "judicial review" (the inverted commas are used in the Act) of claims challenging decisions of the First-tier Tribunal.[129] In these cases, the Upper Tribunal may grant the same judicial review remedies as the High Court.

CORONERS

The Coroners Act 1988 s.13(1) provides that an application may be made **17–043** by or under the authority of the Attorney General where a coroner refuses or neglects to hold an inquest which ought to be held, or "where an inquest has been held by him, that (whether by reason of fraud, rejection of evidence, irregularity of proceedings, insufficiency of inquiry, the discovery of new facts or evidence or otherwise) it is necessary or desirable in the interests of justice that another inquest should be held". The conduct of inquests must, following the Human Rights Act 1998, take into account the requirements of ECHR Art.2 (right to life).[130] The grounds of review under s.13(1) are in effect the same as those that may be deployed on a CPR Pt 54 claim for judicial review,[131] though a wider range of remedial orders will be available on a Pt 54 claim. Before commencing the application in the High Court under s.13, a claimant must obtain the consent of the Attorney General.[132] The criterion applied in each instance is whether there is a reasonable prospect of establishing that it is necessary or desirable in the interests of justice for a fresh inquest to be held.[133]

---

[127] Tribunal, Courts and Enforcement Act 2007 s.11(5). The Lord Chancellor may by Order add to the list of excluded decisions.

[128] Tribunal, Courts and Enforcement Act 2007 s.13.

[129] Tribunal, Courts and Enforcement Act 2007 ss.15–16.

[130] See 7–129; 13–060.

[131] *Terry v East Sussex Coroner* [2001] EWCA Civ 1094; [2002] Q.B. 312 at [21] (Simon Brown L.J.: "the selfsame test should apply under s.13(1)(a) as applies on a judicial review challenge. The court cannot conclude that 'an inquest . . . ought to be held' unless the coroner has misdirected himself in law or his factual conclusion is irrational").

[132] There is no prescribed procedure for obtaining such consent. It should be sufficient to set out a properly reasoned letter supported by a copy of the inquisition, notes of evidence given by witnesses and any material the applicant seeks to rely upon as fresh evidence. The relevant address is: Attorney General's Chambers, 20 Victoria Street, London, SW1H 0NF, telephone 020 7271 2492.

[133] *Hansard* HC, May 20, 1996, col.WA67 and May 2, 1989, col.39WA (adding that "it is not my practice to give a more particular reason"); *R. v Attorney General Ex p. Ferrante, Independent*, April 3, 1995 (CA).

17–044   The procedure on such applications is governed CPR (PD 8, para.19). Claimants sometimes commence a CPR Pt 54 claim for judicial review at the same time as making an application under s.13 of the 1988 Act. The general principle that the court will exercise its discretion to refuse permission to proceed with a CPR Pt 54 claim where there is an alternative remedy available[134] ought to deter claimants whose case could be made under s.13 from using the standard judicial review procedure.[135] Section 13(2) stipulates the remedies available. The High Court may order another inquest be held or, where an inquest has been held, to quash the inquisition on that inquest. There is also an express power to order the coroner to pay "such costs of an incidental to the application as to the court appear just".[136] At the time of writing, the Government is proposing to replace the s.13 procedure with a "simpler, more effective, and accessible appeal process" as part of a wider set of reforms of the coroners' service.[137]

HOMELESS APPEALS

17–045   Also relevant, though not a matter for the Administrative Court, is the right of appeal on point of law to county courts to challenge local housing authorities' decisions relating to homelessness.[138] By the mid-1990s, a third of all judicial review applications to the High Court concerned homelessness decisions; often the dispute was essentially one of fact and primary judgment (was the person intentionally homeless? was the accommodation offered suitable?) rather than of law. The High Court was encouraged to adopt a restrictive stance towards the grant of leave (now called permission) to proceed with such claims.[139] In *Access to Justice*, Lord Woolf recommended that the supervisory jurisdiction over the lawfulness of

---

[134] See 16–014.

[135] *R. v HM Coroner for West Berkshire Ex p. Thomas* [1991] C.O.D. 437 (Bingham L.J. said that he found it "hard to imagine circumstances in which the court would grant relief by way of judicial review if relief is refused under s.13. Where the Attorney General's leave is given, therefore, it seems clear that s.13 is the preferred route for those to challenge a coroner's inquisition".

[136] A protective costs order (see 16–089) may be ordered: see *R. (on the application of Ministry of Defence) v Wiltshire and Swindon Coroner* [2005] EWHC 889, *The Times*, May 5, 2005.

[137] Home Office, *Reforming the Coroner and Death Certification Service: A Position Paper*, Cm. 6159 (2004), para.53; and see the report of the *Death Certification and Investigation in England, Wales and Northern Ireland: The Report of a Fundamental Review 2003*, Cm. 5831 (2003), para.75. A draft bill was published in June 2006.

[138] Housing Act 1996 s.204. The appellant must first seek a review of his request for assistance by the authority (s.202). If he is "dissatisfied with the decision on the review" or the review is not done within the prescribed time limit, he has 21 days to appeal to the county court.

[139] *Puhlhofer v Hillingdon London BC* [1986] A.C. 484 at 518 (Lord Brightman said that it was "not appropriate that . . . judicial review should be used to monitor action of local authorities [in this context] save in exceptional circumstances".

homelessness decision-making should be transferred to the county courts[140] and this was swiftly implemented by Pt 7 of the Housing Act 1996.[141] The grounds of appeal are essentially the same as the grounds for judicial review.[142] The right of appeal does not extend to decisions about the provision of temporary accommodation pending final determination by the local authority or review by the county court; here judicial review continues to be an important method of challenge.[143] The courts have, however, indicated that they will intervene in challenges relating to temporary accomodation only in exceptional circumstances.[144] The existence of an review procedure in the county courts has not taken away the Administrative Court's jurisidction to exercise its judicial review jurisdiction in the context of decisions relating to homelessness, but that jurisdiction will now be used only in exceptional circumstances.[145]

EVALUATION OF JUDICIAL REVIEW PROCEDURES

Any evaluation of the procedural arrangements for the conduct of public law litigation has to take place in the context of the broad objectives which judicial review is intended to serve. Apart from the constitutional role of judicial review which has already been considered,[146] two perspectives can be used to highlight the competing demands that are made on the public law procedural regimes in England and Wales. The first focuses on the adjudicatory role performed by the court. The second views the procedures from the standpoints of the different participants in the judicial review process. To these may be added a third: the principle of proportionate   17–046

---

[140] *Access to Justice: Final Report* (1996), para.16.76. See also *R. v Brighton & Hove Council Ex p. Nacion* (1999) 31 H.L.R. 1095 at 1100–1101 (Lord Woolf M.R.: judicial review not an appropriate method of challenge because the need for relief was often brought at very short notice; applicants often lived far from London; and High Court proceedings were not regarded as the most appropriate forum for resolving the often delicate issues that arose out of local authorities' responsibilities for providing accommodation).

[141] County courts do not have any *general* powers to make quashing orders, prohibiting orders and mandatory orders: County Courts Act 1984 38(3)(a).

[142] *Tower Hamlets LBC v Begum (Runa)* [2003] UKHL 5; [2003] 2 A.C. 430 at [17] (Lord Hoffmann: "Section 204 provides that an applicant who is dissatisfied with a decision on review may appeal to the county court on 'any point of law arising from the decision'. This enables the applicant to complain not only that the council misinterpreted the law but also of any illegality, procedural impropriety or irrationality which could be relied upon in proceedings for judicial review: *Nipa Begum v Tower Hamlets LBC* [2000] 1 W.L.R. 306, CA)".

[143] M. Sunkin *et al.*, "Mapping the Use of Judicial Review to Challenge Local Authorities in England and Wales" [2007] P.L. 545 at 555.

[144] *Nacion* (1999) 31 H.L.R. 1095 (Lord Woolf M.R.: "If an authority refuses even to consider exercising its discretion under s.204(4) then I can understand that judicial review may be an appropriate remedy. Apart from that situation, I have difficulty in envisaging cases where application for judicial review will be appropriate").

[145] *R. (on the application of Lynch) v Lambeth LBC* [2006] EWHC 2737 (Admin); [2007] H.L.R. 15 (defective decision letter could be dealt with by county court procedure).

[146] See 1–006.

dispute resolution—advocated by the courts as well as government—to ensure so far as possible that when disputes arise between the citizen and the State they are resolved in a manner that is timely and cost effective.

The role of the court in judicial review

17-047 On a claim for judicial review and the other forms of judicial review proceedings the court may have to deal with questions of (a) law, (b) fact and (c) policy. CPR Pt 54 claims for judicial review provide an adequate framework for determining questions of law, but it provides a less effective mechanism for dealing with factual and possibly policy issues.

Questions of law

17-048 While questions of law are still decided on the basis of oral argument in court,[147] written arguments now play an increasingly important role in comparison to other types of claims, both for parties[148] and interveners.[149] But whereas in other types of claims, at least at first instance, points of law do not have to be included in the statement of claim, the claimant in judicial review is required to set out both the factual and legal grounds of challenge (supported by authorities) to the decision in question from the very outset. This is a sensible practice since it enables the defendant and the court to make a preliminary assessment of the merits of the claim and if the grounds need amending permission to amend is normally readily granted. So whether the issue of law is statutory or common law, little complaint can be made of the present arrangements. Arrangements introduced by the Tribunals, Courts and Enforcement Act 2007 for "judicial review" to be carried out by the Upper Tribunal,[150] which is a superior court of record, should prove to be a useful in ensuring that points of law relating to fields of administration falling within the ambit of tribunals are determined by judges with expertise in particular statutory regimes (which are often of great complexity) as well as general principles of administrative law.

Questions of fact

17-049 The facts upon which a claim is made are frequently agreed; the court will generally only be concerned with the legal consequences or inferences to be drawn from them. Although it is not generally for the courts on judicial review to alter a public authority's evaluation of issues of fact, a court will often have to satisfy itself, for example, that inferences were reasonably drawn or that conclusions rationally relate to evidence available to a

---

[147] Though provision now exists for determinations without a hearing: see 16-076.
[148] See 16-072.
[149] See 2-064.
[150] See 1-090.

decision-maker.[151] In this situation the existing procedure also works satisfactorily.

Issues of fact are usually decided on written evidence. While cross-examination of people who have given written evidence can be ordered, permission is not often sought to do so.[152] In addition, formal disclosure of documents is seldom ordered; claimants must rely on the defendant public authority to make full disclosure.[153] In the past, any conflict between a claimant's and defendant's evidence normally had to be resolved in the public authority's favour, on the grounds that the claimant has failed to discharge the onus which he is required to satisfy to show that the defendant has acted unlawfully. There is, however, a growing "culture of justification" in which public authorities are expected to explain the factual as well as the legal basis for their decisions.[154] Especially where Convention rights are in issue, this may entail a greater scrutiny of the underlying evidence to consider whether the defendant public authority has acted proportionately,[155] or the factual basis necessary to justify action (such as detention or compulsory treatment) exists,[156] or the court is required to have "full jurisdiction" in order to satisfy the requirements of ECHR Art.6.[157]

17–050

Unfortunately, there are many situations in which there can be disputes as to the assessment of facts between the individual citizen and public authority where there is no or no adequate alternative fact-finding mechanism to the court, such as an appeal body or ombudsman. A written procedure is unsuited to resolve "disguised" appeals as to the merits of the decisions of this nature and the court on judicial review can do no more than decide whether on the evidence which the public authority contends was available it was entitled to come to the decision which it did. Yet such issues continue to form a significant proportion of the public law caseload. There is, therefore, a need for a more effective fact-finding procedure. One alternative would be for the court to be more ready to allow cross-examination and disclosure as happens now when the courts have to determine the existence of precedent fact, but this would involve changing the nature of the ordinary judicial review hearing from a reviewing role and making the procedure more protracted and expensive and adding to the existing delays in obtaining a decision from the court. A preferable solution would be for those cases which regularly give rise to factual issues to have those factual issues initially determined by a tribunal and for its decisions to be subject to review by the court. Alternatively, the High Court could be given the power to refer issues of fact to another body—such as the ombudsmen or the county courts—for determination.

17–051

[151] See 11–036.
[152] See 16–074.
[153] See 16–065.
[154] See 11–004.
[155] See 11–079.
[156] See 13–070; 16–074.
[157] See 7–119.

Questions of policy

17–052   The most acute problems arise where judges are required to make decisions which involve their evaluating public policy considerations. Although it is usually accepted by judges that policy-making is for the administration and should be eschewed by the courts,[158] the courts sometimes need to justify their decisions simply in terms of what is socially desirable rather than on any legal principle. This is perhaps most apparent when a court exercises discretion as to whether to grant a remedy for unlawful action. In judicial review under CPR Pt 54 and applications to quash a remedy does not follow as of right and relief can be refused even if the court finds the action or decision tainted by unlawfulness. Relief has been refused on the ground, for example, that to grant the order sought would result in unacceptable administrative disruption[159] or the absence of prejudice to a claimant. The court, therefore, takes cognisance of the practical impact of their decisions, yet it may not necessarily be fully informed of what this is likely to be.

17–053   It is, therefore, not surprising that it has been argued that at the present time we have the worst of two worlds: a judiciary which is becoming increasingly interventionist which is confined by procedures and practices which exclude from their consideration certain information and factual investigation which would enable them to make more appropriate decisions as to when and how to intervene. A possible solution which has been proposed is the creation of an Advocate-General or Director of Civil Proceedings whose duty would be to present evidence of the public interest to the court,[160] and a movement from adversarial towards inquisitorial procedures.

The different interests of those affected by judicial review

17–054   The different participants involved in proceedings for judicial review may well attach importance to different aspects of the present procedures. The claimant will not be interested in the safeguards which are built into the procedure which are justified by the need to avoid abuse. However, the defendant public authority will attach the greatest importance to their retention since otherwise its activities may be unnecessarily disrupted which would not be in the interests of good administration. The courts are also attaching greater importance to the existence of the safeguards to help them alleviate the problems created by their increasing case load which is subjecting the court system to unwelcome strain.

17–055   Neither the claimant nor the defendant will necessarily welcome the involvement of third parties since their presence may complicate the proceedings and lead to additional expense and delay. However, the

---

[158] See 1–031.
[159] See, e.g. R. v Gateshead BC Ex p. Nichol [1988] C.O.D. 97.
[160] J.A.G. Griffith, "Judicial Decision-Making in Public Law" [1985] P.L. 564; H. Woolf, Protection of the Public: A New Challenge (1990), pp.109–113; Sir Jack Jacob, "Safeguarding the Public Interest in English Civil Proceedings" [1982] C.J.Q. 312, 316–319.

presence of the intervener may be of the greatest assistance to the court since otherwise the court may be totally unaware of a consequence of its decision which would be prejudicial to the public at large.[161]

While the interests of the court, the parties and other interested bodies may appear to be in conflict, closer examination may indicate that their interests are much closer than they realise. A claimant who has a meritorious case usually will have no difficulty in surmounting the hurdle of obtaining permission, but he could be seriously prejudiced if his case is substantially delayed because of the court having to deal with unmeritorious claims which should have been dealt with at the outset by a refusal of permission. The third party who can be affected by the proceedings may have no desire to incur the expense of being involved in the proceedings. His sole concern could well be that the proceedings should be completed as soon as possible so that, for example, a property which is subject to planning blight may be sold.   **17–056**

What is required is a procedure which reconciles these interests to the greatest extent possible. A procedure which allows the citizen ready access to a system of justice that he can afford and provides, where he has been unfairly or unreasonably or unlawfully treated, an effective remedy; a system which, while protecting the public from abuse of power is not so interventionist that it is inconsistent with good administration because it is over-intrusive. Devising a system which reconciles these objectives is by no means easy. It requires a careful balancing of the respective interests involved.   **17–057**

[161] See 2–064.

CHAPTER 18

JUDICIAL REVIEW REMEDIES

SCOPE

This chapter examines the public law remedies—interim and final—that **18–001** may be made on a claim for judicial review and the extent of the court's discretion to withhold them. The Administrative Court has at its disposal a range of powers to grant remedial orders in relation to a claim for judicial review, stemming from statutory and common law sources.

- Supreme Court Act (Senior Courts Act) 1981 s.37 and CPR Pts 25 and 54 govern interim remedies. These include interim injunctions, stays of proceedings and interim declarations.

- Supreme Court Act 1981 (Senior Courts Act) ss.29 and 31[1] and CPR Pt 54 regulate the main types of final remedy in judicial review claims. The various remedies—prohibiting, mandatory and quashing orders, injunctions and declarations—may be granted either singly or in combination.[2]

- The common law may provide a right to damages, restitution or recovery of a sum due where there has been an unlawful administrative act—but only if the elements of a recognised tort (typically negligence, breach of statutory duty and misfeasance of public office) or other cause of action can also be established.[3] In practice, claims for damages and other monetary remedies are usually determined at a separate hearing after the public law issues have been decided.

- The Human Rights Act 1998 s.4 (declarations of incompatibility) and s.8 (damages for actions breaching Convention rights)[4] provide specific remedies in judicial review and other claims in this context.[5]

- European Community law requires additional and modified remedies to be available in order to ensure the full protection of Community law rights.[6]

[1] As amended on May 1, 2004 by The Civil Procedure (Modification of Supreme Court Act 1981) Order 2004 (SI 2004/1033) (which altered the names of the remedies).
[2] Supreme Court Act (Senior Courts Act) 1981 s.31(2).
[3] See Ch.19.
[4] See 19–025.
[5] See 13–045 The text is set out in Appendix F.
[6] See 14–051.

FUNCTION OF REMEDIES

18–002 The modern era of English judicial review is marked by two changes in the way remedial orders are made and thought about. First, prior to the reforms to the judicial review system in 1978,[7] a plethora of technical rules restricted the circumstances in which claimants could be granted remedies in public law. Now the courts are reluctant to let the former intricacies and obscurities hamper the provision of effective redress. The courts adopt a flexible approach—though the willingness to innovate has not extended as far as accepting the radical suggestion that there is no longer any need for remedial orders specific to judicial review.[8]

18–003 Secondly, before the modern era of judicial review, the limits of the High Court's supervisory jurisdiction were defined by placing restrictions on the situations in which the particular remedies of certiorari, prohibition and mandamus could be granted. As we have seen, the approach today is a much broader one: the boundaries of the court's supervisory powers are determined by focusing on the source of legal authority and the character of the function,[9] and whether the subject-matter of the claim is justiciable.[10] Little of the old case law on the reach of each remedy is of much practical relevance.[11] The question to be addressed is therefore no longer, "does certiorari lie against such a decision?" but rather whether the impugned decision is one made by a public authority in the exercise of a public function and is justiciable. Today it can be said that the remedial orders at the disposal of the court perform the subsidiary role of giving practical effect to the judgment of the court.

18–004 The importance of remedies should not, however, be under estimated. In the first of the Hamlyn lectures, published as *Freedom under the Law*, Denning J. saw the biggest challenge facing the judiciary the fashioning of new remedies to protect our freedoms. As this and the next Chapters will make clear, this is one challenge that the judiciary, with the help of Parliament and academics and practitioners, have to a considerable extent successfully met.

REMEDIES AGAINST THE CROWN AND MINISTERS

No coercive remedies against the Crown directly

18–005 The prerogative orders (mandatory, prohibiting and quashing orders) and injunctions cannot be granted against the Crown directly.[12] Declaratory relief is however available. The justification given for this restriction is

[7] See 15–087.
[8] D. Oliver, "Public Law Remedies and Procedures—Do We Need Them?" [2002] P.L. 91.
[9] Ch.3.
[10] See 1–025; 11–014.
[11] There is no need, for example, to inquiry whether the decision was a "judicial one": see Appendix B on the classification of functions.
[12] On the nature of the Crown, see 3–037.

"both because there would be an incongruity in the Queen commanding herself to do an act, and also because disobedience to a writ of mandamus is to be enforced by attachment".[13]

Ministers are officers of the Crown

The restriction on coercive remedies against the Crown presents few **18–006** practical problems as legislation rarely places duties or confers powers on the Crown as such. Most statutory and prerogative powers of central government are exercised by Secretaries of State (who are *officers of the Crown* as distinct from the Crown itself) and coercive judicial review remedies may be granted against ministers in their official capacity.[14]

Interim relief against ministers

The one difficulty that used to face claimants seeking a remedy against a **18–007** minister was that, until relatively recently, Pt II of the Crown Proceedings Act 1947, which restricts the circumstances in which injunctions may be granted against ministers, was held to apply not only to private law proceedings against central government but also to restrict the court's powers to grant injunctions on applications for judicial review. In other words, the 1947 Act, which had been passed to make litigation against central government less hampered by outdated technical protections against "the Crown", was believed to qualify the plain words in s.31 of the Supreme Court Act (Senior Courts Act) 1981 giving power to the court to grant injunctive relief during a claim for judicial review. At the time, the bar on injunctive relief against ministers could pose significant practical difficulties for claimants as injunctions were the only form of remedial order which, on an application for judicial review, the court was able to grant on an interim basis pending the full hearing of the case.[15]

Since the 1990s it is clear, however, that the court does indeed have **18–008** jurisdiction to grant injunctions against ministers on claims for judicial review. First, the House of Lords held, following the European Court of Justice, that the court had power to grant interim injunctions against ministers where this was necessary in order to protect rights under European Community law.[16] Secondly, the House of Lords held that Pt II of the 1947 Act applies only to "civil proceedings," as defined by s.38(2), not to claims for judicial review.[17] Even though it is now clear that the

---

[13] *R. v Powell* (1841) 1 Q.B. 352 at 361 (Lord Denman C.J.), cited with approval in *M v Home Office* [1994] 1 A.C. 377 at 415, HL (Lord Woolf); *cf. Page v Hull University Visitor* [1993] A.C. 682 where the HL appears to have accepted without argument that certiorari could lie against the Queen "as visitor" to a University. See further 3–037.
[14] *R. v Commissioners of Customs and Excise Ex p Cook* [1970] 1 W.L.R. 450 at 455 (Lord Parker C.J.). On the nature of the office of Secretary of State, see 3–003.
[15] Since 1998 the court may grant interim declarations: see 18–021.
[16] See 14–039.
[17] *M v Home Office* [1994] 1 A.C. 377; in relation to the Scottish Executive, see *Davidson v Scottish Ministers* [2005] UKHL 74; 2006 S.C. (H.L.) 41.

courts possess jurisdiction to grant injunctions against ministers and other officers of the Crown, this power is exercised only in the most limited of circumstances. A declaration—in interim or final form—will continue to be regarded as the most appropriate remedy on a claim for judicial review involving officers of the Crown.[18]

INTERIM REMEDIES

18–009   Interim remedies "hold the ring".[19] As in most other types of claim, there may be a need in claims for judicial review for the court to grant an interim remedy to preserve the position of the parties until a final resolution of the legal dispute between the claimant and defendant.[20] Interim relief may be sought at *any* point, including (in urgent cases) before the claimant has obtained permission to proceed with the claim and even after the final judgment has been given.[21] Most typically, however, interim remedies are sought at the permission stage.[22] In practice the form of interim remedy most commonly granted in judicial review claims is an interim injunction and stay of proceedings. Interim declarations are also available, along with a variety of other orders listed in CPR 25.1(1). The defendant public authority may be willing to give an undertaking to the court, so avoiding the need for a formal interim order to be sought and made.

Urgency

18–010   Interim relief will typically be requested by the claimant at the point of applying for permission to proceed with the claim. The determination of an application for permission typically takes in excess of six weeks, not least because the defendant has 21 days to provide an acknowledgment of service. In some cases this length of time would leave a claimant vulnerable, so it is possible to obtain interim remedies before the point at which the court grants permission. CPR Pt 54 is unfortunately silent on how to make urgent applications and the main Practice Direction adds only that "Where urgency makes it necessary for the claim for judicial review to be made outside London or Cardiff, the Administrative Court Office in London should be consulted (if necessary, by telephone) prior to filing the claim form".[23] Following lobbying from practitioners, a Practice Statement and form for "Request of Urgent Consideration" do however now exist.[24]

---

[18] *M v Home Office* [1994] 1 A.C. 377 at 412.
[19] An expression used in *R. v Cardiff City Council Ex p. Barry* [1990] C.O.D. 94 and *M v Home Office* [1992] 1 Q.B. 270 at 139J, CA.
[20] CPR Pt 25 governs claims for judicial review as it does other types of claim.
[21] CPR r.25.2(1).
[22] On permission, see 16–041.
[23] PD 54, para.2.4.
[24] Form N463 is available from HM Court Service website; see also *Practice Statement (Administrative Court: Listings and Urgent Cases)* [2002] 1 W.L.R. 810.

In exceptionally urgent cases, application may be made to the out-of-hours judge.[25] Where a request for an interim remedy is refused on the papers, a practice has developed of allowing the application to be renewed at an oral hearing.[26]

Interim injunctions

An interim injunction is one granted before trial, for the purpose of **18–011** preventing any change in the status quo from taking place until the final determination of the merits of the case and to ensure that any final order that may be made at the full hearing of the claim should not be rendered nugatory. Interim injunctions may be mandatory[27] or prohibitory.

General approach

The general approach to the grant of interim relief in civil claims was **18–012** established in 1975, when the House of Lords held that a claimant need no longer establish a prima facie case, but instead demonstrate that there is a serious issue to be tried, i.e. a claim that is not frivolous or vexatious and discloses a reasonable prospect of success.[28] The claimant having shown that there is, at the least, a serious issue to be tried, the court will then consider whether it is just and convenient to grant an interim injunction. This involves the court assessing the relative risks of injustice by deciding whether there is an adequate alternative remedy in damages, either to the claimant seeking the injunction[29] or the defendant in the event that an injunction is granted against him.[30] The availability of a remedy in damages to the claimant will normally preclude the grant to him of an injunction. Even if damages are available, they may not be an adequate remedy.[31] If there is doubt about either or both the claimant's and/or the defendant's remedy in damages the court will proceed to consider what has become known as the "balance of convenience". The factors to be taken into consideration will vary from case to case. The aim of this approach is to

[25] For a practitioner's view, see K. Marcus, "Urgent Applications, Interim Relief and Costs" [2004] J.R. 256.
[26] *R. (on the application of Q) v Secretary of State for the Home Department* [2003] EWHC 2507 at [10].
[27] See, e.g. *R. (on the application of S) v Norfolk CC* [2004] EWHC 404; [2004] E.L.R. 259 (local education authority ordered to continue funding child's place at a residential college).
[28] *American Cyanamid Co v Ethicon Ltd* [1975] A.C. 396. As the editors of the *White Book* point out, since the coming into force of the CPR the context in which interim remedies are sought has changed, not least because there is now encouragement for the early resolution of issues, and at some point the HL's approach may need to be reconsidered: *White Book 2007*, para.25.0.1.
[29] For example, in the event of the interim injunction being refused, but the claimant succeeding at trial.
[30] For example, if the interim injunction is granted but the claimant fails at trial. The grant of an interim injunction is usually conditional on the claimant giving an undertaking to pay damages in these circumstances.
[31] See, e.g. *R. v Kensington and Chelsea RLBC Ex p. Hammell* [1989] 1 Q.B. 518.

avoid the court having to consider difficult questions of law or fact at the interim stage.

Approach in judicial review claims

18–013 The old prima facie case test continues to apply, in effect, in many judicial review cases[32] because a prerequisite to the grant of an interim injunction is normally the grant of permission, where the threshold often approximates more to the need to show a prima facie case than merely a potentially arguable one.[33] Moreover, questions as to the adequacy of damages as an adequate alternative remedy will usually be less, or not at all, relevant because of the absence of any general right to damages for loss caused by unlawful administrative action per se.[34] It follows that in cases involving the public interest, for example where a party is a public authority performing public duties, the decision to grant or withhold interim injunctive relief will usually be made not on the basis of the adequacy of damages but on the balance of convenience test.[35] In such cases, the balance of convenience must be looked at widely, taking into account the interests of the general public to whom the duties are owed.[36]

18–014 Another difference from private law proceedings is that in judicial review, there is less likely to be a dispute of issues of fact. Where the only dispute is as to law, the court may have to make the best prediction it can of the final outcome and give that prediction decisive weight in resolving the interlocutory issue.[37]

18–015 Others factors that may be taken into account in determining the balance of convenience include the importance of upholding the law of the land and the duty placed on certain authorities to enforce the law in the public interest.[38] In the case of a challenge to the validity of a law, the court should not exercise its discretion to restrain a public authority by interim injunction from enforcing apparently authentic law unless it is satisfied, having regard to all the circumstances, that the challenge to the validity of the law is, prima facie, so firmly based as to justify so exceptional a course being taken.[39] The general principle that expression of opinion or the expression and the dissemination of information will not be restrained by

---

[32] But not all: see, e.g. *R. v Secretary of State for the Home Department Ex p. Doorga* [1990] C.O.D. 109; *Scotia Pharmaceuticals International Ltd v Secretary of State for Health* [1994] C.O.D. 241.

[33] See 16–046.

[34] See Ch.19.

[35] *R. v Secretary of State for Transport Ex p. Factortame Ltd (No.2)* [1991] 1 A.C. 603 at 672–673.

[36] *Factortame (No. 2)* [1991] 1 A.C. 603; and *R. v HM Treasury Ex p. British Telecommunications Plc* [1995] C.O.D. 56; cf. *R. v Secretary of State for Health Ex p. Generics (UK) Ltd* [1997] C.O.D. 294;

[37] *Factortame (No.2)* [1991] 1 A.C. 603 at 660 (Lord Bridge).

[38] *Factortame (No.2)* [1991] 1 A.C. 603 at 672.

[39] *Factortame (No.2)* [1991] 1 A.C. 603 at 673 (Lord Goff).

the courts except on pressing grounds applies as much to a public authority which is under a duty to express an opinion as to a private individual.[40]

The discretionary bars to the award of an injunction[41] are applied with **18–016** particular stringency to the claimant for interim relief, and he is in any event usually required to give an undertaking in damages lest at the trial the interim injunction is shown to have been wrongly granted and the defendant has suffered loss as a result. Many claimants are legally aided and have insufficient means to give an effective undertaking in damages. This is not a bar to the grant of interim relief,[42] for the requirement of a cross-undertaking is a matter of discretion for the court. Neither ministers nor local authorities have any special exemption from giving cross-undertakings in damages, but a court is unlikely to exercise its discretion to require one where an injunction is sought in a law enforcement action.[43]

Stay of proceedings

Under CPR r.54.10(2), the court may grant a stay of proceedings when the **18–017** claimant is granted permission to proceed with a judicial review claim. Authorities are divided as to the scope and effect of such a "stay".[44] The Court of Appeal has held that the term is apt to include executive decisions and the process by which the decision was reached and may be granted to prevent a minister from implementing a decision.[45] The Privy Council has however held, *obiter,* that a stay of proceedings is merely an order which puts a stop to the further conduct of proceedings in court or before a

---

[40] *R. v Advertising Standards Authority Ltd Ex p. Vernons Organisation Ltd* [1993] 1 W.L.R. 1289; cf. *R. v Advertising Standards Authority Ex p. Direct Line Financial Services Ltd* [1998] C.O.D. 20 (interim injunction granted restraining ASA from publishing adjudication).

[41] See 18–048.

[42] *Ex p. Hammell* [1989] 1 Q.B. 518; *Allen v Jambo Holdings Ltd* [1980] 1 W.L.R. 1252 (but note *Belize Alliance of Conservation Non-Governmental Organisations v Department of the Environment (Interim Injunction)* [2003] UKPC 63; [2003] 1 W.L.R. 2839 at [39], where the PC held that *Allen* "should not be taken too far" as "The court is never exempted from the duty to do its best, on interlocutory applications with far-reaching financial implications, to minimise the risk of injustice". In *R. v Secretary of State for the Environment Ex p. Rose Theatre Trust Company* [1990] 1 Q.B. 504 Schiemann J. held the court should be extremely slow to grant an injunction without a cross-undertaking in damages; see also *R. (on the application of Greenpeace Ltd) v Inspectorate of Pollution* [1994] 1 W.L.R. 570 at 574.

[43] *F Hoffmann-La Roche & Co AG v Secretary of State for Trade and Industry* [1975] A.C. 295; *Director General of Fair Trading v Tobyward Ltd* [1989] 1 W.L.R. 517; *Kirklees MBC v Wickes Building Supplies Ltd* [1993] A.C. 227; *Coventry City Council v Finnie* (1997) 29 H.L.R. 658.

[44] The glossary to the CPR states "A stay imposes a halt on proceedings, apart from taking any steps allowed by the Rules or the terms of the stay. Proceedings can be continued if a stay is lifted".

[45] *R. v Secretary of State for Education and Science Ex p. Avon CC* [1991] 1 Q.B. 558 at 561, 563 (Glidewell and Taylor L.JJ.) (decision of minister to make order giving school grant maintained status); and *R. v Secretary of State for the Home Department Ex p. Muboyayi* [1992] 1 Q.B. 244 at 258 (Lord Donaldson M.R declines to express opinion on whether *Avon* will survive an appeal to the HL); *R. v Advertising Standards Authority Ltd Ex p. Vernons Organisation Ltd* [1993] 1 W.L.R. 1289 (application for stay "in truth" a claim for an injunction).

tribunal at the stage which they have reached, the object being to avoid the hearing or trial taking place; and that it could have no possible application to an executive decision which has already been made.[46] The position still awaits clarification by the House of Lords.[47]

18–018   Given the fundamental conflict of authorities over the basic nature of the order, it is difficult to describe with any certainty the principal features of a stay of proceedings. Unlike an injunction it is an order directed not at a party to the litigation but at the decision-making process of the court, tribunal or other decision-maker. It may not, therefore, be an order capable of being breached by a party to the proceedings, or anyone else, and may not be enforceable by contempt proceedings.[48] A decision made by an officer or minister of the Crown can be stayed by an order of the court.[49] Now that it is clear that interim injunctive relief can be ordered against officers and Ministers of the Crown,[50] and the court has power to make interim declarations, this characteristic of the stay is of less importance than it once was. There is much to be said for the view that, in the light of these developments, stays of proceedings may be confined to use in relation to judicial proceedings.[51] It does however, as we point out below, act as an effective brake on administrative action and it is not only the judicial proceedings which are brought to a halt while the stay is in operation.

18–019   Although the court has a general discretion to grant a stay of proceedings subject to any conditions it considers appropriate, cross-undertakings in damages will not normally be required.

18–020   The practical effect of a stay varies depending on the context.[52] Where the public authority has yet to make a final decision, the grant of a stay prohibits them from taking further steps to make that decision. Where a final decision has been made but not yet implemented, a stay will prevent implementation of the decision, which is suspended for the time being and any formal order is treated as temporarily being of no effect. The more

---

[46] *Minister of Foreign Affairs, Trade and Industry v Vehicles and Supplies Ltd* [1991] 1 W.L.R. 550 at 556 (Lord Oliver). The Board was considering s.564B(4) of the Jamaican Civil Procedure Code which was in similar terms to RSC, Ord.53 r.3(10)(a) (now CPR r.54.10(2)). *Ex p. Avon* [1991] 1 Q.B. 558 was neither referred to nor cited in argument.

[47] The Law Commission has recommended that "proceedings" in this context ought to be given a narrow meaning. This is in light of the fact that injunctions are now available against ministers on a claim for judicial review and the suggestion that the court ought to be empowered to grant interim declarations: see Law Com. No.226, para.6.26.

[48] *Vehicles and Supplies Ltd* [1991] 1 W.L.R. 550 at 71 (Lord Oliver).

[49] *Ex p. Avon CC* [1991] 1 Q.B. 558 at 558, 562 (Glidewell L.J.). cf. *R. v Secretary of State for the Home Department Ex p. Kirkwood* [1984] 1 W.L.R. 913; *R. v Secretary of State for the Home Department Ex p. Mohammed Yacoob* [1984] 1 W.L.R. 920. In the two House of Lords' decisions in the *Factortame* cases ((No. 1)) [1990] 2 A.C. 85; (No. 2) [1991] 1 A.C. 603), no mention was made of the question whether the court had power to grant a stay of proceedings against Ministers; it had been suggested that this omission was no accident: see Woolf, *Protection of the Public—a New Challenge* (1990), p.65.

[50] *M v Home Office* [1994] 1 A.C. 377.

[51] C. Lewis, *Judicial Remedies in Public Law*, 3rd edn (2004), para.6–028.

[52] *R. (on the application of H) v Ashworth Hospital Authority* [2002] EWCA Civ 923; [2003] 1 W.L.R. 127 at [45]–[48].

difficult question is whether a stay may be granted where a decision has been both made and implemented. The Court of Appeal has answered this in the affirmative, on the basis that if a final quashing order is eventually made, the decision will be treated as never having had any legal effect and therefore the court should have jurisdiction to say that a decision is without legal effect on a temporary basis.[53]

Interim declarations

Interim declarations were once "unknown to law" and even said to be "a contradiction in terms".[54] Following recommendations by the Law Commission and in Lord Woolf's *Access to Justice* report, an express power to grant interim declarations was included in the CPR when they were enacted in April 1999.[55] So far, the courts have not made a great deal of use of interim declarations in judicial review proceedings. 18–021

Bail

Until April 2004, the High Court exercised a general inherent power (usually heard by a judge in chambers) to grant bail to a person who had been refused bail by a magistrates' court or the Crown Court pending trial or appeal.[56] That general power to grant bail was abolished by s.17 of the Criminal Justice Act 2003.[57] With the abolition of this alternative remedy,[58] now the appropriate course for a person aggrieved by the refusal of bail by a magistrates' court or the Crown Court will often be to apply for judicial review of that refusal, though the court has warned that it will exercise its jurisdiction sparingly.[59] 18–022

FINAL REMEDIAL ORDERS

At the conclusion of the full hearing, a successful claimant may request the court to grant a mandatory order (formally called mandamus),[60] a quashing order (certiorari) or a prohibiting order (prohibition)[61]—a group of 18–023

[53] *Ashworth Hospital Authority* [2002] EWCA Civ 923; [2003] 1 W.L.R. 127 at [46].
[54] *International General Electric Co of New York Ltd v Customs and Excise Comrs* [1962] Ch.784 at 790 (Lord Diplock).
[55] CPR r.25.1(1)(b).
[56] *Sezek v Secretary of State for the Home Department (Bail Application)* [2001] EWCA Civ 795; [2002] 1 W.L.R. 348.
[57] As part of the implementation of Sir Robin Auld's review of the criminal court system; note that s.17(6) provides "Nothing in this section affects any right of a person to apply for a writ of habeas corpus or any other prerogative remedy".
[58] *cf. the position in contempt proceedings where there is a right of appeal to the Court of Appeal Criminal Division which must be exercised in preference to making a claim for judicial review: R. v Serumaga* [2005] EWCA Crim 370; [2005] 2 All E.R. 160.
[59] *R. (on the application of M) v Isleworth Crown Court* [2005] All E.R. (D) 42 (Mar); *R (on the application of Allwin) v Snaresbrook Crown Court* [2005] EWHC 742 (guidance on bringing a claim).
[60] See 18–024.
[61] See 18–026.

remedies for historical reasons known collectively as "prerogative orders".[62] The court may also grant injunctions[63] and declarations.[64] For almost all purposes, the mandatory and prohibiting orders can now be regarded as indistinguishable in their effect from final injunctions:[65] All three remedies "direct any of the parties to do, or refrain from doing, any act in relation to the particular matter".[66] A distinctive feature of all these remedies is that the court has discretion to withhold them from a claimant even if the defendant public authority is held to have acted unlawfully.[67] Remedies may be granted in combination with one and other.

Mandatory orders

18–024 The modern approach to remedies—in which the function of remedial orders is simply to give effect to the judgment of the court on substance of a claim—means that it is no longer necessary at this stage to describe the kinds of decision in which mandatory orders may be granted.[68] If the court has found there to be breach of a duty, a mandatory order may be granted if in all the circumstances that appears to the court to be the appropriate form of relief. Mandatory orders will not lie to compel the performance of a mere moral duty,[69] or to order anything to be done that is contrary to law.

18–025   Many of the narrow technicalities which once applied to the grant of mandamus, for example, that it would not lie for the purpose of undoing that which has already been done in contravention of statute,[70] no longer restrict the remedy. It has long been held to be preferable for the claimant to be able to show that he has demanded performance of the duty and that performance has been refused by the authority obliged to discharge it.[71] A claimant, before applying for judicial review, should address a distinct and

[62] Ch.15. In its 1994 report *Administrative Law: Judicial Review and Statutory Appeals*, the Law Commission argued that the Latin names for the prerogative orders obscured their functions to non-lawyers; it recommended that the Supreme Court Act 1981 be amended to renamed (Law Com. No.226, para.8.3). This suggestion was not supported by Lord Woolf in *Access to Justice*, para.13–065, but did find favour with the Bowman committee (see 15–097) and ss.29 and 31 of the 1981 Act were amended in 2004; see 3–016.

[63] See 18–034.

[64] See 18–038.

[65] *M v Home Office* [1994] 1 A.C. 377, 415E.

[66] Words used in the Australian Administrative Decisions (Judicial Review) Act 1977 s.30 which introduced a flexible range of remedies to replace prerogative writs with a view to freeing "judicial review from its emphasis on the character of the remedy sought, instead allowing the court to consider the substance of the applicant's grievance" (Electoral and Administrative Review Commission, Issues Paper No.4, 1990).

[67] See 18–048.

[68] On issues to do with substance, see e.g. the distinction between mandatory and "directory" duties and powers (see 5–064); whether lack of resources may excuse failure to perform what otherwise would be a duty (see 5–152).

[69] For example, to make good a military officer's pay: *Ex p. Napier* (1852) 18 Q.B. 692.

[70] See the 4th edition of this work, p.542.

[71] T. Tapping, *On Mandamus* (1853), pp.282–286.

specific demand or request to the defendant that he perform the duty imposed upon him.[72] Today this learning is encapsulated in the general obligation on claimants to follow the steps set out in the Pre-Action Protocol for Judicial Review, which includes writing a letter before claim.[73]

Quashing and prohibiting orders

Historically, the orders of certiorari and prohibition had so many charac-   **18–026**
teristics in common that they may, in their modern forms, be discussed together. The one significant difference between them is that a prohibiting order may, and usually must, be invoked at an earlier stage than a quashing order. A prohibiting order will not be granted unless something remains to be done that a court can prohibit. A quashing order will not lie unless something has been done that a court can quash. But it is sometimes appropriate to apply for both orders simultaneously—a quashing order to quash an order made by a tribunal in excess of its jurisdiction, and a prohibiting order to prevent the tribunal from continuing to exceed its jurisdiction.

It has been held that the orders will not issue to persons who take it   **18–027**
upon themselves to exercise a jurisdiction without any colour of legal authority; the acts of usurpers are to be regarded as nugatory. Where a tribunal which had power to grant cinematograph licences adopted a practice of approving building plans before the application for a licence was made, on the understanding that it would later grant the licence if it approved the plans, the courts held that certiorari and mandamus would not go to the tribunal for a refusal to approve plans, since the tribunal had no legal authority whatsoever to make provisional decisions.[74] However, today, in order to remove uncertainty, a court would issue the orders to public authorities that purport to be acting in pursuance of lawful authority. In relation to a void decision, a quashing order *in effect* declares that it was ineffective *ab initio;* in the case of a voidable decision, a quashing order will deprive the decision of legal effect.[75]

It is still not altogether clear what is the earliest stage at which a claim   **18–028**
for a prohibiting order may be made. If want of jurisdiction is apparent, a prohibiting order may be applied for at once. If want of jurisdiction is not apparent, the claim must wait until the tribunal has actually stepped

[72] *cf. R. v Bristol & Exeter Ry* (1843) 4 Q.B. 162, where the only demand made was premature.
[73] See Appendix I.
[74] *R. v Barnstaple Justices Ex p. Carder* [1938] 1 K.B. 385. See also *Re Daws* (1838) 8 A. & E. 936; *R. v Maguire and O'Sheil* [1923] 2 I.R. 58; and *Re Clifford and O'Sullivan* [1921] 2 A.C. 570 (no prohibition to court martial in state of martial law, for it is not a body exercising legal jurisdiction but an instrument for executing the will of the military commander). But for a more satisfactory result see *Steve Dart Co v Board of Arbitration* [1974] 2 E.C. 215 (prohibition issued to a tribunal purporting to act under legislation that did not empower its creation).
[75] On the distinction between void and voidable, see 4–056.

outside its jurisdiction (as by continuing the hearing after an incorrect determination of a jurisdictional fact) or is undoubtedly about to step outside its jurisdiction (as where it has announced its intention to entertain matters into which it has no power to inquire).[76] This is the generally accepted doctrine; but doubts have sometimes been expressed about the power to grant prohibiting orders for an anticipatory excess of jurisdiction.[77] On the other hand, there have been modern decisions in which applications for prohibiting orders have been considered even before the inferior tribunal has had the opportunity to address itself to the disputed question of its jurisdiction.[78] In any event, a doubt as to whether a request for a prohibiting order is premature is likely to be resolved in the claimant's favour if the final order of the tribunal may be protected by statute from challenge.[79]

Remitting the matter back to the decision-maker

18–029   Section 31(5) of the Supreme Court Act (Senior Courts Act) 1981 provides that

"If, on an application for judicial review seeking a quashing order, the High Court quashes the decision to which the application relates, the High Court may remit the matter to the court, tribunal or authority concerned, with a direction to reconsider it and reach a decision in accordance with the findings of the High Court."

18–030   This power to remit is useful in two main circumstances. First, where otherwise—following the quashing of a decision—the claimant would be inconvenienced by having to reapply to the public authority for a decision to be made. Secondly, where a quashing order alone might risk administrative inconvenience if a public authority had to start proceedings against the claimant afresh.

Substituting a decision

18–031   The general principle that a court hearing a judicial review claim does not substitute its decision for the original decision-maker is subject to two specific and limited exceptions, which extend the jurisdiction of the court when quashing orders are sought.

---

[76] *Re Zohrab v Smith* (1848) 17 L.J.Q.B. 174 at 176; *London Corp v Cox* (1867) L.R. 2 HL 239; *R. v Electricity Commissioners* [1924] 1 K.B. 171; *R. v Minister of Health Ex p. Villiers* [1936] 2 K.B. 29. See also *R. v Local Commissioner for Administration for North and East Area of England Ex p. Bradford MCC* [1979] Q.B. 287 (reversed in CA), where on a claim to prohibit a local commissioner from investigating certain matters, a declaration was granted that the Commissioner should not investigate complaints that did not prima facie amount to allegations of maladministration.

[77] *Re Ashby* [1934] O.R. 421 at 431.

[78] *R. v Tottenham & District Rent Tribunal Ex p. Northfield (Highgate) Ltd* [1957] 1 Q.B. 103, 107–108 (Lord Goddard C.J.); But a court may decline to exercise its discretion to issue prohibition before the tribunal has had an opportunity to explore the factual issues upon which its jurisdiction may depend: *Maritime Telegraph and Telephone Co Ltd v Canada Labour Relations Board* [1976] 2 E.C. 343.

[79] *R. v Minister of Health Ex p. Davis* [1929] 1 K.B. 619, DC.

First, where a claimant seeks a quashing order to quash a sentence of a **18–032** magistrates' court or the Crown Court on the grounds that the court had no power to pass the sentence, the Administrative Court may, instead of quashing the sentence and remitting the matter back, pass any sentence which the former courts could have passed.[80] Secondly, CPR r.54.19(3) provides:

> "Where the court considers that there is no purpose to be served in remitting the matter to the decision-maker it may, subject to any statutory provision, take the decision itself. (Where a statutory power is given to a tribunal, person or other body it may be the case that the court cannot take the decision itself)."

A statutory foundation for the power for the court "to take the decision **18–033** itself" was given when the Supreme Court Act (Senior Courts Act) 1981 s.31 was amended by the Tribunals, Courts and Enforcement Act 2007 s.141.[81] On the face of it, CPR 54.19(3) is considerably wider than the power to make substitute orders proposed by the Law Commission in 1994, which would have been confined to situations where the decision-maker was a court or tribunal and expressly limited to errors of law (not procedural impropriety or abuse of discretion) and where there was only one decision which the impugned court or tribunal could properly have reached.[82] The CPR must now be read in the light of the amended s.31 of the Supreme Court Act (Senior Courts Act) 1981, which more closely matches the Law Commission's recommendation. In practice, however, there may be relatively few opportunities for using CPR r.54.19(3).[83] One such may be where the court substitutes words in an inquisition.[84]

Final Injunctions[85]

The jurisdiction of the High Court to grant injunctions on a claim for **18–034** judicial review rests on s.31(2) of the Supreme Court Act (Senior Courts Act) 1981[86] which gives the court power to grant an injunction in any case

---

[80] Supreme Court Act (Senior Courts Act) 1981 s.43; *R. v St Helens Justices Ex p. Jones* [1999] 2 All E.R. 73; *R. v Nuneaton Justices Ex p. Bingham* [1991] C.O.D. 56.
[81] See Appendix E below.
[82] Law Com. No.226, para.8.16.
[83] For an illustration of the type of situation where the "blunt instrument" of the prerogative orders could usefully be supplemented by a power to make a substitute order, see *R. v Tower Hamlets LBC Ex p. Tower Hamlets Combined Traders Association* [1994] C.O.D. 325. See also *Governing Body of the London Oratory School v Schools Adjudicator* [2005] EWHC 1842 (Admin); [2005] E.L.R. 484.
[84] *R. (on the application of Mowlem Plc) v Avon Assistant Deputy Coroner* [2005] EWHC 1359 (Admin).
[85] Detailed references to authorities for basic propositions of law relating to injunctions are omitted: see generally, D. Bean, *Injunctions*, 9th edn (2007).
[86] See s.30 in relation to injunctions restraining a person not entitled to do so from acting in a public office. On the High Court's general jurisdiction to grant injunctions, see s.37.

where it appears just and convenient to do so having regard to: (a) the nature of the matters in respect of which relief may be granted by a prerogative order; (b) the nature of the persons and bodies against whom relief may be granted by such orders; and (c) all the circumstances of the case.

18–035   An injunction is an order of a court addressed to a party requiring that party to do or to refrain from doing a particular act. Hence an injunction may be prohibitory or mandatory. Until late in the 19th century all injunctions were worded in a prohibitory form (e.g. not to allow an obstruction to continue to interfere with the plaintiff's rights), but the direct mandatory form (e.g. to remove the obstruction) may now be used. A final injunction granted on a claim for judicial review is normally indistinguishable in its effect from a prohibiting or mandatory order:[87] injunctions may be granted to prevent ultra vires acts by[88] public bodies and to enforce public law duties.[89] The court may grant an injunction on such terms and conditions as it thinks fit. Although the discretion conferred is very broad, it will be exercised in accordance with recognised principles.

18–036   A final injunction is granted at the conclusion of the proceedings and is definitive of the rights of the parties, but it need not be expressed to have perpetual effect; it may be awarded for a fixed period, or for a fixed period with permission to apply for an extension, or for an indefinite period terminable when conditions imposed on the defendant have been complied with; or its operation may be suspended for a period during which the defendant is given the opportunity to comply with the conditions imposed on him, the plaintiff being given leave to reapply at the end of that time. The elasticity of form and content that characterises the injunction is, indeed, one of its main advantages over mandatory and prohibitory orders.

18–037   In general, a mandatory injunction will not issue to compel the performance of a continuing series of acts—for example, the execution of building or repair works[90] or the operation of a ferry service[91] or the delivery of mail that has been interrupted by an industrial dispute[92]—which the court is incapable of superintending. This rule cannot be expressed without qualification, for the court has jurisdiction to order the abatement of a nuisance although compliance with its order may entail the execution of extensive works over which the court would not be capable of

---

[87] M v Home Office [1994] 1 A.C. 377 at 415E.
[88] See, e.g. R. v North Yorkshire CC Ex p. M [1989] Q.B. 411.
[89] See, e.g. R. v Kensington and Chelsea RLBC Ex p. Hammell [1989] 1 Q.B. 518.
[90] Attorney General v Staffordshire CC [1905] 1 Ch. 336 at 342 (a case where a declaration was sought in respect of liability to maintain and repair a highway).
[91] Attorney General v Colchester Corp [1955] 2 Q.B. 207; cf. Gravesham BC v British Railways Board [1978] Ch. 379 at 403–405. See also Attorney General v Ripon Cathedral (Dean & Chapter) [1945] Ch. 23; Dowty Boulton Paul Ltd v Wolverhampton Corp [1971] 1 W.L.R. 204 at 211–212 (maintenance of airfield; injunction prohibitory in form but mandatory in substance).
[92] Stephen (Harold) & Co Ltd v Post Office [1977] 1 W.L.R. 1172.

maintaining effective superintendence[93] and it can award a prohibitory injunction to restrain the discontinuance of a public service.[94] It is doubtful whether a mandatory injunction will issue at the suit of a private plaintiff to compel a public authority to carry out its positive statutory duties, unless the statute is to be interpreted as giving the plaintiff a private right of action for breach of those duties; the more appropriate judicial remedy (if any) will be a mandatory order.[95]

Declarations

A declaration is a formal statement by the court pronouncing upon the existence or non-existence of a legal state of affairs. It declares what the legal position is and what are the rights of the parties. A declaration is to be contrasted with an executory, in other words, coercive judgment which can be enforced by the courts. In the case of an executory judgment, the courts determine the respective rights of the parties and then order the defendant to act in a certain way, for example to pay damages or to refrain from interfering with the claimant's rights. If the order is disregarded, it can be enforced by official action, usually by levying execution against the defendant's property or by imprisoning him for contempt of court. A declaration, on the other hand, pronounces upon the existence of a legal relationship but does not contain any order which can be enforced against the defendant.[96] The court may, for example, declare that the claimant is a British subject or that a notice served upon him by a public authority is invalid and of no effect. The declaration pronounces on what is the legal position. **18–038**

The fact that a declaration is not coercive is one of its advantages as a public law remedy. Because it merely pronounces upon the legal position, it is well suited to the supervisory role of administrative law in England. In **18–039**

---

[93] See, e.g. *Pride of Derby & Derbyshire Angling Association Ltd v British Celanese Ltd* [1953] Ch. 149. Other limited exceptions to the general rule are mentioned in *Attorney General v Colchester Corp* [1955] 2 Q.B. 207, 216

[94] *Warwickshire CC v British Railways Board* [1969] 1 W.L.R. 1117.

[95] *Glossop v Heston & Isleworth Local Board* (1879) 12 Ch.D. 102; and *Attorney General v Clerkenwell Vestry* [1891] 3 Ch. 527 at 537 (alleged breach of duty in failing to provide proper drainage system). It appears even a claim for mandamus would have been inappropriate because Parliament had provided another specific remedy: *Pasmore v Oswaldtwistle UBC* [1898] A.C. 387. See also *Attorney General v Pontypridd Waterworks Co* [1908] Ch. 388; *Holland v Dickson* (1888) 37 Ch. D. 669 (illustration of a mandatory injunction issuing to compel the performance of a semi-private nature; statutory duty of company to permit stockholder or shareholder to inspect its books); *Meade v Haringey LBC* [1979] 1 W.L.R. 637 (right to sue for damages does not appear to have been regarded as a condition precedent to the award of a mandatory injunction).

[96] *Webster v Southwark LBC* [1983] Q.B. 698 (Forbes J., although there had been only a declaration and no injunction granted and although a declaration was not a coercive order the court had an inherent power to make an order of sequestration where the interests of justice demanded compliance. If, for example, the courts have declared that an individual has the right to remain in this country, it could be contempt for the Home Office to remove him after having had notice of the declaration). This was accepted to be the position by counsel for the Home Secretary in *M v Home Office* [1994] 1 A.C. 377.

addition, by careful draftsmanship the declaration can be tailored so as not to interfere with the activities of public authorities more than is necessary to ensure that they comply with the law. In many situations all that is required is for the legal position to be clearly set out in a declaration for a dispute of considerable public importance to be resolved. It usually relates to events which have already occurred. However, as will be seen, it is increasingly being used to pronounce upon the legality of a future situation and in that way the occurrence of illegal action is avoided. The courts have jurisdiction to grant an anticipatory injunction, *quia timet*, where this is the only way to avoid imminent danger to the plaintiff but the courts are extremely cautious about granting such relief and the necessity for it can be avoided by granting a declaration instead.

18–040   During the 1970s litigants applied with increasing frequency for declarations in order to obtain relief against the activities of ministers and other public authorities. Many of the landmark decisions which Lord Diplock regarded as constituting the "progress towards a comprehensive system of administrative law [which was] the greatest achievement of the English courts in [his] judicial lifetime"[97] were decided in civil proceedings in which the plaintiff sought a declaration. For example, in perhaps the most important decision of all, *Ridge v Baldwin*,[98] Lord Reid concluded his historic speech by announcing: "I do not think that this House should do more than declare that the dismissal of the appellant is null and void and remit the case to the Queen's Bench Division for further procedure". Similarly, in the almost equally important decision of *Anisminic v Foreign Compensation Commission*,[99] in restoring the decision of Browne J. which had been reversed by the Court of Appeal, the House of Lords granted a declaration that a provisional determination by the Commission was made without, or in excess of, jurisdiction and was a nullity.

Negative declarations

18–041   The courts can be unwilling to grant a negative declaration. By a negative declaration is meant a declaration of no right or no liability. It can also be a declaration as to the absence of any right or power in a defendant or defendant. In order to decide whether a declaration is a negative declaration, it is necessary not merely to examine the terms of the declaration but also its substance since by a careful use of language, what is in fact a negative declaration can be drafted in positive terms.

18–042   There are probably two reasons which explain the reluctance of the court to grant negative declarations.[100] The first is very similar to the reason that explains the opposition to granting declarations as to

---

[97] *R. v Inland Revenue Commissioners Ex p. National Federation of Self-Employed and Small Businesses Ltd* [1982] A.C. 617 at 641.
[98] [1964] A.C. 40.
[99] [1969] 2 A.C. 147.
[100] *Guaranty Trust Co of New York v Hannay & Co* [1915] 2 K.B. 536 at 564–565 (Pickford L.J.: "I think that a declaration that a person is not liable in an existing or possible action is

theoretical issues, if the objective is to anticipate possible proceedings, those proceedings may never occur. The second reason is that they can be used for the purposes of forum shopping.[101] Where there are no existing proceedings, the court will usually want to be satisfied that there is some bona fide reason for commencing them but if there is the court will then be prepared to decide on the merits whether declaratory relief should be granted.[102]

Theoretical issues and advisory declarations

If an issue is theoretical, then in ordinary civil proceedings that is a **18–043** compelling factor against the grant of relief and that remains the situation even if one of the parties has a perfectly legitimate reason for seeking clarification of the legal situation.[103] In claims for judicial review, however, there have now been a number of cases in which the courts have given advisory opinions, in the form of a declaration, where it was clearly desirable that they should do so. The declaratory opinions are given in circumstances where no other remedy would be appropriate. Sir John Laws categorises these situations where it is appropriate for the courts to grant declarations as being "hypothetical". They can equally appropriately be described as raising *theoretical* issues. A hypothetical question is a question which needs to be answered for a real practical purpose, although there may not be an immediate situation on which the decision will have practical affect.[104] A "hypothetical" question has to be distinguished from an "academic" question. An academic question is one which need not be answered for any visible practical purpose, although an answer would satisfy academic curiosity, for example, by clarifying a difficult area of the law. Sir John considers that it would be wrong for the court to grant relief in order to answer academic questions.[105]

one that will hardly ever be made, but that in practically every case the person asking it will be left to set up his defence in the action when it is brought"); *Dyson v Attorney General* [1911] 1 K.B. 410 at 417.

[101] *Camilla Cotton Oil Co v Granadex SA* [1976] 2 Lloyd's Rep. 10 and the speech of Lord Wilberforce.

[102] *Rediffusion (Hong Kong) Ltd v Attorney General of Hong Kong* [1970] A.C. 1136 at 1156; *British Airways v Laker Airways* [1985] A.C. 58; *Staffordshire Moorlands DC v Cartwright* (1991) 63 P. & C.R. 285, CA (granted declarations that planning permission had not been implemented by the defendants, but Mustill L.J. indicated that it was an exceptional case and normally resort should be had to enforcement proceedings).

[103] *Sun Life Assurance v Jervis* [1944] A.C. 111 at 114 (Viscount Simon L.C.: "the appellants are concerned to obtain, if they can, a favourable decision from this House because they fear that other cases may arise under similar documents in which others who have taken out policies of endowment assurance with them will rely on the decision of the Court of Appeal, but if the appellants desire to have the view of the House of Lords on the issue on which the Court of Appeal has pronounced, their proper and more convenient course is to await a further claim and to bring that claim, if necessary, up to the House of Lords with a party on the record whose interest it is to resist the appeal").

[104] See, e.g. *R. (on the application of Sacupima) v Newham LBC* [2001] 1 W.L.R. 563 (because of the "considerable practical importance" of the legal issues, the Admin. Ct and CA dealt with a challenge to the lawfulness of provision of temporary accommodation even though the claimant had by the time of the hearings been provided with satisfactory long-term housing).

[105] J. Laws, "Judicial Remedies and the Constitution" (1994) 57 M.L.R. 213, 214–219.

18–044   The court has jurisdiction to make advisory declarations.[106] Advisory declarations have two main functions: first, to reduce the danger of administrative activities being declared illegal retrospectively, and, secondly, to guide public authorities by giving advice on legal questions which is then binding on everyone.[107]

Declarations of incompatibility

18–045 By s.4 of the Human Rights Act 1998, the court has jurisdiction to grant declarations of incompatibility; these are considered in Chapter 13.[108]

CONTEMPT

18–046 Failure to comply with a mandatory or prohibiting order or injunction, or an undertaking given to the court, is punishable as contempt of court. In theory all the normal sanctions are at the disposal of the court— imprisonment, sequestration, fine—in a case where a public authority fails to comply with a court order in judicial review, a mere finding of contempt rather than a penalty may suffice to mark the gravity of the situation.[109]

18–047   In relation to central government, a court contemplating making a finding of contempt must consider the difference in constitutional law between ministers (who are responsible to Parliament for the failings of their departments and cannot delegate their functions to officials) and officials (who are servants of the Crown, not servants or agents of ministers—though they work under the direction of ministers).[110] It is a minister in his official capacity who a party to the judicial review claim, not officials. It is a minister who is primarily responsible to the court for any failure; but if an official is wilful in his disobedience to a court order, his own conduct may expose him to the risk of being held in contempt.[111] The court may order a senior civil servant to attend court to represent a minister when it is delivering its judgment in contempt proceedings, but a compulsory order to appear should not be made against a civil servant unless there is a good reason for doing so.[112]

---

[106] *Equal Opportunities Commission v Secretary of State for Employment* [1995] 1 A.C. 1 at 27, 36.
[107] Zamir and Woolf, *The Declaratory Judgment*, 3rd edn (2002), p.143, cited with approval *R. (on the application of Campaign for Nuclear Disarmament) v Prime Minister* [2002] EWHC 2777; [2003] A.C.D. 36 at [46].
[108] See 13–045.
[109] *M v Home Office* [1994] 1 A.C. 377.
[110] *Carltona Ltd v Commissioners of Works* [1943] 2 All E.R. 560; *Beggs v Scottish Ministers* [2007] UKHL 3; [2007] 1 W.L.R. 455 at [8] (letters to a prisoner from his legal advisers continued to be opened by prison officers despite an undertaking that this unlawful action would cease).
[111] *Beggs* [2007] UKHL 3; [2007] 1 W.L.R. 455 at [11].
[112] *Beggs* [2007] UKHL 3; [2007] 1 W.L.R. 455 at [13], [40].

DISCRETION IN GRANTING AND WITHHOLDING REMEDIES

Presumption in favour of relief

The general approach ought to be that a claimant who succeeds in establishing the unlawfulness of administrative action is entitled to be granted a remedial order. The court does, however, have discretion—in the sense of assessing "what it is fair and just to do in the particular case"[113]—to withhold a remedy altogether[114] or to grant a declaration (rather than a more coercive quashing, prohibiting or mandatory order or injunction which may have been sought by the claimant)[115] or to grant relief in respect of one aspect of the impugned decision, but not others.[116] But the requirements of the rule of law mean that "the discretion of the court to do other than quash the relevant order or action where such excessive exercise of power is shown is very narrow".[117]   **18–048**

The discretion is narrower still—or in some circumstances non-existent—where the claimant has succeeded in demonstrating a directly effective right under European Community law, given the general obligation on the court to provide effective protection under Art.10 of the EC Treaty.[118] Similarly, where Convention rights are in issue, the court will   **18–049**

---

[113] See generally: Lord Justice Bingham, "Should Public Law Remedies be Discretionary?" [1991] P.L. 64, 66.

[114] *R. v Lincolnshire CC and Wealden DC Ex p. Atkinson, Wales and Stratford* (1996) 8 Admin. L.R. 529 at 550 (Sedley J.: "To refuse relief where an error of law by a public authority has been demonstrated is an unusual and strong thing; but there is no doubt that it can be done").

[115] See, e.g. *Great North Eastern Railway Ltd v Office of Rail Regulation* [2006] EWHC 1942 at [96] (challenge to charging regime for track access).

[116] Discretion is an inherent characteristic of the remedies of quashing, mandatory and prohibiting orders, declarations and injunctions. Supreme Court Act (Senior Courts Act) 1981, s.31(6) makes express provision for delay to considered by the court (see Appendix D). Quashing orders under various enactments (see 17–025) are expressed in terms of that the court "may quash", see e.g. Town and Country Planning Act 1990 ss.287–288.

[117] *Berkeley v Secretary of State for the Environment, Transport and the Regions (No.1)* [2001] 2 A.C. 603 (Lord Bingham). *cf. Credit Suisse v Allerdale* [1997] Q.B. 306 at 355 (Hobhouse L.J.: "The discretion of the court in deciding whether to grant any remedy is a wide one"); *R. v HM Coroner for Inner London South District Ex p. Douglas-Williams* [1999] 1 All E.R. 344 at 347 (Lord Woolf M.R.: "When it comes to exercising this discretion I cannot suggest a better test for a court to apply when deciding whether it should give relief than that it should be 'necessary or desirable to do so in the interest of justice'", in a case relating to a inquest, must be read in context of the use of that expression in Coroners Act 1988 s.13, which provides an alternative remedy to judicial review).

[118] See 14–051; and *Berkeley* [2001] 2 A.C. 603 where the HL rejected the argument that relief should be refused since all the environmental information that would have been part of an environmental impact assessment (which had not been conducted at all) was already in the public domain; but later cases make clear that the mere existence of a European Community law right is not necessarily a bar on the exercise of the court's discretion: *Bown v Secretary of State for Transport, Local Government and the Regions* [2003] EWCA Civ 1170; [2004] Env. L.R. 26; *R. (on the application of Rockware Glass Ltd) v Chester City Council* [2006] EWCA Civ 99 (operation of quashing order suspended); *R. (on the application of Gavin) v Harringey LBC* [2004] 2 P. & C.R. 13 at [40]–[41] (delay provisions in SCA 1981 s.31(6) on delay not inconsistent with principles relating to Environmental Impact Assessments);

need to consider the relevance of ECHR Art.13 which, while not incorporated into national law by the HRA, has a pervasive influence in requiring effective remedies for breaches of Convention rights.[119] The writ of habeas corpus, examined in Chapter 17, is not discretionary but should issue if unlawful detention is established.[120] As with other aspects of the judicial review process, the court must give effect to the "overriding objective" of the CPR in its decision-making about remedies.[121]

18–050　　Where the exercise of discretion by a judge at first instance is challenged on appeal, the Court of Appeal will normally intervene only if the judge below proceeded on the basis of the wrong principles.[122]

Delay

18–051　Delay as a ground on which the court may withhold a remedy is expressly recognised in s.31(6) of the Supreme Court Act (Senior Courts Act) 1981 which provides that where there has been undue delay in making a claim for judicial review:

> "the court may refuse to grant—(a) leave [i.e. permission] for making the application [i.e. claim], or (b) any relief sought on the application if it considers that the grant of the relief sought would be likely to cause substantial hardship to, or substantial prejudice to the rights of, any person or would be detrimental to good administration."[123]

18–052　CPR r.54.5(1) states that judicial review claim form must be filed promptly and in any event within three months from the date when grounds for the claim first arose".[124] Delay is thus relevant both at the permission stage and in relation to the grant of relief after the court has determined the merits of the claimant's case. The court regards these as distinct stages and in relation to the latter, delay is a factor to be considered in deciding whether or not to withhold a remedy *only* if to grant relief would be likely to cause hardship, prejudice or detriment to the defendant or a third party within the meaning of s.31(6)(b). At the full hearing the court is not concerned with the question whether there was good reason to extend time for filing the claim form and seeking permission.[125]

18–053　　The courts have tended to avoid formulating any precise description of what constitutes detriment to good administration. This is because claims for judicial review arise in many different situations and the need for

[119] See 13–010.
[120] See 17–010.
[121] See 16–011.
[122] *R. v Islington LBC Ex p. Dignan* (1998) 30 H.L.R. 723, CA.
[123] *R. (on the application of Parkyn) v Restormel BC* [2001] EWCA Civ 330; [2001] 1 P.L.R. 108 at [32] (Sedley L.J., describing the provision as "distracting and unhelpful").
[124] See 16–050.
[125] *R. v Criminal Injuries Compensation Board Ex p. A* [1999] 2 A.C. 330; on good reasons to extend time, see 16–054.

finality may be greater in one context than another. It has, however, been observed that "there is an interest in good administration independently of hardship, or prejudice to the rights of third parties".[126] In relation to the permission stage, a court may take the view that it is self-evident that a delay has caused detriment to good administration without requiring specific evidence that this has in fact occurred,[127] but in relation to withholding relief evidence may be required.[128] Courts should be unwilling to excuse a breach of the standards required by administrative law merely upon the ground that to quash the decision would cause the decision maker administrative inconvenience: "even if chaos should result, still the law must be obeyed".[129] In *R. v Secretary of State for Social Services Ex p. Association of Metropolitan Authorities*[130] Webster J. held that, although the Secretary of State had not complied with his statutory duty to consult, the housing benefit regulations under challenge should not be quashed, as delegated legislation is not normally revoked unless there are exceptional circumstances, and to revoke the existing regulations would result in confusion.[131] Fortunately, however, courts traditionally receive arguments based upon administrative impracticability with scepticism. Except where the difficulty caused to the decision maker is more than inconvenience, and approaches impracticability or where there is an overriding need for finality and certainty,[132] a remedy should not be refused solely upon this basis. Even if, contrary to Lord Atkin's dictum, convenience and justice are

---

[126] *R. v Dairy Produce Quota Tribunal Ex p. Caswell* [1990] 2 A.C. 738; *R. v Monopolies and Mergers Commission Ex p. Argyll* [1986] 1 W.L.R. 763 at 774; *Coney v Choyce* [1975] 1 W.L.R. 422 at 436; *R. v Panel on Takeovers and Mergers Ex p. Guinness Plc* [1990] 1 Q.B. 146 at 177.

[127] *R. v Newbury DC Ex p. Chieveley Parish Council* (1998) 10 Admin.L.R. 676 (unexplained delay in applying out of time for judicial review of major planning proposal).

[128] *R. v Secretary of State for the Home Department Ex p. Oyeleye (Florence Jumoke)* [1994] Imm. A.R. 268 (no evidence of detriment to good administration had been put before the court and accordingly the court could not be satisfied that there was any such detriment).

[129] *R. v Governors of Small Heath School Ex p. Birmingham CC* [1990] C.O.D. 23, CA; *Bradbury v Enfield LBC* [1967] 1 W.L.R. 1311 at 1324 (Lord Denning M.R.).

[130] [1986] 1 W.L.R. 1, DC; and *R. v Gateshead MBC Ex p. Nichol* (1988) 87 L.G.R. 435 (CA refused to quash part-implemented school reorganisation scheme).

[131] Since a large number of local authorities had acted upon the regulations as promulgated by determining claims in accordance with their terms; *R. v Secretary of State for Employment Ex p. Seymour-Smith* [1994] I.R.L.R. 448; *R. v Brent LBC Ex p. O'Malley*; *R. v Secretary of State for the Environment Ex p. Walters* [1998] C.O.D. 121 (CA upheld decision of Schiemann J. that notwithstanding that the extensive consultation process (relating to the redevelopment of council housing estates) carried out by the respondents was flawed, no relief should be granted since there was overwhelming evidence that the granting of review would damage the interests of a large number of other individuals, and it would be "absurd" to ignore such disbenefits); the courts' discretion to refuse relief was said to be a broad one to be exercised in the light of the particular circumstances (see 18–048).

[132] See, e.g. *R. v Monopolies and Mergers Commission Ex p. Argyll Group* [1986] 1 W.L.R. 763 (CA refused to grant a remedy for what was held to be an unlawful delegation of discretion because, among other reasons, commercial considerations dictated that decisions of the MMC should be speedy and final. The CA was influenced, however, by the fact that the unlawful decision had been approved by the minister); *cf. R. v Panel on Takeovers and Mergers Ex p. Datafin* [1987] Q.B. 815, CA.

on speaking terms,[133] conversation between the two should be strictly limited.[134]

Standing

18–054 The extent of the "sufficient interest" of the claimant is a factor to be considered when deciding what, if any, relief to grant.[135] As we have noted, when it comes to deciding in its discretion whether to grant relief—a court is going to be more hesitant in some situations in granting, for example, a mandatory order or an injunction than a declaration.

Remedy would serve no practical purpose

18–055 The court may exercise discretion not to provide a remedy if to make an order would serve no practical purpose. For example, events can overtake proceedings. So a licence, the validity of which is challenged in the proceedings, may have expired by the time the claim is determined by the Administrative Court. Similarly an activity under challenge may have ceased before a remedy has been granted.[136] It may, for instance, be pointless to quash a decision to enable the public to be consulted on data that has become out of date;[137] or to quash a decision to disclose a report which had, by the date of judgment, already been disclosed.[138] Even a declaration may serve little practical purpose in such circumstances.

18–056   The modern purpose of remedies is simply to give effect to the judgment of the court on the substance of the law.[139] In relation to the procedural fairness, however, the courts have in the past sometimes failed to make a clear distinction between (a) holding that a decision is *not unlawful* because the procedural defect is subsequently cured, for example, by an appeal—in which case the claimant has no grounds of complaint, and (b) situations where a ground of review is established but the court nonetheless withholds relief.[140]

---

[133] *General Medical Council v Spackman* [1943] A.C. 627 at 638.
[134] The same principle may be seen in the case law of the ECJ.
[135] See 2–022; see, e.g. *R. v Felixstowe Justices Ex p. Leigh* [1987] Q.B. 582).
[136] In *Williams v Home Office (No.2)* [1981] 1 All E.R. 1211 and [1982] 2 All E.R. 564, a prison unit had closed.
[137] *R. (on the application of Edwards) v Environment Agency (No.2)* [2006] EWCA Civ 877; [2007] Env. L.R. 9 at [126].
[138] *R. v Sunderland Juvenile Court Ex p. G* [1988] 1 W.L.R. 398; *cf. R. v NW Thames Regional Health Authority Ex p. Daniels* [1993] 4 Med. L.R. 364.
[139] See 18–002.
[140] See Ch.8.

Claimant has suffered no harm

In some cases the court has withheld a remedy from a claimant on the basis **18–057**
that he has been caused no harm (the term "prejudice" is often used) by
the unlawful act of the public authority.[141] Under this head, a minor
technical breach of statutory requirement may too insignificant to justify
relief. The court may also take into account the fact that the public
authority would have made the same decision even if the legal flaw had not
occurred.[142] Here it is important to proceed with a considerable degree of
caution. As the Law Commission has pointed out, in assuming inevitability
of outcome the court is prejudging the decision and thus may be in danger
of overstepping the bounds of its reviewing functions by entering into the
merits of the decision itself.[143]

Financial ramifications of a remedy

As we have seen in earlier chapters, the courts have in some cases **18–058**
considered the impact that their judgments may have on resource allocation in deciding whether or not a public authority has acted unlawfully in
the circumstances.[144] At the stage we are concerned with in this chapter—
the grant of remedies—it is submitted that financial considerations ought
not to feature in the calculation of a court deciding whether to grant a
remedial order to a claimant who has demonstrated to the court's
satisfaction that a public authority has acted unlawfully. An award of
damages will have obvious financial implications for a public authority, but
the courts do not have regard to the resources available to the defendant in
a particular case if tort liability has been established.[145] The same approach
should be applied to other remedies available in judicial review claims.

Nullity and ultra vires and discretion

The result of a decision being unlawful is considered fully elsewhere.[146] **18–059**
However, if (which is doubtful) for the purposes of public law a decision
can ever be categorised as being a nullity, then that will be relevant to the

[141] See, e.g. *R. v Dairy Produce Quota Tribunal Ex p. Davies* [1987] 2 C.M.L.R. 399; *R. v
Lambeth LBC Ex p. Sharp* (1988) 55 P. & C.R. 232; *R. v Governors of Small Heath School Ex
p. Birmingham City Council* [1990] C.O.D. 23; *R. v Governors of Bacon's School Ex p. ILEA*
[1990] C.O.D. 414; *R. (on the application of Laporte) v Newham LBC* [2004] EWHC 227.
[142] See, e.g. *Cinnamond v British Airports Authority* [1980] 1 W.L.R. 582; *R. (on the
application of Jones) v Swansea City and CC* [2007] EWHC 213 (Admin), [2007] All E.R. (D)
191 (Feb) at [31] ("virtually inconceivable that the defendant would do other than grant
planning permission").
[143] Law Com No.226, *Administrative Law: Judicial Review and Statutory Appeals*, para.8.18.
See also D. Clark, "Natural Justice: Substance and Shadow" [1975] P.L. 27; *John v Rees*
[1970] Ch. 345 at 402 (Megarry J.).
[144] See 5–124 (relevance of financial considerations).
[145] See Ch.19.
[146] See 4–056; *Anisminic Ltd v Foreign Compensation Commission* [1969] 2 A.C. 147 at 171;
London and Clydeside Estates Ltd v Aberdeen DC [1980] 1 W.L.R. 182 at 189, 203; *Chief
Constable of North Wales Police v Evans* [1982] 1 W.L.R. 1155 at 1163; *Hoffmann-LaRoche
& Co v Secretary of State for Trade and Industry* [1975] A.C. 295.

exercise of discretion to grant or withhold relief. There can be no purpose in purporting to keep alive a decision which is devoid of all content. Subject to there being some purpose in obtaining the decision of a court, if a court comes to the conclusion that a decision is totally invalid and of no effect, it will normally readily be prepared to grant a declaration to this effect. Strictly speaking there is nothing to be achieved in the case of a decision which is a nullity in making a quashing order. You cannot quash something which is already a nullity. However, in practice adopting a pragmatic approach and so avoiding becoming involved in issues as to the quality and status of an invalid administrative decision, the court will be prepared to make a quashing order without resolving the complex issue as to whether or not this is strictly necessary. This is subject to the case being one in which the court would in any event have granted relief, if this were necessary, in the form of a quashing order.

Claimant's motive

18–060 The claimant's motive in making a claim for judicial review—whether it is commercial or otherwise—is not a relevant consideration in the court's decision to grant or withhold a remedy.[147]

---

[147] *R. (on the application of Mount Cook Land Ltd) v Westminster City Council* [2003] EWCA Civ 1346; [2004] C.P. Rep. 12 at [45]–[46] (unless the motive raises questions as to abuse of process).

CHAPTER 19

MONETARY REMEDIES IN JUDICIAL REVIEW

SCOPE

This chapter examines the circumstances in which a claimant for judicial **19–001**
review (or a claimant in civil proceedings alleging that a public authority
has acted unlawfully in a public law sense) may be awarded a monetary
remedy.[1] These are principally where the public authority:

- has committed a tort during the course of exercising its public
  functions;[2]

- is under an obligation to make restitution of money paid by the
  claimant;[3]

- has breached a Convention right, contrary to the duty in s.6 of the
  HRA, and the court considers it is just and appropriate to award
  damages under s.8 of the HRA;[4]

- damages under European Community law are considered in Chapter
  14.[5]

The award of damages serves to compensate but may also act as a sanction
to discourage careless or intentional wrongdoing.[6]

Other sources of compensation

The sums of money recoverable for wrongs done by public authorities in **19–002**
the exercise of their public functions are often relatively modest. In
contrast, the costs of litigation, particularly in the High Court, may be

---

[1] See generally P. Hogg and P. Monahan, *Liability of the Crown*, 3rd edn (2000); D.
Fairgrieve, *State Liability in Tort: A Comparative Law Study* (2003); K. Stanton, P. Skidmore,
M. Harris and J. Wright, *Statutory Torts* (2003); D. Nolan, "Suing the State: Governmental
Liability in Comparative Perspective" (2004) 67 M.L.R. 844; C. Harlow, *State Liability: Tort
Law and Beyond* (2004).
[2] See 19–025.
[3] See 19–075.
[4] See 19–081.
[5] See 14–066.
[6] The role of exemplary (or punitive) damages is considered below at 19–063. Linden argues
that "Tort law is an ombudsman. It can be used to apply pressure on those who wield
political, economic or intellectual power. This is rarely the expressed aim of a tort suit, but it
can be an important side effect" (A. Linden, "Tort Law as Ombudsman" (1973) 51 Can. B.R.
155). In England and Wales many of the tort claims made against the police and prison
services need to be viewed in this light. The impact of tort liability on the behaviour of
officials and public bodies is considered at 19–072.

considerable. One of the overriding objectives of the CPR is to ensure that cases are dealt with in a manner that is proportionate to the amounts of money involved, the complexity and importance of the case.[7] In relation to cases where there is an overlap between maladministration (for example delay or muddle) and breach of a Convention right, the Court of Appeal has emphasised the need for would-be claimants to consider making a complaint to the one of the ombudsmen,[8] who have powers to recommend that compensation be paid to a person who has suffered injustice as a result of maladministration. This approach has much to commend it in all situations in which the real gist of the complaint is maladministration.

19–003   Where there is no statutory or common law right to compensation or restitution for unlawful action, public authorities have discretion in many contexts to make ex gratia payments. Decisions as to whether to make payments of statutory or discretionary compensation, in practice an important source of compensation, may themselves be susceptible to judicial review.[9]

PROCEDURAL ISSUES

19–004   Public authorities, like individual citizens and business enterprises, may be subject to civil liability to compensate or make restitution as a result of their wrongful acts or omissions in different contexts, many of which are unconnected issues of public law. This chapter deals with one aspect of this broad field—monetary claims that are related or ancillary to a claim for judicial review.

19–005   On a CPR Pt 54 claim for judicial review, the Administrative Court may award the claimant "damages, restitution or the recovery of a sum due" if "(a) the application includes a claim for such an award arising from any matter to which the application relates; and (b) the court is satisfied that such an award would have been made if the claim had been made in an action begun by the applicant at the time of making the application".[10] This provision is a procedural one designed to prevent multiplicity of proceedings and does not affect the general rule of substantive law that

---

[7] See 16–011.

[8] On which, see 1–081; *R. (on the application of Anufrijeva) v Southwark LBC* [2003] EWCA Civ 1406; [2004] Q.B. 1124 at [81].

[9] See, e.g. *Tower Hamlets LBC v Chetnik Developments Ltd* [1988] A.C. 858; *R. (on the application of Elias) v Secretary of State for Defence* [2005] EWHC 1435; [2005] I.R.L.R. 788; *R. (on the application of Association of British Civilian Internees (Far East Region)) v Secretary of State for Defence* [2003] EWCA Civ 473; [2003] Q.B. 1397; *Hooper v Secretary of State for Work and Pensions* [2005] UKHL 29; [2005] 1 W.L.R. 1681, HL; [2003] EWCA Civ 813; [2003] 1 W.L.R. 2623, CA; *R. (on the application of O'Brien) v Independent Assessor* [2007] UKHL 10; [2007] 2 W.L.R. 544.

[10] Supreme Court Act (Senior Courts Act)1981 s.31(4), as substituted by the Civil Procedure (Modification of the Supreme Court Act 1981) Order 2004 (SI 2004/1033). Before 2004 the relevant provisions referred only to damages.

there is no right to damages for unlawful administrative action per se. A claimant must identify a tortious liability—typically negligence, breach of statutory duty, misfeasance in public office or trespass—or a right to restitution or recovery of a sum due. The Human Rights Act 1998, s.8 provides the court with power to award damages for breach of Convention rights[11] and damages may also be awarded for serious breach of European Community law.[12]

Civil claim or judicial review?

Prior to the CPR, the relationship between civil actions and applications **19–006** for judicial review was often unhappily the subject of dispute in the courts.[13] Now the case management powers of CPR provide a flexible regime for allocating claims to the most appropriate court and judge.[14] CPR 52.3(2) prohibits a claimant seeking only a monetary remedy in judicial review proceedings—the claim must also include a request for a mandatory, prohibiting or quashing order or a declaration or injunction.[15] Thus where the claimant's sole purpose in resorting to litigation is to obtain damages the appropriate procedure is a CPR Pt 7 civil claim rather than judicial review. Beyond this, a spectrum of different scenarios may arise in which legal advisers and the court need to consider whether a monetary remedy should be sought by way of a claim for judicial review or by a civil claim under CPR Pt 7.

No public law issues

Where there is no public law content to the dispute (for example, if the **19–007** claim concerns the negligent driving of a vehicle), a claim for judicial review is obviously inappropriate. The claim should be determined by the county court or High Court under CPR Pt 7.

Public law issues a background to the dispute

Where public functions provide the background to a dispute (for example **19–008** allegations of failure by a local education authority to provide adequate schooling), a claim for judicial review will be inappropriate where the remedy sought is solely damages[16] and the main issues at stake is whether there has been a tortious wrong. Here again the claim should be determined under CPR Pt 7 in the county court or High Court.

[11] See 19–081.
[12] See 14–066.
[13] See 3–097.
[14] See, e.g. *R. (on the application of Wilkinson) v Broadmoor Special Hospital Authority* [2001] EWCA Civ 1545; [2002] 1 W.L.R. 419 at [62].
[15] Ch.18.
[16] CPR r.54.2(3).

Public law issues must be decided to determine damages claim

19-009 Where questions relating to the unlawfulness of the exercise of a public function (that is, whether the public authority has acted contrary to one of the grounds of judicial review—illegality, irrationality and procedural impropriety) will substantially determine whether the claimant is entitled to a monetary remedy in tort or restitution. Here the claimant's advisers and the court need to decide how to proceed. Recent decisions relating to procedural exclusivity have emphasised the need to consider whether the procedure adopted by the claimant is well-suited to determine the issues rather than rigid conceptual distinctions between public and private law issues.[17] If the sole or main purpose of a CPR Pt 54 claim is merely to "prime the pump" for a damages claim, it has been indicated that the court should refuse permission for a claim for judicial review and transfer the matter to continue as an ordinary civil claim,[18] but this may not always be the case and the court should adopt a pragmatic approach and determine the most advantageous course for the proceedings it is considering—always bearing in mind that "judicial review was not intended to be used for debt collecting".[19] The CPR Pt 54 claim for judicial review procedure is not well suited to determining those monetary claims which turn on factual disputes which are more appropriately dealt with by a detailed statement of claim and oral evidence from witnesses subject to cross-examination.[20] In such cases it may be more convenient for the Administrative Court first to determine the public law issues, and then make an order transferring the issues relating to tortious or other private law liability to proceed as if begun under CPR Pt 7.[21] Among other possible ways of determining issues are: the court may award damages at the judicial review hearing, but leave quantum to be assessed by a Master; where a claim is started in the county court but it is thought that expertise in public law issues is needed, the case may be transferred to the High Court to be heard by a judge with Administrative Court experience, or a High Court judge with Administrative Court expertise may sit as a judge in the county court pursuant to s.5(3) of the County Courts Act 1984.[22]

Claim for damages under s.8 of the HRA

19-010 Where a claim for damages under s.8 of the HRA is made separately from a judicial review claim, and turn on what is in essence a complaint of "maladministration", the Court of Appeal has indicated that this should be

---

[17] See 3–103.
[18] *R. v Blandford JJ. Ex p. Pamment* [1990] 1 W.L.R. 1490 (certiorari to quash order of magistrates refused); *R. v Gloucestershire CC Ex p. P* [1993] C.O.D. 303 (declaration that respondent has delayed unreasonably in providing statement of special educational needs refused). *R. v Ministry of Agriculture, Fisheries and Food Ex p. Live Sheep Traders Ltd* [1995] C.O.D. 297.
[19] *Trustees of the Dennis Rye Pension Fund v Sheffield CC* [1998] 1 W.L.R. 840, 846 (Lord Woolf M.R.).
[20] *D v Home Office* [2005] EWCA Civ 38; [2006] 1 W.L.R. 1003 at [104].
[21] CPR r.54.20 and Pt 30.
[22] See, e.g. *D v Home Office* [2005] EWCA Civ 38; [2006] 1 W.L.R. 1003 at [128].

made to the Administrative Court by an ordinary claim under CPR Pt 7.[23] But this ought not to be regarded as an invariable rule, and attention must always be paid to the overriding objective of the CPR.[24] Where, for example, a claim for damages under s.8 arises in the context of a local authority's duties in relation to children, a claim for damages under s.8 may be more appropriately dealt with by the Family Division.

Interest

In the past there has been uncertainty over whether the court has power to award interest in relation to a monetary remedy awarded in CPR Pt 54 judicial review proceedings, though the better view is that interest may be awarded.[25]   19–011

DEFENDANTS IN MONETARY CLAIMS RELATING TO JUDICIAL REVIEW

In the context with which we are concerned, the person against whom the claim for a monetary remedy is made will usually be the defendant in a judicial review claim or other public law proceeding. However, direct and vicarious liability in tort may make it necessary for some other person to be   19–012

---

[23] R. (on the application of Anufrijeva) v Southwark LBC [2003] EWCA Civ 1406; [2004] Q.B. 1124 at [81]. The CPR do not make clear the presumption that claims for HRA damages should be made to the Administrative Court. See also Practice Direction to Pt 16, para.15 on the requirements of a statement of claim.

[24] See 16–011.

[25] The court's general power to award interest rests on Supreme Court Act 1981 (Senior Courts Act 1981) s.35A. In R. v Secretary of State for Transport Ex p. Sherriff and Sons Ltd, Independent, January 12, 1988 it was held that s.35A did not apply to judicial review proceedings in relation to non-payment of a grant under the Railways Act 1974 (Taylor J.: "In my judgment, the whole tenor of the language used in section 35A confines its application to civil actions in the private law field. Only by the loosest and most stretched use of language could these proceedings be said to be 'for the recovery of a debt'"). This issue was canvassed, but not resolved, in R. v Newham LBC Ex p. Barking and Dagenham LBC [1994] R.A. 13 in relation to a restitutionary award. Late payments of grants made under statutory schemes may, in many contexts, be regarded as giving rise to claims in debt: see, e.g. Trustees of the Dennis Rye Pension Fund v Sheffield CC [1998] 1 W.L.R. 840 (landlord could bring ordinary civil proceedings to recover unpaid grant as an ordinary debt, notwithstanding statutory code); R. v Ministry of Agriculture Fisheries and Food Ex p Lower Burytown Farms Ltd, CO/956/96, February 10, 1998, Laws J. (unrep.) (interest awarded following late payment of "set aside" grant to farmer); cf. Jones v Department of Employment [1989] Q.B. 1. The view that interest is not recoverable is surely misconceived since, if it were not, all a claimant would need to do would be to request the court to direct that the claim should be continued as if started under CPR Pt 7 (see CPR r.54.20 and 30) and then the court would have power to grant interest. The Law Commission recommended in its 1994 report that the court should have the same power to award interest as in ordinary civil proceedings: see Law Com. No.226, para.8.8. In R. (on the application of Kemp) v Denbighshire Local Health Board [2006] EWHC 181 (Admin); [2006] 3 All E.R. 141 the Admin. Ct. accepted it had jurisdiction to award interest on a sum of money reimbursed because a local authority ought to have paid for the claimant's care in a nursing home.

joined as a party where a monetary remedy is sought. The principle espoused by Dicey and Maitland,[26] that an individual official is personally liable for torts committed in the course of his official duties, remains good today.[27] Usually the official's employer will be vicariously, and so jointly and severally, liable;[28] but an employer of an official will not be vicariously liable for a person who is a public officer given independent statutory powers or duties in his or her own right.[29] After some hesitation, it is now clear that a public authority may be vicariously liable for its officers who commit misfeasance in public office providing that the employee is engaged in a misguided and unauthorised method of performing his or her duties rather than an unauthorised act so unconnected with his or her authorised duties as to be quite independent of and outside those duties.[30] Police officers are neither Crown servants nor employees of the local police authority; the Chief Constable of each police force in the United Kingdom is, however, made by statute vicariously liable for the acts and omissions of his officers and any damages awarded against an officer will be paid out of the police fund.[31] Generally, it has been argued that the imposition of personal liability on individual decision makers, or vicarious liability on their employer, may have a detrimental impact on their behaviour and that

[26] See 19–026.
[27] See, e.g. *Lonrho Plc v Tebbit* [1992] 4 All E.R. 280 (minister and officials alleged to have negligently failed to release claimant company from undertakings not to acquire more than 30% of another company following investigation by Monopolies and Mergers Commission). Mr Tebbitt was the Secretary of State for Trade and Industry at the time. In practice, the Crown will pay any damages awarded against a minister or official. *D v Home Office* [2005] EWCA Civ 38; [2006] 1 W.L.R. 1003 at [56] ("there is on the face of it nothing in the slightest bit peculiar about an individual bringing a private law claim for damages against an executive official who has unlawfully infringed his private rights").
[28] See, e.g. *Phelps v Hillingdon LBC* [2001] 2 A.C. 619 (local education authority vicariously liable for educational professionals); *Home Office v Dorset Yacht Co Ltd* [1970] A.C. 1004 (Borstal officers, for whom the Home Office was vicariously liable, owed a duty to take such care as is reasonable in all the circumstances with a view to preventing the boys under their control from causing damage to private property). *cf.* the position of a minister who is not vicariously liable for acts or omissions for civil servants in his department; they are not his employees or agents, but the Crown's.
[29] For example, the council would not have been responsible for their employee, Mr Sharp, the local land charges registrar in *Ministry of Housing and Local Government v Sharp and Hemel Hempstead RDC* [1970] 2 Q.B. 223, Lord Denning M.R.: "In keeping the register and issuing the certificates, [Mr Sharp] is not acting for the council. He is carrying out his own statutory duties [as the 'proper officer' under the Land Charges Act 1925] on his own behalf. So he himself is responsible for breach of those duties and not the council: see *Stanbury v Exeter Corp* [1905] 2 K.B. 838". The council was, however, vicariously liable for the subordinate clerk employed by them who actually carried out the negligent search. The council did not seek to rely on the fact that the minor clerk, although their employee, was seconded to the registrar and so part of his staff.
[30] *Racz v Home Office* [1994] 2 A.C. 45 (ill-treatment at the hands of prison officers); see 19–048.
[31] Police Act 1996 s.88; Police Act 1997 s.42. This rule does not apply to a Chief Constable himself who, in theory at least, remains personally liable for damages arising from his own tortious acts. For a detailed treatment of police liability, see R. Clayton et al., *Civil Actions Against the Police*, 3rd edn (2005).

direct governmental liability is to be preferred in an ideal scheme of remedies.[32]

It has been said that "if a man is required in the discharge of a public **19–013** duty to make a decision which affects, by its legal consequences, the liberty or property of others, and he performs that duty and makes that decision honestly and in good faith, it is . . . a fundamental principle of our law that he is protected"[33] against civil liability in respect of the consequences of that decision. Clearly, however, this proposition is inapplicable to many statutory functions involving the exercise of discretion. The donee of a power may often be held liable in tort for the consequences of an erroneous or negligent exercise of his discretion although he has acted in perfectly good faith.[34] Even where a statute has exempted public officers from liability for acts done "bona fide for the purpose of executing this Act", the courts have held that a negligent act causing damage is nonetheless actionable.[35] Nonetheless the passage quoted may be a correct statement of the rules applicable to the exercise of certain classes of statutory functions. Thus, election officers who had wrongfully refused to accept votes of legally qualified voters were held immune from civil liability unless they had acted in bad faith.[36] The General Medical Council was held not to be liable for having removed a dentist from the register by an improper procedure but in good faith.[37] The common thread running through these cases is the erroneous exercise of judgment on matters immediately affecting the legal rights of individuals.[38] It would appear to be

[32] D. Cohen and J. Smith, "Entitlement and the Body Politic: Rethinking Negligence in Public Law" (1986) 64 Can.B.R. 1, 9, 16; P. Schuck, *Suing Government: Citizen Remedies for Official Wrongs* (1983).

[33] *Everett v Griffiths* [1921] 1 A. C. 631 at 695 (Lord Moulton); *Percy v Hall* [1997] Q.B. 924 (the fact that byelaws were later declared void for uncertainty did not render tortious the actions of police officers who, at the relevant time, reasonably believed that byelaw offences were being committed).

[34] See, e.g. *Evans v Governor of Brockhill Prison (No.2)* [2001] 2 A.C. 19 (tort of false imprisonment was one of strict liability and the fact that the prison governor had acted in good faith was no defence); *cf. Quinland v Governor of Belmarsh Prison* [2002] EWCA Civ 174; [2003] Q.B. 306 (until an order of a court was set aside it justified detention so imprisonment pursuant to that order was not tortious).

[35] *Bullard v Croydon Hospital Group Management Committee* [1953] 1 Q.B. 511 construing National Health Service Act 1946 s.72 (now NHS Act 1977 s.125 as amended by National Health Service and Community Care Act 1990 Sch.2); *cf. Capital & Counties Plc v Hampshire CC* [1997] Q.B. 1004 (CA held that Fire Services Act 1947 s.30 was not apt to establish an implied immunity from proceedings for negligence or breach of statutory duty for fire fighters involved in extinguishing a fire).

[36] *Tozer v Child* (1857) 7 E. & B. 377; *Drewe v Coulton* (1787) 1 East 563n., applying Holt C.J.'s judgment in *Ashby v White* (1703) 2 Ld. Raym. 938. No civil liability is now incurred by election officers for breach of official duty (Representation of the People Act 1983 s.63, as amended by s.24 of the Representation of the People Act 1985). For discussion of bad faith in the context of judicial review, see 5–080.

[37] *Partridge v GMC* (1890) 25 Q.B.D. 90. The authority for this decision is not beyond question, for the GMC's procedural error amounted to a denial of natural justice. *cf. McGillivray v Kimber* (1915) 52 S.C.R. 142.

[38] But the categories of those consensually appointed by the parties who enjoy immunity from liability save for bad faith are more narrowly drawn: *Sutcliffe v Thackrah* [1974] A.C. 727; *Arenson v Arenson* [1977] A.C. 405 (distinguishing arbitrators from valuers). See also *Campbell v Edwards* [1976] 1 W.L.R. 403.

justifiable to infer that members of administrative bodies which exercise functions of a broadly judicial character are not liable in tort for the consequences of erroneous or unreasonable decisions or procedural irregularities within the scope of their jurisdiction, provided that they have not acted in bad faith. Bad faith is here understood to mean intentional usurpation of power, wilful partiality, discrimination motivated by considerations which are incompatible with the discharge of public responsibilities.

19–014 Local authorities are statutory corporations given specific powers to institute and defend any legal proceedings.[39] The now routine use of "contracting out" and other market based mechanisms for the delivery of public services has not yet been followed by the development of any new general principles of civil liability. So on normal principles,[40] where service delivery has truly been contracted out to an independent contractor, the public authority will not be vicariously liable for the tortious acts of that contractor (unless statute provides otherwise).[41] The public authority may, however, owe some non-delegable duty to the claimant in these circumstances. But many "bodies" delivering services, such as executive agencies in central government, directly managed units (DMUs) in the National Health Service and direct service organisations (DSOs) in local government, have no separate legal personality apart from that of their parent organisation which will remain directly liable for tortious acts.

The Crown as a defendant[42]

19–015 As with amenability to judicial review[43] and judicial review remedies,[44] the Crown—as distinct from its servants and agents—needs special consideration in relation to monetary remedies. Following the enactment of the Crown Proceedings Act 1947, many though not all of the Crown's former immunities from suit for damages in contract and tort enjoyed by central government have been removed and to a large extent it now stands in a broadly (but not wholly) similar position to a private person of full age and capacity in relation to its liabilities.[45] The constitutional principle of the rule of law requires that "the Crown (that is the executive government in its various emanations) is in general subject to the same common law obligations as ordinary citizens",[46] unless there is a clearly established exception established by law.

[39] Local Government Act 1972 s.222.
[40] Criticised by E. McKendrick, "Vicarious Liability and Independent Contractors: A Re-Examination" (1990) 53 M.L.R. 770.
[41] Under Criminal Justice Act 1991 s.85, any contracted-out remand prison must have a "controller", a Crown Servant appointed by the Secretary of State; presumably the Crown will be vicariously liable for the tort of this officer under Crown Proceedings Act 1947 s.2(1).
[42] P. Hogg and P. Monahan, *Liability of the Crown*, 3rd edn (2000).
[43] See 3–037.
[44] See 18–005; *M v Home Office* [1994] 1 A.C. 377; *Davidson v Scottish Ministers* [2005] UKHL 74; 2006 S.C. (HL) 41.
[45] Crown Proceedings Act 1947 s.2(1).
[46] *Deutsche Morgan Grenfell Group Plc v Inland Revenue Commissioners* [2006] UKHL 49; [2006] 3 W.L.R. 781, [133].

The 1947 Act "does not work by making the state a potential tortfeasor: **19–016** it works by making the Crown vicariously liable for the torts of its servants".[47] In relation to tort, s.2 of the 1947 Act places the Crown in the same position as other defendants for certain categories of liability, namely: (i) vicarious liability; (ii) direct liability to its employees; (iii) direct liability arising from breaches of duties attaching to the ownership, occupation, possession and control of property; and (iv) direct liability for breach of a statutory duty.[48] This approach has been criticised as it may leave the Crown with unintended immunity where no individual Crown servant is negligent (so the Crown is not vicariously liable), yet the duty owed by the Crown directly does not fall within one of the specified categories.[49] For reasons of policy, not all of them convincing, the Crown continues to benefit from a number of specific immunities by reason of its status:[50]

(a) The 1947 Act makes no alteration to the rule that the Crown is not bound by a statute unless such an intention is express or necessarily implied.[51]

(b) The Crown is not directly or vicariously liable for its servants and agents who are discharging or purporting to discharge "any responsibilities of a judicial nature".[52]

(c) Crown immunity under s.10 of the 1947 Act in relation to the armed services has now been suspended;[53] the Secretary of State may by delegated legislation reinstate it in emergency situations.

(d) The monarch in her personal capacity continues to be immune from suit.[54]

(e) In relation to governmental acts performed outside the jurisdiction on the orders of the Crown, the defence of act of state may be available to the Crown (and its servants) in limited circumstances.[55]

---

[47] *Chagos Islanders v Attorney General* [2004] EWCA Civ 997; *The Times*, September 21, 2004 at [20] (Sedley L.J.).

[48] This does not make the Crown liable for damages for breach of public law statutory duties possessed by it alone; there is liability only in respect of statutory duties "binding also upon persons other than the Crown and its officers": see s.2(2).

[49] P. Hogg and P. Monahan, *Liability of the Crown*, 3rd edn (2000), pp.110–111.

[50] The 1947 Act made no attempt to separate the governmental from the commercial functions of the Crown.

[51] *BBC v Johns* [1965] Ch.D. 32 at 79; *Lord Advocate v Dumbarton DC* [1990] 2 A.C. 580. *cf.* Hogg and Monahan (2000), Ch.6, where it is argued that there is no good reason for this rule.

[52] 1947 Act s.2(5); see 19–018.

[53] Crown Proceedings (Armed Forces) Act 1987; *Mulcahy v Ministry of Defence* [1996] Q.B. 732 (no duty of care existed between soldiers on active service and MoD was not obliged to maintain a safe system of work in battle situations). Section 10 is a substantive limitation rather than a procedural bar to civil liability: *Matthews v Ministry of Defence* [2003] UKHL 4; [2003] 1 A.C. 1163.

[54] 1947 Act s.40(1).

[55] *Nissan v Attorney General* [1970] A.C. 179.

(f) Although bad faith can be imputed to ministers of the Crown, it seems that it cannot be imputed to the Crown itself; but an act done by the Crown may be impugned on the ground that it was done in good faith but for an unauthorised purpose.[56]

19-017 Those who carry on the activities of government in the various bodies which collectively constitute the Crown are servants or agents of the Crown. For the purposes of civil proceedings, the 1947 Act states that, unless the context otherwise requires, "agents" includes an independent contractor employed by the Crown and "officer" in relation to the Crown includes any servant of Her Majesty and accordingly includes a minister of the Crown.[57] In relation to liability of the Crown for tort, the Act provides that an "officer" is someone who has been directly or indirectly appointed by the Crown and who is, at the material time, being paid in respect of his duties as an officer of the Crown solely out of the consolidated fund, monies provided by Parliament, or any other fund certified by the Treasury.[58] In accordance with s.17, the Cabinet Office from time to time publishes a list of authorised government departments for the purpose of identifying the department by and against which civil proceedings may be brought.[59] The list is not exhaustive and where a body, which is part of the Crown, is not identified on the list or where there is doubt as to which of the authorised departments on the list is the appropriate one, the proceedings can be brought against the Attorney General.

Judicial immunity from civil liability[60]

19-018 Many judicial review challenges are against the decisions of judges, magistrates, coroners, tribunals or others taking decisions of a judicial nature. In an important exception to the general principle of treating public officials similarly to private persons, the common law confers an extremely high degree of immunity from tortious liability on those exercising judicial functions.[61] First, as already noted, the Crown enjoys

---

[56] R. v Halliday [1917] A.C. 260; Hudson's Bay Co v Maclay (1920) 36 T.L.R. 469.
[57] 1947 Act s.38(2).
[58] 1947 Act s.2(6).
[59] Sedley L.J. laments that practitioners tend overlook the fact that the list names the "Home Office", not the "Secretary of State for the Home Department", as the relevant name: Akenzua v Secretary of State for the Home Department [sic.] [2002] EWCA Civ 1470; [2003] 1 W.L.R. 741 at [1].
[60] See A. Olowofoyeku, Suing Judges: A Study of Judicial Immunity (1993); M. Brazier, "Judicial Immunity and the Independence of the judiciary" [1976] P.L. 397.
[61] The case law relating to ECHR Art.6 recognises that judicial immunity is a legitimate means of ensuring the proper administration of justice: see, e.g. Mond v United Kingdom (Admissibility) (49606/99) (2003) 37 E.H.R.R. CD 129 (immunity from suit afforded to the Official Receiver was proportionate to the legitimate aim of enabling him to discharge his public duties without fear of litigation); cf. in European Community law, Case C-224/01 Kobler v Austria [2004] Q.B. 848 (subject to conditions, the principle that Member States were obliged to make reparations for the State's breaches of Community law applied to reparations stemming from decisions by a national court of final instance); see 14-066.

complete immunity and is neither primarily nor vicariously liable for any wrongful exercise of power by its judicial officers.[62] Secondly, words spoken in the course of judicial proceedings (including those before some tribunals)[63] are absolutely privileged in the law of defamation which means no action lies even if a statement is made maliciously.[64] Thirdly, those carrying out judicial functions enjoy wide immunity from actions for damages generally.[65] This general immunity from actions for damages attaches to judicial functions, not the person or tribunal and such, and so a judge is not protected when exercising administrative or ministerial powers[66] nor when he is *functus officio* (i.e. having completed his duties in relation to a matter). It is not possible to provide an exhaustive definition of what constitutes a judicial act (as distinct from "administrative" or "ministerial" ones), though they usually involve the evaluation of facts and/or law, resolve disputes between opposed parties and will be determinative of the rights and liabilities of the parties.[67]

[62] Crown Proceedings Act 1947 s.2(5) ("No proceedings shall he against the Crown . . . in respect of anything done or omitted to be done by any person while discharging or purporting to discharge any responsibility of a judicial nature vested in him.").

[63] A narrow conception of "judicial" has prevailed in cases where it has been sought to establish the proceedings of administrative tribunals are judicial proceedings for the purpose of attracting absolute privilege in respect of defamatory statements and reports made to or by them. "The question . . . in every case," it has been said, "is whether the tribunal in question has similar attributes to a court of justice or acts in a manner similar to that in which such courts act": *Conner v Waldron* [1935] A.C. 76 at 81 (Lord Atkin.) It has often been difficult to persuade the courts that administrative tribunals possess judicial characteristics, even when they are determining questions of legal right. In Australia, however, absolute immunity from defamation has been extended to proceedings of a board of inquiry, even though its functions were to investigate and make recommendations to the Governor in Council: *Tampion v Anderson* [1973] V.R. 321 at 715. There is undoubtedly much to be said in favour of denying absolute privilege from defamation actions to parties and witnesses appearing before administrative tribunals, for the proceedings are usually lacking the traditional formality that may tend to deter irresponsible persons from making maliciously untrue statements. This factor does not necessarily apply with equal force to the members of the tribunals themselves, and it is arguable that where membership of a tribunal is deemed to require a degree of judicial detachment that is incompatible with membership of the House of Commons (see House of Commons Disqualification Act 1975 s.1 and Sch.1), it ought to carry with it the same immunity from liability for words spoken in the course of proceedings and statements made in orders or judgments as is enjoyed by members of courts *stricto sensu*.

[64] *Scott v Stansfield* (1868) L.R. 3 Exch. 220. See generally P. Milmo and W. Rogers, *Gatley on Libel and Slander* (2004). Absolute privilege against defamation has also been conferred by statute upon reports made by the Parliamentary Commissioner for Administration and other ombudsmen and certain other communications made in connection with the performance of their functions: see Parliamentary Commissioner Act 1967 s.10(5); Local Government Act 1974 s.32(1).

[65] The old common law "action on the case as for a tort" against magistrates acting within their jurisdiction maliciously and without reasonable and probable cause is obsolete and no longer lies: *Re McC* [1985] 1 A.C. 528.

[66] Thus it was recognised from early times that JPs had ministerial duties and that their immunity from civil liability in respect of the erroneous performance of their judicial functions did not extend to their ministerial functions: *Green v Hundred of Bucclechurches* (1589) 1 Leon. 323 at 324.

[67] On the "classification of functions" see Olowofoyeku (1993), Ch.2.

19–019   Despite legislation which seeks to place magistrates in the same position to other judges with regard to immunity,[68] the distinction between superior courts and inferior courts of limited jurisdiction is so deep rooted in English law,[69] that it is still prudent to deal separately with the position of different types of courts; otherwise it is difficult to make sense of the case law.

Judges of superior courts

19–020   The position of judges in the Court of Appeal and the High Court is not particularly pertinent to the subject matter of this Chapter (liability to provide compensation for loss caused by acts contrary to the principles of judicial review) because judicial review does not lie against these courts. Superior courts have unlimited jurisdiction in that the court constitutes the sole arbiter as to what matters fall within its jurisdiction.[70] When an order of the High Court is set aside on appeal this is merely the correction of an erroneous exercise of that court's inherent jurisdiction in assuming jurisdiction of the matter; it is a valid order unless and until it is so corrected. The Crown Court, though a superior court, is subject to judicial review (though not for matters relating to trial on indictment)[71] and it is conceivable that an aggrieved person might seek damages following the quashing of such a decision. Such a claimant is extremely unlikely to succeed. At common law, immunity extends to all decisions taken within the judge's very wide jurisdiction (in the sense previously defined) even if actuated by malice or corruption.[72] Only if a judge of a superior court acts deliberately or recklessly without any colour of right can an action in tort lie. Thus, "if the Lord Chief Justice himself, on the acquittal of a defendant charged before him with a criminal offence were to say: 'That is a perverse verdict', and thereupon proceed to pass a sentence of imprisonment, he could be sued for trespass".[73]

Magistrates

19–021   Magistrates' courts and justices of the peace are inferior courts with limited jurisdiction and judicial review may lie.[74] With respect to any matter within their jurisdiction, justices of the peace (and justices' clerks exercising the functions of a single justice by virtue of any statutory provision) enjoy immunity from any action for damages in respect to acts or omissions in

---

[68] Courts and Legal Services Act 1990, s.108; see below.
[69] Re McC [1985] 1 A.C. 528 at 550 (Lord Bridge). But see Olowofoyeku (1993), p.19.
[70] Sirros v Moore [1975] Q.B. 118, 139 (Buckley L.J.), approved in Re McC [1985] 1 A.C. 528 at 559 (Lord Templeman).
[71] Supreme Court Act (Senior Courts Act) 1981 s.29(3).
[72] Anderson v Gorrie [1895] 1 Q.B. 668; Olowofoyeku (1993), p.20.
[73] Re McC [1985] 1 A.C. 528 at 540 (Lord Bridge).
[74] Judicial review is often excluded in practice, though not expressly, by reason of the existence of a specific alternative remedy such as an appeal to the High Court by way of case stated or appeal to the Crown Court: see 3–090.

the execution of their duties.[75] For acts or omissions with respect to a matter which is not within a magistrate's jurisdiction an action may lie only if it is proved that he acted in bad faith.[76]

The question of what is within a magistrate's "jurisdiction" for the **19–022** purposes of immunity is difficult to answer.[77] Clearly, as with judges of a superior court, where a magistrate acts entirely without any colour of authority, he will act outside his jurisdiction. Jurisdiction will also be absent where there is no "jurisdiction of the cause[78] i.e. the court has no power to entertain the proceedings at all.[79] A magistrate would certainly also be acting outside his jurisdiction where if guilty of some gross and obvious irregularity of procedure or the rules of natural justice.[80] Where however a justice has merely misconstrued a statute (a type of error considered by the majority in *Anisminic Ltd v Foreign Compensation Commission* to be "jurisdictional"[81]) this is probably insufficient to take him outside his jurisdiction for the purposes of losing immunity from civil actions.[82] Justices and justices' clerks may be indemnified out of local funds for costs, damages or sums payable in reasonable settlement of any proceedings or claim if he acted reasonably and in good faith.[83]

Tribunals

As a matter of common law, no claim of damages will lie against bodies **19–023** such as professional disciplinary tribunals[84] and statutory tribunals where a judicial decision was within the jurisdiction of the body (in the narrow sense described above). In respect to decisions outside their jurisdiction, it is probable that such tribunals stand in a similar position to magistrates and an action may be brought if there is bad faith.[85]

---

[75] Justice of the Peace Act 1997 ss.51–53.

[76] Justice of the Peace Act 1997 s.52.

[77] Formerly Justices of the Peace Act 1979; *R. v Manchester City Magistrates' Court Ex p. Davies (Barry)* [1989] 1 Q.B. 631.

[78] *Marshalsea Case* (1613) 10 Co. Rep. 68b at 76a (Court with jurisdiction limited to members of the King's household had no jurisdiction to entertain a suit between two citizen's neither ofwhom was a member of the King's household. An action lay for false imprisonment).

[79] *Re McC* [1985] 1 A.C. 528 at 536.

[80] *Re McC* [1985] 1 A.C. 528 at 546–547. Lord Bridge was dealing with the statutory formula "without jurisdiction or excess of jurisdiction" in relation to justices of the peace in Northern Ireland. Illustrations offered by Lord Bridge include where one justice absents himself for part of the hearing and relied on another to tell him what happened during his absence or if a justice refused to allow the defendant to give evidence. On the facts of *Re McC*, justices were held to have acted outside their jurisdiction when they failed to inform the defendant of his right to apply for legal aid, as required by legislation, before ordering him to be sent to a training school.

[81] [1969] 2 A.C. 147. On the concept of jurisdiction, see 4–007.

[82] *Re McC* [1985] 1 A.C. 528 at 546 (Lord Bridge).

[83] Justice of the Peace Act 1997 s.54.

[84] See, e.g. *Partridge v General Council* [1890] 25 Q.B.D. 90; *Heath v Commissioner of Police of the Metropolis* [2004] EWCA Civ 943; [2005] I.C.R. 329 (employment tribunal had no jurisdiction to hear a complaint of unlawful sexual discrimination by a police disciplinary board).

[85] Olowofoyeku (1993), p.85.

The reason for immunity

19–024 Judicial immunity has been justified on the utilitarian basis that "if one judge in a thousand acts dishonestly within his jurisdiction to the detriment of a party before him, it is less harmful to the health of society to leave that party without a remedy than that nine hundred and ninety nine honest judges should be harassed by vexatious litigation alleging malice in the exercise of their proper jurisdiction".[86] The immunity of the Crown in this context has been said to stem from the constitutional independence of the judiciary from the executive: "if they are independent no one else can be vicariously answerable for any wrong that they may do".[87] The desirability of finality of legal proceedings and the avoidance of relitigation may also explain the current law. It has, however, been argued that there is no compelling need for a rule of absolute immunity for wrongful acts and omissions within jurisdiction.[88]

NO RIGHT TO DAMAGES FOR UNLAWFUL ADMINISTRATIVE ACTION AS SUCH

19–025 A finding by a court that a public authority, in performing a public function, has breached a ground of judicial review does not of itself provide a basis for entitlement at common law to compensation.[89] Nor does the careless performance of a statutory duty in itself give rise to any cause of action in tort in the absence of a common law duty of care in negligence or a right of action for breach of statutory duty.[90] To recover damages, a recognised cause of action in tort must be pleaded and proved—such as negligence, the tort of breach of statutory duty, misfeasance in public office, false imprisonment or trespass. So while in some cases it may be a necessary[91] condition, it is never a sufficient one for the award of damages that the act or omission complained of be "unlawful" in a public law sense.

19–026 The English common law has generally set its face against the development of a distinct body of rules for the tortious liabilities of officials and government bodies (though until the enactment of the Crown Proceedings Act 1947, certain procedural difficulties stood in the way of a person

[86] *Re McC* [1985] 1 A.C. 528 at 541 (Lord Bridge).
[87] H.W.R. Wade and C. Forsyth, *Administrative Law*, 9th edn (2004), p.825. See however *Maharaj v Attorney General of Trinidad and Tobago* [1979] A.C. 385.
[88] Olowofoyeku, (1993), Chs 6–7.
[89] "Illegality without more does not give a cause of action": *Three Rivers DC v Bank of England (No.3)* [2003] 2 A.C. 1 at 229 (Lord Hobhouse, citing *Lonrho Ltd v Shell Petroleum Co. Ltd (No.2)* [1982] A.C. 173, 189); *X v Bedfordshire CC* [1995] 2 A.C. 633 at 732 and 734–735; *Percy v Hall* [1997] Q.B. 924 at 947.
[90] *Geddis v Proprietors of Bann Reservoir* (1878) 3 App. Cas. 430 as explained by the HL in *X (Minors) v Bedfordshire CC* [1995] 2 A.C. 633.
[91] See 19–045.

wishing to sue the Crown).[92] Where the common law does acknowledge the public status of a defendant in a private law action, this recognition tends merely to be in the form of adaptations to the general framework of the ordinary rules of liability. Professors F.W. Maitland[93] and A.V. Dicey, writing near the start the 20th century, both elevated this characteristic of English law to the status of an aspect of the constitutional principle the rule of law. In Dicey's words, "every man, whatever be his rank or condition, is subject to the ordinary law of the realm and amenable to the jurisdiction of the ordinary tribunals".[94] Dicey then explains that the law reports of his time abounded with cases in which officials were brought before the courts and made, in their personal capacity, liable to the payment of damages for acts done in their official capacity.[95] For Dicey, the function of tortious liability here was principally to provide a mechanism for controlling governmental power.

In modern administrative law in England and Wales, actions for damages 19–027 and restitutionary claims have been eclipsed by the development of principles of judicial review as the main way of controlling executive action within the confines of the law.[96] Today the major question is whether a system of remedies in administrative law can be complete without the provision of rights to compensation and restitution to people harmed by ultra vires acts or omissions of public bodies. If compensation and restitution are to be provided for at least some of the losses caused by such actions of government, the question arises as to how best this can be achieved. The orthodox common law approach, described by Dicey, is still applied with vigour in the courts and enjoys some support among academic writers.[97] Others, however, now question whether this model is appropriate for handling losses caused by governmental action and there have been calls for a distinctively public law of tort.[98]

[92] See 19–015. For an account of the civil liability of the Crown prior to 1947, see J. Jacob, "The Debates behind an Act: Crown Proceedings Reform, 1920–1947" [1992] P.L. 452.
[93] *The Constitutional History of England* (1908), p.484: "We can hardly lay too much stress on the principle that though the King cannot be prosecuted or sued, his ministers can both be prosecuted and sued, even for what they do by the King's express command. Law, especially modern statute law, has endowed [ministers] with a great many powers, but the question whether they have overstepped those powers can be brought before a court of law, and the plea 'this is an official act, an act of state', will not serve them. A great deal of what we mean when we talk of English liberty lies in this".
[94] *Introduction to the Law of the Constitution*, 10th edn (1959), p.193.
[95] *Introduction to the Law of the Constitution*, 10th edn (1959), p.193. In his exposition, Dicey chose to ignore the special position of the Crown and also the existence of judicial immunity.
[96] But see n.6 above.
[97] See, e.g. P. Hogg, *Liability of the Crown*, 2nd edn (1989), p.iv ("in my view, the government ought usually to be subject to the same rules of legal liability as the subject. I reject the European-derived alternative of a distinctive public law of governmental liability, administered by special courts. My approach leads me to criticise most of the immunities and privileges that still apply to the Crown".) and p.119; C. Harlow, *Compensation and Government Torts* (1982), p.80 and *State Liability: Tort Law and Beyond* (2004); H.W.R. Wade, *Constitutional Fundamentals* (1980), p.663.
[98] See, e.g. D. Cohen and J. Smith, "Entitlement and the Body Politic: Rethinking Negligence in Public Law" (1986) 64 Can. B.R. 1 and B. Hepple, Ch.6 in P. Birks (ed.), *Frontiers of Liability*, Vol.II (1994).

RELATIONSHIPS BETWEEN THE GROUNDS OF JUDICIAL REVIEW AND RIGHTS TO A PECUNIARY REMEDY

19–028   The correlation between a finding that a decision of a public authority is, as a matter of public law, flawed and a person's right in private law to damages is not straightforward.

19–029   It is generally neither helpful nor necessary to introduce public law concepts as to the validity of a decision into the question of a public authority's liability at common law for negligence.[99] Nonetheless, issues as to the lawful scope of a public authority's discretion do remain important to questions of tortious liability in relation to negligence, breach of statutory duty, misfeasance in public office and other torts. A duty of care in negligence will not be imposed which will be inconsistent with, or fetter, a statutory duty.[100] In recent years, however, the courts have become markedly more sceptical of claims that imposing a duty of care will have an adverse impact on public authorities' work: the defendant will have to establish that this (the court should not presume it be so) and this is likely to be demonstrated only in exceptional circumstances.[101]

19–030   The English common law has long drawn a distinction between negligently performed actions and alleged negligence in relation to *omissions* to act. Where a statute confers a discretion on a public authority as to the extent to which, and the methods by which, a statutory duty is to be performed, only if the decision complained of is outside the ambit of the lawful discretion may a duty of care be imposed; in relation to "policy" decisions[102] of a public authority, a finding that the act or omission was unlawful is normally viewed as a precondition for common law liability in tort.[103]

19–031   Holding a decision to be unlawful does not involve a finding that it was taken negligently; a decision without legal authority may nevertheless have been the product of very careful consideration by a decision-maker.[104] Unlawfulness (in the judicial review sense) and negligence are conceptually

---

[99] *Phelps v Hillingdon LBC* [2001] 2 A.C. 619 at 653 (Lord Slynn approves approach in *Barett v Enfield LBC* [2001] 2 A.C. 550 that "the fact that acts which are claimed to be negligent are carried out within the ambit of a statutory discretion is not in itself a reason why it should be held that no claim for negligence can be brought in respect of them); *X (Minors) v Bedfordshire CC* [1995] 2 A.C. 633; D. Fairgrieve, "Pushing back the Boundaries of Public Authority Liability: Tort Law Enters the Classroom" [2002] P.L. 288, 297–299.

[100] On fetters to discretion, see Ch.9.

[101] See, e.g. *Phelps v Hillingdon LBC* [2001] 2 A.C. 619 at 653 (no justification for a blanket immunity policy in respect of education officers performing a local authority's functions with regard to children with special educational needs, doubting the approach in *X (Minors) v Bedfordshire CC* [1995] 2 A.C. 633).

[102] The distinction between policy decisions and operational activities of public bodies is considered at 19–041. "Operational" activities are not normally the subject of claims for judicial review.

[103] See 19–031.

[104] P. Craig, "Negligence in the Exercise of a Statutory Power" (1978) 94 L.Q.R. 428, 448.

distinct[105] and so negligence cannot be inferred by a process of "relating back" from a finding of invalidity.[106]

There is no special affinity between any particular grounds of judicial **19–032** review and cause of action for damages; whether there is a cause of action will depend on the particular facts. This may be illustrated in the following ways:

(a) Where a decision-maker takes into account an irrelevant consideration, as well as providing grounds for quashing the decision, this may create a right to damages for misfeasance in public office if it can be proved that the action complained of was done knowingly or maliciously.[107] But the fact that a consideration was taken into account which is irrelevant says nothing about whether the decision-making process which led to the error involved any failure to take reasonable care—a necessary element for recovery in the tort of negligence.[108]

(b) An official's statement, in addition to creating a legitimate expectation[109] according to the principles of judicial review, may possibly, if untrue and given in response to a specific request, also give an action in damages for negligent misstatement.[110]

(c) The failure of a public authority, contrary to the principles of natural justice, to give a person a proper hearing before making a decision does not, of itself, give rise to a cause of action for damages.[111] In order to recover damages in the public law arena, the aggrieved person will need to show that the procedural impropriety

---

[105] *Dunlop v Woollahra Municipal Council* [1982] A. C. 158 at 171–172 (Lord Diplock).

[106] P. Craig,"Compensation in Public Law" (1980) 96 L.Q.R. 413, 425.

[107] See 19–048.

[108] Craig (1978) 94 L.Q.R. 428, 448.

[109] See Ch.12.

[110] See, e.g. *Davy v Spelthorne DC* [1984] A.C. 262. In the past an assurance by a government official addressed to an individual may have been treated as contractual (see *The Amphitrite* [1921] 3 K.B. 500), but today this would almost certainly be approached as a matter of public law and consequently there would be no scope for any claim for damages for breach of contract. In *R. (on the application of Nurse Prescribers Ltd) v Secretary of State for Health* [2004] EWHC 403 (Admin) the court found that a legitimate expectation had been disappointed but held that there was no basis on which to award damages for expenditure wasted as a result of the Department of Health's change of policy on prescribing of saline solution, which had not been communicated to the claimant.

[111] *Dunlop v Woollahra Municipal Council* [1982] A.C. 158 at 171–172, PC and *Welbridge Holdings Ltd v Metropolitan Corp of Greater Winnipeg* [1971] S.C.R. 957 (no duty of care owed to person damnified through reliance on validity of council byelaw later held invalid for breach of natural justice). Quaere whether damages might be awarded under Lord Cairn's Act in lieu of an injunction. cf. *Maharaj v Attorney General for Trinidad and Tobago (No.2)* [1979] A.C. 385, PC (constitutional provision for the redress for breach of fundamental rights held to include award of damages for committal for contempt without complying with the requirements of natural justice). Where a contract exists between the parties, such as a contract of employment, contravention of a principle such as *audi alterem partim* may amount to a breach of an express or implied term of the contract; but where there is a contractual relationship of this sort, judicial review will not normally lie (see 3–056).

or other unlawful administrative action also constituted an actionable breach of statutory duty, misfeasance in public office or other recognised civil wrong.

(d) Delay in making a decision may result in a mandatory order in a claim for judicial review[112] and, possibly, a claim for damages— though delay of itself does not found a cause of action.[113] Negligence or actionable breach of statutory duty will have to be argued.

(e) Although the term "reasonableness" may be used to define both the standard of care imposed by the tort of negligence and as a ground of judicial review, the terminology does not always bear a consistent meaning between the two branches of law. It does not follow that because a decision is held unlawful as *Wednesbury* unreasonable,[114] the decision taker was negligent, i.e. he failed to take reasonable care coming to the decision; it may have been reached after careful deliberation and therefore not contain the arbitrary characteristics normally associated with the irrational or *Wednesbury* unreasonable decision. A court may, however, infer that a decision was so unreasonable that it could only be explained by the presence of malice.[115]

General difficulties

19–033   This section outlines possible grounds for seeking damages in tort against a public authority in circumstances where judicial review may also lie. Many of the difficulties which face any claimant pursuing an action in tort are exacerbated where what is being claimed is compensation for loss due to the activities associated with the public functions of public authorities. This is especially the case where the decisions relate to the allocation of resources, licensing, inspection and other forms of regulation.

---

[112] See, e.g. *R. v Gloucestershire CC Ex p. P* [1993] C.O.D. 303 (alleged unreasonable delay by education authority in providing statement of special educational need under the Education Act 1981 not found on the facts).

[113] See, e.g. *R. v HM Treasury Ex p. Petch* [1990] C.O.D. 19. (Popplewell J. held that there was an implied duty owed to a civil servant under the Superannuation Act 1972 to consider his claim for a pension timeously and failure to do so could give rise to damages for breach of statutory duty and in common law negligence—though on the facts there had been no breach. In an unreported decision on January 15, 1990, the CA dismissed the claimant's appeal on the facts without hearing argument on the law.) In *Calveley v Chief Constable of Merseyside Police* [1989] A.C. 1228, HL police officers were suspended on full pay pending investigation of complaints made against them. They alleged the disciplinary proceedings were misconducted and there had been undue delay. It was held that there was no actionable breach of statutory duty because Parliament did not intend to confer on police officers subject to disciplinary proceedings under the Police (Discipline) Regulations 1977 any right to damages; nor was there a common law duty of care as no loss was foreseeable.

[114] See Ch.12.

[115] See, e.g. *Jones v Swansea City Council* [1990] 1 W.L.R. 1453 at 1461 *et seq.* (misfeasance in public office).

First, the loss suffered by the claimant as a result of a public authority's **19-034** negligent acts or omissions[116] will often be economic loss, which is not consequential on any damage to property or personal injury, a kind of loss in respect of which the courts are reluctant to provide a remedy in the absence of a contract.[117] Secondly, in many cases, the complaint will be that a public authority failed to prevent a third party inflicting loss on the complainant, for instance by approving plans or inspecting buildings[118] (where the breach of duty can be characterised as the failure of a public authority to control the acts or omissions of builders or architects), licensing of financial services (supervision of deposit takers)[119] in the context of the criminal justice system, failing to detect and prevent the acts of criminals.[120] English tort law is generally unreceptive to the idea of imposing a duty of care for acts of independent third parties.[121]

In addition, it is rare for the common law to impose a duty to take **19-035** positive action, in the absence of a special relationship and without the defendant having himself created or contributed to the danger,[122] to protect a stranger from being harmed. In the perennial illustration of this principle, a man may stand by and watch a child drown in a shallow pool without committing any tort. The main policy justifications for distinguishing between failing to act (nonfeasance) and acting wrongfully

[116] The position in relation to negligent misstatements and economic loss is rather different: since *Hedley Byrne & Co Ltd v Heller & Partners Ltd* [1964] A.C. 465 pure economic loss arising from negligent information and advice has, in some circumstances, been recoverable. This cause of action is considered separately, see 19–046.

[117] On economic loss generally, see M. Dugdale and M. Jones, *Clerk and Lindsell on Torts*, 19th edn (2006), para.10–04.

[118] *Anns v Merton LBC* [1978] A.C. 728 (now largely overruled); *Curran v Northern Ireland Co-ownership Housing Association Ltd* [1987] A.C. 718; *Murphy v Brentwood DC* [1991] 1 A.C. 398.

[119] *Yuen Kun-yeu v Attorney General of Hong Kong* [1988] A.C. 175.

[120] *Hill v Chief Constable of West Yorkshire* [1989] A.C. 53 (no duty owed by police to victim for alleged failure promptly to apprehend unknown perpetrator of a crime). The approach in *Hill* was found to be in violation of ECHR Art.6(1) in *Osman v United Kingdom* (2000) 29 E.H.R.R. 245, where the policy factors which led to a denial of a duty of care, along with the practise of striking out claims at a summary hearing as disclosing no triable issue, were held to constitute an "exclusionary rule". This categorisation was "extremely difficult to understand" (*Barrett v Enfield LBC* [2001] 2 A.C. 550 at 558) and see now *Z v United Kingdom* [2001] 2 F.L.R. 612. *Brooks v Commissioner of Police of the Metropolis* [2005] UKHL 24; [2005] 1 W.L.R. 1495 (with hindsight, not every principle in *Hill* could now be supported and a more sceptical approach to the carrying out of all public functions was necessary. However, the core principle of *Hill* had remained unchallenged in domestic and European law for many years and it had to stand).

[121] *Clerk and Lindsell on Torts*, 19th edn (2006), para.2–90; *X (Minors) v Bedfordshire CC* [1995] 2 A.C. 633 at 751G (Lord Browne-Wilkinson: "In my judgment, the courts should proceed with great care before holding liable in negligence those who have been charged by Parliament with the task of protecting society from the wrongdoings of others"); *JD v East Berkshire Community Health NHS Trust* [2005] UKHL 23; [2005] 2 A.C. 373 at [105] (Lord Rodgers of Earlsferry: "For the most part, then, the settled policy of the law is opposed to granting remedies to third parties for the effects of injuries to other people").

[122] *cf.*, e.g. *Kane v New Forest DC (No.1)* [2001] EWCA Civ 878; [2002] 1 W.L.R. 312 at [28] (local authority created source of danger by requiring a footpath with restricted lines of vision to be built, so distinguishing the situation from *Stovin v Wise and Norfolk CC* [1996] A.C. 923).

(misfeasance) are, first, that the imposition of affirmative duties is normally more burdensome on an individual in terms of time, trouble, risk and money than are negative duties and, secondly, the difficulty in some cases of identifying the person to be sued.[123] Over the years, the courts have found it difficult to develop satisfactorily the law in the case of nonfeasance by public bodies. The current state of the law rests on the assumption that it will be unusual (though not impossible) for a public authority to owe a duty of care for foreseeable loss cause by a statutory discretion not being performed.[124] The rationale for this restrictive approach is that the fact that Parliament has conferred a discretion must be some indication that the policy of the Act conferring the power was not to create a common law right to compensation.[125] There is a two-stage approach. To establish a duty of care it must first be shown that it would have been irrational for the public authority not to have exercised its power "so that there was in effect a public law duty to act".[126] Secondly, some exceptional reason must be demonstrated to show that the statute in question requires compensation to be paid to a person who suffers loss because the power was not exercised.[127]

19–036   The causation of damage also creates particular problems in respect of the imposition of tortious liability on public authorities for unlawful administrative action.[128] It is trite law that judicial review is not concerned with the merits of administrative decisions and the court should ordinarily avoid substituting its own opinion for that of the public authority as to how precisely a discretion should be exercised. How, then, is a court to approach a case where, for example, a claimant alleges that a breach of natural justice activated by malice has caused him loss (such as the refusal of a licence to trade) or the decision maker negligently failed to take into account a relevant consideration? The court may avoid second-guessing what decision the public authority would have reached had the decision not been tainted by illegality by saying that the claimant has at most lost an

---

[123] P. Cane (ed.), *Atiyah's Accidents, Compensation and the Law*, 4th edn (2006), p.72, who goes on to argue that there is no really satisfactory reason for distinguishing between misfeasance and nonfeasance: "this distinction is based on irrational misconceptions about causal principles on the one hand, and an exaggerated fear of the burdensomeness of affirmative obligations on the other".

[124] *Stovin v Wise and Norfolk CC* [1996] A.C. 923 (HL, by a 3:2 majority, held that failure to exercise discretionary powers to remove obstructions conferred by Highways Act 1980 s.79 did not give rise to a duty of care); *Calderdale MBC v Gorringe* [2004] UKHL 15; [2004] 1 W.L.R. 1057 (local authority's statutory duty to promote road safety under Road Traffic Act 1988 s.39 did not create common law duty of care; it would be unusual for a duty of care to arise simply from a failure, however irrational, to provide some benefit which a public authority had a duty or power to provide).

[125] *Stovin* [1996] A.C. 923 at 953 (Lord Hoffmann).

[126] *Stovin* [1996] A.C. 923 at 953.

[127] *Stovin* [1996] A.C. 923 at 953.

[128] See generally *Clerk and Lindsell on Torts*, 19th edn (2006), paras 1–08, 5–71, 8–42. In the context of damages in the public law context, see C. Harlow, *Compensation and Government Torts* (1982), p.93. *cf.* Report of the Committee of the Justice/All Souls Review of Administrative Law in the United Kingdom, *Administrative Justice—Some Necessary Reforms* (1988) para.11.86, which did not see causation as a major problem.

opportunity to obtain a benefit. Probability will be defined by, among other facts, the degree of discretion possessed by the decision maker. Whilst in most cases a court may attempt to place a value on a lost chance,[129] special difficulties arise in relation to damages claims associated with judicial review because this exercise would necessarily involve the court substituting its own discretion for that of the decision-maker[130] A solution is to defer the claim for damages until after the outcome of the claim for judicial review is known and the public authority has complied with the decision. However, even if the court considering the damages claim waits for the decision-maker to reconsider the decision in accordance with law, conceptual problems may still arise if a decision is characterised as void (rather than voidable);[131] in these circumstances what will have caused the claimant's loss? One answer, arguably, is the act of taking a void, or the omission to take a valid, decision. If practical steps have been taken to implement a void decision, e.g. by entering onto the claimant's land or seizing his goods, then that physical act may of itself constitute the tort rather than the underlying invalid decision.[132] But often there will be no such steps to execute a decision, e.g. as when a licence to carry on a trade is revoked negligently or in a manner which amounts to misfeasance in public office. In a number of cases, it has been held that a claimant ought to have ignored an invalid decision,[133] with the result that damage has been held to have arisen not from the unlawful administrative decision, but the claimant's own voluntary compliance with it. This approach has rightly been criticised as unrealistic,[134] and the courts have on occasion explicitly or implicitly accepted that a person's act in obeying an invalid order was a reasonable response.[135]

A final difficulty with tort liability for unlawful administrative action lies **19–037** in the application of the rules as to remoteness of damage,[136] particularly in relation to economic damage.[137] Given the fact that governmental actions will often, of their very nature, foreseeably affect a great many people, it is not clear that the applications of ordinary principles on remoteness will

---

[129] See *Chaplin v Hicks* [1911] 2 K.B. 786 (a case in contract); in relation to tort claims, see *Hotson v East Berkshire AHA* [1987] A.C. 750; *Gregg v Scott* [2005] UKHL 2; [2005] 2 A.C. 176.

[130] Again, the *Justice/All Souls* review saw no problem in the court considering whether an authority might validly have refused the benefit and taking that into account in determining damages (1988), para.11.86). *cf.* Craig, (1980) 96 L.Q.R. 413, 438–439.

[131] See 4–056.

[132] See, e.g. *Cooper v Wandsworth Board of Works* (1883) 14 C.B. (N. S.) 180.

[133] See e.g. *Dunlop v Woollahra MC* [1998] 1 W.L.R. 840; *Scott v Gamble* [1916] 2 K.B. 504; *O'Connor v Isaacs* [1956] 2 Q.B. 288.

[134] P. Hogg and P. Monahan, *Liability of the Crown* (2000), p.144, n.185, citing *McClintock v Commonwealth* (1947) 75 C.L.R. 1. See further A. Rubenstein, *Jurisdiction and Illegality* (1965), p.322.

[135] See, e.g. *Farrington v Thomson* [1959] V.R. 286; *Roncarelli v Duplessis* (1959) 16 D.L.R. (2nd) 689 at 708. See further J. McBride, "Damages as a Remedy for Unlawful Administrative Action" [1979] C.L.J. 323.

[136] *Clerk and Lindsell on Torts*, 19th edn (2006) Ch.2.

[137] *Clerk and Lindsell on Torts*, 19th edn (2006) para.2–151.

adequately protect public authorities from being subject to crushing liability.

NEGLIGENCE[138]

19–038   In general, liability for negligent acts and omissions will be imposed by a court where:

(a) the defendant owes the claimant a duty of care. This will exist if (i) the harm suffered by the claimant was reasonably foreseeable; (ii) the relationship between the defendant and claimant was sufficiently "proximate"; and (iii) the imposition of a duty of care would be just and reasonable;[139]

(b) the defendant was in breach of the standard of care required in the circumstances;

(c) the claimant suffered damage as a result of the breach. The damage in question must normally include physical damage to property[140] or the person or economic loss arising from such damage.[141] (The position in relation to economic loss caused by negligent statements is considered separately below.)

19–039   English law has turned its back on the search for general principles of negligence liability, and instead the law is set to develop incrementally, on a case by case basis. In novel situations, arguments based on analogies to previously decided cases, rather than appeals to principle, are likely to find more favour in the courts.[142]

19–040   In many instances, the application of such general rules of liability to public bodies presents little difficulty: when a pedestrian is struck down by a negligently driven van it is of no importance whether the driver is on the business of a commercial enterprise or a public authority. Where, however, allegations of negligence are made in relation to the way in which a public authority has performed some public function—such as the state regulation

---

[138] Charlesworth and Percy on Negligence, 10th edn (2001); C. Booth and D. Squires, *The Negligence Liability of Public Authorities* (2006); B. Markesinis and J. Fedtke, "Damages for the Negligence of Statutory Bodies: The Empirical and Comparative Dimension to an Unending Debate" [2007] P.L. 299.

[139] *Clerk and Lindsell on Torts*, 19th edn, (2000) para.8–17.

[140] On the need to show damage to property other than to the negligently constructed building or manufactured chattel itself, see *Murphy v Brentwood DC* [1991] 1 A.C. 398.

[141] *Clerk and Lindsell on Torts*, 19th edn, para.1–36

[142] See, e.g. *Murphy v Brentwood DC* [1991] 1 A.C. 398 at 461 (Lord Keith); *X (Minors) v Bedfordshire CC* [1995] 2 A.C. 633 at 735D (Lord Browne-Wilkinson); *Phelps v Hillingdon LBC* [2001] 2 A.C. 619 (failure to diagnose a congenital condition such as dyslexia and to take the necessary action, resulting in a child's level of academic achievement being reduced and a consequential loss of wages, could constitute damage for a personal injuries claim).

of financial services, social work or the investigation of crime—greater difficulties may arise. Ultimately any judicial decision on whether to impose a duty of care in a novel situation is one of policy. Because of the nature of public functions which give special powers and impose responsibilities on administrators—some factors not usually relevant, or less important, where the defendant is a private person come into play. Regrettably, much effort has been spent deliberating how such considerations are to be taken into account by the common law, rather than in the examination of what they are and when they are to apply.

Much of the debate in the case law and academic literature has been over **19–041** whether there needs to be a special framework for determining the existence of a duty of care in respect of governmental activities or whether the general test (described above) is sufficiently flexible to be used in this context. In many cases in which the courts have had to decide whether a public authority owes a claimant a duty of care in respect of its public functions, the courts have proceeded simply by the application of the general legal framework.[143] In other cases, the courts have adopted a different and more elaborate approach[144] to determining whether a duty arises in respect of functions which contain an element of "planning" or "policy", as opposed to merely "operational" activities.[145] Those who advocate the need for a special framework suggest it is needed for two broad types of reason. First, the general test is inadequate to accommodate the special policy factors that need to be taken into account in relation to certain public functions. Secondly, application of the general test will, it is thought by some, result in liability being imposed in too many cases,[146] or alternatively that it will result in too large an area of immunity for public bodies.

In *Anns v Merton LBC*[147] Lord Wilberforce distinguished policy aspects **19–042** of a local authority's functions from its operational ones and said that a duty of care was more likely to be imposed in respect of the latter. The terms "policy" and "operational" are misleading in that they may suggest a distinction between making a decision and carrying out a decision. It is

[143] See, e.g. *Phelps v Hillingdon LBC* [2001] 2 A.C. 619; *Jones v Department of Employment* [1989] 1 Q.B. 1 (claim that Adjudication Officer negligently determined entitlement to unemployment benefit); *Welsh v Chief Constable of the Merseyside Police and the Crown Prosecution Service* [1993] 1 All E.R. 692 (claim that Crown Prosecution Service failed to ensure that a magistrates' court was informed that offences for which claimant had been bailed were subsequently taken into consideration by the Crown Court).
[144] Harlow (2004), p.55, describes it as "incredibly complex".
[145] For a critical survey of decisions which have applied, ignored or distinguished the policy/operational text between 1978 and 1985, see S.H. Bailey and M.J. Bowan, "The Policy/Operational Dichotomy—A Cuckoo in the Nest" (1986) 45 C.L.J. 430.
[146] See, e.g. H. Woolf, *Protection of the Public* (1990), p.60.
[147] [1978] A.C. 728; Lord Salmon drew no such distinction in *Anns*, holding more straightforwardly that every person whether discharging a public duty or not, is under a common law obligation to some persons in some circumstances to conduct himself with reasonable care so as not to injure those persons likely to be injured by his lack of care. So far as English law is concerned, the origins of the policy/operational dichotomy lie in Lord Diplock's speech in *Home Office v Dorset Yacht Co Ltd* [1970] A.C. 1004.

clear that some stages of the implementation process involve a policy aspect, and so are unlikely to give rise to a duty of care situation.[148] Various synonyms are used: "administrative" or "business powers"[149] instead of operational; "planning" decisions instead of "policy".

19–043   Where the policy/operational dichotomy has been used, the following have been held to be "operational" decisions:[150] a decision by a local authority to place a boy with known pyromaniac tendencies in an insecure home;[151] the decision of a highway authority not to put up temporary signs warning of the absence of road markings;[152] and a decision of a minister not to release a company promptly from certain undertakings it had been required to give during an investigation by the Monopolies and Mergers Commission.[153] Policy decisions typically involve discretionary decisions on the allocation of scarce resources and the distribution of risks.[154]

19–044   The general status of the House of Lords' decision in *Anns* is now greatly diminished, it now having been overruled by *Murphy* in so far as it was authority for imposing a duty of care in respect of defects in work which has not caused damage to the property or person of the claimant[155] In *Murphy* nothing was said, however, about the policy/operational approach, and it can be assumed that this aspect of the decision was not intended to be overruled.[156] Since then the usefulness of the distinction has been doubted by the Privy Council[157] and various views have been expressed about its cogency in the House of Lords.[158] It has also been suggested that

---

[148] For example, decisions as to the staffing levels at a regulatory agency.
[149] *Rowling v Takaro Properties Ltd* [1988] A.C. 473 at 500.
[150] For further illustrations of the application of the distinction, see: *Clerk and Lindsell on Torts*, 19th edn (2006) para.8–20.
[151] *Vicar of Writtle v Essex CC* (1979) L.G.R. 656.
[152] *Bird v Pearce* [1979] R.T.R. 369.
[153] *Lonrho Plc v Tebbit* [1991] 4 All E.R. 973 (Browne-Wilkinson V.C.); [1992] 4 All E.R. 280, CA.
[154] See now P. Craig, *Administrative Law*, 5th edn (2003), pp.895–899 for a discussion of justiciability in relation to duties of care in tort law.
[155] *Murphy v Brentwood DC* [1991] 1 A.C. 398.
[156] *X (Minors) v Bedfordshire CC* [1995] 2 A.C. 633 at 736C (Lord Browne-Wilkinson acknowledges that this part of the decision in *Anns* has largely escaped criticism in later cases).
[157] In determining the question whether a minister who had allegedly misconstrued regulations so as to cause loss to the claimant was liable, the PC in *Rowling v Takaro Properties Ltd* [1988] A.C. 473 inclined to the views, expressed in the academic literature, that the distinction did not provide a touchstone for liability but rather was expressive of the need to exclude altogether those cases in which the decision under attack is of such a kind that a question whether it had been made negligently was not justiciable. Of course, establishing that a decision is an "operational" one is only a precondition to recovering damages for tort—a duty, breach and damage will have to be proved.
[158] *Phelps v Hillingdon LBC* [2001] 2 A.C. 619 at 658 ("Over-use of the distinction between policy and operational matters so as respectively to limit or create liability has been criticised, but there is some validity in the distinction", Lord Slynn); 673–674 ("the classification may provide some guide towards identifying some kinds of case where a duty of care may be thought to be inapprorpiate", Lord Clyde); 665 ("I have reservations about any attempt to draw a sharp-edged distinction between 'policy' decisions and 'operational' decisions, for the reasons I stated in *Stovin v Wise* [1996] AC 923, 938d–939b", Lord Nicholls); *Stovin v Wise and Norfolk CC* [1996] A.C. 923 (Lord Hoffmann describes the distinction between policy

"there are two areas of potential inquiry": whether the decision is justiciable at all; and "the classic three stage enunciated in *Caparo*".[159]

Wrangling over the dichotomy risks deflecting attention from the heart **19-045** of the matter: what, if any, factors are uniquely or commonly determinative of public bodies' liability in negligence in respect of their public law functions? An exhaustive list of considerations is, of course, impossible, as all the relevant circumstances of a case will need to be considered.[160] Some of the following may be relevant.

(a) The statutory context within which the public authority exercises its powers must be considered to ensure that a common law duty of care will not be imposed which will be inconsistent with the statutory framework.[161] Where the defendant is performing a specific statutory function the purpose for which the power or duty was conferred is regarded as being relevant in determining the existence and extent of any common law duty of care.[162] Thus where the purpose of the duty is to protect health and safety this is seen as impliedly excluding any greater common law duty (e.g. to prevent economic loss arising from a defective building). Arguably this confuses and blurs the boundaries between the tort of negligence and the tort of breach of statutory duty[163] and unduly restricts the development of negligence liability. Since the duty of care in negligence arises from a relationship between the parties, not by virtue of a statute as in breach of statutory duty, the purpose for which the public authority was given certain powers by statute should at most be no more than a matter to be considered as part of the relationship. In any event the pursuit of identifying a precise implicit legislative purpose is often a fruitless exercise as it is relatively easy to ascribe a variety of objects or purposes to statutes conferring powers.

and operation as "inadequate"; it was often elusive—and even if the distinction were clear cut, so leaving no element of discretion in the sense that it would be irrational, in the public law meaning of that word, for a public authority not to exercise its powers, it did not follow that the law should superimpose a common law duty of care). *cf X Minors v Bedfordshire CC* [1995] 2 A.C. 633 where the policy/operation distinction received support.
[159] *Carty v Croydon LBC* [2005] EWCA Civ 19; [2005] 1 W.L.R. 2312 at [28] (Dyson L.J.), [82] (Mummery L.J.) (education officers owed duty of care to child (but had not breached that duty) in relation to decisions about his schooling).
[160] *Rowling v Takaro Properties Ltd* [1988] A.C. 473 (Lord Keith).
[161] See, e.g. *A v Essex CC* [2003] EWCA Civ 1848; [2004] 1 W.L.R. 1881 (adoptive parents claimed local authority negligently failed to convey to them "all relevant information" about a child, but such a duty of care would have been nconsistent with the statutory framework under which adoption agencies were entitled to have policies in place about what information should be disclosed to potential adopters).
[162] *Governors of the Peabody Donation Fund v Sir Lindsay Parkinson and Co Ltd* [1985] A.C. 210, 242 at 245; *X Minors v Bedfordshire CC* [1995] 2 A.C. 633 at 739C; *Stovin v Wise and Norfolk CC* [1996] A.C. 923 at 952 (Lord Hoffmann: "Whether a statutory duty gives rise to a private cause of action is a question of construction. It requires an examination of the policy of the statute to decide whether it is intended to confer a right to compensation for the breach).
[163] See 19–052. See further K. Stanton et al., *Statutory Torts* (2003), para.14–117.

(b) Many powers and duties of a governmental nature must necessarily contain a large "policy" element and it is for the public authority, not the courts, to decide what policy to pursue.[164] This may apply both to the question of whether a duty of care is imposed and the setting of the standard of care required.

(c) It may be desirable for the law of torts and the grounds of judicial review to set broadly consistent standards as to the conduct required of public authorities.[165] For instance, if a decision which is amenable to judicial review is "reasonable" in the *Wednesbury* sense, it may be undesirable to categorise it as negligent. As Harlow has put it, many judges believe that there must be an exact correspondence between negligence liability and "unlawful" exercise of discretionary power in public law.[166] It is unfortunate that the term "unreasonable" is used both in judicial review and negligence; it usually means different things in each context.[167]

(d) Often the damage caused by unlawful administrative action will be pure economic loss not consequential on any physical damage. For a variety of policy reasons the law of negligence in general denies recovery for such loss;[168] many of these are as applicable to determining the liability of public authorities for their public functions as elsewhere.

(e) The concern that exists that the imposition of liability may have a chilling effect on the quality of administrators' actions.[169] In more recent cases, however, there has been a growing scepticism about the likelihood that this will occur.[170] Nonetheless, at least in cases where it is claimed that a public authority has negligently failed to exercise a statutory discretion, it is legitimate for the court to have regard to

---

[164] For an illustration of a situation in which a duty of care was denied because the claimant public bodies were carrying out a public duty involving balancing the public interest, see *Bennett v Commissioner of Police of the Metropolis* [1995] 1 W.L.R. 488 (Secretary of State signing public interest immunity certificate).

[165] See 19–04.

[166] C. Harlow, *Compensation and Government Torts* (1982), p.53.

[167] *X (Minors) v Bedfordshire CC* [1995] 2 A.C. 633 at 736F (Lord Browne-Wilkinson: "I do not believe that it is either helpful or necessary to introduce pubic law concets as the validity of a decision into the question of liability at common law for negligence. In public law a decision can be ultra vires for reasons other than *Wednesbury* unreasonableness (e.g. breach of the rules of natural justice) which have no relevance to the question of negligence"). As Cane points out, it is unclear why *Wednesbury* unreasonableness has been singled out as the only form of ultra vires which can give rise to liability in tort for negligence (P. Cane, "Suing Public Authorities in Tort" (1996) 113 L.Q.R. 13).

[168] *Clerk and Lindsell on Torts*, 19th edn, (2006) para.1–36; *Davis v Radcliffe* [1990] 1 W.L.R. 821 (action by depositors against the Finance Board and Treasury of the Isle of Man) but cf. *Allen v Bloomsbury Health Authority* [1993] 1 All E.R. 651 (action against health authority for economic loss due to failure to sterilise).

[169] See 19–072; e.g. *X (Minors) v Bedfordshire CC* [1995] 2 A.C. 633 at 739D–E, 749H (Lord Browne-Wilkinson).

[170] *Phelps v Hillingdon LBC* [2001] 2 A.C. 619 at 667 (Lord Nicholls): "Denial of the existence of a cause of action is seldom, if ever, the appropriate response to fear of its abuse".

the distorting impact that imposing liability would have on the authority's resource allocation decisions.[171]

(f) The existence or absence of an alternative method of redress for the claimant is often regarded as relevant to determining whether or not a common law duty of care exists. Thus, where the claimant may appeal to a tribunal or official against a decision, and the appellate body has power to order compensation, that will indicate that the court ought not impose a tortious liability on the original decision maker.[172] There are comments in the case law justifying the same inference being drawn because of the existence of the right to apply for judicial review.[173] However, judicial review is available in respect of almost all administrative action and accordingly no special significance can be attached to its availability.

(g) The courts will be slow to regard the misinterpretation of legislation as indicating negligence on the part of the decision-maker.[174] There is often room for more than one construction of a statutory provision and only a court can give a conclusive interpretation.

---

[171] *Stovin v Wise* [1996] A.C. 923 at 958 (Lord Hoffmann); *JD v East Berkshire Community Health NHS Trust* [2005] UKHL 23; [2005] 2 A.C. 373 (health professionals responsible for investigating suspected child abuse did not owe the person suspected of having committed the abuse a duty sounding in damages if they carried out that investigation in good faith but carelessly; Lord Nicholls of Birkenhead at [85] "But when considering whether something does not feel 'quite right', a doctor must be able to act single-mindedly in the interests of the child. He ought not to have at the back of his mind an awareness that if his doubts about intentional injury or sexual abuse prove unfounded he may be exposed to claims by a distressed parent").

[172] See, e.g. *Jones v Department of Employment* [1989] 1 Q.B. 1 (claimant had no cause of action in negligence against an officer who underestimated his entitlement to a welfare benefit. The claimant had successfully appealed against the determination and had received back-payments, though no interest); *X Minors v Bedfordshire CC* [1995] 2 A.C. 633 at 751A-B (in relation to social workers investigating child abuse, a statutory complaints procedure under Children Act 1989 provided means to have grievances investigated (though no compensation) and the Local Government Ombudsman would have power to investigate); *R. (on the application of Rowley) v Secretary of State for Work and Pensions* [2007] EWCA Civ 598; *The Times*, July 6, 2007 (child support); but *cf. Phelps v Hillingdon LBC* [2001] 2 A.C. 619 at 672 (Lord Clyde).

[173] See, e.g. *Rowling v Takaro Properties Ltd* [1988] A.C. 473 at 501–502 (Lord Keith) where it was held that the only effect of the allegedly negligent decision by the minister (in misconstruing legislation and so refusing consent) was delay: "This is because the processes of judicial review are available to the aggrieved party; and assuming that the alleged error of law is so serious that it can properly be described as negligent, the decision will assuredly be quashed by a process which, in New Zealand as in the United Kingdom, will normally be carried out with promptitude." See also *Calveley v Chief Constable of the Merseyside Police* [1989] A.C. 1228 at 1237 ff where, in relation to a claim for breach of statutory duty, Lord Bridge refers to judicial review as an alternative remedy justifying the refusal of tortious liability and *Curran v Northern Ireland Co-Ownership Housing Association Ltd* [1987] A.C. 718.

[174] See, e.g. *Rowling v Takaro Properties Ltd* [1988] A.C. 473 and *Dunlop v Woollahra MC* [1982] A.C. 158.

NEGLIGENT MISSTATEMENT

19–046 Liability for careless false statements of fact and opinion which cause a claimant economic loss is based on somewhat different principles than liability for types of loss caused by careless acts and omissions.[175] In this area of law, no material distinction appears to have been drawn between the liability of public authorities and other persons.[176] It is clear that not every false statement made by a public official will attract liability. A duty of care will be owed only where a statement was both intended to be relied upon for a particular purpose or transaction and it was actually so relied upon and there is a sufficiently proximate relationship between the parties.[177] Even as between private persons the courts are very slow to superimpose a common law duty of care on a defendant who is disseminating information in order to comply with a statutory requirement;[178] a similar approach will certainly be adopted in the public law context. The defendant also had to know that what he said would be communicated to the claimant or a class of persons of which the claimant was a member. In the public law context, liability is most likely to lie against officials giving answers to specific questions.[179] There is unlikely to be a duty of care in relation to the giving of general advice.[180]

19–047   Both in the case of negligent misstatement and other forms of negligence it must be accepted that as a result of the decisions of the House of Lords and the Privy Council already cited, the circumstances in which liability for negligence for administrative default will be limited to special situations. Unless and until there is legislative intervention or a change of heart on the part of the House of Lords, little progress in developing additional situations where damages will be payable can be expected.

---

[175] *Hedley Byrne & Co v Heller* [1964] A.C. 465 and *Caparo Industries Plc v Dickman* [1990] 2 A.C. 605. *cf. James McNaughton Paper v Hicks Anderson* [1991] 2 Q.B. 113 (Neill L.J.: in the light of later decisions, detailed reference to *Hedley Byrne* serves little purpose).

[176] See, e.g. *Ministry of Housing and Local Government v Sharp* [1970] 2 Q.B. 223; cf. though, the *Welbridge Holdings* case. But probably no action will he against the Crown in respect of a negligent statement by one of its servants unless that servant also owed a duty of care (Crown Proceedings Act 1947 s.2(1)(a), proviso).

[177] *Yuen Kun-Yeu v Attorney General of Hong Kong* [1988] A.C. 175 at 194 (Lord Keith).

[178] See, e.g. *Caparo v Dickman* [1990] 2 A.C. 605 accounts audited pursuant to Companies Act); *Deloitte Haskins & Sells v National Mutual Life Nominees Ltd* [1993] 2 All E.R. 1015 (duty to report under Securities Act 1978).

[179] *Davy v Spelthorne BC* [1984] A.C. 262 (planning officers gave erroneous assurances that the operation of an enforcement notice would be suspended for three years); *Welton v North Cornwall DC* [1997] 1 W.L.R. 570 (special relationship between claimant guesthouse owner and environmental health officers which gave rise to a duty to take reasonable care in statements made about extent of alterations needed to comply with law).

[180] See, e.g. *Tidman v Reading BC* [1994] 3 P.L.R. 72 (although local authority had published a document encouraging persons involved in planning matters to seek guidance and advice from planning officers, a person who sought such guidance or advice did not thereby necessarily place the authority in a position where it owed a *Hedley Byrne* duty); *Commissioner of Police of the Metropolis v Lennon* [2004] EWCA Civ 130; [2004] 1 W.L.R. 2594.

MISFEASANCE IN PUBLIC OFFICE[181]

As a general rule, in determining questions of tortious liability the motives **19–048** of the defendant are immaterial, though proof of improper motive maybe fatal to a defence of statutory authority to commit an act that is prima facie tortious.[182] Improper motive (malice and bad faith are often used as synonyms) is however an essential ingredient in the tort of misfeasance in public office, the scope of which has been greatly clarified in recent years.[183] A public authority[184] or person holding a public office[185] may be liable for the tort of misfeasance in public office. There must be a connection between the misconduct complained of and the office of which the misconduct is an alleged abuse (so actions done in an officer's own time may not create a liability).[186]

The tort appears to have its genesis in election corruption actions **19–049** starting in the late 17th century,[187] but it fell into disuse and its elements were crystallised only in recent years.[188] The tort is not confined to those actions or decisions which are capable of being characterised as the exercise of "public" power and extends to decisions taken by a public authority in capacities such as the claimant's landlord or in the exercise of contractual powers.[189] A police officer investigating suspected disciplinary offences alleged to have been committed by another officer who makes a written report to his superior officer was, however, held not to have done

---

[181] See M. Andenas and D. Fairgrieve, "Misfeasance in Public Office, Governmental Liability and European Influences" (2002) 51 I.C.L.Q. 757; S. Hannett, "Misfeasance in public office: the principles" [2005] J.R. 227.

[182] cf. *Westminster Corp v L & NW Ry* [1905] A.C. 426 (where the allegations of improper motives were not, however, made out).

[183] Note also the tort of malicious prosecution and the crime of misconduct in public office (*R. v Bowden (Terence)* [1996] 1 W.L.R. 98; Public Bodies Corrupt Practices Act 1889).

[184] *Three Rivers DC v Bank of England (No.3)* [2003] 2 A.C. 1. After some initial hesitation as to whether a public authority could be vicariously for the misfeasance of its servants, the HL confirmed that they may be: *Racz v Home Office* [1994] 2 A.C. 45.

[185] A person who is paid out of public funds and who "owes duties to members of the public as to how the office shall be exercised": see *Tampion v Anderson* [1973] V.R. 715 at 720. Also *Henley v Mayor of Lyme* (1828) 5 Bing. 91 at 107. Quaere whether the officer has to be paid out of public funds. The term office is to be understood "in a relatively wide sense" (*Cornelius v Hackney LBC* [2002] EWCA Civ 1073; [2003] B.L.G.R. 178 at [13]) and includes e.g. a local authority's exercise of functions as a landlord (*Jones v Swansea City Council* [1990] 1 W.L.R. 1453, HL). But the Society of Lloyd's is not a public officer: *Society of Lloyd's v Henderson* [2007] EWCA civ 930; *The Times*, October 19, 2007.

[186] *Cornelius* [2002] EWCA Civ 1073; [2003] B.L.G.R. 178 at [16].

[187] For a useful account of the historical development of the tort, see R. Evans, "Damages for Unlawful Administrative Action: The Remedy for Misfeasance in Public Office" (1982) 31 I.C.L.Q. 640. Revival of interest in the tort dates from a series of Commonwealth decisions: *Farrington v Thomson and Bridgland* [1959] V.C. 286 (wrongful order to close hotel); *Roncarelli v Duplessis* [1959] S.C.R. 121 (Can.); and *David v Abdul Cader* [1963] 1 W.L.R. 834, PC, Ceylon.

[188] The leading authority is now *Three Rivers DC v Bank of England (No.3)* [2003] 2 A.C. 1.

[189] *Three Rivers DC v Bank of England (No.3)* [2003] 2 A.C. 1 at 191 (Lord Steyn); *cf Jones v Swansea City Council* [1990] 1 W.L.R. 1453 at 1458 (Lord Lowry, *obiter*) (the claimant needed both planning permission and the council's permission as her landlord for the change of use of premises).

an "act" amounting to an exercise of power or authority for the purposes of this tort.[190]

19–050   There are two alternative forms of the tort, depending on the state of mind of the tortfeasor. In both it is necessary "to prove the requisite subjective state of mind of the defendant in relation not only to his own conduct but also its effect on others".[191] In both, the tort concerns deliberate acts—it cannot be committed negligently or inadvertently.[192] In both the defendant has exercised a power which is unlawful—in the sense of that term similar to that used in judicial review. The two forms (or "limbs") of the tort are as follows.

(a) First, there is the situation where the unlawful exercise of the power is motivated by malice targeted at and intending to injure the particular claimant.[193] A power is exercised maliciously if its repository is motivated by personal animosity towards those who are directly affected by its exercise.[194] Bad faith is demonstrated by knowledge of probable loss on the part of the public officer.[195]

(b) Second, there is the situation where a decision-maker acting unlawfully does so "with a state of mind of reckless indifference"[196] or "blind disregard" to the legality of his act,[197] and an awareness that the act will in the ordinary and probable course of events cause injury to a person or a class of persons (who need not be identifiable at the time the tort is committed).[198] There is no need to establish any greater proximity, link or relationship between defendant and claimant than this.[199] Bad faith or dishonesty (synonyms in this

---

[190] *Calveley v Chief Constable of the Merseyside Police* [1989] A.C. 1228 at 1240. Such a report may however give rise to a cause of action for defamation.

[191] *Three Rivers DC v Bank of England (No.3) (Summary Judgment)* [2001] UKHL 16; [2003] 2 A.C. 1 at [164] (Lord Hobhouse).

[192] *Three Rivers (No.3)* [2003] 2 A.C. 1 at 230 (Lord Hobhouse), 235 (Lord Millett); see, e.g. *Ashley v Chief Constable of Sussex* [2005] EWHC 415.

[193] That is, an intent to injure the claimant: see *Bennett v Commissioner of Police of the Metropolis* [1995] 1 W.L.R. 488 at 501. On intention in tort see *Douglas v Hello! Ltd (Trial Action: Breach of Confidence) (No.3)* [2005] EWCA Civ 595; [2006] Q.B. 125 at [159]. In *Weir v Secretary of State for Transport* [2004] EWHC 2772; [2005] U.K.H.R.R. 154, a former minister was cross-examined for over two days in an unsuccessful claim in which it was said that he had deliberately impaired the value of their shareholding in the Railtrack Group, leading to the making of an administration order on October 7, 2001, without paying compensation or seeking the prior approval of Parliament.

[194] In *Roncarelli v Duplessis* [1959] S.C.R. 121 at 141, Rand J. defined malice more widely, as "acting for a reason and purposed knowingly foreign to the administration".

[195] *Three Rivers (No.3)(Summary Judgment)* [2001] UKHL 16; [2003] 2 A.C. 1 at [44] (Lord Hope).

[196] *Three Rivers (No.3)* [2003] 2 A.C. 1 at 192.

[197] *Three Rivers (No.3)* [2003] 2 A.C. 1 at 231 (Lord Hobhouse).

[198] *Three Rivers (No.3)* [2003] 2 A.C. 1 at 191 (Lord Steyn), 228 (Lord Hutton), 230 (Lord Hobhouse), 235 (Lord Millett). And see *Three Rivers DC v Bank of England (No.3) (Summary Judgment)* [2001] UKHL 16; [2003] 2 A.C. 1 at [46] (Lord Hope).

[199] *Akenzua v Secretary of State for the Home Department* [2002] EWCA Civ 1470; [2003] 1 W.L.R. 741.

context) is required on the part of the defendant public officer[200] and is demonstrated by recklessness on his part in disregarding the risk of loss.[201] This is sometimes referred to as the "untargeted malice" form of the tort.

Where misfeasance is alleged against a decision-making body, it is sufficient   19–051
to show that a majority of its members present had made the decision with the object of damaging the claimant.[202] A court will not entertain allegations of bad faith or malice made against the repository of a power unless it has been expressly pleaded and properly particularised.[203] Often there may be no direct evidence of the existence of malice, and in these circumstances the court may make adverse inferences, e.g. from the fact that a decision was so unreasonable that it could only be explained by the presence of such a motive.[204] The claimant must prove that the exercise of power caused loss (financial loss or physical or mental injury)—distress (as opposed to a recognised psychiatric condition), injured feelings, indignation or annoyance are insufficient; it is not a tort actionable per se.[205] Exemplary damages may be awarded in addition to compensatory damages.[206]

BREACH OF STATUTORY DUTY[207]

English law has witnessed "the painful emergence of a nominate tort" of   19–052
breach of statutory duty,[208] where in a limited range of circumstances a breach of a statutory duty, in and of itself and without proof of negligence, or malice, may give rise to an action in damages.

[200] *Three Rivers (No.3)* [2003] 2 A.C. 1 at 228 (Lord Hutton, who prefers the term "bad faith"), 191 (Lord Steyn: it "involves bad faith inasmuch as the public officer does not have an honest belief that his act is lawful").
[201] *Three Rivers (No.3) (Summary Judgment)* [2003] 2 A.C. 1 at 228 (Lord Hutton), 231 (Lord Hobhouse).
[202] *Jones v Swansea City Council* [1990] 1 W.L.R. 1453 at 1458–1459, HL.
[203] *Demetriades v Glasgow Corp* [1951] 1 All E.R. 457 at 460, 461, 463; *Three Rivers (No.3) (Summary Judgment)* [2003] 2 A.C. 1 at [49] (Lord Hope—"In my judgment a balance must be struck between the need for fair notice to be given on the one hand and excessive demands for detail on the other".
[204] *Three Rivers (No.3)* [2003] 2 A.C. 1 at 235–263 (Lord Millett—"The question is: why did the official act as he did if he knew or suspected that the had no power to do so and that his conduct would injure the plaintiff?").
[205] *Watkins v Secretary of State for the Home Department* [2006] UKHL 17; [2006] 2 A.C. 395 (prison officers deliberately and in bad faith opened and read legal correspondence to a prisoner, contrary to Prison Rules). For a broad interpretation, see *Karagozlu v Commissioner of Police of the Metropolis* [2006] EWCA Civ 1691; (2007) 151 S.J.L.B. 29 (loss of liberty, if not a form of physical of physical injury, is at least akin to or analogous to physical injury).
[206] *Kuddus v Chief Constable of Leicestershire* [2001] UKHL 29; [2002] 2 A.C.
[207] See further K. Stanton et al., *Statutory Torts* (2003); *Clerk and Lindsell on Torts*, 19th edn, (2006) Ch.9.
[208] *The Queen in Right of Canada v Saskatchewan Wheat Pool* (1983) 143 D.L.R. (3rd) 9, Dixon J. (Sup. Ct. of Canada). For the purposes of awards of exemplary damages, breaches of different statutory duties are to be regarded as sui generis torts rather than there being a single nominate tort of branch of statutory duty: see *AB v South West Water Services Ltd* [1993] 3 All E.R. 609 at 620 (overruled in other respects by *Kuddus v Chief Constable of Leicestershire* [2001] UKHL 29; [2002] 2 A.C. 122).

19–053   Some statutory provisions expressly create rights of action for damages in tort against public bodies in breach of a statutory duty[209] and here few problems arise. Added difficulty arises in the more common situation where the legislation is silent on the issue whether breach entitles a person who suffers loss due to non-compliance with the statutory duty to commence an action for damages. The question is always approached as one of statutory construction to ascertain whether the legislature intended to provide for such private law claims for monetary compensation and for this reason it is difficult to discuss the tort in terms of generally applicable principles.[210] This judicial technique has rightly been criticised: "The failure of the judges to develop a governing attitude means that it is almost impossible to predict, outside the decided authorities, when the courts will regard a civil duty as impliedly created. In effect the judge can do what he likes, and then select one of the conflicted principles stated by his predecessors in order to justify his decision".[211]

19–054   Most statutory duties in the public law context are owed to the public at large rather than to private individuals.[212] Where the legislation in question establishes an administrative system to promote the social welfare of the community, exceptionally clear statutory language will be needed to show a parliamentary intention to create a right to damages for breach of statutory duty.[213] Categorising a duty as being in broad and general terms in this way is fatal to a claim for damages, even on judicial review. On this basis a breach of s.8 of the Education Act 1944 was held to give no right of action.[214]

19–055   It is therefore a necessary, but not sufficient, precondition to liability to establish that the particular statutory duty was intended to protect a certain class of person (rather than the public at large) from a particular type of damage.[215] Factors which may raise a presumption of no legislative intention to create private rights to compensation include: the existence of a penalty or other remedy (including judicial review) for non-compliance;[216] the fact that the aggrieved person had opportunities to participate in the decision-making process and had appeal rights;[217] by whom the duty is owed;[218] and the anticipated policy consequences of

---

[209] See, e.g. Highways Act 1980 s.57.

[210] *R v Deputy Governor of Parkhurst Prison Exp. Hague* [1992] 1 A.C. 58 at 159 (Lord Bridge).

[211] Glanville Williams, "The Effect of Penal Legislation in Tort" (1960) 23 M.L.R. 233, 246.

[212] On "target" duties, see 5–064.

[213] *X (Minors) v Bedfordshire CC* [1995] 2 A.C. 633 at 731; *Phelps v Hillingdon LBC* [2001] 2 A.C. 619 at 652.

[214] *R. v Inner London Education Authority Ex p. Ali* (1990) 2 Admin. L.R. 822 (local education authority had failed to provide school places for a large number of children in the Stepney area of London).

[215] *Hague* [1992] 1 A.C. 58 at 170 (Lord Jauncey).

[216] See, e.g. *Lonrho Plc v Shell Petroleum Co (No.2)* [1982] A.C. 173; *Hague* [1992] 1 A.C. 58; *Calveley v Chief Constable of the Merseyside Police* [1989] A.C. 1228.

[217] *X (Minors) v Bedfordshire CC* [1995] 2 A.C. 633.

[218] So, if the duty is imposed only on a public authority, rather than also on private persons, there may be a presumption against an intention to create liability in damages; see T. Weir, "Compensation in Public Law" [1989] P.L. 40, 53.

imposing liability.[219] Where the duty in question arises from a statutory instrument, the court will examine the enabling Act to see whether it gives power to the minister to create private rights.[220] By way of illustration, breach of the Prison Rules has been held to give no right of action in damages to a prisoner;[221] nor the Police (Discipline) Regulations to an officer facing disciplinary action;[222] nor duties under the homeless persons legislation.[223]

DEPRIVATION OF LIBERTY: FALSE IMPRISONMENT[224]

Claims for damages arising from unlawful actions which lead to the unlawful confinement of the claimant are most likely to arise in connection with government functions such as the criminal justice system, immigration control and the treatment of the mentally ill. The tort of false imprisonment has two elements:[225] (a) the fact of complete deprivation of liberty for any time, however short;[226] and (b) the absence of lawful authority to justify it for its full duration.[227] It is not necessary to prove physical incarceration; rather the gist of the tort is restraint (over and above that imposed by the general law or a binding contract) so that a person has no liberty to go at all times to all places where he wishes.[228] The tort is one of strict liability.[229] Bad faith is not an ingredient of the tort of false imprisonment, so it is no defence for the official authorising or carrying out the detention to say that he acted in good faith.[230] A claim may also lie for trespass to the person. **19–056**

Where a person has been deprived of liberty, a claim for damages for breach of ECHR Art.5 under s.8 of the HRA may be made.[231] **19–057**

---

[219] *Clegg Parkinson & Co Ltd v Earby Gas* [1896] 1 Q.B. 592.
[220] *Hague* [1992] 1 A.C. 58 at 170 (Lord Jauncey).
[221] *Hague* [1992] 1 A.C. 58.
[222] *Calveley v Chief Constable of the Merseyside Police* [1989] A.C. 1228.
[223] *O'Rourke v Camden LBC* [1998] A.C. 188, HL, overruling *Thornton v Kirklees MBC* [1979] Q.B. 626, CA. Housing Act 1985 Pt III was a social welfare programme intended to confer benefits at public expense pursuant to public policy, which suggested that Parliament did not intend to confer private law rights in relation to it.
[224] *Clerk and Lindsell on Torts*, 19th edn, (2006) para.15–23. See also 17–010 on the writ of habeas corpus.
[225] *Hague* [1992] 1 A.C. 58 at 162 (Lord Bridge).
[226] On deprivation of liberty, see *Re L (R. v Bournewood Community and Mental Health NHS Trust Ex p. L)* [1999] 1 A.C. 458 (L's re-admission to hospital under s.131(1) Mental Health Act 1983 did not amount to the tort of false imprisonment as he had not been deprived of his liberty, since he was not kept on a locked ward and had not made any attempt to leave); L successfully challenged this decision in the ECtHR: *L v United Kingdom* (2005) 40 E.H.R.R. 32 as breaching Art.5(1) and Art.5(4).
[227] *Clerk and Lindsell on Torts*, 19th edn, (2006) in what is now para.15–26, quoted with approval by Lord Jauncey in *Hague* [1992] 1 A.C. 58 at 173;
[228] *Hague* [1992] 1 A.C. 58 at 173 (Lord Jauncey).
[229] *Evans v Governor of Brockhill Prison* [2001] 2 A.C. 19 (the fact that the prison governor had acted in good faith was no defence).
[230] *Evans* [2001] 2 A.C. 19 at [42].
[231] See 13–070 and 19–092.

Lawful authority

19–058 Questions as to whether a person has lawful authority to detain another must, since the coming into force of the HRA, be read subject to the overriding requirements of Art.5; some earlier cases must therefore be read with caution and may not be a reliable guide to what constitutes lawful detention.[232] It is unnecessary for a claimant to obtain a quashing order or declaration in relation to the unlawfulness of the detention; that is a matter that may be determined by the court hearing the tort claim.[233]

19–059 As we have noted, judges of the higher courts have absolute immunity from suit[234] and magistrates may be subject to liability only if it can be proved that he acted both in bad faith and in excess of jurisdiction.[235] A police constable in exercising his discretion to arrest under s.24(6) of the Police and Criminal Evidence Act 1984 is subject to judicial control on *Wednesbury* principles.[236] Immunity may also be conferred by statute on those carrying out detention functions in various contexts, such as caring for the mentally ill.[237]

19–060 Section 12(1) of the Prison Act 1952 provides lawful authority for the restraint of prisoners within the defined bounds of the prison by the governor of the prison. A prisoner has no cause of action for false imprisonment if he is confined for a particular time within a particular part of the prison, for example, he is segregated and held in solitary confinement, even if the restraint was not in accordance with the Prison Rules 1964.[238] Where, however, a prison officer acts in bad faith by deliberately subjecting a prisoner to restraint which he knows he has no authority to impose he may render himself personally liable to an action for false imprisonment.[239] An otherwise lawful imprisonment is not rendered unlawful by reason only of the conditions of detention, however intolerable they may be.[240] Immigration Officers who act unlawfully have no special immunity under Sch.2 to the Immigration Act 1971; the burden of establishing a defence therefore lies upon them.[241]

---

[232] *D v Home Office* [2005] EWCA Civ 38; [2006] 1 W.L.R. 1003 at [67]. On Art.5, see 13–070.

[233] *D v Home Office* [2005] EWCA Civ 38; [2006] 1 W.L.R. 1003 at [120].

[234] See 19–020.

[235] See 19–021.

[236] *Mohammed-Holgate v Duke* [1984] A.C. 437 at 443; *Cumming v Chief Constable of Northumbria Police* [2003] EWCA Civ 1844; [2004] A.C.D. 42 at [43]–[44]; *Paul v Chief Constable of Humberside* [2004] EWCA Civ 308 at [30];

[237] Mental Health Act 1983 s.139.

[238] *Hague* [1992] 1 A.C. 58.

[239] *Hague* [1992] 1 A.C. 58.

[240] *Hague* [1992] 1 A.C. 58.

[241] *D v Home Office* [2005] EWCA Civ 38; [2006] 1 W.L.R. 1003 (asylum seekers held in detention centre).

Procedural considerations

Where a person is allegedly unlawfully detained by a public authority, a **19–061** challenge may be made either in a CPR Pt 54 claim for judicial review or by way of an application for a writ of habeas corpus.[242] In the former proceedings, a claim for damages for false imprisonment may be included; if habeas corpus is sought, a separate claim for damages will have to be commenced. Claims for false imprisonment may be tried by judge and jury.[243]

MEASURE OF DAMAGES IN TORT[244]

Generally, the aim of damages is to compensate the claimant for loss **19–062** caused by the defendant's conduct. In tort, damages put the claimant as nearly as possible into the position he would have been in had the tortious act not occurred. In addition to ordinary damages, exemplary and aggravated may be awarded. Guidelines have been laid down by the Court of Appeal on quantum of damages, in the context of claims against the police.[245]

Exemplary damages

Exceptionally, the court may award exemplary damages in tort to deter **19–063** and condemn the defendant's conduct rather than merely to compensate the claimant. Such damages are generally viewed as anomalous and courts take a restrictive approach, awarding exemplary damages only if the case falls within one of three categories (based on nature of the defendant's tortious conduct) set out by Lord Devlin in *Rookes v Barnard*.[246] The first is "oppressive, arbitrary or unconstitutional action by the servants of the government". In this context, government servants includes all those who by common law or statute are exercising functions of a governmental character such as local authorities and the police as well as Crown servants. Torts committed in the course of carrying out commercial operations, such as the supply of water, fall outside this category.[247] The meanings of oppressive, arbitrary and unconstitutional are not settled, though it is clear that the three elements are to be read disjunctively.[248] Doubt has been

---

[242] See 17–010.
[243] County Courts Act 1984 s.66; Supreme Court Act (Senior Court Act) 1981 s.69.
[244] For a more detailed account of damages generally, see *McGregor on Damages*, 15th edn (1988).
[245] *Thompson v Commissioner of Police of the Metropolis* [1998] Q.B. 498.
[246] *Rookes v Barnard (No.1)* [1964] A.C. 1129.
[247] *AB v South West Water Services Ltd* [1993] Q.B. 507 (overruled in other respects by *Kuddus* [2001] UKHL 29; [2002] 2 A.C. 122.
[248] *Holden v Chief Constable of Lancashire* [1987] Q.B. 380.

expressed in the Court of Appeal as to whether every ultra vires act is unconstitutional and the absence of aggravating features is something which ought to be taken into account in deciding whether to award exemplary damages.[249] Conduct which is merely negligent is probably insufficient.[250] The second category of case is where the defendant committed the tortious act having calculated that the economic benefits to him flowing from the action would be greater than any damages he might be liable to pay. The third category contemplated by Lord Devlin is where there are circumstances in which the award of exemplary damages was expressly authorised by statute, none of which are particularly relevant in the public law context. Exemplary damages may be awarded against a chief constable of police variously liable for actions of his officers under s.88 of the Police Act 1996.[251]

Aggravated damages

19–064 Aggravated damages "compensate the victim of a wrong for mental distress (or 'injury to feelings') in circumstances in which that injury has been caused or increased by the manner in which the defendant committed the wrong, or by the defendant's conduct subsequent to the wrong".[252] Their main purpose, in distinction to exemplary damages, is not punitive. An award of aggravated damages requires "exceptional or contumelious conduct or motive on the part of a defendant in committing the wrong" and "mental distress sustained by the plaintiff as a result".[253]

REFORM FOR TORT LIABILITY

19–065 For many years the law and policy relating to civil liability of public authorities has been regarded as unsatisfactory.[254] Some commentators doubt whether the courts are best placed to provide monetary recompense;[255] certainly it needs to be born in mind that the ombudsmen have

---

[249] *Holden* [1987] Q.B. 380, (Purchas L .J.).
[250] *Barbara v Home Office* (1984) 134 N.LJ. 888.
[251] *Rowlands v Chief Constable of Merseyside* [2006] EWCA Civ 1773; (2007) 151 S.J.L.B. 28 at [48]. But "While it is possible that a Chief Constable could bear a responsibility for what has happened, due to his failure to exercise proper control, the instances when this is alleged to have occurred should not be frequent": *Thompson v Commissioner of Police of the Metropolis* [1998] Q.B. 498 at 512 CA.
[252] Law Commission, Aggravated, Exemplary and Restitutionary Damages (Law Com. No.247).
[253] *Appleton v Garrett* [1996] P.I.Q.R. P1.
[254] In 2004 the Law Commission began a project on monetary remedies in public law, later widened to encompass a broader range of remedies: see *Monetary Remedies in Public Law* (October 2004); *Remedies against Public Bodies: a Scoping Report* (October 2006). For a trenchant critique, see R. Bagshaw, "Monetary Remedies in Public Law—Misdiagnosis and Misprescription" (2006) 26 L.S. 4.
[255] C. Harlow, *State Liability: Tort Law and Beyond* (2004).

powers to recommend compensation for injustice caused by maladministration.[256] There are also concerns about the alleged growth of a "compensation culture" and increased risk aversion,[257] and in this context the deep pockets of public authorities have at times been seen as easy targets.[258] Against this backdrop, s.1 of the Compensation Act 2006 restates in statutory terms the long-standing approach of the common law that

> "A court considering a claim in negligence or breach of statutory duty may, in determining whether the defendant should have taken particular steps to meet a standard of care (whether by taking precautions against a risk or otherwise), have regard to whether a requirement to take those steps might—(a) prevent a desirable activity from being undertaken at all, to a particular extent or in a particular way, or (b) discourage persons from undertaking functions in connection with a desirable activity."

Public authorities are in a different position compared to private-sector businesses and individuals who choose to carry on activities; a statutory duty may lock the public authority into providing services regardless of the risks of litigation. The 2006 Act also provides that "An apology, an offer of treatment or other redress, shall not of itself amount to an admission of negligence or breach of statutory duty".[259]   19–066

Some people take as their starting-point a belief that public authorities and officials should provide compensation for damage caused by their unlawful administrative conduct. Certainly, it can seem unfair that an aggrieved person is left to shoulder loss where a court finds the administrative action which caused it unlawful and grants judicial review. This is especially so where the public authority erred while carrying out a regulatory function (e.g. by means of licensing) designed to benefit the community as a whole and where it was not practicable for the adversely affected person to insure against the risk of damage.[260] In such circumstances why should it not be the community qua taxpayers—rather than the individual who suffers damage as a result of unlawful administration—which bares the loss? The imperfect interface in English law between notions of unlawful acts in judicial review proceedings and rights to damages in tort means that some victims of bureaucratic error currently go   19–067

---

[256] See 1–19–084.

[257] See House of Commons Constitutional Affairs Committee, *Compensation Culture*. HC Paper No.754–I (Session 2205/06).

[258] A high-water mark is *Anns v Merton LBC* [1978] A.C. 728 (now largely overruled) dealing with local authority liability in respect of a homeowner's repair costs following the failure of foundations which had been laid in the absence of adequate inspection.

[259] Compensation Act 2006 s.2.

[260] Many tort actions against central and local government are, in reality, brought by insurance companies exercising their rights of subrogation under policies. T. Weir has argued that claims in respect of damage covered by a solvent insurer should be barred absolutely: see "Governmental Liability" [1989] P.L. 40, 59.

uncompensated,[261] though in the absence of empirical data it is unclear how extensive the problem really is.

19–068   Other concerns point in the opposite direction, to a perceived injustice that there is no common law right to damages for loss caused by unlawful administration action in English law: the regulatory functions of government, improperly carried out, may result in loss of profit; other unlawful action or inaction may result in personal inconvenience or the deprivation of a benefit. The standard judicial review remedies—quashing, prohibiting and mandatory orders—are not necessarily adequate cures.[262]

19–069   Judges, pressure groups and political parties in England have attempted or called for reform but none have yet been successful. In 1966, three members of the High Court of Australia, in a case where the defendant council unlawfully[263] extracted gravel from a river bed thereby preventing the claimant using his right under licence to pump water to irrigate his farmland, asserted the proposition that "by an action for damages upon the case, a person who suffers harm or loss as the inevitable consequence of the unlawful, intentional and positive acts of another, is entitled to recover damages from that other".[264] But this principle has since been rejected by the House of Lords[265] and doubted by the Privy Council,[266] and subsequently overruled by the High Court of Australia.[267]

19–070   In 1988, the Justice/All Souls Review recommended that even in the absence of an actionable tort or other ground for claiming damages in private law, there should be a right to damages for unlawful administrative action or omission which causes a person loss.[268] Four years earlier, the Committee of Ministers of the Council of Europe had also adopted a principle of rights to compensation: "Reparation should be ensured for damage caused by an act due to a failure of a public authority to conduct

[261] See, e.g. *R. v Knowsley MBC Ex p. Maguire, The Times*, June 26, 1992.
[262] One often cited illustration of the low-water mark of English law is *R. v Knowsley MBC Ex p. Maguire* (1992) 90 L.G.R. 653, where the court held that there was no remedy in damages for loss suffered as a result of an unlawfully refused hackney carriage licence.
[263] It had failed to obtain the necessary permit or certificate of authority, contrary to regulations.
[264] *Beaudesert District Shire Council v Smith* (1966) 120 C.L.R. 145 at 156. In line of early English cases damages were awarded on the basis of the unlawfulness of an act in itself, see, e.g. *Ashby v White* (1704) 1 Brown 62 (returning officers liable for rejecting vote of qualified elector without proof of malice).
[265] *Lonrho Ltd v Shell Petroleum (No.2)* [1982] A.C. 173 at 188.
[266] *Dunlop v Woollahra Municipal Council* [1982] A.C. 158.
[267] *Northern Territory of Australia v Mengel* (1995) 60 A.L.J.R. 527.
[268] Report of the Committee of the Justice/All Souls Review of Administrative Law in the United Kingdom, *Administrative Justice—Some Necessary Reforms* 1988), para.11.83: "compensation shall be recoverable by any person who sustains loss as a result of . . . (a) any act, decision, determination, instrument or order of a public authority which materially affects him and which is for any reason wrongful or contrary to law; or (b) unreasonable or excessive delay on the part of any public authority in taking any action, reaching any decision or determination, making any order or carrying out any duty". An earlier report by justice, Administration under Law (1971) had also advocated the power to award damages to persons aggrieved by decisions tainted with procedural or substantive irregularity in circumstances where there is no cause of action for damages under the law as it now stands. *cf.* the criticisms of H. Woolf, *Protection of the Public—A New Challenge* (1990), p.58.

itself in a way which can reasonably be expected from it in relation to the injured person. Such a failure is presumed in case of transgression of an established legal rule".[269]

In 1991 the Institute for Public Policy Research in its draft constitution **19–071** for the UK included provision for an Act of Parliament to provide for "effective remedies (including the payment of compensation) in cases where applications for judicial review are upheld",[270] though this stops short of requiring the creation of a right of action for damages of unlawful administrative action as such. Neither of the major political parties in the UK has made commitments to enacting legislation for compensation in this context. What is most likely to prompt such legislative reform is the growing divergence between rights to compensation for ultra vires acts under European Community law[271] and those in the purely domestic law sphere.

In the absence of new legislation, reform through the courts will be **19–072** difficult: the general principle of "no damage in the absence of a recognised tort" is now probably too entrenched in domestic case law to permit any far-reaching change of direction by the judges. In any event, the dominant judicial attitude during the 1980s and early 1990s has been one of hostility towards attempts to extend any further the liability of public authorities, even within the confines of the current framework of tort law. The main fear appears to be that to do so would inhibit effective decision taking by public bodies. Thus, duties of care have been denied in relation to the work of a financial services regulatory agency,[272] social workers[273] and in respect of investigations by the police[274] in part in concern that liability would lead to "detrimentally defensive" administration. In *Rowling v Takaro Properties Ltd*, Lord Keith spoke of the danger of "overkill"[275] and suggested that following the House of Lord's decision in *Anns v Merton LBC*[276] (where council inspectors carrying out statutory functions of inspection of the safety of new building were held to be negligent in

[269] Principle I contained in Recommendation No.R (84) 15 Relating to Public Liability (adopted by the Committee of Ministers on September 18, 1984 at the 375th meeting of the Ministers' Deputies). The aim of the recommendation, which of course is non-binding, is to encourage uniformity among the Member States of the Council of Europe. The Justice/All Souls Report (1988), para.11.63 argued that this formula probably adds little to the existing heads of liability in English law.
[270] *The Constitution of the United Kingdom*, art.118.1.3.
[271] See 14–066.
[272] *Yuen Kun-yeu v Attorney General of Hong Kong* [1988] A.C. 175 at 196 In England, statutory immunity has in some circumstances been given to those exercising regulatory functions, e.g. under s.187 of the Financial Services Act 1986 and s.14 of the Lloyd's Act 1982.
[273] *X (Minors) v Bedfordshire CC* [1995] 2 A.C. 633.
[274] *Hill v Chief Constable of West Yorkshire* [1988] 1 A. C. 53 (Lord Keith: "The general sense of public duty which motivates police forces is unlikely to be appreciably reinforced by the imposition of such liability so far as concerns their function in the investigation and suppression of crime . . . In some instances the imposition of liability may lead to the exercise of a function being carried out with a detrimentally defensive frame of mind".
[275] [1988] A.C. 473 at 502.
[276] [1978] A.C. 728.

approving defective foundations) the cure had been worse than the disease. Building inspectors of some local authorities had reacted by simply increasing, unnecessarily, the requisite depth of foundations, thereby imposing a substantial and unnecessary financial burden on members of the community.[277] A similar danger, Lord Keith believed, arose in relation to the imposition of a duty of care on a minister (as in Rowling) not to misconstrue legislation. Similar concerns have been expressed extra-judicially.[278] The judicial view is not, however, monolithic.[279] In *Home Office v Dorset Yacht Co Ltd*,[280] Lord Reid had no hesitation in dismissing a policy argument that imposing vicarious liability on the Home Office for damage caused as a result of prison officers negligently allowing borstal boys to escape from custody would curtail continued experimentation with minimum security regimes which were an important aspect of rehabilitation schemes. His experience led him to believe that "Her Majesty's servants were made of sterner stuff" than the public servants of New York who had been granted immunity in *Williams v New York State*.[281]

19–073   A number of questions emerge from the assertion that the further imposition of liability to pay damages for invalid administrative action would have a detrimentally chilling effect on decision-makers. First, the arguments often fail to identify who will be liable and in what sense: is the liability directly that of the public authority, its vicarious liability for the acts of employees, or the personal liability of individual administrators? It has been argued that vicarious and personal liability is undesirable and may indeed have a detrimental impact on decision-making; and that direct state liability is at least disadvantageous.[282] But in practice even if an individual civil servant or minister is a named defendant in a successful action for damages, the award will be paid out of public funds. Any impact on an administrator's behaviour therefore comes not from anxiety of personal financial inconvenience or ruin flowing directly from the damages award as such.

19–074   Why then is the problem of self-protection by administrators more significant in relation to damages awards than public law remedies? A sharp distinction has sometimes been drawn between remedies such as prohibiting and quashing orders, which are said to have a beneficial impact on administrative behaviour, and liability for damages which has an

---

[277] See also G. Ganz, "Public Law and the Duty of Care" [1977] P.L. 306.
[278] H. Woolf, *Protection of the Public—A New Challenge* (1990), p.58.
[279] On the contradictory "academic and judicial musing . . . regarding the instrumental affect of state liability", see further D. Cohen and J.C. Smith, "Entitlement and the Body Politic: Rethinking Negligence in Public Law" (1986) 64 Can.B.R. 1.
[280] [1970] A.C. 1004.
[281] (1955) 127 NE (2nd) 545. See also *Osman v Ferguson* [1993] 4 All E.R. 344.
[282] See D. Cohen and J. Smith (1986) 64 Can.B.R. 1, pp.9, 16; P. Schuck, *Suing Government: Citizen Remedies for Official Wrongs* 1980). These authors point out that the assumptions about rational economic behaviour of private individuals and firms in reaction to tort liability often cannot be applied to government bodies. As Cohen and Smith state succinctly at p.8: "To the extent that private tort law doctrines are premised on deterrent objectives they may be singularly ineffective when applied to the state".

undesirable effect.[283] In its broadest sense, however, "judicial review of administrative action" is not confined to the public law grounds of illegality, procedural propriety and unreasonableness. The present function of tort law is not confined to retrospective compensation for harm inflicted; the substantive rules of tort also set standards of acceptable administrative behaviour and so too would any expanded liability for damages. In the absence of more cogent empirical evidence on the effects of imposing (or not imposing) a more extensive liability to pay damages on public officials than currently exists,[284] it would be rash to oppose damages for unlawful acts on this ground alone. But equally, even if greater compensation for invalid administrative acts is desirable, it does not inevitably follow that creating a new action for damages is the most appropriate mechanism for providing it. Alternatives include greater use of the ombudsmen to recommend, or require, compensation to be paid or the creation of a fund analogous to that administered by the Criminal Injuries Compensation Board to which the victim of unlawful administrative action causing loss may apply.

RESTITUTIONARY AND OTHER CLAIMS FOR RETURN OF MONEY

Statutory rights for return of money paid

Legislation makes express provision for return of money erroneously paid **19–075** to public authorities in some situations, e.g. overpayments of tax.[285] If a statutory provision for the return of money paid gives a discretion to the public authority as to what sum, if any, to repay, the exercise of that discretion will be subject to judicial review.[286] It is a question of construction in each case as to whether the existence of a statutory right to repayment precludes a claimant making a restitutionary claim.[287]

Procedure

As with damages claims in tort, a claim under CPR Pt 7 may be a more **19–076** appropriate route for bringing a dispute about the recovery of money in restitution than a claim for judicial review under CPR Pt 54.[288] It is not

---

[283] See, e.g. the speech of Lord Bridge in *Hague v Deputy Governor of Parkhurst Prison* [1992] 1 A.C. 58 where it was said that "the availability of judicial review as a means of questioning the legality of action purportedly taken in pursuance of the Prison Rules is a beneficial and necessary jurisdiction which cannot properly be circumscribed by considerations of policy or expediency in relation to prison administration"—in contrast to the "wholly different question" of the availability of damages.

[284] A handful of small-scale empirical studies have been carried out in England, see: G. Ganz, "Public Law and the Duty of Care" [1977] P.L. 306; T. Weir, "Government Liability and the Duty of Care" [1989] P.L. 40, 60.

[285] Taxes Management Act 1973 s.33.

[286] See 19–003.

[287] *Deutsche Morgan Grenfell Group Plc v Inland Revenue Commissioners* [2006] UKHL 49; [2006] 3 W.L.R. 781 at [19].

[288] See, e.g. *R. (on the application of Rowe) v Vale of White Horse DC* [2003] EWHC 388; [2003] 1 Lloyd's Rep. 418 (recovery of payments for sewerage charges).

appropriate to use a mandatory order in judicial review proceedings to enforce a civil obligation to make restitution to a third party.[289]

Rights for return of money in restitution

19-077 There are four general elements to a claim for restitution:[290] (a) a benefit must have been gained by the defendant; (b) the benefit must have been obtained at the claimant's expense; it is not necessary for a claimant to have requested a service—this element is satisfied if the defendant has freely accepted or acquiesced in the supply for consideration of the services rendered or in exceptional circumstances the defendant has been incontrovertibly benefited from their receipt; (c) there must exist a factor recognised in law rendering it unjust or the defendant to retain the benefit; and (d) there must be no defence available to extinguish or reduce the defendant's liability to make restitution. There are various situations in the public law context in which restitutionary claims may arise.

19-078 First, where a person makes a payment in response to an unlawful demand for tax he has, on that basis alone, a prima facie right to automatic repayment of the money.[291] The demand had been made under a statutory instrument declared to be ultra vires the Income and Corporation taxes Act 1970.[292] Although it was unnecessary for their Lordships to decide whether this principle extended to cases where the demand was not ultra vires in this narrow sense,[293] but where for example the authority had mis-construed legislation,[294] Lord Goff indicated that it should.[295] In relation to payment of taxes, this ground of restitution also reflects the constitutional prohibition under the Bill of Rights 1689 against taxation without Parliamentary approval.

19-079 Secondly, following the House of Lords' landmark decision in *Kleinwort Benson Ltd v Lincoln City Council*,[296] the long-standing rule that money paid under a mistake of law was not recoverable in restitution no longer

---

[289] *R. v Barnet Magistrates Court Ex p. Cantor* [1999] 1 W.L.R. 334 (claimant sought mandamus to compel clerk to the justices to repay money paid by claimant's mother to settle a £30,000 fine held to have been unlawfully imposed).

[290] See generally G. Virgo, "Restitution from Public Authorities: Past, Present and Future" [2006] J.R. 370.

[291] *Woolwich Equitable Building Society v Inland Revenue Commissioners (No.2)* [1993] 1 A.C. 70. At the time, there was a general rule barring recovery of money paid under a mistake of law.

[292] Decided by the HL in an earlier application for judicial review: *R. v Inland Revenue Commissioners Ex p. Woolwich Building Society* [1990] 1 W.L.R. 1400. The Revenue repaid the sums that had been unlawfully demanded; the restitutionary claim was for interest on that sum.

[293] See 4–010.

[294] Or, e.g. had increased rents for market stalls without proper consultations: see *R. v Birmingham City Council Ex p. Dreger and Paget* [1993] C.O.D. 340. As in many others, although a restitutionary remedy was mooted in this case, it was not pursued because the council, like other responsible defendants, was assumed to be willing to give the necessary refunds that justice demanded in consequence of the quashing of its resolution to increase the rents.

[295] At 177. See also *British Steel Plc v Customs and Excise Commissioners (No.1)* [1997] 2 All E.R. 366.

[296] [1999] 2 A.C. 349 (the case concerned interest rate swaps, not tax).

applies. There is now a general right of recovery in cases of unjust enrichment, subject to defences. The concept of mistake of law is interpreted broadly, and includes a situation in which payment was demanded and paid under a law subsequently held ultra vires. The new approach applies to overpayments payments of tax made under a mistake of law.[297]

A third possible ground for seeking restitution unique to the public law **19–080** context arises from a group of decisions sometimes referred to as the *colore oficii* cases.[298] In these cases, money paid to a person in a public or quasi-public position to obtain performance by him of a duty which he was bound to perform for nothing, or for less than the sum demanded, was recoverable to the extent that the official was not entitled to it.[299] It is not clear whether these cases are to be explained on the basis that refusal to perform a public duty is a special category of duress[300] or whether they were precursors to the now recognised right to recover unlawfully demanded payments per se.[301] In any event, they are probably of no practical importance after the *Woolwich* decision.

COMPENSATION UNDER THE HUMAN RIGHTS ACT

Section 8 of the Human Rights Act 1998 provides:[302]   **19–081**

"8.—(1) In relation to any act (or proposed act) of a public authority which the court finds is (or would be) unlawful, it may grant such relief or remedy, or make such order, within its powers as it considers just and appropriate.

(2) But damages may be awarded only by a court which has power to award damages, or to order the payment of compensation, in civil proceedings.

(3) No award of damages is to be made unless, taking account of all the circumstances of the case, including—

(a) any other relief or remedy granted, or order made, in relation to the act in question (by that or any other court), and (b) the consequences of any decision (of that or any other court) in respect of that act,

---

[297] *Deutsche Morgan Grenfell Group Plc* [2006] UKHL 49; [2006] 3 W.L.R. 781: ECJ held that an aspect of advance corporation tax was contrary to European Community law because it discriminated between national and multi-national groups of companies.

[298] See: *Piggott's case* (cited in *Cartwright v Rowley* (1799) 2 Esp. 723); *Dew v Parsons* (1819) 2 B. & Ald. 562; *Morgan v Palmer* (1824) 2 B. & C. 729; *Steele v Williams* (1853) 8 Exch. 625.

[299] *Woolwich (No.2)*, [1993] 1 A.C. 70, 164 (Lord Goff).

[300] R. Goff and G. Jones, *The Law of Restitution*, 6th edn (2002), pp.310–316.

[301] P. Birks, *An Introduction to the Law of Restitution* (1989 rev. edn), pp.175–176.

[302] For a comprehensive account, see T. Eicke and D. Scorey, *Human Rights Damages, Principles and Practice* (2001, loose-leaf). For an early exposition of relevant principles, see Law Commission, *Damages under the Human Rights Act 1998* (October 2000).

the court is satisfied that the award is necessary to afford just satisfaction to the person in whose favour it is made.

(4) In determining—

(a) whether to award damages, or (b) the amount of an award, the court must take into account the principles applied by the European Court of Human Rights in relation to the award of compensation under Article 41 of the Convention.

(5) A public authority against which damages are awarded is to be treated—

(a) in Scotland, for the purposes of section 3 of the Law Reform (Miscellaneous Provisions) (Scotland) Act 1940 as if the award were made in an action of damages in which the authority has been found liable in respect of loss or damage to the person to whom the award is made;

(b) for the purposes of the Civil Liability (Contribution) Act 1978 as liable in respect of damage suffered by the person to whom the award is made.

(6) In this section —
'court' includes a tribunal;
'damages' means damages for an unlawful act of a public authority; and
'unlawful' means unlawful under section 6(1)."

19–082 Section 9(3) provides: "In proceedings under this Act in respect of a judicial act done in good faith, damages may not be awarded otherwise than to compensate a person to the extent required by Article 5(5) of the Convention." This excludes the award of exemplary damages.

19–083 Two provisions in the ECHR are of particular relevance to s.8. First, Art.13 requires everyone whose rights and freedoms are violated "to have an effective remedy". This article has not expressly been incorporated into national law by the HRA, but has a influence through the requirement for national courts, under s.2 of the HRA, to take account of Strasbourg case law.[303] Secondly, Art.41, referred to in s.8, requires the ECtHR to afford "just satisfaction" to an injured party if this is not provided by a national court.

The Woolf principles

19–084 Writing before the HRA came into force, Lord Woolf outlined eight principles that might guide the courts in the UK in their application of s.8.[304]

---

[303] See 13–034.
[304] Lord Woolf, "The Human Rights Act 1998 and Remedies", Ch.30 in M. Andenas (ed.), *Liber Amicorum in Honour of Lord Slynn of Hadley: Vol.II Judicial Review in International Perspective* (2000). The principles were cited in *R. (on the application of KB) v South London and South and West Region Mental Health Review Tribunal* [2003] EWHC 193 (Admin); [2004] Q.B. 936 at [20].

"The first principle could well be that if there is any other appropriate remedy in addition to damages, that other remedy should usually be granted initially and damages should only be granted if and to the extent that an additional award of damages is necessary to afford just satisfaction. This principle appears to accord with the approach envisaged by section 8 itself. In many cases what will be primarily required is an order which will result in the decision being taken again or an injunction to restrain the unlawful conduct or a declaration to establish the unlawfulness of that conduct. There should be no automatic right to compensation.

The second principle may be that the court should not award exemplary or aggravated damages. This does not mean there should be no award for anxiety, distress, injured feelings or other forms of non-pecuniary loss.

The third principle may be that an award should be of no greater sum than that necessary to achieve just satisfaction. If a public authority is required to take a decision again it may be necessary to adjourn the question of damages until it is known what the new decision is. If, for example, a retrial is necessary of a criminal offence the decision as to whether to make an award of damages could well depend on the outcome of the retrial.

The fourth principle may be that quantum of the award should be moderate.[305]

The fifth principle may be that the court should restrict the award to compensating the victim for what has happened so far as the unlawful conduct exceeds what could lawfully happen. If for example there is a complaint of a failure under Art.6 to provide a public hearing within a reasonable time, the compensation will be limited so that it only applies to the period which exceeds what is reasonable.

The sixth principle is likely to be that any failure of the claimant to take action promptly to remedy or avoid the situation of which complaint is made will reduce the amount of damages payable.

The seventh principle is that there is no reason to distinguish between pecuniary and non-pecuniary loss. What matters is that the loss complained of should be real loss clearly caused by conduct which is contrary to the Act and not whether it is pecuniary loss.

The eighth principle is that our domestic rules as to costs will probably cover any costs or expenses incurred by the complainant."

---

[305] The principle went on to state, "Certainly, the award should not exceed analogous awards made in the case of tortious claims and normally they should be on the low side by comparison to tortious awards". But this was not accepted in *R. (on the application of Bernard) v Secretary of State for the Home Department* [2005] EWHC 452 (Admin) or by the Law Commission, para.4.61 "on the basis that it involved a departure from the principle of full reparation for damage suffered"—an approach accepted by the CA in *KB* [2003] EWHC 193 (Admin); [2004] Q.B. 936 at [73].

19-085 *Anufrijeva* provided the Court of Appeal (presided over by Lord Woolf) with the first opportunity to consider the English courts' approach to s.8 of the HRA.[306] The court pointed out that, for the ECtHR, "any question of compensation will be of secondary, if any, importance"—the main aim of proceedings in Strasbourg being to bring to an end the violation of Convention rights.[307] The ECtHR routinely treats a finding of a violation as in itself providing just satisfaction. In this respect, the approach of the ECtHR in viewing damages as a "last resort" is fundamentally different from that of English courts in adjudicating on tortious claims, where damages are the primary remedy. Referring to the White Paper that preceded the HRA, the court in *Anufrijeva* explained that in "considering whether to award compensation and, if so, how much, there is a balance to be drawn between the interests of the victim and those of the public as a whole".[308] Although in most contexts awards under s.8 are "modest", damages should generally be similar to quantum in tort claims (though exact comparators may not exist); but no regard should be had to the quantum of damages awarded for sex and race discrimination.[309] Especially in cases where there is no similar ECtHR, the English courts should be guided by the framework of the HRA—that damages have to be "just and appropriate" and "necessary".[310] In so doing, the court should take into account "the scale and manner of violation".[311] The court should also have regard to *manner* in which the violation occurred.[312]

19-086 The Court of Appeal in *Anufrijeva* was concerned to ensure that there should be proportionality between the costs of obtaining a remedy and the quantum of damages at stake. To this end, the court suggested:

"i) The courts should look critically at any attempt to recover damages under the HRA for maladministration by any procedure other than judicial review in the Administrative Court.

ii) A claim for damages alone cannot be brought by judicial review (Pt 54.3(2)) but in this case the proceedings should still be brought in the Administrative Court by an ordinary claim.

iii) Before giving permission to apply for judicial review, the Administrative Court judge should require the claimant to explain why it would not be more appropriate to use any available internal complaint procedure or proceed by making a claim to the PCA

---

[306] *R. (on the application of Anufrijeva) v Southwark LBC* [2003] EWCA Civ 1406; [2004] Q.B. 1124 (asylum seekers claimed that local authorities had failed to discharge duties under the National Assistance Act 1948 to arrange for suitable accommodation, contrary to ECHR Art.8).
[307] *Anufrijeva* [2003] EWCA Civ 1406; [2004] Q.B. 1124 at [53].
[308] *Anufrijeva* [2003] EWCA Civ 1406; [2004] Q.B. 1124 at [56].
[309] *KB* [2003] EWHC 193 (Admin); [2004] Q.B. 936 at [74]; *R. (on the application of Greenfield) v Secretary of State for the Home Department* [2005] UKHL 14; [2005] 1 W.L.R. 673 at [18].
[310] *Anufrijeva* [2003] EWCA Civ 1406; [2004] Q.B. 1124 at [66].
[311] *Anufrijeva* [2003] EWCA Civ 1406; [2004] Q.B. 1124 at [67].
[312] *Anufrijeva* [2003] EWCA Civ 1406; [2004] Q.B. 1124 at [68].

[Parliamentary Ombudsmen] or LGO [Local Government Ombudsmen] at least in the first instance. The complaint procedures of the PCA and the LGO are designed to deal economically (the claimant pays no costs and does not require a lawyer) and expeditiously with claims for compensation for maladministration. . . .

iv) If there is a legitimate claim for other relief, permission should if appropriate be limited to that relief and consideration given to deferring permission for the damages claim, adjourning or staying that claim until use has been made of ADR, whether by a reference to a mediator or an ombudsman or otherwise, or remitting that claim to a district judge or master if it cannot be dismissed summarily on grounds that in any event an award of damages is not required to achieve just satisfaction.

v) It is hoped that with the assistance of this judgment, in future claims that have to be determined by the courts can be determined by the appropriate level of judge in a summary manner by the judge reading the relevant evidence. The citing of more than three authorities should be justified and the hearing should be limited to half a day except in exceptional circumstances.

vi) There are no doubt other ways in which the proportionate resolution of this type of claim for damages can be achieved. We encourage their use and do not intend to be prescriptive. What we want to avoid is any repetition of what has happened in the court below in relation to each of these appeals and before us, when we have been deluged with extensive written and oral arguments and citation from numerous lever arch files crammed to overflowing with authorities. The exercise that has taken place may be justifiable on one occasion but it will be difficult to justify again."[313]

The approach outlined in *Anufrijeva* was affirmed by the House of Lords in **19–087** *Greenfield*.[314] In rejecting the view that tort damages were an appropriate yardstick for assessing damages under s.8 of the HRA, Lord Bingham recalled that "the purpose of incorporating the Convention in domestic law through the 1998 Act was not to give victims better remedies at home than they could recover in Strasbourg but to give them the same remedies without the delay and expense of resort to Strasbourg".[315] Nonetheless, "the developing domestic jurisprudence under the Act may lead to modest (but more than nominal) awards of damages in cases of deliberate official wrongdoing, even if it does not occasion monetary loss".[316]

---

[313] *Anufrijeva* [2003] EWCA Civ 1406; [2004] Q.B. 1124 at [81].
[314] *Greenfield* [2005] UKHL 14; [2005] 1 W.L.R. 673: claimant sought damages for breach of Art.6, having been found guilty of a drugs offence by the deputy controller of the private prison in which he was incarcerated. R. Clayton, "Damage Limitation: The Courts and Human Rights Act damages" [2005] P.L. 429.
[315] [2005] UKHL 14; [2003] 1 W.L.R. 673 at [19].
[316] *Watkins v Home Office* [2006] UKHL 17; [2006] 2 A.C. 395, [73] (Lord Walker of Gestingthorpe).

Principles relating to ECHR Art.41

19–088 Although s.8 exhorts the court to take into account "the principles" applied by the ECtHR, the Court of Appeal in *Anufrijeva* noted the difficulty of identifying clear principles governing the award of damages as the ECtHR has chosen not to develop these, especially in relation to "anxiety and distress".[317] Often the ECtHR awards a global sum without differentiating between various heads of damage. The general approach is that the claimant should "insofar as this is possible, be placed in the same position as if his Convention rights had not been infringed".[318] Because compensation is the purpose of any award of damages, "it is in general not the function of an award of damages to mark the court's disapproval of the conduct complained of, or to compel future compliance with the Convention, or to reflect the importance of the right infringed".[319] The ECtHR takes account of any conduct of the applicant that contributed to the damage or injury.[320]

19–089 Different considerations apply to different Convention rights.[321] It is not possible here to provide a comprehensive account of the relevant case law, but illustrations in relation to several Convention rights provide some insight into the courts' approach. In having regard to quantum of damages awarded by the ECtHR in particular cases, the English courts should bear in mind that standards of living vary across Europe and should therefore ensure that any compensation that is awarded in an English court is adequate for a person living in the United Kingdom.[322] The English courts "should not aim to be significantly more or less generous than the [ECtHR] might be expected to be, in a case where it was willing to make an award at all".[323]

Article 2 (right to life)

19–090 *Van Colle v Chief Constable of Hertfordshire*[324] concerned a murder of a witness in a forthcoming criminal trial; the police were aware of threats to intimate witnesses but took no steps to protect the victim. The Chief Constable was held to have acted unlawfully in violation of Arts 2 and 8. The claimants were the victim's parents, acting as personal representatives

---

[317] *Anufrijeva* [2003] EWCA Civ 1406; [2004] Q.B. 1124 at [60].

[318] *Anufrijeva* [2003] EWCA Civ 1406; [2004] Q.B. 1124 at [59]; *Kingsley v UK* (2002) 35 E.H.R.R. 10, para.40.

[319] *KB* [2003] EWHC 193 (Admin); [2004] Q.B. 936 at [50].

[320] See, e.g. *Johnson v UK* (1999) 27 E.H.R.R. 440, para.77 (applicant's negative attitude and lack of co-operation).

[321] *Greenfield* [2005] UKHL 14; [2005] 1 W.L.R. 673 at [7] (Lord Bingham: "There is a risk of error if Strasbourg decisions given in relation to one article of the Convention are read across as applicable to another").

[322] *R. (on the application of KB) v South London and South and West Region Mental Health Review Tribunal* [2003] EWHC 193 (Admin); [2004] Q.B. 936 at [47]; *R. (on the application of Bernard) v Enfield LBC* [2002] EWHC 2282; [2003] H.R.L.R. 4 at [43].

[323] *Greenfield* [2005] UKHL 14; [2005] 1 W.L.R. 673 at [19].

[324] [2007] EWCA Civ 325;[2007] 1 W.L.R. 1821, See generally 13–060.

of his estate and in their own capacity. The Court of Appeal held that the award of £50,000 was excessive and should have been set at no more than £25,000 (£10,000 for the victim's estate and £7,500 for each of his parents).

Article 3 (prohibition of torture, inhumane and degrading treatment)

In *Napier v Scottish Ministers*[325] a prisoner was held on remand for 40 days **19–091** in an overcrowded and inadequately ventilated cell without access to toilet facilities at weekends and at night. His eczema flared up during his detention. Having regard to the relatively short period of time, the finding of a breach of Art.3 and the award of £2,000 solatium (for breach of a common law duty), the court made no further award under s.8 of the HRA.

Article 5 (right to liberty and security)

Article 5(5) expressly states that "Everyone who has been the victim of **19–092** arrest or detention in contravention of the provisions of this article shall have an enforceable right to compensation". This does not, however, mean that damages must be awarded by the ECtHR in all cases in which a breach of Art.5 occurs as Art.5(5) must be read in the broader context of Art.41, under which the ECtHR has a discretion.[326] The practice of the ECtHR is that awards for non-pecuniary loss of any kind are likely to be the exception, not the rule—though the case law does not speak with one voice on this.[327]

In *R. (on the application of KB) v South London and South and West* **19–093** *Region Mental Health Review Tribunal*[328] there were delays in hearings of the claimants' applications for reviews of their detention under the Mental Health Act 1983 by a tribunal, contrary to Art.5(4).[329] The Administrative Court accepted that awards under Art.5 should be broadly comparable to those that may be obtained for the tort of false imprisonment. In this case, the claimants' loss was in essence the loss of an opportunity to present their case to the tribunal at an earlier date and the chance to secure earlier release. The court held that a "claimant who seeks damages on the basis of

---

[325] 2005 1 S.C. 229 at [94] (Lord Bonomy: "It would in any event be extremely difficult to quantify compensation for any element of the petitioner's experience of his conditions which would not be adequately compensated in this way, bearing in mind the role of stress in causing the petitioner's eczema to flare up, the significance that I have already attributed to the conditions of detention in causing that stress, and the account I have taken of his psychological symptoms in assessing solatium"). S. Foster, "Prison Conditions, Human Rights and Art.3 ECHR" [2005] P.L. 35. See generally 13–063

[326] *KB* [2003] EWHC 193 (Admin); [2004] Q.B. 936 at [28], citing *Wassink v The Netherlands* (1253/86).

[327] *KB* [2003] EWHC 193 (Admin); [2004] G.B. 936 at [36].

[328] [2003] EWHC 193 (Admin); [2004] Q.B. 936. See generally 13–070.

[329] "Everyone who is deprived of his liberty by arrest or detention shall be entitled to take proceedings by which the lawfulness of his detention shall be decided speedily by a court and his release ordered if the detention is not lawful".

an allegation that he would have had a favourable decision at an earlier date if his Convention right had been respected must prove his allegation on the balance of probabilities" with convincing evidence.[330] Damages should relate to the period of time between the date when the tribunal should have determined the claimant's case (which may not always be clear) and when it did so; and the court should avoid calculating damages on a rate per day—the task is necessarily impressionistic.[331] Non-pecuniary damages to compensate for frustration and distress may be awarded if that distress is of significant intensity (for example, prompting a note to be made in the claimants' clinical records).[332] Having considered the evidence, the court awarded one of the claimants £4,000, four received £1,000, one £750 and in relation to two of them the finding of a breach was considered to be just satisfaction.

19–094　　The court in *R. (on the application of Bernard) v Secretary of State for the Home Department*[333] held that muddle and misunderstanding had caused delay in referring the claimant's case to the Parole Board but that this did not constitute a breach of Art.5(4). If it had, the court would not have considered it necessary to award damages. There was no evidence—only "very generalised assertions of feelings of frustration and distress"—which did not meet the threshold of significance to justify compensation.

19–095　　In *Austin v Commissioner of Police of the Metropolis*[334] the police responded to a surprise political procession on May Day by detaining thousands of people in a cordon for several hours at Oxford Circus in London in order to prevent a breakdown in law and order. The court held that the claimant's detention was a deprivation of liberty within Art.5(1) but was justified under Art.5(1)(c). The court held, *obiter*, that if the had been a breach of Art.5 no award of damages would have been made under s.8 of the HRA in the light of the guidance laid down in *Anufrijeva*.

19–096　　In *R. (on the application of TH) v Wood Green Crown Court*[335] the claimant was a witness to a serious assault. He provided the police with witnesses statements but was later reluctant to attend court to give evidence for the Crown against the youths he had identified to the police. The judge at trial remanded him in custody under s.4(3) of the Criminal Procedure (Attendance of Witnesses) Act 1965. It was held that there was no breach of Art.5(1). Had there been, a finding of a breach would have been just satisfaction—or if the court was wrong on this the English authorities on false imprisonment indicated that "the measure of damages would be in the hundreds rather than in the thousands of pounds".

[330] [2003] EWHC 193 (Admin); [2004] G.B. 936 at [64].
[331] [2003] EWHC 193 (Admin); [2004] G.B. 936 at [65].
[332] [2003] EWHC 193 (Admin); [2004] Q.B. 936 at [72]–[73].
[333] [2005] EWHC 452 (Admin).
[334] [2005] EWHC 480; [2005] H.R.L.R. 20 at [597].
[335] [2006] EWHC 2683; [2007] H.R.L.R. 2.

In *R. (on the application of Hirst) v Secretary of State for the Home* **19–097**
Department[336] the court found there to be breaches of Art.5(2)[337] and 5(4)
in arrangements for the recall of a life prisoner released on license. The
court held that the claimant had probably served 14 additional days
imprisonment as a result of delays but did not considered damages were
necessary to ensure just satisfaction. The sum of £1,500 was awarded for
distress associated with being detained again after his release.

In *King v Secretary of State for the Home Department*[338] there was a **19–098**
breach of Art.5(4) because of the delay in conducting a review of the
claimant's detention after he had completed the tariff part of a life
sentence; no award of damages was necessary however because it was
"very unlikely there has been loss, or that any annoyance or frustration
suffered would suffice to justify an award of damages".

Article 6 (right to a fair trial)

The first consideration of s.8 of the HRA by the House of Lords took place **19–099**
in *Greenfield*,[339] in which the claimant prisoner had been found guilty of
drugs offences in prison by the deputy controller of the prison and ordered
to serve an additional 21 days (which he had served by the time his judicial
review claim was heard). The defendant conceded that the disciplinary
arrangements breached Art.6(1) as the deputy controller was not an
independent and impartial tribunal and Art.6(3) because the claimant had
been denied legal representation.[340] Their Lordships held that "In the great
majority of cases in which the European Court has found a violation of
Art.6 it has treated the finding of the violation as, in itself, just satisfaction
under Art.41".[341] Where damages have been awarded by the ECtHR, this
has generally been either to compensate for the loss of an opportunity to
put a case and secure a benefit, or for anxiety and frustration. In relation to
the former, in conceptualising the loss caused by a breach of Art.6, the
courts have similar problems as in relation to Art.5(4): "A claim . . . may
be put on the straightforward basis that but for the Convention violation
found the outcome of the proceedings would probably have been different
and more favourable to the applicant, or on the more problematical basis
that the violation deprived the applicant of an opportunity to achieve a
different result which was not in all the circumstances of the case a

---

[336] [2005] EWHC 1480; (2005) 102(40) L.S.G. 27. See generally 7–119.
[337] "Everyone who is arrested shall be informed promptly, in a language which he understands, of the reasons for his arrest and of any charge against him".
[338] [2003] EWHC 2831; [2004] H.R.L.R. 9.
[339] *Greenfield* [2005] UKHL 14; [2005] 1 W.L.R. 673.
[340] In *Ezeh v United Kingdom* (2004) 39 E.H.R.R. 1 the ECtHR held that disciplinary
proceedings in prison were "criminal proceedings" for the purposes of Art.6, so engaging the
range of additional rights set out in Art.6(3)(a)–(e), where the led to the imposition of
additional days as punishment. See further *R. (on the application of Napier) v Secretary of
State for the Home Department* [2004] EWHC 936; [2004] 1 W.L.R. 3056 and the general
discussion of the civil/criminal distinctionin Ch.7.
[341] *Greenfield* [2005] UKHL 14; [2005] 1 W.L.R. 673 at [8].

valueless opportunity".[342] To succeed, the claimant must establish a clear causal connection.[343] In relation to feelings of distress, anxiety and frustration, the ECtHR has been sparing in its awards and awards are not generally made in cases of "structural bias". But "To gain an award under this head it is not necessary for the applicant to show that but for the violation the outcome of the proceedings would, or would probably, or even might, have been different, and in cases of delay the outcome may not be significant at all".[344] The House of Lords held that there were no special features in Greenfield's case which warranted the award of damages.

19-100   In R. (on the application of Napier) v Secretary of State for the Home Department[345] no award of damages was sought or made to the prisoner claimant. As in Greenfield, the violation of Art.6 arose from a refusal of the prison authorities to permit the claimant to have legal representation in disciplinary proceedings about drug misuse. A penalty of 35 additional days was imposed. The defendant accepted that there had been a violation of Art.6(3) and remitted the punishment of additional days, but refused to quash the finding of guilt. The claimant was subsequently allocated to a "closed supervision centre" within a prison; one criterion for being placed there was past adjudicatory findings. The court held that the defendant had both acknowledged the breach of Art.6 and afforded sufficient redress.

Article 8 (right to respect for private and family life)

19-101   In R. (on the application of Bernard) v Enfield LBC[346] the claimants were a severely disabled women and her husband, who lived with their six children in unsatisfactory accommodation. The local authority was held to be in breach of its statutory duties under the National Assistance Act 1948 and the Housing Act 1996; and to be in breach of Art.8. The court held that it was necessary to award damages having regard to the deplorable conditions, "wholly inimical to any normal family life, and to the physical and psychological integrity", which they had endured as a consequence of failures by the local authority over 20 months despite repeated letters urging action from the claimants' solicitor. The court considered awards made by the ombudsmen, which were of "great assistance". The court held that damages should be "at the top of the range" and awarded a total of £10,000.[347]

---

[342] *Greenfield* [2005] UKHL 14; [2005] 1 W.L.R. 673 at [12].
[343] *Greenfield* [2005] UKHL 14; [2005] 1 W.L.R. 673 at [15].
[344] *Greenfield* [2005] UKHL 14; [2005] 1 W.L.R. 673 at [16].
[345] [2004] EWHC 936; [2004] 1 W.L.R. 3056.
[346] [2002] EWHC 2282; [2003] H.R.L.R. 4. See generally 13-084.
[347] [2002] EWHC 2282; [2003] H.R.L.R. 4 at [62] (Sullivan J.: "Although there are two claimants it is important to avoid double counting, and since these damages are intended to give them just satisfaction for a breach of their Art.8 rights, it is sensible to start off with an overall figure to reflect the impact of the breach on their family life together, and then to apportion that figure between the two claimants having regard to the relative effects on their private lives. Bearing all these factors in mind, I conclude that the appropriate figure is £10,000, and I apportion that £8,000 to the second claimant and £2,000 to the first claimant").

In *Anufrijeva*[348] the Court of Appeal heard three appeals from asylum **19–102**
seekers and their families who claimed that their respective local authorities had failed to arrange accommodation and provide benefits to which
they were legally entitled and accordingly had failed in their positive
obligations under Art.8. The court characterised the failings of the local
authorities, in particular their delay, as "maladministration". The court
held that in cases concerning positive obligations under Art.8, in a context
in which public funds were limited, it was important to avoid a situation in
which "the impression is created that asylum seekers whether genuine or
not are profiting from their status, this could bring the Human Rights Act
into disrepute".[349] Because the nature of the administrative failings in these
cases were akin to maladministration, the court suggested that an appropriate point of comparison for quantum of damages would be the (relatively
modest) levels of compensation awarded by the ombudsmen.[350] In relation
to one of the claimants, the court held that

> "Where a public authority commits acts which it knows are likely to
> cause psychiatric harm to an individual, those acts are capable of
> constituting an infringement of Art.8. Maladministration will not,
> however, infringe Article 8 simply because it causes stress that leads a
> particularly susceptible individual to suffer such harm in circumstances
> where this was not reasonably to be anticipated. No lack of respect for
> private life is manifested in such circumstances. The egg-shell skull
> principle forms no part of the test of breach of duty under the HRA or
> the Convention."[351]

In all three appeals, the court held that the local authorities' failings did
not constitute a breach of Art.8.

Article 14 (prohibition of discrimination)

The House of Lords in *R. (on the application of Wilkinson) v Inland* **19–103**
Revenue Commissioners[352] held the Revenue—even though conceding that
their decision was contrary to Art.1 of the First Protocol (peaceful
enjoyment of possessions) and Art.14—had not acted contrary to their
duty under s.6 of the HRA in refusing a widow a tax allowance equivalent
to the widow's bereavement allowance because (in the words of s.6(2))
they "could not have acted differently" under provisions contained in
primary legislation. Although not necessary to do so, the House considered
what award would have been made to ensure "just satisfaction". In the
context of Art.14, what is it necessary for the court to do in order to put

---

[348] [2003] EWCA Civ 1406; [2004] Q.B. 1124.
[349] [2003] EWCA Civ 1406; [2004] Q.B. 1124 at [75].
[350] [2003] EWCA Civ 1406; [2004] Q.B. 1124 at [74].
[351] [2003] EWCA Civ 1406; [2004] Q.B. 1124 at [143].
[352] [2005] UKHL 30; [2005] 1 W.L.R. 1718. Widow's allowance was abolished by the
Finance Act 1999 with effect from April 2000. See generally 13–098.

the claimant in the position he would have been in had the breach of a Convention right not occurred? Lord Hoffmann explained: "In a discrimination case, in which the wrongful act is treating A better than B, this involves forming a view about whether the state should have complied by treating A worse or B better. Normally one would conclude that A's treatment represented the norm and that B should have been treated better. In some cases, however, it will be clear that A's treatment was an unjustifiable anomaly".[353] His Lordship held that had Parliament paid proper regard to Art.14 in this context, it would (as indeed it did) remove the different treatment of widows and widowers by abolishing widow's allowance rather than by extending the allowance to widowers.[354] Lord Browne of Eaton-under-Heywood agreed that Art.14 presents particular difficulties in relation to the award of "just satisfaction": "In any claim against a public authority for financial compensation in respect of past discrimination it must be remembered that the general public (often the general body of taxpayers) will be footing the bill. In determining the requirements of just satisfaction, just as in the application of the Convention as a whole, regard should be had not only to the victim's rights but also to the interests of the public generally".[355]

19–104   In *R. (on the application of Baiai) v Secretary of State for the Home Department*[356] the court considered damages claims following findings that arrangements under which a "certificate of approval" was required (at a cost of £135) before immigrants could marry, unless they planned to do so in an Anglican church ceremony, were incompatible with Art.12 (right to marry) and Art.14. In relation to Art.12, the court rejected the defendant's argument that (in the words of s.6(2) of the HRA) he "could not have acted differently" because he had a discretion whether or not to impose fees. But the defendant *could* have established a system for scrutinising marriages, and charged a fee, which was Convention compliant. The claimants were therefore not entitled to recover the fees as the purpose of compensation was to place the claimants in the same position as if their Convention rights had not been infringed. Moreover, the declaration of incompatibility under s.4 of the HRA did not affect the validity of the provision, so the fee was not unlawful as a matter of domestic law.[357] The court also considered and rejected damages claims for "distress and humiliation". On the evidence, the claimants' reaction had not reached the required level of intensity; there was no evidence of the claimants needing medical treatment for their distress; and in any event the claimants must have been extremely worried about the *general* immigration status of their

---

[353] [2005] UKHL 30; [2005] 1 W.L.R. 1718 at [26].
[354] [2005] UKHL 30; [2005] 1 W.L.R. 1718 at [28].
[355] [2005] UKHL 30; [2005] 1 W.L.R. 1718 at [48].
[356] [2006] EWHC 1035 (Admin) (following on from the judicial review claim in *R. (on the application of Baiai) v Secretary of State for the Home Department* [2006] EWHC 1454 (Admin); [2006] 4 All E.R. 555).
[357] [2005] EWHC 1035 (Admin) at [29].

partners. In relation to Art.14, the court held that the defendant "could not have acted differently" as the provision excluding Anglican marriage ceremonies was contained in primary legislation.

First Protocol, Art.2 (right to education)

In *A v Headteacher and Governors of Lord Grey School*[358] the claimant had **19–105** been excluded from school pending a police investigation into an allegation that he had been involved in arson. The majority of the Lordships held that there was no breach of the claimant's right to education. Baroness Hale of Richmond, allowing the appeal against the claimant on different grounds to their other Lordships, held that it was unnecessary to award damages to afford just satisfaction.[359]

LIABILITY UNDER EUROPEAN COMMUNITY LAW

The liability of public authorities for breaches of European Community law **19–106** is examined in Chapter 14.[360]

---

[358] [2006] UKHL 14; [2006] 2 A.C. 363.
[359] [2006] UKHL 14; [2006] 2 A.C. 363 at [83].
[360] See 14–066.

APPENDICES

A. Notes on citation and use of authorities

B. Classification of Functions

C. Ouster clause contained in the Asylum and Immigration (Treatment of Claimants etc.) Bill

D. Extracts from Supreme Court Act (Senior Court Act) 1981

E. Extracts from Tribunals, Courts and Enforcement Act 2007

F. Extracts from Human Rights Act 1998

G. Civil Procedure Rules Pt 54

H. Civil Procedure Rules: Practice Direction, Judicial Review

I. Pre-Action Protocol for Judicial Review

J. N461 Judicial Review Claim Form

K. N462 Judicial Review Acknowledgment of Service

L. N463 Application for Urgent Consideration

NOTE ON CITATION OF AUTHORITES

Law reports

In written and oral submissions in court,   A–001

(a) citations should be to the official *Law Reports* published by the Incorporated Council of Law Reporting in England and Wales (A.C. Q.B. Ch., and Fam.)[1]

(b) if a case is not, or not yet, reported in the Law Reports, the *Weekly Law Reports* (W.L.R.) or the *All England Reports* (All E.R.) should be cited;[2]

(c) "If a case is not reported in any of these series of reports, a report in any of the authoritative specialist series of reports may be cited. Such reports may not be readily available: Photostat copies of the leading authorities or the relevant parts of such authorities should be annexed to written submissions; and it is helpful if Photostat copies of the less frequently used series are made available in court".[3]

(d) "It is recognised that occasions may arise when one report is fuller than another, or when there are discrepancies between reports. On such occasions, the practice outlined above need not be followed".[4]

(e) "It is always helpful if alternative references are given".

There is a wide range of specialist law reports containing cases of relevance to judicial review. The following are among those referred to in this book.

Journal title	Abbreviation	Publisher
Administrative Court Digest (formerly Crown Office Digest)	A.C.D.	Sweet & Maxwell

---

[1] *Practice Direction (Court of Appeal: Citation of Authorities)* [1995] 1 W.L.R. 1096; *Practice Statement (Supreme Court: Judgments)* [1998] 1 W.L.R. 825.
[2] [1995] 1 W.L.R. 1096; [1998] 1 W.L.R. 825.
[3] [1995] 1 W.L.R. 1096; [1998] 1 W.L.R. 825.
[4] [1995] 1 W.L.R. 1096; [19981 1 W.L.R. 825.

Journal title	Abbreviation	Publisher
Administrative Law Reports	Admin. L.R.	Barry Rose Law Periodicals from 1989 to 1998
Butterworths Human Rights Cases	B.H.R.C.	LexisNexis Butterworths
Butterworths Local Government Reports	B.L.G.R.	LexisNexis Butterworths
Common Market Law Review	C.M.L.R.	Kluwer Law International
Community Care Law Reports	C.C.L. Rep.	Legal Action Group
Crown Office Digest (now called Administrative Court Digest)	C.O.D.	Sweet & Maxwell
Education Law Reports	E.L.R.	Jordan Publishing
Entertainment and Media Law Reports	E.M.L.R.	Sweet & Maxwell
Environmental Law Reports	Env. L.R.	Sweet & Maxwell
European Human Rights Reports	E.H.R.R.	Sweet & Maxwell
Housing Law Reports	H.L.R.	Sweet & Maxwell
Immigration Appeal Reports	Imm. A.R.	
Journal of Planning and Environmental Law	J.P.L.	Sweet & Maxwell
New Property Cases	N.P.C.	
Property and Compensation Law Reports	P. & C.R.	Sweet & Maxwell
United Kingdom Human Rights Reports	U.K.H.R.R,	Sweet & Maxwell

Use of unreported judgments

A–002 On occasion we have referred to unreported judgments. While for academic purposes the fact that a case has or has not been selected to be reported is of little importance, practitioners appearing in the courts of England and Wales have restrictions placed on their use of unreported decisions. In 2001 the Lord Chief Justice (Lord Woolf) gave the following guidance in *Practice Direction. (Citation of Authorities)* [2001] 1 W.L.R. 1001:

"6.1 A judgment falling into one of the categories referred to in paragraph 6.2 below may not in future be cited before any court unless it clearly indicates that it purports to establish a new principle or to extend the present law. In respect of judgments delivered after the date of this Direction [April 9, 2001], that indication must take the form of an express statement to that effect. In respect of judgments delivered before the date of this Direction that indication must be present in or clearly deducible from the language used in the judgment.

6.2 Paragraph 6.1 applies to the following categories of judgment:

- Applications attended by one party only
- Applications for permission to appeal
- Decisions on applications that only decide that the application is arguable
- County Court cases, unless (a) cited in order to illustrate the conventional measure of damages in a personal injury case; or (b) cited in a County Court in order to demonstrate current authority at that level on an issue in respect of which no decision at a higher level of authority is available.

6.3 These categories will be kept under review, such review to include consideration of adding to the categories."

Citation of other categories of judgment

"7.1 Courts will in future pay particular attention, when it is sought to cite other categories of judgment, to any indication given by the court delivering the judgment that it was seen by that court as only applying decided law to the facts of the particular case; or otherwise as not extending or adding to the existing law. A–003

7.2 Advocates who seek to cite a judgment that contains indications of the type referred to in paragraph 7.1 will be required to justify their decision to cite the case."

Methods of citation

"It 8.1 Advocates will in future be required to state, in respect of each authority that they wish to cite, the proposition of law that the authority demonstrates, and the parts of the judgment that support that proposition. If it is sought to cite more than one authority in support of a given proposition, advocates must state the reason for taking that course. A–004

8.2 The demonstration referred to in paragraph 8.1 will be required to be contained in any skeleton argument and in any appellant's or respondent's notice in respect of each authority referred to in that skeleton or notice.

8.3 Any bundle or list of authorities prepared for the use of any court must in future bear a certification by the advocate responsible for arguing the case that the requirements of this paragraph have been complied with in respect of each authority included.

8.4 The statements referred to in paragraph 8.1 should not materially add to the length of submissions or of skeleton arguments, but should be sufficient to demonstrate, in the context of the advocate's argument, the relevance of the authority or authorities to that argument and that the citation is necessary for a proper presentation of that argument."

Judgments given at the permission stage of a claim for judicial review will usually fall within the ambit of paragraph 6.2 and are in any event of only persuasive authority.[5]

Judgments from other jurisdictions

A–005   We draw on experiences from other legal systems,[6] in particular Australia. Canada, India, New Zealand and South Africa. Most citations are from the following sources.

Australia	
Commonwealth Law Reports	C.L.R. (authorised reports)
Australian Law Reports	A.L.R
Online resources	*http://www.austlii.edu.au/*
Canada	
Supreme Court Reports Online resources	S.C.R. (authorised reports) *http://www.lexum.umontreal.ca* *http://www.canlii.org/en*
India	
Supreme Court Reports	S.C.R. (official reports)
Supreme Court Cases	S.C.C.

---

[5] *Clark v University of Lincolnshire and Humberside* [2000] 1 W.L.R. 1988J at [431].
[6] See Ch.1.

Online resources	*http://judis.openarchive.in/* *http://www.judis.nic.in*
New Zealand	
New Zealand Law Reports	N.Z.L.R. (authorised reports)
New Zealand Administrative Reports	N.Z.A.R.
New Zealand Resource Management Appeals	N.Z.R.M.A.
Online resources	*http://www.waikato.ac.nz/library/resources/law/* *http://www.nzlii.org/*
South Africa	
South African Law Reports	S.A.
Online resources	*http://www.saflii.org/*

Practitioners in England and Wales seeking to rely upon overseas case law **A–006** in written or oral submissions in court must heed the guidance set out in *Practice Direction (Citation of Authorities)* [2001] 1 W.L.R. 1001:

"*Authorities decided in other jurisdictions*

9.1 Cases decided in other jurisdictions can, if properly used, be a valuable source of law in this jurisdiction. At the same time, however, such authority should not be cited without proper consideration of whether it does indeed add to the existing body of law.

9.2 In future therefore, any advocate who seeks to cite an authority from another jurisdiction must

i. comply, in respect of that authority, with the rules set out in paragraph 8 above [set out above in relation to unreported judgments];

ii. indicate in respect of each authority what that authority adds that is not to be found in authority in this jurisdiction; or, if there is said to be justification for adding to domestic authority, what that justification is;

iii. certify that there is no authority in this jurisdiction that precludes the acceptance by the court of the proposition that the foreign authority is said to establish.

9.3 For the avoidance of doubt, paragraphs 9.1 and 9.2 do not apply to cases decided in either the European Court of Justice or the organs of the European Convention of Human Rights. Because of the status in English law of such authority, as provided by, respectively, section 3 of

971

the European Communities Act 1972 and section 2(1) of the Human Rights Act 1998, such cases are covered by the earlier paragraphs of this Direction."

New form of naming for judicial review cases

A–007 As part of the justice modernisation programme, the style of naming cases in judicial review changed. Up to January 11, 2001, the format was *R. v Secretary of State for Administrative Affairs Ex p Bloggs* ("Ex parte" in this context meaning "on behalf of the claimant Bloggs). From 2001, claims for judicial review are cited as *R. (on the application of Bloggs) v Secretary of State for Administrative Affairs.*

Neutral citation system

A–008 Between 2001 and January 2002, a "media neutral" citation system was introduced in England and Wales, in which each judgment is given a unique reference number and paragraphs are numbered. This enables cases to be identified and pinpoint references to be given without reliance on a particular series of law reports or a page number of a particular report. The transitional arrangements mean that there are there ways in which a judgment may be cited, depending on when it was handed down.

- Before January 11, 2001: no neutral citations. Reported cases are known only by the law report citations; unreported decisions are referred to by the relevant date and the court.
- Between January 11, 2001 and January 13. 2002: neutral citations to Administrative Court decisions are in the format [2001] EWHC Admin 8. "Admin is an essential part of the neutral citation because each division of the High Court was responsible for allocating sequential numbers to its cases.[7]
- After January 14, 2002: the current neutral citation system came into force.[8] The unique reference numbers are now allocated according across all divisions of the High Court. The format for Administrative Court decisions after this date is therefore [2002] EWHC 5 (Admin). The description "(Admin)" is not an essential part of the citation as no other case will in another division will have been allocated the number 5. "Under these arrangements, it will be unnecessary to include the descriptive word in brackets when citing

[7] *Practice Direction (Judgments: Form and Citation)* [2001] 1 W.L.R. 194 (issued on January 11,2001).
[8] *Practice Direction (Judgments: Neutral Citations)* [2002] 1 W.L.R. 346.

the paragraph number of a judgment. Thus paragraph 59 of *Smith v Jones* [2002] EWHC 124 (QBD) would be cited: *Smith v Jones* [2002] EWHC 124 at [59]".[9]

[9] *Practice Direction (Judgments: Neutral Citations)* [2002] 1 W.L.R. 346 at [3].

APPENDIX B

CLASSIFICATION OF FUNCTIONS

Introduction

As we have noted,[1] for many years the development of English administra- B–001
tive law was impeded by the distinctions made by the courts between
functions which were classified as "legislative", "administrative", "judicial", "quasi judicial" and "ministerial". In particular, natural justice was
reserved for decision-making which was "judicial" or "quasi judicial" in
nature and judicial review as a whole was not considered appropriate for
decisions which were of a "legislative" or "ministerial" character. In the
last edition of this work which he edited (in 1973), de Smith was highly
critical of the "terminological contortions" produced by these classifications. Although he thought that the conceptual problems associated with
the classifications still "appeared to be overwhelming", he regarded them
as "analytically erroneous" and detected some hope that "to an increasing
extent courts exercising powers of judicial review in administrative law are
abandoning servitude to their own concepts and asserting mastery over
them" (p.77).

Abandonment of these classifications

Servitude to these classifications has now largely been abandoned. In B–002
regard to natural justice, the notion that a fair hearing is reserved to a
"judicial" or "quasi-judicial" situation has been firmly "scotched" as a
"heresy".[2] The prerogative remedies of certiorari and prohibition are no
longer confined, as they once were, to the "judicial" functions of public
bodies. The sweeping away of this restriction was helped by the common
procedure established by RSC, Ord.53 in 1978.[3] Today both certiorari and
prohibition (quashing and prohibiting orders) may be granted in relation to
functions which may be regarded as "administrative" or even as "legislative"[4] In cases regarding prison discipline the House of Lords has
disregarded the "fancied distinctions"[5] between "administrative" and

---

[1] See Chs 1 and 6
[2] *R v Gaming Board Ex p. Benaim and Khaida* [1970] 2 Q.B. 417 at 430 (Lord Denning, in
respect of the decision of the HL in *Ridge v Baldwin* [1964] A.C. 40) and *O'Reilly v Mackman*
[1983] A.C. 23 at 279 (Lord Diplock).
[3] See Ch.15.
[4] On review of legislation, see Ch.3.
[5] *Leech v Parkhurst Prison Deputy Governor* [1988] A.C. 533.

"judicial or quasi judicial" distinctions by upholding the possibility of judicial review of the decisions of prison governors. Lord Oliver held that "it is not the label . . . that determines the existence of [the court's] jurisdiction but the quality and attributes of the decision".[6]

B–003   The rejection of the classification of functions as determining the existence or scope of judicial review means it no longer has a place at the start of a book on judicial review. However, its relevance to the history of judicial review is considerable, and it still throws light on the "quality and attributes" of decisions which may render them more or less amenable to judicial review. On the whole the test of "public function"[7] and "justiciability"[8] has replaced that of classification of function as a determinant of the appropriateness of a decision for judicial review.[9] Yet some of the qualities of the old classifications contribute to the identification of a decision's justiciable features. For example, the question may be asked as to whether "managerial"-type decisions, or decisions involving the allocation of scarce resources, are amenable to control by the courts rather than the electorate.[10] Similarly, delegation of powers is less likely to be tolerated in relation to bodies performing judicial-type functions.[11] In some cases a statute may specifically draw a distinction between so-called administrative and judicial functions, for example, in relation to the functions of the ombudsmen.[12] Immunity in tort claims is granted by statute and the common law in respect of acts and omissions in the course of judicial proceedings.[13] To the extent therefore that the classifications are still useful and relevant (and their relevance should by no means be overrated),[14] what follows is an abridged version of Chapter 2 of the 4th edition (1979) of this work, edited by J. Evans.

De Smith on classification of functions

B–004   "We class schools, you see, into four grades: Leading School, First-rate School, Good School, and School." (Evelyn Waugh, *Decline and Fall*.)

[6] [1988] A.C. 533 at 579; and 566 (Lord Bridge).
[7] See Ch.3.
[8] See Chs 1, 5 and 11.
[9] On justiciability, see Chs 1 and 5.
[10] For example, the distinction between managerial and other functions drawn in *R. v Secretary of State for the Environment, ex. p. Hammersmith and Fulham LBC* [1991] A.C. 521.
[11] See Ch.7.
[12] See Ch.1; *R. v Local Commissioner Ex p. Croydon LBC* [1989] 1 All E.R. 1033 at 1043.
[13] See Ch.1; e.g. (a) the Crown Proceedings Act 1947 provides the Crown wit absolute immunity from primary or vicarious liability for its officers' wrongful exercise of judicial power; (b) words spoken in the course of "judicial proceedings" are absolutely privileged in the law of defamation, and (c) those carrying out judicial functions enjoy wide immunity from suit for otherwise tortious acts done within their jurisdiction.
[14] As they were it is submitted, in *R. v Inland Revenue Commissioners Ex p. TC Coombs & Co* [1991] 2 A. C. 283 (Lord Lowry: a "judicial"-type decision could not be held Wednesbury unreasonable); cf. R. v Legal Aid Board Ex p. Bateman [1992] 1 W.L.R. 711 at 719 (Nolan L J.: Wednesbury was "equally appropriate no matter whether the role of the board is regarded as administrative or quasi judicial").

The functions of public authorities may be roughly classified as (a) legislative, (b) administrative (or executive), (c) judicial (or quasi-judicial) and (d) ministerial. In some countries classification raises constitutional issues connected with the separation of powers.

In the United Kingdom this kind of problem does not arise. Hence **B–005** constitutional decisions by the Privy Council and Commonwealth courts on the nature and characteristics of judicial power are only of marginal interest in this country. Those decisions[15] may indeed be positively misleading if taken too seriously; for a decision to the effect that, for constitutional purposes, a power vested in a tribunal is non judicial does not necessarily imply that the tribunal is exempt from a duty to "act judicially" in accordance with natural justice or is immune from control by certiorari and prohibition.[16] English lawyers already have enough to puzzle them as they observe the terminological contortions of courts deciding cases in the field of administrative law.

The meanings attributed by the courts to the terms "judicial", "quasi- **B–006** judicial", "administrative", "legislative" and "ministerial" for administrative law purposes have been inconsistent. Lawyers are, of course, quite familiar with the notion that a legal term may convey a range of meaning and that within that range the meaning appropriate for the resolution of a particular dispute may well depend upon the context which the term has to be applied. Nonetheless, when specific legal consequences flow from the manner of classifying a particular function, the use of the same word to denote different things and different words to denote the same thing is apt to generate confusion. The development of administrative law has provided ample proof of the truth of this proposition, although in recent years English judges have to a large extent succeeded in extricating the law from the state of confusion into which it appeared to have fallen. The statutory admonition that the purpose for which a function is being classified should never be forgotten may go some way at least towards the avoidance of the pitfalls inherent in the limitations of language. Rather than elaborating at great length the problems of classification, an attempt will be made here (a) to state briefly the legal situations in which classification of a function in one category or another may be of material importance; (b) to outline the main approaches to classification adopted by the courts; and (c) to indicate, where possible, *why* the courts have chosen one method of classification rather than another in individual contexts.

---

[15] Among the best-known cases are *Shell Oil Co of Australia Ltd v Federal Commissioner of Taxation* [1931] A.C. 275; and the following appeals from Ceylon (now the Republic of Sri Lanka) before the abolition of PC appeals and the adoption of a republican constitution: *Bribery Commissioner v Ranasinghe* [1965] A.C. 172; *United Engineering Workers' Union v Devanayagam* [1968] A.C. 356; *Ranaweera v Wickramasinghe* [1970] A.C. 951; *Ranaweera v Ramachandran* [1970] A.C. 962.

[16] *Ranaweera v Wickramasinghe* [1970] A.C. 951 at 962; *R. v Trade Practices Tribunal* [1970] A.L.R. 499; cf. *Jayawardane v Silva* [1970] 1 W.L.R. 13651, PC; *Trapp v Mackie* [1979] 1 W.L.R. 377 at 388.

B–007   Certain preliminary points must be stated. First, it is sometimes impossible to discern why a court has characterised a given function as judicial or administrative. Often, it is true, the method of characterisation can be seen as a contrivance to support a conclusion reached on non-conceptual grounds. But in many cases the terms seem to have been used loosely and without deliberation: and in some cases definitions propounded in earlier reported cases appear to have dominated the juristic analysis of the case in hand and indeed the conclusion reached by the court. Although in this "highly acrobatic part of the law"[17] an aptitude for verbal gymnastics is of advantage, a commentator endowed with this attribute is frequently left wondering whether Mr Justice Malaprop's formulation is really more dextrous, more fortuitous, more laboured or simply more ineffectual than his own would have been. Secondly, recent English case law has tended to blur rather than clarify the distinctions between the two most important classes of function, the judicial and the administrative. And thirdly, as distinctions have been blurred, so has their practical importance tended to dwindle. Seldom does the outcome of a case nowadays turn purely on the mode of classifying a function vested in the competent authority. The intrinsic difficulties of the topic under consideration have not diminished, but they are no longer as oppressive as they once were.

Ministerial

B–008   In politics "ministerial" is commonly used as an epithet appertaining to Ministers of the Crown, or, more broadly, to the party in office. We speak of ministerial responsibility, ministerial cheers. As a technical legal term it has no single fixed meaning.

(1) It may describe any duty, the discharge of which involves no element of discretion or independent judgment. Since an order of mandamus will issue to compel the performance of a ministerial act, and since, moreover, wrongful refusal to carry out a ministerial duty may give rise to liability in tort, it is often of practical importance to determine whether discretion is present in the performance of a statutory function. The cases on mandamus show, however, that the presence of a minor discretionary element is not enough to deter the courts from characterising a function as ministerial. Thus although the issue of a warrant for non-payment of rates is usually said to be a ministerial act, the justices must first be satisfied that the rate was properly made, published and demanded, that it has not been paid and that the person on whom it was made was in truth the person rateable; but once satisfied on these points they have no discretion to extend the time for payment.[18] The issue of a warrant for the nonpayment of taxes has

[17] Willis, "Administrative Law and the British North America Act" (1940) 53 Harv L.R. 251. The tendency in recent years for courts in a number of areas to move away from a classifactory approach is discussed by K. Keith (1976–1977) 7 N.Z.U.L.R. 325.
[18] "Discretion not Unlimited" (1949) 113 J.P J. 566; *R. v Middlesex Justices* (1842) 6 J.P. 772 (distress warrant); and *R. v York Justices Ex p. York Corp* [1949] W.N. 72 (order for possession).

been held to be a ministerial act (and therefore not reviewable by certiorari) although the officer issuing the warrant had discretionary power to take proceedings in the courts for the recovery of the taxes.[19] Again, where an authority has erroneously declined jurisdiction over a matter or has failed to exercise a discretion according to proper legal principles, the issue of a mandamus to it has sometime been represented as a remedy forbreach of a ministerial duty, although the determination of such questions may be far from a mechanical operation.[20]

(2) It is often used, more narrowly, to describe the issue of a formal instruction, in consequence of a prior determination which may or may not be of a judicial character, that direct action be taken in relation to another's person or property.[21]

(3) It may describe the execution of such an instruction by an inferior officer (who is sometimes called a ministerial officer).

(4) It is sometimes used loosely to describe any act that is neither judicial nor legislative. In this sense the term is used interchangeably with "executive" or "administrative",[22] So, the function of an assessment committee,[23] the making of slum clearance and compulsory purchase orders under housing legislation,[24] and the assessment of charges to be imposed on the inhabitants of a district in a colony,[25] have all been called ministerial, although their most obvious characteristic is that they involve the exercise of wide discretionary powers. This use of the term is misleading. In the present work the term will be used to refer to the making of decisions, the issue of orders or the execution of acts in which the element of judgment or discretion is either absent or relatively very small.[26]

"Administrative" and "legislative"

The term "administrative" is capable of bearing a wide range of meanings, **B–009** some of which are remote from the problems raised by the classification of statutory functions. In such phrases as "administrative law" "administrative tribunal" and "judicial review of administration action" it refers to broad areas of government activity in which the repositories of power may

---

[19] *Hetherington v Security Export Co* [1924] A.C. 988.
[20] For an analysis of the senses in which the term "ministerial" may be used in different contexts, see A. Rubinstein, *Jurisdiction and Illegality*, (1965) pp.16–20, 98–101, 135–139, 15–159
[21] D. Gordon "Administrative Tribunals and the Courts" (1933) 49 L.Q.R. 94 at 98.
[22] *Haridas v Khan* [1971] 1 W.L.R. 507 at 512; *Dean v District Auditor for Ashton-in-Makerfield* [1960] 1 Q.B. 149 at 156.
[23] *R. v Westminster (City of) Assessment Committee* [1941] 1 KB. 53.
[24] *Errington v Minister of Health* [1935] 1 K.B. 249 at 259; *Robins (E) & Son Ltd v Minister of Health* [1939] 1 K.B. 520 at 534, 535.
[25] *Patterson v District Commissioner of Accra* [1948] A. C. 341 at 349.
[26] *R. v Majewski* [1977] A.C. 443 at 451 (power of registrar to refer appeals to the Court of Appeal (Criminal Division) for summary determination when the point raised is frivolous or vexatious).

exercise every class of statutory function. We need not dwell upon these usages. Nor, at this point, shall we consider the analytical distinctions drawn between administrative and judicial functions; these can conveniently be postponed until we discuss the meanings of "judicial".

B–010   A distinction often made between legislative and administrative acts is that between the general and the particular. A legislative act is the creation and promulgation of a general rule of conduct without reference to particular cases: an administrative act cannot be exactly defined, but it includes the adoption of a policy, the making and issue of a specific direction, and the application of a general rule to a particular case in accordance with the requirements of policy of expediency or administrative practice. Legal consequences flow from this distinction.

B–011   Since the general shades off into the particular, to discriminate between the legislative and the administrative by reference to these criteria may be a peculiarly difficult task, and it is not surprising that the opinions of judges as to the proper characterisation of a statutory function is at variance. If a Minister has power to requisition houses and to delegate his power, and he proceeds to delegate his power to an individual clerk to a local authority, there can be no doubt that this delegation is an administrative act,[27] but if he delegates his power to all clerks to local authorities, is the instrument of delegation a legislative or an administrative order?[28] Fortunately decisions in the courts seldom turn on this type of question alone; and when it arises it is apt to be glossed over.

B–012   Other criteria for distinguishing legislative from administrative acts appear in ordinary linguistic usage. In the first place, every measure duly enacted by Parliament is regarded as legislation. If land is compulsorily acquired by means of a Private Act of Parliament or a Provisional Order Confirmation Act, the acquisition is deemed to be a legislative act; though if the acquisition is effected by means of a compulsory purchase order made under enabling legislation, it will usually be classified as an administrative act. Secondly, departmental instruments or announcements which, although general in application, normally neither create legally enforceable rights nor impose legally enforceable obligations since they are not made pursuant to express statutory authority. Rules of this kind are usually referred to as examples of "administrative action". Circulars issued by the Department of the Environment to local planning authorities on the manner in which they should exercise their statutory powers fall into this category,[29] as do the rules formulated by the Foreign and Commonwealth Office to govern the exercise of the prerogative power over the issue and withdrawal of passports.[30] And the same is true of an announced amnesty

---

[27] *Lewisham LBC v Roberts* [1949] 2 K.B. 608.

[28] For conflicting views on this point, see *Blackpool Corp v Locker* [1948] K.B. 349 (Scott and Asquith L.JJ.); *Lewisham LBC v Roberts* [1949] 2 K.B. 608 621–622 (Denning L.J.).

[29] See, e.g. *Bizony v Secretary of State for the Environment* (1976) 239 E.G. 28l at 283.

[30] *Hansard* HC, Vol.881, col.265WA November 15, 1974.

for illegal immigrants who satisfy certain criteria.[31] Just as the Crown is without authority to alter the general law of the land by prerogative,[32] so are its servants and other public authorities without inherent authority to impose legal duties or liabilities or to confer legally enforceable rights, privileges or immunities on the subject.[33] Hence, the extra-statutory concessions to taxpayers that the Inland Revenue and Customs and Excise authorities announce from time to time cannot be relied upon in any court of law,[34] although they have been styled "administrative quasi-legislation".[35] It must not be assumed, however, that departmental communications issued in the form of circulars, notes for guidance or letters to local and regional authorities, or press notices, are necessarily destitute of legal effect.[36] It is possible that in some circumstances, at least, the promulgation of informal rules or the announcement of a policy must give rise to procedural obligations,[37] or be used as evidence of the matters that may legitimately be considered in the exercise of discretion [38] or even create a form of estoppel. And it may not be totally fanciful to imagine that a public authority may be held to have abused its discretion by clearly misinterpreting its own rules that it purported to apply. In one instance the courts have given legislative effect to what is ostensibly a purely administrative announcement. The Criminal Injuries Compensation Board was created to administer a non-statutory scheme for compensating victims of crimes of violence by *ex gratia* payments out of funds authorised by Parliament. The Board was required to follow a judicial-type procedure and to apply the legal standards contained in the scheme. Although a

---

[31] *Birdi v Secretary of State for Home Affairs, The Times,* February 12, 1975; *Purewal v Entry Clearance Officer* [1977] Imm. A.R. 93 (Immigration Appeal Tribunal: amnesty provisions not within jurisdiction of immigration appellate authorities); *cf. Salemi v MacKellar (No.2)* (1977) 137 C.L.R. 396.

[32] *Case of Proclamations* (1611) 12 Co. Rep. 74; *cf. R. v Criminal Injuries Compensation Board Ex p. Lain* [19671 2 Q.B. 864 at 886–889 (Diplock L.J., for certain qualifications of the general rule).

[33] *cf. Earl Fitzwilliam's Wentworth Estate Ltd v Minister of Town and Country Planning* [1951] 2 K.B. 284 at 311–312 (Denning L .J.); *M'Ara v Edinburgh Magistrates* 1913 S.C. 1059; *R. v Knuller (Publishing etc.) Ltd* [19731 A.C. 435 at 456 (Lord Reid, remarks on an assurance by a Law Officer of the Crown in the House of Commons that a charge of conspiracy to corrupt public morals would not be used to circumvent the statutory defences contained in the Obscene Publications Act 1959).

[34] *R. v Customs—and Excise Commissioners Ex p. Cook* [1970] 1 W.L.R. 450 at 454–455.

[35] R. Megarry, "Administrative Quasi-Legislation (1944) 60 L.Q.R, 125, 218 *Vestey v Inland Revenue Commissioners (No.2)* [1979] Ch. 198 at 202–204 (ad hoc use of this "dispensing power" is strongly criticised).

[36] Thus a decision made solely on the basis of such a rule or policy may be impugned on the ground that the authority had thereby fettered its discretion. A decision made in accordance with announced policy may also be held invalid if the policy included factors that the authority was not statutorily empowered to take into consideration on the proper interpretation of its power.

[37] See, e.g. *R. v Liverpool Corp. Ex p. Liverpool Taxi Fleet Operators' Association* [1972] 2 Q.B. 299; *R. v Home Secretary Ex p. Hosenball* [1977] 1 W.L.R. 766 at 781, 788; *R. v Criminal Injuries Compensation Board Ex p. Ince* [1973] 1 W.L.R. 1334 at 1345; *Salemi v Mackellar (No.2)*

[38] *Bristol DC v Clark* [1975] 1 W.L.R. 1443 at 1451.

claimant has no legally enforceable right to any compensation, he is entitled to obtain certiorari to quash a determination of the Board if the proceedings or determination are tainted by defects that would warrant the award of certiorari to quash a determination of a statutory tribunal.[39]

B–013   There are other acts which, though non-legislative in form, are cognisable by the courts and approximate to legislation in effect. Standard terms embodied in contracts between local authorities and council tenants, between government departments and manufacturers or suppliers.[40] may not differ in substance from byelaws[41] or statutory instruments. A decision of the House of Lords overturning an established judge-made rule can sometimes fairly be represented as unavowed legislation with, moreover, a limited retroactive operation.[42]

"Quasi-judicial"

B–014   In administrative law this term may have any one of three meanings. It may describe a function that is partly judicial and partly administrative, e.g. the making of a compulsory purchase order (a discretionary or administrative act) preceded by the holding of a judicial-type local inquiry and the consideration of objections. It may, alternatively, describe the "judicial" element in a composite function; holding an inquiry and considering objections in respect of a compulsory purchase order are thus "quasi-judicial" acts. Or it may describe the nature of a discretionary act itself where the actor's discretion is not unfettered Seldom is it essential to use this ambiguous term, and it will be avoided here as far as possible.

Judicial

B–015   A judicial decision made within jurisdiction is binding and conclusive in so far as it cannot be impeached in collateral proceedings; and it cannot, in general, be rescinded by the tribunal itself.[43] Words spoken in the course of judicial proceedings are absolutely privileged in the law of defamation; so too, it appears, are fair and accurate newspaper reports of judicial proceedings.[44] On the other hand, it is a contempt to comment on proceedings pending before a court in circumstances that prejudice a fair

[39] *R. v Criminal Injuries Compensation Board Ex p. Lain* [1967] 2 Q.B. 864.
[40] See C. Turpin (1972), *Government Contracts*, Ch. 3. And see *Racal Communications Ltd v Pay Board* [1974] W.L.R. 1149 (interpretation of Fair Wages Resolution passed by House of Commons).
[41] Housing Act 1957s. 12(1) (as amended).
[42] The retroactive effects of judicial decisions have tended to inhibit "judicial law-making"; there have been hints that English courts should be empowered to overrule decisions prospectively: see *R. v National Insurance Commissioner Ex p. Hudson* 944 at 1015, 1026.
[43] See, e.g. *Punton v Ministry of Pensions and National Insurance (No.2)* [1964] 1 W.L.R. 226.
[44] But newspaper reports of proceedings before "any justice or justices of the peace acting otherwise than as a court exercising judicial authority" enjoy only qualified privilege (Defamation Act 1952 Sch. para.10(b)).

trial of the issues. No civil liability is incurred in respect of erroneous or negligent judicial decisions and acts, provided that the officers concerned have acted in good faith and within their jurisdiction.[45] The Crown is immune from liability in tort in respect of anything done or omitted to be done by any person while discharging or purporting to discharge "responsibilities of a judicial nature"[46] even if that person is individually liable. Only in very exceptional circumstances may judicial functions be subdelegated in the absence of express authorisation. In a number of cases courts have refused to entertain appeals from decisions which are not of a judicial character.[47]

We have listed the main contexts in which the courts may have to determine whether to classify the functions of public authorities as judicial; the catalogue is not, however, exhaustive.[48] The meaning is apt to vary according to the purpose for which it has to be defined. For example, a function deemed to be judicial in so far as it is reviewable by certiorari may become "administrative" when an attempt is made to establish that it attracts absolute privilege in the law of defamation.[49] A Minister making a town planning decision may be required to act judicially in the sense of being obliged to observe the rules of natural justice, but if his decision is quashed he will not enjoy the immunity from liability to pay costs that is granted to members of judicial tribunals.[50] When it is said that mandamus will not issue in respect of judicial acts "judicial" is being contrasted with

B–016

[45] A majority of the Court of Appeal in *Siros v Moore* [1975] Q.B. 118 stated that a judicial act or decision bona fide done or made in the purported exercise of jurisdiction was not actionable, even though it turned out to be one that was outside the jurisdiction of the tribunal. Judges of courts stricto sensu are immune from liability for all acts down within jurisdiction, even if they have acted maliciously.

[46] Crown Proceedings Act 1947 s.2(5). The meaning of "judicial" for this purpose may well be held to be as wide as for the purpose of determining the immunity of persons in respect of non-malicious judicial acts.

[47] *Moses v Parker* [1896] A.C. 245; *Kaye v Hunter* 1958 S.C. 208; *Dean v District Auditor for Ashton-in-Makerfield* [1960] 1 Q.B. 149; *Attorney General of the Gambia v N'Jie* [1961] A.C. 617, 633; *R. v Cornwall Q. S. Ex p. Kerley* [1956] 1 W.L.R. 906.

[48] The phrase "judicial officer" has had to be interpreted for the purpose of s.3 of the Judicial Committee Act 1833 (*Lovibond v Governor General of Canada* [1930] A.C. 717), and the phrase "judicial proceedings" for the purpose of the Perjury Act 1911. See also *St Catherine's Flying School Ltd v Minister of National Revenue* [1956] 1 W.L.R. 1336. For the "non judicial" character of the functions exercised by inspectors conducting inquiries into proposals of the former Legal Government Commission, see *Wednesbury Corp v Ministry of Housing and Local Government (No.2)* [1966] 2 Q.B. 275. The provisions of the Tribunals and Inquiries Act 1971 were inapplicable to the exercise of "executive functions" by certain of the tribunals there specified (s.19(4)). The judicial functions of government departments are excluded from the terms of reference of the Parliamentary Commissioner for Administration (Parliamentary Commissioner Act 1967 s.5(1)).

[49] This emerges most clearly in the case on licensing tribunals: see *Royal Aquarium & Summer and Winter Gardens Society v Parkinson* [1892] 1 Q.B. 431; *Attwood v Chapman* [1914] 3 K.B. 275.

[50] *Tysons (Contractors) Ltd v Minister of Housing and Local Government* (1965) 63 L.G.R. 506. And in *R. v Secretary of State for the Environment Ex p. Ostler* [1977] 1 Q.B. 122, the administrative nature of the power to make a compulsory purchase order was one reason given for the court's adoption of a literal interpretation of the statutory limitation upon the availability of judicial review.

ministerial and includes discretionary acts which would ordinarily be called administrative. Similarly, the rules protecting judicial acts within jurisdiction from collateral impeachment and granting exemptions from tortious liability for judicial acts embrace some discretionary functions that are typically administrative:[51]

B–017   These illustrations of terminological vagaries could be multiplied. Some have been deliberately contrived by judges seeking to impose on their decisions a veneer of superficially persuasive legal reasoning. The difficulties posed by these verbal problems have been particularly perplexing in two sets of situations. How does one determine (1) whether a body is required to act in a judicial capacity for the purpose of ascertaining if its acts are reviewable by the orders of certiorari and prohibition and (ii) whether a body is under a duty to act judicially in the sense of being obliged to observe the rules of natural justice? Fortunately, however, recent developments in the law have reduced the importance that these two questions at one time had.

B–018   The two questions overlap, for among the grounds for which certiorari and prohibition will issue is breach of the rules of natural justice. But the questions are also partly distinct, since certiorari and prohibition will issue on other grounds (notably want or excess of jurisdiction) and a person aggrieved by a breach of natural justice may have recourse to other remedies, such as a declaratory order.

B–019   Till the 1960s it was generally assumed that certiorari and prohibition could not issue to a body of persons acting in a purely administrative capacity[52] though in fact the orders had often issued in respect of acts and decisions bearing only a remote resemblance to the judicial. This assumption is now obsolete[53] and, in any event, the introduction of a single procedure an application for judicial review, in which any of the common law forms of relief may be sought, has further diminished the practical significance of having to characterise as judicial the order or decision impugned.

Tests for identifying judicial functions

B–020   The more closely a statutory body resembles a court in the strict sense, the more likely is it that that body will be held to act in a judicial capacity. Indeed, the proceedings of a tribunal will not be held to be judicial for the

---

[51] A. Rubinstein, *Jurisdiction and Illegality* (1965), pp.137–139, 157–160.

[52] See, e.g. *R. v Electricity Commissioners* [1924] 1 K.B. 171; *Nakkuda Ali v Jayaratne* [1951] A. C. 66 *R. v Manchester Legal Aid Committee Ex p. Brand (RA) & Co* [1952] 2 Q.B. 413.

[53] See, e.g. *Ridge v Baldwin* [1964] A.C. 40 at 74–76; *R. v Birmingham City Justices Ex p. Chris Foreign Foods (Wholesalers) Ltd* [1970] 1 W.L.R. 1428: *R. v Liverpool Corp ex p. Liverpool Taxi Operators' Association* [1972] 2 Q.B. 299 at 308–309, 310; *R. v Hillingdon LBC Ex p. Royco Homes Ltd* [1947] Q.B. 720 at 728; *R. v Race Relations Board Ex p. Selvarajan* [1975] 1 W.L.R. 1686 at 1700. *R. v Barnsley MBC Ex p. Hook* [1976] 1 W.L.R. 1052. And in a case decided in part, at least, on the ground that certiorari was not available to impugn the proceedings in question, the old distinction was not revived: *R. v Hull Prison Board of Visitors Ex p. St Germain* [1978] Q.B. 678; rev'd [1979] Q.B. 425, CA.

purpose of attracting absolute privilege unless the tribunal resembles a court very closely. But it must not be assumed that because a body closely resembles a court, each and every one of its functions will be characterised as judicial. Even functions performed by courts are not necessarily characterised as judicial. Thus, it was recognised from early times that justices of the peace had ministerial duties and that their immunity from civil liability in respect of the erroneous performance of their judicial functions did not extend to their ministerial functions[54] and orders of mandamus frequently issue to compel inferior courts to carry out ministerial duties. Courts also exercise a wide variety of discretionary powers.[55] When exercised by courts, these powers are usually called judicial discretions; when exercised by bodies which are not courts they may possibly be called administrative acts.[56] And just as courts and bodies analogous to courts may be held to exercise non judicial functions, so may bodies that are not analogous to courts be held to exercise judicial functions. In short, the answer to the question whether a body is acting in a judicial capacity when performing a particular function does not necessarily depend upon the degree in which that body's general characteristics resemble those of an ordinary court, although the degree of resemblance may be a major factor influencing a decision that the function in question is judicial.

Conclusiveness

The first test that may be applied for distinguishing judicial functions from **B–021** other classes of functions turns upon whether the performance of the function terminates in an order that has conclusive effect. The decisions of courts are binding and conclusive, inasmuch as they have the force of law without the need for confirmation or adoption by any other authority[57] and cannot be impeached (if the court has acted within its jurisdiction) indirectly in collateral proceedings. This characteristic is generally regarded as one of the essential features of judicial power.[58] And a body exercising

---

[54] *Green v Hundred of Bucclechurches* (1589) 1 Leon. 323 at 324; Justice Protection Act 1848 s.l.

[55] I.Jennings, *The Law and the Constitution* (1959) 5th edn App. I.

[56] But a court may hold that it has no discretion when its exercise would require broad political considerations to be weighed: *Lord Advocate v Glasgow Corp*, 1973 S.L.T. 33 at 36.

[57] Where constitutional or statutory provision exists for courts to give advisory opinions, differences of opinion often arise as to whether the advisory jurisdiction is of a truly judicial character. The Judicial Committee of the PC has a special advisory jurisdiction under s.4 of the Judicial Committee Act 1833; its decision in other cases are in effect judgments, but take the form of advisory reports to Her Majesty, which are always promulgated by Order in Council: *Ibralebbe v R.* [1964] A.C. 900.

[58] See, e.g. *Stow v Mineral Holdings (Australia) Pty Ltd* (1977) 51 A.L.J.R. 672, High Ct. Aust.

powers which are of a merely advisory,[59] deliberative[60], investigatory[61] or conciliatory[62] character, or which do not have legal effect until confirmed by another body,[63] or involve only the making of a preliminairy decision,[64] will not normally be held to be acting in a judicial capacity. Nevertheless, the proceedings of bodies exercising functions of this type have sometimes been held to be judicial for the purpose of enjoying absolute privilege in the law of defamation; they are not invariably exempt from the duty to observe natural justice.[65] It must be added that where orders made by an administrative body are given finality by being exempted from judicial review, those orders do not thereby acquire a judicial quality if no other characteristic of judicial power is present. Power to make orders that are binding and conclusive is not, therefore, a *decisive factor*.

Trappings and procedure

B–022 A second test, or group test, for ascertaining whether statutory functions are of a judicial character turns primarily on the presence or absence of certain formal and procedural attributes. The manner in which courts proceed is distinguished by a number of special characteristics. They determine matters in cases initiated by parties; they must normally sit in public[66] they are empowered to compel the attendance of witnesses, who may be examined on oath; they are required to follow the rules of evidence; they are entitled to impose sanctions by way of imprisonment, fine, damages or mandatory or prohibitory orders, and to enforce

[59] *Re Clifford and O'Sullivan* [1921] 2 A.C. 570; *R. v MacFarlane Ex p. O'Flanagan and O'Kelly* (1923) 32 C.L.R. 518; *R. v St Lawrence's Hospital. Caterham, Statutory Visitors Ex p. Pritchard* [1953] 1 W.L.R. 1158.
[60] *R. v Legislative Committee of the Church Assembly Ex p. Haynes-Smith* [1928] 1K.B.411.
[61] See, e.g. *Re Grosvenor & West-End Railway Terminus Hotel Co* (1897) 76 L.T. 337, *Hearts of Oak Assurance Co v Attorney General* [1932] A.C. 392; *O'Conner v Waldron* [1935] A.C. 76; *St John v Fraser* [1935] S.C.R. 441; *Lockwood v Commonwealth* (1954) 90 C.L.R. 177; *Ex p. Mineral Deposits Pty Ltd; re Claye and Lynch* (1959) S.R. (N.S.W.) 167; *R. v Fowler Ex p. McArthur* [1958] Qd.R 41; *R. v Coppel Ex p. Viney Industries Pty Ltd* [1962] V.R. 630; *Testro Bros Pty Ltd v Tait* (1963) 109 C.L.R. 353; *Guay v Lafleur* [1965] S.C.R. 12; *R. v Collins Ex p. ACTU-Solo Enterprises Pty Ltd* (1976) 8 A.L.R. 69l, High Ct Aust.f. *Re Pergamon Press Ltd* [1971] Ch. 388: *cf.*, however, the subsequent decision in *Maxwell v Department of Trade and Industry* [1974] Q.B. 523.
[62] *Ayriss (FF) & Co v Alberta Labour Relations Board* (1960) 23 D.L.R. (2nd) 584; *R. v Clipsham Ex p. Basken* (1965) 49 D.L.R. (2nd) 747; *R. v Race Relations Board Ex p. Selvarajan* [1975] 1 W.L.R 1686.
[63] *R. v Hastings Local Board of Health* (1865) 6B.& S. 401; *Re Local Government Board Ex p. Kingstown Commissioners* (1885)16 L.R.Ir.150; (1886)18 L.R.Ir. 509; *Re Zadrevec and Town of Brampton* (1973) 37 D.L.R. (3rd) 326.
[64] *Jayawardane v Silva* [1970] 1 W.L.R. 1365: *Pearlberg v Varty* [1972] 1 W.L.R. 534 (*cf. Wiseman v Borneman* [1971] A.C. 297).
[65] See e.g. *R. v Kent Police Authority Ex p. Godden* [1971] 2 Q.B. 662; *Committee for Justice and Liberty v National Energy Board* [1978] 1 S.C.R. 369. Alternatively, they may be held to be under a duty to "act fairly". And see generally, on the availability of certiorari to bodies which have no authority to make binding decisions, *R. v Criminal Injuries Compensation Board Ex p. Lain*, [1967] 2 Q.B. 864.
[66] *Scott v Scott* [1913] A.C. 417; *McPherson v McPherson* [1936] A.C. 177; *Stone v Stone* [1949] P. 165.

obedience to their own commands. The fact that a body has been endowed with many of the "'trappings of a court" may not always be sufficient to establish conclusively that it has been invested with judicial power[67] but the presence of such trappings tends to support that conclusion. Thus, in seeking to establish that the proceedings (or the functions) of a statutory body are to be classified as judicial for any given purpose, it maybe material to show that the body is called a "tribunal" which holds "sittings" and makes "decisions" in relation to "cases" before it,[68] that it is empowered to summon witnesses and administer oaths,[69] that it is normally required to sit in public,[70] that its members are debarred from sitting if personally interested in a matter before them,[71] that it has power to award costs[72] or to impose sanctions to enforce compliance with its orders[73].

Perhaps the most obvious characteristic of ordinary courts is that they determine, on the basis of evidence and arguments submitted to them, disputes between two or more parties about their respective legal rights and duties, powers and liabilities, privileges and immunities. "It is a truism that the conception of the judicial function is inseparably bound up with the idea of a suit between parties, whether between Crown and subject or between subject and subject, and that it is the duty of the court to decide the issue between those parties. . ."[74] If, then, the functions of a statutory body include the determination of issues that closely resemble jus inter partes, (rights as between parties) it is to be expected that for most if not all purposes those functions will be classified as judicial. **B–023**

First, when determining a *lis inter partes* (dispute between parties) a court gives a binding decision in relation to the dispute. A body that hears evidence in a dispute between parties will not normally be held to be acting in a judicial capacity unless it has power to give a binding decision. **B–024**

Secondly, in administrative law many of the issues that arise between contending parties are different in character from those typically determined by courts. An applicant may appear before a licensing tribunal to **B–025**

[67] cf. *Shell Co of Australia Ltd v Federal Commission of Taxation* [1931] A.C. 275 at 296–297 (dealing with judicial power under the Australian Constitution).
[68] *Jackson (FE) & Co v Price Tribunal (No.2) [1950]* N.Z.L.R 433 at 448–449: *New Zealand United Licensed Victuallers' Association of Employers v Price Tribunal* [1957] N.Z.L.R. 167 at 204, 207.
[69] And see *Attorney General v BBC* [1978] 1 W.L.R. 477 at 481.
[70] *Copartnership Farms v Harvey-Smith* [1918] 2 K.B. 405 at 411.
[71] *Copartnership Farms* [1918] 2 K.B. 405.
[72] *R. v Manchester Justices* [1899] 1 Q.B. 571; *R. v Sunderland Justices* [1901] 2 K.B.357 at 369.
[73] The power of the Commonwealth Court of Conciliation and Arbitration to impose penalties for breaches or non-observance of its orders and awards was held by the PC in the Boilermakers' case to be "plainly judicial" ([1957] A.C. 288 at 322).
[74] *Labour Relations Board of Saskatchewan v John East Iron Works Ltd* [1949] A. C. 134 at 149. See also *Boulter v Kent Justices* [1897] A.C. 556 at 569; *Huddart Parker & Co Pty Ltd v Commonwealth* (1908) 8 C.L.R. 330 at 357 (Griffith C.J.); Report of the Committee on Ministers' Powers (Cmd.4060 (1932), 73. *cf. Re Rubber Plastic and Cable Making Industry Award* (1963) 8 F.L.R. 396 (Commonwealth Industrial Court exercising judicial power of the commonwealth in interpreting award although no dispute between parties bound by the award).

seek a legal privilege; a member of the public may appear to oppose the application. Superficially the tribunal seems to be deciding a *lis inter partes*; but if it decides to refuse the application it is not deciding only in favour of the objector; it is deciding that it is not in the public interest to grant the licence, and the decision may in effect be in favour of the public at large, who are not directly represented at the hearing.[75] In the context of inquiries relating to administrative orders which *affect* private interests in land, analogies with *lis inter partes* are also questionable. A local authority makes a compulsory purchase order: a property-owner lodges objections to the order; the Minister, who will have to decide whether or not to confirm the order, causes a local inquiry to be held; the local authority and the objector appear before the inspector who conducts the inquiry: the Minister considers the inspector's report and the objections, together with any other materials that appear to him to be relevant, and then makes his decision. He is entitled to disregard the weight of the evidence submitted at the inquiry and to found his decision on broad considerations of national policy. The procedural steps that have to be taken when an objection is lodged have therefore been described (perhaps too readily) as "merely a stage in the process of arriving at an administrative decision".[76]

B–026   These considerations have had some influence on the scope of judicial review. They help to explain why at one time licensing justices were held not to be a "court"[77] and why their proceedings have not been regarded as judicial for the purpose of attracting absolute privileged.[78] They also help to explain why a Minister who had to decide whether or not to confirm an order made by a local authority was not held to be under an obligation to observe the rules of natural justice at certain stages of his functions.[79]

B–027   Nevertheless, functions may become reviewable as "judicial" because of statutory interpolation of a procedure bearing a superficial resemblance to a *lis inter partes*. Thus, the proceedings of licensing bodies that are required to conduct hearings are sufficiently judicial to be amenable to review by certiorari and prohibition and must be conducted in conformity with natural justice. A Minister acting as confirming authority must act judicially in accordance with the rules of natural justice from the moment when

---

[75] *Boulter v Kent Justices* [1897] A.C. 556 at 569 (Lord Herschell); and *R. v Howard* [1902] 2 K.B. 363; *Tynemouth Corp v Attorney General* [1899] A.C. 293 at 307; *R. v Ashton Ex p. Walker* (1915) 85 L J.K.B. 27 at 30.

[76] *Johnson (B) & Co (Builders) Ltd v Minister of Health* [1947] 2 All E.R. 395 at 399 (Lord Greene M.R.); *R. v Canterbury (Archbishop) Ex p. Morant* [1944] K.B. 282 (observations on false analogies with lites inter partes); *Lithgow v Secretary of State for Scotland* 1973 S.L.T. 81; *R. v Medical Appeal Tribunal (Northern Region) Ex p. Hubble* [1958] 2 Q.B. 228 at 239–241; *R. v Deputy Industrial Injuries Commissioner Ex p. Moore* [1965] 1 Q.B. 456 at 472–474, 486, 489–491 (analyses of the inquisitorial functions of tribunals involved in the administration of a social security scheme); *Bushell v Secretary of State for the Environment* [1981] A. C. 75.

[77] *Boulter v Kent Justices* [1897] A.C. 556; cf. *Jeffrey v Evans* [1964] 1 W.L.R. 505; *R. v East Riding of Yorkshire QS* [1968] 1 Q.B. 32.

[78] *Attwood v Chapman* [1914] 3 K.B. 275.

[79] *Johnson and Co (Builders Ltd v Minister of Health* [1947] 2 All E.R. 395.

objections are lodged against the local authority's order, although his functions have been characterised as "purely administrative" before objections have been lodged or if he himself is the initiating authority.[80] Indeed, preoccupation with the pseudo-concept of a *lis*, particularly in the latter class of situation, led to the development of a trend of opinion that a body could *not* be said to be acting in a judicial capacity *unless* it was expressly obliged to hold a hearing in respect of an issue between two or more contending parties. This heresy has been exposed, and the courts have conceded that in certain circumstances a body may be under an *implied* duty to act judicially in accordance with the rules of natural justice although not expressly required to determine a *lis inter partes* or anything resembling a *lis.*[81]

Interpretation and declaration

A typical lis *inter partes* culminates in a decision by a tribunal resolving any   B–028
disputed questions of law or fact; the legal issues are determined by reference to principles and rules already in being. A tribunal or other deciding body is therefore likely to be held to be acting in a judicial capacity when, after investigation and deliberation, it determines an issue conclusively by the application of a pre-existing legal rule or another objective legal standard to the facts found by it. That interpreting, declaring and applying the law are characteristic hallmarks of the judicial function is too elementary a proposition to call for authoritative support.[82] It would, of course, be absurd to insist that these are mechanical operations in which an adjudicator has no freedom to choose between alternative rules or competing interpretations, for judges can and do develop and modify the law when deciding cases before them. And there is another reason why it would be inaccurate to describe the judicial function as being merely to declare pre-existing rights or obligations. P may be guilty of a crime; Q may be entitled to damages for breach of contract; R may be entitled to social security benefit and S to compensation for compulsory acquisition of his land: but until a competent tribunal has pronounced on the law in relation to the facts of these cases, their liabilities and rights are inchoate; they acquire legal recognition by virtue of the judgment or order, which to this extent has a "constitutive" effect.

There is, however, an obvious difference of substance and degree   B–029
between a decision that X is or is not liable to pay a certain tax in respect of a particular transaction, and a decision that it is in the public interest that Y should or should not be granted an office development permit. In the first case the function is typically judicial: in the second the function is

---

[80] *Johnson and Co (Builders Ltd v Ministry of Health* [1947] 2 All E.R. 395.
[81] *Ridge v Baldwin* [1964] A.C. 40; *Maradana Mosque Trustees v Mahmud* [1967] 1 A.C. 13; *Durayappah v Fernando* [1967] 2 A.C. 337.
[82] *Moses v Parker* [1896] A. C. 245; *United Engineering Workers; Union v Devanayagam* [1968] A.C. 356.

typically administrative inasmuch as it entails the exercise of almost unfettered discretionary power. The wider the "public policy'" content of an administrative discretion the more reluctant may the courts be to require the repository of the direction, to "act judicially" according to natural justice.[83]

B–030　Between clearly judicial acts and clearly administrative acts lies an awkward intermediate category, sometimes called judicial discretions. Judges exercise discretion in awarding costs, sentencing prisoners, removing arbitrators and trustees, varying the terms of a trust, permitting applications to be made out of time, and so on. In exercising such powers they may create new rights and duties or otherwise vary the status quo, but the powers are normally called "judicial" discretions, partly because it is customary to call all the non-ministerial powers of courts judicial, and partly because these discretionary powers have to be exercised according to reasonably well-settled principles, which are capable of being formulated and applied as standards by higher courts when entertaining appeals against the manner in which they have been exercised. The difference between a judicial discretion (which need not necessarily be confided in a court *stricto senu*) and an "administrative" discretion in which the subjective elements of policy and expediency loom large, is seldom more than one of degree.[84] But, as has been indicated, the distinction is sometimes of practical importance. If a court is prepared to review the factors on which the exercise of a discretion has been founded, it is apt to label the discretion "judicial"; if it feels that it would be inappropriate or impracticable to embark on review, it may observe that the discretionary power is purely administrative.[85] Although, as we shall see, courts in recent years have been much less reluctant to review the bases upon which administrative discretion has been exercised than they once were.

B–031　When certiorari and prohibition and the rules of natural justice were said to extend only to bodies performing judicial functions, courts were readier so to characterise them where the decisions or orders in question were made on the basis of fact-finding, rule-applying and the exercise of limited discretion. In a number of contexts, however, courts have been prepared to label as "judicial" discretionary acts that would seem more appropriately to be called administrative.

B–032　In addition "judicial" was given a wide meaning in some of the older cases on mandamus. A tribunal or other body may be under a ministerial duty, enforceable by mandamus, to determine a matter or exercise a discretion. But it is not normally under any duty to determine that matter

[83] See, e.g. *R. v Brixton Prison Governor Ex p. Soblen* [1963] 2 Q.B. 243; *Essex CC v Ministry of Housing and Local Government* (1967) 66 L.G.R. 23; *Schmidt v Home Secretary* [1969] 2 Ch. 149.
[84] *R. v Manchester Legal Aid Committee Ex p. Brand (RA) & Co* [1952] 2 Q.B. 413.
[85] See, e.g. *Johnson (B) & Co (Builders) Ltd v Minister of Health* [1974] 2 All E R 395; *Attorney General v Bastow* [1957] 1 Q.B. 514. To this extent what is administrative is non-reviewable, whereas for certain purposes an act may be non-reviewable because it is "judicial".

or exercise its discretion in a particular way, and mandamus will not, therefore, issue to it for such a purpose. When explaining their inability to issue mandamus for these non-ministerial purposes the courts occasionally described the functions concerned as judicial, irrespective of whether they involved the determination of questions of legal right[86] or the exercise of wide discretionary powers.[87]

One may sum up by saying that the courts classified wide discretionary B–033 powers as judicial when they thought such a classification to be necessary or desirable in a particular situation; though power to alter existing rights and obligations is not at all characteristic of the archetypal judicial function. As long as the only alternatives were "ministerial" and "legislative" this latitudinarianism caused few difficulties. But once the distinct concept of "administrative" functions began to emerge, analytical and verbal problems proliferated, and they are likely to persist for some time despite the recent and welcome tendency to belittle the practical importance of classification of functions.

Judicial proceedings and absolute privilege

A narrow conception of "judicial" has prevailed in cases where it has been B–034 sought to establish that the proceedings of administrative tribunals are judicial proceedings for the purpose of attracting absolute privilege in respect of defamatory statements and reports made to or by them. "The question . . . in every case", it has been said, "is whether the tribunal in question has similar attributes to a court of justice or acts in a manner similar to that in which such courts act.[88] It may be sufficient, in order to establish the judicial character of the tribunal, to show either that it decides issues of a type normally decided by the ordinary courts[89] or that its constitution and procedure closely resemble those of ordinary courts.[90] But in this context it has been difficult to persuade the courts that administrative tribunals possess those characteristics,[91] even when they are determining questions of legal right. Thus, in one case it was held that a Court of Referees in determining whether claimants were legally entitled to unemployment benefit was "merely discharging administrative duties" because it was "not a body deciding between parties nor does its decision . . . affect

---

[86] See, e.g. *R. v Law* (1857) 7 E. & B. 366.
[87] See, e.g. *R. v Lichfield (Bishop)* (1734) 7 Mod. 217 at 218; *Staverton v Ashburton* (1855) 4 E. & B. 526 at 531; *Ex p. Cook, re Dyson* (1869) 2 E. & B. 586; *R. v London Justices* [1895] 1 Q.B. 214 at 616.
[88] *O'Connor v Waldron* [1935] A.C. 76 at 81 (Lord Atkin); *Royal Aquarium & Summer and Winter Gardens Society v Parkinson* [1892] 1 Q.B. 431 at 442 (Lord Esher M.R.).
[89] *Keenan v Auckland Harbour Board* [1946] N.Z.L.R. 97 (where the authorities are fully reviewed); *Atkins v Mays* [1974] 2 N.Z.L.R. 459 (proceedings to hear objections to town planning scheme absolutely privileged).
[90] *Copartnership Farms v Harvey Smith* [1918] 2 K.B. 405 at 410.
[91] *Thompson v Turbott* [1962] N.Z.L.R. 298 at 308 (held that hearings before Public Service Board of Appeal were absolutely privileged).

the status of an individuals".[92] In a more recent Australian case,[93] however, immunity was said to extend to the proceedings of a Board of Inquiry, even though its functions were to investigate and make recommendations to the Governor-in-Council. In general the courts have taken the view that it would be contrary to public policy to concede absolute privilege to the proceedings of such bodies and that they are adequately protected by qualified privilege.[94] It is significant that the only English case in which absolute privilege was held to attach to the proceedings of an administrative tribunal[95] concerned a local tribunal set up to determine claims to exemption from militaiy service in wartime.[96] There is undoubtedly much to be said in favour of denying absolute privilege to parties and witnesses appearing before administrative tribunals, for the proceedings are usually lacking in the traditional formality that may tend to deter irresponsible persons from making maliciously untrue statements.[97] This factor does not necessarily apply with equal force to the members of the tribunal themselves, and it is arguable that where membership of a tribunal is deemed to require a degree of judicial detachment that is incompatible with membership of the House of Commons,[98] it ought to carry with it the same immunity from liability for words spoken in the course of proceedings and statements made in orders or judgments as is enjoyed by members of courts *stricto sensu.*[99]

[92] *Collins v Henry Whiteway & Co* [1927] 2 K.B. 378 at 383 (distinguished in *Keenan,* [1946] N.Z.L.R. 97; *Mason v Brewis Bros Ltd* [19381 2 All E.R. 420; *Smith v National Meter Co* [1945] K.B. 453.

[93] *Tampion v Anderson* [1973] V.R. 321 at 715.

[94] *Royal Aquarium, etc. Society v Parkinson* [1892] 1 Q.B. 43l at 447–448. 451; *Attwood v Chapman* [1914] 3 K.B. 275 at 285–286; *Collins v Henry Whiteway & Co* [1927] 2 K.B. 378 at 382–383. Fair and accurate newspaper reports of the proceedings of administrative tribunals held in public also enjoy qualified privilege (Defamation Act 1952s.7 Sch. para.l0(e)).

[95] The courts have been less reluctant to concede absolute privilege to the proceedings of tribunals which, although lacking some of the attributes of courts *stricto sensu.* have not been connected with the administrative process. See *Dawkins v Lord Rokeby* (1873) L.R. 8 Q.B. 225; (1875) L.R. 7 H.L. 744 (military court of inquiry); *Barratt v Kearns* [1905] 1 K.B. 504 (ecclesiastical commission of inquiry); *Bretherton v Kaye and Winneke* [1971] V.R. Ill (board of inquiry into police practices); *Lilley v Roney* (1892) 61 L.J.Q.B. 727; *Addis v Crocker* [1961] 1 Q.B. 11 (Disciplinary Committee of the Law Society); *Bottomley v Brougham* [1908] 1 K.B. 584; *Burr v Smith* [1909] 2 K.B. 306 (reports by official receivers); *Lincoln v Daniels* [1962] Q.B. 237 (*cf. Marrinan v Vibart* [1963] 1 Q.B. 234 at 528) (inquiry by Benchers of an Inn of Court into allegations of professional misconduct); *Tampion v Anderson* [1973] V.R. 321 (inquiry into Scientology). *cf. O'Connor v Waldron* [1935] A.C. 76 (proceedings of Commission of Inquiry under Canadian Combines Investigation Act not protected by absolute privilege).

[96] *Copartnership Farms v Harvey-Smith* [1918] 2 K.B. 405: *Slack v Burr* (1918) 82 J.P. 91 (Scot.) (absolute privilege held to attach to statement by witness before wartime industrial arbitration tribunal); *cf. Keenan v Auckland Harbour Board* [1946] N.Z.L.R. 95; *Trapp v Mackie* [1979] 1 W.L.R. 377.

[97] For this reason the Council on Tribunals recommended that there should be no change in the law (Second Report, 14–15).

[98] House of Commons Disqualification Act 1975 s.l and Sch.l.

[99] Absolute privilege has been conferred by statute upon reports made by the Parliamentary Ombudsman (Parliamentary Commissioner Act 1967 s.10(5)) as well as certain other communications made in connection with the performance of the Commissioner's functions.

Conclusions

Judicial acts may be identified by reference to their formal, procedural or **B–035** substantive characteristics, or by a combination of any of them. An act may be judicial because it declares and interprets pre-existing rights, or because it changes those rights provided that the power to change them is not unfettered. A duty to act judicially in conformity with natural justice may be inferred from the impact of an administrative act or decision on individual rights. Although sometimes used in a narrow sense, the term "judicial" in cases involving review by certiorari and prohibition has generally been used in a very wide sense and has been dropped altogether as a requirement for the availability of these remedies. In natural justice cases, variations in linguistic usage have been particularly spectacular and frequently puzzling; but it is generally more profitable to concentrate on what the court has done than on what it has said. In cases where the absolute privilege accorded to judicial proceedings has been claimed in respect of proceedings before statutory tribunals, the courts have fairly consistently given a narrow interpretation to the term "judicial". Where the meaning of judicial has been brought into issue for other purposes (e.g. tort liability and collateral impeachment), the judgments have been singularly deficient in conceptual analysis, but it would seem that judicial acts are to be understood as including certain discretionary functions that could have been called administrative.

At this point terminological and conceptual problems may appear to be **B–036** overwhelming. However, to an increasing extent courts exercising powers of judicial review in administrative law are abandoning servitude to their own concepts and asserting mastery over them.

APPENDIX C

THE OUTSER CLAUSE CONTAINED IN THE ASYLUM AND IMMIGRATION (TREATMENT OF CLAIMANTS ETC.) BILL

This is the ouster clause—discussed at 1–00and 4–00 above—contained in C–001
the Asylum and Immigration (Treatment of Claimants etc.) Bill during its
passage through Parliament in early 2003. Had it been enacted, it would
have become S.108A of the Nationality, Immigration and Asylum Act
2002. The "Tribunal" is the Asylum and Immigration Tribunal.

Exclusivity and finality of Tribunal's jurisdiction

(1) No court shall have any supervisory or other jurisdiction (whether C–002
statutory or inherent) in relation to the Tribunal.

(2) No court may entertain proceedings for questioning (whether by
way of appeal or otherwise)—

(a) any determination, decision or other action of the Tribunal
(including a decision about jurisdiction and a decision under
section 105A),

(b) any action of the President or a Deputy President of the Tribunal
that relates to one or more specified cases,

(c) any decision in respect of which a person has or had a right of
appeal to the Tribunal under—

(i) section 82, 83 or 109 of this Act, or
(ii) section 40A of the British Nationality Act 1981 (c. 61).

(d) any matter which the Tribunal-

(i) was obliged to determine in accordance with section 86 of this
Act, or
(ii) would have been obliged to determine in accordance with that
section had a right of appeal mentioned in paragraph (c) been
exercised, or

(e) a decision to remove a person from the United Kingdom, a
decision to deport a person or any action in connection with a
decision to remove a person from the United Kingdom or to
deport a person, if the removal or deportation is in consequence of
an immigration decision.

(3) Subsections (1) and (2)—

    (a) prevent a court, in particular, from entertaining proceedings to determine whether a purported determination, decision or action of the Tribunal was a nullity by reason of—

        (i) lack of jurisdiction,
        (ii) irregularity,
        (iii) error of law,
        (iv) breach of natural justice, or
        (v) any other matter, but

    (b) do not prevent a court from—

        (i) reviewing a decision to issue a certificate under section 94 or 96 of this Act or under Schedule 3 to the Asylum and Immigration (Treatment of Claimants, etc.) Act 2004 (removal to safe country). or
        (ii) considering whether a member of the Tribunal has acted in bad faith.

(4) A court may consider whether a member of the Tribunal has acted in bad faith, in reliance on subsection (3)(b)(ii), only if satisfied that significant evidence has been adduced of—

    (a) dishonesty,
    (b) corruption, or
    (c) bias.

(5) Section 7(1) of the Human Rights Act 1998 (c. 42) (claim that public authority has infringed Convention right) is subject to subsections (1) to (3) above.

(6) Nothing in this section shall prevent an appeal under section 2, 2B or 7 of the Special Immigration Appeals Commission Act 1997 (c. 68)(appeals to and from Commission).

(7) In this section "action" includes failure to act.

EXTRACTS FROM SUPREME COURT ACT (SENIOR COURT ACT) 1981

The Supreme Court Act 1981 will be renamed as the Senior Courts Act D–001 1981 when Pt 3 of the Constitutional Reform Act 2005 is brought into force (which is expected in October 2009). That will herald the start of work of the new Supreme Court of the United Kingdom. The change of name is intended to avoid confusion.

Section 29: Orders of mandamus, prohibition and certiorari

(1) The orders of mandamus, prohibition and certiorari shall be known D–002 instead as mandatory, prohibiting and quashing orders respectively.

(1A) The High Court shall have jurisdiction to make mandatory, prohibiting and quashing orders in those classes of case in which, immediately before 1st May 2004, it had jurisdiction to make orders of mandamus, prohibition and certiorari respectively.

(2) Every such order shall be final, subject to any right of appeal therefrom.

(3) In relation to the jurisdiction of the Crown Court, other than its jurisdiction in matters relating to trial on indictment, the High Court shall have all such jurisdiction to make [mandatory, prohibiting or quashing orders] as the High Court possesses in relation to the jurisdiction of an inferior court.

(3A) The High Court shall have no jurisdiction to make [mandatory, prohibiting

or quashing orders] in relation to the jurisdiction of a court-martial in matters relating to—

(a) trial by court-martial for an offence, or
(b) appeals from a Standing Civilian Court;

and in this subsection "court-martial" means a court-martial under the Army Act 1955, the Air Force Act 1955 or the Naval Discipline Act 1957.

(3A) The High Court shall have no jurisdiction to make mandatory, prohibiting or quashing orders in relation to the jurisdiction of the Court Martial in matters relating to—

(a) trial by the Court Martial for an offence; or
(b) appeals from the Service Civilian Court.

(4) The power of the High Court under any enactment to require justices of the peace or a judge or officer of a county court to do any act relating to the duties of their respective offices, or to require a magistrates' court to state a case for the opinion of the High Court, in any case where the High Court formerly had by virtue of any enactment jurisdiction to make a rule absolute, or an order, for any of those purposes, shall be exercisable by mandatory order.

(5) In any statutory provision—

(a) references to mandamus or to a writ or order of mandamus shall be read as references to a mandatory order;
(b) references to prohibition or to a writ or order of prohibition shall be read as references to a prohibiting order;
(c) references to certiorari or to a writ or order of certiorari shall be read as references to a quashing order; and
(d) references to the issue or award of a writ of mandamus, prohibition or certiorari shall be read as references to the making of the corresponding mandatory, prohibiting or quashing order.

(6) In subsection (3) the reference to the Crown Court's jurisdiction in matters relating to trial on indictment does not include its jurisdiction relating to orders under section 17 of the Access to Justice Act 1999.

Section 31: Application for judicial review

D–003

(1) An application to the High Court for one or more of the following forms of relief, namely—

(a) a mandatory, prohibiting or quashing order;
(b) a declaration or injunction under subsection (2); or
(c) an injunction under section 30 restraining a person not entitled to do so from acting in an office to which that section applies,

shall be made in accordance with rules of court by a procedure to be known as an application for judicial review.

(2) A declaration may be made or an injunction granted under this subsection any case where an application for judicial review, seeking that relief, has been made and the High Court considers that, having regard to—

(a) the nature of the matters in respect of which relief may be granted by [mandatory, prohibiting or quashing orders];
(b) the nature of the persons and bodies against whom relief may be granted by such orders; and
(c) all the circumstances of the case,

it would be just and convenient for the declaration to be made or of the injunction to be granted, as the case may be.

(3) No application for judicial review shall be made unless the leave of the High Court has been obtained in accordance with rules of court; and the court shall not grant leave to make such an application unless it considers that the applicant has a sufficient interest in the matter to which the application relates.

(4) On an application for judicial review the High Court may award to the applicant damages, restitution or the recovery of a sum due if—

(a) the application includes a claim for such an award arising from any matter to which the application relates; and

(b) the court is satisfied that such an award would have been made if the claim had been made in an action begun by the applicant at the time of making the application.

(5) [1]If, on an application for judicial review, the High Court quashes the decision to which the application relates, it may in addition—

(a) remit the matter to the court, tribunal or authority which made the decision, with a direction to reconsider the matter and reach a decision in accordance with the findings of the High Court, or

(b) substitute its own decision for the decision in question.

(5A) But the power conferred by subsection (5)(b) is exercisable only if—

(a) the decision in question was made by a court or tribunal,

(b) the decision is quashed on the ground that there has been an error of law, and

(c) without the error, there would have been only one decision which the court or tribunal could have reached.

(5B) Unless the High Court otherwise directs, a decision substituted by it under subsection (5)(b) has effect as if it were a decision of the relevant court or tribunal.

(6) Where the High Court considers that there has been undue delay in making an application for judicial review, the court may refuse to grant—

(a) leave for the making of the application; or

(b) any relief sought on the application,

if it considers that the granting of the relief sought would be likely to cause substantial hardship to, or substantially prejudice the rights of, any person or would be detrimental to good administration.

(7) Subsection (6) is without prejudice to any enactment or rule of court which has the effect of limiting the time within which an application for judicial review may be made.

---

[1] Subsections (5), (5A) and (5B) inserted by Tribunals, Courts and Enforcement Act 2007 s.141.

Section 31A: Transfer of judicial review applications to Upper Tribunal[2]

D–004   (1) This section applies where an application is made to the High Court—

(a) for judicial review, or

(b) for permission to apply for judicial review.

(2) If Conditions 1, 2, 3 and 4 are met, the High Court must by order transfer the application to the Upper Tribunal.

(3) If Conditions 1, 2 and 4 are met, but Condition 3 is not, the High Court may by order transfer the application to the Upper Tribunal if it appears to the High Court to be just and convenient to do so.

(4) Condition 1 is that the application does not seek anything other than—

(a) relief under section 31(l)(a) and (b);

(b) permission to apply for relief under section 31(l)(a) and (b);

(c) an award under section 31(4);

(d) interest;

(e) costs.

(5) Condition 2 is that the application does not call into question anything done by the Crown Court.

(6) Condition 3 is that the application falls within a class specified under section 18(6) of the Tribunals, Courts and Enforcement Act 2007.

(7) Condition 4 is that the application does not call into question any decision made under—

(a) the Immigration Acts,

(b) the British Nationality Act 1981 (c.61),

(c) any instrument having effect under an enactment within paragraph (a) or (b), or

(d) any other provision of law for the time being in force which determines British citizenship, British overseas territories citizenship, the status of a British National (Overseas) or British Overseas citizenship.

---

[2] Inserted by Tribunals, Courts and Enforcement Act 2007 s.19.

EXTRACTS FROM TRIBUNALS, COURTS AND ENFORCEMENT ACT 2007

Section 15: Upper Tribunal's "judicial review" jurisdiction

(1) The Upper Tribunal has power, in cases arising under the law of **E–001** England and Wales or under the law of Northern Ireland, to grant the following kinds of relief—

(a) a mandatory order;
(b) a prohibiting order;
(c) a quashing order;
(d) a declaration;
(e) an injunction.

(2) The power under subsection (1) may be exercised by the Upper Tribunal if—

(a) certain conditions are met (see section 18), or
(b) the tribunal is authorised to proceed even though not all of those conditions are met (see section 19(3) and (4)).

(3) Relief under subsection (1) granted by the Upper Tribunal—

(a) has the same effect as the corresponding relief granted by the High Court on an application for judicial review, and
(b) is enforceable as if it were relief granted by the High Court on an application for judicial review.

(4) In deciding whether to grant relief under subsection (l)(a), (b) or (c), the Upper Tribunal must apply the principles that the High Court would apply in deciding whether to grant that relief on an application for judicial review.

(5) In deciding whether to grant relief under subsection (l)(d) or (e), the Upper Tribunal must—

(a) in cases arising under the law of England and Wales apply the principles that the High Court would apply in deciding whether to grant that relief under section 31(2) of the Supreme Court Act 1981 (c.54) on an application for judicial review, and
(b) in cases arising under the law of Northern Ireland apply the principles that the High Court would apply in deciding whether to grant that relief on an application for judicial review.

(6) For the purposes of the application of subsection (3)(a) in relation to cases arising under the law of Northern Ireland—

(a) a mandatory order under subsection (1)(a) shall be taken to correspond to an order of mandamus,
(b) a prohibiting order under subsection (1)(b) shall be taken to correspond to an order of prohibition, and
(c) a quashing order under subsection (l)(c) shall be taken to correspond to an order of certiorari.

Section 16: Application for relief under section 15(1)

E–002

(1) This section applies in relation to an application to the Upper Tribunal for relief under section 15(1).

(2) The application may be made only if permission (or, in a case arising under the law of Northern Ireland, leave) to make it has been obtained from the tribunal.

(3) The tribunal may not grant permission (or leave) to make the application unless it considers that the applicant has a sufficient interest in the matter to which the application relates.

(4) Subsection (5) applies where the tribunal considers—

(a) that there has been undue delay in making the application, and
(b) that granting the relief sought on the application would be likely to cause substantial hardship to, or substantially prejudice the rights of, any person or would be detrimental to good administration.

(5) The tribunal may—

(a) refuse to grant permission (or leave) for the making of the application;
(b) refuse to grant any relief sought on the application.

(6) The tribunal may award to the applicant damages, restitution or the recovery of a sum due if—

(a) the application includes a claim for such an award arising from any matter to which the application relates, and
(b) the tribunal is satisfied that such an award would have been made by the High Court if the claim had been made in an action begun in the High Court by the applicant at the time of making the application.

(7) An award under subsection (6) maybe enforced as if it were an award of the High Court.

(8) Where—

(a) the tribunal refuses to grant permission (or leave) to apply for relief under section 15(1),

(b) the applicant appeals against that refusal, and

(c) the Court of Appeal grants the permission (or leave),

the Court of Appeal may go on to decide the application for relief under section 15(1).

(9) Subsections (4) and (5) do not prevent Tribunal Procedure Rules from limiting the time within which applications may be made.

Section 17: Quashing orders under section 15(1): supplementary provision

(1) If the Upper Tribunal makes a quashing order under section 15(l)(c) in respect of a decision, it may in addition— **E–003**

(a) remit the matter concerned to the court, tribunal or authority that made the decision, with a direction to reconsider the matter and reach a decision in accordance with the findings of the Upper Tribunal, or

(b) substitute its own decision for the decision in question.

(2) The power conferred by subsection (l)(b) is exercisable only if—

(a) the decision in question was made by a court or tribunal,

(b) the decision is quashed on the ground that there has been an error of law, and

(c) without the error, there would have been only one decision that the court or tribunal could have reached.

(3)Unless the Upper Tribunal otherwise directs, a decision substituted by it under subsection (l)(b) has effect as if it were a decision of the relevant court or tribunal.

Section 18: Limits of jurisdiction under section 15(1)

(1) This section applies where an application made to the Upper Tribunal seeks (whether or not alone)— **E–004**

(a) relief under section 15(1), or

(b) permission (or, in a case arising under the law of Northern Ireland, leave) to apply for relief under section 15(1).

(2) If Conditions 1 to 4 are met, the tribunal has the function of deciding the application.

(3) If the tribunal does not have the function of deciding the application, it must by order transfer the application to the High Court.

(4) Condition 1 is that the application does not seek anything other than—

(a) relief under section 15(1);

(b) permission (or, in a case arising under the law of Northern Ireland, leave) to apply for relief under section 15(1);

(c) an award under section 16(6);

(d) interest;

(e) costs.

(5) Condition 2 is that the application does not call into question anything done by the Crown Court.

(6) Condition 3 is that the application falls within a class specified for the purposes of this subsection in a direction given in accordance with Part 1 of Schedule 2 to the Constitutional Reform Act 2005 (c.4).

(7) The power to give directions under subsection (6) includes—

(a) power to vary or revoke directions made in exercise of the power, and

(b) power to make different provision for different purposes.

(8) Condition 4 is that the judge presiding at the hearing of the application is either—

(a) a judge of the High Court or the Court of Appeal in England and Wales or Northern Ireland, or a judge of the Court of Session, or

(b) such other persons as may be agreed from time to time between the Lord Chief Justice, the Lord President, or the Lord Chief Justice of Northern Ireland, as the case may be, and the Senior President of Tribunals.

(9) Where the application is transferred to the High Court under subsection (3)—

(a) the apphcation is to be treated for all purposes as if it—

  (i) had been made to the High Court, and

  (ii) sought things corresponding to those sought from the tribunal, and

(b) any steps taken, permission (or leave) given or orders made by the tribunal in relation to the application are to be treated as taken, given or made by the High Court.

(10) Rules of court may make provision for the purpose of supplementing subsection (9).

(11) The provision that may be made by Tribunal Procedure Rules about amendment of an application for relief under section 15(1) includes, in particular, provision about amendments that would cause the application to become transferrable under subsection (3). [. . .]

EXTRACTS FROM HUMAN RIGHTS ACT 1998

An Act to give further effect to rights and freedoms guaranteed under the European Convention on Human Rights; to make provision with respect 1o holders of certain judicial offices who become judges of the European Court of Human Rights; and for connected purposes.

[9th November 1998]

BE IT ENACTED by the Queen's most Excellent Majesty, by and with the advice and consent of the Lords Spiritual and Temporal, and Commons, in this present Parliament assembled, and by the authority of the same, as follows:—

Introduction

1.—The Convention Rights.

(1) In this Act "the Convention rights" means the rights and fundamental F–001 freedoms set out in —

(a) Articles 2 to 1 2 and 14 of the Convention,
(b) Articles 1 to 3 of the First Protocol, and
(c) [Article 1 of the Thirteenth Protocol].[1] as read with Articles 16 to 18 of the Convention.

(2) Those Articles are to have effect for the purposes of this Act subject to any designated derogation or reservation (as to which see sections 14 and 15).

(3) The Articles are set out in Schedule 1.

(4) The Secretary of State may by order make such amendments to this Act as he considers appropriate to reflect the effect, in relation to the United Kingdom, of a protocol.

(5) In subsection (4) "protocol" means a protocol to the Convention—

(a) which the United Kingdom has ratified; or
(b) which the United Kingdom has signed with a view to ratification.

(6) No amendment may be made by an order under subsection (4) so as to come into force before the protocol concerned is in force in relation to the United Kingdom.

[1] words substituted by Human Rights Act 1998 (Amendment) Order 2004/1547 art.2(1).

2.—Interpretation of Convention rights.

(1) A court or tribunal determining a question which has arisen in connection with a Convention right must take into account any—

(a) judgment, decision, declaration or advisory opinion of the European Court of Human Rights,

(b) opinion of the Commission given in a report adopted under Article 31 of the Convention,

(c) decision of the Commission in connection with Article 26 or 27(2) of the Convention, or

(d) decision of the Committee of Ministers taken under Article 46 ofthe Convention, whenever made or given, so far as, in the opinion of the court or tribunal, it is relevant to the proceedings in which that question has arisen.

(2) Evidence of any judgment, decision, declaration or opinion of which account may have to be taken under this section is to be given in proceedings before any court or tribunal in such manner as may be provided by rules.

(3) In this section "rules"' means rules of court or, in the case of proceedings before a tribunal, rules made for the purposes of this section—

(a) by [the Lord Chancellor or][2] the Secretary of State, in relation to any proceedings outside Scotland;

(b) by the Secretary of State, in relation to proceedings in Scotland; or

(c) by a Northern Ireland department, in relation to proceedings before a tribunal in Northern Ireland—

  (i) which deals with transferred mailers; and

  (ii) for which no rules made under paragraph (a) are in force.

Legislation

3.—Interpretation of legislation.

(1) So far as it is possible to do so, primary legislation and subordinate legislation must be read and given effect in a way which is compatible with the Convention rights.

(2) This section—

(a) applies to primary legislation and subordinate legislation whenever enacted;

(b) does not affect the validity, continuing operation or enforcement of any incompatible primary legislation; and

[2] words inserted by Transfer of Functions (Lord Chancellor and Secretary of State) Order 2005/3429 Sch. 1 para.3

(c) does not affect the validity, continuing operation or enforcement of any incompatible subordinate legislation if (disregarding any possibility of revocation) primary legislation prevents removal ofthe incompatibility.

4.—Declaration of incompatibility.

(1) Subsection (2) applies in any proceedings in which a court determines whether a provision of primary legislation is compatible with a Convention right.

(2) If the court is satisfied that the provision is incompatible with a Convention right, it may make a declaration of that incompatibility.

(3) Subsection (4) applies in any proceedings in which a court determines whether a provision of subordinate legislation, made in the exercise of a power conferred by primary legislation, is compatible with a Convention right.

(4) If the court is satisfied—

(a) that the provision is incompatible with a Convention right, and
(b) that (disregarding any possibility of revocation) the primary legislation concerned prevents removal of the incompatibility, it may make a declaration of that incompatibility.

(5) In this section "court" means—

(a) the House of Lords;
(b) the Judicial Committee of the Privy Council;
(c) the Courts-Martial Appeal Court;
(d) in Scotland, the High Court of Justiciary sitting otherwise than as a trial court or the Court of Session;
(c) in England and Wales or Northern Ireland, the High Court or the Court of Appeal.

(6) A declaration under this section ("a declaration of incompatibility")—

(a) does not affect the validity, continuing operation or enforcement of the provision in respect of which it is given; and
(b) is not binding on the parties to the proceedings in which it is made.

5.—Right of Crown to intervene.

(1) Where a court is considering whether to make a declaration of incompatibility, the Crown is entitled to notice in accordance with rules of court.

(2) In any case to which subsection (1) applies—

(a) a Minister of the Crown (or a person nominated by him),
(b) a member of the Scottish Executive,
(c) a Northern Ireland Minister,

(d) a Northern Ireland department,

is entitled, on giving notice in accordance with rules of court, to be joined as a party to the proceedings.

(3) Notice under subsection (2) may be given at any time during the proceedings.

(4) A person who has been made a party to criminal proceedings (other than in Scotland) as the result of a notice under subsection (2) may, with leave, appeal to the House of Lords against any declaration of incompatibility made in the proceedings.

(5) In subsection (4)—

"criminal proceedings" includes all proceedings before the Courts-Martial Appeal Court; and
"leave" means leave granted by the court making the declaration of incompatibility or by the House of Lords.

Public authorities

6.—Acts of public authorities.

(1) It is unlawful for a public authority to act in a way which is incompatible with a Convention right.

(2) Subsection (1) docs not apply to an act if—

(a) as the result of one or more provisions of primary legislation, the authority could not have acted differently; or

(b) in the case of one or more provisions of, or made under, primary legislation which cannot be read or given effect in a way which is compatible with the Convention rights, the authority was acting so as to give effect to or enforce those provisions.

(3) In this section "public authority" includes—

(a) a court or tribunal, and

(b) any person certain of whose functions are functions of a public nature, but does not include either House of Parliament or a person exercising functions in connection with proceedings in Parliament.

(4) In subsection (3) "Parliament" does not include the House of Lords in its judicial capacity.

(5) In relation to a particular act, a person is not a public authority by virtue only of subsection (3)(b) if the nature of the act is private.

(6) "An act" includes a failure to act but does not include a failure to—

(a) introduce in, or lay before. Parliament a proposal for legislation; or

(b) make any primary legislation or remedial order.

7.—Proceedings.

(1) A person who claims that a public authority has acted (or proposes to act) in a way which is made unlawful by section 6(1) may—

(a) bring proceedings against the authority under this Act in the appropriate court or tribunal, or

(b) rely on the Convention right or rights concerned in any legal proceedings, but only if he is (or would be) a victim of the unlawful act.

(2) In subsection (1)(a) "appropriate court or tribunal" means such court or tribunal as may be determined in accordance with rules; and proceedings against an authority include a counterclaim or similar proceedings.

(3) If the proceedings arc brought on an application for judicial review, the applicant is to be taken to have a sufficient interest in relation to the unlawful act only if he is, or would be, a victim of that act.

(4) If the proceedings are made by way of a petition for judicial review in Scotland, the applicant shall be taken to have title and interest to sue in relation to the unlawful act only if he is, or would be, a victim of that act.

(5) Proceedings under subsection (1)(a) must be brought before the end of—

(a) the period of one year beginning with the date on which the act complained of took place; or

(b) such longer period as the court or tribunal considers equitable having regard to all the circumstances, but that is subject to any rule imposing a stricter time limit in relation to the procedure in question.

(6) In subsection (1)(b) "legal proceedings" includes—

(a) proceedings brought by or at the instigation of a public authority; and

(b) an appeal against the decision of a court or tribunal.

(7) For the purposes of this section, a person is a victim of an unlawful act only if he would be a victim for the purposes of Article 34 of the Convention if proceedings were brought in the European Court of Human Rights in respect of that act.

(8) Nothing in this Act creates a criminal offence.

(9) In this section "rules" means—

(a) in relation to proceedings before a court or tribunal outside Scotland, rules made by the [the Lord Chancellor or]³ Secretary of State for the purposes of this section or rules of court,

(b) in relation to proceedings before a court or tribunal in Scotland, rules made by the Secretary of State for those purposes,

(c) in relation to proceedings before a tribunal in Northern Ireland—

³ words inserted by Transfer of Functions (Lord Chancellor and Secretary of State) Order 2005/3429 Sch. 1 para.3

> (i) which deals with transferred matters; and
>
> (ii) for which no rules made under paragraph (a) are in force, rules made by a Northern Ireland department for those purposes, and includes provision made by order under section 1 of the Courts and Legal Services Act 1990.

(10) In making rules, regard must be had to section 9.

(11) The Minister who has power to make rules in relation to a particular tribunal may, to the extent he considers it necessary to ensure that the tribunal can provide an appropriate remedy in relation to an act (or proposed act) of a public authority which is (or would be) unlawful as a result of section 6(1), by order add to—

> (a) the relief or remedies which the tribunal may grant; or
>
> (b) the grounds on which it may grant any of them.

(12) An order made under subsection (11) may contain such incidental, supplemental, consequential or transitional provision as the Minister making it considers appropriate.

(13) "The Minister" includes the Northern Ireland department concerned.

8.—Judicial remedies.

(1) In relation to any act (or proposed act) of a public authority which the court finds is (or would be) unlawful, it may grant such relief or remedy, or make such order, within its powers as it considers just and appropriate.

(2) But damages may be awarded only by a court which has power to award damages, or to order the payment of compensation, in civil proceedings.

(3) No award of damages is to be made unless, taking account of all the circumstances of the case, including—

> (a) any other relief or remedy granted, or order made, in relation to the act in question (by that or any other court), and
>
> (b) the consequences of any decision (of that or any other court) in respect of that act, the court is satisfied that the award is necessary to afford just satisfaction to the person in whose favour it is made.

(4) In determining—

> (a) whether to award damages, or
>
> (b) the amount of an award,

the court must take into account the principles applied by the European Court of Human Rights in relation to the award of compensation under Article 41 of the Convention.

(5) A public authority against which damages are awarded is to be treated—

> (a) in Scotland, for the purposes of section 3 of the Law Reform (Miscellaneous Provisions) (Scotland) Act 1940 as if the award were

made in an action of damages in which the authority has been found liable in respect of loss or damage to the person to whom the award is made;

(b) for the purposes of the Civil Liability (Contribution) Act 1978 as liable in respect of damage suffered by the person to whom the award is made.

(6) In this section—

"court" includes a tribunal;
"damages" means damages for an unlawful act of a public authority; and
"unlawful" means unlawful under section 6(1).

9.—Judicial acts.

(1) Proceedings under section 7(1)(a) in respect of a judicial act may be brought only—

(a) by exercising a right of appeal;
(b) on an application (in Scotland a petition) for judicial review; or
(c) in such other forum as may be prescribed by rules.

(2) That does not affect any rule of law which prevents a court from being the subject of judicial review.

(3) In proceedings under this Act in respect of a judicial act done in good faith, damages may not be awarded otherwise than to compensate a person to the extent required by Article 5(5) of the Convention.

(4) An award of damages permitted by subsection (3) is to be made against the Crown; but no award may be made unless the appropriate person, if not a party to the proceedings, is joined.

(5) In this section—

"appropriate person" means the Minister responsible for the court concerned, or a person or government department nominated by him;
"court" includes a tribunal;
"judge" includes a member of a tribunal, a justice of the peace and a clerk or other officer entitled to exercise the jurisdiction of a court;
"judicial act" means a judicial act of a court and includes an act done on the instructions, or on behalf, of a judge; and
"rules" has the same meaning as in section 7(9).

Remedial action

10.—Power to take remedial action.

(1)This section applies if—

(a) a provision of legislation has been declared under section 4 to be incompatible with a Convention right and, if an appeal lies—

1011

(i) all persons who may appeal have stated in writing that they do not intend to do so;

(ii) the time for bringing an appeal has expired and no appeal has been brought within that time; or

(iii) an appeal brought within that time has been determined or abandoned; or

(b) it appears to a Minister of the Crown or Her Majesty in Council that, having regard to a finding of the European Court of Human Rights made after the coming into force of this section in proceedings against the United Kingdom, a provision of legislation is incompatible with an obligation of the United Kingdom arising from the Convention.

(2) If a Minister of the Crown considers that there arc compelling reasons for proceeding under this section, he may by order make such amendments to the legislation as he considers necessary to remove the incompatibility.

(3) If, in the case of subordinate legislation, a Minister of the Crown considers—

(a) that it is necessary to amend the primary legislation under which the subordinate legislation in question was made, in order to enable the incompatibility to be removed, and

(b) that there are compelling reasons for proceeding under this section, he may by order make such amendments to the primary legislation as he considers necessary.

(4) This section also applies where the provision in question is in subordinate legislation and has been quashed, or declared invalid, by reason of incompatibility with a Convention right and the Minister proposes to proceed under paragraph 2(b) of Schedule 2.

(5) If the legislation is an Order in Council, the power conferred by subsection (2) or (3) is exercisable by Her Majesty in Council.

(6) In this section "legislation" does not include a Measure of the Church Assembly or of the General Synod of the Church of England.

(7) Schedule 2 makes further provision about remedial orders.

Other rights and proceedings

11.—Safeguard for existing human rights.

A person's reliance on a Convention right does not restrict—

(a) any other right or freedom conferred on him by or under any law having effect in any part of the United Kingdom; or

(b) his right to make any claim or bring any proceedings which he could make or bring apart from sections 7 to 9.

12.—Freedom of expression.

(1) This section applies if a court is considering whether lo grant any relief which, if granted, might affect the exercise of the Convention right to freedom of expression.

(2) If the person against whom the application for relief is made ("the respondent") is neither present nor represented, no such relief is to be granted unless the court is satisfied—

(a) that the applicant has taken all practicable steps to notify the respondent; or
(b) that there are compelling reasons why the respondent should not be notified.

(3) No such relief is to be granted so as to restrain publication before trial unless the court is satisfied that the applicant is likely to establish that publication should not be allowed.

(4) The court must have particular regard to the importance of the Convention right to freedom of expression and, where the proceedings relate to material which the respondent claims, or which appears to the court, to be journalistic, literary or artistic material (or to conduct connected with such material), to—

(a) the extent to which—
   (i) the material has, or is about to, become available to the public; or
   (ii) it is, or would be, in the public interest for the material to be published;
(b) any relevant privacy code.

(5) In this section—

"court" includes a tribunal; and
"relief" includes any remedy or order (other than in criminal proceedings).

13.—Freedom of thought, conscience and religion.

(1) If a court's determination of any question arising under this Act might affect the exercise by a religious organisation (itself or its members collectively) of the Convention right to freedom of thought, conscience and religion, it must have particular regard to the importance of that right.

(2) In this section "court" includes a tribunal.

Derogations and reservations

14.—Derogations.

(1) In this Act "designated derogation" means any derogation by the United Kingdom from an Article of the Convention, or of any protocol to

the Convention, which is designated for the purposes of this Act in an order made by the [Secretary of State][4].

(3) If a designated derogation is amended or replaced it ceases to be a designated derogation.

(4) But subsection (3) does not prevent the [Secretary of State][5] from exercising his power under subsection (1) to make a fresh designation order in respect of the Article concerned.

(5) The [Secretary of State][6] must by order make such amendments to Schedule 3 as he considers appropriate to reflect—

(a) any designation order; or
(b) the effect of subsection (3).

(6) A designation order may be made in anticipation of the making by the United Kingdom of a proposed derogation.

15.—Reservations.

(1) In this Act "designated reservation" means—

(a) the United Kingdom's reservation to Article 2 of the First Protocol to the Convention; and
(b) any other reservation by the United Kingdom to an Article of the Convention, or of any protocol to the Convention, which is designated for the purposes of this Act in an order made by the [Secretary of State][7].

(2) The text of the reservation referred to in subsection (1)(a) is set out in Part II of Schedule 3.

(3) If a designated reservation is withdrawn wholly or in part it ceases to be a designated reservation.

(4) But subsection (3) does not prevent the [Secretary of State][8] from exercising his power under subsection (1)(b) to make a fresh designation order in respect of the Article concerned.

(5) The [Secretary of State][9] must by order make such amendments to this Act as he considers appropriate to reflect—

(a) any designation order; or
(b) the effect of subsection (3).

[4] words substituted by Secretary of State for Constitutional Affairs Order 2003/1887 Sch 2 para.10(1)
[5] words substituted by Secretary of State for Constitutional Affairs Order 2003/1887 Sch. 2 para.10(1)
[6] words substituted by Secretary of State for Constitutional Affairs Order 2003/1887 Sch. 2 para.1O(1)
[7] words substituted by Secretary of State for Constitutional Affairs Order 2003/1887 Sch. 2 para.10(1)
[8] 8 words substituted by Secretary of State for Constitutional Affairs Order 2003/1887 Sch. 2 para.10(1)
[9] words substituted by Secretary of State for Constitutional Aflairs Order 2003/1887 Sch. 2 para.10(1)

16.—Period for which designated derogations have effect.

(1) If it has not already been withdrawn by the United Kingdom, a. designated derogation ceases to have effect for the purposes of this Act, at the end of the period of live years beginning with the date on which the order designating it was made.

(2) At any time before the period—

(a) fixed by subsection (1), or

(b) extended by an order under this subsection,

comes to an end, the [Secretary of State][10] may by order extend it by a further period of five years.

(3) An order under section 14(1) ceases to have effect at the end of the period for consideration, unless a resolution has been passed by each House approving the order.

(4) Subsection (3) does not affect—

(a) anything done in reliance on the order; or

(b) the power to make a fresh order under section 14(1).

(5) In subsection (3) "period for consideration" means the period of forty days beginning with the day on which the order was made.

(6) In calculating the period for consideration, no account is to be taken of any time during which—

(a) Parliament is dissolved or prorogued; or

(b) both Houses are adjourned for more than four days.

(7) If a designated derogation is withdrawn by the United Kingdom, the [Secretary of State][11] must by order make such amendments to this Act as he considers are required to reflect that withdrawal.

17.—Periodic review of designated reservations.

(1) The appropriate Minister must review the designated reservation referred to in section 15(1)(a)—

(a) before the end of the period of five years beginning with the date on which section 1 (2) came into force; and

(b) if that designation is still in force, before the end of the period of five years beginning with the date on which the last report relating to it was laid under subsection (3).

(2) The appropriate Minister must review each of the other designated reservations (if any)—

(a) before the end of the period of five years beginning with the date on which the order designating the reservation first came into force; and

[10] words substituted by Secretary of State for Constitutional Affairs Order 2003/1887 Sch. 2 para.10(1)
[11] words substituted by Secretary of State Constitution Affairs Order 2003/1887 Sch. 2 para.10(1)

(b) if the designation is still in force, before the end of the period of five years beginning with the date on which the last report relating to it was laid under subsection (3).

(3) The Minister conducting a review under this section must prepare a report on the result of the review and lay a copy of it before each House of Parliament.

Parliamentary procedure

19.—Statements of compatibility.

(1) A Minister of the Crown in charge of a Bill in either House of Parliament must, before Second Reading of the Bill—

(a) make a statement to the effect that in his view the provisions of the Bill are compatible with the Convention rights ("a statement of compatibility"); or

(b) make a statement to the effect that although he is unable to make a statement of compatibility the government nevertheless wishes the House to proceed with the Bill.

(2) The statement must be in writing and be published in such manner as the Minister making it considers appropriate.

SCHEDULE 1
THE ARTICLES

Section 1(3)

PART I

THE CONVENTION RIGHTS AND FREEDOMS

Right to life

Article 2

1. Everyone's right to life shall be protected by law. No one shall be deprived of his life intentionally save in the execution of a sentence of a court following his conviction of a crime for which this penalty is provided by law.

2. Deprivation of life shall not be regarded as inflicted in contravention of this Article when it results from the use of force which is no more than absolutely necessary:

(a) in defence of any person from unlawful violence;
(b) in order to effect a lawful arrest or to prevent the escape of a person lawfully detained;
(c) in action lawfully taken for the purpose of quelling a riot or insurrection.

Prohibition of torture

Article 3

No one shall be subjected to torture or to inhuman or degrading treatment or punishment.

Prohibition of slavery and (forced labour

Article 4

No one shall be held in slavery or servitude.

No one shall be required to perform forced or compulsory labour.

For the purpose of this Article the term "forced or compulsory labour" shall not include:

(a) any work required to be done in the ordinary course of detention imposed according to the provisions of Article 5 of this Convention or during conditional release from such detention;
(b) any service of a military character or, in case of conscientious objectors in countries where they are recognised, service exacted instead of compulsory military service;
(c) any service exacted in case of an emergency or calamity threatening the life or well-being of the community;
(d) any work or service which forms part of normal civic obligations.

Right to liberty and security

Article 5

1. Everyone has the right to liberty and security of a person. No one shall be deprived of his liberty save in the following cases and in accordance with a procedure prescribed by law:

(a) the lawful detention of a person after conviction by a competent court;
(b) the lawful arrest or detention of a person for non-compliance with the lawful order of a court or in order to secure the fulfilment of any obligation prescribed by law;

1017

(c) the lawful arrest or detention of a person effected for the purpose of bringing him before the competent legal authority on reasonable suspicion of having committed an offence or when it is reasonably considered necessary to prevent his committing an offence or fleeing after having done so;

(d) the detention of a minor by lawful order for the purpose of educational supervision or his lawful detention for the purpose of bringing him before the competent legal authority;

(e) the lawful detention of persons for the prevention of the spreading of infectious diseases, of persons of unsound mind, alcoholics or drug addicts or vagrants;

(f) the lawful arrest or detention of a person to prevent his effecting an unauthorised entry into the country or of a person against whom action is being taken with a view to deportation or extradition.

2. Everyone who is arrested shall be informed promptly, in a language which he understands, of the reasons for his arrest and of any charge against him.

3. Everyone arrested or detained in accordance with the provisions of paragraph 1 (c) of this Article shall be brought promptly before a judge or other officer authorised by law to exercise judicial power and shall be entitled to trial within a reasonable time or to release pending trial. Release may be conditioned by guarantees to appear for trial.

4. Everyone who is deprived of his liberty by arrest or detention shall be entitled to take proceedings by which the lawfulness of his detention shall be decided speedily by a court and his release ordered if the detention is not lawful.

5. Everyone who has been the victim of arrest or detention in contravention of the provisions of this Article shall have an enforceable right to compensation.

Right to a fair trial

Article 6

1. In the determination of his civil rights and obligations or of any criminal charge against him, everyone is entitled to a fair and public hearing within a reasonable time by an independent and impartial tribunal established by law. Judgment shall be pronounced publicly but the press and public may be excluded from all or part of the trial in the interest of morals, public order or national security in a democratic society, where the interests of juveniles or the protection of the private life of the parties so require, or to the extent strictly necessary in the opinion of the court in special circumstances where publicity would prejudice the interests of justice.

2. Everyone charged with a criminal offence shall be presumed innocent until proved guilty according to law.

3. Everyone charged with a criminal offence has the following minimum rights:

(a) to be informed promptly, in a language which he understands and in detail, of the nature and cause of the accusation against him;

(b) to have adequate time and facilities for the preparation of his defence;

(c) to defend himself in person or through legal assistance of his own choosing or, if he has not sufficient means to pay for legal assistance, to be given it free when the interests of justice so require;

(d) to examine or have examined witnesses against him and to obtain the attendance and examination of witnesses on his behalf under the same conditions as witnesses against him;

(e) to have the free assistance of an interpreter if he cannot understand or speak the language used in court.

No punishment without law

Article 7

1. No one shall be held guilty of any criminal offence on account of any act or omission which did not constitute a criminal offence under national or international law at the time when it was committed. Nor shall a heavier penalty be imposed than the one that was applicable at the time the criminal offence was committed.

2. This Article shall not prejudice the trial and punishment of any person for any act or omission which, at the time when it was committed, was criminal according to the general principles of law recognised by civilised nations.

Right to respect for private and family life

Article 8

1. Everyone has the right to respect for his private and family life, his home and his correspondence.

2. There shall be no interference by a public authority with the exercise of this right except such as is in accordance with the law and is necessary in a democratic society in the interests of national security, public safety or the economic well-being of the country, for the prevention of disorder or crime, for the protection of health or morals, or for the protection of the rights and freedoms of others.

1019

Freedom of thought, conscience and religion

Article 9

1. Everyone has the right to freedom of thought, conscience and religion, this right includes freedom to change his religion or belief and freedom, either alone or in community with others and in public or private, to manifest his religion or belief, in worship, teaching, practice and observance.

2. Freedom to manifest one's religion or beliefs shall be subject only to such limitation as are prescribed by law and arc necessary in a democratic society in the interests of public safety, for the protection of public order, health or morals, or for the protection of the rights and freedoms of others.

Freedom of expression

Article 10

1. Everyone has the right to freedom of expression. This right shall include freedom to hold opinions and to receive and impart information and ideas without interference by public authority and regardless of frontiers. This Article shall not prevent States from requiring the licensing of broadcasting, television or cinema enterprises.

2. The exercise of these freedoms, since it carries with ii duties and responsibilities, may be subject to such formalities, conditions, restrictions or penalties as are prescribed by law and are necessary in a democratic society, in the interests of national security, territorial integrity or public safety, for the prevention of disorder or crime, for the protection of health or morals, for the protection of the reputation or rights of others, for preventing the disclosure of information received in confidence, or for maintaining the authority and impartiality of the judiciary.

Freedom of assembly and association

Article 11

1. Everyone has the right to freedom of peaceful assembly and to freedom of association with others, including the right to form and to join trade unions for the protection of his interests.

2. No restrictions shall be placed on the exercise of these rights other than such as are prescribed by law and are necessary in a democratic society in the interests of national security or public safety, for the

1020

prevention of disorder or crime, for the protection of health or morals or for the protection of the rights and freedoms of others. This Article shall not prevent the imposition of lawful restrictions on the exercise of these rights by members of the armed forces, of the police or of the administration of the State.

Right to marry

Article 12

Men and women of marriageable age have the right to marry and to found a family, according to the national laws governing the exercise of this right.

Prohibition of discrimination

Article 14

The enjoyment of the rights and freedoms set forth in this Convention shall be secured without discrimination on any ground such as sex, race, colour, language, religion, political or other opinion, national or social origin, association with a national minority, property, birth or other status.

Restrictions on political activity of aliens

Article 16

Nothing in Articles 10, 11 and 14 shall be regarded as preventing the High Contracting Parties from imposing restrictions on the political activity of aliens.

Prohibition of abuse of rights

Article 17

Nothing in this Convention may be interpreted as implying for any State, group or person any right to engage in any activity or perform any act aimed at the destruction of any of the rights and freedoms set forth herein or at their limitation to a greater extent than is provided for in the Convention.

Limitation on use of restrictions on rights

Article 18

The restrictions permitted under this Convention to the said rights and freedoms shall not be applied for any purpose other than those for which they have been prescribed.

PART II

THE FIRST PROTOCOL

Protection of property

Article 1

Every natural or legal person is entitled to the peaceful enjoyment of his possessions. No one shall be deprived of his possessions except in the public interest and subject to the conditions provided for by law and by the general principles of international law.

The preceding provisions shall not, however, in any way impair the right of a State to enforce such laws as it deems necessary to control the use of property in accordance with the general interest or to secure the payment of taxes or other contributions or penalties.

Right to education

Article 2

No person shall be denied the right to education. In the exercise of any functions which it assumes in relation to education and to teaching, the State shall respect the right of parents to ensure such education and teaching in conformity with their own religious and philosophical convictions.

Right to free elections

Article 3

The High Contracting Parties undertake to hold free elections at reasonable intervals by secret ballot, under conditions which will ensure the free expression of the opinion of the people in the choice of the legislature.[12]

[12] substituted by Human Rights Act 1998 (Amendment) Order 2004/1574 art. 2(3)

PART III

[Article 1 of the Thirteenth Protocol]

Abolition of the death penalty

The death penalty shall be abolished. No one shall be condemned to such penalty or executed.][13]

---

[13] substituted by Human Rights Act 1998 (Amendment) Order 2004/1574 art. 2(3)

CIVIL PROCEDURE RULES PT 54

I JUDICIAL REVIEW

Scope and interpretation

54.1—(1) This Section of this Part contains rules about judicial review.   **G–001**
  (2)   In this Section—

(a) a 'claim for judicial review' means a claim to review the lawfulness of—
    (i) an enactment; or
    (ii) a decision, action or failure to act in relation to the exercise of a public function.
(b) revoked
(c) revoked
(d) revoked
(e) 'the judicial review procedure' means the Part 8 procedure as modified by this Section;
(f) 'interested party' means any person (other than the claimant and defendant) who is directly affected by the claim; and
(g) 'court' means the High Court, unless otherwise stated.

(Rule 8.1(6)(b) provides that a rule or practice direction may, in relation to a specified type of proceedings, disapply or modify any of the rules set out in Part 8 as they apply to those proceedings)

When this Section must be used

54.2 The judicial review procedure must be used in a claim for judicial review where the claimant is seeking—

(a) a mandatory order;
(b) a prohibiting order;
(c) a quashing order; or
(d) an injunction under section 30 of the Supreme Court Act 1981(1) (restraining a person from acting in any office in which he is not entitled to act).

When this Section may be used

54.3—(1) The judicial review procedure may be used in a claim for judicial review where the claimant is seeking—

(a) a declaration; or
(b) an injunction

(Section 31(2) of the Supreme Court Act 1981 sets out the circumstances in which the court may grant a declaration or injunction in a claim for judicial review)

(Where the claimant is seeking a declaration or injunction in addition to one of the remedies listed in rule 54.2, the judicial review procedure must be used)

(2) A claim for judicial review may include a claim for damages, restitution or the recovery of a sum due but may not seek such a remedy alone.

(Section 31(4) of the Supreme Court Act sets out the circumstances in which the court may award damages, restitution or the recovery of a sum due on a claim for judicial review)

Permission required

54.4 The court's permission to proceed is required in a claim for judicial review whether started under this Section or transferred to the Administrative Court.

Time limit for filing claim form

54.5—(1) The claim form must be filed—

(a) promptly; and
(b) in any event not later than 3 months after the grounds to make the claim first arose.

(2) The time limit in this rule may not be extended by agreement between the parties.

(3) This rule does not apply when any other enactment specifies a shorter time limit for making the claim for judicial review.

Claim form

54.6—(1) In addition to the matters set out in rule 8.2 (contents of the claim form) the claimant must also state—

(a) the name and address of any person he considers to be an interested party;
(b) that he is requesting permission to proceed with a claim for judicial review; and
(c) any remedy (including any interim remedy) he is claiming.

(Part 25 sets out how to apply for an interim remedy)

(2) The claim form must be accompanied by the documents required by the relevant practice direction.

Service of claim form

54.7 The claim form must be served on—

(a) the defendant; and
(b) unless the court otherwise directs, any person the claimant considers to be an interested party,

within 7 days after the date of issue.

Acknowledgment of service

54.8—(1) Any person served with the claim form who wishes to take part in the judicial review must file an acknowledgment of service in the relevant practice form in accordance with the following provisions of this rule.

(2) Any acknowledgment of service must be—

(a) filed not more than 21 days after service of the claim form; and
(b) served on—
   (i) the claimant; and
   (ii) subject to any direction under rule 54.7(b), any other person named in the claim form,

as soon as practicable and, in any event, not later than 7 days after it is filed.

(3) The time limits under this rule may not be extended by agreement between the parties.

(4) The acknowledgment of service—

(a) must—
   (i) where the person filing it intends to contest the claim, set out a summary of his grounds for doing so; and
   (ii) state the name and address of any person the person filing it considers to be an interested party; and
(b) may include or be accompanied by an application for directions.

(5) Rule 10.3(2) does not apply.

Failure to file acknowledgment of service

54.9—(1) Where a person served with the claim form has failed to file an acknowledgment of service in accordance with rule 54.8, he—

(a) may not take part in a hearing to decide whether permission should be given unless the court allows him to do so; but
(b) provided he complies with rule 54.14 or any other direction of the court regarding the filing and service of—

      (i) detailed grounds for contesting the claim or supporting it on additional grounds; and

     (ii) any written evidence,

may take part in the hearing of the judicial review.

(2) Where that person takes part in the hearing of the judicial review, the court may take his failure to file an acknowledgment of service into account when deciding what order to make about costs.

(3) Rule 8.4 does not apply.

Permission given

54.10—(1) Where permission to proceed is given the court may also give directions.

(2) Directions under paragraph (1) may include a stay of proceedings to which the claim relates.

(Rule 3.7 provides a sanction for the non-payment of the fee payable when permission to proceed has been given)

Service of order giving or refusing permission

54.11 The court will serve—

(a) the order giving or refusing permission; and
(b) any directions, on—
    (i) the claimant;
   (ii) the defendant; and
  (iii) any other person who filed an acknowledgment of service.

Permission decision without a hearing

54.12—(1) This rule applies where the court, without a hearing—

(a) refuses permission to proceed; or
(b) gives permission to proceed—
    (i) subject to conditions; or
   (ii) on certain grounds only.

(2) The court will serve its reasons for making the decision when it serves the order giving or refusing permission in accordance with rule 54.11.

(3) The claimant may not appeal but may request the decision to be reconsidered at a hearing.

(4) A request under paragraph (3) must be filed within 7 days after service of the reasons under paragraph (2).

(5) The claimant, defendant and any other person who has filed an acknowledgment of service will be given at least 2 days' notice of the hearing date.

Defendant etc. may not apply to set aside

54.13 Neither the defendant nor any other person served with the claim form may apply to set aside an order giving permission to proceed.

Response

54.14—(1) A defendant and any other person served with the claim form who wishes to contest the claim or support it on additional grounds must file and serve—

(a) detailed grounds for contesting the claim or supporting it on additional grounds; and

(b) any written evidence,

within 35 days after service of the order giving permission.

(2) The following rules do not apply—

(a) rule 8.5 (3) and 8.5 (4)(defendant to file and serve written evidence at the same time as acknowledgment of service); and

(b) rule 8.5 (5) and 8.5(6) (claimant to file and serve any reply within 14 days).

Where claimant seeks to rely on additional grounds

54.15 The court's permission is required if a claimant seeks to rely on grounds other than those for which he has been given permission to proceed.

Evidence

54.16—(1) Rule 8.6 (1) does not apply.

(2) No written evidence may be relied on unless—

(a) it has been served in accordance with any—
   (i) rule under this Section; or
   (ii) direction of the court; or

(b) the court gives permission.

Court's powers to hear any person

54.17—(1) Any person may apply for permission—

(a) to file evidence; or

(b) make representations at the hearing of the judicial review.

(2) An application under paragraph (1) should be made promptly.

Judicial review may be decided without a hearing

54.18 The court may decide the claim for judicial review without a hearing where all the parties agree.

Court's powers in respect of quashing orders

54.19—(1) This rule applies where the court makes a quashing order in respect of the decision to which the claim relates.

(2) The court may—

(a) remit the matter to the decision-maker; and
(b) direct it to reconsider the matter and reach a decision in accordance with the judgment of the court.

(3) Where the court considers that there is no purpose to be served in remitting the matter to the decision-maker it may, subject to any statutory provision, take the decision itself.

(Where a statutory power is given to a tribunal, person or other body it may be the case that the court cannot take the decision itself)

Transfer

54.20 The court may

(a) order a claim to continue as if it had not been started under this Section; and
(b) where it does so, give directions about the future management of the claim.

(Part 30 (transfer) applies to transfers to and from the Administrative Court)

II STATUTORY REVIEW UNDER THE NATIONALITY, IMMIGRATION AND ASYLUM ACT 2002

Scope and interpretation

54.21—(1) This Section of this Part contains rules about applications to the High Court under section 101(2) of the Nationality, Immigration and Asylum Act 2002 for a review of a decision of the Immigration Appeal Tribunal on an application for permission to appeal from an adjudicator.

(2) In this Section—

(a) 'the Act' means the Nationality, Immigration and Asylum Act 2002;
(b) 'adjudicator' means an adjudicator appointed for the purposes of Part 5 of the Act;
(c) 'applicant' means a person applying to the High Court under section 101(2) of the Act;
(d) 'other party' means the other party to the proceedings before the Tribunal; and
(e) 'Tribunal' means the Immigration Appeal Tribunal.

Application for review

54.22—(1) An application under section 101(2) of the Act must be made to the Administrative Court.

(2) The application must be made by filing an application notice.

(3) The applicant must file with the application notice—

(a) the immigration or asylum decision to which the proceedings relate, and any document giving reasons for that decision;

(b) the grounds of appeal to the adjudicator;

(c) the adjudicator's determination;

(d) the grounds of appeal to the Tribunal together with any documents sent with them;

(e) the Tribunal's determination on the application for permission to appeal; and

(f) any other documents material to the application which were before the adjudicator.

(4) The applicant must also file with the application notice written submissions setting out—

(a) the grounds upon which it is contended that the Tribunal made an error of law; and

(b) reasons in support of those grounds.

Time limit for application

54.23—(1) The application notice must be filed not later than 14 days after the applicant is deemed to have received notice of the Tribunal's decision in accordance with rules made under section 106 of the Act.

(2) The court may extend the time limit in paragraph (1) in exceptional circumstances.

(3) An application to extend the time limit must be made in the application notice and supported by written evidence verified by a statement of truth.

Service of application

54.24—(1) The applicant must serve on the Asylum and Immigration Tribunal copies of the application notice and written submissions.

(2) Where an application is for review of a decision by the Tribunal to grant permission to appeal, the applicant must serve on the other party copies of—

(a) the application notice;

(b) the written submissions; and

(c) all the documents filed in support of the application, except for documents which come from or have already been served on that party.

(3) Where documents are required to be served under paragraphs (1) and (2), they must be served as soon as practicable after they are filed.

Determining the application

54.25—(1)The application will be determined by a single judge without a hearing, and by reference only to the written submissions and the documents filed with them.

(2) If the applicant relies on evidence which was not submitted to the adjudicator or the Tribunal, the court will not consider that evidence unless it is satisfied that there were good reasons why it was not submitted to the adjudicator or the Tribunal.

(3) The court may—

(a) affirm the Tribunal's decision to refuse permission to appeal;

(b) reverse the Tribunal's decision to grant permission to appeal; or

(c) order the Asylum and Immigration Tribunal to reconsider the adjudicator's decision on the appeal.

(4) Where the Tribunal refused permission to appeal, the court will order the Asylum and Immigration Tribunal to reconsider the adjudicator's decision on the appeal only if it is satisfied that—

(a) the Tribunal may have made an error of law; and

(b) there is a real possibility that the Asylum and Immigration Tribunal would make a different decision from the adjudicator on reconsidering the appeal (which may include making a different direction under section 87 of the 2002 Act).

(5) Where the Tribunal granted permission to appeal, the court will reverse the Tribunal's decision only if it is satisfied that there is no real possibility that the Asylum and Immigration Tribunal, on reconsidering the adjudicator's decision on the appeal, would make a different decision from the adjudicator.

(6) The court's decision shall be final and there shall be no appeal from that decision or renewal of the application.

Service of order

54.26—(1) The court will send copies of its order to—

(a) the applicant, except where paragraph (2) applies;

(b) the other party; and

(c) the Asylum and Immigration Tribunal.

(2) Where—

(a) the application relates, in whole or in part, to a claim for asylum;

(b) the Tribunal refused permission to appeal; and

(c) the court affirms the Tribunal's decision,

the court will send a copy of its order to the Secretary of State, who must serve the order on the applicant.

(3) Where the Secretary of State has served an order in accordance with paragraph (2), he must notify the court on what date and by what method the order was served.

(4) If the court issues a certificate under section 101(3)(d) of the Act, it will send a copy of the certificate together with the order to—

(a) the persons to whom it sends the order under paragraphs (1) and (2); and

(b) if the applicant is in receipt of public funding, the Legal Services Commission.

Costs

54.27—The court may reserve the costs of the application to be determined by the Asylum and Immigration Tribunal.

III APPLICATIONS FOR STATUTORY REVIEW UNDER SECTION 103A OF THE NATIONALITY, IMMIGRATION AND ASYLUM ACT 2002

Scope and interpretation

54.28—(1) This Section of this Part contains rules about applications to the High Court under section 103A of the Nationality, Immigration and Asylum Act 2002 for an order requiring the Asylum and Immigration Tribunal to reconsider its decision on an appeal.

(2) In this Section—

(a) 'the 2002 Act' means the Nationality, Immigration and Asylum Act 2002;

(b) 'the 2004 Act' means the Asylum and Immigration (Treatment of Claimants, etc.) Act 2004;

(c) 'appellant' means the appellant in the proceedings before the Tribunal;

(d) 'applicant' means a person applying to the High Court under section 103A;

(e) 'asylum claim' has the meaning given in section 113(1) of the 2002 Act;

(ea) 'fast track case' means any case in relation to which an order made under section 26(8) of the 2004 Act provides that the time period for making an application under section 103A(1) of the 2002 Act or giving notification under paragraph 30(5) of Schedule 2 to the 2004 Act is less than 5 days;

(f) 'filter provision' means paragraph 30 of Schedule 2 to the 2004 Act;

(g) 'order for reconsideration' means an order under section 103A(1) requiring the Tribunal to reconsider its decision on an appeal;

(h) 'section 103A' means section 103A of the 2002 Act;

(i) 'Tribunal' means the Asylum and Immigration Tribunal.

(3) Any reference in this Section to a period of time specified in—

(a) section 103A(3) for making an application for an order under section 103A(1); or

(b) paragraph 30(5)(b) of Schedule 2 to the 2004 Act for giving notice under that paragraph,

includes a reference to that period as varied by any order under section 26(8) of the 2004 Act.

(4) Rule 2.8 applies to the calculation of the periods of time specified in—

(a) section 103A(3); and

(b) paragraph 30(5)(b) of Schedule 2 to the 2004 Act.

(5) Save as provided otherwise, the provisions of this Section apply to an application under section 103A regardless of whether the filter provision has effect in relation to that application.

Representation of applicants while filter provision has effect

54.28A—(1) This rule applies during any period in which the filter provision has effect.

(2) An applicant may, for the purpose of taking any step under rule 54.29 or 54.30, be represented by any person permitted to provide him with immigration advice or immigration services under section 84 of the Immigration and Asylum Act 1999.

(3) A representative acting for an applicant under paragraph (2) shall be regarded as the applicant's legal representative for the purpose of rule 22.1 (Documents to be verified by a statement of truth) regardless of whether he would otherwise be so regarded.

Service of documents on appellants within the jurisdiction

54.28B—(1) In proceedings under this Section, rules 6.4(2) and 6.5(5) do not apply to the service of documents on an appellant who is within the jurisdiction.

(2) Where a representative is acting for an appellant who is within the jurisdiction, a document must be served on the appellant by—

(a) serving it on his representative; or

(b) serving it on the appellant personally or sending it to his address by first class post (or an alternative service which provides for delivery on the next working day),

but if the document is served on the appellant under sub-paragraph (b), a copy must also at the same time be sent to his representative.

Application for review

54.29—(1) Subject to paragraph (5), an application for an order for reconsideration must be made by filing an application notice—

(a) during a period in which the filter provision has effect, with the Tribunal at the address specified in the relevant practice direction; and

(b) at any other time, at the Administrative Court Office.

(2) During any period in which the filter provision does not have effect, the applicant must file with the application notice—

(a) the notice of the immigration, asylum or nationality decision to which the appeal related;

(b) any other document which was served on the appellant giving reasons for that decision;

(c) the grounds of appeal to the Tribunal;

(d) the Tribunal's determination on the appeal; and

(e) any other documents material to the application which were before the Tribunal.

(2A) During any period in which the filter provision has effect, the applicant must file with the application notice a list of the documents referred to in paragraph (2)(a) to (e).

(3) The applicant must also file with the application notice written submissions setting out—

(a) the grounds upon which it is contended that the Tribunal made an error of law which may have affected its decision; and

(b) reasons in support of those grounds.

(4) Where the applicant—

(a) was the respondent to the appeal; and

(b) was required to serve the Tribunal's determination on the appellant,

the application notice must contain a statement of the date on which, and the means by which, the determination was served.

(5) Where the applicant is in detention under the Immigration Acts, the application may be made either—

(a) in accordance with paragraphs (1) to (3); or

(b) by serving the documents specified in paragraphs (1) to (3) on the person having custody of him.

(6) Where an application is made in accordance with paragraph (5)(b), the person on whom the application notice is served must—

(a) endorse on the notice the date that it is served on him;

(b) give the applicant an acknowledgment in writing of receipt of the notice; and

(c) forward the notice and documents within 2 days

(i) during a period in which the filter provision has effect, to the Tribunal; and

(ii) at any other time, to the Administrative Court Office.

Application to extend time limit

54.30 An application to extend the time limit for making an application under section 103A(1) must—

(a) be made in the application notice;
(b) set out the grounds on which it is contended that the application notice could not reasonably practicably have been filed within the time limit; and
(c) be supported by written evidence verified by a statement of truth.

Procedure while filter provision has effect

54.31—(1) This rule applies during any period in which the filter provision has effect.

(2) Where the applicant receives notice from the Tribunal that it—

(a) does not propose to make an order for reconsideration; or
(b) does not propose to grant permission for the application to be made outside the relevant time limit,

and the applicant wishes the court to consider the application, the applicant must file a notice in writing at the Administrative Court Office in accordance with paragraph 30(5)(b) of Schedule 2 to the 2004 Act.

(2A) The applicant must file with the notice—

(a) a copy of the Tribunal's notification that it does not propose to make an order for reconsideration or does not propose to grant permission for the application to be made outside the relevant time limit (referred to in CPR rule 54.31(2));
(b) any other document which was served on the applicant by the Tribunal giving reasons for its decision in paragraph (a);
(c) written evidence in support of any application by the applicant seeking permission to make the application outside the relevant time limit, if applicable;
(d) a copy of the application for reconsideration under section 103A of the 2002 Act (Form AIT/103A), as submitted to the Tribunal (referred to in Rule 54.29(1)(a)).

(3) Where the applicant—

(a) was the respondent to the appeal; and
(b) was required to serve the notice from the Tribunal mentioned in paragraph (2) on the appellant,

the notice filed in accordance with paragraph 30(5)(b) of Schedule 2 to the 2004 Act must contain a statement of the date on which, and the means by which, the notice from the Tribunal was served.

(4) A notice which is filed outside the period specified in paragraph 30(5)(b) must—

(a) set out the grounds on which it is contended that the notice could not reasonably practicably have been filed within that period; and

(b) be supported by written evidence verified by a statement of truth.

(5) If the applicant wishes to respond to the reasons given by the Tribunal for its decision that it—

(a) does not propose to make an order for reconsideration; or

(b) does not propose to grant permission for the application to be made outside the relevant time limit,

the notice filed in accordance with paragraph 30(5)(b) of Schedule 2 to the 2004 Act must be accompanied by written submissions setting out the grounds upon which the applicant disputes any of the reasons given by the Tribunal and giving reasons in support of those grounds.

Procedure in fast track cases while filter provision does not have effect

54.32—(1)This rule applies only during a period in which the filter provision does not have effect.

(2) Where a party applies for an order for reconsideration in a fast track case—

(a) the court will serve copies of the application notice and written submissions on the other party to the appeal; and

(b) the other party to the appeal may file submissions in response to the application not later than 2 days after being served with the application.

Determination of the application by the Administrative Court

54.33—(1) This rule, and rules 54.34 and 54.35, apply to applications under section 103A which are determined by the Administrative Court.

(2) The application will be considered by a single judge without a hearing.

(3) Unless it orders otherwise, the court will not receive evidence which was not submitted to the Tribunal.

(4) Subject to paragraph (5), where the court determines an application for an order for reconsideration, it may—

(a) dismiss the application;

(b) make an order requiring the Tribunal to reconsider its decision on the appeal under section 103A(1) of the 2002 Act; or

(c) refer the appeal to the Court of Appeal under section 103C of the 2002 Act.

(5) The court will only make an order requiring the Tribunal to reconsider its decision on an appeal if it thinks that—

(a) the Tribunal may have made an error of law; and

(b) there is a real possibility that the Tribunal would make a different decision on reconsidering the appeal (which may include making a different direction under section 87 of the 2002 Act).

(6) Where the Court of Appeal has restored the application to the court under section 103C(2)(g) of the 2002 Act, the court may not refer the appeal to the Court of Appeal.

(7) The court's decision shall be final and there shall be no appeal from that decision or renewal of the application.

Service of order

54.34—(1) The court will send copies of its order to—

(a) the applicant and the other party to the appeal, except where paragraph (2) applies; and
(b) the Tribunal.

(2) Where the appellant is within the jurisdiction and the application relates, in whole or in part, to an asylum claim, the court will send a copy of its order to the Secretary of State.

(2A) Paragraph (2) does not apply in a fast track case.

(3) Where the court sends an order to the Secretary of State under paragraph (2), the Secretary of State must—

(a) serve the order on the appellant; and
(b) immediately after serving the order, notify—
   (i) the court; and
   (ii) where the order requires the Tribunal to reconsider its decision on the appeal, the Tribunal,

on what date and by what method the order was served.

(4) The Secretary of State must provide the notification required by paragraph (3)(b) no later than 28 days after the date on which the court sends him a copy of its order.

(5) If, 28 days after the date on which the court sends a copy of its order to the Secretary of State in accordance with paragraph (2), the Secretary of State has not provided the notification required by paragraph (3)(b)(i), the court may serve the order on the appellant.

(5A) Where the court serves an order for reconsideration under paragraph (5), it will notify the Tribunal of the date on which the order was served.

(6) If the court makes an order under section 103D(1) of the 2002 Act, it will send copies of that order to—

(a) the appellant's legal representative; and
(b) the Legal Services Commission.

(7) Where paragraph (2) applies, the court will not serve copies of an order under section 103D(1) of the 2002 Act until either—

(a) the Secretary of State has provided the notification required by paragraph (3)(b); or

(b) 28 days after the date on which the court sent a copy of its order to the Secretary of State,

whichever is the earlier.

Costs

54.35 The court shall make no order as to the costs of an application under this Section except, where appropriate, an order under section 103D(1) of the 2002 Act.

Continuing an application in circumstances in which it would otherwise be treated as abandoned

54.36—(1) This rule applies to an application under section 103A of the 2002 Act which—

(a) would otherwise be treated as abandoned under section 104(4A) of the 2002 Act; but

(b) meets the conditions set out in section 104(4B) or section 104(4C) of the 2002 Act.

(2) Where section 104(4A) of the 2002 Act applies and the applicant wishes to pursue the application, the applicant must file a notice at the Administrative Court Office—

(a) where section 104(4B) of the 2002 Act applies, within 28 days of the date on which the applicant received notice of the grant of leave to enter or remain in the United Kingdom for a period exceeding 12 months; or

(b) where section 104(4C) of the 2002 Act applies, within 28 days of the date on which the applicant received notice of the grant of leave to enter or remain in the United Kingdom.

(3) Where the applicant does not comply with the time limits specified in paragraph (2), the application will be treated as abandoned in accordance with section 104(4) of the 2002 Act.

(4) The applicant must serve the notice filed under paragraph (2) on the other party to the appeal.

(5) Where section 104(4B) of the 2002 Act applies, the notice filed under paragraph (2) must state—

(a) the applicant's full name and date of birth;

(b) the Administrative Court reference number;

(c) the Home Office reference number, if applicable;

(d) the date on which the applicant was granted leave to enter or remain in the United Kingdom for a period exceeding 12 months; and

(e) that the applicant wishes to pursue the application insofar as it is brought on grounds relating to the Refugee Convention specified in section 84(1)(g) of the 2002 Act.

(6) Where section 104(4C) of the 2002 Act applies, the notice filed under paragraph (2) must state—

  (a) the applicant's full name and date of birth;

  (b) the Administrative Court reference number;

  (c) the Home Office reference number, if applicable;

  (d) the date on which the applicant was granted leave to enter or remain in the United Kingdom; and

  (e) that the applicant wishes to pursue the application insofar as it is brought on grounds relating to section 19B of the Race Relations Act 1976 specified in section 84(1)(b) of the 2002 Act.

(7) Where an applicant has filed a notice under paragraph (2) the court will notify the applicant of the date on which it received the notice.

(8) The court will send a copy of the notice issued under paragraph (7) to the other party to the appeal.

CIVIL PROCEDURE RULES: PRACTICE DIRECTION 54, JUDICIAL REVIEW

SECTION I—GENERAL PROVISIONS RELATING TO JUDICIAL REVIEW

1.1 In addition to Part 54 and this practice direction attention is drawn to: H–001

- section 31 of the Supreme Court Act 1981; and
- the Human Rights Act 1998

The Court

2.1 Part 54 claims for judicial review are dealt with in the Administrative Court.

2.2 Where the claim is proceeding in the Administrative Court in London, documents must be filed at the Administrative Court Office, the Royal Courts of Justice, Strand, London, WC2A 2LL.

2.3 Where the claim is proceeding in the Administrative Court in Wales (see paragraph 3.1), documents must be filed at the Civil Justice Centre, 2 Park Street, Cardiff, CF10 1ET.

Urgent applications

2.4 Where urgency makes it necessary for the claim for judicial review to be made outside London or Cardiff, the Administrative Court Office in London should be consulted (if necessary, by telephone) prior to filing the claim form.

Judicial review claims in wales

3.1 A claim for judicial review may be brought in the Administrative Court in Wales where the claim or any remedy sought involves:

(1) a devolution issue arising out of the Government of Wales Act 1998; or
(2) an issue concerning the National Assembly for Wales, the Welsh executive, or any Welsh public body (including a Welsh local authority) (whether or not it involves a devolution issue).

3.2 Such claims may also be brought in the Administrative Court at the Royal Courts of Justice.

Rule 54.5—Time limit for filing claim form

4.1 Where the claim is for a quashing order in respect of a judgment, order or conviction, the date when the grounds to make the claim first arose, for the purposes of rule 54.5(1)(b), is the date of that judgment, order or conviction.

Rule 54.6—claim form

Interested parties

5.1 Where the claim for judicial review relates to proceedings in a court or tribunal, any other parties to those proceedings must be named in the claim form as interested parties under rule 54.6(1)(a) (and therefore served with the claim form under rule 54.7(b)).

5.2 For example, in a claim by a defendant in a criminal case in the Magistrates or Crown Court for judicial review of a decision in that case, the prosecution must always be named as an interested party.

Human rights

5.3 Where the claimant is seeking to raise any issue under the Human Rights Act 1998, or seeks a remedy available under that Act, the claim form must include the information required by paragraph 15 of the practice direction supplementing Part 16.

Devolution issues

5.4 Where the claimant intends to raise a devolution issue, the claim form must:

(1) specify that the applicant wishes to raise a devolution issue and identify the relevant provisions of the Government of Wales Act 1998, the Northern Ireland Act 1998 or the Scotland Act 1998; and

(2) contain a summary of the facts, circumstances and points of law on the basis of which it is alleged that a devolution issue arises.

5.5 In this practice direction 'devolution issue' has the same meaning as in paragraph 1, schedule 8 to the Government of Wales Act 1998; paragraph 1, schedule 10 to the Northern Ireland Act 1998; and paragraph 1, schedule 6 of the Scotland Act 1998.

Claim form

5.6 The claim form must include or be accompanied by—

(1) a detailed statement of the claimant's grounds for bringing the claim for judicial review;

(2) a statement of the facts relied on;

(3) any application to extend the time limit for filing the claim form;

(4) any application for directions.

5.7 In addition, the claim form must be accompanied by

(1) any written evidence in support of the claim or application to extend time;
(2) a copy of any order that the claimant seeks to have quashed;
(3) where the claim for judicial review relates to a decision of a court or tribunal, an approved copy of the reasons for reaching that decision;
(4) copies of any documents on which the claimant proposes to rely;
(5) copies of any relevant statutory material; and
(6) a list of essential documents for advance reading by the court (with page references to the passages relied on).

5.8 Where it is not possible to file all the above documents, the claimant must indicate which documents have not been filed and the reasons why they are not currently available.

Bundle of documents

5.9 The claimant must file two copies of a paginated and indexed bundle containing all the documents referred to in paragraphs 5.6 and 5.7.
    5.10 Attention is drawn to rules 8.5(1) and 8.5(7).

Rule 54.7—service of claim form

6.1 Except as required by rules 54.11 or 54.12(2), the Administrative Court will not serve documents and service must be effected by the parties.

Rule 54.8—acknowledgment of service

7.1 Attention is drawn to rule 8.3(2) and the relevant practice direction and to rule 10.5.

Rule 54.10—permission given

Directions

8.1 Case management directions under rule 54.10(1) may include directions about serving the claim form and any evidence on other persons.
    8.2 Where a claim is made under the Human Rights Act 1998, a direction may be made for giving notice to the Crown or joining the Crown as a party. Attention is drawn to rule 19.4A and paragraph 6 of the Practice Direction supplementing Section I of Part 19.
    8.3 A direction may be made for the hearing of the claim for judicial review to be held outside London or Cardiff. Before making any such direction the judge will consult the judge in charge of the Administrative Court as to its feasibility.

Permission without a hearing

8.4 The court will generally, in the first instance, consider the question of permission without a hearing.

Permission hearing

8.5 Neither the defendant nor any other interested party need attend a hearing on the question of permission unless the court directs otherwise.

8.6 Where the defendant or any party does attend a hearing, the court will not generally make an order for costs against the claimant.

Rule 54.11—service of order giving or refusing permission

9.1 An order refusing permission or giving it subject to conditions or on certain grounds only must set out or be accompanied by the court's reasons for coming to that decision.

Rule 54.14—response

10.1 Where the party filing the detailed grounds intends to rely on documents not already filed, he must file a paginated bundle of those documents when he files the detailed grounds.

Rule 54.15—where claimant seeks to rely on additional grounds

11.1 Where the claimant intends to apply to rely on additional grounds at the hearing of the claim for judicial review, he must give notice to the court and to any other person served with the claim form no later than 7 clear days before the hearing (or the warned date where appropriate).

Rule 54.16—evidence

12.1 Disclosure is not required unless the court orders otherwise.

Rule 54.17—court's powers to hear any person

13.1 Where all the parties consent, the court may deal with an application under rule 54.17 without a hearing.

13.2 Where the court gives permission for a person to file evidence or make representations at the hearing of the claim for judicial review, it may do so on conditions and may give case management directions.

13.3 An application for permission should be made by letter to the Administrative Court office, identifying the claim, explaining who the applicant is and indicating why and in what form the applicant wants to participate in the hearing.

13.4 If the applicant is seeking a prospective order as to costs, the letter should say what kind of order and on what grounds.

13.5 Applications to intervene must be made at the earliest reasonable opportunity, since it will usually be essential not to delay the hearing.

Rule 54.20—transfer

14.1 Attention is drawn to rule 30.5.

14.2 In deciding whether a claim is suitable for transfer to the Administrative Court, the court will consider whether it raises issues of public law to which Part 54 should apply.

Skeleton arguments

15.1 The claimant must file and serve a skeleton argument not less than 21 working days before the date of the hearing of the judicial review (or the warned date).

15.2 The defendant and any other party wishing to make representations at the hearing of the judicial review must file and serve a skeleton argument not less than 14 working days before the date of the hearing of the judicial review (or the warned date).

15.3 Skeleton arguments must contain:

(1) a time estimate for the complete hearing, including delivery of judgment;

(2) a list of issues;

(3) a list of the legal points to be taken (together with any relevant authorities with page references to the passages relied on);

(4) a chronology of events (with page references to the bundle of documents (see paragraph 16.1);

(5) a list of essential documents for the advance reading of the court (with page references to the passages relied on) (if different from that filed with the claim form) and a time estimate for that reading; and

(6) a list of persons referred to.

Bundle of documents to be filed

16.1 The claimant must file a paginated and indexed bundle of all relevant documents required for the hearing of the judicial review when he files his skeleton argument.

16.2 The bundle must also include those documents required by the defendant and any other party who is to make representations at the hearing.

Agreed final order

17.1 If the parties agree about the final order to be made in a claim for judicial review, the claimant must file at the court a document (with 2 copies) signed by all the parties setting out the terms of the proposed agreed order together with a short statement of the matters relied on as justifying the proposed agreed order and copies of any authorities or statutory provisions relied on.

17.2 The court will consider the documents referred to in paragraph 17.1 and will make the order if satisfied that the order should be made.

17.3 If the court is not satisfied that the order should be made, a hearing date will be set.

17.4 Where the agreement relates to an order for costs only, the parties need only file a document signed by all the parties setting out the terms of the proposed order.

PRE-ACTION PROTOCOL FOR JUDICIAL REVIEW

INTRODUCTION

This protocol applies to proceedings within England and Wales only. It I–001 does not affect the time limit specified by Rule 54.5(1) of the Civil Procedure Rules which requires that any claim form in an application for judicial review must be filed promptly and in any event not later than 3 months after the grounds to make the claim first arose.(¹)

1 Judicial review allows people with a sufficient interest in a decision or action by a public body to ask a judge to review the lawfulness of:

- an enactment; or
- a decision, action or failure to act in relation to the exercise of a public function.(²)

2 Judicial review may be used where there is no right of appeal or where all avenues of appeal have been exhausted.

Alternative dispute resolution

3.1 The parties should consider whether some form of alternative dispute resolution procedure would be more suitable than litigation, and if so, endeavour to agree which form to adopt. Both the Claimant and Defendant may be required by the Court to provide evidence that alternative means of resolving their dispute were considered. The Courts take the view that litigation should be a last resort, and that claims should not be issued prematurely when a settlement is still actively being explored. Parties are warned that if the protocol is not followed (including this paragraph) then the Court must have regard to such conduct when determining costs. However, parties should also note that a claim for judicial review 'must be filed promptly and in any event not later than 3 months after the grounds to make the claim first arose'.

3.2 It is not practicable in this protocol to address in detail how the parties might decide which method to adopt to resolve their particular dispute. However, summarised below are some of the options for resolving disputes without litigation:

- Discussion and negotiation.
- Ombudsmen—the Parliamentary and Health Service and the Local Government Ombudsmen have discretion to deal with complaints relating to maladministration. The British and Irish Ombudsman Association provide information about Ombudsman schemes and other complaint handling bodies and this is available from their website at www.bioa.org.uk . Parties may wish to note that the Ombudsmen are not able to look into a complaint once court action has been commenced.
- Early neutral evaluation by an independent third party (for example, a lawyer experienced in the field of administrative law or an individual experienced in the subject matter of the claim).
- Mediation—a form of facilitated negotiation assisted by an independent neutral party.

3.3 The Legal Services Commission has published a booklet on 'Alternatives to Court', CLS Direct Information Leaflet 23 (www.clsdirect.org.uk/legalhelp/leaflet23.jsp), which lists a number of organisations that provide alternative dispute resolution services.

3.4 *It is expressly recognised that no party can or should be forced to mediate or enter into any form of ADR.*

4 Judicial review may not be appropriate in every instance.

Claimants are strongly advised to seek appropriate legal advice when considering such proceedings and, in particular, before adopting this protocol or making a claim. Although the Legal Services Commission will not normally grant full representation before a letter before claim has been sent and the proposed defendant given a reasonable time to respond, initial funding may be available, for eligible claimants, to cover the work necessary to write this. (See Annex C for more information.)

5 This protocol sets out a code of good practice and contains the steps which parties should generally follow before making a claim for judicial review.

6 This protocol does not impose a greater obligation on a public body to disclose documents or give reasons for its decision than that already provided for in statute or common law. However, where the court considers that a public body should have provided *relevant* documents and/or information, particularly where this failure is a breach of a statutory or common law requirement, it may impose sanctions.

This protocol will not be appropriate where the defendant does not have the legal power to change the decision being challenged, for example decisions issued by tribunals such as the Asylum and Immigration Tribunal.

This protocol will not be appropriate in urgent cases, for example, when directions have been set, or are in force, for the claimant's removal from the UK, or where there is an urgent need for an interim order to compel a public body to act where it has unlawfully refused to do so (for example, the failure of a local housing authority to secure interim accomodation for a homeless claimant) a claim should be made immediately. A letter before claim will not stop the implementation of a disputed decision in all instances.

7 All claimants will need to satisfy themselves whether they should follow the protocol, depending upon the circumstances of his or her case. Where the use of the protocol is appropriate, the court will normally expect all parties to have complied with it and will take into account compliance or non-compliance when giving directions for case management of proceedings or when making orders for costs.([3]) However, even in emergency cases, it is good practice to fax to the defendant the draft Claim Form which the claimant intends to issue. A claimant is also normally required to notify a defendant when an interim mandatory order is being sought.

The letter before claim

8 Before making a claim, the claimant should send a letter to the defendant. The purpose of this letter is to identify the issues in dispute and establish whether litigation can be avoided.

9 Claimants should normally use the suggested standard format for the letter outlined at Annex A.

10 The letter should contain **the date and details of the decision, act or omission being challenged and a clear summary of the facts** on which the claim is based. It should also contain the **details of any relevant information** that the claimant is seeking and an explanation of why this is considered relevant.

11 The letter should normally contain the **details of any interested parties** ([4]) known to the claimant. They should be sent a copy of the letter before claim **for information. Claimants are strongly advised to seek appropriate legal advice when considering such proceedings and, in particular, before sending the letter before claim to other interested parties or making a claim.**

12 A claim should not normally be made until the proposed reply date given in the letter before claim has passed, unless the circumstances of the case require more immediate action to be taken.

The letter of response

13 Defendants should normally respond within 14 days using the *standard format* at Annex B. Failure to do so will be taken into account by the court and sanctions may be imposed unless there are good reasons.([5])

14 Where it is not possible to reply within the proposed time limit the defendant should send an interim reply and propose a reasonable exten-

sion. Where an extension is sought, reasons should be given and, where required, additional information requested. **This will not affect the time limit for making a claim for judicial review** (⁶) nor will it bind the claimant where he or she considers this to be unreasonable. However, where the court considers that a subsequent claim is made prematurely it may impose sanctions.

15 If the claim is being conceded in full, the reply should say so in clear and unambiguous terms.

16 If the claim is being conceded in part or not being conceded at all, the reply should say so in clear and unambiguous terms, and:

(a) where appropriate, contain a new decision, clearly identifying what aspects of the claim are being conceded and what are not, or, give a clear timescale within which the new decision will be issued;

(b) provide a fuller explanation for the decision, if considered appropriate to do so;

(c) address any points of dispute, or explain why they cannot be addressed;

(d) enclose any **relevant** documentation requested by the claimant, or explain why the documents are not being enclosed; and

(e) where appropriate, confirm whether or not they will oppose any application for an interim remedy.

17 The response should be sent to *all interested parties*(⁷) identified by the claimant and contain details of any other parties who the defendant considers also have an interest.

ANNEX A   LETTER BEFORE CLAIM

SECTION 1.   INFORMATION REQUIRED IN A LETTER BEFORE CLAIM

Proposed claim for judicial review

1 To

(Insert the name and address of the proposed defendant—see details in section 2)

2 The claimant

(Insert the title, first and last name and the address of the claimant)

3 Reference details
(When dealing with large organisations it is important to understand that the information relating to any particular individual's previous dealings with it

may not be immediately available, therefore it is important to set out the relevant reference numbers for the matter in dispute and/or the identity of those within the public body who have been handling the particular matter in dispute—see details in section 3)

4 The details of the matter being challenged

(Set out clearly the matter being challenged, particularly if there has been more than one decision)

5 The issue

(Set out the date and details of the decision, or act or omission being challenged, a brief summary of the facts and why it is contented to be wrong)

6 The details of the action that the defendant is expected to take

(Set out the details of the remedy sought, including whether a review or any interim remedy are being requested)

7 The details of the legal advisers, if any, dealing with this claim

(Set out the name, address and reference details of any legal advisers dealing with the claim)

8 The details of any interested parties

(Set out the details of any interested parties and confirm that they have been sent a copy of this letter)

9 The details of any information sought

(Set out the details of any information that is sought. This may include a request for a fuller explanation of the reasons for the decision that is being challenged)

10 The details of any documents that are considered relevant and necessary

(Set out the details of any documentation or policy in respect of which the disclosure is sought and explain why these are relevant. If you rely on a statutory duty to disclose, this should be specified)

11 The address for reply and service of court documents

(Insert the address for the reply)

12 Proposed reply date

(The precise time will depend upon the circumstances of the individual case. However, although a shorter or longer time may be appropriate in a particular case, 14 days is a reasonable time to allow in most circumstances)

SECTION 2. ADDRESS FOR SENDING THE LETTER BEFORE CLAIM

Public bodies have requested that, for certain types of cases, in order to ensure a prompt response, letters before claim chould be sent to specific addresses.

- **Where the claim concerns a decision in an Immigration, Asylum or Nationality case:**
  - Judicial Review Unit,
    Immigration and Nationality Directorate,
    St Anne's House
    20–26 Wellesley Road
    Croydon CR9 2RL
- **Where the claim concerns a decision by the Legal Services Commission:**
  - The address on the decision letter/notification; and
  - Policy and Legal Department
    Legal Services Commission
    85 Gray's Inn Road
    London WC1X 8TX
- **Where the claim concerns a decision by a local authority:**
  - The address on the decision letter/notification; and
  - Their legal department([8])
- **Where the claim concerns a decision by a dapartment or body for whom Treasury Solicitor acts and *Treasury Solicitor has already been involved in the case* a copy should also be sent, quoting the Treasury Solicitor's reference, to:**
  - The Treasury Solicitor,
    One Kemble Street,
    London WC2B 4TS

In all other circumstances, the letter should be sent to the address on the letter notifying the decision.

Section 3. Specific Reference Details Required

Public bodies have requested that the following information should be provided in order to ensure prompt response.

- **Where the claim concerns an Immigration, Asylum or Nationality case, dependent upon the nature of the case:**
  - The Home Office reference number
  - The Port reference number
  - The Asylum and Immigration Tribunal reference number
  - The National Asylum Support Service reference number
    Or, if these are unavailable:
  - The full name, nationality and date of birth of the claimant.

- Where the claim concerns a decision by the Legal Services Commission:
  — The certificate reference number.

ANNEX B RESPONSE TO A LETTER BEFORE CLAIM

INFORMATION REQUIRED IN A RESPONSE TO A LETTER BEFORE CLAIM

Proposed claim for judicial review

1 The claimant

(Insert the title, first and last names and the address to which any reply should be sent)

2 From

(Insert the name and address of the defendant)

3 Reference details

(Set out the relevant reference numbers for the matter in dispute and the identity of those within the public body who have been handling the issue)

4 The details of the matter being challenged

(Set out details of the matter being challenged, providing a fuller explanation of the decision, where this is considered appropriate)

5 Response to the proposed claim

(Set out whether the issue in question is conceded in part, or in full, or will be contested. Where it is not proposed to disclose any information that has been requested, explain the reason for this. Where an interim reply is being sent and there is a realistic prospect of settlement, details should be included)

6 Details of any other interested parties

(Identify any other parties who you consider have an interest who have not already been sent a letter by the claimant)

7 Address for further correspondence and service of court documents

(Set out the address for any future correspondence on this matter)

ANNEX C   NOTES ON PUBLIC FUNDING FOR LEGAL COSTS IN JUDICIAL REVIEW

Public funding for legal costs in judicial review is available from legal professionals and advice agencies which have contracts with the Legal Services Commission as part of the Community Legal Service. Funding may be provided for:

- *Legal Help* to provide initial advice and assistance with any legal problem; or
- *Legal Representation* to allow you to be represented in court if you are taking or defending court proceedings. This is available in two forms:
  - *Investigative Help* is limited to funding to investigate the strength of the proposed claim. It includes the issue and conduct of proceedings only so far as is necessary to obtain disclosure of relevant information or to protect the client's position in relation to any urgent hearing or time limit for the issue of proceedings. This includes the work necessary to write a **letter before claim** to the body potentially under challenge, setting out the grounds of challenge, and giving that body a reasonable opportunity, typically 14 days, in which to respond.
  - *Full Representation* is provided to represent you in legal proceedings and includes litigation services, advocacy services, and all such help as is usually given by a person providing representation in proceedings, including steps preliminary or incidental to proceedings, and/or arriving at or giving effect to a compromise to avoid or bring to an end any proceedings. Except in emergency cases, a proper *letter before claim* must be sent and the other side must be given an opportunity to respond before Full Representation is granted.

Further information on the type(s) of help available and the criteria for receiving that help may be found in the Legal Service Manual Volume 3: *"The Funding Code"*. This may be found on the Legal Services Commission website at:

www.legalservices.gov.uk

A list of contracted firms and Advice Agencies may be found on the Community Legal Services website at:

www.justask.org.uk

FOOTNOTES

1   While the court does have the discretion under Rule 3.1(2)(a) of the Civil Procedure Rules to allow a late claim, this is only used in exceptional circumstances. **Compliance with the protocol alone is unlikely to be sufficient to persuade the court to allow a late claim.**

2   Civil Procedure Rule 54.1(2).

3   Civil Procedure Rules Costs Practice Direction.

4   See Civil Procedure Rule 54.1(2)(f).

5   See Civil Procedure Rules Pre-action Protocol Practice Direction paragraphs 2–3.

6   See Civil Procedure Rule 54.5(1).

7   See Civil Procedure Rule 54.1(2)(f).

8   The relevant address should be available from a range of sources such as the Phone Book; Business and Services Directory, Thomson's Local Directory, CAB, etc.

N461 JUDICIAL REVIEW CLAIM FORM

| Click here to reset form | Click here to print form | J–001 |

Judicial Review
Claim Form

In the High Court of Justice
Administrative Court

Notes for guidance are available which explain
how to complete the judicial review claim
form. Please read them carefully before you
complete the form.

For Court use only	
Administrative Court Reference No.	
Date filed	

Seal

SECTION 1 Details of the claimant(s) and defendant(s)

Claimant(s) name and address(es)

name

address

Telephone no.

Fax no.

E-mail address

Claimant's or claimant's solicitors' address to which documents should be sent.

name

address

Telephone no.

Fax no.

E-mail address

Claimant's Counsel's details

name

address

Telephone no.

Fax no.

E-mail address

1st Defendant

name

Defendant's or (where known) Defendant's solicitors' address to which documents should be sent.

name

address

Telephone no.

Fax no.

E-mail address

2nd Defendant

name

Defendant's or (where known) Defendant's solicitors' address to which documents should be sent.

name

address

Telephone no.

Fax no.

E-mail address

SECTION 2 Details of other interested parties

Include name and address and, if appropriate, details of DX, telephone or fax numbers and e-mail

name

address

Telephone no.

Fax no.

E-mail address

name

address

Telephone no.

Fax no.

E-mail address

SECTION 3 Details of the decision to be judicially reviewed

Decision:

Date of decision:

Name and address of the court, tribunal, person or body who made the decision to be reviewed.

name

address

SECTION 4 Permission to proceed with a claim for judicial review

I am seeking permission to proceed with my claim for Judicial Review.

Is this application being made under the terms of Section 18 Practice Direction 54 (Challenging removal)? ☐ Yes ☐ No

Are you making any other applications? If Yes, complete Section 7. ☐ Yes ☐ No

Is the claimant in receipt of a Community Legal Service Fund (CLSF) certificate? ☐ Yes ☐ No

Are you claiming exceptional urgency, or do you need this application determined within a certain time scale? If Yes, complete Form N463 and file this with your application. ☐ Yes ☐ No

Have you complied with the pre-action protocol? If No, give reasons for non-compliance in the space below. ☐ Yes ☐ No

Does the claim include any issues arising from the Human Rights Act 1998?
If Yes, state the articles which you contend have been breached in the space below. ☐ Yes ☐ No

SECTION 5 Detailed statement of grounds

☐ set out below ☐ attached

SECTION 6 Details of remedy (including any interim remedy) being sought

SECTION 7 Other applications

I wish to make an application for:-

SECTION 8 Statement of facts relied on

Statement of Truth

I believe (The claimant believes) that the facts stated in this claim form are true.

Full name _____

Name of claimant's solicitor's firm _____

Signed _____ Position or office held _____

       Claimant ('s solicitor)   (if signing on behalf of firm or company)

1060

SECTION 9 Supporting documents

If you do not have a document that you intend to use to support your claim, identify it, give the date when you expect it to be available and give reasons why it is not currently available in the box below.

Please tick the papers you are filing with this claim form and any you will be filing later.

☐ Statement of grounds   ☐ included   ☐ attached

☐ Statement of the facts relied on   ☐ included   ☐ attached

☐ Application to extend the time limit for filing the claim form   ☐ included   ☐ attached

☐ Application for directions   ☐ included   ☐ attached

☐ Any written evidence in support of the claim or
application to extend time

☐ Where the claim for judicial review relates to a decision of
a court or tribunal, an approved copy of the reasons for
reaching that decision

☐ Copies of any documents on which the claimant
proposes to rely

☐ A copy of the legal aid or CSLF certificate *(if legally represented)*

☐ Copies of any relevant statutory material

☐ A list of essential documents for advance reading by
the court *(with page references to the passages relied upon)*

If Section 18 Practice Direction 54 applies, please tick the relevant box(es) below to indicate which papers you are filing with this claim form:

☐ a copy of the removal directions and the decision to which   ☐ included   ☐ attached
the application relates

☐ a copy of the documents served with the removal directions
including any documents which contains the Immigration and   ☐ included   ☐ attached
Nationality Directorate's factual summary of the case

☐ a detailed statement of the grounds   ☐ included   ☐ attached

Reasons why you have not supplied a document and date when you expect it to be available:-

Signed _____ Claimant ('s Solicitor)_____

Click here to print form

1062

N462 JUDICIAL REVIEW ACKNOWLEDGMENT OF SERVICE

Judicial Review
Acknowledgment of Service

Click here to reset form

In the High Court of Justice
    Administrative Court

Name and address of person to be served

name

address

Claim No.	
Claimant(s) *(including ref.)*	
Defendant(s)	
Interested Parties	

SECTION A

Tick the appropriate box

1. I intend to contest all of the claim   ☐
2. I intend to contest part of the claim   ☐   } complete sections B, C, D and E
3. I do not intend to contest the claim   ☐   complete section E
4. The defendant (interested party) is a court or tribunal and **intends** to make a submission.   ☐   complete sections B, C and E
5. The defendant (interested party) is a court or tribunal and **does not intend** to make a submission.   ☐   complete sections B and E

Note: If the application seeks to judicially review the decision of a court or tribunal, the court or tribunal need only provide the Administrative Court with as much evidence as it can about the decision to help the Administrative Court perform its judicial function.

SECTION B

Insert the name and address of any person you consider should be added as an interested party.

name

address

Telephone no.   Fax no.

E-mail address

name

address

Telephone no.   Fax no.

E-mail address

SECTION C

Summary of grounds for contesting the claim. If you are contesting only part of the claim, set out which part before you give your grounds for contesting it. If you are a court or tribunal filing a submission, please indicate that this is the case.

2 of 3

1064

SECTION D

Give details of any directions you will be asking the court to make, or tick the box to indicate that a separate application notice is attached.

SECTION E

	*(I believe)(The defendant believes) that the facts stated in this form are true. *I am duly authorised by the defendant to sign this statement.	(if signing on behalf of firm or company, court or tribunal)	Position or office held
*delete as appropriate			

(To be signed by you or by your solicitor or litigation friend)

Signed _____

Date _____

Give an address to which notices about this case can be sent to you

name _____

address _____

Telephone no. _____ Fax no. _____

E-mail address _____

If you have instructed counsel, please give their name address and contact details below.

name _____

address _____

Telephone no. _____ Fax no. _____

E-mail address _____

Completed forms, together with a copy, should be lodged with the Administrative Court Office, Room C315, Royal Courts of Justice, Strand, London, WC2A 2LL, within 21 days of service of the claim upon you, and further copies should be served on the Claimant(s), any other Defendant(s) and any interested parties within 7 days of lodgement with the Court.

3 of 3

1065

N463 APPLICATION FOR URGENT CONSIDERATION

| Click here to reset form | Click here to print form | l–001 |

Judicial Review
Application for urgent consideration

This form must be completed by the Claimant or the Claimant's advocate if exceptional urgency is being claimed and the application needs to be determined within a certain time scale.

The claimant, or the claimant's solicitors must serve this form on the defendant(s) and any interested parties with the N461 Judicial review claim form.

To the Defendant(s) and Interested party(ies) Representations as to the urgency of the claim may be made by defendants or interested parties to the Administrative Court Office by fax - 020 7947 6802

In the High Court of Justice	
Administrative Court	
Claim No.	
Claimant(s) *(including ref.)*	
Defendant(s)	
Interested Parties	

SECTION 1 Reasons for urgency

SECTION 2 Proposed timetable *(tick the boxes and complete the following statements that apply)*

☐ a) The application for interim relief should be considered within _____ hours/days

☐ b) The N461 application for permission should be considered within _____ hours/days

☐ c) Abridgement of time is sought for the lodging of acknowledgments of service

☐ d) If permission for judicial review is granted, a substantive hearing is sought by _____ (date)

SECTION 3 Interim relief *(state what interim relief is sought and why in the box below)*

A draft order must be attached.

> *(empty box)*

SECTION 4 Service

A copy of this form of application was served on the defendant(s) and interested parties as follows:

Defendant   **Interested party**

☐ by fax machine to   time sent   ☐ by fax machine to   time sent
  ┌Fax no.─────────┐ ┌time──────┐   ┌Fax no.─────────┐ ┌time──────┐

☐ by handing it to or leaving it with   ☐ by handing it to or leaving it with
  ┌name───────────────────────┐   ┌name───────────────────────┐

☐ by e-mail to   ☐ by e-mail to
  ┌e-mail address─────────────┐   ┌e-mail address─────────────┐

Date served   Date served
  ┌Date───────────┐   ┌Date───────────┐

Name of claimant's advocate   Claimant (claimant's advocate)
  ┌name───────────────────────┐   ┌Signed───────────────────────┐

INDEX